THE OXFORD H

JAPANESE
PHILOSOPHY

THE OXFORD HANDBOOK OF

JAPANESE

PHILOSOPHY

Edited by

BRET W. DAVIS

Oxford University Press is a department of the University of Oxford. It furthers
the University's objective of excellence in research, scholarship, and education
by publishing worldwide. Oxford is a registered trade mark of Oxford University
Press in the UK and certain other countries.

Published in the United States of America by Oxford University Press
198 Madison Avenue, New York, NY 10016, United States of America.

© Oxford University Press 2020

First issued as an Oxford University Press paperback, 2022.

CIP data is on file at the Library of Congress
ISBN 978-0-19-994572-6 (hardback)
ISBN 978-0-19-765058-5 (paperback)

For Toshi and Koto, always

CONTENTS

PART III PHILOSOPHIES OF JAPANESE CONFUCIANISM AND BUSHIDŌ

PART IV MODERN JAPANESE PHILOSOPHIES

THE KYOTO SCHOOL

OTHER MODERN JAPANESE PHILOSOPHIES

PART V PERVASIVE TOPICS IN JAPANESE PHILOSOPHICAL THOUGHT

PREFACE

WHEN Peter Ohlin of Oxford University Press first approached me in 2011 about submitting a proposal for this *Handbook of Japanese Philosophy*, my first thought was that it was indeed high time for such a volume to be produced. The timing was especially fortuitous, given the impending publication of *Japanese Philosophy: A Sourcebook* (2011), edited by James Heisig, Thomas Kasulis, and John Maraldo, which would for the first time make accessible in a single volume a wide selection of key texts in translation from the entire history of philosophical thinking in Japan. In the belatedly burgeoning field of Japanese philosophy, what was called for next, it seemed to me, was a *Handbook* that would, in effect, complement the *Sourcebook*. That is to say, what was called for was a collection of interpretive elucidations and critical engagements with a selection of the most important topics, figures, schools, and texts from the entire history of philosophical thinking in Japan.

My second thought, however, was how daunting the task of producing such a *Handbook* would be. As I began to envision the range of material that would need to be covered and to draft a table of contents, I quickly realized that the project could be done properly only if I were able to assemble a veritable "dream team" of contributors. In the end, after just a bit of groveling and arm twisting, almost every one of the scholars I contacted on account of their unparalleled expertise and acumen graciously agreed to collaborate. Although I regret not having been able to include in this project a few other established and upcoming scholars, I am very grateful to those who contributed for carving time out in their busy schedules and for their willingness to work closely with me on what has, I think, turned out to be a remarkably coherent and comprehensive volume. They proved willing to write not just outstanding articles that could each be savored independently but, moreover, articles that were contentiously composed as chapters with the vision of the volume as a whole in mind.

Japanese philosophy is now a flourishing field, with thriving societies, conferences, and journals dedicated to it in North America and Europe as well as in Japan—not to mention an ever-growing library of translations, books, and articles. However, it is still a relative newcomer on the academic landscape. In particular, after having long been confined to fields such as Asian Studies and Religious Studies, it is still finding its legs in the field of Philosophy. Accordingly, it seemed exigent to begin this *Handbook* with an extensive introductory chapter that addresses head-on the many complex and controversial issues enfolded in the deceptively simple question, "What is Japanese Philosophy?"

One of the main questions addressed in the Introduction is that of the semantic and historical range of "Japanese philosophy." Of course, the material presented in the

Modern Japanese Philosophies section, which constitutes nearly half the volume, is unquestionably and recognizably "philosophical." True, the style of most modern Japanese philosophers may be more familiar to students and scholars trained in the continental rather than analytic tradition since modern Japanese philosophers have typically engaged continental European, especially German, philosophy more than they have Anglo-American analytic philosophy. In any case, no one doubts that modern Japanese philosophy is philosophy.

Potentially controversial, however, is the inclusion of coverage of "premodern" discourses in this *Handbook*. Did "philosophy" exist in Japan prior to the Japanese encounter with and appropriation of Western philosophy in the final decades of the nineteenth century? While this question continues to be debated (and these debates are discussed at length in the Introduction), it is *at least* incontrovertible that premodern Japanese discourses are replete with profoundly significant *sources* for philosophical thinking. In other words, the question of whether the writings of Kūkai, Shinran, Motoori Norinaga or Ogyū Sorai should themselves be called "philosophy" can be debated; but, regardless of the outcome of that debate, they are unquestionably valuable sources for any contemporary philosopher who wishes to expand his or her horizon beyond the borders of the Western tradition. Western philosophers have long been accustomed to drawing insights and ideas from literature, religious writings, political speeches, and other texts that need not be considered philosophy to be considered philosophically significant. Why limit these sources of philosophy to one tradition? Whether or not the reader is willing to rethink the definition of philosophy in light of premodern Japanese discourses, there can be no doubt that his or her philosophizing will be all the broader and better for having engaged with the discourses discussed in the first half of this *Handbook*—which consists of sections on Shintō and the Synthetic Nature of Japanese Philosophical Thought, Philosophies of Japanese Buddhism, and Philosophies of Japanese Confucianism and Bushidō.

These sections on the philosophical dimensions of premodern Japanese thought are followed by the large section on Modern Japanese Philosophies. After a substantial chapter on the initial decades of the Japanese encounter with and appropriation of Western philosophy, this section is divided into one subsection on the most well-known group of twentieth-century Japanese philosophers, The Kyoto School, and a second subsection on the no less interesting and important array of Other Modern Japanese Philosophies. Rounding out the volume is a section on Pervasive Topics in Japanese Philosophical Thought, which includes topics that span a range of schools and time periods. In this final section, the reader will find chapters on language, nature and freedom, ethics, aesthetics, and a concluding chapter that returns to a key issue first addressed in the Introduction: the controversial cultural identity of Japanese philosophy. The selection of chapter topics is discussed in greater detail at the end of the Introduction. Readers can explore the thematic interconnections among the chapters by consulting the detailed index at the back of this volume.

The most enjoyable part of completing a large and lengthy project such as this one is the opportunity afforded me to express my gratitude to the many people who made it possible. During the course of the composition of the chapters of this *Handbook*, it was a great pleasure and a great learning experience to work closely with the contributors, either per email or in person. Peter Ohlin, Cecily Berberat, Laura Heston, Madeleine Freeman, Lane Berger and the other and the other editors at Oxford University Press who ushered me through the process were always very responsive and very helpful, as were Anitha Alagusundaram and the rest of the highly competent and cordial copyeditors and print production team. I am very grateful for the support I receive from my home institution, Loyola University Maryland. I began this project in Kyoto during one sabbatical and finished it in Baltimore during a second one. In between, summer research grants from LUM enabled me concentrate on it while spending valuable time back in Japan.

I'd like to take this opportunity to sincerely thank the many teachers, colleagues, and students in Japan, the United States, and Europe who have guided or accompanied me on my journey through the thickets and into the clearings of Japanese philosophy. Allow me to single out a number of benefactors. During the decade I spent in Kyoto, my main teachers were Horio Tsutomu at Ōtani University, Fujita Masakatsu at Kyoto University, and Ueda Shizuteru at Shōkokuji and elsewhere. Supplementing my philosophical studies, I have had the great fortune of being able to practice Zen at the Rinzai Zen training monastery of Shōkokuji under the guidance of Tanaka Hōjū Rōshi from 1996 until 2006, and, since he passed away in 2008, with Kobayashi Gentoku Rōshi. Other teachers and mentors in Kyoto have included Ōhashi Ryōsuke, Hase Shōtō, Keta Masako, Mori Tetsurō, Okada Katsuaki, Ōkōchi Ryōgi, Matsumaru Hisao, Mine Hideo, Hanaoka Eiko, Arifuku Kōgaku, Ogawa Tadashi, Kōsaka Shirō, and, on a memorable visit to his home, Tsujimura Kōichi. Colleagues and conversation partners in Kyoto have included Uehara Mayuko, Akitomi Katsuya, Minobe Hitoshi, Matsumoto Naoki, Sugimura Yasuhiko, Thomas Kirchner, Terao Kazuyoshi, Yoshie Takami, Mizuno Tomoharu, Wu Guanghui, Sugimoto Kōichi, Tanaka Yoshiko, Kawabata Shinsuke, Andrea Leonardi, Miyano Makiko, Takehana Yōsuke, Ōta Hironobu, and Nakajima Yūta. Over the years I have benefitted from conversations about Japanese philosophy at international conferences, during research sojourns in Japan and Germany, and per email with numerous other mentors and colleagues, including John Maraldo, James Heisig, Thomas Kasulis, Rolf Elberfeld, Graham Parkes, Michiko Yusa, Agustín Jacinto Z., Jan Van Bragt, Arisaka Yōko, Tani Tōru, Inoue Katsuhito, Tanaka Yū, Victor Sōgen Hori, Kobayashi Yasuo, Noé Keiichi, Paul Swanson, Mark Blum, Dennis Hirota, Chris Goto-Jones, John Krummel, Gereon Kopf, Itabashi Yūjin, Abe Hiroshi, Nakajima Takahiro, Kajitani Shinji, Steffen Döll, Rein Raud, Ralf Müller, Matteo Cestari, Raquel Bouso, Bernard Stevens, Curtis Rigsby, Lam Wing-keung, Cheung Ching-yuen, Morisato Takeshi, Ishihara Yūko, Leah Kalmanson, Enrico Fongaro, Andrew Whitehead, Hans Peter Liederbach, Anton Luis Sevilla, Jason Wirth, Brian Schroeder, Erin McCarthy, Mark Unno, Melissa Anne-Marie Curley, Brad Park, Steve Lofts, David Johnson, Jacynthe Tremblay, David Jones, Frank Perkins, Elizabeth Tyler, Jan Gerrit Strala, Leon Krings, Inutsuka Yū, Kuwayama Yukiko, James Mark Shields, Brook Ziporyn, Sarah Flavel, Lucy Schultz, and Carolyn Culbertson. Closer to home, I am ever appreciative of the weekly hours of shared silence as well as engaging discussion with members of the Heart of Zen Meditation Group, including Ethan Duckworth, Ed Stokes, Janet Preis, Mickey Fenzel, Janet Maher, Susan Gresens, John Pie, Rhonda Grandy, Bess Garrett, Jeffrey McGrath, Rick Boothby, Steve DeCaroli, and Drew Leder. Among students, let me single out, in memoriam, a special one who took my first seminar on Japanese philosophy at Loyola University Maryland in 2005: Luke Dorsey. Despite what he called my rusty English that first semester back in the States, Luke nevertheless managed to get hooked on studying Dōgen and Watsuji and on practicing *zazen*.

As always, I would like express my heartfelt gratitude to my family. As distant as they are geographically, my three brothers, Peter, Chris, and Sean are always near in spirit, as is the shared memory of our tirelessly supportive mother. Photos and stories exchanged via the Internet and occasional family gatherings with my brothers and their clans are a great source of often lighthearted yet always deeply felt joy. My nearest and dearest support continues to come from my wife, Naomi, and from our two children, Toshi and Koto. Naomi's positive energy radiates through our home and her *vita activa* enables not only my *vita contemplativa* but also the eventful school, soccer, and social lives of our two youngsters. Toshi and Koto are growing up so fast and yet, thankfully, also so well. Even in the midst of these admittedly at times trying preteen and teen years, I am often surprised to discover how they are helping me grow up along with them. Both of them can already easily sprint past me on the track, and it may not be long before they cruise past me in the lifelong maturity marathon as well. In any case, perhaps they are now old enough to appreciate having a book dedicated to them—if, that is, I can get them to glance at it on their way from school to soccer practice.

Note on names and terms: Throughout this volume, Japanese names are generally written in the Japanese order of family name first, followed by given name. This convention is also followed for the names of Japanese contributors, except in the cases of those who work and publish *primarily* in a Western language. To avoid any confusion, in the list of contributors on pages xv–xxv, the family names of all contributors appear in small caps. Unless otherwise specified, italicized non-English terms are Japanese. The following abbreviations for languages are used: Ch. = Chinese, Gk. = Greek, Jp. = Japanese, Sk. = Sanskrit. As is customary, diacritical marks are not used in well-known place names such as Kyoto and Tokyo or in some anglicized terms such as sutra.

For the most part, modern Japanese forms of *kanji* (sinographs or Chinese characters) are used throughout the book, however in some contexts traditional forms are used.

Contributors

Akitomi Katsuya is Professor at Kyoto Institute of Technology, President of the Nishida Philosophy Association, and Chairman of the Board of Directors at the Japanese-German Cultural Institute in Kyoto. He received his undergraduate and doctoral degrees from Kyoto University and studied at Munich University as a Humboldt Fellow. In additional to numerous articles on Nishida Kitarō, Nishitani Keiji, and other figures in the Kyoto School, he is author of *Geijutsu to gijutsu: Haidegga no toi* [Art and Technology: Heidegger's Question] and co-translator with Ōhashi Ryōsuke of Heidegger's *Beiträge zur Philosophie (Vom Ereignis)*.

Yoko Arisaka (Jp. Arisaka Yōko, born in Japan in 1962 and moved to the United States in 1980) received her PhD in Philosophy from the University of California, Riverside (1996). She was Associate Professor of Philosophy in the Philosophy Department as well as at the Graduate Faculty at the Center for the Pacific Rim, both at the University of San Francisco (1996–2007). During the fall of 1997, she was a CNRS research associate at the École des Hautes Études en Sciences Sociales in Paris. Since 2005, she has lived in Hannover, Germany. She was a Fellow at the Forschungsinstitut für Philosophie Hannover (2009–11). She is currently an adjunct faculty member at the University of Hildesheim, Germany. Her fields of research include political philosophy (including philosophy of race and gender issues), modern Japanese philosophy, phenomenology, and ethics. Her publications include *Prophetischer Pragmatismus: Eine Einführung in das Denken von Cornel West*, by Jürgen Manemann, Yoko Arisaka, Volker Drell, Anna Maria Hauk (2012) and *Kitaro Nishida in der Philosophie des 20. Jahrhunderts*, edited by Rolf Elberfeld and Yoko Arisaka (2014). Website: http://www.arisaka.org.

Robert E. Carter is Professor Emeritus at Trent University. He studied at Tufts and Harvard Universities, and at the University of Toronto. He is the author/editor of several books, including *Dimensions of Moral Education* (1984); *God, the Self and Nothingness* (1990); *Becoming Bamboo: Reflections Eastern and Western* (1992); *Encounter with Enlightenment: A Study of Japanese Ethics* (2001); *Rinrigaku: Ethics in Japan*, with Yamamoto Seisaku (1996); *The Nothingness Beyond God: An Introduction to the Philosophy of Nishida* (1997); *The Japanese Arts and Self-Cultivation* (2008), and *The Kyoto School: An Introduction* (2012). Dr. Carter has visited Japan on nine occasions to research and teach, living in Japan for two years as an Invited Professor at Kansai Gaidai University in Japan. He has also been an Invited Professor at the University of Hawai'i. He is a poet and musician and currently plays trumpet in two big-bands. He is married with two children and one grandson, and he lives in Peterborough, Ontario, Canada.

Melissa Anne-Marie Curley is Assistant Professor of Comparative Studies at Ohio State University. Her research focuses on modern Japanese Buddhism, particularly the interaction between sectarian Pure Land thinkers and Japanese philosophers. She is author of *Pure Land, Real World: Modern Buddhism, Japanese Leftists, and the Utopian Imagination* (University of Hawai'i Press, 2017) and co-editor of a book on the Kyoto School entitled *Neglected Themes and Hidden Variations* (Nanzan Institute for Religion and Culture, 2008). Recent articles include "Prison and the Pure Land: A Buddhist Chaplain in Occupied Japan" (*Journal of Buddhist Ethics*, 2018) and "Dead Matter and Living Memory: Three Ways of Looking at the Higashi Honganji Hair Ropes" (*Japanese Religions*, forthcoming). She is currently completing a collaborative translation of Kyoto School philosopher Keta Masako's *Philosophy of Religious Experience: An Elucidation of the Pure Land Buddhist World*.

Bret W. Davis is Thomas J. Higgins, S.J. Professor of Philosophy at Loyola University Maryland. He attained a PhD in philosophy from Vanderbilt University and has spent more than a dozen years in Japan, during which time he studied Buddhist thought at Otani University, completed the coursework for a second PhD in Japanese philosophy at Kyoto University, and trained as a lay practitioner at Shōkokuji, a Rinzai Zen monastery in Kyoto. In addition to publishing more than sixty articles in English and in Japanese on various topics in Japanese, continental, and cross-cultural philosophy, he is the author of *Heidegger and the Will: On the Way to Gelassenheit* (2007); editor of *Martin Heidegger: Key Concepts* (2014); and co-editor of *Sekai no naka no Nihon no tetsugaku* [Japanese philosophy in the world] (2005), *Japanese and Continental Philosophy: Conversations with the Kyoto School* (2011), and *Engaging Dōgen's Zen: The Philosophy of Practice as Awakening* (2017). His translations from German and Japanese include Martin Heidegger's *Country Path Conversations* (2010), Dōgen's "Genjōkōan: The Presencing of Truth" (2009), and Ueda Shizuteru's "Language in a Twofold World" (2011). He serves on the editorial board of several journals and is coeditor of Indiana University Press's book series in World Philosophies.

Steffen Döll is Numata Professor for Japanese Buddhism at the University of Hamburg. He studied Japanology, Sinology, and Religious Studies in Munich and Kyoto. His master's thesis, published in 2005, was the first monograph on contemporary philosopher Ueda Shizuteru (1926–2019) to appear in a Western language. His dissertation was published in 2010 and studies the role of Chinese emigrant monks in the transmission of Chan Buddhism to Japan as well as in the subsequent processes of institutionalization during the thirteenth and fourteenth centuries. In 2015, he was appointed to his current position in the Numata Center for Buddhist Studies at Hamburg University. He is currently pursuing research projects focusing on the entangled histories of religion and literature in East Asia; the construction of sacred spaces and topographies, for example in the form of Buddhist monastic architecture or landscape narratives; and the question of the function and potency of writing in East Asia.

Rolf ELBERFELD is Professor of Philosophy of Culture at Hildesheim University, Germany. He is author of *Kitaro Nishida (1870–1945): Moderne japanische Philosophie und die Frage nach der Interkulturalität; Phänomenologie der Zeit im Buddhismus: Methoden interkulturellen Philosophierens; Sprache und Sprachen: Eine philosophische Grundorientierung;* and *Philosophieren in einer globalisierten Welt.* His edited volumes include *Komparative Ästhetik: Künste und ästhetische Erfahrungen in Asien und Europa; Komparative Ethik: Das Gute Leben zwischen den Kulturen; Was ist Philosophie? Programmatische Texte von Platon bis Derrida;* and *Philosophiegeschichtsschreibung in globaler Perspektive.* He is translator of Ōhashi Ryōsuke's *Kire: Das Schöne in Japan,* and, with Ōhashi Ryōsuke, editor and translator of *Dōgen, Shōbōgenzō: Ausgewählte Texte: Anders Philosophieren aus dem Zen.*

Peter FLUECKIGER is Professor of Japanese at Pomona College. He received his Ph.D. in East Asian Languages and Cultures from Columbia University. He has also been a research student at the University of Tokyo and a visiting researcher at International Christian University. His work focuses on the intersection of literary thought with political and ethical philosophy in eighteenth-century Japanese National Learning (kokugaku) and Confucianism. He is the author of *Imagining Harmony: Poetry, Empathy, and Community in Mid-Tokugawa Confucianism and Nativism* (Stanford University Press, 2011), as well as a number of articles, book chapters, and translations.

FUJITA Masakatsu is Emeritus Professor of Philosophy at the Graduate School of Advanced Integrated Studies in Human Survivability and the inaugural Chair of the Department of the History of Japanese Philosophy at Kyoto University. He received doctoral degrees from Bochum University and Kyoto University, and he is author of *Philosophie und Religion beim jungen Hegel; Gendai shisō toshite no Nishida Kitarō* [Nishida Kitarō as a Modern Thinker]; *Nishida Kitarō: Ikiru koto to tetsugaku* [Nishida Kitarō: Being Alive and Philosophy]; *Nishida Kitarō no shisaku sekai* [Nishida Kitarō's World of Thought]; *Tetsugaku no hinto* [Hints of Philosophy]; and *Nihon tetsugaku-shi* [The History of Japanese Philosophy]. He edited *Tanabe Hajime tetsugaku sen* [Selected Works of Tanabe Hajime's Philosophy]; and, with Kosaka Kunitsugu, the new edition of *Nishida Kitarō zenshū* [Complete Works of Nishida Kitarō]. His other edited volumes include *Nihon kindai shisō wo manabu hito no tame ni* [For Students of Modern Japanese Thought]; *Kyōto gakuha no tetsugaku* [The Philosophy of the Kyoto School]; *Higashiajia to tetsugaku* [East Asia and Philosophy]; *Shisō-kan no taiwa: Higashi ajia ni okeru tetsugaku no juyō to tenkai* [Dialogue Between Ways of Thinking: The Reception and Development of Philosophy in East Asia]; and, with Bret W. Davis, *Sekai no naka no Nihon no tetsugaku* [Japanese Philosophy in the World].

Chris GOTO-JONES was educated at Cambridge, Keiō, and Oxford University. He was Professor of Modern Japan Studies and Professor of Comparative Philosophy at Leiden University before becoming Dean of Humanities and Professor of Philosophy at the University of Victoria, where he is also Honorary Professor in Asian Studies at the University of British Columbia. He has published in the fields of ethics, philosophy of mind, and comparative political thought: *Political Philosophy in Japan: Nishida, the Kyoto School, and Co-Prosperity* (2005); *Re-Politicising the Kyoto School as Philosophy* (ed., 2008). Recent interests are in the intersections between performance, embodiment, ethics, and self-cultivation: *Conjuring Asia: Magic, Orientalism and the Making of the Modern World* (2016); *The Virtual Ninja Manifesto: Fighting Games, Martial Arts and Gamic Orientalism* (2016). In terms of popularizing publications, he is author of *A Very Short Introduction to Modern Japan* (2009), which has been translated into many languages worldwide.

Steven HEINE is Professor of Religious Studies and History and Director of Asian Studies at Florida International University. Previously he taught religious traditions of East Asia at Pennsylvania State University. He has published more than two dozen books on Zen Buddhism and Japanese religions, including *Existential and Ontological Dimensions of Time in Heidegger and Dōgen* (1985), *Dōgen and the Kōan Tradition* (1994), *Shifting Shape, Shaping Text* (1999), *The Kōan* (2000), *Opening a Mountain* (2001), *Did Dōgen Go To China?* (2006), *Zen Skin, Zen Marrow* (2008), *Sacred High City, Sacred Low City* (2011), *Like Cats and Dogs* (2013), *Dōgen: Textual and Historical Studies* (2014), and *From Chinese Chan to Japanese Zen* (2017). In 2007, he received the Order of the Rising Sun award bestowed by the government of Japan for a lifetime of service to Japanese cultural studies.

James W. HEISIG completed doctoral studies at Cambridge University in 1973 and subsequently lectured at graduate schools in Chicago and Mexico for several years before moving to Japan, where he has been a permanent fellow at the Nanzan Institute for Religion and Culture in Nagoya, Japan, since 1978. His books, translations, and edited collections, which have appeared in 12 languages, total more than 70 volumes. They include *El cuento detrás del cuento: Un ensayo sobre psique y mito*; *Imago Dei: A Study of C. G. Jung's Psychology of Religion*; *Philosophers of Nothingness: An Essay on the Kyoto School*; *Dialogues at One Inch Above the Ground*; *El gemelo de Jesús: Un alumbramiento al budismo*; *Nothingness and Desire: An East-West Philosophical Antiphony*; and *Much Ado About Nothingness: Essays on Nishida and Tanabe*. He is the general editor of the nineteen-volume series *Nanzan Studies in Religion and Culture* and *Essays in Japanese Philosophy*; co-editor of Nanzan Library of Asian Religion and Culture; an Italian series on Japanese philosophy, Tetsugaku; and a series of volumes on Korean Religions. Together with Thomas P. Kasulis and John C. Maraldo, he edited the comprehensive anthology *Japanese Philosophy: A Sourcebook*.

Dennis HIROTA is Professor of Shin Buddhist Studies, Emeritus, and senior research fellow at Ryukoku University, Kyoto. He is the Head Translator of *The Collected Works of Shinran* (1997) and has published books and articles in both Japanese and English on Japanese Pure Land Buddhist tradition, particularly the thought of Shinran and Ippen. He has served as Visiting Professor at the International Research Center for Japanese Studies, Kyoto (1996–1997) and Numata Visiting Professor of Buddhist Studies at Harvard Divinity School (1999, 2008). His books include *Asura's Harp: Engagement* *with Language as Buddhist Path* (2006), *Toward a Contemporary Understanding of Pure Land Buddhism* (2000), *Shinran: Shūkyō gengo no kakumeisha* [Shinran and Religious Language] (1998), and *No Abode: The Record of Ippen* (1986, 1997). He is co-author, with Ueda Yoshifumi, of *Shinran: An Introduction to His Thought* (1989) and has published on Buddhism in the aesthetic thought of Japan, including *Wind in the Pines: Classic Writings of the Way of Tea as a Buddhist Path* (1995). He is currently completing a book on the thought of Shinran in the light of Heidegger.

Victor Sōgen Hori is retired professor in the School of Religious Studies at McGill University. He received his doctoral degree in philosophy from Stanford University in 1976 and that same year was ordained a Zen monk in Kyoto. After devoting the next thirteen years to training at monasteries in Japan, he returned to the academic life in 1990. His publications include *Zen Sand: The Book of Capping Phrases for Kōan Practice* (2003), a translation of *The Ten Oxherding Pictures: Lectures by Yamada Mumon Roshi* (2004), and several articles on Zen Buddhism.

Iwasawa Tomoko is Professor of Comparative Religions at Reitaku University in Chiba, Japan. She received her MA and PhD in philosophy of religion from Boston University. Her publications include *Tama in Japanese Myth: A Hermeneutical Study of Ancient Japanese Divinity* (2011), "Transcendence and Immanence, West and East: A Case Study of Japanese Divinity" in *Existenz* (2018), and "Philosophical Faith as the Will to Communicate: Two Case Studies in Intercultural Understanding" in *Philosophical Faith and the Future of Humanity* (2012).

Leah Kalmanson is Associate Professor in the Department of Philosophy and Religion at Drake University. She received her PhD in philosophy from the University of Hawai'i at Mānoa. Her work in comparative philosophy has appeared in *Comparative and Continental Philosophy, Continental Philosophy Review, Hypatia, Journal of World Philosophies, Philosophy East and West,* and *Shofar: An Interdisciplinary Journal of Jewish Studies*. She is co-editor of collections including *Confucianism in Context* (with Wonsuk Chang, 2010), *Levinas and Asian Thought* (with Sarah Mattice and Frank Garrett, 2013), *Buddhist Responses to Globalization* (with James Mark Shields, 2014), *Ineffability: An Exercise in Comparative Philosophy of Religion* (with Tim Knepper, 2017), and *Comparative Studies in Asian and Latin American Philosophies* (with Stephanie Rivera Berruz, 2018). She currently serves as Assistant Editor at the *Journal of Japanese Philosophy* (SUNY).

Thomas P. Kasulis is University Distinguished Scholar and Professor Emeritus of Comparative Studies at the Ohio State University (OSU), where he has taught philosophy, religious studies, and East Asian studies. At OSU he has chaired the departments of Comparative Studies and of East Asian Languages and Literatures and has directed the Center for the Study of Religion. Former president of the Society for Asian and Comparative Philosophy and of the American Society for the Study of Religion, Kasulis has been a visiting professor at Harvard, the University of Chicago, and in Japan at both Ōsaka and Ōtani Universities. He has written dozens of scholarly articles on Japanese philosophers and religions, comparative philosophy, and the philosophy of religion. His books from the University of Hawai'i Press include *Zen Action/Zen Person* (1989); *Intimacy or Integrity: Philosophy and Cultural Difference* (2002) [based on the 1998 Gilbert Ryle Lectures]; *Shinto: The Way Home* (2004); the co-edited *Japanese Philosophy: A Sourcebook* (2011); and *Engaging Japanese Philosophy: A Short History* (2018). For SUNY Press, he coedited a three-volume series comparing Asian and Western ideas of self, coedited *The Recovery of Philosophy in America: Essays in Honor of John Edwin Smith* (1997), and edited (as well as co-translated) Yuasa Yasuo's *The Body: Toward an Eastern Mind–Body Theory* (1987).

Rikki KERSTEN is Dean of the School of Arts at Murdoch University in Western Australia. She has research interests in modern Japanese political thought and in contemporary Japanese foreign and security policy. She has a particular interest in the nexus between democracy and security in postwar Japanese political discourse and policy. She is the author of *Democracy in Postwar Japan: Maruyama Masao and the Search for Autonomy* (1996). Her recent publications include "Assumptions About Alliances: Australia, Japan and the Liberal International Order," in M. Heazle and A. O'Neill's *China's Rise and Australia-Japan-US relations* (2018), and "Contextualising Australia-Japan Security Cooperation: The Normative Framing of Japanese Security Policy" in the *Australian Journal of International Affairs* (2016).

KOBAYASHI Yasuo (born 1950 in Tokyo) is Emeritus Professor of Culture and Representation at the Graduate School of Arts and Sciences at the University of Tokyo, Komaba, and the Director of the University of Tokyo Center for Philosophy (UTCP). He graduated from the Department of French Studies at the University of Tokyo in 1974, and he completed his PhD in Semiotics under the direction of Claude Abastado at the University of Paris X Nanterre in 1981. He taught at the University of Electro-Communications in Chōfu starting in 1982, and he joined the faculty of the University of Tokyo, Komaba, in 1986. From 2001 to 2002, Professor Kobayashi served as a councilor at the University of Tokyo, and, in 2002, he received the Ordre de Palme Academique Chevalier from the Republic of France. From 2002 to 2017, he was Director of UTCP, under the auspices of the Twenty-First-Century and Global COE Programs of the Ministry of Education (Monkashō). Professor Kobayashi has published on a wide range of subjects. His publications include: *Hyōshō no kōgaku* [The Optics of Representation] (2003), *Chi no Odysseia* [The Odyssey of Savoir] (2009), *Rekishi no deconstruction* [The Deconstruction of History] (2010), and *Kokoro no aporia* [The Aporia of Kokoro] (2013). He has also translated a number of French authors, including Derrida, Levinas, and Duras.

John W. M. KRUMMEL is Associate Professor in the Department of Religious Studies at Hobart and William Smith Colleges in Geneva, New York. He has a PhD in Philosophy from the New School for Social Research and a PhD in Religion from Temple University. He is author of *Nishida Kitarō's Chiasmatic Chorology: Place of Dialectic, Dialectic of Place* (2015). His writings on topics such as Heidegger, Nishida, Reiner Schürmann, imagination, and Buddhist philosophy, among others, have appeared in a variety of philosophy journals and books. He is also the editor of *Contemporary Japanese Philosophy: A Reader* (forthcoming) and co-translator of and author of the introduction for *Place and Dialectic: Two Essays by Nishida Kitarō* (2011). He has translated other works from Japanese and German into English. He is Co-Editor for *Social Imaginaries*, Assistant Editor of *The Journal of Japanese Philosophy*, and the President of the International Association for Japanese Philosophy.

John C. Maraldo is Professor Emeritus of Philosophy and Distinguished Professor at the University of North Florida. He earned a Doctor of Philosophy degree from the University of Munich with a dissertation on *Der hermeneutische Zirkel: Untersuchungen zu Schleiermacher, Dilthey und Heidegger* (1974, 1984), and then spent several years in Japan studying Japanese philosophy and Zen Buddhism. He has been a guest professor at the University of Kyoto and the Catholic University in Leuven, and, in 2008–09, held the Roche Chair in Interreligious Research at Nanzan University, Nagoya, Japan. His interests include Japanese and comparative philosophy, phenomenology and hermeneutics, Buddhist notions of history and of practice, and the sense and significance of non-Western philosophy. He is the co-author of a translation and study of *Heidegger: The Piety of Thinking* (1976) and is co-editor of *Buddhism in the Modern World* (1976), *Rude Awakenings: Zen, the Kyoto School, & the Question of Nationalism* (1994), and *Japanese Philosophy: A Sourcebook* (2011). His volume of essays, *Japanese Philosophy in the Making 1: Crossing Paths with Nishida*, appeared with Chisokudō Publications in 2017.

Graham Mayeda is Associate Professor in the Faculty of Law, Common Law Section of the University of Ottawa, Canada. He completed his PhD on Watsuji Tetsurō, Kuki Shūzō, and Martin Heidegger at the University of Toronto. He has an interest in contemporary Japanese philosophy, phenomenological ethics, political philosophy, and legal philosophy. He is the author of *Time, Space, and Ethics in the Thought of Watsuji Tetsurō, Kuki Shūzō, and Martin Heidegger* (2006) as well as of numerous articles on law and on Japanese philosophy.

Erin McCarthy is Professor and Chair of the Philosophy Department at St. Lawrence University, where she has taught since 2000. She teaches Asian, feminist, continental, and comparative philosophies in the Philosophy Department, Gender and Sexuality Studies Program, and the Asian Studies Program. Author of the book *Ethics Embodied: Rethinking Selfhood through Continental, Japanese and Feminist Philosophies* (2010), her work has been published in several anthologies and journals in both French and English, and she regularly presents her scholarship both nationally and internationally. She was an inaugural recipient of the Frederick P. Lenz Foundation Residential Fellowship for Buddhist Studies and American Culture and Values at Naropa University in 2009. Dr. McCarthy sits on the editorial boards of the journals *Comparative and Continental Philosophy*, *The Journal of Japanese Philosophy*, *Body and Religion*, and she is Co-editor of the *ASIANetwork Exchange: A Journal for Asian Studies in the Liberal Arts*.

She has also served as Chair of the Board of Directors of ASIANetwork (a consortium of more than 170 North American colleges). In addition to her research in comparative feminist philosophy, she also writes on contemplative education.

Mara MILLER professor of philosophy and Japanese art and literature, teaches at the University of Hawai'i at Manoa and is a Visiting Scholar at their Center for Biographical Research. She is the author of *The Garden as an Art* (SUNY Press), *Terrible Knowledge* (reflections on the atomic bombings, forthcoming), and six dozen articles on feminist, Asian, and environmental philosophy; aesthetics; and selfhood, in *The Monist*, *Philosophy and Literature*, *The Journal of Aesthetics and Art Criticism*, and Oxford's *Encyclopedia of Aesthetics* and *Handbooks of World* and *Japanese Philosophy*. Miller was a fellow at the University of Canterbury, the Folger Library, and Rutgers University's Center for Historical Analysis. Her doctorate, in philosophy, is from Yale University.

MINOBE Hitoshi is Professor at Meiji University in Tokyo, Japan. He received his PhD from Kyoto University with a dissertation on Fichte after studying for two years in Wuppertal, Germany, on a DAAD scholarship. His research focuses on German Idealism and on the Kyoto School. He has published numerous articles in these areas, including "Shinichi Hisamatsu – Die Philosophie des Erwachens" (2004) and "Die Stellung des Seins bei Fichte, Schelling und Nishida" (2003), and he is the editor of *Hisamatsu Shin'ichi's Kaku no tetsugaku* [Philosophy of Awakening] (2002).

MORI Tetsurō is Professor of Philosophy and Religion at Kyoto Sangyo University in Japan. After studying at Kyoto University in Japan and Tübingen University in Germany, he was an assistant to Ueda Shizuteru at Kyoto University for three years before taking a position at Kyoto Sangyo University in 1990. His research focuses on German Idealism, especially Schelling; on Zen Buddhism; and on modern Japanese philosophy, especially Nishida Kitarō and Nishitani Keiji. His publications include numerous articles, the edited volume *Sekai-shi no riron: Kyōto-gakuha no rekishi tetsugaku ronkō* [Theories of World History: The Kyoto School's Treatises on the Philosophy of History] (2000), and the coedited volumes *Keiken to kotoba* [Experience and Language] (1995) and *Zen to Kyōto tetsugaku* [Zen and Kyoto Philosophy] (2006).

Shigenori NAGATOMO received a PhD in Philosophy from the University of Hawai'i in 1985, where he studied comparative philosophy focusing on Asian and European traditions. He has been interested in the mind–body problem, with a particular emphasis on Yogic, Buddhist (Zen), and Daoist meditation methods, and he supplements these with Jungian psychology and research on ki-energy. He is the co-author of *Science and Comparative Philosophy* (with David E. Shaner and Yuasa Yasuo, 1989), and author of *Attunement Through the Body* (1992), *A Philosophical Investigation of Miki Kiyoshi's Concept of Humanism* (1995), and *The Diamondsūtra's Logic of Not and a Critique of Katz's Contextualism: Toward a Non-dualist Philosophy* (2006). He has also translated many books, including Yuasa Yasuo's *The Body: Toward an Eastern Mind Body Theory* (with Thomas P. Kasulis, 1987); Yuasa Yasuo's *The Body, Self-Cultivation, and Ki-Energy* (with Monte Hull, 1993); Yuasa Yasuo's *Overcoming Modernity: Synchronicity and Image-Thinking* (with John Krummel, 2009); Nishida Kitarō's *Place and Dialectic: Two Essays of Nishida Kitarō* (with John Krummel, 2011); Hiroshi Motoyama's *The Buddha's Satori* (2010); and Hiroshi Motoyama's *Being and the Logic of Interactive Function* (with John Krummel, 2009). He has been teaching for thirty years in the department of religion at Temple University where he is Professor of Comparative Philosophy and East Asian Buddhism.

ŌHASHI Ryōsuke is a contemporary Japanese philosopher. After graduating from Kyoto University, he went on to receive his doctorate and later Habilitation from universities in Germany. He held several professorships in Japan, most recently at Osaka University and Ryūkoku University, and he was a guest professor at universities and institutes in Europe (in Germany: Cologne, Hildesheim, Hannover, Tübingen; in Austria: Vienna; in Switzerland: Basel). Currently, he is Director of the Japanese–German Cultural Institute in Kyoto. He is the author of numerous books on philosophy and aesthetics, including *Ekstase und Gelassenheit: Zu Schelling und Heidegger* (in Japanese and German); *Zeitlichkeitsanalyse der Hegelschen Logik: Zur Idee einer Phänomenologie des Ortes* (in Japanese and German); *Kire: Das "Schöne" in Japan* (in Japanese and German); *Nihon-tekina mono, Yōroppa-tekina mono* [Things Japanese and Things European]; *Nishida-tetsugaku no sekai* [The World of Nishida Philosophy]; and *Japan im interkulturellen Dialog*; and *Phänomenologie der Compassion* (in Japanese and German). He is a co-editor of the Japanese complete works of Heidegger and is editor of such works as *Kyōtogakuha no shisō* [The Thought of the Kyoto School], *Die Philosophie der Kyōto-Schule* and *Heidegger wo manabu hito no tame ni* [For Students of the Philosophy of Heidegger].

Graham PARKES was born and raised in Glasgow, Scotland. He taught Asian and comparative philosophy for thirty years at the University of Hawai'i before moving to University College Cork, in Ireland, where he founded the Irish Institute for Japanese Studies. He is now Professorial Research Fellow at the University of Vienna. Among his publications are *Heidegger and Asian Thought* (ed., 1987), *Nietzsche and Asian Thought* (ed., 1991), *Composing the Soul: Reaches of Nietzsche's Psychology* (1994), and translations (with commentaries) of Detlet Lauf's *Secret Doctrines of the Tibetan Books of the Dead* (1974), Nishitani Keiji's *The Self-Overcoming of Nihilism* (1990), Reinhard May's *Heidegger's Hidden Sources: East-Asian Influences on His Work* (1996), François Berthier's *Reading Zen in the Rocks: The Japanese Dry Landscape Garden* (2000), and Friedrich Nietzsche's *Thus Spoke Zarathustra* (2005). He is also the author of more than a hundred journal articles and book chapters on topics in Chinese, Japanese, and European philosophies. He recently is finished a book with the working title *Coping with Global Warming: A Philosophical Approach to Ousting the Obstructors, Reforming Democracy, Cooperating with China, and Enjoying Better Lives.*

Paul L. SWANSON is a Permanent Research Fellow at the Nanzan Institute for Religion and Culture in Nagoya, Japan, where he is editor of the *Japanese Journal of Religious Studies*. He has a PhD in Buddhist Studies from the University of Wisconsin–Madison. His major fields of research include Shugendō, a Japanese mountain religion, and the textual and philosophical study of the Buddhist Tiantai/Tendai tradition. His publications include *Foundations of T'ien-t'ai Philosophy* (1989); *Pruning the Bodhi Tree* (co-edited with Jamie Hubbard, 1997); *Nanzan Guide to Japanese Religions* (co-edited with Clark Chilson, 2006); an annotated translation of the complete *Mohe zhiguan* (Jpn. Makashikan), one of the most important texts of the Tiantai tradition (2017); and *In Search of Clarity: Essays on Translation and Tiantai Buddhism* (2018).

TANI Tōru was born in 1954. He studied Philosophy at Keiō University in Tokyo and completed a doctoral course there in 1985. He was awarded a PhD from Tōhoku University in 1998. He taught Philosophy at various colleges and universities in Japan and has been Professor of Philosophy at Ritsumeikan University in Kyoto since 2003. His main research interests are the phenomenology of nature and the phenomenology of interculturality. Major books in Japanese are *Ishiki no shizen* [Physis of Consciousness] (1998), a systematic and encyclopedic study of Husserl's phenomenology and its subsequent development; and *Kore ga genshōgaku da* [This Is Phenomenology] (2002), an introduction to phenomenology. He is also the author of numerous articles in foreign languages, including English-language papers such as "Beyond Individuality, This Side of Totality," in *Phenomenological Approaches to Moral Philosophy* (2002), and "Reading and Rereading the *Ideen* in Japan," in *Husserl's Ideen* (2013). He is the founder and present leader of the Research Center for Intercultural Phenomenology at Ritsumeikan University (2008~).

TERAO Kazuyoshi was born in Osaka, Japan, and graduated from Waseda University in Tokyo. He received a doctoral degree in theology from Nanzan University in Nagoya. He currently holds a post as Professor at St. Catherine University in Matsuyama, and he is a research associate of the Nanzan Institute for Religion and Culture in Nagoya. He has authored numerous academic essays on theology, religion, and philosophical anthropology, among them "The Hermeneutical Advance from Existential Communion to the Consolation of the Spirit of the Dead: Tanabe Hajime and Kimura Hisao" (in Japanese, 2007).

John A. TUCKER is Professor of History at East Carolina University. He completed his doctoral degree at Columbia University under the direction of Wm. Theodore de Bary, with guidance from Wing-tsit Chan and faculty and students participating in the Columbia Neo-Confucian seminar. Earlier, he completed two MA's at the University of Hawai'i, one in Asian philosophy and the other in Asian history. He has conducted research at the Institute for Research in the Humanities at Kyoto University, the Institute for Advanced Studies in the Humanities and Social Sciences at Taiwan National University, and the Institute for Religion and Culture at Nanzan University. He is author of *Itō Jinsai's Gomō jigi and the Philosophical Definition of Early-Modern Japan* (1998), *Ogyū Sorai's Philosophical Masterworks: The Bendō and Benmei* (2006), and editor of the four-volume anthology, *Critical Readings in Japanese Confucianism* (2013). He is coeditor of another volume, with Huang Chun-chieh of National Taiwan University, *Dao Companion to Japanese Confucian Philosophy*, published by Springer.

Mark UNNO is Associate Professor of East Asian Buddhism, Department of Religious Studies, University of Oregon. His research specializations include Classical Japanese Buddhism, Comparative Religion, and Buddhism and Psychotherapy. He is the author of *Shingon Refractions: Myōe and the Mantra of Light* (2004) and editor of *Buddhism and Psychotherapy Across Cultures* (2006), as well as of articles on Zen and Pure Land Buddhism, comparative religious thought, and Buddhism and depth psychology. He is the recipient of the Thomas F. Herman Faculty Achievement Award for Distinguished Teaching.

YAMASAKI Kōji is Associate Professor at the Center for Ainu and Indigenous Studies, Hokkaido University. He is co-curator of the 2009 exhibit Teetasinrit Tekrukoci: The Handprints of Our Ancestors: Ainu Artifacts Housed at Hokkaido University and co-author of the catalogue. He specializes in cultural anthropology and museum studies. His research in collaboration with the Ainu people focuses on modern meanings and uses of museum materials.

Michiko YUSA, PhD, is Professor of Japanese Thought and Intercultural Philosophy at Western Washington University. She received a BA from International Christian University in Tokyo and a PhD from the University of California at Santa Barbara with a dissertation entitled *Persona Originalis: Jinkaku and Personne According to the Philosophies of Nishida Kitarō and Jacques Maritain* (1983), written under the guidance of Raimon Panikkar. Her field of research extends from Nishida's philosophy to aesthetics and women's spirituality, and, more recently, female philosophers. Her other interests include music and the study of languages. Among her numerous publications are *Zen and Philosophy: An Intellectual Biography of Nishida Kitarō* (2002), *Denki Nishida Kitarō* [A Biography of Nishida Kitarō] (1998), *Basic Kanji* (1989), and *The Bloomsbury Research Handbook of Contemporary Japanese Philosophy* (ed., 2017). Her *Japanese Religious Traditions* (2002) has been translated into several languages.

Brook ZIPORYN is Professor of Chinese Philosophy, Religion and Comparative Thought at the Divinity School of the University of Chicago. His research interests focus on Chinese Buddhism, especially the Tiantai tradition, as well as philosophical traditions within Classical Confucian and Daoist thought. His publications include *Evil and/or/as the Good: Omnicentrism, Intersubjectivity and Value Paradox in Tiantai Buddhist Thought* (2000), *The Penumbra Unbound: The Neo-Taoist Philosophy of Guo Xiang* (2003), *Being and Ambiguity: Philosophical Experiments with Tiantai Buddhism* (2004), *Zhuangzi: The Essential Writings, with Selections from Traditional Commentaries* (2009), *Ironies of Oneness and Difference* (2011), *Beyond Oneness and Difference* (2013), and *Emptiness and Omnipresence: An Essential Introduction to Tiantai Buddhism* (2016).

INTRODUCTION

What Is Japanese Philosophy?

BRET W. DAVIS

WHAT is Japanese philosophy? This is not just a difficult question to answer; the very question itself is questionable. Each part of it calls for careful consideration. First of all, what do we mean by asking: *What is* Japanese philosophy? Second, what is *philosophy*? That is to say, what is the genus "philosophy" of which Japanese philosophy would be a specific subset? And, finally, what makes a philosophy specifically *Japanese*? Our question thus contains in fact three questions: What does it mean to ask, *what is* Japanese philosophy? What is Japanese *philosophy*? And, what is *Japanese* philosophy? This introduction aims to provide an orientation to the subject matter of this volume by critically reflecting on these matters. It begins with the "What is" aspect, then proceeds to take up the "philosophy" aspect, and ends by addressing the "Japanese" aspect of our leading question. Yet, while our inquiry will advance roughly in this order, and while it will be helpful to bear in mind the distinctions between the three aspects of the question, we will also find them to be interconnected, such that we will often need to meander back and forth between them.

WHAT DOES IT MEAN TO ASK: *WHAT IS JAPANESE PHILOSOPHY?*

What does it mean to ask after the definition of something, or to define something, such as Japanese philosophy? Is there a single thing called Japanese philosophy with a definite and definable essence? Is there one universally and eternally correct answer to this question? What ontology and view of language are implied in the assumption that there is a definite substance or fixed referent corresponding to such a locution? Are we already "speaking Greek" when we ask "what is" (*ti esti*) Japanese philosophy and look for a substantial essence (*ousia*) underlying all of its accidental manifestations? Is there a Platonic Form of Japanese philosophy?

Or, does "Japanese philosophy" mean many different things to many different people, such that we should ask rather: What are the various complementary and/or competing conceptions of Japanese philosophy? Following Wittgenstein's suggestion that "the meaning of a word is its use in the language,"[1] perhaps we should look at how this phrase has been used and describe the "family resemblances" among these usages. Yet, should we in fact merely seek to *describe*, from the presumed standpoint of an external observer, what "Japanese philosophy" means for Anglophones and what "*Nihon tetsugaku*" (日本哲学)[2] means for Japanophones? Or, should we normatively *prescribe* as well as neutrally describe what is meant by these terms? I will argue that all of us who use the terms "philosophy," "*tetsugaku*" (哲学), "Japanese philosophy," and "*Nihon tetsugaku*" are more or less implicated in the ongoing historical process of semantic reiteration and revision of what they mean and that we should attempt to contribute to this process in a critically self-aware manner.[3]

In order to make informed contributions to this process of semantic reiteration and transformation, we need to be cognizant of how these terms have been and are being used by others. Let us therefore begin with some dictionary definitions that reflect how "philosophy" and "*tetsugaku*" are currently used in English and in Japanese. Webster's online dictionary gives us three definitions for philosophy: "[1] the study of ideas about knowledge, truth, the nature and meaning of life, etc.; [2] a particular set of ideas about knowledge, truth, the nature and meaning of life, etc.; [3] a set of ideas about how to do something or how to live."[4] Although "*tetsugaku*" is not used in colloquial Japanese as frequently as is "philosophy" in colloquial English, these definitions roughly correspond to some contemporary Japanese usages of *tetsugaku*. A standard

---

[1] Ludwig Wittgenstein, *Philosophical Investigations*, 3rd ed., trans. G. E. Anscombe (New York: Macmillan, 1958), 20 (§43). Wittgenstein writes elsewhere that what he calls "the craving for generality," or the "tendency to look for something in common to all the entities which we commonly subsume under a general term"—which he associates with "our preoccupation with the method of science" and with "the contemptuous attitude toward the particular case"—"is the real source of metaphysics, and leads the philosopher into complete darkness" (*The Blue and Brown Books* [New York: Harper & Row, 1958], 17–18). I agree that an overgrown philosophical desire for general definitions can lead us to overgeneralize and stereotype and, at worst, to posit suprahistorical, homogenizing, and exclusivistic essences. Of course, in order to understand the "particular case" at all we cannot entirely avoid generalizations, and yet we can use such generalizations as "Japanese philosophy" to refer to the ongoing historical development of a group of texts, ways of thinking, and ideas that share overlapping and mobile "family resemblances" (rather than some eternal Platonic Form).

[2] Rather than "*Nihon tetsugaku*" (日本哲学), some scholars write "*Nihon no tetsugaku*" (日本の哲学). Linguistically, the difference is merely that the possessive implied in the former expression is made explicit in the latter. I have not found there to be any consistent semantic differences in usage.

[3] The philosopher, too, is ineluctably a participant, and so I do not agree with Wittgenstein that "Philosophy really *is* 'purely descriptive'" (*The Blue and Brown Books*, 18). Description is always more or less redescription, and it usually entails some degree of implicit prescription.

[4] At http://www.merriam-webster.com/dictionary/philosophy, accessed August 2, 2016.

Japanese dictionary (*Kōjien*) gives two definitions of *tetsugaku*.[5] The *second* definition given reads (in translation): "In popular usage, [*tetsugaku* means] a view of life and the world acquired by means of accumulated experience and so forth. Also, [it means] a fundamental way of thinking that pervades the entirety of something." The *first* definition given, however, begins by stating that *tetsugaku* is a translation of the English word "philosophy," which itself derives from the ancient Greek word *philosophia*, meaning "love of wisdom." It goes on to explain how, in the late nineteenth century, Nishi Amane translated this Western term first as *kitetsugaku* (希哲学, literally "the study that aspires to wisdom"), then in abbreviated form as *tetsugaku* ("the study of wisdom").[6] Next, the entry briefly describes the Western history of the term, which ostensibly at first had a more encompassing sense of intellectual inquiry, yet in modern times came to have the more specific sense of an inquiry into the foundations of the sciences and the fundamental principles of the world and human life. In fact, *philosophia* already had this sense for Aristotle. In any case, the *Kōjien*'s definition of *tetsugaku* is generally consistent with

---

[5] *Kōjien*, sixth edition (Tokyo: Iwanami, 2008), under "tetsugaku." All translations in this chapter are my own unless otherwise noted.

[6] Asakura Tomomi argues that the abbreviation of *kitetsugaku* to *tetsugaku* was unfortunate since, in effect, the "philo" was eliminated from "philosophy" and with it the implicit critique of the sophists (who purported to already *possess* wisdom) and the sense of philosophy as a "*desire* for wisdom" (*aichi* 愛知 or *chie no aikyū* 知恵の愛求) (Asakura 2014, 31–40; see also Kida 2014, 44). One could argue, however, that the *ki* (aspiration) was somewhat redundant insofar as *gaku* (study) expresses the action of learning something one does not already possess. In any case, Asakura understands "philosophy" above all in the modern Western sense initiated by Francis Bacon and established by Descartes; namely, as a "foundationalism" or establishment of rational grounds that criticizes rather than relies on tradition, to which he contrasts, borrowing Hegel's phrase, "Asian stagnation" (Asakura 2014, 3–29). Asakura agrees with Maruyama Masao that "dialectics," in the sense of a genuine dialogue and debate between schools of thought, is lacking in East Asian traditions and even still in post-Meiji Japan (Maruyama 1961; Asakura 2004, 37–40). If they are right, the difference between philosophy and *tetsugaku* would reiterate to some extent the (Western conception of the) difference between Western philosophy as an unending quest for a wisdom that one does not yet possess, a quest that proceeds by way of critical debate, and the so-called *wisdom traditions* of non-Western cultures in which sages pass along to disciples the wisdom they have received and realized. To be sure, we can acknowledge there to be some element of truth to this otherwise all too stereotypical contrast. Like an Upanishadic sage, a Confucian scholar and a Zen master do indeed purport to have attained a wisdom that they can help others in turn attain. And yet, their writings often evince a vibrant spirit of critical inquiry along with didactic generosity. And there have been great debates both within and between schools of the Buddhists and Confucian traditions. (Asakura does allow for the innovativeness of Mahāyāna Buddhism and in particular the fact that, in Zen, the student is called on to surpass the master [Asakura 2014, 28].) Conversely, we find "schools" and "traditions" throughout the history of Western philosophy, and it is not only the scholastics who have based much of their thinking on that of their predecessors. Moreover, do not philosophers in the Western tradition, starting with Socrates (see Davis 2013a, 65–66), claim to have attained some knowledge or wisdom ("human wisdom" if not "absolute knowing") that they can convey to others, as opposed to simply pursuing what they don't already possess or "carrying out their education in public" (as Hegel quipped of Schelling)? Indeed, Hegel's self-professed intent was to "help bring philosophy closer to the form of science, to the goal where it can lay aside the title 'love of knowing' and be actual knowing" (*Hegel's Phenomenology of Spirit*, trans. A. V. Miller [New York: Oxford University Press, 1977], 3). One cannot, after all, simply contrast the professed "seeking of wisdom" of Western philosophers with the purported "possessing of wisdom" of Eastern sages.

Webster's definition of "philosophy," other than the fact that the English dictionary did not find it necessary to indicate, much less forefront, the cultural-historical origin of the term.

This similarity and difference is unsurprising given that the term *tetsugaku* is a neologism in Japanese, fashioned by Nishi Amane as a translation of the Western term "philosophy."[7] Yet, the fact that Nishi and others also used Neo-Confucian terms such as "*rigaku*" (理学, literally "the study of principles") to translate "philosophy" raises the crucial and still controversial question: Was there "philosophy" in Japan prior to the importation of Western philosophy by Nishi and others in the late nineteenth century? One of modern Japan's foremost Indologists and comparative philosophers, Nakamura Hajime, rejects the prevalent tendency to assume that "Japanese philosophy ... started with the Meiji Restoration [in 1868] and with the entrance of Western culture into Japan." He claims that "even prior to the Meiji Restoration there was a long history of philosophy in Japan."[8]

However, the answer to the question of whether there was "philosophy" in premodern (in the sense of pre-Meiji[9]) Japan depends, of course, on what definition of philosophy one is using. H. Gene Blocker and Christopher L. Starling distinguish between broad and narrow senses of philosophy. What they call the broad sense of philosophy is an implicit or explicit "expression of cultural values," such that every culture has its philosophy or philosophies. Yet while this sense of the term corresponds to Webster's second and third definitions, it does not correspond to the "narrow" or "technical" sense used by academic philosophers today, defined by Blocker and Starling as "a critical, reflective, rational, and systematic approach to questions of a very general interest."[10] Did the

---

[7] See Chapter 15 in this volume. On Nishi Amane's pivotal contributions to the introduction of Western philosophy to Japan and his translation of key concepts into Japanese, see also Havens 1970; Piovesana 1997, 1–18; Ōhashi 1992, 35–52; and Steineck 2014.

[8] Nakamura 2002, v.

[9] By "pre-Meiji" and "post-Meiji" I mean, respectively, before and after the Meiji Restoration in 1868. In this introduction, I sometimes use the terms "premodern" and "modern" to denote "pre-Meiji" and "post-Meiji," respectively. While for convenience sake and following convention I also sometimes use the adjective "traditional" to mean pre-Meiji, it should be borne in mind that modern or post-Meiji discourses are also part of the ongoing development of Japanese tradition. We also need to keep in mind that Japan has in many respects developed its own "alternative modernity" in response to its encounter with Western modernity. On the philosophical relevance of the contemporary discourse of "multiple modernities," see Elberfeld 2017a, 224–72. While the periods of Japanese history are traditionally designated by either the capitals where the emperor or shōgun resided or by the reign of individual emperors, modern Japanese historians also use the following periodization: "ancient ages" (*kodai* 古代) = Asuka (593–710), Nara (710–784), and Heian (784–1185) periods; "middle ages" (*chūsei* 中世) = Kamakura (1185–1333) and Muromachi (1336–1573) periods; "early modern ages" (*kinsei* 近世) = Azuchi-Momoyama (1573–1603) and Edo (or Tokugawa) (1603–1868) periods; "modern age" (*kindai* 近代) = Meiji (1868–1912), Taishō (1912–1926), and early Shōwa (1926–1945) periods; and "present age" (*gendai* 現代) = post-war Shōwa (1945–1989), Heisei (1989–2019), and now Reiwa (2019–) periods. Maruyama Masao has argued that a number of thinkers (Ogyū Sorai in particular) in the Edo period initiated a "modernization" that paved the way for Westernization (Maruyama 1974; discussed in Chapter 33 in this volume).

[10] Blocker and Starling 2001, 16.

Japanese tradition contain anything corresponding to this narrow sense of philosophy before importing it from the West in the late nineteenth century?

Nakae Chōmin famously declared in 1901 that, "from ancient times to the present, there has been no philosophy in Japan."[11] However, Blocker and Starling reject Nakae's claim for the following reasons. First of all, Nakae, who in Japan was dubbed "the Eastern Rousseau," had a particular conception of philosophy—an atheistic materialism with a sociopolitical Enlightenment agenda—and this "specific ideal of philosophy leads him to an assertion that, taken as a general statement, is false."[12] Second, they reject the criticism made by Nakae and others that Japanese intellectuals over the centuries have only "imported and imitated" first Chinese and, more recently, Western philosophies. They point out that the Japanese adoption of foreign philosophies has always involved critical and creative adaptation. "Japanese Buddhism and Japanese Confucianism differed from their antecedents on account of the initial selection of what to assimilate, specific local interpretations of what was imported, and all the subsequent refashioning of these philosophies within Japan itself."[13]

The same can be said of modern Japanese receptions of Western philosophies. In fact, the same can be said of "German philosophy" or "French philosophy," which do not have autochthonous origins but rather developed through their reception of ancient Greek and medieval Latin philosophy. For that matter, the same could be said of ancient Greek philosophy. As Nietzsche wrote: "Nothing would be sillier than to claim an autochthonous development for the Greeks. On the contrary, they invariably absorbed other living cultures," especially, he acknowledges, those of "the Orient." If we admire the achievements of the Greeks, it should be because—as Nietzsche puts it—"they knew how to pick up the spear and throw it onward from the point where others had left it."[14] This statement by Nietzsche on the Greeks can be compared to a statement made in 1938 by Nishida Kitarō, whom many consider to be the most important progenitor of modern Japanese philosophy. Nishida claimed that Japan has a "musical culture," without fixed form, whose excellence lies, not in creating from scratch, but rather in "taking in foreign cultures as they are and transforming itself" by way of synthesis.[15]

A few years earlier, in 1935, Watsuji Tetsurō wrote of the "layers" (jūsō 重層) of Japanese culture. According to him, it is precisely the contemporaneous coexistence

---

[11] *Nakae Chōmin zenshū* (Tokyo: Iwanami, 1983–1986), vol. 10, p. 155. Nishi Amane also complained that there was little in Japan and China that could be called "philosophy" in the Western sense; namely, critical reason unadulterated by religion (see Fujita 2000b, 6–7). Yet Nishi also often noted the similarities between Chinese and Japanese Confucian thought and Western philosophy, and he called for a development of the former by bringing it into contact with the latter (see Steineck 2014).

[12] Blocker and Starling 2001, 186. As Takeuchi Seiichi points out, however, even though Nakae Chōmin did take Western philosophy as a model, he understood philosophy in terms of independent rational thinking and so was sharply critical of Meiji philosophers who wanted to simply import Western philosophy without learning to think on their own (Takeuchi 2015, 177–78).

[13] Blocker and Starling 2001, 186.

[14] Friedrich Nietzsche, *Philosophy in the Tragic Age of the Greeks*, trans. Marianne Cowan (Washington DC: Regnery Publishing, 1962), 29–30.

[15] Nishida 1987–89, 14: 416–17. See Davis 2011, 34–5.

of such cultural layers, rather than an exclusive replacement of one with another, that characterizes Japanese culture.[16] In his introduction to *Nihon shisōshi gairon* (An Overview of the History of Japanese Thought), without mentioning Nishida or Watsuji, Ishida Ichirō also speaks of the "amazing power of cultural synthesis" possessed by the Japanese. He lists, as the three distinctive characteristics of the history of Japanese thought (1) its preservation of traditional culture; (2) its attempt to compensate for its relatively late development by appropriating foreign cultures, namely first from China and more recently from Europe and the United States; and (3) the formation of a "two layered structure" wherein the older traditional culture is the platform on which the newer foreign culture is introduced and wherein they mutually transform one another such that a distinctive culture is produced.[17] Whereas Watsuji stresses the coexistence of cultural layers, Ishida stresses their mutual transformation. One can easily find examples of both just by walking down the street in Japan and seeing, next door to one another, a Family Mart *konbini* (a very Japanese version of an American convenience store) and a Shintō shrine that hasn't changed much over the centuries.

Japan is certainly not the only culture to have developed by means of cultural synthesis. All European cultures, for example, developed on the basis of a hybridization of radically different Greco-Roman and Judeo-Christian cultures, as well as through the subsequent blending of this synthesis with the indigenous cultures of what became the various European nations. Japan does differ, relatively speaking, with regard to the extent to which earlier and later historical layers are allowed to contemporaneously coexist. This has meant, for example, that some modern Japanese philosophers, in particular some associated with the Kyoto School, could commute between modern Western style universities and still very traditional Zen monasteries. And this commuting has indeed allowed them to develop a distinctive type of Japanese philosophy of religion.[18]

Just as Japanese monastics and scholars in the past not only *adopted* but also *adapted* Chinese Buddhism, Confucianism, and Daoism, Japanese academics in modern times set about critically and creatively appropriating currents of Western philosophy. Kūkai, Dōgen, Shinran, and Nichiren were especially innovative Buddhist thinkers,[19] just as Hayashi Razan, Yamaga Sokō, Itō Jinsai, and Ogyū Sorai developed significantly new interpretations of Confucianism.[20] And all the modern Japanese philosophers treated in this volume were highly original thinkers, most of whom critically confronted as well as creatively drew on aspects of both Western and Eastern traditions of philosophical thinking.

[16] Watsuji 2002, 239–46.

[17] Ishida 1963, 3–4.

[18] See Davis 2004 and 2006a. In comments on a draft of this introduction, Rolf Elberfeld rightly pointed out that it would be fruitful to compare—and contrast—this "commuting" with that of Christian theologians and philosophers today who think out of a movement back and forth between the practices that take place in traditional ecclesiastical institutions and modern universities.

[19] In this volume, on Kūkai, see Chapter 5; on Dōgen, see Chapters 8 and 9; and on Shinran, see Chapter 6. On Nichiren, see Heisig, Kasulis, Maraldo 2011, 86–91; Kasulis 2018, 173–77.

[20] See Chapters 12 and 13 in this volume.

Blocker and Starling make another crucial point with regard to what they call the broader and more narrow or technical senses of philosophy:

> It is true that philosophy in the technical sense sets out to critique the ambient world view, that is, what we may call philosophy in the broad sense, pressing for justification, pointing out contradictions, demanding clarity in vague areas, and so on. But in doing so it also reflects the cultural preconceptions of its exponents and in that sense tends to sustain an already existing set of beliefs, values, and attitudes. Thus, philosophy in the narrow sense both critiques and reflects philosophy in the broad sense.[21]

In other words, philosophy as an *expression* of cultural values and philosophy as a *critique* of cultural values are inevitably intertwined. Not only are they "rarely independent," as Blocker and Starling state; they are, in fact, at all times interdependent. Such, I contend, is the inexorable condition of human philosophizing, which always takes place *between* particular and universal as *a particular approach to universality*.

WAS THERE ANY PHILOSOPHY IN PREMODERN JAPAN?

We have seen that, rather than looking for an eternally unchanging and homogeneous essence of Japanese philosophy, we need to ask: What was, is, and will be Japanese philosophy, and for whom? To begin with, in order to understand the contested meanings that the term "Japanese philosophy" has today, and in order to decide how we should contribute to the meanings it will have in the future, we need to ask: What was Japanese philosophy in the past? Yet, as we have seen, even this question is vexed, insofar as the existence of philosophy in Japan prior to its importation from the West has been frequently denied by Japanese as well as Western scholars.

In order to delve deeper into the question of whether there was any philosophy in premodern Japan—and, if so, what kind—let us very briefly sketch the intellectual history of Japan. Although the prehistory of human culture on the Japanese archipelago goes back thousands of years, recorded Japanese intellectual history begins with the importation of writing, along with Buddhism, Confucianism, and Daoism, from China (sometimes via Korea) beginning in the fifth century CE. Buddhism became the dominant philosophical and religious tradition by the Nara (710–784) period and stayed that way for roughly a millennium during the Heian (784–1185), Kamakura (1185–1333), and Muromachi (1336–1573) periods. From the seventeenth to the mid-nineteenth centuries, during the Azuchi-Momoyama (1573–1603) and Edo or Tokugawa (1603–1868) periods, Confucian and Neo-Confucian schools of philosophy flourished with the support of

---

[21] Blocker and Starling 2001, 11.

the shogunate government. In reaction to the prominence of the "foreign" traditions of Buddhism and Confucianism, a renaissance study of ancient indigenous poetry and Shintō texts arose in the late eighteenth century. A century later, this National Learning or Native Studies (*kokugaku* 国学) exerted an influence on the rise of the ethnocentric ultranationalism that culminated in the Pacific War.

The first Christian missionaries, led by the Jesuit Francis Xavier, arrived in Japan in 1549. However, starting in 1587, this proselytizing and politically unsettling foreign faith was strictly forbidden by the shogunate government. By 1640, Christian converts had been brutally forced to apostatize or go underground as missionaries were expelled along with most merchants and other Westerners.[22] For more than two centuries, Japan isolated itself in response to the threat of the kind of Western imperialism and colonization that was in fact taking place in the Philippines and elsewhere in Asia and around the world at the time. Only a small Dutch trading post on an artificial island near Nagasaki was kept open, allowing some Japanese scholars of "Dutch learning" (*rangaku* 蘭学) to study Western developments in such areas as technology and medicine during this period of relative "national isolation" (*sakoku* 鎖国). This isolationist period lasted until American warships forced the reopening of Japan to trade and international relations in 1853/54. In the wake of this event, the country of Japan, which had been divided into various fiefdoms, was reunited and the emperor was officially restored to power.

With the Meiji Restoration in 1868 began the "modern" history of Japan, during which Japan strove to build a modern nation-state capable of withstanding the threat of imperialism and colonization and, indeed, capable of competing with Western nations and itself becoming an imperial power and colonizer of Korea, Taiwan, and Manchuria (in northeast China) leading up to and continuing during the Pacific War. Together with its political travails during this modern period, including the caesura of defeat in 1945, the attempt that began in the Meiji period (1868–1912)—namely, to adopt and adapt the fruits of Western culture while at the same time preserving and developing its own traditional culture—pervades the history of modern Japan in the Taishō (1912–1926), Shōwa (1926–1989), and Heisei (1989–2019) periods.

With this historical sketch in mind, let us return to the question of philosophy. In the Meiji period, Japanese intellectuals ardently imported and appropriated Western fields of academic inquiry, including "philosophy." Since the end of the nineteenth century, after an initial interest in French and British empiricism, positivism, utilitarianism, and liberal political philosophy had subsided, German philosophy from Kant through Heidegger became, and at least until recently has remained, the most influential Western tradition of philosophy in Japan.[23] According to Itō Tomonobu, the standard view in

---

[22] On Christian missions in Japan and elsewhere in Asia in the context of Western imperialism, see K. M. Panikkar, *Asia and Western Dominance* (New York: Collier Books, 1969), 279–97. Today, only about 1% of the Japanese population is Christian (compared with, for example, with around 30% of South Koreans). Nevertheless, Christian thinkers have played a relatively prominent role in the intellectual history of modern Japan (see Chapter 26 in this volume).

[23] On the early reception of Western philosophy in Japan, see Chapter 15 in this volume; Piovesana 1997; Kasulis 2018, 403–441.

Japan is that, "with regard to philosophy [*tetsugaku*], Japanese modernity begins with the reception of Western philosophy."[24] There may be reason to question the validity of this view, but it is unquestionably the standard—and usually unquestioned—view today in Japan. This was not always the case. During the Meiji period, significant debates took place over the question of whether the traditional (i.e., pre-Meiji) intellectual traditions of Japan could be considered to be "philosophy" (*tetsugaku*). Some Japanese philosophers in the Meiji period adopted Nakae Chōmin's view that "from ancient times to the present, there has been no philosophy in Japan," while others, most notably Inoue Tetsurō and Inoue Enryō, reconstructively presented Confucianism and Buddhism as "philosophy."[25]

While the former view has prevailed in Japan, the latter has prevailed in China and Korea. The Chinese and Koreans adopted the translations of Western terms into sinographs (*kanji* 漢字) made by Japanese scholars in the late nineteenth and early twentieth centuries, including Nishi's translation of "philosophy" as 哲学 (*tetsugaku*), pronounced "*zhéxué*" in Mandarin and "*cheolhak*" in Korean. Yet, in Chinese and Korean, *zhéxué* and *cheolhak* are used still today to refer not only to Western and Western-influenced discourses but also to traditional schools of Buddhist, Confucian, and Daoist thought. "Chinese philosophy" (*Zhōngguó zhéxué* 中国哲学) is a mainstay of many philosophy departments and publications in mainland China, including Hong Kong, as well as in Taiwan and Singapore. The situation is similar in Korea, where the philosophy department at Seoul National University teaches "Oriental philosophy" alongside "Western philosophy," and where the phrase "Korean philosophy" (*Hanguk cheolhak* 韓國哲學) is used mainly to refer to traditional Confucian and Buddhist thought.[26] (Analogous to the cases of China and Korea, in India, certain discourses of traditions such as Hinduism and Buddhism are referred to as "philosophy" and are studied alongside Western ones in most philosophy departments.[27])

In contrast not only to the uses of the "same term" in China and Korea, but also to the manner in which pre-Meiji discourses are often included in the category of "Japanese philosophy" in Europe and the United States, in contemporary Japan, *tetsugaku* is mainly used to refer to Western philosophy and to post-Meiji academic discourses in Japan that engage with the texts and ideas of Western philosophy. In contrast

---

[24] Itō 1990, 112. Itō goes on to note, however, that the first time "philosophy" (*fuirosofuia* フィロソフィア) appears in a Japanese text is 1591, in the context of a discussion of Christian theology, and that there are other precedents leading up to Nishi's importation and translation of the concept.

[25] See Chapters 12, 13, and 15 in this volume.

[26] See Back and Ivanhoe 2017. In fact, in sharp contrast to the situation in Japan, Jin Park is having to work to have more attention paid to *modern* figures under the rubric of "Korean philosophy" (see her chapter in Back and Ivanhoe 2017, and also Park 2017).

[27] According to Arun Iyer, a philosophy professor at the Indian Institute of Technology Bombay, "most philosophy curricula in major Indian universities contain an Indian component comprised of the schools of Hindu philosophy (*aastika* schools) and those of non-Hindu philosophy (the *naastika* Buddhist, Jaina, and Carvaka). Very few Indian universities neglect the teaching of Indian philosophy" (email correspondence, May 3, 2018).

to many books published in English, German, and other Western languages with "Japanese Philosophy" or some such locution in their titles that treat both traditional (pre-Meiji) and modern (post-Meiji) discourses,[28] books published in Japanese with "*Nihon tetsugaku*" (Japanese philosophy) in their titles generally treat only post-Meiji discourses.[29]

A telling example of the still Eurocentric conception of "philosophy" in Japan is the fact that in a 2010 issue of the journal *Nihon no tetsugaku* (Japanese Philosophy) devoted to the theme "What is philosophy?" (*Tetsugaku to wa nanika*), all five essays addressing the theme assume an Occidental definition of "philosophy" (*tetsugaku*).[30] This journal is associated with the Department of the History of Japanese Philosophy at Kyoto University, which was created in 1995 as the first and still only one of its kind in Japan. The departmental website states: "The department makes as its primary focus of research the formation and development of Post-Meiji period Japanese Philosophy, within which Japanese thinkers encountered and deeply engaged Western Philosophy."[31] Although it also goes on to say "The department . . . also recognizes the great importance that should be attributed to the connection between the East-Asian tradition and Japanese Philosophy," traditional East-Asian thought is notably not referred to as "philosophy." As one of the first three students in the doctoral program of this department, I was in fact able to take seminars on Dōgen's *Shōbōgenzō* as well as on modern Japanese philosophers who explicitly draw on traditional Japanese, Chinese, and Buddhist texts.

[28] See Paul 1993; Pörtner and Heise 1995; Brüll 1993; González Valles 2000; Blocker and Starling 2001; Nakamura 2002; Heisig, Kasulis, and Maraldo 2011; Steineck, Weber, Lange, and Gassmann 2018. French scholars tend to be more conservative and Eurocentric, if not indeed Euromonopolistic, in their use of the term "*philosophie*." Even M. Dalissier, S. Nagai, and Y. Sugimura—while expressing great appreciation for the "incredible richness" of traditional premodern Japanese "*pensée*," and while devoting much of their introduction and a fourth of their anthology to what they call an "*archéologie de la pensée japonaise*"—follow the Japanese and French tendency to use "*philosophie*" and "*tetsugaku*" in the "strict sense" to refer only to discourses of the Western tradition and of non-Western peoples like the modern Japanese who have appropriated that tradition. To be sure, they are careful to point out that, while "philosophy" is a Western term, the act of philosophizing itself transcends the fixtures of any tradition; yet they suggest that the modern Japanese had to learn this manner of philosophical tradition-transcending from the West (Dalissier, Nagai, and Sugimura 2013, 13–17). Nevertheless, when they speak of it in terms of a "gesture of infinite emptying of the self" (*geste infini d'évidement de soi*), an East Asian Buddhist influence in their understanding of "Japanese philosophy" is implied, and indeed they cite in this context a work by the contemporary Pure Land Buddhist philosopher Hase Shōtō (16). One Italian author argues that the term "*filosofia giapponese*" should be applied to premodern as well as modern Japanese discourses (Arena 2008), whereas another hesitates to apply it to pre-Meiji discourses, writing: "While in a certain sense it is true that there was no 'philosophy' [in Japan] before the second half of the 19th century, it is also true that philosophy-*tetsugaku* was not born out of nothing but arose in relation to something that was already there": namely, traditional Japanese thought (Forzani 2006, 19; I thank Raquel Bouso García for information on these two Italian sources).

[29] See Tsunetoshi 1998; Tanaka 2000; Kumano 2009; Higaki 2015; Fujita 2018; and my own coedited Fujita and Davis 2005.

[30] *Nihon no tetsugaku*, vol. 11 (2010).

[31] At https://www.bun.kyoto-u.ac.jp/japanese_philosophy/jp-aboutus_en/, accessed on October 3, 2018.

Yet, in my experience, the term *tetsugaku* was generally applied only to Western philosophy and its modern appropriations in places such as Japan and was generally not applied to pre-Meiji "thought" (*shisō* 思想) and "religion" (*shūkyō* 宗教)—even though, as I would annoyingly remind my colleagues, these terms are also translations of Western concepts and categories that should not be uncritically applied to pre-Meiji discourses.

In philosophy departments at Japanese universities, mainly what is taught is the history and contemporary discourses of Western philosophy. As in Western countries, Japanese and other Asian traditions of "thought" are generally studied in other departments.[32] As in the West, in Japan what one typically means by "philosophy" (*tetsugaku*) is first and foremost "Western philosophy" (*seiyōtetsugaku* 西洋哲学).[33]

[32] Kyoto University used to have a department of the History of Indian Philosophy (*Indo-tetsugaku-shi* インド哲学史) and still does have a department of the History of Chinese Philosophy (*Chūgoku-tetsugaku-shi* 中国哲学史), although both of these are housed in the school of Philological and Cultural Studies rather than in that of Thought and Cultural Studies, which houses the departments of Philosophy, the History of Western Philosophy, and the History of Japanese Philosophy. In my experience, the relative lack of communication between these small departments inhibits cross-fertilization as well as critical discussion of topics such as the definitions of "philosophy" and "*tetsugaku*." The University of Tokyo Center for Philosophy has two specialists of "Chinese philosophy" on its faculty (Nakajima Takahiro and Ishii Tsuyoshi), yet the main Department of Philosophy at the University of Tokyo focuses exclusively on Western philosophy (including specialists in "the history of Western philosophy" but none in non-Western—including Japanese—philosophical traditions). Separate departments exist at the University of Tokyo for "Chinese Thought and Culture" (which until 1990 was called "Chinese Philosophy") and "Indian Philosophy and Buddhist Studies." "The History of Japanese Thought" (*Nihon-shisō-shi* 日本思想史) is a major field of study in Japan, and the books devoted to it could fill many bookcases. Those books tend to include a wide range of discourses on "literature," "art," "politics," and "religion," and tend to focus more on pre-Meiji material but also include at least a final section on modern discourses, including "philosophy [*tetsugaku*]" (see Ishida 1963; Imai and Ozawa 1979; Sagara 1984; and Karube and Kataoka 2008). Some Japanese scholars do refer to "Daoist philosophy" and "Buddhist philosophy." See, for example, Ōhama Akira, *Rōshi no tetsugaku* [The Philosophy of Laozi] (Tokyō: Keisō Shobō, 1962) and *Sōshi no tetsugaku* [The Philosophy of Zhuangzi] (Tokyō: Keisō Shobō, 1966), and, more recently, Takemura Makio, *Zen no tetsugaku* [The Philosophy of Zen] (Tokyo: Chūsekisha, 2002) and *Tetsugaku toshite no Bukkyō* [Buddhism as Philosophy] (Tokyo: Kōdansha, 2009). Also see Kopf 2019.

[33] There are, of course, exceptions in the West as well as in Japan. Prior to the restriction of "philosophy" to the Western tradition in the late eighteenth century (see Park 2013; Bernasconi 1997 and 2003; Wimmer 2017), many Enlightenment thinkers looked to China, and Romantic thinkers to India, for "philosophies" that could serve as what J. J. Clarke calls a "corrective mirror" for self-critique (Clarke 1997, 37–70). Of course, as Clarke recognizes, even though much of the Orientalism directed at East Asia—as opposed to the Orientalism directed at the Near and Middle East that was the primary focus of Edward Said's landmark *Orientalism* (New York: Vintage, 1978)—has praised rather than denigrated its object, it has by no means been free of distortions and questionable motivations (see Davis 2009, 15–17). In the twentieth century, Jaspers spoke of there being "three independent origins" of philosophy during what he called the "axial age" (800–200 BCE) in China, India, and Greece (Jaspers 1976, 37, 135–6). In his *The Great Philosophers,* he put Buddha, Confucius, Laozi, and Nāgārjuna on par with foundational Western figures (*Die Großen Philosophen* [Munich: Piper, 1957]). Yet even Jaspers betrays an all too familiar lack of familiarity and thus appreciation for the rigor and depth of those Asian traditions when he writes: "As thus far accessible to us in translations and interpretations, Chinese and Indian philosophy seem far inferior to Western philosophy in scope, in development, and in inspiring formulations.... Only in Western philosophy do we find the clear distinctions, the precise formulations of problems, the scientific orientation, the thorough discussions, the sustained thought, which to us are indispensable" (Karl Jaspers, *Way to Wisdom: An Introduction to Philosophy,* trans. Ralph Manheim [New Haven: Yale

Sueki Fumihiko notes that, while the terms "Indian philosophy" (*Indo-tetsugaku* インド哲学) and "Chinese philosophy" (*Chūgoku-tetsugaku* 中国哲学) have been used in Japan, the "model" by which they are interpreted has been Western philosophy. Moreover, he notes that the trend lately has been to speak more "loosely" of "Indian thought" (*Indo-shisō* インド思想) and "Chinese thought" (*Chūgoku-shisō* 中国思想).[34] In any case, Sueki agrees with the consensus in Japan that it is better to speak of pre-Meiji discourses in terms of a "history of thought" rather than a "history of philosophy," arguing that *tetsugaku* begins in Japan through the creative appropriation of Western philosophy by Meiji scholars and that one significant difference between "*tetsugaku*" and "philosophy" is that the former is informed by Asian and in particular Japanese traditions as well as by Western traditions.[35] Although this is a partially compelling way of thinking about post-Meiji Japanese *tetsugaku*, insofar as it allows us to mark continuities with as well as the departures from both Western philosophy and pre-Meiji "thought," there is a wide variety of degrees in which the discourses of *tetsugaku* are "informed by Asian and in particular Japanese traditions" (later, I will draw a broad distinction between "Japanese philosophy" and "philosophy in Japan").

While distinguishing between "philosophy in the narrow sense" and a more general sense of "thought" can sometimes be useful, it strikes me as problematic that, while scholars often note the Western and specifically Greek origins of "philosophy," they do

University Press, 1954], 190–1). Surely Jaspers could not have made such remarks about Chinese and Indian philosophy had he read the literature now available; for example: Radhakrishnan and Moore 1957; Chan 1963; Graham 1989; Carr and Mahalingham 1997; Ivanhoe and Van Norden 2005; Garfield and Edelglass 2009; and Emmanuel 2013. And if he could have read some of the monographs and anthologies now available on "world philosophies" (Deutsch and Bontekoe 1997; Smart 1999; Garfield and Edelglass 2011), he would have needed to take into consideration current discussions regarding African and Latin American philosophy. Of course, if one looks for strict parallels to Western philosophy in other traditions, what one finds will appear second rate at best. Whereas the Indian philosophical tradition bears many resemblances to the Western tradition, the East Asian traditions pose greater challenges to a Westerner's or a Westernized non-Westerner's sense of the methods as well as the content of the philosophical endeavor. Clarke notes that some continental as well as analytic philosophers in the twentieth century have not been as closed-minded as their colleagues about the potential contributions of non-Western traditions. He quotes Merleau-Ponty as writing: "Western philosophy can learn [from India and China] to rediscover the relationship to being, and to estimate the possibilities we have shut ourselves off from in becoming 'Westerners,' and perhaps reopen them" (Clarke 1997, 114). And Clarke quotes Nozick as writing: "The treatment for philosophical parochialism, as for parochialism of other sorts, is to come to know alternatives . . . . There may even be ways of catapulting oneself, at least temporarily, into different philosophical perspectives, e.g. from Eastern thought" (114).

[34] Sueki 2012, 10. Kida Gen expresses a discomfort with the terms "Chinese philosophy" and "Indian philosophy," as well as "Japanese philosophy," insofar as he views these as part of the legacy of colonialism; that is, as the projection of a Western concept ("philosophy") on non-Western ways of thinking (Kida 2014, 45–6). Most Indian, Chinese, and Korean scholars do not share Japanese scholars' discomfort with the application of either the term "philosophy" or its translations to their traditions of thought, preferring to *appropriate and modify* rather than disown the concept. Min Ou Yang even argues that the neologism used to translate "philosophy," *zhéxué*, need not mean the same thing as "philosophy" does in the West ("There Is No Need for Zhongguo Zhexue to Be Philosophy," *Asian Philosophy* 22:3 [2012]: 199–223).

[35] Sueki 2012, 11–13. See also Fujita 2018, 1, 13.

not attend to the fact that "thought" (translated as *shisō*), too, is originally a Western concept. The problem here is that it is a concept often applied more "loosely" to discourses that are viewed as lacking the "rigor" of "philosophy proper" or "philosophy in the strict sense." For example, although one might have expected Derrida's "deconstruction" of the "ethnocentric metaphysics" of Western "logocentrism"[36] to enable and encourage an interest in and appreciation of non-Western traditions,[37] at a meeting in China Derrida himself repeated—with a reference to Hegel's claims regarding the Greek origins of philosophy proper—the trope that "China does not have any philosophy, only thought."[38] In response to his perturbed hosts, Derrida went on to clarify that what he meant was that "Philosophy is related to some sort of particular history, some languages, and some ancient Greek invention . . . . It is something of European form." Like Heidegger, we could say, Derrida is particularizing rather than universalizing Western philosophy. Nevertheless, in the "only thought" of his initial remark is ironically iterated an ignorant and arrogant claim that is often implicitly or explicitly made by the "ethnocentric metaphysics of logocentrism" that he himself seeks to deconstruct. The claim is that: From within my discourse of "philosophy" I can understand your discourse of "thought" (*pensée*) and rank it beneath my own; but your discourse has neither a name for, nor the capacity to understand, mine.[39]

Derrida's remark would not have been as unwelcome in Japan. While an increasing number (even if perhaps still a minority) of Western philosophers have begun to recognize some traditional non-Western discourses as "philosophy," the trend appears to be moving even further in the opposite direction in Japan: the terms "Indian philosophy" and "Chinese philosophy" are progressively being replaced by "Indian thought" and "Chinese thought."[40] Even when traditional Indian, Chinese, and Japanese schools of thought have been treated as *specific* areas of philosophical inquiry defined—that

[36] Jacques Derrida, *Of Grammatology*, translated by Gayatri Chakravorty Spivak (Baltimore: The Johns Hopkins University Press, 1976), 79.

[37] See Davis 2013a, 74–5; *Buddhisms and Deconstructions*, edited by Jin Park (Lanham, MD: Rowman and Littlefield, 2006).

[38] Du Xiaozhen and Zhang Ning, *Delida zai Zhongguo jiangyanlu* [Lectures by Derrida in China] (Beijing: Zhongyang Bianyi, 2002), 139, cited in Carine Defoort and Ge Zhaoguang, "Editors' Introduction," *Contemporary Chinese Thought* 37: 1 (Fall 2005): 3 and 9n14. See also Asakura 2014, v; Van Norden 2017, 25.

[39] Derrida was presumable implying that the Chinese tradition never constructed what needs to be deconstructed, given his stated appreciation for the "largely nonphonetic scripts like Chinese or Japanese" as testifying to "a powerful movement of civilization developing outside of all logocentrism" (*Of Grammatology*, 90). Yet Derrida's appreciation was apparently not strong enough for him to ever learn much more about these languages and their purportedly non-logocentric traditions. For a critique of Derrida's Orientalism, see Jin Suh Jirn, "A Sort of European Hallucination: On Derrida's 'Chinese Prejudice,'" *Situations* 8:2 (2015): 67–83. Karatani Kōjin argues that what Derrida calls "phonologocentrism" is not exclusively found in the Western tradition since something akin to it can be found in Japan, most explicitly in the phonocentric nationalism of the scholars of National Learning. See Karatani Kōjin, "Nationalism and *Écriture*," in Heisig, Kasulis, Maraldo 2011, 1093–9.

[40] Although Asakura's book is written in a spirit of protest against that idea that "there is no philosophy in East Asia," his main intent is to argue that the post-Meiji Kyoto School along with the contemporaneous New Confucianism of Xiong Shili and Mou Zongsan are exemplars of "East Asian

is to say, delimited—by their cultural-religious-linguistic moorings, when one speaks of "pure philosophy" (*junsui tetsugaku* 純粋哲学) in Japan, one means philosophy as it originated in ancient Greece and is practiced in the modern West as well as in modernized/Westernized countries, such as Japan, into which these sources and methods have been imported. Writing in 1969 for a then controversial collection entitled *Nihon no tetsugaku* (Japanese Philosophy), Hashimoto Mineo unequivocally asserts that "philosophy" originated in Greece and was imported to Japan in the Meiji period. While he acknowledges that "philosophy" can mean a "worldview" or "view of life," insofar as it means "logical scholarly knowledge," he claims that " 'thought' first becomes 'philosophy' by means of 'logic' or 'method' and the intent to formulate a 'system.' " And, Hashimoto goes on to say, "we must clearly acknowledge that the Japanese first attained philosophy as a scholarly discipline starting in the Meiji period." "Theorists who claim that pre-Meiji Buddhism and Confucianism are philosophy," he avers, "are ignoring or slighting the logical and scholarly aspect of philosophy."[41] Although not uncontested, this view—namely, the view that "philosophy" is a universal discourse that originated and matured in the West and was first imported to Japan in the Meiji period, a view that, as we have seen, was first expressed in Japan more than a half-century earlier by Nakae Chōmin—has prevailed.

Fujita Masakatsu suggests that the main reason Japanese scholars from Nakae Chōmin to present times have preferred to speak of pre-Meiji Japanese "thought" (*shisō*) rather than "philosophy" (*tetsugaku*) is that traditional Buddhist, Confucian, and other thinkers have been insufficiently critical vis-à-vis authoritative figures and texts in their respective traditions.[42] However, not only has this distinctively European Enlightenment devaluation of "authority" and "tradition"—a devaluation which, we should note, can and has been used to disqualify or marginalize much of Medieval Western philosophy as well—been called into question by hermeneutical philosophers such as Gadamer,[43] it is also not the case that there was no rigorous argumentation and debate in pre-Meiji Japan. Although they do not make a case for the existence of "philosophy" per se in pre-Meji Japan, a group of scholars of "the history of Japanese thought" led by Imai Jun and Ozawa Tomio do set out in their volume, *Nihon shisō ronsō-shi*

philosophy," and he in fact supports the recent trend in Japan to refer to the traditional discourses of Confucianism, Daoism, and Buddhism as "Chinese thought" (*Chūgoku shisō*) rather than as "Chinese philosophy" (*Chūgoku tetsugaku*) (Asakura 2014, 36). While this may indeed be the trend of the times, in response to papers I gave at the 2015 meeting of the Nishida Tetsugakkai (The Nishida Philosophy Association) in Kyoto and at a symposium in 2018 at the University of Tokyo Center for Philosophy on the theme of "Sekai tetsugaku toshite no Ajia shisō" (Asian Thought as World Philosophy), I found that at least some philosophers in Japan (albeit among the type that attend such meetings) are open to revisiting the question of the semantic and historical scope of "*Nihon tetsugaku*" (see Davis 2015, 2019*b*).

[41] Hashimoto Mineo, "Keijijōgaku o sasaeru genri" [The Principle Supporting Metaphysics], in Furuta and Ikimatsu 1972, 55–57.

[42] Fujita 2018, 11–12.

[43] See Hans-Georg Gadamer, *Truth and Method*, 2nd revised ed., translated by Joel Weinsheimer and Donald Marshall (New York: Crossroad Publishing, 1989), 277–285.

(A History of Disputations in Japanese Thought), to debunk the stereotype that the traditional Japanese stress on "harmony" (*wa* 和) prevented pre-Meiji thinkers from engaging in rigorous intellectual contestation and argumentation.[44]

Moreover, there are different ways of debating views, some more confrontational and some more conciliatory. Thomas Kasulis contrasts "refutation" as the dominant mode of argumentation in the Western tradition with what he calls argument by "relegation" wherein "the preferred theory accepts intact a new or opposing theory but only by consigning it to a subordinate position within an enlarged version of itself." "When we disagree in the relegation form of argument, I do not say that you are wrong. To the contrary, I agree that your position is correct although limited and I assert that my position includes yours in some way."[45] One finds examples of argument by relegation throughout the history of philosophical thinking in Japan, a classical pre-Meiji example being Kūkai's theory of the ten mindsets (*jūjūshinron* 十住心論), which attempts to take into account "all philosophies known in Japan at the time, showing each to be included in, but subordinate to, the mindset of Shingon Buddhism." A paradigmatic modern example is Nishida Kitarō's theory of enveloping "places" (*basho* 場所). By thinking of the ultimate place in East Asian Buddhist terms of "the place of absolute nothingness" (*zettai mu no basho* 絶対無の場所), Nishida sought to "absorb western philosophies, accepting their truth, but showing them to be partial when compared with his own theory."[46] Kasulis notes that relegation is not simply conciliatory, since "we will indeed be competing over which position can relegate which."[47] Nevertheless, argument by relegation does seek to accommodate different perspectives rather than vanquish them.

Indeed, we need to question the manner in which—and the metaphors through which—we tend to understand not only different forms of argumentation but the practice of philosophy more generally. Sarah Mattice has drawn attention to the tendency in the Western tradition to understand this practice in metaphorical terms of "combat" between adversaries who are seeking to defeat one another by winning an argument.[48] By contrast, A. S. Cua argues that disputation in early Chinese philosophy is "conducted in a context of common concern. It is a cooperative enterprise." Contentiousness (Ch. *zhēng* 爭) is avoided, not merely because it brings about disharmony, but also because it "betrays the lack of concern with a matter of common interest."[49] When philosophers converse in a competitive rather than a cooperative spirit, victory can take precedence over veracity. The aim of the enterprise is no longer that of reaching a better understanding of the shared matter at issue, but rather that of "defeating" one's "opponent" and

---

[44] Imai and Ozawa 1979, 18.

[45] Kasulis 2018, 38–39.

[46] Kasulis 2018, 38.

[47] Kasulis 2018, 39.

[48] Mattice 2014, chapter 2.

[49] A. S. Cua, *Ethical Argumentation: A Study in Hsun Tzu's Moral Epistemology* (Honolulu: University of Hawaii Press, 1985), 8; quoted in Mattice 2014, 26.

being recognized by one's peers as the "victor" of the debate. Drawing on Gadamer's hermeneutics, cognitive linguists, and feminist philosophy as well as on classical Chinese philosophy, Mattice explores the difference it would make if we understood the philosophical endeavor in metaphorical terms of "play" or "aesthetic experience" rather than "combat."[50] To be sure, the case can be made that the "agonistic" approach to philosophy bequeathed to us by the ancient Greeks has borne much fruit and continues to have its advantages. The point is not to deny this, but rather to suggest that it may be complemented (not simply replaced) by East Asian approaches to philosophical thinking and dialogue that sometimes (but by no means always) stress over contestation or accommodation over elimination.

Philosophers can and should continue to discuss methodological and metaphilosophical questions such as the advantages and disadvantages of various metaphorical conceptions of the discipline, the nature of logical analysis and rational argumentation and their relation to hermeneutical reflection and phenomenological description, and the proper roles (or lack thereof) to be played by authority, tradition, faith, meditative experience and so on in the practice of philosophy. But surely one should not *a priori* exclude others, or even entire traditions, from this discussion merely because one does not find useful, or is not used to, their views on such methodological and metaphilosophical questions. The proper method and understanding of philosophy should, after all, be matters of ongoing philosophical discussion. It would thus be better to argue that a discourse about the nature of the self, the world, or how the self should live in the world is "bad philosophy" than to *a priori* exclude it from consideration, that is, from participation in the ideally worldwide field of philosophical contestation and cooperation by claiming that it is "not philosophy."

Unfortunately, by confining the study of traditional Japanese discourses on recognizably philosophical topics to the separate discipline of "the history of Japanese thought" (*Nihon shisō-shi* 日本思想史), Japanese scholars and academic institutions have largely prevented these discourses from contributing to the (re)shaping of the discipline of "philosophy" (*tetsugaku*) in Japan. To this day, the discipline of philosophy in modern Japan remains oddly, yet obstinately, Eurocentric. Even when Japanese scholars do admit that other philosophical traditions exist in at least India and perhaps also in China, they tend to measure these by the yardstick of Western philosophy. A prominent example can be found in the entry for *tetsugaku* in the widely used *Iwanami tetsugaku shisō jiten* (Iwanami Dictionary of Philosophy and Thought), published in 1998. The entry is divided into two parts, the first dealing with Western philosophy and the second with Indian philosophy. There is no section for Chinese philosophy, much less one for Japanese philosophy. In the section on Western philosophy, Watanabe Jirō writes:

> Of course, if we understand philosophy in a broad sense that covers various thoughts pertaining to "views of life" (Lebensanschauungen) and a "worldviews"

---

[50] Mattice 2014, chapters 3 and 4.

(Weltanschauungen), then, to be sure, philosophy has been developed from ancient times in Asia too, namely in India, China, and Japan, in Buddhism, Confucianism, Daoism, and other currents of thought. However, in contemporary times it is undeniably the case that, in all countries of the world, the basic character of philosophy is understood to be the intellectual quest for a "logical foundation" of a unified and holistic view of life and the world, a quest that is carried out in the strictly logical manner that originated above all in Western philosophy.[51]

In the section on Indian philosophy, Marui Hiroshi introduces that tradition in terms of concepts that share some commonalities with, but also evince differences from, the Western term "philosophy" (namely *darśana* and *ānvīkṣikī*).

The Eurocentric, or indeed "Euromonopolistic" assumption adopted by most post-Meiji philosophers in Japan is that the Western philosophical tradition, and it alone, has transcended—or at least has self-consciously taken on what Husserl calls the "infinite task" of transcending—its cultural-linguistic particularities in its search for universal truth.[52] While other traditions of intellectual inquiry can be relegated to this or that particular field of "area studies," such as Asian Studies or Japanese Studies (*Japanologie*), Western philosophy is held to be a universal field of inquiry that cannot be confined to "Occidental Studies." Here, as elsewhere, Western arrogance problematically dovetails with Japanese deference. In philosophy departments, the self-colonizing mission of some Meiji intellectuals to "escape Asia and enter Europe" (*datsu-a nyū-ō* 脱亜入欧) lives on, and, along with it, the problem that Karl Löwith pointed out when he wrote that Japanese intellectuals "live as if on two levels [or floors, *Stockwerken*]: a lower, more fundamental one, on which they feel and think in a Japanese way; and a higher one, on which the European sciences [*Wissenschaften*] from Plato to Heidegger are lined up."[53] Unfortunately, during his five years in Japan, Löwith learned neither the Japanese language nor much about Japanese philosophy, and so, at the time, he knew little about the Kyoto School and other Japanese philosophers who were intensely working to bring Eastern and Western traditions into critical and creative dialogue with one another.

---

[51] Hiromatsu 1998, 1119.

[52] Edmund Husserl, *The Crisis of the European Sciences and Transcendental Phenomenology*, trans. David Carr (Evanston: Northwestern University Press, 1970), 289. It is for this reason that Husserl claims that, while all non-Western peoples are rightly motivated to Europeanize themselves, "we [Europeans], if we understand ourselves properly, would never Indianize ourselves" (275). For a recent defense of the idea that "European philosophy" is a tautology, see Gasché 2009. For critiques, see Perkins 2011; Davis 2017.

[53] Karl Löwith, *Martin Heidegger and European Nihilism*, ed. Richard Wolin, trans. Gary Steiner (New York: Columbia University Press, 1995), 232. For an account of and critical response to Löwith's critique, see Davis 2011.

DISLODGING PHILOSOPHICAL
EUROCENTRISM AND EUROMONOPOLISM

In the West, claims that there is no philosophy outside the Western tradition—claims, that is, of not just "philosophical Eurocentrism" but what I am calling "philosophical Euromonopolism"—more often than not simply betray an ignorance of other traditions.[54] Is Dignāga's and Dharmakīrti's Buddhist logic any less rigorous than that of Aristotle or Aquinas? Are Fazang's and Dōgen's ruminations on the nature of being and time any less profound than those of Augustine, Bergson, or Heidegger? Are the ethical debates in China and across East Asia among Confucians, Mohists, Daoists, and Buddhists any less thoughtful and thought-provoking than debates in the Western tradition among proponents of virtue ethics, divine command theory, natural law theory, consequentialism, and deontological ethics? There are no doubt vast differences between various methods of investigation and argumentation, but we can also find analogous differences among Western philosophers such as Heraclitus, Epictetus, Kierkegaard, and Wittgenstein—and yet we don't hesitate to call them all philosophers.

Most Japanese philosophers today continue to echo the more conservative Eurocentric and even Euromonopolistic views of their Western colleagues in refusing to refer to any pre-Meiji Japanese discourses as philosophy. In the West, on the other hand, and especially in the United States, the presumption that "pure philosophy" can be found only in the Western tradition and its modern offshoots is becoming increasingly untenable. This is the case not only among postcolonial critics and among the growing

---

[54] For example, in the introduction to one of his major works, Slavoj Žižek remarks, parenthetically and without argument, that philosophy is synonymous with Western philosophy (*Less than Nothing: Hegel and the Shadow of Dialectical Materialism* [London/New York: Verso, 2012], 5). Neither there nor in the ensuing thousand-plus pages of his text does he make any attempt to justify this exclusionary claim. This is especially odd given that the main opponent—the near enemy, so to speak—of his entire project is clearly Buddhism: "The only other school of thought that fully accepts the inexistence of the big Other is Buddhism" (129); and yet, "This book tries to demonstrate that the Freudian drive cannot be reduced to what Buddhism denounces as desire" (3). Although Žižek returns again and again to distinguish his position from that of his characterizations (or caricatures) of Buddhism (see, for example, 38, 108–10, 123, 129–35, 928, 945), his text and footnotes contain no references whatsoever to scholarly works on Buddhism, much less to any texts from the various Buddhist traditions themselves. The apex of Western philosophy for Žižek is Hegel, and Žižek inherits the Eurocentrism of his philosophical *Meister*. Yet Hegel at least bothered to keep up with the growing literature of his day on Buddhism and Hinduism and to keep his mind open enough such that "Reading the memoirs of [Henry Thomas] Colebrooke actually led this denigrator of things Indian to go back on his previous judgments in the course of the last years of his education in Berlin, from 1827 to 1831 . . . . For example, he wrote that speculative Indian thought, such as Colebrooke made known, 'completely deserves to be called philosophy [Sehr wohl den Namen Philosophie verdient]'!" Roger-Pol Droit, *The Cult of Nothingness: The Philosophers and the Buddha*, trans. David Streight and Pamela Vohnson (Chapel Hill: The University of North Carolina Press, 2003), 71; Droit is quoting Hegel's *Berliner Schriften*, in *Werke*, vol. 11 (Frankfurt: Suhrkamp, 1970), 144.

number of philosophers who are trained in (or even just sufficiently exposed to) a non-Western tradition, but more widely still among those continental philosophers who are trained in hermeneutical, deconstructive, or genealogical approaches to the Western tradition, as well as among those analytic philosophers who have discovered or been made to recognize the rigorous argumentation to be found in non-Western traditions. Philosophical Euromonopolism is untenable not only because a complete transcendence of cultural-linguistic particularities is unachievable in the West or anywhere else, but also because other traditions, in their own manners, have self-critically and rigorously pursued universal truths and not merely cultural self-expression or doctrinal systematization.

In a provocative article published in 2016 in *The New York Times*, Jay Garfield (a specialist in Buddhist and comparative philosophy) and Bryan W. Van Norden (a specialist in Chinese and comparative philosophy) point out that "The vast majority of philosophy departments in the United States offer courses only on philosophy derived from Europe and the English-speaking world" and that "The profession as a whole remains resolutely Eurocentric," perpetuating "the perception that philosophy departments are nothing but temples to the achievement of males of European descent." "Our recommendation is straightforward," they write: "Those who are comfortable with that perception should confirm it in good faith and defend it honestly . . . . We therefore suggest that any department that regularly offers courses only on Western philosophy should rename itself 'Department of European and American Philosophy.'"[55] In other words, if philosophy departments are going to continue to refuse to diversify and relegate the study of, for example, Asian philosophical traditions to Asian Studies departments, then Ameri-Eurocentric and especially Ameri-Euromonopolistic philosophy departments should confess to being themselves a field of area studies. This suggestion is certainly meant to be ironic since almost everyone would agree that to confine philosophy to a field of area studies would entail philosophical suicide. It would entail either an abandonment of the quest for universal truth (including the universal truth about which kinds of things are culturally relative), or the ignorant and arrogant claim that only the Western tradition has been interested in thoughtfully seeking truths whose validity transcends the boundaries of its own cultural tradition.

In response to an earlier reactionary retrenchment in the United States revolving around questions of diversifying our college curriculums, Martha Nussbaum argued against conservative critics of multicultural education such as Allan Bloom, who ignorantly asserted that "only in the Western nations, i.e. those influenced by Greek philosophy, is there some willingness to doubt the identification of the good with one's own way."[56] In fact, this claim is not just ironic but indeed oxymoronic, in that

---

[55] Garfield and Van Norden 2016. For Garfield's and Van Norden's responses to the many shockingly aggressive and ignorantly parochial criticisms they received, see Van Norden 2017, xi–xxi, 8–12. See also Davis 2019a.

[56] Allan Bloom, *The Closing of the American Mind* (New York: Simon and Shuster, 1987), 36; quoted in Martha Nussbaum, *Cultivating Humanity: A Classical Defense of Reform in Liberal Education* (Cambridge, MA: Harvard University Press, 1997), 132.

by identifying the "good" capacity for self-critique exclusively with the Western tradition, Bloom demonstrates precisely the closed-minded conceit he attributes to others. Nussbaum, herself a renowned scholar of Greek and Roman philosophy, recognizes that "One of the errors that a diverse education can dispel is the false belief that one's own tradition is the only one that is capable of self-criticism or universal aspiration."[57]

Decisions regarding the bestowal of the honorific monikers "philosophy" and "philosopher" seems to have more to do with cultural chauvinism and the politics of academia than they do with the rigor of reasons. Just as "the acceptance of continental thought in the English-speaking world has, for the most part, taken place outside of philosophy departments"[58] for reasons that have to do with how one particular tradition has tended to monopolize the way that the methods and canon of philosophy are defined vis-à-vis other academic disciplines, the treatment of non-Western philosophical traditions has often been relegated to fields such as Asian studies, religious studies, or comparative literature. Those who engage in the study and development of Japanese or other non-Western philosophies should respond to this situation, as Simon Critchley has done on behalf of continental philosophy, by calling for a robust philosophical pluralism that recognizes "that philosophy has more than one tradition and that assertions of philosophical exclusivism result, at best, in parochialism and, at worst, in intellectual imperialism."[59]

In his article "Philosophy's Paradoxical Parochialism: The Reinvention of Philosophy as Greek," Robert Bernasconi points out that the dogma that "philosophy proper" begins in ancient Greece and was developed solely in the Western tradition—a dogma that still largely shapes our philosophy departments, curricula, and conference programs—was actually first formulated in the late eighteenth century, when, rather abruptly, it replaced the long-standing recognition that the ancient Greeks had drawn on Egyptian and other Eastern sources and that different yet recognizably philosophical thinking can be found in India, China, and elsewhere. "What is one to make," Bernasconi provocatively asks, "of the apparent tension between the alleged universality of reason and the fact that its upholders are so intent on localizing its historical instantiation?" This is what he calls "the paradox of philosophy's parochialism."[60] Elsewhere he writes:

> It is necessary to expose the tension between, on the one hand, the belief in the universality of reason, truth, and philosophy, and, on the other hand, the parochialism, the specificity of the geographical location of the peoples whose philosophy is alone heard in the vast majority of European and North American philosophy departments.[61]

---

[57] Nussbaum, *Cultivating Humanity*, 11.
[58] Critchley 1998, 5.
[59] Critchley 1998, 14.
[60] Bernasconi 1997, 215–16.
[61] Bernasconi 1995, 252.

It could be added: Even were one to maintain that logic—understood as the set of fundamental rules or patterns of rational thinking and argumentation—is universal (which is itself a controversial claim that some philosophers in Japan and elsewhere would not uncritically accept[62]), it cannot be denied that the phenomenological and hermeneutical sources from which philosophical arguments necessarily draw their content are far more richly varied than those found in the West alone. Hence, the neglect or refusal to include non-Western cultures and traditions in the field of philosophy is an impoverishing omission as well as an illegitimate exclusion. At the very least, pre-Meiji "thought" should be understood as containing valuable sources for contemporary philosophical thinking not only in Japan, but in any country where philosophers are interested in moving beyond the Ameri-Eurocentric parochialism that ironically continues to plague our conceptions of philosophy as well as our philosophy departments, societies, and publication venues.

If I myself used and encouraged the use of "thought" (or the perhaps conciliatory term "philosophical thought") in places in this *Handbook*, it is because I wanted to include a wide range of "sources of philosophy" without committing to referring to all these sources—for example, the *Kojiki* (see Chapter 2) or Bashō's comments on poetry (see Chapter 33)—as themselves philosophy. Yet, while I wish to reopen rather than foreclose discussion of the distinction between "thought" and "philosophy," I am inclined to think that we should let at least some discourses of pre-Meiji "thought"—for example, those of Kūkai (see Chapter 5) or Ogyū Sorai (see Chapter 13)—challenge and potentially even contribute to a transformation of our definition of "philosophy."

---

[62] Gregor Paul is among those who insist that logic—beginning with the laws of identity, contradiction, and the excluded middle—is universal, the same in all languages, cultures, and philosophical traditions, including the Buddhist discourses on causality found in Japan (Paul 1993, 4–5, 16, 164–95). But some contemporary philosophers and logicians in fact dispute the principle of noncontradiction. Notable in this regard is the analytic philosopher Graham Priest, who often refers to Buddhist philosophy and especially to Nāgārjuna. See Graham Priest, J. C. Beall, and Bradley Armour-Garb (eds.), *The Law of Non-Contradiction: New Philosophical Essays* (New York: Oxford University Press, 2007); and Graham Priest, *Beyond the Limits of Thought* (New York: Oxford University Press, 2002), 249–70 (a chapter written with Jay Garfield). John Maraldo notes that Nishitani Keiji claims that "the classical law of contradiction abstracts from reality and cannot accommodate actual contradictions in it," his point being not so much about the laws of formal logic themselves but rather "that the restriction to atomic propositions in abstract, formal logic is precisely what precludes an ability to grasp concrete, continually transforming reality and the relationship between things and human selves" (Maraldo 1997, 814). Whether or not Nāgārjuna's deconstructive arguments, certain Zen kōans, Nishida's logic of "absolutely contradictory self-identity" (*zettai mujun-teki jiko-dōitsu* 絶対矛盾的自己同一; see Chapters 17 and 18 in this volume), or D. T. Suzuki's "logic of is/not" (*soku hi no ronri* 即非の論理; see Chapter 11) should be understood as violations of and/or replacements for the law of noncontradiction, and regardless of whether we can identify certain very basic rules of rational thought that are universally accepted, in any case, there surely remains much room for significant and even radical variation between philosophical traditions, analogous to the way in which basic facts of human biology such as the need to eat do not detract from the great variety among culinary customs and the basic facts of visual perception tell us next to nothing about the affective and symbolic significance of colors in different cultures.

At the same time, we need to be wary of patronizingly projecting our understanding of philosophy on others. Among the scholars who do speak of pre-Meiji "philosophy," some do so in the still Eurocentric manner of searching for parallels to Western philosophy.[63] One can, no doubt, abstract the elements of "logical reasoning" from out of the "religious" context of Buddhist texts. One can show that "even the Japanese" wrote many commentaries on the "pure philosophical reasoning" found in the Buddhist logic of causality (Sk. *hetu-vidyā*; Jp. *immyō* 因明). But one has already begged all the interesting questions when one begins by stating "it makes little sense to speak of philosophy if one does not distinguish it from mythos, religion, and theology," and when one preemptively defines "religion" as a "mythical" "belief in God."[64] If its concepts and practices are from the start reductively translated into modern Western ones, Japanese Buddhism cannot help but appear as a quasi-religion with a quasi-philosophy. In the present age of (the criticism of) Eurocentrism, it is surely "necessary to rethink the terms of 'religion,' 'philosophy,' as well as the relation of 'religion and philosophy,'"[65] especially when explicating a non-Western tradition.[66]

Some scholars attempt to overcome Ameri-Eurocentrism by looking for universal patterns of philosophical thinking in non-Western and Western traditions alike. Nakamura Hajime even claims that "Japanese philosophers grappled with the same kinds of problems as did philosophers in the West, in India, and in China, and the history of Japanese philosophical thought follows much the same course of development

[63] Gregor Paul claims that ancient "Japanese philosophers mostly raised the same questions as European philosophers, and also indicated numerous answers in the same directions as the solutions sought for in Europe" (Paul 1993, 14; see also 341). He does acknowledge that the "dharma theory" of Buddhism "is very different from almost all ontologies of the European tradition" (348); nevertheless, criticizing numerous Japanese and Western scholars, he refuses to acknowledge, for example, that there is any significant sense in which a "unity of nature and human" has been a distinguishing characteristic of Japanese culture (2, 345–7). See, however, Chapter 33 in this volume. And, in contrast to Paul's downplaying of the philosophical significance of linguistic differences (5, 15–17), see Chapter 32 in this volume.

[64] Paul 1993, 7.

[65] Mineshima Hideo (ed.), *Hikakushisōjiten* [Dictionary of Comparative Thought] (Tokyo: Tokyoshoseki, 2000), 235.

[66] I have elsewhere argued that it is the Buddhist requirement of extending rational discourses into holistic practices (especially meditation), rather than a "leap of faith" into the acceptance of a rationally groundless doctrine of revelation, that both challenges and is challenged by the presuppositions and limits of modern Western philosophy. And this challenge is reflected in the Kyoto School's "philosophies of religion" (*shūkyō-tetsugaku* 宗教哲学). See Davis 2004, 2006a. In his provocatively original account of the origins of Western philosophy in Ionia rather than Athens, Karatani Kōjin argues that, "As long as we follow the contemporary classifications that separate religion, philosophy, and science, we will never be able to recognize the world-historical leap in the sixth and fifth centuries BCE" carried out independently by Buddha, Laozi and Confucius, Ezekiel and other Jewish prophets in Babylonian exile, and the Ionian "Presocratic" thinkers (Karatani 2012, 10). In Karatani's Neo-Marxist interpretation, this leap entailed the emergence of a new mode of exchange (rather than, as Marx would have it, a new mode of production), one that recovers in a sublated form the freedom and equality found in the communities of nomadic hunter-gatherers that preceded the rigid systems of reciprocity found in agricultural clan societies (138).

as that found elsewhere."[67] By contrast, the chapters in the present volume frequently attend to the ways in which Japanese philosophies challenge our accustomed understanding of the methods and aims, as well as the content of philosophy, while, at the same time, they are careful to avoid a pendulum swing into a hardened relativism that precludes not only any quest for universal truth but even any meaningful dialogue and mutual exchange.

What Is Western Philosophy?

By questioning what it means to ask "*What is* Japanese philosophy?" we have come to see that it makes little sense to look for an unchanging universal essence and more sense to examine how the phrases "Japanese philosophy" and "*Nihon tetsugaku*" have been and are being used. This in turn enables us to participate in the determination of how these phrases will be used in the future. This enterprise can hardly be restricted to a narrow field of area studies since asking "What is Japanese *philosophy*?" requires that we address the broader question "What is philosophy?" Let us delve still deeper into this second aspect of our leading question.

When judgments are made concerning whether there was philosophy in pre-Meiji Japan or in other places and times, it is important to clarify exactly what definition of philosophy is being explicitly or implicitly presupposed. The simple answer is that it tends to be Western philosophy; that is, philosophy as it has been conceived of and practiced in the Western tradition. But is there a univocal definition of "philosophy" in the Western tradition? In fact, the meanings and methods of "philosophy" have been discussed, disputed, and repeatedly redefined throughout the Western tradition from the ancient Greeks to recent proponents of the contending contemporary schools of analytic, pragmatist, continental (including phenomenological, hermeneutical, deconstructive, Neo-Marxist, feminist, etc.), and other modes of philosophizing.[68]

---

[67] Nakamura 2002, v–vi. On Nakamura's universalistic approach to comparative philosophy, in contrast to Izutsu Toshihiko's more relativistic approach, see Chapter 25 in this volume. For other approaches to comparative and cross-cultural or intercultural philosophy, see Halbfass 1988; Larson and Deutsch 1988; Clarke 1997; Elberfeld 1999, 2004, 2017a; Mall 2000; Davis 2009; Ma and van Brakel 2016; Chakrabarti and Weber 2017.

[68] For an excellent anthology of texts that reveal the great diversity of definitions of "philosophy" throughout the Western tradition, see Elberfeld 2006. Elberfeld's anthology is meant to prepare us to engage with "texts from Asia and other non-European cultures" (243), a dialogical engagement that will challenge us to once again radically rethink the self-image of philosophy (248). At the end of his historical survey of the myriad ways in which "philosophy" has been defined in the Western tradition, Regenbogen (2014) argues that, while "intercultural philosophy" is a problematic concept insofar it presupposes rigid borders across which philosophical dialogue must be established, "it makes more sense to understand philosophizing as a *trans*cultural practice in heterogeneous cultures of knowledge . . . . The comparison between philosophical traditions is an everyday occurrence, since there is not 'the philosophy' but rather a pluralism worth maintaining of philosophical questions and arguments" (39). For a thought-provoking cross-cultural typology of philosophers, see Smith 2016. Smith concludes that "there are simply too many different and only partially overlapping activities to warrant any unified and all-purpose definition of 'philosophy' that will be of service across different times and places" (237).

Heidegger,[69] Deleuze and Guattari,[70] and other recent philosophers have written books and articles on the question "What is philosophy?" and, as with other central questions of philosophy, there is little agreement among them.[71] Some stress the clarity and rigor of

[69] In his *What Is Philosophy?* Heidegger claims that "Occidental-European philosophy is, in truth, a tautology.... the statement that philosophy is in its essence Greek says nothing more than that the Occident and Europe, and only these, are, in the innermost course of their history, originally 'philosophical'" (Heidegger 1956, 31, trans. mod.). However, it is important to note that Heidegger equates "philosophy" with Western "metaphysics," which he himself is trying to overcome or recover from. Hence, he speaks of "the end of philosophy and the task of thinking" and writes: "The thinking that is to come is no longer philosophy because it thinks more originally than metaphysics—a name identical to philosophy" (Martin Heidegger, *Pathmarks*, ed. William McNeill [Cambridge: Cambridge University Press, 1998], 276). And with regard to this non-metaphysical "thinking," Heidegger was intensely interested in dialogue with East-Asian traditions (see Davis 2013*b*; and Bret W. Davis, "East-West Dialogue After Heidegger," in *After Heidegger?*, edited by Gregory Fried and Richard Polt [London: Rowman & Littlefield, 2018], 335–45). Kida Gen argues that Heidegger belongs among a litany of Western thinkers since Nietzsche who have "relativized 'philosophy'" such that "philosophy" is no longer seen as a matter of "universal knowledge" that should be found everywhere (even if, factually, it is not found everywhere: hence the supposed superiority of the West over the Rest). "Philosophy," according to Kida, is a "particular manner of thinking" that is historically limited to the Western tradition that starts with the metaphysics of Plato (not the Presocratics), was taken up by Christianity, and continues to determine the modern scientific-techonological worldview (Kida 2014, 48–50). The other figure Kida draws heavily on is Merleau-Ponty, who, in one of his final writings, referred to his own thought—and indeed to the age of thought as a whole that began after Hegel—as that of "*anti-philosophie*" or "*non-philosophie*" (see Maurice Merleau-Ponty, "Philosophy and Non-Philosophy Since Hegel," trans. Hugh Silverman, in *Philosophy and Non-Philosophy Since Merleau-Ponty*, ed. Hugh Silverman [Evanston: Northwestern University Press, 1997]; see also Kida 2004, 2–3). However, Kida acknowledges that "philosophy" is for him an ambiguous word that can be used, on the one hand, in a more specific sense to mean the tradition of Western metaphysics from Plato to modern science and technology, and, on the other hand, in a more general sense that includes the project of "anti-philosophy" (*han-tetsugaku* 反哲学) that he suggests Japanese thinkers are well positioned to inherit from Heidegger, Merleau-Ponty, and other recent Western thinkers (Kida 2014, 51). Regardless of whether one agrees with the specifics of Kida's interpretation of the history of Western philosophy and anti-philosophy, it does seem that we are left with the ambiguity of "philosophy" understood, on the one hand, as synonymous with "Western philosophy" and, on the other hand, as an (initially Western) expression intended to encompass, and thus allow us to compare and contrast, critically reflect on, and creatively develop, the various manners of thinking about fundamental questions to be found in various cultures, languages, and traditions. The problem that Heidegger, Kida, and others alert us to is the perhaps unavoidable conflation of these two senses. Yet, even if such a conflation cannot simply be avoided, it can be critically reflected upon as we allow other ways of thinking to contribute to a multilateral dialogue on the methods and aims, as well as the content, of philosophy.

[70] In their *What Is Philosophy?* Deleuze and Guattari define philosophy as "the art of forming, inventing, and fabricating concepts" on a "plane of immanence" that is itself "like a section of chaos and acts like a sieve" (Deleuze and Guattari 1994, 2, 42). Although in places they repeat the Euromonopolistic trope that "philosophy" is essentially Greek in origin (43, 93), in a footnote they do seem to attribute to Dōgen "the supreme act of philosophy: not so much to think THE plane of immanence as to show that it is there, unthought in every plane [... as ...] that which cannot be thought and yet must be thought" (59–60). In this regard, they refer to "the Zen text of the Japanese monk Dôgen, which invokes the horizon or 'reserve' of event: *Shôbôgenzô*" (220*n*2). In another footnote, Deleuze and Guattari refer to a translation of texts by Dōgen and to an anthology of Japanese literature as manifestations of "Japanese philosophy," which they include—alongside Jewish, Islamic, Hindu, and Chinese philosophy—among the ways in which "Today, by freeing themselves from Hegelian or Heideggerian stereotypes, certain authors are taking up the specifically philosophical question on new foundations" (223*n*5).

[71] Carel and Gamez 2004 consists of eighteen essays by philosophers approaching the definition of philosophy from various analytic and continental perspectives. The editors claim that "The book

linguistic analysis and logical argumentation; others the depth and richness of phenomenological insight and description; others a hermeneutical, deconstructive, or genealogical engagement with traditional texts and their historical effects on the present; and still others the power dynamics or pragmatic potentials involved in all of the above. Often proponents of one approach to philosophy accuse proponents of other approaches of deviating from the true path of philosophy. Both analytic and continental philosophers tend to trace their lineages to Kant, yet they disagree on how to read him and on the sense of his philosophical legacy.[72] A range of Western philosophers in the latter half of the twentieth century claimed that philosophy had come to an end, while others claimed that it was undergoing a transformation; yet there was little agreement on precisely what either of these claims mean.[73] Perhaps we might at least be able to get proponents of the various streams and schools of Western philosophy to agree that it is today, more than ever, necessary for philosophers to address the meta-philosophical question regarding the nature of philosophy.[74]

portrays the nature and state of philosophy at the beginning of the twenty-first century, capturing its features on a particular day, at a specific age, as it appears in a certain historical context" (2). Evidently, no Asian traditions are woven into that historical context, for, even though it contains one illuminating chapter on African philosophy and another on Latin American philosophy, there are no chapters on Indian, Buddhist, Chinese, or Japanese philosophy (the existence of Chinese philosophy is merely acknowledged in passing in the introduction). For another noteworthy collection of essays by some contemporary representatives of the analytic, pragmatist, and continental streams of Western philosophy reflecting on the meta-philosophical question of the nature and aims of philosophy, see Ragland and Heidt 2001.

[72] For a remarkable attempt to explain the divergence of continental and analytic streams of philosophy in terms of a disagreement over how to move beyond the concept/intuition dualism of Kant's epistemology, and over how to inherit his four great questions (What can I know? What should I do? What may I hope? What is man?), see Cutrofello 2005, 1–29, 396–418. He argues that the division is not at the level of a philosophical controversy, but rather at the meta-philosophical level of "a controversy about the nature of philosophical controversies" (5, see also 402), which entails a "meta-antinomy about what it means to respond philosophically to antinomies" (413). He asks, with Russel, should we treat apparent paradoxes as logical puzzles to be solved, or, with Derrida, should we treat at least some of them as aporias in which we have a duty to "interminably persist" (404–7)? Cutrofello concludes that the real problem is not that "analytic and continental philosophers have been unable to agree about the nature of the highest philosophical good"; rather, it is that "they have been unable to [figure out a way to] *argue* about their respective conceptions of the philosophical enterprise." To do that, they need to find a way to discuss "Kant's fifth question, namely, 'What is philosophizing good for and what is its ultimate end?'" (416).

[73] For a selection of key texts from analytic, continental, and pragmatist philosophers on this topic, see Baynes, Bohman, and McCarthy 1987. For attempts to clarify and/or reconcile the continental-analytic divide, see James Chase and Jack Reynolds, *Analytic Versus Continental: Arguments on the Methods and Value of Philosophy* (Montreal: Mcgill-Queen's University Press, 2010); and *Beyond the Analytic-Continental Divide: Pluralist Philosophy in the Twenty-First Century*, ed. Jeffrey A. Bell, Andrew Cutrofello, Paul M. Livingston (New York: Routledge, 2015).

[74] Yet even this agreement may be difficult to obtain. C. P. Ragland and Sarah Heidt state, on the one hand, that "the question 'What is Philosophy?' does seem to be a necessary part of philosophy." And yet, on the other hand, they claim that "The nature of philosophy is not a preeminent philosophical question,

It should be stressed that each of the three main streams of contemporary Western philosophy—analytic, continental, and pragmatist—is itself quite diverse, including divisions regarding the very nature and purpose of philosophy. H. O. Mounce argues that there are two essentially different pragmatisms, one stemming from Peirce's realism and the other getting its start in James's misunderstanding of Peirce and reaching its apex in Rorty's anti-realism.[75] While analytic and continental philosophers often seem certain in their metaphilosophical pronouncements that the other camp is not really doing philosophy, or at least not doing it properly, there is little agreement *within* each camp about the topics, methods, and aims of philosophy. Regarding analytic philosophy, Fraser MacBride writes:

> It doesn't have a subject matter to call its own . . . . And despite its name, analytic philosophy has no distinctive method either. Not all analytic philosophers commit themselves to a programe of analysis, whether of language or thought, and even if they do what they have in mind to do is often very different. Some analytic philosophers make it their business to analyse words and phrases of the languages we already speak whilst others dedicate themselves to inventing new languages that improve upon the old ones.[76]

In *Twentieth-Century Analytic Philosophy*, Avrum Stroll writes: "Many scholars would agree with [Hans] Sluga that there is no single feature that characterizes the activities of all those commonly known as analytic philosophers."[77] Stroll does note, however, that in addition to a widely shared concern with articulating the meaning of certain concepts (such as "knowledge" and "justification"), one frequently finds an espousal of "scientism"—"the doctrine that only the methods of the natural sciences give rise to knowledge"—among analytic philosophers, including those who "hold

and philosophers can be great without writing essays on meta-philosophy." Why, they ask, should we "suppose that philosophers need to inquire into the nature of philosophy any more than artists need to ponder the nature of art?" (Ragland and Heidt, 3–4). Yet, one could turn this analogy around to point out that, in modern and contemporary times, at least, when the definition and purpose of art has fallen into question, most "great artists" are in fact deeply involved in the question of what it is that they are doing. At least in times of crisis, revolution, renaissance, and innovation—in other words, in times when philosophy is most called for—meta-philosophy does indeed seem to be a preeminently philosophical endeavor.

[75] H. O. Mounce, *The Two Pragmatisms: From Peirce to Rorty* (New York: Routledge, 1997).

[76] Fraser MacBride, "Analytic Philosophy and its Synoptic Commission: Towards the Epistemic End of Days," in O'Hear 2014, 221.

[77] Stroll 2000, 7–8. Hans-Johann Glock finds "geo-linguistic, historiographical, formal, material and 'ethical' conceptions of analytic philosophy" to be wanting, yet he argues that "analytic philosophy" can be coherently defined as "a historical tradition held together by ties of influence on the one hand, family resemblances on the other" (Glock 2008, 204, 231). While he is somewhat more optimistic about the possibility of a methodological definition of analytic philosophy in terms of the shared use of a "toolbox" of a variety of "conceptions and techniques of analysis," in the end, agrees Michael Beaney, "the only way to answer the question, 'What is analytic philosophy?' is to provide a history of the analytic tradition" (Beaney 2013, 29).

that philosophy should deal with normative or valuative questions, as opposed to science, which is a wholly descriptive, fact-finding activity."[78] Joseph Margolis claims that over the past century "analytic philosophy has been engaged in testing … the limits of every form of scientism," and, in his view, scientism has consistently failed the test.[79] Of course, there are a number of prominent analytic philosophers who reject scientism, including Wittgenstein, Moore, Gilbert Ryle, Bernard Williams, and Thomas Nagel.[80]

In his introduction to *A Companion to Continental Philosophy*, Simon Critchley admits that "continental philosophy is a highly eclectic and disparate set of intellectual currents that could hardly be said to amount to a unified tradition."[81] Nevertheless, he does attempt to delineate some common views of philosophy shared by most continental philosophers (including, of course, those working in the United States and elsewhere), such as "the recognition of the essential historicity of philosophy (and philosophers)" and an engagement in a transformative practice of critique.[82] Critchley suggests that continental philosophy's "most salient and dramatic difference from analytic philosophy" is its "anti-scientism," by which he means "the dual belief that (i) the procedures of the natural sciences cannot and, moreover, should not provide a model for philosophical method and (ii) that the natural sciences do not provide our primary or most significant access to the world."[83] Critchley concedes that at times continental philosophy's aversion to reductive scientism leads it to run the risk of "obscurantism," and he writes that "In my view, the two poles that are to be avoided in philosophy are scientism and obscurantism."[84] Many (certainly almost all continental) philosophers would agree, yet those (mostly analytic) philosophers who embrace scientism obviously would not.[85] It should be pointed out that, recently, a number of philosophers working out of continental traditions have called for an end to continental philosophy's

[78] Stroll 2000, 1–2.

[79] Joseph Margolis, *The Unraveling of Scientism* (Ithaca, NY: Cornell University Press, 2003), 16. For a leading contemporary phenomenologist's arguments against scientism, see Schmitz 2018.

[80] See Thomas Nagel's clear rejection of scientism in *The View from Nowhere* (New York: Oxford University Press, 1986), 9–10. On Wittgenstein's and Williams's rejection of scientism, see Glock 2008, 119, 161, 245. Although his treatment of continental philosophies is often unfairly polemical, Glock rightly points out that the realism versus anti-realism/constructivism/relativism debates over the nature of science cannot be equated with debates between analytic versus continental camps in philosophy since there are also numerous anti-realist, constructivist, or relativist analytic philosophers (235–38).

[81] Critchley 1998, 5.

[82] Critchley 1998, 10.

[83] Critchley 1998, 12–13.

[84] Critchley 2001, xiii–xiv.

[85] Relatively few modern Japanese philosophers avow scientism, although many traditional and modern Japanese philosophers have been accused of indulging in obscurantism. Without denying that some may be guilty as charged, and while affirming that clarity and various kinds of rigor are very often very important virtues in philosophy, let me also point out that *forced clarity* obscures, especially when the matter under investigation itself involves ambiguities, ambivalences, indistinctness, paradoxes, and even aporias. In such cases, rather than force reality into our clear and distinct concepts, it is arguably the task of the philosopher to be as clear as possible about what is inherently unclear. Dōgen, for example,

long-standing antipathy to naturalism. While still warning against falling into a reductive scientism or naïve realism, some have sought to develop a "speculative realism" or "transcendental materialism" that hinges in large part on taking seriously developments in the sciences.[86]

In short, the myriad topics, methods, and styles of doing philosophy that get facilely lumped together into the two supposedly antagonistic and incommensurable camps of analytic philosophy and continental philosophy are too varied and too overlapping to sustain any simplistic binary opposition. Dan Zahavi compellingly concludes that

> it is a mistake to carve up the philosophical landscape into two distinct (and incommensurable) traditions. The mistake is both one of oversimplification and reification. There are far more than two traditions (let us not forget the existence of Asian philosophical traditions) and, when it comes to analytical philosophy and continental philosophy neither (set of) tradition(s) is monolithic.[87]

BEYOND MODERN
EUROMONOPOLISTIC PHILOSOPHY

In fact, Asian philosophical traditions are not only frequently forgotten, they also have often been intentionally excluded. Despite the many deep disagreements among modern and contemporary analytic, continental, and pragmatic philosophers regarding the nature and purpose of philosophy, they are often in agreement that philosophy is a unique legacy of the ancient Greeks. Yet even this would-be Pax Philosophica is disturbed by a number of factors, beginning with the fact that the solely Greek origins of Western philosophy have been contested by scholars who emphasize ancient Greece's intellectual indebtedness to Egypt, Persia, and India. For example, Pythagoras, who is

---

would probably say that, even in his most dense and playfully convoluted prose, he was being precisely as clear as possible and as appropriate to the matter at hand. He adamantly rejected the idea that Zen kōans are "beyond logic and unconcerned with thought" and reproached monks who hold such views: "the illogical stories [*murikaiwa* 無理会話] mentioned by those bald-headed fellows are only illogical for them, not for buddha ancestors." Dōgen, *Shōbōgenzō*, edited by Mizuno Yaoko (Tokyo: Iwanami, 1990), vol. 2, p. 190; *Treasury of the True Dharma Eye: Zen Master Dogen's Shobo Genzo*, ed. Kazuaki Tanahashi (Boston: Shambhala, 2012), 157. On kōans as used in Rinzai Zen practice, see Chapter 10 in this volume. On Dōgen's philosophy of language, see Chapters 9 and 32.

[86] See Peter Gratton, *Speculative Realism: Problems and Prospects* (New York: Bloomsbury, 2014), 135–6. See also *The Speculative Turn: Continental Materialism and Realism*, edited by Levi Bryant, Nick Srnicek, and Graham Harman (Melbourne: re.press, 2011).

[87] Zahavi 2016, 92. Zahavi notes parallels between the transcendental character of both Husserlian phenomenology and analytic philosophy of language, but also indicates a divergence between the former's bracketing of the "natural attitude" and recent attempts by analytic philosophers of mind to "naturalize phenomenology."

credited with the invention of the word *philosophia*, spent time in Egypt and Babylonia, where he evidently learned and adopted the Indian doctrines of reincarnation and vegetarianism. We need to bear in mind that Greek philosophy was not born in Athens but rather in the intensely cross-cultural setting of the Greek colonies in Asia Minor. Thomas McEvilley demonstrates that the "period of unimpeded contact [with India] through the medium of Persia lasted approximately from 545 till 400," that is, precisely during the time of the development of pre-Socratic philosophy. Decades of meticulous research leads him to conclude that "there is a relationship between early Greek philosophy and early Indian philosophy as clear as that between, say, early Greek sculpture and Egyptian sculpture."[88]

Despite what many have been taught—and what many still teach—in their introductory philosophy courses, the doctrine of the exclusively Greek origins of philosophy is, in fact, a fairly recent convention. Franz Martin Wimmer and Peter Park have thoroughly documented how it was only "in the late eighteenth century that historians of philosophy began to claim a Greek beginning for philosophy" and "to deny that African and Asian peoples were philosophical."[89] Moreover, Park and Bernasconi have convincingly argued that this formation of an exclusionary definition and canon of philosophy was to a significant degree driven by ethnocentric and racist motives.[90] To be sure, an ethnocentric view of the exclusively Greek origin of philosophy can be traced back at least to Diogenes Laertius (3rd century CE), who opens his influential *Lives and Opinions of Eminent Philosophers* with the claim: "There are some who say that the study of philosophy had its beginning among the barbarians. . . . These authors forget that the achievements which they attribute to the barbarians belong to the Greeks, with whom not merely philosophy but the human race [*genos anthrōpōn*] itself began."[91] In the twentieth century, we find Levinas supplementing this astonishingly ethnocentric anthropological claim with the equally shocking statement: "I often say, although it is a dangerous thing to say publically, that humanity consists of the Bible and the Greeks. All the rest can be translated: all the rest—all the exotic—is dance."[92] Levinas, the great thinker of ethical openness to the other, is appallingly dismissive of traditions other than those of the Bible and the Greeks and even of the humanity of the adherents to those traditions.

[88] McEvilley 2002, 18. In the second half of his monumental book, McEvilley shows how the Greeks, having been on the receiving end during the pre-Socratic period, exerted a counter-influence on the development of Indian philosophy during the Hellenistic period. See also Elberfeld 2017a, 21–59.

[89] Park 2013, 1–2; see also Wimmer 2017.

[90] In addition to Park 2013, see Bernasconi 1995, 1997, 2003.

[91] Diogenes Laertius, *Lives and Opinions of Eminent Philosophers*, translated by R. D. Hicks (Cambridge, MA: Harvard University Press, 1972), vol. 1, p. 5.

[92] Emmanuel Levinas in Raoul Mortley, *French Philosophers in Conversation* (London: Routledge, 1991), 18. On this and other such comments by Levinas, see Robert Bernasconi, "Who Is My Neighbor? Who Is the Other? Questioning 'the Generosity of Western Thought,'" in *Emmanuel Levinas: Critical Assessments*, vol. 4, edited by Claire Katz with Lara Trout (London: Routledge, 2005), 5–30; Bret W. Davis, "Ethical and Religious Alterity: Nishida After Levinas," in *Kitarō Nishida in der Philosophie des 20. Jahrhunderts*, edited by Rolf Elberfeld and Yōko Arisaka (Freiburg/Munich: Alber Verlag, 2014), 337–41.

European philosophers did not always hold such Eurocentric, much less Euromonopolistic views of philosophy. From the French *philosophes* to Leibniz and Wolf, for example, many were intensely interested in "Chinese philosophy," just as Schelling and Schopenhauer were in "Indian philosophy."[93] Johann Jakob Brucker was the first modern scholar to attempt to write a comprehensive account of the history of philosophy. Both the German version (1731–1736) and the Latin version (1742–1744) of his multivolume history included coverage of the "philosophies" of, among others, the Hebrews, Chaldeans, Persians, Indians, Arabs, Phoenicians, Egyptians, Moors, Celts, Chinese, Japanese, and Iroquois as well as the Greeks, Romans, and later Europeans.[94] Indeed, prior to the last decade of the eighteenth century, the "opinion of most early modern historians of philosophy (including the ones who imitated Diogenes) was that philosophy emerged first in the Orient."[95] This view was still held in the early nineteenth century by prominent philosophers such as Friedrich Ast, who "designated Indian philosophy as the primeval philosophy (*Urphilosophie*), placing it in the first major period of history along with the philosophies of the Chinese, Tibetans, Chaldeans, Persians, and Egyptians," relegating Greek philosophy to the second period of the history of philosophy.[96]

Park traces the turn to what I am calling the Euromonopolistic conception of philosophy back to a now obscure German scholar, Christoph Meiners (1747–1810).[97] The "racist arguments of this half-forgotten anthropological writer" were developed in a "racist feedback loop" with the anthropological writings of Kant and later adopted by Hegel. As a result, the now forgotten writings of Meiners can be said to "lay at the origin of the exclusion of Africa and Asia from modern histories of philosophy."[98] Up to the end of the eighteenth century, histories of philosophy generally still treated non-European traditions under the rubric of *philosophia barbarica* and *philosophia exotica*. In the wake of Kant's claim that "Philosophy is not to be found in the whole of the Orient," along with his shockingly racist reasons for thinking that only the European "race of the whites" is capable of philosophy,[99] it was the Kantian historians of philosophy Dieterich Tiedemann (in 1791) and Wilhelm Gottlieb Tennemann (in 1798) who first simply eliminated a discussion of non-Western traditions from their accounts

---

[93] See Clarke 1997, chapters 3 and 4.

[94] Johann Jakob Brucker, *Historia critica philosophiae a mundi incunabulis ad nostrum usque aetatem deducta*, 5 vols. (Leipzig: Christoph Breitkopf, 1742–1744). For an abridged English edition, see Johann Jakob Brucker, *The History of Philosophy, from the Earliest Times to the Beginning of the Present Century*, two volumes, trans. William Enfield (London: W. Baynes, 1791).

[95] Park 2013, 70; see also Park 2013, 2.

[96] Park 2013, 9.

[97] Park 2013, 76–82.

[98] Park 2013, xi, 94, 149–50.

[99] For a concise collection of Kant's racists assertions to the effect that "Chinese, Indians, Africans, and the Indigenous peoples of the Americas are congenitally incapable of philosophy," see Van Norden 2017, 21–23. For a translation of the relevant texts, see *Kant and the Concept of Race*, edited by Jon M. Mikkelsen (Albany: State University of New York Press, 2013).

so as to develop not merely a Eurocentric but, as Wimmer puts it, a "Euroequating" (*euräqualistische*) history and definition of philosophy.[100]

Although it is being increasingly challenged, this Euroequating or Euromonopolistic conception of philosophy and the history of philosophy remains, even today, the dominant paradigm in the Western academy.[101] The dominance of this Euromonopolistic paradigm is generally maintained by means of either a rhetoric of dismissive tropes or a sigetics of silent omission. Ironically, in the long wake of the European Expansion, this Euromonopolistic paradigm has been adopted by many non-Western—including most Japanese—philosophers themselves. While we should not discount the power of ideas, we should also not naïvely overlook the sociological forces of cultural colonization at work in this process of philosophical globalization qua Westernization.[102]

In this regard, it is important to note the time period when the Japanese imported Western philosophy. The end of the nineteenth century was perhaps the zenith of philosophical Euromonopolism in Europe. If the Japanese had imported Western philosophy a century earlier or a century later, they would have been much less likely to adopt Nakae Chōmin's 1901 claim that "from ancient times to the present, there has been no philosophy in Japan," since at the end of the eighteenth century most Western philosophers recognized the existence of pre-Meiji "Japanese philosophy," as do an increasing number of Western philosophers today.

Even during the two centuries in which philosophical Euromonopolism was the norm, some Western as well as non-Western philosophers were able to think outside the Euromonopolistic box.[103] A noteworthy example from the early twentieth century is Georg Misch's *Der Weg in die Philosophie*, first published in 1926. A substantially revised and expanded English version of the first part of this book appeared in 1951 under the title *The Dawn of Philosophy: A Philosophical Primer*. According to Misch, a student and son-in-law of Dilthey, philosophy originates precisely in the experience of breaking through the cultural assumptions that congeal to form what he

---

[100] Wimmer 2017, 167, 169, 172, 180; on Tiedemann and Tennemann, see also Park 2013, 82–87.

[101] For a dismal account of the minimal representation or nonrepresentation of non-Western traditions in graduate programs in the United States, see Van Norden 2017, 2–3, 162–3.

[102] Indeed, a global sociology of philosophy is called for (see Collins 1998), one which would include an investigation of the sociological reasons that many academic philosophers insist on a Eurocentric or Euromonopolistic conception of philosophy. In Japan, this would involve analyzing how philosophers (*tetsugakusha*) occupy a position within the hybrid society of modern Japan as representatives of Western culture vis-à-vis other positions, such as those occupied Buddhist priests, teachers of traditional artistic Ways, and other representatives of traditional Japanese culture. The social prestige of philosophy professors in Japan is manifested, for example, in the rhetorical power they wield by having a command of Western terms and texts. To suggest a delimitation of the purview of those terms and texts is in effect to threaten to delimit the prestige of the professors. Of course, a sociology of philosophy would also need to examine the social motives others have for wanting to incorporate non-Western (such as pre-Meiji Japanese) traditions into the field of philosophy.

[103] For a survey of works in Western languages over the past century that have sought to reopen the field of philosophy to non-Western traditions, see Elberfeld 2017c, 286–323.

calls, borrowing a term from Husserl, "the natural attitude." Misch uses this term to indicate the meaning-bestowing and value-laden worldview that we unquestioningly assume to be "natural" and in which we "go about our business and pursue our aims" without reflecting on the horizonal limits that structure those activities.[104] As examples of such philosophical breakthroughs, Misch begins his book with citations from the *Zhuangzi*, the life of the Buddha, Spinoza, and Plato's Allegory of the Cave. Helping break the mold of more than a century of avowedly or unquestioningly Eurocentric or Euromonopolistic philosophy, Misch writes: "The assumption that Greek-born philosophy was the 'natural' one, that the European way of philosophizing was the logically necessary way, betrayed that sort of self-confidence which comes from narrowness of vision."[105]

Moreover, as I have been arguing, there is no single unequivocal "European way of philosophizing." Even were one to stubbornly maintain that philosophy originated exclusively in ancient Greece and developed solely within the Western tradition, the definition of the philosophical endeavor that the ancient Greeks are said to have bequeathed to the Western tradition has itself long been contested *within* this tradition. Writing at the start of the twentieth century, in a treatise titled *The Essence of Philosophy (Das Wesen der Philosophie)*, Dilthey commented that "The term 'philosophy' or 'philosophical' has so many meanings according to time and place . . . that it can seem that the different times have attached the fine word formulated by the Greeks, philosophy, onto always different intellectual images."[106] Is there a unifying thread to all of Western philosophy? Dilthey suggests that the answer to this question is no. "There are philosophies, but not philosophy"; there is no system, but only various systems of philosophy, each with "a different content and compass."[107]

Indeed, even in ancient Greece, "philosophy" never had a univocal definition. The fifth-century commentator Ammonius, in his attempt to synthesize Platonic and Aristotelian conceptions of the discipline, could whittle the definitions of philosophy down to no fewer than six: "knowledge of being as being" (see Aristotle, *Metaphysics* IV.1–3), "knowledge of what is divine and what is human," "becoming like God, so far as this is possible for humans" (see Plato, *Theatetus* 176b), "to attend to death" and thus to "the separation of the soul from the body" (see Plato, *Phaedo* 67b–d), "the art of arts and the science of sciences" (see Aristotle, *Metaphysics* I.2), and "the love of wisdom" (attributed to Pythagoras). Ammonius ends by saying: "There are still other definitions of philosophy, but these will suffice."[108] How many contemporary

---

[104] Georg Misch, *The Dawn of Philosophy: A Philosophical Primer* (Cambridge: Harvard University Press, 1951), 9.

[105] Misch, *The Dawn of Philosophy*, 44. See also Eric S. Nelson, *Chinese and Buddhist Philosophy in Early Twentieth-Century German Thought* (New York: Bloomsbury, 2017), chapter 5.

[106] Wilhelm Dilthey, *Das Wesen der Philosohie*, as excerpted in Elberfeld 2006, 196.

[107] Dilthey, *Das Wesen der Philosohie*, in Elberfeld 2006, 197.

[108] Ammonius, "Die Definitionen der Philosophie," German translation by Rainer Thiel, in Elberfeld 2006, 80–91.

academic philosophers would accept the Platonic definitions of philosophy as a matter of "becoming like God" and "practicing dying" by separating the soul from the body?

The definition of philosophy as a rational inquiry into the eternal order of the cosmos, undertaken for its own sake, can in part be traced back to an Aristotelian conception of *theoria*, which some see as prefiguring the purportedly disinterested inquiry of modern theoretical science. However, we should bear in mind both that Aristotle says that the contemplative activity of *theoria* should be pursued because it constitutes the highest human happiness (*eudaimonia, Nicomachean Ethics* 10.7–8), and that many contemporary philosophers would dispute the claim that the practice of science is disinterested, noting its intimate connection with the desire for technological control over the environment. Regardless, in a polemically and rather defensively entitled book, *But Not Philosophy: Seven Introductions to Non-Western Thought,* George Anastaplo supports the claim that the "European tradition that began in ancient Greece is superior to other traditions of thought" insofar as purportedly it alone discovered a universal order of "nature as distinguished from custom or convention."[109] In his critique of Anastaplo's book, John Maraldo suggests that it should be seen "in light of the greater project of University of Chicago scholars" who, in the wake of Allan Bloom, pursue an agenda "to counter the expansion of the general education curriculum at American universities beyond western classics." In any case, Maraldo judiciously continues, this challenge can at least indirectly help those interested in Japanese philosophy to raise and reflect on some important questions:

> Do we find in Japanese traditions evidence of inquiry pursued for its own sake, or hints of such a basis for theoretical science? Is there an explicit, consciously formed notion of nature as opposed to human convention? Are these features necessary conditions of philosophy proper, philosophy as it is traditionally delimited? It would seem to me that the alternatives—inquiry for the sake of spiritual transformation, for example, or theory necessarily informed by practice, or human cultivation as part of nature—are not only instructive but perhaps constitutive of a more developed definition of philosophy.[110]

In other words, allowing pre-Meiji Japanese "thought" into discussions of "philosophy" may enrich our critical considerations not only of the specific content but also of the general framework within which such discussions take place. In helping us to recover from the myopia that results from an exclusive immersion in contemporary Western views, it may also help us to recover previous Western ways as well as introduce non-Western ways of philosophizing.

---

[109] George Anastaplo, *But Not Philosophy: Seven Introductions to Non-Western Thought* (Lanham, MD: Lexington Books, 2002), xvi–xvii.

[110] Maraldo 2004, 223–4.

THE PRACTICE OF PHILOSOPHY AS A
LIBERATING WAY OF LIFE

According to Pierre Hadot, what most of all separates modern from ancient Western philosophies is that we no longer think—as the Greeks and Romans did—of philosophy as an existentially transformative "way of life."[111] Rolf Elberfeld writes in this regard:

> One could even propose the provocative thesis that it is precisely modern philosophy, with its ideal of becoming a strict science, that has lost sight of the proper tasks of classical philosophy—e.g., the love of *wisdom*, the training for death, and the task of ethical transformation; and it would thus be modern philosophy that is not philosophy in the strict sense.[112]

Hadot agrees with the idea that the Occidental "ancients were perhaps closer to the Orient than we are," insofar as they thought of philosophy as a soteriological practice of a way of life. "The 'philosopher,' or lover of wisdom," in the sense that Hadot seeks to recover, "can therefore seek models of life in the oriental philosophies, and these will not be so very far from the ancient [occidental] models."[113] However, elsewhere, Hadot acknowledges a crucial difference; namely, that the ancient Greek and Roman practices of philosophy did not explicitly entail *embodied* practices in the way that Asian traditions such as Buddhism do. "Unlike the Buddhist meditation practices of the Far East," Hadot writes, "Greco-Roman philosophical meditation is not linked to a corporeal attitude but is a purely rational, imaginative, or intuitive exercise."[114]

Plato's conception of philosophy in the *Phaedo* as a "practice of dying" (*Phaedo* 64–65), understood as a practice of separating the soul from the body, is an extreme example of a persistent tendency in the West to view the body as an obstacle to, rather than as a vehicle for, the practice of philosophy. John Maraldo has argued that "a detachment from everyday life accompanied the distancing from the body in ancient Greek philosophy" and that, in general, "Greek-based Western philosophy often displays a double

---

[111] Hadot 1995 and 2002.

[112] Elberfeld 2017a, 161–2. Kasulis contrasts "engaged knowing" with "detached knowing" and argues that the former is stressed in Greek as well as in traditional Asian philosophies, whereas the latter is stressed in modern academic philosophy as developed in the West and adopted by most modern Japanese philosophers (Kasulis 2018, 20–32, 575–7). There are, of course, exceptions. John Krummel has argued that Heidegger, Nishida, and Nishitani share an understanding of "philosophy" as a quest for the meaning of existence in the face of mortality and the experience of something—or rather "nothing"—that exceeds our horizons of meaning (Krummel 2017). Yet, although Krummel makes a good case for this being a compelling way of understanding "philosophy," one that links at least some Western and Japanese philosophers, it would be difficult to argue that this definition of philosophy is universally shared across historical periods and traditions.

[113] Hadot 2002, 279.

[114] Hadot 1995, 59.

detachment, from everyday life and from embodied existence. In contrast, Japanese Buddhist and Confucian philosophies evince an appreciation of embodied existence in the ordinary world."[115] Several modern Japanese philosophers have sought to incorporate the psychosomatic practices of Zen and other Japanese traditions into their thinking in such a manner as to supplement, as well as challenge, the exclusively cerebral practice of philosophy in the Western tradition.[116]

The founder of the Kyoto School, Nishida Kitarō, claims that "the motivation for philosophy must be that of a profound sense of the sorrows (*hiai* 悲哀) of life," and not only the desire for intellectual knowledge evoked by Aristotle's "astonishment" or "wonder" (*thaumazein*).[117] Heidegger claims that all philosophizing arises out of a particular "fundamental attunement" (*Grundstimmung*) and that another fundamental attunement would be required to spawn an "other inception" of philosophy.[118] Whereas Greek philosophy was born out of the attunement of wonder, which can lead to a disengaged quest for objectivity, one hears in Nishida's remark an echo of Buddhist philosophy, which has its impetus and remains embedded in a holistic quest for a release from suffering.[119]

Among modern authors, Nishida's student and Zen philosopher Hisamatsu Shin'ichi is surely the most outspoken critic of the expulsion of the religious quest for existential liberation from academic philosophy understood as a disinterested pursuit of knowledge. In the opening lines of his *Eastern Nothingness*, Hisamatsu emphatically writes:

> A so-called pure scholar pursues academic study for the sake of academic study or engages in scholarly endeavors in order to become a scholar. But I have not undertaken nor have I wanted to undertake these pursuits with such intentions. Indeed, academic scholarship is neither my ultimate aim nor my original concern. For me there exists a problem on which my life is staked. This is not merely a problem

---

[115] Maraldo 2013, 21, 31.

[116] See Chapters 11, 21, 22, and 27 in this volume; Davis 2004 and 2019. Drawing on American transcendentalist and pragmatist philosophers as well as on continental phenomenologists such as Merleau-Ponty, Richard Schusterman has attempted to reincorporate somatic exercises into the practice of philosophy, and he has made some compelling connections between his project and East Asian philosophies and practices such as those of Zen Buddhism. See his *Thinking Through the Body: Essays in Somaesthetics* (Cambridge: Cambridge University Press, 2012), especially chapter 13, "Somaesthetic Awakening and the Art of Living: Everyday Aesthetics in American Transcendentalism and Japanese Zen Practice." Nevertheless, while the pragmatic and aesthetic aims of his "somaesthetics" may intersect with, they are not the same as the soteriological or rather liberative aims of Zen. See Bret W. Davis, "Toward a Liberative Phenomenology of Zen," in *Yearbook for Eastern and Western Philosophy*, vol. 2, edited by Hans Feger, Xie Dikun, and Wang Ge (Berlin: De Gruyter, 2017), 304–20.

[117] Nishida 1987–89, 6: 116.

[118] In the 1920s, Heidegger suggested that anxiety or profound boredom could trigger the step back from immersion in a predetermined understanding of beings required for philosophical thinking. In the 1930s, he thought that the "other inception" of thinking will be attuned by "shock, reticence, and awe." And, in the 1940s, after turning decisively away from a willful resoluteness, he spoke of a nonwillful "releasement" (*Gelassenheit*) of letting-be as the most proper attunement for philosophical thinking. See Bret W. Davis, *Heidegger and the Will: On the Way to Gelassenheit* (Evanston: Northwestern University Press, 2007).

[119] See Elberfeld 2004, 57–84.

for academic study. It is rather one that presses upon me in the manner of a life or death decision . . . . It is not an intellectual academic problem for one segment of my life, but rather a living problem that engages my life in its entirety.[120]

If the meaning of "philosophy" were restricted to a purely rational discourse that does not address the whole human being, then Hisamatsu would turn the tables on Nakae Chōmin and celebrate the fact that "from ancient times to the present, there has been no philosophy in Japan."[121]

Different attitudes toward embodiment and everyday life—and indeed different conceptions of the impetuses, aims, and practices of philosophy—are some of the more provocative ways in which some aspects of the Japanese tradition may, if we let them, challenge us to rethink not only the content but even the methods and purposes of the practice of philosophy.

NON-WESTERN RELIGION, ART, AND PHILOSOPHY: NAVIGATING THROUGH THE DILEMMA OF INCLUSIONARY VERSUS EXCLUSIONARY VIOLENCE

Before looking at other ways in which Japanese thinkers may enrich our understanding of philosophy, let us examine one potentially legitimate reason for refraining from referring to non-Western traditions as philosophy. The question is, Does applying the label "philosophy" to other ways of thinking, such as those of pre-Meiji Japan, entail forcing them into a Western mold? The inclusion of non-Western traditions within the category of "philosophy" does seem to present us with a dilemma in which other traditions are either *included and distorted* or they are *excluded and dismissed*.

Robert Bernasconi writes of the "double bind" that exponents of African philosophy are placed in:

> when African philosophy takes Western philosophy as its model, then it seems to make no distinctive contribution and so effectively disappears, but when its specificity is emphasized then its credentials to be considered genuine philosophy are put in question and it is dismissed either as religion or as wisdom literature.[122]

---

[120] *Hisamatsu Shin'ichi chosakushū* (Tokyo: Risōsha, 1970), vol. 1, p. 11. On Hisamatsu, see Chapter 11 in this volume. On Nishitani Keiji's understanding of practicing philosophy as a matter life and death, see Chapter 21.

[121] *Nakae Chōmin zenshū* (Tokyo: Iwanami, 1983), vol. 10, p. 155.

[122] Bernasconi 2003, 572.

Sarah Mattice reiterates the point in her study which draws on Chinese as well as Western philosophy:

> The philosophical double bind occurs in judging what is or who has philosophy; when judged from the perspective of Greece or western philosophy, either the work of the other is so similar as to be uninteresting, or so different as to not count as philosophy.[123]

A parallel double bind exists in the case of deciding whether to include non-Western traditions in the category of "religion." Bernasconi writes:

> We seem to be faced with a choice between two violences: on the one hand the violence of imposing the category "religion" on practices (and perhaps also beliefs) even though those practices and beliefs do not readily fit the model of religion and are thereby distorted, misjudged, and found wanting in the process, and on the other hand, the violence of refusing the term religion to such practices because that denial can also be regarded as demeaning so long as the still dominant framework of the Western tradition remains intact.[124]

Kant claimed that there can be only one religion, and, predictably, it was found exclusively in Christianity.[125] Analogously, philosophy has been thought to be found only—or at least most purely and properly—in the Western tradition. Once this assumption is made, we do violence to other traditions *either* by excluding them from philosophy altogether *or* by including and yet marginalizing and misunderstanding them within this field.

Even if, today, on balance we find it more appropriate to include non-Western traditions in—rather than exclude them from—the categories of philosophy and religion, we must also recognize that there is no quick and easy way through the dilemma: there is a *violence of inclusion* as well as a *violence of exclusion*, and navigating the difficult path through the horns of this dilemma requires what Bernasconi calls "a constant process of negotiation."[126] We in the West need to begin by recognizing that hermeneutical processes of navigation and negotiation have long been under way in places like Japan, places in which people have not only adopted but also adapted originally Western categories such as philosophy, religion, and art.

Jason Ānanda Josephson has argued that, "while the discourse on religion emerged in the context of Western Christendom, it is no longer exclusively Western in its current formulations. Rather, the concept was reformulated in the *interstices*, the

---

[123] Mattice 2014, 30.

[124] Robert Bernasconi, "Must We Avoid Speaking of Religion: The Truths of Religions," *Research in Phenomenology* 39/2 (2009): 222.

[125] Bernasconi, "Must We Avoid Speaking of Religion," 215.

[126] Bernasconi, "Must We Avoid Speaking of Religion," 223.

international—in the spaces between nations and cultures."[127] He has shown in detail how the concept of "religion"—translated by repurposing a relatively rare term that had traditionally been used to indicate the main teachings of a sect (*shūkyō* 宗教)—was imported and reformulated in Japan in response to domestic exigencies as well as under foreign influence. Hence, "the category of religion was not a mere imposition" since "the Japanese were far from passive recipients or imitators."[128] Josephson goes so far as to claim that the "combined pressure of non-European actors . . . has begun to strain religion as a category, leading to our current moment, in which the term religion lacks any analytic cohesion and is in the process of disintegration."[129] This is no doubt a contentious claim, but he is surely right to point out the pressure that non-Abrahamic "religions" exert on the very concept of religion to undergo a semantic transformation into a more inclusive and less hierarchical category. The question is never asked whether Christianity is a religion, but the question of whether Buddhism or Confucianism are truly religions has frequently been raised. This reveals that there is a center and there are margins within the category of religion. The survival of the concept of religion presumably depends on its transformation and specifically on whether it can be reformulated so as to decenter Christianity and demarginalize as well as decolonize traditions such as Buddhism and Confucianism.

Something similar could be said of the concept of "art." As with "philosophy" and "religion," the modern concept of "art" bears a metamorphic genealogy. There have been significant shifts in the historical development of the Western terms and concepts for "art" (*techne, ars, Kunst,* etc.) on the way to the modern conception of "fine art" as what is paradigmatically found in museums and galleries and set in contrast to "primitive art," "religious or ceremonial art," and "craft art."[130] This modern Western conception shapes the lenses through which we perceive, understand, and judge non-Western as

---

[127] Josephson 2012, 5. On the Christian and Eurocentric history of the concept of "world religions," see Tomoko Masuzawa, *The Invention of World Religions: Or, How European Universalism Was Preserved in the Language of Pluralism* (Chicago: The University of Chicago Press, 2005). It is important to bear in mind that *"religio"* was a Latin concept with no Greek equivalent and that the plural "religions" becomes commonly used only starting in the seventeenth century.

[128] Josephson 2012, 257. Specifically, Josephson demonstrates, "Japanese officials translated pressure from Western Christians into a concept of religion that carved out a private space for belief in Christianity and certain forms of Buddhism, but also embedded Shintō in the very structure of the state and exiled various 'superstitions' beyond the sphere of tolerance" (21). Before the importation of Western categories, the general term *oshie* (教え) or *kyō* (教) was used to refer to the teachings of Buddhism, Confucianism, and Shintō, yet it covered a wide "combination of what we might call education, politics, religion, science, and ethics" (257). The term that came to be used in the Meiji period as a translation of "religion," *shūkyō* (宗教), a term that originally referred to the main teachings of a sect, came signify "effectively what was left over from *oshie* after politics, education, and knowledge had been removed" (257). This meant that the three pre-Meiji "*oshie*—Buddhism, Shintō, and Confucianism—were fractured in new ways. Buddhism became a religion, Shintō was divided into religious and secular political forms, and Confucianism became a philosophy" (258).

[129] Josephson 2012, 257.

[130] See Larry Shiner, *The Invention of Art: A Cultural History* (Chicago: University of Chicago Press, 2003).

well as premodern Western artifacts that are deemed as, more or less, conforming to "art."[131] We might compare, on the one hand, what happens to (this or that person's experience of) a painting of the Virgin Mary when it is taken out of its original setting in a tenth-century Italian Basilica and hung up for viewing in a New York art museum with, on the other hand, what happens to (this or that person's experience of) a fourteenth-century woodcarving of Amida Buddha when it is removed from its original setting in a Japanese temple and put up for sale in a San Francisco art gallery.[132] When we consider these displacements, we should be wary of uncritically employing an expression such as "religious art." The problem is not only that this expression imputes to them the character of "religious" as if "religion" were simply an ahistorical and universal concept, but also that it is an anachronistic expression formulated to distinguish such artifacts from "pure art" or "art for art's sake" (l'art pour l'art, originally an early nineteenth-century French expression intended to distinguish fine or pure art from artifacts that serve a utilitarian or didactic function). How, to take a particularly difficult yet also prominent example, should we categorize what we call the Japanese "Tea Ceremony" (a phrase with which we translate both the "Way of Tea" [chadō or sadō 茶道] and a meeting for the enactment of this Way [chakai 茶会 or chaseki 茶席])? Is it a kind of "participatory performance art," a "religious ceremony," a "spiritual discipline," or—in order to distinguish it from purportedly purer forms of art and more serious activities of religion—should we just call it a "cultural ritual"? While each of these expressions may help an unfamiliar Westerner to hermeneutically approach the activity, each says both too much and too little.[133]

[131] For rebuttals by contemporary representatives of "analytic aesthetics" to the claim—which is said to be "so pervasive in enclaves of the humanities outside philosophy" (23)—that non-Western traditions of "art" do not conform to modern Western definitions, see the final two chapters in *Theories of Art Today*, edited by Noël Carroll (Madison: University of Wisconsin Press, 2000): Stephen Davies, "Non-Western Art and Art's Definition" (199–216) and Denis Dutton, "'But They Don't Have Our Concept of Art'" (217–38). While Davies and Dutton do point out some excessive and otherwise questionable claims made by certain ethnographers and anthropologists, the problem with attempts such as theirs to define "art" in a manner that includes artifacts and practices from all times and places is not just that these definitions end up being so general as to be rather indefinite; the more serious problem is that they inevitably end up privileging or "centering on" a certain kind of art—the kind one finds in modern Western museums and galleries: "Fine or High Art ... art with a capital A," as Davies writes (202)—and *de jure* or at least *de facto* marginalizing and to some extent misunderstanding, if not excluding, significant artifacts and practices of non-Western as well as premodern Western cultures. In their attempts to be inclusive, they fail to sufficiently attend to the violence of inclusion and to self-critically allow their own paradigmatically modern Western conception of art to be called into question and potentially modified by the artifacts and practices they deign to include.

[132] In this regard, see the admirable, if only moderately successful, attempt by Japanese and American craftsmen in 1909 to recreate a Japanese temple ambience for the Buddhist statues removed from Japan to the Museum of Fine Arts Boston (https://www.mfa.org/collections/featured-galleries/japanese-buddhist-temple-room).

[133] For an attempt by a Western philosopher to approach the Way of Tea and other "Japanese arts" own their terms, see Carter 2008 and Chapter 34 in this volume. Carter begins his book by stating: "Art, philosophy, and religion are intertwined in Japanese culture" (1). However, he might have prefaced this with the phrase: "What we call, from a modern Western perspective, art, philosophy, and religion ...."

In a series of important anthologies, Michele (Michael) Marra has shown how questions of how to translate "art" and "aesthetics" and how to apply these to Japanese artifacts and activities have been intensely and repeatedly grappled with by scholars in Japan from the Meiji period to the present.[134] Insofar as "modern aesthetics" and "Western aesthetics" are both—at least initially in their strict senses—tautologies,[135] the question has been what it means to speak of "Japanese aesthetics" and also whether using this Western conceptual lens necessarily leads to a distorted interpretation of artifacts and activities of pre-Meiji Japan. In posing such questions, Marra takes his bearing in part from the concerns raised by Heidegger in his "Dialogue Between a Japanese and an Inquirer on Language." Heidegger writes: "The name 'aesthetics' and what it names grow out of European thinking, out of philosophy. Consequently, aesthetic consideration must ultimately remain alien to Eastasian thinking."[136] Yet, whereas Heidegger spoke at times of the three centuries Westerners require to properly prepare for "the inevitable dialogue with the East Asian world,"[137] Marra's anthologies reveal the intensity with which the Japanese have been critically and creatively engaging in this dialogue for more than a century. The result is that concepts such as *bijutsu* (美術) and *bigagku* (美学), while beginning as neologisms used to translate the Western concepts "fine arts" and "aesthetics," have in the meantime taken on a life of their own in Japanese language and thought. The expression "Japanese aesthetics" is thus not an oxymoron, but rather "refers to a process of philosophical negotiation between Japanese thinkers and Western hermeneutical practices in the creation and development of images of Japan."[138] Mara Miller, in effect, concurs with this view when she writes: "Ever since Japanese writers began studying Western aesthetics in the Meiji . . . they have both studied its applicability to their own preexisting concepts and phenomena, and used it in their own ways."[139]

This kind of intercultural hermeneutical negotiation is the approach I am suggesting that we take to the evolving definition of "Japanese philosophy." Only thus can we find a way through the horns of the dilemma of exclusionary versus inclusionary violence. Only thus can the bilateral breaking of old molds result in the cooperative creation of new pots, of new provisional containers for practicing philosophy in our contemporary contexts.

Just as the very concepts of "religion" and "art" must change when non-Abrahamic and non-Western traditions are included in these categories, so does the concept of "philosophy" need to undergo metamorphoses as non-Western traditions are included. In fact, philosophers can learn from their art historian and religious studies colleagues since their fields are further along in the process of de-Eurocentralization. Whereas

---

[134] Marra 1999, 2001, 2002.
[135] Marra 1999, 1–2.
[136] Heidegger 1971, 2; see Marra 2001, 4.
[137] See Davis 2013*b*, 461.
[138] Marra 1999, 2.
[139] Miller 2011. This view informs the approach Miller takes in Chapter 35 of this volume.

non-Western traditions still tend to be *marginalized within* the academic fields of art history and religious studies, they still tend to be *excluded from* the field of philosophy. We need not only to include non-Western traditions but also to take them seriously. Henceforth in our philosophical discourses and discussions, I think we must allow non-Western traditions to contribute not just new concepts, theses, narratives, descriptions, and arguments, but also new conceptions of the philosophical endeavor itself. This will appear both new and old to the Western philosophical tradition, which has, after all, repeatedly redefined itself. From the ancient Greeks to twentieth-century philosophers such as James, Wittgenstein, Heidegger, and Derrida, the very definition of philosophy has been almost incessantly disputed and transformed.[140] Why should not other, non-Western voices be allowed into this transformational dialogue and debate?

Two things have tended to happen when the term "philosophy" (or *tetsugaku*) is applied to non-Western discourses such as those found in pre-Meiji Buddhist or Confucian schools of thought. One is an orientalist or otherwise colonial imposition of a Western category and conceptual framework that covers over differences. This problem is simply repeated, rather than resolved, by applying another Western term such as "religion" and is at best evaded by employing a bland and more inclusive, yet also thereby depreciating, term such as "thought." After all, "Buddhism" and "Confucianism" are Western terms, and the curious debates over whether these are "(quasi-)religions" or "(quasi-)philosophies" tell us as much about Western categories and frameworks as they do about the different manners in which people in these traditions think about what it is that they are doing. And so a conscientious scholar understandably might maintain that we should refer to these traditions in their own terms: the study of the "Buddha Dharma" (*buppō* 仏法) and the practice of the "Buddha Way" (*butsudō* 仏道) rather than "Buddhism," or "the study of rational principles" (*rigaku* 理学) and "scholar-sage learning" (*jugaku* 儒学) rather than "Confucianism." In order to counteract our conceptual prejudices, it may even be helpful to experimentally view Western philosophies as "quasi-*buppō*" or as "quasi-*rigaku*."[141]

But there is something else we can do: We can apply the moniker "philosophy" to some discourses found in non-Western traditions, knowing that we are running the risk of colonial distortion, but also with the intention of expanding or developing our own definition and practices of philosophy. Indeed, philosophy, as it has been practiced heretofore in the Western tradition, resists definition—resists, that is, the establishment of unquestioned concepts and methods, insofar as it remains open to critical reflection on and revision of those very concepts and methods. And so Western *philosophy*, if it

---

[140] In addition to earlier sections of this introduction, see Elberfeld 2006.

[141] Blocker and Starling write: "Perhaps Hindu scholars asked Alexander's generals whether there were any *rishis* among the Greeks. We can imagine Marco Polo trying to satisfy the curiosity of Yuan dynasty Confucian administrators concerning the presence or absence in Europe of *zi*" (Blocker and Starling 2001, 14). See also Leah E. Kalmanson, "Dharma and Dao: Key Terms in the Comparative Philosophy of Religion," in *Ineffability: An Exercise in Comparative Philosophy of Religion*, edited by Timothy D. Knepper and Leah E. Kalmanson (New York: Springer, 2017), 248–9.

stays true to its own process of self-critical self-understanding, cannot remain merely *Western* philosophy.

COMPETING DEFINITIONS
OF JAPANESE PHILOSOPHY

In June of 2004, scholars from around the world convened at the Nanzan Institute for Religion and Culture in Nagoya, Japan, for a conference on the topic of "Japanese Philosophy Abroad."[142] This gathering also included the first of several international meetings to plan a volume that was eventually published seven years later: *Japanese Philosophy: A Sourcebook*, a monumental anthology of translations of primary texts from all periods of Japanese intellectual history from the seventh through the twentieth centuries, edited by James Heisig, Thomas Kasulis, and John Maraldo.[143] A major topic of debate during that first meeting in 2004 was whether to refer to the pre-Meiji material as "thought" or as "philosophy." A Francophone scholar insisted that it be called *pensée*, while a German scholar countered that, for reasons of content as well as academic politics, it should be designated *Philosophie*. The rest of us took positions somewhere on the spectrum between these two views, and, in the end, a truce was drawn with the suggestion that the question could be left open and up to readers to ponder, insofar as there can be little doubt that the pre-Meiji discourses to be included belong among the "sources of Japanese philosophy" and so belong in a *Sourcebook*.

At the time they composed their introduction to the *Sourcebook*, it seems that some differences remained even among the three editors over the question of whether to apply the term "philosophy" to the pre-Meiji selections in the book. Differences seemed to remain in particular between the views of Kasulis and Maraldo.[144] On the one hand, in a section presumably drafted by Kasulis, we read:

---

[142] The conference papers were later published as Heisig 2004.

[143] Heisig, Kasulis, and Maraldo 2011. See also the Spanish edition: Heisig, Kasulis, Maraldo, and Bouso Garcá 2016. The present *Handbook* complements the *Sourcebook*. Whereas the *Sourcebook* consists mainly of a wide-ranging sampling of primary texts in translation, the *Handbook* is devoted to explicating and interpreting a selection of the most significant and influential figures, schools, and sources of Japanese philosophy in a manner that allows them to address and contribute to contemporary philosophical discussions. Another noteworthy complement to the *Sourcebook*, as well as to the present *Handbook*, is Kasulis 2018, which offers an engaging interpretation of seven paradigmatic Japanese philosophers (Kūkai, Shinran, Dōgen, Ogyū Sorai, Motoori Norinaga, Nishida, and Watsuji) along with their cultural and intellectual contexts.

[144] This was confirmed by Kasulis and Maraldo at a conference in April of 2015 at Ohio State University commemorating Kasulis's retirement. At that time, in response to my paper, "Was There Philosophy in Pre-Meiji Japan?" Maraldo expressed sympathy with the idea of referring to some pre-Meiji discourses as "philosophy." Kasulis expressly applies the term "philosophy" to pre-Meiji as well as post-Meiji discourses in Kasulis 2018 and 2019. In his book on the Kyoto School, James Heisig writes that "if one understands philosophy in its stricter sense as the particular intellectual tradition that began in Athens" and developed in the Western tradition, a tradition that has "never been broken,

As a work on Japanese philosophy, the *Sourcebook* aims both to challenge the limitations of the prevailing definitions of "philosophy" and to demonstrate by its selection of texts some distinctively Japanese alternatives. In other words, it is presented as textual support for the thesis that long before the term *tetsugaku* was coined in the mid-nineteenth century to designate the imported academic discipline of philosophy, Japan already had in place a solid philosophical tradition rooted in an intellectual history that provided it with resources comparable to but very different from those that have sustained western philosophy.[145]

On the other hand, elsewhere in the introduction, in a section presumably drafted by Maraldo, we read that "the principle of selection at work in this *Sourcebook* inclines to" a definition of "Japanese philosophy" that

acknowledges that philosophical methods and themes are principally western in origin, but insists that they can also be applied to premodern, prewesternized, Japanese thinking. Those who practice Japanese philosophy in this sense understand it primarily as an endeavor to reconstruct, explicate, or analyze certain themes and problems that are recognizably philosophical when viewed objectively.[146]

While Maraldo surely would not want to conflate viewing matters "objectively" with viewing them from a Western perspective, the suggestion here does seem to be that, while pre-Meiji thinking can be productively *reconstructed* as an alternative philosophizing *from the perspective of Western philosophy*, it is not in and of itself an alternative way of philosophizing.

In this section of the introduction to the *Sourcebook*, Maraldo is drawing on a seminal article of his in which he isolates four senses in which the notion of "Japanese philosophy" has been used: (1) Western philosophy as it happens to be practiced by Japanese scholars; (2) traditional Japanese thought (Confucian, Nativist, Buddhist, etc.) as it was formulated prior to the introduction of Western philosophy; (3) a form of inquiry which has methods and themes that are Western in origin but that can be applied to pre-modern, pre-Westernized, Japanese thinking; and (4) a kind of thought that has "a distinctive eastern or Japanese originality or character." In that article, Maraldo argues for the superior viability of the third of these conceptions, in part because it pays due hermeneutical attention to the Greek origins of the heretofore prevailing methods and themes of "philosophy." And yet, crucially, he also stresses that the very methods

---

spliced, enlarged, or seriously challenged by Asian thought," then the groundbreaking achievement of the Kyoto School is to have been the first to break this Eurocentric mold by developing original "world philosophies" that draw on East Asian and Buddhist sources as well as on Western ones (Heisig 2001, 7–8). However, the momentous cross-cultural achievements of the Kyoto School notwithstanding, there have in fact been earlier episodes in the "entangled histories" (*Verflechtungsgeschichten*) of the Asian and Western philosophical traditions. See McEvilley 2002; Clarke 1997; Elberfeld 2017*a*, 21–127.

[145] Heisig, Kasulis, and Maraldo 2011, 17.
[146] Heisig, Kasulis, and Maraldo 2011, 20–1.

and themes of philosophy are essentially always "in the making" and that the production of "Japanese philosophy" will have to "strike a balance between reading (predefined) philosophy into [Japan's traditional] texts and reading alternatives out of them, constructing contrasts to that [pre-defined] philosophy [of the West]."[147]

I agree that the first of these definitions is unduly restrictive in that it freezes philosophy in its Western mold and does not allow for its development through contact with non-Western traditions in Japan and elsewhere. I also agree that the second definition is unduly restrictive in that it limits the Japanese tradition to what existed prior to the Meiji period. The second definition is not only ideologically conservative, it is also hermeneutically naïve insofar as it lacks a "critical awareness of its own reconstructive nature."[148] Regarding the fourth definition, I agree that it can lead, and has led, scholars into the pitfall of an "inverted Orientalism" that celebrates an ideologically homogenized and romanticized reconstruction of Japanese thought, usually at the expense of an equally homogenized yet conversely caricatured image of Western thought. It is true that much of what passes as *Nihonjin-ron* 日本人論 (theories of Japanese uniqueness) can be characterized as an ideologically motivated inverted Orientalism.[149] Nevertheless, as Maraldo would agree, some Japanese thinkers who can be fit into the mold of *Nihonjin-ron*—indeed some who, like Motoori Norinaga, D. T. Suzuki, and Watsuji,[150] preformed or formed this mold—are too influential and their ideas too philosophically rich and provocative (including provoking critique) to ignore. Moreover, many Japanese philosophers who assert that there is in some sense "a distinctive eastern or Japanese originality or character," including at times Nishida Kitarō and subsequent philosophers associated with the Kyoto School, cannot simply be dismissed as promulgating an inverted or reverse Orientalism.[151]

After all, how many Western philosophers have suggested that Western culture and philosophy have distinctive and valuable ideas and practices that can, and even should, be offered to the rest of the world? The crucial question is how that "offering" takes place (e.g., imperialistically or dialogically). Certainly, many Western philosophers have been all too eager to teach others while being much more reluctant to learn anything from them, especially when that learning would involve self-criticism. Nevertheless, surely we want to have at least some artists, authors, and philosophers cultivate and contribute

---

[147]   Maraldo 2004, 238–44; see also Heisig, Kasulis, Maraldo 2011, 19–21; Krummel 2017, 206–14.

[148]   Heisig, Kasulis, Maraldo 2011, 20.

[149]   For more on the problem of ethnocentrism and chauvinism in *Nihonjin-ron* discourses, see Chapter 36 in this volume. Also see Dale 1986; Sakai 1997; Kasaku Yoshino, *Cultural Nationalism in Contemporary Japan: A Sociological Enquiry* (New York: Routledge, 1992); Harumi Befu, *Hegemony of Homogeneity: An Anthropological Analysis of Nihonjinron* (Melbourne: Trans Pacific Press, 2001).

[150]   In this volume, on Motoori Norinaga, see Chapter 3; on Suzuki, see Chapter 11; and on Watsuji, see Chapter 23.

[151]   On this I disagree with critics such as Peter Dale (1986) and Bernard Faure (see his "The Kyoto School and Reverse Orientalism," in Fu and Heine 1995, 245–81). See Davis 2011 and 2013. On the controversial cultural and political writings of Kyoto School philosophers, see Chapters 16, 19, 20, and 36 in this volume. For an overview of the issues, see section 4 of Davis 2019c. For an array of in-depth treatments, see Heisig and Maraldo 1995 and Goto-Jones 2008.

the best of what their respective traditions have to offer, just as we want others to cross borders, facilitate dialogue, and creatively cross-pollinate.

If I am sympathetic with yet not entirely convinced by Maraldo's preference for his third definition of Japanese philosophy, it is because that definition devalues if not excludes potentialities of the second and fourth definitions. Regarding the second definition, while we certainly should attend to the manner in which the concepts and methods of Western philosophy inform our interpretive understanding of pre-Meiji discourses, this does not mean that those discourses cannot call into question and make claims on us, claims not just regarding this or that idea within philosophy but also regarding the very definition of what it means to philosophize. In other words, while Maraldo is certainly right to point out that to speak of pre-Meiji discourses as "philosophy" or "*tetsugaku*" is to bring them into an originally Occidental framework, it is possible to do so in such a way that those discourses are allowed to exert a counter-effect (what Nishida would call a "counter-determination," *gyaku-gentei* 逆限定) on the framework itself. A properly hermeneutical encounter is always, after all, a two-way street.[152]

GENERALIZATIONS
ABOUT JAPANESE PHILOSOPHY

In a passage that can be understood as providing reasons for not judging the *other ways of philosophizing* practiced in pre-Meiji Japan to be *otherwise than philosophy*, Heisig, Kasulis, and Maraldo write the following:

> The traditional modern western philosophical cannon has more or less systematically assumed a universal logic that is conducive to theoretical science pursued for its own

---

[152] In response to a draft of this introduction, John Maraldo informed me that he, too, had come to view his earlier formulation of the third definition (i.e., the definition of Japanese philosophy as "a form of inquiry which has methods and themes that are Western in origin, but that can be applied to pre-modern, pre-Westernized, Japanese thinking") as too restrictive. He pointed out that, in the *Sourcebook*, he added the following: "A small number of Japanese philosophers in Japan allow for the kind of balanced dialogue where the critique is allowed to run in both directions. These thinkers ... not only read traditional Japanese texts in light of modern philosophy; they also use premodern concepts and distinctions to illuminate contemporary western philosophy and to propose alternative ways to solve modern or contemporary philosophical problems. Whether these endeavors unearth philosophy retrospectively from traditional Japanese thought, or go further to use that thought as a resource for current philosophical practice, their air is inclusion: making the Japanese tradition part of an emerging, broader tradition of philosophy" (Heisig, Kasulis, Maraldo 2011, 20; see also Maraldo 2017, 6–11). Nevertheless, Maraldo rightly stresses that all of our reflections on what "Japanese philosophy" was, is, and can be "proceed from a contemporary standpoint in which Japan has already imported 'Western' philosophy and developed *tetsugaku*" (email correspondence, 7 August 2018). I concur that while we can, as it were, make the hermeneutical street run in two directions, we cannot simply reverse its direction. In other words, we can allow pre-Meiji discourses to modify our current understandings of philosophy, but we cannot label those discourses "philosophy" without at least provisionally projecting upon them modern Western and modern Japanese understandings of what is meant by that term.

sake.... [Yet] whereas [Western] philosophy has traditionally been considered timeless, reflective, discursive, analytical, rational, skeptical, aimed at clarity through opposition, focused on principles, and deriving definite conclusions through sound inference or deduction, engagement with Japanese philosophy needs to allow for a style of thinking that rather puts the emphasis on being organic, generative, allusive, relational, syncretic, aimed at contextual origins and underlying obscurities, and negation as a way to transforming perspective.[153]

They go on to make the following generalizations about Japanese philosophy: a preference for internal rather than external relations; a tendency to think in terms of a holographic relation of whole and parts; argument by "relegation" (i.e., "opposing positions are treated not by refuting them, but by accepting them as true, but only true as part of the full picture"); and a preference for philosophizing in *media res*, that is, by beginning "in the gaps left by abstract concepts about reality" and seeking to uncover an "experiential ground out of which the abstractions of philosophy emerge and to which they must answer."[154]

Expanding on and adding to these generalizations, we could say that many Japanese philosophies criticize and/or provide alternatives to ontological and epistemological subject–object dualisms, view human beings as intimately related with one another and with the natural world, and espouse process rather than substance ontologies. Many are suspicious of the reifying and dichotomizing effects of certain kinds or uses of language, if not of language as such, and many are informed by and/or articulate a metaphysical or religious sensibility that inclines toward what Nishida calls "immanent transcendence" (*naizai-teki chōetsu* 内在的超越),[155] as distinct from both a dualistic transcendence and a reductive immanence.

Whereas the Western tradition has tended to privilege *being* over *becoming* and to define being in terms of what is unchanging or what Heidegger calls "constant presence" (*ständige Anwesenheit*), the Japanese tradition has tended to understand reality in terms of "impermanence" (*mujō* 無常). Insofar as humans desire permanence, this desire is at odds with reality and is thus understood to be a primary cause for sorrow. Yet a keen sense of the finitude and frailty of things is poetically cultivated by Motoori Norinaga and others in terms of an aesthetics of "the pathos of things" (*mono no aware* もののあわ れ).[156] For example, cherry blossoms are experienced as poignantly beautiful because of,

153 Heisig, Kasulis, and Maraldo 2011, 23; see also Maraldo 2004, 244–5.
154 Heisig, Kasulis, and Maraldo 2011, 25–8. See also Kasulis 2019 and chapter 1 of Kasulis 2018.
155 See Nishida 1987–89, 11: 434, 458; Nishida 1987, 99, 118.
156 See Chapter 3 in this volume. While duly recounting his fervent nationalism, Blocker and Starling write that "Motoori uses philosophy to challenge philosophy, and in a way that has postmodern resonances" (Blocker and Starling 2001, 186). In his critique of what he sees as Chinese abstract rationalizations of human suffering, and in his defense what he sees as the honest and sincere emotionalism of indigenous Japanese poetry, Motoori is said to help us "see more clearly that this perennial debate between the head and the heart is not a debate between East and West, but within philosophy, both Eastern and Western" (Blocker and Starling 2001, 110). Ueyama Shunpei claims that Japanese Buddhism and Japanese Confucianism also evince a critique of excessive rationality and

not despite, their ephemerality.[157] A subtle appreciation of the evanescence and imperfection of things is cultivated by artists and by tea masters such as Sen no Rikyū in terms of an aesthetic of "rustic simplicity and quiet solitude" (*wabi sabi* 侘寂). Moreover, insofar as we can liberate ourselves from the inordinate desire for an illusory permanence, Zen master Dōgen teaches that we can affirm that "impermanence is itself buddha nature" (*mujōsha sunawachi busshō nari* 無常者即仏性也).[158]

Whereas the Western tradition has tended to think in terms of independent substances, the Japanese tradition has tended to think in terms of interdependent processes. This tendency can be found already in indigenous strands of thought, such as in the key Shintō concept of *musuhi* or *musubi* ("the vital force motivating whatever comes into being," generating and "binding together" all the interconnected processes of being).[159] It can also be found in the Neo-Confucian idea of the psycho-physical "generative force" (Ch. *qi*; Jp. *ki* 気) that pervades, forms, and reforms all things.[160] And it can, of course, also be traced back to the principal ontological teaching of Buddhism, namely "interdependent origination" or "conditioned co-arising" (Sk. *pratītya samutpāda*; Jp. *engi* 縁起).[161] Both traditional and modern Japanese philosophers have tended to understand relations among humans beings and between humans and the natural world in fluidly dynamic and nondualistically interrelational terms.[162]

civilization, a critique that corresponds to a return to "naturalness" (*jinen* 自然) and "simplicity" (*soboku* 素朴). He says that this movement can be called a radical "negation of philosophy" (*tetsugaku hitei* 哲学否定) (Ueyama 1972, 1–2). Kida Gen reads Nietzsche, Heidegger, Merleau-Ponty, Derrida, and other recent Western philosophers as developing an "anti-philosophy" (*han-tetsugaku* 反哲学) that seeks to overcome the metaphysical tradition that runs from Plato to the materialistic and mechanized view of nature in modern science and technology, and he suggests that the Japanese, whose tradition was not based on such a metaphysical delimitation and denigration of nature, are well positioned to take up this project of overcoming the supernatural legacy of Western philosophy as metaphysics and recovering a more positive and holistic sense of nature (Kida 2014, 50–1).

[157] Charles Inoyue writes in this regard: "The syllogism that brings evanescence and sorrow together to yield something more 'positive' would go something like this: A: Life is evanescent and, as a result, sorrowful. B: Sorrow heightens the beauty of things. C: Therefore, evanescent life is beautiful" (Inoyue 2008, 85). Inoyue shows that "a Japanese sensitivity to 'all things changing all the time' predates Buddhism's entry into the country in the sixth century," and his book is a remarkable interpretation of "the tendency toward the formal"—whether it is ritualized commemorations of seasonal changes or formalized social behavior—in Japanese culture as "an effort to give meaning to a constantly changing reality. In Japan, radical form balances radical change" (215). Rather than seeking eternal forms that transcend the transient processes of nature, however, the Japanese have often looked for form within the changing world, that is to say, within what Inoyue calls "the order of here-and-now" as opposed to "the transcendental order" (51–65).

[158] Dōgen, *Shōbōgenzō*, 1: 90; *Treasury of the True Dharma Eye*, 243.

[159] See Chapter 2 in this volume. Motohisa Yamakage (Jp. Yamakage Motohisa) writes that the etymology of *musubi* is related also to the sense of "to bind together" (*musubu*). And he says that "the basic religious idea of Shintō is the continuous process of creation" (Yamakage 2006, 125–6).

[160] See Chapter 12 in this volume.

[161] See Chapters 4 and 5 in this volume.

[162] See Chapters 23, 30, 33, and 34 in this volume.

Many of these generalizations apply not only to Japanese philosophies but also to their Chinese and Buddhist predecessors. Yet most of them are more pronounced in East Asia than in South Asia, and some more in Japan than in China. Tachikawa Musashi traces how, during the course of the development of Mahāyāna Buddhism in India and then in East Asia, the positive, world-reaffirming aspects of the teaching of "emptiness" (Sk. śūnyatā; Ch. kong; Jp. kū 空) became ever more pronounced. According to Tachikawa, whereas the notion that "form is emptiness" was initially understood mainly as a warning not to cling to impermanent phenomena, later, especially in East Asia and most adamantly in Japan, it also came to mean that phenomenal forms are as such the true face of reality (Jp. shohō-jissō 諸法実相).[163]

As one manner in which Japanese Confucians did not merely adopt but also critically adapted Chinese Neo-Confucianism, Blocker and Starling highlight the following:

> Japanese Confucianists … rejected en masse Zhu Xi's leading idea that the ultimate reality is something abstract, immaterial, eternal, and unchanging, existing apart from material qi and individual things. If there is anything that is peculiarly Japanese in Japanese Confucianism, or indeed in Japanese philosophy in general, it is surely this preference for what is immediate, immanent, sensuous, changing, material, and naturalistic, along with a correlative suspicion and lack of sympathy for anything exclusively intellectual, transcendental, abstract, immaterial, unchanging, ethereal, and so on.[164]

The reader of the second half of this Handbook will find that many of the traditional Japanese sensibilities and philosophical proclivities sketched here inform many modern Japanese philosophies as well. To be sure, there are also many differences and debates among Japanese philosophies, traditional as well as modern, and each of them calls for careful and critical examination.

It is important to keep in mind that the "generalizations" given here, even if accurate, are decidedly not "universalizations." Kasulis reminds us that "a generalization is not the same as a universal qualifier.... A generalization, by its very nature, always has

---

[163]   Tachikawa Musashi, Kū no shisōshi: Genshibukkyō kara Nihon kindai e [A History of the Thought of Emptiness: From Early Buddhism to Modern Japan] (Tokyo: Kōdansha, 2003), 6, 324–9. For a more detailed examination of the "positive" manner in which the doctrine of emptiness is developed in Japan, see Tamura 1982. Tamura discusses the challenge of "affirming actual reality" (genjitsu kōtei 現実肯定) when "actual reality" ambiguously means both impermanence and samsaric existence on the one hand and the ignorance and psychic defilements that cause and characterize suffering on the other. Whereas some Tendai monks fell into a licentious brand of "original enlightenment thought" (hongaku shisō 本覚思想), and whereas Hōnen called for a rejection of actual reality and an aspiration for birth in a transcendent Pure Land, according to Tamura, Shinran, Dōgen, and Nichiren attempted to somehow sublate or unify the two standpoints such that ignorance and psychic defilements were negated and yet this world of impermanence and finitude is affirmed (Tamura 1982, 896–7). Such subtleties are not recognized by the so-called Critical Buddhists of late who reject anything resembling "original enlightenment thought" and "affirmation of actual reality" as purportedly un-Buddhist (see Hubbard and Swanson 1997, Shields 2011, and Chapter 4 in this volume).

[164]   Blocker and Starling 2001, 71.

exceptions."[165] Just as one could point to Heraclitus, Hegel, and the Christian notion of the Trinity as exceptions to the Western tradition's tendency to think in terms of independent substances, and to Socrates, Epictetus, and Foucault as Western philosophers who understand the practice of philosophy as a practice of caring for the self, it is certainly not the case that *all* Japanese philosophies reflect *all* of the generalizations sketched here. Nor do all Japanese philosophers—and certainly not all post-Meiji Japanese philosophers (not even all of those associated with the Kyoto School)—regard or wish to rethink the practice of philosophy as a liberating way of life connected to psychosomatic practices such as Zen meditation.

While it can be said that the textual history of Japanese philosophy begins in 604 CE with the attempt to *synthetically harmonize* Buddhist, Confucian, and native Shintō ideas in the *Seventeen-Article Constitution* attributed to Prince Shōtoku,[166] there have been plenty of disagreements and debates in the intellectual history of Japan. For example, Zen and Pure Land Buddhists have argued over whether the road to nirvāna is best traveled by means of "self-power" (*jiriki* 自力) or "other-power" (*tariki* 他力).[167] Many Confucian and Neo-Confucian philosophers—who otherwise debated among themselves—were often united in their criticism of what they saw as Buddhism's otherworldliness and lack of commitment to family and society.[168] Readers of the second half of this *Handbook* will find even greater differences among modern Japanese philosophies. Members of the Kyoto School, for example, not only shared but also debated the meaning of terms such as "absolute nothingness" (*zettai mu* 絶対無). Indeed, the Kyoto School was not formed merely by followers of "Nishidan philosophy" (*Nishida-tetsugaku* 西田哲学), but rather through formative debates between Nishida Kitarō and his junior colleague Tanabe Hajime.[169] Much more variety can be found among the other modern Japanese philosophers treated in this *Handbook*, not

---

[165] Kasulis 2002, 8; see also Kasulis 2018, 41–2. I agree with Kasulis that, even though "generalizations are always distortions," insofar as they are selective, highlight some things or facets of things and leave out or marginalize others, and so on, we can use them—indeed, we cannot help but use them heuristically in scholarship as in daily life.

[166] See Chapter 1 in this volume.

[167] Pure Land Buddhists distinguish themselves from practitioners of Zen and other schools of Buddhism who purportedly rely on their own efforts with practices such as meditation. Arguing the futility of such a reliance on self-power given our thoroughly corrupt nature, they argue that the only possible path to nirvāna left open to us is an utter reliance on the other-power of Amida (Sk. Amitābha or Amitāyus) Buddha. However, the opposition between at least Shinran's interpretation of Pure Land Buddhism and Zen is not as clear-cut as such polemics make it out to be, and these apparently rival schools of Japanese Buddhism in fact share some profound commonalities, the ideal of "naturalness" (*jinen* 自然) among them. See Bret W. Davis, "Naturalness in Zen and Shin Buddhism: Before and Beyond Self- and Other-Power," *Contemporary Buddhism* 15/2 (July 2014): 433–47. On Shinran's Shin Buddhism, see Chapters 6 and 7 in this volume.

[168] See Chapters 12 and 13 in this volume.

[169] See Chapters 16 and 19 in this volume; Davis 2019c; Sugimoto Kōichi, "Tanabe Hajime's Logic of Species and the Philosophy of Nishida Kitarō: A Critical Dialogue within the Kyoto School," in *Japanese and Continental Philosophy: Conversations with the Kyoto School*, edited by Bret W. Davis, Brian Schroeder, and Jason M. Wirth (Bloomington: Indiana University Press, 2011), 52–67.

to mention among those who belong to the wider field of what I will call "philosophy in Japan," of which what I am calling "Japanese philosophy" is mainly a subset. Before elaborating on that distinction, however, let me now address head-on the third aspect of our leading question: What is meant by *"Japanese* philosophy"?

JAPANESE PHILOSOPHY AS A SET
OF PARTICULAR APPROACHES
TO UNIVERSALITY

Whether one calls some pre-Meiji discourses about the nature of the world and our place in it "Japanese philosophy" (*Nihon tetsugaku*) or whether one follows the custom in Japan of restricting the application of this contested phrase to the narrower sense of modern Japanese philosophy (*kindai Nihon tetsugaku* 近代日本哲学), one in any case needs to address the question of what it means to characterize a thinking or a philosophizing that aims to discover and articulate *universal* truths with a *particularizing* adjective such as "Japanese." What does it mean, after all, to speak of *Japanese* (or, for that matter, of *Greek, German*, etc.) philosophy?

Ueda Shizuteru, the central figure of the third generation of the Kyoto School, writes:

> Since philosophers have often spoken of Greek philosophy, French philosophy, English philosophy, American philosophy, and so on, it would seem plausible to speak of "Japanese philosophy." Nevertheless, until about twenty or thirty years ago, philosophers in Japan generally did not take this to be a philosophically meaningful locution . . . . If one did speak expressly of "Japanese philosophy," this tended to be understood as stressing the "Japanese" character of the philosophy in question, and this was deemed inappropriate to the scholarly nature of philosophy as an objective and universal discipline. The universality of philosophy was implicitly understood to mean the scholarly nature of Western philosophy.[170]

As we have seen, post-Meiji Japanese philosophers have tended to import Eurocentrism along with European philosophy, and this importation has included the paradoxical yet persistent claim that only Europe, or at least Europe in particular, has aimed to overcome its particularity and attain to universal truths. Ueda, for his part, goes on to write:

> The turn away from the previous identification of European philosophy with philosophy as such, and the development of world philosophy will no doubt advance a philosophical thinking that is no longer restricted to the specific "love of wisdom" and "science of principles as the science of sciences" that originated in the West.

---

[170] Ueda 2011, 19.

Contact between different traditions promises to help shed light on shared fundamental structures of human existence, and it will encourage new ways of bringing to awareness the understandings of the world and the self found in our various manners of being-in-the-world.[171]

What Ueda means by "world philosophy" (*sekai tetsugaku* 世界哲学) clearly does *not* mean that there will be one style of philosophy practiced all around the world. Indeed, for Ueda, such a philosophical homogenization would be another lamentable phenomenon in what he calls "the grim global reality of today," namely "the formation of a mono-world which renders meaningless differences between East and West, and which thus invalidates the historic undertaking of [Japanese philosophers such as] Nishida and Nishitani."[172] What Ueda refers to as "world philosophy" is evidently not a particular standpoint or style, but rather the cooperative cultivation of a heterogeneous space of dialogue among particular standpoints and styles.

Yet what, then, does it mean to speak of *Japanese* philosophy, or for that matter of *German* philosophy or even of *Western* philosophy? Is it legitimate for philosophy to be delimited with such geographical, cultural, or linguistic adjectives? Hashimoto Mineo goes so far as to say that the expression "Japanese philosophy" is a "contradictory descriptor," insofar as philosophy is "an academic discipline that above all must take universality to be its essence."[173] Kant claimed that there cannot be more than one philosophy, since there is only one human reason.[174] While one might want to challenge the specifics and specificity of Kant's conception of "human reason," there is certainly an important point being made here. If one sets out to articulate a Japanese or a Greek or an American philosophy, it might seem that one is either not searching for universal truth or that one is assuming from the start that this or that particular tradition or culture has a privileged access to universal truth. Yet, insofar as philosophy involves self-questioning rather than mere self-assertion, it must entail critically reflecting on the horizonal limits of one's own cultural tradition rather than just rearticulating and venerating the contours of those limits. Although a colloquial sense of the term "philosophy" does lend itself to being used in the sense of a "cultural worldview," surely what is meant by "Japanese philosophy" should be more than and different from assertions of a Japanese worldview or set of values, such as one uses the term "philosophy" on the mission statement of a business enterprise to refer to its principles, policies, and purposes. Philosophy, in the sense we are concerned with, *questions* rather than simply *asserts* cultural limits; it *critiques* rather than merely *attacks or defends* worldviews.[175]

---

[171] Ueda 2011, 20.

[172] Ueda 2011, 30. On Ueda, see Chapter 22 in this volume.

[173] Hashimoto Mineo, "Keijijōgaku wo sasaeru genri" [The Principles Supporting Metaphysics], in Furuta and Ikimatsu 1972, 53; see also Fujita 2011, 993–4.

[174] Kant, *Die Metaphysik der Sitten*, excerpted in Elberfeld 2006, 152–3.

[175] Compare in this regard the longstanding debates in the field of African philosophy over the notion of "ethnophilosophy." See D. A. Masolo, *African Philosophy in Search of an Identity* (Bloomington: Indiana University Press, 1994).

Hence, there is something disturbing about the term "Western philosophy" as well. The troubling question is: Can philosophy belong to *any* culture or tradition? To be sure, there are those who think that the West is *uniquely* defined by its thrust toward universality. As discussed earlier, the claim is that, at its philosophical core, Western culture is paradoxically defined by its perpetual transcendence of cultural limits; in other words, Western culture is purportedly defined only by its incessant transgressing of definition. The West would be the only particular that has taken upon itself the "infinite task" of transcending its particularity.[176] Yet, for anyone who has seriously studied non-Western traditions of philosophical thought, such as those found in South and East Asia, it is hard not to hear in this claim an arrogance based on ignorance. Have not great Asian philosophers also engaged in critique of cultural beliefs and practices and in self-critical searches for universal truth?

It may nevertheless be true that the attempt to search for truth outside the strictures of allegiance to any cultural tradition or religious institution is an especially predominant feature, if not of the Western philosophical tradition as a whole (in which ancient, medieval, and contemporary philosophers have more often than not associated themselves with a particular school, tradition, religion, or philosopher), then at least of an understanding of philosophy that attained prominence during the seventeenth- and eighteenth-century European Enlightenment. Ironically, however, many Enlightenment philosophers sought to question the prejudices of the European Church, society, and tradition by looking to what they thought of as the *philosophies* of China.[177] Moreover, and more to the point, we would do well to recall Gadamer's critique of the Enlightenment's "prejudice against prejudice itself."[178] Gadamer points out that learning takes place by foregrounding and correcting or modifying ones prejudices or "pre-judgments" (*Vor-urteile*), not by pretending to be able to simply do away with them. A presuppositionless philosophy is not only impossible, but, even if it were possible, it would leave us disoriented and bereft of a starting point for thought and experience. We may agree with Habermas that Gadamer goes too far in the other direction when he claims that "the self-awareness of the individual is only a flickering in the closed circuits of historical life,"[179] such that the individual philosopher would hardly be able to step outside of his or her own historical tradition in order to carry out a rational critique of it.[180] Nevertheless, not only hermeneutically sensitive philosophers of the continental

---

[176] See note 52.

[177] See Clarke 1997, 43–50.

[178] Hans-Georg Gadamer, *Truth and Method* (second edition), trans. Joel Weinsheimer and Donald Marshall (New York: Crossroad, 1989), 270.

[179] Gadamer, *Truth and Method*, 276.

[180] Jürgen Habermas sees Gadamer's revival of the "authority of tradition" as having gone too far in limiting the critical resources of the Enlightenment that enable us to uproot the prejudices of the tradition. See his "A Review of Gadamer's *Truth and Method*," in *The Hermeneutic Tradition*, ed. Gayle L. Ormiston and Alan D. Schrift (Albany: State University of New York Press, 1990), 213–44. Keta Masako argues that Gadamer fails to fully account for the aspect of religious experience that exceeds reabsorption into the enveloping continuity of tradition and its structure of understanding/interpretation. See her *Nihirizumu no shisaku* [Thinking of Nihilism] (Tokyo: Sōbunsha, 1999), 112.

tradition, but also pragmatist and analytic philosophers today mostly agree that we have no absolute access to a "view from nowhere." This acknowledgment does not abandon us to relativism in the sense that we would each be hermetically locked up within the horizon of our own culture, language, and tradition. As Gadamer has pointed out, "the closed horizon that is supposed to enclose a culture is an abstraction" since our horizons and the prejudices that form them are inherently open to modification, revision, expansion, and fusion with other horizons through intercultural dialogue.[181] It is not that truth is entirely relative, but rather that all our approaches to truth are conditioned by the perspectival orientations made available to us through our languages, cultures, and traditions. Thus, it could be said that each act of philosophizing enacts *a particular approach to universality*, and we have no access to universality that would bypass these particular approaches.

There is no free-floating universal reason beyond or beneath particular attempts to think rationally by means of the medium of this or that language, culture, and tradition. Hilary Putnam tersely puts the point thus: "Tradition without reason is blind; reason without tradition is empty."[182] Putnam goes on to say that "actual reasoning is necessarily situated within one or another historical tradition." I would add that it also can—and in its philosophically most fecund moments often does—take place in the encounter between two or more historical traditions. Putnam would seem to agree: "To be sure, members of different traditions can and do enter into discussion and debate. But (as Dewey also stressed) in such discussions we typically find ourselves forced to renegotiate our understanding of reason itself." Indeed, "reason calls for such endless renegotiation."[183] As philosophers, we are always more or less rooted in one or more tradition—and yet we are never completely determined by them. Hence, we are neither entirely free of nor completely bound to the adjectives that describe the origins and orientations of our philosophizing. This is a basic insight of continental philosophers such as Gadamer as well as pragmatist and analytic philosophers such as Putnam and Nagel.[184]

Philosophy thus always takes place in between the particular and the universal. For example, if I say that humans are mortal, I am not just saying that humans who speak my language and who belong to my culture and tradition are mortal. I am attempting to state a universal truth. And yet, the sense and significance of "mortality," not to mention specific views of how to live in the face of our universal condition of mortality, will always be colored by the particularities of our languages, cultures, and traditions. This is

---

[181] Gadamer, *Truth and Method*, 304–7. On the potential and limits of Gadamer's contribution to cross-cultural philosophy, see Davis 2013a, 68–71; Bret W. Davis, "Sharing Words of Silence: Panikkar After Gadamer," *Comparative and Continental Philosophy* 7/1 (2015): 52–68.

[182] Hilary Putnam, "Must We Choose Between Patriotism and Universal Reason?" in Martha C. Nussbaum, *For Love of Country?* (Boston: Beacon Press, 2002), 94. Putnam seems here to answer his own question of a few years earlier: "Why can we not just be philosophers without an adjective?" (quoted in Chase and Reynolds, *Analytic Versus Continental*, 4).

[183] Putnam, "Must We Choose," 94.

[184] See Nagel, *The View from Nowhere*, 3–12.

not to say that we are locked in the horizons of these particularities, but it does mean that we always begin to philosophize from somewhere. From there, we may transgress and transform our horizons in philosophical dialogue with others and their other horizons. Such cross-cultural philosophical dialogue enables us not only to learn from one another about our present differences and commonalities, but also to cultivate and/or alter these differences and commonalities in novel ways that strike us as fruitful and compelling. A sophist or an apologist might enter a debate with a fixed standpoint that he or she merely asserts and tries to defend, but to enter into a philosophical dialogue, it seems to me, one must be open to the possibility of philosophical conversion. One has to be willing to put one's cards on the table—that is, to put one's particular understanding of matters up for questioning and possible revision. At the very least, one must be willing to allow one's particularity to be set within a wider field of universality—that is, to understand one's particularity as one determination qua delimitation of that wider field.

Particular and universal are, after all, correlative terms, and so it does not make sense to speak of one without the other. One cannot speak of particular differences without some sense of a shared universality. This is so even if that sense often remains unclarified and unarticulated in the background. It may be the case, as some Japanese philosophers have argued, that the ultimate universal is essentially unarticulable (that is to say, unspecifiable) since to articulate or specify it would turn it into a particular. Nishida calls the ultimate universal which encompasses all particular beings "the place of absolute nothingness" (*zettai mu no basho* 絶対無の場所); it is the only universal or "medium" (*baikaisha* 媒介者) capable of encompassing unique singularities or "true individuals" (*shin no kobutsu* 真の個物).[185] But Nishida also attends—especially after his confrontation with Tanabe's "logic of species" (*shu no ronri* 種の論理)—to the many levels in between the singular individual and the ultimate universal; that is, to the many specific universals or "places of being" (*u no ippansha* 有の場所) such as the languages and cultures in which we dwell.[186]

It may be the case that human beings in different cultures and traditions think differently. Yet, even this statement is a claim to a universal truth about our diversity. To begin with, it claims that it is universally true that different human beings think differently. The fact that we are different is, of course, not the only universal truth we share. Difference, after all, logically implies sameness, just as sameness implies difference. The statement that human beings in different cultures think differently posits or presupposes a horizon

[185] See Nishida 1987–89, vols. 4–7. On Nishida's idea of the place of absolute nothingness, see Chapters 17 and 18 in this volume.
[186] On Nishida's confrontation with Tanabe over the question of "species" in between individual and universal, see Sugimoto, "Tanabe Hajime's Logic of Species and the Philosophy of Nishida Kitarō." On Nishida's potential contributions to as well as actual ventures and misadventures in cross-cultural philosophy, see Chapter 36 in this volume; Davis 2006b and 2014, 175–82; Bret W. Davis, "Nishida's Multicultural Worldview: Contemporary Significance and Immanent Critique," *Nishida Tetsugakkai Nenpō* [The Journal of the Nishida Philosophy Association] 10 (2013): 183–203; Elberfeld 1999; Gereon Kopf, "Ambiguity, Diversity and an Ethics of Understanding: What Nishida's Philosophy Can Contribute to the Pluralism Debate," *Culture and Dialogue* 1/1 (2011): 21–44; Kopf 2014.

of commonalities (humanity, thinking, culture) in terms of which specific differences can be discussed. A cross-cultural philosopher wants to know not only what makes us different, but also what nevertheless unites us in our diversity. In Nishida's parlance, the desideratum of cross-cultural philosophy should not be understood in either/or terms of one *or* many, universal sameness *or* particular differences, but rather in both/and terms of "one-qua-many/many-qua-one" (*issokuta–tasokuitsu* 一即多・多即一), in other words, unity-in-diversity and diversity-in-unity.

The genuine cross-cultural philosopher, in my mind, is not only interested in disclosing differences; he or she also wants to know what we can learn from our differences. For example, were someone to be merely interested in theories of Japanese uniqueness, were someone concerned only with asserting what makes the Japanese different from other peoples, then I would hesitate to call that person a philosopher. Yet, if someone were interested in showing how some peculiarity of Japanese thought, culture, or language can shed light on a universal human potentiality that has been especially actualized in Japan, and in showing how other people can learn from this, then that person is doing something philosophically very interesting and important. This is what I suggest we should be trying to do when we study, and participate in the ongoing development of, Japanese philosophy.

Japanese Philosophies as Contributions to Cross-Cultural Philosophical Dialogue

In a text on Nishitani Keiji's philosophy, Ueda Shizuteru insightfully addresses the question of the adjective "Japanese" as follows:

> If we are to use the characterization "Japanese," this does not signify merely a particularity of Japan, but rather must be understood in the sense that a certain area of universal primal human possibility has been historically realized particularly in Japan. Hence, "European" does not straightaway mean "global," but rather that a certain area of universal primal human possibility has been historically realized particularly in Europe . . . . If we understand ourselves as the particularization of something universal, this means, at the same time, that we can understand others as different particularizations of something universal. Only then, with the communication between particular and particular, can something universal come to be realized.[187]

---

[187] Ueda Shizuteru, "Nishitani Keiji: Shūkyō to hishūkyō no aida" [Nishitani Keiji: Between Religion and Non-Religion], in Nishitani Keiji, *Shūkyō to hishūkyō no aida* [Between Religion and Non-Religion], edited by Ueda Shizuteru (Tokyo: Iwanami, 1996), 309.

This manner of understanding the relation between cultural particulars and human universals means, on the one hand, that we cannot comprehend one cultural worldview in the terms of another and, on the other hand, that we are not locked in our particular cultural worldviews but can enter into dialogue and learn from one another. It is through such a dialogue among persons whose thought is shaped by certain particularities that we can best approach an understanding of the universal (or, to use a traditional East Asian term, *ri* 理) that encompasses and engenders these particularities (or *ji* 事). If we want to understand "food," we need to compare various foods. Analogously, if we want to understand "human being," we need to engage in a dialogue among various human beings.

In "The Significance of Japanese Philosophy," Fujita Masakatsu, the founding head of the Department of the History of Japanese Philosophy at Kyoto University (succeeded in 2013 by Uehara Mayuko), reflects on this issue as follows. To begin with, he recognizes the tension we have been discussing between the universal thrust and the particular roots of any endeavor to philosophize. "While on the one hand, philosophy is a discipline that stresses universality, such that it does not matter where a philosopher lives, this is only part and not the whole truth of the matter."[188] Not only is what Watsuji spoke of as "the impact of geographical setting and climate (*fūdo* 風土)" important,[189] the influence of language on thinking is also momentous.[190]

As an example, Fujita discusses Nishida's response to Descartes. Nishida agrees with Descartes's method of "doubting whatever can be doubted," and yet Nishida doubts precisely what Descartes ultimately claims is indubitable: "that there is a possessor of consciousness existing prior to consciousness."[191] By contrast, Hobbes, in his critical response to Descartes's denial of the corporeity of the *res cogitans* (thinking thing), nevertheless in passing agrees with Descartes on our supposed "inability to conceive an act without its subject." "We cannot," Hobbes agrees, "conceive of jumping without a jumper, of knowing without a knower, or of thinking without a thinker."[192] Thus, writes Fujita,

> Descartes unquestionably shares with Hobbes the assertion that all acts belong to a "subject" (i.e., substratum or hypokeimenon). But it is precisely with regard to this point that Nishida could not agree with Hobbes or Descartes . . . . According to Descartes, it is impossible to think of experience without there being a subject (substratum) of experience . . . . Nishida's philosophy of "pure experience," on the other hand, is based on a criticism of this understanding of experience.[193]

---

[188] Fujita 2013, 7. See also Fujita 2011.
[189] See Chapter 23 in this volume.
[190] See Chapter 32 in this volume.
[191] Fujita 2013, 16.
[192] *The Philosophical Writings of Descartes*, trans. John Cottingham, Robert Stoothoff, and Dugald Murdoch (Cambridge: Cambridge University Press, 1985), vol. 2, p. 122.
[193] Fujita 2013, 16.

According to Nishida's early philosophy, prior to the constitution of the individual subject who thinks about or represents objects, experience is not dichotomized into subject and object: "there is not yet a subject or an object, and knowing and its object are completely unified."[194] This doctrine of "pure experience" is, to be sure, only the starting point of Nishida's philosophical journey.[195] The point Fujita is making in "The Significance of Japanese Philosophy" is that this starting point, this questioning of an assumption unquestioningly shared by Descartes and Hobbes, as well as arguably by most (though certainly not all) other Western philosophers,[196] was apparently enabled or at least stimulated by Nishida's linguistic and cultural background—not to mention his practice of Zen. Whereas in European languages the grammatical subject is generally an ineradicable part, and indeed the most prominent part of a sentence (either as a noun, a pronoun, or as expressed in the conjugation of verbs such as *cogito*), in a Japanese sentence a verb or a verbal adjective is central and the subject often does not appear. And so, "given this grammatical structure, from the vantage point of the Japanese language the understanding shared by Descartes and Hobbes—namely the idea that 'we cannot conceive of an act without its subject'—does not of necessity arise."[197]

It is important to point out that Fujita is not asserting a kind of linguistic or cultural relativism according to which one's thought would be strictly determined by one's language and culture such that there would be no reason for, or even any possibility of, cross-cultural dialogue. Rather, quite to the contrary, his point is that it is because our cultural and linguistic backgrounds do strongly influence our thinking that cross-cultural philosophical dialogue is so significant and potentially so fruitful. Fujita concludes:

> If the contrasting claims of Descartes and Nishida presuppose different manners of experience and different structures of language, then, by way of comparison, that is

---

[194] Nishida 1990, 3–4.

[195] See Chapter 17 in this volume.

[196] John Maraldo rightly points out (in an email correspondence dated 7 August 2018) that some Western philosophers, notably Nietzsche, have also doubted the existence of a substantial ego-subject that preexists the act of thinking. Nevertheless, I think it is noteworthy that Nietzsche suggests that this "prejudice of philosophers" may stem from the particularities of the grammar of Indo-European languages (Friedrich Nietzsche, *Beyond Good and Evil*, trans. Walter Kaufmann [New York: Vintage, 1966], 23–4). Moreover, Nietzsche goes on to speculate that "It is highly probable that philosophers within the Ural-Altaic languages [a now contested language family that includes Japanese] (where the concept of the subject is least developed) look otherwise 'into the world,' and will be found on paths of thought different from those of the Indo-Germanic peoples and the Muslims" (27–8). However, Maraldo notes that Pierre Gassendi had objected directly to Descartes that one cannot infer the existence of an agent that thinks merely from the existence of the operation of thinking. See section 3 of Saul Fisher, "Pierre Gassendi," *The Stanford Encyclopedia of Philosophy* (Spring 2014 Edition), Edward N. Zalta (ed.), URL = <https://plato.stanford.edu/archives/spr2014/entries/gassendi/>. Other Western thinkers before and after Nietzsche, including Georg Lichtenberg and William James, also made similar objections. Thus, while we might agree with Fujita that the philosophies of Descartes and Nishida were likely *influenced* by the grammars of their respective languages, it is not the case that grammar strictly *determines* the parameters of what can be thought and what can be questioned.

[197] Fujita 2011, 17. See also Chapter 32 in this volume.

to say, by way of letting each be reflected in the mirror of the other, we can shed light on both of their presuppositions. We can examine whether each of their philosophies is established on the basis of questionable preconceptions, and, if so, we can remove these and rethink the problem at issue. This is what I have in mind when I stress the importance of dialogue in my lectures on the history of Japanese philosophy. It is, after all, the creative dialogue engendered in this manner that enables philosophy to progress along its path of radical inquiry.[198]

This is why Fujita entitled a Japanese text that reiterated these thoughts: "*'Taiwa' toshite no tetsugaku* 「対話」としての哲学 [Philosophy as 'dialogue']."[199]

Philosophy, I have been arguing, always takes place in between a particular and the universal. A particular philosopher or philosophical school or even an entire philosophical tradition can never reach the universal, but they can also never stop trying. This attempt to reach the universal is not a flight from particularity, but rather an attempt to understand one's own particularity and that of others by situating them within the wider context that enables them to be what they are in their similarities and differences. There are no universal human beings floating free of any language, culture, and tradition. And so, in order to better understand the universal humanity that unites us in and mediates our differences, we need to engage in an ongoing dialogue among singular individuals who are situated in—and also move between—particular cultural spheres, spheres which are themselves modified in the processes. "Japanese philosophy," I am suggesting, best names a set of approaches to universality that draw significantly on the sources of Japanese language, culture, and tradition, sources that are themselves continually being formed and reformed in the historical movement of intra- and inter-traditional interaction and dialogue.

Japanese Philosophy as (Mainly) a Subset of Philosophy in Japan

Before concluding this introduction, it behooves us to make a distinction—even if it is one that needs to be kept porous and malleable—between the more specific topic of this volume, "Japanese philosophy," and the more general category of "philosophy in Japan." I hold that the former is best understood as mainly a subset of the latter. The distinction I am proposing between the broader concept of "philosophy in Japan" and the more specific concept of "Japanese philosophy" is a heuristic one and is not meant to reflect a rigid or absolute difference. Moreover, we should remain wary of nationalistic or other ideological attempts to essentialize Japanese philosophy. As a subset of philosophy

---

[198] Fujita 2013, 18. Fujita has recently revised and published his lectures on the history of modern Japanese philosophy (Fujita 2018).

[199] Fujita Masakatsu, *Tetsugaku no hinto* [Hints of philosophy] (Tokyo: Iwanami, 2013), 1–16.

in Japan, Japanese philosophy, too, is a historically fluid category open to international and cross-cultural influences. Nevertheless, there is an important difference between, on the one hand, the text of a Japanese philosopher who explicitly draws on the cultural, linguistic, literary, and religious heritage of Japan and, on the other hand, the text of a Japanese philosopher who merely elucidates and comments on a Western discourse without reflecting on the difference it makes to do this in the Japanese language and cultural milieu. Many philosophers in Japan today do the latter. Indeed, most of the philosophy that is studied, taught, and written about today in Japan is not what most scholars would call Japanese philosophy.[200]

[200] The in other respects informative anthology, *Begriff und Bild der modernen japanischen Philosophie* (Steineck, Lange, Kaufmann 2014a), suffers from a failure to effectively recognize this distinction between Japanese philosophy and philosophy in Japan. Moreover, the editors fail to conceive of a positive conception of "Japanese philosophy" as philosophy that critically and creatively draws on the intellectual, linguistic, cultural, religious, and other sources of Japanese tradition and instead tend to paint all such "Japanese philosophies" with the broad polemical brush of ethnocentric Japanism. As a result, they misleadingly censure the editors of *Japanese Philosophy: A Sourcebook* (Heisig, Kasulis, and Maraldo 2011), as well as the *Frontiers of Japanese Philosophy* series published under Heisig's direction, for purportedly operating under a "cultural relativistic conception of philosophy" (Steineck, Lange, and Kaufmann 2014b, 30). The editors of *Begriff und Bild* are right to stress the diversity of modern Japanese philosophies, and they rightly point out that the development of modern Japanese philosophy can be exclusively characterized "neither in the direction of a dialectical materialism on the one hand nor as a specifically Asian thinking on the other." They stipulate the aim of their volume as that of bringing the full breadth of modern Japanese philosophy to light by offering a "corrective" to what they see as "the predominant reduction in Western literature of modern Japanese philosophy to its Japanistic, self-orientalizing streams" (34–5). Yet their own "corrective" is often as problematic as what they aim to criticize. For example, just prior to this passage, they lump the Kyoto School together with "the long dominant apologetical 'state philosophy' in the line of Inoue Tetsujirō," against which they pit a variety of Japanese philosophers who stood for the "political independence of philosophy" (34). This is a mischaracterization or at best a gross oversimplification of the complexity of the political writings of the Kyoto School philosophers and the controversy surrounding them (see note 151). The editors of *Bild und Begriff* complain that works such as *Sourcebook for Modern Japanese Philosophy* (Dilworth, Viglielmo, Zavala 1998) unduly restrict the scope of (modern) Japanese philosophy to thinkers more or less affiliated with the Kyoto School. They also lodge this complaint against some Japanese works (Fujita 1997; Tsunetoshi 1998), and they could have mentioned many others (Tanaka 2000; Fujita and Davis 2005; Kumano 2009; Higaki 2015). It is indeed the case that attention given to the Kyoto School both in Japan and abroad has overshadowed other interesting and important modern Japanese philosophies, many of which are featured in the second part of the present volume's section on "Modern Japanese Philosophies." However, although the title of their volume speaks of "modern Japanese philosophy," its contents are better characterized as "philosophy in modern Japan" or, indeed, as "the reception of currents of modern Western philosophy in modern Japan." Even though they begin by stating that the "Occidentalization" of philosophy in modern Japan—such that it has tended to be done "in a Western key"—is regrettable, their editorial decision to categorize the main "philosophical streams in Japan" in terms of the reception of Western streams, and so to commission chapters on empiricism, German idealism, phenomenology, existentialism, environmental philosophy, and analytic philosophy as they have been taken up by Japanese philosophers, perpetuates and exacerbates the problem. As informative as those chapters are on aspects of *philosophy in modern Japan* that get marginalized in works that, like the present one, focus on *Japanese philosophy*, presenting "modern Japanese philosophy" as merely a

I suggest that we call Japanese philosophy *any rigorous reflection on fundamental questions that draws sufficiently and significantly on the intellectual, linguistic, cultural, religious, literary, and artistic sources of the Japanese tradition.* Japanese philosophy is thus mainly only a subset of philosophy done in Japan since much of the philosophizing done in Japan today does not sufficiently or significantly draw on these sources—albeit, precisely what counts as "sufficient and significant" should remain open for debate, just as should the parameters of what counts as part of the Japanese tradition.

In fact, based on arguments I have been making in this introduction, the following caveats to this definition are immediately called for. Exactly what the fundamental questions of philosophy are, and what it means to rigorously reflect on them, should remain open for discussion. We need to bear in mind the problems I have addressed regarding the application of terms like "art" and "religion" to non-Western traditions such as that of Japan; these terms are provisionally used here to indicate the range of the sources of Japanese philosophy. Cultures, languages, and traditions are not hermetically sealed and stagnant boxes. Rather, they are streams that never stop changing and interrelating; they are continually in the process of development, often under the influence of, and sometimes in confluence with, other cultures, languages, and traditions.[201] Cultures, languages, and traditions are not monolithic entities but rather the variegated

set of receptions of currents of Western philosophy paints an Ameri-Eurocentric—albeit also an anti-Japanistic—picture of modern Japanese philosophies as mere branches of Western trees. In effect, they oversimplify and exaggerate the pervasiveness of Japanism and counter it with an unrecognized retrenchment of Eurocentrism. In the introduction to his anthology of contemporary philosophy in Japan, Hans Peter Liederbach (2017a) is sharply critical of the editors of *Begriff und Bild* for their lack of attention to the hermeneutical situatedness of philosophies in Japan or elsewhere (but see the critiques of both ironically ethnocentric universalisms as well as cultural essentialisms articulated in Steineck and Lange 2018). Yet he is also wary of claims made by Kyoto School philosophers such as Nishitani and Ueda (and philosophers working in their lineage, such as myself) to be able to draw on Japanese traditions in order to develop a post-metaphysical philosophy that fruitfully responds to the critiques of Western metaphysics by philosophers such as Nietzsche and Heidegger (Liederbach 2017b). In effect, like the editors of *Begriff und Bild*, Liederbach is suggesting that such claims are cut from the same cloth as the cultural ideology of *Nihonjin-ron* theorists. To my mind, however, these critics themselves ironically make the same kind of error as do the cultural ideologues they purport to criticize; in both cases, the cultural cart is put before the philosophical horse. What matters most is not whether a proponent of Japanese philosophy argues for the compelling quality of certain Japanese ideas, but whether he or she argues for them *because they are Japanese* OR *because they are philosophically compelling.* Nishitani and Ueda (and I) are surely intending to do the latter.

[201] The modern concept of culture first came to prominence in the middle of the eighteenth century. Along with the concept of civilization, until the mid-nineteenth century, the concept of culture was only used in the singular (i.e., as a *singulare tantum*). Even Herder, in his influential writings about the differences among countries, peoples, languages, and religions, only used *Kultur* in the singular. It was apparently first Burckhart and then Nietzsche who developed a plural understanding of *Kulturen*. Since the mid-nineteenth century, the plural concept of cultures has served as a means of criticizing Eurocentric conceptions of "progress" as entailing cultural imperialism (see Elberfeld 2017a, 222–4). However, after Spengler's controversial yet influential organistic conception of essentially separate cultures, there has been a persistent tendency to reify different cultural spheres or civilizations into incommensurable monoliths (see, for example, Samuel Huntington's *Clash of Civilizations* [New York: Touchstone, 1996]). Rather, we need to understand cultures as having interwoven histories; we need to understand cultures as fluid and porous spheres that repeatedly enter into a variety of relations of influence and sometimes confluence with other fluid and porous spheres. Japanese culture,

and variable media through which individuals express themselves. Cultures, language, and traditions both shape (determine) and are shaped (counter-determined) by the expressive acts of individuals. Individuals also shape and are shaped by subcultures within a culture, and those subcultures have various relations—some complementary and some antagonistic—with one another. Individuals can and, today more than ever, many do take part in two or more cultures, language, and traditions (being bilingual usually also means being bicultural), such that cross-cultural dialogue is for them an intra- as well as interpersonal affair.

Several pitfalls must be avoided when we define Japanese philosophy as philosophy that draws on Japanese language, culture, and tradition. We must constantly beware of the error many so-called theories of Japaneseness (*Nihonjin-ron*) make[202] insofar as they attempt to essentialize Japanese culture by claiming that there is some unchanging essence such as the "indigenous Japanese spirit" (*yamato-damashī* 大和魂) that would be the exclusive property of the Japanese nation and the ethnically Japanese people.[203] This is to ignore the historicity and the synthetic nature of the Japanese tradition which, like all great traditions, has changed over time, often by critically and creatively appropriating other traditions. Despite past ideologies of "Japanese spirit together with Chinese techniques" (*wakon-kansai* 和魂漢才) and later "Japanese spirit together with Western techniques" (*wakon-yōsai* 和魂洋才), the spiritual, intellectual, and cultural traditions of Japan have been largely shaped and modified by earlier appropriations of Chinese traditions and more recent appropriations of Western traditions. Hence, the adjective "Japanese" in the phrase "Japanese philosophy" should not be taken to imply a cultural essentialism; like all such cultural markers, it refers to a shape-shifting place of critical and creative hybridization. Rein Raud well expresses this point:

> The "Japanese" in the compound "Japanese philosophy" thus does not refer to some hypothetical pure beginning or unchanged cultural quality that is continuous throughout history, but to a specific way of blending cultural flows, in which the later stages contain the memory of the previous ones without necessarily abiding by them.[204]

---

often singled out for its purported uniqueness, is in fact a shape-shifting sphere of iterating patterns that has been formed and reformed over the course of its history, most notably through its formative contacts in the past with Chinese cultural streams and more recently with Western cultural streams.

[202] See note 149.

[203] Here I agree with Gregor Paul that the locution "Japanese philosophy" has at times been used and abused, usually alongside such expressions as "Japanese spirit" (*nippon seishin* 日本精神) and "indigenous Japanese spirit" (*yamato damashii*), in a politically nefarious manner (Paul 1993, 14). Although I do not agree with Paul's portrayal of Nishida and the Kyoto School as mere ideologues of Japanism (136), it is true that Nishida's student Kōyama Iwao, and, to a lesser extent, Nishida himself, at times fell into the trap of essentializing Japanese culture (see Davis 2006*b*, 227–38).

[204] Raud 2017, 19. See also Davis 2011.

Moreover, "Japanese philosophy" is only *mainly* a subset of "philosophy in Japan" since it can, has been, and is being done by philosophers living outside Japan. Not only are there many ethnically Japanese philosophers living and working abroad, there are also a number of ethnically non-Japanese scholars who write about and contribute to the development of Japanese philosophy—in some cases even in the Japanese language. Thus, "Japanese philosophy" should not be taken to refer exclusively to works produced by philosophers who are ethnically Japanese. If Japanese philosophy were the exclusive possession of ethnically Japanese persons, or were it to exclusively address and concern ethnically Japanese persons, then it would not be worthy of being called philosophy, insofar as philosophy aims at universally valid truths (including truths about how to understand particular differences) and not merely at cultural self-expression, much less at self-aggrandizing assertions of cultural superiority. When ethnically Japanese philosophers or ethnically non-Japanese participants in the development of Japanese philosophy concern themselves with the Japanese tradition, it is not merely, and certainly not primarily, for the sake of expressing the particularity of this tradition; it is, or should be, mainly for the sake of making an original contribution to the nascent dialogue of worldwide philosophy. By "worldwide philosophy" I mean a practice of philosophizing that is open to contributions from any and all cultural or intellectual traditions and that refuses to confine the hermeneutical horizon of philosophy to one tradition, such as the Western tradition. Japanese philosophy should be understood as a specific set of contributions to such a worldwide dialogue of philosophy.

Hence, "Japanese philosophy" can be defined as any rigorous reflection on fundamental questions that draws on the intellectual, linguistic, cultural, religious, literary, and artistic heritage of Japan. But this in no way means that it is restricted in practice or in application to persons born and raised in Japan or of ethnically Japanese ancestry, any more than Greek philosophy only applies to and can only be engaged in by Greeks, or German philosophy only applies to and can only be engaged in by Germans.

Another pitfall that must be avoided is the assumption that "Japanese philosophy" is always more valuable than other areas of "philosophy in Japan." To be sure, it is fair to say that any philosopher should attend at least in part to his or her own linguistic and cultural context at least insofar as he or she should strive to become aware of his or her own preconceptions and motivations.[205] On the first day of an introductory philosophy course, Japanese students may learn that, according to Socrates, philosophy involves heeding the imperative to "know thyself" (Gk. *gnōthi seauton*). And yet, in many such ironically Eurocentric philosophy courses in Japan, connections are not drawn to Dōgen's

---

[205] See Kasulis 2018, 578–80, for a trenchant critique of the Ameri-Eurocentrism of postwar academic philosophy in Japan. Claiming that most modern academic philosophers in Japan are in effect acting as accomplices of their own cultural and intellectual colonization, ignoring both Socratic and traditional Japanese injunctions to "know thyself," Kasulis accuses them of "denying their own philosophical heritage" as they "do their technical work as if they were western philosophers working in outposts of European or American departments of philosophy" (578–9).

dictum: "To learn the Buddha Way is to learn the self"[206] or to Daitō Kokushi's characterization of Zen as an "investigation into the self" (己事究明 *koji-kyūmei*). Can one learn to philosophize on one's own two feet if one never looks down? Yet another Zen dictum is applicable here: "Illuminate what lies directly underfoot!" (*shōko-kyakka* 照顧 脚下). It is fair to say that Japanese philosophers, like those of other lands, philosophize best when they spend at least part of their time reflecting on their own situatedness in the ongoing development of the cultural and intellectual history of the Japanese tradition.

On the other hand, the introduction, elucidation, and critical appropriation of foreign philosophical texts and ideas often make very valuable contributions to one's local context of philosophizing. Philosophers often manage to upset the status quo and reshape the intellectual landscape by introducing perspectives that are (at least initially) foreign. The history of philosophical thinking in Japan is replete with examples of this: many pre-Meiji and post-Meiji Japanese philosophers have made indelible contributions to the ongoing development of the Japanese tradition by introducing and appropriating Buddhist, Chinese, and Western ideas and practices. Analogously, many philosophers in Western countries have made in the past, and are making today, significant contributions to the ongoing development of their traditions by critically and creatively appropriating non-Western ideas and practices. Indeed, the chapters of the present volume aspire to be involved in this process. Yet, just as we would generally not refer to these chapters on Japanese philosophy as in and of themselves already instances of Anglo-American philosophy, we need not consider much of the valuable philosophizing that goes on in Japan today as instances of Japanese philosophy. Of course, if and when and to the extent that these appropriations do make a sufficient impact on a tradition, then it would make sense to refer to them as integral parts of that tradition. In fact, all Japanese philosophies arose out of critical and creative appropriations of Buddhist, Chinese, and Western traditions; even the earliest Shintō texts, after all, were written in the Chinese script and in light of Chinese ideas.[207]

In the beginning of this introduction, I heeded Wittgenstein's advice and looked for the definitions of "Japanese philosophy" and "*Nihon tetsugaku*" not in some realm of eternal essences, but rather in the way these terms are used in English and Japanese. It may be that, like the "language games" that Wittgenstein analyzes, there are only "family resemblances" rather than a single essence shared by all that has gone under the name of "philosophy" in the Western tradition and under the names *tetsugaku* and *Nihon tetsugaku* in post-Meiji Japan. To bring this diversity and these family resemblances into view, one can follow Wittgenstein and "don't think, but look!"[208] However, I have not in fact merely looked at and described how the terms "Japanese philosophy" and "*Nihon tetsugaku*" have been and are being used for the reason that languages are always developing and *we are participants in their development*. We are called on not simply to be

---

[206] Dōgen goes on to say that "to learn the self is to forget the self" and that "to forget the self is to be verified by the myriad things of the world." See Chapter 8 in this volume.

[207] See Chapters 1, 2, and 15 in this volume.

[208] Wittgenstein, *Philosophical Investigations*, 31 (§66).

bystanders and observers, but rather to take part in reformulating as well as playing the language game; we are called on not just to play along but to critically think about how the rules and terms of the game have been determined and how they perhaps should be revised. In our case, the question is not just how the terms "Japanese philosophy" and "*Nihon tetsugaku*" have been used in the past and how are they being used today, but also how they should be used in the future. What manner of using these terms would be most faithful to the facts of the past and present as well as most fair and fruitful to possibilities for the future?[209]

Accordingly, I have not only tried to take stock of how "Japanese philosophy" and "*Nihon tetsugaku*" have been and are being used and contested in English (and other Western languages) as well as in Japanese; I have also critiqued these usages and made some suggestions for how we might modify our usage in the future. In particular, while noting attendant problems and pointing out other possibilities, I have suggested that we include at least some pre-Meiji discourses in the category of "philosophy" and "*tetsugaku*." At the very least, I have argued, they should be read and discussed by students and scholars as valuable sources of philosophy. The reasons I have given are both political and philosophical. They are political insofar as I believe the exclusion of non-Western traditions from—or at best marginalization within—departments of philosophy and in general the academic category of "philosophy" in Western countries has been politically motivated. Philosophers are by no means exempt from the all-too-human inclinations to ethnocentrism and racism, and established and influential professors (including those who are neither especially ethnocentric nor racist) do not like to be told that they should include within their fiefdom experts on something they know little to nothing about.

Yet the reasons I have given for including non-Western traditions within the field of philosophy are also strictly philosophical, not only because these traditions harbor discourses that are recognizably philosophical, and not only because they can contribute new ideas, but also insofar as the meta-philosophical question of the nature of philosophy has always been and should always be a welcome part of the practice of philosophizing. Philosophers in various traditions have not only thought and argued about the nature of humans and the world and about how the former should act within the latter; they have also thought and argued about the best way to think and argue about such things. We need a discursive and dialogical field in which the very definition of "philosophy" is open to question and that means open to the possibility of being redefined in light of non-Western traditions. Rather than retreating into a de facto field

---

[209] Rather than simply describing the world, I believe that philosophers are called on to critique, redescribe, and participate in its transformation. Philosophy, I believe, should be prescriptive as well as descriptive, normative as well as analytical. Here I find myself at odds with Wittgenstein (see *The Blue and Brown Books*, 18; also note 3 above), yet in accord both with most continental philosophies, insofar as engagement in a transformative practice of critique is a distinctive trait of that tradition (Critchley 1998, 10), and with most Japanese (and more generally Asian) philosophies, insofar as transformative and liberative practices are also a prominent characteristic of them.

of area studies, the field of hitherto Ameri-Eurocentric or Ameri-Euromonopolistic philosophy is called on to become worldwide philosophy in the sense of a worldwide forum for philosophical dialogue, including dialogue about the very nature of philosophical dialogue.

ON SELECTING TOPICS FOR THIS HANDBOOK

One could restrict the scope of a handbook such as this one to post-Meiji "modern Japanese philosophy" by using the yardstick of modern Western definitions of academic philosophy. This would follow the tendency during the past century in Japan to restrict the use of the term *tetsugaku* in this manner. I have not done this, however, because such a restriction is questionable for both political and philosophical reasons and also because traditional Japanese discourses are manifestly replete with *sources* of philosophical thinking, even if one does not consider those discourses to be themselves sufficiently philosophical. Even the narratives and doctrines of the Shintō tradition, which may well strike one as more "mythological" than philosophical, are nevertheless replete with "philosophical implications" that can be explicated and brought to bear on issues in comparative philosophy of religion and culture (Chapter 2).[210] Regardless of whether readers are convinced that the pre-Meiji source material treated in this or that chapter should be labeled "philosophy," all the chapters in this volume are certainly philosophical treatments of their topics that aim to contribute to contemporary philosophical

---

[210] See also Carter 2001; Kasulis 2004; and Iwasawa 2011. Moreover, note the manner in which modern philosophers such as Watsuji Tetsurō (see Chapter 23 in this volume), Kuki Shūzō (Chapter 24), and Sakabe Megumi (see Chapters 30 and 31) draw on the philosophical resources embedded in Japanese linguistic usage (Chapter 32) and literary texts without claiming that these resources are themselves philosophy. For a contemporary attempt to draw out the philosophical implications of indigenous Japanese words and expressions (*yamato-kotoba* やまと言葉), see Takeuchi 2012 and 2015. Takeuchi's endeavor is based on the idea that, as Nishida Kitarō puts it, "Insofar as philosophy entails coming to a logical self-awareness of our life, it must have an ethnic character to it" (Nishida 1987–1989, 13: 217; Takeuchi 2015, 186), and he repeatedly echoes Watsuji's call for Japanese philosophers to philosophize on the basis of their everyday experience as expressed in everyday language (Watsuji 2011, 90–1; Takeuchi 2015, 3, 165, 209). Takeuchi affirms Watsuji's definition of philosophy as an "academic discipline that attempts to clarify our self-understanding that precedes reflection" (Takeuchi 2015, 9, 169). Yet, on its own, this is surely an insufficient definition of philosophy insofar as this *phenomenological and hermeneutical* endeavor to "clarify" what Heidegger calls our everyday "pre-ontological understanding" must be combined with a *critical* endeavor that runs in both directions, seeking to correct pernicious habits or implicit biases (such as racism) embedded in our everyday experience and language as well as to reformulate abstract concepts that cover over and distort our more concrete experiences of reality. In emphasizing the task of philosophy as an elucidation of prereflective self-understanding, Takeuchi's project must take care not to repeat an ethnically reductive and relativistic conception of philosophy that sees it as primarily the expression of "the genius of an ethnic nation" (see Takeuchi 2015, 185), not to mention the assertions of superiority and exclusionary nationalism of the eighteenth-century scholars of National Learning (see Takeuchi 2015, 8).

discussions. While the chapters in each section proceed roughly in chronological order and aim to cover the most significant and influential topics and figures of (the sources of) philosophical thinking in Japan from the seventh through the beginning of the twenty-first century, the chapters are designed to be individually engaging to contemporary philosophers and students of philosophy and not merely to students and scholars interested in the intellectual history of Japan. History matters for philosophy, but it matters most for how it determines the present and contributes to the future.

While I have been less restrictive than some scholars may have wished by including treatments of pre-Meiji discourses that are either in themselves philosophical or at least contain rich sources for philosophy, other scholars may wish that I would have been even less restrictive, including even more pre-Meiji and post-Meiji figures and discourses. My principle of selection favored figures and discourses that made original and distinctively Japanese contributions to philosophical thinking. Again, the general criterion I have used to determine whether a text is a significant contribution to *Japanese* philosophy is the extent to which the author implicitly or explicitly draws on and makes original and fruitful contributions to the ongoing development of the Japanese tradition of thinking deeply and rigorously about fundamental matters.[211] Hence, for instance, the chapters in the "Philosophies of Japanese Buddhism" section start with Saichō's Tendai (Chapter 4) and Kūkai's Shingon (Chapter 5), rather than with the earlier Nara schools since those earlier schools were importations that do not yet evince much originality.[212] The complexity, depth, and originality of Zen master Dōgen's philosophical writings,

---

[211] While I agree with many of his points and appreciate his efforts to foster attention to the wider field of "Japanese thought," I think that Richard Calichman goes too far when he claims in his introduction to *Contemporary Japanese Thought* that "there seems to be little reason to determine thought on the basis of its geographical or cultural background" (Calichman 2005, 2). What sense would it make to call something "Japanese thought" if it has nothing to do with the Japanese archipelago or with the cultures that have developed there? Does Calichman renounce the legitimacy of the title of his book when he questions "the very possibility of assigning to thinkers and their thoughts any fixed regional properties" (2)? Perhaps not, if we highlight the qualifier "fixed." I agree with Calichman that the editor of a book such as his, or this one, of necessity participates in the ongoing (re)definition of terms such as "Japanese thought" and "Japanese philosophy." But I do not think of this participation in the apparently voluntaristic and explicitly decisionistic terms of Calichman. What he calls "the departure point of phenomenology" is in fact more of an existential voluntarism: "that things in their natural existence are meaningless in and of themselves; objective meaning is something that can by right be *arrived at* only through the participation of consciousness in its repeated acts of inscription" (12). "Japan is *nothing*," he quotes Takeuchi Yoshimi as writing, "meaning in this context that no substantial reality can precede the operation in which Japan comes to be temporarily inscribed or marked up as meaningful" (12). Yet, in terms of Heidegger's early phenomenological ontology, this is to overly stress our *projection* (*Entwerfen*) of meaning without sufficiently attending to our *thrownness* (*Geworfenheit*) in a world already provisionally determined by historicity and facticity. To be sure, "Japan" was never a "substantial reality" endowed with ahistorical essences. But neither was it ever merely "nothing"; there was never a blank slate upon which the first theorist of Japan Studies arbitrarily inscribed a definition of this term. "Japan" was not invented *ex nihilo*, such that a theorist could just as effectively have decided to inscribe the same meanings on the factical givenness—or, as Watsuji would say, on the "climate-and-culture" (*fūdo* 風土)—of, for example, what has come to be called "Iceland."

[212] See Matsunaga and Matsunaga 1976, 1: 26–137.

and the influence they have exerted and continue to exert on modern Japanese philosophy, called for the treatment of his thought in more than one chapter (Chapters 8 and 9). Although space did not allow for the inclusion of chapters on the many noteworthy individual Rinzai Zen masters such as Musō Kokushi, Ikkyū Sōjun, Takuan Sōhō, Bankei Yōtaku, and Hakuin Ekaku, the Rinzai tradition is otherwise well represented with one chapter devoted to the philosophical implications of Rinzai Zen *kōan* training (Chapter 10), another to the three most prominent modern Rinzai Zen thinkers—D. T. Suzuki, Hisamatsu Shin'ichi, and Abe Masao (Chapter 11)—and yet another to the topic of freedom and nature in Zen and related streams of Japanese thought (Chapter 33). Alongside Zen Buddhism, the other most prominent and philosophically influential school of Japanese Buddhism is Shin Buddhism, founded by the thirteenth-century Pure Land Buddhist reformer Shinran. Accordingly, one chapter has been devoted to the philosophical implications of Shinran's writings themselves (Chapter 6) and another to his two most prominent and philosophically astute modern interpreters, Kiyozawa Manshi and Soga Ryōjin (Chapter 7).

The main figures and lines of thought in Japanese Confucianism are treated in two substantial chapters. The first emphasizes the differences between Japanese Neo-Confucianism and Chinese and Korean Neo-Confucianism by highlighting the distinctive relationships between Japanese Neo-Confucianism, Christianity, and Shintō (Chapter 12). The second shows how, even though the scholars of Ancient Learning (*kogaku* 古学) purported to carry out a revival of classical Confucianism, their criticisms of Zhu Xi and other Neo-Confucians in fact reflected their own involvement in the learning of Neo-Confucianism rather than merely their departure from it (Chapter 13). This section of the book also includes a chapter on *bushidō* (Chapter 14), a varied and influential, yet also highly controversial set of discourses on "the way of the warrior" that was developed from strands of Zen Buddhist, Shintō, and Confucian thought in the Edo/Tokugawa period (Chapter 14). This chapter shows how the reconstructive codification of *bushidō* in the early twentieth century informed not only the ideology of militarism but also, in a different key, the ethical and spiritual discourses of modern Japanese martial arts.

The "Modern Japanese Philosophies" section makes up approximately half the book. It begins with a substantial chapter on the introduction of Western philosophy to Japan at the end of the nineteenth century and beginning of the twentieth, a chapter which revisits in greater detail some of the issues discussed in this introduction (Chapter 15). For the remainder of this large section I commissioned chapters on what I judged to be the most significant and original contributions to philosophical thinking in post-Meiji Japan. I did this rather than, for example, commissioning chapters on the intellectual history of how various Western philosophers and schools of philosophy—such as Kant and Neo-Kantianism, German idealism, Marxism, Heidegger, existentialism, post-structuralism, and, more recently, Anglo-American analytic philosophy[213]—have been

---

[213] It can be said that "Anglo-American 'analytic' philosophy of the 1950s and '60s scarcely made a dent in Japanese consciousness" (Blocker and Starling 2001, 189) and, in general, that "the influence of

received in modern Japan. In cases such as Christian philosophies (Chapter 26), the political philosophies of Marxism and liberalism (Chapters 20 and 28), feminist philosophy (Chapter 29), and phenomenology (Chapter 30), it seemed to me that sufficiently original and distinctively Japanese contributions have been made to warrant inclusion chapters devoted to these topics. In the case of some other topics—such as Japanese contributions to environmental philosophy (Chapters 23 and 33) and the philosophy of embodiment (Chapters 5, 20, 27, and 29)[214]—treatment was divided among two or more chapters.

The Kyoto School has undoubtedly been the most prominent group of post-Meiji Japanese philosophers (Chapter 16). While there is some variety in the manners in which scholars define the Kyoto School and its membership,[215] it is a coherent enough set of philosophers to merit grouping them together and separately from other prominent post-Meiji philosophers; although it should be noted that some of the latter—especially Watsuji Tetsurō (Chapter 23), Kuki Shūzō (Chapter 24), and Yuasa Yasuo (Chapter 27)— also had close ties to the Kyoto School. The founder of the Kyoto School, Nishida Kitarō, is widely accepted to be the first truly original and still today the most influential philosopher of modern Japan. His philosophy is accordingly treated in two chapters, one tracing the development of his thought (Chapters 17) and another discussing the contemporary relevance of some of his central ideas (Chapter 18). Although space did not allow for extensive coverage of all the noteworthy philosophers associated with the Kyoto School,[216] subsequent chapters in this subsection focus on the most prominent

Anglo-American analytic philosophy has lagged behind the impact of European thinking on modern Japanese philosophy" (Maraldo 1997, 828). As in other places in the "globalizing" world, however, Anglo-American analytic philosophy presently appears to be gaining popularity in Japan. The Tokyo Forum for Analytic Philosophy, at which papers are given in English, was first formed in 2012. Yamaguchi Shō goes so far as to claim that analytic philosophy is "the most intensively received and researched" current of philosophy in Japan today ("Analytische Philosophie," in Steineck, Lange, and Kaufmann 2014a, 269). (One of the main figures Yamaguchi presents as representative of analytic philosophy in Japan is Ōmori Shōzō, an original thinker whose work in fact defies easy categorization. He is treated in Chapter 31 of the present volume.) Yet Toda Takefumi, in the same volume, gives a more commonly heard and probably more accurate portrayal: "Still today philosophy in the Anglo-Saxon tradition is a minority in Japan" ("Empirismus," in Steineck, Lange, and Kaufmann 2014a, 155). Among the reasons for this, Toda notes the predominant influence of German philosophy in Japan since the Meiji period.

[214] For a recent anthology of Japanese environmental philosophy, see Callicott and McRae 2017. For a substantial discussion of Japanese bioethics (*seimei rinrigaku* 生命倫理学), see Heisig, Kasulis, and Maraldo 2011, 1231–45.

[215] In addition to Chapter 16 in this volume, see Davis 2019c.

[216] Chapter 16 includes brief treatments of Tosaka Jun, Kōyama Iwao, Mutai Risaku, Shimomura Toratarō, and other philosophers associated with the Kyoto School who are not treated extensively elsewhere in this volume. Tosaka has received much attention from Neo-Marxist intellectual historians, and his interventions certainly played a very important role in the modern intellectual history of Japan (see *Tosaka Jun: A Critical Reader*, edited by Ken C. Kawashima, Fabian Schafer, and Robert Stolz [New York: Cornell University Press, 2014]). Nevertheless, although his leftist credentials are more ambiguous, Miki Kiyoshi is surely the most original and philosophically influential of the Marxist philosophers associated with the Kyoto School (see Chapter 20; on some significant postwar Marxist philosophers, see Chapter 28).

among them: Tanabe Hajime (Chapter 19), Miki Kiyoshi (Chapter 20), Nishitani Keiji (Chapter 21), and Ueda Shizuteru (Chapter 22).

Even less could all of the great variety of modern Japanese philosophers working more or less outside the orbit of the Kyoto School be covered in the second subsection of "Modern Japanese Philosophies" (Chapters 23–31). The best that could be done is to treat a broad range of some of the most significant and influential of these, with apologies to readers who do not find their favorite modern Japanese philosophers or topics receiving their due attention.[217] Following the chapters already mentioned, this second subsection on "Other Modern Japanese Philosophies" closes with a chapter on four noteworthy philosophers who taught at the Komaba campus of the University of Tokyo: Hiromatsu Wataru, Sakabe Megumi, Ōmori Shōzō, and Inoue Tadashi (Chapter 31). While not claiming that they formed a "school," the chapter does demonstrate how each of these four philosophers drew on the conceptual resources of the Japanese language—specifically on the homonyms *koto* (こ と, occurrence) and *koto* (こ と, word or language)—to articulate an ontology according to which occurrence and language are inseparable.

The final section of this *Handbook* is dedicated to significant topics that span a range of time periods and schools of thought. It includes chapters on the philosophy of language (Chapter 32), nature and freedom (Chapter 33), ethics (Chapter 34), and aesthetics (Chapter 35). This final section, and the book as a whole, ends with a chapter on the controversial cultural identity of Japanese philosophy, a chapter which substantially supplements the initial treatment of this thorny issue in the present introduction (Chapter 36).

As for drawing chronological lines, it made the most sense to begin with the legendary Prince Shōtoku's *Seventeen-Article Constitution* of 604 CE (Chapter 1), not only because of its antiquity and influence, but also because it clearly presents the synthetic origins of philosophical thinking in the Japanese tradition. On the other end of the temporal spectrum, it seemed best to limit coverage to philosophers who had published their main body of work by the beginning of the twenty-first century. While not purporting to be an Owl of Minerva that can discern in hindsight the essential thinkers and thoughts of the past, even less can I claim to have a grasp on everything significant that is happening in contemporary Japanese philosophy.[218] In any case, the future of Japanese philosophy

---

[217] Inevitably, some noteworthy recent philosophers, such as Nakamura Yūjirō (see Pörtner and Heise 1995, 385–9; Heisig, Kasulis, and Maraldo 2011, 952–7) and Karatani Kōjin (see Karatani 2017 as well as notes 39 and 66 above and Chapter 36 in this volume), did not receive as much attention as they probably deserve; nor arguably did certain topics and movements, for example, debates over "Critical Buddhism" (see Hubbard and Swanson 1997, Shields 2011, and Chapter 4 in this volume) and developments of "clinical philosophy" (see Kimura and Noe 2014, and Chapter 30 in this volume).

[218] For a range of other contemporary work being done in Japanese philosophy and/or philosophy in Japan, see Maraldo 1997; Calichman 2005; Steineck, Lange, and Kaufmann 2014; Liederbach 2017a; Yusa 2017; Krummel 2019; the *Frontiers of Japanese Philosophy* series published by Nanzan Institute for Religion and Culture (http://nirc.nanzan-u.ac.jp/en/publications/ejp/); *Studies in Japanese Philosophy* series published by Chisokudō Publishing (http://chisokudopublications.com/); the *Tetsugaku Companions to Japanese Philosophy* series published by Springer; *Journal of Japanese Philosophy*; *European Journal of Japanese Philosophy*; and the Japanese journals: *Nihon no tetsugaku*,

depends in large part on what we all make of its past and present, and my hope is that this *Handbook* will serve philosophers working both inside and outside of the geographical and cultural spaces of Japan—or somewhere in between—as a platform for that future.

Bibliography and Suggested Readings

Abe, Masao. (1997) "Buddhism in Japan." In *Companion Encyclopedia of Asian Philosophy*, edited by Brian Carr and Indira Mahalingam. New York: Routledge, 746–91.

Arena, Leonardo Vittorio. (2008) *Lo spirito del Giappone: La filosofia del Sol Levante dalle origini ai nostri giorni*. Milano: RCS Libri.

Arisaka, Yoko. (2014) "Modern Japanese Philosophy: Historical Contexts and Cultural Implications." In *Philosophical Traditions*, edited by Anthony O'Hear. Cambridge: Cambridge University Press, 3–25.

Asakura Tomomi. (2014) *"Higashi Ajia ni tetsugaku wa nai" no ka* [Is it True that "There Is No Philosophy in East Asia"?]. Tokyo: Iwanami.

Back, Youngsun, and Philip J. Ivanhoe, eds. (2017) *Traditional Korean Philosophy: Problems and Debates*. Lanham, MD: Rowman and Littlefield.

Baynes, Kenneth, James Bohman, and Thomas McCarthy, eds. (1987) *After Philosophy: End or Transformation?* Cambridge, MA: The MIT Press.

Beaney, Michael. (2013) "What Is Analytic Philosophy?" In *The Oxford Handbook of the History of Analytic Philosophy*, edited by Michael Beaney. New York: Oxford University Press, 3–29.

Bernasconi, Robert. (1995) "Heidegger and the Invention of the Western Philosophical Tradition." *Journal of the British Society for Phenomenology* 26/3: 240–55.

Bernasconi, Robert. (1997) "Philosophy's Paradoxical Parochialism: The Reinvention of Philosophy as Greek." In *Cultural Readings of Imperialism: Edward Said and the Gravity of History*, edited by Keith Ansell-Pearson, Benita Parry, and Judith Squires. London: Lawrence and Wishart, 212–26.

Bernasconi, Robert. (2003) "Ethnicity, Culture, and Philosophy." In *The Blackwell Companion to Philosophy* (second expanded edition), edited by Nicholas Bunnin and E. P. Tsui-James. Oxford: Blackwell, 567–81.

Blocker, H. Gene, and Christopher L. Starling. (2001) *Japanese Philosophy*. New York: State University of New York Press.

Bocking, Brian. (1997). "The Origins of Japanese Philosophy." In *Companion Encyclopedia of Asian Philosophy*, edited by Brian Carr and Indira Mahalingam. New York: Routledge, 709–29.

Bodart-Bailey, B. M. (1997) "Confucianism in Japan." In *Companion Encyclopedia of Asian Philosophy*, edited by Brian Carr and Indira Mahalingam. New York: Routledge, 730–45.

Bouso, Raquel, and James W. Heisig, eds. (2009) *Frontiers of Japanese Philosophy 6: Confluences and Cross-Currents*. Nagoya: Nanzan Institute for Religion and Culture.

Brüll, Lydia. (1993) *Die japanische Philosophie: Eine Einführung* (second edition). Darmstadt: Wissenschaftliche Buchgesellschaft.

Nihontetsugakushi kenkyū, and *Nishida tetsugakkai nenpō*. Also see the websites of the following societies devoted to Japanese philosophy: Nishida Philosophy Association (http://nishida-philosophy.org/); European Network for Japanese Philosophy (https://enojp.org/); and International Association of Japanese Philosophy (https://iajp.weebly.com/).

Calichman, Richard F., ed. (2005) *Contemporary Japanese Thought*. New York: Columbia University Press.

Callicott, J. Baird, and James McRae, eds. (2017) *Japanese Environmental Philosophy*. New York: Oxford University Press.

Carel, Havi, and David Gamez, eds. (2004) *What Philosophy Is: Contemporary Philosophy in Action*. New York: Continuum.

Carr, Brian, and Indira Mahalingam, eds. (1997) *Companion Encyclopedia of Asian Philosophy*. New York Routledge.

Carter, Robert E. (2001) *Encounter with Enlightenment: A Study of Japanese Ethics*. New York: State University of New York Press.

Carter, Robert E. (2008) *The Japanese Arts and Self-Cultivation*. New York: State University of New York Press.

Chakrabarti, Arindam, and Ralph Weber, eds. (2017) *Beyond Comparative Philosophy*. New York: Bloomsbury Academic.

Chan, Wing-Tsit, ed., trans. (1963) *A Sourcebook in Chinese Philosophy*. Princeton, NJ: Princeton University Press.

Cheung, Ching-Yuen, and Wing-Keung Lam, eds. (2017) *Globalizing Japanese Philosophy as an Academic Discipline*. Göttingen: Vandenhoeck & Ruprecht.

Clarke, J. J. (1997) *Oriental Enlightenment: The Encounter Between Asian and Western Thought*. New York: Routledge.

Collins, Randall. (1998) *The Sociology of Philosophies: A Global Theory of Intellectual Change*. Cambridge, MA: Harvard University Press.

Critchley, Simon. (1998) "Introduction: What Is Continental Philosophy?" In *A Companion to Continental Philosophy*, edited by Simon Critchley and William R. Schroeder. Malden: Blackwell, 1–17.

Critchley, Simon. (2001) *Continental Philosophy: A Very Short Introduction*. New York: Oxford University Press.

Cutrofello, Andrew. (2005) *Continental Philosophy: A Contemporary Introduction*. New York: Routledge.

Dale, Peter. (1986) *The Myth of Japanese Uniqueness*. New York: St. Martin's Press.

Dalissier, M., S. Nagai, and Y. Sugimura, eds. (2013) *Philosophie japonaise: Le néant, le monde et le corps*. Paris: Vrin.

Davis, Bret W. (2004) "Provocative Ambivalences in Japanese Philosophy of Religion: With a Focus on Nishida and Zen." In *Japanese Philosophy Abroad*, edited by James W. Heisig. Nagoya, Japan: Nanzan Institute for Religion and Culture, 246–74.

Davis, Bret W. (2006a) "Rethinking Reason, Faith, and Practice: On the Buddhist Background of the Kyoto School." *Shūkyōtetsugaku kenkyū* (Studies in the Philosophy of Religion) 23: 1–12.

Davis, Bret W. (2006b) "Toward a World of Worlds: Nishida, the Kyoto School, and the Place of Cross-Cultural Dialogue." In *Frontiers of Japanese Philosophy*, edited by James W. Heisig. Nagoya: Nanzan Institute for Religion and Culture, 205–45.

Davis, Bret W. (2009) "Step Back and Encounter: From Continental to Comparative Philosophy." *Comparative and Continental Philosophy* 1/1: 9–22.

Davis, Bret W. (2011) "Dialogue and Appropriation: The Kyoto School as Cross-Cultural Philosophy." In *Japanese and Continental Philosophy: Conversations with the Kyoto School*, edited by Bret W. Davis, Brian Schroeder, and Jason M. Wirth. Bloomington: Indiana University Press, 33–51.

Davis, Bret W. (2013a) "Opening Up the West: Toward Dialogue with Japanese Philosophy." *Journal of Japanese Philosophy* 1: 57–83.

Davis, Bret W. (2013b) "Heidegger and Asian Philosophy." In *The Bloomsbury Companion to Heidegger*, edited by François Raffoul and Eric S. Nelson. New York: Bloomsbury Academic, 459–71.

Davis, Bret W. (2014) "Conversing in Emptiness: Rethinking Cross-Cultural Dialogue with the Kyoto School." In *Philosophical Traditions*, edited by Anthony O'Hear. Cambridge: Cambridge University Press, 171–94.

Davis, Bret W. (2015) "Nihon-tetsugaku no teigi ni tsuite" [On the Definition of Japanese Philosophy]. *Nishidatetsugakkai Kaihō* [Bulletin of the Nishida Philosophy Association] 7: 5–7.

Davis, Bret W. (2017) "Gadfly of Continental Philosophy: On Robert Bernasconi's Critique of Philosophical Eurocentrism." In *Dislodging Eurocentrism and Racism from Philosophy*, a special issue of *Comparative and Continental Philosophy* 9/2: 119–29.

Davis, Bret W. (2019a) "Beyond Philosophical Euromonopolism: Other Ways of—not otherwise than—Philosophy." *Philosophy East and West* 69/2.

Davis, Bret W. (2019b) "Nihon-tetsugaku to wa nanika: Sono teigi to han'i wo saikō suru kokoromi" [What Is Japanese Philosophy? Rethinking Its Definition and Scope]. *Nihontetsugakushi Kenkyū* [Research in the History of Japanese Philosophy] 16: 1–20.

Davis, Bret W. (2019c) "The Kyoto School." *The Stanford Encyclopedia of Philosophy* (Summer 2019 Edition), edited by Edward N. Zalta. https://plato.stanford.edu/archives/sum2019/entries/kyoto-school/.

Davis, Bret W., Brian Schroeder, and Jason M. Wirth, eds. (2011) *Japanese and Continental Philosophy: Conversations with the Kyoto School.* Bloomington: Indiana University Press.

Deleuze, Gilles, and Félix Guattari. (1994) *What Is Philosophy?* translated by Hugh Tomlinson and Graham Burchell. New York: Columbia University Press.

Deutsch, Eliot, and Ron Bontekoe, eds. (1997) *A Companion to World Philosophies.* Malden, MA: Blackwell Publishers.

Elberfeld, Rolf. (1999) *Kitarō Nishida: Modern japanische Philosophie und die Frage nach der Interkulturalität.* Amsterdam: Rodopi.

Elberfeld, Rolf. (2004) *Phänomenologie der Zeit im Buddhismus: Methoden interkulturellen Philosophierens.* Stuttgart: Frommann Holboog.

Elberfeld, Rolf, ed. (2006) *Was ist Philosophie? Programmatische Texte von Platon bis Derrida.* Stuttgart: Reclam.

Elberfeld, Rolf. (2017a) *Philosophieren in einer globalisierten Welt.* Freiburg: Verlag Karl Alber.

Elberfeld, Rolf, ed. (2017b) *Philosophiegeschichtsschreibung in globaler Perspektive.* Hamburg: Felix Meiner Verlag.

Elberfeld, Rolf. (2017c) "Geschichtsschreibung zur Philosophie in Japan in westlichen Sprachen seit dem 20. Jahrhundert." In *Philosophiegeschichtsschreibung in globaler Perspektive*, edited by Rolf Elberfeld. Hamburg: Felix Meiner Verlag, 151–63.

Elberfeld, Rolf. (2017d) "Ansätze globaler Philosophiegeschichtsschreibung: Kommentierender Überblick anhand von Textpassagen und Inhaltsverzeichnissen." In *Philosophiegeschichtss chreibung in globaler Perspektive*, edited by Rolf Elberfeld. Hamburg: Felix Meiner Verlag, 281–340.

Emmanuel, Steven, ed. (2013) *A Companion to Buddhist Philosophy.* West Sussex, UK: Wiley-Blackwell.

Forzani, Giuseppe Jisô. (2006) *I fiori del vuoto: Introduzione a la filosofia giapponese.* Torino: Bollati Boringhieri.

Fu, Charles Wei-Hsun, and Steven Heine, eds. (1995) *Japan in Traditional and Postmodern Perspectives*. New York: SUNY Press.

Fujita Masakatsu, ed. (1997) *Nihon kindai shisō o manabu hito no tame ni* [For Students of Modern Japanese Thought]. Kyoto: Sekaishisōsha.

Fujita Masakatsu, ed. (2000*a*) "*Chi no zahyōjiku: Nihon ni okeru tetsugaku no keisei to sono kanōsei* [Coordinate Axes of Knowledge: The Formation and Possibilities of Philosophy in Japan]. Kyoto: Kōyō Shobō.

Fujita Masakatsu. (2000*b*) "Nihon no tetsugaku?" [Japanese Philosophy?]. In "*Chi no zahyōjiku: Nihon ni okeru tetsugaku no keisei to sono kanōsei* [Coordinate Axes of Knowledge: The Formation and Possibilities of Philosophy in Japan], edited by Fujita Masakatsu. Kyoto: Kōyō Shobō, 3–19.

Fujita Masakatsu. (2011) "The Question of Japanese Philosophy," translated by John C. Maraldo. In *Japanese Philosophy: A Sourcebook*, edited by James W. Heisig, Thomas P. Kasulis, and John C. Maraldo. Honolulu: University of Hawai'i Press, 993–1001.

Fujita Masakatsu. (2013) "The Significance of Japanese Philosophy," translated by Bret W. Davis. *Journal of Japanese Philosophy* 1: 5–20.

Fujita Masakatsu. (2018) *Nihon-tetsugaku-shi* [The History of Japanese Philosophy]. Kyoto: Shōwadō.

Fujita Masakatsu, and Bret Davis, eds. (2005) *Sekai no naka no Nihon no tetsugaku* [Japanese Philosophy in the World]. Kyoto: Shōwadō.

Furuta Hikaru, and Ikimatsu Keizō, eds. (1972) *Nihon no tetsugaku* [Japanese Philosophy]. Tokyo: Iwanami.

Garfield, Jay, and William Edelglass, eds. (2009) *Buddhist Philosophy: Essential Readings*. New York: Oxford University Press.

Garfield, Jay, and William Edelglass, eds. (2011) *The Oxford Handbook of World Philosophy*. New York: Oxford University Press.

Garfield, Jay L., and Bryan W. Van Norden. (2016) "If Philosophy Won't Diversify, Let's Call It What It Really Is." *The New York Times*, May 11, 2016. http://www.nytimes.com/2016/05/11/opinion/if-philosophy-wont-diversify-lets-call-it-what-it-really-is.html?emc=eta1&_r=1

Gasché, Rodolphe. (2009) *Europe, or the Infinite Task: A Study of a Philosophical Concept*. Stanford: Stanford University Press.

Glock, Hans-Johann. (2008) *What Is Analytic Philosophy?* New York: Cambridge University Press.

Goto-Jones, Chris, ed. (2008) *Re-politicising the Kyoto School as Philosophy*. London: Routledge.

González Valles, Jusús. (2000) *Historia de la filosofía japonesa*. Madrid: Tecnos.

Graham, A. C. (1989) *Disputers of the Tao: Philosophical Argument in Ancient China*. Chicago: Open Court.

Hadot, Pierre. (1995) *Philosophy as a Way of Life: Spiritual Exercises from Socrates to Foucault*, edited by Arnold I. Davidson, translated by Michael Chase. Oxford: Blackwell.

Hadot, Pierre. (2002) *What Is Ancient Philosophy?* translated by Michael Chase. Cambridge, MA: Belknap Press.

Halbfass, Wilhelm. (1988) *India and Europe: An Essay in Understanding*. Albany: State University of New York Press.

Havens, Thomas R. H. (1970) *Nishi Amane and Modern Japanese Thought*. Princeton, NJ: Princeton University Press.

Heidegger, Martin. (1958) *What Is Philosophy?* translated by William Kluback and Jean T. Wilde. New Haven, CT: College and University Press.

Heidegger, Martin. (1971) "Dialogue Between a Japanese and an Inquirer on Language." In *On the Way to Language*, translated by Peter D. Hertz. New York: Harper & Row, 1–54.

Heisig, James W. (2001) *Philosophers of Nothingness: An Essay on the Kyoto School*. Honolulu: University of Hawai'i Press.

Heisig, James W., ed. (2004) *Japanese Philosophy Abroad*. Nagoya, Japan: Nanzan Institute for Religion and Culture.

Heisig, James W., ed. (2006) *Frontiers of Japanese Philosophy*. Nagoya: Nanzan Institute for Religion and Culture.

Heisig, James W., Thomas P. Kasulis, and John C. Maraldo, eds. (2011) *Japanese Philosophy: A Sourcebook*. Honolulu: University of Hawai'i Press.

Heisig, James W., Thomas P. Kasulis, John C. Maraldo, and R. Bouso García, eds. (2016) *La filosofía japonesa en sus textos*. Barcelona: Herder.

Heisig, James W., and John C. Maraldo, eds. (1995) *Rude Awakenings: Zen, the Kyoto School and the Question of Nationalism*. Honolulu: University of Hawai'i Press.

Heisig, James W., and Rein Raud, eds. (2010) *Frontiers of Japanese Philosophy 7: Classical Japanese Philosophy*. Nagoya: Nanzan Institute for Religion and Culture.

Heisig, James W., and Uehara Mayuko, eds. (2008) *Frontiers of Japanese Philosophy 3: Origins and Possibilities*. Nagoya: Nanzan Institute for Religion and Culture.

Higaki Tatsuya. (2015) *Nihon tetsugaku genron josetsu* [Prolegomenon to a Groundwork of Japanese Philosophy]. Kyoto: Jinbun Shoin.

Hiromatsu Wataru et al., eds. (1989) *Iwanami tetsugaku shisō jiten* [Iwanami Dictionary of Philosophy and Thought]. Tokyo: Iwanami.

Hori, Victor Sōgen, and Melissa Anne-Marie Curley, eds. (2008) *Frontiers of Japanese Philosophy 2: Neglected Themes and Hidden Variations*. Nagoya: Nanzan Institute for Religion and Culture.

Huang, Chun-chieh, and John Allen Tucker, eds. (2014) *Dao Companion to Japanese Confucian Philosophy*. New York: Springer.

Hubbard, Jamie, and Paul L. Swanson, eds. (1997) *Pruning the Bodhi Tree: The Storm Over Critical Buddhism*. Honolulu: University of Hawai'i Press.

Imai Jun, and Ozawa Tomio, eds. (1979) *Nihon shisō ronsō-shi* [A History of Disputations in Japanese Thought]. Tokyo: Perikan-sha.

Inouye, Charles Shirō. (2008) *Evanescence and Form: An Introduction to Japanese Culture*. New York: Palgrave Macmillan.

Ishida Ichirō. (1963) *Nihon-shisō-shi gairon* [Overview of the History of Japanese Thought]. Tokyo: Yoshikawa Kōbun-kan.

Itō Tomonobu. (1990) "Kindai Nihon-tetsugakusha no keifu" [Genealogy of Modern Japanese Philosophers]. In *Gendai Nihon no tetsugakusha* [Contemporary Japanese Philosophers], a special issue of *Risō* 646: 112–23.

Ivanhoe, Philip J., and Bryan W. Van Norden, eds. (2005) *Readings in Classical Chinese Philosophy* (second edition). Indianapolis: Hackett.

Iwasawa, Tomoko. (2011) *Tama in Japanese Myth: A Hermeneutical Study of Ancient Japanese Divinity*. Lanham, MD: University Press of America.

Jacinto Zavala, Agustín, ed. (1995) *Textos de la filosofía japonesa moderna*. Michoacán: El Colegio de Michoacán.

Jacinto Zavala, Agustín. (1997) *La otra filosofía japonesa*. Michoacán: El Colegio de Michoacán.

Jaspers, Karl. (1976) *Was ist Philosophie? Ein Lesebuch*. Munich: Piper.

Josephson, Jason Ānanda. (2012) *The Invention of Religion in Japan*. Chicago: University of Chicago Press.

Karatani, Kōjin. (2017) *Isonomia and the Origins of Philosophy*, translated by Joseph A. Murphy. Durham, NC: Duke University Press.

Karube Tadashi, and Kataoka Ryū, eds. (2008) *Nihon-shisō-shi handobukku* [Handbook of the History of Japanese Thought]. Tokyo: Shinsho-kan.

Kasulis, Thomas P. (2002) *Intimacy or Integrity: Philosophy and Cultural Difference*. Honolulu: University of Hawai'i Press, 2002.

Kasulis, Thomas P. (2004) *Shintō: The Way Home*. Honolulu: The University of Hawai'i Press.

Kasulis, Thomas P. (2018) *Engaging Japanese Philosophy: A Short History*. Honolulu: The University of Hawai'i Press.

Kasulis, Thomas P. (2019) "Japanese Philosophy." *The Stanford Encyclopedia of Philosophy*.

Kida Gen. (2004) *Tetsugaku to han-tetsugaku* [Philosophy and Anti-philosophy]. Tokyo: Iwanami.

Kida Gen. (2014) "'Tetsugaku' to wa nan de atta no ka" [What Was "Philosophy"]. In *Kida Gen: Keimyō shadatsu na han-tetsugaku* [Kida Gen: Lambent and Unconstrained Anti-philosophy]. Tokyo: Kawade Shobō Shinja, 40–52.

Kimura Bin, and Noe Keiichi, eds. (2014) *Rinshō tetsugaku to wa nanika* [What is Clinical Philosophy?]. Nagoya: Kawai Bunka Kyōiku Kenyūsho.

Koizumi, Takashi. (1997) "Morals and Society in Japanese Philosophy." In *Companion Encyclopedia of Asian Philosophy*, edited by Brian Carr and Indira Mahalingam. New York: Routledge, 792–809.

Kopf, Gereon. (2014) "Philosophy as Expression: Towards a New Model of Global Philosophy." *Nishida Tetsugakkai Nenpō* 11: 155–81.

Kopf, Gereon, ed. (2019) *Dao Companion to Japanese Buddhist Philosophy*. New York: Springer.

Krings, Leon. (2017) "Materialien und Auswahlbibliographie zur japanischsprachigen Philoso phiegeschichtsschreibung." In *Philosophiegeschichtsschreibung in globaler Perspektive*, edited by Rolf Elberfeld. Hamburg: Felix Meiner Verlag, 341–64.

Krummel, John W. M. (2017) "Philosophy and Japanese Philosophy in the World." *European Journal of Japanese Philosophy* 2: 189–222.

Krummel, John W. M., ed. (2019) *Contemporary Japanese Philosophy: A Reader*. New York: Roman & Littlefield International.

Kumano Sumihiko. (2009) *Nihon tetsugaku shōshi* [A Short History of Japanese Philosophy]. Tokyo: Chūōkōron Shinsha.

Lam, Wing-keung, and Cheung Ching-yuen, eds. (2009) *Frontiers of Japanese Philosophy 4: Facing the 21st Century*. Nagoya: Nanzan Institute for Religion and Culture.

Larson, Gerald James, and Eliot Deutsch, eds. (1988) *Interpreting Across Boundaries: New Essays in Comparative Philosophy*. Princeton, NJ: Princeton University Press.

Liederbach, Hans Peter, ed. (2017a) *Philosophie im gegenwärtigen Japan*. Munich: Iudicium.

Liederbach, Hans Peter. (2017b) "Philosophie im gegenwärtigen Japan: Eine Problemskizze." In *Philosophie im gegenwärtigen Japan*, edited by Hans Peter Liederbach. Munich: Iudicium, 9–34.

Ma, Lin, and Jaap van Brakel. (2016) *Fundamentals of Comparative and Intercultural Philosophy*. Albany: State University of New York Press.

Mall, Ram Adhar. (2000) *Intercultural Philosophy*. New York: Rowman & Littlefield.

Maraldo, John C. (1997) "Contemporary Japanese Philosophy." In *Companion Encyclopedia of Asian Philosophy*, edited by Brian Carr and Indira Mahalingam. New York: Routledge, 810–35.

Maraldo, John C. (2004) "Defining Philosophy in the Making." In *Japanese Philosophy Abroad*, edited by James W. Heisig. Nagoya, Japan: Nanzan Institute for Religion and Culture, 220–45.

Maraldo, John C. (2013) "Japanese Philosophy as a Lens on Greco-European Thought." *Journal of Japanese Philosophy* 1: 21–56.

Maraldo, John C. (2017) *Japanese Philosophy in the Making 1: Crossing Paths with Nishida*. Nagoya: Chisokudō.

Marra, Michele. (1999) *Modern Japanese Aesthetics: A Reader*. Honolulu: University of Hawai'i Press.

Marra, Michael F., ed., trans. (2001) *A History of Modern Japanese Aesthetics*. Honolulu: University of Hawai'i Press.

Marra, Michael F., ed. (2002) *Japanese Hermeneutics: Current Debates on Aesthetics and Interpretation*. Honolulu: University of Hawai'i Press.

Maruyama, Masao. (1961) *Nihon no shisō* [Japanese Thought]. Tokyo: Iwanami Shinsho.

Maruyama, Masao. (1974) *Studies in the Intellectual History of Tokugawa Japan*, translated by Mikiso Hane. Tokyo: University of Tokyo Press.

Matsunaga, Daigan, and Alicia Matsunaga. (1976) *Foundation of Japanese Buddhism*. 2 volumes. Los Angeles/Tokyo: Buddhist Books International.

Mattice, Sarah A. (2014) *Metaphor and Metaphilosophy: Philosophy as Combat, Play, and Aesthetic Experience*. Lanham: Lexington Books.

McEvilley, Thomas. (2002) *The Shape of Ancient Thought: Comparative Studies in Greek and Indian Philosophies*. New York: Allworth Press.

Miller, Mara. (2011) "Japanese Aesthetics and Philosophy of Art." In *The Oxford Handbook of World Philosophy*, edited by Jay Garfield and William Edelglass. New York: Oxford University Press, 317–33.

Miyoshi, Masao, and H. D. Harootunian, eds. (1989) *Postmodernism and Japan*. Durham, NC: Duke University Press.

Morisato, Takeshi, ed. (2008) *Critical Perspectives on Japanese Philosophy: Frontiers of Japanese Philosophy 8*. Nagoya: Nanzan Institute for Religion and Culture.

Morisato, Takeshi, ed. (2015–) Book series: *Studies in Japanese Philosophy*. Nagoya: Chisokudō Publishing.

Nagatomo, Shigenori. (1997) "Contemporary Japanese Philosophy." In *A Companion to World Philosophies*, edited by Eliot Deutsch and Ron Bontekoe. Malden, MA: Blackwell Publishers, 523–30.

Najita, Tetsuo, and Irwin Scheiner, eds. (1978) *Japanese Thought in the Tokugawa Period 1600–1868*. Chicago: University of Chicago Press.

Nakamura, Hajime. (2002) *History of Japanese Thought 592–1868: Japanese Philosophy before Western Culture Entered Japan*. London: Kegan Paul.

Nihon no tetsugaku [Japanese Philosophy]. (2000–) An annual journal edited by the *Nihon tetsugakushi fōramu* [Forum of the History of Japanese Philosophy]. Kyoto: Shōwadō.

Nihontetsugakushi kenkyū [Studies in the History of Japanese Philosophy]. (2003–) An annual journal edited and published by the Department of the History of Japanese Philosophy at Kyoto University.

Nishida Kitarō. (1987–1989) *Nishida Kitarō zenshū* [Complete Works of Nishida Kitarō]. Tokyo: Iwanami.

Nishida Kitarō. (1990) *An Inquiry into the Good*, translated by Masao Abe and Christopher Ives. New Haven, CT: Yale University Press.

Nishida Kitarō. (1987) *Last Writings: Nothingness and the Religious Worldview*, translated with an Introduction and Postscript by David A. Dilworth. Honolulu: University of Hawai'i Press.

Nishida tetsugakkai nenpō [Journal of the Nishida Philosophy Association]. (2005–) An annual journal published by the *Nishida Tetsugakkai* (Nishida Philosophy Association).

Nishitani Keiji, ed. (1967) *Gendai Nihon no tetsugaku* [Contemporary Japanese Philosophy]. Kyoto: Yūkon-sha.

Noe, Keiichi, Ching Yuen Cheung, and Wing Keung Lam. (2019–) Book series: *Tetsugaku Companions to Japanese Philosophy*. New York: Springer.

Ōhashi Ryōsuke. (1992) *Nihon-tekina mono, Yōroppa-tekina mono* [Things Japanese, Things European]. Tokyo: Shinchō-sha.

Ohashi, Ryôsuke, ed. (2014) *Die Philosophie der Kyôto Schule* (third edition). Freiburg: Karl Alber.

O'Hear, Anthony, ed. (2014) *Philosophical Traditions*. Cambridge: Cambridge University Press.

Park, Jin. (2017) "Philosophizing and Power: The East-West Encounter in the Formation of Modern East Asian Buddhist Philosophy." *Philosophy East and West* 67/3: 801–24.

Park, Peter K. (2013) *Africa, Asia, and the History of Philosophy: Racism in the Formation of the Philosophical Canon, 1780–1930*. Albany: State University of New York Press.

Paul, Gregor. (1993) *Philosophie in Japan von den Anfängen bis zur Heian-Zeit: Eine kritische Untersuchung*. München: Iudicium.

Perkins, Franklin. (2011) "Europe and the Question of Philosophy: A Response to Rodolfe Gasché, *Europe, or the Infinite Task*." *Comparative and Continental Philosophy* 3/1: 34–43.

Piovesana, Gino K. (1997) *Recent Japanese Philosophical Thought, 1862–1996: A Survey*. Revised edition including a new survey by Naoshi Yamawaki: "The Philosophical Thought of Japan from 1963 to 1996." Richmond, UK: Japan Library (Curzon Press Ltd).

Pörtner, Peter, and Jens Heise. (1995) *Die Philosophie Japan: Von den Anfängen bis zur Gegenwart*. Stuttgart: Alfred Kröner Verlag.

Radhakrishnan, Sarvepalli, and Charles A. Moore, eds. (1957) *A Sourcebook in Indian Philosophy*. Princeton, NJ: Princeton University Press.

Ragland, C. P., and Sarah Heidt, eds. (2001) *What is Philosophy?* New Haven, CT: Yale University Press.

Raud, Rein. (2017) "What Is Japanese About Japanese Philosophy?" In *Rethinking "Japanese Studies,"* edited by Mayuko Sano and Liu Jianhui. Kyoto: Nichibunken, 15–27.

Regenbogen, Arnim. (2014) "Philosophiebegriffe." In *Disziplinen der Philosophie*, edited by Horst D. Brandt. Hamburg: Felix Meiner Verlag, 9–42.

Sagara Tōru, ed. (1984) *Nihon-shisō-shi nyūmon* [Introduction to the History of Japanese Thought]. Tokyo: Perikansha.

Sakai, Naoki. (1997) *Translation and Subjectivity: On "Japan" and Cultural Nationalism*. Minneapolis: University of Minnesota Press.

Schmitz, Hermann. (2018) *Wozu philosophieren?* Freiburg: Verlag Karl Alber.

Shields, James Mark. *Critical Buddhism: Engaging with Modern Japanese Buddhist Thought*. Burlington, VT: Ashgate.

Smart, Ninian. (1999) *World Philosophies*. New York: Routledge.

Smith, Justin E. H. (2016) *The Philosopher: A History in Six Types*. Princeton: Princeton University Press.

Steineck, Raji C. (2014) "Der Begriff der Philosophie und seine taxonomische Funktion bei Nishi Amane." In *Begriff und Bild der modernen japanischen Philosophie*, edited by Raji C. Steineck, Elena Louisa Lange, and Paulus Kaufmann. Stuttgart-Bad Cannstatt: Frommann-holzboog, 41–61.

Steineck Raji C., and Elena Louisa Lange. (2018) "Introduction: 'What is Japanese Philosophy?'" In *Concepts of Philosophy in Asia and the Islamic World, Vol. 1: China and Japan*, edited by Raji C. Steineck, Ralf Weber, Elena Louisa Lange, and Robert H. Gassmann. Leiden and Boston: Brill Rodopi, 459–81.

Steineck, Raji C., Elena Louisa Lange, and Paulus Kaufmann, eds. (2014a) *Begriff und Bild der modernen japanischen Philosophie*. Stuttgart-Bad Cannstatt: Frommann-holzboog.

Steineck, Raji C., Elena Louisa Lange, and Paulus Kaufmann. (2014b) "Moderne japanische Philosophie—historiographische Ansätze und Probleme." In *Begriff und Bild der modernen japanischen Philosophie*, edited by Raji C.Steineck, Elena Louisa Lange, and Paulus Kaufmann. Stuttgart-Bad Cannstatt: Frommann-holzboog, 1–37.

Steineck, Raji C., Ralf Weber, Elena Louisa Lange, and Robert H. Gassmann. (2018) *Concepts of Philosophy in Asia and the Islamic World, Vol. 1: China and Japan*. Leiden and Boston: Brill Rodopi.

Strala, Jan Gerrit, and Takeshi Morisato, eds. (2016–) *European Journal of Japanese Philosophy*. Nagoya: Chisokudō.

Stroll, Avrum. (2000) *Twentieth-Century Analytic Philosophy*. New York: Columbia University Press.

Sueki Fumihiko. (2012) *Tetsugaku no genba: Nihon de kangaeru to iu koto* [The Site of Philosophy: Thinking in Japan]. Tokyo: Transview.

Synthesis Philosophica No. 37 (2004). Zagreb, Croatia. Special issue on "Japanische Philosophie."

Takeuchi Seiichi. (2012) *Yamato kotoba de tetsugaku suru* [Philosophizing in the Indigenous Japanese Language]. Tokyo: Shunjūsha.

Takeuchi Seiichi. (2015) *Yamato kotoba de "Nihon" o shisō suru* [Thinking "Japan" in the Indigenous Japanese Language]. Tokyo: Shunjūsha.

Tamura Yoshirō. (1982) "Nihon shisō ni okeru kū" [Emptiness in Japanese Thought]. In *Kū* [Emptiness] (part 2), *Bukkyō shisō* [Buddhist Thought], vol. 7, edited by Bukkyō shisō kenkyūkai [Research Group for the Study of Buddhist Thought]. Kyoto: Byōrakuji Shoten, 881–906.

Tanaka Kyūbun. (2000). *Nihon no "tetsugaku" o yomitoku* [Reading Japanese "Philosophy"]. Tokyo: Chikuma Shinsho.

Tremblay, Jacynthe, ed. (2010) *Philosophes japonais contemporains*. Montreal: Montréal University Press.

Tsunetoshi Sōzaburō, ed. (1998) *Nihon no tetsugaku o manabu hito no tame ni* [For Students of Japanese Philosophy]. Kyoto: Sekaishisō-sha.

Tsunoda, R., and W. T. de Bary, eds. (1958) *Sources of Japanese Tradition*. 2 Volumes. New York: Columbia University Press.

Tucker, John Allen, ed. (2013) *Critical Readings in Japanese Confucianism*. 4 Volumes. Leiden: Brill.

Ueda Shizuteru. (2000) "Nihon no tetsugaku" [Japanese Philosophy]. *Nihon no tetsugaku* [Japanese Philosophy] 1: 3–4.

Ueda Shizuteru. (2011) "Contributions to Dialogue with the Kyoto School," translated by Bret W. Davis. In *Japanese and Continental Philosophy: Conversations with the Kyoto School*, edited by Bret W. Davis, Brian Schroeder, and Jason Wirth. Bloomington: Indiana University Press, 19–32.

Uehara Mayuko, ed. (2013–) *Japanese Philosophy*. A journal published by State University of New York Press.

Ueyama Shunpei. (1972) "Shisō no Nihon-teki tokushitsu" [The Distinctively Japanese Character of Thought]. In *Nihon no tetsugaku* [Japanese Philosophy], edited by Furuta Hikaru and Ikimatsu Keizō. Tokyo: Iwanami, 1–51.

Van Norden, Bryan W. (2017) *Taking Philosophy Back: A Multicultural Manifesto*, with a foreword by Jay L. Garfield. New York: Columbia University Press.

Wakabayashi, Bob Tadashi, ed. (1998) *Modern Japanese Thought*. Cambridge: Cambridge University Press.

Watsuji Tetsurō. (2002) *Shinpen Nihonseishinshi kenkyū* [New Edition of Studies in the Intellectual History of Japan], edited by Fujita Masakatsu. Kyoto: Tōei-sha.

Watsuji Tetsurō. (2011) "The Japanese Language and the Question of Philosophy," translated by Michael F. Marra. In *Japan's Frames of Meaning: A Hermeneutics Reader*, edited by Michael F. Marra. Honolulu: University of Hawai'i Press, 51–91.

Wimmer, Franz Martin. (2017) "Unterwegs zum euräqualistischen Paradigma der Philosophiegeschichte im 18. Jahrhundert: Barbaren, Exoten und das chinesische Ärgernis." In *Philosophiegeschichtsschreibung in globaler Perspektive*, edited by Rolf Elberfeld. Hamburg: Felix Meiner Verlag, 167–94.

Yamakage Motohisa. (2006) *The Essence of Shintō: Japan's Spiritual Heart*, edited by Paul de Leeuw and Aidan Rankin, translated by Mineko S. Gillespie, Gerald L. Gillespie, and Yoshitsugu Komuro. New York: Kodansha International.

Yusa, Michiko, ed. (2017) *The Bloomsbury Research Handbook of Contemporary Japanese Philosophy*. New York: Bloomsbury.

Zahavi, Dan. (2016) "Analytic and Continental Philosophy: From Duality Through Plurality to (Some Kind of) Unity." In *Analytic and Continental Philosophy: Methods and Perspectives*, edited by Sonja Rinofner-Kreidl and Harald A. Wiltsche. Berlin: De Gruyter, 79–93.

PART I

SHINTŌ AND
THE SYNTHETIC
NATURE OF JAPANESE
PHILOSOPHICAL
THOUGHT

CHAPTER 1

....

PRINCE SHŌTOKU'S *CONSTITUTION* AND THE SYNTHETIC NATURE OF JAPANESE THOUGHT

....

THOMAS P. KASULIS

JAPAN's reputation for blending the new with the traditional applies as much to its philosophies as its other cultural domains. When foreign ideas or theories have entered Japan, its intellectuals have usually not resisted them as alienating or threatening (as Hegelianism would predict), but instead quite the opposite. Like today's electronics consumers who queue up at the retail store to be the first to acquire the latest break-through in technological gadgetry, Japanese thinkers throughout history have generally been eager to consume the latest idea or theory from abroad. I use the term *consume* advisedly because the Japanese reaction to the foreign has generally been not to view it from a detached standpoint with the voyeuristic gaze associated with Western ori-entalism, but instead, whether the new theory from abroad be Chinese Confucianism, Zen Buddhism, or German idealism, Japanese thinkers have tended to judge the new by intellectually ingesting it. If it does not sit well, they can spew it out and avoid it in the future. If it is promising but still unsettling in some way, they might try to season it ac-cording to local tastes or perhaps try to find a local item with which to blend its flavor. How far back can we trace this propensity in Japanese philosophy?

I suggest we find it already in one of the oldest extant Japanese documents, the *Seventeen-Article Constitution* (604 C.E.?), attributed to Prince Regent Shōtoku (574?–622?). For the same reason Aristotle named Thales as the first Hellenic philosopher, we can legitimately argue Shōtoku was the first Japanese philosopher. In his *Metaphysics* I.3, Aristotle selected Thales not because he was the first to have a philosophical idea, nor even because his theories were particularly detailed or brilliant, but rather because he introduced *a way of doing philosophy* that later philosophers, including Aristotle him-self, followed. Specifically, Aristotle claimed Thales was the first to base his views about reality not on myths about gods but on what could be deduced through observation and reason. My parallel claim is that Shōtoku developed innovative theories by analyzing, assimilating, and transforming newly introduced foreign ideas and, in so doing, set a pattern that most subsequent Japanese philosophers have followed.

To describe Japanese philosophy as simply "syncretistic" or "synthetic" does not do justice to the variety of approaches taken by its thinkers over the centuries. The philosophically interesting issue is not the syncretism itself, but instead *how* philosophers were able to blend the new and foreign with the traditional and local. I will begin, therefore, by describing three major strategies Japan's thinkers have employed: what I will call *allocation, hybridization*, and *relegation*. In recognizing those approaches as alternative paths to syncretistic innovation, the reader of Japanese philosophy can better appreciate and evaluate the various philosophies developed throughout its history. The second part of this chapter will focus on the *Seventeen-Article Constitution* itself, analyzing which of those strategies Shōtoku applied in his own syncretistic philosophical analysis.

STRATEGIES FOR ASSIMILATING THE NEW AND FOREIGN

Allocation embraces the new by giving it a specified role alongside already accepted theories. There is no attempt to create a new theory melding the two, but rather the old and new are allowed to coexist by granting each its own domain or function. Allocation does not require creating new ideas or theories, but simply determines how to make the old and new complementary. A classic case of allocation is the adage concerning the roles of Shintō, Confucianism, and Buddhism in Japanese life: Japanese are born Shintō, live out their family lives and careers as Confucians, and die as Buddhists. Tradition attributes to Shōtoku himself an organic metaphor for the allocation of roles: Shintō represents the roots of Japanese culture, Confucianism its trunk and branches, and Buddhism its fruit. In the nineteenth century, a popular slogan for Japan's modernization was that it should represent "Japanese spirit and Western ingenuity" (*wakon yōsai* 和魂洋才), itself an echo of a motto from a millennium earlier when the imported ideas were coming from a different direction: "Japanese spirit and Chinese ingenuity" (*wakon kansai* 和魂漢才). As those examples show, allocation keeps intact at least part of the old and at least part of the new, sealing off the pair from each other by allotting them mutually exclusive spheres. The second way integrating old and new—hybridization—is different in that it dissolves rather than preserves the integrity of each position.

Hybridization cross-pollinates ideas from different traditions to create a new theory or way of thinking. A thinker who was particularly clear about the difference between allocation and hybridization was Ninomiya Sontoku (1787–1856). He claimed to have developed a philosophical "medicine" for the health of the Japanese nation and its individual people, a "round pill" consisting of one-half the "essence" of Shintō, one-quarter the essence of Confucianism, and one-quarter the essence of Buddhism. When asked the function of each (as if they had been allocated discrete roles), Sontoku laughed and said, "When I mentioned that the pill was round, I meant that it well combines and harmonizes the ingredients so that one does not know what the pill actually contains."[1]

Insofar as a hybrid is a complete entity in itself with its own qualities, it may disguise its genealogical parentage and seem unique. For example, a loganberry is a species in itself, although a botanist knows it came into existence as a hybrid between a blackberry and a raspberry. The Way of the Warrior (*bushidō* 武士道) has its own ideology, but a genealogical study of its heritage clearly shows it cross-bred elements of Confucian virtue and hierarchy, Buddhist discipline and self-control, and Shintō purity and sincerity.[2] Modern Japanese philosophy presents us with many hybrids born of the cross-pollination of Western ideas with traditional Japanese ideas resulting in a new theory, no longer simply Asian or simply Western. The ethical system of Watsuji Tetsurō (1889–1960) is a good example insofar as it is a hybrid of Confucian collectivism, existential individualism (a la Heidegger), and a Buddhist dialectic of emptiness.[3] Through hybridization, two or more integrated philosophies lose their former integrity as independent theories to become a new holistic system. Despite their difference as to whether they preserve or dissolve the discrete character of the original theories, allocation and hybridization do share one trait: the traditional, already accepted ideas and the newly introduced ones are kept on roughly equal footing; neither is fully subordinated by the other. That is not the case with the third common Japanese option for assimilation, namely, relegation.

Relegation rejects the segregation of traditions found in allocation but does not go as far as hybridization in creating something completely new. In relegation, the preferred (usually "traditional") theory accepts intact a new or opposing theory but only by consigning it to a subordinate position within an enlarged version of itself. Relegation preserves the other, but only by saying it is already covered by the original (preferred) system of thought, thereby establishing a clear hierarchy. Relegation's inclusive and expansive character is especially effective in developing holistic or systematic theories that absorb rather than exclude opposing ideas under its umbrella. Relegation's hierarchical ordering does not reject the competing view—indeed, it affirms the competing view as *completely* true but simply not as the *whole* truth. An example of relegation is in the answer a Tendai Buddhist monk gave when I asked why the Lecture Hall in his temple on Mt. Hiei contained images of Hōnen, Shinran, Dōgen, Eisai, and Nichiren—medieval figures who each broke away from Tendai to found new Buddhist schools of their own. After all, I said, one does not find statues of Luther, Calvin, Wesley, and Knox in St. Peter's Basilica. His response was that each Japanese innovator had been trained initially as a Tendai monk and then each focused exclusively on one aspect of the tradition

---

[1] From the translation by John Allen Tucker in Heisig, Kasulis, and Maraldo 2011, p. 451.

[2] On *Bushidō*, see Chapter 14; on Confucianism, Chapters 12 and 13; on Shintō, Chapters 2 and 3; and on Buddhism, Chapters 4–11 in this volume.

[3] On Watsuji, see Chapter 23 in this volume.

(Amidism, meditation, reverence for the *Lotus Sutra*, etc.), raising it to the highest level of development. As such, each contributed to improving a part of Tendai's all-inclusive, comprehensive system. In other words, each medieval reformer was completely right about a part, but only that part, of the whole truth, that whole truth being found only in Tendai.

With its ability to integrate apparently competing views into a single system, relegation has been popular throughout Japanese intellectual history. We find it as early as the ninth century in the system of the ten mindsets (*jūjūshinron* 十住心論) that Kūkai used to characterize all philosophies known in Japan at the time, showing each to be included in, but subordinate to, the mindset of Shingon Buddhism. In terms of praxis, Japanese esoteric Buddhism also accepted the indigenous Shintō *kami*, but only by relegating them to being no more than the surface manifestations of the more profound pantheon of buddhas (a relegating hermeneutic called *honji suijaku* 本地垂跡). Even a bit earlier in the Nara period, the very paradigm of relegation had been introduced by the imported philosophy of the Chinese Huayan (Jp. Kegon 華厳) school which placed teachings of other schools into lower tiers of its own inclusive system.

On the other end of the historical spectrum, we find relegation at work in such modern philosophers as Nishida Kitarō (1870–1945) when he attempted to find a "place" within his system for all the major modern philosophical perspectives, such as Western empiricism and idealism.[4] In his "logic of place" (*basho no ronri* 場所の論理) system, Nishida consigned all other philosophies to their respective loci, each subordinate to the most inclusive locus called *absolute nothingness*. Viewed in that light, Nishida used the Buddhist notion of nothingness to absorb Western philosophies, accepting their truth but showing them to be partial when compared with his own theory.

Allocation, assimilation, and relegation all represent ways of assimilating new ideas from outside, welcoming them in one way or another into one's own cultural and intellectual tradition. Of course, the new or foreign does not have to be so welcomed; it might be outright rejected. The most straightforward way of doing so is through *refutation*.

As a form of analysis and argument, refutation is not nearly as common in Japan as it is in the West (or even in India). Indeed, refutation is so widely accepted in the West as the established mode of argument that its assumptions often go unanalyzed. So it merits a brief discussion here. First of all, refutation often serves to support an opposing position. An emblematic example of that usage is the form of argument known as *reductio ad absurdum*. If I am making a *reductio* argument, I affirm the truth of my initial thesis by assuming its opposite and then demonstrating the latter to be false, usually because it entails a contradiction. Therefore, goes the argument, my original thesis must be true. Such an argument applies two Aristotelian principles of logic: the laws of no contradiction and of the excluded middle. Formally speaking, I begin by taking my original thesis x and formulating its contradictory, *not-x*. By the law of no contradiction, x and *not-x* cannot both be true in the same way at the same time, and, by the law of excluded

---

[4] On Nishida, see Chapters 17 and 18 in this volume.

middle, there is no third possibility. It follows that either one of the theses *x* or *not-x* must be true. Hence, if I disprove *not-x*, *x* is affirmed. In Western philosophy, we find this argumentative form as far back as the Socratic dialogues and the legalist arguments of the Greek sophists. Aristotle's two laws merely made theoretically explicit what was already assumed in argumentative practice.

As a technique, refutation is not limited to the rarefied forms of proof we find in symbolic logic or geometry. On the contrary, it is at the heart of our everyday arguments with colleagues, friends, family, and strangers. As long as we are disagreeing in a rational, cool-headed way, when you and I argue about the truth of a position, the protocol is as follows. If I believe your view is wrong, we break it down into its propositional premises, some (even most) of which I accept as true. Then we can isolate the precise pivotal point (or points) of disagreement wherein I find I hold position *x* and you position *not-x*. With that logical binary, only one of us can be right, but it turns out in practice that it is usually easier to prove something false rather than true (to be false, it need only be proven false in some one respect; to be shown to be true, however, it needs to be demonstratively true in all respects). So once the argument gets fully under way, most of our time is spent in your trying to refute my position *x* and my trying to refute your *not-x*. This process is so inculcated in the Western tradition as to be second nature. Indeed, it seems to most Westerners to define the very essence of what argument is.

Yet, for the most part, this refutative form of argument and analysis is not the dominant one in Japan. What alternative is there?[5] We have already seen three from traditional Japan: allocation, hybridization, and relegation. For allocation, we look not to refute the other position but to find out how, in certain contexts, for some purposes, it is right. "Oh, if you are talking about an umpire's judgment in a ball game and not a judgment in a court of law, I can agree with you about how judgments are made." By such allocation, each type of judgment is given its own domain or application. Hybridization tries to take the two positions and, instead of opposing them so as to choose between

[5] When Western philosophy had its major impact on Japan starting in the latter half of the nineteenth century, a number of Japanese philosophers adopted Hegelian dialectic as a new assimilative alternative to refutation. An interesting twist, however, is that the Japanese form of dialectical reasoning often progressed from differentiation and opposition *back* to a preceding unity rather than *forward* to a synthetic unity, what I have called a dialectic of *whence* rather than *whither*. See Kasulis 1989.

A second strategy for assimilating opposing ideas in the modern period was developed first by Inoue Enryō and Inoue Tetsujirō, picked up by D. T. Suzuki (see the first part of Chapter 11 in this volume), and formulated further within the Kyoto School of Nishida Kitarō. It draws on the copula-like function of a Chinese word pronounced *soku* (即) in Japanese that is sometimes used in classical Buddhist texts to establish a relation of identity with difference or difference with identity. Thus, some philosophers affiliated with the Kyoto School, following the terminology of its founder, spoke of a "logic of *soku*" or a "logic of *soku-hi* (即非)" (i.e., a "logic of *is/not*" or "a logic of *sameness/difference*") as part of a system of field or *basho* (場所). To my knowledge, no Japanese philosopher ever developed this idea to the extent of examining whether a formal logical system could be conceived in which *soku* could function like other logical operators such as "if-then," "and," "or," "if," "if and only if," and so forth. An American philosopher has, however, successfully outlined what the basics of such a logical system might look like. See Jones 2004.

them, melds them into a new position. "Let's see, if we take these aspects of your position and blend it with these from mine, we've a new theory that improves on both." Relegation accepts the other position but argues it is only part of the larger truth that my position represents. "I couldn't agree with you more, but that is only part of the whole story. Let me explain . . . ."

Of course, I am not saying that Japanese philosophers never use refutation and Western philosophers never use allocation, hybridization, or relegation. I am speaking in generalities, and generalities not only have exceptions, they *must* have exceptions (otherwise, they would be universalizations not generalities). But if we are looking to the Shōtoku *Constitution* as an indicator of an early step in what would become the general direction of the evolution of Japanese philosophizing, a generalization is all we need. Having concluded these preliminaries about assimilation and refutation, let us now turn to Shōtoku's *Constitution*.

BACKGROUND AND PURPOSE
OF THE CONSTITUTION

Tradition dates the *Seventeen-Article Constitution* at 604 C.E. Although recent scholarship raises questions about its true authorship, since at least the early eighth century, it has been widely assumed to be Shōtoku's document. As a result, almost all philosophers throughout Japanese history have thought of the *Constitution* as Shōtoku's work and tradition treats him as the father of the Japanese state. Meanwhile, in folk religious belief starting about a century after his death, Shōtoku has been revered as an incarnation of the bodhisattva of compassion, Kannon. Such hagiographical appreciation can make it difficult to separate legend from fact. For convenience, since we are focusing on the thought in the *Constitution* and not its authorship, I will proceed as if Prince Shōtoku, serving as regent to his aunt Empress Suiko (524–628), actually wrote the document or at least presided over its writing in the way a chief of state uses speechwriters for formal proclamations today.

In Shōtoku's time, Japan's national identity was only beginning to solidify. The country had as yet no orthography for writing its native language, no stable central government, and no well-formulated and institutionalized religion (only a set of native beliefs, myths, and simple practices I will call "proto-Shintō"). The kinship group known as the Yamato had risen to prominence, becoming the foundation for the imperial family as it exists up to today, but the political structure during this era was not yet fully an imperial system, although it was clearly moving in that direction. Yet, even within the Yamato kinship group there was dissension and intrigue. Suiko had become empress via a sequence of events that began with the victory of her family led by Soga no Umako (?–626) over its major competitor, the Mononobe in 587, a conflict triggered in part by an imperial succession dispute. As family head, Umako then installed his nephew on the throne.

Unhappy with his lack of obedience, Umako had him assassinated two years later, replacing him with his niece Suiko in 593. Given that gruesome history, the *Constitution's* opening line of "Take harmony to be of the highest value and take cooperation to be what is most honored" (Article 1)[6] was as much a plea for sanity as a political ideal.

To the modern Western eye, the text does not read as we would expect a constitution to read, seeming to be more an edifying document addressed to courtiers, charging them to behave responsibly and virtuously in carrying out their official duties. Although called a "constitution" (*kenpō* 憲法), it lacks any detailed discussion of government organization, the duties and privileges of ordinary people, or legal procedures. It is not that Shōtoku was disinterested in government organization—he did put in place a system for ranking court officials (the twelve-cap system), for example. And, within a few decades, Japan had formalized penal and civil codes based on Chinese models. Those were followed by various codes in the medieval period established by regional barons (*daimyō*) as the rule of law for their domains. Yet no other legal document or code was called a *kenpō* until the 1890 Meiji Constitution. It might be best, therefore, to think of the *Seventeen-Article Constitution* as a preamble to all later Japanese legal documents rather than a document that itself lays out the parameters of law.

Since there was no method for writing the Japanese language at the onset of the seventh century, all documents, including the *Constitution*, were written in Chinese. In some ways, this was advantageous for the blossoming of philosophy in Japan because the introduction of the Chinese language a little more than a century prior to the writing of the *Constitution* gave Japan access to almost two millennia of philosophical and literary works in Chinese, especially Confucian and Buddhist. Shōtoku's project in the *Constitution*, therefore, was to draw on ideas foreign and domestic to build a Japanese national identity, the earliest documented case of Japanese philosophical thinking as assimilating ideas from abroad.

SHŌTOKU'S USE OF CONFUCIAN AND BUDDHIST INTELLECTUAL RESOURCES

Scholars often assume that Confucianism, rather than Buddhism or proto-Shintō, was the guiding light behind the document. Shōtoku had not only a large collection of Chinese texts, but also a cadre of trusted advisors and teachers (mainly Korean immigrants trained as Chinese literati well versed in the Confucian tradition) who could help him navigate those texts and their ideas. Like the Koreans, the Japanese aristocracy admired the cultural and political accomplishments of China, and a widespread belief was that if Japan were ever to become a unified state, the imperial system and

---

[6] Quotations from the *Constitution* are from the Roger T. Ames translation found in Heisig, Kasulis, and Maraldo 2011, 36–39.

philosophical teachings of China—especially Confucianism—offered an excellent template. Thus, Shōtoku could call on officials to be true to their appointed roles: "persons should each have their charge and manage what is appropriate to their office" (Article 7). If the officials would adhere to the principal Confucian virtue of observing "ritual propriety," the nation will be "properly ordered of its own accord" (Article 4). Above all, the status of the emperor as the final authority must go unquestioned:

> On receiving imperial commands, execute them. The lord is the sky and the ministers are the earth. When the sky covers and shelters all and the ministers provide their support, the cycle of the four seasons turns smoothly and all of the life forces in nature flourish. (Article 3)

In such passages, we find the traditional Confucian motifs, diction, and exhortations, enough for many to consider the *Constitution* primarily Confucian in inspiration. If that were the case, however, we would need to account for why two pillars of classical Confucian ideology are missing. First, the document lacks any mention of the Confucian pedagogical agenda, the foundation of its praxis. The traditional Confucian was to study the classics so as to learn the Way of the ancient Chinese sage kings that Confucius himself emphasized as the basis for his philosophy. Second, there is no mention of the authority of the ruler as deriving from the mandate of heaven (Ch. *tianming*; Jp. *tenmei* 天命). That doctrine stated that the power to rule with the charisma needed for a harmonious society derives from a source beyond the individual, namely, heaven (Ch. *tian*; Jp. *ten* 天). Of course, one might suspect Shōtoku's readers would assume those two points to such an extent that there was no need to be explicit about them. That theory would be more convincing if it were not for Shōtoku's treatment of Buddhism in the text.

The very next article following the opening call to harmony is strikingly *not* Confucian. As such, we need give it careful analysis.

> Revere in earnest the three treasures: the Buddha, the Dharma, and the Sangha, for these are the final refuge for all sentient beings and are the most sacred and honored objects in the faith of all nations. What persons in what age would fail to cherish this Dharma? There are few persons who are truly wicked. Most can be instructed and brought into the fold. Without repairing to these three treasures, wherein can the crooked be made straight? (Article 2)

Most notably, we see that Shōtoku is here treating Buddhism as a state religion, implying in fact that this should be so everywhere as Buddhism is "most honored in the faith of all nations." Three facts help explain why there might be such a strong non-Confucian and pro-Buddhist emphasis in the document.

First, a point of contention between the Mononobe and Soga in their war had been religious, with the Soga favoring Buddhism and the Mononobe being put in charge of court rituals related to the proto-Shintō *kami*. The Mononobe had, in fact, predicted the retaliation of the *kami* and a national disaster if Buddhism would continue to enjoy the imperial sponsorship advocated by the Soga. The Soga victory and lack of divine retribution therefore seemed to affirm Buddhism's superiority over its contenders. Second, the Chinese Sui Dynasty, with which Shōtoku and Suiko's court maintained close contact, was particularly partial to Buddhism. Emperor Wu, the founder of the Sui, had been raised by Buddhist nuns, supported Buddhist scholarship, and, in his later years, tried to bring Buddhist principles to his rulership. Thus, at Shōtoku's point in history, being both a sinophile and a Buddhist was a natural mixture in light of the situation in imperial China. Last, another text attributed to Shōtoku is a commentary on the *Queen Śrīmālā Sutra,* a sutra which characterizes the virtue of a Buddhist monarch who brings peace and prosperity by applying Buddhist, not Confucian, principles of compassion and the promulgation of Buddhism as part of her political rule.

This does not imply that Shōtoku was anti-Confucian, of course. Rather, he wanted to place Confucianism and Buddhism in their own appropriate spheres. The *Constitution* advocates Confucianism for its hierarchical social order and the virtues to be exemplified by court officials. That is, it stresses Confucian *social order* and *behavior.* In Article 2, however, and in the *Constitution's* general discussion of Buddhism, the *Constitution* speaks more *psychologically* about "faith" and about using Buddhism to make straight the wicked, a comment about *developing moral character.* The overall vision seems to be that if you want to know how to act or if you want to know how to order a society or a government, let Confucianism be your guide; but if you want to understand your inner drives and transform your character, Buddhism has the answer. The allocation is clear: both Confucianism and Buddhism are kept intact, but they are given different roles or domains. We might even say Shōtoku believes Japan would be best served by a Buddhist populace fulfilling their duties as defined by Confucianism. Why did he not simply advocate Confucianism with its pedagogical nurturing of virtues (as in the *Analects*) or simply advocate Buddhism with its Buddhist principles of monarchical rule (as in the *Queen Śrīmālā Sutra* or in the tradition of the Dharma-wheel-turning King)? Why did he favor allocation rather than any other option, including the possibility of refuting one or the other tradition?

The key to answering that question may be in the following lines:

> And there is no guarantee that we are the sages and that they [those with whom we disagree] are the fools. We are all just ordinary people. How cans anyone set a rule for what is right and what is wrong? We all have our share of wisdom and of foolishness like an endless circle. (Article 10)

As we have seen, Shōtoku's *Constitution* respects the Confucian social ideal of hierarchy and differentiation: those above should take care of those below, while those below should respect and be loyal to those above. Yet it advocates that system only as a hierarchy of *roles,* not a hierarchy of personal worth or virtue. Social order demands a chain of command, but working with other people requires recognizing our commonalities. In our social roles—ruler–subject, senior–junior, husband–wife, and so forth—we are different, but as human beings we are the same. Whether correctly or not, Shōtoku associates Confucianism with hierarchy and Buddhism with egalitarianism.

We see that link between Buddhism and egalitarianism in other aspects of Shōtoku's storied career. When he built the Buddhist Temple of the Four Heavenly Kings (Shitennōji) in gratitude for the Soga victory over the Mononobe, the complex included not only meditation and study halls, but also a school and a hospital. That suggests Shōtoku understood Buddhism as having a social mission, a calling to help the people, perhaps a reason for his later identification with the Bodhisattva of Compassion. I have already mentioned that tradition attributes to Shōtoku a commentary on the *Queen Śrīmālā Sutra*, but there are also two other sutras on which he wrote commentaries, the *Vimalakīrti Sutra* and the *Lotus Sutra*.[7] The three share—indeed, are particularly well-known for—the claim that enlightenment is equally available to anyone, whether male or female, whether clergy or layperson. Again, we find a link in his mind between Buddhism and an egalitarian potential for enlightenment, wisdom, and virtue.

That egalitarian view of wisdom helps explain the concluding article of the *Constitution*:

> Important matters of state should not be decided unilaterally; they must be discussed, as needed, with others. Small affairs are less important and do not require such consultation. It is only in coming to discuss weighty matters where there is a worry something might go amiss that such affairs should become a matter of shared deliberation, thereby guaranteeing the right outcome. (Article 17)

That vision of administration seems more like a board meeting headed by the CEO than Confucius's image in *Analects* 2.2 wherein the virtuous ruler is compared to the North Star around which all others revolve. Shōtoku maintained, as the aforementioned Article 3 insisted, that the absolute and final authority must rest with the emperor or empress. Again, administration requires a clear chain of command. Article 17 adds, however, that the ruler should recognize his or her own shortcomings and depend on consultation with others. No doubt, the Confucian emperor would have his own consultants, but the difference is that Shōtoku understood the Japanese imperial advisors as neutralizing the emperor's personal limitations, ego, and inadequate wisdom. As noted in the aforementioned Article 10, sagely wisdom might come from anyone. Shōtoku's Buddhist philosophical anthropology is that the seeds of enlightenment are in everyone, but it is also the case that each individual, even the ruler, is susceptible to delusion.

Throughout the *Constitution*, Shōtoku calls on his officials to be reflective about their motivations, damping their anger, and bridling their ego's inclination toward self-interest. He wants his Confucian officials—with their ritual propriety, trust, and deference to hierarchy—to be good Buddhists who practice introspection and control their inner drives. And he wants no contentious arguments driven by ego:

---

[7] For a brief discussion of the relation between Shōtoku's Buddhist commentaries and the *Constitution* see Kasulis 2018, 63–71.

Contain the fury; rein in the irate glare. Do not respond with anger at personal differences. People all have their own mind and all hold their own opinions. What is right for us can be wrong for them; what is wrong for them can be right for us . . . . How can anyone set a rule for what is right and what is wrong? . . . [Even] though others glare at us irately, let us instead worry about our own failings. And even though we alone are in the right, let us go along with the multitude and offer them our support. (Article 10)

It seems Shōtoku is wary of refutation as a mode of argument in decision-making. To insist that one's own view can be the only right one brings ego into the discussion, allows logical rules to overshadow interpersonal human civility, and leads to rancor rather than concord. The last line of Article 10 even suggests that, for the sake of harmony, we should concede our personal viewpoints when necessary to achieve consensus.

I noted previously a second point at which the *Constitution* diverges from classical Confucian political ideology: the lack of any reference to justifying imperial rule as deriving from the mandate (or will) of heaven. How, then, does Shōtoku understand the source of imperial rule? Proto-Shintō beliefs may be a factor here.

A HYBRID HEAVEN?

Although there is no mention of any heavenly mandate, the *Constitution* does mention the traditional Chinese binary of heaven (or sky, Ch. *tian*) and earth in the already quoted Article 3. If we disengage from the usual way of interpreting such passages and think about the words themselves, a provocative question arises: How do we know the word "heaven" (written 天) is the Chinese *tian* (pronounced in Japanese, *ten*) and not the native Japanese sense of heaven, namely, *ama* (which is written with the same sinograph, 天)? It is fruitful to explore the possibility that 天 in the *Constitution* may be a hybrid of the Chinese *tian* and the Japanese *ama*, a sense of *heaven* derived from both traditions rather than exclusively one or the other.

There is no doubt that, a century after the *Constitution*, the two official chronicles, *Kojiki* and *Nihon shoki*, explicitly claim that the Japanese emperor's authority derives from heaven in the Japanese sense of *ama*, specifically from the "Heaven Illuminating One," the Sun Kami Amaterasu (天照), progenitrix of the Yamato imperial family. Those chronicles themselves claim that their mythicohistorical narratives coincide with accounts that were part of the Japanese tradition much earlier. Were they part of the common literature in Shōtoku's time? I think it likely. In addition to the *Constitution* and three Buddhist commentaries, *Nihon shoki* mentions that Shōtoku had commissioned two chronicles called *Record of the Emperors* (*Tennōki*) and *Record of the Country* (*Kokki*), and they in turn were said to be partly based in still older written texts, *Ancient Matters* (*Kyūji*) and *Imperial Records* (*Teiki*). Unfortunately, we have no extant versions of any of those texts, so we can only speculate whether they contained the narrative about the heavenly source of the imperial family's right to rule. We cannot be certain of the answer, but it is not only possible but even likely. What implications would that assumption about the divinely conferred imperial rule have for interpreting the *Constitution*?

The difference between ruling through a Chinese-style heavenly mandate (Ch. *tianming*; Jp. *tenmei* 天命) and by the directive of the Heaven Illuminating One is that the latter involves a *blood relation*. Mencius, the Chinese Confucian of the third-century C.E., had argued (in *Mencius* 1B8) that when a ruler does not rule as a ruler should, an attack on him is justified. That is because a ruler who does not act as a ruler is not a true ruler, but an imposter. Such an argument had little relevance to Japan because its emperor's tie to heaven was not by mandate, but by blood relation, something that cannot be withdrawn.

Of course, this line of analysis assumes Shōtoku, the ardent Buddhist, did revere the *kami* as well. What do we know of his attitude toward the native *kami*? Historical accounts indicate that Shōtoku supported an annual proto-Shintō ritual and even made a formal proclamation that the *kami* should be revered. Yet, if indeed Shōtoku saw imperial authority including that of the Yamato lineage specifically as deriving at least to some extent from the *kami*, why did he not say so in his *Constitution*? First, if there were already imperial chronicles that gave the *kami*-derived narrative for imperial authority, it may not have been thought necessary to state the obvious in the *Constitution*. That is, the *Constitution* does not reference the heavenly mandate doctrine because it was irrelevant to the understanding of imperial rule already operative in Japan. Moreover, the word "heaven" or "sky" occurs only in Article 3, where it simply expresses the distinction between heaven and earth and the need for them to be in accord. That idea is genuinely both Confucian and proto-Shintō (as represented in the oldest extant narratives). Perhaps the concept of "heaven" was already to some extent hybridized into a new idea with roots in both Japan and China. As with the loganberry, the genealogy may be disguised, but if we investigate it, we find the hierarchy of the Confucian heaven hybridized with the Japanese heaven in such a manner that the heavenly mandate has been cross-bred out of the concept.

CROWNING SHŌTOKU

Given this analysis of Shōtoku and his *Constitution*, we can justify his coronation as "Japan's first philosopher" as Aristotle had crowned Thales in his own tradition. We find Shōtoku struggling to make a coherent whole of ideas both foreign and domestic and using that new system to address the pressing issues of his day. In his project, we find the allocation of Buddhism and Confucianism to their own specific domains, a rejection of refutation as a mode of analysis (at least in government councils), and a possible case of creative hybridization in understanding the relation between heaven and earthly rule. Relegation does not appear in this historical period (although its spirit might be implicit in the imported *Lotus Sutra,* which claims to be the One Way that subordinates all other Ways). Yet, relegation would become a major philosophical strategy used by esoteric Buddhism as in, for example, Kūkai's system of the ten mindsets and the hermeneutic of Buddhist-Shintō praxis called *honji suijaku.* Relegation requires a sophisticated level of philosophical systemization, and Japanese thinkers would not be equipped to undertake such a complicated creative process for another couple of centuries after Shōtoku.

In the final analysis, by distinguishing allocation, hybridization, relegation, and refutation, we have come to a revealing way of understanding what is sometimes covered under the single umbrella of "Japanese syncretism." With our enriched understanding of different paths to synthesis, it is now too simplistic to say the *Constitution* is "Confucian," or that it is "Buddhist," or even that it is a "synthesis." To appreciate Japanese philosophy in all its historical manifestations, we should pay close attention to *how* ideas are being harmonized, *how* foreign ideas are being Japanized. To the extent we do so, we are implicitly recognizing in Japan a process that we can trace back to Japan's "first philosopher," Shōtoku.

BIBLIOGRAPHY AND SUGGESTED READINGS

Anesaki, Masaharu. (1948) *Prince Shōtoku: The Sage Statesman.* Tokyo: Boonjudo.

Como, Michael. (2008) *Shōtoku: Ethnicity, Ritual, and Violence in the Japanese Buddhist Tradition.* New York: Oxford University Press.

Deal, William E. (1999) "Hagiography and History: The Image of Prince Shōtoku." In *Religions of Japan in Practice,* edited by George J. Tanabe, Jr. Princeton, N.J.: Princeton University Press, 316–333.

Heisig, James W., Thomas P. Kasulis, and John C. Maraldo (eds.). (2011) *Japanese Philosophy: A Sourcebook.* Honolulu: University of Hawai'i Press.

Jones, Nicholas J. (2004) "The Logic of *Soku* in the Kyoto School," *Philosophy East and West* 54/3: 302–321.

Kasulis, Thomas P. (1989) "Whence and Whither: Philosophical Reflections on Nishitani's View of History." In *The Religious Philosophy of Nishitani Keiji: Encounter with Emptiness,* edited by Taitetsu Unno. Berkeley: Asian Humanities Press, 259–278.

Kasulis, Thomas P. (2018) *Engaging Japanese Philosophy: A Short History.* Honolulu: University of Hawai'i Press.

Nakamura Hajime. (1988) *Shōtoku Taishi.* Tokyo: Shunjūsha,

Nakamura, Hajime. (2002) "The Idea of a Universal State and Its Philosophical Basis: Prince Shōtoku and His Successors." In *History of Japanese Thought 592–1868: Japanese Philosophy Before Western Culture Entered Japan* (chapter 1). London: Kegan Paul, 1–38.

Piggott, Joan R. (1997) *The Emergence of Japanese Kingship.* Stanford, CA: Stanford University Press.

Shōtoku Taishi, and Mark W. Dennis. (2011) *Prince Shōtoku's Commentary on the Śrīmālā Sutra.* Berkeley: Bucky Dendō Kyōkai America, Inc.

Shōtoku Taishi, and Jamie Hubbard. (2012) *Expository Commentary on the Vimalakirti Sutra.* Berkeley: Bukkyō Dendō Kyōkai America, Inc.

Terry, Charles S. (1978) "Legend and Political Intrigue in Ancient Japan: Shōtoku Taishi." In *Great Historical Figures of Japan*, edited by Murakami Hyōe and Thomas J. Harper. Tokyo: Japan Culture Institute.

Yoshida, Kazuhiko. (2003) "Revisioning Religion in Ancient Japan," *Japanese Journal of Religious Studies*. Nagoya, Japan: 30/1–2: 1–26.

CHAPTER 2

··

PHILOSOPHICAL IMPLICATIONS OF SHINTŌ

··

IWASAWA TOMOKO

"What is Shintō?" is an enigmatic question, for the fundamental problem of how to define "Shintō" is still in debate. This debate has unfolded especially in the field of history.
First, we need to determine when the concept of Shintō emerged in Japanese history, and
then we can address the more fundamental question of "What is Shintō at all?" The term
"Shintō" appeared for the first time in the *Nihon shoki* (completed in 720 CE) in contrast
to Buddhism, which was introduced to Japan in the sixth century. Based on this fact,
some scholars maintain that, although we had to wait until its appearance in the *Nihon
shoki* for its conceptualization, Shintō has been *the* primal religion of Japan, one that has
existed since before the introduction of Buddhism. Others insist that the term used in
that text simply shows the then emperor's intention of promulgating this concept as a
new political idea designating "the way of the emperor as a god" and thus of establishing
a strong system of state cult in the seventh and eighth centuries. Still others contend that
Shintō as a word designating a coherent religious system was introduced for the first
time in the fifteenth century by Yoshida Kanetomo, the founder of Yoshida Shintō.[1] Last,
there is another influential thesis, maintained by historian Kuroda Toshio in the twentieth century, that Shintō, as the distinct and autonomous religion as we know today, is
an invention of nineteenth-century Japanese ideologues and that Shintō in its earliest
usage in the *Nihon shoki* was a referent not for the Japanese indigenous system of belief
but, rather, for Daoism.[2] Given this controversy over the question "What is Shintō?,"
how can we start discussing the "philosophical implications of Shintō" at all?

---

[1] Nelly Naumann, "The State Cult of the Nara and Early Heian Periods," in *Shintō in History: Ways of
the Kami*, edited by John Breen and Mark Teeuwen (Honolulu: University of Hawai'i Press, 2000), 64.
[2] Kuroda Toshio, "Shintō in the History of Japanese Religion," in *Religion & Society in Modern
Japan*, edited by Mark R. Mullins, Shimazono Susumu, and Paul L. Swanson (Asian Humanities Press,
1993), 7–30.

The central issue raised in these debates might be summarized as follows: (1) can Shintō claim its changelessness that has continued in an unsevered line from prehistoric times to the present? (i.e., the question of changeless continuity); and (2) is Shintō indigenous—that is, is it uniquely Japanese, being independent from other religious traditions, such as Buddhism, Daoism, and Confucianism? (i.e., the question of indigenousness and uniqueness). To both questions, this chapter answers "No," but in a different manner from the views introduced earlier. First, many shrines, priestly lineages, and forms of *kami* worship and rites in Japan *do* show a remarkable degree of continuity over a very long period of time. We cannot ignore this continuity, even though it has not been accomplished without change. At various historical stages, Shintō has absorbed various elements of other religious traditions, such as Buddhism, Daoism, Confucianism, or other imported practices, and dynamically synthesized these elements to make an enduring religious structure. As Michael Pye asserts, "the essential parameters of Shintō as primal religion have not been changed as such, but . . . many adjustments have taken place in order to maintain its position in developing, and indeed [in] highly developed socio-political circumstances."[3] We may define such Shintō as an "adjusted primal religion"[4] that has exerted no small influence on Japanese religious experience since ancient times. This definition does not negate Shintō's continuity, and yet it simultaneously acknowledges its susceptibility to change and constant adjustment.

Setting this as a premise, this chapter tries to elucidate Shintō's *primal* worldview as its concept first emerged in the eighth century. An important fact of that time was that two texts were officially compiled to record the ancient myths of Japan: the *Kojiki* (古事記, *Record of Ancient Events*, completed in 712 CE) and the *Nihon shoki* (日本書記, *Chronicle of Japan*, 720 CE). Composed under the auspices of Emperor Tenmu (reigned 673–686 CE), these two texts laid the foundation of Shintō as a state cult, providing its worldview through mythic narratives, some of which were later developed into important Shintō beliefs and rituals. By way of examining these primal texts, this chapter will clarify how Shintō propounds the relationships among the divine, the human, and the world—a worldview that makes a remarkable contrast to that of Western theism.

THE JAPANESE COSMOGONY: *KAMI* AS *MUSUHI*

"Shintō" (*shintō* 神道) literally means "the way of *kami*." The word *kami* has often been translated as "god." But if we regard *kami* as a transcendent, almighty, personified God as in the case of Western theism, we will misunderstand the essence of Japanese religious

---

[3] Michael Pye, "Shintō, primal religion and international identity," in *Marburg Journal of Religion*: volume 1, no. 1 (April 1996), 5.

[4] Ibid., 5.

experience. The following statement by a Western scholar clearly shows a perplexity that Western people typically experience when attempting to understand the Japanese concept of *kami*: "Humanity is descended from the *kami*, not created by them. This fact puts the Japanese mythology into a unique category and demonstrates how different it is from the Judeo-Christian myths, for example. It is not a mythology of creation in the Western sense ... What indeed is a *kami*?"[5] As properly indicated by this statement, what most markedly separates the Japanese from the Judeo-Christian myth is the concept of creation; there is no creation in the Japanese myth. Then how does it explain the origin of being and of the cosmos? In order to answer this, we will explore the Japanese cosmogony in contrast to the Western. Before examining its details, however, let us first clarify what *creation* means for the Judeo-Christian monotheistic tradition. In this examination, we will apply Paul Ricoeur's analytical framework from *The Symbolism of Evil* because his analysis is particularly cogent and complete as a basis for comparison and contrast of the Judeo-Christian and the Japanese traditions.

In his interpretation of the ancient Near Eastern and Mediterranean myths that foreshadow the problem of evil in monotheistic religions, Paul Ricoeur seeks to create a typology concerning the origin and the end of evil. He maintains that the development of Western mythical consciousness represents the salvation process constantly engaged in the elimination of evil. What is the evil so persistently opposed in Western culture? Ricoeur answers this question by providing three archetypal myths that represent three major moments of consciousness respectively: defilement, sin, and guilt. Among these three, he analyzes the notion of *defilement* as the most primordial experience informing the origin of evil.

The first type representing the schema of defilement is the Mesopotamian creation myth, the *Enuma elish*, in which evil was experienced as the primordial chaos that existed before god's creative activity. According to Ricoeur, the central theme of *Enuma elish* is "the final victory of order over chaos,"[6] the theme that goes on to underlie the Judeo-Christian cosmogony. Here, "creation" means "creating order (the cosmos)." The god's work consists in founding the world, in creating the cosmos; what disturbs this cosmos-creation is regarded as chaotic, irrational, and uncontrollable, and, therefore, evil. The god's purpose is to eliminate these chaotic elements to make the world intelligible and logically coherent. Ricoeur calls this eliminating process *salvation*, which liberates humans from the blindness inherent in the primordial chaos. In the *Enuma elish*, this primordial chaos is symbolized by Tiamat, who, being the disordered and the irrational, is ultimately slain and exterminated by Marduk, her offspring. Ricoeur says that this overwhelming irrationality of Tiamat provokes "a specific sort of fear that blocks reflection,"[7] a fear that is closely connected with the sense of defilement. In it, the concept of evil still does not take on a psychological connotation but is experienced

---

[5] Picken 1994, 63–64.

[6] Paul Ricoeur, *The Symbolism of Evil*, translated by Emerson Buchanan (Boston: Beacon Press, 1967), 175.

[7] Ibid., 25.

more straightforwardly as something physically defiling; a "stain," an "objective event" that "infects by contact." The only possible way of improving this situation is to get rid of this stain. Removing the stain is possible because, insofar as it is a stain, the defilement is not inherent but something put on from outside. This metaphor of the stain captures the fundamental characteristic of evil for the Judeo-Christian consciousness. Evil is something other than oneself; it is not inherent in the true self but is instead a heterogeneity that should be abhorred and exterminated.

This primordial experience of "defilement" takes on a totally different mode for the Japanese mythical consciousness. In Japanese myth, "defilement" appears not as the origin of evil, but rather as a process necessary for the reinvigoration and reorganization of being. Here, we should note that the Japanese understanding of "being" is different from that of the Judeo-Christian. The Japanese cosmogony that marks the beginning of the *Kojiki,* the oldest recorded myth of Japan, describes the origin of being as follows:

> At the time of the beginning of heaven and earth, there came into existence in Takama-no-hara a deity named Ame-no-mi-naka-nushi-no-kami; next, Taka-mi-musuhi-no-kami, next, Kami-musuhi-no-kami. These three deities all came into existence as single deities, and their forms were not visible. Next, when the land was young, resembling floating oil and drifting like a jellyfish, there sprouted forth something like reed-shoots. From these came into existence the deity Umashi-ashi-kabi-hiko-ji-no-kami; next, Ame-no-toko-tachi-no-kami. These two [pillars of] deities also came into existence as single deities, and their forms were not visible. The five [pillars of] deities in the above section are the Separate Heavenly Deities.[8]

This opening sharply contrasts with Genesis, which proclaims: "In the beginning God created the heavens and the earth." According to Genesis, there was nothing before God; as later Jewish and Christian metaphysics asserts, God is the prime mover, the first principle, and cosmic governor. Every being is therefore created by God *ex nihilo.* In the Japanese cosmogony, by contrast, what existed in the beginning was not God, nor even nothingness, but *Taka-ma-no-hara* (the Plain of High Heaven), which was already there without being created. Upon this plain appeared the triad of *kami* (deities): *Ame-no-mi-naka-nushi-no-kami* (The Deity Who Is Lord of the Sacred Center of Heaven), *Taka-mi-musuhi-no-kami* (High Deity of *Musuhi),* and *Kami-musuhi-no-kami* (Divine Deity of *Musuhi).* Interestingly, these deities took no positive action. Unlike the Western God, they created nothing but concealed themselves after their emergence. As its name indicates, the first deity is supposed to be lord of heaven, and therefore, of the entire cosmos that will come into being. In spite of this seemingly central role, this deity appears only in this opening remark and is never mentioned in the rest of the text. In contrast with the mysterious character of this deity, the following two deities embody *musuhi,* the core principle dominating the Japanese cosmogony.

---

[8] Philippi 1995, 47.

The Japanese word *musuhi* consists of two parts: *musu* and *hi*. *Musu* is a verb that primarily means "to come into being" (*musu* 生す) as well as "to give birth" (*musu* 産す). The word is also used in the sense of "steaming" (*musu* 蒸す), and, further, is associated with the concept of "breathing" (*musu* 息). Uniting these multiple meanings, the word *musu* suggests the primordial image of *constant appearing*; that is, the ever-proliferating process of being. Also, the *hi* of *musu-hi* embraces various meanings, such as "the sun" (*hi* 日), "fire" (*hi* 火), and, more abstractly, "awe-inspiring mysterious divine power" (*hi* 霊). In sum, we may understand *musuhi* as "the vital force motivating whatever comes into being" or "the awe-inspiring mysterious divine power that is the origin of all beings." By introducing these *musuhi* deities at the very beginning, the Japanese myth provides a contrasting worldview to the Judeo-Christian one.

The Judeo-Christian cosmogony is characterized by the concept of *creation*, which is based on the duality of the creator and the created. By contrast, being indifferent to this kind of duality, the Japanese cosmogony describes the image of an organism's dynamic process of emerging, growing, and proliferating, revealing how the Japanese mythical consciousness has understood the fundamental principle of "being (*aru* 有る1)." The concept of being has never meant for the Japanese "to exist absolutely or eternally," as is the case of the Judeo-Christian tradition. Rather, the Japanese have understood "being" through such process phenomena as "being born (*nari-ideru* 生り出る)," "becoming (*naru* 変化)," and "being matured (*nari-owaru* 成り終わる)"; in other words, "being" means a phenomenon in which something concealed has come to "appear (*aru* 現る)."[9] This concept of constant appearing—that is, the ever-proliferating process of being—has constituted the most fundamental experience of "being" and, therefore, of *kami* for the Japanese. In Shintō, the phenomenon of this divine appearing is called "*mi-are*" (御阿礼 or 御生れ), the appearance of *kami*, which corresponds to "epiphany"), and all the Shintō rituals and festivals are intended to make this "*mi-are*" happen.

As the force that brings about this process of appearing, the concept of *musuhi* has become a basic symbol of worship, underlying the deepest stratum of Shintō's religious experience. *Musuhi* is the life force permeating all living beings. In the *Kojiki*, this abstract concept of *musuhi* is given the concrete image of *Umashi-ashi-kabi-hiko-ji-no-kami* (Excellent Reed-shoots Male Deity), a deity appearing right after the opening triad of *musuhi* deities. It is a deification of vital force symbolized by the reed-shoots sprouting up vigorously in spring and regarded as an apparent symbolization of *musuhi*. It is this biocentric notion of *musuhi* that the Japanese concept of *kami* originated from. *Kami* for the Japanese never means a transcendent, extracosmic, absolute god, but rather the intracosmic divine essence that gives constant dynamism to all beings in the world. The Japanese concept of *kami* as *musuhi* thus reveals how strongly the philosophy of Shintō focuses on life and its dynamism.[10]

---

[9] Maruyama 1995, 298.
[10] "Life" in Japanese is "*i-no-chi*," which originally meant "the power (*chi*) of breath (*iki*)."

IZANAMI, THE MOTHER GODDESS

In the *Kojiki*, this opening cosmogony is followed by the myth of Izanagi and Izanami, the first couple who give birth to numerous beings in the world. Different from Genesis, where God creates all beings through His Word, the Japanese myth describes the birth of all beings as a result of this couple's procreative activity. They first give birth to the numerous islands of Japan and then to multitudes of deities who represent the elements of the natural world: stones, water, wind, trees, mountains, fields, and foods. Here, too, the metaphor of "giving birth" suggests the idea of natural proliferation, making a contrast to the Judeo-Christian concept of controlled "creation." This peaceful scene of abundant procreation of Izanagi and Izanami, however, is suddenly disrupted by a happening: the appearance of the fire-god whose birth kills Izanami, the first death introduced in the *Kojiki*. Because of this death, Izanami hereafter becomes the symbol of "defilement" in Japanese myth.

Now let us compare the death of Izanami with that of Tiamat. An inquiry into how Japanese myth describes Izanami's death will elucidate what "defilement" means for the Japanese mythical consciousness. First, Izanami, the mother goddess, passes away not by being killed but by giving birth to "fire," which, in the mythical narrative, is often regarded as the symbol of "culture." As such, this story describes not only the mother goddess's death but also the origin of fire (i.e., of culture) in Japanese mythology. In fact, after giving birth to fire, out of Izanami's deceased body appear multiple deities representing cultural activities such as mining, earthenware producing, and irrigation. Izanami's death thus symbolizes the end of pristine nature (i.e., that humans start cultivating the land and controlling nature). Unlike Tiamat, who was slain by her own offspring, Izanami's death was a self-sacrifice, one that abundantly benefited humans. Here, the mother goddess in Japanese myth is not regarded as an abhorred enemy/primordial chaos that humans should overcome by eliminating it, but as the merciful source of all beings, by which even the realm of culture was produced. Second, Izanami becomes the symbol of defilement not because she is regarded as inherently evil, but just because she has eaten at the hearth of Yomi; that is, she has been contaminated by sharing the cooking fire in the realm of the dead. Stated differently, what Japanese myth regards as "defilement" is not the mother goddess herself, but the very phenomenon of death. Unlike Tiamat, Izanami was not eliminated from the world after all, for she continues to exist in the Land of the Dead as its ruler. Later in the myth, this Land of the Dead is also called the Mother Land or the Nether Land, which is regarded as the place where all the souls ultimately return.

In the Izanagi-Izanami myth, Izanami (the chthonic)'s death symbolism does not necessarily contradict Izanagi (the uranic)'s life symbolism. Rather, death is an inescapable phase of the life cycle. In other words, the myth presents not a dualistic opposition of life and death but a monistic encompassing of those two elements. This nonexclusionary tension between life and death is impressively described in the resolution that Izanagi and Izanami make when breaking their marriage. After their battle in the Land of the Dead, Izanagi does not slay the defiled Izanami but confines her to the nether world by placing a boulder between the realms of the dead and the living. Enraged by this separation, Izanami endeavors to kill a thousand people a day, to which Izanagi responds by begetting a thousand and five hundred people a day. This results in a "victory" of life over death, leaving five hundred more infants than corpses—a mythical explanation for the natural phenomenon of population increase. The formula 1,500 − 1,000 = 500 does not ignore but acknowledge the daily presence of death.

The difference between *Enuma elish* and the Izanagi-Izanami myth lies in how they treat the chthonic Mother. Tiamat is finally slain and overcome by Marduk, whereas Izanami continues to exist as the one dominating the realm of the dead. In Japanese myth, the realm of the chthonic is neither negated nor annulled; rather, in the Japanese folkloric tradition, the chthonic became an object of worship that was believed to provide the realm of the living with tremendous power. The defiled, the chthonic, is indeed abhorred and negated; but this tremendous power has the possibility of being transformed into a positive power that, if handled properly, introduces dynamism into a rigid reality.

What is the principle that enables such transformation between the opposing forces of the chthonic? The etymology of the Japanese word for "defilement," *kegare* (穢れ), gives an answer. Tanikawa Kotosuga, a nineteenth-century scholar, suggested that *kegare* originated from the similarly pronounced 気枯れ, which means "the decline of *ki* (気)."[11] *Ki* denotes the unfathomable force behind all natural transformations, a life-giving force in nature as well as within humans. It is the power encompassing both energy and matter; it is the psychophysiological force associated with blood and breath and can thus be translated as "vital force." It is a concept that opposes the mechanistic view of the body emphasized by mind-body dualism and instead suggests that we can develop the potencies of the body so as to produce a new mode of being. In Japanese, the physically as well as mentally healthy state is called "*gen-ki*" (元気), literally "the original state of *ki*." As this word shows, *ki* undergoes increase and decrease, but the original state of *ki* is supposed to be full of vigor; it is the state that one can realize by uniting oneself with the *ki* of the world (i.e., the ebb and flow of vital force in nature).

According to Tanikawa's etymological analysis, the Japanese concept of "defilement" (*ke-gare*) was defined by the ebb and flow of *ki*. Among various types of defilement, the Japanese have traditionally viewed the defilement of death (called *kuro-fujyō* 黒不浄, the black defilement) and that of blood (called *aka-fujyō* 赤不浄, the red defilement) as the two primary aspects of *kegare*. When *ki* leaves one's body, the typical case of which is death, one is regarded as defiled.[12] Bloodshed, too, shows the energy, represented by blood, departing from one's body. In these cases, defilement means a condition lacking

---

[11] Tanikawa Kotosuga, *Wakun no shiori* [A Dictionary of Japanese Words] (Gifu: Seibidō, 1898), 435.

[12] According to Orikuchi Shinobu, the Japanese word "*shi-nu* (死ぬ, to die)" was derived from '*shi-nu* (萎)—the condition that life force waned—which was later pronounced "*shi-na-fu* (萎ふ)." See Orikuchi 1996, 12–13.

in *ki*. One of Shintō's important rituals—the purification ritual—is also understood from this perspective; it is a symbolic reenactment of transforming one's defiled condition (i.e., the condition of *kegare*, in which one's vital force waned) into a revitalized pure state that might produce health, vigor, good fortune, and long life. What is unique about this purification ritual is that it brings about this pure state not by eliminating the defiled, but by utilizing its power in an opposite manner that leads toward an increase of potencies. This transformation is possible because the philosophy of *ki* presupposes the ever-circulating system of life in which defilement is an inescapable phase of the life cycle. In this philosophy, defilement is no longer a "stain" or an "otherness" to be annihilated, as in the Judeo-Christian tradition, but a process necessary for the reinvigoration and reorganization of being.

AMATERASU AND THE HARVEST FESTIVAL

Ricoeur regards the Adamic Vision of Sin and Myth of the Fall as the paradigmatic myth elucidating the Western notion of "sin." In it, the concept of sin entails that a human confronts God, the moral lawgiver, who is the source and foundation of an ethics of prohibition, condemnation, and forgiveness. In Japanese mythology, the archetypal myth underlying the notion of sin is the myth of Amaterasu and Susanowo, which comes right after the Izanagi-Izanami myth. Amaterasu and Susanowo are two of the three deities that were born out of Izanagi's purification ritual, which was performed after his battle with Izanami in the Land of the Dead. Amaterasu is the Sun Goddess born out of Izanagi's left eye, and Susanowo is the Storm God born out of his nose. In this Japanese myth, the sinner is symbolized by Susanowo, who sins against Amaterasu. This Sun Goddess, however, is not necessarily depicted as a moral lawgiver. Then what is Amaterasu? How does Susanowo sin against her? What is the meaning of "sin" in this Japanese context?

The central episode of the Amaterasu-Susanowo myth is Amaterasu's concealment in the rock-cave, which was caused by Susanowo's violent conduct. His lawless acts dissolve the order of things, one after another. To take concrete examples, he broke down the ridges between the rice paddies of Amaterasu and covered up the ditches. Also, he defecated and scattered the excrement in the hall where Amaterasu was celebrating the harvest festival. Moreover, he opened a hole in the roof of this sacred hall and dropped down into it the sacrificial pony that he had skinned from its tail. These destructive behaviors of Susanowo eventually made Amaterasu so angry that she hid herself in the rock-cave, which brought complete darkness to the world.

Scholars have proposed that this episode provides the genesis of the Japanese concept of sin because a historical document entitled the *Engi-shiki*, a compilation of laws and minute legal regulations completed in the tenth century, introduces the Japanese word for "sin" (*tsumi* 罪) for the first time by defining the brutal conduct of Susanowo as the "Heavenly Sins" (*ama-tsu-tsumi* 天つ罪). The climax of the Amaterasu-Susanowo myth comes when Amaterasu hides in the rock-cave, which metaphorically expresses her death. Without her, the Plain of High Heaven was completely dark, and all kinds of calamities arose. The eight-hundred myriads of gods assembled to discuss how to lure her out of the cave. They collected cocks, whose crowing precedes the dawn, and hung a mirror and *maga-tama* jewels in front of the cave. Then the goddess Ame-no-uzume began a dance on an upturned tub, partially disrobing herself. This so delighted the assembled gods that they roared with laughter. Amaterasu became curious as to how the gods could make merry while the world was plunged into darkness, and she was told that outside the cave there was a deity more glorious than she. She peeped out, saw herself reflected in the mirror, heard the cocks crow, and was thus drawn out of the cave. Now the world was filled with light and brought to life again. The myth finally tells that Susanowo was punished and expelled forever from the heavenly realm of the divine.

It is said that this episode is the model for the Shintō renewal ritual, one of the most important rituals in the Shintō tradition to this day. We have already observed that Susanowo interrupted the harvest festival. This festival corresponds to the *Niiname-sai* (新嘗祭),[13] the festival celebrating new crops of rice. Susanowo's repeated lawless acts, therefore, indicate the violation of the social order expressed symbolically by this Shintō festival, the *Niiname-sai*. In ancient Japan, rice harvest rituals, modeled after folk harvest rituals of the time, became the official rituals at the imperial court. In the early agricultural society of Japan, the leaders, including the early emperors, were magico-religious leaders, whose political powers rested on an ability to call forth supernatural powers to ensure good crops. The agricultural cosmology and ritual, therefore, became the bulwark of the ancient imperial system, which laid the foundation of Shintō.

On one level, the *Niiname-sai* symbolizes a cosmic gift exchange in which new crops of rice are offered to the deities in return for the original seeds of rice given by the deities to the first emperor.[14] According to Japanese myth, at the time of his descent from the Heavenly to the Earthly realm, Amaterasu gives her grandson Ninigi-no-mikoto (Prince Ninigi) the original rice grains that she had harvested from the two fields in Heaven. With these original seeds given to him, Ninigi transforms a wilderness into a country of rice stalks with succulent ears of rice (*mizuho* 瑞穂) and abundant grains of five kinds (*gokoku* 五穀). Here, "Ninigi" means "rice stalks with succulent grains" (i.e., the source of life force [*musuhi*] for the Japanese), and this deity is hereafter regarded as the ancestral symbol of the successive emperors of Japan. The *Niiname-sai* is partly a ritualization of this myth, which tells the origin of the emperor and the meaning of his existence. In this ritual, the emperor offers new crops of rice to the deities, taking the form of co-eating them between the deities and himself, so that the emperor, as the symbol of the country and its people, can be replenished with new power of *musuhi* that can ensure good crops for the next year.

---

[13] In Japanese, "*niiname*" means 'the tasting of new crops (*name* "to taste"; *nii* "new").

[14] See Ohnuki-Tierney 1993, 44–62.

This religious cum political cum economic nature of the Shintō harvest festival can be interpreted on another level, too. The *Niiname-sai* intends "the driving out of the old year and the coming of the new year." Here, the "new year" means the birth of a new mode of existence in the spiritual sense, not only for individuals, but also for society as a whole. Human lives wane unless they are replenished with new life force. Humans and their communities, therefore, must rejuvenate themselves by periodically harnessing the positive power of the divine. The ancient Japanese most vividly experienced this sacred moment—the transition from the old to the new existence, or, more metaphorically, the transition from death to rebirth—at the winter solstice. In ancient Japanese agricultural society, the concept of fertility was conceived within the rhythm of the seasons and developed to the idea of periodic regeneration that occurs once a year, most symbolically on the winter solstice when the sun experiences its metaphorical death.

This idea of "death and rebirth" constitutes another core aspect of the *Niiname-sai*. The *Niiname-sai* is preceded by the important ritual called *Chinkon-sai* (鎮魂祭, which is also called "*Tama-furi*," i.e., the invigoration of soul/spirit), which is held on the day before the winter solstice. The central theme of the *Chinkon-sai* is to experience imitative death and rebirth—the theme depicted in the Japanese myth as the concealment and unconcealment of the Sun Goddess Amaterasu. Previous studies describe that, when this ritual was held in the Imperial Court, the emperor first lay on the sacred bedding covered with *madoko-ou-fusuma* (真床覆衾), which was like a robe or a net that seemingly functioned as a magical covering under which the emperor performed imitative death.[15]

The emperor's concealing himself in the *madoko-ou-fusuma* may be interpreted as symbolizing the return to the womb. In *Myth and Reality*, Eliade discusses the symbolic meaning of this concept:

> From the structural point of view, the return to the womb corresponds to the reversion of the Universe to the "chaotic" or embryonic state. The prenatal darkness corresponds to the Night before Creation and to the darkness of the initiation hut.... The initiation myths and rites of *regressus ad uterum* [return to the womb] reveal the following fact: the "return to the origin" prepares a new birth, but the new birth is not a repetition of the first, physical birth. There is properly speaking a mystical rebirth, spiritual in nature—in other words, access to a new mode of existence. The basic idea is that, to attain to a higher mode of existence, gestation and birth must be repeated; but they are repeated ritually, symbolically.[16]

This statement can apply to the Japanese myth and its ritual. In the Japanese myth, Amaterasu conceals herself in a cave, which appears to symbolize the womb. In the *Chinkon* ritual held every year, the emperor re-enacts this return to the womb mythically performed by Amaterasu. This point should be emphasized as a striking

---

[15] See Orikuchi 1995, 187–189; also, Matsumae 1996, 212–245.
[16] Mircea Eliade, *Myth and Reality* (New York: Harper & Row, 1963), 80–81.

difference between the Japanese and the Mesopotamian mythical consciousness. The Mesopotamian New Year's festival consisted in the ceremonial recitation of Marduk's paradigmatic recreation of the cosmos (the scene of *Enuma elish* in which Marduk slays Tiamat and recreates the cosmos). By contrast, the Japanese myth and its ritual dramatize the return to the womb, not the negation of the womb as represented by Marduk's slaying of Tiamat. The Japanese mythical consciousness emphasizes the "womb," "death," or "the Night before Creation," regarding it as what conceives the origination of life, the source of energies on which life in the universe depends. After death comes rebirth; after the emperor conceals himself in the *madoko-ou-fusuma*, the *Chinkon* ritual brings about the rebirth of the emperor by reinvigorating his life force. A court lady in front of the *madoko-ou-fusuma* stands on an overturned box and strikes the box ten times with a halberd. This performance, which the Japanese myth depicts as Ame-no-uzume's dancing in front of the cave, represents the act of calling in life force from outside and attaching it to the emperor's body so that it can rejuvenate his life again.

What is expressed in the Amaterasu-Susanowo myth is this motif of "the Dying and Reviving Deity." Hardly unique to the Japanese, this motif is similarly observed in the worship and myths of Osiris, Adonis, Attis, Dionysus, and Demeter, as Frazer pointed out. Yet it is extremely important that the Japanese myth made this "Dying and Reviving Goddess" the central figure of its pantheon. The Central Deity of the Japanese myth dies and revives; what she symbolizes is the vicissitudes of being and its eternal recurrence. In this recurrent cycle, the transformation of being is realized not by overcoming the physical and transcending to the metaphysical, but by returning to the "womb," to the origin of being where the physical and the metaphysical are not yet separated. The theme of the return to the womb thus permeates the myth of Amaterasu, who is the source of the constantly rejuvenated circle of life. Interestingly, the Japanese emperor, who re-enacts Amaterasu's role at the *Chinkon-sai* every year, is nothing but the symbolic embodiment of this principle. Ultimately, the constant rejuvenation and reinvigoration of our being (including the being of *kami*) becomes the central theme of Shintō; this rejuvenation is accomplished not by negating and exterminating the chthonic in us, but by meaningfully resuscitating it so that it can bring dynamism into our rigid reality.

SUSANOWO AND THE CHTHONIC DIALECTIC

Now the meaning of Susanowo and that of "sin" in Japanese myth must be analyzed from this perspective. Susanowo's outrageous conduct indeed caused the death of Amaterasu. But it is this same conduct of Susanowo that provided the world with its dynamism. In fact, to regard Susanowo as the archetypical sinner, and so as the symbol of evil, has not been accepted in the Japanese tradition. On the contrary, in Japanese folk religion, Susanowo has long been worshipped as a vital god who brings about fertility. How can he be both sinner and the god of fertility? To answer this, we need to inquire into how differently the Japanese and the Judeo-Christian understand the notion of sin. According to Ricoeur, the category dominating the Judeo-Christian notion of sin is that of "before God"; sin is the concept that defines the relationship of a finite human facing the infinite God. To provide a concrete image of sin, Ricoeur analyzes Hebrew words in the Bible that constitute the primordial experience of sin for the Jew or Christian: *chattat* meaning "missing the target," *'awon* meaning "a tortuous road," *pesha'* meaning "revolt," and *shagah* meaning "being lost." From these, Ricoeur concludes that the Judeo-Christian notion of sin originates in such images as "missing the mark, deviation, rebellion, and straying from the path"[17]—the path that should go straight to meet the infinite demands of God.

When we compare this image of sin with that of the Japanese, we find a totally different view. In the first place, in Japanese myth, the original sinner Susanowo is not a human. The Japanese myth has no clear distinction between the human and the divine and, therefore, no conflict between them. Susanowo is a deity, so his conduct is not a rebellion against God. Rather, his "sinful" act is regarded as an aspect embodied in the divine itself. In Susanowo, the values of good and evil co-exist simply as different modes of being. Or, more precisely, the Japanese traditionally have not made a value judgment on these two elements as good and evil but instead regarded them as the co-existence of *ara-mi-tama* (荒御魂, the wild soul) and *nigi-mi-tama* (和御魂, the peaceful soul), which are believed to constitute two necessary, innate elements of being (i.e., the ebb and flow of vital force in nature). Susanowo, whose name literally means the "Raging Male," was also the Storm God, not only because he was unruly and destructive, but because his excessive vigor simultaneously represented the extraordinary power originating life. With the images of thunder and rain, the Storm God Susanowo symbolizes the epiphany of force and violence, the necessary source of energies on which life in the universe depends.

Different from the monotheistic Western tradition, "sin" in the Japanese cosmogony is not a descent from original innocence into chaos, leading eventually, through an essentially linear mode of progression, to redemption and salvation, but rather it signals the recurring and never-ending cycle of order and disorder. This is typically expressed by the story of Amaterasu and Susanowo. Susanowo's sin is that he brings chaos with him through his every action, but he is also a *chthonic kami* who destroys fields yet also simultaneously fertilizes them with his feces. Amaterasu, by withdrawing to her cave and concealing herself within it, permits disorder to reign in the now darkened world outside her cave. Her action symbolizes death, and yet, by the time she exits the cave, it has become transformed from a realm of death into one offering life—a womb. The conflicts or dualisms in Japanese myth do not resolve themselves into a synthesis; rather, they remain unresolved and, as such, present us with a *chthonic dialectic* that is not Western (i.e., that is not linear but circular and never-ending). It is an unresolved dialectic of order and chaos, being and becoming, good and evil, each constantly being transformed into the other. Here, order and harmony are not permanent states, but rather moments of equilibrium in a process of continual change.

---

[17] Ricoeur, *The Symbolism of Evil*, 74.

As Ricoeur observes, the monotheistic Western tradition created its own dialectic by suppressing and eliminating the chthonic so that this dialectic could culminate in the Unitary One. By contrast, Japanese mythical consciousness has incorporated the chthonic into its dialectical system as a positive occasion that can reinvigorate and reorganize being. The Japanese myth repeatedly dramatizes the moment of death or "the return to the womb," in Eliade's phraseology. By making us repeatedly encounter the phenomena of death and rebirth, the Japanese myth emphasizes that death is not an end, but a passing to a new existence. The chthonic is not an enemy outside us, but an absolutely necessary source for the reinvigoration of our being. Here, the chthonic is not merely decried as defiled, irrational, or evil. Rather, it is revered as a power revealing the complexity and contradiction of human existence irreducible either to the ideational or to the sensible, to the pure or to the impure, to the good or to the evil. The chthonic in Japanese myth manifests itself, on the one hand, as monstrous and dreadful, but also, on the other hand, as the primal giver of affluent creativity and empathy. It is through the powerful manifestation of this complexity and contradiction of humanity that the Japanese concept of the chthonic poses a crucial question: "why do we live?"—in other words, "what is the meaning of being in this world?"

In the Shintō philosophy based on this eternal recurrence of life force, opposite powers do not exclude each other; instead, they require the other for their own existence because this opposition itself is the very element that motivates the dynamism of the life cycle. As discussed earlier, Ricoeur contended that the theme underlying the Western cosmogony was "the final victory of order over chaos." What supports this Western theme is the historical consciousness that posits a linear progress toward the realization of a universal, transcendental order that is never affected by the changes in the phenomenal world. The Japanese mythological consciousness clearly opposes this progressive worldview. In the Japanese context, order does not mean that which is attained by destroying and overcoming chaos; rather, it indicates a momentary balance and equilibrium realized in the dynamic circulation of opposite powers. In this cyclical worldview, order is never fixed or eternal, but is constantly determined by the ever-changing interdependent whole that forever repeats the dynamic recurrence of life, death, and rebirth.

Is such a worldview unique to Shintō's religious experience, or does it have any contemporary significance today? This author contends that the meaningful resuscitation of the chthonic in us, rather than an elimination of it, might be required for the final liberation of our being, which has long been agonized over, split into mind and body, metaphysical and physical, good and evil. An analysis of Shintō's worldview thus provides an important perspective to the program of comparative philosophy, one that should create new values from out of ever-developing dialogues.

BIBLIOGRAPHY AND SUGGESTED READINGS

Aston, W. G., trans. (2011) *Nihongi: Chronicles of Japan from the Earliest Times to A.D. 697.* New York: Routledge.

Breen, John, and Mark Teeuwen, eds. (2000) *Shintō in History: Ways of the Kami.* Honolulu: University of Hawai'i Press.

Eliade, Mircea. (1963) *Myth and Reality.* New York: Harper & Row.

Grapard, Allan G. (1992) *The Protocol of the Gods: A Study of the Kasuga Cult in Japanese History.* Berkeley: University of California Press.

Inoue, Nobutaka, ed. (2003) *Shintō—A Short History.* London & New York: Routledge Curzon.

Iwasawa, Tomoko. (2011) *Tama in Japanese Myth: A Hermeneutical Study of Ancient Japanese Divinity.* Lanham, MD: University Press of America.

Kasulis, Thomas P. (2004) *Shintō: The Way Home.* Honolulu: University of Hawai'i Press.

Matsumae Takeshi. (1996) "Chinkon-sai no genzō to keisei" [The Original Image of *Chinkon* Ritual and Its Transformation]. In *Matsumae Takeshi chosakushū* [Collected Works of Matsumae Takeshi]. Vol. 6. Tokyo: Ōfū.

Maruyama Masao. (1995) "Rekishi-ishiki no kosō" [The Ancient Stratum of Historical Consciousness]. In *Chūsei to hangyaku* [Faith and Rebellion]. Tokyo: Chūō kōronsha.

Mullins, Mark, Shimazono Susumu, and Paul L. Swanson, eds. (1993) *Religion & Society in Modern Japan.* Asian Humanities Press.

Nelson, John K. (1996) *A Year in the Life of a Shintō Shrine.* Seattle: University of Washington Press.

Ohnuki-Tierney, Emiko. (1993) *Rice as Self: Japanese Identities through Time.* Princeton, NJ: Princeton University Press.

Orikuchi Shinobu. (1995) "Daijōsai no hongi" [The True Meaning of the *Daijōsai*]. In *Orikuchi Shinobu zenshū* [Collected Works of Orikuchi Shinobu]. Vol. 3. Tokyo: Chūō kōronsha.

Orikuchi Shinobu. (1996) "Genshi shinkō" [Ancient Belief]. *Orikuchi Shinobu zenshū* [Collected Works of Orikuchi Shinobu]. Vol. 19. Tokyo: Chūō kōronsha.

Philippi, Daniel L., trans. (1995) *Kojiki.* Tokyo: University of Tokyo Press.

Picken, Stuart D. B. (1994) *Essentials of Shintō: An Analytical Guide to Principal Teachings.* Westport, CT: Greenwood Press.

Sonoda Minoru. (1990) *Matsuri no genshō-gaku* [Phenomenology of Japanese Festivals]. Tokyo: Kōbundō.

Ricoeur, Paul. (1967) *The Symbolism of Evil,* translated by Emerson Buchanan. Boston: Beacon Press.

Tamaru, Noriyoshi, and David Reid, eds. (1996) *Religion in Japanese Culture: Where Living Traditions Meet a Changing World.* New York: Kodansha International.

CHAPTER 3

NATIONAL LEARNING

Poetic Emotionalism and Nostalgic Nationalism

PETER FLUECKIGER

NATIONAL Learning (*kokugaku* 国学) was an intellectual and literary movement in Tokugawa Japan dedicated to the recovery of purely native Japanese forms of language, literature, religion, and government, which National Learning scholars believed had become corrupted and obscured by centuries of foreign, particularly Chinese, cultural influence. These figures depicted ancient Japan as a harmonious society governed by the emperor in accordance with the forces of nature or the will of the gods and the ancient Japanese as honest, emotionally sensitive, and spontaneously ethical. These qualities had been lost, they argued, with the adoption of foreign ideologies that replaced Japan's original artlessness with duplicity and didactic rationalism, resulting in a socially fragmented world lacking in the ties of empathy needed to truly unite people.

The study of Japanese texts from the past played a central role for National Learning scholars because they believed that these texts were a repository of forms of language and spirit that had been lost in their contemporary world but that could be recovered through the application of proper hermeneutics. They focused primarily on works of the Nara (710–784) and Heian (794–1185) periods, including, among others, the *Kojiki* (Records of Ancient Matters), an eighth-century mythohistory that recounts the deeds of the gods and the early Japanese emperors; courtly romances of the Heian period, such as the *Ise monogatari* (Tales of Ise) and *Genji monogatari* (Tale of Genji); and anthologies of *waka* 和歌 poetry, such as the eighth-century *Man'yōshū* (Collection of Ten Thousand Leaves) and the tenth-century *Kokinshū* (Collection of Japanese Poetry of the Past and Present). *Waka* translates literally as "Japanese song"; it can refer narrowly to the 31-syllable form with lines of 5, 7, 5, 7, and 7 syllables that was most common in these anthologies and, more broadly, to other traditional forms as well, such as the *chōka* 長 歌 ("long song"). *Waka* poetry played a prominent role for National Learning scholars because they saw it not only as uniquely capable of expressing and communicating authentic human emotions, but also as the purest form of the Japanese language and the most transparent window onto the spirit of the Japanese past. Poetry offered a means to inhabit the Japanese past, then, and to recreate the forms of community that they imagined had existed then. These roles of poetry were particularly emphasized by Kamo no Mabuchi (1697–1769) and Motoori Norinaga (1730–1801), the National Learning scholars who are the focus of this chapter.

Defining Japan's Native "Way"

A central mission of National Learning scholars was to demonstrate that Japan possessed its own native "Way" (*michi* 道), distinct from such foreign Ways as Confucianism and Buddhism, for bringing harmony and order to society. In doing so, they were taking a position in a long-standing debate among Tokugawa intellectuals over how to regard the foreign origins of Confucianism in relation to its application to Japanese society, an issue that rose to the forefront as Confucianism came to dominate moral and political philosophy in Japan from the seventeenth century onward.[1] Japanese thinkers' different responses to this dilemma were tied to a basic division within Confucian discourse itself between those who viewed the Confucian Way as an expression of metaphysical truths and those who saw it as a product of human history and culture.

For Tokugawa followers of the Song dynasty Confucian Zhu Xi (1130–1200), who equated the Confucian Way with a metaphysical "principle" (Ch. *li*; Jp. *ri* 理), it was possible to argue that Confucian teachings had no inherent connection to any particular time or place and that it was merely a historical accident that they had first appeared in China. Whereas Confucianism as a textual tradition may be foreign, then, the content of its teachings is culturally neutral, so that following them does not involve any abandonment of Japanese identity. Some Japanese, such as Yamazaki Ansai (1618–1682), went a step further, claiming that even before importing Confucian texts, Japan in fact exhibited Confucian virtues more perfectly than China itself. According to this view, whereas Confucian texts have an important role to play, they are merely one possible vehicle for transmitting certain universal values. Another such vehicle, Ansai and others argued, was Shintō, whose teachings they claimed were ultimately identical with those of Confucianism.

A very different approach can be seen in Ogyū Sorai (1666–1728), who denied that the Confucian Way was a transcendent metaphysical truth, instead arguing that it was a human creation of specific sage kings of ancient China, consisting of such things as political institutions, ritual, and music. This makes the Confucian Way inseparable from its concrete historical origins, meaning that Japan could not have had any access to this Way without actually importing teachings from China. An extreme version of Sorai's Sinocentrism is presented by his disciple Dazai Shundai (1680–1747) in *Bendōsho*

[1] For a discussion of the many ways in which Tokugawa Confucian scholars addressed this issue, see Kate Wildman Nakai, 1980, "The Naturalization of Confucianism in Tokugawa Japan: The Problem of Sinocentrism," *Harvard Journal of Asiatic Studies* 40(1): 157–199.

(A Treatise on the Way), where he claims that ancient Japan was a barbaric country utterly lacking any norms for governing society. Its people lived in a brutal state of nature governed only by force, he writes, and were unaware of the most rudimentary ethical teachings, with even the imperial family engaging in incestuous relationships. It was only by receiving Confucian teachings from China, he maintains, that the Japanese were able to achieve any kind of civilization.[2]

Mabuchi's *Kokuikō* (Reflections on the Meaning of Our Country), his most important statement on the Japanese Way, attacks the views presented by Shundai in his *Treatise on the Way* while also providing a more general critique of what Mabuchi sees as the flaws of Confucian thought. Mabuchi describes Japan's native culture as in harmony with the vast and unfathomable workings of heaven and earth, the fluid and vital character of which cannot be reduced to the rigid, artificial categories imposed by foreign ideologies, especially Confucianism. Central to Mabuchi's philosophy is the idea that human reasoning is inherently limited in its ability to grasp the fullness of nature. The seductiveness of Confucianism, he argues, lies in the fact that, as a product of human reasoning itself, it is completely understandable by human reason. This comforting sense of adequacy with our own cognitive powers, though, blinds us to the limitations of Confucian theorizing. He claims that because Japan's native values were not articulated through the kind of rational conceptual apparatus offered by Confucianism, the ancient Japanese fell easy prey to its superficial plausibility, causing them to lose touch with their original connection to the forces of heaven and earth.

As one example of the difference between Japanese and Chinese ways of thinking, Mabuchi points to the Chinese practice of choosing rulers based on virtue, which he contrasts with the Japanese emphasis on simply maintaining the imperial lineage. Although the Chinese method may be easier to justify rationally, he argues, the historical record shows that it has led to constant chaos and usurpations in Chinese history, while Japan was governed peacefully until the introduction of foreign teachings. This argument is part of a more general idea of Mabuchi's that virtues should be allowed to manifest themselves spontaneously rather than being imposed forcefully through artificial categories. For example, Shundai claimed that the lack of native Japanese terms for Confucian virtues is proof that these virtues did not exist in ancient Japan and that Japanese only came to practice them after learning from Chinese teachings, but Mabuchi, echoing Daoist critiques of Confucianism, counters by asserting, "These five [Confucian] virtues exist naturally in the world, though, just like the four seasons. . . . Things end up becoming constrained because humans . . . create particular names such as humaneness, rightness, ritual propriety, and wisdom. It is better to do without such names and just go along with the heart of heaven and earth."[3] He describes Japan's native

[2] Dazai Shundai, *Bendōsho* [A Treatise on the Way], in *Nihon rinri ihen* [Collection of Japanese Ethical Texts], vol. 6, edited by Inoue Tetsujirō and Kanie Yoshimaru (Tokyo: Ikuseikai, 1902), 223–224.

[3] Kamo no Mabuchi, *Kokuikō* [Reflections on the Meaning of Our Country], in *Kinsei shintōron • zenki kokugaku* [Early Modern Shintō Theory and Early National Learning], *Nihon shisō taikei* [Anthology of Japanese Thought], no. 39, edited by Taira Shigemichi and Abe Akio (Tokyo: Iwanami Shoten, 1972), 383–384; Flueckiger 2008, 251–252.

ethics as based on the quality of being "straightforward" (*naoshi* 直し), which he defines not as absolute moral perfection, but rather as complete honesty and transparency. He comments, "People's hearts are diverse, so bad things do occur, but since even bad things are done with a straightforward heart, people do not conceal them. Not being concealed, they do not develop into anything major and come to an end after only a momentary disturbance."[4] The Confucian quest for moral perfection is not only unrealistic, he charges, but also causes people to hide their misdeeds, introducing a gap between surface appearances and reality that eats away at the fabric of society. He sees this fate as having befallen Japan after the importation of foreign teachings and cultural practices in the Nara period, leading to a situation in which "while on the surface everything became elegant, there came to be many people with wicked hearts."[5]

Norinaga presents a similar defense of Japan's native Way in *Naobi no mitama* (The Upright Spirit), which served as the preface to the *Kojiki den* (Transmission of the *Records of Ancient Matters*), a massive commentary on the *Kojiki* that he completed over the course of thirty-five years. Much like Mabuchi, he argues that ancient Japan was originally governed peacefully without Confucian teachings; although people followed the Confucian virtues, they did so spontaneously and without any need to explicitly identify and name these virtues. With the importation of Chinese books, though, this original simplicity was corrupted: "Casting aside the superior Way of Japan, people copied and revered the superficially sophisticated and argumentative thought and behavior of the Chinese. Thus their minds and deeds, at one time so honest and pure, became contrived and filthy."[6] Norinaga shares Mabuchi's idea that the ultimate basis behind Japan's native Way is unfathomable by human reason, but he differs in identifying this Way as a creation of the Japanese gods, rather than a product of the impersonal forces of heaven and earth. In Norinaga's view, the gods are responsible for both the good and the bad in the world, but they must be obeyed unconditionally, without judging their actions in any way, and the same obedience must be extended to the emperors as descendants of the gods. It should be noted, though, that whereas in the nineteenth century National Learning eventually did become involved in the movement for imperial restoration, neither Mabuchi nor Norinaga translated their nostalgic paeans to ancient imperial rule into a challenge to the Tokugawa status quo in which the emperor was a figurehead, with real power held by the shogun.

Mabuchi and Norinaga are similar to figures like Yamazaki Ansai to the extent that they argue that Confucian virtues were practiced more perfectly in ancient Japan, even in the absence of Confucian textual teachings, than in China. Where they differ, though, is in their conscious distancing of themselves from Confucianism as a philosophical tradition. For Mabuchi and Norinaga, what is distinctly "Confucian" is not simply the

---

[4] Kamo no Mabuchi, *Kokuikō*, 382; Flueckiger 2008, 250.

[5] Kamo no Mabuchi, *Kokuikō*, 377; Flueckiger 2008, 244.

[6] Motoori Norinaga, *Naobi no mitama* [The Upright Spirit], in *Motoori Norinaga zenshū* [Collected Works of Motoori Norinaga], vol. 9, edited by Ōno Susumu and Ōkubo Tadashi (Tokyo: Chikuma Shobō, 1968), 53; Nishimura 1991, 31.

content of what Confucianism teaches, such as filial piety and loyalty, which they, too, see as desirable to practice. Rather, it is a certain rationalistic and didactic mindset that they see as the distinguishing feature of Confucianism and that they contrast with the honesty and spontaneity of Japanese culture. They see these distinctly Japanese qualities as epitomized by Japanese poetry, their views on which we turn to next.

POETRY, EMOTIONS, AND HUMAN NATURE

National Learning scholars argued that poetry should be a spontaneous expression of genuine emotions and that these emotions should not be subject to moral judgments of right and wrong. They presented this vision of poetry as a challenge to the Confucian theory that poetry should serve as a moral teaching for "encouraging virtue and chastising vice" (Ch. *quanshan cheng'e*; Jp. *kanzen chōaku* 勧善懲悪), a view rooted in Zhu Xi's formulation of the relationship between emotions and moral virtues. According to Zhu Xi's metaphysics, all things are made up of a combination of an abstract metaphysical "principle" and a physical "material force" (Ch. *qi*; Jp. *ki* 気). Principle is perfectly virtuous and ties together all things in the cosmos into the unified moral order of the Way (Ch. *dao*; Jp. *michi* 道), whereas material force can be morally good or morally bad, depending on whether it facilitates or impedes the manifestation of principle. In humans, principle is represented by the "original nature" (Ch. *benran zhi xing*; Jp. *honzen no sei* 本然之性), which consists of such virtues as humaneness (Ch. *ren*; Jp. *jin* 仁) and rightness (Ch. *yi*; Jp. *gi* 義), whereas material force is represented by the emotions (Ch. *qing*; Jp. *jō* 情), which can serve as an outward expression of these inner virtues but can also obscure them, such as when we are led astray by immoral desires. Confucian cultivation, then, becomes a process of achieving correctness in our emotions in order to gain access to the virtue that is latent in our original nature but hidden from us.

Zhu Xi's philosophy allows for a variety of views of the relationship between literature and the Confucian Way, as can be seen among his Tokugawa followers. To the extent that literature expresses immoral emotions, it can be seen as a corrupting force, as Yamazaki Ansai charged, whereas to the extent that it expresses moral emotions, it can be a tool for conveying the Way, as described by Hayashi Razan (1583–1657). According to the theory of "encouraging virtue and chastising vice," though, which can be seen, for example, in Andō Tameakira's (1659–1716) interpretation of the *Tale of Genji*, both moral and immoral emotions expressed in literature aid in the moral cultivation of the reader; morality in literature serves as a model and, at the same time, depictions of immorality serve as a warning against the consequences of wrongdoing. Although this view tolerates the presence of immoral emotions in literature, it only values these to the extent that they ultimately serve as a path toward morality.[7]

---

[7] The literary thought of these and other figures is discussed in Nakamura Yukihiko, "Bakusho

In one of his early writings on poetry, Mabuchi objects to the idea that a morally defined "principle" should be the measure of poetry, arguing that such a notion of principle
fails to grasp humans in the fullness of their being: "The Song Confucians discussed
poetry only in terms of rational principle and claimed that the sole purpose of poetry
was to encourage virtue and chastise vice. Although rational principle may generally
apply in the world, one cannot govern solely by reason. Poetry expresses the true nature
of people, and true emotions expressed just as they are felt do not necessarily follow
reason."[8] In his later works, he situates Japanese poetry within the framework of his notion of "straightforwardness," opening *Ka'ikō* (Reflections on Poetry) by stating, "In ancient times, people's hearts were direct and straightforward . . . . When emotions rose
up in their hearts, they would put them into words and would sing, and they called this
'poetry.' . . . Their words were in ordinary, straightforward language, so they flowed and
were well ordered without any conscious effort to make them so. Poetry was simply the
expression of a single heart, so in the past there was no particular differentiation between those who were poets and those who were not."[9] Ancient Japanese poetry, then,
is the linguistic manifestation of the perfect honesty and interpersonal transparency of
humans in their natural, uncorrupted state.

Norinaga similarly argues for pure emotionality, free from moral didacticism, as
the essence of poetry, writing, "Poetry, unlike other writings, is not something that
should posture about everything, saying it should be like this or that. Instead, it should
simply be the feelings in the heart just as they are, whether good or bad."[10] He stresses
the emotional vulnerability at the core of human nature, commenting that although in
people's everyday lives they often suppress their feelings for the sake of appearances,
poetry manifests emotions without reserve, thus revealing people in their true humanity. He also presents this emotional authenticity in gendered terms, contrasting
the artificial self-control of men with the free emotional outpourings of women. For
example, he describes the stoic demeanor of fathers upon the death of a child as "an

Sōgakushatachi no bungaku kan" [The Literary Views of Early Tokugawa Scholars of Song
Confucianism], in *Kinsei bungei shichō kō* [Reflections on Early Modern Literary Thought]
(Tokyo: Iwanami Shoten, 1975), 1–31. For excerpts from Yamazaki Ansai's and Andō Tameakira's writings
on literature, see Haruo Shirane, ed., *Early Modern Japanese Literature: An Anthology, 1600–1900*
(New York, Columbia University Press, 2002), 359–362.

 [8] Kamo no Mabuchi, *Futatabi kingo no kimi ni kotaematsuru fumi* [Another Reply to Tayasu
Munetake], in *Nihon kagaku taikei* [Anthology of Japanese Poetics], vol. 7, edited by Sasaki Nobutsuna
(Tokyo: Kazama Shobō, 1957), 155; Shirane, *Early Modern Japanese Literature*, 605, translation
modified.

 [9] Kamo no Mabuchi, *Ka'ikō* [Reflections on Poetry], in *Kinsei shintōron • zenki kokugaku* [Early
Modern Shintō Theory and Early National Learning], *Nihon shisō taikei* [Anthology of Japanese
Thought], no. 39, edited by Taira Shigemichi and Abe Akio (Tokyo: Iwanami Shoten, 1972), 349; Shirane,
Early Modern Japanese Literature, 607.

 [10] Motoori Norinaga, *Isonokami sasamegoto* [Ancient Whisperings], in *Motoori Norinaga shū* [Works
of Motoori Norinaga], *Shinchō Nihon koten shūsei* [Shinchō Collection of the Japanese Classics], no. 60,
edited by Hino Tatsuo (Tokyo: Shinchōsha, 1983), 413.

outward appearance they put on by suppressing their feelings of sadness," whereas "the way that mothers pay no heed to the eyes of others, drenching themselves with tears, may appear to be womanly and shameful, but it is this that constitutes unadorned, true emotions."[11]

Norinaga most famously describes the emotionality of poetry and *monogatari* 物語 (tales) through the term *mono no aware* ものののあはれ (or just *aware* あはれ), which can be rendered in English very roughly as "pathos," and which he describes as "feeling deep emotions in response to things seen, heard, or done."[12] He sees *mono no aware* as providing a set of norms distinct from those of Confucian and Buddhist morality, explaining this multiplicity of value systems by noting that "all judgments of good and bad differ depending on the relevant Way."[13] He writes that "Confucianism and Buddhism are Ways that instruct and guide people, so sometimes they conflict with human emotions and severely reprimand people."[14] When judging literary writings according to the measure of *mono no aware*, though, "what is considered good and bad is simply the distinction between what is in keeping with human emotions and what is not."[15] For Norinaga, the problem with using Confucianism and Buddhism to judge poetry and *monogatari* is not that these value systems are invalid per se but rather that such interpretations overstep the proper purview of these teachings and fail to appreciate the distinctive character of literary writings, which must be judged by their own standards. Norinaga often discusses the conflicts between *mono no aware* and Confucian and Buddhist morality, even going so far as to say that it is illicit sexual relationships that bring out the most profound emotions, but he defends himself against potential charges of promoting immorality by writing, "I do not value amorousness as something wonderful, but rather value knowing *mono no aware*."[16] He goes on to compare the immorality in which *mono no aware* flourishes to the muddy water in which a lotus grows: "Although one does not value the muddy pond, one values the great purity of the lotus flowers, so one sets aside the fact that the muddy pond is clouded."[17] In other words, the function of poetry and *monogatari* is not to invert or supplant conventional morality but to provide a space within which moral concerns can be temporarily set aside, allowing for the unfettered expression and cultivation of the depths of human emotionality.

---

[11] Motoori Norinaga, *Isonokami sasamegoto*, 412.

[12] Motoori Norinaga, *Isonokami sasamegoto*, 297.

[13] Motoori Norinaga, *Shibun yōryō* [The Essence of the *Tale of Genji*], in *Motoori Norinaga shū* [Works of Motoori Norinaga], *Shinchō Nihon koten shūsei* [Shinchō Collection of the Japanese Classics], no. 60, edited by Hino Tatsuo (Tokyo: Shinchōsha, 1983), 82; Shirane, *Early Modern Japanese Literature*, 619, translation modified.

[14] Motoori Norinaga, *Shibun yōryō*, 83; Shirane, *Early Modern Japanese Literature*, 619.

[15] Motoori Norinaga, *Shibun yōryō*, 83; Shirane, *Early Modern Japanese Literature*, 619.

[16] Motoori Norinaga, *Shibun yōryō*, 159.

[17] Motoori Norinaga, *Shibun yōryō*, 159.

POETIC CLASSICISM AND EMOTIONAL
SELF-CULTIVATION

Despite National Learning scholars' extolling of genuine emotions, their guidelines for poetic composition demanded the close imitation of a restricted set of models taken from the Japanese poetry of the past. They believed that the Japanese of their day had become alienated from the authentic emotionality and poetic modes of expression that had existed in the past, so that if they simply composed whatever they felt in whatever language came naturally to them, their poetry would be inauthentic and vulgar. It is not difficult to find a basic contradiction in encouraging people to express authentic emotions by copying others, but this aspect of National Learning scholars' poetics was more than just a failure to carry through their emotionalism to its proper conclusions or to break free from traditional poetic forms; it was rooted in their notion of the "real" Japan as a normative concept that could not simply be equated with the empirical reality of Japan in their day. This real Japan remained hidden from sight to varying degrees and needed to be recovered not only by investigating ancient texts, but also by cultivating the self emotionally through the mediation of the classics.

Mabuchi asserts the universality of the sentiments expressed in ancient poetry by declaring that "ancient poetry is the true heart (magokoro 真心) of all people."[18] Describing the later deterioration of poetry, he writes, "In recent times the feelings and words of poetry have become different from ordinary feelings and words. In poetry, people distort their proper heart and seek words to describe this distortion . . . . How could the words chosen and uttered by the clouded and filthy hearts of people of later times fail to be soiled?"[19] Mabuchi does not draw a strict line between the poetry of the Man'yōshū and the Kokinshū, pointing out the internal diversity of both anthologies, but, for the most part, he sees the Man'yōshū as exemplifying the authenticity of ancient poetry and the Kokinshū as representing the beginning of the decline of Japanese poetry, which he often describes in gendered terms as a shift from the "manly" (masurao 丈夫) to the "effeminate" (taoyame 手弱女) style, a marked contrast with how Norinaga would later, as we have seen, praise the authenticity of feminine emotions.[20] In order to recover poetic authenticity, Mabuchi argues, people of his own time must study ancient poetry and compose their own poetry in imitation of it, after which "the ancient style will naturally be absorbed into one's own heart, and one will surely grasp the lofty and manly spirit of the ancients, whose straightforward hearts and courtly words had not a speck of filth or dust."[21] He put his poetic ideals into practice by himself composing

---

[18] Kamo no Mabuchi, Niimanabi [An Introduction to Learning], in Kinsei shintōron • zenki kokugaku [Early Modern Shintō Theory and Early National Learning], Nihon shisō taikei [Anthology of Japanese Thought], no. 39, edited by Taira Shigemichi and Abe Akio (Tokyo: Iwanami Shoten, 1972), 361.

[19] Kamo no Mabuchi, Ka'ikō, 349; Shirane, Early Modern Japanese Literature, 608.

[20] See, for example, Kamo no Mabuchi, Niimanabi, 358.

[21] Kamo no Mabuchi, Ka'ikō, 351; Shirane, Early Modern Japanese Literature, 609.

in the *Man'yōshū* style and promoting it among his students, leading to a proliferation of neo-*Man'yōshū* poetry in the late eighteenth century. This represented a repudiation of the literary ideals of the aristocratic court poets, whose aesthetic was rooted in the *Kokinshū*. The court poets had virtually monopolized the teaching and practice of *waka* poetry prior to the Tokugawa period, relying on both privileged access to manuscripts and the authority of carefully guarded secret teachings to uphold their prestige. The spread of printing and the relative democratization of learning in the Tokugawa period led to a weakening of the court poets' position, but they still remained influential rivals against which National Learning scholars staked out their own vision of *waka* poetry, which involved claiming the Japanese poetic tradition as the cultural inheritance of all Japanese, not just those of a specific social class.

Whereas Mabuchi relies on a kind of naïve primitivism in exhorting his contemporaries to recover the simple purity of ancient times, Norinaga gives much more attention to the distance between the past and present and to the contradictions involved in achieving spontaneity and authenticity through imitation and conscious effort. Norinaga draws a distinction, for example, between two senses in which we can speak of genuine emotions in poetry: the first refers to poetry that expresses whatever we happen to spontaneously feel, whereas the second refers to poetry that expresses the truth of our human nature. He comments, "Japanese poetry since middle antiquity does not contain genuine emotions; it is all false. But this falseness is different from that of Chinese poetry, as the falseness of Japanese poetry is composed from learning the genuine emotions of the past. While it is false, then, it is the truth of human emotions."[22] In other words, it is false in the sense that it does not reflect our spontaneous emotions, but it is true in that it reflects what we ought to feel as humans. A similar normative approach to emotionality can be seen in how Norinaga speaks not only of *mono no aware* but also of "knowing *mono no aware*" (*mono no aware o shiru* もののあはれを知る), which he defines as "discerning the essence of events that should make one feel joyful or sad upon encountering these events."[23] According to this formulation, *mono no aware* as an emotional and literary ideal is not just about deep feeling, but also about feeling the right emotions at the right times.

A process of historical decline and infiltration by foreign cultures, argues Norinaga, has alienated us from our true human nature, so that if people of the present "just composed based on the state of their own heart, this would create extremely vulgar poetry."[24] Instead, it is necessary to "immerse our hearts in the poetry composed by the ancients, and become accustomed to it on a daily basis, so that our emotions will naturally be transformed, and the elegant intentions of the ancients will arise in our own hearts."[25]

---

[22] Motoori Norinaga, *Ashiwake obune* [A Small Boat Punting Through the Reeds], in *Kinsei zuisō shū* [Collection of Early Modern Essays], *Shinpen Nihon koten bungaku zenshū* [New Edition of the Collected Works of Classical Japanese Literature], no. 82, edited by Suzuki Jun and Odaka Michiko (Tokyo: Shōgakukan, 2000), 350–351.

[23] Motoori Norinaga, *Shibun yōryō*, 282.

[24] Motoori Norinaga, *Ashiwake obune*, 303.

[25] Motoori Norinaga, *Ashiwake obune*, 306.

When this happens, the two types of "genuineness" will be reunited because we will spontaneously feel the emotions that reflect our true human nature. Norinaga presents the resulting immediacy of expression, though, as bearing certain traces of its mediated origins, such as in his departure from Mabuchi's primitivism in his approach to poetic composition. One difference from Mabuchi is that Norinaga's primary aesthetic ideal is taken from the *Kokinshū* and other imperially commissioned anthologies of the Heian period, rather than from the earlier *Man'yōshū* (although he did see the study and imitation of the *Man'yōshū* as important in philological training, an additional role of poetry discussed later). More importantly for the issue at hand, he recommends that his contemporaries not imitate the poetry of these Heian anthologies directly but instead model their poetry on the later *Shinkokinshū* (New Collection of Japanese Poems of Past and Present), dating from the early thirteenth century, which he values for how "its poems are composed by immersing the heart in the style of the past,"[26] a reference to its frequent use of such techniques as *honkadori* 本歌取 (drawing on a source poem), in which a poem is composed as a variation on one or more poems from the past. When Norinaga tells poets of his own day to emulate the *Shinkokinshū*, then, this is not so much a stylistic imitation as an imitation of the process through which the poems of the *Shinkokinshū* were produced, in which the poet's expression is self-consciously mediated through a literary tradition that he is at a distance from.

Norinaga's discussion of the different types of "genuineness" in poetry was connected to a broader Tokugawa debate, originating in Confucian discourse, over the relationship between human nature and the normative Way for governing society. Followers of Zhu Xi saw the Way as latent in the original nature of humans due to their possession of a universal metaphysical principle, and they defined "genuineness" (Ch. *zheng*; Jp. *sei/makoto* 誠) as that which expresses this perfectly virtuous original nature. Sorai denied the existence of such an innately perfect human nature, though, and saw the Way as a cultural creation that is external to and shapes human nature, meaning that cultivation in the Way requires not, as for Zhu Xi, that people uncover their true inner nature but rather that they assimilate to something originally foreign to them. For Sorai, "genuineness" refers to whatever people do spontaneously, whether as an expression of their raw human nature or as a result of training to the point where certain learned behavior becomes as if natural. Unlike for Zhu Xi, then, "genuineness" can describe any kind of behavior, whether in keeping with the Confucian Way or not, as long as this behavior comes naturally, thus making "genuineness" itself a normatively empty concept. When Confucian texts exhort people to achieve genuineness, he argues, this is in reference not to genuineness in the abstract but specifically to the process of absorbing the Confucian Way, in which "when one studies the Way of the ancient kings and is transformed by it over a long period of time, so that learned customs become as if they were the heaven-endowed inborn nature, then that which at the beginning could not be known or done can now be achieved without conscious thought, and be correct without

---

[26] Motoori Norinaga, *Ashiwake obune*, 267.

effort."[27] Norinaga is similar to Sorai in how he presents two types of "genuineness," a similarity that is connected to how both thinkers share a conception of culture as a source of norms that must be learned to the point at which it becomes second nature. The important difference, though, is that for Norinaga the cultural norms of Japanese poetry reflect the essence of human nature itself, so that the mastery of these norms ultimately represents not the acquisition of something new, as in Sorai's philosophy, but a return to a self (and a Japan) that was always already there but that people of his own time had lost touch with.

The appeal to the Japanese past as a source of norms was tied to another role of poetic classicism among National Learning scholars, which was its connection to philological training. These scholars considered the culture of the Japanese past to be accessible in their own day primarily through its textual legacy, and they saw the Japanese poetic tradition as playing a unique role in unlocking this legacy by bridging the gap between past and present. They claimed that this poetry was a repository of older and purer forms of the Japanese language and, at the same time, that it embodied a certain mindset and spirit that were at the core of the purely native Japanese culture of the past. In order to make the language and spirit of the poetry of the past truly one's own, they believed it was necessary not only to study it, but also to compose poetry in imitation of it, which would in effect transform the student himself into one of the ancients. Their incorporation of poetry into their philological project drew heavily on the methodology of Sorai, who saw the study and composition of Chinese poetry as the key to grasping the ancient Chinese language and inhabiting the mental world of the ancient Chinese, which would in turn make it possible to properly understand the ancient texts in which the Confucian Way is recorded.

National Learning scholars defined their philological methodology in relation to two main sets of opponents among their Tokugawa contemporaries. The first of these were the aristocratic court scholars, who relied on the authority of received tradition, passed down from teacher to student through a properly sanctioned scholarly lineage, as the basis for valid interpretation. National Learning scholars rejected this reliance on institutional and class-based authority but, at the same time, they denied that the isolated individual, employing nothing but his own powers of reasoning, could qualify as a competent reader of texts from the Japanese past. An excessive reliance on subjective reasoning was the flaw they saw in their second main target: those scholars, like Yamazaki Ansai, who used Confucian, especially Song Confucian, theoretical frameworks to understand ancient Japanese texts. Mabuchi, for example, criticizes those who "construct theories about everything" and "explain things as if they could be determined exhaustively with the human heart."[28] Norinaga, writing about the same kinds of Confucian interpreters of Japanese texts, complains about how "fettered by their exclusive reliance on Chinese-style logic, they do not realize that they should search for the spirit

---

[27] Ogyū Sorai, *Benmei*, in *Ogyū Sorai* [Ogyū Sorai], *Nihon shisō taikei* [Anthology of Japanese Thought], no. 36, edited by Yoshikawa Kojirō et al. (Tokyo: Iwanami Shoten, 1973), 93.

[28] Kamo no Mabuchi, *Kokuikō*, 381–382; Flueckiger 2008, 249.

of ancient times."[29] To properly understand these texts, he argues, one must cultivate one's "Japanese spirit" (*yamato-damashii* 大和魂) and cleanse oneself of the "Chinese heart" (*karagokoro* 漢意). For Mabuchi and Norinaga, then, a precondition for valid interpretation is that the reader mentally inhabit the world of the Japanese past, which they imagined as a cultural whole that transcends and grounds the subjectivity of those who belong to it.

POETRY AND COMMUNITY

For National Learning scholars, the cultivation of emotions through poetry was not just an individual matter, but was also tied to a vision of community as rooted in emotional bonds. The question of the social value of Japanese poetry rose to prominence in the Tokugawa period with a famous debate that erupted over *Kokka hachiron* (Eight Essays on Japanese Poetry), a work by Kada no Arimaro (1706–1751). Arimaro was the nephew of Kada no Azumamaro (1669–1736), a renowned scholar of Shintō and classical Japanese literature, and was employed as Assistant in Japanese Studies (*wagaku goyō* 和学御用) to Tayasu Munetake (1715–1771), second son of the shogun Tokugawa Yoshimune (1684–1751, r. 1716–1745). The aspect of Arimaro's work that gave rise to the greatest controversy was his claim that poetry is simply a form of amusement that "is of no use in governing the realm, nor is it of any benefit to everyday life," a statement meant as a repudiation of Confucian ideas on the benefits of poetry to government and personal cultivation.[30] Munetake took issue with Arimaro's dismissal of the moral and social benefits of poetry, drawing on Zhu Xi's philosophy to argue that poetry plays an important moral function through its role in "encouraging virtue and chastising vice."[31] When Munetake called on Mabuchi to present his views on the issues under debate, Mabuchi agreed with him on the basic idea of the social benefits of poetry but argued that these benefits come not from serving as a medium for moral cultivation, but from facilitating the emotional understanding and emotional regulation needed for a smoothly functioning society. He describes poetry as able to reach into the depths of people's hearts to change their customs and behavior, as a tool for rulers to grasp the

[29] Motoori Norinaga, *Uiyamabumi* [First Steps into the Mountains], in *Motoori Norinaga* [Motoori Norinaga], *Nihon shisō taikei* [Anthology of Japanese Thought], no. 40, edited by Yoshikawa Kōjirō, Satake Akihiro, and Hino Tatsuo (Tokyo: Iwanami Shoten, 1978), 519; Nishimura 1987, 463.

[30] Kada no Arimaro, *Kokka hachiron* [Eight Essays on Japanese Poetry], in *Karonshū* [Works on Poetic Theory], *Nihon koten bungaku zenshū* [Collected Works of Classical Japanese Literature], no. 50, edited by Hashimoto Fumio, Ariyoshi Tamotsu, and Fujihira Haruo (Tokyo: Shōgakukan, 1975), 540; Shirane, *Early Modern Japanese Literature*, 602.

[31] Tayasu Munetake, *Kokka hachiron yogen* [My Views on the *Eight Essays on Japanese Poetry*], in *Nihon kagaku taikei* [Anthology of Japanese Poetics], vol. 7, edited by Sasaki Nobutsuna (Tokyo: Kazama Shobō, 1957), 199–200; Shirane, *Early Modern Japanese Literature*, 604.

emotions of their subjects, and as a way to temper and moderate emotions that would otherwise go out of control and lead to strife.[32]

Despite Mabuchi's objection to the strictly moral approach to poetry associated with the Confucianism of Zhu Xi, his views on the social benefits of poetry as expressed in the debate over the *Eight Essays on Japanese Poetry* were tied to other strains of Confucian thought, as he himself notes when he comments, "In government it is important to make the people spontaneously follow. Therefore when the sages governed in China, they took into consideration that which cannot be reached by principle and rules, and so created music, and used it among the households and among the feudal states in order to change the customs of the people and harmonize their hearts."[33] As touched on earlier, a basic division can be made within Confucianism between those who, like Zhu Xi, see the Confucian Way in terms of a metaphysical moral rationalism, and those who see it as a cultural force that operates through such mechanisms as ritual and music. It is the latter tendency in Confucianism that Mabuchi draws on here, one that was represented in Tokugawa Japan most notably by Ogyū Sorai. As we have seen, though, in his later works Mabuchi became not only stridently anti-Confucian, but also harshly critical of the Confucian culture promoted by Sorai and his school, characterizing it as artificial and forced—as opposed to how Japanese culture is an outgrowth of nature—and blaming it for the loss of the original "straightforward heart" that the Japanese possessed in ancient times. The recovery of this straightforward heart through the study of ancient poetry, he argues, would restore interpersonal relations based on complete honesty and transparency, which would create a harmonious society without the need for relying on explicit regulations or the use of force by rulers.

A distinctive feature of Norinaga's explanation of the social benefits of poetry is his focus on poetic composition as a fundamentally communicative act, such as when he writes, "When we feel *aware* very deeply, composing alone will not satisfy our heart, so we have a person listen to us and are comforted . . . . This is the nature of poetry, so having someone listen is truly the essence of poetry and not an accidental aspect of it."[34] Norinaga sees the linguistic "design" (*aya* 文) of poetic language, such as its meter and rhetorical devices, as arising out of this same need for communicability. He comments, "Those who fail to understand this principle say that true poetry consists simply of saying what we feel, just as we feel it, whether well or poorly, and that the aspect that relates to the listener is not true poetry . . . . It is important that poetry be heard by another who sympathizes, so it is the essential nature of poetry that we create design in our words."[35] By making their emotions known to each other, he argues, people are

---

[32] Kamo no Mabuchi, *Kokka hachiron yogen shūi* [Gleanings from *My Views on the "Eight Essays on Japanese Poetry"*], in *Nihon kagaku taikei* [Anthology of Japanese Poetics], vol. 7, edited by Sasaki Nobutsuna (Tokyo: Kazama Shobō, 1957), 117–118.

[33] Kamo no Mabuchi, *Kokka hachiron yogen shūi*, 117.

[34] Motoori Norinaga, *Isonokami sasamegoto*, 312–313; Shirane, *Early Modern Japanese Literature*, 616–617.

[35] Motoori Norinaga, *Isonokami sasamegoto*, 313; Shirane, *Early Modern Japanese Literature*, 617.

able to move beyond the narrow confines of their own experience and empathize with others: "Those who do not know *mono no aware* have no sympathy for anything and are often hard-hearted and cruel. Because they have no encounters with various matters, they do not understand them. The rich do not know the hearts of the poor, the young do not know the hearts of the aged, and men do not know the hearts of women . . . . But when people deeply understand the hearts of others, they naturally act so as not to harm society or other people. This is another benefit of making people sensitive to *mono no aware*."[36] Norinaga is adamant that the content of poetry not be judged in terms of virtue and vice, but, at the same time, emotional communication does take on a strongly ethical character for him because it leads people to behave properly, but without needing to resort to the rationalism and explicit didacticism of Confucian teachings, which he sees as ultimately counterproductive.

Whereas on one level Norinaga depicts poetry as a way for people to communicate their personal emotional experiences to those who are different from themselves, we should remember that he denies the validity of the spontaneous emotions felt by people of his own day, instead demanding that they learn to feel according to the emotional norms embodied in a canon of Japanese poetry. The interpersonal differences that are overcome through poetic communication, then, exist within the framework of a shared cultural sphere that forms the ultimate ground of communicability, a cultural sphere that is absolutized by being equated not only with Japaneseness, but also with human nature itself.

CONCLUSION

For National Learning scholars, Japanese poetry was the key to overcoming the social fragmentation of their day and recovering the spontaneous harmony that they imagined had existed in ancient Japan. One way they claimed it did this was by allowing people to express the emotional core of their human nature and bond with others through ties of empathy, thus creating deeper human connections than were possible through the rules of Confucian morality, which they saw as artificial and excessively rationalistic. Another way was by embodying and transmitting the cultural and linguistic norms from the past through which these scholars defined Japanese identity. National Learning scholars saw both of these roles of poetry as indispensable to the formation of community; cultural norms that do not engage people on an emotional level remain an external imposition and, at the same time, emotions in the absence of cultural norms fail to rise beyond the level of mere personal inclination. Japanese poetry, for National Learning

---

[36] Motoori Norinaga, *Isonokami sasamegoto*, 444–446; Shirane, *Early Modern Japanese Literature*, 618.

scholars, is able to embody both cultural norms and authentic emotions without these contradicting each other, something made possible by how they define "authenticity" itself as a normative concept, in which it is only those emotional responses authorized by a canon of Japanese poetry that are considered truly authentic. In this way, eighteenth-century National Learning was a precursor to modern Japanese nationalist ideologies that insisted on an erasure of the distinction between public and private and an identification of the Japanese self as the only true self.

Bibliography and Suggested Readings

Burns, Susan. (2003) *Before the Nation: Kokugaku and the Imagining of Community in Early Modern Japan.* Durham, NC: Duke University Press.

Caddeau, Patrick. (2006) *Appraising "Genji": Literary Criticism and Cultural Anxiety in the Age of the Last Samurai.* Albany: State University of New York Press.

Flueckiger, Peter. (2008) "Reflections on the Meaning of Our Country: Kamo no Mabuchi's *Kokuikō*," *Monumenta Nipponica* 63(2): 211–263.

Flueckiger, Peter. (2011) *Imagining Harmony: Poetry, Empathy, and Community in Mid-Tokugawa Confucianism and Nativism.* Stanford: Stanford University Press.

Harootunian, H. D. (1988) *Things Seen and Unseen: Discourse and Ideology in Tokugawa Nativism.* Chicago: University of Chicago Press.

Marra, Michael. (1998) "Nativist Hermeneutics: The Interpretive Strategies of Motoori Norinaga and Fujitani Mitsue," *Japan Review* 10: 17–52.

Marra, Michael. (2007) *The Poetics of Motoori Norinaga.* Honolulu: University of Hawai'i Press.

Maruyama, Masao. (1974) *Studies in the Intellectual History of Tokugawa Japan*, translated by Mikiso Hane. Princeton, NJ: Princeton University Press.

Matsumoto, Shigeru. (1970) *Motoori Norinaga, 1730–1801.* Cambridge, MA: Harvard University Press.

McNally, Mark. (2005) *Proving the Way: Conflict and Practice in the History of Japanese Nativism.* Cambridge, MA: Harvard University Asia Center.

Najita, Tetsuo. (1991) "History and Nature in Eighteenth-Century Tokugawa Thought." In *The Cambridge History of Japan, Volume 4: Early Modern Japan*, edited by J. W. Hall. Cambridge, UK: Cambridge University Press, 596–659.

Nishimura, Sey. (1987) "First Steps into the Mountains: Motoori Norinaga's *Uiyamabumi*," *Monumenta Nipponica* 42(4): 449–493.

Nishimura, Sey. (1991) "The Way of the Gods: Motoori Norinaga's *Naobi no mitama*," *Monumenta Nipponica* 46(1): 21–41.

Nosco, Peter. (1981) "Nature, Invention, and National Learning: The *Kokka hachiron* Controversy, 1742–46," *Harvard Journal of Asiatic Studies* 41(1): 75–91.

Nosco, Peter. (1990) *Remembering Paradise: Nativism and Nostalgia in Eighteenth-Century Japan.* Cambridge, MA: Council on East Asian Studies, Harvard University.

Sakai, Naoki. (1991) *Voices of the Past: The Status of Language in Eighteenth-Century Japanese Discourse.* Ithaca, NY: Cornell University Press.

Teeuwen, Mark. (1997) "Poetry, Sake, and Acrimony: Arakida Hisaoyu and the Kokugaku Movement," *Monumenta Nipponica* 52(3): 295–325.

Thomas, Roger. (2008) *The Way of Shikishima: Waka Theory and Practice in Early Modern Japan*. Lanham, MD: University Press of America.

Wehmeyer, Ann. (1997) *Motoori: Kojiki-den, Book 1*. Ithaca, NY: Cornell East Asia Series.

Yoda, Tomiko. (1999) "Fractured Dialogues: *Mono no aware* and Poetic Communication in *The Tale of Genji*," *Harvard Journal of Asiatic Studies* 59(2): 523–557.

PART II

PHILOSOPHIES OF JAPANESE BUDDHISM

CHAPTER 4

SAICHŌ'S TENDAI

In the Middle of Form and Emptiness

PAUL L. SWANSON AND BROOK ZIPORYN

PART I BY PAUL SWANSON

SAICHŌ (最澄, 767–822) was the founder of the Japanese Tendai (天台) school of Buddhism on Mt. Hiei (near the capital of Kyoto), which involved transmitting the Chinese Tiantai as well as other aspects of the East Asian Mahāyāna Buddhist tradition. The Tendai school grew to be one of the largest Buddhist organizations through much of Japanese history and served as the womb for the movements that make up most of the current traditional Buddhist schools in Japan (the Pure Land schools of Hōnen and Shinran, the Zen schools of Eisai and Dōgen, the Lotus schools of Nichiren, and so forth). Saichō was not a creative genius on a par with Kūkai, the other pre-eminent Buddhist figure of the time, one who transmitted and founded the esoteric Shingon tradition. And yet Saichō had the insight to recognize the importance of the Tiantai texts that had been brought to Japan by Ganjin (688–763, a precepts master who had also trained in the Tiantai tradition). Among these texts, which Saichō discovered of special significance, was the encyclopedic *Mohezhiguan* (Jp. *Makashikan* 摩訶止観) of Zhiyi (Jp. Chigi 智顗, 538–597), which would later become one of the primary textbooks of the Tendai curriculum. Thus inspired, Saichō arranged to travel to Tang China to learn and transmit these important teachings; hence, his posthumous title Dengyō Daishi (伝教大師, Great Master Who Transmitted the Teachings). In the first part of this chapter, we begin by looking at the teachings that were transmitted by Saichō, as they form the basis of his thought; then we examine some developments in his own teachings with regard to Buddha-nature and the bodhisattva precepts; and, finally, we look at his legacy in terms of how his ideas developed in "original enlightenment" texts that were produced after his life but later attributed to him.

The Threefold Truth of Tiantai Buddhism as the Foundation of Saichō's Thought

Tiantai Buddhism was established by Zhiyi (538–597), whose comprehensive system attempted to incorporate all aspects of Buddhism, a vast tradition of teachings and practices that had been introduced haphazardly to China from India through Central Asia. The "one vehicle" rhetoric of the *Lotus Sutra*, that all people are ultimately destined for Buddhahood, along with the concept of "skillful means" (Jp. *hōben* 方便; Sk. *upāya*), was utilized to explain seeming contradictions in the Buddhist teachings and to provide a hierarchy of methods and teachings. A threefold (or fourfold) pattern was identified as the key to basic Buddhist teachings and practice: that all things arise through a confluence of causes and conditions and therefore are empty of substantial being, and yet all phenomena have significance as being temporary or conventionally existent; to realize these two aspects as identical and equally significant is the Middle Way.

This basic Mahāyāna Buddhist insight is most succinctly expressed in verse 24:18 of the *Middle Treatise* of Nāgārjuna:[1]

> All things that arise through conditioned co-arising
> I explain as emptiness;
> Again, they are conventional designations;
> Again, this is the meaning of the Middle Path.

First is the basic Buddhist insight that all phenomena consist of a confluence of innumerable causes and conditions, that everything is a result of the flux of conditioned co-arising (Jp. *innen* 因縁 or *engi* 縁起; Sk. *pratītya-samutpāda*). In other words, there is no unchanging "substance" or "self" within phenomena or at the core of the person. All things are "empty" (Jp. *kū* 空; Sk. *śūnyatā*) of unchanging or eternal "being," and this is the most fundamental attribute of all of reality (often referred to as "thusness" or "suchness," *shinnyo* 真如). Nevertheless, as phenomena arise through the confluence of causes and conditions, they have significance as temporary, conventional, or provisional existence (*kemyō* 仮名) or "forms." As they are experienced by us, given conventional designations, and are thus "named," they "exist" provisionally. Thus, though empty of an eternal and unchanging substance, human beings (and other phenomena) are significant and worthy of attention and, insofar as they experience suffering, are deserving of compassion. To realize the emptiness of all things and their conventional existence is two different ways of expressing the same truth of conditioned co-arising; this is the wisdom of the "Middle Way" (*chūdō* 中道), the insight of a Buddha.

This basic Mahāyāna Buddhist pattern is perhaps most famously seen in the short phrase that is the heart of the *Heart Sutra*, the short *Prajñāpāramitā* ("perfection of wisdom") text that presents the gist of the teaching of "emptiness," that "form is emptiness

---

[1] For a more detailed explication, see Swanson 1989, 1–17.

and emptiness is form" (*shiki soku ze kū kū soku ze shiki* 色即是空空即是色). What we experience as having "form"[2]—our physical bodies, the chair we sit on, the apple we eat, the rose we smell—is empty of eternal or substantial being since these phenomena are made up of an almost infinite variety of interconnected causes and conditions. And yet "emptiness" is not an alternate reality or something apart from the forms we experience in their temporary existence and conventionally named appearances. Emptiness is inseparable from these forms, and the mundane world of temporary forms is where we live and move and have our being. Again, these two phrases form a set, and the affirmation of both aspects is the "Middle Way."

This fourfold pattern—the first item of "conditioned co-arising" added to the threefold truth of emptiness, conventionality, and the Middle—is also reflected in the categories by which Zhiyi classified the entire corpus of Buddhist teachings in what was probably the most successful of the many Chinese attempts at Buddhist "doctrinal classification." First, the "Tripitaka Teachings," represented by the *Āgama* sutras and considered from the Mahāyāna perspective to be somewhat inferior "Hīnayāna" teachings adhered to by the earlier disciples of the Buddha, focused on the teaching of dependent co-arising. Second, the "Shared Teaching" (common to both Mahāyāna and Hīnayāna) was characterized by an emphasis on "emptiness" and was most developed in the *Prajñāparamitā* sutras. Third, the "Distinct Teaching," unique to Mahāyāna, emphasized the importance of conventional reality and involvement in this mundane world through compassion as represented in a variety of Mahāyāna texts (such as the *Flower Garland* [Ch. *Huayan*; Jp. *Kegon* 華厳] and *Vimalakīrti* sutras). Fourth and finally, the "Perfect Teaching" (represented by the *Lotus Sutra* and also somewhat by the *Mahāyāna Parinirvāṇa Sutra*) went beyond the "skillful means" of the earlier teachings by providing a Middle Way in which it was recognized that all people have the capacity (Buddha-nature) to attain Buddhahood and for which Buddhahood was the ultimate goal for all through a "direct path" (*jikidō* 直道) to enlightenment. These concepts played a central role in Saichō's thought.

Saichō and Tendai Buddhism: Buddha-nature and the Mahāyāna Bodhisattva Precepts

Saichō travelled to T'ang China in 803, with the support of the Imperial court, and returned to Japan in 805, having in this short period visited Mt. Tiantai and received training and official transmissions not only in Tiantai proper but also in the Zen Buddhism of the Ox Head school, in the esoteric Buddhist tradition, and in the bodhisattva precepts based on the *Bonmōkyō* (Ch. *Fan wang sutra* 梵網経; *Brahmajāla-sūtra*,

---

[2] The Sanskrit *rūpa* is rendered in Chinese and Japanese as 色 (Jp. *shiki*); literally, "color," or "visible form," but this implies and represents not only the experiences of sight but also includes the other senses such as hearing, scent, touch, and so forth.

The Sutra of Brahmā's Net).[3] Thus, it is traditionally said that the Tendai school founded by Saichō on Mt. Hiei is based on four pillars: (1) esoteric Buddhism (*mikkyō* 密教), (2) Zen (禅), (3) bodhisattva precepts (*bosatsukai* 菩薩戒), and (4) the "perfect teachings" of Tiantai proper (*tendai engyō* 天台円教). Although Saichō's activity and thought encompassed a wide variety of ideas and practices—the Tiantai tradition, after all, was an attempt to include the entire scope of Buddhism—here, we will look closely at two aspects of his thought: the debate over Buddha-nature with the Hossō (Yogācāra) monk Tokuitsu (徳一), in which Saichō supported the idea of universal Buddhahood in contrast to Tokuitsu's traditional Hossō teachings that some people have no "seeds" or potential and can never attain Buddhahood, and Saichō's concern to establish the Mahāyāna bodhisattva precepts as part of the "direct path" to Buddhahood. Both of these aspects reflect Saichō's concern with the idea of universal Buddhahood, that all people have the capacity to become a Buddha, and, indeed, are destined for Buddhahood, as expressed in traditional Mahāyāna Buddhist terms such as the "one vehicle" (Jp. *ichijō* 一乗; Sk. *ekayāna*), "Buddha-nature" (*busshō* 仏性), *tathāgata-garbha* (*nyoraizō* 如来蔵), and, later, as "original enlightenment" (*hongaku* 本覚).

Saichō's Debate with Tokuitsu over Buddha-nature

One of the most important events in Saichō's career was his extended debate with the Hossō monk Tokuitsu over various aspects of Tendai versus Hossō (Yogācāra) teachings, including the crucial question about Buddha-nature and the basic nature of human beings and their relationship to the "absolute."[4] What is human nature? Do all people have the capacity to attain enlightenment or Buddhahood? The debate over this question consisted more of appeal to authority ("proof" texts from the sutras and other authoritative sources) than philosophical argument. For example, Tokuitsu assumed that the teachings of the *Lotus Sutra*—that all people were capable of attaining Buddhahood—were tentative "skillful" means and that in fact different people have different capabilities, and he quoted texts that supported this idea. In Buddhist terms, Tokuitsu championed the Hossō position that the capabilities of people can be categorized into five types (Sk. *gotra*), including that of the lowly and hopeless *icchantika* whose evil deeds have resulted in "burnt" or "tainted" seeds (or lack any "untainted seeds" to begin with) and thus preclude any possible attainment of enlightenment in the future. Saichō, on the other hand, assumed that the *Lotus Sutra* was the final, perfect teaching and all other texts were tentative means leading up to the real promise of Buddhahood for all, and he quoted texts that supported this idea. In Buddhist terms, he recognized that the various goals and earlier (pre-*Lotus*) teachings on various other paths or vehicles (sravaka, pratkekabuddha, bodhisattva) were "skillful means" (Sk. *upāya*; Jp. *hōben* 方便)

---

[3] For details see Groner 1984, 39–64.
[4] Ibid., 91–106.

and that there is ultimately only one vehicle for all—that of Buddhahood (*sanjō hōben* 三乗方便; *ichijō shinjitsu* 一乗真実; · *sangon ichijitsu* 三権一実). Thus, the debate revolved around philosophical assumptions supported by reliance on scriptural authority rather than on logically arguing the merits of provable hypotheses. Nevertheless, these assumptions (and their presumed conclusions) were crucial.

On the basis of everyday experience, it can be argued that the Hossō position is more "realistic" and that Saichō's position is more "idealistic" or "optimistic." Anyone with any experience in the world will readily agree that there are more people who appear to fit into the category of an *icchantika* than there are bodhisattvas and Buddhas, and so the ideal of universal Buddhahood may seem unrealistic. Nevertheless, although disagreements and discussion on this topic continued beyond Saichō and Tokuitsu's debate, it was Saichō's ideal of universal Buddhahood that eventually became the accepted norm and dominant assumption for most of Japanese Buddhism.

The Establishment of the Mahāyāna Bodhisattva Precepts

Saichō's goal to construct an official platform for ordaining priests on Mt. Hiei using only the Mahāyāna bodhisattva precepts is often explained in terms of the political and institutional need for the Tendai school to gain independence from the Nara Buddhist establishment. These were certainly important factors, and yet it must be pointed out that a preference for the Mahāyāna bodhisattva precepts was also a natural development based on the teachings and ideas of universal Buddhahood and bodhisattva activity promoted by Saichō. There certainly was a political and social necessity for an independent precept platform, but this was not a merely institutional development—the idea of universal Buddhahood undergirds the need for "bodhisattva precepts" that reflect the Mahāyāna bodhisattva ethos. And the acceptance of the Mahāyāna precepts—with its emphasis on the spirit more than the letter of the rules—was, in turn, an important factor for the ideas of Buddha-nature and original enlightenment to become core concepts in Japanese Tendai thought.[5]

The Mahāyāna precepts that were promoted by Saichō referred primarily (although not exclusively) to the bodhisattva precepts in the *Bonmōkyō*. As we shall see, these sources emphasize more the "spirit" of the law rather than the detailed do's and don'ts of the traditional Hīnayāna precepts in the Vinaya, such as the 250 precepts for monks and 348 precepts for nuns as expounded in the *Four Part Vinaya* (*Shibunritsu* 四分律).

The Mahāyāna precepts of the *Bonmōkyō* consist of ten major and forty-eight minor (or "light") precepts. These ten major precepts overlap somewhat but are again different from the ten traditional basic precepts of the ordained monks and nuns and the ten "good actions" kept by the laypeople, as taught in the so-called Hīnayāna

---

[5] See, for example, Shirato 1987 on "Inherent Enlightenment (*hongaku shisō*) and Saichō's acceptance of the Bodhisattva Precepts," and Groner 2014.

rules.[6] The opening four precepts are common to all these lists and basic to any moral system: prohibition against killing, stealing, lust, and lying. The remaining prohibit handling alcohol, speaking of the faults of others, praising oneself and disparaging others, stinginess, being resentful, and denigrating the three treasures (of Buddha, Dharma, and Sangha). The forty-eight minor precepts are more general than the 250 precepts of the Hīnayāna rules and are concrete examples of what should be expected of one living a Bodhisattva-like life and aiming for Buddhahood: do not show disrespect to teachers, do not eat meat, do not miss the chance to attend Dharma lectures, do not turn your back on the Mahāyāna and regress to the Hīnayāna, do not seek to gain political influence, do not fail to care for the sick, do not amass weapons, do not make groundless accusations, do not earn your living improperly, do not receive guests improperly, do not pursue personal gain, do not teach the precepts to the wrong people, and so forth.

Another source that Saichō used to support the idea of bodhisattva precepts was the *Lotus Sutra*. There are no lists of precepts as such in the *Lotus Sutra*, and it may seem strange to use this text in this context, but the *Lotus Sutra* provided support for the idea that all people should seek Buddhahood as the final goal and live the altruistic life of a bodhisattva. Saichō referred particularly to the fourteenth chapter of the *Lotus Sutra*, on "peaceful practices" (or, "actions that will result in serene peace"; *anrakugyōbon* 安楽行品), which describes how bodhisattvas are to act in our "degenerate era," when it is difficult to lead a strict moral life. Again, rather than detailed lists of specific rules, these actions were described in general terms of a moral life under the fourfold rubric of physical, verbal, intentional (mindful), and vow-based actions. For example, one is to be "gentle, agreeable, good, and acquiescent, not given to fits of violence, nor at heart becoming alarmed,"[7] and so forth, as well as avoiding familiarity with kings and princes, followers of non-Buddhist teachings, and social outcasts, presumably to avoid the entanglements and temptations that such contacts would entail. The emphasis, however, is on following the "spirit" of a bodhisattva in order to take the path to enlightenment.

This "path to enlightenment" was the "direct path" (*jikidō* 直道) of the Mahāyāna bodhisattva. The *Lotus Sutra* expresses this in many ways, such as in the parable of the conjured city, where a guide must use skillful means such as a "conjured city" as a waystation while leading the (Hīnayāna-type) people in a roundabout way to the final goal, rather than on a direct route.[8] The *Makashikan*, following up on this parable, frequently uses the phrase "leading directly to the place of enlightenment" (*jikishi dōjō* 直至道場) to describe the way of the Perfect Teaching, the direct (and quick) way to Buddhahood. Indeed, the last, closing words of the *Makashikan* (T 46.140c17–18) encourage the reader: "Riding on the one great vehicle, you will traverse the four

---

[6] For details, see the entries under these categories in the Digital Dictionary of Buddhism (http://www.buddhism-dict.net/ddb/).

[7] See Hurvitz, *Lotus Sutra*, 1976, 208–224.

[8] See the seventh chapter of the *Lotus Sutra*, Hurvitz 1976, 130–155.

directions directly to the place of enlightenment, and fulfill right awakening." The inferior Hīnayāna way is a "warped" or "round-about way" compared to the "direct" way to Buddhahood offered by Mahāyāna. Saichō picks up on the term "direct path" to argue for the importance of living a bodhisattva-like life and going directly to Buddhahood rather than keeping detailed moralistic rules over long eons of practice.

Thus we can see that although Saichō himself led a strictly moral life and kept the traditional Vinaya rules, his advocacy of a more general morality in terms of maintaining the spirit and living the bodhisattva life was in tune with the idea of universal Buddha-nature. This idea was to be developed in the post-Saichō Tendai tradition in terms of "original enlightenment" (*hongaku* 本覚) and become a major part of his legacy.

Saichō's Legacy in the Development of Original Enlightenment Thought

The term "original enlightenment" played a special role in the development of Japanese Buddhist thought as a nonsectarian concept that represents Japanese variations on the theme of realizing enlightenment. It is in line with the idea of Buddha-nature as an expression of the potential of all people to realize Buddhahood. Developments of this idea in the Japanese Tendai tradition in particular involved a special oral transmission of ideas now called "original enlightenment thought" (*hongaku shisō* 本覚思想), a set of ideas based on the belief that all sentient being (or, indeed, all things, even nonsentient things such as rocks and trees) inherently have the potential to become an enlightened Buddha. Eventually, this idea reached its apex in the conclusion that all beings are already endowed with enlightenment, that they are Buddha just as they are.

This radical idea—that all beings are Buddha just as they are—has been called "absolute nonduality," the complete identity of opposites.[9] This is not just nonduality in the traditional Mahāyāna sense of the necessary interrelationship between opposites, such as big and small, or light and dark, or the unity of seemingly opposing concepts such as form and emptiness, or ignorance and enlightenment. In this traditional sense, each side of the pair of opposites "depends" on the other in that there is no "big" without "small," and there is enlightenment because there is ignorance, and so forth. For Zhiyi, the founder of Tiantai philosophy, such opposites are "neither one nor two, and both one and two," "neither completely different nor totally the same," "nondual yet distinct." In the original enlightenment tradition of absolute nonduality, however, there is a total identification of opposites: ignorance *is* enlightenment; the passionate defilements *are* the wisdom of the Buddha; this anxiety-ridden cycle of birth-and-death *is* nirvāna; this defiled world *is* the Pure Land, just as it is. This is the logic of a total and simple identity of opposites, the most radical extension of the idea of "original enlightenment."

---

[9] See, for example, Tamura Yoshirō's essay in Tada et al. 1973, 477–598; and Tamura 1965 and 1987.

Original and Acquired Enlightenment in *The Awakening of Faith*

The term "original enlightenment" appears for the first time in the influential treatise *The Awakening of Faith in the Mahāyāna*, a text attributed to the famous Indian poet Aśvagoṣa but almost certainly composed in China around the fifth or sixth century as an indigenous interpretation of the doctrine of "Buddha-nature in all living beings" extolled in the *Mahāyāna Parinirvāṇa Sutra*. The term is paired with, and defined along with, the idea of "incipient enlightenment" (*shikaku* 始覚) or enlightenment that is actualized or acquired. Thus, there is "original enlightenment," understood as either the innate potential to become enlightened or as the "original" state of all beings as inherently enlightened, and there is "incipient enlightenment," understood as the enlightenment that is actualized or acquired through practice by someone who "realizes" enlightenment. The key, if also cryptic passage on these ideas in the *Awakening of Faith* can be rendered as follows:

> The meaning of "enlightenment": The essence of mind is free from actual thoughts. The characteristics of being free from thoughts is to be like the realm of empty space, everywhere and yet not in any one place, the one single characteristic of reality, the undifferentiated Dharma-body of the Tathāgata. Grounded on the Dharma-body, it is called "original enlightenment." Why? Because the meaning of original enlightenment is explained in contrast to acquired enlightenment, and acquired enlightenment is in fact identical with original enlightenment. The meaning of acquired enlightenment is this: grounded on original enlightenment, there is the actual state of non-enlightenment. Because there is non-enlightenment, we can speak of acquiring enlightenment.
>
> [T 32. 576b, trans. Swanson]

Although interpreted variously over the years, it is clear that "original" and "acquired" enlightenment are not independent of each other and can be seen as radically nondual. Eventually, in the Japanese Tendai tradition, this radical nonduality was interpreted to mean that all things are enlightened just as they are.

Later Tendai Hongaku Texts Attributed to Saichō

Although many later texts extolling the idea of *hongaku* were attributed to Saichō, in texts that can safely be attributed to him, he did not cite the Awakening of Faith and rarely used the term *hongaku* (preferring, as we have seen, the term "Buddha-nature"). Original enlightenment thought, however, was especially prominent in the later Tendai school, where we find an identifiably independent movement called the "gate of original enlightenment" (*hongaku-mon* 本覚門) or "Tendai original enlightenment thought" (*Tendai hongaku shisō* 天台本覚思想). Texts devoted to the theme of original enlightenment appear in the late Heian and Kamakura periods (tenth to thirteenth century), many of them attributed to prominent Tendai figures such as Saichō, Ryōgen 良源 (912–985), and Genshin 源信 (942–1017). Although these are not, as they claim, texts that can be said to have been compiled directly by the hand of Saichō himself, they were later attributed to him and represent developments of his ideas and thus can be considered part of his legacy. Such texts include *The Great Cord of Essential Truth* (*Honri daimōshū* 本理大網集), which interprets the most important Tendai teachings in terms of original enlightenment, and *Private Notes on the Transmission from Xiucha-si* (*Shuzenji sōden shiki* 修禅寺相伝私記; or *Shuzenjiketsu* 修禅寺決), which purports to contain the teachings learned by Saichō at one of the temples he visited during his travels in China; it contains details on the oral transmissions of original enlightenment ideas, practices, and lineages. In these texts emphasis was placed on oral transmissions, with their accompanying lineages, and involved a subjective hermeneutics of understanding and of realizing enlightenment through the "mind of contemplation" or "contemplating the mind" (*kanjin* 観心). For example, the *Shuzenjiketsu* explains:

> One who practices calming-and-contemplation should calmly settle in a basic understanding of what the teaching and practice of calming-and-contemplation consists. Each and every dust-like phenomenon is simultaneously empty, conventionally existent, and the middle, completely independent of emotional thoughts. When the sublime truth of this threefold contemplation is clearly discerned, one realizes that there is nothing to practice and nothing to realize. At the time of practice and realization, what is there to discuss with regard to "beginnings" or "origins"? The internal and external are both mysteriously undifferentiated; external conditions and internal insight or contemplation are mutually quiescent. All thoughts arise in association with objects of sense experience, you should not become attached to them. One who dwells in threefold contemplation without a second thought is a true practitioner of calming-and-contemplation. In this way one should dwell securely in a basic understanding of threefold contemplation without attachment and not taking it as something to be attained . . . . The practitioner who contemplates this is, in his own body, the sublime body of the realm of enlightenment, that is, he is a Buddha; he is forever liberated from the aspects of a common, ignorant person, and quickly abandons the nature of an ordinary person.
>
> (Tada et al. 1973, 44–45, trans. Swanson)

Thus, building on the Mahāyāna idea of the identity (interrelatedness and inseperability) of this world of suffering (samsāra) and the bliss of enlightenment (nirvāna), and on Saichō's promotion of universal Buddhahood (Buddha-nature) and a morality based on an altruistic bodhisattva spirit, original enlightenment thought evolved into an ethos of absolute nonduality and a total affirmation of the conventional, mundane world just as it is. This ideal was perhaps best expressed in the phrase (or some variation thereof) claiming that "the grasses, trees, and land all attain Buddhahood" (*sōmoku kokudo shikkai jōbutsu* 草木国土悉皆成仏), a phrase that turns up almost incessantly in Japanese literature, art, theatre, and Buddhist philosophy. This religious idea constituted an unchallenged assumption for most of Japanese Buddhist intellectual history and continues to dominate today as an unexamined supposition in the wider Japanese worldview.

PART II BY BROOK ZIPORYN

The Paradoxes of the Unconditioned in Early Buddhism and its Paradoxical Solutions

The idea of original enlightenment, although seeming to fly in the face of the most basic premises of Buddhism, is viewed in Tiantai thinking—strange as it may seem— as an inevitable logical development of the basic teachings of Buddhism. The founding claim of all Buddhism is that whatever is *conditional* is ipso facto *impermanent* and, for that reason, devoid of "self" and unavoidably saturated with suffering. The only possible freedom from suffering was to be sought, therefore, in an *unconditional* state. The problem in early Buddhism, however, is that this unconditional state is supposed to be something that does not yet exist or that some beings are not currently enjoying: it is something that must be achieved through the cessation of all conditioned states. This unconditioned state is called *nirvāna*, and early Buddhist texts are careful not to give it any positive description because anything that can be positively described is ipso facto conditioned, inasmuch as positive attributes can only have any meaning when they are defined as one way rather than another; they must contrast with and exclude some other possible attribute, which means that they are conditioned by the excluded state not presently obtaining. "Conditioned" means "applying only under the right conditions, thus in some cases, times, and places, not in all cases, times, and places." But an unconditional state must, by definition, then be something that applies in all cases, at all times and places; otherwise, it would be "conditioned" by it being the case that some particular state or time or place obtains. Nirvāna would only apply "on the condition" that one has destroyed the defilements and successfully practiced the Buddhist path; that it obtains is "conditioned" by so doing, which makes nirvāna into just one more conditional state, hence also impermanent, suffering, and therefore *not nirvāna*. To be unconditional means not to be obstructed by any conditional state, but to obtain no matter what. The idea of original enlightenment sees that nirvāna, *by definition*, must obtain simultaneously with all states, in all times and places; otherwise, it would not really be unconditional.

But the proposition that everything in the universe, just as it is, is already perfect and unimprovable, that all existence is always already instantiating the highest possible value, has a number of seemingly paradoxical properties of its own. If taken in its full radical literalness, it seems to imply that nothing needs to be done to change or improve anything. This makes some feel that this proposition is useless at best: if true, it seems unnecessary and appears to make all effort and endeavor, including Buddhism itself, pointless. It seems to have talked itself out of a job.

Worse, the proposition seems to some to imply a self-contradiction that invalidates it. Since it is after all making a claim, it is itself doing something, producing a change. Inasmuch as it seems to convey information, it implies that this information was lacking until it was conveyed and that there was some reason to convey it. To say nothing needs to be done is, after all, not the same as not saying anything about whether anything needs to be done because nothing needs to be done. The statement "nothing needs to be corrected" seems to be correcting something.

The complications continue when we further note that "the impulse to change something that exists" is itself something that exists. If everything that exists is perfect just as it is, then this desire to change things is also perfect just as it is. Furthermore, the erroneous view that things are not perfect, which is the premise of this desire, must also be perfect. The same goes for the actual action of changing things: this, too, must be perfect just as it is.

Tiantai/Tendai's Embrace and Utilization of Value Paradox

It is characteristic of the peculiar Tiantai way of thinking that it regards precisely these intricacies implicit in the proposition—the exacerbation of its inner contradictions— as the very mechanism that, if fully thought through, will resolve these very problems and which give it its great meaning for Buddhist practice, pointing to something deeply important for the human condition. On close examination, we discover that these intrinsic complexities of the doctrine of original enlightenment provide the structural basis of the variations evidenced in the contrasting Japanese Tendai and Chinese Tiantai versions of the doctrine as described earlier: everything just as it is "is identical to" Buddhahood (Tendai), and everything just as it is "is both identical to and different from" Buddhahood (Tiantai). In fact, if we factor in the basic Tiantai/Tendai ontological position on the nature of sameness and difference, these two claims amount to the same thing, with different rhetorical emphases.

This sort of claim, and the paradoxes it embodies in any of its versions, is not a mere logical puzzle: it has profound existential and ethical implications. These implications differ radically in different ideological contexts. In a monotheistic context, the claim that all creation is perfect might be meant to point to the perfect goodness and power of the world's creator and serve as a justification for encouraging praise and fealty to this deity. In a pantheistic context, it might serve as a discouragement of the positing of transcendental realms of value and being above those of the immanent world of nature. In a politically conservative context, it might serve as a discouragement of reform and innovation. The Tiantai and Tendai doctrine of original enlightenment is a claim for inalienable perfection of all being, made under the auspices of two key ideological contexts: Mahāyāna Buddhism and traditional Chinese ethics, especially those of Daoism.

In the Buddhist context generally, the claim represents a surprisingly thoroughgoing reversal of the most basic premises of basic Buddhism as displayed in the so-called Hīnayāna teaching: that all forms of conditional existence, such as constitute all of mortal existence, are through and through suffering, of no lasting value, and need to be completely abandoned and transcended. The original enlightenment idea claims the opposite: it affirms this world and this life exactly as it is and rejects the need to transcend or abandon or indeed even transform it. Now, early Buddhism held that the root cause of the intrinsic suffering was desire. Desire, however, is intrinsically desire to change something. Indeed, all desire is on this view always the desire to reduce or eliminate suffering by more or less intelligent or self-defeating methods. So, the cause of suffering—of the fact that everything needs to be changed—is precisely the desire to change things. Suffering is caused by trying to eliminate suffering. In this sense, the apparently directly opposed early Buddhist claim, which denied any value to the world, ends up being identical to the Tiantai/Tendai claim: the cause of suffering is the very attempt to evade suffering (i.e., desire). In this sense, the full radical acceptance of everything exactly as it is *makes* the world acceptable, for the only thing that initially made the world unacceptable was, on Buddhist premises, desire (i.e., the desire to change something). We see here again that the original enlightenment claim that nothing needs to be done is itself doing something, is proposing a huge change: for the default condition before this claim is made is that the entire world is thoroughly permeated and indeed constituted by precisely desire (i.e., by the desire to change what is the case). The world accepted-as-it-is is the perfect antithesis of the world-as-it-is prior to this acceptance, for the latter is nothing but the nonacceptance of the world-as-it-is. Absolute world-denial morphs into absolute world-acceptance via the thinking through of the most fundamental of pan-Buddhist premises, and this can be equally validly described as either a total acceptance of the world as it is or as a total rejection of the world as it is.

Ethical Implications and the Chinese Background

The ethical implications of this move are premised on a traditional Chinese attitude toward ethics, which we might call motive-ethics rather than deontological rule-based ethics, or virtue ethics. Motive-ethics might be considered a subspecies of consequentialism, and one which dovetails fruitfully with the pragmatic ethics of Buddhism, which views actions as good only insofar as they contribute to the specific consequence of leading to the end of suffering. The goal in traditional Chinese motive-ethics, in some (although not all) prominent strains of both Confucianism and philosophical Daoism, is not primarily to restrict or control ethically undesirable deeds, but to focus instead on finding cognitive or behavioral ways to root out the conditions that motivate these behaviors in the first place. The implication is that once someone actually wants to do them, it is too late to cure the problem in a fundamental or lasting way. Instead, attention is given to how to make ethically desirable behavior spontaneously desirable and desired, to reorient desire itself. In the Daoist cases that influence Tiantai thinking most profoundly, there is another wrinkle to this shared premise: the root cause of moral problems is moral preaching itself. It is the attempt to permanently fix the problems of the world, which would otherwise be blips on the screen in the normal cycles of fluctuation between positive and negative states, that encourages the state of mind of attempting to control and dominate the world, which in turn exacerbates the problem, leading to an escalating vicious cycle. Ideals, especially moral ideals, are the cause of the world's problems, for ideals interfere with the natural tendency to self-regulation and balance, which is the most basic characteristic of pre-deliberate existence. Deliberate endeavors motivated by conscious ideals encourage a rigid distinction between self and world, as controller and controlled, while simultaneously severing the desirable states from the nondesired substratum of world that is viewed as their real source. The sense of opposition between the valued and the disvalued is itself the cause of the proliferation of the disvalued; the sense of their mutual dependence, on the contrary, allows the full flourishing of the valued. We see something of this attitude also embodied in the Tiantai insistence on the nonduality of saṃsāra and nirvāṇa as a specifically moral stance, which is crucial to actual progress in the Buddhist path to nirvāṇa, and then toward the compassionate embrace of the world in all its diverse states. In this spirit, Zhiyi asserts in the *Mohezhiguan* that regarding delusion and enlightenment as mutually exclusive opposites encourages viewing them as "strangers to one another," who may be expected to respond to any conflict between them with hatred and violence, whereas stressing the commonality between them situates them in a relationship analogous to family members who are kind to one another even when they have superficial conflicts. There is thus, surprisingly, a strong pragmatic rhetorical dimension to the teaching of the nonduality of delusion and enlightenment.

Full Acceptance of the Given as Transcendence of the Given

We have seen that the straightforward claim of total identity between delusion and enlightenment, as characterizing Japanese Tendai, already entails the paradoxical character and ethical implications made more central to the earlier Chinese claim of both identity and difference. This should not surprise us. After all, in Tiantai/Tendai thought, identity always implies difference, and difference always implies identity: this statement is indeed a shorthand rendering of the threefold truth. As we saw earlier, this is the claim that all existence is simultaneously empty of any independent being and thus incapable of being anything at all definitively on its own and yet also conventionally existing as one thing rather than another; and furthermore, that these are really just two alternate descriptions of the same fact. But this means that any identifiable entity, X, is only what it is because it is always also something other than X. The most basic condition of any being is a fundamental sameness-and-difference *even with itself.* To be X is, in this view, definitionally to be both X (conventional existence) and other-than-X (non-X, emptiness), and to be the synonymity of being-X and being-non-X (the middle). Simply to be itself is already also to be otherwise. Each thing is not only different from other things (conventionally) and identical to them (ultimately); it is also, radically, different from itself (ultimately) and identical to itself (conventionally)—and it must be remembered that the distinction and hierarchy between conventional and ultimate is precisely what is denied by the Tiantai threefold truth. This doctrine is a radicalization of the basic Buddhist notion that all existence is intrinsically impermanent and empty, which is to say that its being is constituted by its always already being in the process of becoming otherwise, such that its otherwiseness is in no way separable from its being what it is. We saw also that one way this basic condition of always-becoming-otherwise is manifest is precisely as the desire of all existence to be otherwise than it currently is, which is just another way of describing the thoroughgoing suffering of all existence (for suffering is nothing but the desire to be otherwise, and all being desires to be otherwise, is precisely the desire to be otherwise).

We should thus recognize clearly that it is not just the factual world, as divorced from human desire, that is affirmed just as it is; desire—desire for things to be different— is also affirmed just as it is. This is why Tiantai affirms more than just the identity of samsāra and nirvāna, which might be taken to imply that these terms refer to one reality which can be viewed either deludedly (rendering it as samsāra) or enlightenedly (rendering it as nirvāna). This would still suggest that there is a dualism between the two alternate views of this one reality: the subjective states of delusion and enlightenment might still be viewed dualistically, as would desire and desirelessness. There would be a dualism between viewing this ultimate reality as nirvāna or as samsāra, between desiring to change or escape it and not desiring to change or escape it. Thus, Tiantai also affirms the nonduality of delusion and enlightenment, of wrong view and right view, of desire and desirelessness, not merely the nondualism of that which is rightly or wrongly viewed or desired. All subjective states are just as nondual as all objective states.

The ethical implications of this sameness-as-difference of delusion and enlightenment can be gleaned from the following passage from the Chinese Tiantai master Siming Zhili (960–1014):

> Desire is a defiling disturbance, and thus we speak of getting free of it. But desire is also a Dharma-gate, so we speak of dwelling within it. To get free of it is precisely to dwell within it; one completely frees oneself from it, and also completely dwells within it. The more deeply free of it we get, the more deeply we dwell within it. The most complete freedom from it is also the most complete dwelling within it. (T34.946a, trans. Ziporyn)

The dynamism of the Tiantai notion of full-acceptance is amply in evidence here. For desire-as-we-think-of-it is, in fact, like any other subjective or objective entity according to Tiantai ontology, never really all of what desire really is. Desire is also much more than desire: it is non-desire as well. To dwell in something, to fully accept it, is to change our initial apprehension of that thing and reveal more about what it is. Since this "more" always involves a negation of the originally conceived thing, this fuller dwelling is at the same time a getting free of the original dualistically conceived entity (i.e., thought of as mutually exclusive with other entities that are putatively not it). In fact, the Tiantai claim is that each entity really inherently includes all other possible entities, and it is only the full realization of this entity just as it is—as it really is—that reveals this vast all-inclusive nature and each and every other entity entailed in it. Desire inherently includes all non-desire things, including the ending of desire, including nirvāna, including Buddhahood.

It should be noted here that this means "being more or less fully what it already is" always applies in the full acceptance of everything exactly as it is, for, according to Tiantai ontology, there is no such thing as something simply being what it is, full stop. Buddhahood is really just the full realization of what everything already is. But this also means that what anything already is is only realized in Buddhahood. The Buddha is more X than any X, more chairlike than any chair, more demonic than any demon, more you than you. To become a Buddha is just to become more thoroughly—more unconditionally, more absolutely—you as you are right now. To become more fully you is to become a Buddha. This also means that you are only sketchily, putatively "you" right now; you have not yet fully dwelt in being you, not yet fully accepted you-as-you-are. If you did that, if you became fully you, you would be a Buddha. So Buddhahood is both radically different from you as you are right now and radically identical to it: Buddha is more identical to you-as-you-are than you are.

This has another surprising consequence in Tiantai ontology. For this idea of become "more X" also means "becoming more non-X," which is to say, "becoming more fully every particular non-X, every other entity." That means that as you become more "you," you also become more everyone and everything else. This process of more and more deeply "getting free of" and "dwelling within" what anything is, manifesting more fully the vastness of its being, is not just a manifestation of one entity to the exclusion of others; rather, the more manifest any one of them becomes (the more freed-from as empty, the more dwelt within as ineradicable), the more manifest all others become and the more manifest the intersubsumption between these originally seemingly mutually exclusive (dualistic) entities becomes. The more you become ordinary, the more you become a Buddha and the more you become a demon, a chair, a dung beetle, a pencil, a president. The more you accept yourself just as you are, the more you accept the world just as it is, the more you accept that all the other states of the world, and of all possible worlds, are just further aspects of you and yourself as aspects of them. This, too, entails the surprising end of desire right in the midst of the affirmation of desire. For, in accepting just as it is the desire itself, accepting just as you are you in your present desiring state, you manifest this desire also as all other states, including the originally desired state. Since your desire has intrinsically already reached what it desires, it is no longer desire. Precisely by being more thoroughly what it is—desire—it is also the end of desire, the nirvāna of a Buddha.

Bibliography and Suggested Readings

Andō Toshio and Sonoda Kōyū, eds. (1974). *Saichō*, Nihon Shisō Taikei 4. Tokyo: Iwanami Shoten.

Groner, Paul. (1984). *Saichō: The Establishment of the Japanese Tendai School*. Berkeley: Berkeley Buddhist Studies Series 7.

Groner, Paul. (2014). "The Lotus Sutra and the Perfect-Sudden Precepts," *Japanese Journal of Religious Studies* 41(1): 103–131.

Heisig, James W., Thomas P. Kasulis, and John C. Maraldo, ed. (2011). *Japanese Philosophy: A Sourcebook*. Honolulu: University of Hawai'i Press. (esp. "Original Enlightenment Debates," pp. 92–103).

Hurvitz, Leon (1962 [1980]). *Chih-i (538–597): An Introduction to the Life and Ideas of a Chinese Buddhist Monk*. Mélanges Chinois et Bouddhiques XII, Burxelles: Institut Belge des Hautes Études Chinoises.

Hurvitz, Leon, transl. (1976). *Scripture of the Lotus Blossom of the Fine Dharma (The Lotus Sūtra)*. New York: Columbia University Press.

Robert, Jean-Noël, tr. (2007). *Quatre courts traité sur la Terrasse Céleste*. Paris: Fayard.

Shirato Waka. (1987). "Inherent Enlightenment (*hongaku shisō*) and Saichō's Acceptance of the Bodhisattva Precepts," *Japanese Journal of Religious Studies* 14(2–3): 113–127.

Stone, Jacqueline I. (1999). *Original Enlightenment and the Transformation of Medieval Japanese Buddhism*. Kuroda Institute Studies in East Asian Buddhism 12. Honolulu: University of Hawai'i Press.

Swanson, Paul L. (1989). *Foundations of T'ien-t'ai Philosophy: The Flowering of the Two Truths Theory in Chinese Buddhism*. Nanzan Studies in Religion and Culture. Berkeley: Asian Humanities Press.

Swanson, Paul L., trans. (1995). *Collected Teachings of the Tendai Lotus School*. BDK English Tripiṭaka 97–II. Berkeley: Numata Center for Buddhist Translation and Research.

Tada Kōryū, Ōkubo Ryōjun, Tamura Yoshirō, and Asai Endō, eds. (1973). *Tendai hongakuron* [Tendai Original Enlightenment Texts]. Nihon Shisō Taikei 9. Tokyo: Iwanami Shoten.

Tanabe, George J., Jr., ed. (1999). *Religions of Japan in Practice*. Princeton Readings in Religions. Princeton: Princeton University Press.

Tokiwa Daijō. (1973, reprint). *Busshō no kenkyū* [Studies on Buddha-nature]. Tokyo: Kokusho Kankōkai.

Tamura Yoshirō. (1965). *Kamakura shinbukkyō no kenkyū* [Studies on New Kamakura Buddhism]. Kyoto: Heirakuji Shoten.

Tamura Yoshirō. (1987). "Japanese Culture and the Tendai Concept of Original Enlightenment," *Japanese Journal of Religious Studies* 14(2–3): 203–210.

Ziporyn, Brook. (2000). *Evil and/or/as the Good: Omnicentrism, Intersubjectivity and Value Paradox in Tiantai Buddhist Thought*. Cambridge: Harvard University Press.

Ziporyn, Brook. (2004). *Being and Ambiguity: Philosophical Experiments with Tiantai Buddhism*. Chicago: Open Court.

Ziporyn, Brook. (2016). *Emptiness and Omnipresence: The Lotus Sutra and Tiantai Buddhism in Contemporary Philosophical Perspective*. Bloomington: Indiana University Press.

CHAPTER 5

....

KŪKAI'S SHINGON

Embodiment of Emptiness

....

JOHN W. M. KRUMMEL

KŪKAI (774–835), the founder of Shingon (真言) Buddhism, was an important and in-fluential figure in Japanese intellectual history. His philosophy is distinct in bringing together what initially seem to be concepts of opposite significance—body (*shin* 身, *karada* 体) and emptiness (*kū* 空). It does so in the context of formulating a complex system of cosmology-ontology that is inseparable from religious practice. On the one hand, bodies are empty. But, on the other hand, emptiness is also the place for bodies and their interactions. And, in turn, that empty place is a cosmic body comprising a manifold of bodies. The cosmos is one giant empty body enfolding an infinity of empty bodies in its space. For Kūkai, the body is of central significance to one's being vis-à-vis the world as the environing *wherein* of embodiment. This is evident when examining his concepts of "becoming a buddha in this very body" (*sokushinjōbutsu* 即身成仏), "the embodiment of the dharma preaching the dharma" (*hosshin seppō* 法身説法), "the three mysteries" (*sanmitsu* 三密), and "empowerment and retention" (*kaji* 加持). Through our bodies, we find ourselves implaced—embodied—within the world, in interactivity with the environment. We are who we are through our bodily interactions. But the cosmos is also a body that we, in turn, mirror as its microcosms, and this intermirroring between the individual qua microcosm and the cosmic whole qua macrocosm is played out via bodily interrelations. In accordance with Mahāyāna philosophy, however, inter-activity, intermirroring, interdependence precisely is the meaning of emptiness; that is, the lack of substantiality, the absence of ontological independence. Kūkai thus develops the formula taken from the *Heart Sutra* that "form is emptiness, emptiness is form" in a direction that involves the body qua empty body and embodied emptiness. Moreover, a third key factor that plays into this relationship between embodiment and emptiness for Kūkai is language, for the body is the medium for communicating this dharma—that is, the truth of emptiness in its nonduality with embodiment.

Of Kūkai's theoretical works, the ones providing expositions of Shingon cosmology, including the significance of embodiment, are *On Becoming a Buddha in This Very Body* (*Sokushinjōbutsugi*); *On the Meaning of Voice, Letter, and Reality* (*Shōjijissōgi*); and *On the Meaning of the Letter Hūṃ* (*Unjigi*), grouped together as the "Three Writings" (*Sanbu-sho*), all of which he composed in succession between 821 and 824. The first text explicates the concept of *sokushinjōbutsu*. The latter two explicate the concept of *hosshin seppō*. All of these "Three Writings" in fact deal with the embodied realization of the dharma—the truth—but from different perspectives. In the following, I discuss the role that embodiment plays in Kūkai's system and its relationship to emptiness as explicated mainly in these three works

BODY

The concept of the body possesses a manifold and universal significance in Kūkai's Buddhism. He explains the concept of the body (*shin*) in *On Becoming a Buddha in This Very Body* as referring to one's own body, the bodies of other beings, sentient and otherwise. It can mean the entire cosmos as the "realm of the dharma" (Sk. *Dharmadhātu*; Jp. *hokkai* 法界), which in turn is identified as the body of the "Great Sun" Buddha (Sk. *Mahāvairocana*; Jp. *Dainichi* 大日) that personifies the "embodiment of the dharma" (Sk. *Dharmakāya*; Jp. *hosshin* 法身). The dharma (Jp. *hō* 法) here should be taken in the sense of the truth. It can also mean the various manifestations of this cosmic Buddha-body, the elements making up that cosmic body, as well as the various "bodies" involved in ritual practice symbolizing the dharma, such as the figures of Sanskrit letters (*ji* 字), the gestural symbols (*in* 印) of *mudrās* (Jp. *ingei* 印契; body-postures and hand-gestures), and *maṇḍalas* (Jp. *mandara* 曼荼羅; geometrical diagrams or patterns), as well as one's expressive demeanor or countenance (*gō* 業).[1] These senses are all interrelated to comprise one cosmic webwork that in itself is the body of the Buddha Dainichi as the embodiment of the dharma—a universal medium allowing for the concretization of universal enlightenment. Thus, in *On the Meaning of Voice, Letter, and Reality*, Kūkai cites lines from the *Avatamsaka Sūtra* that "all lands are in the body of the Buddha," or that "each hair [of the Buddha] contains myriad lands as vast as oceans." We might understand "body" then to mean the very "stuff" of the world and of reality in general, including one's self. That bodiliness of reality here is not limited to the physical but encompasses the mental as well. But it cannot be reduced to the mind. Kūkai's philosophy in this respect is distinct from the "mind-only" (Sk. *vijñāpti-mātra*; Jp. *yuishiki* 唯識) doctrine of the Yogācāra school of Buddhism. For Kūkai, the mental and the material are equally interpenetrating aspects of the dharma. His perspective is neither merely idealist nor merely materialist but takes a third standpoint that integrates the material and the mental or spiritual as all "body."

[1] Kūkai 1972*a*, 232; 1972*b*, 212–213; 1983, 246–247.

The cosmos as such—as Dainichi's body and as embodying the dharma—is made up of six universal elements (*rokudai* 六大): five material elements (earth, water, fire, air/wind, and space) and consciousness or mind.[2] The *Mahāvairocana sūtra* (Jp. *Dainichikyō* 大日経) discusses the first five material elements, but to these Kūkai adds consciousness to underscore the nonduality of the material and the mental (*shikishin funi* 色心不二).[3] Their dynamic but harmonious interplay constitute the "timeless yoga" or *samadhi* (*jō* 定) of Dainichi's body-and-mind. The cosmic body (i.e., "body-and-mind") as such embraces every thing-event in the cosmos as composed of these elements, interfused in different ways. It takes the figure of a mandala. In other words, its pattern in shape and movement is represented in the mandalas used in Shingon ritual.[4] The cosmos is a flowering of the dharma preached by Dainichi—this is the concept of "the embodiment of the dharma preaching the dharma" (*hosshin seppō*)—as it spreads out to beings receiving it in various degrees in accordance with their understanding. The mandala is the form this flowering takes. Correspondingly, the mind of the practitioner is also supposed to take on the form of a mandala through practice to realize its nonduality with the mandalic *hosshin*. In envisioning reality as a mandala, the practitioner realizes his own nature—in body and mind—as the Buddha existing in that mandalic reality and expressing itself in mandalic form. But this involves engagement of not the mind alone, but also of the body. All material bodies—each in its own way—manifest that cosmic embodiment of the dharma (*hosshin*). And it becomes manifest to greater degrees through one's successful bodily practice and consequent enlightenment (i.e., "becoming Buddha"). Truth as such—the dharma—therefore cannot simply be what constitutes the mind alone. It comprises the material as well as the mental. It involves both mind and matter, knower and known, subject and object, as interdependent, nondual aspects of reality, *always already* encompassing and permeating everything, including the body-and-mind of each of us and constituting the body-and-mind of the Buddha Dainichi.[5] In summary, Kūkai reveals the nondual reality behind three kinds of apparent duality: the duality within each of us (mind-body), the duality in our relations with other things (mind-matter, subject-object, self-other), and the duality in our relations with the very cosmos wherein we exist (individual-universe).

Our own bodies (bodies-and-minds) are thus dynamically interrelated with the cosmos as a whole. Microcosmos and macrocosmos touch and mirror one another via the body. Embodiment in this sense is the medium or vehicle of our implacement within the greater body that is the universe, mediating our relationship to everything else. The function of the *hosshin* is equated with all movements and change that

---

[2] Kūkai 1972*a*, 229; 1972*b*, 202, 205–206; 1983, 231, 235.

[3] Miyasaka Yūshō, *Kūkai: shōgai to shisō* [Kūkai: Life and Thought] (Tokyo: Chikuma shobō, 2003), 68.

[4] The mandala is a diagram or picture, usually a painting, that in Shingon Buddhism pictures the doctrines expounded in the two major esoteric scriptures, *Dainichikyō* and *Kongōchōgyō*. It visually depicts the manifestation of enlightenment in the universe and serves as a map for one's journey to enlightenment.

[5] See Kūkai 1972*a*, 231; 1972*b*, 206, 209; 1983, 236, 242.

occur in the cosmos. And, as Dainichi expresses the dharma through his movements, the cosmos is also the place for his sermonizing of the dharma; in other words, "the dharma-embodiment's dharma-preaching" (*hosshin seppō*). Kūkai categorizes such cosmic alterations, the functions of the *hosshin*, in three ways in terms of visible form (e.g., loco-motion or change of place and transformation or change in shape), the audible (sound), and the mental (the thinking process). Visible alterations are movements of Dainichi's body, audible alterations are movements of Dainichi's speech, and mental alterations are movements of Dainichi's thoughts. Together they are called the "three mysteries" (*sanmitsu*). The "three mysteries" are at work in all thing-events and are ultimately nondualistic with the corresponding movements of ourselves. In being bodily, we take part in the living body of Dainichi, in its cosmic interplay. We are always already participating in its movements in our mental states and in our bodily actions. Implaced within the cosmos, our individual bodies as microcosmic mirrors of the macrocosm thus serve as locales for the self-manifestation of the cosmic Buddha. The body as such, both microcosmically and macrocosmically, is no mere dead matter—*Körper* in German—but rather *alive, Leib*. Rather than the corporeal body, it means the embodied existence of body-and-mind as a dynamic whole, embodiment as *life*. And such lived and living embodiment makes the experiential verification of our Buddha-nature (*busshō* 佛性), its *realization*, possible.

It is this significance of embodiment that leads Kūkai to recognize the inseparability of *theoria* and *praxis*. Kūkai's major contribution to Japanese Buddhism, which filled a lack in Nara Buddhism, was to bridge the gap between doctrine and practice. He provided a systematic rationale for the esoteric rituals and explained the connections between text, ritual, and icon[6] previously left unexplained by the orthodox Nara schools. And he did this with his notion of embodiment in its multiple levels. On the basis of that theory, bodily *praxis* becomes essential for self-realization and, in this respect, possesses religious significance. Kūkai expresses this with his motto, "becoming a Buddha in this very body" (*sokushinjōbutsu*), which he explicates in *On Becoming a Buddha in This Very Body*. His claim is that the esoteric teachings of Shingon, as direct revelations from Dainichi himself expressing his enlightenment through the very "material" media of the world—*hosshin seppō*—enables the immediate realization of one's own innate Buddhahood through one's presently lived embodied existence. Kūkai here is referring to the Mahāyāna notion of "original enlightenment" (*hongaku* 本覚), the idea that all sentient beings have an original potential for enlightenment (Buddhahood) due to their inherent but unrealized Buddha-nature. But his understanding of enlightenment is distinct from what was taught in the orthodox Nara schools of Japanese Buddhism, according to which enlightenment involves a long and gradual process over countless eons of rebirths.

The idea of Buddha-nature goes back to the Mahāyāna doctrine of the *tathāgatagarbha* (Jp. *nyoraizō* 如来藏), the "womb of the realizer of suchness." But the *garbha* here that

---

[6] Abe 1999, 11.

means "womb" can also mean "matrix," as well as "embryo" or "seed." As the seed or womb for realizing reality (hence, enlightenment), it signifies the universal potential for Buddhahood. But as a matrix, the womb could also mean the very cosmos *wherein* we evolve and grow toward enlightenment. As a seed, the *tathāgatagarbha* is *within* each of us, but as the cosmic womb or matrix, we are *within* it. Kūkai thus connects this essential ambiguity with the notion that the cosmos itself is the body of Dainichi that we mirror in our own bodies. By drawing out the implications, Kūkai can thus explicitly connect the doctrine of "original enlightenment" with embodied existence itself, involving the bodily reciprocity among Buddha, man, and cosmos. That is to say that the potential for enlightenment is *within* one's own body, which in turn is the microcosmic embodiment or expression of cosmic enlightenment itself. But, as such, one is also *within* the cosmic embodiment of enlightenment, the living cosmic body of Dainichi. Kūkai expresses this reciprocity with the expression, "Buddha enters me and I enter Buddha" (*nyūga ganyū* 入我我入).[7] As Dainichi preaches the dharma through all phenomena, we ourselves are the bodies through which this preaching takes place. This means precisely that we are enabled to realize the cosmic *samadhi* that our bodies-and-minds express. In this respect, the two exemplary concepts of Shingon Buddhism—*hosshin seppō* ("the embodiment of the dharma preaching the dharma") and *sokushinjōbutsu* ("becoming a Buddha in this very body")—are nondual. The latter can then signify the realization of the universal Buddhahood of *all* beings, not only one's self.[8] In these manifold ways, Kūkai reworks the traditional Mahāyāna notion of inherent Buddhahood so as to underscore the bodiliness involved in the nonduality among Buddha, cosmos, and sentient being.

That significance of the body, then, underlies Kūkai's prescriptions of specific forms of ritual behavior as the *technē* for realizing the intermirroring of microcosm and macrocosm, self and Buddha. The practice involves a "symbolic mimesis" of the three modalities of the cosmos, through the "three acts" (*sangō* 三業) of our own body, speech, and mind: taking on certain bodily postures (especially involving mudra-making[9]), engaging in specific oral-verbal utterances (mantra-incantations, *dhāraṇī*-recitations[10]), and performing certain mental exertions (including *yoga, samādhi*-concentration, *maṇḍala*-visualization).[11] Thereby, Kūkai not only provides a coherent explanation of the relationship between theory and practice, but he also provides a concrete method for realizing through bodily experience original enlightenment. Kūkai's elaborate system of ritual *praxis* underscores both the ontological and the epistemological significance of bodily interactivity with the environment and the nonduality between those ontological and epistemological senses. That is to say that in *knowing through the body*, one *is*

---

[7] Kūkai 1984, 41.

[8] Miyasaka, *Kūkai*, 65.

[9] These are special hand gestures with intricate positionings of the fingers.

[10] *Mantras* are vocal formulas, and *dhâraṇīs* are verses and hence longer than the former, although Kūkai employs *dhâraṇīs* as in themselves *mantras*. The Japanese term "*shingon*" ("true word") translates this Sanskrit word *mantra*.

[11] Kūkai 1972*a*, 220, 230; 1972*b*, 208; 1983, 137, 240–241.

through the body. The dharma reveals itself without end, but it is never unembodied, never without form,[12] and hence we must realize this through our embodiment.

EMPTINESS

The body or materiality in general in Kūkai, however, cannot be understood in terms of *substance*. Rather, it must be underscored that the body for Kūkai—inheriting the basic Mahāyāna concept of emptiness (Sk. *śūnyatā*; Jp. *kū*)—is empty of substantantility. Now the six elements comprising the cosmic body are said to be interdependent (*rokudai engi* 六大縁起, "codependent origination of the six universals") and mutually nonobstructing (*rokudai muge* 六大無礙, "nonobstruction amongst the six universals"). Each element, as a microcosm of the macrocosm, manifests the very truth embodied in the cosmos. That truth or dharma, one might say, is the "suchness" (Sk. *tathatā*; Jp. *nyojitsu* 如実) of their interdependent origination (*engi* 縁起), which had already been equated by the Chinese Huayan (Jp. Kegon 華厳) and Tiantai (Jp. Tendai 天台) Buddhists with the emptiness of all. Because each thing is relative to, dependent upon, contingent to other things, nothing is substantial; that is, nothing is ontologically independent. Rather, as dependent, everything is empty. And the very elements that constitute each thing are themselves empty. The entire cosmic web of interdependence and mutual nonobstruction then means a cosmic emptiness—the absence of any substantiality to guarantee permanence or stability.[13] The cosmic body in this sense embodies the dharma qua emptiness, it is an embodiment of emptiness, an empty body. Moreover, that interdependence and mutual nonobstruction is not only horizontal, between the elements or bodies situated within the cosmos. It also obtains vertically between whole and part, Dainichi and beings. The whole is what it is in virtue of its parts, just as the parts are what they are in partaking of the whole. This entails microcosmic and macrocosmic correlativity. It is another way of putting the intermirroring of microcosmic and macrocosmic bodies. In mirroring each other, they are both equally *as such* and *empty*, desubstantialized and yet equally existing, and that is their dharma, the nonduality of suchness and emptiness. Although the *hosshin* is the embodiment of emptiness, it is nothing other than the physical, verbal, and mental forms of the cosmos.[14] Through such radical relationality, Kūkai treads a middle path that avoids the reification of individuals as substances as well as their absorption into a universal totality as a cosmic substance. And through the nonduality of emptiness and suchness, he treads a

---

[12]   Pamela D. Winfield, *Icons and Iconoclasm in Japanese Buddhism: Kūkai and Dōgen on the Art of Enlightenment* (New York: Oxford University Press, 2013), 76.

[13]   In fact, the very name, "Kūkai," which he took on when he converted to Buddhism, means "the sea of emptiness" or "empty sea."

[14]   Winfield, Icons and Iconoclasm, 74.

middle path that precludes any sort of reification or hypostatization, on the one hand, as well as any kind of annihilation into utter nothingness on the other.

In this respect, a proper comprehension of Kūkai's nonsubstantialism as designated in the Mahāyāna concept of emptiness is a key to understanding his notion of embodiment. The body is significant, yet not to be reified, whether human or cosmic, material or ideal, as monistic whole or as isolated monad. For it is formed only in its interrelations and, as such, is empty of substance. Embodiment entails the cosmic webwork of interrelations, in vertical and horizontal correlativity, on both micro and macro levels. And dependent origination in Mahāyāna thought means the emptiness of substantiality (ontological independence). So the embodiment of the truth in the cosmos—*hosshin* qua *hokkai*—signifies a universal emptiness that permeates that cosmic body. The cosmic body's essence is this cosmic emptiness. And that emptiness, in addition, means "vast space" for its graph also signifies space.[15] The ontological ground of all beings is an empty space, an unground, that engulfs all. The cosmic body in its endless vastness is a space embracing everything, a space of nonobstruction, allowing for their emergence without obstruction via interdependence. The cosmic body as empty is an open space permitting interrelationships with others, in contrast to being a self-enclosed monad or solidity. In its emptiness, it makes room for the myriad beings of the world. Within it, everything is equally empty. And each bodily being implaced within this cosmic body-place, as its microcosmic mirror, is likewise an empty place allowing for its nonobstructed interrelations with other beings and with the cosmos itself. The cosmic body comprising interdependent thing-events embodies the dharma qua emptiness. In virtue of this embodied emptiness or empty bodiliness, man and Buddha and cosmos are hence nondual. The dharmic truth of emptiness as such is embodied everywhere. It is not abstract but concrete, embodied, even if empty. It is not simply transcendent as the truth preached by Dainichi to the world. For it is, in fact, immanent to the very world, embodied in the world as its emptiness, the interdependent origination of its elements. Kūkai thus reads the *Prajñāpāramitā Heart Sutra*'s maxim, "form is emptiness, emptiness is form," to mean the embodiment of emptiness or the body *as* empty. The dharma as such entails the nonduality of emptiness and embodiment, nothing and being. This acknowledgment of concrete embodiment on the one hand and emptiness on the other hand is in the spirit of Mahāyāna, which treads the middle path avoiding substantialism and nihilism.

LANGUAGE

Kūkai's theories of embodiment and emptiness cannot be divorced from his linguistic theory. Through the interdependent elements of the universe, the embodiment of truth,

---

[15] The same Chinese character 空 is used to designate both "emptiness" and "space."

the *hosshin*, personified in the Buddha Dainichi, is continuously omnipresencing everywhere. Kūkai characterizes this as the *hosshin's* expounding of the dharma—*hosshin seppō*. In virtue of the omnipresence of the dharma, everyone has the inherent ability to recognize the universal Buddha-nature within. All phenomena are true expressions of universal emptiness. On this basis, we can realize our original enlightenment. Kūkai claims in his *Treatise on the Difference Between Esoteric and Exoteric Teachings* (*Benkenmitsu nikkyōron*) that his own "esoteric" brand of Buddhism is based directly on that dharma preached by Dainichi,[16] a "sermon" that is happening through all phenomena, material and mental, through bodily, verbal, and mental media—configurations, resonances, and patterns—permeating the cosmos. That is to say that the sermon itself is the dynamic process involving the cosmos' continual transformation. Kūkai explains how all thing-events serve as the "voice" of Dainichi's preaching and as "letters" of his cosmic text. He expresses this in the term *shōjijissō* (声字実相) or "voice, letter, and reality," which he explicates in his *On the Meaning of Voice, Letter, and Reality* (*Shōjijissōgi*). *Shō* (声), meaning "sound" or "voice," is the breath of Dainichi, the vibrations of the five material elements in their interplay that resonate sounds through the air. *Ji* (字), meaning "sign," "word," "letter," or "graph," is sound in its signifying character as naming or meaning something. It provides the material base for fixing the sign's distinction (*shabetsu* 差別) from other signs to specify its meaning. Every phenomenon of the cosmos, being empty of substantiality, is what it is through its interdependent origination. This also means that every thing—rocks, mountains, ants, and all—is what it is in mutual distinction with everything else. And this differentiation occurs vis-à-vis other thing-events in an endless chain of mutually referring (and differing) correlative thing-events. In reference to others and without substantial self-presence, each thing-event is hence empty. On this basis, all phenomena, as constituted by the intervibrations of the material elements and through their mutual distinctions, serve as letters of the cosmic (con)text, all signifying in different ways the dharma qua emptiness. The world itself, ordered into distinct and discrete things and events, thus emerges in the articulation of this dharmic text through mutual differentiations. And *jissō* (実相) means that "reality" is what is thus named, intended, meant, referred to, as evoked by *shō* becoming *ji*. The ultimate referent of the world as text is the dharma spontaneously embodied in the cosmos while serving as its source of reality and meaning.

The gist of Kūkai's linguistic theory here is that the entirety of all beings is language, a symbolic expression of meaning in all things. The cosmos in that significance is the original cosmic body-text embodying the *Dainichi-kyō* (*Mahāvairocana Sūtra*), of which the Sanskrit text is only a derivative translation into human language. And the cosmos as such is one big cosmic mantra, as the monologue of the embodiment of the dharma—*hosshin*—preaching the dharma—*hosshin seppō*—of the suchness of things qua emptiness. In fact, it is an audiovisual text, a mantra in its significance and a mandala in its visual aspect. The mantra (*shingon* 真言) as used in Shingon practice symbolizes the

---

16 Kūkai 1972*a*, 151; 1983, 149.

vocalization of this cosmic sermon, immanent throughout the universe.[17] The language of this cosmic text requires deciphering, and, depending on how one "reads" that text or "hears" its sermon, the language of the cosmos can guide one to enlightenment or deceive one into delusion.[18] Its meaning can only be discerned through a religious practice that makes evident the dharma. Proper decipherment would involve the practitioner's experiential realization of the Buddha's threefold cosmic activities of body, speech, and mind—"the three mysteries" (*sanmitsu*)—through his own body, speech, and mind.[19]

Kūkai further explicates the linguistic or mantric significance of the dharma in terms of "primal nonorigination" (or "originally unborn," *honpushō* 本不生), as designated specifically by the Sanskrit letter *A*. By "nonorigination" (or "unborn"), he means the "nonarising" aspect of the perpetually "born" and co-arising thing-events; that is, their emptiness and their differential referentiality that is without beginning or end.[20] It is the origin of all in their ongoing and beginningless dependent origination—their "origin of no origin." Each thing-event, as a sign referring to the rest of the cosmic text, mirroring the infinity of all other mutually referring and differing thing-events and their emptiness, points to that primal nonorigination of all. The writing of the cosmic text—a cosmogony qua cosmology—is not only ongoing but endless, continuously being reworked. Shingon ritual practice attempts to trigger the realization of that dharma through mantric pronunciations of Sanskrit syllables that emulate Dainichi's utterance and attune the practitioner to the interresonance of the basic elements of the cosmos. Their incomprehension make explicit the materiality and dynamic process involved in the emergence of signs and undermines any linguistic assumption of the substantiality of things.[21] But, of these syllables, it is the first Sanskrit letter, *A*, that for Kūkai specifically symbolizes that primal nonoriginating character of all being qua emptiness. *A* stands for the Sanskrit words for "origin" (*ādi*) and for "unborn" (*anutpāda*), combined in the Sanskrit *ādyanutpāda* (Jp. *honpushō*) or "primal nonorigination." The mantra *A* (*aji shingon* 阿字真言), as "the mother of all sounds,"[22] is thus taken to be the first sound uttered from Dainichi's mouth.[23] The Sanskrit *A* is also a prefix expressing negation, annihilation, and nothingness, that would undo reification into substances. But *A* is also the source of all sounds, as suggested by its being the first letter of the Sanskrit alphabet. For the absence of substantiality, emptiness, is precisely the interdependent origination of all. The negative here is also positive. *A*, in that respect, represents the nonduality of emptiness and form, nothingness and being, or, put differently, embodied emptiness, empty bodies. In symbolizing the nonoriginating emptiness that would undo any reification anywhere, *A* also means the original enlightenment of the embodiment of the dharma (*hongaku*

---

[17] Kūkai 1972a, 239, 245; 1983, 272–273, 293. On the cosmos as mantra, also see Abe 1999, 282, 298, 299.

[18] See Kūkai 1972a, 242; 1983, 279.

[19] Kūkai 1972a, 230; 1972b, 208; 1983, 240.

[20] Kūkai 1972a, 239, 249; 1972b, 214; 1983, 249–250, 273, 305.

[21] See Abe 1999, 297–298.

[22] Kūkai 1972a, 247; 1983, 302.

[23] See also Izutsu Toshihiko's reading of this in his *Ishiki to honshitsu* [Consciousness and Essence] (Tokyo: Iwanami, 2001), 232–233.

hosshin 本覚法身)—the Buddha-nature pervading everywhere—that we ourselves, all sentient beings, are endowed with. This gives us hope for the realization of the enlightenment of all. These manifold meanings are all combined in Shingon's *mantric* use of *A* to represent the primal vocalization of the *hosshin*.

PRAXIS

On the basis of the preceding discussion, we might summarize Kūkai's philosophy with the basic point that the whole of being—the entire cosmos—is a *body* that embodies the truth and is, at the same time, a *text* that communicates that truth. It is a body made up of manifold bodies that likewise embody that truth and that serve as letters or symbols of that truth. And that truth or dharma it embodies and communicates is its emptiness and suchness via its interdependent origination with its constituent bodies, the primal nonorigination of all in their interreferentiality that criss-crosses the vertical and the horizontal dimensions. Implaced within this cosmic body, which is in fact a dynamic webwork, participating in its movements, its articulations of the dharma, we are all endowed with the originally enlightened body of truth (*hongaku hosshin*).[24] Buddhahood as such then is not something we achieve or attain, but that we rather *realize* as inherent to ourselves. This is the idea behind the Shingon practice of the "three acts" (*sangō*) of our body, speech, and mind—taking certain bodily postures (e.g., mudra-making), engaging in specific oral-verbal utterances (e.g., mantra-incantations), and performing certain mental exertions (yoga, *samādhi*-concentration, focusing on Sanskrit letters, mandala-visualization, etc.)—as a "symbolic mimesis" of the three cosmic modalities of the auditory, the visual, and the mental.[25] Hence, "attaining Buddhahood in this very body" (*sokushinjōbutsu*) would mean precisely the *realization* of one's inherent enlightenment through such bodily-and-mental mimesis, putting one's own microcosmic body-and-mind in interresonance with the macrocosmic body-and-mind of the *hosshin*, to read correctly the cosmic text in its phonic, gestural, and graphic languages and discern the dharma. One thus realizes the empty mirror nature of one's own body as embodying that dharma in mutual intermirroring with the "great mirror wisdom" of Dainichi,[26] whereby "Buddha enters me and I enter Buddha" (*nyūga ganyū*).[27] But if one can practice that "symbolic mimesis" in a natural setting, even outside of its usual ritualized context, "without form" (*musō* 無相) as opposed to "with form" (*usō* 有相), in one's everyday movements, utterances, and thinking, one has come to truly spontaneously mirror the *hosshin*, realizing one's nonduality with the truth one embodies. If the point of the practice of the "three acts" is to intentionally accord with,

---

[24] Kūkai 1972a, 245; 1983, 293.

[25] Kūkai 1972a, 200, 230; 1972b, 208; 1983, 137, 240–241.

[26] See Kūkai 1972a, 231, 234; 1972b, 209, 215; 1983, 241, 253.

[27] Kūkai 1984, 41.

or interresonate with, Dainichi's movements, to do the same unintentionally and spontaneously outside of the ritual context, but with the same awareness, would be an even higher level of realization.

Kūkai also expresses the dynamic correspondence between Buddha Dainichi and practitioner with the term *kaji*, meaning their "empowerment and retention." The reference is to the mutual encounter between the Buddha's compassion and the practitioner's effort and aspiration. *Ka* (加), literally "addition" or "increase," designates Dainichi's compassionate power that pours down to illuminate like sunrays the practitioner's mind. And *ji* (持), literally "retaining" or "holding," designates the practitioner's effort to retain and absorb that power like the illuminated water surface reflecting the sunlight. Shingon ritual bodily training is meant to express this bidirectionality, whereby the practitioner strives to ascend "upward" to meet Dainichi's compassionate descent "downward." The *hosshin*'s centrifugal preaching of the dharma (*hosshin seppō*) is to be met by the practitioner's centripetal return to that dharmic source. As such, *kaji* also expresses the mutuality and correspondence obtained between *hosshin seppō*, descending from the summit and spreading out from the center, and *sokushinjōbutsu*, raising the practitioner from below and gravitating him toward the center, as two ways of conceiving from different angles the same interrelationality. But this is really a metaphorical way of expressing the single movement of intermirroring or interpermeation between the "three mysteries" (*sanmitsu*) of the macrocosmic body and the "three acts" (*sangō*) of the microcosmic body. That is, our own bodily, verbal, and mental activities are *already* expressions of the three mysteries of the *hosshin*. *Kaji* designates this realization that one's self and activity is a microcosmic manifestation of the macrocosmic activity of the cosmos itself. In realizing the integration of the Buddha's "three mysteries" and one's own "three acts," *kaji* entails an embodied and existential—rather than merely intellectual—comprehension of the dharma, verifying the dharma the *hosshin* preaches in one's own be*ing*. In Shingon praxis, one's striving thus *is* the grace of the Buddha. The "always already" nonduality of these two directions of movement—up and down, centripetal and centrifugal, self-power and other-power—is realized by degrees in enlightenment, whereby "Buddha enters me and I enter Buddha" (*nyūga ganyū*) and one "becomes Buddha."[28]

CONCLUSION

In summary, both emptiness and embodiment mean for Kūkai neither a reifying realism, whether monistically or atomistically, nor an annihilating nihilism. The body, for Kūkai, both microcosmically and macrocosmically is empty in the following senses: (1) as a medium of interrelationality and interdependent origination; (2) as nonsubstantial,

[28] See Kūkai 1972*a*, 230, 232; 1972*b*, 208, 212; 1983, 240–241, 245–246; 1984, 26–27, 34.

without any self-contained essence that would obstruct its relations; and (3) as open and mutable, shaped through its interrelations. It cannot be reduced to mere material substantiality, but neither can it be reduced to a chimera of the mind. In this respect, he treads the Mahāyāna middle path that would avoid materialism on the one hand and idealism on the other. Moreover, that body, macrocosmically, is the text and, microcosmically, is the letters or signs communicating the meaning of that text, the dharma of emptiness that is the suchness of all. The universality of this embodied emptiness on both macrocosmic and microcosmic levels, mirroring one another, is what allows for the realization of this dharma; that is, for the realization of the nonduality between the preaching of the embodiment of the dharma (*hosshin seppō*), on the one hand, and one's becoming enlightened in this very body (*sokushin jōbutsu*) on the other.

What relevance does Kūkai's philosophy of the body as empty have for us today? Despite the common prejudice that would relegate Kūkai's thinking to the realm of superstitious and magical religiosity, his thinking concerning embodiment and emptiness is in fact a wellspring of ideas that could be of interest to philosophers today. To recognize the fundamental significance of the body in its relation to the vaster body of the cosmos, both as *living* and *lived* rather than as *dead* matter, might open a vista to tackling the existential question of identity befalling contemporary humans in regard to their place in the world of difference and opposition. Miyasaka Yūshō, for example, regards Kūkai's philosophy to be a "logic of integrative co-existence" (*sōgōteki kyōson no ronri* 綜合的共存の論理) that makes our multisided and comprehensive relationality evident, as opposed to a logic of power.[29] It is precisely a standpoint of multisided integration that avoids the dichotomy of materialism and idealism and their mutual exclusion. Kūkai's philosophy of embodied emptiness offers an alternative to the mind-body dualism that struggles to dislodge the self from the world or from the body. And it is also an alternative to the humans versus nature dualism that would set us apart from nature as its conqueror. The inadequacies of both types of dualism have already been made obvious by countless authors with the winding down of modernity. In showing our bodies to be ephemeral yet concrete media of intersection within the cosmic web, Kūkai's thought can help turn us away from and provide an alternative to the hubris of modern subjectivity.

Bibliography and Suggested Readings

Abe, Ryūichi (1999). *The Weaving of the Mantra: Kūkai and the Construction of Esoteric Buddhist Discourse*. New York: Columbia University Press.

Gardiner, David (2008). "Metaphor and Mandala in Shingon Buddhist Theology," *Sophia: International Journal for Philosophy of Religion, Metaphysical Theology and Ethics* 47(1): 43–55.

Ingram, Paul O. (1993). "The Jeweled Net of Nature," *Process Studies* 22(3): 134–144.

[29] Miyaska, *Kūkai*, 126.

Kasulis, Thomas (1988). "Truth Words: The Basis of Kūkai's Theory of Interpretation." In *Buddhist Hermeneutics*, edited by Donald S. Lopez, Jr. Honolulu: University of Hawai'i.

Kasulis, Thomas (1990). "Kūkai (774–835): Philosophizing in the Archaic." In *Myth and Philosophy*, edited by Frank Reynolds and David Tracey. Albany, NY: SUNY Press, 257–272.

Kasulis, Thomas (1995). "Reality as Embodiment: An Analysis of Kūkai's *Sokushinjōbutsu* and *Hosshin Seppō*." In *Religious Reflections on the Human Body*, edited by Jane Marie Law. Bloomington: Indiana University Press, 166–185.

Kasulis, Thomas (2000). "Kūkai." In *Concise Routledge Encyclopedia of Philosophy*. London: Routledge.

Krummel, John W. M. (2010). "Kūkai." In *Stanford Encyclopedia of Philosophy*. http://plato. stanford.edu/entries/kukai/

Kūkai (1972a). *Kūkai: Major Works Translated, with an Account of His Life and a Study of His Thought*, translated by Yoshito Hakeda. New York: Columbia University Press.

Kūkai (1972b). "Kūkai's *Sokushin-jōbutsugi* [Principle of Attaining Buddhahood with the Present Body]," translated by H. Inagaki. *Asia Minor: A British Journal of Far Eastern Studies* 17(2): 190–215.

Kūkai (1973). *Kōbō daishi Kūkai zenshū* [Kōbō Daishi Kūkai Collected Works]. Vol. 1. Tokyo: Chikuma shobō.

Kūkai (1983). *Kōbō daishi Kūkai zenshū* [Kōbō Daishi Kūkai Collected Works]. Vol. 2. Tokyo: Chikuma shobō.

Kūkai (1984). *Kōbō daishi Kūkai zenshū* [Kōbō Daishi Kūkai Collected Works]. Vol. 4. Tokyo: Chikuma shobō.

Kūkai (1985). *Sokushinjōbutsugi* [Becoming a Buddha in This Very Body], translated into modern Japanese by Kanaoka Shūyō. Tokyo: Taiyō shuppan.

Kūkai (2004). *On the Differences Between the Exoteric and Esoteric Teachings; The Meaning of Becoming a Buddha in This Very Body; The Meanings of Sound, Sign, and Reality; The Meanings of the Word Hûm; and The Precious Key to the Secret Treasury*. In *Shingon Texts*, translated by Rolf W. Giebel. Berkeley, CA: Bukkyō Dendō Kyōkai and Numata Center for Buddhist Translation and Research.

Parkes, Graham (2013). "Kūkai and Dōgen as Exemplars of Ecological Engagement," *Journal of Japanese Philosophy* 1: 85–110.

Shaner, David Edward (1985). *The Bodymind Experience in Japanese Buddhism: A Phenomenological Perspective of Kūkai and Dōgen*. Albany, NY: SUNY Press.

Snodgrass, Adrian (1984–86). "The Shingon Buddhist Doctrine of Interpenetration," *Religious Traditions: A Journal in the Study of Religion* 7–9: 53–81.

Yamasaki, Taiko (1988). *Shingon: Japanese Esoteric Buddhism*, translated by Richard and Cynthia Peterson. Boston: Shambhala.

CHAPTER 6

PHILOSOPHICAL DIMENSIONS OF SHINRAN'S PURE LAND BUDDHIST PATH

DENNIS HIROTA

SHINRAN (1173–1263) is widely recognized as one of the most original and seminal figures in the Japanese intellectual tradition. As with other Buddhist thinkers, the specifically philosophical interest of his work lies in the thinking given to the most basic questions of the Buddhist path: What is the nature of awakening or reality, and in what mode of human life does it come to manifestation? Shinran's importance in the Buddhist tradition turns on his insight into the recalcitrance of self-attachment that persists even in religious discipline and on his self-reflective exploration of unenlightened, conditioned existence in vigorous engagement with the Buddhist path. These enable him to trace, from an existential perspective, the nonduality of the karmically created and the uncreated that is taught to characterize wisdom or reality in Mahāyāna tradition. Furthermore, many of the pivotal themes of his thought—self-will or "self-power" (*jiriki* 自力), "calculative thinking" (*hakarai* はからひ), the linguisticality of human existence, "provisional" and "true" hermeneutical modes of Buddhist engagement, temporality, "naturalness" or the self-giving of reality (*jinen* 自然), and "the attainment of supreme awakening by the person who is evil" (*akunin jōbutsu* 悪人成仏)—resonate with focal concerns of recent Western thought.

At the age of twenty-nine, after two decades of monastic study and training in the Enryakuji temple complex on Mount Hiei, Shinran abandoned the Tendai Pure Land practice that he had conscientiously but fruitlessly pursued. In his quest for genuine realization, he turned instead to the teaching of the learned monk Hōnen (1133–1212) that was newly spreading among the populace and joined Hōnen's following in the foothills of the mountain. Six years later, amid persecution by the established temples, Hōnen and several disciples, including Shinran, were stripped of their priesthood by the secular authorities and banished from the capital to scattered locations. Although all were pardoned after nearly five years in exile, Shinran chose to remain in the countryside for more than twenty years longer, transmitting the teaching to ordinary people, often illiterate peasants, villagers, or lower-class samurai, whose access to Buddhism had long been restricted by the political authorities. He returned to Kyoto only when past sixty and lived the remainder of his long life in relative obscurity, devoting himself to completing his major work and providing guidance to his following in the Kanto region through letters, hymns, and short commentaries.

Despite the modest circumstances of his life and his lengthy absence from Kyoto, the center of Buddhist learning and ecclesiastical power, the religious path Shinran established through his propagation and writings—the Shin Buddhist tradition (*Jōdo shinshū* 浄土真宗)—grew into one of the most dynamic and influential temple institutions in Japanese society in the fifteenth century, and it remains among the largest Buddhist movements in the world today. It is based on the teaching of the Buddha Amida (Sk. Amitābha, Amitāyus, "Immeasurable Light and Life"), who appears in sutras dating from the first century CE, the period of the redaction of the *Prajñāpāramitā, Lotus,* and other major Mahāyāna sutras. According to the *Sutra of the Land of Bliss* (Sk. *Suhkāvatīvyūha sūtra*; Jp. *Muryōjukyō* 無量寿経, referred to below as the *Larger Sutra*), Amida, as the bodhisattva Dharmākara, aspired to actualize perfect wisdom-compassion by enabling every living being to attain enlightenment. To accomplish this, he established and fulfilled a vow to make his own attainment of Buddhahood contingent upon his amassing the virtues needed to bring all who say his Name, entrusting themselves to his compassionate working, to birth into the buddha-field generated by his awakening (known as the "Pure Land"). There, they are themselves able to realize perfect enlightenment. In the East Asian Pure Land tradition, the Name of Amida is understood to be the formula "Namu-amida-butsu" (literally, "I take refuge in Amida Buddha"), and both the Buddha-Name and its utterance are termed the *nenbutsu*.

READING SHINRAN

Shinran's Stance

The philosopher Nishitani Keiji succinctly identifies Shinran's contribution to the broad sweep of Buddhist intellectual history and to Japanese Buddhist thought in particular:

> Shinran's significance lies in his unprecedented accomplishment of rooting up the whole set of previous Pure Land concepts from their mythological foundation and transplanting them in the ground which had been common to the other Mahāyāna schools since Nāgārjuna, a ground lying in . . . [Śākyamuni] Buddha's life and mind . . . . Pure Land Buddhism . . . became, thanks to Shinran, something to be interpreted "existentially."[1]

---

[1] Shinran 1973, xi. Volume 1 of this work includes a translation of the first four chapters of Shinran's major work (omitting the final two), together with editors' notes, some of which are relevant passages

Two distinctive, intertwined aspects of Shinran's engagement with the Pure Land teaching are indicated here. First, he reflects on the Pure Land path by delving to its wellsprings, what Nishitani terms "the Buddha's life and mind." This is the awakening of Śākyamuni, which Shinran regards as the historical unfolding of "true reality" (jissō 実相 or shinjitsu 真実; Shinran employs as synonymous such terms as nirvāna, suchness, dharma-nature [hosshō 法性], Buddha-nature [busshō 仏性], etc.). From it, the teaching of Amida's Vow emerges to enable and in fact guide all beings to share in this same realization. Through the Pure Land path, that which is beyond conceptual grasp "summons" forth beings' awareness and enters into their existence.[2] Thus, Shinran identifies the sources of his own writings: "How joyous I am, my heart and mind being rooted in the Buddha-ground of [Amida's] universal Vow and my thoughts and feelings flowing within the dharma-ocean beyond comprehension."[3]

Second, through the presentation of the scriptural tradition in his writings, Shinran seeks to engender in his readers a mode of apprehending and engaging the Pure Land path that is open to its dynamic, a comportment that he characterizes as "overturning self-power" and becoming "free of calculative thinking." Above all, he seeks to communicate the nature and significance of what he calls attaining or realizing "entrustment" (shinjin 信心; lit., entrustment-mindedness or awareness), a term which, in its ordinary usage, is often rendered "faith" or "trust." In Shinran's case, however, it might better be left untranslated for he seeks to overturn common understandings of faith as an attitude one generates and embraces within oneself and safeguards from external challenges. For Shinran, attainment of genuine entrustment signifies not the subjective state of an individual but the arising, in one thought-moment, of an entire world of meaning in which the former self and world have been transformed without being nullified, pervaded by a dimension beyond conceptuality. One discovers oneself already carrying on one's life within such a world of entrustment, but there is nothing that one has or could have accomplished to achieve entry. Furthermore, once a person has entered that world, the transformation is decisive, so that there is no return to what one had been.

Shinran's writings are often read as discursive arguments or systematic expositions set forth by marshalling prooftexts from the tradition. Indeed, his major work consists largely of arrangements of scriptural quotations. In essence, however, his strategy turns not on the persuasiveness of doctrinal coherence or the authority of traditional texts, but rather on effecting a radical alteration in the reader's stance in relation to the teaching. This is because he understands genuine engagement with the Buddhist path to occur only with the relinquishment of endeavor to appropriate the teaching within the frameworks of conventional understanding.

---

drawn from Suzuki's writings; volume 2 includes a number of important essays by Suzuki on Pure Land topics.

[2] Shinran 1997, I: 38. Translations from Shinran's works are frequently modified in this chapter for the sake of clarity in context.

[3] Shinran 1997, I: 291.

Hōnen and the Historical Context of Shinran's Thought

The characteristic quality of Shinran's thought and writings may be grasped by considering them in relation to the work of his teacher. Hōnen had devoted his major composition, *Senchakushū*, to a systematic, scholastic argument intended to present to the institutional Buddhist order of his day a comprehensive formulation of his nenbutsu teaching and to establish it, on the basis of scriptural texts and transmission lineages, as a legitimate tradition of praxis among the other historically recognized schools stemming from Śākyamuni.[4] Furthermore, citing various accounts of cosmic devolution, Hōnen argues that the Pure Land path alone remains effective for persons who share the adverse conditions of the present age, increasingly remote as it is from Śākyamuni's enlightening influence.

According to Hōnen, saying the nenbutsu has been determined as *the* act that brings about birth in the Pure Land. This is not, however, because of its inherent efficaciousness in cultivating virtue, but because it is easily available to all. Precisely for this reason it has been compassionately "selected" by Amida as the conduit of his own merits to even those spiritually inept or intellectually unaccomplished. In other words, the Pure Land path fulfills the highest ideal of Mahāyāna wisdom-compassion, for in it Amida Buddha has effected the practical means to render his attainment of awakening through arduous practice inseparable from the awakening of all beings.

The nenbutsu that accords with Amida's Vow is therefore to be performed in relinquishment of all assertion of one's own virtue, with a trust that acknowledges one's incapacity to achieve awakening oneself, being possessed of ignorance and unwholesome emotions. Without entrusting one's attainment to the Buddha's already fulfilled virtue, reciting the nenbutsu remains merely another among the myriad forms of praxis taught in various sutras, dependent on one's own aptitude for religious dedication and discipline ("self-power") for whatever merit that may accrue. Thus Hōnen states that the nenbutsu practitioner should become "a dull and foolish person ... free of any pretensions to wisdom."[5] The entrusting of oneself wholly to Amida's Vow is crucial in order that one's saying of the nenbutsu be the act designated and empowered by the Buddha's wisdom-compassion, which transcends discrimination of self and other. In the East Asian tradition, it is termed "Other Power (*tariki* 他力)," meaning beyond the horizon of dichotomous thinking.

Hōnen's heavily doctrinal exposition in his central work and the necessity for wholehearted trust have led to the view that Japanese Pure Land Buddhism advocates a dogma of "salvation by faith alone," in contrast to praxis or "works," and to frequent comparison with Protestant Christian tradition (e.g., Karl Barth).[6] Nevertheless, Shinran's thought evinces a development in the conception of "entrustment," moving from notions of

---

[4] See Hōnen 1998. Hōnen's title may be understood: "On the recitation of the nenbutsu ('Namu-amida-butsu'), selected as the appropriate act of practice for beings by Amida Buddha in his Primal Vow."

[5] From "The One-Page Testament of Hōnen" (*Ichimai kishōmon*), translated in Hirota 1989, 71.

[6] See Hirota 2000, 35–38.

steadfast reliance and personal commitment to one centered on the defusing of all attachment to the ego-self. Although modern interpretations of Shinran often treat his work as chiefly a refinement of Hōnen's teaching and a rebuttal of criticisms of the master, the focus of his thought lies rather in his elucidation of the transformative shift in mode of existence that forms the core of his Pure Land path.

Shinran's Aims

Shinran explores the nature of the self in relationship with Amida. If utterance of the nenbutsu is effective wholly because it embodies the power of Amida's pure practice, precisely how does the Buddha's virtue—the power to realize awakening—become our own in our saying the Name? If it is wholehearted trust that makes one's utterance not merely a personal act but the Buddha's practice, how is it possible to give rise to such trust, underpinned as it must be by elimination of all trace of one's own deep-rooted, compulsive egocentricity? How can one fulfill the nenbutsu if it requires that, as Nishida Kitarō puts it in a brief essay on Shinran, one "let go from the cliff's ledge and come back to life after perishing"?[7] Shinran himself borrows a phrase from a Chinese master and reinterprets it to characterize the realization of entrustment-mindedness (*shinjin*, the entrustment of oneself to Amida's Vow): "in the preceding moment, life ends . . . in the next moment [of entrustment], you are immediately born" (i.e., are grasped by the Buddha's wisdom-compassion).[8] In Shinran's probing of such questions, the Pure Land teaching ceased to be understood simply eschatologically—as a superlative method of praxis to reach an exalted status in an afterlife—and became instead an exposition of the contours of ongoing existence within the disclosure of what is true and real.

Shinran's aim in his writings is that the reader be brought to an apprehension of the true and real through engaging the verbal transmission of its historical emergence. Such an encounter takes place as a profound shift in perspective. Thus, Nishitani's comment cautions us against the assumption that Shinran's carefully structured writings are primarily an effort to set forth a persuasive system of doctrinal propositions. Viewing Shinran's Buddhism as conforming to a commonplace notion of faith as belief obscures the nature of his accomplishment. Nishitani states elsewhere, regarding a passage from *Tannishō*, a record of Shinran's spoken words:

> In seeking to come to an understanding of the words [of Shinran], it is above all important that the attitude taken be one of an existential grasp, rooted in one's own self existing here and now, for this was precisely the attitude of Shinran himself as expressed in them. We must avoid as far as possible approaching them through a merely conceptual or doctrinal understanding.[9]

[7] Nishida 1995, 243.
[8] Shinran 1997, I: 594.
[9] Nishitani 1978, 13, translation modified.

Shinran's endeavor from the outset is to convey an "existential grasp" of the path of nenbutsu as awakening or reality that has emerged in his own life "here and now." He employs terms and writings of the tradition in the service of a phenomenological elucidation and, for this reason, at crucial points radically transmutes the standard interpretations of the texts he quotes.[10]

Organizational Motifs of Shinran's Writings

Shinran's major writing, *A Collection of Passages on the True Teaching, Practice, and Realization of the Pure Land Way* (hereafter *Teaching, Practice, and Realization*), is a lengthy (200 printed pages in Chinese), meticulously crafted and tightly organized work. It is his first, and indeed, his life-work. A draft was made in 1224, when he was already at the age of fifty-two. In addition to the twenty years of monastic practice and six years of study with Hōnen in Kyoto, he had passed more than fifteen years in reflection and propagation activity in the harsh conditions of the countryside. Nevertheless, he continued to revise his work, particularly after his return to Kyoto at about the age of sixty. It was not until he was seventy-five that he allowed a close disciple to copy it, and, except for marginal annotations on copied sutras, all his other extant writings, including letters, hymns in *kanbun* (classical Chinese read in a Japanese manner) and Japanese, and commentaries in Japanese on important passages from the canon in Chinese, postdate this point. Even after turning to other kinds of composition, he continued to make minor revisions in his text almost until his death when more than ninety.

Teaching, Practice, and Realization is highly distinctive in form, particularly as the fundamental statement of a major, radically innovative religious thinker. It is a collection of passages, ranging from a few words to many pages, from the Buddhist scriptural and commentarial tradition in Chinese, painstakingly selected and arranged to convey the Pure Land path as Shinran had come to understand it. Fully ninety percent of the work is quoted text, ranging from Pure Land sutras in multiple Chinese translations to the past masters from India to East Asia whom he regarded as vital to the historical disclosure of the path, including his teacher Hōnen and extending to near contemporaneous writings from the Korean peninsula.

Shinran's method throughout almost all of his writings is to communicate his thinking by assembling and arranging, translating, interpreting, and annotating passages from the textual tradition.[11] This mode of composition reflects Shinran's view that the words of the teaching emerge in human history from reality or awakening itself, manifesting and effecting the work of wisdom-compassion, and thus that they reveal their truth to reflective reading or genuine "hearing." In the case of *Teaching, Practice, and Realization*, the quotations are not ordered to function primarily as prooftexts, demonstrating or

[10] See Shinran 1997, II: 23–25, for a discussion of Shinran's interpretive practice.
[11] See Ueda and Hirota 1989, 47–55.

enabling an intellectual mastery over the teaching, but rather juxtaposed so that their significance becomes discernible through reflection. His is thus a probing, disclosive engagement with the language of the teaching, unfolding its implications for a person's existence through weighing each word, rather than through a discursive pursuit of conceptual relationships.

The underlying principles of organization are crucial for grasping Shinran's stance. The body of the work is in six chapters of widely varying length: I. "A Collection of Passages Revealing the True Teaching of the Pure Land Way" (titles abbreviated hereafter); II. "True Practice"; III. "True Entrustment"; IV. "True Realization"; V. "True Buddha and Buddha-land"; and VI. "Transformed Buddha-bodies and Buddha-lands." There are three overarching organizing motifs by which Shinran structures the whole:

1. The true and real (Chapters I–V) as opposed to the provisional and accommodated (Chapter VI);
2. The two aspects of Amida Buddha's working in beings: that for bringing them to birth into the Pure Land and to simultaneous attainment of enlightenment (Chapters I–IV, §1–13), and that enabling them to return immediately to the topos of samsaric existence to compassionately guide others to awakening (Chapter IV, §14 to end);
3. The individual aspects of "the true and real" as it manifests itself in relation to a person's existence (Chapter I–V): (1) the teaching, (2) practice, (3) entrustment, (4) realization, and (5) Buddha and buddha-field of the Pure Land path.

Each of these three overlapping structural configurations is employed to explore central philosophical themes of a person's engagement with the Pure Land path. The first involves hermeneutical issues of the nature of engagement with the teaching; the second, the ontological and temporal structure of the relationship between Buddha and self; and the third, aspects of the existential and ethical situation of the nenbutsu practitioner. We will consider these in turn.

SHINRAN'S HERMENEUTICS: DISTINGUISHING MODES OF ENGAGEMENT

Provisional and True Engagement with the Path

In his writings, both in scholarly Chinese and in the vernacular, Shinran turns from Hōnen's core issues of establishing the Pure Land teaching as a legitimate school and the act of vocal nenbutsu as its complete, perfectly realized practice. Shinran's authorial purpose lies less in guiding readers *to* the Pure Land path than in probing the nature of genuine engagement *within* it. In other words, his deepest concern is the stance of the person already involved with the Pure Land teachings. It arises from his awareness of the deep-seated, often hidden, traces of self-attachment that persist in and irredeemably infect human endeavors, including religious praxis.

Shinran proceeds by distinguishing two modes of engagement—the provisional and the true. With each, he elucidates its dual aspects: not only the teaching as expounded and apprehended, but also the attitude of the practitioner. On the one hand: "In the Pure Land teaching, there is the true and the provisional. The true is the selected Primal Vow [in which Amida determined nenbutsu as the act in accord with the Vow]. The provisional teaches . . . various meditative and nonmeditative practices."[12] The latter includes contemplative exercises focused on features of the Pure Land or the observance of precepts and performance of rituals and meritorious acts. On the other, there are "two kinds of people who seek birth in the Pure Land: those of Other Power and those of self-power."[13]

The contrasting terms "Other Power" and "self-power" had been used since the sixth century to distinguish the Pure Land path, which teaches that attainment occurs through Amida's Vow ("Other Power"), from all other Buddhist paths, which encourage personal endeavor ("self-power") in diverse forms of practice. Shinran, however, brings these terms to bear on Pure Land engagement itself, so that their contrast highlights the transformative shift that occurs between a preliminary, provisional involvement (continuing "self-power [attitudes] even within the Other Power [path]"[14]) and authentic encounter (being "grasped" by wisdom-compassion; attaining "entrustment that is itself Other Power").

Shinran's distinction indicates that engagement with the path is at the same time a matter of hermeneutical grasp. The two types of Pure Land practitioners possess different paradigms for understanding the nature of the path and its goal and, more crucially, different perceptions of the self. Thus, for Shinran, a single Pure Land text may harbor both "an explicit meaning [corresponding to the provisional] and an implicit, hidden, inner meaning" that is the disclosure of the true apprehended in realization of entrustment.[15] The rift between these two kinds of meaning and awareness gives rise to Shinran's sometimes radical departures from the established, literal readings of scriptural texts in order to manifest the true (an example will be given later).

Two points may be noted regarding Shinran's distinction between the provisional and true. First, the provisional, both in the gist of the teaching and in the attitude of the practitioner, reflects a commonsense understanding within the causal and instrumental frameworks of everyday life. Practitioners determine and endeavor to perform morally

---

[12] Shinran 1997, I: 524.
[13] Shinran 1997, I: 525.
[14] Shinran 1997, I: 548.
[15] Shinran 1997, I: 212.

and religiously good acts that will advance them toward their ends. Thus, Shinran states that they pursue their goals "according to their own particular circumstances and opportunities,"[16] and they aspire to images of attainment that correspond to their own objectified projections, what Shinran terms "provisional" Buddha-lands. Hence, "Since there are thousands of differences in the causes of birth in the provisional Buddha-lands, there are thousands of differences in those lands."[17]

By contrast with such incorporation of the path within the horizons of ordinary, purposive consciousness, the "true" encompasses an apprehension of the limits of one's conceptual understanding and the distortions of the perceptions of the ego-self as a subject purportedly standing at the center of the world. While provisional Buddha-lands are depicted with palaces, landscapes, and bodhi-trees of precious substances and numerically quantified dimensions, the true land "is infinite, like space, vast and boundless."[18] True attainment cannot be conceived as paradisial or achieved as a consequence of one's moral reckoning; rather, "All receive the body of naturalness (*jinen*) or of emptiness, the body of boundlessness."[19]

The second significant point is that, in Shinran's understanding, the Pure Land path itself functions to draw beings from a notion of linear progress to a "crosswise leap" (*ōchō* 横超) or transcendent shift of awareness. One is led from a provisional mindset reflecting the self's presuppositions within conventional frames of thought to true engagement, in which the self itself stands illumined in its finitude. A close disciple of Shinran notes: "That we set aside the provisional and adopt the true is [Shinran's] *fundamental intent*."[20] Furthermore, Shinran declares: "It is not attainment of ... enlightenment that is difficult; the genuine difficulty is realizing true and real *shinjin* [entrustment]. Why? Because this realization ... comes about wholly through the power of great compassion and all-embracing wisdom."[21]

Shinran's Buddhist Anthropology

To characterize the attitude of practitioners who take up the Pure Land path in its provisional "self-power" mode, Shinran adopts the traditional term "doubt," quoting the *Larger Sutra*:

> There are sentient beings who, with minds full of doubt, aspire to be born in the [Pure] Land through meritorious acts. Unable to realize Buddha-wisdom, the inconceivable wisdom ... they doubt these wisdoms and do not entrust themselves.

---

[16] Shinran 1997, I: 525.
[17] Shinran 1997, I: 203.
[18] Shinran 1997, I: 203, quoting Vasubandhu.
[19] Shinran 1997, I: 154, quoting the *Larger Sutra*.
[20] Shinran 1997, I: 679; Hirota 1982, 129.
[21] Shinran 1997, I: 79.

Believing [instead in the recompense of] evil and good, they aspire to be born in that land through cultivating roots of good.[22]

For Shinran, doubt here is not vacillation regarding Pure Land doctrines, to be dispelled through commitment or assent. It is at once more specific and encompassing in meaning, pointing to a fundamental quality of human awareness.

In Shinran's understanding, doubt most importantly signifies acceptance of Pure Land teachings while presupposing the ego-self and its capacities to determine and pursue virtuous action that will lead to attainment. It manifests itself in both expectancy and anxiety regarding one's efforts to fulfill the conditions for birth in the Pure Land. Thus: "Self-power is ... the endeavor to make yourself worthy through mending the confusion in your acts, words, and thoughts, confident of your own powers and guided by your own calculative thinking."[23] Shinran's synonym for doubt or self-power here is "calculation" or "designing." He follows general Buddhist thinking in viewing ignorance—the blind clinging to a delusional, reified construct of self—as the wellspring of the "afflicting passions" (bonnō 煩悩) of craving, aversion, and foolishness that drive samsaric existence. With the concept of calculative thinking, he identifies the way in which this fundamental ignorance is problematized and finally broken through, though not eliminated, in the Pure Land path.

The realization of entrustment is precisely the dissolution of the horizon of one's calculative thinking, occurring at the point at which the incessant operation of afflicting passions in one's perceptions and judgments arises to awareness. At the same time, it is the dissolution of the reifying dualism of the practitioner as subject objectifying the elements of the path. Thus Shinran states incisively, "Other Power means to be free of any form of calculation."[24] In personal terms:

I know nothing at all of good or evil [regarding attainment of entrustment]. For if I could know thoroughly, as is known in the mind of Amida, that an act was good, then I would know the meaning of "good." If I could know thoroughly, as Amida knows, that an act was evil, then I would know "evil." But for a foolish being filled with blind passions, in this fleeting world—this burning house—all matters without exception are falsehoods and gibberish, totally without truth and sincerity. The nenbutsu alone is true and real.[25]

Shinran's insight into the final emptiness of his pronouncements of good and evil is not relativism or license, but the recognition of the partialities and contingencies that inevitably warp and debase his own moral discernment. Furthermore, in confessing his ignorance, he transposes into linguistic terms the dichotomous determinations that

[22] Shinran 1997, I: 209.
[23] Shinran 1997, I: 525.
[24] Shinran 1997, I: 537.
[25] Shinran 1997, I: 679; Hirota 1982, 44.

inform teleological will and order social life. He characterizes as "falsehoods and gibberish" (*soragoto, tawagoto*) the historically conditioned, perspectival judgments of conventional life that shore up the notion of self as subjective center and autonomous agent. In this way, he indicates the linguisticality at the heart of human understanding.

Shinran does not explicitly thematize language in his works, but his references to its role in human life make it clear that he follows much of Mahāyāna tradition in viewing ordinary language use as typified by discriminative, falsely substantializing thought and perception. Commenting on phrases from the *Larger Sutra*, he states: "People of this world have only thoughts that are not real, and those who wish to be born in the Pure Land have only thoughts of deceiving and flattering. Even those who renounce this world have nothing but thoughts of fame and profit."[26] Shinran indicates two kinds of discord here: epistemological ("what is spoken and what is thought are not real") and moral ("what is in the mind and what is said are at variance").[27] Linguistic practice harbors both pitfalls.

The linguisticality of human existence is thus closely intertwined with the Buddhist concept of evil (*aku* 悪, *zaiaku* 罪悪) as meaning any act, even a solely mental one, that leads not to awakening but to further pain in samsaric existence for self and others. The Buddhist path functions precisely to break the attachments of discriminative perception. Shinran parts from traditions of contemplative practice in rejecting as ultimately self-defeating all meditative endeavors aimed at stilling mental and linguistic activity. The bedrock of Shinran's religious anthropology is an acknowledgment of the ineluctable linguisticality of human existence. That language is constitutive of the world of experience and social interactions means, for Shinran, that human existence is pervaded by the reification of and delusional absorption with the historically conditioned constructs of the ego-self. Thus: "Our desires are countless, and anger, wrath, jealousy, and envy are overwhelming, arising without pause; to the very last moment of life they do not cease, or disappear, or exhaust themselves."[28] Nevertheless, it is through engagement with the Pure Land path that this insight can arise, and, when it does, the force of afflicting passions is broken and their obsessions defused, though not eliminated.

SHINRAN'S ANTI-SUBJECTIVISM

Relocating Practice Beyond Discriminative Thought

If even the practitioner's determinations of good and evil directed to spiritual well-being lie within the domain of self-attachment, how is advance toward liberation possible? With his thoroughgoing critique of the self-willed appropriation of practice and

---

[26] Shinran 1997, I: 466.
[27] Shinran 1997, I: 466.
[28] Shinran 1997, I: 488.

discipline as inescapably blighted by complacency, Shinran seeks to bring to awareness, and thereby undermine, the dichotomous, instrumentalist thinking that reifies
the subject as autonomous agent. This may appear to contradict the frequent Buddhist
exhortations to endeavor in practice. The Japanese Pure Land tradition is sometimes
assumed to reject "works" and denigrate practice in favor of a notion of "faith alone."
But, in fact, the concept of practice remains vital in Shinran's thinking, as is evident from
his dedication of a pivotal chapter of *Teaching, Practice, and Realization* to "true and
real practice." Rather, he raises a critical issue regarding the conception of practice in
Buddhist tradition as a whole by inquiring into its nature and what enables it to occasion awakening. Taking a rigorous stance, he refuses the assumption that effort in self-
discipline can naturally mature into the eradication of self-attachment instead of lapsing
into a deepening sense of self-satisfaction. In his view, the sources and motives of authentic practice as action that leads toward liberation must themselves be uncorrupted
by the assertion of ego-self.

As Shinran notes, in Mahāyāna teachings Buddhas and awakened bodhisattvas who
have plumbed the "samadhi of non-action" that is "attained through stilling [discrim-
inative] thought, so that there is no mental activity grasping this and that"[29] are paradoxically enabled, for this very reason, to perceive each being as "one's only child" and
accomplish genuinely selfless compassionate action. The person born in the Pure Land
becomes a bodhisattva who, "in saving ... perceives no object of salvation.... Although
one saves countless sentient beings, in reality there is not a single sentient being who
realizes nirvāna. Manifesting the act of saving sentient beings is thus like play."[30] Amida,
as the archetypal bodhisattva Dharmākara, is depicted in the *Larger Sutra*: "He never
harbored a single thought of greed, anger, or folly; ... he cherished no thought of
form ... or tangible thing."[31]

Engagement with the path within the frameworks of one's habitual perspective in
daily life leads to arrogation of the teaching, utilizing Pure Land piety and nenbutsu recitation for gratifying the ego-self. How can authentic practice be generated by a being
immersed in the ignorance of discriminative awareness? In Pure Land terms, how can
one's embrace of the teaching and utterance of the nenbutsu escape being infected by
self-will? Shinran advances Pure Land thought precisely by grappling with this issue. In
his view, practice in the Buddhist sense—action possessed of the power to break reifying
attachments—is the dynamic of wisdom or reality itself taking effect in beings' samsaric
existence. In the Pure Land path, authentic practice is conceived as set in motion by
Dharmākara, whose attainment of Buddhahood as Amida is fused with disseminating
the liberating power to all beings. Moreover, this emergence occurs through language,
as the hearing and saying of the Name; that is, the medium of the bondage of human ignorance itself becomes the topos of transformative encounter.

---

[29] Shinran 1997, I: 325.
[30] Tanluan, quoted in Shinran 1997, I: 174.
[31] Quoted in Shinran 1997, I: 96.

Displacing Subject–Object Reciprocity

Hōnen's notion of the nenbutsu in accord with the Vow as unalloyed Other Power eluded many among his followers, who tended to lapse into concern with proper engagement: either exclusive devotion to vocal nenbutsu or cultivation of wholehearted trust in Amida's Vow. This difference manifested itself in distinct forms of dedication in daily life. Adherents emphasizing practice (*gyō* 行) called for moral vigilance and diligence in nenbutsu recitation, in anticipation of entrance into the Pure Land at death; those emphasizing trust (*shin* 信) stressed recognition of personal moral incapacity, utter reliance on Amida, and acceptance of the Vow's assurance of future attainment, even if a person says the nenbutsu only once. Mutual criticism across this divide, particularly in terms of self-discipline or laxity in daily life, arose even while Hōnen was alive. The master, however, was unable to convey the coherence of the path and maintain the unity of his movement.

In Shinran's view, the root of the problem lies in construals of the path that remain captive to the presuppositions of conventional thought and thus to the "provisional." In seeking to assimilate the concepts and elements of the path within the parameters of subject-centered thinking, such practitioners objectify them as means for self-benefit. They then seek to overcome the rift they have imposed and establish a relationship with Other Power. An example of such an attempt often borrowed in the Japanese tradition is Shandao's enumeration of "three relationships" (*san'en* 三縁) linking the person of nenbutsu and Amida Buddha through a notion of reciprocity: when persons calls the Name, Amida hears them; when persons bows in reverence, Amida sees them; when persons constantly think on the Buddha, Amida is aware of them.

While Hōnen and a number of his disciples adopt Shandao's images of mutual interpersonal relatedness, Shinran does not, for he perceives the deeper issue.[32] Once subject–object dualism has been asserted regarding the practitioner's relation to Amida or his Name, subsequent efforts to overcome the duality, whether through faith or practice, become self-defeating. Such endeavor is inevitably engulfed in the web of calculative thinking, as shown by the bitter intrasectarian disputation over "many-calling" (emphasis on continuous praxis) versus "once-calling" (emphasis on complete trust) that plagued Hōnen's following.

The Givenness of Practice and Entrustment

Shinran's resolution of this issue is expressed in the second of the major structural features of *Teaching, Practice, and Realization*. It involves penetrating the horizons of ordinary thought into a dimension of interaction that transcends the comprehension

---

[32] For the thinking of another of Hōnen's followers, Shōkū of the Seizan Pure Land school, and its later developments, see Ippen 1997, especially xlvi–lxxi.

of the path in terms of the subject–object dichotomy and that is always already at work prior to any conscious engagement with it. The opening chapter of his work begins:

> Reflecting on the true essence of the Pure Land way, we find [Amida's] twofold *directing of virtue* (ekō 回向) to sentient beings. One aspect enables our departure [from samsaric existence]; the second, our return [to the world of samsāra to liberate all beings]. In relation to the first, we are provided with the true teaching, practice, *shinjin* [entrustment], and realization.[33]

In Buddhist tradition the basic "pillars" of the path—sometimes formulated as "teaching, practice, and realization," as in Shinran's title—have been viewed as constituting a progression so that the practitioner advances from enquiry into the dharma, through stages of incorporating the teachings into one's life in praxis, to final attainment of awakening. Trust or faith is assumed vital to one's initial study of the teaching and immersion in practice. For Shinran, however, these elements, when genuinely encountered, are not stepping stones to be successively traversed. The crucial conversion in the Pure Land path occurs, as we have seen, in the shift from the thinking and endeavor of "provisional" teachings and practices to the true. The "true teaching, practice, entrustment, and realization" are not serially acquired through resolute advance, but rather temporally simultaneous facets of the Buddha's activity of wisdom-compassion as it manifests itself in one's existence.

Shinran articulates this activity through his radical reinterpretation of the term *ekō* ("directing virtue"), which occurs in the *Larger Sutra* passage in which Śākyamuni teaches the fulfillment of Amida's Vow of birth through the nenbutsu. In Mahāyāna tradition, *ekō* signifies redirecting the merits derived from one's virtuous actions, which would normally accrue to oneself in the course of karmic existence, either toward other beings or toward one's transcendence of samsaric life. It is frequently used to express the bodhisattva's compassionate "transference" of merit to others or as synonymous with aspiration for birth in the Pure Land. The latter is the meaning in the passage as traditionally understood. Śākyamuni's words read, according to Hōnen's interpretation:

> If sentient beings hear his Name and, *trusting and rejoicing, say the nenbutsu even one time* while single-mindedly and *wholeheartedly transferring their merits* (ekō) in the aspiration for birth in his land, *then* they will attain birth and dwell in nonretrogression [in the Pure Land].[34]

This passage is significant for its reiteration of the Vow's conditions for attaining birth in the Pure Land, and, in Hōnen's writings, it functions as a prooftext verifying that the Vow has indeed been fulfilled. Shinran, however, diverges radically from the interpretation he learned from Hōnen as well as from the literal surface of the text. For Shinran,

---

[33] Shinran 1997, I: 7.
[34] Hōnen 1998, 79.

the significance of the passage lies not in confirming the Vow, but rather in providing a key for interpreting and apprehending its vital meaning. His reading may be rendered:

> All sentient beings, as they hear the Name, *realize even one thought-moment of entrustment (shinjin) and joy*. This, [Amida] has directed to them *from the true mind* [of enlightenment]. Aspiring to be born in that land, they *immediately* attain birth and dwell in nonretrogression [in the present].[35]

Shinran introduces several critical departures from the traditional interpretation (relevant phrases in italics). Most crucially, he inverts the relationship of practitioner and Amida by indicating the Buddha, not the practitioner, as the agent of "directing virtue (*ekō*)" (italicized phrases). He thereby relocates the dynamism of engagement to the dimension of nondichotomous wisdom or reality. In terms of the Pure Land teaching, Amida "directs" or imparts to beings the Buddha's nondiscriminative wisdom or "true mind," which opens forth in them as entrustment or the falling away of calculative thinking. For this reason, realizing genuine entrustment holds the significance of attaining the bodhisattva stage of "nonretrogression," meaning that, after the emergence of the Buddha-mind in a person, he or she never lapses from its full unfolding in perfect enlightenment. For Shinran, this occurs when one's karmic bonds in this life are severed at death. In the present, one's samsaric existence, while continually agitated by afflicting passions, at the same time has become fused with the dimension of nirvāna: "When the waters—the minds, good and evil, of foolish beings— / Have entered the vast ocean / Of Amida's Vow of wisdom, they are immediately / Transformed into the mind of great compassion."[36] Thus, the central attainment in the path occurs when one is touched by wisdom or reality in the realization of entrustment and "immediately attains birth."[37]

Twofold Temporality: One Thought-Moment and the Dynamism of *Jinen*

At the core of Shinran's conception of the givenness of the power that disrupts the thinking of ordinary life and enables awakening is a Mahāyāna Buddhist understanding of nonduality formulated as the "twofold dharma-body" in Pure Land tradition. As stated by Tanluan:

> All Buddhas and bodhisattvas have dharma-bodies of two dimensions: [formless, nonconceptual] "dharma-body as dharma-nature" and "dharma-body as compassionate means" [that manifests form]. The latter emerges [in the world of historical

---

[35] Quoted and translated according to Shinran's annotations, Shinran 1997, I: 80.
[36] Shinran 1997, I: 408.
[37] For a detailed discussion of Shinran use of the expression, "immediately attain birth," see Ueda 1984.

meaning] from the former; the former arises [to human awareness] by means of the latter. These two dimensions of dharma-body [or true reality] differ but are not separable; they are one but not identical.[38]

Shinran adopts Tanluan's conception of reality as the nondiscrimination of the inconceivable (suchness, wisdom) on the one hand and form (meaning, Buddha available to human apprehension) on the other, applying it to both ontological and temporal dimensions. He expresses both the dynamism and the abiding nonduality: "From [reality as formless] oneness, form was manifested, taking the name of Bodhisattva Dharmākara, who ... became Amida Buddha."[39] Further: "Appearing in the form of light, ... [Amida] is without color and without form, that is, identical with the dharma-body as dharma-nature, dispelling the darkness of ignorance."[40]

Furthermore, Shinran's attention to temporality—one of the most distinctive characteristics of his thought—reflects a similar motif of nonduality. His treatment stems in part from his rejection of the presuppositions of the "provisional" stance of self-will. During the Heian and Kamakura periods, people hoping to reach Amida's Buddha-land commonly looked to the moment of death as crucial and decisive. Based on sutra descriptions of Amida's appearance to the dying, deathbed rites were devised to aid practitioners in maintaining their devotion and composure at the very end. The underlying conception of time was unilinear and eschatological. The practitioner's concerns were mapped temporally, in terms of anxiety over past actions and hopefulness of the future. Shinran, however, states unequivocally:

> The expectancy of "Amida's coming" [to receive one into the Pure Land] at the moment of death is held by people who seek to gain birth there by doing various practices.... The moment of death is of central concern to them because they have not yet attained true entrustment.[41]

The person who has genuinely realized entrustment "need not wait in anticipation for the moment of death.... At the time entrustment becomes settled, one's birth in the Pure Land becomes settled,"[42] for entrustment is the unfolding as a person's existence of the nonduality of the formless and the karmically created existing in time. As such nonduality, the realization of entrustment occurs in "one thought-moment." As Nishitani states, it is "time occurring where the sharp tip of eternity pierces time, or eternity occurring where the sharp tip of time pierces eternity."[43] While the practitioner continues temporal, karmic existence as a being of ignorance and afflicting passions,

---

[38] Shinran 1997, I: 165.
[39] Shinran 1997, I: 486.
[40] Shinran 1997, I: 461.
[41] Shinran 1997, I: 523.
[42] Ibid.
[43] Nishitani 1978, 18.

"the heart of the person of entrustment already and always resides in the Pure Land."[44] This is the nontemporal or transtemporal dimension of entrustment. Shinran states:

> Nirvāna, called ... the uncreated, ... Buddha-nature ... pervades the countless worlds; it fills the minds of the ocean of all beings. Thus, plants, trees, and land all attain Buddhahood. It is with this mind of all sentient beings that they entrust themselves to the Vow; ... hence, their entrustment is none other than Buddha-nature.[45]

According to Shinran, Buddha-mind or reality in its liberative functioning emerges in history through Śākyamuni's enlightenment as the teaching of Amida in the *Larger Sutra*: "The Primal Vow is the true intent of this sutra; the Name of Amida Buddha is its essence." The Name calls beings to the realization of entrustment. This, Shinran explains, is the meaning of "hear" in the sutra passage on the Vow's fulfillment quoted earlier: "Sentient beings, having heard how the Buddha's Vow arose—its origin and fulfillment—are altogether free of doubt,"[46] that is, free of the bonds to calculative thinking. Without narrative and Name, the path is not available to be traversed and lived; but without its contraction into a moment of hearing, entrance upon the path does not occur. Shinran also explains: "one thought-moment refers to the *ultimate brevity and expansion* of the length of time in which one attains the mind and practice [i.e., entrustment and nenbutsu] that result in birth in the Pure Land."[47] The moment of entrustment expands to transfuse and transform each moment of one's karmic existence. One cannot contrive to bring about such hearing, which occurs as the falling away of self-will and teleological intent. Thus, "In entrusting ourselves to the Vow and saying the Name once, necessarily, *without seeking* it, we are brought to receive the supreme virtues, and *without knowing* it, we acquire the great and vast benefit."[48]

Late in life, Shinran adopts the term *jinen* ("of itself-ness," "spontaneous making-become-so," "naturalness") by which to indicate reality in both its dimensions: formless suchness or nirvāna ("Supreme Buddha is formless, and because of being formless is called *jinen*") and the temporal dynamic of all the elements of the path in their self-giving. For practitioners, Shinran speaks of "awaiting" the occurrence of attaining entrustment, implying a mode of attentiveness to the motions of one's egocentric passions and reflection on the teaching. *Jinen* manifests itself as the dissolving of calculation and disarming of self-will:

> *Jinen* signifies "being made to become so from the very beginning." Amida's Vow is, from the very beginning, designed to bring each of us to entrust ourselves to it— saying "Namu-amida-butsu"—and to receive us into the Pure Land; none of this is through our calculation.[49]

[44] Shinran 1997, I: 528.
[45] Shinran 1997, I: 461.
[46] Shinran 1997, I: 112.
[47] Shinran 1997, I: 298.
[48] Shinran 1997, I: 481.
[49] Shinran 1997, I: 427.

In the present, "having waited upon and attained the moment when entrustment becomes settled ... one has parted forever from samsaric existence."[50]

SHINRAN'S PHENOMENOLOGY OF RELIGIOUS LIFE: NENBUTSU AS MINDFULNESS

The title of Shinran's major work speaks of "the true and real teaching, practice, and realization," sometimes referred to as the "three pillars" of the Buddhist path; his first four chapter titles, however, indicate the themes of "teaching," "practice," "entrustment," and "realization." Shinran's variance from traditional formulations, his surprising placement of the theme of "entrustment" *following* practice, and the discrepancy between the structure of the work and its title have been topics of debate in Shin scholastics.[51]

Broadly viewed, Shinran's development and positioning of an independent chapter on entrustment may be understood in part as deconstructing the teleological view of the path based on aspiration for the Pure Land through learning, resolution, and endeavor. For Shinran, the exposition of genuine entrustment develops naturally in its givenness to beings out of the Buddha's practice. The nenbutsu practice prepared for beings, as Name, in fact beckons them. It wakens the Buddha-mind that fills them as entrustment, becoming the wellspring of utterance that manifests practice that is genuine. Through the interaction of nenbutsu and entrustment revealed in the structure of his work, Shinran removes both from the sphere of self-will and subjective intent.

Each element of the Pure Land path in its authentic aspect shares the fundamental twofold and nondual structure of reality, in which the world of form and time opens onto the inconceivable and timeless at its roots. They emerge together in the practitioner's present simultaneously with the collapse of calculative thinking through awakening to the impervious egocentricity of one's existence. The true and real teaching, as language and meaning, emerges from Śākyamuni's immersion in the nondiscrimination of "the samadhi of great tranquility,"[52] the "supreme enlightenment" "where all Buddhas abide."[53] Further, "Amida, who attained Buddhahood in the infinite past, ... took the form of Śākyamuni Buddha"[54] to appear in human history and transmit the teaching. Indeed, Amida himself, conceptually apprehensible as Vow and Name, "comes forth from [formless] suchness and manifests various bodies"[55] to convey the Pure Land path. Thus, despite the sutra's account of Amida's attainment of Buddhahood, "he seems

---

[50] Shinran 1997, I: 381.
[51] See Shinran 1997, II: 19–23 for a discussion of these issues.
[52] Shinran 1997, I: 339.
[53] Shinran 1997, I: 7–8.
[54] Shinran 1997, I: 349.
[55] Shinran 1997, I: 153.

more ancient than kalpas countless as particles."[56] The vectors of historical narrative and emergence into conceptual meaning intersect and interact dialectically.

In the same way, the other elements of the Pure Land path all share a dual nature, at once rooted in formless reality and at the same time emerging in the historical world of human meaning, imparted to beings as the unfolding of enlightened compassion. *Practice*, as the saying of the Name, is "the treasure ocean of virtues that is suchness or true reality."[57] *Entrustment* "is itself Other Power"[58] and "none other than Buddha-nature."[59] *Realization* in the Pure Land path also shares this dual structure, for at the moment in ongoing life that one realizes entrustment, reality as wisdom-compassion floods one's existence and one's full enlightenment in the future becomes settled, even as one continues life in ignorance, afflicted by egocentric emotions and perceptions. Shinran expresses, in addition to the joy of other passages, the ever deepening self-discernment that is part of this complex religious consciousness:

> I myself am floundering in an immense ocean of desires and attachments, and am overwhelmed and astray in vast mountains of fame and advantage, so that I rejoice not at all ... at coming near the realization of true enlightenment. How ugly it is! How wretched![60]

With the arising of the path in the religious existence of Pure Land practitioners, their acts of craving and self-will emerge to self-awareness. Shinran speaks of his realization that "hell is decidedly my abode."[61] Although illumined in the practitioner's "constant mindfulness" through the Buddha's working, unwholesome acts do not lose their karmic force. Nevertheless, "without the practitioner's calculating in any way whatsoever, all that person's past, present, and future evil karma is transformed into the highest good."[62] "Transformed" means that one's acts of evil, "without being nullified or eradicated," simultaneously come to embody the Buddha's virtues, tempering the force of one's blind passions and moving one toward full awakening. Thus, "gentleheartedness and forbearance surely arise through the [Vow's] spontaneous working (*jinen*)."[63]

Furthermore, the practitioners themselves come to participate in the dynamism of wisdom-compassion, for entrustment, as the Buddha-mind, is also the "mind that aspires to save all sentient beings."[64] Conscious, deliberate accomplishment of Buddha-work awaits their own complete liberation, but "when persons attain enlightenment [at death in this world], with great love and great compassion immediately reaching

[56] Shinran 1997, I: 340.
[57] Shinran 1997, I: 13.
[58] Shinran 1997, I: 365.
[59] Shinran 1997, I: 99.
[60] Shinran 1997, I: 125.
[61] Shinran 1997, I: 662.
[62] Shinran 1997, I: 453.
[63] Shinran 1997, I: 676.
[64] Shinran 1997, I: 113.

their fullness in them, they return to the ocean of birth-and-death to save all sentient beings."[65] Even in this life, persons of entrustment gain "the benefit of constantly
practicing great compassion,"[66] for the elements of the path manifest themselves in their
existence without their knowing or seeking it. Their world comes to be informed by the
nenbutsu, and "to say Namu-amida-butsu is to repent all the karmic evil one has committed since the beginningless past ... to give this virtue to all sentient beings ... to
adorn the Pure Land."[67]

Among the people of the countryside in thirteenth century Japan, Shinran effected a
radical innovation in Buddhist tradition, one that remains remarkable amid the essentially monastically centered lineages across Asia. Rooted in the heritage of Mahāyāna
thought, Shinran brought critical strains of Buddhist insight into the everyday lives
of ordinary people, including those customarily discriminated against. At the major
turning point in his religious practice, when he abandoned monastic life, he was
encouraged by a verse received in contemplative vision:[68]

> Buddhist practicer! Should you, impelled by your inborn past, come to violate
>   [the precept against sexual contact with] a woman,
> I (Kannon) will become incarnate as a virtuous woman and bear the violation.
> Throughout your lifetime, I will actively adorn [your life of practice],
> And at the end of life guide you to birth in the buddha-field of bliss.

The actuality of human life intimated here—co-existing with others in engagement with
the world—takes place within a horizon bounded and also informed by inconceivable
reality, the dynamic of *jinen*, and thus elicits both gratitude and profound repentance.
This is the hallmark of Shinran's Buddhist path. Relinquishing all claim to personal
goodness or virtue and recognizing the deficiency of any performance of practice he
might accomplish, Shinran abandoned celibacy and married while continuing Buddhist
life, wearing monk's robes and spreading the dharma.

In his late years, Shinran shared his feelings of attachment to life with a disciple:[69]

> It is hard for us to abandon this old home of pain, where we have been transmigrating
> for innumerable kalpas down to the present, and we feel no longing for the Pure Land
> of peace, where we have yet to be born. Truly, how powerful our blind passions are!

Here again, he is able to acknowledge the ineradicable depth of such fundamental
human passions as sexual desire and sorrow at death, for by being ever more deeply

---

[65] Shinran 1997, I: 454.

[66] Shinran 1997, I: 112.

[67] Shinran 1997, I: 504.

[68] The single dream recorded in *Shinran Muki* [Shinran's Dream Record, n.d.], which survives in
a copy by Shinran's disciple Shinbutsu; in *Jōdo shinshū seiten zensho* [Complete Scriptures of Jōdo
Shinshū], edited by Kyōgaku Dendō Kenkyū Senta (Kyoto: Honganji Shuppansha, 2011), volume 2, 1008.

[69] Shinran 1997, I: 666.

illumined as they are, they cease to be obstructive. In its cultivation of such self-awareness, its rejection of self-serving moralism, and its tempering of the drive to absolutize and impose on others one's own conditioned perceptions of the world, Shinran's Buddhist path retains a cogent message in the present.

Finally, in reflecting on the thought of Shinran, it is useful to bear in mind that, despite the long-powerful temple institutions that have enshrined him, his intention was never to found a new school or lineage. He had no direct involvement whatever in establishing the Honganji complex—except as ash remains interred there—and had expressed instead the wish: "When my eyes have closed for good, put me in the Kamo River and give me to the fish."[70] If a tradition is sought as his native milieu, it is that of the nenbutsu *hijiri* or "holy men" who populate the medieval landscapes and marketplaces as wandering priests and village teachers of dharma.[71]

References

Hirota, Dennis. (1982) *Tannishō: A Primer.* Kyoto: Ryukoku University.

Hirota, Dennis. (1989) *Plain Words on the Pure Land Way: Sayings of the Wandering Monks of Medieval Japan. A Translation of Ichigon hōdan.* Kyoto: Ryukoku University.

Hirota, Dennis, ed. (2000) *Toward a Contemporary Understanding of Pure Land Buddhism.* Albany: State University of New York Press.

Hōnen. (1998) *Hōnen's Senchakushū: Passages on the Selection of the Nembutsu in the Original Vow*, translated and edited with an introduction by Senchakushū English Translation Project. Honolulu: University of Hawai'i Press.

Ippen. (1997) *No Abode: The Record of Ippen*, translated, with an introduction and notes, by Dennis Hirota. Honolulu: University of Hawai'i Press.

Nishida Kitarō. (1995) "Nishida's 'Gutoku Shinran,'" translated with an introduction by Dennis Hirota, *The Eastern Buddhist* 28:2, 231–244.

Nishitani Keiji. (1978) "The Problem of Time in Shinran," translated by Dennis Hirota, *The Eastern Buddhist* 11:1, 13–26.

Shinran. (1973) *The Kyōgyōshinshō: The Collection of Passages Expounding the True Teaching, Living, Faith and Realizing of the Pure Land*, translated by D. T. Suzuki; foreword by Nishitani Keiji. Kyoto: Shinshū Ōtaniha.

Shinran. (1997) *The Collected Works of Shinran*, translated, with introductions, glossaries, and reading aids, by Dennis Hirota et al., 2 vols. Kyoto: Honpa Hongwanji.

Ueda Yoshifumi. (1984) "The Mahāyāna Structure of Shinran's Thought," translated by Dennis Hirota. *The Eastern Buddhist* 17:1, 57–78 (Part one) and 17:2, 30–54 (Part two).

Ueda Yoshifumi and Dennis Hirota. (1989) *Shinran: An Introduction to His Thought.* Kyoto: Hongwanji International Center.

---

[70] *Gaijashō* 16, in *Jōdo Shinshū Seiten Chūshaku-ban [Annotated Scriptures of Jōdo Shinshū]*, edited by Shinshū Seiten Hensaniinkai (Kyoto, 1988), 937.

[71] See Hirota 1989.

FURTHER READING

Amstutz, Galen. (1997) *Interpreting Amida: History and Orientalism in the Study of Pure Land Buddhism*. Albany: State University of New York Press.

Bloom, Alfred. (1965) *Shinran's Gospel of Pure Grace*. Ann Arbor, MI: Association for Asian Studies.

Bloom, Alfred, ed. (2004) *Living in Amida's Universal Vow: Essays in Shin Buddhism*. Bloomington, IN: World Wisdom.

Blum, Mark L., and Robert F. Rhodes, eds. (2011) *Cultivating Spirituality: A Modern Shin Buddhist Anthology*. Albany: State University of New York Press.

Dobbins, James C. (2002) *Jōdo Shinshū: Shin Buddhism in Medieval Japan*. Honolulu: University of Hawai'i Press.

Hirota, Dennis. (1993) "Shinran's View of Language," *The Eastern Buddhist*, 26:1, 50–93 (Part one) and 26:2, 91–130 (Part two).

Hirota, Dennis. (2006) *Asura's Harp: Engagement with Language as Buddhist Path*. Heidelberg: Universitätsverlag Winter.

Hirota, Dennis. (2008) "Shinran and Heidegger on Truth." In *Boundaries of Knowledge in Buddhism, Christianity, and the Natural Sciences*, edited by Paul Numrich. Göttingen: Vandenhoeck and Ruprecht, 59–79.

Hoshino Genpō. (1994–1995) *Kōkai Kyōgyōshinshō* [A Commentary on *Teaching, Practice, and Realization*], 5 vols. Kyoto: Hōzōkan.

Nishida Kitarō. (1986–1987) "The Logic of Topos and the Religious Worldview," translated by Michiko Yusa, *The Eastern Buddhist* 19:2, 1–29 and 20:1, 81–119.

Shigaraki Takamaro. (2013) *Heart of the Shin Buddhist Path: A Life of Awakening*, translated by David Matsumoto. MA, Somerville: Wisdom Publications.

Shigaraki Takamaro et al., eds. (1988–1989) *Shinran Taikei: Shisō-hen* [Shinran Collection: On Shinran's Thought], 13 vols. Kyoto: Hōzōkan.

Suzuki, D. T. (2015) *Selected Works of D.T. Suzuki*. Volume II: *Pure Land*, edited by James Dobbins. Oakland: University of California Press.

Takeuchi Yoshinori. (1983) "Centering and the World Beyond." In *The Heart of Buddhism: In Search of the Timeless Spirit of Primitive Buddhism*, edited by James W. Heisig. New York: Crossroad, 48–60.

Tanabe Hajime. (1986) *Philosophy as Metanoetics*, translated by Takeuchi Yoshinori with Valdo Viglielmo and James W. Heisig. Berkeley: University of California Press.

Unno, Taitetsu. (1998) *River of Fire, River of Water: An Introduction to the Pure Land Tradition of Shin Buddhism*. New York: Doubleday.

CHAPTER 7

MODERN PURE LAND THINKERS

Kiyozawa Manshi and Soga Ryōjin

MARK UNNO

KIYOZAWA Manshi (1863–1903) and Soga Ryōjin (1875–1971) were Pure Land Buddhist thinkers who emerged in the context of Japan's tumultuous transition to modernity during the Meiji Period (1868–1912). Although they both contributed to the systematic articulation of Pure Land thought from the late nineteenth to the mid-twentieth centuries, their prominence as thinkers was due as much to the idea that they lived their philosophies. Thus, their philosophical significance needs to be considered within a larger triangulation: Kiyozawa and Soga themselves as individual religious seekers, their attempts at institutional reform, and their work as constructive religious thinkers. To begin, however, some background knowledge on Shin Buddhism, their particular form of Pure Land Buddhism, is in order for those who are unfamiliar.

BACKGROUND OF SHIN BUDDHISM

Kiyozawa and Soga were scholar-priests of Higashi Honganji, which, along with Nishi Honganji, is one of the two largest branches of Jōdo Shinshū (True Pure Land Sect), known as Shin Buddhism in the West. Shin Buddhism is based on the thought of the founder Gutoku Shinran ("Bald-Headed Fool Shinran" 1173–1262) and his articulation of Pure Land Buddhism.[1]

---

[1] Unno 2005. See also Chapter 6 in this volume for a fuller treatment of Shinran's thought. Here, the key terms relevant for understanding Kiyozawa and Soga are introduced along with the "concepts" versus "narrative" hermeneutical distinction applied for the purposes of the present.

Shinran, along with his teacher Hōnen, were part of a movement away from the dominant monastic institutions of their day and toward a more lay-centered approach to Buddhist life and practice. Shinran, who had spent two decades at the monastic center of the Tendai Sect on Mount Hiei northeast of the ancient capital of Kyoto, abandoned his vows and was the first Japanese Buddhist monk to openly marry. He and his wife Eshinni, a laywoman who took a Buddhist nun's name and is usually depicted wearing the robes of a religious, had six children and lived for nearly three decades ministering among peasants in the Kanto region (present-day Tokyo area). He had originally left the Kyoto area exiled for his heretical views and practices but, even when pardoned, chose to live among the farmers and fishermen whom he considered more down to earth and sincere than the wealthy intellectual class, both ecclesiastical and lay, in the aristocratic culture of Kyoto. Shinran returned to Kyoto for the final three decades of his life, choosing to live in his brother's house, never to inhabit a temple again, where he wrote prolifically until he passed away at the age of ninety. His magnum opus was the *Kyōgyōshinshō* (Teaching, Practice, True Entrusting, and Realization;),[2] in which he articulated much of his philosophical understanding.

Shin Buddhism: Key Concepts

As a follower of Mahāyāna Buddhism, Shinran subscribed to the twofold truth of conventional and highest truth, form and emptiness (Sk. *śūnyatā*), where conventional truth was defined as the realm of discursive concepts and forms and highest truth as freed from or empty (Sk. *śūnya*) of any rigid or dogmatic views based on a referential view of language.[3] As long as one understood these as twofold—that is, not as separate truths but as two sides of the same coin—one could abide in the discursive realm without getting caught in a kind of naïve realism in which one mistook one's own ideas about self and reality for the things themselves.

Shinran was concerned for himself and others, both lay and monastic, as inextricably caught up in the world of attachments to preconceived notions about reality. Thus, he expressed the twofold truth in terms of the state of attachment and liberation from that attachment. This is the dynamic of blind passion (*bonnō* 煩悩) and boundless compassion (*daihi* 大悲), foolish being (*bonbu* 凡夫) and the awakening of infinite light (Amida Buddha; Jp. *Amida Butsu*), where blind passion and foolish being correspond to the one who is entangled in attachment to form, on the one hand, and boundless compassion and Amida Buddha to emptiness, on the other. These expressions are drawn from the tradition of Pure Land Buddhism, originating in India around the beginning of the Common Era. Later Chinese interpreters would expand upon them, using such terms as "self-power" (Ch. *zili*; Jp. *jiriki* 自力) to denote the deluded ego-centered force of the foolish being, and "other power" (Ch. *tali*; Jp. *tariki* 他力) to signify the power

---

[2] CWS 8-341.
[3] Unno 2005.

other than ego, the power of boundless compassion.[4] The foolish being is the one who is blinded by his attachments from seeing reality-as-it-is (Sk. *tathatā*; Jp. *shinnyo* 真如). Yet, illuminated, embraced, and dissolved into the flow of the truth of emptiness/oneness, he realizes unbounded freedom. Just as conventional truth does not exist apart from highest truth or form apart from emptiness, so too, blind passion and the boundless compassion of emptiness that releases blind passion are also inseparable. One still has attachments, but these attachments lose their power. One still suffers, but this suffering is no longer overwhelming or overriding. In fact, the deeper one delves into one's own suffering, the more one discovers the deep bonds with all others who also suffer. Thus, the suffering of blind passion is transformed into the realization of boundless compassion. Shinran likened this to water and ice: "The greater the ice [of blind passion], the greater the water [of great compassion]."[5] Emptiness in and of itself has no identifiable characteristics: it is formless, tasteless, odorless. Yet the release from blind passions is positively experienced as a freeing into, or feeling with, reality as such; hence, its expression as boundless compassion (*mugai no daihi* 無蓋の大悲, *muen no ji* 無縁 の慈).[6]

The central practice of Shin Buddhism is the intoning or chanting of the Name of Amida Buddha, the Cosmic Buddha of Infinite Light and Infinite Life. In Japanese, this is Namu Amida Butsu, a transliteration of what in Sanskrit is *Namō Amitābha Buddha* ("I bow and give myself over to the Buddha of Infinite Light"). Yet Amida Buddha is not an external being in a transcendent realm. Rather, Amida Buddha is the true nature of the self, the embodiment of emptiness realized as boundless compassion and infinite illumination in the here and now. Since, ultimately, the true nature of the self is emptiness/oneness with all beings and all reality, the chanting of Namu Amida Butsu represents the dynamic nonduality of the foolish being with the boundless realization of emptiness, the one who suffers from the ego delusion of separateness and independence, on the one hand, and the true self of oneness and interdependence, on the other. Thus, Namu Amida Butsu may be more accurately rendered, "I entrust myself to the awakening of infinite light." Furthermore, the Name ultimately issues from emptiness/ oneness, not the ego self; thus, chanting Namu Amida Butsu is realized as the call of Amida from the depths of being beyond the ego.

The act of entrusting the self (Jp. *shinjin* 信心) appears at first glance to come from the practitioner as an individual but is ultimately regarded as issuing from Amida as the deepest reality of the self. Both Kiyozawa and Soga frequently referenced key concepts such as "entrusting," "self-power," and "other power," as well as "emptiness/oneness" and "great compassion," but Kiyozawa remained more focused on key concepts while Soga often turned to the narrative dimensions of Pure Land Buddhist expression.

---

[4] The terms *zili* and *tali*, "self-power" and "other power," were first enunciated in the Pure Land tradition by the Chinese master Tanluan (*Jingtu lunzhu* [*Commentary on the Treatise on the Pure Land*], T. vol. 40, p. 826).

[5] SCZ 429; CWS 371

[6] SCZ 14, 328

Shin Buddhism: Narratives

Key narratives of Shin Buddhism are found in the *Three Pure Land Sutras* as identified by Shinran, especially the *Larger Sutra of Eternal Life* (Sk. *Sukhāvatī-vyūha-sūtra;* Jp. *Daimuryōjukyō*).[7] This Mahāyāna scripture begins with the story of a king who renounces his throne to set out on his quest to attain awakening. This initiates his career as Dharmākara Bodhisattva, a spiritual aspirant who refuses to attain awakening unless all others also attain awakening since their suffering is inseparable from his own. In order to realize such a cosmic oneness, Dharmākara formulates forty-eight bodhisattva vows that define the ideal parameters of a realm of emptiness in which all beings realize oneness in boundless compassion.

The fulfillment of these vows culminates in Dharmākara Bodhisattva becoming Amida Buddha, and the world of suffering is transformed into the Pure Land of awakening. The realization of Amida Buddha and the Pure Land is presented as fully realized, as the expression of cosmic oneness. The foolish being, however, cannot see or feel this oneness due to her blind passions. Thus, the practice of chanting the Name, Namu Amida Butsu, is paradoxical; it is *already* but *not yet*: the oneness of boundless compassion is already here, but the foolish being has yet to realize it. This is the paradox of the Primal Vow of Amida (Jp. *Mida no Hongan* 弥陀の本願), so called because it is the realization of Amida's power of boundless compassion as the fulfillment of the vows made originally or at the primal level as a bodhisattva.

In much of Mahāyāna Buddhism, higher truth is expressed as both personal and impersonal, yet neither personal nor impersonal. Thus, emptiness/Amida Buddha are both personal and impersonal; ultimately, they are beyond any preconceived categories, such that they are neither personal nor impersonal, dissolved in the illumination of infinite awakening. Blind passion and the unfolding of boundless compassion, Dharmākara Bodhisattva and Amida Buddha, and the realization of Namu Amida Butsu all are at the core of both Kiyozawa and Soga's understanding of Shin Buddhism. As we shall see, Kiyozawa places special emphasis on Amida and the infinite; Soga finds a particular significance in Bodhisattva Dharmākara and the *process* of realization.

KIYOZAWA AND SOGA: INDIVIDUAL RELIGIOUS SEEKERS

Some examination of Kiyozawa and Soga as religious persons is essential to understanding their philosophical thought. There are two reasons for this. First, the power

[7] T #360; 12.365

of their philosophical thinking is attributable in part to the notion that they lived according to their ideas. Second, there are problems of philosophical understanding that can be beneficially illuminated by reference to these thinkers' lives.

Both Kiyozawa and Soga were ordained as Shin Buddhist priests at a young age, they were independent thinkers and practitioners who were willing to risk life and career to seek out their religious paths, they suffered censure and exile for expressing their views and taking a stand, and yet they came to be seen as religious leaders in their communities and institutions. There are resonances here with the founding figure Shinran who also set out on his own path at greatest risk to his own life, was exiled for his views, but eventually came to be seen as leader and founder of one of the largest developments of Japanese Buddhism. This does not mean that they were perfect; they would be the first to reject any label of perfection or sainthood. As self-professed "foolish beings," they had many limitations; nevertheless, these very limitations became, for them, portals to deeper insight and realization, such that they inspired many to follow the path of Shin Buddhism.

Kiyozawa Manshi

Kiyozawa Manshi (1863–1903) was born Tokugawa Mannosuke, the son of a samurai or warrior of lower status who lost his employ during the tumult of the Meiji restoration as Japan made its transition to parliamentary government and a modern nation state.[8] One way to obtain both financial means and education was to become ordained and enter into the sectarian fold of a Buddhist institution. Thus Mannosuke became ordained at the age of fifteen and enrolled in a sectarian high school of the Higashi Honganji.

Mannosuke excelled academically and advanced onto the preparatory division of Tokyo Imperial University and then onto the undergraduate division of the college of arts and letters of what is today the University of Tokyo, where he focused on Western philosophy. Many intellectuals faced personal crises during the late nineteenth to the mid-twentieth centuries, caught between the deluge of Western thought and culture that seemed to be overwhelming traditional values and outlooks, on the one hand, and the need to maintain a connection with existing intellectual, cultural, and religious sources, on the other. This was not just an intellectual dilemma but a visceral one. During the early to mid-twentieth century, many literati and intellectuals committed suicide, unable to bridge this cultural and spiritual divide.

Kiyozawa was one of these intellectuals who experienced this tension but attempted to engage it creatively to synthesize his own self-understanding. As he intensified his self-inquiry, he became increasingly disenchanted with the institutional status quo of

[8] The biographical information on Kiyozawa herein, as well as the information included in the section on institutional reform, has been gleaned from Hashimoto Hōyū, ed., *Kiyozawa Manshi—Suzuki Daisetsu*, Nihon no meicho 43 (Tokyo: Chūōkōronsha, 1984), 13–32, 499–503.

Higashi Honganji and came to see his fellow priests as preoccupied with rank and social status at the expense of any real sense of commitment to the Buddhist Way:

> Ministers today debase the dignity of being the Buddha's disciples and look for sympathy from worldly people. They go so far as to flatter and fawn upon people in order to win their favor. But do they want to make a beggar out of the liberator of mankind? Do they want the leader of humanity [the Buddha] to be a slave? They are seriously lacking in self-esteem! . . . Buddhist teaching is only dignified when articulated by a dignified person. It becomes superficial when spoken of by a superficial person [who only thinks of rank and status].[9]

As we shall see, his study of Western philosophy would enable him to grapple with the intellectual bases of the influx of foreign culture he was experiencing. Furthermore, he found sources of renewal and inspiration for reimagining what he had come to see as the decadent thought and institutions of his own religious tradition.

Yet his vision was not philosophical merely in a conceptual sense. Rather, he took a three-pronged approach to deepen his inward realization, to reformulate the core of Shin Buddhist thought incorporating key concepts from Western philosophy, and to initiate a movement toward institutional reform. The philosophical thrust of this three-pronged approach is apparent from early on in his career:

> My readers may have noticed that my criticism of servility and my appeal for self-esteem are not intended to encourage aloofness or indifference . . . . In my opinion, a Buddhist must live in two worlds at once . . . . They are the supramundane world and the mundane world, the world of oneness and the world of diversity . . . . These worlds may be described as the Absolute (Jp. *zettai* 絶対) and the relative (*sōtai* 相対), or the Infinite (*mugen* 無限) and the finite (*yūgen* 有限) . . . . The two most outstanding spiritual features of a Buddhist are, first, that he *mentally* transcends the world of diversity (or secularity) and enters into the world of oneness (or supreme truth), from which point he views the world of diversity; and second, that he *physically* stays in the world of diversity, from which point he views the world of oneness, while striving to liberate and benefit others.[10]

For Kiyozawa, what he described as mental transcendence into the world of oneness was no mere conceptual cognition but a commitment of one's whole being to turn toward inward realization. Before this inward turn, in 1888, at the age of twenty-five and at the request of the leadership of Higashi Honganji, he had become the principal of a sectarian high school and married into the prestigious Kiyozawa temple family of Saihōji of Higashi Honganji.

---

[9] Haneda 1984, 63–64.
[10] Haneda 1984, 64–65

Yet, dissatisfied with the state of his inner spiritual realization, he abruptly resigned his position as principal in 1890, just two years into his appointment, and entered a period of severe asceticism that he termed an experiment in the "Minimum Possible." He abandoned Western clothing, wore simple Buddhist robes, gave up all luxuries including the Western cigars he favored, became vegetarian, and eventually reduced his diet to just pine needles and resin. He visited Buddhist monks and masters, and he focused his study on Buddhist classics such as the early Buddhist *Āgama* or sacred teachings of the historical Buddha Śākyamuni; the *Tannishō*, a posthumous collection of sayings by Shinran as well as commentary on them; and the *Discourses* of Epictetus, the Greek Stoic philosopher. He later came to call these his three sacred scriptures.

Kiyozawa's asceticism eventually led him to fall gravely ill with tuberculosis, to the point where his life was in danger. At the urging of family and friends, he began to eat more regularly, take rest, and eventually recovered. It was at the low point, however, that he had a religious awakening he would later describe as like having passed through death and letting go of ego: "Since what I ... have been is dead, this corpse is at your disposal" (Haneda 1984, 84). The brink of physical death also meant the demise of ego-driven self-power, the giving up of self to other power:

> When I am aware of liberation through other power, the way to live my life becomes clear to me. When I forget liberation through other power, the way to live my life becomes uncertain ....
>
> Ah, liberation through other power! How my awareness of it frees me from this world of delusion and suffering! How it makes me enter the Pure Land of peace and tranquility!
>
> At this very moment I feel myself being liberated through my awareness. If it had not been for (Shinran's) teaching about liberation through other power, I would never have avoided confusion and despair.[11]

Outwardly, he would spend the rest of his career seeking institutional reform, experiencing periods of rejection and ostracism alternating with brief of moments recognition. Yet he garnered the loyalty of a coterie of disciples and followers who would carry on his work and become the leaders of the very institution whose authority Kiyozawa rejected and that stripped him of his authority: Higashi Honganji. At one point, Kiyozawa began to refer to himself as useless as a fan in the cold of December, even titling his personal journal, *December Fan* (1898–1899).[12] Due to the physical ravages of his experiment with the "minimum possible" and resulting illness, the taxing nature of his efforts at institutional reform, and the generally harsh life that he led, Kiyozawa eventually retreated to his wife's temple Saihōji, where his tuberculosis relapsed. Few congregants turned out to listen to his lectures, which were perceived to be more like

[11] Haneda 1984, 46–47

[12] Kiyozawa 2008.

difficult philosophical disquisitions than sermons, and during which he would expel tubercular discharge into a spittoon. Kiyozawa died at Saihōji at the young age of thirty-nine (1903).

Soga Ryōjin

Soga Ryōjin (1875–1971) was born the third son of a Shin Buddhist priest at Entokuji temple in Niigata prefecture, on the Japan Sea side of the northern part of the main island of Honshū.[13] Like Kiyozawa, he married into a temple that lacked a male heir. He thus entered Jōonji temple and took on his wife's surname, changing from Tomioka to Soga. Soga did not leave a record of his personal quest for religious understanding and realization in the way that Kiyozawa did, but, like Kiyozawa and as one of his followers, Soga sought to reinvigorate Shin Buddhism both philosophically and through institutional reform. He became a member of Kiyozawa's inner circle upon enrollment (1901) at the new Shinshū Daigaku (Shinshū University) for Shin Buddhist studies for which Kiyozawa had taken his appointment as president.

Soga eventually became a professor of Shinshū Daigaku (1904) but resigned when it was moved to Kyoto in 1911, where it would go back to close administrative supervision under Higashi Honganji and was eventually renamed Ōtani University. Like Kiyozawa, Soga refused to compromise and either willingly resigned or was forced out of positions numerous times, including multiple appointments at Shinshū Daigaku/Ōtani University, where he concluded his career in 1967. Soga was well known for his intense, serious lecture style that inspired faculty and students alike, and he remained active in lecturing and publishing until almost the end of his life in 1971.

INSTITUTIONAL REFORM

For both Kiyozawa and Soga, institutional reform was based on what they viewed as the spirit of the founder Shinran. For them, as it was for Shinran, there could be no compromise in commitment to religious truth and their religious paths. This meant rejection of the institutional status quo, which they regarded as both doctrinally and administratively corrupt insofar as fundamentalist doctrinal orthodoxy was used to maintain the authority of administrators and their privileged lifestyles, both at

---

[13] The biographical information on Soga herein, as well as in the section on institutional reform, has been gleaned from Robert Rhodes, "Soga Ryōjin: Life and Thought," in Blum and Rhodes 2011, 101–106; and Itō Emyō, "Shinchi no shizenjin," in *Jōdo Bukkyō no shisō* 15. *Suzuki Daisetsu, Soga Ryōjin, Kaneko Daiei*, edited by Bandō Shōjun, Itō Emyō, and Hataya Akira (Tokyo: Kōdansha, 1993), 127–260.

Higashi Honganji as the mother temple and at Shinshū Daigaku/Ōtani University. In the Mahāyāna spirit of skillful adaptation (Sk. *upāya;* Jp. *hōben* 方便) to the changing circumstances of time, culture, and the capacities of Buddhist followers, Kiyozawa and Soga sought to return to the spirit of Shinran's Shin Buddhism through doctrinal innovation. For both of them, advances in doctrine were philosophical expressions of their quests for individual self-realization as well as their attempts at institutional reform. The fact that the Higashi Honganji eventually incorporated their ideas into its core doctrinal understanding did not necessarily mean that Kiyozawa and Soga succeeded in the wholesale transformation of institutional culture; nevertheless, their ideas continued to inform and enliven the religious thought of Higashi Honganji and Ōtani University in later generations.

Kiyozawa Manshi

Kiyozawa's advancement through the most prestigious educational institutions of his day, including his study of Western philosophy at Tokyo Imperial University, brought him to the attention of sectarian leaders, and he received increasingly prestigious appointments within the order. It was in the midst of being groomed for leadership within the academic ranks of Higashi Honganji that Kiyozawa became critical of institutional corruption and entered his experimental period of "minimum possible" to attain religious realization.

After he recovered sufficiently from his tuberculosis, he began an institutional reform movement in 1894, and he was stripped of all official standing within Higashi Honganji for insubordination. In 1898, he founded Kōkōdō, a private academy and austere religious practice center in Tokyo. There, he mentored a small group of dedicated students, many of whom would later become leading sectarian scholars and leaders. He also founded the journal *Seishinkai* (Spiritual World) to publish his and his students' criticisms of the status quo, their own vision of Shin Buddhism as religious thought and as a movement. This movement would come to be known as *seishinshugi* (精神主義), which can be rendered roughly as "promoting true spirit." In 1901, the same year that he began publication of *Seishinkai*, he was appointed president of Shinshū Daigaku but resigned only a year later.

Kiyozawa had insisted that Shinshū Daigaku be an institution for the pure pursuit of religious understanding, not for career advancement. In some ways, his ideal of Shin Buddhist education was altogether impractical. When some students petitioned him to allow for a school teacher certification program, he steadfastly refused, and when faculty joined in with the petitioning students, Kiyozawa submitted his resignation. Although there was a countermovement to retain him as president, he made it clear that his decision to resign was final. A controversial figure to be sure, and radical in his actions and lifestyle, the intensity of Kiyozawa's religious quest, philosophical inquiry, and attempts at institutional reform injected renewed vigor into the religious thought and institutional development of Higashi Honganji.

Soga Ryōjin

In his youth, Soga had been a brilliant student, finishing grade school in just three years, and he advanced to Shinshū Daigaku to continue his studies in Shin Buddhism. It was serendipitous that he did so immediately before Kiyozawa became president there and had it moved to Tokyo (1901), away from the immediate control of the theocrats at Higashi Honganji, and that Soga was able to follow Kiyozawa and study intensively with him. In 1903, Soga joined a small group of disciples in intensive study at Kōkōdō. By this time, Kiyozawa had already resigned his presidency at Shinshū Daigaku and had returned to his wife's temple. Nevertheless, Kiyozawa continued to influence Soga indirectly through the former's followers in the intimate, intensive learning environment of Kōkōdō.

Eventually, Soga was appointed professor of Shinshū Daigaku, but he resigned when it was moved from Tokyo back to Kyoto under close supervision of Higashi Honganji in 1911. He then moved back to his wife's temple of Jōonji where he wrote the essay, "A Savior on Earth: The Meaning of Dharmākara Bodhisattva's Advent" (*Chijō no kyūshu: Hōzō Bosatsu shutsugen no igi*), which was published in *Seishinkai* (1913). This work, in which he reinterprets the significance of the Dharmākara narrative as expressing the arising of entrusting to other power from within the depths of the practitioner's mind, became a central theme throughout Soga's Buddhist thought.

He became a professor at Tōyō University and became the editor of *Seishinkai*. Finally, in 1925, he agreed to return to Shinshū Daigaku, which had been renamed Ōtani University. Yet, following the publication of his controversial work, *Nyorai hyōgen no hanchū to shite no sanshin kan* (The View of the Three Minds [of Amida] as Categories of the Tathāgatha's [Buddha's] Self-Expression), in which he reinterpreted traditional Shin Buddhist views of Dharmākara Bodhisattva in light of early Mahāyāna Buddhist views of mind, Soga was forced to resign (1930). This caused a revolt among both faculty and students, but Soga did not return to Ōtani University for more than a decade.

During this hiatus, Soga, along with another former Kiyozawa follower, Kaneko Daiei, and others in Kiyozawa's lineage, such as Yasuda Rijin, founded Kōbō Gakuen (Academy for Upholding the Dharma), a small private academy for Shin Buddhist studies. Just as Soga had benefitted from the intimate learning environment of Kōkōdō, he now served as mentor to serious Shin seekers at Kōbō Gakuen. Soga returned to Ōtani University in 1941 and eventually became President of Ōtani University (1961), a post he held until his retirement (1967).[14]

Soga's reformulation of Shin thought, his sense of intellectual and ethical independence and integrity, his commitment to mentoring sincere seekers, and his rise to

[14] Recently, there has been some discussion of the complicity of Soga and Kaneko in the militaristic rhetoric of World War II. See, for example, the upcoming monograph by Jeff Schroeder, *The Revolution of Buddhist Modernism: Jōdo Shin Thought and Politics, 1888–1956*. Mark Blum, in his discussion of this matter, tends to regard this as a less significant issue (see his "Shin Buddhism in the Meiji Period," chapter 1 in Blum and Rhodes 2011).

institutional prominence through the perceived merits of his personification of the Shin path and philosophical contributions, formed key strands in the development of his efforts at institutional reform.

PHILOSOPHICAL INNOVATION

Kiyozawa Manshi

Kiyozawa's personal quest for religious realization and his attempts at institutional reform were driven by his quest for truth and integrity in the face of what he perceived to be institutional hypocrisy and corruption. From a Western philosophical perspective, it can be said that he was seeking the basis of his total existence: metaphysical, epistemological, and ethical. His ethical struggle is especially apparent in the foregoing descriptions of his efforts to live his own life and his reform attempts within the institutional ranks of Higashi Honganji. Yet he says very little about exactly what does constitute a truly ethical life. In fact, he makes a startling statement in his essay "My Faith" (*Waga shinnen*), that purports to express the core of his realization:

> How does Tathāgata [Buddha], the infinite compassion, enable me to attain peace of mind? In no other way than by assuming the burden of my every responsibility. Nothing, not even the worst evil, can hinder the working of Tathāgata. There is no need for me to deliberate on what is good or evil, right or wrong. There is nothing I cannot do. I act as I please and do as I am inclined. There is no need for me to be concerned about my every action, even if it turns out to be a mistake or a crime.[15]

At first glance, this seems to be a statement of ethical abdication rather than ethical responsibility, of abandoning any sense of right or wrong and ceding all moral agency to the unseen and unknown agency of the "Buddha," even to the extent of lacking concern for committing crimes.

Yet, paradoxically, for Kiyozawa, this statement is at the heart of his ethico-religious self-understanding. Kiyozawa clarifies his view of the relation and difference between the ethical and religious planes of existence in his *Lectures on Spirit* (*Seishin kōwa*). He divides his discussion into three lectures: "Repose Beyond Ethics," "Basis Beyond Ethics," and "Negotiating the Divide Between Religious Morality and Conventional Morality".[16] The key points he makes are as follows: Conventional morality and the religious life each have their own legitimate spheres of activity, independent from each other. Conventional morality is necessarily particularistic and relative, fraught with conflict and contradiction. Religious repose and freedom are attained through renouncing

---

[15] Haneda 1984, 10.
[16] Hashimoto 1984: 210–225.

and letting go of the need to achieve an ethically consistent life, leading to the realization of non-self or non-ego (*muga* 無我) and complete trust in the infinite compassion (Amida Buddha) of the absolute, which is beyond all conception. Once one has attained the freedom of the absolute, there is no need to worry about what one does on the relative plane of conventional morality because the freedom of the absolute cannot be hindered or obstructed by the standards of conventional morality.

As an illustration of the ethical life, he cites the medieval Japanese feudal lord, Taira no Shigemori, who is said to have lamented, even to the extent of contemplating ending his own life, "If one wishes to be loyal, then one cannot be filial; if one wishes to be filial, one cannot be loyal. Whether I, Shigemori, seek to advance or retreat, I end up here."[17] According to this view, there are too many instances where one cannot simultaneously be faithful to one's feudal lord and be filial to one's parents. For example, suppose that a feudal lord commands one of his soldiers to join the fight at the front lines, but the soldier has just learned his mother is dying. He wishes to return home and be a good, filial son, but he is bound to stay by his lord's side, even if it should mean losing his life in the midst of battle.

According to Kiyozawa, it is easy enough to see that the ethical demands of these virtues, which are among the most pervasive and most highly valued, conflict on a regular basis. This is emblematic of the relative, particular character of all ethics and thus of their limitations. In a sense, this is Kiyozawa's way of stating an aspect of the First Noble Truth of Buddhism, that all is suffering; one cannot escape the ethical plane, yet it is inherently self-contradictory.

Although one cannot escape the ethical plane, one can live above or beyond it, as it were, by rooting one's subjective awareness in the religious plane, by giving up any hope of resolving the ethical plane, and attaining the inner freedom of infinite compassion, of the absolute. This is the plane of spiritual repose beyond ethics, and it forms the ultimate basis of authentic subjectivity rooted in the absolute. One lives in the ethical realm but is not of it and is instead rooted in the absolute. Yet significant questions remain. When should one make ethical decisions, and when should one release into the infinite freedom of the absolute? That is, how should one negotiate the divide between the ethical and religious planes of existence? For Kiyozawa, the very fact that one is asking such questions only betrays one's failure to let go of ego and release one's attachments to the finite self. The proper negotiation between the relative, ethical self and the absolute, religious self entails letting go of the former to realize the latter.

Kiyozawa never really answers the question of how one ought to live on the ethical plane of existence. In part, one could argue that this reflects a perspective that has existed throughout much of Buddhist history. The historical Buddha renounced the ethical plane by going outside of the existing social order, the caste system in place in ancient India. His quest for nirvāna was not an ethical quest; rather, he sought liberation

[17] Hashimoto 1984, 210.

from suffering that he defined as pervading all of existence, as the endless round of death and rebirth, or *saṃsāra*. In other words, earthly existence itself is the problem, and the realization of nirvāna is to live above or beyond the inevitable confusion of samsaric existence.

Such a view, however, contains obvious dangers. It can easily devolve into a rationalization to do as one wishes. In Shin Buddhism, this is called the problem of "pride in the Primal Vow" (*hongan bokori* 本願誇り), that one can commit any transgression and not worry because the Primal Vow of Amida unconditionally embraces the foolish being filled with blind passions.[18] In the *Tannishō*, the founder Shinran addresses this by saying that one "should not take poison simply because there is a cure."[19] The unconditionality of the Vow concerns the path to spiritual liberation and does not absolve one of having to face karmic consequences in this life: moral, social, legal, and otherwise. For Kiyozawa, inward renunciation of worldly desires opens the way to the attainment of nirvāna or the realization of infinite compassion. Although the intent is thus spiritual liberation, one can see that this does have a bearing on the ethical life; namely, one cannot simply cling to ego-desires and realize Buddhist non-self, infinite compassion. Still, questions remain. While traditionally Buddhist teachings have provided ethical guidelines for all Buddhists, lay and ordained, and the concept of karma has been instrumental in delineating the moral consequences of one's actions, Kiyozawa really does not provide clear ethical guidelines for his followers or invoke a karmically based view of ethics.

Philosophically, Kiyozawa adapted Hegelian dialectics to express his view of the realization of the absolute. In his *Skeleton for a Philosophy of Religion*,[20] he sets up the contradiction between the subjective and objective standpoints and their synthesis, or *aufhebung*, as the absolute. The objective is the realm of science, ethics, and society. The subjective is the realm of religious self-awareness. What appear to be objective in the conventional worlds of science, ethics, and society turn out upon closer inspection to be contingent and accidental. Through renunciation in inward subjectivity, the false sovereignty of the objective comes to light. This, then, allows one to live in the objective world with the freedom of the absolute. The resulting synthesis is to live in the objective world with subjective awareness in the light of infinite compassion and freedom. Furthermore, the authentic ethical life is to bring to liberation those who falsely live in the world of conventional ethics. In the conclusion of the *Skeleton for a Philosophy of Religion*, Kiyozawa states,

> In the [Pure Land] Path of other power ... at the moment of attaining spiritual repose, the relation between the finite and the infinite is brought clearly into relief, and the existence of the finite within the larger framework of the infinite becomes clear.

---

[18]   Unno 1996, 21.
[19]   Unno 1996, 22.
[20]   Hashimoto 1984, 47–78.

One realizes the basis of the finite as such. On the one hand, one completes one's relation to the absolute; on the other, one recognizes one's ethical relation to other finite [beings]. From a religious perspective, one comes to rejoice in the embrace of other power. From an ethical perspective one walks the Great Path with the peoples of the world.[21]

This movement of renunciation away from the objective, visible world toward the realm of infinite subjective awareness and the life that ensues is a synthesis: living in the world but not being of it. This is the common thread that unites what Kiyozawa came to regard as his three sacred texts: the early Buddhist *sutta* of the *Āgama*, more commonly known as the *Nikāya* literature, that tells the story of the historical Buddha's life of renunciation; the *Tannishō*, containing the Shin teachings of Shinran, that emphasizes the impossibility of overcoming karmic forces greater than oneself and the need to entrust the self to infinite other power; and the *Discourses* of Epictetus that emphasize Stoic serenity in the face of a world beyond one's control. These works also share similarity of genre: as the teachings of each thinker presented in dialogue with disciples and interlocutors, they are practical texts that respond to the pressing religious and philosophical needs of living seekers. As much as Kiyozawa was a philosophical innovator, he was first and foremost a religious seeker and teacher, one whose legacy is reflected in the direct personal impact he had on his students and colleagues.

Soga Ryōjin

Whereas Kiyozawa emphasized the core concepts of Shin Buddhism and their renewed articulation within the larger international context of religious thought, Soga emphasized a reconceptualization of the narrative of Dharmākara Bodhisattva as presented in the *Larger Sutra of Eternal Life*. He did so through two main ideas: "Dharmākara Bodhisattva is/becomes me," and "Dharmākara Bodhisattva is/becomes the storehouse consciousness." As a matter of intellectual history, Soga developed the ideas in this order, but, philosophically, it is easier to understand them in reverse, as forming a kind of syllogism:

Dharmākara Bodhisattva is/becomes the storehouse consciousness.
Dharmākara Bodhisattva is/becomes me.
The storehouse consciousness is/becomes me.

The storehouse consciousness (Sk. *ālaya-vijñāna*) is the eighth and deepest layer of mind according to the Yogācāra or Mind-Only school (Sk. *Cittamātra, Vijñapti-mātratā*)

---

[21] Hashimoto 1984, 78.

of Buddhism, in which there is a base stream of causally interrelated mental events or thought-moments.[22] Each thought-moment is like a seed (Sk. *bīja*) that influences and bears consequences later on. In one sense, it is a theory of karma expressed in terms of a theory of mind. When the seed bears the force of deluded self-grasping or ego-attachment (Sk. *manas*), suffering results. When the seed releases the liberating force of its true nature (Sk. *pariniṣpanna*) without conceptual entanglements, liberation is attained. This true nature is akin to emptiness (Sk. *śūnyatā*) understood as pure consciousness. Thus, the same stream of storehouse consciousness appears differently depending on one's mode of cognition. When one's mind is in its grasping mode, one becomes lost in delusion. When one's mind is in its mode of non-grasping, then the true nature of consciousness as liberation or emptiness becomes manifest.

For Soga, the Shin Buddhist narrative of Dharmākara Bodhisattva who becomes Amida Buddha is the story of the transformation of the suffering of sentient beings caught in the web of delusions, blind passions, and attachments into the liberation of boundless compassion that is signified by the Buddha of Infinite Light. The base consciousness is unchanged as the infinite mind-store, or *ālaya-vijñāna*, but manifests variously as ego delusion or as compassionate liberation depending on the impelling force of realization, as either ego blindness or as boundless compassion:

> The dynamism of our momentary impulses is caused by *manas*, the all-ignorant self-consciousness which takes hold of the basic *ālaya-vijñāna* as its own ego. *Ālaya-vijñāna* accepts all manner of differentiation and limitation as they come, yet never loses its [true] identity [as pure nature]. For as the ultimate subjectivity, *ālaya-vijñāna* is the eternal Mind itself, communing in the depths with all sentient beings, submerged as they may be in the darkness of ignorance . . . . This innermost Mind is none other than the mind of aspiration expressed by Dharmākara Bodhisattva . . . . It is none other than the Original Vow [of Amida].[23]

The key point here is that the *ālaya-vijñāna* accepts all thoughts, both deluded and liberating, but that its true nature as pure, *pariniṣpanna*, is disclosed only if allowed to unfold as such. In Soga's Shin Buddhist rendering, this is the force of the original or primal vow of Amida that is *originally* expressed as the fundamental or *primal* movement of the mind of emptiness, the basis for the narrative of Dharmākara Bodhisattva.

The question remains, however, as to when or how this transformation actually occurs, from delusion, blind passion, and suffering on the one hand, to awakening and boundless compassion on the other. This is where the second statement comes into view: "Dharmākara Bodhisattva is/becomes me." That is, the mind of pure

---

[22] For an excellent explication of the eight layers of consciousness in the Yogācāra, especially of the *bīja* or seed-action of consciousness and the overturning (*paratantra*) of discriminating consciousness (*parikalpita*) to disclose pure consciousness (*pariniṣpanna*), see Robert Gimello, *Chih-yen and the Foundation of Hua-yen Philosophy*, Ph.D. Dissertation (New York: Columbia University, 1976).

[23] Soga 1991, 227.

consciousness, of the *ālaya-vijñāna* as Dharmākara Bodhisattva, must be manifest in the life of the Shin follower or Buddhist practitioner.

This manifestation has two aspects. The first is that it must be embodied; it is a mind–body realization in which the mind of awakening is embodied in the practitioner:

> Many years ago I called the *ālaya-vijñāna*, this supraconsciousness in which all *dharmas* are stored, this "storehouse consciousness," "Dharmākara-consciousness" . . . . it is a storehouse in the sense that the *ālaya-vijñāna* contains the seeds of all things within itself . . . .
>
> Here I should call attention to the fact that our fleshly body as such is the embodiment of *ālaya-vijñāna*, for not only does it refer to the consciousness that stores infinite potentiality, but also to our actual fleshly body. Consciousness and body are totally identified in *ālaya-vijñāna*. In fact, one's salvific self-realization as a person can only take place in the unity of consciousness and body. Salvation takes place only when one realizes this unity personally according to the teachings of Dharmākara Bodhisattva and *ālaya-vijñāna*. We then become completely aware of the reality we are living.[24]

For Soga, the philosophical understanding of Shin Buddhism needed first and foremost to be validated in one's own life. He saw in the life of his mentor Kiyozawa and his cohorts at the private academy of Kōkōdō the embodiment of awakened consciousness, one that rejected the delusions of the status quo and that sought the purity of the religious life.

The second aspect is the emphasis on the subjective moment of appropriation in the present. This is the moment of transformation in the here-and-now, when the primal vow of boundless compassion is realized as "*for me.*"

Soga describes the time in which this became clear to him in his essay, "A Savior on Earth: The Significance of Dharmākara Bodhisattva's Appearance in This World." He states that the meaning of the oneness of Amida Buddha and the Shin follower as the foolish being filled with blind passions only became clear to him when he understood this as the process of Dharmākara becoming one with self, as the movement of the primal vow of boundless compassion that dispelled the darkness and delusion of the Shin follower as foolish being:

> It was in early June of last year [1912] . . . that I at last gained an insight into that exceptional phrase, *Nyorai wa ware nari* . . . "The Tathāgata [Buddha] becomes [one with] me" And then in late August at Akegarasu Haya's place [in Kanazawa], I came around to understanding, *Nyorai ware to narite ware o sukui au* . . . . "It is through the Tathāgata becoming [one with] myself that the Tathagata manages to save me" Then, around October I realized what was meant by *Nyorai ware to naru to wa bosatsu ryūtan no koto nari,* "That the Tathāgata becomes one with me

---

[24] Soga 1991, 228.

signifies the emergence or birth of [Dharmākara] Bodhisattva [in my own heart and mind]."[25]

In 1913, Soga published this essay in *Seishinkai*, the journal founded by Kiyozawa. At that point, Soga did not know whether he would spend the rest of the days as a Shin priest in his wife's temple in the remote area of Niigata or whether he would ever have another opportunity to share his ideas with the broader world under terms he would find acceptable. Yet, on the occasion of his eighty-eighth birthday, in 1963, Soga gave a lecture on Dharmākara Bodhisattva as President of Ōtani University: "The *ālaya-vijñāna* is the true 'I.' The pure 'I' . . . . The true nature of the self is the *ālaya-vijñāna* . . . . However, when one becomes attached to a fixed notion of self, . . . asserting one's power over others . . . by making claims about 'mine,' and what 'belongs to me,' one ends up losing the greatest gift that has been given to one."[26]

This view of *ālaya-vijñāna* becoming self is significant in at least three ways. First, it represents Soga's attempt to reinterpret the path of Shin Buddhism within the larger scope of Mahāyāna Buddhism. Second, it may be seen as his attempt to demythologize the narrative of Dharmākara Bodhisattva in philosophically acceptable terms. And, arguably, the converse may also be true in that it may be regarded as his attempt to remythologize Shin Buddhism, to bring the story of Dharmākara Bodhisattva becoming Amida Buddha down to earth so that it might inhabit the hearts and minds of Shin followers. This latter perspective is evident in his emphasis on the central practice of Shin Buddhism, that of invoking or chanting the Name of Amida Buddha, "Namu Amida Butsu":

> Dharmākara Bodhisattva comes to life as [the saying of] Namu Amida Butsu. There is no Buddha without "Namu Amida Butsu." The Buddha manifests because of Namu Amida Butsu . . . . It is not the case that we have Namu Amida Butsu because of the primal vow; rather, the primal vow [unfolds] because of Namu Amida Butsu.[27]

If the conclusion of Soga's work had simply been, "The *ālaya-vijñāna* becomes me," then his contribution could be regarded as a philosophical reinterpretation of the core of Shin thought. However, the fact that this formed the basis for his rearticulation of Shin Buddhist "theology" or "dharmalogy" as a matter of religious praxis indicates his basic orientation as a religious thinker and seeker.

There are many other aspects to Soga's contributions to Shin Buddhist thought. However, his distinctive reformulation of the process of realizing the Shin path in terms of Dharmākara Bodhisattva, *ālaya-vijñāna*, and the realization of the pure "I" stands out as the core of his philosophical originality, creativity, and innovation. This constellation

---

[25] Soga n.d., 1; T 2.7. For another translation, see Blum and Rhodes 2011, 107–8.
[26] Soga 1977, 30.
[27] Soga 1972, 218–219.

of ideas emerged in response to his awareness of the global scope of Buddhism, the necessity of formulating a narrative or process view of Shin Buddhism in the face of the modernized, Westernized world now defined in terms of historical narratives, and his own religious awareness in the face of the vastness of corruption: social, institutional, and interior to his own subjectivity.

CONCLUSION

For both Kiyozawa and Soga, their philosophical understanding of Shin Buddhism needed first and foremost to be validated in their own lives. As they saw it, they rejected the deluded, corrupt view of the status quo and sought to realize the absolute other power of Amida Buddha or Dharmākara-consciousness, respectively, in their own lives first and then to seek institutional reform. Yet such institutional reform entailed a necessary awareness of and confrontation with the global scope of religious and philosophical discourse. While Kiyozawa and Soga both looked back to earlier Buddhist traditions and forward to new formulations of Shin Buddhist thought appropriate to the modern age, Kiyozawa launched himself into the constructive philosophical project of synthesizing traditional Shin Buddhist thought with Western philosophy, and Soga focused more on the problem of reformulating the narrative of Dharmākara Bodhisattva in light of earlier Mahāyāna thought, in particular that of the Yogācāra.

BIBLIOGRAPHY AND SUGGESTED READINGS

Abbreviations Used

CWS. (1997) *Collected Works of Shinran*. Dennis Hirota. Head Translator. Kyoto: Honganji International Center.

SCZ. (1964) *Shinran chosaku zenshū* [Collected Works of Shinran]. Kaneko Daiei. General Editor. Kyoto: Hōzōkan.

T. (1924–1932) *Taishō shinshū daizōkyō*. Takakusu Junjirō and Watanabe Kaigyoku. Editors. Tokyo: Taishō Issaikyō Kankōkai.

Other Works

Blum, Mark L. and Robert F. Rhodes, eds. (2011) *Cultivating Spirituality: A Modern Shin Buddhist Anthology*. Albany: State University of New York Press.

Buddhabhadra and Paoyun, trans. *Wuliang shou jing* [Sutra of Eternal Life]. T #360; 12.365.

Haneda Nobuo. (1984) *December Fan: The Buddhist Essays of Manshi Kiyozawa*. Kyoto: Higashi Honganji.

Hashimoto Hōyū, ed. (1984) *Kiyozawa Manshi, Suzuki Daisetsu*. Nihon no Meicho 43. Tokyo: Chūō Kōronsha.

Kiyozawa Manshi. (2008) *Rōsenki chūshaku* [December Fan *with Notes*], edited by Ōtani Daigaku Shinshū Sōgō Kenkyūjo. Kyoto: Hōzōkan.

Oldfather, W.A., trans. (1925, 1928) *Epictetus: Discourses*, Books 1–2; 3–4. Loeb Classical Library. Cambridge: MA: Harvard University Press.

Soga Ryōjin. (1972) *Hongan ni ikiru* [Living in the Vow]. Tokyo: Chikuma Shobō.

Soga Ryōjin. (1977) *Hōzō Bosatsu* [Dharmākara Bodhisattva]. Kyoto: Hōzōkan.

Soga Ryōjin. (1991) "Dharmākara Bodhisattva." In *The Buddha Eye: An Anthology of the Kyoto School* edited by Frederick Frank. Bloomington, IN: World Wisdom, 229–240.

Soga Ryōjin. (n.d.) "The Savior on Earth: The Significance of Dharmākara Bodhisattva's Appearance in This World," translated by Wayne Yokoyama. *Shin Dharma Net*. Accessed March 14, 2015 http://www.shindharmanet.com/wp-content/uploads/2012/pdf/Ryojin-Savior.pdf

Tanluan. *Jingtu lunzhu* [Commentary on the Treatise on the Pure Land]. T #1819; 40.826.

Unno, Mark. (2005) "Shinran." *Encyclopedia of Philosophy*. New York: Macmillan.

Unno, Taitetsu, trans. (1996) *Tannishō: A Shin Buddhist Classic*. 2nd Edition. Honolulu, HI: Buddhist Study Center Press.

CHAPTER 8

THE PHILOSOPHY OF ZEN MASTER DŌGEN

Egoless Perspectivism

BRET W. DAVIS

Carrying the self forward to verify-in-practice the myriad things is delusion; for the myriad things to come forth and verify-in-practice the self is enlightenment. . . .

. . . When a person verifies-in-practice the Buddha Way, attaining one thing he or she becomes thoroughly familiar with that one thing; encountering one activity he or she [sincerely] practices that one activity. Since this is where the place [of the presencing of truth] is and the Way achieves its circulation, the reason that the limits of what is knowable are not known is that this knowing arises and proceeds together with the exhaustive fathoming of the Buddha Dharma.[1]

DŌGEN Kigen (1200–1253), founder of the Japanese Sōtō school of Zen Buddhism, is undoubtedly one of the most philosophically original and profound thinkers in Japanese history.[2] The focus of this chapter will be on Dōgen's *Genjōkōan*, which can be translated

[1] Dōgen 1990a, 1: 54, 59; Davis 2009, 256, 258; compare Dōgen 2002, 40, 44. Most of my primary references will be to Dōgen 1990a, a reliable and readily available Japanese edition of the *Shōbōgenzō* in four volumes. Although all translations of quoted passages from Dōgen's texts will be my own, for the reader's convenience I will cross-reference available English translations in addition to citing the original Japanese texts.

[2] An earlier version of this chapter was published in *The Oxford Handbook of World Philosophy*, edited by Jay Garfield and William Edelglass (New York: Oxford University Press, 2011), 348–360.

as "The Presencing of Truth."[3] This key text for understanding Dōgen's thought is the core fascicle of his major work, *Shōbōgenzō* (Treasury of the True Dharma Eye). It is the "treasury of the true Dharma eye" that Śākyamuni Buddha (ca. 500 B.C.E.) is said to have transmitted to his successor, Mahākāshyapa, by silently holding up a flower. This event is held to mark the beginning of the Zen tradition, which is believed to have been characterized by Bodhidharma (ca. 500 C.E.) as "a special transmission outside all doctrines; not depending on any texts; directly pointing to the human mind; seeing into one's true nature and becoming a Buddha." Like Bodhidharma, who is said to have sat in meditation for nine years after bringing Zen (Ch. Chan) from India to China, Dōgen, too, placed great emphasis on the silent practice of "just sitting" (*shikantaza* 只管打坐).[4]

Yet Dōgen's writings are not just expedient means to practice and enlightenment, fingers pointing at the moon; they are also literary and philosophical masterpieces in their own right. Indeed, Dōgen is considered by many to be the greatest "philosopher" in the tradition of Zen Buddhism.[5] Rather than merely insist on the limits of language and reason, he poetically and philosophically manifests their expressive potential. The "entangled vines" (*kattō* 葛藤) of language are not treated simply as impediments to be cut through with the sword of silent meditation and ineffable insight. Instead, they are understood to have the potential to become "expressive attainments of the Way" (*dōtoku* 道得) that manifest perspectival aspects of the dynamic Buddha-nature of reality.[6]

Dōgen accepts the delimited and delimiting nature of language and of thought in general. And yet he does not think that the perspectival limits of all perception, feeling, understanding, and expression are as such antithetical to enlightenment. Rather than an

---

[3] For a full translation of this text, together with an explanation of the title, see Davis 2009, 254–259. Other translations of *Genjōkoan* include "Manifesting Suchness" (Waddell and Abe 2002), "Manifesting Absolute Reality" (Cook 1989), "The Realized Universe" (Nishijima and Cross 2007–2008), "Actualizing the Fundamental Point" (Tanahashi 2012), and "Offenbarmachen des vollen Erscheinens" (Ōhashi and Elberfeld 2006).

[4] For an explication of Dōgen's instructions for and understanding of meditation, see Davis 2016.

[5] Dōgen was first treated as a "philosopher" in Japan in the early twentieth century, most notably by Watsuji Tetsurō (1889–1960) (Watsuji 2011) and by Tanabe Hajime (1885–1962) (Tanabe 1963). Prior to that, the study of his texts had been confined to Sōtō sectarian exegesis, starting with Dōgen's own disciple Senne together with his follower Kyōgō and culminating in a detailed and influential commentary by Nishiari Bokusan (1821–1910), published posthumously in 1930 (Nishiari 1965 and 2011). Recent commentaries by Zen masters include those by Shunryu Suzuki (in Nishiari et al. 2011, 95–125), Kosho Uchiyama (in Nishiari et al. 2011, 149–223), Yasutani Hakuun (1996), and Shohaku Okumura (2010). Philosophical studies of Dōgen in the West include Abe 1992; Heine 1985 and 2012; Kim 2004 and 2007; Kasulis 1981; Kopf 2002; Steineck 2002; and Wirth, Schroeder, and Davis 2016. Kim 2007 and Heine 2012 are especially pertinent to the content of the present chapter. The latter contains an excellent commentary and response to recent Japanese reinterpretations of the *Genjōkoan*'s line, "When verifying one side, the other side is obscured," which stress the finitude of enlightened as well as delusory perception (Kurebayashi 1992; Yoshizu 1993; Ishii 1997; Matsumoto 2000). Although the original version of the present chapter appeared earlier, in general, I find myself in agreement with Heine's attempt to split the difference between the traditional interpretation and these recent reinterpretations.

[6] See Chapter 9 in this volume; Dōgen 1999, 163–172, 179–184; Heine 1994, 243–249; Cook 1989, 101–106; and Davis 2019a.

overcoming of perspectivism, enlightenment for Dōgen entails a radical reorientation and qualitative transformation of the process of perspectival delimitation. Nietzsche once wrote "Egoism is the law of perspective applied to feelings."[7] Dōgen would say that "egoistic perspectivism" well describes a state of delusion. Enlightenment, on the other hand, is precisely a matter of shedding the egoistic will to posit oneself as the fixed center of the world. Nevertheless, according to Dōgen, enlightenment does not supplant perspectival knowing with an omniscient "view from nowhere." Rather, it involves an ongoing nondual engagement in a process of letting the innumerable perspectival aspects of reality illuminate themselves. Enlightenment thus entails an egoless and nondual perspectivism.

Dōgen would agree with Heidegger that any manifestation of truth always involves both a revealing and a concealing.[8] As Dōgen puts it, "When verifying one side, the other side is obscured [*ippō o shō suru toki wa ippō wa kurashi* 一方を証するときは一方は くらし]"[9] This epistemological principle is one of the central themes of his thought, and it can be found at work already in the famous opening section of the *Genjōkōan*. Since the programmatic yet laconic first four sentences of this text are often thought to contain the kernel of Dōgen's philosophy of Zen, let us begin by quoting and explicating them. As we shall see, these few lines can be read as a compact history of the unfolding of Buddhist thought from its foundational teachings through Mahāyāna philosophies to Dōgen's Zen.

THROUGH BUDDHISM TO ZEN

When the various things [*dharmas*] are [seen according to] the Buddha's teaching [Buddha Dharma], there are delusion and enlightenment; there is (transformative) practice; there is birth/life; there is death; there are ordinary sentient beings; and there are Buddhas.

When the myriad things are each [seen as] without self [i.e., as without independent substantiality], there is neither delusion nor enlightenment; there are neither Buddhas nor ordinary sentient beings; and there is neither birth/life nor death.

Since the Buddha Way originally leaps beyond both plenitude and poverty, there are arising and perishing; there are delusion and enlightenment; and there are ordinary sentient beings and Buddhas.

---

[7] Friedrich Nietzsche, *The Gay Science*, translated by Walter Kaufmann (New York: Vintage Books, 1974), p. 199 (§162); see also Friedrich Nietzsche, *The Will to Power*, translated by Walter Kaufmann and R. J. Hollingdale (New York: Vintage Books, 1967), p. 340 (§637). On Nietzsche's ambivalently egocentric perspectivism, see Davis 2018, 124–126.

[8] See Martin Heidegger, "The Essence of Truth," in *Pathmarks*, edited by William McNeill (Cambridge: Cambridge University Press), 136–154. On Heidegger's thought in relation to Zen's nonegocentric perspectivism, see Davis 2019b.

[9] Dōgen 1990a, 1: 54; compare Davis 2009, 256, and Dōgen 2002, 41.

And yet, although this is how we can say that it is, it is just that flowers fall amid our attachment and regret, and weeds flourish amid our rejecting and loathing.[10]

While the first sentence speaks from the temporal perspective of "*when* the various things are [seen according to] the Buddha's teaching . . . ," the second sentence speaks from that of "*when* the myriad things are each [seen as] without self. . . . " That which is affirmed in the first sentence is strikingly negated in the second. What is Dōgen doing here in this overturning alteration of perspective? While the first sentence sets forth several fundamental distinctions which constitute the basic teachings of Buddhism— such as that between ordinary sentient beings and their delusion on the one hand and Buddhas and their enlightenment on the other—the second sentence, by focusing now on the central teaching of no-self (Sk. *anātman*; Jp. *muga* 無我), goes on to negate *the reification of* these oppositional designations. For readers familiar with Mahāyāna Buddhism's Perfection of Wisdom literature, such self-deconstructive negations in a Buddhist text do not come as too much of a surprise. *The Heart Sutra*, for example, radicalizes the early Buddhist doctrine of no-self into that of the emptiness (Sk. *śūnyatā*; Jp. *kū* 空; i.e., the lack of independent substantiality) of all phenomenal elements of existence (Sk. *dharmas*; Jp. *shohō* 諸法) and linguistic conventions, even to the point of a systematic negation of (a reified misunderstanding of) traditional Buddhist teachings themselves, including the Four Noble Truths and the Eightfold Path. *The Heart Sutra* also speaks of no-birth, no-death, and no-attainment, rather than of nirvāna as the attainment of a release from samsāra as the cycle of birth and death.[11]

Furthermore, readers familiar with Madhyamaka Buddhist philosopher Nāgārjuna's notion of the "emptiness of emptiness" (i.e., the idea that emptiness itself is not an independently substantial entity, but rather is the nature of events of interdependent origination [Skt. *pratītya-samutpāda*; Jp. *engi* 緣起]),[12] and with Tiantai (Jp. Tendai) Buddhist philosopher Zhiyi's development of the doctrine of Two Truths (i.e., the conventional truth of provisional designations and the ultimate truth of emptiness) into the Three Truths of "the provisional, the empty, and the middle,"[13] will be prepared for the third sentence of the *Genjōkōan*. No longer qualified by a "when . . . ," the "middle" perspective expressed here resolves the tension between the first two perspectives so as to make possible the reaffirmation of distinctions, but now without reification. In fact, in its teaching of the ontological middle way of interdependent origination, Buddhism has always rejected nihilism and annihilationism along with substantialism and eternalism. The Buddhist account of the interdependent and dynamic nature of reality and the self is not subject to the "all or nothing" dilemma that plagues an ontology of independent and eternal substances. As Dōgen says here, "the Buddha Way originally leaps beyond

---

[10] Dōgen 1990a, 1: 53; Davis 2009, 256; compare Dōgen 2002, 40.
[11] See Nhat Hanh 1988 and Lopez 1988.
[12] See Garfield 1995, 312–321. On this and other senses of "emptiness" in Zen, see Davis 2013.
[13] See Chapter 4 in the present volume and Swanson 1995.

both plenitude [i.e., substantial being] and poverty [i.e., nihilistic void]." Affirmatively thought, using the language of the Three Truths, the Buddhist *middle* way embraces the nondual polarity of the *provisional* "plenitude" of differentiated being and the "poverty" or substantial *emptiness* of ubiquitous interdependent origination.

It is possible to relate these first three sentences of the *Genjōkōan* not only to the Three Truths of Tiantai (Tendai) philosophy, but also to Chan Master Weixin's famous three stages on the way to enlightenment, according to which a mountain is first seen as a mountain (i.e., as a conceptual reification), then not as a mountain (i.e., as empty of independent substantiality and linguistic reification), and finally really as a mountain (i.e., in the suchness of its interdependent origination).[14] The path of the Buddha Way ultimately leads one back to the here and now.

Be that as it may, and although we should bear in mind that Dōgen was first of all trained as a Tendai monk and was intimately familiar with doctrines such as the Three Truths, it is also important to recall that he was from an early age dissatisfied with the then prevalent doctrine of "original enlightenment" (*hongaku* 本覚). What concerned the young Dōgen was that a premature and blanket affirmation of the self and the world of distinctions *as they are* tends to deny or at least downplay the importance of transformative practice (*shugyō* 修行). This dissatisfaction and concern finally induced him to come down from Tendai's Mt. Hiei on a path that led him to Zen.[15]

The primary and ultimate standpoint of Dōgen's Zen is most directly expressed in the climactic—and, in a sense, intentionally anticlimactic—fourth sentence of the *Genjōkōan*. Here, Dōgen calls for a return from the heights of reason (*ri* 理) to the basis of fact (*ji* 事), that is, to the non-idealized here and now of concrete experience, where "flowers fall amid our attachment and regret, and weeds flourish amid our rejecting and loathing." I would suggest that this crucial sentence, like so many in Dōgen's often polysemous texts, can be read in at least two ways. On the one hand, as an expression of the concrete experiences of enlightened existence, it signifies that nirvāna is not somewhere beyond the trials and tribulations of samsāra (the realm of desire and suffering). Rather, it is a matter of "awakening in the midst of the deluding passions" (*bonnō soku bodai* 煩悩即菩提). Zen enlightenment is not an escapist *dying to*, but rather a wholehearted *dying into* a liberated and liberating engagement in the human life of emotional entanglements.

On the other hand, I think that this fourth sentence can also be read—on a less advanced but certainly no less significant level—as an acknowledgment that no amount of rational explanation of the nonduality of samsāra and nirvāna can bring about an actual realization of this truth. In *Fukanzazengi*, Dōgen writes: "From the beginning the Way circulates everywhere; why the need to verify it in practice? . . . And yet, if there is the slightest discrepancy, heaven and earth are vastly separated; if the least disorder

---

[14] However, just as each of Tiantai's Three Truths is affirmed as a view of the truth, many traditional commentators (including Nishiari) stress that each of the first three sentences of the *Genjōkōan* ultimately has its own unassailable validity as a perspectival expression of the whole truth.

[15] See Davis 2016, 202–204.

arises, the heart and mind get lost in confusion."[16] And he tells us in *Bendōwa*: "Although the truth [Dharma] amply inheres in every person, without practice, it does not presence; if it is not verified, it is not attained."[17] Religious practice is necessary, which, for Dōgen, involves not just the practice of meditative concentration but also the practice of thoughtful discrimination. Hence, after the opening section of the *Genjōkōan*, he proceeds to concretely describe the conversion from a deluded/deluding to an enlightened/enlightening comportment to the world.

VERIFICATION: THE PRACTICE
OF ENLIGHTENMENT

A deluding experience of the world, according to Dōgen, occurs when one "carries the self forward to verify-in-practice (*shushō* 修証) the myriad things." On the other hand, "for the myriad things to come forth and verify-in-practice the self is enlightenment."[18] In order to appreciate this explanation of delusion and enlightenment, we need to first discuss Dōgen's peculiar notion of *shushō*. In this term, Dōgen conjoins two characters to convey the inseparable nonduality of "practice" and "enlightenment (verification)."[19] This key aspect of Dōgen's teaching is memorably expressed in the concluding section of the *Genjōkōan*, where the action of the Zen master fanning himself (practice) is demonstrated to be one with the truth that the wind (Buddha-nature) circulates everywhere.

> As Chan Master Baoche of Mount Mayu was using his fan, a monk came and asked, "It is the wind's nature to be constantly abiding and there is no place in which it does not circulate. Why then, sir, do you still use a fan?"
> The master said, "You only know that it is the nature of the wind to be constantly abiding. You don't yet know the reason [more literally: the principle of the way] that there is no place it does not reach."
> The monk said, "What is the reason for there being no place in which it does not circulate?"
> At which time the master just used his fan.
> The monk bowed reverently.
> The verifying experience of the Buddha Dharma and the vital path of its true transmission are like this. To say that if it is constantly abiding one shouldn't use a fan, that even without using a fan one should be able to feel the wind, is to not know [the meaning of] either constantly abiding or the nature of the wind.[20]

---

[16] Dōgen 1990b: 171; compare Dōgen 2002, 2–3.

[17] Dōgen 1990a, 1: 11; compare Dōgen 2002, 8; also see Dōgen 1985, 87.

[18] Dōgen 1990a, 1: 54; Davis 2009, 256; compare Dōgen 2002, 40.

[19] See Dōgen 1990a, 1: 28; Dōgen 2002, 19. On Dōgen's key teaching of the "oneness of practice and enlightenment," see Davis 2016, 207–215.

[20] Dōgen 1990a, 1: 60; Davis 2009, 259; compare Dōgen 2002, 44–45.

Enlightenment, for Dōgen, is found neither in inactive detachment, nor in a passive acceptance of the way things are, but rather in the midst of a holistic participation—an engaged playing of one's part—in the world.

The character for *shō* 証, which is Dōgen's favored term for enlightenment, normally means to verify, prove, attest to, confirm, or authenticate something. As a synonym for enlightenment, *shō* is a matter of *verifying* ("showing to be true" and literally "making true") and hence *realizing* (awakening to and thus actualizing) the fact that one's true self (*honbunnin* 本分人), one's "original part," is originally part and parcel of the dynamically ubiquitous Buddha-nature. In the *Busshō* fascicle of the *Shōbōgenzō*, Dōgen famously rereads the *Mahāparinirvāna Sūtra*'s claim that "all sentient beings have the Buddha-nature" to mean that "Buddha-nature is all that is" (*shitsu-u wa busshō nari* 悉有は仏性なり).[21] Enlightenment is a matter of *verifying-in-practice* this fundamental fact. It is a matter of *authentication*, of truly becoming what one in truth is: a unique expression of a universally shared Buddha-nature.

LEARNING TO FORGET THE SELF

The self is a participant in the dynamically interconnected matrix of the world. Delusion occurs when the self egoistically posits itself as the single fixed center—rather than existing as one among infinitely many mutually reflective and expressive focal points—of the whole.[22] In delusion, the myriad things are seen, not according to the self-expressive aspects through which they show themselves, but rather only as they are forced into the perspectival horizon of the self-fixated and self-assertive ego. To borrow the language of Kant, the deluded and deluding ego willfully projects its own forms of intuition and categories of understanding onto the world. In contrast, through practicing the Buddha Way, one comes to realize the empty (i.e., open and interdependent) nature of the true self.

Dōgen describes the steps of this process of practice and enlightenment in three of the most frequently cited lines of the *Genjōkōan*:

> To learn the Buddha Way is to learn the self.
> To learn the self is to forget the self.
> To forget the self is to be verified by the myriad things [of the world].[23]

---

[21] Dōgen 1990a, 1: 73; compare Dōgen 2002, 61.

[22] As with much of Zen thought, Dōgen's perspectivism is heavily influenced by Huayan (Jp. Kegon) philosophy, which in turn draws on the *Avatamsaka Sūtra*'s image of the "jewel net of Indra" wherein each jewel reflects all the others (see Chang 1971; Cook 1977; Davis 2018, 128–131).

[23] Dōgen 1990a, 1: 54; Davis 2009, 256; compare Dōgen 2002, 41.

The study of Buddhism, according to Dōgen's Zen, involves more than a cognitive grasp of the truth of the Buddhist teachings (Buddha Dharma; *buppō* 仏法). It involves a holistic practice of a way of life (Buddha Way; *butsudō* 仏道).[24] The central practice of the Buddha Way for Dōgen, and for the Zen tradition in general, is seated meditation (*zazen* 坐禅)[25] rather than study of scriptures, performance of esoteric rituals, or calling on the grace of a transcendent savior. According to Zen, "what comes through the gate [i.e., from outside of oneself] is not the treasure of the house"; the truth must be discovered within. Dōgen thus speaks of meditation as a practice of taking a radical "step back that turns the light around."[26]

The light of our unenlightened minds is generally directed outward, shining its objectifying gaze on things and on a projected image of the ego itself. Things and other persons become objects of attachment or aversion, purported possessions or enemies of a reified conception of the self as ego-subject. But things and persons change and otherwise refuse to obey one's will, ever slipping from the grasp of the ego, which is itself constantly subject to mutation and otherwise fails to live up to its self-constructed image of itself. Hence, repeatedly disappointed and frustrated, the ego suffers the resistance of the world and, out of greed, hate, and delusion, inflicts suffering on others. Ironically, the Buddha Dharma itself, as with any teaching, can be turned into just another object of dogmatic and even fanatic attachment, diverting us from the root of the problem: namely, a false conception of ourselves and our relation to the world. Therefore, the Buddha Way first of all requires a penetrating examination of the self.

Yet when one turns the light around to reflect on the deepest recesses of the self, what one ultimately finds is—nothing. There is no substantial ego-subject underlying our thoughts, feelings, and desires. But neither is this nothingness—or emptiness—a nihilistic void. Rather, the ungraspable no-thingness of the self is the very source of the open-minded, open-hearted, and creatively free activity of the true self. The true self is an open engagement with others. A thoroughgoing "learning of the self" thus paradoxically leads to a "forgetting of the self" as an independent and substantial ego-subject.

Dōgen speaks of this "forgetting" most radically in terms of his own enlightenment experience of "dropping off the body-mind" (*shinjin-datsuraku* 信心脱落). Note that Dōgen does not speak dualistically of freeing the mind from the body. In fact, he explicitly rejects the mind–body dualism of the so-called Senika heresy and speaks of the "oneness of body–mind" (*shinjin ichinyo* 身心一如) along with the nonduality of the "one mind" with the entire cosmos.[27] Insofar as we have identified ourselves with a dualistic and reified conception of the mind, however, along with the body this, too, must be shed.

[24] Note the terminological shift from "Buddha Dharma" to "Buddha Way" in the first section of the *Genjōkōan*. In Japan, the terms traditionally used for "Buddhism" (now *bukkyō* 仏教) were *buppō* (仏法, Buddha Dharma or Law, which refers to the Buddhist teachings or the truth indicated by those teachings) and *butsudō* (仏道, Buddha Way, which refers to the practice of the way of the Buddha).

[25] The very word "Zen" (Ch. *Chan* 禅) derives from the Sanskrit *dhyāna*, meaning meditation.

[26] Dōgen 1990b, 170; compare Dōgen 2002, 3.

[27] See Dōgen 2002, 21–23, and Dōgen 1994, 41–46. On the notion of "body–mind" in Dōgen, see Yuasa 1987, 111–123; Nagatomo 1992, 105–129; and Shaner 1985, 129–155.

Only through a radical experience of letting go of all reifications of and attachments to the mind as well as the body does one become open to the self-presentation of the myriad things of the world.

Yet this openness must be realized, and this realization is neither static nor simply passive. When Dōgen says that "things come forth and verify-in-practice the self" (elsewhere he even claims that "original practice inheres in the original face of each and every thing"[28]), he is countering the willful self-assertion of unenlightened human subjectivity by calling attention to the "objective side" of the "total dynamism" or "undivided activity" (*zenki* 全機) of a nondual experience of reality. He speaks of the *nonduality* of this experience as follows: "When you ride in a boat, body-and-mind, self-and-environs, subjectivity-and-objectivity are all together the undivided activity of the boat. The entire earth as well as the entire sky are the undivided activity of the boat."[29] For our part, in order to authentically participate in this nondual event—and hence to verify or realize this or that aspect of reality—we must not only liberate ourselves from a self-assertive fixation on our body–mind by letting it drop off; we must also spontaneously pick up the body–mind again in an energetic yet egoless "total exertion" (*gūjin* 究尽) of "rousing the [whole] body–mind to perceive forms, rousing the [whole] body–mind to listen to sounds."[30]

Let us pause for a moment to review the pivotal paradoxes involved in Dōgen's path of Zen. (1) Turning to and from ourselves: by way of initially turning the light of the mind away from (a deluded view of) external reality and back toward ourselves, we discover an emptiness at the heart of the self that opens us up to an enlightened experience of the myriad things of the world. (2) Utter detachment and total involvement: This process of enlightenment entails a radical "dropping off the body–mind" that leads, not to a state of mindless disembodiment, but rather to a holistic integration of the body–mind and its unattached yet wholehearted employment in nondual events of enlightening perception and understanding.

NONDUAL PERSPECTIVISM

The intimately engaged yet egoless perception and understanding that Dōgen speaks of are never shadowless illuminations of all aspects of a thing. The epistemology implied in Dōgen's understanding of enlightenment is plainly not that of simultaneous

---

[28] Dōgen 1990*a*, 1: 18; compare Dōgen 2002, 14.

[29] Dōgen 1990*a*, 2: 84; compare Dōgen 1999, 174.

[30] Dōgen 1990*a*, 1: 54; Davis 2009, 256; compare Dōgen 2002, 41. There are contrasting interpretations of this passage. Along with traditional scholars, I have interpreted this "rousing the [whole] body–mind to perceive and listen" in terms of enlightenment. Some recent scholars, however, have argued for reading it in terms of delusion (Ishii 1997, 235; Ueda 2002, 287–291).

omniscience.[31] Enlightenment does not entail the achievement of an instantaneous all-knowing view from nowhere, but rather the realization of being on an endless path of illuminating the innumerable aspects of reality, an ongoing journey of appreciating the "inexhaustible virtues" of things. Enlightenment is not a state of final escape to another world, but rather a never self-satisfied process of enlightening darkness and delusion within this world. Indeed, setting out on this never-ending Way of enlightenment entails awakening to the ineradicable play of knowledge and nescience. And thus, once again paradoxically, Dōgen tells us: "When the Dharma does not yet saturate the body-mind, one thinks that it is sufficient. If the Dharma fills the body-mind, one notices an insufficiency."[32]

Dōgen makes this epistemological point most clearly and forcefully in the section of *Genjōkōan* where he speaks of the inexhaustible aspects and virtues of the ocean.

> For example, if one rides in a boat out into the middle of the ocean where there are no mountains [in sight] and looks in the four directions, one will see only a circle without any other aspects in sight. Nevertheless, the great ocean is not circular, and it is not square; the remaining virtues of the ocean are inexhaustible. It is like a palace [for fish]. It is like a jeweled ornament [to gods]. It is just that, as far as my eyes can see, for a while it looks like a circle. It is also like this with the myriad things. Although things within and beyond this dusty world are replete with a variety of aspects, it is only through a cultivated power of vision that one can [intimately] perceive and apprehend them. In order to hear the household customs of the myriad things, you should know that, besides appearing as round or square, there are unlimited other virtues of the ocean and of the mountains, and there are worlds in all four directions. And you should know that it is not only like this over there, but also right here beneath your feet and even in a single drop [of water].[33]

When Dōgen speaks of a human being sitting on a boat in the middle of the ocean, looking out in all four directions and seeing only a vast empty circle, he is perhaps also speaking metaphorically of a meditative experience of emptiness. We might refer in this regard to the empty circle or "circular shape" (*ensō* 円相) that appears as the eighth of the *Ten Oxherding Pictures*,[34] which is often interpreted as a symbol for the absolute emptiness of the Dharmakāya (the Truth Body of the Buddha), or the Buddha-nature (*busshō* 仏性) understood—as Dōgen and other Zen masters sometimes do—in terms of *mu-busshō* (無仏性, "no-Buddha-nature" or the "Buddha-nature-of-Nothingness").[35]

---

[31] On Chinese Huayan and Zen perspectivism in relation to earlier Indian Buddhist doctrines of omniscience, see Davis 2018, 126–131. The early Daoist text *Zhuangzi* is a major influence on the development of Zen's perspectivism in China (see Davis forthcoming).

[32] Dōgen 1990a, 1: 57; Davis 2009, 257; compare Dōgen 2002, 43.

[33] Dōgen 1990a, 1: 57–58; Davis 2009, 258; compare Dōgen 2002, 43.

[34] See Yamada 2004; Davis 2022, chap. 24.

[35] See Dōgen 1990a, 1: 81–90; Dōgen 2002, 69–75.

In any case, what is crucial is that neither the *Ten Oxherding Pictures* nor Dōgen's Zen stops at the empty circle. It may be necessary to pass through an experience of emptiness as a "great negation" of the ego and its reifying attachments, and as the realization of absolute equality and equanimity. But even emptiness must not be grasped as a purportedly "perspectiveless perspective" in which one abides. In the all-embracing "one taste" of perfect equality, the differences between singular things are obscured. Here, too, "emptiness must empty itself" and allow for distinctions, such that true nonduality is a matter of "neither one nor two" (*fu-ichi fu-ni* 不一不二). The universal truth of emptiness is not an overarching perspective that negates, but rather a pervading principle that enables the interplay between unique yet interconnected beings. In its "suchness," each thing, person, animal, or event is neither an independent substance nor an indistinct portion of an undifferentiated totality: rather, it is a unique perspectival opening within the dynamically interweaving web of the world.

Hence, even though one may perceive the ocean (or world) as a vast empty circle, Dōgen goes on to write: "Nevertheless, the great ocean is not circular, and it is not square; the remaining virtues [or qualities] of the ocean are inexhaustible. It is like a palace [for fish]. It is like a jeweled ornament [to gods]. It is just that, as far as my eyes can see, for a while it looks like a circle." Dōgen is drawing here on the traditional Buddhist notion that different sentient beings experience the world in different manners, depending on the conditioning of their karma. He is likely alluding specifically to the following commentary on the *Mahāyāna-saṃgraha*: "The sea itself basically has no disparities, yet owing to the karmic differences of devas, humans, craving spirits, and fish, devas see it as a treasure trove of jewels, humans see it as water, craving spirits see it as an ocean of pus, and fish see it as a palatial dwelling."[36] Dōgen writes elsewhere that one "should not be limited to human views" and naively think that what you view as water is "what dragons and fish see as water and use as water."[37]

The epistemology implied in Dōgen's view of enlightenment as an ongoing practice of enlightening, as an unending path of discovery, is thus what I would call an engaged yet egoless, a pluralistic yet nondual perspectivism. It is a perspectivism insofar as it understands that reality only shows itself one aspect and focal point at a time. But while, on the one hand, in a deluded/deluding comportment to the world this aspect and focus get determined by the will of a self-fabricating ego that goes out and posits a horizon that delimits, filters, and schematizes how things can reveal themselves (namely, as objects set in front of a subject who represents and manipulates them), in an enlightened/enlightening comportment to the world, on the other hand, things are allowed to reveal themselves through nondual events in which the self has "forgotten itself" in its pure activity of egoless engagement. This engagement is neither simply passive nor simply active; for, originally, we are not detached ego-subjects who subsequently encounter (either passively or actively) independently subsisting objects. The original

---

[36] Quoted in Dōgen 2002, 43; see also Dōgen 1990*a*, 1: 440.
[37] Dōgen 1990*a*, 2: 198.

force at work in experience is neither "self-power" (*jiriki* 自力) nor "other-power" (*tariki* 他力). Rather, writes Dōgen, the "continuous practice" (*gyōji* 行持) one participates in is "pure action that is forced neither by oneself nor by others."[38] At every moment of enlightened/enlightening experience there is—for the time being—but a single nondual middle-voiced event of "being-time" (*uji* 有時)[39] as a self-revelation of a singular aspect of reality. Enlightenment is a matter of realizing that the world is in truth made up of such nondual self-revelatory events. And just as these interconnected yet unique events are infinite, so is the path of their verification-in-practice.

Bibliography and Suggested Readings

Abe, Masao. (1992) *A Study of Dōgen: His Philosophy and Religion,* edited by Steven Heine. Albany: State University of New York Press.

Bein, Steve. (2011) *Purifying Zen: Watsuji Tetsurō's Shamon Dogen.* Honolulu: University of Hawai'i Press.

Chang, Garma C. C. (1971) *The Buddhist Teaching of Totality: The Philosophy of Hwa Yen Buddhism.* University Park: The Pennsylvania State University Press.

Cook, Francis H. (1977) *Hua-yen Buddhism: The Jewel Net of Indra.* University Park: The Pennsylvania State University Press.

Cook, Francis H. (1989) *Sounds of Valley Streams: Enlightenment in Dōgen's Zen.* Albany: State University of New York Press.

Cook, Francis H. (2002) *How to Raise an Ox: Zen Practice as Taught in Zen Master Dogen's Shobogenzo.* Somerville, MA: Wisdom Publications.

Davis, Bret W. (2009) "The Presencing of Truth: Dōgen's *Genjōkōan*." In *Buddhist Philosophy: Essential Readings,* edited by William Edelglass and Jay L. Garfield. Oxford: Oxford University Press, 251–259.

Davis, Bret W. (2013) "Forms of Emptiness in Zen." In *A Companion to Buddhist Philosophy,* edited by Steven Emmanuel. West Sussex: Wiley-Blackwell, 190–213.

Davis, Bret W. (2016) "The Enlightening Practice of Nonthinking: Unfolding Dōgen's *Fukanzazengi*." In *Engaging Dōgen's Zen: The Philosophy of Practice as Awakening,* edited by Tetsuzen Jason M. Wirth, Shūdō Brian Schroeder, and Kanpū Bret W. Davis. Somerville, MA: Wisdom Publications, 199–224.

Davis, Bret W. (2018) "Zen's Nonegocentric Perspectivism." In *Buddhist Philosophy: A Comparative Approach,* edited by Steven M. Emmanuel. West Sussex: Wiley-Blackwell, 123–143.

Davis, Bret W. (2019a) "Expressing Experience: Language in Ueda Shizuteru's Philosophy of Zen." In *Dao Companion to Japanese Buddhist Philosophy,* edited by Gereon Kopf. New York: Springer Publishing, 713–38.

Davis, Bret W. (2019b) "Knowing Limits: Toward a Versatile Perspectivism with Nietzsche, Heidegger, Zhuangzi and Zen." *Research in Phenomenology* 49/3: 301–334.

Davis, Bret W. (2022) *Zen Pathways: An Introduction to the Philosophy and Practice of Zen Buddhism.* New York: Oxford University Press.

Dōgen. (1985) *Flowers of Emptiness: Selections from Dōgen's Shōbōgenzō,* translated by Hee-Jin Kim. Lewiston, ME: Edwin Mellen Press.

---

[38] Dōgen 1990a, 1: 297; compare Dōgen 1999, 114.

[39] In the *Uji* fascicle (Dōgen 1990a, 2: 46–58; Dōgen 2002, 48–58), Dōgen famously reads the compound *uji*, not simply as "for the time being," but as a nondual event of "being-time." On this philosophically impactful aspect of his thought, see Heine 1985; Stambaugh 1990; and Elberfeld 2004.

Dōgen. (1985) *Flowers of Emptiness: Selections from Dōgen's Shōbōgenzō*, translated by Hee-Jin Kim. Lewiston, ME: Edwin Mellen Press.

Dōgen. (1990a) *Shōbōgenzō* [Treasury of the True Dharma Eye], edited by Mizuno Yaoko. 4 vols. Tokyo: Iwanami.

Dōgen. (1990b) *Dōgen Zenji goroku* [Recorded Words of Zen Master Dōgen], edited by Kagamishima Genryū. Tokyo: Kōdansha.

Dōgen. (1992) *Rational Zen: The Mind of Dōgen Zenji*. Boston: Shambhala.

Dōgen. (1995) *Moon in a Dewdrop: Writings of Zen Master Dogen*, edited by Kazuaki Tanahashi. New York: North Point Press.

Dōgen. (1999) *Enlightenment Unfolds: The Essential Teachings of Zen Master Dōgen*, edited by Kazuaki Tanahashi. Boston: Shambhala.

Dōgen. (2002) *The Heart of Dōgen's Shōbōgenzō*, translated by Norman Waddell and Masao Abe. Albany: State University of New York Press.

Dōgen. (2004) *Dōgen's Extensive Record: A Translation of the Eihei Kōroku*, translated by Taigen Dan Leighton and Shohaku Okumura. Boston: Wisdom.

Dōgen. (2007–2008) *Shōbōgenzō: The True Dharma-Eye Treasury*. 4 vols. translated by Gudo Wafu Nishijima and Chodo Cross. Berkeley, CA: Numata Center for Buddhist Translation and Research.

Dōgen. (2012) *Treasury of the True Dharma Eye: Zen Master Dogen's Shobo Genzo*, edited by Kazuaki Tanahashi. Boston: Shambhala.

Elberfeld, Rolf. (2004) *Phänomenologie der Zeit im Buddhismus*. Stuttgart: Frommann Holzboog.

Garfield, Jay. (1995) *Fundamental Wisdom of the Middle Way: Nāgārjuna's Mūlamadhyamakakārikā*. New York: Oxford University Press.

Heine, Steven. (1985) *Existential and Ontological Dimensions of Time in Heidegger and Dōgen*. Albany: State University of New York Press.

Heine, Steven. (1994) *Dōgen and the Kōan Tradition: A Tale of Two Shōbōgenzō*. Albany: State University of New York Press.

Heine, Steven. (2012) "What Is on the Other Side? Delusion and Realization in Dōgen's 'Genjōkōan.'" In *Dōgen: Textual and Historical Studies*, edited by Steven Heine. New York: Oxford University Press, 42–74.

Ishii Seijun. (1997) "Shōbōgenzō 'Genjōkōan' no maki no shudai ni tsuite" [On the Main Theme of the *Genjōkōan* Chapter of *Shōbōgenzō*]. *Komazawa Daigaku Bukkyō Gakuburonshū* 28: 225–239.

Kasulis T. P. (1981) *Zen Action/Zen Person*. Honolulu: University of Hawai'i Press.

Kim, Hee-Jin. (2004) *Dōgen: Mystical Realist*. Boston: Wisdom.

Kim, Hee-Jin. (2007) *Dōgen on Meditation and Thinking: A Reflection on His View of Zen*. Albany: State University of New York Press.

Kopf, Gereon. (2002) *Beyond Personal Identity: Dōgen, Nishida and a Phenomenology of No-Self*. Richmond, UK: Routledge.

Kurebayashi Kōdō. (1992) *Genjōkōan o kataru: Ima o ikiru Shōbōgenzō kōsan* [Talks on the *Genjōkōan*: Lectures on the *Shōbōgenzō* for Living in the Present]. Tokyo: Daihōrinkan.

LaFleur, William R., ed. (1985) *Dōgen Studies*. Honolulu: University of Hawai'i Press.

Lopez, Donald S., Jr. (1988) *The Heart Sūtra Explained*. Albany: State University of New York Press.

Matsumoto Shirō. (2000) *Dōgen shisōron* [On Dōgen's Thought]. Tokyo: Daizō Shuppan.

Nagatomo, Shigenori. (1992) *Attunement Through the Body*. Albany: State University of New York Press.

Nhat Hanh, Thich. (1988). *The Heart of Understanding: Commentaries on the Prajñaparamita Heart Sutra*. Berkeley, CA: Parallax Press.

Nishiari Bokusan. (1965) *Shōbōgenzō keiteki* [*Shōbōgenzō*: Right to the Point]. Tokyo: Daihōrinkaku.

Nishiari Bokusan. (2011) "Commentary on the Genjo Koan," translated by Sojun Mel Weitsman and Kazuaki Tanahashi. In *Dōgen's Genjo Koan: Three Commentaries*, edited by Nishiari et al. Berkeley, CA: Counterpoint, 11–90.

Nishiari Bokusan et al. (2011) *Dōgen's Genjo Koan: Three Commentaries*. Berkeley, CA: Counterpoint.

Ōhashi, Ryōsuke and Rolf Elberfeld. (2006) *Dōgen Shōbōgenzō: Ausgewählte Schriften*. Tokyo: Keio University Press.

Okumura, Shohaku. (2010) *Realizing Genjokoan: The Key to Dogen's Shobogenzo*. Boston: Wisdom Publications.

Shaner, David Edward. (1985) *The Bodymind Experience in Japanese Buddhism: A Phenomenological Study of Kūkai and Dōgen*. Albany: State University of New York Press.

Stambaugh, Joan. (1990) *Impermanence Is Buddha-Nature: Dōgen's Understanding of Temporality*. Honolulu: University of Hawai'i Press.

Steineck, Christian et al., eds. (2002) *Dōgen als Philosoph*. Wiesbaden: Harrassowitz Verlag.

Swanson, Paul. (1995) *Foundations of T'ien-T'ai Philosophy: The Flowering of the Two Truths Theory in Chinese Buddhism*. Berkeley, CA: Asian Humanities Press.

Tanabe Hajime (1963) "*Shōbōgenzō* no tetsugaku shikan" [My Philosophical Perspective on the *Shōbōgenzō*]. In *Tanabe Hajime zenshū* [Complete Works of Tanabe Hajime]. Tokyo: Chikuma, vol. 5, pp. 443–494.

Ueda Shizuteru. (2002) "'Genjōkōan' to shizen" [Genjōkōan and Nature]. In *Ueda Shizuteru shū* [Ueda Shizuteru Collection]. Tokyo: Iwanami, 9: 239–294.

Watsuji Tetsurō. (2011) *Shamon Dōgen*, translated by Steve Bein. In *Purifying Zen: Watsuji Tetsurō's Shamon Dogen*. Honolulu: University of Hawai'i Press, 25–117.

Wirth, Tetsuzen Jason M., Shūdō Brian Schroeder, and Kanpū Bret W. Davis, eds. (2016) *Engaging Dōgen's Zen: The Philosophy of Practice as Awakening*. Somerville, MA: Wisdom Publications.

Yamada, Mumon. (2004) *Lectures on the Ten Oxherding Pictures*, translated by Victor Sōgen Hori. Honolulu: University of Hawai'i Press.

Yasutani, Hakuun. (1996) *Flowers Fall: A Commentary on Zen Master Dōgen's Genjōkōan*, translated by Paul Jaffe. Boston: Shambhala.

Yoshizu Yoshihide. (1993) "Ippō o shō suru toki ha ippō wa kurashi' no ikku no kaishaku ni tsuite" [On Interpreting the Phrase, "When verifying one side, the other side is obscured"]. *Shūgaku kenkyū* 35: 12–17.

Yuasa, Yasuo. (1987) *The Body: Toward an Eastern Mind–Body Theory*, translated by Nagatomo Shigenori and T. P. Kasulis. Albany: State University of New York Press.

CHAPTER 9

....

DŌGEN ON THE LANGUAGE
OF CREATIVE TEXTUAL
HERMENEUTICS

....

STEVEN HEINE

PERHAPS the most useful and thought-provoking analysis of Dōgen's philosophy of language produced in Western scholarship remains one of the earliest essays on the topic, written by Hee-Jin Kim, "The Reason of Words and Letters: Dōgen and Kōan Language." This article was originally delivered as a lecture in the early 1980s, and it was published a few years later in a conference volume edited by William LaFleur.[1] Kim, who was already well known at the time for pioneering the field of Dōgen studies in the West with a monograph comprehensively covering Dōgen's life and thought released a decade earlier,[2] was particularly inspired by a seminal study in Japanese of the Zen master's method of appropriating passages from Chinese Chan-recorded sayings texts in addition to Mahāyāna sutras. Kagamishima Genryū, the leading specialist in research on Dōgen during the post-World War II period in Japan, published that work in 1965.[3]

By carefully examining various examples from Dōgen's major collection of epistles and sermons dealing with Chan prose and poetic comments on kōans, the *Shōbōgenzō* (*Treasury of the True Dharma Eye*) that was composed over a twenty-year period from the early 1230s when he opened his first temple in Kyoto to the end of his career in the early 1250s when he resided at Eiheiji Temple in the Echizen mountains, Kim demonstrates various ways that Dōgen creatively uses language to disclose the dharma. In his interpretations, written in the vernacular Japanese of Kamakura-era Japan, of kōan cases reflecting the puzzling and paradoxical repartee and philosophical games of one-upmanship evoked by Song-dynasty Chinese masters, Dōgen exhibits a kind of alchemical capacity to alter literature significantly by twisting and even distorting

[1] Kim, 1985.
[2] Kim, 1975.
[3] Kagamishima, 1965.

conventional expressions in order to uncover the underlying theoretical significance embedded in speech acts.

By refashioning words and phrases from Chinese sources through drawing out philosophical puns and wordplay based on Japanese syntax and pronunciations, Dōgen adopts an expansive view of the role of language in the quest for enlightenment. This was quite different from or even opposed to the mainstream approach to Zen meditation in Song China that stressed a minimalist use of words in deference to the powerful significance of silence. Kim suggests that, as "a superb master of language, appreciating it not for its rhetorical use-value, but rather for its appeal to reason and rationality" because "the interior and exterior of language were the very fabric of existence," Dōgen is able to "change word order, shift syntax, indicate alternate meanings, create new expressions, and revive forgotten symbols."[4]

I wholeheartedly agree, and I wish to apply and extend the core of Kim's theory to highlight that Dōgen uses language as coterminous with, instead of as a means—or, contrariwise, an obstacle—to the realization of Zen enlightenment, which represented the more typical approaches to the role of discourse. This method of magnifying the impact of rhetorical eloquence does not at all reflect what Heidegger has referred to as the inauthentic mode of "idle chatter" or speaking a great deal without revealing very much. Nor is the approach a matter of moving rhetorically in arbitrary and chaotic directions without an underlying conceptual plan or pattern.

Rather, by drawing from Chinese literary styles and motifs contained in the first great kōan collection published in 1128, the *Biyanlu* (Jp. *Hekiganroku, Blue Cliff Record* 碧巖 錄), Dōgen is in accord with the Chan notion of "live words," which are compelling and fulfilling in their intricacy, as opposed to "dead words," which are merely descriptive in a way that leaves little to the imagination. Dōgen's approach also recalls classic Daoist philosopher's Zhuangzi's notion of ever-resourceful "goblet words," or the words of no-words in that their meaning is not fixed but fluid and flexible. This linguistic function allows one to communicate endlessly and productively without having exhausted the topic through simultaneously constructing and deconstructing multiple perspectives unconstrained by attachment or partiality. As Zhuangzi has said, "I wish to meet someone who has forgotten words, so that I might have a word with that person!"

CONTEXTUALIZING DŌGEN'S APPROACH TO LANGUAGE

In this chapter, I first discuss the intellectual historical context of Chan/Zen Buddhist debates regarding the appropriate uses of language in twelfth- and thirteenth-century China and Japan that helped shape the formation of Dōgen's philosophy. Then, I focus

---

[4] Kim, 1985, 79.

on a case study of Dōgen's innovative way of dealing with the so-called Mu Kōan, in which master Zhaozhou responds to a query from an anonymous monk about whether a dog possesses the universal spirituality of the Buddha-nature. Although the mainstream approach cites the version of the case in which Zhaozhou simply answers *Mu* (Ch. *Wu* 無, literally "No") to emphasize the truth of absolute nothingness beyond speech and logic, in the "Buddha-nature" ("Busshō") fascicle of the *Shōbōgenzō*, Dōgen cites an alternate version of the kōan in which the answer is both *Mu* and *U* (Ch. *You* 有, literally "Yes"). Each of the responses in this version, also featured in the kōan collection the *Congronglu* (Jp. *Shōyōroku* 從容録, *Record of Serenity*) of 1224, has a quixotic follow-up dialogue between Zhaozhou and the perplexed novice. This is done to emphasize a relativist view of reality characterized by the interplay of truth and untruth that innovatively explores various meanings of *Mu* in relation to absence, nihility, and denial by displaying the contingency of nonbeing and being or negation and affirmation.

However, I suggest a modification of Kim's analysis that stresses the role of "reason," by which he refers to the term *dōri* (道理, literally, "logic of the way"). According to Kim, "Dōgen reveals himself to be exceedingly conscious of language, and in this respect, astonishingly modern. And yet, despite the evidence of a deliberate rhetorical component in his writing, his foremost concern is ultimately rational rather than rhetorical; he believes that reason, not eloquence, is paramount for the attainment of the way."[5] In forcing Dōgen into the mold of modernization while apparently seeking to contradict the view of D. T. Suzuki, who famously argued that Zen discourse is fundamentally irrational,[6] Kim seems to skew the point that Dōgen is first and foremost an inventive transmitter/interpreter of Chan texts, including kōan, recorded sayings, and transmission of the lamp collections compiled during the Song dynasty.

In the vernacular writings of the *Shōbōgenzō* and the Sino-Japanese (*kanbun* 漢文) writings of the *Eihei kōroku* (*Dōgen's Extensive Record*), Dōgen's approach, I maintain, is not necessarily rational. Instead, it is preferable to see Dōgen performing the creative hermeneutic function of offering the interconnected elements of exegesis, in transmitting and explicating Chinese sources for a Japanese audience, and eisogesis, by incorporating his distinctive vision of the inner meaning of these passages. Through integrating the objective and impersonal component of exegesis with the subjective and personal component of eisogesis, while operating at the intellectual historical crossroads of Song Chinese and Kamakura Japanese forms of expressiveness, Dōgen further takes license to intrude upon and imaginatively change and transform the original words so as to capture multiple rhetorical elements that disclose the source passage's implications and significance.

---

[5] Kim, 1985, 56.
[6] C. Lawson, Crowe, "On the 'Irrationality of Zen,'" *Philosophy East and West* 15, 1(1965): 31–36.

DŌGEN'S EXPANSIVIST OUTLOOK

When Dōgen arrived in China in 1223, at the beginning of a pilgrimage that would last four years before he returned to spread the dharma of the Sōtō (Ch. Caodong) sect to his native land, he encountered two main, very much opposed philosophical outlooks regarding the role of language. One was the expansionist approach found in the *Biyanlu*, produced by master Yuanwu and based on the notion that language consists of entangled vines or *kattō* (Ch. *geteng* 葛藤), which reveal reality through the process of unraveling and disentangling their inner complexity. The other was the reductionist approach endorsed by Yuanwu's foremost but contentious disciple Dahui (who was said to have burned the xylographs of his mentor's kōan collection) and based on the notion that language should be reduced to minimal catchphrases or *watō* (Ch. *huatou* 話頭) that convey absolute nothingness and silence. The term *Mu* in the case about the dog's Buddha-nature was the primary example of the catchphrase outlook.

The *kattō* outlook was refined and transformed by Dōgen, who injected into his commentaries on kōans innovative rhetorical styles, including extended textual hermeneutics based on explicating Japanese elocutions of Chinese terms. Dōgen strongly disagrees with Dahui by stressing in the "Entangling Vines" ("Kattō") fascicle of the *Shōbōgenzō* that language should be continually explored as a process of "disentangling vines through the intricate play of entangled vines."[7] Rather than stressing the response of "No" as supreme, in a *Eihei kōroku* sermon he argues, "Whether you say 'Yes' or 'No,' either one is slander. If the person were to ask 'What?,' at the very moment of his speaking he would be hit with my stick."[8]

Dōgen's approach is based on the view that each and every aspect of the universe in its daily activity preaches the dharma verbally or nonverbally, and, in the "Mountains and Rivers Sutras" ("Sansuikyō") fascicle he maintains, "mountains and rivers themselves are the sound of the sutras." His interpretative stance is a deliberately meandering scenic-route that seems to be striving for a middle way between sacramentalism and iconoclasm, metaphor and criticism, or mythos and logos. Dōgen maintains the necessity of perpetually "expressing the Way" (*dōtoku* 道得) through "disclosing mind/disclosing nature" (*sesshin sesshō* 説心説性), and he consistently affirms rather than denies the efficacy of all forms of discourse, including anecdotes, parables, metaphors, and logical analysis, as essential means of revealing the experience of enlightenment. In "Explaining a Dream Within a Dream" ("Muchūsetsumu"), he suggests that metaphorical words are

---

[7] Dōgen is known for his scathing critique of Dahui in the "Self-Fulfilling Samadhi" ("Jishō zammai") fascicle, where he goes so far as to question Dahui's enlightenment, and elsewhere, especially "Disclosing Mind, Disclosing Nature" ("Sesshin sesshō"); but he also occasionally praises the Chinese master for his dedication and perseverance and apparently borrows the title of *Shōbōgenzō* (Ch. *Zhengfayanzang*) from one of his kōan collections of 661 cases.

[8] *Dōgen zenji zenshū*, 3: 214; *Dōgen's Extensive Record*, 301.

not merely "figures of speech" (*hiyu* 比喩), but are also the "true form of reality" (*shohō jissō* 諸法實相).

Dōgen's expansionist approach is expressed in *Eihei kōroku* 2.128, where he cites a story in which Danxia, an important monk in the Caodong lineage, points out that master Deshan, from whom the Yunmen and Fayan lineages were descended, said to his assembly, "There are no words or phrases in my school, and also not a single Dharma to offer to people."[9] Danxia comments, "He was endowed with only one single eye . . . [but] in my school there are words and phrases (*goku*) . . . . The mysterious, profound, wondrous meaning is that the jade woman becomes pregnant in the night." According to Dōgen, this saying did not go far enough because, "Although Danxia spoke in this way . . . (i)n my school *there are only words and phrases* (*yui goku* 唯語句) [emphasis added]." He thereby supports the unity of Zen and language that is expressed with a more sustained although partisan argumentation in "Mountains and Rivers Sutras" and elsewhere.

The interpretative approach of the *Shōbōgenzō* is dependent on but distinct from various kinds of Song Chinese Chan writings. To consider briefly the considerable literary connections, the texts that first appeared in the eleventh century in China—especially transmission of the lamp histories and recorded sayings—contain hagiographical elements borrowed from other kinds of Chinese Buddhist collections treating the lives of eminent monks by focusing on the ineffable truth embodied by the charismatic personality of a great master who carefully initiates a chosen successor.[10] The *Biyanlu* and other kōan compilations are centered on interpreting a number of traditional cases, which are usually encounter dialogues culled from one of the previously developed genres, to which are added extensive prose and verse commentaries alluding to related anecdotes, parables, and legends. A feature shared by Dōgen's *Shōbōgenzō* and the major kōan collections is an emphasis on admonishing disciples against the traps and pitfalls of misinterpreting cases through a faulty appropriation of silence, leading either to an overabundance or a paucity of interpretative discourse.

Unlike the multilayered style of Song commentaries that interpret a particular core dialogue surrounded by prose and verse comments, in addition to the hybrid prose-poetic capping phrase (*jakugo* 著語) remarks, the literary structure of the *Shōbōgenzō* revolves around doctrinal themes for which various cases and related sayings are summoned as part of the remarks on the main topic. Nearly every fascicle sets up a key Mahāyāna or Zen notion of philosophy or practice and uses various kōan cases and sutra passages, which are generally overlooked by Chan collections that see themselves as outside the scriptures, as sources for elaborating on the meaning and significance of doctrine. Thus, the dialogue that constitutes the core literary unit of a kōan record around which comments revolve is subsidiary in Dōgen's novel and inventive interpretative standpoint, referred to here as the "hermeneutics of intrusion." In contrast to the

---

[9] *Dōgen zenji zenshū*, 3: 72–74; *Dōgen's Extensive Record*, 155.

[10] See John R. McRae, *The Northern School and the Formation of Early Ch'an Buddhism* (Honolulu: University of Hawai'i Press, 1986), 73–100.

Biyanlu, Dōgen does not use capping phrase comments in "Buddha-nature" because he developed other innovative ways of commenting on kōan records in the *Shōbōgenzō*.[11]

In addition to its highly refined literary quality borrowed, in part, from Japanese rhetorical techniques, Dōgen's writings reflect some degree of influence from Abhidharma or sastra literature in its use of line-by-line analysis exploring some of the metaphysical and psychological implications of doctrine. The fluidity and open-endedness of Dōgen's informal sermons, originally delivered to a small ring of disciples and later edited and published, makes the text less conservative in structure than the major kōan collections in that it allows for or even demands taking license with tradition in accord with the spirit and intention of the Tang-dynasty Chan masters' original (supposedly) spontaneous and irreverent utterances.

MULTIPLE CITATIONS OF THE MU KŌAN

Although Dōgen is best known for commenting on the Mu Kōan in the "Buddha-nature" fascicle, in which he examines the notion of universal spirituality in relation to negation and nothingness from nearly every imaginable angle, throughout his collected works, he actually uses a couple of different renditions of the case with various interpretations. These include those favored by Dahui and additional variations. Table 9.1 shows the seven instances of Dōgen's references to the kōan by listing the text and its date of composition, along with a brief overview of which version and type of comment is included.

Note that Dōgen does cite the Mu-only response on two occasions—the first and sixth—but the latter example contains the follow-up dialogue that is found in Zhaozhou's recorded sayings. When referring to the version with both *Mu* and *U* responses, he is somewhat inconsistent regarding the sequence of the positive and negative replies, as well as whether or not the complete or partial version is cited.[12]

As the longest and most complex fascicle in the *Shōbōgenzō* and the one with the most sustained and consistent argumentation concerning a single doctrinal topic (although, like most other fascicles, it does not have a systematic sequential organization), "Buddha-nature" offers a vivid demonstration of constructive and deconstructive rhetorical elements. Whereas Dahui further contracts the abbreviated version of the kōan in order to highlight the power of doubt generated by the *watō* consisting of the single syllable Mu, Dōgen's *kattō*-based approach emphasizes the power of disclosure so as to intrude upon and alter the multiple meanings and implications of the relativist version.

---

[11] In fact, this interpretative style is limited in Dōgen's corpus to just a small handful of the Sino-Japanese (*kanbun*) sermons in the *Eihei kōroku*.

[12] See Kagamishima Genryū, et. al., ed., *Dōgen no in'yō goroku no kenkyū* [Studies of Dōgen's Citations of Recorded Sayings] (Tokyo: Sōtōshū shūgaku kenkyūsho, 1995), 282–284; this work is a revised and expanded version of sections of Kagamishima, 1965.

Table 9.1. Dōgen's Citations of the Mu Kōan

Text by Year	How Case Is Cited
1. Gakudōyōjinshū (1234)	Mu response only, which "cannot be grasped"
2. Mana Shōbōgenzō (1235)	Mu and U full dialogues, basis for "Busshō" version
3. Eihei Kōroku 9.73 (1236)	U and Mu full dialogues, with two verse comments
4. Shōbōgenzō "Busshō" (1241)	Mu and U full dialogues, with interlinear commentary
5. Eihei Kōroku 3.226 (1247)	U and Mu abbreviated, with brief prose comment
6. Eihei Kōroku 4.330 (1249)	Mu only and dialogue, with brief prose comment
7. Eihei Kōroku 6.429 (1251)	Mu and U alluded, with verse comment

Dōgen rethinks and rewrites the case along with other anecdotes and dialogues through a dazzling display of inventive reversals, ingenious puns, and dialectical formulas, which thereby disallows a reader from being trapped or limited to a fixed position. In the end, there is no distinction between right and wrong, winner and loser; or, rather, everyone who scores a triumph also suffers defeat and vice-versa.

While emphasizing the parity of affirmation and negation, Dōgen does not overlook the critical and subversive aspect of language whose foundation is the insubstantiality of nothingness or no-Buddha-nature (*mu-busshō* 無佛性), a notion he prefers to the denial of Buddha-nature (*busshō-mu* 佛性無) or the termination of discussion in regard to the implications of doctrine. Yet, each time Dōgen speaks of the merits of *Mu*, he quickly reverses himself and relativizes this standpoint through an emphasis on *U*. Therefore, by the time he deals with the Mu Kōan in the thirteenth (or penultimate) section of the "Buddha-nature" fascicle, he has already extensively commented upon and defused various misconceptions, an effort that serves as a crucial basis for his way of interpreting the Zhaozhou dialogue. Viewing the case record as part of a rich textual tradition is diametrically opposed to Dahui, who insists on extricating *Mu* from any sort of conceptual context that might represent a deadly distraction.

It is clear that Dōgen enjoyed a special relationship with Zhaozhou's works, including several dialogues that are not included in the canonical version of the Tang master's recorded sayings and that Dōgen cites several dozen times: the *Sanbyakusoku Shōbōgenzō* (*300-Case Treasury of the True Dharma-Eye*) has nearly two dozen examples of citations, the *Shōbōgenzō* features Zhaozhou's dialogues in at least fourteen fascicles,[13] and the *Eihei kōroku* also contains numerous references throughout the collection. The last section of "Entangling Vines" evokes Zhaozhou as a precursor for embracing the notion of

[13] Dōgen cites Zhaozhou extensively in the following fourteen fascicles as included according to the numbering scheme in the seventy-five-fascicle version of the *Treasury of the True Dharma-Eye*: 3 "Buddha-nature" ("Busshō"); 9 "Ancient Buddha-mind" ("Kobusshin"); 16 "Sustained Exertion" ("Gyōji"); 28 "Praying and Gaining the Marrow" ("Raihaitokuzui"); 30 "Reading the Sutras" ("Kankin");

literary embellishment. Of a famous dialogue in which Bodhidharma tries to choose a successor by requesting that each of his four main disciples demonstrate his or her (one was a nun) knowledge of Zen enlightenment, the typical view is that the monk who remains silent, Huike, has the deepest understanding because he is anointed the second ancestor. Like Dōgen, however, Zhaozhou finds truth as well as untruth embedded in every one of the four responses without an evaluative ladder being presumed. Instead of seeing a hierarchy leading from the use of metaphor reflecting skin as the most superficial element through the flesh and bones of indirect communication as somewhat deeper, and ultimately to the marrow of reticence, which is profoundly true and ultimately real, the Tang Chinese and Kamakura Japanese masters agree that trainees must realize that if they "do not get the skin" they will also not get the marrow, but, at the same time, getting the marrow requires not abandoning the skin.[14]

DŌGEN'S HERMENEUTICS OF INTRUSION IN "BUDDHA-NATURE"

The groundwork is thus laid for Dōgen's hermeneutics of intrusion, which represents a transgressive discourse aimed at transcending stale interpretations by transmitting the essential ingredients underlying diverse standpoints through employing the following interpretative elements: understanding the comprehensive scope of citations; atomizing key passages; introducing multiperspectival standpoints; creating inversions of ordinary meaning; and developing imaginative ways of encroaching on the conceptual space of source dialogues. After offering a sweep of Mahāyāna Buddhist and Zen approaches regarding the topic of Buddha-nature, along with a detailed investigation of particular phrasings coupled with a variety of views of negation that foster discursive reversals, Dōgen takes license to rework the exchanges themselves. He modifies the core conversations by making suggestions and countersuggestions in the spirit of a Tang-dynasty Chan master's irreverent creativity, aimed at enhancing the contemporaneous significance of the case for disciples who were at the time in training under his tutelage.[15]

---

33 "Expressing the Way" ("Dōtoku"); 38 "Entangling Vines" ("Kattō"); 40 "Cypress Tree" ("Hakujushi"); 41 "Triple World Is Mind-Only" ("Sangai yuishin"); 56 "Seeing Buddha" ("Kenbutsu"); 59 "Everyday Life" ("Kajō"); 60 "Thirty-seven Methods of Realization" ("Sanjūshichihon bodai bunpō"); 73 "Reading Other's Minds" ("Tajintsū"); and 74 "A King Requests Saindhava" ("Ōsaku sendaba"). Other masters frequently cited by Dōgen include Bodhidharma, Dongshan, Huike, Huineng, Linji, Mazu, Nanyue, and Yuanwu, in addition to Sakyamuni and Mahakasyapa, as well as predecessors Hongzhi and Rujing, who receives by far the greatest number of citations.

14 *Dōgen zenji zenshū*, 1: 420.

15 Some of this argument is included in *Like Cats and Dogs: Contesting the Mu Kōan in Zen Buddhism* (New York: Oxford University Press, 2013).

Comprehensive Scope

The comprehensive scope of the "Buddha-nature" fascicle refers to the abundance of citations, references, and allusions developed from the Chan Buddhist canon filtered through Dōgen's own reflections and speculation. Dōgen functions as a textual historian or a one-man fountain of knowledge who disseminates Chan literature, which is turned upside down and pulled inside out by the remaining hermeneutic elements. Dōgen examines more than a dozen dialogues concerning causality, temporality, language, life-and-death, illusion, and practice in regard to the notion of universal spirituality. Beginning with the famous opening passage in which he twists on its head the *Nirvāṇa Sutra* passage implying that Buddha-nature is a possession that one "has" (U) by showing that the kanji 有, like 無, has a double meaning and can also suggest that one "is" or, more holistically, indicates "*being*-Buddha-nature," Dōgen refutes numerous fallacies. He repudiates views that hypostatize Buddha-nature either as an objectifiable entity or supramundane perfection, a teleological goal or a prior possession, a phenomenon evolving in time or a realm that is beginningless and eternal, and a reality beyond illusion or an idealistic projection.

These delusions tend to either identify truth with the ordinary world or presuppose a realm beyond concrete existence, thereby violating the middle path. Dōgen seeks to subvert and surpass delusions that are based on a false sense of duality with positive notions encompassing a unity of opposites. These notions include *shitsuu* ("whole-being" 悉有), which overcomes the conflict between anthropocentrism and otherworldliness by integrating all entities, whether human or nonhuman, sentient or insentient into a unified reality; *shingen* ("manifesting body" 真現), which overcomes the opposition of cosmology and substantiality by suggesting that the truth is ever manifest through concrete particularities that are fundamentally contingent and variable yet disclosive of the whole; and *gyō* ("activity" 行), which surpasses teleology versus potentiality by eliminating the sense of past and future or, rather, by fusing the three tenses of time into the dynamic present moment of one's everyday effort to practice the spiritual path that links background or intentions with goals or purpose.

Additional philosophically innovative notions used by Dōgen to upend delusions derived from polarities include *setsu* ("symbolic disclosure" 説), which overcomes ineffability versus reason by highlighting the ways that each and every form of verbal and nonverbal expression, whether or not it reflects a fully enlightened state, conveys at least partially the diverse perspectives and meanings of Buddha-nature; *mujō* ("impermanence" 無常), which surpasses time versus eternity by indicating that evanescent temporality is not lacking but, in its fleeting manifestations, captures the fullness of reality or "eternal now" encompassing anticipation and arrival; *i* ("dependence" 衣), which overcomes causation versus liberation by suggesting that all interconnected beings are able to attain freedom by virtue of the web of mutual conditioning that makes them inseparable; and *gabyō* ("painted rice-cake" 画餅), which surpasses the conflict between reality and illusion by asserting that ideas and impressions generated by the imagination are, when appropriately understood, just as viable and powerful as seemingly actual things that in their own way may well be illusory or less than real.

Atomization

Through the atomization of words and phrases made in his interlinear comments, Dōgen also serves as a linguist/grammarian/philologist and poet who zeroes in on particular passages with a rhetorical flair and razor-sharp analytic precision that reflects his crucial role at the historical juncture of transforming Song Chan texts through the incorporation of Kamakura Japanese pronunciations as well as indigenous literary devices and related forms of expression. The primary theme that emerges underlying various repudiations and revisions is the fundamental issue of the nothingness of Buddha-nature. Of the fourteen sections in the fascicle, more than half deal directly with this topic, including the commentary on the Mu Kōan. In laying the basis for examining the dog dialogue, Dōgen develops a detailed focus on diverse meanings of *Mu*, embracing while sublating the notions of denial, negation, nonexistence, nihility, and emptiness in terms of the direct and immediate yet continuing experience of no-Buddha-nature.

Mu is one of the multiple ways of expressing the notion of no-Buddha-nature, which must not be absolutized in the sense of becoming one more reified metaphysical notion or an abstraction that is static and fixed; instead, it is to be perpetually explored through considering alternative perspectives and associated views of negation that, Dōgen says, cause a "reverberating echo circulating through Zhaozhou." Citing several early Chan leaders, he argues, "The words, 'no [or: nothingness] Buddha nature (*mu busshō*),' are discussed far beyond the ancestral chamber of the Fourth Ancestor. They originated in Huangmei, circulated to Zhaozhou, and were taken up in Dayi [Guishan]. You must unfailingly concentrate on the words 'no Buddha nature' "[16]

In his analysis of several dialogues that took place between the fourth and fifth Chan patriarchs, Dōgen maintains that the nothingness of no-Buddha-nature is the primary concern pervading Zhaozhou's *Mu*, which is not a matter of denial, in that emptiness is the foundation of expressing no. On the other hand, no-Buddha-nature does not merely represent an ironic confirmation because the categories of affirmation and negation must be subverted and broken through. In hearing mention of the doctrine of universal spirituality, Dōgen maintains, the average person fails to consider what it truly means and remains preoccupied with "such things as the existence or non-existence of Buddha-nature." He stresses that to comprehend the truth of no-Buddha-nature, "one must not think of it in terms of the nothingness of being and nothingness, and ask instead, 'What is the very Buddha-nature?' "

The same is true for an atomized focus on *U* that Dōgen shows literally means "having" but philosophically implies "being" in a sense that is beyond the dichotomies

---

[16] *Dōgen zenji zenshū*, 1: 19; see also *The Heart of Dōgen's Shōbōgenzō*, 71.

of possession and absence or acquisition and loss. In highlighting Zhaozhou's affirmative response, Dōgen argues that the doctrine of being-Buddha-nature (*u-busshō* 有佛性) is not a possession or an inherent potentiality that exists in contrast to no-Buddha-nature. Of Zhaozhou's *U*, he writes, "it is not the 'has' posited by the Sarvastivadans [an early Buddhist school of 'realism'] . . . The being of Buddha is the being of Zhaozhou. The being of Zhaozhou is the being of the dog. The being of the dog is being-Buddha-nature."[17]

Multiperspectivism

Dōgen also demonstrates agility with putting forth multiple perspectives through exploring dissimilar or even conflicting and contradictory readings of various cases. This outlook embodies a Nietzschean theoretical facility, which was in turn influenced by various strains of Mahāyāna Buddhist thought, of never acquiescing to a particular standpoint without considering complementary and competitive points of view. The initial query of the Mu Kōan, "Does the dog have Buddha-nature or not?," is generally seen as an unfortunate, idle, speculative question, begging to be rebuffed or dismissed, about whether a being that lacks self-reflective consciousness possesses the potential to be enlightened.

Dōgen comments, "The meaning of this question must be clarified. It neither asks whether the dog has or does not have Buddha-nature. It is a question of whether an iron [enlightened] man continues to practice the Way." As Robert Aitken puts it in his modern commentary, "The monk sitting before Zhaozhou cannot acknowledge his own Tathagata. At a deep level he is asking, 'Do I really have Buddha-nature as they say?'"[18] Dōgen further remarks that this question is so disturbing and penetrating that Zhaozhou is taken aback; he at first feels threatened and blunders his way into poisonous territory, an image that could also be interpreted to refer to the way the master outsmarts the naïve inquirer who is trapped in the complication of words.

When the query is somewhat stubbornly restated by the novice as, "All sentient beings have Buddha-nature, so why not the dog?," Dōgen argues, "The real meaning of this is, if all sentient beings are nothingness (*mu*), then Buddha-nature must be nothingness, and the dog must be nothingness as well. The real meaning is such, the dog and Buddha-nature manifest nothingness as such[ness]." That is, Dōgen rereads the question, "Why does not the dog have it?," as the statement, "the dog is such nothingness," or "the dog is no[-Buddha-nature]." By elevating rhetoric beyond the conventional distinctions of truth and error, the supposedly deluded question is coterminous with the master's

[17] *Dōgen zenji zenshū*, 1: 39–41, for this and the following passages on the Mu Kōan in *Shōbōgenzō* "Busshō"; see also *The Heart of Dōgen's Shōbōgenzō*, 91–94.
[18] Robert Aitken, trans., *The Gateless Barrier: The Wu-Men Kuan (Mumonkan)* (New York: North Point Press, 1991), 11.

enlightened response in disclosing a wellspring of nothingness-as-suchness from which all expressions derive.

This approach to interpretation can also be referred to as "hermeneutics beyond slander" in that all views, whether representing truth or untruth, are allowed to stand conterminously, without judgment or preference. Dōgen disputes Baizhang, who suggests that freedom from extreme views is gained through the denial of each standpoint by saying that "to preach sentient beings have . . . or do not have the Buddha-nature slanders Buddha." In contrast, Dōgen argues, "Despite such disparagement, you cannot avoid explaining something . . . Although it slanders, is the Buddha-nature disclosed, or not? If the Buddha-nature is disclosed, it is penetrated by the teacher and at the same time it is heard by the listener."[19] This view of affirming the need for discourse ironically complements the seemingly opposite notion that whether one says "Yes" or "No" to the question about the dog slanders the dharma. There is no set position regarding the use and/or abandonment of words and phrases to express the meanings of Buddha-nature, which can and should be analyzed from every possible perspective.

Inversion

The inversion of conventional readings of the source record is accomplished whereby Dōgen becomes a kind of postmodern Dadaist who makes use of the alchemy of words, to cite a Rimbaud phrase, in order to flip back and forth by diverting and discontinuing or cutting off or extending the path of any given discourse. Dōgen suggests that the *Mu* response to the question of the dog's Buddha-nature is perplexing and subject to diverse interpretations. *Mu* has various negative implications, including, but not limited to, "What a foolish question, for the Buddha-nature is not a possession and a dog cannot be enlightened," and from a very different angle that is similar to *watō*, a diamond-cutting or lion's roaring silence that puts an end to all manner of speculation. *Mu* can also paradoxically indicate an affirmation in that there is no Buddha-nature apart from concrete existence, as symbolized by the dog, and, from the standpoint of emptiness, the dog as well as each and every phenomenon in the universe manifests Buddha-nature.

According to Dōgen, Zhaozhou answered both *Mu* and *U* because these terms are interchangeable yet distinct ways of expressing no-Buddha-nature. This approach stands in contrast to the *watō*-based interpretation. In addition, Dōgen interprets in positive terms Zhaozhou's ironic reply, "This is because it has awareness of karma." Therefore, he contends that the *watō* method fosters subtle yet devastating dichotomies between means and end, practice and realization, and illusion and truth. Because causality is inseparable from noncausality and vice versa, affirming the dog's awareness of karma and its consequences indicates that the problem of the dog's Buddha-nature is oriented in terms of "the nothingness of the dog and the nothingness of Buddha-nature." The

[19] *Dōgen zenji zenshū*, 1: 21; see also *The Heart of Dōgen's Shōbōgenzō*, 88.

phrase *kushi-mu bussho-mu nari* 狗子無佛性無なり can also be read as "no-dog and no-Buddha-nature," "dog-nothingness and Buddha-nature-nothingness," or "dog-*mu* and Buddha-nature-*mu*."

Intrusion

These rhetorical elements reveal Dōgen surveying different approaches to Buddha-nature so that he can isolate and analyze examples of Zhaozhou's response in a way that captures multiple meanings and encompasses paradoxes and conceptual reversals. Disruptive discursive techniques contribute to and converge in the hermeneutics of intrusion that delve further into and alter the source dialogue itself as Dōgen transmutes any and all words and phrases through modifying, sometimes overtly and in other instances with a beneath-the-surface subtlety of expression, the original wording but not the intention of the kōan case record. This approach is demonstrated by the way Dōgen transforms a seemingly innocent phrase, "Since it already has," in the monk's retort to Zhaozhou's positive response: "Since it already has [Buddha-nature], why does it enter into this skin-bag?" According to Dōgen's distinctive interpretation, this phrase, "since it already has," deliberately implies both the implications of "given that" and "from the time that." This is the same "since," used here as an affirmation, that is evoked in some of Dahui's *watō*-based passages in order to highlight, ironically enough, what he considers to be a recognized truth that there is no Buddha-nature since the phrasing is understood in a negative sense.

Dahui suggests, "Since it [the dog] has (Ch. *jiyou*; Jp. *kiu* 既有) no [or: does not have] Buddha-nature, as Zhaozhou has stated," disciples should "simply pick up this statement of 'No' as in 'the dog has no Buddha-nature,'" because "it is necessary to use only the one character *Mu* [in training]," as "this functions as a sword that extricates from the path of life and death so that when illusions arise you only need the word *Mu* to cut through them."[20] Note that in this sequence of remarks there is an avoidance of the implications found in the *Mu–U* version of the case, which includes as part of one of the subdialogues the phrase, "Since it has . . . ," rather than "does not have," the Buddha-nature. The significance of this deviation from the double-response rendition, as Dōgen brings out in his interlinear commentary, is that it loses sight of Zhaozhou's style of expression, which indicates ontological rather than physical time. There is an original condition that precedes and is thus unfettered by the contradiction of neither strictly having nor not having a primordial spiritual endowment.

Dōgen's interpretation of the full "Yes" subdialogue indicates, "This monk asks whether Zhaozhou's response refers to what is currently existing, previously existing, or already existing." Dōgen suggests that "since it has" or "since it is" must be broken down to distinguish it from other temporal indicators, that is, from the ordinary sense

---

20 Cited from *Taishō shinshū daizōkyō*, 47: 896a; see also *Taishō*, 47: 903c.

of past as opposed to present or of present in contrast to future. Here, he endorses a view of primordial temporality that is discussed in numerous other fascicles, especially "Being-Time" ("Uji"), by making a claim that, "already existing might seem to indicate one of several forms of existence, but in fact already existing shines alone." Thus, "since"-cum-already-existing now refers to a foundational level of being surpassing divisions. Therefore, Zhaozhou's phrasing is not a mere pointer to but rather is synonymous with the truth of Buddha-nature.

Dōgen then questions whether "already existing should be understood as something that enters into or does not enter into [a skin-bag]," since this discrepancy implies a duality of spiritual and physical dimensions, which he considers to be misleading. The very words "entering into," he suggests, are superfluous because there is no distinction between immanence and transcendence or manifesting and not manifesting in the flesh. In any event, "the act of entering into this skin-bag is not committed erroneously or in vain" and can help lead to an awakening, in that mundane existence is inseparable from nirvāna.

By asserting the unity of spiritual and physical realms, Dōgen maintains, "The treasure concealed in the daily activity of liberation is concealed in self and others." Alluding to a passage from the *Jingde chuandenglu* (*Jingde Transmission of the Lamp Record*) volume 2, he admonishes, "Having referred to [concealment], this is not intended to mean that you are not yet free of ignorance. That would be like someone who puts a donkey in front of a horse!" To foster multiple perspectives that are liberating in that they each touch base with the multiple meanings of Buddha-nature, by alluding to an obscure passage attributed to Yunju from the *Liandeng huiyao* (*Essential Lamps Merged*) volume 22, Dōgen asserts, "Even if you have a partial, halfway understanding of the Buddha Dharma that has long been in error for days or even months on end, it still cannot be anything but the dog entering into a skin-bag."

Furthermore, in his analysis of this part of the *U* dialogue, Dōgen remarks that knowing better yet willfully choosing transgression is a common colloquial expression that had become known in Chan circles through Zhaozhou's utterance, but "it is none other than being-Buddha-being." He then alludes to a saying attributed to Shitou in the *Jingde chuandenglu* volume 30 by asserting, "If you want to know the Undying Man in his hermitage, you must not leave your own skin-bag!" In addition, Dōgen indicates in typical paradoxical fashion that, "'It knows better yet willfully chooses this transgression' is not necessarily 'entering into a skin-bag,' and 'entering into a skin-bag' is not necessarily 'It knows better yet willfully chooses this transgression.'"

Dōgen's textual hermeneutics of intrusion, however compelling and imaginative, could easily be seen as capricious and arbitrary because he willfully alters and distorts the source passages. However, a careful analysis of how he treats the Chinese Chan source passages in his Japanese vernacular appropriations, as undertaken by Hee-Jin Kim and Kagamishima Genryū, shows that this criticism is avoided because the creativity of the effort is based on a textual hermeneutical method that enables the unfolding of the tangled webs of words and phrases that at least partially reveal truth; this is inseparable from untruth that, in turn, discloses in an indirect way what is real. Or, it could be said that there is no truth like untruth and that untruth is no truth at all.

Bibliography and Suggested Readings

Abe, Masao. (1994) *Dōgen: His Philosophy and Religion*, edited by Steven Heine. Albany, NY: State University of New York Press.

Bein, Steven. (2011) *Purifying Zen: Watsuji Tetsurō's Shamon Dogen*. Honolulu: University of Hawai'i Press.

Bielefeldt, Carl. (1988) *Dōgen's Manuals of Zen Meditation*. Berkeley: University of California Press.

Bodiford, William M. (1993) *Sōtō Zen in Medieval Japan*. Honolulu: University of Hawai'i Press.

Dōgen. (1988–1993) *Dōgen zenji zenshū* [Collected Works of Zen Master Dōgen], 7 vols., edited by Kawamura Kōdō, et. al. Tokyo: Shunjūsha.

Dōgen. (1985) *Moon in a Dewdrop: Writings of Zen Master Dogen*, translated by Kazuaki Tanahashi. San Francisco, CA: North Point Press.

Dōgen. (2002) *The Heart of Dōgen's Shōbōgenzō*, translated by Norman Waddell and Masao Abe. Albany, NY: State University of New York Press.

Dōgen. (2004) *Dōgen's Extensive Record: A Translation of the Eihei Kōroku*, translated by Taigen Dan Leighton and Shohaku Okumura. Boston: Wisdom.

Dōgen. (2012) *Treasury of the True Dharma Eye: Zen Master Dogen's Shobo Genzo*, edited by Kazuaki Tanahashi. Boston: Shambhala.

Dumoulin, Heinrich. (1998) *Zen Buddhism: A History. Volume 2: Japan*, translated by James Heisig and Paul F. Knitter. New York: Macmillan.

Heine, Steven. (1994) *Dōgen and the Kōan Tradition: A Tale of Two Shōbōgenzō Texts*. Albany, NY: State University of New York Press.

Heine, Steven, trans. (1997) *The Zen Poetry of Dōgen: Verses from the Mountain of Eternal Peace*. Boston: Tuttle.

Heine, Steven. (2006) *Did Dōgen Go to China? What He Wrote and When He Wrote It*. New York: Oxford University Press.

Heine, Steven, ed. (2012) *Dōgen: Textual and Historical Studies*. New York: Oxford University Press.

Kagamishima Genryū. (1965) *Dōgen zenji to in'yō kyōten-goroku no kenkyū* [Studies of Dōgen's Citations of Sutras and Recorded Sayings]. Tokyo: Mokujisha.

Kim, Hee-Jin. (1975) *Dōgen Kigen: Mystical Realist*. Tucson: University of Arizona Press. Revised edition (2004): *Eihei Dōgen: Mystical Realist*. Boston: Wisdom.

Kim, Hee-Jin. (1985) "'The Reason of Words and Letters: Dōgen and Kōan Language." In *Dōgen Studies*, edited by William R. LaFleur. Honolulu: University of Hawai'i Press, 54–82.

Kim, Hee-Jin. (2007) *Dōgen on Meditation and Thinking: A Reflection on His View of Zen*. Albany, NY: State University of New York Press.

Kodera, Takashi James. (1980) *Dogen's Formative Years in China*. Boulder, CO: Prajna Press.

CHAPTER 10

RINZAI ZEN KŌAN TRAINING

Philosophical Intersections

VICTOR SŌGEN HORI

> To approach Zen as if it is a philosophy is to begin in a wrong way from the very beginning.
>
> —Osho[1]

IN Rinzai Zen monasteries in Japan today, Buddhist monks still continue the kōan practice. A kōan is a paradoxical question upon which the Rinzai Zen monk focuses his attention while sitting in meditation. The standard beginner's kōan (called "first barrier" kōan) include the famous *Mu* kōan:

> A monk once asked Jōshū, "Does a dog have Buddha-nature?"
> Jōshū answered, "No [*mu*]."

There is also Hakuin's well-known kōan:

> You know the sound of two hands clapping, what is the sound of one?

as well as Original Face:

> What is your original face before your father and mother were born?

The beginning monk attempts to answer the kōan question as he would any other question. He expects there is some way to interpret the words of the kōan so that it can be given a reasonable answer. The Zen teacher, however, gives the advice, "Don't think about the kōan. Become one with the kōan itself." Not knowing what it means to

---

[1] Osho Online Library (www.osho.com/online-library-zen-philosophy-mind-fded3115-60b.aspx), accessed June 25, 2013.

"become one with the kōan," the beginning Zen monk spends his hours in meditation full of doubt and uncertainty. Rinzai Zen kōan meditation practice is thus quite unlike the meditation practices of other branches of Buddhism, which usually aim at stillness and calmness of mind.

Textbooks on Zen usually start with the quotation of what has become known as "Bodhidharma's verse," a verse that has been used to identify the Chan/Zen school since the Song Dynasty (960–1279 CE) in China:

> A separate transmission outside the teaching,
> Not founded on words and letters.
> Point directly at the human mind
> See one's nature and become a buddha.[2]

Generations of Zen teachers have quoted this verse to explain that one cannot comprehend Zen through hearing a verbal explanation; one can only comprehend Zen, they say, through direct personal experience. Although the word "philosophy" does not occur in these lines, clearly, the verse implies that Zen cannot be intellectually comprehended, and, if there is no intellectual comprehension of Zen, then Zen is not accessible to philosophy.[3]

Despite this warning, many people (including Zen monks) have written "words and letters" about Zen. And since written texts are eminently accessible to philosophy, these writings have stimulated attempts to apply philosophical concepts to Zen in an attempt to understand (and, more recently, to deconstruct) Zen claims about the awakening experience and about kōan practice. In this chapter, I examine some attempts to apply Western philosophical concepts to Zen kōan practice and compare this philosophical analysis with my own personal experience of kōan practice. In 1976, after receiving a Ph.D. in philosophy from Stanford University, I was ordained as a Rinzai Zen monk and spent the years from 1977 to 1990 in monastic kōan practice under several Zen teachers in Japan. In this chapter, I assume both the outsider stance of an academic scholar and the insider stance of a Rinzai Zen monk. (I will have more to say later about the distinction between insider and outsider.)

---

[2] Albert Welter has argued that the lines of this verse originally circulated independently and were collected together only during the Song period (960–1279 CE) to make a four-line verse that was then attributed to Bodhidharma, who was supposed to have lived in fifth–sixth century CE (Welter 2000, 79). The line "a separate transmission outside the teaching" was, however, especially contentious. During the Tang period (618–907 CE), Chan Buddhism still thought of itself as text-based, as did the other schools of Buddhism. However, in the early Song period, a movement to distinguish Chan from the other schools arose based on the claim that Chan was "not founded on words and letters" but was instead the recipient of the direct enlightenment experience. This new image was projected back in history as if it were true of the Chan during the Tang period (Welter 2000).

[3] On whether Zen is a philosophy, see Rosemont 1970b.

RINZAI KŌAN TRAINING

My report as a Rinzai monk constitutes an autoethnography. The first point to make is that for a monk in kōan practice, a moment of insight—an "experience"—is essential to progress in the training. This is an empirical statement, the collective observation of those who have undergone the Rinzai kōan training. (I realize that the term "experience" is a contentious term in Western scholarship, but here it is an emic term, translating a concept that Rinzai Zen practice communities themselves use, *taiken* 體驗 or *taitoku* 體得.) The beginning monk wants to follow the master's advice to "become one with the kōan" but does not know what this means. The least he can do is to continuously repeat to himself the kōan, "sound of one hand, sound of one hand" during the hours of meditation, wondering all the while what it means. At first, he has to remind himself to stay focused, but, in time, he discovers that whenever his attention is not focused on some immediate task at hand, the words "sound of one hand, sound of one hand" repeat themselves in his head. This is an important half-step in kōan training because it shows clearly that it is not his conscious self that is keeping the words repeating in his head; some other activity of mind has started to operate. Finally, if the monk is lucky, there comes a moment of insight. It may take a great deal of time; it certainly requires committed effort, and not everyone is capable.[4] Suddenly, the monk knows "It's me!" This "it's me!" can be a powerful ecstatic convulsion lasting days or just a plain momentary "Aha!"[5] But after this moment, the kōan starts to make sense and the monk starts to "pass kōan." When the monk has had this experience, the Zen master will say that he has "seen the kōan" (*kōan o mita* 公案を見た).

What is it to see a kōan? There is little emic vocabulary to analyze this moment, partly because monks are told not to discuss their kōan practice with others. But at least we can say, in the moment of seeing, the monk *became one with the kōan*. Here, I revert to my scholarly persona to offer an explanation of this moment. At first, the monk searched for the sound of one hand as if it were a definite object. The constant repetition imprinted itself on his mind so that the words "sound of one hand" repeated themselves without his willing it. As he sank deeper into meditation, he was no longer directing the search for the sound of one hand; on the contrary, the search for the sound of one hand had taken on a momentum of its own, had become an independent activity and was more and more consuming him. At some point, the sound of one hand overwhelmed the seeking self, sweeping away the ground underfoot, so to speak. At that point, the seeking self realized that it itself was the sound of one hand. That is why the monk said, "It's me" but

---

[4] I have a longtime friend who is the head monk of a monastery with many branch zendōs. She has literally introduced hundreds of people to the kōan practice. She reports that of the many people who wish to enter into kōan practice, some people are "allergic to the kōan" and never have insight to a kōan. Perhaps a third of new students are unsuited to working with kōan.

[5] The Zen teacher Albert Low records his own very dramatic *kenshō* experience with the kōan "Mu" in Low 2013, 207–221.

the speaker of those words was, so to speak, the sound of one hand itself. One could just as easily say the sound of one hand realized that it was "I." On reflection, one can see that "one hand" refers to the experience of a unity. The "sound of one hand" at first was an object for which the monk was seeking. It then turned out to be the seeking activity itself. It is both the object of the seeking and the subject of the seeking. The monk "realizes" this in two senses of the word: first, he "makes real" the unity of subject and object by himself becoming an instance of that unity, and, second, he has cognitive comprehension of that fact.[6] He "becomes the kōan." He himself *is* the sound of one hand.

The insight the monk has had in seeing the kōan may be shallow or deep, confident or hesitant, once-and-for-all or in need of constant recharging. To gauge the depth and strength of his insight and to push the monk to explore his insight more deeply, the Zen teacher asks "checking questions" (*sassho* 拶処).

1. Having heard the sound of one hand, what is your proof?
2. When you hear the sound of one hand, it is said you become a buddha. How do you become a buddha?
3. After you have turned to ash, what do you hear? (Or, what is the sound of one hand after you have died?)
4. Can the Suimō Sword cut the sound of one hand?[7]
5. Why can't the Suimō sword cut the sound of one hand?
6. Bring me that which pervades the universe.
7. The sound of one hand before you were born?
8. The sound of one hand atop Mount Fuji?
9. Capping phrase for the sound of one hand atop Mount Fuji?
10. Did you hear it from the front or from the back?
11. Having heard the sound of one hand, what will you do with it?
12. Such a valuable treasure; let me hear it, too.
13. That sound of one hand, how far does it reach?
14. What is the sound of one hand before the fifteenth of the month, after the fifteenth of the month, and right on the fifteenth of the month?
15. What is the subtle sound of one hand?
16. What is the silent sound of one hand?
17. The true "realm" (*kyōgai*) of the sound of one hand?
18. The root-origin of the sound of one hand?
19. Capping phrase.
20. Capping phrase.[8]

---

[6] Nishitani Keiji discusses these two meanings of "realize" (Nishitani 1982, 5–6).

[7] The Suimō Sword is a famously sharp sword. *Suimō* means "blown hair." A hair blown against the blade of this sword would be cut into two. See the kōan "Pa Ling's Blown Hair Sword," Case 100 of the *Blue Cliff Record* (Cleary and Cleary, 1977), 636–640.

[8] Hau Hōō 1970, 78–82.

Checking questions also help to expose cheating. Beginning monks sometimes learn from older monks the answer to a kōan. To test whether a monk has had his own insight, all the Zen master needs to do is ask a few checking questions. A monk without his own experience of the sound of one hand will not be able to respond.

Within this list of checking questions are capping phrases, *jakugo* (着語, 著語; numbers 9, 19, and 20). A capping phrase is a verse that expresses the point of the kōan or of the checking question just passed. Monks search through handbooks of verses specially designed for Zen kōan practice. The verses are taken from Chinese Chan texts, Tang and Song period Chinese poetry, Confucian and Daoist classics, Chinese histories, and other Chinese literature. The Zen monk selects the verse that expresses the insight he has had. Even though Zen declares it is not founded on words and letters, nevertheless there is literary study in Zen kōan practice. The practice of capping phrases constitutes the beginning of this literary study.[9]

At advanced stages, the Zen monk will be asked to write an essay on the kōan just passed, called *kaki-wake* (書き譯; literally "writing the rationale"). In the essay, he expounds the surface of *kotoba* (言葉; the words); that is, he identifies proper names, explains literary references, provides historical context as in ordinary academic scholarship, and then, finally, he explains the *kokoro* 心 (the inner heart; i.e. the Zen import) of the kōan. This is the *hōri* (法理), the dharma rationale, of the kōan. In writing this essay, he consults dictionaries, Buddhist sutras, Zen texts such as the "transmission of the lamp" histories (*dentō-roku* 傳統録), the "recorded sayings" of past Zen masters (*goroku* 語録) and many other texts. Over the years, the monk becomes quite familiar with the texts of traditional Zen scholarship. Kōan practice begins with an experience beyond words and letters, but, in the later stages of practice, the monk learns how to talk about what cannot be talked about. The monk writes this essay with a brush in black ink on rice paper, and the Zen teacher marks the paper with a red pen as would an academic professor grading student papers.

After the *kaki-wake* essay, the monk is asked to compose a four-line verse in Chinese style, called *nenrō* (拈弄), to express his insight on that particular kōan. I call this exercise "deft play" because the monk is supposed to display creativity and originality, to show his individual way of seeing and handling the kōan.

The kōan that comprise the basic body of the kōan curriculum are taken from the standard collections such as the *Gateless Barrier* (*Mumonkan*), the *Blue Cliff Record* (*Hekigan-roku*), and the *Entangling Vines Collection* (*Kattō-shū*). At very advanced stages, the Zen teacher may present kōan taken from some nonstandard text, such as the *One Hundred Alternate and Additional Cases of Master Kidō* (*Kidō Oshō Hyakusoku Daibetsu*) or the *Record of Master Daitō* (*Daitō-roku*). The curriculum contains several hundred kōan. The order in which they are presented to the monk and the choice of the very advanced kōan texts varies with the Zen master's lineage. A monk who resides in the monastery twelve months a year and maintains a regular meditation schedule

---

[9] Hori 2003 is a full study of capping phrases and literary study in Zen kōan practice.

of several hours a day will need ten to fifteen years to complete the curriculum. The product of the kōan training is a mature Zen monk—a monk who not only can explain Buddhist teachings in words and letters but who also fully embodies them in person.

THE PERFORMATIVE APPROACH

As scholars in the West became increasingly familiar with Zen texts, they saw many examples of Chan/Zen masters giving answers that appeared quite irrelevant to the question posed:

> Great Master Ma was unwell. The temple superintendent asked him, "Teacher, how has your health been in recent days?" The Great Master said, "Sun Face Buddha, Moon Face Buddha."[10]

> Mu Chou asked a monk, "Where have you just come from?" The monk immediately shouted. Mu Chou said, "I've been shouted at by you once." Again the monk shouted. Mu Chou said, "After three or four shouts, then what?" The monk had nothing to say. Mu Chou then hit him and said, "What a thieving phoney you are?"[11]

> A monk asked Tung Shan, "What is Buddha?" Tung Shan said, "Three pounds of hemp."[12]

When Western scholars saw the "crazy wisdom" behavior of Chan/Zen masters, some were quick to suggest that the words of the Zen master were to be taken not literally but performatively. Thus, Henry Rosemont wrote:

> The Zen master's intent in performing these perlocutionary speech acts is to bring about a specific enlightenment "response" in his students. Questions like "What is the sound of one hand clapping?" or "What was your face like before you were born?" have no cognitive answer whatever, so a fortiori they have no answer that might express some principle of Zen Buddhism transcendent or otherwise . . . . Mondō and kōan sentences have no truth value, nor, except incidentally, do they have literary value; they can have, for the Zen apprentices, great shock value.[13]

The performative approach reflected a major trend in the first half of the twentieth century—the so-called *linguistic turn*—in which analytical philosophy turned to language as the way to solve traditional philosophical problems. Ludwig Wittgenstein suggested in the *Tractatus Logico-Philosophicus* that philosophical problems be treated

---

[10] Case 3, *Blue Cliff Record*. Cleary and Cleary 1977, 18.
[11] Case 10, *Blue Cliff Record*. Cleary and Cleary 1977, 66.
[12] Case 12, *Blue Cliff Record*. Cleary and Cleary 1977, 81.
[13] Rosemont 1970a, 118.

in a logically precise formal language. An atomic proposition would "picture" an atomic fact. The entire structure of propositions in the language would isomorphically map the entire structure of facts of the world. However, in his later phase, Wittgenstein rejected the formal approach and, in the *Philosophical Investigations*, devoted himself to explaining how natural language worked instead. He rethought what it meant for a word to have meaning. Rather than depicting meaning as picturing, he said "For a *large* class of cases—though not for all—in which we employ the word 'meaning' it can be defined thus: the meaning of a word is its use in the language."[14] Instead of meaning as simply denotation or reference or representation, Wittgenstein proposed that meaning is use. This perspective set the agenda for analytical philosophy during the mid-century as philosophers explored the idea that meaning is use. In particular, J. L. Austin developed a theory of speech-acts or performatives[15] that Henry Rosemont Jr. then applied to the Zen kōan.

The performative approach looks especially promising because, in many kōan, the Chan/Zen master frequently responds to questions by performing an action such as slapping the monk, kicking over a water pitcher, blowing out a candle, twisting the monk's nose, and more. But from an insider's Zen practice perspective, there are two problems with Rosemont's analysis. First, he says that the words of the Zen master have neither cognitive content nor truth value. Their only function is to shock the Zen monk into some kind of insight. But this statement cannot be true. Our autoethnographic report shows that after the monk sees a kōan, the Zen master then poses checking questions, requests capping phrases, and assigns a *kaki-wake* essay in which the monk explains the *hōri* or dharma rationale of the kōan. All these practices clearly assume that the words of the Chan/Zen master have cognitive content and truth value. Second, although Rosemont's performative analysis captures an essential feature of kōan practice, it accounts for only one kind of performance. Rosemont is quite justified in saying that the words of the Zen teacher constitute a perlocutionary performative, a speech-act that triggers (or is meant to trigger) an act or event. But it is not just the teacher who is performing; in kōan training, the monk is also performing. The monk cannot proffer a merely verbal answer for his kōan; he must "be" the sound of one hand. That is, he performs his *kenge* (見解), his understanding of his insight, in action and does not describe it in words. His answer to the kōan is the performance of an action that expresses the unity he experienced when he first uttered "It's me." This act of presenting one's answer to the kōan is not performative in the perlocutionary sense. Rather, it is similar to Austin's illocutionary performative because one performs the act *in* saying something (but is dissimilar in that no illocutionary verb such as "I promise," "I apologize," "I declare" is used).[16] Nevertheless, the utterance of the words has illocutionary force because

---

[14] Wittgenstein 1958, §43.

[15] Austin 1962.

[16] Austin distinguished two kinds of performatives, illocutionary and perlocutionary. "Illocutionary" refers to the "performance of an act *in* saying something" (Austin 1962, 99) as, for example when I say "I promise" or "I apologize"; in uttering the words, I perform the act of promising or apologizing. In a perlocutionary performative, one performs an act *by* saying something (Austin 1962, 109), as

the utterance of the words in itself performs an act; it *realizes* (makes real) the sound of one hand.

This performance ritually recreates his original moment of insight, the moment when he himself was nondually one with the sound of one hand. It is important that he pour himself totally into the act. If there is hesitation or self-consciousness or less than total effort, the Zen teacher rings his bell dismissing the monk. The teacher is not judging the correctness of his words; he is judging the monk's performance. He is judging the monk's *kyōgai* (境涯)—the level of intensity or seriousness with which he performs.[17]

Thus, Rosemont's early attempt to offer a performative analysis of the kōan did highlight an essential feature of kōan training—that a monk's *kenge* or "answer" to a kōan was not an explanation or a description but a performance—but his analysis fell short on two fronts. First, we need a more articulated concept of performance that would include both the perlocutionary speech-act of the Zen master and the illocutionary speech-act of the Zen monk. They are both performances but in different senses. Second, in kōan training, there is more than performance. There is also considerable literary study. After he passes his kōan, at advanced stages, the Zen monk must explain in writing the *hōri* or dharma rationale of the kōan. A proper analysis of the kōan training must include both the noncognitive performance aspect and the cognitive intellectual aspect.

Pure Experience

Dale Wright identifies "a fundamental component of Western-language interpretations of Zen experience—the idea that Zen enlightenment is an undistorted, 'pure experience' of 'things as they are' beyond the shaping power of language."[18] William James' essay, "A World of Pure Experience,"[19] provides the *locus* for this term in recent scholarship. In 1911, Nishida Kitarō (1870–1945), Japan's first modern philosopher, published his maiden work *Zen no kenkyū* (*Inquiry into the Good*) taking the standpoint of pure experience. "To experience means to know facts just as they are, to know in accordance with facts by completely relinquishing one's own fabrications. What we usually refer to as experience is adulterated with some sort of thought, so by pure I am referring to the state of experience just as it is without the least addition of deliberative discrimination."[20] Nishida in his early years carried on a kōan practice,[21] and, within the Kyoto School, he is associated

---

for example, when I say "Shoot her!" Austin says that "the perlocutionary act always includes some consequences" (Austin 1962, 107), thus implying that the utterance ("Shoot her!") is a separate event from the consequent act (presumably the act of shooting). See also Searle 1979 for a typology of illocutionary utterances.

17 On the concept of *kyōgai*, see Hori 2000, 286–295.
18 Wright 1992, 113.
19 James 1904.
20 Nishida 1990, 3.
21 Heisig 2001, 29.

more with Zen than with Pure Land Buddhism. It is thus easy to assume that when he talks about pure experience, he is talking about the Zen awakening experience. In actual Rinzai monastery kōan practice, however, no one ever talks of "pure experience." "Pure experience" is a stereotype imposed on Zen; it is useful to investigate why people want to impose this stereotype.

In the twentieth century, the concepts of mystical experience, religious experience, and pure experience have been subjected to rigorous scrutiny. Proponents of mystical experience in a variety of different religious and cultural contexts are wont to claim that, in mystical experience, one comes into direct contact with the infinite; such experience is "pure" in the sense that it transcends conventional language and theological doctrine. In several studies, Steven Katz and colleagues examined reports of such "mystical experience" and showed that, contrary to claim, reports of mystical experience do not transcend texts so much as affirm them; they support theological doctrine rather than flout them.[22] His conclusion was "There are no pure (unmediated) experiences."[23]

Wayne Proudfoot studied the claim, made by Friedrich Schleiermacher and Rudolf Otto, that religious experience is ineffable, that the experience of the infinite transcends language and conceptual thought. In Proudfoot's analysis, the term "ineffable" is not a descriptive; it is a disguised prescriptive whose function is to disqualify any descriptions people might try to apply to the experience. This prescriptive function is part of a larger "protective strategy."[24] Both Schleiermacher and Otto were seeking to protect Christianity from secular critics. By saying that the critics had never had religious experience, they could claim the critics had no understanding of religion and therefore were not qualified to criticize it. Robert Sharf has extended Proudfoot's critique to Buddhism in general and to Zen in particular. The vocabulary of meditation in Buddhism, says Sharf, does not function ostensively to denote states of consciousness. "Rather, such discourse turns out to function ideologically and performatively—wielded more often than not in the interests of legitimation and institutional authority" (Sharf 1995a, 228). Both Proudfoot and Sharf emphasize that it is not the content of statements about "experience" that counts: it is their ideological function that is important.

Dale Wright has argued that the "pure experience" conception of Zen awakening is conceptually incoherent by showing that it leads to a *reductio ad absurdum*. The ordinary person experiences the world dualistically, falsely seeing everything in either-or categories when things in themselves are nondual. Only the mind of the awakened one in Zen has broken through to pure consciousness and is able to perceive things in their nondual unity. This explains the Zen master's freedom of action. Instead of being locked into habitual dualistic responses, the Zen master can choose to respond in the usual dualistic way or to respond in an awakened nondual way. Wright takes this stereotypical picture of Zen awakening to its absurd conclusion. Nonduality itself is a dualistic concept. When the Zen master chooses to act nondually, he is making a dualistic choice. He

---

[22] Katz 1978, 1983.
[23] Katz 1978, 25–26. For a recent review of this literature, see Komarovsky 2012.
[24] Proudfoot 1985, 199.

has not really escaped duality; he has merely traded duality at one level for duality at a higher level. In fact, he has saddled himself with a duality unknown to the ordinary unawakened person.

Is seeing a kōan in Rinzai kōan practice a moment of pure experience? The short answer is "no" because the seeing of a kōan contains conceptual comprehension. As Nishitani explains, this moment "realizes" in two senses. First, the sound of one hand realizes (makes real) itself in the mind of the seeking monk, and, second, the monk realizes (comprehends) this fact.[25] It is an experience of nonduality within conceptual cognition.

SEEING AS

We can see now that the attempt to explain the language of a kōan as a performative and the idea of Zen awakening as pure experience presuppose the same philosophical paradigm. In this paradigm, human knowledge divides into two layers. First, the bottom foundational layer is constituted by the unmediated data of direct perception; on top of that is an upper layer, the intellectual or conceptual activity that produces an organized conception of the world. The upper layer is also the source of error or uncertainty in human knowledge. The Zen moment of seeing a kōan is then depicted as a breakthrough back to the immediate. Dumoulin is typical of many commentators: "The essence of the kōan is to be rationally unresolvable and thus to point to what is arational. The koan urges us to abandon our usual thought structures and step beyond our usual state of consciousness in order to press into new and unknown dimensions. This is the common purpose of all kōan no matter how much they may differ in content or literary form."[26] This paradigm—sometimes referred to as the "myth of the given"—motivated Descartes in his search for a starting point that could not be doubted and the British empiricists in their privileging of sensation as the foundation of human knowledge. However, another stream of modern philosophy, running from Kant through Heidegger and Gadamer, has argued for an alternative vision of human knowledge. They insist that although one can theoretically separate the data of sensation from conceptual thought, in fact all experience is the synthesis of the two; there is no basic foundation of immediate experience devoid of conceptual discrimination. In *The Critique of Pure Reason*, Kant stated, "Without sensibility no object would be given to us, without understanding, no object would be thought. Thoughts without content are empty, intuitions without concepts are blind."[27] Continuing in a similar vein, Heidegger argued that even the most basic perception has an "as-structure."[28] We inhabit an everyday world in which we move about,

---

[25] Nishitani 1982, 5.
[26] Dumoulin vol. 1 1988, 246.
[27] Kant 1929, A51 = B75.
[28] Heidegger 1962, 188–203.

handle objects, interact with people, in a totally matter-of-fact way. We hear a ringing and straightway say "Answer the telephone." We come to a door and without thinking turn the door knob. We sit down without asking "What is a chair?" We hear a ringing *as* a telephone. We see that round protrusion *as* a doorknob. We see that object *as* a chair. All seeing is seeing as. Even in the crudest prereflective experience, concepts—"telephone," "doorknob," "chair"—organize our sensations and give them meaning. If one could do the impossible and subtract all conceptual structure to get back to "pure experience," everyday experience would degenerate into a confusion of shapes, noises, color patches, and sensations without significance. This is not the consciousness of Zen. As Wright points out, even a Zen master sees the lines on the wall and knows "door," hears the ringing and knows "telephone," drinks from a mug and tastes "coffee."[29]

Hindsight allows us to see that Western philosophical attempts to understand the kōan embroiled it in the ongoing debate about whether human knowledge has a nonconceptual foundation or is conceptualized right from the start. The Western philosopher immediately wants to know if the Zen experience of "seeing a koan" is an example of pure experience, in the sense of James and Nishida (it is not) or is an example of mediated experience, in the sense of Heidegger (it is). But these are not the categories the Zen kōan tradition itself uses for talking about the experience of seeing a kōan. When a monk appears before the Zen master and proffers a *kenge* based on interpreting the words of the kōan, the master will scold the monk for using *rikutsu* (理屈), intellectualizing. But instead of instructing the monk to bring an example of pure experience, the master instructs the monk to become one with the kōan, whether it be the sound of one hand, "Mu," or his original face before father and mother were born. Here, I create a technical term to capture this point: *embodiment*. He must embody the kōan itself. He must *be* the kōan. When the Zen master employs the rhetoric of ineffability ("not founded on words and letters"), he is measuring the monk's insight on a scale with *rikutsu* at one end and embodiment at the other end. He is not worried about whether and how much experience is "pure" or "impure," mediated or not mediated by concepts.

Recent attempts to analyze Zen in terms of the Western concept of "pure experience" turn out to be irrelevant to Rinzai monastic kōan training practice. "Pure experience" is a concept foreign to both the Zen master and the Zen monk. Rather, the application of the concept of "pure experience" reflects ongoing debates among philosophers.

ZEN EXPERIENCE

In the past two decades, Robert Sharf has leveled a strong critique against the entire received picture of Zen Buddhism. In his view, it is incorrect to conceive of modern

---

[29] Wright 1992, 122.

Zen Buddhism as a school of Buddhism with a long history in East Asia; he says that, basically, it was invented by D. T. Suzuki at the beginning of the twentieth century and projected back into history.[30] Suzuki, he says, got his ideas for a new version of Zen from Paul Carus. As a young man, Suzuki had spent the years from 1897 to 1909 in Illinois working as an assistant to Carus and absorbed his vision of a "Religion of Science."[31] Sharf says Suzuki also learned of William James's idea of pure experience and transmitted it to the philosopher Nishida, who then used it as the standpoint for his book, *Zen no kenkyū* (*An Inquiry into the Good*).[32] Thus, he concludes D. T. Suzuki's Zen, "with its unrelenting emphasis on an unmediated inner experience, is not derived from Buddhist sources so much as from his broad familiarity with European and American philosophical and religious writings."[33] In addition, Sharf says that, in historical fact, Zen monks were not committed to the search for enlightenment and did not emphasize the practice of meditation.[34] The language of "experience" cannot be found in premodern Chinese or Japanese texts.[35] Some of Sharf's remarks are highly demeaning. Comparing Buddhist accounts of the experience of enlightenment with reports of alien abduction, he asks "Is there any reason to assume that the reports of experiences by mystics, shamans, or meditation masters are any more credible as 'phenomenological descriptions' than those of the abductees?"[36]

Sharf's criticisms are so complex, it is not possible to deal with them all in this short chapter. Let us, instead, focus on the last statement. If the reports of meditation masters are not credible, then neither will be the report of a former Rinzai Zen monk describing kōan practice. If Sharf is correct, then my insider's autoethnography will be no more credible than a report of alien abduction. My account also would be guilty of "phenomenological reduction," the assumption that the vocabulary of Zen enlightenment and of Buddhist meditation in general refers to states of inner experience. Sharf denies that the vocabulary of meditation refers to states of consciousness and argues instead that it is used ideologically in statements to legitimize vested interests and to confer or deny authority.[37] Let's think about that. If it is reductionist to *always* interpret "He has had *satori*" as a phenomenological description of a person's state of consciousness, it is equally reductionist to *always* interpret "He has had *satori*" as an ideological statement about that person's authority or legitimacy. The performative analysis of language in twentieth-century philosophy shows that reductionism in general is a mistake; it is wrong to always insist that words *always* get their meaning in one and only one way. The reductionist mistake is the same regardless of whether that one and only one way is thought to be phenomenological or ideological.

[30] Sharf 1993, 3–6.
[31] Sharf 1993, 17.
[32] Sharf 1993, 22.
[33] Sharf 1998, 101.
[34] Sharf 1995a, 241–243.
[35] Sharf 1993, 21–22; 1998, 102.
[36] Sharf 1998, 110.
[37] Sharf 1993, 22.

All language can be used ideologically. Consider, for example, "objectivity," the essential element in defining the academic outsider's stance to the study of religion. The word "objectivity" functions in academic communities exactly parallel to the way the word "experience" functions in a Zen community. Objectivity is held to be a state of mind—as is Zen experience. According to the rhetoric of objectivity, an objective mind sees things as they are without imposing its own slanted point of view—as does Zen experience (and Buddhist wisdom in general). However, skeptics doubt that there is such a thing as an objective mind—as is the case with Zen experience. Most important, objectivity is used ideologically, as in the case of Zen experience. Objectivity is used to draw an exclusionary line between those who are qualified to do scholarship because they are "objective" (e.g., scholars of religion) and those who are not "objective" (e.g., practitioners of a religion). It is not merely Schleiermacher and Otto who deploy a "protective strategy." Following Sharf's logic, we should conclude that ethnographic evidence belies the notion that the rhetoric of academic objectivity functions ostensively; the word "objectivity" does not really point to a state of mind. Rather, such discourse turns out to function ideologically and performatively—wielded in the interests of legitimation and institutional authority. The ideological critique leveled against the insider can also be leveled against the outsider.

CONCLUSION

Bodhidharma's verse, as usually interpreted, insists that Zen insight is founded not on words and letters but on direct personal experience. The verse asserts the specialness of Zen, but it is worthwhile remembering that not just Zen insight but all of personal experience is unspeakable. To one who has never tasted coffee, no amount of explanation will fully convey that flavor. To one who lacks the experience, a migraine headache, the joy of mathematics, the appreciation of Jacqueline du Pré's performance of Elgar's *Cello Concerto* cannot fully be explained in words. But the other side of the coin is that people who share an experience can speak to each other about it and carry on a conversation. If this is so generally, then two people who share Zen insight should be able to talk about it with each other and carry on a conversation. Does this not open up a space for the application of philosophical concepts to Zen? This chapter has examined some attempts by Western scholars to apply philosophical concepts to Zen. Not surprisingly, because these scholars were outside observers, their attempts did not capture very much Zen but did reflect the disputes internal to philosophy. What is needed now is philosophical reflection by Zen practitioners themselves.[38]

---

[38] Ueda Shizuteru is both a Zen practitioner with long experience in Rinzai kōan training and a professional philosopher who has written on language in Zen. See Davis 2019 for a full discussion with references.

BIBLIOGRAPHY AND SUGGESTED READINGS

Cleary, Thomas, and J. C. Cleary, trans. (1977) *The Blue Cliff Record*. Boulder, CO: Shambhala.

Davis, Bret W. (2019) "Expressing Experience: Language in Ueda Shizuteru's Philosophy of Zen." In *Dao Companion to Japanese Buddhist Philosophy*, edited by Gereon Kopf. New York: Springer, 713–38.

Dumoulin, Heinrich. (1988) *Zen Buddhism: A History. Vol. 1: India and China; Vol. 2: Japan*. New York: Macmillan.

Gimello, Robert. (1983) "Mysticism in Its Contexts." In *Mysticism and Religious Traditions*, edited by Steven T. Katz. Oxford: Oxford University Press, 61–88.

Hau Hōō. (1970) *Gendai Sōjizen Hyōron*. Tokyo: Mizuho Shobō.

Heidegger, Martin. (1962) *Being and Time*, translated by John Macquarrie and Edward Robinson. New York: Harper Collins.

Heisig, James, W. (2001) *Philosophers of Nothingness: An Essay on the Kyoto School*. Honolulu: University of Hawai'i Press.

Hori, Victor Sōgen. (2000). "Kōan and Kenshō in the Rinzai Zen Curriculum." *The Kōan*, edited by Steven Heine and Dale S. Wright. New York: Oxford University Press, 280–315.

Hori, Victor Sōgen. (2003) *Zen Sand: The Book of Capping Phrases for Zen Kōan Practice*. Honolulu: University of Hawai'i Press.

James, William. (1904) "A World of Pure Experience." *Journal of Philosophy, Psychology, and Scientific Methods* 1: 533–543, 561–570.

Kant, Immanuel. (1929) *Critique of Pure Reason*, translated by Norman Kemp Smith. London: Macmillan and Co.

Katz, Steven T., ed. (1978) *Mysticism and Philosophical Analysis*. Oxford: Oxford University Press.

Katz, Steven T., ed. (1983) "The 'Conservative' Character of Mystical Experience." In *Mysticism and Religious Traditions*, edited by Steven T. Katz. Oxford: Oxford University Press, 3–60.

Katz, Steven T., ed. (1992) *Mysticism and Language*. Oxford: Oxford University Press.

Komarovsky, Yaroslav. (2012) "Buddhist Contributions to the Question of (Un)mediated Mystical Experience." *Sophia* 51.1: 87–115.

Low, Albert. (2013) *What More Do You Want? Zen Questions, Zen Answers*. Tokyo: Tuttle Publishing.

Nishida Kitarō. (1990) *An Inquiry into the Good*, translated by Masao Abe and Christopher Ives. New Haven, CT: Yale University Press.

Nishitani Keiji. (1982) *Religion and Nothingness*, translated by Jan Van Bragt. Berkeley: University of California Press.

Proudfoot, Wayne. (1985) *Religious Experience*. Berkeley: University of California Press.

Rosemont, Henry Jr. (1970a) "The Meaning is the Use: Koan and Mondo as Linguistic Tools of the Zen Masters." *Philosophy East and West* 20.2: 109–119.

Rosemont, Henry Jr. (1970b) "Is Zen Buddhism a Philosophy?" *Philosophy East and West* 20.1: 63–72.

Searle, John R. (1979) *Expression and Meaning: Studies in the Theory of Speech Acts*. Cambridge: Cambridge University Press.

Sharf, Robert. (1993) "The Zen of Japanese Nationalism." *History of Religions* 33.1: 1–43.

Sharf, Robert. (1995a) "Buddhist Modernism and the Rhetoric of Meditative Experience." *Numen* 42.3: 228–283.

Sharf, Robert. (1995b) "Sanbōkyōdan: Zen and the Way of the New Religions." *Japanese Journal of Religious Studies* 22.3–4: 417–458.

Sharf, Robert. (1998) "Experience." In *Critical Terms for Religious Studies*, edited by Mark C. Taylor. Chicago: University of Chicago Press, 94–116.

Suzuki, D. T. (1956) *Zen Buddhism: Selected Writings of D. T. Suzuki*, edited by William Barrett. Garden City, NY: Doubleday and Co.

Suzuki, D. T. (1961) *Essays in Zen Buddhism: First Series*. New York: Grove Press/Evergreen.

Suzuki, D. T. (1972) *What is Zen?* New York: Harper and Row/Perennial Library.

Welter, Albert. (2000) "Mahākāśyapa's Smile: Silent Transmission and the Kung-an (Kōan) Tradition." In *The Kōan: Texts and Contexts in Zen Buddhism*, edited by Steven Heine and Dale S. Wright. Oxford/New York: Oxford University Press, 75–109.

Welter, Albert. (2008) *The Linji lu and the Creation of Chan Orthodoxy: The Development of Chan's Records of Sayings Literature*. Oxford/New York: Oxford University Press.

Wittgenstein, Ludwig. (1922) *Tractatus Logico-Philosophicus*. London: Kegan Paul, Trench, Trubner.

Wittgenstein, Ludwig. (1958) *Philosophical Investigations*. Oxford: Basil Blackwell.

Wright, Dale S. (1992) "Rethinking Transcendence: The Role of Language in Zen Experience." *Philosophy East and West* 42.1: 113–138.

CHAPTER 11

··

MODERN ZEN THINKERS

D. T. Suzuki, Hisamatsu Shin'ichi, and Masao Abe

··

MORI TETSURŌ, MINOBE HITOSHI, AND STEVEN HEINE

THIS chapter consists of three parts, each of which presents the philosophical contributions of an influential modern Japanese thinker closely affiliated with Rinzai Zen Buddhism: D. T. Suzuki or Daisetz Teitaro Suzuki (Jp. Suzuki Daisetsu, 1870–1966), Hisamatsu Shin'ichi (1889–1980), and Masao Abe (Jp. Abe Masao, 1915–2006).[1] Suzuki is well known for having introduced Zen Buddhism to the West in his prolific writings, translations, and lectures in English throughout his long life.[2] Hisamatsu was a student of Nishida Kitarō. Although he is less known in the West, like Suzuki, he engaged in dialogue with major Western thinkers such as Martin Heidegger[3] and Paul Tillich,[4] and he has exerted much influence on practitioners of Zen and the artistic "ways" associated with Zen—especially the Way of Tea (*sadō* or *chadō* 茶道) and also the Way of Calligraphy (*shodō* 書道)—as well as on philosophers with an interest in Zen and these artistic ways.[5] Abe, a student of Hisamatsu, continued Suzuki's endeavor to introduce Zen to a Western audience, carrying out numerous profound and provocative discussions in print and in person regarding Zen in relation to Western philosophies and theologies.[6] Along with

---

[1] The first part of this chapter is authored by Mori Tetsurō, the second by Minobe Hitoshi, and the third by Steven Heine. The first two parts were translated from Japanese by Bret W. Davis, who also wrote this introductory section.

[2] See Suzuki 1964, volume one of Suzuki 2015–16, and the many works by Suzuki listed in the bibliography at the end of this chapter. More recently, Suzuki's relation to wartime Japanese nationalism and militarism has been the subject of some debate; see the articles by Brian Taizen Victoria and by Kemmyō Taira Satō in collaboration with Thomas Kirchner in volume 41/2 (2010) of *The Eastern Buddhist*.

[3] See Heidegger and Hisamatsu 1989*a* and 1989*b*, and Suzuki 1989.

[4] See Tillich and Hisamatsu 1971–1973.

[5] See Hisamatsu 1960, 1982*a*, 1982*b*, 2002; and Ives 2010.

[6] See Abe 1985, 1990, 1994, 1995, 2003; Cobb and Ives 1990; and Mitchell 1998.

Nishitani Keiji[7] and Ueda Shizuteru,[8] Suzuki, Hisamatsu, and Abe have been the most important Japanese contributors to the philosophical articulation of the thought and practice of Zen Buddhism (including the practice of transcending the limits of certain kinds of thought) in modern times.

Although Suzuki's prolific writings in English are well known throughout the world, lesser known outside of Japan are his even more numerous writings in Japanese, as well as the influence these writings continue to exert on lay practitioners as well as priests and Zen masters in Japan. Suzuki's writings also continue to influence some academic philosophers in Japan, especially those associated with the Kyoto School who are also practitioners of Zen, including the author of the first part of this chapter.[9] Mori Tetsurō focuses on the kernel of Suzuki's "Zen thought," namely, the "logic of *is/not*" (*soku-hi no ronri* 即非の論理) that Suzuki gleans from *The Diamond Sutra* and views as the "logic" underlying Zen koāns such as Dongshan's instruction to "go to that place where there is no cold or heat" and Zen teachings such as Bankei's "Unborn Buddha Mind."

The second part of this chapter is also written by a Japanese philosopher affiliated with the Kyoto School, one who is a practitioner of the Way of Tea as well as of Zen. After sketching Hisamatsu's path from studying philosophy under Nishida to taking up the practice of Zen, Minobe Hitoshi focuses on the key themes of Hisamatsu's thought: his understanding of the "true self" in terms of a formless and thus completely unobjectifiable "absolute nothingness" (*zettai no mu* 絶対の無) and his claim that this true self is "absolutely autonomous" (*zettai jiritsu* 絶対自律). Unlike Suzuki and Nishida,[10] Hisamatsu showed little admiration for the Pure Land Buddhist path of "other-power" (*tariki* 他力),[11] much less for Christian conceptions of God as "wholly other" and as a higher power on which one can rely for salvation. Hisamatsu's Zen is strictly and solely aimed at "awakening" (*kaku* 覚) to the radical freedom of the true self.

The third part of this chapter is written by one of the foremost Western scholars of Zen who has also worked closely with Masao Abe, editing several of his books. Steven Heine provides an overview of Abe's sustained and significant contributions to the philosophical analyses of Zen texts and teachings as well as to *intrafaith* dialogue (especially between Zen and Pure Land schools of Japanese Buddhism) and *interfaith* dialogue (especially between Mahāyāna Buddhism and Christianity). He ends by showing how, late in life in three books written in Japanese, Abe developed an original philosophical interpretation of the central Mahāyāna Buddhist concept of "emptiness" (Skt. *śūnyatā*; Jp. *kū* 空) in the context of interfaith dialogue.

---

[7] See Chapter 21 in this volume.

[8] See Chapter 22 in this volume.

[9] For an excellent elucidation of the range and content of Suzuki's writings on Zen from the perspective of a Western scholar of religious studies, see Richard M. Jaffe's editor's introduction to volume one of Suzuki 2015–16, ix–lvi.

[10] See Suzuki 1998; Nishida 1990, 150, 170; and Nishida 1987, 79–80, 96–97.

[11] See Chapters 6 and 7 in this volume.

PART ONE: D. T. SUZUKI'S LOGIC OF *IS/NOT* AS ZEN PRAXIS (BY MORI TETSURŌ)

D. T. Suzuki or Daisetz Teitaro Suzuki (Jp. Suzuki Daisetsu) is well known as a "Zen thinker" who introduced a novel version of traditional Zen Buddhism as "Zen" to the West. Yet, at the same time, Suzuki, like his lifelong friend and pioneering "world philosopher" Nishida Kitarō (1870–1945), was a creative intellectual giant who went well beyond the confines of Buddhist studies and philosophy in their narrow senses to develop his own original thought. This thought revolved around such notions as "Japanese spirituality" (*Nihon-teki reisei* 日本的霊性), "the nature of the great earth" (*daichisei* 大地性), "the discrimination of non-discrimination" (*mufunbetsu no funbetsu* 無分別の分別), and "the logic of *is/not*" (*soku-hi no ronri* 即非の論理), also translatable as "the logic of affirmation/negation" or as "the logic of sameness/difference." Suzuki lived to be ninety-six years old, spending one-third of his life abroad. He was truly a citizen of the world as well as of Japan. Borrowing his own terms, we can say that he was a "rare person" (*ke-u no nin* 稀有の人) who was able to express in the form of his own life the "outwardly broad and inwardly deep" (*soto wa hiroi, uchi wa fukai* 外は広い、内は深い) insights he attained through the mediums of both Eastern and Western cultures. Suzuki's thought strongly resonates with that of Nishida, which unfolded in stages marked by the key ideas of "pure experience" (*junsui keiken* 純粋経験), "self-awareness" (*jikaku* 自覚), and "place" (*basho* 場所) before reaching his final standpoint of "absolutely contradictory self-identity" (*zettai mujun-teki jiko-dōitsu* 絶対矛盾的自己同一).[12] In what follows, let us examine the formation of Suzuki's conception of the "person" (*nin* 人) in the context of "Zen experience, Zen consciousness, and Zen thought" (*Zen keiken, Zen ishiki, Zen shisō* 禅経験・禅意識・禅思想),[13] with a focus on "the logic of *is/not*" as a matter of "Zen praxis" (*Zen kōi* 禅行為).

The Mountain Is/Not the Mountain

The Zen sect has traditionally claimed to "not be founded on words and letters" and to be "a special transmission outside doctrines." While on the one hand heeding the essentially translinguistic dimension of Zen, Suzuki transgressed the framework of this traditional claim and, professing that "words and letters are also the Way" (*moji mo mata michi* 文字も亦道),[14] pursued an innovative path of expression. Furthermore, in his quest for a universal religiosity beyond the strictures of any particular religious sect,

---

[12] See Chapters 17 and 18 in this volume.

[13] Suzuki also uses traditional terms for these: "Zen state-of-being, Zen mindset, Zen principles" (*Zen kyō, Zen i, Zen ri* 禅境・禅意・禅理). See Suzuki 1999–2003, 15: 259.

[14] Suzuki 1999–2003, 18: 249.

what he came to mean by "Zen" (in distinction from "the Zen sect") was the ultimate dimension of living religious experience also found in religions other than Buddhism. Zen could thus be found everywhere. "Zen is life, life is Zen, and we are living Zen itself." Yet "it is not enough to live *in* Zen; humans must live *by* [*ni yotte* によって] Zen."[15] This "consciousness of living in Zen"[16] is what he means by the "Zen consciousness" (or "self-awareness") that goes beyond mere "Zen experience." And this is what Suzuki develops into "Zen thought" as "the logic of *is/not*" in order to go beyond tradition and address the contemporary world.

Suzuki first wrote of "the *prajñā* logic of *is/not*" (*hanya soku-hi no ronri* 般若即非の 論理) in the final chapter of the first edition of *Japanese Spirituality* (*Nihon-teki reisei*, 1944), entitled "The Zen of the *Diamond Sutra*" (*Kongōkyō no Zen*). The basic idea of the logic of *is/not* along with the expression "*is/not*" (*soku-hi* 即非) stem from the following lines in chapter 13 of the *Diamond Sutra*: "The Buddha taught the Perfection of Wisdom, which is not [即非] the Perfection of Wisdom; thus it is called the Perfection of Widsom."[17] According to Suzuki, "this can be formalized as 'That A is A means that A is not A, and therefore A is A.'" He explains this as matter of "affirmation being negation and negation being affirmation." And he says that "this is the essential logic of the thought found in the Perfection of Wisdom Sutras; it is the logic of Zen and of Japanese spirituality."[18]

Put in terms of the famous saying by the Song Chan (Zen) Master Qingyuan Weixin (ninth cent.)—according to which before the practice of Zen he saw the mountain as a mountain, during the practice of Zen he no longer saw the mountain as a mountain, and after Zen practice he once again saw the mountain as a mountain[19]—the logic of *is/not* can be succinctly expressed as: "The mountain is not a mountain; therefore, the mountain is a mountain."[20] The negation entailed in saying that it is "*not* a mountain" cannot be explained in linguistic or epistemological terms, for example, as indicating a difference between phenomenon and substance. Moreover, while the logic can be formulated in terms of a movement from an affirmation of commonsensical "discriminations" (*funbetsu* 分別), through the incomprehensible negation involved in a "non-discrimination" (*mufunbetsu* 無分別), to a "discrimination of non-discrimination" (*mufunbetsu no funbetsu* 無分別の分別) that returns to the initial affirmation,[21] it should decidedly not be understood in dialectical terms of a process with stages. The mysterious contradiction of "the mountain is not a mountain" is not a mere verbal or theoretical game but rather is based on the Zen experience of a "spiritual intuition" that

---

[15] Suzuki 1999–2003, 12: 268.

[16] Suzuki 1999–2003, 12: 269, emphasis added.

[17] Suzuki uses Xuanzang's Chinese translation: 仏説般若波羅蜜。即非般若波羅蜜。是名般若波羅蜜, formulating it into Japanese *Kanbun* as: 般若波羅蜜は、即ち般若波羅蜜ではない。それでこれを般若波羅蜜と名づける。

[18] Suzuki 1999–2003, 5: 381.

[19] See Suzuki 1999–2003, 13: 176.

[20] Suzuki 1999–2003, 5: 381.

[21] Suzuki 1999–2003, 13: 176.

sees that "the mountain is the self and the self is the mountain," an intuition that in an instant simultaneously manifests both the negation of "the non-discrimination of discrimination" and the affirmation of "the discrimination of non-discrimination."

Suzuki's logic of *is/not* has a number of dimensions, including the metaphysical or mystical religious dimension of divine love in which "God is not God, therefore God is God."[22] At bottom, however, it is meant to elucidate the core of Buddhism expressed in such phrases as "samsāra is nirvāna" (*shōji soku nehan* 生死即涅槃) and "deluding afflictions are enlightening wisdom" (*bonnō soku bodai* 煩悩即菩提) as well as the existential concretization of these ideas in the Zen praxis of "the doing of non-doing" (*musa no sa* 無作の作).

The Place Where There Is/Not Birth and Death

In Case 43 of the *Blue Cliff Records*, "Dongshan's No Cold or Heat," we find the following exchange. A monk asked Dongshan (807–869), "When beset by cold and heat, how can I evade them?" In effect he is asking: When faced with the great matter of life and death, that is, the great matter of samsāra, what am I to do?" Dongshan answered, "Why don't you go to that place where there is no cold or heat?" In other words, he is saying: You should go to the world where there is no birth and death. The monk responded, "What is this place where there is no cold or heat?" Dongshan immediately replied, "When it is cold, the cold kills you; when it is hot, the heat kills you." In other words: When it is cold, it is just cold; when it is hot, it is just hot; when you are born, you are just born; and when you die, you just die. When it is cold, it is just cold; there is not even a "self" there who feels the cold: "Oh it's cold!"—that alone. Killed by the cold, the self that has died to itself does not "evade" the cold but rather dives right into its midst. If one can die into the experience, becoming one with the matter directly at hand, a dimension opens up that transcends life and death (i.e., samsāra). This is what Suzuki means when he says that "the logic of is/not is praxis itself."[23]

In this way, the conjunction of "the place of no cold or heat" with "being killed by the cold when it's cold, being killed by the heat when it's hot" illuminates the fundamental matter of human existence; namely, the *is/not* of "birth and death are not birth and death, and no birth and death are birth and death." The *not* (*hi* 非) of *is/not* indicates the "fundamental contradiction"; that is to say, "the clash between things which absolutely exclude one another in the world of birth and death, in the world of cold and heat."[24] The *is* (*soku* 即) indicates that "these things which absolutely exclude one another are as such moving within a field of unity." "The *not* is as such the *is*, in other words, absolute mutual negation (*hi*) is at once sameness (*soku*). The *is* and the *not* are, just as they are, united."[25]

[22] Suzuki 1999–2003, 12: 268.
[23] Suzuki 1999–2003, 13: 464.
[24] Suzuki 1999–2003, 13: 274.
[25] Suzuki 1999–2003, 13: 275.

Here, we can see the proximity of Suzuki's logic of *is/not* to Nishida's "world of absolutely contradictory self-identity."[26]

> Sameness [*soku*] itself is nowhere to be found [by means of intellectual discrimination]. When reality is discovered, the world of sameness disappears. Sameness arises as the sameness of difference [*hi*], and difference arises as the differentiation of sameness. Sameness exists in the midst of difference, and difference exists in the midst of sameness. Sameness is difference and difference is sameness. This is the nature of factual human experience as such.[27]

In this way, Buddhism emphasizes the "self-identity of the contradictory concepts of differentiation and equality," yet rather than speculate by means of logic or "intellectual discrimination" (*funbetsu* 分別) on the sameness (*soku*) or "non-discrimination" (*mu-funbetsu* 無分別) at issue, it urges us to attain a "spiritual intuition" of the fact that "in everyday experience non-discrimination permeates discriminations."[28]

However, if this *is/not* or *sameness/difference* is misunderstood, the tendency arises to equate the sameness (*soku*) at issue here with an antiquated and problematic conception of the Buddhist "view of equality" (*byōdōkan* 平等観). The praxis of *is/not* is manifested by way of breaking through such a theoretical and monotonous spatiality of "equality" and plunging into the midst of "differentiations" (*shabetsu* 差別). Suzuki writes that "*is/not* is the logic that is the truest to life, and so, in terms of religion and personhood, it is a direct expression of the conjunction of great compassion and great wisdom."[29] Nishida, at the time he was composing his final essay on religion,[30] wrote in a letter to Suzuki: "I want to derive the person [*nin* 人], that is, personhood [*jinkaku* 人格]" from "what I call absolutely contradictory self-identity, in other words, from the logic of *is/not*, and I want to connect this with the reality of the historical world."[31] This was indeed Suzuki's own ultimate standpoint, and we can approach the core of his logic of *is/not* in this direction.

In his lectures to the emperor and empress of Japan the year after Nishida's death, published as *The Essence of Buddhism* (*Bukkyō no daihi* [The Great Compassion of Buddhism], 1946), Suzuki takes up Nishida's indications and writes the following:

> The self-identity of things that exclude one another [i.e., what Nishida calls "absolutely contradictory self-identity"], that is to say, the non-discrimination of discriminations, has proven to be a difficult problem for all kinds of thinkers, and yet at the same time it is the most fundamental of all matters . . . . Buddhists came up with an original formulation for this, namely "inconceivable liberation" (Jp. *fukashigi-gedatsu* 不可思議解脱; Skt. *acintya moksha*). It is also what is meant by

26 Suzuki 1999–2003, 13: 280.
27 Suzuki 1999–2003, 13: 281.
28 Suzuki 1999–2003, 7: 14.
29 Suzuki 1999–2003, 13: 282.
30 Nishida 1987–89, 11: 371–464; Nishida 1987, 47–123.
31 Nishida 1987–89, 19: 399. See also Nishida 1987–89, 11: 398; Nishida 1987, 70.

"no-mind" (*mushin* 無心) or no-thought (*munen* 無念). Intellectually, it is a matter of opening the eye of wisdom. Volitionally speaking, it is a matter of plunging into the very midst of contradictions themselves. Why is a hand called a hand, how could a single hand make a noise? It is only when one enters the center of that thing itself, rather than looking at it from the outside, that the problem is resolved.[32]

Suzuki goes on to say that this is what is referred to as "the resolution of nonresolution" (*mu-kaishō no kaishō* 無解消の解消) and "the thinking of not-thinking" (*fushiryō no shiryō* 不思量の思量). "Logic and thought do not enter into this region" of inconceivable liberation. Zen adepts "do not look in on and interpret problems of life from without, rather they plunge into the midst of life itself." And yet, he stresses, this "*is/not* of Zen praxis" is precisely the "*prajñā* [wisdom] that is not *prajñā* and therefore is *prajñā*."[33]

Religious experience is "experience of suffering," and, "because it is this experience, liberation from suffering is possible."[34] However, this liberation is not possible by means of the discriminations of affect or intellect, but only by way of coming into contact with "spirituality" (*reisei* 霊性) as "the heart-mind of great love and great compassion" (*daiji-daihi no kokoro* 大慈大悲の心). The "logic of *is/not*" is manifested in the spiritual awakening to the "mystery" of the fact that "the contradiction of karma and non-karma is, just as it is, a self-identity"[35]; in other words, it is an "awakening to the fact that, even as one truly realizes the workings of karmic conditioning, the originary wellsprings of our existence are not bound by this conditioning."[36]

We have seen how the misunderstanding of the *is* (*soku*) of *is/not* (*soku-hi*) results in an erroneous view of equality that obfuscates differences. On the other hand, we find an example of a misunderstanding of the *not* (*hi*) of *is/not* in the phrase "not falling into causality" (*furaku-inga* 不落因果) as it is used in the famous wild fox kōan (the second kōan in the *Gateless Barrier*).[37] If one thinks that by practicing Zen one will, for example, "not die even if one dies," then one is regarding causality as something outside of oneself and, if queried about falling into or not falling into causality, one will display a misunderstanding of the *not* (*hi*) of intellect and spirit. The truly liberating response of "not obscuring causality" (*fumai-inga* 不昧因果) evinces precisely a realization of the *is/not* of "causality is not causality and therefore it is causality."[38] In other words, "if one becomes causality then there is no causality, and so there is no question of falling or

[32] Suzuki 1999–2003, 7: 25.

[33] Suzuki 1999–2003, 7: 25.

[34] Suzuki 1999–2003, 7: 32.

[35] Suzuki 1999–2003, 7: 34.

[36] Suzuki 1999–2003, 7: 32.

[37] See Zenkei Shibayama, *The Gateless Barrier: Zen Comments on the Mumonkan* (Boston: Shambhala, 1974), pp. 32–41. This kōan tells the story of an abbot who was reborn as a wild fox for five hundred lifetimes after having told a monk that an accomplished practitioner "does not fall into causality" (*furaku-inga*). He was finally freed from the fox body after being taught that such a practitioner "does not obscure causality" (*fumai-inga*).—*Tr.*

[38] Suzuki 1999–2003, 7: 40.

not falling, obscuring or not obscuring."[39] Suzuki adds: "When one does not fall into causality, one has already fallen into it" and "to fall into causality is, on the contrary, not to fall into it; to go yet further, not falling is not obscuring, and not obscuring is not falling."[40] Intimated in what Wumen (Jp. Mumon) calls the "five hundred happy blessed lives as a fox"[41] is a deep appreciation for the extraordinary naturalness of a life lived in what we might call "the freedom of the *is/not*."

Bankei's Unborn Buddha-Mind as the Field of the Is/Not

Suzuki discovered the core of Japanese spirituality at work in the founders of the two strands of Pure Land Buddhism in Japan, Hōnen (1133–1212) and Shinran (1173–1263) (the essential concord between whom Suzuki insightfully perceived), as well as in modern exemplars of Shin Pure Land Buddhist piety (*myōkōnin* 妙好人).[42] He also found it at work in the Zen teaching of Bankei (1622–1693), whom he placed on par with Dōgen (1200–1253) and Hakuin (1686–1768).[43] The spiritual world of radical freedom pervades both the "entrusting heart" (*shinjin* 信心) of Shinran's Shin Buddhism and the "Unborn" (*fushō* 不生) of Bankei's Zen. Concerning the freedom of the *is/not* that is vividly apparent in the latter, Suzuki writes the following:

> The Unborn is not set in opposition to birth but rather to arising-and-perishing or birth-and-death, in other words, to samsāra. That is to say, as opposed to the discrimination of birth and death, it is a matter of the discrimination of non-discrimination. That is the Unborn. Hence, the Unborn resolves the contradiction between birth or life (*sei* or *shō* 生) and death, such that it is a matter of "birth is death and death is birth—and that is the Unborn." This is the essence of enlightenment.[44]

Suzuki writes that the Unborn is the name of the field (*ba* 場) in which "the discriminating nature of consciousness and the non-discriminating nature of supra-consciousness" come into contact with one another.[45] He writes:

> Birth and death are birth and death in the field of the Unborn . . . . Seeing birth and death apart from the Unborn is delusion, and enlightenment occurs when they are returned to the field of the Unborn. Yet we have never left this field . . . . The Buddha-mind and living Buddhas are all pointing to this field of the Unborn, this

---

[39] Suzuki 1999–2003, 7: 41.

[40] Suzuki 1999–2003, 7: 41.

[41] *The Gateless Barrier*, 33.

[42] See Chapters 6 and 7 in this volume.

[43] On Dōgen, see Chapters 8 and 9, and, on Rinzai Zen kōan practice as institutionalized by Hakuin, see Chapter 10 in this volume.

[44] Suzuki 1999–2003, 1: 483.

[45] Suzuki 1999–2003, 1: 20.

field which is not outside of birth and death (i.e., saṃsāra) but which is birth and death themselves.[46]

Suzuki quotes Bankei's words: "Among the people who are here right now, there is not a single unenlightened one; each and every one of you is the Unborn Buddha-mind."[47] At the same time as they are the happening of each moment, birth and death are but the "logic of discrimination." Yet "non-discriminating wisdom makes possible discrimination," and the field of the Unborn, Suzuki writes, is also a "metaphysical concept" that entails a "logical structure"; namely the structure of *is/not*, according to which there are "the discrimination of non-discrimination and the non-discrimination of discrimination—and life and death are as such the Unborn."[48] Nevertheless, since "humans habitually turn non-discrimination into discrimination, making the Unborn into birth and death and birth and death into the Unborn … there is no way around the fact that Zen experience (*Zen keiken* 禅経験) has to become Zen consciousness (*Zen ishiki* 禅意識)."[49] It was, according to Suzuki, Bankei's teaching of the Unborn that helped raise Zen experience to the level of "Zen thought" (*Zen shisō* 禅思想).

In 1957, at the age of eighty-seven, at Erich Fromm's seminar in Mexico, Suzuki spoke of the Unborn in terms of a "cosmic unconsciousness" (*uchū-teki muishiki* 宇宙的無意識) and an originary wellspring for "the manifestation of a great activity" (*taiyū genzen* 大用現前). He professed that anyone can, by breaking through the bedrock of the discriminating intellect by means of the tremors of the will, come into contact with this unconsciousness and thereby become an "artist of life" who uses his or her own embodied existence to freely express him- or herself. Thus is indicated an originary freedom that does not even need to be labeled "Zen."[50] In the great work of his later period, *The Fundamental Thought of Linji* (*Rinzai no kihon shisō*, 1949), Suzuki locates Linji's (d. 866) core teaching in the "person" (*nin* 人) of his famous phrase, "the true person of no rank" (*mu-i no shinnin* 無位の真人). When Linji speaks of "becoming the master wherever one is" and of "the one who is right here and now clearly listening to the discourse on the Dharma," he is, for Suzuki, stressing the great activity of "the person of spiritual awakening."

As evidence for the Unborn Buddha-mind, Bankei points to the "chirping of birds which can be heard even though one does not consciously try to hear" or "the pain of being pricked by an awl." In reference to this Suzuki writes:

Suppose I am in the midst of writing with pen in hand and, suddenly and unintentionally, someone sticks me from behind with an awl. "Ouch!" This *one who says*

---

[46] Suzuki 1999–2003, 1: 484.
[47] Suzuki 1999–2003, 1: 483.
[48] Suzuki 1999–2003, 1: 483.
[49] Suzuki 1999–2003, 1: 486.
[50] Suzuki 1960.

"ouch!" is *the Unborn as such*, the master who sees, hears, and otherwise perceives; this is the *person* of whom Linji speaks.[51]

Speaking of an experience of my own, once when I was in a crowded subway I inadvertently stepped on the foot of another passenger. Without thinking, I—the one who had inflicted the pain—cried out "ouch!" At that moment, the other passenger smiled rather than getting angry. Cannot even such a happening reveal the endlessly interesting world of an interpersonal (in Linji's sense) encounter? In the last years of his life, one of Suzuki's favorite words was the *myō* in the Mahāyāna Buddhist phrase "true emptiness, wondrous being" (*shinkū myōu* 真空妙有). As a translation of this word, Suzuki suggested the "good" in the English phrase "good morning." He noted the resonances between Meister Eckhart's saying, "Every morning is a good morning" and Zen master Yunmen's (860–949) saying, "Every day is a good day." In saying *"Good morning!"* one person encounters another by wishing him or her well. At the heart of such a commonplace greeting can be felt the ultimate reaches of Zen.

PART TWO: HISAMATSU SHIN'ICHI'S AWAKENING TO THE TRUE SELF (BY MINOBE HITOSHI)

Hisamatsu's Context and Concerns

Hisamatsu Shin'ichi was a professor of Buddhist Studies at Kyoto University and, in that respect, can be regarded as a scholar. Yet in the preface to his first book, *Eastern Nothingness* (*Tōyō-teki mu*), he writes:

> A so-called pure scholar pursues academic study for the sake of academic study or engages in scholarly endeavors in order to become a scholar. But I have not undertaken nor have I wanted to undertake these pursuits with such intentions. Indeed, academic scholarship is neither my ultimate aim nor my original concern. For me there exists a problem on which my life is staked. This is not merely a problem for academic study.[52]

In an autobiographical essay entitled "Memories of Life as a Student," Hisamatsu writes that what he desired was "to live in absolute truth."[53] While attempting to live in absolute truth, in his actual life, Hisamatsu had to face many difficulties. In his youth, he had

---

[51] Suzuki 1999–2003, 3: 520, emphasis added.
[52] Hisamatsu 1994–96, 1: 11.
[53] Hisamatsu 1994–96, 1: 416.

considered becoming a Buddhist monk, yet he felt that he could not attain salvation within the strictures of an established religion and so he decided instead to enter Kyoto University and study philosophy under Nishida Kitarō.

In studying philosophy, however, Hisamatsu's malaise, his psychological distress, was not resolved but only deepened. When he was nearing graduation, he confided in Nishida that he felt unable to continue his studies. In response, Nishida arranged for him to meet the Zen master of Myōshinji, Ikegami Shōzan, under whose direction Hisamatsu began his Zen practice.

Soon thereafter, Hisamatsu's malaise was fundamentally resolved. At his first intensive meditation retreat (*ōzesshin* 大摂心), he reportedly had the experience of awakening to "the true self" (*shin no jiko* 真の自己).[54] This was a decisive experience for him, after which all the activities of his life were said to be performed from out of this true self.

After Hisamatsu began to teach at Kyoto University in 1935, he devoted himself, on the one hand, to a scholarly elucidation of the true self and, on the other hand, to guiding students in the praxis of awakening to it. Hisamatsu held the Way of Tea (*chadō* or *sadō* 茶道) to be a particularly effective form of this praxis,[55] and, in 1941, *Shinchakai*, a group dedicated to awakening to the true self through the practice of the Way of Tea, was established under Hisamatsu's direction on the grounds of Kyoto University. Also under his direction, and also on the grounds of Kyoto University, in 1944 *Gakudō Dōjō* was formed, a group that aimed at awakening to the true self both through praxis, especially that of seated meditation (*zazen* 坐禅), as well as through study (*gaku* 学). This group was later renamed FAS Kyōkai, the acronym standing for the threefold purpose of the group: (1) to awake to the Formless self, (2) to stand on the standpoint of All mankind, and (3) to create Superhistorical history.

The time period during which Hisamatsu taught at Kyoto University was filled with turmoil. In 1941, the Pacific War broke out and quickly escalated. In 1943, students, who up to that point had been exempted from the draft, began to be enlisted and sent off to the front lines. As is evident from the many written accounts that remain, to go to the battlefield at that time meant that one had to be prepared to go to one's death. Hisamatsu saw many of his students go off to war. After the defeat in 1945, some of them returned to the university with wounded hearts as well as bodies. Such was the historical context in which Hisamatsu lectured to a great number of people about the true self and strove to revitalize Zen in a manner appropriate to the modern age.

---

[54] Hisamatsu 1994–96, 1: 433.

[55] See his *The Philosophy of the Way of Tea* (*Chadō no tetsugaku*), reprinted as Hisamatsu 1994–96, vol. 4.

The True Self Is Absolute Nothingness

What exactly does Hisamatsu mean by the "true self"? To begin with, what was the problem that was resolved upon awakening to the true self? In "Memories of Life as a Student," Hisamatsu writes that he had been plagued by a feeling that his life was "deceitful" (*kyogi* 虚偽); in other words, that he was living a lie. He includes in this essay a letter he wrote to Nishida at the time, which in part said:

> The more deeply I introspect, the more loudly and clearly screams out the realization that the way I had been living my life was deceitful . . . . I had been living a strictly moral life, yet was this moral life issuing from the free demands of my innermost heart? . . . In the train had I not been unable to give my seat to an elderly person or a small child out of fear that others would think I was trying to show off my good deed, even though I had felt sorry for the elderly person or small child, and even though on other occasions I had indeed tried to show off my good deeds in front of others?[56]

It seems that Hisamatsu felt that his life was being ruled, not by himself, but by the eyes of those around him. This was presumably not simply a matter of living a life of self-sacrifice so that he could win the praises of society, for he was not trying to suppress his own desires in order to be complimented by others. Rather, it seems that the problem was that he could not discover a rule for his life other than the judgments of society. Insofar as this was the case, what was plaguing him was a kind of nihilism.

The judgments of society are relative. They change depending on the person making them, or depending on the time and place in which they are made. It could be said that what afflicted the young Hisamatsu was that he could not discover something to guide his life other than such relative judgments of society; in other words, he could not find something absolute within himself.

By discovering through meditation the absolute "true self," Hisamatsu was liberated from his malaise. That is to say, he overcame his malaise by discovering the reality of the self in a place beyond relative postulates of meaning such as the judgments of society—and since all postulates of meaning are relative, this was a place beyond all postulates of meaning.

Because the true self is something formless (*katachi no nai mono* 形の無いもの) beyond all postulates of meaning, Hisamatsu designated it with the word "nothingness" (*mu* 無). According to Hisamatsu, the radical source (*kongen* 根源) of the self has no form. Although we are living within a world constituted by relative postulates of meaning, our radical source is a "nothingness" that transcends this world. He was fond of explaining this with the metaphor of water and waves, a metaphor that has been used since ancient times in Buddhism.[57] Our selves are like waves. Although each wave has

---

[56] Hisamatsu 1994–96, 1: 427–428.

[57] This metaphor is commonly used in East Asian Buddhism. It stems in part from the seminal sixth-century text, *The Awakening of Faith in Mahāyāna*, on which Hisamatsu wrote a commentary. See *The Awakening of Faith*, trans. Yoshito S. Hakeda (New York: Columbia University Press, 1967); and Hisamatsu 1994–96, vol. 9.—*Tr.*

its own limited form and exists in relation to other relative waves, originally it is form-less water. Water transcends the relativity of waves and exists absolutely. Waves arise out of and return to water. In this sense, while our selves have a relative meaning within the world, they are at the same time an absolute nothingness (*zettai no mu* 絶対の無). In a passage where he uses this metaphor of water and waves, Hisamatsu writes:

> All waves ... arise from water and do not depart from water; they disappear and return to water without leaving any trace whatsoever .... Looked at from the water, waves are the movement of water; water is non-dually one with waves, and yet the arising and perishing of waves does not entail the arising and perishing or the increasing and decreasing of water. Water arises and perishes as waves and yet, as water, neither arises nor perishes.[58]

Someone who understands the self only as the form of a wave does not know the radical source of the self. Someone who does not know the radical source of the self is unable to dwell at peace in the self. Hisamatsu thought that only when one comes to realize that the self is originally and absolutely the water that neither arises nor perishes does one become able to absolutely affirm the self and find peace of mind.

Absolute Autonomy and Suffering

This absolute nothingness, which Hisamatsu claims is the radical source of the self, and which he compares to the water that neither arises nor perishes, is not a nihilistic nothingness. Just as the water is non-dualistically one with waves, absolute nothing-ness is one with our individual selves. That the radical source of our selves is an absolute nothingness means that our selves are formed from this absolute nothingness which is, Hisamatsu emphasizes, not static but rather creative.

Moreover, he stresses that the workings of this creativity are none other than the workings of our selves. This is because the fact that our selves are formed from absolute nothingness means that our selves freely form themselves from absolute nothingness. Hisamatsu refers to this freedom with the concept of "absolute autonomy" (*zettai jiritsu* 絶対自律), which he says is the essential characteristic of the true self. As long as any element of heteronomy can still be found within the self, that is not the true self. One gets the sense that Hisamatsu felt that any heteronomously lived life still contains some degree of deception. He was thus sharply critical, for example, of dialectical theology's conception of God as a "wholly other" (*Ganz-Anderes*). He thought that as long as there remains an element of alterity to God, who can be said to be the very life of our own selves, then our life cannot truly become our own, and thus we cannot truly be saved. A heteronomous life, for Hisamatsu, is not a true life.

---

[58] Hisamatsu 1994–96, 1: 65.

Yet is it in fact possible for the self to be absolutely autonomous? Is it not the case that, in reality, each one of us suffers from the fact that the self is limited by what persons and things outside ourselves do, such that one's self is not always how one wishes it to be? Could it not be said that to think that the self is absolutely autonomous and so is not subject to psychological suffering is, at best, a wishful fantasy and, at worst, a hubristic conflation of human being with some kind of divine being? If the individual self were thought to be absolutely autonomous, then this would indeed be a wishful fantasy or hubristic delusion. Such a way of thinking would result in relativism and nihilism. However, this was not in fact Hisamatsu's way of thinking. He recognized the reality of the sufferings of the individual self. His point, however, is that the individual self that suffers needs to realize that he or she is one form of the self-determination of absolute nothingness. This requires that one depart from the manner of being an individual self, that one gain distance from one's individual self, and see it from its radical source; that is, from absolute nothingness. When the self sees the individual self as the self-determination of absolute nothingness, the self is, while standing in relative relation to other things and persons, at the same time an absolutely singular person. This manner of being a self is what Hisamatsu means when he speaks of being absolutely autonomous.

To view the self as absolutely autonomous means, concretely speaking, that one does not attribute the causes of one's suffering—one's distresses and worries (*nayami* 悩み)—to something or someone other than oneself, but rather fully takes responsibility for resolving them oneself. If one lives in such a manner, one neither detests others nor falls into despair. The worries of the self are then none other than the worries of the world. That is to say, they are worries about what to do with the world. This is how Hisamatsu conceived of the way of being of the true self.

In an interview late in life, Hisamatsu remarked that he had no worries. Yet he did not mean that in his actual daily life he did not have anything to worry about. Rather, he explains:

> I don't actually have any worrisome thoughts . . . . Even though I do engage in what people usually refer to as worrying, for me this is not really worrying . . . . This is because it is the worry-free subject who is worrying. I really think that this kind of worrying is not what is usually regarded as worrying.[59]

It is not that Hisamatsu never had worries. Rather, without making excuses, he fully accepted and, from the radical source of the self, thoroughly addressed his worries. Yet, because he worried from the radical source of the self, these were no longer "his own" worries. To thus engage in life's daily troubles from the radical source of the self, for Hisamatsu, was to live in absolute truth.

---

[59] Hisamatsu 1994–96, 9: 476–477.

PART THREE: MASAO ABE'S CONTRIBUTIONS TO MODERN JAPANESE BUDDHIST PHILOSOPHY (BY STEVEN HEINE)

This section of the chapter examines some of the main accomplishments of Masao Abe (Jp. Abe Masao) in the field of Buddhist and comparative philosophical studies. These include his expositions of classic and contemporary Zen philosophy as a primary representative of this tradition, his ongoing involvement in constructive dialogue between Buddhism and Western religions as well as various ideological factions within Japanese Buddhism, and his distinctive approach to articulating an innovative philosophy for the current age based primarily on a critical view of Buddhist approaches to metaphysics and ethics. Perhaps best known in the West for his contributions to interfaith dialogue, toward the end of his career, Abe's several new publications in Japanese developed a unique view of the Buddhist notion of emptiness in relation to modern philosophical issues.

Abe's Major Achievements

During the course of a remarkable career spanning nearly six decades of exhaustive philosophical engagement, beginning with his training under Zen teacher Hisamatsu Shin'ichi at Myōshinji Temple in Kyoto and going on to lecture at various institutions and numerous conferences while publishing extensively both in Japan and the West, Abe became known for several important accomplishments in disseminating Buddhist thought in comparative perspectives and global contexts. These include his expositions of classic and contemporary Zen philosophy as a primary representative of this tradition, his ongoing involvement in constructive dialogue between Buddhism and Western religions as well as various ideological factions within Japanese Buddhism, and his distinctive approach to articulating an innovative philosophy for the current age based primarily on a critical view of Buddhist approaches to metaphysics and ethics.

In particular, Abe gained prominence as an exponent of traditional Zen Buddhism and presenter of this philosophy to the modern West. It is often said that, with the death of D. T. Suzuki in 1966, the mantle of leadership was then passed to Abe, who became the main figure at the end of the past century, playing the role of transmitter whose own theoretical outlook embodied the open-ended and multiperspectival standpoint of Zen thought. A major part of this development was Abe's considerable contributions to the teaching and mentoring of several dozen Western scholars who became prominent figures in the fields of Buddhist and cross-cultural philosophical studies.

A major corollary achievement was Abe's translation and interpretation of eminent Zen Buddhist thinkers, both traditional and modern. Abe is especially known for his work on Dōgen, the thirteenth-century founder of the Sōtō Zen sect, and Nishida Kitarō, the leading figure in modern Japanese philosophy and originator of the Kyoto School, of which Abe is considered a prominent member. Abe's renderings and hermeneutic discussions of Dōgen and Nishida remain among the best known and most frequently cited commentaries in the respective fields.[60]

For many scholars and theologians east and west, perhaps Abe's foremost accomplishment is his vigorous participation in and lifelong commitment to interfaith dialogue, primarily involving Buddhist–Christian studies, in addition to exchanges with Jewish thinkers and discussions of related thematic issues, such as the encounter of religion and science or the impact of the Holocaust on comparative ethics. The hallmark of the Kyoto School is a comparison of Japanese Buddhism and Western thought. However, Abe went much further than predecessors and colleagues in personally seeking out and getting to know while exchanging ideas with dialogue partners from among the leading theologians and philosophers of religion in the West representing a wide range of Christian and, to a lesser extent, Jewish traditions.[61]

While Abe is probably most widely known for his contribution to the East–West philosophical encounter, a crucial aspect of his effort to establish *interfaith* dialogue was the undertaking of a multifaceted *intrafaith* exchange involving various factions of Japanese Buddhist thought, especially Zen and Pure Land as well as, within the context of the former, the Rinzai and Sōtō sects. The two dimensions of dialogue—interfaith and intrafaith—complement, reinforce, and enhance each other. The base of Abe's overall dialogical project is Zen thought. But before (in an ontological rather than chronological sense) he turns to examining other traditions, he clarifies the meaning of his own tradition. Therefore, intrafaith dialogue is the necessary building block that makes possible the construction of the larger interfaith edifice, or the micro-element needed for the macro-structure. Or, to use a naturalist metaphor favored by a host of Eastern thinkers, it represents the roots that allow the growth of the branches.

The first level of exchange, which exists on the borderline between inter and intrafaith dialogue, deals with dialogue between Zen and its apparent ideological opposite within Buddhism, the Pure Land school. This intrafaith dialogue particularly involves the two leading thinkers of Kamakura-era Japan, Dōgen and his contemporary Shinran in the early thirteenth century, the founder of the Jōdo Shin-shū sect of Pure Land Buddhism.[62] Zen is known as the path of self-power (*jiriki* 自力) and Pure Land as the path of other-power (*tariki* 他力). Zen stresses an inner, contemplative realization of the Unborn (*fushō* 不生) moment in this life, while Pure Land emphasizes attainment through humility and faith in Amida Buddha of rebirth in the next life.

Yet, in the respective approaches to such issues as naturalism and causality, Abe shows underlying similarities between Zen and Pure Land, which both derive their philosophies from the Mahāyāna doctrines of the universality of the Buddha-nature

---

[60] Abe 1994 and 2003.
[61] Mitchell 1998.
[62] See Chapters 6, 8, and 9 in this volume.

(*busshō* 仏性) and original enlightenment (*hongaku* 本覚). He also demonstrates how and why the two schools of thought should dispense with polemics and creatively encounter each other in a modern context on the issues of human nature as well as the potentials and obstacles for soteriological fulfillment in relation to the primordial potentiality of Buddha-nature in order to reach a higher degree of self-understanding. In comparing Dōgen and Shinran, Abe's methodology stresses that although contemporary reason allows us to set up a critical contrast, "we cannot help but confront the issues ... when we subjectively inquire into the religious attainment of the two thinkers in terms of our own existential realization rather than objectively compare them by putting our self outside of their experiences."[63] That is, Abe's approach is never merely comparative in an abstract speculative sense, but, by drawing on yet surpassing the critical approach of objective scholarship, he incorporates into the dialogue the dimension of Zen subjectivity with its deeply existential awareness of identity and difference to creatively empathize with alternative viewpoints.

Abe as an Original Zen Thinker

The question that arises from an analysis of Abe's overall scholarly production and publications, including major works not yet translated, is whether and to what extent Abe can be considered an original thinker, and, if so, what is his special contribution to the Kyoto School and cross-cultural religious philosophy in a broader sense. In reflecting on this issue, I have often thought about an episode that took place a few years ago, when I requested permission from a journal to reprint an article in a collection of Abe's work that I was editing for a new publication. The editor's response in consenting to the request included the comment that he considered Abe's contribution to Buddhist studies to be "not a secondary, but a primary source."

What did this remark mean? I believe there are two possibilities. One possibility, on the more critical side, is that Abe does not present Buddhism in an objective, historical fashion and is thus not worthy of being referred to as a secondary source, which in a sense has more validity than the approach he represents. The positive side of the journal editor's comment is that Abe's work offers a distinctively original interpretation that is part of the continuing construction of Buddhist thought for the modern world. Following this line of understanding, my tentative answer to the question of whether Abe is an original thinker is "yes." A major reason for my saying this is based on the fact, of which the editor was not aware, that Abe rather late in his life was producing books in Japanese for an audience in Japan rather than the West.[64]

In three volumes published between 1996 and 2000, Abe began to develop what he innovatively called "sunyata-ology," or a systematic discussion of the root meaning and

---

[63] As stated in conversation in Kyoto, July 1998.
[64] Abe 1996, 2000*a*, and 2000*b*.

far-ranging philosophical implications of the Mahāyāna Buddhist doctrine of *śūnyatā* or emptiness. This term is often used interchangeably with the notion of nothingness (*mu* 無) in relation to or in contrast with nihilism, nihility, and negation. Like his Kyoto School predecessor Nishitani Keiji, who was in turn greatly influenced by Western philosophers Friedrich Nietzsche and Martin Heidegger, the mission of overcoming nihilism at its root must be the central goal of modern thought, according to Abe, who believes that the Kyoto School and Zen in particular is best equipped to accomplish this philosophical task.

Abe's original thought can also be found by exploring themes that are expressed in his English-language publications, and for this I will focus on two of his essays, one dealing with dialogue and the other with the issue of nihilism. The first essay is "Spirituality and Liberation: A Buddhist-Christian Conversation (with Paul F. Knitter),"[65] and the second is "Evil, Sin, Falsity, and the Dynamics of Faith,"[66] which I translated for *Zen and the Modern World* from a piece originally published in *Kyogi to kyomu*.

The interfaith dialogue with Knitter is one of the more fascinating examples of Abe's cross-cultural exchanges. Knitter brings to the discussion a background and sympathy for Zen as a co-translator of Heinrich Dumoulin's monumental two-volume history of Zen from German to English in the 1980s,[67] in addition to his interest in Liberation Theology and the need for religious commitment to social causes. Knitter's criticism of Buddhism from a Christian perspective can be summed up by two expressions he coins. The first is that in Buddhism, "You cannot change the world unless you sit," and the second is that in Christianity, "You cannot sit unless you change the world." For Knitter, the second approach, which is active and socially aware, is clearly preferable because the Buddhist view can lead to either an ethical lethargy or a decline into antinomianism, long the bane of utopian mystical philosophies.

Abe's rebuttal emphasizes that Knitter uses the term "sit" in two different ways that ignore the dynamism of Buddhist meditation, which avoids complacency. More significantly, he argues that Knitter's corollary, which is that in Christianity "We do before we know," is an unfair comment in relation to Buddhism because it ignores the true meaning of "before." Here, Abe makes a metaphysical move in casting doubt on Knitter's Christian approach, which is not sensitive to the notion that "before" should not be understood in a simple sequential or chronological sense but as a primordial activity of "knowing" that underscores and enhances "doing" each and every moment. In this exchange, we get a glimpse of Abe's originality, although his response to Knitter's ethical challenge is still somewhat abstract and lacking in specificity.

Abe's distinctive thought regarding the religious quest is especially evident in the second essay, "Evil, Sin, Falsity, and the Dynamics of Faith." Here, he documents a progression of self-awareness about human limitations that moves from the most abstract

---

[65] Abe 1995, 223–242.

[66] Abe 2003, 119–126.

[67] Heinrich Dumoulin, *Zen Buddhism: A History*, 2 vols., trans. James Heisig and Paul Knitter (New York: Macmillan, 1988).

level of understanding to the existential dynamics of accomplishing the core spirituality of Mahāyāna Buddhism through the awakening of faith, yet also moves beyond conventional devotion or commitment to the divine. Abe begins by analyzing the notion of evil, which is an ontological category that exists whether or not an individual is aware of participating in its effects, and moves to the category of sin, a theological category whereby self-limitation becomes apparent.

Following this, Abe's next category is the phenomenological notion of falsity as prelude to the religious quest for spiritual fulfillment that cannot escape from and must always acknowledge and come to terms with the world of illusion and disappointment. On this level of nihility in relation to faith, Abe stresses the role of the authentic realization of nothingness attained through exploring self-doubt to its ultimate conclusion and transformation as a key to the overcoming of nihilism. According to Abe:

> By entering into a relation with God, however, the self overcomes nothingness encountered in the failure of morality and becomes the religious self, but at this moment it is drawn again into the dark abyss of groundlessness or nothingness because of the inevitable failure of faith to transcend falsity. Therefore, we must say that the awareness of falsity, along with being unified with the awareness of nothingness in and of itself, is an awareness in which the falsity that is surpassed by faith is thus made opposite to itself and is transformed into a twofoldness by being directly aware of itself once again. Now, if we call the awareness of nothingness due to the failure of morality a kind of nihilism based on the awareness of evil, this would imply the possibility of the self being overcome by believing in a transcendental divinity mediating with the human being as the nothingness faced at the very moment of the failure of immanent human reason.[68]

In this passage, we find a superb example of the originality of Abe's thought regarding Zen in relation to worldwide religiosity that stands beyond his accomplishments in the field of dialogue and perhaps surpasses his approach to ethics. He demonstrates that the Buddhist notion of emptiness is a universal category that encompasses and explains the dynamics of faith arising from the self-realization of the failure of human reason to experience nothingness in a genuine way.

Human inability, usually understood in terms of undergoing doubt, anxiety, and despair as a necessary existential awareness of the abyss of the dark night of the soul, leads at first to nihilism, which represents a limited and partial view of emptiness that does not transcend falsity. In order to overcome such a pessimistic worldview by questioning and seeking to resolve the origins of the expressions of falsity along with the performance of misguided actions that plague their existence, people often look for comfort to the notion of a transcendental divinity or make a Kierkegaardian leap of faith by trying to embrace a higher power that fills the inescapable void. However, it is just this level of understanding that gives way to a deeper turnabout experience, whereby *śūnyatā*

---

[68] Abe 2003, 125.

unfolds as the true basis of delusory thoughts and deeds and, therefore, opens up the possibility for reconciliation with human nature resulting in a realization of the fundamental groundless ground of nothingness that at once causes and overcomes evil, sin, and falsity.

Therefore, the apparent experience of the divine through faith is exposed as yet another chimera based on inauthenticity that releases humans to become aware of the true meaning of emptiness expressed in various Zen sayings and other sources, one that is unbound by the conventional oppositions of pessimism and optimism or truth and falsity. In this way, Abe insightfully shows the origins and limits of various kinds of theology so as to pave the way for what he refers to elsewhere as sunyata-ology. This profound yet flexible notion was primarily articulated in two books published in Japanese in 2000 that, unfortunately, have not yet been translated. Those works reveal the core of an impressively original Japanese thinker associated with the Kyoto School culminating a lifelong mission to engage Buddhism critically yet constructively by virtue of absolute nothingness (*zettai mu*) with worldwide traditional religious thought and modern existential philosophy of religion.

Parts One and Two Translated from the Japanese by Bret W. DAVIS

REFERENCES

Abe, Masao. (1985) *Zen and Western Thought*, edited by William R. LaFleur. Honolulu: University of Hawai'i Press.

Abe, Masao. (1990) "Kenotic God and Dynamic Sunyata." In *The Emptying God: A Buddhist-Jewish-Christian Conversation with Masao Abe on God, Kenosis, and Sunyata*, edited by John B. Cobb, Jr. and Christopher Ives. Maryknoll, NY: Orbis Books, 3–65.

Abe, Masao. (1994) *Dōgen: His Philosophy and Religion*, edited by Steven Heine. Albany: State University of New York Press.

Abe, Masao. (1995) *Buddhism and Interfaith Dialogue*, edited by Steven Heine. Honolulu: University of Hawai'i Press.

Abe Masao. (1996) *Kongen kara no shuppatsu* [Emerging From the Root]. Kyoto: Hōzōkan.

Abe, Masao. (1997) *Zen and Comparative Studies*, edited by Steven Heine. Honolulu: University of Hawai'i Press.

Abe Masao. (2000a) *Kyogi to kyomu: Shūkyōteki jikaku ni okeru nihilizumu no mondai* [Falsehood and Emptiness: The Problem of Nihilism in Religious Consciousness]. Kyoto: Hōzōkan.

Abe Masao. (2000b) *Hibutsu hima: Nihirizumu to akuma no mondai* [Neither Buddha nor Devil: The Problem of Nihilism and the Devil]. Kyoto: Hōzōkan.

Abe, Masao. (2003) *Zen and the Modern World*, edited by Steven Heine. Honolulu: University of Hawai'i Press.

Cobb, John B. Jr., and Christopher Ives, eds. (1990) *The Emptying God: A Buddhist-Jewish-Christian Conversation with Masao Abe on God, Kenosis, and Sunyata*. Maryknoll, NY: Orbis Books.

Heidegger, Martin, and Shinichi Hisamatsu. (1989a) "Wechselseitige Spiegelung." In *Japan und Heidegger*, edited by Harmut Buchner. Sigmaringen: Thorbecke, 189–192.

Heidegger, Martin, and Shinichi Hisamatsu. (1989*b*) "Die Kunst und das Denken: Protokoll eines Colloquiums am 18. Mail 1958." In *Japan und Heidegger*, edited by Harmut Buchner. Sigmaringen: Thorbecke, 211–215.

Hisamatsu Shin'ichi. (1960) "The Characteristics of Oriental Nothingness," translated by Richard DeMartino. *Philosophical Studies of Japan* 2: 65–97.

Hisamatsu Shin'ichi. (1982*a*) *Zen and the Fine Arts*, translated by Gishin Tokiwa. Tokyo: Kodansha.

Hisamatsu Shin'ichi. (1982*b*) *Bokkai: Hisamatsu Shin'ichi no sho* [Hisamatsu Shin'ichi's Calligraphy]. Kyoto: Tōeisha.

Hisamatsu Shin'ichi. (1994–96) *Hisamatsu Shin'ichi chosakushū* [Collected Works of Hisamatsu Shin'ichi], 9 vols. Kyoto: Hōzōkan. This is the newer edition of Hisamatsu's *Collected Works*.

Hisamatsu Shin'ichi. (2002) *Critical Sermons of the Zen Tradition*, edited and translated by Christopher Ives and Tokiwa Gishin. New York: Palgrave.

Mitchell, Donald W. (1998) *Masao Abe: A Zen Life of Dialogue*. Boston: Tuttle.

Nishida Kitarō. (1987) *Last Writings: Nothingness and the Religious Worldview*, translated with an Introduction and Postscript by David A. Dilworth. Honolulu: University of Hawai'i Press.

Nishida Kitarō. (1987–1989) *Nishida Kitarō zenshū* [Complete Works of Nishida Kitarō], 19 vols. Tokyo: Iwanami.

Nishida Kitarō. (1990) *An Inquiry Into the Good*, translated by Masao Abe and Christopher Ives. New Haven, CT: Yale University Press.

Suzuki, D. T. (1960) "Lectures on Zen Buddhism." In *Zen Buddhism and Psychoanalysis*, edited by D. T. Suzuki, Erich Fromm, and Richard De Martino. New York: Harper & Brothers, 1–76.

Suzuki, D. T. (1964) *An Introduction to Zen Buddhism*. Forward by Carl Jung. New York, Grove Press.

Suzuki, Daisetsu T. (1989) "Erinnerungen an einen Busuch bei Martin Heidegger (1953)," translated by Elmar Weinmayr. In *Japan und Heidegger*, edited by Harmut Buchner. Sigmaringen: Thorbecke, 169–172.

Suzuki, Daisetz T. (1998) *The Buddha of Infinite Light: The Teachings of Shin Buddhism, the Japanese Way of Wisdom and Compassion*. Boston: Shambhala.

Suzuki Daisetsu. (1999–2003) *Suzuki Daisetsu zenshū* [Complete Works of D. T. Suzuki], 40 vols. Tokyo: Iwanami.

Suzuki, D. T. (2015–16) *Selected Works of D. T. Suzuki*, 3 vols. edited by Richard M. Jaffe. Oakland: University of California Press.

Tillich, Paul, and Hisamatsu Shin'ichi. (1971–1973) "Dialogues East and West: Paul Tillich and Hisamatsu Shin'ichi." Published in three installments in *The Eastern Buddhist* 4/2 (1971): 89–107; 5/2 (1972): 107–128; and 6/2 (1973): 87–114.

FURTHER READING

Bankei. (2000) *The Unborn: The Life and Teachings of Zen Master Bankei (1622–1693)*, revised edition. Translated and with an introduction by Norman Waddell. New York: North Point Press.

Fujiyoshi Jikai, ed. (1983) *Hisamatsu Shin'ichi no shūkyō to shisō* [Hisamatsu Shin'ichi's Religion and Thought]. Kyoto: Zen Bunka Kenkyū-sho.

Fujiyoshi Jikai, and Kurasawa Yukihiro, eds. (1985) *Shin-nin Hisamatsu Shin'ichi* [Hisamatsu Shin'ichi: A True Person]. Tokyo: Shunjūsha.

Harr, Francis, and Masao Abe, eds. (1995) *A Zen Life: D. T. Suzuki Remembered*. New York: Weatherhill.

Hisamatsu Shin'ichi. (1969–80) *Hisamatsu Shin'ichi chosakushū* [Collected Works of Hisamatsu Shin'ichi], 8 vols. Tokyo: Risōsha. This is the older edition of Hisamatsu's *Collected Works*.

Hisamatsu, Shin'ichi. (1975) *Die Fülle des Nichts*, translated by Hirata Takashi and Johanna Fischer. Pfullingen: Neske.

Hisamatsu, Shin'ichi. (1990) *Philosophie des Erwachens*, translated by Nobert Klein and Takizawa Katsumi. Berlin: Theseus-Verlag.

Hisamatsu, Shin'ichi. (1990–91) *Hisamatsu Shin'ichi Bukkyō kōgi* [Hisamatsu Shin'ichi's Lectures on Buddhism], 4 vols. Kyoto: Hōzōkan.

Hisamatsu, Shin'ichi. (2012a) "Eine Erläuterung des Lin-chi-(=Rinzai)-Zen," translated by Tsujimura Koichi and Hartmut Buchner. In *Die Philosophie der Kyoto-Schule*, third edition, edited by Ohashi Ryôsuke. Freiburg/Munich: Alber, 218–221.

Hisamatsu, Shin'ichi. (2012b) "Kunst und Kunstwerke im Zen-Buddismus," translated by Geza S. Dombrady. In *Die Philosophie der Kyoto-Schule*, third edition, edited by Ohashi Ryôsuke. Freiburg/Munich: Alber, 222–234.

Hisamatsu, Shin'ichi. (2012c) "Selbst-Bild," translated by Tsujimura Koichi and Hartmut Buchner. In *Die Philosophie der Kyoto-Schule*, third edition, edited by Ohashi Ryôsuke. Freiburg/Munich: Alber, 235–236.

Hisamatsu, Shin'ichi, and Yagi Seiichi. (1980) *Kaku no shūkyō* [Religion of Awakening]. Tokyo: Shunjūsha.

Ives, Christopher. (1992) *Zen Awakening and Society*. Foreword by Masao Abe and John Hick. Honolulu: University of Hawai'i Press.

Ives, Christopher. (2010) "True Person, Formless Self: Lay Zen Master Hisamatsu Shin'ichi." In *Zen Masters*, edited by Steven Heine and Dale S. Write. New York: Oxford University Press, 217–238.

Linji. (2009) *The Record of Linji*, translated by Ruth Fuller Sasaki, edited by Thomas Yūhō Kirchner. Honolulu: University of Hawai'i Press.

Suzuki, D. T. (1927, 1949, 1958) *Essays in Zen Buddhism, First Series*. London: Luzac and Co., Rider and Co.

Suzuki, D. T. (1930) *Studies in the Lancavatara Sutra*. London: George Routledge & Sons.

Suzuki, D. T. (1933, 1950, 1958) *Essays in Zen Buddhism, Second Series*. London: Luzac and Co., Rider and Co.

Suzuki, D. T. (1934, 1953, 1958) *Essays in Zen Buddhism, Third Series*. London: Luzac and Co., Rider and Co.

Suzuki, D. T. (1949) *The Zen Doctrine of No-Mind: The Significance of the Sutra of Hui-neng (Wei-lang)*. London: Rider.

Suzuki, D. T. (1956) *Zen Buddhism: Selected Writings of D. T. Suzuki*, edited by William Barrett. Garden City, NY: Doubleday, 1956.

Suzuki, D. T. (1957) *Mysticism: Christian and Buddhist*. London: Allen and Unwin.

Suzuki, D. T. (1962) *The Essentials of Zen Buddhism: Selected from the Writings of Daisetz T. Suzuki*, edited by Bernard Phillips. New York: E. P. Dutton.

Suzuki, Daisetz Teitaro. (1972) *Japanese Spirituality*, translated from the Japanese by Norman Waddell. Tokyo: Japanese Society for the Promotion of Science.

Suzuki, D. T. (1972) *Living by Zen*. York Beach, Maine: Samuel Weiser.

Suzuki, D. T. (1980) *The Awakening of Zen*, edited by Christmas Humphreys. Boulder, CO: Prajna Press.

Suzuki Daisetsu. (2001) *Suzuki Daisetsu Zen senshū* [Selected Writings on Zen by D. T. Suzuki], 12 vols. Tokyo: Shunjūsha.

Suzuki, Daizetz T. (2010). *Zen and Japanese Culture*. Princeton: Princeton University Press.

Suzuki, D. T., Erich Fromm, et al. (2006) *Zen Buddhism and Psychoanalysis*. New York: Harper and Brothers.

Ueda Shizuteru, and Horio Tsutomu, eds. (1998) *Zen to gendai sekai* [Zen and the Contemporary World]. Kyoto: Zen Bunka Kenkyū-sho.

Ueda Shizuteru, Kitano Hiroyuki, and Mori Tetsurō, eds. (2006) *Zen to Kyōto tetsugakku* [Zen and Kyoto Philosophy]. Kyoto: Tōei-sha.

PART III

PHILOSOPHIES OF JAPANESE CONFUCIANISM AND BUSHIDŌ

CHAPTER 12

....

JAPANESE NEO-CONFUCIAN
PHILOSOPHY

....

JOHN A. TUCKER

CONFUCIANISM refers to a multifaceted set of ideas, texts, practices, and forms of self-cultivation expressed multidimensionally as philosophy, religion, literature, history, ideology, and intellectual history, as well as combinations and recombinations thereof. Confucianism began in ancient China with the teachings of Kongfuzi, later Romanized as Confucius, but spread to Korea, Japan, and Southeast Asia, forming one layer of East Asian culture and civilization over time. Many of its ethical notions, such as humaneness, filial piety, and justice, remain current today even though their Confucian roots might have been forgotten over time. Although much criticized early on during the modern transformation of East Asia, Confucianism remains a powerful substratum of ethical thinking, practice, and prognosis at the individual, social, and political levels. Despite its regional ties, it typically addresses issues at a cosmic if not universal level, thus making its claims relevant to "all under heaven" and precluding petty parochialism.

Here, however, Confucianism is examined as a Japanese philosophical expression, one distinctive to Japan and its cultural subjectivities even while drawing on earlier and contemporaneous developments in China and Korea. More specifically, the focus is on later Confucianism, often called Neo-Confucianism in the West, that appeared during the Song dynasty in China and then spread throughout the region in later centuries, forming the final wave of traditional philosophical thinking to inform East Asian life prior to the internalization of Western philosophy in the nineteenth century and beyond. Neo-Confucianism was "neo" because its content was highly innovative, its praxis largely unprecedented, and its texts so novel that even East Asians discussing it referred to it as "later Confucianism," "Song Confucianism," "Song-Ming Confucianism," "the School of Human Nature and Principle," or "the School of the Way." Appellations were many but nevertheless united in differentiating later Confucianism from its ancient, classical expressions. The difference between Confucianism and Neo-Confucianism might be compared to that between Theravāda Buddhism, conveying the early teachings of Siddhārtha Gautama, the historical Buddha, and Mahāyāna Buddhism, the later more universalistic and multifaceted teachings that spread throughout Asia. As with Mahāyāna, Neo-Confucianism also traveled farther and deeper than the earliest expressions of the tradition, pervading the region as a common form of higher learning conveying a far more secular, realistic, and commonsense-oriented approach to philosophical problems than had characterized the preceding age of Buddhist dominance when Mahāyāna notions of emptiness, nirvāna, reincarnation, and a glorious Pure Land as opposed to a hell of endless reincarnation and karmic punishment permeated the spiritual and philosophical culture of the day.

The Song master Zhu Xi (1130–1200) is generally recognized as the "premier" philosopher of Neo-Confucianism, in large part because he was able to synthesize so many ideas advanced earlier by a series of forerunners including Zhou Dunyi (1017–1073), Zhang Zai (1020–1077), Cheng Hao (1032–1085), and Cheng Yi (1033–1107), each of whom developed highly innovative understandings of Confucianism. With every wave of new thinking, new texts were authored or old ones emended, thus conveying the new thinking in largely unprecedented ways. In the process, the old Confucian curriculum of the Five Classics—including the *Book of Changes*, the *Book of History*, the *Book of Poetry*, the *Spring and Autumn Annals*, and the *Records of the Rites*—although still studied, was de-emphasized. The new curriculum that emerged consisted primarily of the Four Books: the *Great Learning*, the *Analects* of Confucius, the *Mencius*, and the *Doctrine of the Mean*, as well as the commentaries of Zhu Xi and others on them. In many respects, elevation of the Four Books simplified Confucian literature, making it more accessible for most students due to their relative brevity compared to the Five Classics of ancient Confucian thought. Two of the Four Books, for example, were little more than chapters taken from the *Book of Rites*, yet the two chapters were now designated by Song philosophers (including Zhu Xi) as books, each in their own right. Such textual innovation continued with newly emended passages and textual insertions in the first of the Four Books, the *Great Learning*, now elevated as the gateway to learning. This rearrangement of Confucian literature privileging the Four Books over the Five Classics was one of many innovations distinguishing Song and post-Song Confucianism from ancient Confucianism.

CONFUCIANISM AND PHILOSOPHY: ORIGINS

A few words about the study of Confucianism as philosophy are in order. Western discussions of Confucianism as philosophy have a deep and fascinating history, beginning with the Jesuit work, *Confucius Sinarum Philosophus* (*Confucius: The Philosopher of China*), published in Paris in 1687, under the auspices of King Louis XIV. That work, the first major presentation of Confucius' thought to the West, cast Confucius, significantly enough, neither as a religious teacher nor simply as a thinker, but instead as a philosopher. *Confucius Sinarum Philosophus* included translations from three of the Four Books—the *Great Learning*, the *Doctrine of the Mean*, and the *Analects*—omitting only the *Mencius* because Mencius' ideas were so different from those of Confucius, even though the *Mencius* had been considered, in China, an orthodox expression of what was otherwise called "Confucianism." Ironically, the authors of *Confucius Sinarum Philosophus* sought to differentiate what they thought they were presenting—ancient Confucianism, which they thought was theistic—from what they had seen in seventeenth-century China: the legacy of Song Confucianism or Neo-Confucianism, which they deemed atheistic. Despite their efforts, which ultimately misrepresented the religious thinking of both halves of the Confucian tradition, their presentations remained Neo-Confucian in accepting the Four Books as the basic texts of the tradition. The quality of their hermeneutics aside, the Jesuit authors of *Confucius Sinarum Philosophus* provided Western students of Confucian and Neo-Confucian thinking with one of the most seminal interpretive approaches to those forms of learning, seeing it as philosophy and interpreting it philosophically.

From the Jesuit work, in Latin, soon came vernacular translations into French and English. Once the Enlightenment began and philosophes such as Voltaire appeared, the view of Confucius as a rationalist thinker, perhaps now more deistic than theistic, was widely affirmed. Even Hegel, the grand continental philosopher of the early nineteenth century, included Confucius the moralist as one of the Oriental philosophers he considered, albeit with clear condescension. Hegel's scant respect for Confucius, however, had considerable consequences. Later, the young Meiji intellectual Inoue Tetsujirō (1855–1944), after studying philosophy in Germany from 1884 to 1890, returned to Japan for an appointment as the first Japanese professor of philosophy at Tokyo Imperial University. Over the next fifteen years, Inoue published a number of works describing what he called "Japanese philosophy," or *Nihon tetsugaku*. The latter he saw as a subset of *Tōyō tetsugaku* or Asian philosophy. One of Inoue's most famous works was a trilogy, authored between 1895 and 1905, the years corresponding to the Sino-Japanese and Russo-Japanese Wars. The trilogy included *Nihon Shushigakuha no tetsugaku* (*The Philosophy of the Japanese School of Master Zhu Xi*), *Nihon Yōmeigakuha no tetsugaku* (*The Philosophy of the Japanese School of Wang Yangming*), and *Nihon kogakuha no tetsugaku* (*Philosophy of the Japanese School of Ancient Learning*). Although the term "Neo-Confucianism" had yet to come into common usage, Inoue clearly understood the distinction between the ancient Confucianism of Confucius and the later Confucianism of Zhu Xi, Wang Yangming (1472–1529), and others. Indeed, at least two of the three schools of philosophy Inoue identified are widely considered today as Neo-Confucian.

The third school, that of Ancient Learning, was arguably a Neo-Confucian school as well, and surely was the most distinctively Japanese one; however, it is classified. The trilogy has distinctive Hegelian echoes, with the Zhu Xi School serving as the thesis, the Wang Yangming as the antithesis, and the Ancient Learning as the synthesis, sublating all before in a new and powerful statement of Confucian thought. Much as Japan was emerging as the military power of East Asia, capable of overcoming Qing China and Czarist Russia, so did the Ancient Learning thinkers go well beyond the earlier Chinese schools of Neo-Confucian philosophy. Inoue's analyses, like so many from that time, reveal much national and military pride. In the decades following his trilogy, Inoue took

Confucian and Neo-Confucian notions further down the path of ultra-nationalism and imperialism with publications on "National Morality" (*kokumin dōtoku* 国民道徳) and "the way of the warrior" (*bushidō* 武士道). Inoue's reworking of Confucianism along ideological lines only came to a conclusion in 1944, the year of his demise. In the postwar years, as an unfortunate consequence of Inoue's elevation of Confucianism as the beginning point of Japan's philosophical tradition and his integration of Confucianism into his later work on *kokumin dōtoku* and *bushidō*, scholars such as Maruyama Masao rejected the notion that Confucianism, Neo or otherwise, was anything more than ideology designed tragically to hoodwink Japanese into the worst of fates. Although Confucianism and Neo-Confucianism continued to be studied in Japan, it was as anything but philosophy.

CONFUCIANISM AND *TETSUGAKU*

The disassociation of Confucian and Neo-Confucianism from what the postwar Japanese academe referred to as *tetsugaku* (哲学) or philosophy is ironic considering that the term *tetsugaku*, coined as a translation of the Western notion, "philosophy," derives most conspicuously from the Confucian lexicon, with both *tetsu*, meaning "wise," and *gaku*, meaning "study" or "learning," having lengthy histories in Confucian and Neo-Confucian writings. These words were not typically combined as a compound, but, individually, they appear in many Confucian passages. Zhou Dunyi, a Song Confucian philosopher, did, however, speak of *kitetsugaku*, or a "search for wisdom." Yet it was only in the Meiji period that Nishi Amane (1829–1897), a leading translator of Western philosophical literature into Japanese, offered *tetsugaku* as a gloss for philosophy. That rendition gained wide acceptance in Japan among scholars and eventually in China and Korea as well, where the same characters used to write *tetsugaku* were used to convey the modern Chinese and Korean words for philosophy. Nishi's early education had been in Confucianism, making it natural enough that he would draw on its lexicon in offering a rendering for the word. Although Nishi never suggested that Confucianism was philosophy, nor did he claim that Japan had developed philosophy prior to its introduction from the West, his use of Confucian terms to render the notion suggested that Confucianism was at least proximate to philosophy. Inoue's position on the matter was even stronger: in no uncertain terms, he identified Japanese Confucianism with Japan's first expression of philosophy.

Western scholars, relatively unaware of Inoue's fuller legacy or perhaps willing to disregard the ideological in favor of Inoue's often-solid scholarship, have in part led the way in reviving the study of Confucianism and Neo-Confucianism as an important—if not the first—expression of Japanese philosophy. James Heisig, Thomas Kasulis, and John Maraldo, editors of *Japanese Philosophy: A Sourcebook*, contributed significantly to this by including a substantial Confucian section in their sourcebook. Introductory volumes on Japanese philosophy now regularly include recognition of Japanese Confucianism.

The University of Hawai'i's Department of Philosophy and the East-West Philosophers' Conferences it sponsors have long since endorsed the notion as well. The University of Tokyo Center for Philosophy has also advanced discussions of Japanese Confucianism as philosophy, recognizing that the Japanese philosophical tradition is not simply a post-Meiji development.

ZEN ORIGINS AND BEYOND

Neo-Confucian philosophical thought appeared in Japan not long after Zhu Xi's day, largely due to the efforts of Japanese Zen monks bringing back religio-philosophical literature from China. In medieval Japan, however, Neo-Confucian ideas were not, by and large, advanced outside Zen temples, where they were taught as integral components in syncretic texts including Buddhism, Confucianism, and Shintō and/or Daoism. It was only after Toyotomi Hideyoshi's (1536–1598) attempted conquest of Ming China in the 1590s that new texts entered Japan along with Korean scholars taken as prisoners of war. Under Korean POW tutelage, a few Japanese students of the new texts began to affirm that Neo-Confucian teachings were, in many significant respects, quite opposed to Buddhism. During the early Tokugawa period, the fortunes of Neo-Confucian thinking rose in part due to increasing samurai patronage, as well as due to developments in woodblock printing, an extended period of peace, and an urban-based civil culture. Neo-Confucian philosophical ideas also appeared as powerful influences on non-samurai urban thinkers such as Itō Jinsai (1627–1705), Ishida Baigan (1685–1644), and their successors. In short order, the Japanese digested the new Chinese philosophical system along secular lines and began to articulate their own multifaceted variations of it.

In part, this process of creative re-expression was facilitated by the multiple iterations of Neo-Confucian thought that entered Japan during this period, ranging from the late-Song through the Yuan and Ming. What the Japanese discovered was a multiplicity of solutions offered to philosophical problems; they responded with more of the same, presenting new multidimensional answers of their own. Ironically enough, although Neo-Confucianism was a profoundly novel development, in China, Korea, and Japan, it was not typically cast as creative thought so much as a return to the original teachings of Confucius and Mencius. This was true with Zhu Xi and his predecessors who charted lineages leading back to Confucius, as well as with Tokugawa thinkers who, despite their continued originality in philosophical expression, claimed to be returning to the beginnings and articulating a faithful and true account of Confucianism.

Neo-Confucianism is often imagined as some monolithic, uniform set of doctrines if not dogmas, lacking in variation or change. To the contrary, however, it brimmed with variety, debate, discussion, disagreement, doubt, and skepticism—often enough expressed by one Neo-Confucian and directed at one another. In Song times, Zhu Xi and Lu Xiangshan (1139–1192) were known for their debates over the nature and functions of the human mind. But no one would suggest that Lu was any less a Neo-Confucian for having disagreed with Zhu on these matters. Japanese critics of Zhu Xi were no less Neo-Confucians for their criticisms. Nakae Tōju (1608–1648), an advocate of Wang Yangming's philosophy, criticized Hayashi Razan (1583–1657) not simply because Razan was a proponent of Zhu Xi's ideas, but also due to Razan's willingness to comply with shogunal demands that he shave his head as if he were a Buddhist teacher of Zhu Xi's thought in service to the shogun, rather than present himself as a Confucian in attire and grooming who taught the same. Tōju's harsh words made him no less a Neo-Confucian than was Razan in shaving his head. Their common participation in a movement emphasizing individual pursuit of authentic truth, corroborated by and for oneself, entailed this kind of critical exchange, making its presence a reflection of the vitality of the movement rather than cause for ostracism or exclusion of one by another. Neo-Confucian thinking about learning, debate, and even skepticism coincided with patterns of European thought advocated by Descartes and others developing new philosophical and scientific methods. Not surprisingly, the rise of Neo-Confucian thinking in early seventeenth-century Japan has been construed as the essential moment when distinctively philosophical thinking in Japan began and when the beginnings of at least the vocabulary of science and modernity in advanced learning crystallized.

THE FOUR BOOKS

Perhaps the strongest ties binding Tokugawa Neo-Confucians were the Four Books, especially as explained by Zhu Xi, whose commentaries on them were most widely known and well-respected. One form of philosophical engagement with the Four Books involved making them accessible in Japanese, either by punctuating the Chinese for reading as Sino-Japanese (*kanbun* 漢文) or paraphrasing their contents in classical Japanese (*bungo* 文語). Razan oversaw an early woodblock publication of Zhu's commentaries, now presented in *kanbun* and marketed in the major urban areas: Kyoto, Edo, and Osaka. Razan also authored primers on the texts, in *bungo* with ample syllabic *kana*, explaining key passages via vernacular translations. Razan's broad learning additionally prompted his punctuation and publication of an early Tokugawa *kanbun* edition of the Five Classics, texts that Zhu Xi commented on as well. One of Razan's students, Yamaga Sokō (1622–1685), similarly took up the task and offered his own readings of the Four Books, continuing a line of philosophical scholarship earlier pioneered by Zhu Xi and his Song predecessors, and then furthered in Japan by Razan and others. Yamazaki Ansai (1619–1682) also published a Sino-Japanese version of the Four Books and Five Classics differing significantly at points with Razan's earlier work. Itō Jinsai wrote commentaries on three of the Four Books, but then argued in successive essays that the first of the Four Books, the *Great Learning*, was not in fact a Confucian text at all due to thematic, semantic, and linguistic differences between it and other well-established texts of the Confucian philosophical tradition. Ogyū Sorai (1666–1728) had no use for the *Mencius*, seeing it as a polemical, inconsistent work. Otherwise, he recognized, with Zhu Xi, the fundamental legitimacy and integrity of three of the Four Books, and he praised the Five Classics regularly as the texts that should be the ultimate foundations of right philosophical thinking. Beyond Jinsai and Sorai, later Tokugawa philosophers continued to engage the Four Books and the Confucian canon, explaining and re-explaining that literature, but rarely simply repeating verbatim what had been said before. Nevertheless, their disagreements no more set them apart than had Zhu Xi's disagreements with his predecessors over philosophical positions and nuances. Far more important than shared conclusions on any one topic was the shared concern for a form of learning revived in the wake of a period of Buddhist dominance, a learning that had always invited critical, probing thought rather than dealing in dogmas and demands for blind faith.

Neo-Confucianism, Christianity, and Shintō

Although many Song Neo-Confucians practiced Buddhism early in life, their increasing opposition to it as a wrongheaded heterodoxy became, especially in China and Korea, the dominant position. In Japan, by early Tokugawa times, much the same was true, with Neo-Confucian leaders such as Fujiwara Seika (1561–1619) and Hayashi Razan moving away from their Buddhist upbringings and toward Neo-Confucianism, often with a concomitant hostility toward Buddhism in particular and otherworldly forms of thinking in general. The introduction of Christianity into Japan in the 1550s presented the newly emerging Neo-Confucians, entering the philosophical stage mostly in the late 1590s and early 1600s, with potential competition of a spiritual and philosophical sort. Needless to say, Neo-Confucians, like the newly risen samurai rulers leading the Tokugawa shogunate, were obliged to take a stand in relation to Christianity as well, either embracing, tolerating, or opposing it. In Edo, Hayashi Razan, a scholar-philosopher serving the Tokugawa shogunate, emerged early on as one of the more outspoken critics of the foreign heterodoxy, as he called it. Matsunaga Sekigo (1592–1657), a private scholar teaching in Kyoto, similarly criticized Christianity as a set of deceptive and misleading teachings that would undermine if not destroy the social and political order of Japan. Writing shortly after the Shimabara Uprising of 1637–38, which was in part inspired by Christianity, Sekigo willingly found common ground among Neo-Confucianism, Shintō, and Buddhism, but identified Christianity as a dangerous if not evil heterodoxy that had already caused the deaths of myriad Japanese. Attempting to further the fight against Christianity by philosophical means, Sekigo advanced his version of Neo-Confucian syncreticism, accommodating Shintō and Buddhism for the sake of building a united religio-philosophical front against the foreign heterodoxy. In many respects, subsequent affirmations of Neo-Confucianism in Japan were meant to preempt the appeal of Christianity philosophically, much as temple registration requirements imposed on the Japanese populace by the Tokugawa shogunate did so at the mundane level. A succession of later Neo-Confucian scholars, including Kumazawa Banzan (1619–1691) and Arai Hakuseki (1657–1725), readily continued the critical attacks on the barbarian heterodoxy.

Many Japanese Neo-Confucians, however, found room for Shintō. Hayashi Razan, drawing on medieval ideas about the unity of the three teachings—Confucianism, Buddhism, and Shintō—omitted Buddhism while emphasizing the extent to which Shintō resonated with Neo-Confucianism, especially texts such as the *Book of Changes* and other works conveying a naturalistic metaphysics or cosmology. Razan often paired the notions yin and yang with spiritual dichotomies found in Shintō, such as the primordial deities, Izanami and Izanagi. Razan was not unique in this regard: Yamazaki Ansai (1619–1682), a Kyoto thinker whose ideas eventually spread to Edo as well, founded a teaching called Suika Shintō (垂加神道), matching Shintō ideas with Neo-Confucian notions, especially those from the *Book of Changes*, and establishing their mutuality rather than opposition. An early Tokugawa Neo-Confucian work of uncertain authorship, the *Kana seiri* (*Human Nature and Principle for Japanese*), similarly suggested that the Sun Goddess Amaterasu, in providing for all, exemplified the "mind of the way," a notion Zhu Xi extolled and contrasted with the more ethically precarious "mind of humanity."

Combining Neo-Confucian notions with Shintō was not a universal trait of Japanese Neo-Confucianism, but neither was it an aberration. Rather, this was one way in which the Chinese teachings were naturalized and made more familiar and acceptable to Japanese. This tendency continued throughout the Tokugawa period, becoming especially conspicuous toward its end with the development of Mito thinking, a combination of Neo-Confucianism and nativistic Shintō, with increasingly well-developed appeals to the sanctity of the nation.

Dealing with Metaphysical Ambiguities

A grand ambiguity in Zhu Xi's metaphysics arose from his occasional equivocation over the relationship of principle (Ch. *li*; Jp. *ri* 理) and generative force (Ch. *qi*; Jp. *ki* 氣). Zhu recognized a rational and ethical structure to reality, one "above form," or "metaphysical," invisible at the empirical level but perceivable and comprehensible by the mind through focused inquiry deliberative study, and reflection. This structure, commonly known as "principle" in translation, constituted an ideal dimension, one sometimes compared to Plato's forms (*eidos*). Although often spoken of in reference to a single, particular thing, Zhu Xi affirmed that through understanding one principle, one could understand all principles informing reality and its processes of becoming. Furthermore, Zhu identified principle with human nature (Ch. *xing*; Jp. *sei* 性) and heaven (Ch. *tian*; Jp. *ten* 天), suggesting an intimate bond between people and the cosmos. Principle not only provided unity to the universe, but moreover its essential goodness, ethically speaking, reinforced the Mencian tenet that human nature is good, and encouraged the view that the cosmos is as well. In recognizing a vital material dimension, Zhu Xi posited "generative force" (often translated as material force) as the stuff of reality that, as present within form, constitutes the substantial nature of things. Depending on the clarity or turbidity of generative force, principle is, to a greater or lesser degree, transparent and efficacious in relation to generative force, enabling the best possible realization of the latter or a distorted one due to the clouded, perhaps opaque relationship between rational principle and transformative generative force. Although Zhu Xi did not prefer to discuss principle and generative force in terms of their relative standing or order, when pressed to do so by his disciples, he allowed that principle appeared prior and generative force secondary. Zhu added that such characterizations should not confuse the essential interrelatedness of principle and generative force. Nevertheless, after conceding that principle was in some sense prior, Zhu's philosophy was increasingly referred to as "the School of Principle," privileging, in the minds of many, the ideal over the actual, principle over the material.

Japanese Neo-Confucians, like those in China and Korea, typically either emphasized, metaphysically, principle and its multifaceted significance, as with Yamazaki Ansai and many of his followers, or they privileged generative force, as did Hayashi Razan, Itō Jinsai, Kaibara Ekken, and other "materialists." Jinsai, in particular, despite his proclaimed return to the *Analects* and *Mencius*, advanced a systematic metaphysics elevating his notion of a monistic generative force (*ichigenki* 一元気), one not found in either the *Analects* or *Mencius*. As proof, Jinsai did not cite passages from either ancient text, but rather offered a thought experiment, one in which a box maker makes a box with wood. Even when a top is added and the box is sealed, Jinsai relates, the inside of the box is full of generative force. Proof is found in the white mold that will soon spontaneously grow inside the box. Jinsai then likens heaven and earth to the box, and the myriad things of existence to the white mold growing inside. He adds that nothing created generative force as such, nor did it come from somewhere else. It simply exists as the transformative, generative substance of reality. There is no principle prior to it. Instead, principle, to the extent that it can be recognized, is simply the rationale existing within generative force, not something outside of or prior to it.

Jinsai was not alone in affirming generative force. Kaibara Ekken (1630–1714) and a number of other philosophers did the same. Jinsai is highlighted here, however, because his ideas are often cast as fundamentally opposed to Neo-Confucianism, so much so that they are grouped as part of another movement, that of Ancient Learning, devoted to a faithful return to the ancient classics of Confucianism. Admittedly, Jinsai claimed that he was doing as much. But, then again, Zhu Xi never claimed to be creating a new form of Confucianism. His expressed concern was to revive Confucianism in opposition to Buddhism. Considered in that light, both Zhu and Jinsai saw their teachings as reviving ancient Confucianism. Also, regardless of Jinsai's proclaimed return to ancient texts, one finds no metaphysical discussions of the relationship of generative force and principle in them. The metaphysical discourse that Jinsai participated in was one largely defined, ambiguously or otherwise, by Zhu Xi and those Neo-Confucians who came after him. Later Confucians did not always agree with Zhu, but in addressing the philosophical problems that he did and in developing the categories that he helped pioneer, such as principle and generative force, later Confucians were inevitably Neo-Confucians as well.

PRINCIPLE AND QUIET SITTING

Alongside philosophical study and learning, Zhu Xi endorsed "quiet sitting" (Ch. *jingzuo*; Jp. *seiza* 靜坐) as a meditative practice conducive to focusing the mind; intuiting human nature and its original, undisturbed goodness; and preparing the individual for active engagement with things. Zhu's references to this practice, however, were only occasional. They hardly characterized his commentaries on the Four Books. Here again, Zhu's equivocation led to multiple subsequent positions, for and against the practice, with some advancing it as a defining feature of their thinking. Satō Naokata (1650–1719), a follower of Yamazaki Ansai, extolled the practice as an approach to nourishing, preserving, and cultivating the inborn ethical nature. Ansai had practiced Zen before turning to Neo-Confucianism, and perhaps his appraisal of quiet sitting drew on his experiences with Zen meditation. Razan, however, also started his philosophical journey as a Zen Buddhist, but later, as a Neo-Confucian, he reacted against the quietism that he deemed intrinsic to quiet sitting. Zhu Xi spent years studying Chan (Zen) Buddhism before turning away from it and toward Neo-Confucianism. Zhu's equivocation vis-à-vis quiet sitting, sometimes praising it and sometimes remaining silent about it, perhaps reflected his multifaceted philosophical and spiritual past. Other Tokugawa Neo-Confucians, such as Sokō and Jinsai, although they did not begin life as Zen monks, knew of Zen and Buddhist teachings. In quiet sitting, they ultimately saw a crypto-Buddhist practice that deadened one with quietism and stillness rather than energizing the self through active engagement in and with the spheres of humanity and nature. Naokata is an interesting case because he had no background in Buddhism and yet seems to have had a far greater distaste for and intolerance of it than did Jinsai. But Naokata was perhaps the single most energetic advocate of quiet sitting in Tokugawa Japan. Moreover, his political philosophy recognized the legitimacy of overthrowing abusive tyrants who posed as rulers. That such a position would issue from a practitioner of quiet sitting suggests that the latter encouraged some practitioners to a degree of readiness for political activism rarely seen among philosophers of any stripe.

REFLECTIONS ON THINGS AT HAND

Of the many texts associated with Neo-Confucianism, Ansai's school considered the anthology edited by Zhu Xi and Lü Zuqian, the *Jinsilu* (*Reflections on Things at Hand*), to be among the most authoritative. A distinctive feature of the *Jinsilu* is its opening presentation of Zhou Dunyi's (1017–1073) *Taiji tushuo* (*Explanation of the Great Ultimate*), a brief but hardly intuitive cosmological account of the origins of all becoming. Zhou's text begins with the statement, "The ultimate of non-being and yet the great ultimate" (Ch. *wuji er taiji* 無極而太極). The "ultimate of non-being" is often explained as referring to the infinite possibilities inherent in future, as yet unrealized potential becoming, whereas the "great ultimate" refers to the principles informing all things that are in a process of ongoing generation and transformation. From these emerge yin and yang, the five elements, and the transformation of the myriad things. Essentially, one can see these accounts as providing for a cosmology affirming the substantial, dynamic, and limitless metaphysical reality of the world, one responding to Buddhist claims about the emptiness and illusory nature of the world. Ansai, following Zhu Xi and the great Korean Neo-Confucian, Yi T'oegye (1501–1570), accepted the validity of the great ultimate and the ultimate of nonbeing as the two ultimate sources of the real world of becoming. Apart from their rather abstruse metaphysical nature, these notions were either questioned or criticized by many thinkers on the other side of the Neo-Confucian fence, including Razan, Ekken, Sokō, Jinsai, and Sorai, as heterodox and inappropriate to Confucian philosophizing. In their minds, notions such as the *wuji* were of Daoist origin and, as heterodox concepts, had no place in Confucian discourse of any kind. Even Zhu Xi had reservations about including Zhou's text at the opening of the *Jinsilu*, thinking that it would be a puzzling turnoff that might distance students rather than engage them. Again, Zhu's equivocations here left ample room accommodating various philosophical positions that emerged among Japanese Neo-Confucians.

Along with Zhou Dunyi's *Taiji dushuo*, the *Jinsilu* also included Zhang Zai's (1020–1077) "Western Inscription," a brief but important text setting forth a quasi-utopian vision of the cosmos as family. Zhang's text opens with the declaration that heaven is his father and earth, his mother, while the ten thousand things of existence are his brothers and sisters. With this brief line, Zhang presented the cosmos as a familial force uniting humanity, as well as all things organic and inorganic, as essentially one, bound together by their common parents and so sharing family relations as children of the cosmos. This vision overlapped with others offered by Neo-Confucians prior to Zhu Xi and reiterated in Japan by diverse followers, affirming that the Confucian virtue, humaneness, manifested itself fully in an individual's realization of his oneness with "the ten thousand things of the world." Such a perspective, in turn, led some Neo-Confucians to refrain from cutting the grass outside their windows because they saw its vitality as an expression of its very integrity as a living entity toward which self-serving violence should never be done. Although this thinking might be cast as mysticism, it could also be construed as a forerunner of the deep ecology philosophy advanced by Arnes Naess in the late twentieth century. Zhu Xi affirmed this line of thought, but not as enthusiastically as did others. In Japan, however, the vision of Zhang Zai's "Western Inscription" was widely affirmed, at one level or another, and appreciated for the cosmic and natural commonality it affirmed. Kumazawa Banzan even authored an exposition of Zhang Zai's text, "The Japanese Western Inscription" (*Yamato seimei* 大和西銘), expanding upon and thus popularizing Zhang Zai's text in vernacular Japanese.

CHEN BEIXI'S PHILOSOPHICAL LEXICOGRAPHY

A number of Japanese Neo-Confucians were influenced by an important post-Zhu Xi work: Chen Beixi's (1159–1223) *Xingli ziyi* (*The Meanings of Human Nature and Principle*). This text, attributed to Beixi but recorded by his disciples, presents analytic accounts of the meanings of more than two-dozen terms central to Neo-Confucianism as developed by Zhu Xi, Beixi's teacher. Rather than a faithful recapitulation of Zhu Xi's thinking on every topic, Beixi omitted many notions and nuances while giving others far greater priority than Zhu had. Although acknowledging principle and generative force, Beixi, for example, readily assigned greater and more primary significance to the unitary generative force infusing everything. When he addressed principle as a discrete notion, Beixi, unlike Zhu Xi, had relatively little to say.

Beixi most likely never imagined that his thoughts would be subjected to the scrutiny of scholars over the centuries. Whether he meant to establish a philosophical genre—that of the philosophical lexicon—that would offer later Neo-Confucians a format for redefining their understandings of Neo-Confucianism, is open to question, but that was an undeniable consequence of Beixi's *Ziyi*. Early on, Hayashi Razan admired the *Ziyi* and authored a classical Japanese explication of it, the *Seiri jigi genkai* (*Vernacular Explanation of the Meanings of Human Nature and Principle*), published in 1659. Even earlier, Razan had punctuated a copy of the 1553 Korean edition and oversaw its woodblock publication in 1632. Decades later, philosophical masterworks such as Sokō's *Seikyō yōroku* (*Essential Records of the Sagely Teachings*), Itō Jinsai's *Gomō jigi* (*The Meanings of Terms in the Analects and Mencius*), and Ogyū Sorai's *Benmei* (*Distinguishing Terms*) were written in the same genre—that of the philosophical lexicon—as Beixi's *Ziyi*, even as each text defined a profoundly different understanding of Neo-Confucian philosophy.

It would be easy to characterize these works as exercises in philological learning. If so, one must understand philology and the concern for right meaning in its philosophical context: that of Confucian thinking as set forth in the *Analects*. There, when asked what he would do first if given charge of government of the state of Wei, Confucius responded that he would "rectify names" (*zheng ming* 正名), explaining to his disciple that if names did not correspond with realities, then language would become disordered, and social and political chaos and anarchy would ensue. Confucius thus emphasized the importance of keeping words in accordance with their right meanings, observing that the ruler is careful about his use of words. Considered in this context, Tokugawa thinkers who defined their understandings of Confucianism along lexicographic lines, ordering their concepts for analysis much as Beixi had, were equally defining the philosophical bases of a new political order as they imagined it should have been defined. In effect, their philosophical lexicographies were works of political philosophy. In Meiji Japan, politically concerned Japanese, even in remote areas, drafted constitutions as statements of what they thought the emerging new political order ought to consist. In the Tokugawa, arguably, philosophical lexicography served a similar function.

THE IMPORTANCE OF DOUBT

One conspicuous difference between Chinese Neo-Confucianism and Japanese is that whereas many Chinese philosophers accepted a metaphysics privileging the notion of principle over generative force, in Japan, beginning with Hayashi Razan, the tendency was to privilege generative force over principle, insisting that principle exists only within generative force. Also, Chinese Neo-Confucians more readily accepted the notions of the great ultimate and the ultimate of nonbeing, whereas Japanese philosophers often argued, citing textual evidence, that the latter notion in particular was of heterodox origin and therefore inappropriate for Confucian discussions. In this respect, perhaps, Chinese Neo-Confucianism was more idealistic than Japanese wherein emphasis on generative force resulted in a more materialistic and substance-oriented metaphysics. This was true of Razan and far more so with later scholars who expressed disagreement with Zhu Xi over the matter, denying that principle could exist apart, in any sensible way, from generative force. Philosophical thinkers such as Itō Jinsai, Kaibara Ekken, and Ogyū Sorai, as well as a number of eighteenth-century Neo-Confucian scholars, were of this mind.

In expressing their disagreements, Japanese Neo-Confucians often simultaneously emphasized another of Zhu Xi's teachings regarding the importance of doubt and questioning. In doing so, their critical logic resonated with that of Zhu Xi and a host of later Neo-Confucians who questioned Zhu's thinking. On this count, apart from Zhu himself, perhaps the most important figure in Tokugawa Japan was the Ming thinker Luo Qinshun (1465–1547), author of the *Kunzhiji* (*Knowledge Painfully Acquired*). As with so many important Neo-Confucian texts, Hayashi Razan played a leading role in its dissemination, hand copying the *Kunzhiji* and overseeing its Sino-Japanese publication in an early woodblock edition. In the *Kunzhiji*, Luo records his heartfelt doubts about Neo-Confucian metaphysics and especially its privileging of principle over generative force. This kind of doubt-ridden approach appears to have shaped the thinking of Hayashi Razan, Itō Jinsai, and Kaibara Ekken—just to name the luminaries—who later more explicitly vented similar misgivings about Neo-Confucian metaphysics.

Razan adumbrated this dimension of Neo-Confucian philosophy in his *Santokushō* (*Selections on the Three Virtues*). There, Razan paraphrased Zhu Xi's remarks on the importance of having doubts about questionable matters in relation to making authentic progress in learning. Razan paraphrased Zhu in noting that without doubts, one makes no progress. With a few doubts, one makes minor progress. With major doubts, one makes major progress in learning. Razan sanctioned, even encouraged, this strategy, presumably realizing that many Neo-Confucian teachings would seem questionable to Japanese upon first hearing. Very possibly, Zhu Xi realized the same about his ideas. Rather than dogmatically declare their teachings beyond doubt, Zhu and later Razan invited doubt, questioning, and scrutiny in the hopes that realization of the deeper significance of the notions advocated would produce a more informed and in-depth appreciation of them.

With Yamaga Sokō's *Seikyō yōroku* (*Essential Records of the Sagely Confucian Teachings*), this emphasis on doubt took the form of systematic questioning of Zhu's thinking even as Sokō offered, in tandem, what sometimes sounded like a new paraphrase of the same. Sokō has often been classified as an "Ancient Learning" thinker rather than as a Neo-Confucian because of his omnibus criticisms of Song and Ming Confucians. However, the conclusion that Sokō's critiques of Song and Ming thinkers landed him in another philosophical lineage only makes sense if one assumes that Neo-Confucians could not criticize one another and still be Neo-Confucians. If Zhu's and later Razan's advocacy of doubt are considered in relation to one's thinking about what constitutes a Neo-Confucian, Sokō all the more embodies the Neo-Confucian philosophical ethos of critically probing matters, with authentic doubt and skepticism, rather than standing as one who broke with the fold because he doubted. That Sokō appealed to ancient Confucians such as the Duke of Zhou and Confucius was not different from what Zhu Xi had done in tracing the transmission of the way to ancient sages such as Fuxi, long before Confucius.

Much the same can be said regarding the systematic doubts expressed by other Tokugawa thinkers such as Kaibara Ekken in his *Taigiroku* (*Record of Great Doubts*), Itō Jinsai in his *Gomō jigi*, and Ogyū Sorai in his *Bendō* (*Distinguishing the Way*) and *Benmei*. These thinkers expressed their doubts about earlier Neo-Confucian philosophical expressions, primarily Zhu Xi's, and then offered their own understandings of the teachings in light of their prolonged study of the ancient foundations of the Confucian philosophical tradition. In disagreeing, they were authentically embodying the ethic of Neo-Confucianism—a philosophical search for truth—rather than repeating dogma meant to be accepted without question.

JITSUGAKU

Neo-Confucian philosophers agreed with Karl Marx in holding that philosophy should seek to change the world, not simply interpret it. In defining cosmological terms,

Neo-Confucians held that right language, meaning, and usage could effectively trans-form the world, whereas wrongheaded language and usage would bring chaos and up-heaval. Others were more explicit in addressing day-to-day realities and the practical problems challenging those governing. Both sets of thinkers participated, arguably, in *jitsugaku* or "practical learning." *Jitsugaku* was practical in that it typically addressed social, political, and economic problems with the goal of solving rather than simply theorizing about them. In his *Daigaku wakumon* (*Questions and Answers on the Great Learning*), Kumazawa Banzan (1619–1691) opened his discussion of the *Great Learning*, a text about governing and bringing peace and prosperity to all below heaven, by first explaining the function of the ruler in terms of his appointment by heaven to serve as the father and mother of the people by enacting humane government. If successful in this, heaven favors him; if unsuccessful, he loses heaven's favors and presumably his le-gitimate position as ruler. Banzan next shifts to a discussion of practical issues such as the loss of forests due to castle construction and the rebuilding of temples, shrines, and other construction projects. Understanding the egregious consequences of losing nat-ural resources for both the shogunate and the realm at large, Banzan advocated shogunal sponsorship of systematic reforestation and moratoria on major construction projects until new forest plantings could become established. Although his suggestions were not well received, Banzan made evident one way in which Japanese Neo-Confucians were concerned with the real and practical problems facing the people and the natural realm they inhabited.

Ogyū Sorai only recorded his political proposals after being asked for them by the shogun Yoshimune. In his *Seidan* (*Discourse on Government*), Sorai addressed the so-cioeconomic crisis of his day: increasing samurai debt and burgeoning castle towns as urban centers of conspicuous consumption where debilitating vices, especially among samurai, were bred. Sorai's most memorable solution to the problem was returning the samurai to the countryside to dwell among the rural elements of society, where the challenges of life would once again strengthen them as warrior leaders of society. As long as samurai dwelt in castle towns and indulged in costly leisurely activities, they would fall into more debt and lose their ability to fight and their moral authority to lead. Nothing less than systematic relocation of the samurai to the countryside was needed to bring Tokugawa Japan out of its decline into debt-ridden decadence. Sorai made this proposal in part on the basis of his recognition of the value of his own early expe-rience in exile with his father and family. During their decade in exile, Sorai had not been distracted by Edo's diversions and so devoted himself to Neo-Confucian study and learning while many of his peers wasted their energies on idle pleasures. Although Sorai's proposals were never enacted, that he was asked for his thoughts indicates the de-gree to which scholars were as invested in the practical project of governing as they were in book learning.

Another Neo-Confucian who devoted much of his thinking to practical affairs was the Mito scholar, Aizawa Seishisai (1781–1863). Active in the final decades of the Tokugawa, when Western gunboats began undermining the raison d'être of samurai rule, Aizawa alerted his students to the dangers that foreigners posed to Japan's *kokutai* or "national essence." Defense of Japan, however, required that it allow relations with the West so as to internalize Western strengths and then use them to repel Western threats to Japan. Aizawa's *Shinron* (*New Theses*) was an inspiring text for many who later participated in the *sonnō jōi* (尊皇攘夷), "revere the emperor and repel the barbarian" movement that eventually contributed to the downfall of the Tokugawa shogunate and the establishment of the new Meiji imperial regime. As with the phrase, *sonnō jōi*, the politically charged atmosphere of the late Tokugawa was brimming with rhetoric taken from Confucian works, especially those with Neo-Confucian commentaries. The long-standing political focus of Confucianism served those active in the final years of samurai rule as a multifaceted practical discourse that could be drawn upon for defense of the realm and the challenges facing it.

NEO-CONFUCIANISM FOR WOMEN

One of the new dimensions of Neo-Confucianism was its concern with women. Ancient Confucianism had relatively little to say on this count. Overall, the teachings admittedly affirm a male-dominated sociopolitical world. The *Jinsilu*, however, includes a chapter addressing the moral way for families. In it, Zhu Xi and Lü Zuqian (1137–1181) suggest that sons should obey their mothers with tenderness so that their mothers might realize righteousness in their lives. The chapter also quotes the account that Cheng Yi (1033–1107), one of Zhu Xi's predecessors, gave of his parents. There, Cheng Yi notes how his mother and father "mutually waited on each other as a host would a guest." Cheng Yi praised his mother as one who was "humane, altruistic, tolerant, and generous" in dealing with others, including the children of her husband's concubines. He praised her for "governing the family methodologically, with orderliness but without severity." These remarks suggest that Cheng Yi, a well-known Neo-Confucian presented in the *Jinsilu*, neither disdained nor degraded women as subservient.

Japanese Neo-Confucians also authored texts such as the *Onna daigaku* (*Great Learning for Women*), setting forth the way for women. Unfortunately, the *Onna daigaku* hardly reflects the best Neo-Confucian thinking about women, or at least not that of the *Jinsilu*, so much as the mores of a samurai-dominated world in which women had relatively few options other than submissive obedience to male authority. Far more than the *Jinsilu*, the *Onna daigaku* teaches subordination and duty. At the same time, it does recognize women as human beings deserving of an education and worthy of being taught their own moral way. Compared to Buddhist views of women, the *Onna daigaku* appears progressive. Significantly, the *Onna daigaku* also established a starting point from which Meiji thinkers, such as Fukuzawa Yukichi in his *Shin onna daigaku* (*New Great Learning for Women*), were able to succeed in defining more egalitarian thinking about women.

THE FREEDOM AND PEOPLE'S RIGHTS MOVEMENT AND BEYOND

During the Meiji period, Western ideas of all sorts—philosophical, religious, scientific, literary, and historical—entered Japan. Some of the most influential notions were those related to political philosophy, especially those revolutionary ideas expressed in works such as John Locke's *Two Treatises on Government*, Rousseau's *Social Contract*, the "Declaration of the Rights of Man and of the Citizen," and the American "Declaration of Independence." These works helped fuel the Freedom and People's Rights Movement (*Jiyū minken undō* 自由民権運動) of the late 1870s and 1880s, when politically minded Japanese called for popular rights and freedoms. One of the challenges in authoring such works was translating notions such as "freedom," "rights," "natural rights," and so on. As often as not, Japanese theorists found in the Neo-Confucian lexicon an ample supply of words with nuances that approximated those to be incorporated into Japanese. Although Neo-Confucian discourse qua Neo-Confucianism fell out of favor among avant-garde intellectuals, most leaders of the movement for popular rights had first been educated in Neo-Confucian thinking and so cast their new thinking about human rights and liberty in idioms that derived clearly from Neo-Confucianism. In much the same way, the discipline of philosophy itself was rendered into Japanese via combining the notions *tetsu* and *gaku* drawn from ancient and Neo-Confucian writings.

This progressive legacy of Neo-Confucian discourse in modern Japan was countered, however, by an arguably more powerful usage of traditional Confucian notions for inculcating what came to be called by Inoue Tetsujirō and others following his ideas imperial Japan's "national ethics" (*kokumin dōtoku*). Although sounding innocuous enough perhaps, this ethical system increasingly emerged as so much philosophically nuanced national propaganda meant to further imperial Japan's military ambitions in East Asia. With defeat, the tragic consequences prompted many to harbor exceptional distrust of the system of ideas that had informed so much of the educated cultural traditions of Japanese history. Neo-Confucianism continued to be studied but more often than not as an "ideology" than as a living philosophy relevant to contemporary society. That aside, some external observers, such as E. O. Reischauer, saw beyond the postwar reaction against Neo-Confucian thinking and into the very ethics of daily life, concluding that, at a certain level, virtually all Japanese are Confucians, even though hardly any claim as much.

BIBLIOGRAPHY AND SUGGESTED READINGS

Boot, W. J. (1982) *The Adoption and Adaptation of Neo-Confucianism in Japan: The Role of Fujiwara Seika and Hayashi Razan*. University of Leiden Dissertation.

Chen, Beixi. (1986) *Xingli ziyi. Neo-Confucian Terms Explained*, translated by Wing-tsit Chan. New York: Columbia University Press.

De Bary, William Theodore, and Irene Bloom, editors. (1979) *Principle and Practicality: Essays in Neo-Confucianism and Practical Learning*. New York: Columbia University Press.

Fukuzawa, Yukichi. (1988) *Fukuzawa Yukichi on Japanese Women*, translated by Eiichi Kiyooka. Tokyo: University of Tokyo Press.

Huang, Chun-chieh, and John Allen Tucker, editors. (2014) *Dao Companion to Japanese Confucian Philosophy*. Dordrecht: Springer.

Itō, Jinsai. (1998) *Itō Jinsai's Gomō jigi and the Philosophical Definition of Early Modern Japan*, translated by John Allen Tucker. Leiden: Brill.

Kumazawa, Banzan. (1938) "*Daigaku wakumon*: A Discussion of Public Questions in the Light of the *Great Learning*," translated by Galen Fisher. *Transactions of the Asiatic Society of Japan*, Second Series, 16: 259–356.

Luo, Qinshun. (1987) *Kunzhiji. Knowledge Painfully Acquired: The K'un-chih chi by Lu Ch'in-shun*, translated by Irene Bloom. New York: Columbia University Press.

McMullen, Ian James. (1999) *Idealism, Protest and the Tale of Genji: The Confucianism of Kumazawa Banzan (1619–91)*. Oxford: Oxford University Press.

Najita, Tetsuo. (1998) *Visions of Virtue in Tokugawa Japan*. Chicago: University of Chicago Press.

Ng, Waiming. (2000) *The I Ching in Tokugawa Thought and Culture*. Honolulu: University of Hawai'i Press.

Ogyū, Sorai. (1999) *Ogyū Sorai's Discourse on Government*, translated by Olof G. Lidin. Wiesbaden: Harrassowitz Verlag.

Ogyū, Sorai. (2006) *Ogyū Sorai's Philosophical Masterworks: The Bendō and Benmei*, translated by John Allen Tucker. Honolulu: University of Hawai'i Press.

Paramore, Kiri. (2009) *Ideology and Christianity in Japan*. London: Routledge.

Tucker, John Allen, editor. (2013) *Critical Readings in Japanese Confucianism*, vols. 1–4. Leiden: Brill.

Tucker, Mary Evelyn. (2007) *The Philosophy of Qi: The Record of Great Doubts*. New York: Columbia University Press.

Wakabayashi, Bob Tadashi. (1986) *Anti Foreignism and Western Learning in Early-Modern Japan: The New Theses of 1825*. Cambridge: Harvard East Asian Monographs.

Watanabe, Hiroshi. (2012) *A History of Japanese Political Thought, 1600–1901*, translated by David Noble. Tokyo: International House of Japan.

Yoshikawa, Kōjirō. (1983) *Jinsai, Sorai, Norinaga: Three Classical Philologists of the Tokugawa Period*. Tokyo: Tōhō gakkai.

CHAPTER 13

··

ANCIENT LEARNING

The Japanese Revival of Classical Confucianism

··

JOHN A. TUCKER

INOUE Tetsujirō (1855–1944), the first Japanese professor of philosophy at Tokyo Imperial University, was also the first to state that there had been, in Japanese philosophical history, a revival of classical Confucianism advocated by the Japanese school of Ancient Learning (*Nihon kogakuha* 日本古学派). Inoue cast *kogaku*, "ancient learning," as a dynamic philosophy (*tetsugaku* 哲学) that in three successive waves opposed earlier statements of Japanese Neo-Confucianism in favor of a proclaimed return to more ancient, classical philosophical foundations of Confucian thinking. Inoue identified numerous champions of *kogaku*, but focused primarily on three major figures, Yamaga Sokō (1622–1685), Itō Jinsai (1627–1705), and Ogyū Sorai (1666–1728), the leaders of sequential expressions of the movement. Before Inoue, there were no philosophical histories describing a *kogaku* school in anything approximating the detail found in his philosophical narrative. Indeed, before Inoue there were no systematic accounts of Japanese philosophical history. If anything, those addressing the question of philosophy in Japan concluded that there had been none. It was Inoue who first formulated the narrative affirming that Japan had a long-standing philosophical tradition of its own and that *kogaku* figured prominently within it.

Rather than a set of dated notions irrelevant to modern Japan, Inoue saw in Yamaga Sokō's thinking seminal ideas worthy of study by Japanese trying to come to terms with modernity via their own traditions. Inoue's views on *kogaku* informed his later writings on "national ethics" (*kokumin dōtoku* 国民道徳), a set of teachings meant to instill in Japanese an understanding of ethics that would underpin the sociopolitical order of imperial Japan. The mixing of Inoue's thinking about *kogaku* and his later work on *kokumin dōtoku* ultimately resulted in a postwar reaction against both, as well as against Inoue's view that Japan had achieved philosophy prior to its interaction with the West. Yet even one of Inoue's most compelling opponents, Maruyama Masao (1914–1996), salvaged the outlines of the interpretive narrative Inoue proposed, including the central role attributed to the *kogaku* school, and used it in his own analyses that were otherwise so opposed to Inoue's. Western scholarship on Japanese Confucianism, for the most part, also endorsed the triadic framework of Inoue's narrative, although with little understanding that the narrative began with Inoue. Recent critiques of Maruyama's ideas have increasingly prompted questions or relative silence about *kogaku* and the narrative as a whole. Instead, Sokō, Jinsai, and Sorai are more often studied independently, as thinkers worthy of consideration in their own right and on their own terms. This essay proposes an interpretation of Sokō, Jinsai, and Sorai as revisionist Neo-Confucians challenging earlier iterations but remaining engaged with the *problématique* addressed by Neo-Confucianism throughout East Asia: the nature of humanity, ethics, the polity, and the cosmos as a whole. As will be shown, there are good methodological reasons—and ones related to philosophical genre—for interpreting *kogaku* in this way, if at all.

INOUE'S NARRATIVE AND OTHERS

Inoue presented his thoughts about *kogaku* in *Nihon kogakuha no tetsugaku* (*The Philosophy of the Japanese Ancient Learning School*), published in 1902. That study, the second volume of his monumental trilogy, traced the dialectical progression of Japanese philosophy before Japan's encounter with the West. In the 1880s, Inoue had studied in Germany, focusing on German idealism and especially Hegel's thought. Like Hegel, Inoue saw Confucianism as an expression of "Asian philosophy" (*tōyō tetsugaku* 東洋哲学). Unlike Hegel, who had scant respect for Asian thought,[1] Inoue sought to present positively at least the Japanese philosophical traditions.

In his quasi-Hegelian trilogy, Inoue suggested that although two schools of Japanese Confucianism—the Zhu Xi (1130–1200) school and the Wang Yangming (1472–1529) school—emerged from earlier Chinese developments, there was yet another, *kogaku*, which overcame them much as a thesis generates an antithesis, and then both are sublated through a new synthesis. In *Nihon Shushigakuha no tetsugaku* (*The Philosophy of the Japanese Zhu Xi School*), published in 1905, Inoue dismissed the Japanese Zhu Xi school as offering a relatively slavish repetition of earlier Chinese thinking, one lacking in original development. In *Nihon Yōmeigakuha no tetsugaku* (*The Philosophy of the Japanese Wang Yangming School*), published in 1900, Inoue spoke better of the Japanese Wang Yangming school for having transformed the Chinese teaching along Japanese lines, but recognized simultaneously its limitations especially when considered in relation to later developments of Japanese philosophy.

With the third school, Inoue posited an intellectual force that had not been noticed as such previously in studies of Tokugawa Confucianism. The *kogaku* school, Inoue claimed, was bound together by its common opposition to the Zhu Xi school's emphasis on rational principle (*li* 理) over generative force (*qi* 氣). *Kogaku* scholars were also

---

[1] Georg Wilhelm Friedrich Hegel, *Lectures on the Philosophy of Religion*, ed. Peter C. Hodgson (Berkeley: University of California Press, 1987), vol. II, 547–558.

united in opposing the supposed quietism of the Zhu Xi school in contrast to the more activistic metaphysics advocated by *kogaku* thinkers. *The kogaku* school supposedly opposed the Zhu Xi school's appeals to abstract ontological notions such as the ultimate of nonbeing (*mukyoku* 無極), a term *kogaku* scholars traced to heterodox texts. No doubt there was shared philosophical ground among *kogaku* thinkers, but more than a few of the *kogaku* objections were also shared by Neo-Confucians in good standing, such as Hayashi Razan (1583–1657).

A major problem of Inoue's narrative is that the three major figures of the movement, Sokō, Jinsai, and Sorai, never refer to each other as allies in a common theoretical cause. Of the three, Sokō is most problematic because neither Jinsai nor Sorai so much as mention him in their writings. Jinsai never broaches Sorai's thought, although Sorai criticized Jinsai to no end, taking every opportunity in his *Benmei* (*Distinguishing Names*) to explain how Jinsai erred. On several occasions, Sorai suggested that Jinsai's ideas were ultimately no different from those of Zhu Xi and his followers, the very thinkers Jinsai often identified as his opposition. In offering this evaluation of Jinsai, Sorai proposed an insightful criticism that could easily be expanded into an alternative narrative that effectively undermined the notion of a *kogaku* school significantly opposed to Neo-Confucian philosophizing. One thing, however, is certain: each of the *kogaku* scholars began their philosophical development as followers of Zhu Xi, and early on authored what would be considered, by any standard, Neo-Confucian texts.

Sorai's criticism of Jinsai is affirmed here as an interpretive line that applies equally to his, Sorai's, thought and that of Sokō, the other major philosopher who supposedly defined the contours of the school. This essay suggests that, just as Sorai saw Jinsai as a thinker who, despite his proclaimed return to ancient Confucianism essentially remained in the camp of later Confucians—i.e., Neo-Confucians—in his post-Buddhist engagement with philosophical issues, much the same applies to Sokō and Sorai as well. Neo-Confucianism here refers to a variety of names used by Sokō, Jinsai, and Sorai such as "later Confucians," "Song Confucians," and "advocates of human nature and principle," in reference to post-Buddhist expressions of Confucianism that indeed also reaffirmed ancient Confucianism in responding to religio-philosophical challenges earlier posed by Buddhism. Although there was never a rigid orthodoxy in Japan, the Zhu Xi school's teachings most approximated that status, making them prime, but not exclusive, exemplars of Neo-Confucianism. Doctrinally, Zhu Xi and his followers affirmed the reality of the world, its rational and material nature, and its generative and life-affirming character. Zhu Xi schoolmen affirmed, at the human level, the reality of the self, the mind, human feelings, and, most importantly, ethically good natures with which all are endowed from the start. Neo-Confucians generally affirmed the continuity between human nature and the natural world, leading to the conclusion that the world, too, is inherently good. Mahāyāna Buddhists purportedly denied these positions in favor of their ultimate truth of emptiness. In opposition to Buddhist claims, Zhu Xi's teachings defined a different worldview, one acknowledging the reality and essential goodness of everyday life, as well as rational, common-sense approaches to the real challenges presented therein. Neo-Confucians were not, however, necessarily followers of Zhu Xi; many who participated in the "later Confucian" movement criticized Zhu and his followers at length, especially over matters such as the relative priority of rational principle vis-à-vis generative force or the legitimacy of the ultimate of nonbeing as an ontological notion in Confucian discourse. Yet, in engaging such issues, these critics of Zhu Xi's thought made authentic their philosophical participation in the larger Neo-Confucian movement which, as much as anything, encouraged doubt, questioning, criticism, discussion, and thoughtful reflection geared toward realization of the true way of things.

Sokō, Jinsai, and Sorai each launched their scholarly careers with writings that expounded Zhu Xi's learning. Over time, they developed their own thinking about the problems of Confucian philosophy and established schools where they could teach others the conclusions they had come to. In this respect, they were modern theorists, despite the fact that they remained uneasy about acknowledging precisely what they were doing: formulating their own interpretations. In calling for a return to ancient Confucianism, they were hardly breaking with Neo-Confucianism so much as matching its rigorous demands for honest doubt and personal attainment of authentic understandings of Confucian teachings. In pursuing philosophical truth, teaching others to do the same, and setting down in words their manifest comprehensions of Confucianism, Sokō, Jinsai, and Sorai were arguably founders of innovative and distinctively Japanese forms of Neo-Confucianism.

If Inoue's narrative is historically contextualized, it can be read as an expression of the national pride realized in the late-Meiji, a pride heightened by Japan's victory over Qing dynasty China in the Sino-Japanese War, followed by another over czarist Russia in the Russo-Japanese War. Publication of the first volume, on the philosophy of the Japanese school of Wang Yangming, followed the first victory by five years, appearing in 1900. The triumphant volume, Inoue's study of the philosophy of *kogaku*, was published in 1902, the year the Anglo-Japanese Alliance linked Britain and imperial Japan, marking a new, more egalitarian period in Japanese diplomatic history. Inoue's last volume, on the Japanese Zhu Xi school, was published in 1905, the year of Japan's victory over Russia. Inoue's narrative hints that the emergence of a Japanese expression of Confucianism, *kogaku*, signaled, even in the Tokugawa period, Japan's burgeoning philosophical prevalence over China, much as imperial Japan militarily prevailed over China and then Russia in the late Meiji.

Inoue's view that *kogaku* surpassed the Zhu Xi and Wang Yangming schools resonated with claims voiced earlier by Sokō. In his *Chūchō jijitsu* (*The True Central Dynasty*), Sokō affirmed that imperial Japan had proved itself to be the real "central dynasty" or "China" by manifesting loyalty to its imperial line, unbroken and sacrosanct, while China, despite priding itself on being the central dynasty, had shown, by repeatedly overthrowing its dynastic lines, that it hardly deserved such status. This evaluation seemed compelling in Sokō's day following the overthrow of the Ming in 1644. Inoue's trilogy revived this motif in a philosophical narrative that presented *kogaku* as the victor over earlier Chinese expressions of Neo-Confucianism.

KOGAKU, BUSHIDŌ, AND NATIONAL ETHICS

Inoue's accounts of Japan's philosophical traditions soon morphed into writings on "national ethics" (*kokumin dōtoku* 国民道徳), a mix of philosophical notions and nationalistic ideology highlighting essentially Confucian virtues that supposedly distinguished Japan and its subjects as a superior nation and people. Inoue also published widely on a subdivision of "national ethics," *bushidō* (武士道), or "the way of the warrior." Nitobe Inazō's (1862–1933) work, *Bushido: The Soul of Japan*, published in 1900, following Japan's victory over China and the same year as Inoue's study of Japan's Wang Yangming school, rapidly emerged as an international best-seller, quickening discourse on a suddenly hot topic not notably developed previously. Nitobe's work claimed that *bushidō*, like the English Constitution, was an "unwritten code," but one that every Japanese absorbed through the air they breathed. Nitobe's book was originally written in English for a Western audience fascinated with little Japan's defeat of huge China. It was later published in Japanese but to considerably less acclaim. Critics such as Inoue challenged Nitobe's assertion that *bushidō* had no written tradition. In later volumes on *bushidō* and those on *kogaku*, Inoue identified Yamaga Sokō as "the constitutional theorist of *bushidō*," praising him for first expounding that code. In later writings, Inoue added more, presenting *bushidō* as a deeply rooted philosophical ethic, one sprung from the depths of Japanese antiquity.

Objections were raised by Basil Hall Chamberlain (1850–1935), a professor of Japanese language and philology at Tokyo Imperial University, in his brief study, *The Invention of a New Religion*, published in 1912. Chamberlain argued that a new belief system, centered on the emperor and the nation and undergirded by the ethic of *bushidō*, had been manufactured in the Meiji as a means of indoctrinating Japanese in unprecedented ways. Contrary to those praising Japan's unbroken imperial line, Chamberlain declared that few countries had been more cavalier in dealing with their monarchs. Regarding *bushidō*, he noted that the word appeared in no significant dictionary, encyclopedia, or account of Japan prior to 1900, the year Nitobe's book was published. According to Chamberlain, the ethic of *bushidō* had been "fabricated out of whole cloth."[2]

Chamberlain's objections were directed at both Nitobe's book and Inoue's efforts to identify a tradition of literature explaining *bushidō*. Inoue published prodigiously on *bushidō*, beginning with *Bushidō sōsho* (*Bushidō Library*), in three volumes, co-edited with Arima Sukemasa (1873–1931) and published in 1905. In 1912, Inoue published *Kokumin dōtoku gairon* (*An Outline of National Ethics*), extolling the Japanese imperial throne, military spirit, and moral virtues. Inoue continued with similar publications over the next three decades, moving from defining the contours of Japanese Confucian philosophy to affirming an increasingly militaristic version of Japan's national ethics with substantial portions coming from Confucianism and the thought of Sokō. Inoue's

---

[2] Basil Hall Chamberlain, *The Invention of a New Religion* (London: Watts and Company, 1912), 1–27.

death in 1944 spared him from the tragic harvest of his work. The academy of defeated Japan soon shunned Inoue's claims about national ethics as egregiously wrongheaded propaganda. Although Inoue's insights regarding Confucianism and the beginnings of Japan's philosophical traditions had some merits, they were dismissed in favor of the claims that real philosophy was Western philosophy and its appearance in Japan, a Meiji development.

INOUE, MARUYAMA, AND *KOGAKU*

Inoue's triadic narrative of Confucian philosophy survived in the writings of a powerful critic. The young Maruyama Masao, writing in the early 1940s, significantly revised the appraisals developed in Inoue's quasi-Hegelian accounts but affirmed the framework of three major schools, the Zhu Xi, the Wang Yangming, and the Ancient Learning, with the latter presiding even more heroically than ever over the dissolution of all expressions before it. Read historically, Maruyama's hermeneutic might be construed as echoing imperial Japan's conquest of Republican China and its creation of a "New Order in East Asia" much as Inoue's had earlier echoed Meiji Japan's victory over czarist Russia. Maruyama did not, however, praise Sokō's thought but instead cast Sorai as the protagonist of his narrative. For Inoue, Sorai was problematic because he extolled the ancient Chinese language, Chinese culture, and Chinese philosophy rather than anything Japanese. Sorai called himself an "eastern barbarian" and disparaged Japan in relation to China. Sorai exalted the ancient sages as the creators of civilization and denied, moreover, that there had been any sages since those of ancient China. In Inoue's view, such claims amounted to China worship. Maruyama found Sorai's thinking far less objectionable.

Inoue did recognize philosophical aspects of Sorai's thought. For example, Inoue allowed that Sorai conceptualized ethics in terms of what contributed to peace and prosperity for everyone, prompting Inoue to see Sorai as a utilitarian anticipating positions formulated by nineteenth-century British philosophers Jeremy Bentham and John Stuart Mill. Yet Inoue saw little that was positive in Sorai's utilitarianism because it did not enhance Japan's *kokutai* 国体, or national essence, a sacrosanct dimension of *kokumin dōtoku*. Doing what was best for *kokutai* might, after all, not bring peace and happiness to the majority, but it could entail considerable sacrifice. In the end, Inoue's quasi-Hegelian tripartite analysis of *kogaku* was inverted, with the first figure, Sokō, emerging as the most meaningful and abiding. Sokō won high honors from Inoue for his ideas on *shidō* 士道, or the samurai way, and for his admiration of imperial Japan as the true central dynasty.

Sorai, on the other hand, extolled the ancient Chinese sages who had created civilization. Sorai also disparaged the Japanese imperial line and questioned the historical integrity of Shintō. Consequently, Inoue could hardly view the final expression of *kogaku* as its most perfect. Maruyama, who witnessed Japan's wartime fortunes, had little use for glorifications of the Japanese emperor, Shintō, or romantic notions about the grandeur

of the nation and its people. In these respects, he had no problems with Sorai and perhaps shared considerable common ground with him. Maruyama also claimed to find
in Sorai's thought meaningful positions, such as Sorai's supposed distinction between
"public" and "private" spheres and his praise for the "logic of invention," positions that
marked the beginnings of a modern political consciousness for Japan. In these respects,
Maruyama claimed, Sorai went well beyond the traditionalistic, naturalistic Zhu Xi
mode of thought and, in doing so, decisively contributed to the downfall of the latter.

Despite the originality of many of his claims, Maruyama endorsed via repetition
Inoue's interpretive narrative divvying Japanese Confucianism into the schools of
Zhu Xi, Wang Yangming, and *kogaku*. Maruyama thus contributed to the continued
longevity of Inoue's broader analyses through the second half of the twentieth century. Nowhere was this more true than in the West, where Mikiso Hane's (1922–2003)
translation of Maruyama's *Nihon seiji shisōshi kenkyū* as *Studies in the Intellectual
History of Tokugawa Japan* helped gain for Maruyama's ideas a revered standing as the
starting points for further research on Tokugawa intellectual history, philosophical
or otherwise—and this despite the fact that, in the preface to the English translation,
Maruyama himself admitted that his text included a number of substantial interpretive and factual errors. Ironically, Inoue—the source of so much in Maruyama—
receded from the forefront of research agendas addressing *kogaku* and Japanese
Confucianism.

QUESTIONING *KOGAKU*

Prior to Inoue's trilogy, one finds no mention of *kogaku* as a movement comprising the
three giants, Sokō, Jinsai, and Sorai, and their followers. True, Jinsai often referred to
kogi 古義, or "ancient meanings," in his writings; Jinsai's school has also been called the
Kogidō 古義堂, or "the Hall of Ancient Meanings"; and he was known posthumously
as the *kogaku sensei*, or the "teacher of Ancient Learning." But to transfer the notion
of *kogaku* to Sokō first and then to Sorai as well is anachronistic and inappropriate.
Sorai characterized his work as *kobunjigaku* 古文辞学, or "studies of ancient words and
phrases." To posit school relations between the two seems lacking in appreciation for
philosophical variety and nuance. An early account of Tokugawa Confucianism, Hara
Nensai's (1774–1820) *Sentetsu sōdan*, published in 1817, includes entries on seventy-
two Confucian scholars. Although Jinsai and Sorai are included, Nensai recognized
no school relationship between them. In fact, Jinsai's entry opened the fourth volume,
but the entry for Sorai appears at the beginning of the sixth. Nensai notes that Jinsai
was called "*kogaku sensei*," but mentions no connection with Sorai. When discussing
Sorai, Nensai relates that Sorai criticized Jinsai but says nothing about them belonging
to the same school. Nensai situates Sorai in an intellectual genealogy by tracing Sorai's
kobunji ideas to two Ming literary theorists, Li Panlong (1514–1570) and Wang Shizhen

(1526–1590), rather than to Sokō and Jinsai.[3] Judging from this late-Tokugawa compilation, there is no hint that *kogaku* was viewed, prior to the late-Meiji, as a movement including Sokō, Jinsai, and Sorai.

Equally far-fetched is the notion that Jinsai and Sorai continued a lineage that began with Sokō. *Sentetsu sōdan* does not include Sokō among the seventy-two luminaries presented as the leading Confucian thinkers of Tokugawa Japan. When Sokō is introduced in a follow-up volume, the *Sentetsu sōdan kōhen* (*Sequel to Discussions of Earlier Wise Men*), edited by Tōjō Kindai (1795–1878) and published in 1827, he is not cast as the *kogaku* pioneer whose ideas led to those of Jinsai and Sorai but rather as a philosopher of the second order, influential on the Akō rōnin and their vendetta, perhaps, but not at the headwaters of a movement broader than his own.[4]

One of Sokō's writings, the *Seikyō yōroku* (*Essential Teachings of Sagely Confucianism*), offended high-ranking shogunal officials including Hoshina Masayuki, a student of Yamazaki Ansai's highly orthodox Zhu Xi school. Consequently, Sokō was exiled from Edo for nearly a decade, and his learning was left with the stigma of criminality. For the remainder of the Tokugawa, few other than his scattered followers in later generations had praise for it. However, one of Sokō's followers, Yoshida Shōin, kept Sokō's teachings—or at least his understanding of them—alive as a counterculture philosophy, appealing to those in remote "outer" (*tozama*) domains such as Chōshū, where concerns for shogunal approval were often low to negative. That Sokō and his ideas had once been banished virtually damned them in Edo even while enhancing their appeal in *tozama* domains. Other than in *tozama* domains, however, Sokō was not a philosopher much cited or discussed. If there were ties among Sokō, Jinsai, and Sorai, they were not ones affirmed in writing.

Admittedly, Sokō, Jinsai, and Sorai did advocate returning to ancient Confucian texts in purported opposition to positions advanced by the Japanese Zhu Xi school. However Sokō, Jinsai, and Sorai hardly agreed on which texts were most authoritative. For Sokō, the return was to Confucius' thinking, especially as advanced in the *Analects*. But as often as not, Sokō's ideas paraphrased either Zhu Xi or other post-Zhu Xi Neo-Confucian philosophers. Sokō's proclaimed return to ancient texts was thus more rhetorical than real. With Jinsai, the purported return was to the *Analects* and *Mencius*, but, as with Sokō, Jinsai advanced many ideas and methods found in the works of Zhu Xi or his later followers. Jinsai's rejection of the Zhu Xi teachings was thus more selective than comprehensive and his return to the *Analects* and *Mencius* more announced than actual. Sorai claimed to return to the ancient Six Classics: the *Book of History*, the *Book of Poetry*, the *Book of Changes*, the *Book of Rites*, and the *Spring and Autumn Annals* (the *Book of Music*, the sixth classic, was long lost). Yet again, Sorai's rejection of the Zhu Xi school teachings was only partial and polemical, and his continued participation in its discourse far more substantial and conspicuous than he admitted. The criticism

---

[3] Hara Nensai, "Itō Jinsai," *Sentetsu sōdan*, ed. Tsukamoto Tetsuzan (Tokyo: Yūhōdō shoten, 1920), vol. 4, 176–190. Hara, "Ogyū Sorai," *Sentetsu sōdan*, vol. 6, 329–346.

[4] Tōjō Kindai, "Yamaga Sokō," *Sentetsu sōdan kōhen* (Edo: Suharaya, 1830), 2/1a-2/6b.

that Sorai directed at Jinsai—that Jinsai remained a practitioner of the Zhu Xi school teachings despite his criticisms of Zhu Xi—might well be applied to Sorai equally.

Most significantly, the strategy of calling for a return to ancient Confucian teachings—rhetorical or real—was one that Zhu Xi, his predecessors, and his followers, all affirmed. Indeed, that was precisely what they claimed they were doing. Zhu Xi's teachings first emerged in Song China in reaction against Buddhism and, in doing so, called for a return to the ancient Confucian teachings constituting the bedrock of right understanding. Thus, Zhu Xi and his followers wrote commentary after commentary on the *Analects*, the *Mencius*, and the Six Classics attempting to revive Confucianism over and against the prevalence of Buddhism. In this respect, the Zhu Xi school can be viewed as the first expression of *kogaku*, or, alternatively, the *kogaku* movement can be seen as a later, revisionist expression of the thinking of Zhu Xi and his followers. To accept Sokō, Jinsai, and Sorai's proclaimed return to ancient texts as a move that completely broke with the Zhu Xi mode of philosophizing seems patently naïve. In the end, Zhu Xi and his followers, later Neo-Confucians, as well as Sokō, Jinsai, and Sorai were more formulating their own ideas than returning to the past; however, rather than say as much, they billed their thinking as a return to ancient classics, presumably thereby taking the ego and its conceits out of their ideas.

Reviving *Kogaku*: Words, Right Meaning, and Governing

There are good grounds, however, for grouping Sokō, Jinsai, and Sorai as three of a kind, linked by a shared genre and methodology used in authoring their masterworks. The methodology can be called philosophical lexicography and the genre that of the philosophical lexicon. The two involve systematic analyses of a set of terms, concepts, and notions of high-level philosophical importance, with the outcome being a comprehensive philosophical vision or worldview. Philosophical lexicography has deep roots in ancient Confucian thinking. The *Analects* 13/3 presents Confucius being asked by a disciple what he would do if given the reins of government in the state of Wei. Confucius responded that he would first rectify names (Ch. *zheng ming*; Jp. *seimei* 正名). When his disciple, dumbfounded, questioned this, Confucius explained that right understanding and usage of words are essential to good government. He added that if names, words, and language were not correct, then everything would go awry, with chaos and anarchy resulting. Rightly ordered language and its usage, Confucius affirmed, are essential keys to a rightly ordered state. The masterworks by Sokō, Jinsai, and Sorai reveal this methodology in systematic practice. Understood in light of Confucius' remarks, their masterworks appear as expressions of philosophical lexicography that indeed have intrinsic political significance. This reveals that these thinkers were not simply engaging in philological or semantic commentary; they were defining the philosophical foundations of a rightly ordered polity. Their work was, in that respect, both concerned with defining terms and the fundamentals of a just polity, comparable in those respects to Plato's *Republic* and Hobbes's *Leviathan* in form if not content.

Whereas Confucius' remarks in the *Analects* explain the political significance of rectifying terms, that approach to philosophizing was made manifest by a late-Song philosophical lexicon, the *Xingli ziyi* (*The Meanings of Human Nature and Principle*), compiled by followers of Chen Beixi (1159–1223), one of Zhu Xi's last disciples. Deployed even as Mongol forces advanced their conquest of the Song, Beixi's methodology both meant to simplify a complex system for beginners and yet also define the right foundations of good government so as to provide for the philosophical defense of the realm. Although the Mongols prevailed, Beixi's work survived in various East Asian editions over the centuries, including the 1553 Korean edition. Copies of the latter entered Japan during Toyotomi Hideyoshi's (1536–1598) invasions of Korea in the 1590s. Thereafter, the text became an important one in early Tokugawa Japan, with a punctuated Japanese edition, based on the 1553 Korean, appearing in 1632. Hayashi Razan was its most enthusiastic advocate, authoring a colloquial translation-commentary on the work entitled *Seiri jigi genkai* (*Japanese Explanation of the Meanings of Human Nature and Principle*), published in 1659. Other than the Four Books, no work was as important to Razan's understanding of Zhu Xi's thought. Through Razan's colloquial account of Beixi's text, Sokō, Jinsai, and Sorai, among others, came to understand Beixi's genre, methodology, and philosophical restatement of many if not all of Zhu Xi's ideas. It was from this lineage, the Zhu Xi–Beixi–Korean 1553–Razan line, that the ideas of Sokō, Jinsai, and Sorai emerged.

Sokō studied with Razan as a youth and learned of Beixi's text early on. The latter is discussed often in Sokō's *Yamaga Gorui* (*Classified Conversations of Yamaga Sokō*),[5] leaving no doubts as to whether Sokō knew the text. The conceptual organization and methodology of Sokō's *Seikyō yōroku* recall Beixi's text in form and structure, and Sokō's allusions to notions and remarks in Beixi's text are many. The contents of the texts often differ, with Sokō proclaiming, at least, his opposition to Song and Ming thinkers and his return to the ideas of the Duke of Zhou and Confucius. Although this might sound like a rupture with Neo-Confucianism, all is not as it might seem. Sokō proceeds to convey his return to the Duke of Zhou and Confucius by analyzing mostly the core stock of terms that Beixi had examined, often giving accounts that differed from Beixi's only in relatively minor ways. When one considers that Zhu Xi encouraged his followers to doubt and question philosophical problems that troubled them and that, in Japan, Razan did the same, Sokō's critical doubts were arguably not so much a break with the movement as they were a fuller participation in it. Given that Song and Ming thinkers such as Lu Xiangshan (1139–1192), Wang Yangming, and Luo Qinshun (1465–1547) criticized Zhu Xi at length and yet remained respected participants in Neo-Confucianism, Sokō's

---

[5] Yamaga Sokō, *Yamaga gorui* [*Classified Conversations of Yamaga Sokō*] (Tokyo: Kokusho kankōkai, 1912), 170, 178, 187, 197–198, 201, 222, 330, 332, 335, 339–340, 359, 362–363, 383, 397, 406, 410, 415.

criticism of Zhu Xi's thought can equally be viewed as a revisionist expression of the same. Razan, one of the founding fathers of Neo-Confucianism in early modern Japan, also expressed doubts, questions, and criticisms of Beixi's text and Zhu Xi's ideas. Doing so authenticated one's participation in the movement by revealing the extent to which one had confirmed for himself solutions to philosophical problems.

KOGAKU VIEWS ON GHOSTS AND SPIRITS

One example illustrating how the lexicographies of Sokō, Jinsai, and Sorai were less grounded in ancient literature than in that of Neo-Confucian lexicography appears in their thinking about ghosts and spirits (*kishin* 鬼神). These terms, seldom discussed by Confucius, figured prominently in Beixi's discussions. Indeed, Beixi's accounts of ghosts and spirits, which he explained as manifestations of generative force (*qi* 気) and *yin* and *yang*, were the lengthiest in his lexicon. The terms also occupied considerable space in the works of Sokō, Jinsai, and Sorai.

Sokō explains ghosts and spirits as "mysterious but omnipresent entities," a characterization clarified via paraphrasing some standard Neo-Confucian accounts of ghosts and spirits otherwise found in Beixi's text. Sokō thus relates, "the spiritual energies of *yin* and *yang*" are "traces of ghosts and spirits." Sokō also explains that heaven, earth, humanity, and all things manifest the traces of ghosts and spirits. Ghosts, Sokō continues, are associated with *yin*, whereas spirits are associated with *yang*. Sokō next reveals that his understanding of Confucius' thinking extends well beyond the *Analects*. Sokō adds that ghosts and spirits have the same generative force that humans do. Sokō further observes, along Neo-Confucian lines found in Beixi's *Ziyi*, that "the heavenly components of the soul (*kon* 魂) belong to *yang*, and spirits are their spiritual forces, while the earthly components of the soul (*haku* 魄) belong to *yin*, and ghosts are their spiritual forces." Sokō briefly explains how ghostly visions occur, observing that while humans are alive, ghosts and spirits reside within them, but with their demise, ghosts and spirits flow about "producing aberrations in the creative work of the universe. It is the wandering of the heavenly components of the soul (*yūkon* 遊魂) that produces these aberrations." Alternatively, Sokō explains that, just as myriad things are rooted in heaven, so are people rooted in their ancestors. Offering sacrifices to one's ancestors and kin should therefore be an integral aspect of human life. Moreover, Sokō affirms that ancestors who are worshiped by their descendants respond to them because they share a common generative force with their descendants.[6]

Apparently, Sokō downplayed the *Analects'* (7/21) statement that Confucius did not discuss "spirits." Had he done otherwise, he might have refrained from such detail about

---

[6] Yamaga Sokō, "Ghosts and Spirits," *Seikyō yōroku*, ed. Tahara Tsuguo and Morimoto Junichirō, *Yamaga Sokō* (Tokyo: Iwanami shoten, 1970), 21–22. Chen Beixi, "Ghosts and Spirits," *Xingli ziyi* (1632 ed.), 73b–76b.

ghosts and spirits that was not, after all, based in ancient Confucian texts. Most significant here is not that Sokō paraphrased Beixi, but that his philosophizing repeatedly engaged Neo-Confucianism, as presented by Beixi, in a revisionist way, revising mostly via summarizing and recapitulating, rather than reviving, in any authentic, compelling manner, classical Confucianism.

Jinsai's analyses of ghosts and spirits in his *Gomō jigi* (*The Meanings of Terms in the Analects and Mencius*), like Sokō's, take as their starting point views explained in Beixi's *Ziyi*. This is hardly surprising because Jinsai's first draft of the *Gomō jigi* dates from a time when he was delivering evening lectures on Beixi's *Ziyi*. As with most Neo-Confucians, Jinsai holds that ghosts and spirits refer to the spirits of heaven, earth, mountains, rivers, ancestral temples, and the deities of the five sacrifices, as well as to spiritual beings capable of causing good and bad fortune. Jinsai recalls how "Master Zhu" explained, "ghosts are spiritual forces of yin, while spirits are the spiritual forces of yang." Jinsai then relates, "Master Zhu articulated what can be called an authentic Confucian account of ghosts and spirits." In acknowledging Zhu Xi's position with muted approval, Jinsai is some distance from classical Confucianism and far closer to Neo-Confucian thinking than he allows.

Overall, Jinsai accepts the accounts in the *Analects* as authentic representations of Confucius' thinking but rejects those in the *Book of Rites*. Jinsai acknowledges that in the *Analects*, Confucius rarely discusses ghosts and spirits and that in the *Mencius* they are not broached. Jinsai adds that the ancient sage kings often indulged people, doing as they did and following them in practices related to ghosts and spirits rather than leading them along the right path. Confucius, however, led rather than followed. In doing so, he cautioned people against obsessive interest in ghosts and spirits. Because Confucius taught so little about ghosts and spirits, Jinsai concludes that the *Book of Rites* passages are "apocryphal tales fabricated by Han scholars, not authentic Confucian teachings." The remainder of Jinsai's discussions of ghosts and spirits pertains to divination and its intrinsic wrongheadedness. Although he presents a number of arguments against divination, the most compelling is that neither the *Analects* nor the *Mencius* sanctioned divination as a practice people should follow.[7] On the other hand it should be added that, neither the *Analects* nor the *Mencius* actually discusses the rightness of divination at all. However, in their commentaries on the *Book of Changes*, Neo-Confucians often did discuss divination, thus making Jinsai's concern for the topic not nearly as classical as it might seem.

Jinsai's opening accounts of ghosts and spirits endorse some basic Neo-Confucian teachings but then quickly switch to reticence. In this regard, Jinsai was arguably returning somewhat to ancient Confucian themes. Yet even the final section of Beixi's accounts of ghosts and spirits addresses the *Analects'* passage (6/20) where Confucius is described as one who revered ghosts and spirits but kept them at a distance. This approach, Beixi reports, is the most perfect and one that Zhu Xi equally extolled.

---

[7] Itō Jinsai, "Ghosts and Spirits," *Gomō jigi*, ed., Yoshikawa Kōjirō and Shimizu Shigeru, Itō Jinsai/Itō Tōgai (Tokyo: Iwanami shoten, 1971), 83–86. Tucker (1998), *Itō Jinsai's Gomō jigi*, 203–207.

It should be added, moreover, that in Beixi's lexicon appeals to the *Analects* are common. The shared ground then suggests continuities among classical Confucianism, Neo-Confucianism, and Jinsai, rather than rupture or dissolution.

Sorai's accounts of ghosts and spirits in his lengthy philosophical lexicon, the *Benmei*, have little use for the naturalistic accounts of Song Confucians explaining ghosts and spirits in terms of *yin* and *yang*. Instead, Sorai asserts literally that "ghosts" refer to "human ghosts," whereas "spirits" refers to "heavenly spirits." Sorai states that the Song Confucian views of ghosts and spirits as the traces of the transformations of heaven and earth, or as *yin* and *yang*, are based on misunderstandings of the *Book of Changes*. Sorai allows that Jinsai's account of ghosts and spirits as "the spirits of heaven and earth, mountains and streams, the ancestral temples and the five sacrifices, and moreover all beings that have spiritual powers and that are capable of causing good fortune or misfortune to mankind" is correct. But Sorai then faults Jinsai for otherwise following the mistakes of the Song Neo-Confucians on ghosts and spirits. Much of the confusion on the topic, Sorai suggests, results from discussions of whether ghosts and spirits actually exist. Sorai declares that there is only one answer: the sages established these notions and so their existence must be accepted. Rather than follow personal opinions on such matters, people should have faith in the sages and their teachings.[8]

Sorai dismisses Song Confucian accounts of ghosts and spirits based on the *Book of Changes* by arguing that the passages cited are taken out of context and given mistaken interpretations. Sorai shines as a critic, but in offering positive positions, his thoughts are less compelling. He declares, for example, "the sage kings revered ghosts and spirits throughout the three dynasties." He then suggests that they could not be mistaken because they are sages, and sages are not given to error. Contrary to Jinsai who argued against divination at length, Sorai does not question the practice and instead states, "divination transmits the words of ghosts and spirits. If there were no ghosts and spirits, neither would there be divination. There are ghosts and spirits; thus there is divination." Whereas Sorai claims to have insight into the sage kings and even divination, he ultimately asserts that "spirits are unfathomable," at least for the common lot. In ancient times, the sages understood ghosts and spirits and authored the *Book of Changes* as a means of comprehending them through divination. Moreover, because ghosts and spirits "do not have deliberative, striving minds," the sages formulated rites for the sake of interacting with them. If ritual services are held for them, wandering ghosts and heavenly spirits will not cause calamities. At one point, Sorai suggests that "the rites all involve returning ghosts and spirits to heaven," but he then insists that the sages never dared to simplify things so crudely. In refraining from such, they exhibited perfect reverence.[9]

[8] Ogyū Sorai, "Heaven, Fate, Lord-on-High, and Ghosts and Spirits," *Benmei*, trans. Tucker, *Ogyū Sorai's Philosophical Masterworks* (Honolulu: University of Hawai'i Press, 2006), 271–279.
[9] Ogyū Sorai, "Heaven, Fate, Lord-on-High, and Ghosts and Spirits," *Benmei*, trans. Tucker, *Ogyū Sorai's Philosophical Masterworks*, 271–279.

Sorai's thinking on ghosts and spirits is more removed from Zhu Xi and most expressions of Neo-Confucianism than are the views of Sokō and Jinsai. Yet even Sorai, in presenting his exposition of ghosts and spirits within a work—the *Benmei*—otherwise devoted to analyzing systematically the meanings of philosophical terms, conspicuously continues a philosophical genre and methodology that links it to the Song Neo-Confucian school of Zhu Xi via Chen Beixi. In terms of genre and method, the ancient Confucian classics offer nothing comparable to what is found in Sorai's *Benmei*. Through these dimensions—genre and method—Sorai, like Sokō and Jinsai, remains a participant in Neo-Confucian discourse far more than a proponent of new and independent schools of thought intent on authentically reviving classical Confucianism.

LATER CRITIQUES AND MEIJI DEVELOPMENTS

The *kogaku* masterworks of Sokō, Jinsai, and Sorai elicited many critical responses perhaps because their genre revealed to contemporaries the political significance of their works. That they were more than philological studies made them potentially threatening to the powers that were, and so, arguably, dangerous. Indeed, shortly after publication of Sokō's *Seikyō yōroku*, which ostensibly was an outspoken critique of Zhu Xi's thought, Sokō was summoned before shogunal authorities and exiled from Edo to the distant hinterlands of Akō domain. Although pardoned nearly a decade later and permitted to return and teach on a small scale at his residence in Edo, Sokō, a tired and broken man, essentially lived under house arrest for the remainder of his years. After Sokō, *kogaku* thinkers did not publish their writings during their lifetimes. Nevertheless, posthumous critics were many, coming from all corners. Most criticisms were directed at Sorai. Goi Ranshū (1697–1762) and Nakai Chikuzan (1730–1804), two thinkers from the Kaitokudō merchant academy in Osaka, defended Jinsai's thought against Sorai's earlier criticisms. Ranshū and Chikuzan objected to Sorai's ruler-centered focus, endorsing instead Jinsai's political thinking, which more emphasized the importance of the people. Yamagata Bantō (1748–1821), who studied under Nakai Chikuzan and Nakai Rikken (1732–1817) at the Kaitokudō, pointedly rejected Sorai's claims that ghosts and spirits exist, advocating instead atheism. Nativist thinkers such as Kamo Mabuchi (1697–1769) questioned Sorai's claims about the importance of the sages in the creation of ethical standards, suggesting that ethical values and virtues existed in all places, in all times, and certainly were not the exclusive creations of the ancient Chinese sages. Ishida Baigan (1685–1744), founder of the Shingaku movement emphasizing mind cultivation, criticized Sorai's insistence that external rites alone were sufficient for controlling the mind. Andō Shōeki (1703–1762), an independent thinker, lambasted "sages," from the ancient Chinese sage kings to the Buddha, as robbers and thieves who ate without tilling the soil. The Kansei Ban on Heterodoxy, meant to exclude "heterodox" (i.e., non-Zhu Xi) teachings such as Jinsai's and Sorai's from shogunal schools, was arguably the culmination of broad-based opposition primarily to Sorai's teachings. That the shogunal ban targeted Sorai is ironic because the overall thrust of Sorai's learning was indeed most suited for rulers.

By the late Tokugawa, Sorai's teachings had markedly declined. It is noteworthy, however, that Jinsai's did not. Jinsai's five sons played instrumental roles in advancing their father's thought as a family profession, enabling his thinking, as modified incrementally by later generations, to remain a force in Kyoto throughout the Tokugawa period. In the early Meiji, Jinsai's school contributed to the development of one of the most progressive thinkers of the age, Fukuzawa Yukichi (1835–1901). Fukuzawa's father had been a student of the thought of Itō Tōgai (1670–1736), Jinsai's eldest son and first successor. Admittedly, Sorai's ideas garnered attention from Katō Hiroyuki (1836–1916), president of Tokyo Imperial University, but did not find champions among many other Meiji intellectuals.

Sokō's philosophical fortunes, however, soared during the Meiji period. In part this resulted from the rise to power of ex-samurai from Chōshū domain who had studied with Yoshida Shōin (1830–1859), a hereditary instructor of the Yamaga teachings. Shōin's impact was also strong on Inoue Tetsujirō, creator of the *kogaku* philosophical narrative and admirer of Sokō's teachings. Through Inoue's trilogy, Sokō's teachings came to impress General Nogi Maresuke (1849–1912) who, as head of the Peer's School, promoted Sokō's ideas there as well as in his teachings to the future Shōwa emperor, Hirohito (1901–1989). When Nogi and his wife committed suicide following the passing of the Meiji emperor, Inoue interpreted their deeds as authentic expressions of Sokō's philosophy on loyal service. In these ways, Inoue established for *kogaku* learning a new level of respectability as part of the emerging philosophy of *kokumin dōtoku*. The fortunes attained by *kogaku* through Inoue's *kokumin dōtoku*, however, ultimately led, as discussed earlier, to its eventual postwar decline. Whereas philosophical narratives such as Maruyama's salvaged *kogaku* as an interpretive category, it seems best to approach Sokō, Jinsai, and Sorai as three independent thinkers whose revisionist approaches to Neo-Confucian learning took them not so much outside the fold as to the very boundaries of orthodoxy and heterodoxy. In going there, however, those thinkers were acting upon philosophical strategies encouraged by Zhu Xi and his followers, those recognizing the value of doubt and criticism, as well as the importance of coming to one's own scholarly comprehension of learning and practice. In this respect, Sokō, Jinsai, and Sorai were arguably authentic Neo-Confucians.

BIBLIOGRAPHY AND SUGGESTED READINGS

Ansart, Olivier. (1998) *L'empire du rite: La pensée politique d'Ogyū Sorai, Japon 1666–1728.* Geneva: Librairie Droz.

Chen Beixi. (1986) *Neo-Confucian Terms Explained*, translated by Wing-tsit Chan. New York: Columbia University Press.

De Bary, William Theodore, and Irene Bloom. (1979) *Principle and Practicality: Essays in Neo-Confucianism and Practical Learning.* New York: Columbia University Press.

Gardner, Daniel K. (1986) *Chu Hsi and the Ta-hsueh: Neo-Confucian Reflection on the Confucian Canon*. Cambridge: Council on East Asian Studies, Harvard University.

Huang, Chun-chieh, and John A. Tucker, editors. (2014) *Dao Companion to Japanese Confucian Philosophy*. Dordrecht: Springer.

Inoue Tetsujirō. (1900) *Nihon Yōmeigakuha no tetsugaku* [*The Philosophy of the Japanese Wang Yangming School*]. Tokyo: Fuzanbō.

Inoue Tetsujirō. (1902) *Nihon kogakuha no tetsugaku* [*The Philosophy of the Japanese Ancient Learning School*]. Tokyo: Fuzanbō.

Inoue Tetsujirō. (1905) *Nihon Shushigakuha no tetsugaku* [*The Philosophy of the Japanese Zhu Xi School*]. Tokyo: Fuzanbō.

Itō Jinsai. (1998) *Itō Jinsai's* Gomō jigi *and the Philosophical Definition of Early Modern Japan*, translated by John Allen Tucker. Leiden: Brill.

Lidin, Olof G. (1973) *Life of Ogyū Sorai: A Tokugawa Confucian Philosopher*. Lund, Sweden: Studentlitteratur.

Maruyama, Masao. (1974) *Studies in the Intellectual History of Tokugawa Japan*, translated by Mikiso Hane. Princeton: Princeton University Press.

McEwan, J. R. (1962) *The Political Writings of Ogyū Sorai*. Cambridge: Cambridge University Press.

Minear, Richard. (1976) "Ogyū Sorai's *Instructions for Students*: A Translation and Commentary," *Harvard Journal of Asiatic Studies* 36: 5–81.

Najita, Tetsuo. (1998) *Visions of Virtue in Tokugawa Japan*. Chicago: University of Chicago Press.

Ogyū Sorai. (1994) *Master Sorai's Responsals: An Annotated Translation of* Sorai sensei tōmonsho, translated by Samuel Hideo Yamashita. Honolulu: University of Hawai'i Press.

Ogyū Sorai. (1999) *Ogyū Sorai's Discourse on* Government, translated by Olof G. Lidin. Wiesbaden: Harrassowitz Verlag.

Ogyū Sorai. (2006) *Ogyū Sorai's Philosophical Masterworks: The* Bendō *and* Benmei, translated by John Allen Tucker. Honolulu: University of Hawai'i Press.

Spae, Joseph John. (1967) *Itō Jinsai: A Philosopher, Educator, and Sinologist of the Tokugawa Period*. New York: Paragon Book Reprint Corp.

Tucker, John Allen, editor. (2013) *Critical Readings in Japanese Confucianism, vols. 1–4*. Leiden: Brill.

Watanabe Hiroshi. (2012) *A History of Japanese Political Thought, 1600–1901*, translated by David Noble. Tokyo: International House of Japan.

Yoshikawa Kōjirō. (1983) *Jinsai, Sorai, Norinaga: Three Classical Philologists of the Tokugawa Period*. Tokyo: Tōhō gakkai.

CHAPTER 14

....

BUSHIDŌ AND PHILOSOPHY

Parting the Clouds, Seeking the Way

....

CHRIS GOTO-JONES

THERE are few aspects of Japanese cultural and intellectual history more iconic than the construct known today as *bushidō* (武士道). The so-called Way of the Warrior (or sometimes, more romantically, the "Way of the Samurai") has emerged as a distinctive and resilient pillar of the "Japanese ideology," informing many interpretations of Japanese society and history. However, despite (or perhaps because of) their deliberate simplicity, icons are complicated things; the most popular and contagious constructions of *bushidō* appear to obscure (rather than reveal) a rich and multifaceted philosophical landscape that should be of great value to philosophers today. This chapter proceeds in the spirit of the famous calligraphy of Funakoshi Gichin (1868–1957, founder of *Shōtōkan karate-dō* 松濤館空手道): *hatsuun jindō* (抜雲尋道, parting the clouds, seeking the Way).

Some of the most persistent clouds that require parting involve the construction of an interpretive context for the texts of *bushidō* that privileges Orientalist, essentialist, romantic, exotic, or esoteric readings. Such a context has been supported since the twentieth century by an industry of popular translations that deliberately emphasizes these commercially attractive features. While this work has done a great deal to bring *bushidō* into mainstream public discourse, another result has been the compression of technical, philosophical terms and concepts into vague, cloudy categories, which in turn serves to make the texts seem more inscrutable and mysterious. One of the difficulties for the translator is the extent to which many of these texts are deeply embedded in the religious and philosophical conventions of Mahāyāna Buddhism, Daoism, Shintō, Neo-Confucianism, and (later) also the Kyoto School. Making a translation accessible to audiences unschooled in these traditions without copious notes and explanations will inevitably result in some level of simplification and conceptual vulgarity. Outside Japan, such translations and their popular associations appear to have undermined scholarly will to take the field seriously.

To the extent that scholars have paid attention to *bushidō*, it has appeared as a feature (or sometimes as a symptom) of discourses about Japanese uniqueness (*Nihonjin-ron*

日本人論).[1] Since the first half of the twentieth century in Europe and North America, historians have devoted persistent critical energy to revealing the ways in which *bushidō* was invented as a tradition in the Meiji and Taishō periods, in the context of Japan's confrontation with modernity and the ideological project of Japanese imperialism.[2] Despite the critical force of this valuable historical work, popular understandings and representations of *bushidō* remain staunchly Orientalist, inextricably intertwined with the romance of the image of the samurai and the mystique of ancient tradition. In fact, part of the mystery of *bushidō* seems to be precisely the way in which it excites a popular imagination that resists scholarly intervention.

In this context, one fascinating aspect of the popular appropriation of *bushidō*, especially as it features in the various subcultures that have formed around the martial arts, is the emphasis placed on authenticity and antiquity in specific lineages and schools. Indeed, the rhetoric of competition between styles of martial arts often pivots around claims to more ancient pedigrees, sometimes tracing roots back to divine transmission or to the Shaolin Temple in Henan, China.[3] Hence, the stakes involved in debates about the politics of knowledge and the invention of tradition are serious, creating a volatile and sometimes violent encounter. In some circles, to call *bushidō* in general (or a specific style of martial art in particular) an "invented tradition" is literally fighting talk; in such circles this claim amounts to a simple accusation that practitioners (or perhaps "believers") have been duped into an inauthentic pursuit.

---

[1] In his classic analysis of the *Nihonjin-ron* genre, Peter Dale unpacks Kuki Shuzō's aesthetic concept of *iki* (いき) as a "commingling [of] the ethical idealism of *Bushidō* with the religious irrealism of Buddhism," seeing this as a balance of "military honour and stoic resignation" (Dale 1986, 70, 71; on Kuki's interpretation of *iki*, see Chapter 24 in this volume; on *Nihonjin-ron*, see the Introduction and Chapter 36). Dale's thesis ties *iki* to a grander process of the invention of Japanese uniqueness that he claims characterized Japan's encounter with modernity during the Meiji period. He observes that, as early as 1912, the prominent British Japanologist, Basil Hall Chamberlain (1850–1935) had already "raised a cry of alarm at the mass falsification of the past being enacted by the Meiji bureaucracy" in order to create an imperial cult that incorporated the invented tradition of *bushidō* (Dale 1986, 210). Dale sites Chamberlain's skepticism that any "modern researcher had so much as heard of the word *Bushidō* until the turn of the century" (Dale 1986, 210–211). In this way, Dale (like Chamberlain) relies on the work of Nitobe Inazō (1862–1933) who claimed to have coined the term *bushidō* in his famous (English language) book, *Bushido: The Soul of Japan* (2002, first published in 1900). Although Nitobe's work was marginal to the discourse on *bushidō* in Japan, it was massively influential internationally, accomplishing its ideological task of tying the idea of *bushidō* essentially and uniquely to the ethnic and cultural nationalism developing in Japan in that period. As Dale notes, Nitobe insisted on using the Japanese word *bushidō* in his English book because "a teaching so circumscribed and unique, engendering a cast of mind and character so peculiar, so local, must wear the badge of its singularity on its face" (Dale 1986, 205).

[2] Perhaps the first to uncover this, in 1912, was Basil Hall Chamberlain 1971, esp. pp. 531–544. See also Chamberlain 1912. The most recent and most sustained intervention in this spirit, a century later, is the excellent work of Benesch 2014.

[3] The place of the Shaolin Monastery in the history of the martial arts is much debated and is beyond the scope of this chapter, but the place of Shaolin in the history of Chinese martial arts is beautifully evoked in Shahar 2008.

While this kind of reaction reveals an important misunderstanding about the nature and meaning of the idea of an "invented tradition," it also reveals something of the intensity of the contemporary relationship between certain subcultures (both within and outside Japan) and the idea of *bushidō*.[4] Indeed, there is a sense in which this relationship approximates that between a believer and a religion.[5] To some extent, this should be unsurprising because the term *dō*（道）refers to a "path" or "way" of life; indeed, *dō* was appended to a whole range of Japanese arts in the modern period precisely to suggest that their practice could involve a form of self-cultivation that approached the spiritual.[6]

What might be surprising, however, is the fact that the people who self-identify as practitioners of this "way" today are located in all walks of life all around the world. Far from being the historical preserve of the Tokugawa period samurai or the Imperial Japanese Army, *bushidō* is alive and well as a transnational philosophy of life today.[7] In other words, experience today reveals very clearly that whatever else *bushidō* might be (or might have been), it is at least *also* a body of thought, belief, and practice in which people who are neither samurai nor even Japanese can participate (or can *believe* that they participate). The fact that this is a controversial claim in itself reveals that *bushidō* is not only an international philosophical terrain, but that it also involves an intricate ideological landscape of values and judgments that do indeed maintain various requirements of social, cultural, and ethnic identity. In these terms, it is contestable whether or not those people outside the boundaries of a "unique Japan" (or a "traditional Japan") can make any claim to participation in *bushidō*. My point here is simply that this contestation must itself be seen as a feature of the landscape of *bushidō* today.

The complicated question of the authenticity of the relationship between these diverse groups and *bushidō* is confronted quite explicitly in movies like *Ghost Dog* (Jim Jarmusch, 1999), in which Forest Whitaker constructs himself as the eponymous urban samurai and mafia hitman in a nameless American city (that closely resembles Jersey

---

[4] The notion of the "invented tradition" is conventionally associated with the work of Hobsawm and Ranger 1983. With particular focus on Japan, Vlastos 1998. A popular misunderstanding is that an "invented tradition" is not a "real tradition." Rather, the study of the process of the invention of tradition is supposed to reveal the ideological mechanisms and imperatives behind the transformation of elements of history into "traditions" in the modern period.

[5] The idea that the *bushidō* or *budō*（武道）can take on religious qualities is not new. Recent work has also suggested that specific martial arts can take the place of religion in practitioners' lives. Jennings, Brown, and Sparkes 2010.

[6] A meaningful discussion of this is Inoue Shun, "The Invention of the Martial Arts: Kanō Jigorō and Kōdōkan Judō," in Vlastos 1998. See also Yamada 2011. Much of this literature focuses on the ways in which the work of D. T. Suzuki encouraged the perception of a union between the martial arts and Zen in the West. It is noteworthy that Suzuki's major work in this trajectory appeared (in English) during the 1930s, when there was intensive debate about *bushidō* in Japan. Suzuki 1938, especially pp. 54–100. On the Japanese "ways" as paths of spiritual cultivation, see Chapter 34 in this volume.

[7] Intriguingly, this pattern of identification is not limited to military personnel or even to people who practice martial arts of various kinds; such identification is also spreading to include other cultures, such as video gamers (Goto-Jones 2016). Elements of so-called *bushidō* are taught in ethics classes at military academies around the world (French 2003).

City). Ghost Dog appears to have a rather tenuous claim to authenticity as a samurai. Indeed, his claim appears to rely on his repeated reading of a battered copy of a popular, partial, English translation of the seventeenth-century Japanese classic of *bushidō*, the *Hagakure* of Yamamoto Tsunetomo (1659–1719). As far as we know, Ghost Dog has never encountered Japan directly nor has he been in the tutelage of a samurai (a historical impossibility in the twentieth century). Instead, Ghost Dog's actions are themselves an argument that the true authenticity of the *bushi* (武士, warrior) resides not in texts or doctrines per se, but rather in the constant endeavor to reside in and embody a specific philosophy of life (no matter how distant he may be from anything that might be considered an authentic initiation into that way of life).

In fact, as we'll see, this sense that *bushi* (warrior) is a category to which people attain through disciplined training (*shugyō* 修行) rather than a category that is ascribed by birth is a critique common in texts of the *bushidō* corpus. Indeed, this emphasis on the potential for any individual to transform themselves into an ethically and spiritually superior being through persistent and consistent effort (*kufū* 工夫) resides at the core of many *bushidō* texts—Miyamoto Musashi (1584–1645) calls this the *dokkōdō* (独行道, Self-Made Way); it is one of the ways in which these texts show the influence of Zen Buddhism.[8] So, whatever else we might think about Ghost Dog, the sincerity of his training and his effortful, intentional self-transformation do place him within the orbit of *bushidō* as a life philosophy, even if they cannot transform him into a Tokugawa samurai.

This raises the possibility of a fascinating provocation: Is it possible that Ghost Dog is a better (or even a more authentic) *bushi* than were many samurai? One of the implications of this would be that *bushidō* contains the possibility that *bushi* is a nonchauvinistic, ideal category (like master or sage or saint) to which seekers of spiritual development anywhere might aspire.[9] Indeed, such a reading would be consistent with some of the classic texts of *bushidō*, such as Miyamoto Musashi's famous *Gorinsho* (*The Book of Five Rings*, c. 1645), which offer critiques of the conduct of historical samurai by comparing them with the ideal conduct and values of *bushi*, often judging samurai as unworthy of consideration in this category.[10]

---

[8] One of the distinguishing features of Zen Buddhism is its tendency toward an emphasis on self-power (*jiriki* 自力) rather than a reliance on other-power (*tariki* 他力) as a means to attain enlightenment in this life. The influence of Zen in the *bushidō* literature is powerful and often explicit, such as in the work of Takuan Sōhō (1573–1645). It is also pervasive in various technical ways, such as in the persistent use of terms like *shugyō* and *kufū* (Ch. *kung fu*) to describe disciplined training that leads to spiritual transformation. Nonetheless, many *bushidō* authors are careful to emphasize that *bushidō* is its own way (i.e., that it is not Buddhism). Miyamoto Musashi, for instance, admonishes his readers about maintaining fidelity to the Way of the Martial Arts (*heihō no michi* 兵法の道), cautioning them that while this involves paying respect to the Buddhas and Kami, it also means that they should rely on their own power and not on the power of Buddhas or Kami. Miyamoto Musashi 2004, 164–166.

[9] Neville 1978 suggests that the "soldier" is one of (at least) three models of spiritual perfection, common to myriad cultures around the world. The soldier represent the accomplishment of psychic integrity through self-discipline.

[10] The implication is that *samurai* is a historical category while *bushi* is an ideal category.

THE DIMENSIONS OF *BUSHIDŌ*

Aside from the issue of the invention of tradition, one of the basic dilemmas confronting a philosophical engagement with *bushidō* is the question of how we draw its conceptual parameters. In fact, these are twin dilemmas since one of the pillars of the position that *bushidō* is an invented tradition is the observation that the term itself only develops a consistent pattern of usage in the twentieth century.[11] Before that time, there appears to be no coherent discourse or accepted tradition of debate around the term *bushidō*. Many of the texts that are seen as central to *bushidō* literature today make no mention of this term at all, while others use it interchangeably (sometimes inconsistently) with other terms such as *budō* (武道, martial ways), *heihō no michi* or *heihōdō* (兵法道, ways of martial conduct), *kassen no michi* or *kassendō* (合戦道, the way of conflict), *tachi no michi* or *tachidō* (太刀道, the way of the sword), *bugei no michi* or *bugeidō* (武芸道, the way of warrior arts), *bushi no hō* (武士の法, the laws of warriors), and *heihō no shindō* (兵法の真道, the true way of martial conduct).[12]

A crucial landmark in the development of the contours of *bushidō* as a philosophical tradition was the assembly of the *Bushidō zensho* (Collected Works of *Bushidō*, 11 volumes) in 1942.[13] The principal editors of this important collection, Inoue Tetsujirō (1855–1944) and Saeki Ariyoshi (1867–1945), took great pains to explain that while *bushidō* might find its origins in ancient Japan, scholarship about *bushidō* was only in its infancy in the modern period.[14] Hence, they saw it as their responsibility to collect together the central texts of the tradition as a service to the nation of Japan at a time of great military and spiritual need. Both are clear that *bushidō* is unique to Japan and an essential feature of the national polity (*kokutai* 国体).[15] Inoue, who was already famous for making the case that Confucianism was a form of philosophy indigenous to Japan even before the arrival of European philosophy in the nineteenth century, is emphatic that *bushidō* is itself a kind of philosophy, drawing on the fundamental knowledge of

---

[11] It is conventional to ascribe the start of this usage to Nitobe Inazo in around 1900. However, Oleg Benesch 2014 makes a convincing case that the term took on its modern meaning in the earlier work of Ozaki Yukio (1858–1954), probably in the 1880s.

[12] All of these terms appear in Miyamoto Musashi, *Gorinsho*.

[13] Inoue, Saeki, Ueki, and Inobe 1942. Hereafter abbrieviated as BZ.

[14] Inoue argues that even though his contemporaries generally maintain that *bushidō* finds its origins in the Kamakura period, its true roots are in the time of the first emperor, Jinmu Tennō (mythic, 711–585 BCE), and traces can be seen in the most ancient of Japanese texts, like the *Kōjiki* (712), *Nihon shoki* (720), and the *Man'yōshū* (c. 759). BZ 1: 3. Saeki appears to disagree with Inoue's sense of the mythic roots of *bushidō*; he argues that the start of *bushidō* is later than the Kamakura period, in the Pax Tokugawa. For Saeki, *bushidō* really takes form when Confucian scholars like Yamaga Sokō start to write about millitary education (*Bukyō shōgaku*, 1657) and the duties of samurai as "gentlemen" (*shi*). BZ 1: 7.

[15] Inoue dismisses the idea that *bushidō* is comparable with European chivalry (*kishidō* 騎士道), arguing that chivalry is essentially a cult for the worship of women (*joseisūhai* 女性崇拝). *Bushidō*, on the other hand, is essentially about crushing the strong and helping the weak (*tsuyoki o kujiki, yowaki o tasukeru* 強きを挫き弱きを助ける). BZ 1: 2.

a rich, indigenous textual tradition.[16] Not only that, however; Inoue also suggests that philosophical *bushidō* is itself a form of practice (*jissen* 実践).[17] That is, *bushidō* is a form of practical philosophy (*jissen tetsugaku* 実践哲学), or perhaps practice-philosophy. Properly studied, he argues, *bushidō* should protect the power of Japan and transform individuals at the same time.[18]

The *Bushidō zensho* contains a diverse range of texts from various historical periods reaching back to the fourteenth century.[19] It is interesting to observe that most of them make no mention of *bushidō* at all. Again, we see *budō, heihō, bukyō* (武教, military teachings), *gunsho* (軍書, military texts), *shidō* (士道, the way of the samurai/gentleman), *bunbu nidō* (文武二道, the dual ways of culture and conflict), *hōkōnin no michi* or *hōkōnindō* (奉公人道, the way of retainers), and other allied terms.

One of the things that is revealed by this unapologetically ideologically driven attempt at canon formation is that the category of *bushidō* as a species of practical philosophy is bounded by concerns for Confucian-influenced issues of service, loyalty, piety, and moral courage on the one hand and Buddhist-influenced issues of intentional self-transformation, existential questions, ethics and salvation, and concerns about death on the other. At the same time, Shintō influences are evident in the theme of imperialism and appeals to the native Japanese spirit (*yamato-damashii* 大和魂). Daoist influences are suggested in the themes of the unity of thought and action, in the freedom of spontaneity, and in the cultivation of *ki* (気) energy. And the whole appears to be wrapped in a practical concern for military skill, martial competence, strategic advantage, and confrontation with (mortal) danger.

In other words, far from being a simple list of instructions, code of conduct, or a "few maxims"[20] that ostensibly directed the actions of samurai or soldiers in the imperial army, *bushidō* emerges as a complex philosophical landscape, rich with contestation and competing trajectories of thought. Rather than pulling its component elements apart and arguing that it offers nothing other than, say, Confucianism and Buddhism,

---

[16] In his early career, Inoue was centrally concerned with establishing the credentials of Confucianism as an indigenous intellectual and ethical tradition that could confront Western philosophy in terms of its power and sophistication. He attempted this in a trilogy of influential works at the turn of the century: 1897/1900, 1902/1945, and 1905/1918. See Chapters 13 and 15 in this volume. In Chapter 13, John Tucker introduces *bushidō* in the context of the development of the Confucian tradition in Japan.

[17] BZ 1: 2.

[18] BZ 1: 1.

[19] For instance, Yagyū Munemori's *Heihō kadensho* appears in volume 2 together with Takuan Sōhō's *Fudōchi shinmyōroku* and Daidōji Yūzan's *Budō shoshinshū*; Yamaga Sokō's *Bukyō shōgaku* and *Shidō* appear in volume 3; Miyamoto Musashi's *Gorinsho* appears in volume 4; while the *Hagakure* of Yamamoto Tsunetomo appears in book 6. Significantly, despite including a significant number of modern texts (especially in volumes 5 and 8), the work of Nitobe Inazo does not appear in this collection. Indeed, Inoue was outspoken in his criticism of Nitobe, not only because he felt the statesman had a superficial understanding of *bushidō* but also because Nitobe's *Bushido* (2002, first published in 1900) appears to deny that there could be a written canon, asserting that "it is not a written code; at best it consists of a few maxims handed down from mouth to mouth" (5). In some ways, the *Bushidō zensho* is Inoue's emphatic refutation of the relevance of Nitobe.

[20] Nitobe 2002, 5.

it is helpful to see *bushidō* as the creative and dynamic nexus at which a range of other traditions intersect and interact in the service of meta-concerns about martial arts, self-cultivation, ethics, violence, duty, and death. Whether or not we are interested in the question of *bushidō*'s modern invention *qua* tradition, this body of work and concerns hangs together in a coherent and valuable manner that is worthy of philosophical inquiry today.

Bushidō and Ideology

It is one of the most resilient mysteries of *bushidō* that it remains controversial (and even inflammatory) to make relatively uncontroversial observations about its history. One of the most powerful myths about *bushidō*, for instance, is that it describes the historical conduct of the samurai. Indeed, the association between *bushidō* and the samurai is generally represented as so intimate and essential that the term *bushidō* is frequently translated as the Way of the Samurai.[21]

There are at least two ways in which this myth can be exploded, neither of which should be controversial. The first way is to observe, with Cameron Hurst and others, that the equation of *bushidō* with samurai behavior affects a category mistake. This is the "classic mistake of assuming that a system of normative ethics describes an actual field of behavior."[22] As Karl Friday puts it, this amounts to a "fairly overt historian's sleight of hand."[23] The second way is to observe, with Karl Friday and others, that while some of the historical samurai may have aspired to the kinds of conduct codified in the texts of *bushidō*, many were simply self-serving opportunists and profiteers acting out of self-preservation rather than selfless honor.[24] That is, no matter how much we'd like to believe that that samurai were moral paragons and exquisitely expert swordsmen, living in accordance with the ideals of *bushidō* (whatever those turn out to be), most of them were not. Not only that, but most of the texts we now recognize as central to the *bushidō* tradition were written during the Pax Tokugawa—a period in which the samurai class was no longer involved in warfare and was prohibited from private combat. In other words, the connection of *bushidō* with the samurai (and perhaps even with martial conduct in general) is romantic and ideological rather than descriptive.[25]

---

[21] As we will see, rather than being a mistranslation per se, rendering *bushidō* as the "way of the samurai" amounts to an ideological assertion. Not incidentally, Ghost Dog's refrain about being a samurai also appears to emerge from the ideological positioning of the particular translation of the *Hagakure* that he reads, which has an invented editorial subtitle added to it to direct Anglophone readers: *Hagakure—the Book of the Samurai* (trans. Wilson 1979/2002).

[22] Hurst 1990, 517.

[23] Friday 1994, 340.

[24] Friday 1994, 342.

[25] To the extent that we can talk about the existence of *bushidō* in the Tokugawa period (rather than the existence of various unconnected texts that would later be recognized as the *bushidō* tradition in the twentieth century), it seems most likely that it served as an ideological device to bolster the prestige

A parallel case can be made to confront one of the other resilient representations of *bushidō*, that it describes the ruthless and appalling actions of members of the Japanese imperial army who perpetrated atrocities against humanity during the so-called Great East Asia War of the 1930s and early 1940s. Indeed, *bushidō* was intermittently invoked by defendants as a justification for various actions (including the practice of beheading prisoners with a sword) during the International Military Tribunal for the Far East (IMTFE), and it features prominently in a number of accounts of these atrocities.[26]

The character of *bushidō* that we see on trial at the IMTFE, shrouded in the wartime propaganda of both Imperial Japan and the victorious allies, appears significantly different from the ideals of honor and discipline to which the historical samurai so often failed to adhere. Indeed, in the modern period, when *bushidō* was invented as a national tradition for Japan, *bushidō* could no longer be a code of aspirational virtues tied to the conduct of the samurai class since the samurai had already been abolished during the Meiji Restoration; whatever *bushidō* was in the 1940s, it had little to do with the historical samurai.[27]

This leaves us with a fascinating question about the dimensions and scope of *bushidō* as a body of thought: Is it the case that the samurai and/or the Imperial army were wrong about *bushidō* (i.e., that what they took from this "tradition" to justify their actions did violence to it in some way)? Or could it be the case that one or the other (or both) were right about *bushidō* (i.e., that our understanding of the landscape of *bushidō* today must at least also encompass the possibility that it provokes or promotes atrocity)? My tendency is to reject the former in favor of the latter, not only (but also) because to make the claim that there is a "true *bushidō*" away from which the samurai and/or the Imperial army veered too far is to claim a new ideological position in itself. The debate over the

(and self-identity) of a social class whose actual function in society was decreasingly clear. In the vast majority of cases, the Tokugawa samurai would have little or no opportunity to enact the military aspects of *bushidō* or to die on the sword of another samurai. A powerful study of the function of samurai values in this period is Ikegami 1995.

[26] Especially influential in this respect is Russell 1958. In fact, the visceral abhorrence occasioned by the decapitation of prisoners by Japanese officers led to a fixation on the idea that one of the principles of *bushidō* was the endorsement of *tsujigiri* (辻斬り), the practice of testing one's new sword on a random passer-by at a crossroads. This practice seemed so unequivocally abhorrent that Mary Midgely 1981/2003 used it as the centerpiece for her powerful argument against what she called "moral isolationism" (the position that it is wrong to judge morally the conduct of other cultures): some things, like *bushidō*, are simply wrong, and we should not be afraid to say so. In fact, as we'll see shortly, far from being simply endorsed, the practice of *tsujigiri* is deeply problematic and contested within the *bushidō* tradition. Indeed, it is a primary case for testing ethical theory in *bushidō*, as well as an instance of radical moral and existential crisis.

[27] The significance and meaning of the abolition of samurai for the dimensions and integrity of *bushidō* were hotly debated during the first half of the twentieth century in Japan, including by leading philosophers of the time such as Inoue Tetsujirō (who saw this as the occasion for the generalization of the *bushidō* ethic from a single class to the whole nation) and the cultural philosopher Watsuji Tetsurō ([1889–1960], who saw the universalism inhernet in this event as a basic condition for the possibility of *bushidō* itself; i.e., before the abolition of the samurai, there was no *bushidō*).

meaning of "true *bushidō*" is already a central (and fascinating) feature of this conceptual terrain.

Before delving into some of the core texts in a little more detail, in the following subsections I'd like to consider the ideological dimensions of *bushidō*, first during the Tokugawa period and then during the modern period.

Bushidō, Samurai Ideology, and Peace

One fascinating implication of the fact that most of the texts in today's *bushidō* canon date from a period in which the samurai were not involved in combat (indeed, during which their involvement in combat was prohibited) is that it situates *bushidō* as a life philosophy for a time of *peace* rather than *war*. Given the explicit emphasis of many of the texts on military affairs, martial training, and the willingness to die in service, the idea that *bushidō* might be of most interest during peacetime seems counterintuitive, but it is worthy of consideration.

Just as the "late *bushidō* boom"[28] was gripping Japan, in 1910 William James penned an essay for *McClure's Magazine* in the United States, "The Moral Equivalent of War."[29] James, who was such an inspiration for modern Japanese philosophers,[30] appears to be partially inspired by Japan in this important essay; he writes of his ignorance "of the innermost recesses of Japanese mentality" but expresses great interest in the need to understand military (and militarist) thinking in Japan specifically.[31] Indeed, while a self-proclaimed pacifist himself, James is concerned that anti-militarist mentalities are causing the United States to degenerate, leaving it imperiled. He is not advocating militarism, but argues that pacifist opposition to militarism involves "two unwillingnesses of the imagination, one aesthetic, and the other moral."[32]

For James, pacifist arguments fail to convert people from militarism because they are phrased as "merely negative criticism" and offer no engaging, exciting, or thrilling alternative to war as a means to energize individuals and society, leaving mankind only "its weaker and more cowardly self." That is, pacifists appear naïve about the power of the "aesthetical and ethical point of view of their opponents"; he laments this as a form of utopianism.[33]

---

[28] Benesch describes the period between 1905 and 1914 as the "late *bushidō* boom" (2014, 111–149).

[29] Originally published in August 1910, reprinted in *The Popular Science Monthly*, October, 1910, and then, in the immediate wake of the end of World War II, in James 1947. Quotations are from the latter.

[30] The influence of James on key figures within the Kyoto School of Philosophy, especially on Nishida Kitarō, is well documented. James's openness to and familiarity with Asian traditions of thought, especially in his work on religious experience, is also well known.

[31] James 1947, 318. James cites Japan (in the Pacific) and Germany (in Europe) as nations with potentially dangerous military ambitions that threaten the international peace.

[32] James 1947, 320.

[33] James 1947. The idea that a nation requires an enemy (and war) to energize it is probably drawn from Hegel. In a move that would be deeply unpopular today, James adds an intriguing twist when he suggests that a better target for these sentiments would be a war against the impersonal forces of Nature rather than the personal forces of another nation.

More concretely, James argues that "so long as anti-militarists propose no substitute for war's disciplinary function, no *moral equivalent* of war … so long they fail to recognize the full inwardness of the situation."[34] James' "unwillingnesses" revolve around a form of denial that society can thrive without the kind of aesthetic and moral qualities that are usually associated with military training—by neglecting these dynamic and contagious forces, the anti-militarists will always appear less attractive, less vital, and more naïvely utopian than the militarists.

However, his point is not that the militarists are correct, but rather that the anti-militarists (who seek to live in peace rather than war) must find the aesthetic and moral *equivalent* of war to energize their position, their followers, and ultimately their society: any condition of peace will only persist for as long as its defenders can stand persuasively against those who advocate for war.

> All these beliefs of mine put me squarely into the anti-militarist party. But I do not believe that peace either ought to be or will be permanent on this globe, unless the states pacifically organized preserve some of the old elements of army-discipline. A permanently successful peace-economy cannot be a simple pleasure-economy. In the more or less socialistic future towards which mankind seems drifting we must still subject ourselves collectively to those severities which answer to our real position upon this only partially hospitable globe. We must make new energies and hardihoods continue the manliness to which the military mind so faithfully clings. Martial virtues must be the enduring cement; intrepidity, contempt of softness, surrender of private interest, obedience to command, must still remain the rock upon which states are built … the martial virtues, although originally gained by the race through war, are absolute and permanent human goods.[35]

In fact, by making the case that martial virtues are among the greatest of human ideals and by claiming that such virtues can (and should) be both cultivated and exercised even in the absence of military action or war, James joins an established tradition of Western thinkers who thought likewise.[36] Continuing in this tradition, Robert Neville makes the case that the ideal soldier is a model of psychic integrity across myriad cultures around the world. He argues that the "soldier is the archetype for the development of the spirited part of the soul" in Plato's tripartite model (which consists of a spirited part, a rational

---

[34] James 1947,321.

[35] James 1947, 323.

[36] There is a strong thread of such thought running through the Stoic tradition, including in its reinvigorated form in the modern period. We might also consider the work of John Milton, "Of Education" (1644), in which Milton advocates training with the sword as an essential component of a great and noble education, without which a nation might perish: "The Exercise which I commend first, is the exact use of their Weapon, to guard and to strike safely with edge, or point; this will keep them healthy, nimble, strong, and well in breath, is also the likeliest means to make them grow large and tall, and to inspire them with a gallant and fearless courage, which being temper'd with seasonable Lectures and Precepts to them of true Fortitude and Patience, will turn into a native and heroick valour, and make them hate the cowardise of doing wrong."

part, and an appetitive part).[37] Through arduous physical and mental training, the soldier forges his (or her) own will, and it is the power of this will that enables the soldier to act with integrity, devotion, and selflessness even in the conduct of life-threatening tasks, in the face of death.

In this philosophical context, we might recognize the Tokugawa literature of *bushidō* as precisely this kind of engagement with martial virtues as means to cultivate individuals and energize a peaceful society. Indeed, it is revealing to note that a great many of the texts of *bushidō* are training manuals of various kinds, prevailing on their readers to live their lives in constant, disciplined readiness for the battles for which their training ostensibly prepares them. Texts like the *Hagakure* famously argue that the important work of discipline and cultivation is done in preparation for battle (whether or not battle ever transpires); the desired result of training is the possibility of correctly conditioned, spontaneous action without the need for discrimination or calculation. Training *is* the act of devotion, not merely a rehearsal for it; victory (which need not be over an Other) can be won even without a fight: *shishō gosen* (始勝後戦, first win, then fight).

There is a powerful sense in which this "living in readiness" every day comprises a way of being in itself. Living every moment as though in confrontation with one's own death, as advocated in many of the most influential texts, is both the method and the goal of the training, whether or not one ever comes face to face with an opponent's blade.[38] The occurrence of an actual fight or the experience of real danger at some point in the future is only pertinent as an idea that motivates correct conduct (and sincerity in training) in the present.[39] With some notable exceptions, most training in the martial arts involves no real danger at all, only disciplined exercises and the imagination of danger as a device

---

[37] Neville 1978, 7.

[38] The deployment of a confrontation with death as a device to focus the mind on the present moment is a feature of various Buddhist traditions, especially those that make use of the *Satipatthana Sutta* (Discourse on the Cultivation of Mindfulness). Indeed, the "Nine Cemetery Contemplations" in the *Satipatthana Sutta* are extremely graphic depictions of bodily death and decay, which are sometimes shocking to modern practitioners. In recent years, this method (and text) has become associated with (mindfulness-based) cognitive-behavioral therapy. One interesting question provoked by this is to what extent the martial flavor and direction of training in *bushidō* might appropriately be seen as an analogy, much as various Buddhist sources talk of cultivation as a means to combat (mental and spiritual) demons.

[39] The *Hagakure*, for instance, asserts that the martial arts (*budō*) are concerned with "morning after morning, the practice of death [*shin-narai* 死慣], considering whether it will be here or there, imagining the most unsightly way of dying, and putting one's mind firmly in death" (2005, 122–23). Later on, it continues: "meditation on inevitable death should be performed every day. Every day when one's body and mind are at peace, one should meditate upon being ripped apart by arrows, rifles, spears and swords, being carried away by surging waves, being thrown into the midst of a great fire, being struck by lightning, being shaken to death by a giant earthquake, falling from thousand-foot cliffs, dying of disease or committing *seppuku* at the death of one's master. And every day without fail one should consider himself as dead" (282–83). Finally, the *Hagakure* explicitly advocates that there is nothing other than the present moment: "If one fully understands the present moment, there will be nothing else to do, and nothing else to pursue. Spend your life nourishing the integrity of the here and now" (2005, 112–13). The *Hagakure* is not unique in this kind of position. The *Gorinsho*, for instance, explains that the essence of its "fire" scroll is "about diligent daily training, about valuing each moment as though it were the decisive one, and about never letting the mind go slack" (2004, 23–24).

to forge the will. There's a very real sense in which sincere, disciplined training is itself the embodiment of *bushidō* as a life philosophy.

Bushidō, Imperial Ideology, and War

A second important set of ideological parameters around *bushidō* relies on the political context of Japanese Imperialism in the modern period. It represents a kind of militarization of *bushidō*. In particular, the legacy of *bushidō* from this period is associated with the codification of the *kokutai* (国体, national polity) of Japan and its (conceptual, cultural, and military) confrontation with the West. Indeed, the *Kokutai no hongi* (Fundamental Principles of the National Polity, 1937), which was by far the most influential and widespread of the official *shūshinsho* (修身書, ethics textbooks), included a number of explicit statements about the centrality of *bushidō* to the Japanese spirit, giving rise to the phrases *kokutai no bushidō* (国体の武士道) as a variation on *kinnō bushidō* (勤皇武士道, imperial *bushidō*). The *Kokutai no hongi* sold millions of copies and was required reading for all teachers and students in middle and higher schools in Japan by 1943: "*Bushidō* can be seen as expressing the most remarkable feature of our national morality . . . . To embrace life and death as one, to fulfill the Way of Loyalty [to the Emperor], that is our *bushidō*."[40]

Kokutai no hongi did little to add to the conceptual sophistication of *bushidō*, but rather it served as an official endorsement of a particular ideological construction of it. *Kokutai no bushidō* placed emphatic emphasis on absolute loyalty to the emperor as its primary virtue, identifying the emperor as the embodiment of divine will and morality, and as the locus of obligation and duty. The nuanced philosophy of authenticity through confrontation with (the idea of) one's own death collapsed into a more vulgar call for instrumental self-sacrifice in the interests of an Other (i.e., the emperor). In this way, *kokutai no bushidō* affected a form of Confucian-Shintō synthesis in the interpretation of *bushidō*, a synthesis that was already characteristic of the imperial *bushidō* propagated by Inoue Tetsujirō, which he constructed as the exemplary form of *shinmin no michi* (臣民の道, the way of subjects). Although Inoue's seminal collection, *Bushidō zensho*, appeared after *Kokutai no hongi*, his earlier *Bushidō sōsho* (Selected Works of *Bushidō*) appeared in 1905.[41] In other words, Inoue's emphasis on the centrality of the Confucian thinker Yamaga Sokō (1622–1685) as *bushidō*'s most characteristic ideologue was already well-known and widely accepted, as was his assertion that the roots of *bushidō* were found in the divine foundations of the Japanese empire, in the time of the first emperor Jinmu Tennō.[42]

---

[40] Itō 1937, 110–11.

[41] Inoue 1905.

[42] BZ:1, p. 3. It is notworthy that Sokō himself was an early advocate of Japan's cultural superiority over China, identifying the centrality of the "middle kingdom" as a myth but the divine origins of the Japanese imperial line (coeval with heaven and earth) as historical.

Sokō's *bukyō* (warrior teachings) and *shidō* (way of the samurai/gentleman) represent a rejection of the emphasis placed on contemplation and introspection in Neo-Confucianism (in the work of his teacher Hazashi Razan, 1583–1657) and also in Zen. Instead, he argues for a reversion to the teachings of Confucius himself and an emphasis on *gi* (義, rightness, duty) as received hierarchically in a feudal system; samurai should behave with absolute loyalty, always placing their self-interest as subordinate to the principle of loyalty and obedience to their lords. Unlike the Neo-Confucians (especially Wang Yangming/Ōyōmei, 1472–1529) who maintained that reflection and contemplation (including via meditation, *meisō* 瞑想 or, more commonly for Neo-Confucian practice, *seiza* 静座) could reveal the "pure knowledge" of rightness that is innate in all of us, Sokō emphasized that principles of rightness are received through study of the classics and instruction from one's lord.

Sokō had little patience for contemplation and saw the way of the samurai as a way of educated (dutiful, selfless) action.[43] Rather than finding rightness in spontaneous or intuitive action of the kind advocated by Neo-Confucians in the unity of knowledge and action (*chigyō gōitsu* 知行合一), Sokō emphasized the importance of *chisen kōgo* (知先行後, knowledge first, action later). Controversially, Inoue suggested that Sokō's approach provided the ethical foundations for the actions of the *Akō rōnin*, who had famously committed ritual suicide after carefully executing a detailed plan to exact vengeance on the man whom they believed had killed their master.[44] As we will see, the legend of *Chūshingura* and the forty-seven *Akō rōnin* was very popular throughout the early years of the twentieth century, but it provides a flash point for debate and contestation in the *bushidō* tradition, even in the 1940s. The *Hagakure*, for instance, is scathingly critical of the *Akō rōnin* for having waited for knowledge before action instead of moving instantly with a spontaneous and intuitive kind of freedom.[45]

The appeal to the Imperial Japanese government of this construction of *bushidō* as a national ethic of absolute loyalty to the nation and the emperor should be obvious. One of the conceptually interesting features of this ideology was the deliberate conflation of filial piety (the traditional priority in Chinese Confucianism) with loyalty in

---

[43] That said, Sokō was also consistent in his attempts to divorce *bushidō* from its emphasis on combat and was instrumental in its transformation into a systematic, ethical system that could be learned and passed on through education and scholarship.

[44] Inoue 1912. For an excellent analysis of the unreliability of this version of the story of the influence of Yamaga Sokō's work on the *rōnin*, see Tucker 2002.

[45] In fact, as we have seen, the moral philosophy of the *Hagakure* rests upon the cultivated ability to act skillfully without deliberation or calculation. Yamamoto states clearly: "calculating people (*kanjōsha* 勘定者) are contemptible. The reason for this is that calculation deals with loss and gain, and the loss and gain mind never stops. Death is considered loss and life is considered gain," which prevents the *bushi* from acting with freedom in the present moment (Yamamoto 2005, 72–73). In turn, the *Gorinsho* also advocates spontaneous, noncalculating action as the basis of morality. In the "emptiness" (*kara*) scroll, Musashi argues that the way of emptiness is the gateway to the way of truth because disciplined practice results in an empting of the calculating mind, resulting in spontaneous action, ability, and strength. "The Way of the Martial Arts is natural freedom" (2004, 25). On the concept of "natural freedom," see Chapter 33 in this volume.

the slogan *chūkō ippon* (忠孝一本, loyalty and filial piety as one).[46] The authors of the *Kokutai no hongi* attribute this to the samurai ideologue Yoshida Shōin (1830–1859), the *sonnō jōi* (尊皇攘夷, revere the emperor and expel the barbarians) insurgent and one of the progenitors of the Meiji Restoration. In fact, Shōin was an important figure for Inoue—the pivotal text *Shiki shichisoku* (1856, Seven Precepts for Samurai/Gentlemen) was included in the seventh volume of the *Bushidō zensho*. For Inoue, Shōin provides a crucial stepping stone on the path of *bushidō*'s continuous development from before the arrival of Buddhism in Japan in the sixth century (placing it alongside Shintō as the in- digenous ethical foundation of the nation) to its ultimate form in the twentieth century as a *chūkun aikoku* (忠君愛国, loyalty and patriotism).

For Inoue, the sequence from piety through loyalty to patriotism was constructed as a progressive development in scale and grandeur. This stance is clearly echoed in the *Kokutai no hongi*: "At the time of the Meiji Restoration, *bushidō* discarded feudalism's anachronisms [*hōken no kyūtai* 封建の旧態], increased in radiance, and became the Way of loyalty and patriotism [*chūkun aikoku no michi* 忠君愛国の道]."[47] In other words, for Inoue and the ideologues of *Kokutai no bushidō*, the significance of the Meiji Restoration and the abolition of the samurai was not a shift in *kind* but merely a shift in the *scale* of *bushidō*; it marked the moment at which the ideal qualities of the samurai became the ideal qualities of Japan as a whole, and especially of the common soldiers in the Imperial Japanese army.[48] Hence, for Inoue, the modern period opened up the possibility of the ultimate expression of loyalty and patriotism to *every soldier*—*jibaku* (自爆, self-destruction) in the name of the emperor. In a text of 1941, Inoue explains to soldiers that *bushidō* is a national treasure of Japan and that practices like *jibaku* distin- guish the glorious Japanese army from the military forces of other, lesser nations.[49] That is, *bushidō* is a vital source of moral energy that will enable Japan to "overcome moder- nity" and overcome the Western powers.[50]

[46] Variations on this slogan included *chūkō ichidō* (忠孝一道, loyalty and piety are one path, or the way of loyalty and piety as one), *chūkō muni* (忠孝無二, loyalty and piety are non-dual), and *chūkō itchi* (忠孝一致, loyalty and piety are one). James McMullen deftly demonstrates that the Chinese Confucian emphasis on filial piety is gradually overthrown by a Japanese emphasis on loyalty (or on the unity of the two) in the work of Yamaga Sokō and Asami Keisai (1652–1711). McMullen 1987.

[47] Itō 1937, 111.

[48] Even in the 1940s, though, this hegemonic position had opponents. Watsuji Tetsurō for instance, argued that, far from merely being a change in *scale*, the shift from loyalty to patriotism was a radical shift in *kind*. Indeed, for Watsuji it makes no sense to talk about *bushidō* at all before this shift. The significance of the Meiji Restoration was not to grow *bushidō* from a smaller to a larger constituency; rather, it was one of the conditions for the possibility of *bushidō* itself (Goto-Jones 2008, 47–50).

[49] Inoue Tetsujirō, *Senjinkun* (1941), which was issued to soldiers in the imperial army in the name of Tōjō Hideaki, then Minister of War.

[50] The idea that Japan could confront the material wealth and power of Britain and the United States with the force of its spiritual cultivation (a position that eventually found expression in institutions such as the *kamikaze*, 神風) was central to public debates in the early 1940s about Japan's place in world history ("*Sekaishitekai tachiba to Nihon*," *Chuōkōron*, January 1942, pp. 150–92) and the possibility that modernity was a phenomenon that could be overcome by Japan (Kawakami and Takeuchi 1979).

In other words, the conceptual and ideological contours of imperial *bushidō* are relatively clear, and it is this form of total ideology that is so deeply enmeshed in the idea of the "total defeat" of Japan after total war. This constituted a deliberate and specific construction of *bushidō* as an ethic of absolute loyalty to the point of ruthless violence and self-destruction. In James's terms, it involved an aesthetic of violence and an ethic of duty. It was also a radically chauvistic ideology, rooted essentially in an ethnic story of Japaneseness and thus inaccessible (and inapplicable) to anyone else.

There is a powerful and popular sense in which imperial *bushidō* was defeated and discredited by the unconditional surrender of the Japanese Empire on August 15, 1945, and then found guilty of perpetrating crimes against humanity in the IMTFE. Hence, (imperial) *bushidō* forms part of the cultural matrix that postwar Japan has struggled to understand and to reconcile with its postwar identity. This is the *bushidō* that people fear as ethically, politically, or culturally dangerous; in a clear statement along these lines, Shigeno Saburō has written *Against Bushidō*, arguing that it is little more than an anachronistic and dangerous ideology that fetishizes violence and has no place in a peaceful modern democracy.[51] He laments the way in which (this kind of) *bushidō* has become part of the basic toolkit with which the world seeks to explain Japanese society, Japanese business practices, and Japanese culture.

In fact, Shigeno is not the first to lament the international popularity of *bushidō* in the postwar period, observing that its resilience as part of the popular representation of Japan casts a heavy shadow over the ability of other (non-*bushidō*) aesthetics and ethics to prosper as central elements of Japanese identity. Such sentiments might have been recognisable to Kawabata Yasunari (1899–1972), Japan's first winner of the Nobel Prize for Literature (1969), who self-consciously sought to represent the Japan that was lost in the war as a gently tragic, beautiful, elegaic, poetic land. Kawabata deliberately eschewed the aesthetic of violence preferred by his friend Mishima Yukio (1925–1970), whose life and works celebrated what he saw as Japan's lost martial virtues, culminating in his dramatic ritual suicide by *seppuku*（切腹）in the office of the commandant of the Ichigaya camp of the Japan Self-Defence Forces after a failed attempt at a *coup d'etat* and imperial restoration. Mishima spectacularly misjudged public opinion in Japan, which was not ready for this kind of radical revisionist vision of Japanese identity in 1970. However, similar sentiments (albeit in dramatically less committed, less sophisticated, and less elegant forms) simmer along in right-wing and revisionist popular culture in Japan today, for instance in the work of *manga-ka* Kobayashi Yoshinori.[52]

In fact, Mishima's vision of Japanese aesthetics and ethics might also be seen as part of a postwar attempt in Japan to reject imperial *bushidō* as a corruption of a more romantic Tokugawa *bushidō*.[53] As we have seen, however, this tendency to appeal to an idealized

---

[51] Shigeno 2014.

[52] Kobayashi 1995–2003.

[53] Benesch argues that "after 1945, many scholars dismissed what they regarded as the corrupting modern developments in *bushidō* and turned to re-examining the historical samurai to draw conclusions regarding 'traditional' Japanese culture and behavioural patterns" (Benesch 2014, 3).

vision of the samurai involves participation in a different area of *bushidō*'s ideological landscape. Between them, samurai ideology and imperial ideology set out many of the most important markers around the territory of *bushidō*.

Bushidō, *Budō*, and Philosophical Dispute

Without question, Mishima's favourite text from *bushidō* literature was the *Hagakure*, which is also one of the most philosophically complex and nuanced texts in the tradition.[54] In his own book about the *Hagakure*, Mishima recalls that he first read it during the war, when he kept it with him at all times. Writing in 1967, he recalls that it is the only book he has continued to re-read for the twenty years since then, feeling that it shines from within him like a light. He explains how it was extraordinarily popular during the war, even though (or because) it was a paradoxical book (*gyakusetsu-teki na hon* 逆説的な本). While it shone as a brilliant object in open daylight during the war, Mishima feels that its true light can only be seen in the darkness of its neglect in the postwar period.[55]

Mishima was quite right that the *Hagakure* was widely read (and much contested, even) during the war. Indeed, in some ways, it represents a philosophical battleground within what at first appears to be the uniform territory of imperial *bushidō*. The *Hagakure* is ecclectic and strangely organized, but it contains sections that are deeply speculative, conceptually innovative, and metaphysically provocative. Within the context of debates about *bushidō*, it was a preferred text of modern philosophers like Watsuji Tetsurō, who saw Yamamoto Tsunetomo rather than Yamaga Sokō as defining the philosophical foundations of *bushidō*.[56] Meanwhile, its speculative, metaphysical nature and emphasis on the ethical unity of knowledge and action garnered little attention or approval from Confucian ideologues such as Inoue Tetsujirō. The *Hagakure* seemed to resonate more closely with Buddhist-inspired (or-influenced) texts in the corpus, such as those by Takuan Sōhō, which placed much more emphasis on *bushidō* as an approach to self-transformation and personal salvation than on the idea that duty was instrumental for an external agent.

One of the most challenging ideas in the *Hagakure* is the possibility that there is a site in which duty and loyalty are at one with the idea of spontaneous freedom. Yamamoto

---

[54] Henry Scott Stokes (1974/1999, 264–266) reveals that this was partly because of the overt endorsement of homosexuality in the text and partly because of the aesthetic pairing of love and death.

[55] Mishima 1967, 8–9.

[56] This argument is elaborated in Goto-Jones 2008. Together with Furukawa Tetsushi, Watsuji Tetsurō published a modern Japanese translation of the *Hagakure* in three volumes in 1941 (reprinted, Tokyo: Iwanami shoten, 2003). Watsuji was also involved with the committee that drew up the *Kokutai no hongi*, but the clearest statement of his own philosphy of *bushidō* is Watsuji Tetsurō, "Nihon no shindō," in Watsuji Tetsurō 1961–92, 14: 297–312.

suggests that the *bushi* has no need for loyalty or devotion per se. Indeed, there is a realm in which being loyal means little more than obedience—it manifests a form of contemptible calculation of gain and loss for the self. However, with disciplined training, duty and loyalty can be subsumed into the ethical realm of spontaneous freedom—that is, the *bushi* acts without calculation or discrimination in a manner unified with the demands of duty. The cultivation of being-in-the-face-of-death becomes the basic foundation of both freedom and service.[57]

For Sōhō, the mind that lingers on calculation or profit or discrimination is the same as the mind that gets stuck on the blade of an opponent—it is a form of affliction, and it leads to sickness or even death. It is the unbalanced mind (*henshin* 偏心), the confused mind (*mōshin* 妄心), or the existent mind (*ushin* 有心). The purpose of training is to cultivate the "mind that doesn't stop at anything . . . that is energized from the place of no-abiding."[58] Even concepts like loyalty or duty become afflictions if your mind adheres to them.[59] For Sōhō, the martial arts provide a way to cultivate a "standpoint of ignorance" (*mumyō jyūchi* 無明住地) from which skilful yet spontaneous freedom becomes possible; the confrontation with (and constant contemplation of) death is a means to sever the bonds between the mind and its afflictions.

Indeed, there is a strong sense in Sōhō that the martial arts are merely expedient means (*hōben* 方便) to assist samurai in the pursuit of self-emancipation and enlightenment.[60] That is, swordsmanship emerges from Sōhō's writings largely as an analogy that enables the Zen monk to explain principles of Buddhist cultivation to an audience preoccupied by their relationship with the sword. In fact, this assertion of hierachy (in which technical training is in the service of spiritual ends) is one of the key differences between Sōhō's work and that of the legendary swordsmaster Yagū Munemori (1571–1646), whose *Heihō kandensho* is usually seen as a response to or even continuation of Sōhō.[61] While Sōhō maintains that disciplined training in the martial arts may (and ideally should) lead to spiritual accomplishment, Munemori is keen to invert this hierachy and argue that spiritual accomplishment results in superior martial skills. Indeed, the balance and priority given to ethical accomplishments and technical accomplishments (both of which should apparently emerge through training) is one of the key issues of debate in the *bushido* literature.

---

[57] "In the martial arts (*budō*), if one uses discrimination, he will fall behind. One needs neither loyalty nor devotion, but simply to become desperate (*shingurui* 死狂ひ) in the way of the warrior (*bushidō*). Loyalty and devotion are one with themselves within that" (Yamamoto 2005, 72–73, 74–75).

[58] Takuan Sōhō 2004, 67.

[59] Sōhō draws a distinction between the Great Loyalty (*daichū* 大忠) and the Little Loyalty of everyday actions. Great Loyalty is realized only in the moment of self-forgetting and spontaneous freedom that creates moral action—it is loyalty to something that transcends the idea of agency (2004, 86).

[60] Early on in *Fudōchi shinmyōroku*, Sōhō is explicit that he is trying to explain complex Buddhist concepts in a language that his (samurai) reader will understand (e.g., 2004, 25).

[61] Yagyū Munemori (1571–1646), *Heihō kadensho*, is included in the *Bushidō zensho* volume 2.

The *Hagakure*, for instance, is deeply skeptical about the apparent obsession with skill and special techniques in swordsmanship and the martial arts. Indeed, it states clearly that this obsession is a form of attachment and sickness. Yamamoto laments the *[bu] geisha* ([武]芸者, artists) who master various techniques and take on many students, believing that they have become warriors; he states that they have not fulfilled the stature of *bushi*. Rather, they are simply artists or technicians.[62] Later, he calls them fools and worthless people. While not as scathing, Musashi shares similar sentiments in *Gorinsho*, suggesting that those who focus entirely on skill and technique are not masters of the martial creed (*heihō no tatsujin* 兵法の達人) or *bushi* but simply martial artists (*heihōsha* 兵法者) who have reduced their lives to commodities for sale like a form of theater.[63] They have reduced their "ways" into merchandise.

While the *Hagakure* and *Gorinsho* scorn practitioners who focus their efforts on the acquisition of skills without a sense of disciplined cultivation appropriate to the *bushi*, Sōhō goes even further to argue that such people actually commit evil (*ashiki* 悪). Indeed, the only way for a martial artist to perform his or her techniques (which bring about pain, injury, and death) without committing evil is if these techniques arise out of the spontaneous freedom of no-mind no-thought (*mushinmunen* 無心無念), without any intervention of the self, the will, discrimination, or calculation. Acting out of duty is not enough, just like acting for profit is not enough. For Sōhō, the purpose of correct training is precisely to reach the highest levels of technical competence and ethical competence simultaneously: "in this way, completely forget about the mind and then you'll reach the highest competence in all you do ... when you cannot completely abandon the mind, all your conduct/movements (*shosa* 所作) will result in evil (*ashiki*)."[64]

What this reveals is that, even during the hegemonic period of imperial or *kokutai no bushidō*, the overall landscape of *bushidō* was already more complex, more nuanced, and more sophisticated than that ideological construction suggests. In fact, even the *Bushidō zensho* included a range of texts that had the potential to trouble and contest the hegemonic narrative. *Hagakure* was only one such text. The work of Takuan Sōhō was relatively exogenous to the hegemonic ideology despite appearing in the emerging canon. In the postwar period, this hidden territory in the overall landscape of *bushidō*, which we might call *jitsuzon-teki bushidō* (実存的武士道, existential *bushidō*) became increasingly important and visible.

This approach to *bushidō* is also deeply enmeshed in a cluster of texts that found no place in the *Bushidō zensho*, despite emerging during the same period, but which have become central to the field after the war. These additional texts are those of the modern *budō* tradition, written by practicing martial artists (rather than professional critics or academics) in the twentieth century. Such texts by the likes of founder of Shotokan Karate-dō, Funakoshi Gichin (1868–1957); founder of Aikidō, Ueshiba Morihei (1883–1969); and the founder of Jūdō, Kanō Jigorō (1860–1938), are the closest thing

62 Yamamoto 2004, 59, 67.
63 Miyamato 2004, 15.
64 Sōhō 2004, 75. *Ashiki* suggests both technical and moral poverty.

we have to new primary texts in the tradition of those penned by samurai swordsmen in the Tokugawa period or earlier.[65] The emphasis on the ethical and spiritual purpose of *budō* in the work of these author-practitioners was consistent and clear. They each drew on the emerging tradition of *bushidō* for resources to describe their own practices and practice-philosophies, producing texts that resonated with some of the more practical volumes in the *Bushidō zensho*, such as the Musashi's *Gorinsho*, which took pains to describe the correct conduct of martial techniques alongside advocating disciplined training in these techniques as a form of self-cultivation.[66]

We might speculate that Inoue Tetsujirō and the ideologues of military *bushidō* would have omitted attention to this important and popular body of work by martial arts instructors (who were already teaching these new *budō* in universities, police colleges, and military academies) because of their desire to represent *bushidō* as a system of "philosophy" at a time when the meaning and integrity of "philosophy" was bound up with purely textual traditions. Despite writing *about* the importance of martial discipline and training, most of the ideologues were rather sedentary academics. Hence, the idea that Funakoshi, Ueshiba, or Konō might actually be the most authentic possible representatives of *bushidō* as a philosophical practice would have seemed very radical (and possibly threatening). Indeed, the status of performance, embodiment, and practice in philosophy today remains exciting but controversial; it is clear that the *bushidō* tradition

---

[65] Funakoshi Gichin's influential *Shōtōkan nijū-kun* (21 Precepts of Shotokan) were printed for the first time in Nakasone 1938. Funakoshi's masterwork, *Karatedō kyōhan* had already appeared in 1935. While the former is entirely dedicated to the ethical and spiritual goals of training in *Karate-dō*, the latter mixes writings about spiritual development with illustrations and photographs designed to help students to learn the techniques. Funakoshi's precepts present Karate as a practice-oriented life-philosophy, emphasizing self-development, spiritual training, and the courage to defend principles of justice. In terms of the priority given to mental and spiritual accomplishments in Funakoshi's karate, this is made clear in precept 5: *Hitotsu, gijutsu yori shinjutsu* (一つ、技術より心術, one! mentality over technique!).

Ueshiba Morihei's early texts are even more emphatic about the necessary connection between *budō* and spiritual transformation, presenting techniques as forms of philosophical and spiritual expression in their own right. Like those of Funakoshi, Ueshiba's key texts were also published in the 1930s: *Budō renshū* (Tokyo, 1933) and *Budō* (Tokyo, 1938).

Kanō Jigorō published a wide range of articles (in Japanese and English) throughout the 1930s, presenting Judō as a modernization of unarmed methods of samurai fighting, emphasizing its benefits for health, well-being, and character development, including through carefully controlled competition. Indeed, Kanō's work at this time opened the doors to the transformation of *budō* (and *bujutsu* 武術) into sports, wherein the ostensibly "martial" origins of various techniques would be practiced and performed in the safety of friendly competition.

[66] It seems likely that Kanō developed the belt system of grades in Judō (which then influenced Funakoshi's system in Karate) inspired by Takuan Sōhō's description of the way that training in the martial arts begins with innocent, skilless, spontaneous action (i.e., the white belt), develops through increasing levels of technical competency but with concomitant loss in spontaneity (i.e., the black belt), but then with enough disciplined training, these skills become sublimated and internalized until the point when they are expressed spontaneously (i.e., when the black silk is worn off the belt by continuous use, revealing the white hessian core).

has much to teach us about it.[67] The *Gorinsho* talks of the "heart of direct transmission" (*chokutsū no kokoro* 直通の心) residing in the way that constant, diligent training enables "martial arts to become inherent in your body."[68]

CONCLUSION: CONTEXTS AND CONTOURS
FOR *BUSHIDŌ* AS PHILOSOPHY

There are many clouds around the *bushidō* tradition, some of which form elements of the tradition itself. Rather than seeking to offer a comprehensive survey of this iconic field, which I think would be impossible in this space, I have sought merely to part those clouds and reveal some of the richness and diversity of the landscape beyond.

One of the first revelations for me is the tension between the various ideological constructions of *bushidō*. For instance, consider the tension between the radical particularism of Inoue Tetsujirō's construction of imperial *bushidō*, which inextricably wove *bushidō* into the ethnic and cultural fabric of Japaneseness, and the philosophical universalism of Watsuji Tetsurō's construction of existential *bushidō*, which threw *bushidō* into the global mix of ideas for the use of any who find it useful.

There are other tensions between historical models of *bushidō*. On the one hand, the romantic image of the samurai and, on the other, the horrors of imperial atrocities. There are questions of aesthetics and violence. There are questions of ethics. There are metaphysical issues and radical provocations about the relationship between performance, embodiment, action, and the enterprise of philosophy itself. There are grand epistemological dilemmas around rationality, intuition, and the unity of knowledge and action. And there are sweeping problematics about the nature of war and peace and the kinds of behavior appropriate to each.

In the end, far from being a simple code of conduct for samurai, *bushidō* emerges as a distinctive field of philosophical inquiry in its own right. It may indeed be a modern invented tradition, but that does not make that tradition any less interesting for us today.

BIBLIOGRAPHY AND SUGGESTED READINGS

Allen, Barry. (2015) *Striking Beauty: A Philosophical Look at the Asian Martial Arts.* New York: Columbia University Press.
Benesch, Oleg. (2014) *Inventing the Way of the Samurai: Nationalism, Internationalism, and Bushidō in Modern Japan.* Oxford: Oxford University Press.

[67] The move toward the embrace of the body as integral to philosophical practice is powerfully provoked by Lakoff and Johnson 1999.
[68] Miyamoto 2004, 73. The idea of "direct transmission" has been used by some authors to mystify these texts, suggesting that it refers to secret techniques or teachings. However, reading the *bushidō* tradition as a form of embodied philosophy enables this simpler and more effective reading.

Brown, Roger. (2013) "Yasuoka Masahiro's 'New Discourse on Bushidō Philosophy': Cultivating Samurai Spirit and Men of Character for Imperial Japan." *Social Science Japan Journal* 16/1: 107–129.

Chamberlain, Basil Hall. (1912) *The Invention of a New Religion*. London: Rationalist Press.

Chamberlain, Basil Hall. (1971) *Japanese Things*. Reprint Tokyo: Charles Tuttle.

Dale, Peter. (1986) *The Myth of Japanese Uniqueness*. London & New York: Routledge.

French, Shannon. (2003) *The Code of the Warrior: Exploring Warrior Values Past and Present*. Oxford: Rowman & Littlefield.

Friday, Karl. (1994) "*Bushidō* or Bull? A Medieval Historian's Perspective on the Imperial Army and the Japanese Warrior Tradition." *The History Teacher*, 27/3.

Funakoshi Gichin. (1935/1958) *Karatedō kyōhan* [Karate-dō the Mastertext]. Tokyo: Jitsugetsusha.

Funakoshi Gichin. (1956/2004) *Karatedō ichiro* [The One Way of Karate-dō]. Okinawa: Gajumru shorin.

Goto-Jones, Chris. (2008) "The Way of Revering the Emperor: Imperial Philosophy and Bushidō in Modern Japan." In *The Emperors of Modern Japan*, edited by Ben Ami-Shillony. Boston: Brill.

Goto-Jones, Chris. (2016) *The Virtual Ninja Manifesto: Fighting Games, Martial Arts, and Gamic Orientalism*. London & New York: Rowman & Littlefield International.

Hobsawm, Eric, and Terence Ranger, eds. (1983) *The Invention of Tradition*. Cambridge: Cambridge University Press.

Hurst, Cameron, III. (1990) "Death, Honor, and Loyalty: The Bushidō Ideal." *Philosophy East & West* 40/4: 511–527.

Ikegami, Eiko. (1995) *The Taming of the Samurai: Honorific Individualism and the Making of Modern Japan*. Cambridge, MA: Harvard University Press.

Inoue Shun. (1998). "The Invention of the Martial Arts: Kanō Jigorō and Kōdōkan Judō." In *Mirror of Modernity: Invented Traditions of Modern Japan*, edited by Stephen Vlastos. Berkeley: University of California Press, 163–173.

Inoue Tetsujirō. (1987/1900) *Nihon yōmei gakuha no tetsugaku* [The Philosophy of the Japanese School of Wang Yangming]. Tokyo: Fuzanbō.

Inoue Tetsujirō. (1902/1945) *Nihon shūshi gakuha no tetsugaku* [The Philosophy of the Japanese School of Chu Hsi]. Tokyo: Fuzanbō.

Inoue Tetsujirō (1905/1918) *Nihon kogakuha no tetsugaku* [The Philosophy of the Japanese School of Kogaku]. Tokyo: Fuzanbō.

Inoue Tetsujirō, ed. (1905) *Bushidō sōsho* [Selected Works of Bushidō]. Tokyo: Hakubunkan.

Inoue Tetsujirō. (1912) *Kokumin dōtoku gairon* [Outline of the National Morality]. Tokyo: Sanseidō.

Inoue Tetsujirō, Saeki Arioshi, Ueki Naoichirō, and Inobe Shigeo, eds. (1942) *Bushidō zensho* [Collected Works of Bushidō]. 11 vols. Tokyo: Jidaisha.

Itō Enkichi. (1937) *Kokutai no hongi* [Fundamentals of the National Polity]. Tokyo: Monbushō.

Ives, Christopher. (2009) *Imperial-Way Zen: Ichikawa Hakugen's Critique and Lingering Concerns for Buddhist Ethics*. Honolulu: University of Hawai'i Press.

James, William. (1947) *Essays on Faith and Morals*. New York & London: Longmans, Green, and Co.

Jarmusch, Jim. (1999) *Ghost Dog: The Way of the Samurai*. Artisan Entertainmnent.

Jennings, George, David Brown, and Andrew Sparkes. (2010) " 'It Can Be a Religion if You Want': Wing Chun Kung Fu as a Secular Religion." *Ethnography* 11/4:533–557.

Kawakami Tetsutarō and Takeuchi Yoshimi, eds. (1979) *Kindai no chōkoku* [Overcoming Modernity]. Tokyo: Fuzanbō.

King, Winston. (1993) *Zen and the Way of the Sword: Arming the Samurai Psyche*. New York & Oxford: Oxford University Press.

Kobayashi Yoshinori. (1995–2003) *Shin gōmanizumu sengen special: Sensō ron* [New Gomanism Manifesto Special: On War]. 3 vols. Tokyo: Gentōsha.

Lakoff, George, and Mark Johnson. (1999) *Philosophy in the Flesh: The Embodied Mind and Its Challenge to Western Thought*. New York: Basic Books.

McMullen, James. (1987) "Rulers or Fathers? A Casuistical Problem in Early Modern Japanese Thought." *Past and Present* 116: 56–97.

Midgely, Mary. (1981/2003) "Trying Out One's New Sword." In *Heart and Mind: The Varieties of Moral Experience*. London & New York: Routledge.

Mishima Yukio. (1967) *Hagakure nyūmon* [Introduction to the *Hagakure*]. Tokyo: Shinchosha.

Mishima Yukio. (1977) *On Hagakure: The Samurai Ethic and Modern Japan*, translated by Kathryn Sparling. New York: Basic Books.

Miyamoto Musashi. (2004) *Gorinsho* [Book of Five Rings], edited by Watanabe Ichirō. Tokyo: Iwanami shoten.

Miyamoto Musashi. (2001) *Gorinsho: The Book of Five Rings (bilingual edition)*, translation by William Scott Wilson. Tokyo & New York: Kodansha International.

Nakasone Genwa (ed.). (1938/1948) *Karatedō taikan* [Encyclopedia of Karate-dō]. Tokyo: Kanbukan Shuppanbu.

Neville, Robert. (1978) *Soldier, Sage, Saint*. New York: Fordham University Press.

Nitobe Inazō. (2002) *Bushido: The Soul of Japan*. Tokyo & New York: Kodansha International.

Lord Russell of Liverpool. (1958) *The Knights of Bushido: A Shocking History of Japanese War Atrocities*. New York: EP Dutton.

Shahar, Meir. (2008) *The Shaolin Monastery: History, Religion, and the Chinese Martial Arts*. Honolulu: University of Hawai'i Press.

Shigeno Saburō. (2014) *Han bushidō ron* [Against Bushidō]. Tokyo: Bungeisha.

Smith, Henry, II. (2003) "The Capacity of Chushingura." *Monumenta Nipponica* 58/1: 1–42.

Stokes, Henry Scott. (1974/1999) *The Life and Death of Yukio Mishima*. New York: Cooper Square Press.

Suzuki, D. T. (1938) *Zen Buddhism and its Influence on Japanese Culture*. Kyoto: Otani Buddhist College.

Takuan Sōhō. (1970/2004) *Fudōchi shinmyōroku* [Mysterious Records of Immovable Wisdom], edited by Ikeda Satoshi. Tokyo: Tokuma Shoten.

Tucker, John. (2018) *The 47 Rōnin: The Vendetta in History*. Cambridge: Cambridge University Press.

Tucker, John. (2002) "Tokugawa Intellectual History and Prewar Ideology: The Case of Inoue Tetsujirō, Yamaga Sokō, and the Forty-Seven Rōnin." *Sino-Japanese Studies Journal* 14: 35–70.

Ueshiba, Morihei. (1933) *Budō renshū* [Training in Budō]. Tokyo.

Ueshiba, Morihei. (1938) *Budō* [Budō]. Tokyo.

Various. (1942) "Sekaishiteki tachiba to Nihon [Japan and the Standpoint of World-history]." *Chuōkōron* January: 150–192.

Varley, Paul. (1994) *Warriors of Japan as Portrayed in the War Tales*. Honolulu: University of Hawai'i Press.

Victoria, Brian. (1997) *Zen at War*. New York & Tokyo: Weatherhill.

Vlastos, Stephen, ed. (1998) *Mirror of Modernity: Invented Traditions of Modern Japan.* Berkeley: University of California Press.

Watsuji Tetsurō. (1961–1992) *Watsuji Tetsurō zenshū* [Collected Works of Watsuji Tetsurō], 27 vols. Tokyo: Iwanami shoten.

Yamada, Shoji. (2011) *Shots in the Dark: Japan, Zen and the West.* Chicago: University of Chicago Press.

Yamamoto, Tsunemoto. (1941/2003) *Hagakure* [Hagakure], edited by Watsuji Tetsurō & Furukawa Tetsushi, 3 volumes. Tokyo: Iwanami Shoten.

Yamamoto, Tsunetomo. (2005) *Hagakure: The Book of the Samurai (bilingual edition),* translation by William Scott Wilson. Tokyo & New York: Kodansha International.

Yamamoto, Tsunetomo. (1979/2002) *Hagakure: The Book of the Samurai,* translated by William Scott Wilson. Tokyo & New York: Kodansha International.

PART IV

MODERN JAPANESE
PHILOSOPHIES

CHAPTER 15

....

THE JAPANESE ENCOUNTER
WITH AND APPROPRIATION
OF WESTERN PHILOSOPHY

....

JOHN C. MARALDO

THE appropriation of Western philosophy in Japan came about through a transformation of the Japanese language. The encounter with Western philosophy in the late Tokugawa and the Meiji Periods, stretching from about 1853 to 1912, occasioned a new way of articulating thought that allowed Japanese to make philosophy their own, a discipline proper to the continual formation of their culture. This appropriation redefined Japan's past intellectual traditions as well, interpreting them in the light of Western philosophical concepts and problems. Outside Japan, it has facilitated an understanding of Japanese thought as properly belonging to the history of philosophy. Philosophers, theologians, and scholars of religion worldwide now incorporate philosophical insights that originated in East Asian thought.

The fact that Japanese scholars had to transform their written language in order to appropriate and make sense of Anglo-European philosophical texts gives evidence that people of different cultures historically have thought differently.[1] To indicate how they changed their language may also uncover historical and cultural presuppositions in discussions of the universality of philosophy. Momentous changes in Japanese linguistic expression had occurred before, of course, first in the fifth century and then in

---

[1] See Heisig, Kasulis, and Maraldo 2011, 1. Evidence that peoples of different cultures have actually thought differently does not, however, support the conclusion (advanced by Steineck, Lange, and Kaufmann 2014, 30) that the concept of philosophy is therefore rendered relative to particular cultures. Indeed, the transmission of traditions and translation of texts mean that conceptions of philosophy move and develop both across and within cultures and languages, as shown by examples cited later from both European and Japanese history.

the sixteenth. In the fifth century, Japanese began to appropriate Chinese writing along with Chinese and Korean Buddhism and Confucianism. The adoption of Chinese writing, or sinographs (漢字, pronounced *kanji* in Japanese), gave Japanese peoples a way to write their own dialects and enabled them to think in new ways with new words—in essence to think in a foreign language. After phonetic symbols were eventually added to express Japanese syntax, Chinese words continued to infuse the gradually unifying Japanese language with non-native ideas. By medieval times, Japanese versions of classical Chinese and hybrid forms of the written language were both well defined.

Then in the mid-1500s Japanese encountered Europeans on their shores, among them Pedro Gómez, a Spanish Jesuit missionary who taught scholastic philosophy in the Jesuit College of Funia in eastern Kyūshū. His Latin Compendium, completed in 1593 and translated into early modern Japanese, consisted of a Thomistic adaptation of Aristotle's De Anima—focusing on free will and the rational, eternal soul—as well as a work on astronomy as natural theology and a catechism of Tridentine "Catholic Truth."[2] Gómez's work was probably the very first to introduce Western philosophy and science into Japan. The unprinted Japanese version remained the basis for lectures at Jesuit schools at least until 1616, but during this era of the persecution of Christians, Gómez's work was eventually lost until the twentieth century. Its effect on Japanese language and learning in general would have been extremely limited. Still, the translations of some terms foretell the linguistic challenges that later scholars would face. *Philosophia* was usually rendered phonetically, but a literal translation (*kōgaku* 好學), love of knowledge or wisdom, also appears. More telling is that Latin terms like *potentia, actus, essentia, forma, causa* and *anima* each had multiple translations, often adapting Buddhist vocabulary or inventing now obsolete expressions.[3] It is probable that the sense of these foreign concepts became clear only in lengthy discussions; the trans-lation of European thought required extensive dialogue across languages and a willingness to experiment.

By the 1640s, the newly formed Tokugawa shogunate had expelled the Jesuit missionaries and Portuguese traders, but allowed Dutch traders to stay on a tiny artificial island off Nagasaki.Except for trade with Holland and China, Japan remained relatively closed to the outside world for the next two centuries. The Dutch brought medical and scientific knowledge as well as guns and other inventions, and the appropriation of that knowledge required a few Japanese scholars to learn Dutch and, eventually, smatterings of English and German.

---

[2] See Frédéric Girard, "On the Translation of the *De Anima* of Aristotle and its *Commentary* by Thomas Aquinas, in the *Compendium Catholicae Veritatis* of Pedro Gómez (1595)," *Tōyō kenkyū* 192 (2014): 149–164.

[3] For a list of examples see Frédéric Girard, 「ペド ロ•ゴ メ ズ の 『講義要綱』 の和譯 (1595年)と日本宗教」 [The Japanese Translation of Pedro Gómez's *Compendium*], *Tōyō no shisō to shūkyō* 28 (2011): 1–53.

From the standpoint of linguistics, European languages differed from native forms of Japanese—before writing was introduced—hardly any more than Chinese had.[4] But by the time of Japan's encounter with Europeans, originally Chinese concepts and ways of thinking had long been assimilated, and the linguistic expressions of the Europeans were as alien as their customs and technology. Beginning in the 1720s, with relaxed government control, Japanese scholars established "Dutch Studies" to translate Dutch texts, absorb new concepts such as *science*, and apply as best they could what they learned of human anatomy, the natural world, global geography, and the worlds made visible through telescopes and microscopes. Consistent with its interest in technology and science, Dutch Studies (also called "Western Learning") reflected the Japanese Confucian penchant for practical thinking. Scholars rendered the relatively few writings on liberal arts that made their way into Japan with a mix of Confucian terms and untranslated Dutch words. Only one instance of a native philosophical treatise is known from that era: the medical and military scholar Takano Chōei's "Theories of Western Sages" of 1835, a brief and very incomplete survey of ancient Greek and modern European philosophers and experimental scientists.[5] For all its Confucian residues, however, Dutch Studies prepared the way for the next momentous change.

THE DISCOVERY OF THE IDIOM OF PHILOSOPHY BY JAPANESE ENLIGHTENMENT THINKERS

In 1853, four American steamships, two of them armed with massive cannons, sailed into Tokyo harbor and took Japan by surprise. This encounter initiated Japan's reopening to trade and the exchange of ideas with Western nations. Ideas, unlike commercial objects, could not be conveyed apart from linguistic expression, and their appropriation once again required a long and arduous process of transforming the Japanese language. Philosophical texts began to stream into Japan in the 1860s and 1870s and, soon afterward, were studied by Japanese scholars visiting Europe or America. To understand the logic and language of these texts meant once again to learn and partially adapt a foreign language.

In philosophical Japanese today, the traces of its alien and exotic origins are largely invisible due in part to the use of traditional Chinese characters or sinographs to translate terminology. One feature of the use of the Chinese-infused written language made it relatively easy to try out various translations to convey the nomenclature of Western

---

[4] See Chapter 32 in this volume for further clarification of the Japanese language and its relation to Chinese.

[5] See Heisig, Kasulis, and Maraldo 2011, 554–555, for a summary and translation of an excerpt.

disciplines: single sinographs, each with its own semantic content, could be combined in virtually unlimited ways to form new compounds of two or more sinographs.[6] Reading the translations and treatises of Meiji-era scholars, one might encounter several different compounds meant to render the same Western term, "contradiction," for example.[7] Many compounds have gone out of use; others are now so commonplace that it is forgotten they were neologisms at the time. And where Meiji translators were at a loss to convey a meaning or felt the construction of new words to be inadequate, they could simply transcribe a foreign term in one of the two phonetic scripts in Japanese or even use sinographs purely phonetically to render a pronunciation of a foreign name. *Philosophia*, for example, was at first simply transcribed, although later replaced by a new compound. *Ideorogī* (ideology), *tōtorojī* (tautology), and *tēma* (theme) are examples of transcribed words whose usage in philosophy still predominates over Sino-Japanese constructions to translate the original.

The nearly invisible transformative effects of translation are by no means unique to philosophy in Japan, however. The Greek and Latin origins of many Western terms lie hidden to the untrained eye. Indeed, the journey of philosophy through the ages in the Western hemisphere had required equally momentous changes in European languages. The translation of Greek philosophy into Latin vocabulary and grammar lost the subtlety of the middle voice and transformed many concepts. *Hypokeimenon*, for example, became *subiectum*, the "subject." Latin transmuted into modern European languages, erasing significant differences between cognates or giving new meanings to old terms. Even when roots were retained, connotations changed. The difference disappeared between *sacer*, awe-inspiring, and *sacred* in the sense of holy or the opposite of secular, for example. The Roman theatrical mask indicating the role played by a character, called *persona*, in the guise of "person" took on the meaning of an individual, living human being. In the seventeenth century, Descartes and Leibniz continued to write in Latin as well as in their native tongues, thus marking the gap between scholars and other literate people. By the 1700s, written language in Europe, however, was much closer to the colloquial idiom than was the case with the Japanese language throughout the Meiji Period. To appropriate Western philosophy in Japan meant to model Japan's written language

---

[6] Suzuki Hideo points out that, in the Meiji era, compounds of Chinese characters (*kango* 漢語) came to outnumber originally Japanese words in the written language as a result of compounds created or adapted to indicate imported things, ideas, and concepts. "The primary factors for the emergence of new vocabulary and grammar are newly introduced cultures and the translation done to import them." *"Meijiki no nihongo—furusa to atarashisa no konzai"* (Meiji period Japanese language—an intermingling of the old and the new), *Eurika* (November 1984), 277–278. Of course, the new words in the Meiji era translated Western, not Chinese, ideas.

[7] The Meiji philosopher Kiyono Tsutomu's comments (in Senuma 1974, 86) on the compilation of philosophical lexica and the reformation of language mentions as an example two translations of the "principle of contradiction" that have since fallen out of use: *dōchaku shugi* (撞着主義, the doctrine of inconsistency or conflict) and *shokugen no genri* (食言の原理, the principle of retracting one's words). The term for "contradiction" that eventually became standard, but is not mentioned in Kiyono's 1888 article, is *mujun* (矛盾), an ancient Chinese compound of the sinograph for a halberd (that could penetrate anything) and the sinograph for an (impenetrable) shield, together also used to mean "taking up arms and going to war."

after the idiom of philosophy in the West.[8] Even the grammatical structure of the typical written sentence—a designated topic followed by a comment—was often modified to reflect more clearly the subject-predicate structure of Indo-European languages.[9] Notably, some contemporary philosophers argue that the way the Japanese language was transformed—by creating new words based on Chinese sinographs and adapting a Westernized conception of grammar—actually hampered the possibility of doing philosophy in a manner more expressive of native Japanese.[10]

In the 1870s, several scholars schooled in Confucian texts and trained in Dutch Studies established a society called Meiji Six (named after its founding in the sixth year of the Mejii era) to discuss newly imported ideas and to urge state officials to modernize Japan. Many of its members helped form Japan's first university out of their private academies, taught at the University of Tokyo, and became government functionaries. Collectively, they became known as the *keimō gakusha* (啓蒙学者), scholars of the Enlightenment. In line with their ideal of liberalizing education in Japan, they decided to write in a prose more accessible to the general reading public than was the literary style of their Confucian predecessors. One founding member, Mori Arinori, at one point went so far as to urge that the Japanese language be replaced by English, or at least that it be written phonetically in Roman letters in order not only to engage in commerce, but also to further the march of civilization in Japan.[11] In retrospect, the style that prevailed in their philosophical works seems archaic if innovative, somewhere between traditional Confucian discourse and the prose of twentieth-century Japanese philosophers. No one was more adept than Nishi Amane (1829–1887) in creating new words to express alien Western concepts, "philosophy" among them.

The word Nishi eventually settled on to translate "philosophy" was the Confucian-sounding neologism, *tetsugaku* (哲学), roughly, the learning of the sages, *tetsujin* (哲人). Nishi had encountered this strange kind of learning in the course of his Dutch studies and initially deemed it superior even to Zhu Xi's "explanations of the principles of human nature and life."[12] Understanding the methods and content of "philosophy" required some sort of mediation, and Confucian ideas, particularly the concept of *ri* (理),

---

[8] In Maraldo 2017: 11–14, I argue that philosophy can be understood as a textually transmitted practice involving the transference of texts from one natural language to another, as well as the transformation of textually embedded problems, methods, and terminologies both across and within languages.

[9] The Flemish scholar Willy Vande Walle writes that "By the time Nishida [Kitarō] was publishing his *Zen no kenkyu* [in 1911], the Japanese language had already undergone a deep change, equipping it with a syntax that came much closer to that of Western languages . . . . In a sense, in order to make translations of Western works into Japanese faithful, the Japanese language had to mimic the source languages." Introduction to his edited volume, *Dodonaeus in Japan: Translation and the Scientific Mind in the Tokugawa Period* (Leuven, Belgium: Leuven University Press, 2001), 19–20.

[10] Sakabe Megumi (1936–2009) made this argument in 1987, in his book "Shutai no kagami to busshin" toshite no kotoba [Language as "Mirror and Fetish of the Subject"]. For a partial translation, see Heisig, Kasulis, and Maraldo 2011, 979–992. Thomas Kasulis succinctly summarizes the issue in *Engaging Japanese Philosophy: A Short History* (University of Hawai'i Press, 2018), 569–573. We might question whether there remains enough of a "native Japanese" language to actualize Sakabe's hope to recreate philosophy with it.

[11] Ivan Parker Hall, *Mori Arinori* (Cambridge, MA: Harvard University Press, 1973), 189, 194.

[12] Heisig, Kasulis, and Maraldo 2011, 556.

served as the medium of comparison. At first, Nishi parsed *tetsugaku* with Confucian terms such as *rigaku* (理学), aligning it with the Neo-Confucian "study of principles," but, by 1873, he tended to distinguish *philosophia* from Confucian studies and to use *tetsugaku* exclusively.[13] Still, for two more decades among Nishi's contemporaries, "philosophy" also went by the name of *rigaku*. In another permutation, *rigaku* came to designate the natural sciences. Nishi spent much effort in making sense of the *ri* of the East Asians and the rationality of the Europeans.[14] Polysemous as it was, *ri* (meaning pattern, principle, reason, or truth) served as a bridge term that allowed Nishi and others to move between the Confucian ground on which they were raised and the European ground they confronted. It was as if an earthquake had destabilized both sides, throwing traditional studies into doubt but also leaving unsettled the translation of the new. Some terms they invented for *philosophy, religion,* and other European notions have gone by the wayside. Others proposed by Nishi, such as *tetsugaku* and words for *sensibility, induction, deduction, idea,* and *concept,* survived several variations and are now standard terms in the philosophical lexicon in Japan.

Nishi deepened his understanding of philosophy during two years of study at Leiden University in Holland, where he encountered August Comte's system of positivism unifying all sciences and John Stuart Mill's utilitarian ethics and system of inductive logic. These were the philosophical schools he introduced to Japan, along with Western legal and economic theories and military science—all consonant with his predilection toward studies that had practical consequences. Ultimately, he included Chinese thought in the province of philosophy and suggested that "objective contemplation," the forte of Western philosophy, needed to be supplemented by the "subjective contemplation" in which Eastern philosophers have excelled. Nishi used the English words here, and the quaint Japanese expressions he chose to gloss them suggest a playful spirit in interpreting ideas that had no counterparts in Japanese.[15]

A fellow scholar of the Meiji Six Society, Nishimura Shigeki (1828–1902), imitated Nishi's penchant for inventing terms and echoed his view of the strengths and weakness of Western and Eastern thought. He wrote that thinkers of the Zen School and Chinese Confucians like Wang Yangming excelled in "inner contemplation" (*naikan* 内観) and in *synthesis* (*sōgō* 総合), whereas thinkers in the West excel in "outer contemplation" (*gaikan* 外観) and *analysis* (*bunseki* 分析)—all either neologisms or old words with new meanings. His writings leave open the question of whether past Confucian

---

[13] Steineck (2014, 59–60) argues that Nishi ultimately conceived *rigaku* as an overarching category that included both *tetsugaku*, as developed by European traditions, and *jugaku* or Confucian studies. In tension with his suggested taxonomy, however, Steineck also points out that Nishi thought the East Asian Confucian tradition needed to develop the critical reflection found in European philosophy and become more like it, that is, more *"tetsugaku-teki"* or "philosophical."

[14] Heisig, Kasulis, and Maraldo 2011, 583–588. See also 555–559 for more texts and commentary than can be offered in this chapter.

[15] Nishi Amane, *Seisei hatsu-un* [The Relationship Between the Physical and the Spiritual, i.e., between physiology and psychology, 1871–1873], in Senuma 1974, 8. Nishi proposed that both Chinese and European traditions originally evinced a turn to the subject (see Steineck 2014, 49), although the

and Buddhist thought should count as philosophy proper. Nishimura's discussion seems future-oriented, and in fact it foreshadows contemporary debates about the nature of consciousness. He proclaimed it necessary to research the nature of mind holistically and internally as well as analytically in physiology and in the study of observable mental phenomena.[16]

Critics outside the circles of the "Enlightenment" movement continued debating whether the East, and Japan in particular, ever had philosophy, that is, *tetsugaku*. In the context of this chapter, we may note that, whichever side they took, their style and terminology reflected the unstable stage of transition visible in the Enlightenment thinkers. Miyake Seturei (1860–1945) argued for a qualified recognition of Eastern philosophy and cautioned against uncritical imitation of Western ideas. He associated Western philosophy with logical and causal investigations, Indian philosophy with intention or will (意), and Chinese philosophy with feeling (情).[17] Nakae Chōmin (1847–1901) advocated Rousseau's egalitarian philosophy and derided University of Tokyo philosophy professors as epigones and elitists. His *Digging Up the Hidden and Profound Truths of Philosophy,* published in 1886, was the first popular outline of philosophy in Japan. It mixed some terms that eventually became standard with invented and unusual sinograph compounds to treat various "isms" such as sensationism (*kankaku-setsu* 感覚説), idealism (*ishō-setsu* 意象説), pantheism (*shinbutsuittai-setsu* 神物一体説), mysticism (*shinjinkangō-setsu* 神人感合説), materialism (*jisshitsu-setsu* 実質説), and skepticism (*kaigi-setsu* 懐疑説). There was, he famously proclaimed, "no such thing as philosophy in Japan," but past Western philosophers who believed in God or immortality were also deluded.[18] Both Setsurei and Chōmin spoke freely of philosophy (writing both *tetsugaku* and *rigaku*) as if it were a commonplace idea. Yet, although their views appear quite modern, their arguments were still couched in a rhetoric of classical grammar replete with old, Confucian-tinged terminology.

A recognizably twentieth-century philosophical idiom had to wait for thinkers like Ōnishi Hajime (1864–1900) and Nishida Kitarō (1870–1945). The gifted Christian philosopher Ōnishi was conversant with Chinese and Japanese classics; gained facility in English, German, French, Latin, and Greek; and published a history of Western philosophy in 1895. In 1898, he visited Wilhelm Wundt's Institute for Experimental Psychology in Leipzig. His *Logic*, written somewhat earlier, presents the discipline as universal and

---

latter came to excel in objective observation as well as in critical reflection. Noteworthy is Nishi's use of the Western categories *subjective* and *objective* to depict this history.

[16] Nishimura Shigeki, *Jishiki roku* [A record of self-knowledge, 1899], in *Senuma* 1974, 23.

[17] *Tetsugaku kenteki* [Philosophical Trifles, 1889], partially translated in Heisig, Kasulis, and Maraldo 2011, 563.

[18] Heisig, Kasulis, and Maraldo 2011, 564, 605. Contrary to Chōmin's famous repudiation in 1901, the pioneer of logical studies Kiyono Tsutomu had written in 1883 "one cannot say that since olden times there has never been any *philosophia* in the many countries of the Orient … That statement could pertain only to a discipline corresponding to logic." *Kakuchi tetsugaku choron*, cited in Nakamura Hajime, Takeda Kiyoko, et al., eds., *Tetsugaku-shisōka jiten* [Dictionary of Philosophers and Thinkers] (Tokyo: Tokyo shoseki,1982), 209. Apparently Kiyono did not include India, with its long traditions of logic, among his "countries of the Orient."

autonomous, unaffected by experimental sciences. It includes a critique of deductive argumentation and detailed analyses of Buddhist and Confucian reasoning (or the lack of it). He sought a universal position in his *Ethics* as well and forcefully argued against the authoritarian Confucian ideology still evident in the new Japanese state.[19] His writings are noted for lucid thinking and clearly defined positions. Much of that clarity derives from the modern idiom he adapted.

Nishida Kitarō's pathbreaking *Inquiry into the Good* appeared in 1911. With few exceptions, his idiom was unmistakably different, in style and terminology, from the language of those who had begun to appropriate Western philosophy in Meiji-era Japan. The frequently cited judgment that this work initiated original Japanese philosophy cannot be separated from the force of Nishida's language.[20] Nishida's philosophy will be treated in subsequent chapters in this volume. The sketches that follow focus on a few of his many predecessors who deserve consideration in Japan's early appropriation of philosophy.

FUKUZAWA YUKICHI: THE INVENTION OF CIVILIZATION

In the Foreword to *An Outline of Theories of Civilization* Fukuzawa Yukichi (1835–1901) refers repeatedly to the sudden jolt and massive disturbance Japanese people experienced when they encountered the startlingly different culture and superior technology of America and European nations in the 1850s. Fukuzawa took personally this rude awakening on a national scale and decided to learn all he could about these alien peoples and their exotic ideas. By the time he published *An Outline* in 1875, he was a recognized expert in the "conditions of the West," the title of three popular books he wrote between 1867 and 1870. He had produced an English-Japanese dictionary in 1860 by adding Japanese pronunciations to a Cantonese-English phrasebook he found in San Francisco earlier the same year.[21] He became a consummate translator and paraphraser of works ranging from the *Declaration of Independence* to Francis Wayland's *Moral Science* of 1835 and John Hill Burton's *Political Economy* of 1852. He progressed to become an independent thinker and wrote *An Encouragement of Learning* (alternatively translated *A Recommendation of Science*),[22] advocating "national independence through personal

---

[19]   Heisig, Kasulis, and Maraldo 2011, 631–635, translates an excerpt of his argument that the Confucian ideals of filial piety and loyalty could not serve as a basis for ethics. Reitan 2010, 94–97, summarizes Ōnishi's debate with Inoue Tetsujirō and other defenders of the 1890 Imperial Rescript on Education. Piovesana 1997, 43–47, gives a summary of his activities. More complete Western-language treatments of Ōnishi's philosophy are sorely lacking.

[20]   Heisig, Kasulis, and Maraldo 2011, 573–576, summarizes early appraisals of Nishida's work.

[21]   Craig, 9.

[22]   *Gakumon no susume* (学問のすすめ), published in seventeen volumes between 1872 and 1876. See Fukuzawa 2013.

independence." He made a case for individualism, a free and competitive exchange of ideas, and methodic doubt and selective judgment—all ideas that challenged authoritarianism in general and what he saw as Confucian practices in particular.[23] But the treatise called *An Outline of Theories of Civilization* also questioned assumptions commonly held in the premier academy of Dutch Studies where Fukuzawa had studied. It denigrated reliance on Buddhist and Shintō beliefs and customs as well. It was a broadside—if cautious—attack on nearly all intellectual traditions in Japan.

Fukuzawa found it necessary to use Western concepts and discursive methods to argue for the Western ways that could, he was convinced, advance the people and nation of Japan. The language he employed to pursue his agenda cannot be said to be as disquieting as Japan's confrontation with Western culture and technology. In fact, he attempted to express ideas in a language accessible to most educated people in Japan. But even that aim was unconventional for a scholar like Fukuzawa, and, to accomplish it, he marshaled novel distinctions, an unusual use of hortatory argumentation, and what Derrida has called "paleonomy": giving old terms new meanings. As bland as his texts in translation seem today, his early readers must have experienced a certain "shock of the new."

The most important term in Fukuzawa's *Outline* is a word with a foreign meaning: *bunmei* (文明), a translation of "civilization" from the English and the French. People today do not give the word a second glance, but when it first appeared with this new meaning in the 1870s, it was unfamiliar and in need of explanation, even if easily understandable with its overtones of letters or literary arts (*bun* 文) and illumination (*mei* 明), rather than of *civis*, the inhabitants of a city and their culture.[24] By the early 1900s, the frequent use of the word had made it seem an ordinary part of the Japanese language. The notion that *bunmei* always entailed "progress" became a matter of dispute,[25] but the word retained one undisputed meaning: it referred foremost to the advanced level of social, technological, and individual development characteristic of European peoples. Fukuzawa believed that Japan, too, could—indeed must—achieve that level.

The word *bunmei* opens Fukuzawa's treatise: "Civilization-theory means a discussion of the development of a people's spirit."[26] He had used the word before, in several senses, in his popular *Conditions of the West*, and in *An Outline* it sometimes carries connotations of what we would call a people's *culture*. The predominant reference,

---

[23] Perhaps Fukuzawa's understanding of Confucian ideals was skewed by Confucian practitioners in his day. John A. Tucker insists on the positive role that doubt and skepticism played in traditional Confucianism. Heisig, Kasulis, and Maraldo, 292. See also Chapters 12 and 13 in this volume.

[24] Nishimura Shigeki, "An Explanation of Twelve Western Words" (1875), in Braisted, 446–449.

[25] Carol Gluck, *Japan's Modern Myths: Ideology in the Late Meiji Period* (Princeton, NJ: Princeton University Press, 1985) 253–255 and 381, note 19. The word for "progress" (*shinpo* 進歩) had been used earlier in the Tokugawa era, but the idea of progress that Fukuzawa imported "was revolutionary because it so totally contravened [the] conventional wisdom" of Confucian Japan. Craig, 3.

[26] Fukuzawa Yukichi, *Bunmei ron no gairyaku* [An Outline of Theories of Civilization] (Tokyo: Iwanami Shoten, 1931, 1984), 9.

however, is to an advanced stage in the historical development of a people. Fukuzawa adopted this meaning from American geography textbooks that, in turn, had inherited it from Scottish philosophers and scholars later associated with the European Enlightenment. Some of them also wrote of an "enlightened" stage, to indicate either an aspect of the "civilized" stage or, depending on the author, a stage even more advanced. Fukuzawa took the two words in apposition and again gave a new meaning to an obscure Japanese term to translate "enlightened": *kaika* (開化), with overtones of "opening" (*kai*) and "change" (*ka*).[27] *Bunmei kaika* became the standard expression that gets translated back into English as "civilization and enlightenment." This composite term also names the school of thinkers mentioned earlier and the historical movement they initiated in early Meiji Japan. In Fukuzawa, the composite term refers to the progressive, scientific, and intellectual achievements evident in Europe and America and thus to the ideal that Japan must achieve if it is to survive.[28] As a result of its fortuitous encounter with Western powers, according to Fukuzawa, Japan in fact was already in transition to this stage.

Often using the single term *bunmei* in his *Outline*, Fukuzawa adapted its European meaning to Japan's unique historical situation in the 1870s:

> Contemporary Japanese culture [*bunmei*] is undergoing a transformation in essence, like the transformation of fire into water, like the transition from non-being to being. The suddenness of the change defies description in terms of either reformation or creation. Yet, as a result of the jolt to the mind of Japanese people, their sights are now being reset on the goal of elevating Japanese civilization to parity with the West, or even of surpassing it . . . . We have the advantage of being able directly to contrast our own personal pre-Meiji experience with Western civilization . . . . We can attest to the changes of history through the more reliable witness of personal experience. This actual experience of pre-Meiji Japan is the accidental windfall we scholars of the present day enjoy.[29]

Fukuzawa effectively reinvented the idea of civilization. So momentous was his creative adaptation that one American scholar urges us to reassess Fukuzawa "as a Western as well as a Japanese thinker," because he

> dealt with complex Western ideas more extensively and with greater facility than most of his compatriots, and found in them a significance that had escaped their original authors. He used the Western idea of "stages of history" prescriptively to plot

---

[27] See Craig, 39–46, for an illuminating account of Fukuzawa's sources. In *An Outline*, Fukuzawa also relied on the 1846 English translation of François Guizot's *Histoire de la civilisation en Europe* and Henry Thomas Buckle's *History of Civilization in England* (1857).

[28] Fukuzawa's evaluation was reversed in the discourse on "overcoming modernity" in the early 1940s: "civilization and enlightenment" became a term of derision symbolizing decadent western values. For examples, see Richard F Calichman, *Overcoming Modernity: Cultural Identity in Wartime Japan* (New York: Columbia University Press, 2008), viii, 31, 98, 168, 191–194.

[29] Fukuzawa 2009, 3.

Japan's future course, and descriptively to analyze its past and present. In so doing he logically extended Enlightenment thought in a direction unexplored by Western thinkers, and with a greater facility and rigor than any other non-Western thinker.[30]

There is a distinct irony, however, in Fukuzawa's extension of the meaning of "civilized and enlightened." He adapted an idea that in the West was intended to exclude non-Western cultures from the ranks of the civilized. He accepted as globally demonstrated the Scottish Enlightenment's division of peoples into categories like primitive, semi-developed, and civilized.[31] Civilized people had framed the laws of the universe, discovered the basis of invention, learned self-control, spontaneously cultivated virtue, and refined their knowledge.[32] Today, this sort of classification may seem utterly naïve and biased, but Fukuzawa's use of it exposed its latent Eurocentrism and opened it to a more global and relative viewpoint. At the same time, he neglected to mention the way that European nations had attempted to civilize other peoples through imperialism and colonization, a practice that Japanese government officials saw as a threat to their own nation and one that they would emulate from the 1890s to the 1940s. When Fukuzawa wrote "we cannot be satisfied with the present level of attainment of the West,"[33] he envisioned a future in which the West could learn from Japan.[34] In the pursuit of imperialism, however, it was the other way around.

Fukuzawa extended not only the range of peoples who would count as civilized. His treatise also implied an extension of the way to progress. A people could progress not only along a gradual, linear path to civilization (i.e., by inheriting and improving on the achievements of their predecessors). A people like the Japanese could reach and even surpass the level achieved by Europeans because a new way had opened to them, the way of *experience*: they had lived through the experience of confronting an alien civilization. Fukuzawa used the word *keiken* (経験), his translation of the English *experience* and the same word that Nishida Kitarō would later select to speak of "pure experience."[35]

[30] Craig, ix.

[31] Fukuzawa 2009, 17–18. A more common scheme in the Scottish writers and American geographers included four stages, adding "barbarous" after "savage" (Craig, 35). Part of the confusion generated by the encounter with Western powers was due to the opinion, widespread since the sixteenth-century contact with Portuguese traders and missionaries, that Europeans were barbarians. In the 1860s, Fukuzawa's views competed with those of rebels who would "revere the emperor, expel the barbarians," as the popular slogan had it.

[32] Translation by Craig, 104.

[33] Fukuzawa 2009, 20.

[34] Some scholars today suggest that future has arrived: the Harvard historian Niall Ferguson asks "if we can come up with a good explanation for the West's past ascendancy [from the fourteenth to the twenty-first-centuries], can we then offer a prognosis for its future? Is this really the end of the West's world and the advent of a new Eastern epoch? Put differently, are we witnessing the waning of an age when the greater part of humanity was more or less subordinated to the civilization that arose in Western Europe?" *Civilization: The West and the Rest* (New York: Penguin Books, 2011), xv.

[35] Although I cannot be sure that Nishida read Fukuzawa's *Outline*, it is evident that as a high school student he had at least read parts of *An Encouragement of Learning* and continued to admire Fukuzawa. See Michiko Yusa, *Zen and Philosophy: An Intellectual Biography of Nishida Kitarō* (Honolulu: University of Hawai'i Press, 2002), 26, 64, 346 note 60.

The argument and style, as much as the content, of *An Outline* demonstrated that Japan was on its way to its own distinct form of civilization. Chapter 1 sets out a basis for argumentation: establish a point of view, compare and contrast, use common sense. "People can judge for themselves" the strengths and weaknesses of old and new theories.[36] Fukuzawa teaches his readers how to argue in this fashion by employing these methods himself. He is explicit about his own point of view: "My own criterion [for judgment] . . . will be that of Western civilization."[37] Further on in chapter 2, he illustrates how one can sweep away "blind attachments" to old practices. In an answer to his critics a year later, he added "methodic doubt and selective judgment" to these procedures, noting that the West had "advanced its civilization by systematically doubting established truths" and by following a "zig-zag course between competing interpretations."[38] In his *Outline*, he refers to historical tensions that encourage "dissident thought and the play of reason" that will enable Japan to outpace China in adapting Western ways.[39] The mark of his argumentation is to eschew all traditional Confucian and Buddhist appeals to authority and to directly express his own thoughts in a style that captures his sense of *enzetsu* (演説), a word he adapted to translate the concept of a public speech.[40]

Fukuzawa also made a case for Western thinking by employing novel distinctions. A central chapter of *Outline* is devoted to the distinction between knowledge or wisdom (*chi* 智) on the one hand and virtue (*toku* 徳) on the other. Earlier chapters had linked the two concepts to argue that the progress of civilization depends on the development of both capacities in a people. In chapter 6, Fukuzawa felt the need to draw a line between wisdom and virtue. Why? It seems that the civilization he advocated required a different sort of wisdom, an intellectual knowledge quite distinct from moral virtue, and he wanted to make that crystal clear.

The Confucian precedent had been to present wisdom as one of the virtues. Knowledge or the exercise of wisdom was ultimately practical and connected to the moral life of humans. Fukuzawa's distinction contradicted that tradition and promoted instead a distinctly modern Western view of knowledge. The meanings of several terms are at stake here, with no direct correspondence between Fukuzawa's English lexicon and his Japanese terms. In colloquial English, we tend to distinguish intelligence as a mental capacity, wisdom as a sense of good judgment acquired through experience, and knowledge as the content of what we have learned. Fukuzawa tends to use his terms more or less synonymously and to blend these meanings. He begins with the standard Confucian term *chi*, by which he says he means *chi-e* (智恵) and gives the Latin

---

[36] Fukuzawa 2009, 9.

[37] Fukuzawa 2009, 20.

[38] The first quotation is Craig's paraphrase; the second is his translation of Fukuzawa. Craig, 108.

[39] Craig, 113; Fukuzawa, *Bunmei no gairyaku*, 35.

[40] In *Yukichi Fukuzawa: The Making of the Modern World* (Hampshire, NY: Palgrave, 2002, 43), Alan Macfarlane claims that Fukuzawa invented the now common word *enzetsu* (演説), but Suzuki Hideo (p. 279) says it is an old word given new meaning to translate *speech*, just as *jiyū* (自由) was used anew to translate *liberty*.

derivative "intellect" as a synonym. Let us call it simply "knowledge." Tactful in his challenge to the Confucian tradition, he then expands the distinction at stake to include the difference between private and public, which can qualify both knowledge and virtue. The public manifestation of knowledge is what counts for civilization, and its development from private knowledge requires *sōmei eichi* (聡明叡知), roughly, "the wisdom of intelligence." In the popular understanding of the terms, Fukuzawa writes, the "wisdom [of intelligence] should not be called a virtue."[41] I would surmise that, for Fukuzawa, the traditional virtue of personal, moral wisdom bore little resemblance to the disinterested, objective kind of knowledge he found to be the basis of Western civilization.[42] Public knowledge was far more crucial than virtue, private or public, to the progress of civilization.[43] Here, Fukuzawa differed sharply with one proposed way to modernize the nation by combining "Japanese spirit and Western technology."

It is also telling that Fukuzawa showed little interest in other aspects often considered central to a civilization: the arts, music, and literature—"high culture" in other words. He mentions literature in a broad sense (*bungaku* 文学) as one of its aspects, but paid little heed to the "nonpractical" aspects of Western civilization.[44] This was not because he overlooked civilization's "spiritual" dimension, as his frequent invocation of the intangible but pervasive "spirit" of a people or civilization makes clear.[45] Yet the aspects of "the civilization that first appeared in the West" most important to Fukuzawa were its sciences, technology, inventions, and political systems. His disinterest in the aesthetic accomplishments of his own culture mirrors that of his fellow Enlightenment thinkers. It was left to the American Ernest Fenollosa, in the 1880s one of the first philosophy professors at the University of Tokyo, to foster appreciation of Japan's arts in that country and abroad. Fukuzawa Yukichi's interest lay in promoting the art of governing a free and independent people with universal equal rights.

[41] Fukuzawa 2009, 101.

[42] As far as I know, Fukuzawa does not invoke the new term *kyakkan-teki* (客観的), the translation of "objective" later used by Inoue Tetsujirō and Inoue Enryō that is standard today. He does, however, clarify that intelligence "deals with external things," "functions in reference to external circumstances and . . . is the exact opposite of morality." Fukuzawa 2009, 107.

[43] Fukuzawa does, to be sure, contend that "knowledge and virtue, together, are as necessary for civilized society" as fish and meat (along with grains and vegetables) are for the bodily nourishment. Fukuzawa 2009, 105. He makes clear, however, that the reason for Japan's low level of civilization is the relative lack of knowledge or "outward-directed intelligence."

[44] Craig, 89.

[45] See Craig, 106, for one of the explanations Fukuzawa gives of spirit or "ethos" (*kifū* 気風), and Craig, 102, on Fukuzawa's limited admiration of Western civilization.

Katō Hiroyuki: The Evolution of the Individual and Human Rights

Katō Hiroyuki (1836–1916) was, like Fukuzawa, born into a samurai family, steeped first in Confucian classics and then in Dutch Studies, and participated in the discussions of the "Meiji Six" Enlightenment thinkers. Unlike Fukuzawa, he drew his ideas primarily from German texts, eventually became a government functionary and advisor, and served as an administrator of the academy of Western studies that became the University of Tokyo, where he taught and served as president. He was, in turn, loyal to the Tokugawa shogunate at the end of its reign, supportive of Japan's opening to the West, and an advocate of a strong, central government in the Meiji Era. His primary questions included the proper role of government; the origin and nature of morality, laws, and rights; and the method for establishing the truth about the nature of human beings. In the late 1870s, he was exposed to the theory of evolution and its purported relevance for social development, and he became convinced that the proper method for establishing truth was empirical science; it alone could explain all matters of significance. On the way to this position of naturalism—the reduction of philosophical issues to the "facts" established by the natural sciences—Katō was forced to frame his questions in terms that were by no means transparent to his readers.

An example is the question of "rights." As much contemporary debate as there is concerning the nature and origin of human rights, in the twenty-first century we share an understanding of the term that was not available to nineteenth-century Japanese. The term they eventually used to translate the Dutch word *regt* and its European cognates was a neologism, *kenri* (権利). As usual with such neologisms, the term was a compound of sinographs that both independently and in other combinations carried familiar nuances, in this case, implications of power or authority (権) and of advantage or benefit (利). Singly, the sinographs were common enough, but the new compound *kenri*, and more so the idea behind it, were puzzling.[46] The familiar idea was that of obligations (*giri* 義理), which were relative to particular relationships between people and therefore relatively flexible. There was no notion of "rights" as an entitlement due exclusively to one party of a relationship. The distinction between rights and duties would have made little sense to Confucian-educated Japanese, for although duties were by nature reciprocal, if unequal, and varied according to the relationship between parties, everyone had duties, just as we today might think that everyone has rights.[47] Understanding what "human rights" meant was also difficult, I suspect, because the conception of the individual assumed in the Western notion of human rights was lacking. Such rights are often ascribed to a person simply by virtue of their being a human being, an individual person.

[46] On the difficulty of the meaning, see Yanabu, 151–172.

[47] Contributing to the difficulty of distinguishing the two was Fukuzawa's early translation of "rights" as *tsūgi* (通義) in his *Conditions of the West,* which uses the sinograph that usually denotes duties (義). In *An Encouragement of Learning* Fukuzawa uses the apposition *kenri tsūgi* (権理通儀) to translate "rights,"

The idea of "the individual" or "individual person" posed serious challenges to the early Japanese translators. *Kojin* (個人), the combination of sinographs that Fukuzawa settled on and the translation that has become standard, implied a solitary or singled out human being who in fact always exists in relationships with others. The Japanese term *jin* or *hito* (人) bore no hint of the autonomy and self-subsistence of the individual person more or less taken for granted in the Western notion.[48] One recent scholar, perhaps overstating the case, explains the difficulty:

> [In Japan] an individual is *not considered to be an independent entity*. Rather, *his interest is absorbed in the interest of the collectivity* to which he belongs, and the interest of the collectivity is recognized as having primary importance … there is no place for the concept of the individual as an independent entity equal to other individuals.[49]

This observation is clear enough in English, but it would have been obtuse to the early Japanese compilers of dictionaries. Similarly, we read without batting an eye Fukuzawa's statement that the "equality [of people] means equality in essential [or universal] human rights,"[50] but the term he used for rights, *kenri*, would have caught the notice of his readers in the mid-1870s. He used the new word only after circumscribing its meaning several times in expressions such as "not obstructing or hindering one another." He also took care to distinguish from any sense of selfishness his notions of rights and of freedom and independence (*jiyū jizai* 自由自在). In adopting this old Japanese phrase, he faced the difficulty of the convoluted meanings of *jiyū*, which in popular usage could connote selfish indulgence, but could also recall the sense in Zen texts of an unhindered mind in action—both of which differed from the modern Western political sense of individual freedom from oppression that he wished to convey.[51]

writing the sinograph 理 instead of 利 that became standard for *ri* in *kenri*, the usual term for "rights" today (*Gakumon no susume* [Tokyo: Iwanami shoten, 1978], 21). Katō's later discussions of egoism (*riko* 利己) and altruism (*rita* 利他) also use 利, connoting benefit. The Korean Confucian Yu Kil-chun (1856–1914), influenced by Fukuzawa, also used the term 通義 (pronounced *t'ong'ŭi* in Korean) to refer to the rights of the people, but understood it in terms of universally recognized duties, writing for example that "one has to control the overuse of liberty [自由] with *t'ong'ŭi* [通義] as it can teach indulgence." Cited in Yeonsik Choi, "Yu Kil-chun's Moral Idea of Civilization and Project to Make All People Gentlemen," *Asian Philosophy* 24.2 (May 2014): 113. Nishi Amane had also attempted to differentiate rights and duties. See Koizumi Takashi's extensive article *"Genpōteikō" ni okeru Nishi Amane no kenri shisō: Fukuzawa Yukichi no tenpu-jinken shisō to hikaku shite* [Nishi Amane's Ideas of Rights in Comparison with Fukuzawa Yukichi], *Shimane Journal of North East Asian Research* 14–15 (March 2008), 87–102.

[48] Similarly, *jinkaku* (人格), the standard translation of the philosophical term "person" and of the German *Persönlichkeit* (personality or personhood), originally connotes the class (格) to which humans (人) belong.

[49] Kawashima Takeyoshi, "The status of the individual in the notion of law, right, and social order in Japan," in Moore 1968, 431 and 440.

[50] Fukuzawa 2013, 13.

[51] Yanabu (175–191) discusses the various senses of *jiyū* (freedom), noting that it often had a socially negative meaning. At the end of the Tokugawa Period, for example, the Dutch word *vrijheid* (freedom) had been translated as *wagamama* (我がまま), that is, selfishness (Yanabu 178). But the positive meaning of the classical Chinese Zen terms *jiyū* and *jiyū jizai* (自由自在), which connoted functioning in a spontaneous, natural, and unobstructed way, also differed from the modern political sense. Yanabu 179;

Katō Hiroyuki never defined human rights (which he abbreviated to *jinken* 人権) in the abstract, but he must have anticipated that his readers would be able to gather the meaning of rights from the context and the specific examples he mentioned, such as the right to life and security of property, or the right to vote. Katō refers to the "startling idea," unprecedented in China and Japan, "that men are by nature equal, that they are endowed by Heaven with Natural Rights."[52] But his thinking about human rights underwent an evolution of its own. Several distinctions are at stake in untangling his views. The question of whether rights were natural or not depended on several senses of "natural," not all of them evident to the discussants. Early in his career, Katō wrote of "human rights endowed by Heaven" (*tenpu jinken* 天賦人権), but he stripped the Confucian notion of Heaven of any sense of a transcendent power. Still, if we retranslate his term as "natural rights," we need to avoid the connotation that rights derive somehow from the "nature" or dignity of each individual and his or her natural desire for happiness. Katō's "natural rights" also differed from anything ascribable to the "state of nature" imagined by Western thinkers like Hobbes, who proposed that the individual's natural right was to "use his own power ... for the preservation of his own Nature."[53] Katō rejected the idea of any such state of nature at the beginning of human history as empirically unverified and so entirely specious. By the time he published the influential essay "A New Theory of Human Rights" in 1882, he also repudiated the notion of heavenly endowed rights as a useless illusion.

Katō nevertheless left open another sense of natural rights, although he would not have called it that. Rights, he argued, naturally evolved through history when "superior entities" suppressed their own power in order to serve their own best interests. He adopted the general principle "superiors win, inferiors lose," but with a distinct twist from the Darwinist idea of survival of the fittest. Katō proposed that natural evolution led to the social evolution of humans who progressed in intellectual prowess and social and political ability. The state, too, was a product of natural and social evolution, and its power and rights superseded those of its individual members. The view that rights evolve was Katō's distinct contribution to the discussion about natural rights. As debatable as it may be, his view offers an alternative to another distinction he recognized to be relevant to discussions about the origin of ethics, namely that between natural (*tennen*

Iriya Yoshitaka and Koga Hidehiko, eds., *Zengo jiten* [Dictionary of Zen Terms] (Kyoto: Shibunkaku, 1991), 180.

[52] David Abosch, "Katō Hiroyuki, and the Introduction of German Political Thought in Modern Japan: 1868–1883," Ph.D. dissertation, University of California, Berkeley, 1964, 324, cited in W. Davis, 11. In the following, I draw from the lucid summary of Katō's views in W. Davis, who explains the European sources of Katō's theories as well as the opposing view of Ueki Emori, a leader of the Freedom and People's Rights Movement in the 1880s.

[53] Hobbes, *Leviathan* 1, XIV. Bob Tadashi Wakabayashi has exposed the Confucian roots of Katō's early formulations and their difference from Western Enlightenment views of natural rights. He seems, however, to overlook the problem of invoking the notion of "the individual." See his article "Katō Hiroyuki and Confucian Natural Rights, 1861–8170," *Harvard Journal of Asiatic Studies* 44/2 (1984): 469–492.

天然) and artificial (*jin-i* 人為). For later Katō, morality is neither entirely a natural phenomenon nor an offspring of human nature, nor is it merely a human invention. Morality rather is a product of natural and social selection.[54]

Two distinctions central to modern Western ethics were missing in Katō's later discussions: the distinction between *is* and *ought*, and that between *morality* and *law*. Katō put the latter two in apposition in his work of 1910, *The Progress of Morality and Law*, which distinguished various forms of egoism and altruism.[55] Katō's conflation of the moral and the legal was entirely consistent with his philosophical naturalism that reduced values to facts. For a naturalist like him, a distinction between *what is* and *what ought to be* would assume an unbridgeable difference between the status quo and a desirable state of affairs, but that difference is leveled in the natural and social evolution of human civilization. Morality (and law) are but the objective, social expressions of subjective egoism and altruism, and consideration for the interests of others is but a naturally evolved form of the self-interest that Katō saw evident in animals and "primitive" humans. Individualism, by implication, is a primitive form of human evolution. At least by connecting egoism and altruism, Katō differed from Darwin and Spencer and anticipated the evolutionary naturalism of contemporary philosophers like Daniel Dennett.[56] Katō's views also sparked a debate with his younger colleague at the University of Tokyo, Inoue Tetsujirō, who argued for the autonomy of altruism and of ethics.[57]

What these discussions and debates obscure is the problematic nature of the notion of "the individual" for the Meiji Enlightenment figures. Early on, Katō had been the first to distinguish private and public rights, and, like Fukuzawa, he continually invoked terms that we retranslate as the individual or person. But their struggle to gain acceptance of their views was in part an effort to make clear for themselves the scope of the Western notions.

INOUE TETSUJIRŌ: THE CREATION OF HISTORICAL AND SYSTEMATIC PHILOSOPHY IN JAPAN

Inoue Tetsujirō (1855–1944), along with the unrelated Inoue Enryō (1858–1919), deserve credit for formulating Japanese intellectual traditions as "philosophy" and for

---

[54] Katō's evolved position also resolves the "contradiction" that Wakabayashi, 409, finds in his earlier views: on the one hand, Katō declared that Heavenly endowed rights stem from "natural desires for unrestricted independence," but, on the other hand, he asserted that the state, for its own best interests, endows people with rights.

[55] Katō Hiroyuki, "*Dōtokuhōritsu no shinpo*," excerpted in Senuma 1974, 27–30.

[56] See Daniel C. Dennett, *Freedom Evolves* (New York: Viking, 2003).

[57] For a summary of this debate, see W. Davis, 43–51. For a sample of the general debate between the two, see Heisig, Kasulis, and Maraldo, 566–567.

developing philosophical systems of their own.[58] Both appropriated Western philosophical categories to recast old traditions and renew them as relevant for a modernized Japan. Inoue Tetsujirō also shared some interests with Katō Hiroyuki, his senior professor and administrator at the newly renamed Imperial University of Tokyo. Like Katō, he was concerned with the nature of morality, the role of government, and the proper method for establishing truths about human beings and the world they live in. He, too, became an outspoken advocate of state power over individual rights. Inoue's theory of a "national morality," his increasing nationalism, and his construction of bushidō or the "way of the samurai," are topics that deserve separate treatment.[59] With the exception of a growing political conservatism, however, Inoue differed significantly from Katō in his philosophical training and convictions. After an education in the Chinese classics, he mastered English; studied in Germany from 1884 to 1890 with Eduard von Hartmann, Wilhelm Wundt, and others; and then became the first Japanese to hold a chair in philosophy at the University of Tokyo. He lectured on Western philosophy in general but specialized in German thought and—as he came to call them—the philosophies of Confucian thinkers.

Inoue rejected Katō's philosophical materialism and naturalism and engaged in written debates with Katō about the scope of philosophy and science. He presented philosophy as a systematic investigation of things in general, with methods not limited to establishing facts, as is the case with the specialized, empirical sciences. Only philosophy can achieve a unified view of the world. Unlike the sciences and mathematics, moreover, philosophy aims at spiritual peace or unperturbed mind.[60] Inoue seems to have drawn this goal, philosophy's "loftiest ideal," from the Eastern traditions he studied, and this conception helped him make a case that they were as philosophical—if not more so—than modern Western philosophies.

Inoue's agenda to establish Eastern thought as tetsugaku began early in his career. Katō Hiroyuki had ensured that Indian and Chinese studies were represented at the University of Tokyo, but it was Inoue Tetsujirō who promoted them as legitimate areas of philosophy. Even before going to Germany, he supplemented his early works, such as Lectures on Western Philosophy and the eclectic New Theory of Ethics, with a History of Eastern Philosophy, and he gave lecture courses on Chinese and Eastern philosophies. This general endeavor culminated in a monumental three-volume work suggesting a tripartite division in Japanese Confucian schools: The Philosophy of the Japanese Wang

---

[58] Tsuchida Kyōson claimed that Katō Hiroyuki was the first in Japan to construct a system of philosophy of his own. Kyoson Tsuchida, Contemporary Thought of Japan and China (London: Williams and Norgate, 1927), 41. W. Davis (107–109) also regards Katō's mature thought as "a philosophical system" but considers Katō a derivative thinker at best.

[59] See Chapters 13 and 14 in this volume, and also Heisig, Kasulis, and Maraldo 2011, 1104–1105; Reitan 2010; Johann Nawrocki, Inoue Tetsujirō (1855–1944) und die Ideologie des Götterlandes (Hamburg: Lit Verlag, 1998); Piovesana 1997, 38–39; and Winston Davis, "The civil theology of Inoue Tetsujirō," Japanese Journal of Religious Studies 3.1 (March 1976).

[60] "A Bit of My Worldview," published in Japan's first journal of philosophy, Tetsugaku zasshi in 1884, partially translated by Clinton Godart in Heisig, Kasulis, and Maraldo 2011, 611–618.

Yangming School (1900), *The Philosophy of the Japanese Zhu Xi School* (1906)—both focusing on Japan's versions of traditions we now call Neo-Confucianism—and *The Philosophy of the Japanese Ancient Learning School* (1902), focusing on thinkers like Itō Jinsai and Ogyū Sorai who returned to ancient Confucian thought and analyzed its basic concepts in their lexicons. Inoue's work came at a time when Japanese intellectuals debated whether there ever was such a thing as philosophy in Japan—or in China for that matter.[61] The appellation *tetsugaku* that he applied to the Chinese and Japanese traditions could by no means be taken for granted. But rather than present arguments that these schools of thought deserve the name of philosophy, Inoue cast them as philosophical in two ways.

First, Inoue presented their teachings historically, as investigations and debates among individuals in search of truth. These mostly Confucian Chinese and Japanese thinkers influenced one another through the centuries both in the content and the terms of their discussions. Implicitly for Inoue, their appeal to authority was not a fallacy or shortcoming of independent thinking, but rather a recognition of the historical and contextual nature of philosophizing. One way, then, that Inoue made these thinkers into philosophers, *tetsugaku-sha* (哲学者), was by placing them in a historical context, in a word, by historicizing them. This effort echoed the endeavors in Japan, starting about 1890, to establish the existence and field of "Japanese literature" by writing its history and to establish Buddhism as a legitimate academic field and a worthwhile philosophy in its own right by subjecting it to historical and philological studies. Inoue's effort also reminds us of similar endeavors in China, on the part of Hu Shih in 1919 and Feng Youlan in 1934, to authenticate Chinese thought as "philosophy" (also written in China with Nishi Amane's neologism as 哲学) by writing its history. For the Chinese historians, as for Inoue, the philosophy of these national traditions relativized Western philosophy. Inoue argued that if the philosophy of a nation was to remain alive, however, it needed renewed thinking in light of both East and West. By historicizing Japanese intellectual traditions, Inoue was not relegating them to a past that was overcome by a new, international Japan. Rather, he took his work as a demonstration that Japan had been and could remain an authentic philosophical force in the world. At this point, his philosophical concerns intersected with his nationalist political interests.

Inoue was able to cast Japanese intellectual traditions as philosophy in another manner as well, by presenting them systematically in the terms of Western schools of thought. Often, the Western terms allowed definition of the Japanese schools by way of contrast. Inoue contrasted the Yōmei or Japanese Wang Yangming School, for example, with the individualistic ethics and utilitarianism that were the first forms of Western philosophy to enter modern Japan. He invoked "idealism," "realism," "materialism," and "epistemological objectivism" and "subjectivism" to describe Japanese as well as Western philosophical positions, even where he contrasted the two traditions. The Japanese

---

[61] My "Overview, "Beginnings, Definitions, Disputations," in Heisig, Kasulis, and Maraldo 2011, 553–582, gives a summary of these debates. In Chapter 12 in the present volume, John Tucker discusses Inoue's contribution to the formation of Japanese Confucian thought as philosophy.

translations of these terms were still unsettled, although many eventually became standard and are still used. The irony of rendering familiar Japanese Confucian thought in enigmatic Western categories should not go unnoticed. We tend to forget the neoteric tone they must have had in the early Meiji era. For the most part, the translations were neologisms, new combinations of traditional sinographs that carried nuances remote from the connotations of Western philosophical vocabulary. Some translations partially borrowed Buddhist terms but were tweaked to suggest new or additional meanings.

The terms for subject, subjective, and subjectivism in the epistemological sense, for example—as for object, objective, and objectivism—were words with age-old reverberations: *shukan* (主観) for "subject," literally suggesting the viewpoint of a host or owner, and *kyakkan* (客観) for "object," suggesting a guest or recipient's view, or perhaps things outside one's own purview. To get a hint of the oddity of the new Japanese terms, we might imagine rendering the English term "subject" as "the under-cast" to retranslate the Latin *subjectum* that in turn translated the Greek *hypokeimenon*, "that which lies beneath." Japanese philosophers eventually complicated—or rather clarified—matters by introducing a distinction among three senses of "subject": the cognitive subject, *shukan*; the embodied or integral subject, *shutai* (主体); and the grammatical subject, *shugo* (主語). Only the first of these, *shukan*, was prevalent among the early Meiji philosophers.

It is important to remember that Inoue and his fellow translators confronted more than two millennia of Western philosophical vocabulary telescoped into two or three decades. They set about their chosen task of appropriating Western philosophy and redefining Japanese traditions as philosophical by compiling philosophical dictionaries, often with Inoue in the lead. Nishi Amane had begun the project of defining terms,[62] but Inoue and his collaborators systematized it in their editions of a *Dictionary of Philosophy* published in 1881, 1894, and 1912.[63] The final version added German and French translations to the first edition's English terms of definition and often supplemented the single Japanese translations with alternatives. That critics pointed out numerous errors[64] is another sign that philosophical language was still quite volatile. In 1909, a more comprehensive dictionary began appearing as part of a massive *Encyclopedia Japonica* that

---

[62] Nishi's efforts indicate a period of rapidly changing trial and error in the history of philosophical translation. His *Hyakugaku renkan* (System of one hundred sciences) of 1870 includes terms long since abandoned, such as *chichigaku* (致知学) for *logic* (*ronrigaku* 論理学 today), *ritaigaku* (理体学) for *ontology* (*sonzai ron* 存在論 today), and *meikyōgaku* (名教学) for *ethics* (*rinrigaku* 倫理学 today). In 1883, Kiyono Tsutomu was still using *kakuchi tetsugaku* (格致哲学) to translate *logic*, "the study that accounts for the greatest principles of how the human mind functions," but he soon replaced that neologism with the now standard term *ronrigaku*. For a fascinating account of attempts to translate the term "aesthetics," see Hamashita Masahiro, "Nishi Amane on Aesthetics: A Japanese Version of Utilitarian Aesthetics," in Marra 2002, 89–96. For a Japanese history of the translation of much philosophical vocabulary, see Ishizuka and Shibata 2013.

[63] *Tetsugaku ji-i* (哲学字彙) (Tokyo: Tokyo Daigaku, 1881) and Tetsujiro Inouye, Yujiro Motora, and Rikizo Nakashima, *Dictionary of English, German, and French Philosophical Terms with Japanese Equivalents* (Tokyo: Maruzen, 1912).

[64] Piovesana 1997, 42.

covered medicine, manufacturing, education, economics, and agriculture.[65] Inoue was one of about 75 professors who contributed the philosophical entries now supplemented by biographies, bibliographies, and scholarly comments. The headings under which this *Great Dictionary of Philosophy* organized its entries are indicative of the envisioned scope of philosophy and the other fields whose terms it defined: in addition to philosophy and its history, logic and theory of knowledge, and ethics and aesthetics, we find Eastern philosophy and Eastern ethics, Indian philosophy, the philosophy of Shintō, Buddhist philosophy, Christianity and Judaism, psychology, child studies, religion, sociology and law, linguistics, pedagogy, biology, anthropology, and psychiatry. Biographies of Eastern as well as Western philosophers were appended.[66] By the 1920s, philosophical terminology was fairly well established. Japanese words for standard Western terms either replaced the early translations or veiled the Confucian and Buddhist flavor detectable in many of them. An example is the word *kannen ron* (観念論), which replaced Inoue's Buddhist-flavored *yuishin ron* (唯心論), literally the theory of mind-only, to translate "idealism."[67]

Inoue appropriated Western philosophy and recreated Japanese philosophy by systematizing their types as well as their terms. The tripartite division of Japanese Confucian schools of thought mentioned earlier was largely his own invention and application of Hegelian dialectics.[68] His efforts to establish the critical study of Japanese and other Asian traditions in the University of Tokyo's Department of Philosophy ultimately came to no avail. More than one hundred years later, as of 2019, there is but

[65] The massive encyclopedia was called *Dai nihon hyakka jisho* (大日本百科辭書).

[66] *Tetsugaku dai jisho* (哲學大辭書) (Tokyo: Dōbunkan, 1909), with three volumes of entries, one supplement, and one index. A "much better philosophical dictionary" (Piovesana 1997, 79–80), published in 1922, was Miyamoto Wakichi et al., eds., *Iwanami tetsugaku jiten* (岩波哲學辭典) (Tokyo: Iwanami Shoten), followed in 1930 by a smaller one, compiled by Itō Kichinosuke, the several editions of which became the standard for many years. A dozen or so dictionaries of philosophy have since appeared, including the *Dictionary of Contemporary Philosophy* (*Gendai tetsugaku jiten* 現代哲学辞典), edited by Miki Kiyoshi (Tokyo: Nihon Hyōronsha, 1936), that includes an entry by Kanba Toshio on Japanese philosophy and its particular characteristics, as well as the philosophy of the Meiji Era, post-World War I philosophy, and "philosophy for a time of emergency."

[67] See the entry for "idealism" in Inoue's dictionaries and his "A Bit of My Worldview," 148–149. As a traditional term, *yuishin* referred to the Buddhist theory that the world ordinarily perceived is a projection of one's own deluded mind. Inoue used the term *kannen ron* to denote the more inclusive position which, in its various versions, proposed that the objective world is a product of the knowing subject, in contrast to the view of the realist school (*jitsuzai ha* 実在派). In other words, Inoue's *yuishin ron* or "idealism" was but one type of what we generally designate as philosophical idealism.

[68] Tucker, in Heisig, Kasulis, and Maraldo (291), mentions that there is "scant documentary ground for Inoue's triadic approach to Tokugawa Confucianism." In another work, Tucker interprets Inoue's tripartite division in terms of a Hegelian thesis, antithesis, and synthesis, with a twist: Inoue resurrected the name Ancient Learning and interpreted its school as the higher synthesis of the other two schools that historically came later; but then—reflecting his nationalism and valorization of *bushidō*—he also presented the views of the seventeenth-century Japanese initiator of the Ancient Learning School, Yamaga Sokō, as its crowning achievement. John A Tucker, *Ogyū Sorai's Philosophical Masterworks* (Honolulu: Association for Asian Studies and University of Hawai'i Press, 2006), 103–104; see also Chapters 12 and 13 in this volume.

one chair in Japanese philosophy in all of Japan, and that is at Kyoto University. In the 1920s, the University of Tokyo established independent departments of Chinese philosophy and of Indian philosophy together with Buddhist Studies, with the latter including Japanese Buddhism. Professors of history, ethics, and religion in their own departments sometimes presented the history of Japanese Confucian thought—often using Inoue's tripartite division. But the University of Tokyo did not formally recognize "Japanese philosophy."

Inoue's organization of Western philosophy served both to appropriate Eastern thought into the domain of *tetsugaku* and to define the position he staked out as his own. An essay of 1884 titled "A Bit of My Worldview" offers a hint. Using standard Western categories, he starts off by dividing philosophy according to method and content. Logic defines the method of all philosophy and underlies all authentic worldviews. Inoue implies thereby that a logic can be discovered in traditional Eastern as well as Western thinkers, as is evident in his own treatment of their positions. He presents and then refutes the Vedantic "idealist" position, for instance, by citing its classic example of fallible consciousness and then explaining it differently. We mistake a rope lying on the ground for a snake, and that kind of mistake is what happens over and over again when we live deluded and unenlightened lives. So says Vedānta philosophy. Suppose, however, that we take a realist position and limit "truth" to what is governed by causality. Then the corroborating causes of what I took initially to be a snake would be missing, and I would see that this "snake" does not move or bite; hence, I would recognize my initial mistake—all within the ordinary world governed by the law of cause and effect. Only if the law of cause and effect turns out to be an illusion would the Vedantic position make sense. It is more likely that the extreme idealist position of Vedānta is the mistake.[69] This is Inoue's argument.

Inoue's organization of philosophy according to content likewise follows a traditional Western division: philosophy studies the true, the good, and the beautiful. Knowledge has to do with the truth, will or intention with the good, and feelings and emotions with the beautiful. The inquiry into the true focuses on the nature of mind, matter, and reality. Only such inquiry counts as "pure" or theoretical philosophy, and only it asks skeptically whether truth can be attained at all. Practical philosophy in the form of ethics and political philosophy discusses the good, and, in the form of aesthetics, it studies the beautiful. This organization sounds like the beginning of a rather time-worn and stereotypical introductory course on philosophy, until we again recall the relative novelty of Inoue's terms and distinctions for his Japanese readers. Even the word now common for "truth," *shinri* (真理), was unsettled, and the notion that humans may be incapable of attaining any truths at all was unsettling and probably unprecedented in Japanese thought.

Inoue followed the general path that we can indeed have knowledge. He advocated a position he described as a kind of realism as opposed to idealism. His position claimed that the phenomena we perceive are real "objects outside the subject" and not merely appearances behind which true reality lies. The opposing position earned an imaginative

---

[69] See Godart's translation in Heisig, Kasulis, and Maraldo, 618.

name for Inoue, the theory of "reality beyond the world [of experience]" (*kakyō-teki jitsuzai* 過境的実在) and apparently described Kant's transcendental philosophy of "things-in-themselves." The theory he preferred (and shared with Inoue Enryō, Kiyozawa Manshi, and Miyake Setsurei) used the Buddhist conjunction *soku* (即) to connect phenomena that "at the same time are" reality—"phenomena *qua* reality." They related this theory to the "*Identitätstheorie*" or "*Identitätsrealismus*" they found in German idealist philosophers. The notion of reality differing from appearances, or being identical with it, did have precedents in Japanese Buddhist thought, perhaps most explicitly in Indian Yogācāra theory as it was taken up by Buddhist scholars of the Hossō (法相) school in the eighth century who taught the reality or truth (*hō* 法) of all forms (*sō* 相) of the manifest world, once mental constructs are eliminated. But the modern Western epistemological problem was divorced from the psychological pathology of the knower and disconnected from any soteriology. The history of Western philosophy that Inoue taught his students thus placed the problem in a very different context. One can only imagine the challenge Inoue faced in making sense of "the problem of reality" to his University of Tokyo students; it likely appeared both strangely familiar yet oddly foreign. Eventually, certainly by the mid-twentieth century, it became common for Buddhist scholars to overlook the difference in context and use classifications such as "realism" and "idealism" to describe Buddhist philosophies.[70]

"A Bit of My Worldview" purported to represent the "world of thought of the Orient and Occident as a whole, and not to classify it in terms of West and East." Inoue defined his own position as a part of world philosophy. His epistemological position gives no hint of the role of historicity in knowledge, nor of the historical consciousness he must have gained in his acquaintance with Paul Deussen and Wilhelm Dilthey in Berlin.[71] But a strong sense of history, along with a keen ability to analyze terms and categories, enabled Inoue not only to appropriate Western philosophy in Japan but also incorporate Eastern thought into its province.

INOUE ENRYŌ: THE CONSTRUCTION OF BUDDHISM AS PHILOSOPHY AND PHILOSOPHY AS A BUDDHIST THEORY

Inoue Enryō (1858–1919) equaled if not surpassed Inoue Tetsujirō in casting the net of philosophy over Japanese traditions and defining new fields in Japan's modern academic

---

[70] An example is Junjiro Takakusu, *The Essentials of Buddhist Philosophy* (Honolulu: University of Hawai'i, 1947).

[71] Nawrocki, 113, note 274, cites the quoted statement and on page 96 mentions Inoue's "friendship" with Deussen, Dilthey, and Eduard von Hartmann.

institutions.[72] He promoted "pure" or theoretical philosophy and refashioned Buddhist thought in its terms.[73] Ordained a priest in the True Pure Land School at age thirteen, Enryō eventually left behind his childhood devotion to become one of Japan's great modernizers of the religion, seeking to demonstrate its scientific and philosophical nature. He was already well-versed in Chinese classics and "Western learning" and proficient in both English and German by the time he entered the newly established University of Tokyo in 1881 to study philosophy under Ernest Fenollosa, among other foreign professors. German speculative philosophy, along with Herbert Spencer's evolutionism, had by then replaced positivism and utilitarianism as the predominant interest of Japanese intellectuals and came to inform the philosophy that Enryō defined as his own. An ardent teacher and public lecturer, he traveled to China, Korea, and Okinawa, as well as throughout Japan, giving lectures that ranged from the folly of superstitious beliefs to the need to revitalize Buddhism in a critical period after its persecution. He also made excursions to the United States, Europe, and South Asia in 1888–89 and again in 1902–03, and in 1911–12 he journeyed to continents in the southern hemisphere as well. In 1887, Enryō started a private Academy of Philosophy in Tokyo to promote philosophical education more widely and later designed a "Temple Garden of Philosophy" to portray the organization of philosophical fields and present them to the general public; it included a temple to "the four sages," Confucius, Buddha, Socrates, and Kant. In 1906, his institute became Tōyō University; in 2011, its International Research Center for Philosophy was established. In another area of Tokyo, the Temple Garden still provides respite from the cacophony of the city.

Enryō shared Tetsujirō's nationalism and advocation of national morality[74] and paralleled Tetsujirō in rejecting Christianity as unscientific. Yet he considered religion in a much more positive light. Within Asian traditions, his focus was on Buddhism in general, not Japanese Confucianism, and he made Buddhism into philosophy not so much by historicizing it as by systematizing it in nontraditional terms. Both Inoues proved adept at classifying *tetsugaku* and defining it as a way of reaching truth retrospectively applicable to Eastern thought. And both forged their own syncretic philosophies. Eventually, Enryō claimed a priority for Eastern philosophy's "logic of mutual inclusion"—actually his own position that he also called "enryō philosophy," after the sinographs for his Buddhist name, meaning "circle" and "complete."[75]

[72] The most comprehensive treatment of Enryō in English is Reiner Schulzer, *Inoue Enryo: A Philosophical Portrait*. Albany: SUNY Press, 2019.

[73] For a more complete treatment, see the excellent discussion of Sueki Fumihiko, *"Junsei tetsugaku to bukkyō"* [Pure philosophy and Buddhism] in his book *Meiji shisōka ron* [The Theories of Meiji Thinkers] (Tokyo: Transview, 2004), 43–61. Sueki has also pointed out that Enryō qualified his alignment of Buddhism with philosophy and found them to be different in orientation although sharing a devotion to elucidating truth. *Newsletter of the Toyo University International Research Center for Philosophy* 7 (March 2014): 6.

[74] Two of many writings that give evidence of Enryō's nationalist stance are his *Nihon rinrigaku an* (Japanese Ethics: A Proposal), published in 1890, and his *Sensō tetsugaku ichihan* (A Fragment of a Philosophy of War), published when the Sino-Japanese war broke out in 1894.

[75] See the translation by Clinton Godart of an excerpt of Enryō's *View of the Cosmos*, in Heisig, Kasulis, and Maraldo 2011, 626.

Along his path to visualize the circle of his own philosophy, Enryō struggled to draw a coherent picture of the maze of positions he encountered in his studies, as puzzling for their method as for their content. His witty Preface to *An Evening of Philosophical Conversation* of 1886 samples several descriptions of this "new kind of discipline that has come from the West." It concludes with the quip that, since the descriptions of this new discipline all differ and show only that its nature is not yet known, *tetsugaku* is just that: "whatever we cannot know." Assuming the role of teacher, Enryō settles the matter by saying the differences in views arise precisely because the interlocutors do not know. In the dialogue proper, Enryō intrigues them with metaphysical questions of the relation between matter and mind, the substantiality of the divine, and the nature of truth. By the end, he has defined an early formulation of his ultimate position, a perfect harmony of differences.

The method and content of Enryō's dialogue deserve more explanation than is possible here,[76] but we may note the problem of language he faced. Like the other pioneers of philosophy in Japan, Enryō was compelled to invent a new language whose novelty is easily hidden to contemporary readers of nearly all his writings, particularly in translation. Philosophical terms perfectly familiar to us today were strange and puzzling to readers in Enryō's day. The contemporary reader of Enryō's Japanese will be aware of its archaic style, reminiscent of a Confucian lesson, but may still be oblivious of the originally neoteric tone of many terms and distinctions. Some terms were easily understandable. Enryō's lesson first mentions the difference between things with form, studied by the physical sciences, and things without, studied by philosophy. This paraphrases the distinction Fukuzawa had presented in his *Encouragement of Learning* and echoes much older Buddhist and Chinese language about form and the formless. Readers of Aristotle will recognize its parallel in the difference between *physics* and *metaphysics*. But there the veil of familiarity ends. For examples of the study of things without form, Fukuzawa had used compounds whose meaning often requires the reader's imagination. Without going into details, we may note that, at this stage of the appropriation of philosophy, the variety of terms used to translate standard Western categories belies the exotic and often enigmatic notions they were meant to convey.

A prime example of the Western philosophical problems that preoccupied Enryō is the relation between matter and mind, between things with form and something that is formless. To define this problem, he used the novel term *busshin* (物心), roughly "matter and mind," that, in a different context, could be read *monogokoro*, meaning *discretion*. Separately, the sinographs were as polysemous as the English words "thing" and "mind." Enryō's Temple Garden laid out one area in the shape of the sinograph for matter, another in the shape of that for mind, meant to express materialism and idealism, respectively. As a stable part of the history of modern philosophy in the West, this problem, now so familiar to us, would have seemed abstract and bizarre to Enryō's students. Does

---

[76] Wargo 2005, 11–17, gives a lucid summary and critique of the dialogue and shows its relevance to Nishida's philosophy. My translation of Enryō's Preface appears in Heisig, Kasulis, and Maraldo 2011, 561–562.

reality consist solely of matter (or matter-energy as we would say today), or is there room for a spiritual or immaterial reality that does not reduce to the material? Perhaps the material world itself is a mental construction. Perhaps the mind is an epiphenomenon or mere appearance arising from the material brain. There were remote precedents to these questions in Japanese Confucian debates regarding the relation between *ki* energy (気) and *ri* (理) or principle, with *ki* designating what we would call the physical dimension of reality and *ri* its rational, moral dimension. But the Confucians did not attempt to reduce one to the other. Indian Buddhist theories of consciousness in their Chinese and Japanese forms also prefigured the Western problem, but European philosophers took up the issue as purely theoretical, lacking the practical dimension of breaking through delusion and reaching enlightenment. The issue appears as one of the pressing concerns of philosophy around the globe today. Often called the "hard problem," it concerns the relation between the brain and consciousness.

In Enryō's vision, the problem was a contest between the equally one-sided views that took either the spiritual or the material aspects of reality as illusory. In one essay published in 1887, he sketched no less than eleven versions of the general problem.[77] Although the different positions bore unusual names, part of his classification reflects a Buddhist fourfold scheme. Matter and mind serve tentatively as dualistic explanatory principles, where one is affirmed and the other denied, in theories of (1) "matter only—no mind" and (2) "mind only—no matter." Complementing these positions are theories of (3) "neither matter nor mind" and (4) "both mind and matter." But Enryō complicates this scheme by subdividing the first three into unusual variations, such as materialism (*bushitsu ron* 物質論) and (oddly enough) mentalism (*shinsei ron* 心性論) as varieties of theory 1, consciousness-theory (*ishiki ron* 意識論) and self-awareness-theory (*jikaku ron* 自覚論) as varieties of 2, and sensualism (*kankaku ron* 感覚論) and nihilism (*mugenron* 無元論) as varieties of theory 3. He also adds the theory of matter and mind in concurrence, in its idealist version (*risō ron* 理想論), as well as in the theory of endless cyclical change (*junka ron* 循化論). The last mentioned was Enryō's own version of evolutionary theory.

We should keep in mind that Enryō placed the problem in all its versions in a soteriological context that aimed at the transformation of the viewer as well as at a true account of how things are.

We find one succinct statement of how Enryō resolves the differences in this bewildering variety in an essay of 1917:

> If we examine matter comprehensively, we end up back at mind, and if we examine mind comprehensively, we end up back at matter. Matter is one extreme and mind the other extreme. We might say that this union of the two extremes is what classical materialism and idealism have demonstrated clearly. The claim that either materialism or idealism is the truth is biased. Viewed from the outside, both are nothing

[77] *Tetsugaku yōryō* [The Gist of Philosophy], part two, *Inoue Enryō Senshū* [Selected Works] I (Tokyo: Tōyō University, 1987), 150–215.

other than two extremes of one and the same thing, two aspects of a single thing . . . .
I have called this the "theory of mutual containment and inclusion." . . . [It is] a
theory unknown in the West . . . [and] yet another point on which Eastern philosophy is one step ahead.[78]

The ultimate resolution of differences in "enryō philosophy" presents contradictions
as merely partial aspects of the truth in a logic proven "by the history of philosophy
East and West." But Eastern traditions better illustrate this resolution. Enryō sees this
resolution intimated in the familiar Chinese symbols of *yin* and *yang* that each contain the other.[79] We may note that it also reflects the Buddhist "middle way" between
extremes that he mentions in the *Evening of Philosophical Conversation*, and it mirrors
the unmentioned "interpenetration of all things in each other" (*jijimuge* 事事無礙) in
Kegon or Huayan Buddhism if we substitute philosophical positions for "things" (事).
Echoing the persuasion of Japanese Zen thinkers like Dōgen and Shingon thinkers like
Kūkai, Enryō affirms as real the very world we live in and can interpret from various
viewpoints. He approximates the reconciliation of contradictories in Hegel but refuses
Hegel's dialectical resolution in a higher synthesis and his historical progression toward a telos. Enryō's inclusion of an evolutionary perspective may come from Herbert
Spencer's ideas, but Enryō's evolution is circular or cyclical, with no hint of linear progress. It recalls instead the ancient Chinese theory of perpetual cosmic change. "Enryō
philosophy" also finds a place in the long Japanese tradition of promoting harmony that
stretches from Prince Shōtoku's *Seventeen-Article Constitution* of 604 to the nationalist
tracts of the 1930s, but Enryō recognizes distinctions rather than try to abolish them as
nationalists later did.[80] Notwithstanding all these influences, Enryō's theory of mutual
containment and inclusion is, I think, a coherent and innovative philosophical position. Its shortcoming was that it failed to explain just how the extreme of one position,
such as materialism, completed its circle in its opposite, such as the position of mind-
only. If we apply the standards of logic adopted by later Japanese philosophers, it seems
that Enryō's theory ultimately remained an assertion without sufficiently supportive
argument.

   If we consider Enryō's place in the history of Japanese philosophy, however, the matter
of logical argumentation may be set aside to throw light on another of his contributions.
Along with Inoue Tetsujirō, Enryō not only classified the various branches of Western
philosophy but also defined and promoted "pure philosophy." In contradistinction to
the practical interest of nearly all premodern Japanese philosophers, "pure philosophy"
meant purely theoretical philosophy. The very distinction between theoretical (*rironteki*
理論的) and practical (*jissenteki* 実践的 or *jissaiteki* 実際的) was relatively novel if not

---

[78] Translated by Clinton Godart, in Heisig, Kasulis, and Maraldo, 625–626. The original is *Inoue Enryō
Senshū* 2 (Tokyo: Tōyō Daigaku, 1987), 238, 240.

[79] Heisig, Kasulis, and Maraldo, 626.

[80] Compare Ono Seiichirō's statement "harmony consists in *not making distinctions*," interpreting the
Kokutai no hongi [Fundamental Principles of the National Polity] of 1937, cited in Kawashima, 431.

unprecedented in Japanese thought. Tetsujirō's dictionaries also used "pure philosophy" as a translation of "metaphysics," but for both Inoues it included what we would call epistemology, metaethics, and logic. Perhaps they were thinking of Kant's "pure philosophy," that is, metaphysics as "reason's knowledge derived purely from concepts."[81] The term was not widely used by the Western philosophers they read, but in Japan it acquired a momentum of its own. It became a synonym (or perhaps a synecdoche) for Western philosophy in general—minus ethics and aesthetics—in the designation of academic departments and journals, but it was current outside the academy as well. For Kuwaki Genyoku (1874–1946), successor to Inoue Tetsujirō, pure philosophy came to refer primarily to speculative German philosophy that excluded approaches like pragmatism and utilitarianism. For the Pure Land Buddhist philosopher Kiyozawa Manshi (1863–1903), pure philosophy referred to ontology. Writing in 1889 in a classical style but using unsettled vocabulary, he defined it as "the investigation of reality undergoing change," where reality referred to "all manifest beings in the universe," and change referred to their arising and perishing. Kiyozawa's notion had a distinct epistemological bent: "unlike the other disciplines that originate from the lack of clarity in things and principles, pure philosophy originates from contradictions between ideas or anticipations and the facts of experience."[82] For Inoue Enryō, pure philosophy is the field that investigates "the principles of the various disciplines, the truth of things, the rules of thought, and the like." Its goal is to "demonstrate and elaborate the foundations and principles of ethics, psychology, and other disciplines," in a word, to "investigate the truth of all matters."[83]

In the Preface to the *Evening of Philosophy Conversation*, Enryō informs his audience that "people are more or less familiar with psychology, logic, and so forth, but when it comes to pure philosophy, people haven't the slightest idea of what it is."[84] What could be said of *tetsugaku* twenty years earlier apparently still applied to the themes and questions usually taken as the most central to modern Western philosophy. The new interest in foundations changed the direction of philosophy in Japan. Nishi Amane had, of course, presented *tetsugaku* as an inquiry into principles, reminiscent of Confucian discourse on *ri* (理). He championed British utilitarian and French positivist philosophies, however, for their practical significance and culmination in science, respectively. Still rooted in a Confucian mindset that oriented all inquiry toward practical spiritual and

[81] Kant, *Metaphysische Anfangsgründe der Naturwissenschaft, Vorrede*, 1786. www.susannealbers. de/03philosophie-literatur-Kant6.html

[82] Kiyozawa Manshi, *Junsei tetsugaku* [Pure Philosophy], in Senuma 1974, 63. The translation of the term *ontology* was unsettled until about 1935. Kiyozawa used the term *jitsuzai ron* (実在論), now standard for "realism. "Reality" in the quoted statement renders his term *jittai* (實躰), traditionally used as the opposite of illusion (*maboroshi* 幻) but later as the standard translation of "substance." Kiyozawa's contributions to the appropriation of Western philosophy deserve a much more extensive treatment than can be given here; see Chapter 7 in the present volume.

[83] *Inoue Enryō Senshū* 1, 435. Enryō's essays on pure philosophy are copious and take up much of volumes 1, 2, and 7 of his *Selected Works*.

[84] Enryō continues: "Pure *tetsugaku*, as the study of the pure principles of *tetsugaku*, must be called the study that inquires into the axioms of truth and the foundation of the disciplines." Heisig, Kasulis, and Maraldo 2011, 561.

political ends, Nishi represents a path now relatively forgotten in the writings of modern Japanese philosophers.

For all his emphasis on pure philosophy, however, throughout his career, Enryō also emphasized the practical uses of philosophy and was committed to popularizing philosophy among the general public. He taught that philosophy benefits society as well as the mind by teaching people to appreciate intangible things and to value education and achievements in politics, morals, and arts. Indeed, the elimination of tyranny and the development of civilization depend on philosophical education.[85] Enryō did not discuss a possible discrepancy between his interest in "pure, theoretical philosophy" and his commitment to making philosophy practical. His philosophy of "mutual inclusion and containment" does not mention "theoretical" and "practical" as opposing approaches to be reconciled. Yet perhaps he assumed that the search for fundamental principles, characteristic of pure philosophy, formed the core of practical education for all people and so implicitly offered an alternative to the traditional Western distinction between theoretical and practical. In this regard, Enryō differed from Inoue Tetsujirō, for whom genuine philosophy was no discipline for the masses. In their promotion of pure philosophy, both Inoues represent a new phase in appropriating philosophy in Japan, but in their view of its purpose, they differed fundamentally.

Inoue Enryō and Inoue Tetsujirō also differed in the way they appropriated Japanese traditions into the domain of philosophy. Enryō, of course, focused on showing how Buddhism is philosophical, whereas Tetsujirō historically constructed the philosophy of Confucian schools. But Enryō took an ahistorical approach and located the problems treated by pure philosophy within Buddhist schools of thought. He sketched, for example, "Buddhist scientific theories" (*bukkyō rika* 仏教理科) of time, space, the cosmos, and cosmogeny, along with dozens of other theories, non-Buddhist as well, ranging from astronomy and meteorology to causation and existence. "Pure or theoretical philosophy" seems at times to become merely a collection of theories (*ron* 論) with no common basis. Once again, the significance of Enryō's work lies not so much in any rigor it displays as in its vision of the scope of philosophy. Taking the opposite direction from the philosophy department at the University of Tokyo, he expanded "pure philosophy" to include Indian, Chinese, Persian, and Egyptian *tetsugaku*, in addition to Buddhist theories.[86] Laozi and Zhuangzi contributed to pure philosophy, as did Dōgen and Shinran.[87] Enryō was probably the first to see Dōgen as engaging in *tetsugaku*.

[85]   Torano Ryō, "Tetsugaku no tsūsokuka to wa nanika" [What Is the Popularization of Philosophy?] *International Inoue Enryō Research* 2 (2014), 276. See also Enryō's *Tetsugakujō ni okeru yo no shimei* (My Mission in Philosophy), in *Yokai gendan* (Arcane Talks on the Mysterious), edited by Takemura Makio (Tokyo: Daitō Publishing, 2011), 282–289.

[86]   "Junsei tetsugaku kōgi" [Lectures on Pure Philosophy], in *Selected Works*, volume 7.

[87]   *Zenshū tetsugaku joron* [Prolegomenon to the Philosophy of the Zen School], 1893, and *Shinshū tetsugaku joron* [Prolegomenon to the Philosophy of the True Pure Land School], 1892, in *Selected Works*, volume 6, 247–326 and 179–246. See also Ralf Müller, "Die Entdeckung von Sprache im Zen: Inoue Enryōs *Prolegomena zur Philosophie der Zen-Schule von 1893*," in Steineck, Lange und Kaufmann, 63–105.

Many of Enryō's terms and classifications have become obsolete; other expressions, like "Buddhist idealism" or the "philosophy of Dōgen," are now commonplace. His theory of mutual containment and inclusion is largely forgotten. In formulating it, he cast a Buddhist-tinged net over Western philosophical positions, yet he also opened a way to regard Buddhism as genuinely philosophical. His *Evening of Philosophical Conversation* was a guiding inspiration for Nishida Kitarō, whose endeavors to uncover the ground of distinctions owe their initial spark to Enryō. After four decades of Meiji thinkers surveying the landscape of philosophy and defining myriads of terms, Nishida's return to experience must have seemed like a breath of fresh air. But the atmosphere that gave life to his early philosophical education was created by Inoue Enryō and his contemporaries in the Meiji Era.

BIBLIOGRAPHY AND SUGGESTED READINGS

Asou Yoshiteru. (2008) *Kinsei nihon tetsugaku shi* [History of Early Modern Japanese Philosophy]. Tokyo: Shoshi shinsu.

Braisted, Willian R. (1976) *Meiroku Zasshi: Journal of the Japanese Enlightenment*. Cambridge, MS: Harvard University Press.

Craig, Albert M. (2009) *Civilization and Enlightenment: The Early Thought of Fukuzawa Yukichi*. Cambridge, MA: Harvard University Press.

Davis, Winston. (1996) *The Moral and Political Naturalism of Baron Katō Hiroyuki*. Japan Research Monograph 13. Berkeley: University of California Center for Japanese Studies.

Fukuzawa Yukichi. (2009) *An Outline of a Theory of Civilization*, translated by David A. Dilworth with an introduction by Takenori Inoki. New York: Columbia University Press.

Fukuzawa Yukichi. (2013) *An Encouragement of Learning*, translated by David A. Dilworth with an introduction by Shunsaku Nishikawa. New York: Columbia University Press.

Funayama Shin'ichi (1959) *Meiji tetsugakushi kenkyū* [Studies in the History of Meiji Philosophy]. In *Funayama Shin'ichi Chosakushū* [Collected Writings of Funayama Shin'ichi] 6. Tokyo: Kobushi Shobō.

Havens, Thomas H. (1970) *Nishi Amane and Modern Japanese Thought*. Princeton, NJ: Princeton University Press.

Heisig, James W., Thomas P. Kasulis, and John C. Maraldo, eds. (2011) *Japanese Philosophy: A Sourcebook*. Honolulu: University of Hawai'i Press.

Ishizuka Masahide, and Shibata Takayuki. (2013) *Tetsugaku-shisō honyakugo jiten* [Dictionary of the Translation of Philosophical and Intellectual Terms]. Tokyo: Ronsōsha.

Kōsaka Masaaki. (1958) *Japanese Thought in the Meiji Era*, translated by David Abosch. Tokyo: Pan-Pacific Press. 2017

Maraldo, John C. (2017) *Japanese Philosophy in the Making I: Crossing Paths with Nishida*. Nagoya: Chisokudō Publications.

Marra, Michael F., ed. (2002) *Japanese Hermeneutics: Current Debates on Aesthetics and Interpretation*. Honolulu: University of Hawai'i Press.

Moore, Charles A., ed. (1968) *The Status of the Individual in East and West*. Honolulu: University of Hawai'i Press.

Piovesana, Gino K. (1997) *Recent Japanese Philosophical Thought 1862–1996: A Survey, with a New Survey by Naoshi Yamawaki 1963–96*. London and New York: RoutledgeCurzon.

Reitan, Richard M. (2010) *Making a Moral Society: Ethics and the State in Meiji Japan*
Honolulu: University of Hawai'i Press.

Schulzer, Rainer. (2019) *Inoue Enryo: A Philosophical Portrait.* Albany: State University of New
York Press.

Senuma Shigeki, ed. (1974) *Meiji tetsugaku shisō shū* [Collection of Meiji Philosophy and
Thought]. *Meiji bungaku zenshū* [Collected Works of Meiji literature] 80. Tokyo: Chikuma
Shobō.

Steben, Barry. (2012) "Nishi Amane and the Birth of 'Philosophy' and 'Chinese Philosophy'
in Early Meiji Japan." In John Makeham, ed., *Learning to Emulate the Wise: The Genesis
of Chinese Philosophy as an Academic Discipline in Twentieth-Century China.* Hong
Kong: Chinese University Press. (http://www.academia.edu/1928534/Nishi_Amane_And_
The_Birth_of_Philosophy_and_Chinese_Philosophy_in_Early_Meiji_Japan)

Steineck, Raji C., Elena Louisa Lange and Paulus Kaufmann, eds. (2014) *Begriff und Bild der
modernen japanischen Philosophie.* Stuttgart/Bad Cannstatt: Frommann-Holzboog.

Steineck, Raji C. (2014) "Der Begriff der Philosophie und seine taxonomische Funktion bei
Nishi Amane." In Steineck, Lange, and Kaufmann, eds., *Begriff und Bild der modernen
japanischen Philosophie.* Stuttgart/Bad Cannstatt: Frommann-Holzboog.

Wargo, Robert J. J. (2005) *The Logic of Nothingness: A Study of Nishida Kitarō.*
Honolulu: University of Hawai'i Press.

Yanabu Akira. (1982) *Honyakugo seiritsu jijō* [On Establishing the Translation of Terms].
Tokyo: Iwanami Shinsho.

THE KYOTO SCHOOL

CHAPTER 16

···

THE KYOTO SCHOOL

Transformations Over Three Generations

···

ŌHASHI RYŌSUKE AND AKITOMI KATSUYA

THE aim of this chapter is to provide an introduction to the Kyoto School (*Kyōto-gakuha* 京都学派) of modern Japanese philosophy.[1] It begins with a historical overview of the formation of various images of the School. It then briefly examines the controversial political engagements of members of the School during the Pacific War. The central sections of the chapter introduce the main figures and ideas of the first, second, and third generations of the School. The concluding section offers some reflections on how the School may contribute to a contemporary philosophical critique of technology and to a renewed dialogue between Eastern and Western traditions.

VARIOUS IMAGES OF THE KYOTO SCHOOL

···

Ever since Tosaka Jun (1900–1945),[2] a student of Nishida Kitarō (1870–1945)[3] who was also a Marxist, first employed the appellation "Kyoto School" in an essay in 1932,[4] various images of the Kyoto School have arisen and undergone transformations. In his essay, Tosaka treats Tanabe Hajime (1885–1962)[5] and Miki Kiyoshi (1897–1945)[6] as well

---

[1] The first two sections of this chapter were written by Ōhashi Ryōsuke, and the remaining sections were written by Akitomi Katsuya. Notes, references, and suggestions for further reading have been provided for the most part by the translator.

[2] See *Tosaka Jun: A Critical Reader*, edited by Ken C. Kawashima, Fabian Schafer, and Robert Stolz (New York: Cornell University Press, 2014).

[3] On Nishida's philosophy see Chapters 17 and 18 in this volume; also see the critical discussion of Nishida's political and cultural philosophy in Chapter 36.

[4] Reprinted in Tosaka 1966, 171–176.

[5] On Tanabe, see Chapter 19 in this volume.

[6] On Miki, see Chapter 20 in this volume.

as Nishida as belonging to the School. This shows how, at the time, Miki's *Philosophy of History* (1932)[7] was in part expected to take up the mantle of the "Nishida School."

By the late 1930s and early 1940s, four students of Nishida and Tanabe came to be seen as representative of the Kyoto School: Kōsaka Masaaki (1900–1969), Nishitani Keiji (1990–1990),[8] Kōyama Iwao (1905–1993),[9] and Suzuki Shigetaka (1907–1988). Emblematic is the participation of these four scholars in two symposia. The first of these, called *Overcoming Modernity* (*Kindai no chōkoku*), took place in 1942 and was organized and published by the journal *Bungaku-kai* (The World of Literature).[10] The second was in fact a series of symposia that were published at first serially in the journal *Chūōkōron* in 1942–1943, and then together as a book in 1943 under the title *The World Historical Standpoint and Japan* (*Sekaishi-teki tachiba to Nihon*).[11] In addition to Kōsaka, Nishitani, Kōyama, and Suzuki, Shimomura Toratarō (1902–1995) also took part in the *Overcoming Modernity* symposium. The ultra-right nationalist proponents of the so-called Imperial Way ideology (*kōdō-shugi* 皇道主義) severely attacked the symposia published as *The World Historical Standpoint and Japan*, as well as their four participants, for their "world" oriented viewpoint. Yet, after the War the Kyoto School was denounced for having purportedly "cooperated in the War" (*senso kyōryoku* 戦争協力). Although, as will be discussed later, this image of the Kyoto School was to be largely corrected through the discovery of the "Ōshima Memoranda," for fifty years after the War the image of the Kyoto School as having cooperated in the War spread and became the norm.

However, prior to the end of the Pacific War, Marxist materialists were included among Nishida's students; they in fact formed one group of those following in the wake of his thought. Just as in Germany one speaks of the "Hegelian Left" (*die Hegelsche Linke*), one might speak of "the Kyoto School Left" (*Kyōto-gakuha saha* 京都学派・左派), the central figures of which were Tosaka and Kakehashi Akihide (1902–1996). These leftist intellectuals were not only verbally attacked by the ultra-right nationalists, they were forcefully suppressed; Tosaka died in prison just before the end of the War. The liberal Miki was also persecuted, and, just after the end of the War, he too died in prison.

After the War, the shifting political winds brought Marxism into prominence, and some Kyoto School scholars underwent a reverse intellectual conversion (*tenkō* 転向)[12] to Marxist materialism. Exemplary among them was Yanagida Kenjūrō (1893–1983); Mutai Risaku (1890–1974)[13] could perhaps also be included among this group of

---

[7] Miki 1966, vol. 6.

[8] On Nishitani, see Chapter 21 in this volume.

[9] See Kōyama 2001*a* and 2001*b*.

[10] A translation can be found in Calichman 2008.

[11] A translation (or "English-friendly rendering") can be found in Williams 2014.

[12] The term *tenkō* was used to describe the "intellectual conversion" some scholars underwent during the War from leftist or liberal positions to right wing nationalism, and so Ōhashi is calling these postwar conversions to the left a *tenkō* in the opposite direction.

[13] See Mutai 2000.

converts. These figures are saddled with both images of the Kyoto School, yet their work is partially distorted when made to conform to either image.

The development of the image of the Kyoto School after the War split in general into two different directions. The image fashioned by so-called leftist intellectuals took as its basic motif denouncing the School's "cooperation in the War." The other image set the School in the context of the history of philosophy and assessed its value in terms of its ability to engage in dialogue with European philosophy. This viewpoint was presumably enabled and even necessitated by the fact that Nishida and the other members of the School had absorbed what might be called the disposition of Buddhist thought. This orientation continued to grow after the War. Their writings contained fewer of the kind of statements on current affairs they made prior to the end of the War and increasingly moved in the direction of the philosophy of religion. This can be seen, for example, in Tanabe's "philosophy as metanoetics" (*zangedō toshite no tetsugaku* 懺悔道としての哲学),[14] Hisamatsu Shin'ichi's (1889–1980) "philosophy of awakening" (*kaku no tetsugaku* 覚の哲学),[15] and Nishitani's philosophy of "emptiness" (*kū* 空).[16] This image of the Kyoto School does not enter the purview of discourses from the postwar period of the 1950s that treat the School merely as the object of ideology critique.

Be that as it may, what exactly should be seen as central to the philosophy of the Kyoto School remains in question. The School has left its mark in the fields of philosophy of history, philosophy of science, philosophy of art, and phenomenology. With regard to the last of these, the approach phenomenologists have taken to Nishida's philosophy since the 1990s deserves special mention. This liberated Nishida research from the strictures of the previous approach of ideology critique and, to exaggerate a bit, established a situation in which all scholars of Japanese philosophy make reference to Nishida. (Nevertheless, the ideology critique has continued in recent years, especially in the USA but also in Japan.)

We have thus far, however, been discussing only the first and second generations of the Kyoto School. After that, a third generation of figures arose who were confined neither to the geographical location of Kyoto nor to a lineage based on a teacher–student relation. On the one hand, this effected a "diffusion" of the image of the School, yet, on the other hand, its "pluralization." This is depicted in the German volume I (Ōhashi) edited, *Die Philosophie der Kyōto-Schule: Texte und Einführung*. Together with the various historical transformations of the image of the Kyoto School, the issues addressed by its thinkers also necessarily became more diverse. Still, today, the image of the School has not settled into a fixed determination. Rather, along with the School's ongoing dialogue with the 2,500-year history of Western philosophy, it continues to develop.

---

[14] Tanabe 1986.
[15] Hisamatsu 2002. For more on Hisamatsu, see Chapter 11 in this volume.
[16] See Nishitani 1982.

THE "ŌSHIMA MEMORANDA"

Taking the long view and seeing the Kyoto School from the perspective of the philosophical dialogue with the Western tradition, however, should not entail diverting attention away from the recent events of the Pacific War. Understanding how the members of the School comported themselves toward the War is necessary for understanding the nature of their thought.[17] A primary source for understanding this aspect of the Kyoto School is the abovementioned document, dubbed the "Ōshima Memoranda." After I (Ōhashi) unexpectedly discovered this document, I published a transcription of it with commentary in 2001.[18] The name "Ōshima" refers to Ōshima Yasumasa (1917–1989), who was an assistant professor of philosophy at Kyoto University during the Pacific War. The document narrates the following history: From February of 1942 through July of 1945—that is, throughout almost the entire period of the Pacific War—a group of scholars centered on the Kyoto School philosophers, in part at the bequest of and in cooperation with the Navy, held top secret meetings once or twice a month to analyze and reflect upon current events. Regular participants included Kōyama Iwao, Kōsaka Masaaki, Nishitani Keiji, Kimura Motomori (1895–1946), and Suzuki Shigetaka. Guest participants included the future Nobel Prize–winning physicist Yukawa Hideki (1907–1981) and the erudite scholar of Asian history Miyazaki Ichisada (1901–1995).

In alliance with the Navy, the intent of the meetings was to correct the war-bound course on which the Army was steering the country—hence the top secret nature of these meetings that were, in effect, working within the establishment against the establishment. An offhand remark made by the Minister of the Interior reveals the dire situation at the time: "There can be no guarantee for the life of anyone, including a cabinet official, who works for peace in opposition to the policies of the nation."[19] The impact exerted by this comment is illustrated by the fact that it led to the resignation of the Minister of Foreign Affairs of the first Konoe administration, Ugaki Kazushige, in 1937, five years before the secret meetings began. Had the Army-led government found out about these meetings and their intent to correct the bellicose policies of the Army, the participants would have surely met with the same fate as did Tosaka and Miki. Ōshima Yasumasa not only planned the dates of the meetings, he also wrote down and secretly preserved a record of what was said at them.

Ōshima himself later wrote the following about his record of the meetings:

---

[17] In addition to the treatment of this issue in the present chapter, see Chapters 19, 20, and 36 in this volume. For a variety of views on this still contentious topic, see Heisig and Maraldo 1994, Goto-Jones 2008, Maraldo 2006, and most recently Osaki 2019. For an overview, see section 4 of Davis 2019. For a vigorous defense of the wartime political writings of the Kyoto School and a counter-critique of the racist imperialism of the West, see Willliams 2014. For a severe critique of the scholarship of the critics, see Parkes 1997 and 2011. For recent Neo-Marxist critiques, see Murthy, Schafer, and Ward 2017.

[18] Ōhashi 2001.

[19] *Takagi Sōkichi: Nikki to jōhō* [Takagi Sōkichi: Diary and Information], edited by Itō Takashi (Tokyo: Misuzu Shobō, 2000), vol. 2, p. 516.

In retrospect we can divide the meetings into three broad phases. At the very beginning the theme was how to prevent war from breaking out. Yet it was already too late for that. ... Just thirteen days after the symposium on "The World-historical Standpoint and Japan," which was to be published in the journal *Chūōkōron* in order to sway public opinion, the Japanese attack on Pearl Harbor sparked off the War between Japan and the United States. From that point until the autumn of 1944, the main theme of the meetings, as recorded in the memoranda, was how to bring the War to a favorable end as soon as possible by way of rationally persuading the Army. Toward that end, the necessity of somehow toppling the Tōjō regime and reestablishing the Yonai regime, as well as various means of doing so, were discussed. The theme changed once again in the meetings from the end of 1944 to immediately after the capitulation in 1945. Since, according to information leaked to the group from the Navy, defeat was clearly imminent, the meetings focused on how to deal with postwar issues.[20]

The collection of memoranda actually discovered informs us that the main topics of discussion in the meetings were the intellectual conditions within Japan and abroad; the prospects for the current state of affairs and an analysis of its historical background; the search for a meaning to the War and recommendations for correcting government policy; later on, plans for toppling the regime of Prime Minister Tōjō Hideki, who with the Army had pressed for war with the United States; and, at the end of the War, the outlook on the postwar situation, including the mental state of citizens of a defeated nation.

Philosophy and politics have existed in an inseparable relation since the time of Plato. It is, of course, possible for philosophers to shut their eyes to present actualities and to immerse themselves in textual research within the purely academic world. Indeed, for a long time after the War, that is the stance taken by the academy of philosophers in Japan. Yet, at times, such a withdrawn stance itself recedes and philosophy takes up a political bearing. The thinkers of the Kyoto School, while on the one hand assuming the rational standpoint of Western philosophy, on the other hand attempted to comprehend the historical position and actuality of modern Japan. As in the case of Plato, here, too, philosophy and actuality were involved in an originally inseparable yet nevertheless strange and strained relationship, and the result was that the philosophers became engulfed in the muddy waters of the times. It cannot be said that their historical judgments were without error. Yet that fact cannot be used to justify remaining secluded in a politically innocuous ivory tower.

THE FIRST GENERATION: NISHIDA KITARŌ AND TANABE HAJIME

While teaching high school in Kanazawa, for a decade, Nishida both continued his study of philosophy and intensely engaged in the practice of Zen. It was on the basis of

---

[20] Ōshima 2000, 282. Ōshima's text was originally published in the journal *Chūōkōron* in August of 1965.

that study and practice that he wrote his first book, *An Inquiry into the Good* (*Zen no kenkyū*).[21] Just prior to its publication in January 1911, Nishida took up a position of assistant professor of philosophy at Kyoto University, in August 1910. This, in effect, was the first step toward the formation of what later became known as the Kyoto School.

In *An Inquiry into the Good*, the worldview and conception of the self that had long been cultivated in the traditions of Buddhism and Confucianism were for the first time given philosophical foundation in a manner that enabled them to be brought into dialogue with Western philosophy on the same footing. This was the first truly original philosophical book written in Japan, and it received a great deal of attention, not only from scholars but also from the general public in Japan. As a result, many students gathered around Nishida in Kyoto. Nishida's philosophical labors continued unabated after his maiden work, and, in time, he produced his original thinking of "place" (*basho* 場所), which came to be known as "Nishidan philosophy" (*Nishida-tetsugaku* 西田哲学).

Nishida himself had no intentions of or interest in forming a school. But after his successor in the department of philosophy, Tanabe, developed his own original philosophy through a confrontation with Nishida's thought, their two philosophical oeuvres together in effect laid the foundations for the formation of the Kyoto School. Having first looked up to Nishida as his teacher, in time, Tanabe became critical of his philosophical standpoint. Although it is questionable whether all of Tanabe's criticisms of Nishida hit their mark, in response to them Nishida further developed his thinking, and, in turn, Tanabe modified his own critical standpoint.[22] The sharp critical exchanges that unfolded between Nishida and Tanabe—with their display not only of the tension that exists between philosophical standpoints, but also of the rigor and discipline of philosophical thinking—could not help but influence the students who studied under both of them. Indeed it could be said that this philosophical antagonism between the two founding figures of the Kyoto School became the driving force behind the ways in which the figures of the next generation inherited and developed their thought.

Because at the heart of their dispute lay the notion that Nishida placed at the heart of his philosophy—namely, "absolute nothingness" (*zettai mu* 絶対無)—this concept became the philosophical core of the Kyoto School. Although not every member employed this term per se, it could nevertheless be said that a concern with absolute nothingness, and the inheritance and development of this concept became the defining characteristic of the School.

Nishida's orientation to absolute nothingness is already implied in the central concept of *An Inquiry into the Good*, namely, "pure experience" (*junsui keiken* 純粋経験). As can be seen in the first line of the book—"To experience means to know facts just as they are"[23]—pure experience refers to a moment prior to the division of facts and knowledge, object and subject, a moment in which Nishida locates the source of the self. *An*

---

[21] Nishida 1990.
[22] See Sugimoto 2011.
[23] Nishida 2002–2009, 1: 9; Nishida 1990, 3.

Inquiry into the Good is an attempt to explain everything, starting with such pure experience as the sole reality. Yet, through his confrontation with the rigorous logical and scientific standpoints of contemporary schools of philosophy such as Neo-Kantianism and Husserlian phenomenology, Nishida realized that his philosophy of pure experience had yet to deal satisfactorily with the problem of reflection. The question was whether the higher order thinking involved in reflecting on pure experience could itself be a pure experience. By way of dealing with this question, in *Intuition and Reflection in Self-Awareness* (*Jikaku ni okeru chokkan to hansei*, 1917),[24] Nishida's notion of pure experience developed into that of "self-awareness" (*jikaku* 自覚).

Self-awareness is a matter of "the self knowing the self," yet, given the never objectifiable activity of the self, Nishida understood this to entail "the self mirroring the self within itself" (*jiko ga jiko ni oite jiko wo utsusu koto* 自己が自己において自己を映すこと). At the base of the acting self, there is a mirroring self, a seeing self. This is a seeing without a seer, a self without a self. The place-self is none other than this self that, being itself nothing, mirrors everything else. The volume *From that which Acts to that which Sees* (*Hataraku mono kara miru mono e*, 1927), which contains the essay "Place" (*Basho*),[25] exhibits this development in Nishida's thinking. There, Nishida came to locate the foundation of his philosophy in this standpoint of "place" and, through a confrontation with Western philosophy, proposed a "logic of place" (*basho no ronri* 場所の論理). This logic involved enveloping layers of "places," the ultimate of which is a place that enables all beings to be just as they are without itself being any kind of being; thus Nishida conceives of it as "the place of absolute nothingness" (*zettai mu no basho* 絶対無の場所). This idea provided a philosophical foundation for religion, which Nishida always held to be the consummation of philosophy.[26] After establishing his philosophy of place, Nishida continued to deepen and develop it, making it more concrete by rethinking place in terms of the world as "the dialectical universal" (*benshōhō-teki ippansha* 弁証法的一般者), such that the historical world is conceived of in terms of a mutual determination of self and world.[27]

However, when Nishida conceived of the place-like self as "that which sees without a seer" and of the ultimate place as "the place of absolute nothingness," Tanabe accused him of tilting toward mystical intuition and of turning philosophy into a matter of religion.[28] According to Tanabe, philosophy must always and ceaselessly endeavor to understand irrational reality. From that point on, Tanabe connected his increasingly severe criticism of Nishida's philosophy with the development of his own original philosophy, which he called a "logic of species" (*shu no ronri* 種の論理).[29] In traditional logic,

---

[24] Nishida 1987*a*.

[25] A translation of "Place" is included in Nishida 2012.

[26] See Nishida 1987*b*.

[27] See Nishida 1970.

[28] See Tanabe's essay, "Nishida-sensei no oshie o aogu" [Requesting Instruction from Professor Nishida] (Tanabe 1964, 4: 305–328).

[29] Tanabe 1969.

the species is situated between the genus and the individual; in terms of historical reality, it refers to the nation or the ethnic group. According to Tanabe, Nishida had an insufficient grasp of the species; the individual stressed by Nishida is not understood to be mediated by the historical substance of the ethnic group and so is unable to become a real agent of concrete action. For Tanabe, the dialectic capable of grasping irrational historical actuality is not a "logic of nothingness" that encompasses everything; rather, absolute nothingness must be grasped from a standpoint of dynamic mediation, that is to say, in terms of an "absolute mediation" (*zettai baikai* 絶対媒介) based on action. Nishida gave serious consideration to Tanabe's critique, and, as the Japanese nation become embroiled in the turbulence of world history, he, too, grappled with matters of the nation and the ethnic group such that the gap between their philosophical standpoints narrowed.

Although Nishida died just before the end of the War, Tanabe lived on. Retiring the year the War ended, Tanabe moved to Kitakaruizawa in Gunma Prefecture, where, thinking in isolation, he penned *Philosophy as Metanoetics* (*Zangedō toshite no tetsugaku*)[30] and *A Philosophy of Death* (*Shi no tetsugaku*).[31] In such works, religious themes became prominent, and Tanabe once again came into proximity to the standpoint of Nishida whom he had once so severely criticized.

THE SECOND GENERATION: HISAMATSU SHIN'ICHI, MIKI KIYOSHI, NISHITANI KEIJI, KŌYAMA IWAO, KŌSAKA MASAAKI, SHIMOMURA TORATARŌ, AND SUZUKI SHIGETAKA

Most of the members of the second generation of the Kyoto School studied under both Nishida and Tanabe, and the fierce debate that unfolded between their teachers meant that each of them had to not only carefully consider both philosophical standpoints, but also go on to establish his own.

After retiring in 1928, Nishida began to spend spring and fall in Kyoto and summer and winter in Kamakura. During the time Nishida spent in Kyoto, it became customary for his former students to periodically gather to hear and discuss the latest developments in his thinking. Occasionally, Nishida and Tanabe would directly confront one another. Marxism had become very influential at the time, and their Marxist students would also attend these gatherings. Nishida's poem from 1929 recalls the spirit of those times: "Again discussing Marx into the wee hours; because of Marx I cannot

---

[30]   Tanabe 1986.
[31]   Tanabe 2000, 316–429. See also Tanabe 1959.

sleep." The formation of the Kyoto School as a community of thought took place through frank discussions and lively debates that bridged one generation and the next.

What characterizes the standpoint of the second generation of the Kyoto School is a focus on history. While, as we have seen, Nishida and Tanabe had turned their attention to the historical world and its logic, the second generation of thinkers also directly experienced how the Japanese nation was itself being caught up in the turbulent whirlpool of world history. History was no longer merely an object of philosophical reflection; it was experienced as an actuality that sweeps one up into its movement. The members of the second generation of the School shared in common an interest in grasping the meaning of world history while standing right in the midst of its movement.

A primary example of this is the book by Miki Kiyoshi referred to earlier, *The Philosophy of History*. The facts that he turned to Marxism, never taught at Kyoto University, later became a journalist, and finally died in prison may seem like reasons not to think of Miki as belonging to the Kyoto School. Yet Miki's enduring respect for Nishida and his desire to critically come to terms with Nishida's philosophy, his employment of Nishida's terminology such as "action-intuition" (*kōi-teki chokkan* 行為的 直観) and "poiesis" in his own discourses on imagination and technology, and the fact that he continued to be concerned with the issue of "nothingness" demonstrate the qualities on the basis of which he should unquestionably be counted among members of the School.

A concern with the philosophy of history was also shared by Kōsaka Masaaki. Kōsaka was a professor at Kyoto University before the War, yet after the War he (along with the following three scholars discussed in this section) was purged from his position at this public university on account of the fact that he had participated in the *Overcoming Modernity* and *The World Historical Standpoint and Japan* symposia discussed in the first section of this chapter. Since the publication of his prewar and wartime books, *The Historical World* (*Rekishi-teki sekai*, 1937)[32] and *Introduction to the Philosophy of History* (*Rekishi-tetsugaku josetsu*, 1943), Kōsaka's constant concern was with understanding history, including the endeavors of thinking in the midst of history. In particular, he focused his attention on elucidating the history of Western philosophy and the history of Japanese thought in the Meiji period.[33]

While an assistant professor working under Tanabe starting in the 1930s, Kōyama Iwao was a prolific author of *The Study of Cultural Types* (*Bunka ruikei-gaku*, 1939),[34] *Philosophy of World History* (*Sekai-shi no tetsugaku*, 1942),[35] and other systematic works. In 1946, he succeeded Tanabe as professor and chair of the philosophy department at Kyoto University. That same year, however, he was purged from his position and never again taught at Kyoto University. When the ban was lifted five years later, Kōyama published *The Logic of Place and the Principle of Correspondence* (*Basho-teki ronri to koō*

---

[32] Kōsaka 2002.
[33] Kōsaka 1999.
[34] Kōyama 2001*a*, 6–169.
[35] Kōyama 2001*b*.

no genri, 1951),[36] in which he sets forth his own conception of Nishida's logic of place in terms of what he calls "the principle of correspondence" (*koō no genri* 呼応の原理).

Suzuki Shigetaka was a historian specializing in the medieval period of European history. Prior to being purged from his position after the War, he was an assistant professor at Kyoto University. Although he was not a philosopher, from early on he was engaged in studying Leopold von Ranke (1795–1886), in whom Nishida was also very interested, and from Ranke he learned how to cultivate a wide-angled approach to world history that enquires into the very nature of world history, Europe, and modernity. Suzuki's postwar works, *The Formation of Europe* (*Yōroppa no seiritsu*, 1947) and *The Industrial Revolution* (*Sangyō-kakumei*, 1950),[37] were also written from this wide-angled viewpoint. He was a thinker who could not be confined to the common framework of positivistic historical research.

The fourth member of the Kyoto School to be purged from his position at a public university after the War was Nishitani Keiji. Although Nishitani also published works on the philosophy of history during the War,[38] his major and unique contributions lay in deepening our understanding of how matters of history are related to the issues of religion that had been of concern to Nishida and Tanabe. In Nishitani's thought, "absolute nothingness" is rethought as "emptiness" (*kū* 空; Sk. *śūnyatā*). Although Nishitani's early thought revolved around the idea of absolute nothingness, in his magnum opus, *What Is Religion?* (*Shūkyō to wa nanika*, 1961, translated as *Religion and Nothingness*),[39] by way of passing through a confrontation with Western philosophy, Nishitani sets forth his own philosophical standpoint of emptiness. Behind the need Nishitani felt to use the language of "emptiness" was the experience of "nihilism" (*nihirizumu* ニヒリズム), which he stipulated as his philosophical starting point. Yet in order to understand a human being's experiential encounter with nihility (*kyomu* 虚無) in terms of the philosophical concept of nihilism, it was necessary to thoroughly confront the European modernity that had given rise to this concept. Recognizing the defeat in World War II as a hiatus in modern Japanese history, Nishitani delved into an investigation of European nihilism and, four years after the end of the War, published *Nihilism* (*Nihirizumu*, 1949, translated as *The Self-Overcoming of Nihilism*).[40] At the same time as it was an investigation of European nihilism, the book shone light on the peculiar growth of nihilism in Japan. This growth was rooted in the contradiction that lay at the core of modern Japan; namely, the fact that, in the process of being pushed to modernize by means of Westernizing, the Japanese had to experience a severance from their own intellectual and spiritual traditions.

Having thus far carried out a confrontation with Western philosophy and religion from the standpoint of absolute nothingness, with Nishitani, the Kyoto School

---

[36] Kōyama 2001*a*, 172–391.

[37] Both are contained in Suzuki 2000.

[38] See Nishitani 1986–1995, vol. 4.

[39] Nishitani 1982.

[40] Nishitani 1990.

encountered the problem of nihilism. One way of putting this is to say that the notion of "absolute nothingness" (*zettai mu*), with its Buddhist background, came face to face with the "nothingness" (*mu*) that, of necessity, arose from out of the midst of the history of Christianity. Like Nietzsche and Heidegger, who enquired into the essence of nihilism in order to figure out how to overcome it, the overcoming of nihilism became the central theme of Nishitani's thought. In the Buddhist tradition that was being lost in the process of Japanese modernization, he found the idea of emptiness, and he sought to draw from out of it the philosophical possibility of overcoming the historical reality of nihilism. When the Buddhist concept of emptiness was introduced into the arena of a confrontation with the concepts of Western philosophy, a major advance was made in the development of the philosophy of the Kyoto School. After the postwar ban on their teaching in public universities was lifted, Nishitani was the only Kyoto School philosopher who returned to Kyoto University to resume a professorship of philosophy, and the momentous consequences of this can be seen in the influence that he exerted on almost all of the members of the third generation of the School.

With regard to developments in the philosophy of religion, Nishitani's senior colleague Hisamatsu Shin'ichi deserves special mention. Hisamatsu was among the first generation of Nishida's students at Kyoto University. Although he was more committed to Zen praxis than to academic research, he taught at Kyoto University and elsewhere, and he developed an original manner of thinking based on the standpoint of Zen. For Hisamatsu, absolute nothingness is the source of philosophical theory; it is the "formless self" (*musō no jiko* 無相の自己) found at the level of living praxis. The metaphysical formulation of this in the Eastern tradition Hisamatsu called "Eastern nothingness" (*tōyō-teki mu* 東洋的無).[41] He produced a great number of philosophical treatises, but his most inimitable works are those in which, writing from the standpoint of a Zen adept, he elucidates the arts of Zen and the Way of Tea (*chadō* or *sadō* 茶道).[42] Moreover, Hisamatsu sought to liberate Zen from its institutional tradition and make it available to all humanity in the modern world. During the War, Hisamatsu established *Gakudō dōjō* (学道道場, Center for Study and Praxis) at Kyoto University as a forum for academic study and spiritual praxis, and he later developed this organization into the FAS Society (FAS stands for formless self, all mankind, and superhistorical history). Here again we see a concern with history.

Another direction of investigating history was pursued by Shimomura Toratarō. Shimomura began by studying the history and philosophy of science, moved on to study the Renaissance, and, in his later years, published a book on Jacob Burkhardt (1818–1897). All of these studies were characterized by Shimomura's unique stance toward "intellectual history" (*seishin-shi* 精神史). Whether it was ancient mathematics, modern physics, or Renaissance art, he depicted these formative movements within history as developments of the human spirit (*ningen seishin* 人間精神).[43] Although Shimomura

[41] See Hisamatsu 1960.
[42] See Hisamatsu 2003.
[43] See Shimomura 2000, 2003.

did not hold a position at Kyoto University, the manner in which his investigations into science and art were clearly undergirded by an awareness of the philosophical issues at stake was manifestly inherited from Nishida and Tanabe.

As the preceding synopsis illustrates, each of the thinkers of the second generation of the Kyoto School, while on the one hand attending to Nishida's standpoint of absolute nothingness, on the other hand dedicated themselves to their own investigations into matters of philosophy, intellectual history, and history. They also made remarkable contributions to research on specific philosophers; exemplary in this regard are Nishitani's work on Meister Eckhart and Nietzsche, Kōyama's work on Hegel, Kōsaka's work on Kant, and Shimomura's work on Leibniz. The works by Kōyama, Kōsaka, and Shimomura on these figures were included in a series edited by Tanabe and continued to be read even long after the end of the War.

THE THIRD GENERATION: TAKEUCHI YOSHINORI, ABE MASAO, TSUJIMURA KŌICHI, UEDA SHIZUTERU, ŌMINE AKIRA, HASE SHŌTŌ, KIMURA BIN, AND ŌHASHI RYŌSUKE

In comparison to the members of the second generation, not only do the thinkers who can be considered to belong to the third generation of the Kyoto School span a greater number of years, the content of their work is also less unified.

As distinct from the works of Kōsaka, Shimomura, Kōyama, and others of the second generation, in the philosophies of Takeuchi Yoshinori (1913–2002),[44] Abe Masao (1915–2006),[45] Tsujimura Kōichi (1922–2010),[46] Ueda Shizuteru (1926–2019),[47] Ōmine Akira (1929–2018),[48] and Hase Shōtō (b. 1937),[49] an inheritance of the traditions of Mahāyāna Buddhism is once again clearly manifest: Pure Land Buddhism in the cases of Takeuchi, Ōmine, and Hase, and Zen Buddhism in the cases of Abe, Tsujimura, and Ueda.[50] All these thinkers pursue the kind of philosophy of religion or religious

---

[44] See Takeuchi 1983, 1999.

[45] See Abe 1985, 1990, 2003. For more on Abe, see Chapter 11 in this volume.

[46] See Tsujimura 1971, 1991, 2008, 2011.

[47] See Ueda 2001–2004, 2011c. For more on Ueda, see Chapter 22 in this volume.

[48] See Ōmine 2008, 2009.

[49] See Hase 2003, 2005, 2010.

[50] Hanaoka Eiko, another member of the third generation of the Kyoto School, brings together Zen and Christianity; see Hanaoka 2009.

philosophy (*shūkyō-tetsugaku* 宗教哲学) developed by Nishida and Tanabe and their successors Hisamatsu and Nishitani.

What characterizes the endeavors of these thinkers is not so much the presentation of original ideas as it is the manner in which, based on the Eastern traditions behind the ideas of absolute nothingness and emptiness, they engage in dialogues and confrontations with Western philosophy from this fresh perspective. Whether it was Takeuchi on Hegel, Tsujimura on Heidegger, Ueda on Eckhart, Ōmine on Fichte, or Hase on Ricoeur, in each case a critical dialogue was undertaken with a major figure of Western philosophy. While their manners of engaging with these interlocutors varied, what they shared in common was the fact that, in the course of their textually grounded and meticulous interpretations of these Western philosophers, the standpoint of Mahāyāna Buddhism inevitably came into play, leading to a radical dialogue and confrontation that aimed at the very core of the philosophical encounter between Eastern and Western traditions. At the same time, their endeavors served to widen the scope of the philosophy of absolute nothingness. "Absolute nothingness" is a key term in both Tsujimura's interpretation of Heidegger and in Ueda's interpretation of Eckhart. Moreover, Ueda's original conception of the "twofold world" (*nijū sekai* 二重世界) was not only developed out of his critical reception of Heidegger's idea of "being-in-the-world," but also clearly reflects his attempt to reformulate Nishida's "place of absolute nothingness" and Nishitani's "field of emptiness" (*kū no ba* 空の場).[51] Because Abe Masao published much of his work in English and spent many years lecturing in various universities in the United States, he is better known there than in Japan. As a successor of Hisamatsu's thought, Abe has done much to introduce the philosophy of the Kyoto School to a Western readership.

While much of the Kyoto School's philosophy of religion leans heavily in the direction of Zen Buddhism, Takeuchi, Ōmine, and Hase stand out for having clearly set forth an orientation to Pure Land Buddhism.[52] Ōmine and Hase are especially interested in thinking about language in connection with the "Name" (*myōgō* 名号) of Amida Buddha recited by adherents of Pure Land Buddhism. Together with Ueda's approach to language from the perspective of Zen,[53] their pursuits characterize the philosophy of language developed by members of Kyoto School.

In contrast to the general tendency of the thinkers of the third generation of the Kyoto School to focus on the philosophy of religion, Kimura Bin (b. 1931) stands out for working in the field of psychiatry.[54] Alongside his clinical practice, from early on, Kimura studied European psychiatry together with Husserl's, Heidegger's, and also Nishida's philosophies. Especially by way of appropriating in his own fashion Nishida's ideas of "pure experience" and "action-intuition," he then developed a unique standpoint

---

[51] See Ueda 2001–2004, vols. 3 and 9; 2011c, chap. 3.
[52] The recently retired Professor and Chair of Religious Studies at Kyoto University, Keta Masako, should also be mentioned in this regard; see Curley, Main, and Coughlin 2017.
[53] See Ueda 2011b.
[54] See Kimura 1995, 2001, 2011.

of psychiatry while teaching as a professor of Kyoto University's Faculty of Medicine. Since he does not consider himself to be a philosopher, Kimura does not think of himself as belonging to the Kyoto School. Nevertheless, his work can be regarded as an extension of the potential of Nishida's philosophy in a new field and is thus certainly a development of the philosophy of the Kyoto School.

Turning our attention back to the field of philosophy, my co-author of this chapter, Ōhashi Ryōsuke (b. 1944), is currently in the process of developing the tradition of the Kyoto School in new directions. Ōhashi's prolific work in the areas of philosophy and aesthetics is based on the one hand on his in-depth investigations into Western philosophy—Hegel and Heidegger in particular—and on the other hand on his appropriation of the philosophy of the Kyoto School, especially the standpoints of Nishida and Nishitani.[55] His edited volume mentioned earlier, *Die Philosophie der Kyōto-Schule* (first edition 1990, revised and expanded edition 2011, third edition 2014), helped introduce the Kyoto School to the German-speaking world, and Ōhashi today continues to lecture frequently in Germany and to publish in German as well as Japanese. He is formulating his own philosophical standpoint in terms of the concept of "compassion" (*hi* 悲).[56] Compassion is also a central concept of Mahāyāna Buddhism, but Ōhashi does not so much propose it as a third concept alongside absolute nothingness and emptiness, but rather as an attempt to reformulate these inherited formulations of the standpoint of the Kyoto School through a confrontation with the philosophical problems of the contemporary world.

TOWARD A NEW IMAGE OF THE
KYOTO SCHOOL

We have recounted the intellectual development of the Kyoto School in some detail. Yet the question of what the School was in the past is inseparable from the question of what it can become in the future.

Technology as a Central Issue of the Contemporary World

We have seen that "history" has been a main theme running through the development of the Kyoto School. If we turn our attention to the contemporary age in this regard, the "technology" that drives the contemporary historical world appears as a central and urgent matter. Ōhashi's work has been motivated in part by a concern with technology.[57]

---

[55] See Ōhashi 1995.

[56] See Ōhashi 1998, 2011*b*, 2018, 2019.

[57] See Ōhashi 1995, 128–141.

Yet we should also attend, from a contemporary standpoint, to the manner in which this most pressing issue of our times was already addressed by previous generations of the Kyoto School.

It was Nishida who first clearly brought this issue to the fore. In the course of developing his philosophy of the place of absolute nothingness, Nishida came to conceive of this place more concretely as the historical world, and he explained the movement of this actual world in terms of the mutual determination of self and world. He referred to this mutual determination with his signature phrases such as "action-intuition" and "from what is made to what makes" (*tsukurareta mono kara tsukuru mono e* 作られた ものから作るものへ). For Nishida, the world itself is creative, and the self is a "creative element of the creative world" (*sōzō-teki sekai no sōzō-teki yōso* 創造的世界の創造的 要素). The technological activity of human beings is also understood in this context.[58]

It was Miki who developed a "philosophy of technology" from Nishida's point of view. Although Miki never completely developed his thinking about his central problematic of the "imagination" (*kōsōryoku* 構想力), he conceived of it as having a technological character, and he exposed the close connection that exists between technology and imagination.[59] Although, as mentioned earlier, there has been some question over whether Miki should be regarded as belonging to the Kyoto School, present and future reconsiderations of the School are likely to discover new significance in his conception of technology.

While Nishida and Miki both died the year the War ended and thus did not experience the technological developments of the postwar era, Nishitani lived on for many years to experience and reflect in a penetrating and original manner on the issue of technology. Nishitani was constantly concerned with the relation between science and religion,[60] and his later writings make frequent reference to technology, fathoming the negative side of modern technology in connection with the problem of nihilism. Yet how modern technology could be rethought from the standpoint of emptiness is a question that Nishitani himself did not fully explore. This could be understood as a task that he left for us.

Another thinker who should be reconsidered in this light is Shimomura. As mentioned earlier, Shimomura began his career with a philosophical examination of the history of science starting with ancient Greece and then investigated the contemporary significance of the intellectual history of the Renaissance, an age in which science and art were not yet separated. When this intellectual history of the West is reexamined with a focus on the question of technology, and in terms of the connection between science and art, we can perhaps gain new indications for how to deal with technology now and in the future.

---

[58] See Nishida 2012, 103–174.
[59] See Miki 1966, vol. 8, 2001, 2011.
[60] See Nishitani 2004.

Toward a Renewed Dialogue with Western Thought

In order to form a new image of the Kyoto School that is appropriate to our contemporary age, in addition to the problem of technology, we should focus on the possibility of intercultural dialogue. As we have seen, starting with Nishida's and Tanabe's conceptions of "absolute nothingness" and subsequently in, for example, Nishitani's notion of "emptiness," the intellectual tendency of the Kyoto School has been to bring philosophical standpoints stemming from Mahāyāna Buddhism into dialogue with Western philosophy and religion as well as science and art. Such an engagement in intercultural dialogue is especially pronounced in the thinkers of the third generation of the School, many of whom wrote and published articles and books in Western languages as well as in Japanese.

Moreover, in the wake of the expansion and especially the internationalization of research on the philosophy of Nishida and the Kyoto School that began in the 1980s, foreign scholars have been directly engaging in dialogue with the philosophical standpoints of the Kyoto School. The first big step in this direction was the translation of texts by the philosophers of the School into Western and East Asian languages. In an age of globalization, in which the very meanings of philosophy and religion are being questioned, the philosophies of the Kyoto School are surely capable of offering non-Japanese scholars many valuable possibilities for thought, given that they have engaged in dialogue and confrontation with Western philosophy on the basis of their rootedness in the non-Western tradition of East Asian thought and, in particular, East Asian Mahāyāna Buddhism.

It is important to recognize, however, that this East–West dialogue of thought can today no longer remain within the strictures of Buddhist–Christian dialogue. Nishitani's understanding of nihilism began with a recognition of having been severed from tradition, and from there he proceeded to look to the future by way of recovering possibilities embedded in tradition. The same condition can be said to exist in the West. The question is, once both Easterners and Westerners find themselves in the predicament of having lost their respective traditions, once they have shed, so to speak, what has heretofore been established, what possibilities might be discovered? It is precisely then and there that the Kyoto School philosophies of "nothingness" and "emptiness" may be able to contribute something. The contemporary potential of the Kyoto School presumably depends on what these philosophies of "nothingness" and "emptiness" may offer us in these troubled times.

Translated from the Japanese by Bret W. Davis

REFERENCES[61]

Abe, Masao. (1985) *Zen and Western Thought*, edited by William R. LaFleur. London: Macmillan (published in North America by University of Hawai'i Press).

---

[61] References and suggestions for further reading have been compiled by the translator. For more extensive bibliographies on the Kyoto School, see Heisig 2001, Ohashi 2014, and Davis 2019.

Abe, Masao. (1990) "Kenotic God and Dynamic Sunyata." In *The Emptying God: A Buddhist-Jewish-Christian Conversation with Masao Abe on God, Kenosis, and Sunyata*, edited by John B. Cobb, Jr. and Christopher Ives. Maryknoll, NY: Orbis Books, 3–65.

Abe, Masao. (2003) *Zen and the Modern World*, edited by Steven Heine. Honolulu: University of Hawai'i Press.

Calichman, Richard F., ed. and trans. (2008) *Overcoming Modernity: Cultural Identity in Wartime Japan*. New York: Columbia University Press.

Curley, Melissa Anne-Marie, Jessica L. Main, and Melanie Coughlin. (2017) "The Self-Awareness of Evil in Pure Land Buddhism: A Translation of Contemporary Kyoto School Philosopher Keta Masako," *Philosophy East and West* 67/1: 192–228.

Davis, Bret W. (2019) "The Kyoto School." In *The Stanford Encyclopedia of Philosophy* (Summer 2019 Edition), Edward N. Zalta (ed.), forthcoming URL = <https://plato.stanford.edu/archives/sum2019/entries/kyoto-school/>.

Goto-Jones, Christopher S., ed. (2008) *Re-politicising the Kyoto School as Philosophy*. London: Routledge.

Hanaoka, Eiko. (2009) *Zen and Christianity: From the Standpoint of Absolute Nothingness*. Kyoto: Maruzen.

Hase Shōtō. (2003) *Yokubō no tetsugaku: Jōdokyou sekai no shisaku* [Philosophy of Desire: An Inquiry into the World of Pure Land Buddhism]. Kyoto: Hōzōkan.

Hase Shōtō. (2005) *Kokoro ni utsuru mugen: Kū no imāju-ka* [The Infinite Reflected in the Heart-Mind: The Imaging of Emptiness]. Kyoto: Hōzōkan.

Hase Shōtō. (2010) *Jōdo to wa nanika: Shinran no shisaku to do ni okeru chōetsu* [What Is the Pure Land? The Thought of Shinran and Transcendence on Earth]. Kyoto: Hōzōkan.

Heisig, James W. (2001) *Philosophers of Nothingness: An Essay on the Kyoto School*. Honolulu: University of Hawai'i Press.

Heisig, James W., and John C. Maraldo, eds. (1994) *Rude Awakenings: Zen, The Kyoto School, and the Question of Nationalism*. Honolulu: University of Hawai'i Press.

Hisamatsu Shin'ichi. (1960) "The Characteristics of Oriental Nothingness," translated by Richard DeMartino. *Philosophical Studies of Japan* 2: 65–97.

Hisamatsu Shin'ichi (2002). *Kaku no tetsugaku* [Philosophy of Awakening], edited by Minobe Hitoshi. Kyoto: Tōeisha.

Hisamatsu Shin'ichi (2003). *Geijutsu to cha no tetsugaku* [Philosophy of Art and Tea], edited by Kurasawa Yukihiro. Kyoto: Tōeisha.

Kimura Bin. (1995) *Zwischen Mensch und Mensch: Strukturen japanischer Subjektivität*, translated by Elmar Weinmayr. Darmstadt: Wissenschaftliche Buchgesellschaft.

Kimura Bin. (2001) *Kimura Bin chosakushū* [Collected works of Kimura Bin]. Tokyo: Kōbundō.

Kōsaka Masaaki. (1999) *Meiji shisō-shi* [An Intellectual History of the Meiji Period], edited by Minamoto Ryōen. Kyoto: Tōeisha.

Kōsaka Masaaki. (2002) *Rekishi-teki sekai* [The Historical World], edited by Hase Shōtō. Kyoto: Tōeisha.

Kōyama Iwao. (2001*a*) *Bunka ruikei-gaku, Koō no genri* [The Study of Cultural Types, The Principle of Correspondence], edited by Saitō Giichi. Kyoto: Tōeisha.

Kōyama Iwao. (2001*b*) *Sekai-shi no tetsugaku* [The Philosophy of World History], edited by Hanazawa Hidefumi. Tokyo: Kobushi Shobō.

Maraldo, John C. (2006) "The War Over the Kyoto School." *Monumenta Nipponica* 61/3 (Autumn): 375–401.

Miki Kiyoshi. (1966) *Miki Kiyoshi zenshū* [Complete Works of Miki Kiyoshi]. Tokyo: Iwanami Shoten.

Miki Kiyoshi. (2001) *Sōzō suru kōsōryoku* [Creative Imagination], edited by Ōmine Akira. Kyoto: Tōeisha.

Miki Kiyoshi. (2011) "Towards a Logic of Imagination," translated by Gereon Kopf. In *Japanese Philosophy: A Sourcebook*, edited by James W. Heisig, Thomas P. Kasulis, and John C. Maraldo. Honolulu: University of Hawai'i Press, 705–707.

Murthy, Viren, Fabian Schafer, and Max Ward, eds. (2017) *Confronting Capital and Empire: Rethinking Kyoto School Philosophy*. Boston: Brill Academic.

Mutai Risaku. (2000) *Shakai sonzai no ronri* [The Logic of Social Existence], edited by Kitano Hiroyuki. Kyoto: Tōeisha.

Nishida Kitarō. (1970) *Fundamental Problems of Philosophy*, translated by David A. Dilworth. Tokyo: Sophia University Press.

Nishida Kitarō. (1987a) *Intuition and Reflection in Self-Consciousness*, translated by Valdo Viglielmo. New York: State University of New York Press.

Nishida Kitarō. (1987b) *Last Writings: Nothingness and the Religious Worldview*, translated by David A. Dilworth. Honolulu: University of Hawai'i Press.

Nishida Kitarō. (1990) *An Inquiry into the Good*, translated by Masao Abe and Christopher Ives. New Haven, CT: Yale University Press.

Nishida Kitarō. (2002–2009) *Shin Nishida Kitarō Zenshū* [New Complete Works of Nishida Kitarō], edited by Fujita Masakatsu, Kosaka Kunitsugu, Takeda Atsushi and Klaus Riesenhuber. Tokyo: Iwanami.

Nishida Kitarō. (2012) *Place and Dialectic: Two Essays by Nishida Kitarō*, translated by John W. M. Krummel and Shigenori Nagatomo. New York: Oxford University Press.

Nishitani, Keiji. (1982) *Religion and Nothingness*, translated by Jan Van Bragt. Berkeley: University of California Press.

Nishitani Keiji. (1986–1995) *Nishitani Keiji chosakushū* [Collected Works of Nishitani Keiji]. Tokyo: Sōbunsha.

Nishitani Keiji. (1990) *The Self-Overcoming of Nihilism*, translated by Graham Parkes with Setsuko Aihara. Albany, NY: SUNY Press.

Ōhashi Ryōsuke. (1995) *Nishida-tetsugaku no sekai* [The World of Nishida Philosophy]. Tokyo: Chikuma.

Ōhashi Ryōsuke. (1998) *Hi no genshōron josetsu: Nihontetsugaku no roku tēze yori* [Prolegomenon to a Phenomenology of Compassion: From Six Theses of Japanese Philosophy]. Tokyo: Sōbunsha.

Ōhashi Ryōsuke. (2001) *Kyōtogakuha to Nihon-kaigun: Shinshiryō "Ōshima memo" wo megutte* [The Kyoto School and the Japanese Navy: On the Newly Found Historical Document "The Ōshima Memoranda"]. Kyoto: PHP Kenkyūsho.

Ōhashi Ryōsuke. (2011b) "A Phenomenoetics of Compassion," translated by James W. Heisig. In *Japanese Philosophy: A Sourcebook*, edited by James W. Heisig, Thomas P. Kasulis, and John C. Maraldo. Honolulu: University of Hawai'i Press, 792–798.

Ohashi Ryôsuke, ed. (2014) *Die Philosophie der Kyōto-Schule*, 3rd edition. Freiburg: Karl Alber.

Ohashi, Ryôsuke. (2018) *Phänomenologie der Compassion: Pathos des Mitseins mit den Anderen*. Freiburg/Munich: Karl Alber.

Ōhashi Ryōsuke. (2019) *Kyōsei no patosu: Kompashiōn (Hi) no genshōgaku* [The Pathos of Being Together: A Phenomenology of Compassion]. Tokyo: Kobushi.

Ōmine Akira. (2008) *Jōdo no tetsugaku* [Philosophy of the Pure Land]. Kyoto: Honganji Shuppansha.

Ōmine Akira. (2009) *Shinjin no dentō* [The Tradition of the Entrusting Heart]. Kyoto: Honganji Shuppansha.

Osaki, Harumi. (2019) *Nothingness in the Heart of Empire: The Moral and Political Philosophy of the Kyoto School in Imperial Japan*. Albany: State University of New York Press.

Ōshima Yasumasa. (2000) "Daitōasensō to Kyōtogakuha: Chishikijin no seijisanka ni tsuite" [The Pacific War and the Kyoto School: On the Political Participation of Intellectuals]. In *Sekaishi no riron: Kyōtogakuha no rekishigaku ronkō* [Theory of World History: The Kyoto School's Writings on History], edited by Mori Testurō. Kyoto: Tōeisha, 274–304.

Parkes, Graham. (1997) "The Putative Fascism of the Kyoto School and the Political Correctness of the Modern Academy." *Philosophy East and West* 47/3: 305–336.

Parkes, Graham. (2011) "Heidegger and Japanese Fascism: An Unsubstantiated Connection." In *Japanese and Continental Philosophy: Conversations with the Kyoto School*, edited by Bret W. Davis, Brian Schroeder, and Jason M. Wirth. Bloomington: University of Indiana Press, 247–65.

Shimomura Toratarō. (2000) *Seishin-shi no naka no Nihon kindai* [Japanese Modernity within Intellectual History], edited by Ōhashi Ryōsuke. Kyoto: Tōeisha.

Shimomura Toratarō. (2003) *Seishin-shi toshite no kagaku-shi* [History of Science as Intellectual History], edited by Noe Keiichi. Kyoto: Tōeisha.

Sugimoto Kōichi. (2011) "Tanabe Hajime's Logic of Species and the Philosophy of Nishida Kitarō: A Critical Dialogue within the Kyoto School." In *Japanese and Continental Philosophy: Conversations with the Kyoto School*, edited by Bret W. Davis, Brian Schroeder, and Jason M. Wirth. Bloomington: University of Indiana Press, 52–67.

Suzuki Shigetaka. (2000) *Yōroppa no seiritsu, Sangyō-kakumei* [The Formation of Europe, The Industrial Revolution], edited by Kawakatsu Heita. Kyoto: Tōeisha.

Takeuchi Yoshinori. (1983) *The Heart of Buddhism*, edited and translated by James W. Heisig. New York: Crossroad.

Takeuchi Yoshinori. (1999) *Takeuchi Yoshinori chosakushū* [Collected Works of Takeuchi Yoshinori]. Kyoto: Hōzōkan.

Tanabe, Hajime. (1959) "Todesdialektik." In *Martin Heidegger zum siebzigsten Geburtstag: Festschrift*, edited by Günther Neske. Pfullingen: Neske, 93–133.

Tanabe Hajime. (1964) *Tanabe Hajime zenshū* [Complete Works of Tanabe Hajime]. Tokyo: Chikuma Shobō.

Tanabe Hajime. (1969) "The Logic of Species as Dialectics," translated by David Dilworth and Satō Taira. *Monumenta Nipponica* 24/3: 273–288.

Tanabe Hajime. (1986) *Philosophy as Metanoetics*, translated by Takeuchi Yoshinori. Berkeley: University of California Press.

Tanabe Hajime. (2000) *Zangedō toshite no tetsugaku—Shi no tetsugaku* [Philosophy as Metanoetics, The Philosophy of Death], edited by Hase Shōtō. Kyoto: Tōeisha.

Tosaka Jun. (1966) "Kyoto-gakuha no tetsugaku" [The Philosophy of the Kyoto School]. In *Tosaka Jun zenshū* [Complete Works of Tosaka Jun]. Tokyo: Keisō Shobō, vol. 3, 171–176.

Tsujimura Kōichi. (1971) *Haideggā ronkō* [Heidegger Studies]. Tokyo: Sōbunsha.

Tsujimura Kōichi. (1991) *Haideggā no shisaku* [Heidegger's Thought]. Tokyo: Sōbunsha.

Tsujimura, Kōichi. (2008) "Martin Heidegger's Thinking and Japanese Philosophy," translated by Richard Capobianco and Marie Göbel, *Epoché* 12/2: 349–57

Tsujimura Kōichi (2011). "All-in-One East and West," translated by James W. Heisig. In In *Japanese Philosophy: A Sourcebook*, edited by James W. Heisig, Thomas P. Kasulis, and John C. Maraldo. Honolulu: University of Hawai'i Press, 758–764.

Ueda Shizuteru. (2001–2004) *Ueda Shizuteru shū* [Collected Writings of Ueda Shizuteru]. Tokyo: Iwanami.

Ueda Shizuteru. (2011b) "Language in a Twofold World," translated by Bret W. Davis. In *Japanese Philosophy: A Sourcebook*, edited by James W. Heisig, Thomas P. Kasulis, and John C. Maraldo. Honolulu: University of Hawai'i Press, 766–784.

Ueda Shizuteru. (2011c) *Wer und was bin ich: Zur Phänomenologie des Selbst im Zen-Buddhismus.* Freiburg: Verlag Karl Alber.

Williams, David. (2014) *The Philosophy of Japanese Wartime Resistance: A Reading, with Commentary, of the Complete Texts of the Kyoto School Discussions of "The Standpoint of World History and Japan."* New York: Routledge.

FURTHER READING

Carter, Robert E. (2013) *The Kyoto School: An Introduction*, with a forward by Thomas P. Kasulis. Albany: State University of New York Press.

Davis, Bret W. (2002) "Introducing the Kyoto School as World Philosophy," *The Eastern Buddhist*, 3 4/2: 142–170.

Davis, Bret W. (2011) "Dialogue and Appropriation: The Kyoto School as Cross-Cultural Philosophy." In *Japanese and Continental Philosophy: Conversations with the Kyoto School*, edited by Bret W. Davis, Brian Schroeder, and Jason M. Wirth. Bloomington: University of Indiana Press, 33–51.

Davis, Bret W., Brian Schroeder, and Jason M. Wirth, eds. (2011) *Japanese and Continental Philosophy: Conversations with the Kyoto School.* Bloomington: University of Indiana Press.

Dilworth, David A., and Valdo H. Viglielmo with Agustín Jacinto Zavala, eds. (1998) *Sourcebook for Modern Japanese Philosophy: Selected Documents.* Westport, CT: Greenwood Press.

Frank, Fredrick, ed. (2004) *The Buddha Eye: An Anthology of the Kyoto School and Its Contemporaries.* Bloomington, IN: World Wisdom.

Fujita Masakatsu, ed. (2001) *Kyōtogakuha no tetsugaku* [The Philosophy of the Kyoto School]. Kyoto: Shōwadō.

Fujita Masakatsu, ed. (2018) *The Philosophy of the Kyoto School*, translated by Robert Chapeskie with John W. M. Krummel. Singapore: Springer.

Goto-Jones, Christopher S. (2005) *Political Philosophy in Japan: Nishida, The Kyoto School, and Co-Prosperity.* London: Routledge.

Heisig, James W. (1998) "Kyoto School." In *Routledge Encyclopedia of Philosophy*, edited by E. Craig. London: Routledge.

Heisig, James W., Thomas P. Kasulis, and John C. Maraldo, eds. (2011) *Japanese Philosophy: A Sourcebook.* Honolulu: University of Hawai'i Press.

Hisamatsu Shin'ichi. (1994–1996) *Hisamatsu Shin'ichi chosakushū* [Collected Works of Hisamatsu Shin'ichi]. Kyoto: Hōzōkan.

Kasulis, Thomas. (1982) "The Kyoto School and the West." *The Eastern Buddhist* 15/2: 125–145.

Kimura Bin. (2011) "Time and Self," translated by John W. Krummel. In *Japanese Philosophy: A Sourcebook*, edited by James W. Heisig, Thomas P. Kasulis, and John C. Maraldo. Honolulu: University of Hawai'i Press, 958–972.

Maraldo, John C. (2005) "Ōbei no shiten kara mita Kyōtogakuha no yurai to yukue" [The Whence and Whither of the Kyoto School from a Western Perspective], translated by Azumi Yurika. In *Sekai no naka no Nihon no tetsugaku* [Japanese Philosophy in the World], edited by Fujita Masakatsu and Bret Davis. Kyoto: Shōwadō, 31–56.

Maraldo, John C. (2006) "The War over the Kyoto School," *Monumenta Nipponica* 61/ 3: 375–401.

Mori Testurō, ed. (2000) *Sekaishi no riron: Kyōtogakuha no rekishigaku ronkō* [Theory of World History: The Kyoto School's Writings on History]. Kyoto: Tōeisha.

Nishida Kitarō. (1987–1989) *Nishida Kitarō zenshū* [Complete Works of Nishida Kitarō]. Tokyo: Iwanami.

Nishitani Keiji. (1991) *Nishida Kitarō*, translated by Yamamoto Seisaku and James W. Heisig. Berkeley: University of California Press.

Nishitani Keiji. (2004) "Science and Zen," translated by Richard de Martino. In *The Buddha Eye: An Anthology of the Kyoto School and Its Contemporaries*, edited by F. Frank. Bloomington, IN: World Wisdom, 107–135.

Ōhashi Ryōsuke, ed. (2004) *Kyōtogakuha no shisō* [The Thought of the Kyoto School]. Kyoto: Jinbun Shoin.

Ōhashi Ryōsuke. (2011a) "Philosophy as Auto-Bio-Graphy: The Example of the Kyoto School," translated by Jason M. Wirth. In *Japanese and Continental Philosophy: Conversations with the Kyoto School*, edited by Bret W. Davis, Brian Schroeder, and Jason M. Wirth. Bloomington: University of Indiana Press, 71–81.

Tosaka Jun. (1998) "Is the 'Logic of Nothingness' Logic? On the Method of Nishida's Philosophy," translated by D. Dilworth and V. H. Viglielmo. *Sourcebook for Modern Japanese Philosophy: Selected Documents*, edited by David A. Dilworth, Valdo H. Viglielmo, and Agustín Jacinto Zavala. Westport, CT: Greenwood Press, 362–371.

Ueda, Shizuteru. (1965) *Die Gottesgeburt in der Seele und der Durchbruch zu Gott. Die mystische Anthropologie Meister Eckharts und ihre Konfrontation mit der Mystik des Zen Buddhismus*. Gütersloh: Gütersloher Verlagshaus Gerd Mohn. (In 2018, a new edition of this work appeared from Verlag Karl Alber in Freiburg/Munich.)

Ueda Shizuteru. (1994) "Nishida, Nationalism, and the War in Question," translated by Jan Van Bragt. In *Rude Awakenings: Zen, The Kyoto School, and the Question of Nationalism*, edited by James W. Heisig and John C. Maraldo. Honolulu: University of Hawai'i Press, 77–106.

Ueda Shizuteru, ed. (2006) *Zen to Kyoto-tetsugaku* [Zen and Kyoto Philosophy]. Kyoto: Tōeisha.

Ueda Shizuteru. (2011a) "Contributions to Dialogue with the Kyoto School," translated by Bret W. Davis. In *Japanese and Continental Philosophy: Conversations with the Kyoto School*, edited by Bret W. Davis, Brian Schroeder, and Jason M. Wirth. Bloomington: University of Indiana Press, 19–32.

Unno, Taitetsu, ed. (1989) *The Religious Philosophy of Nishitani Keiji*. Berkeley, CA: Asian Humanities Press.

Unno, Taitetsu, and James W. Heisig, eds. (1990) *The Religious Philosophy of Tanabe Hajime*. Berkeley, CA: Asian Humanities Press.

CHAPTER 17

....

THE DEVELOPMENT OF
NISHIDA KITARŌ'S
PHILOSOPHY

Pure Experience, Place, Action-Intuition

....

FUJITA MASAKATSU

NISHIDA Kitarō's (1870–1945) first book, *An Inquiry into the Good* (*Zen no kenkyū*, 1911), is a monumental work that marks the beginning of the independent development of philosophy as an academic discipline in Japan, following the period of its importation from the West. From that point in time until his death in 1945, Nishida continued to think and write prolifically about a variety of issues, thus contributing greatly to the establishment and growth of Japanese philosophy. This chapter addresses the query: What was the central problematic of Nishida's thought over those many years? In other words, what was his fundamental question?

This query, however, contains a paradox, insofar as Nishida's thought, together with the times in which he lived,[1] underwent major transformations. In his 1936 preface to the republication of *An Inquiry into the Good*, Nishida himself reflected on the development of his thought as follows:

> In *Intuition and Reflection in Self-Awareness* [*Jikaku ni okeru chokkan to hansei*, 1917], through the mediation of Fichte's standpoint of *Tathandlung* (deed-act), the standpoint of pure experience [*junsui keiken* 純粋経験] was developed into the standpoint of absolute will [*zettai ishi* 絶対意志]. Then, in the second half of *From That Which Acts to That Which Sees* [*Hataraku mono kara miru mono e*, 1927], through the mediation of Greek philosophy, it underwent a conversion into the thought of "place" [*basho* 場所]. At that point I acquired an initial sense of how to make my

---

[1] On Nishida's cultural and political thought leading up to and during the Pacific War, see Fujita 2011, 193–273; Kosaka 2001, 8–15, 30–99; Elberfeld 1999; Goto-Jones 2005; Davis 2006 and 2013; the chapters by Ueda Shizuteru and Yusa Michiko in Heisig and Maraldo 1994; as well as Chapters 16 and 36 in this volume.—*Tr.*

thought logical. Next, the thought of "place" was made more concrete as "the dialectical universal" [*benshōhō-teki ippansha* 弁証法的一般者], and then the dialectical universal was made more immediate as "action-intuition" [*kōi-teki chokkan* 行為的 直観]. That which I call in the present book the world of direct or pure experience I have now come to think of as the world of historical reality. The world of action-intuition—the world of *poiesis*—is truly the world of pure experience.[2]

In this way Nishida both acknowledges a transformation in his thinking at the same time as he claims that it is pervaded by something that remained constant. Also in his 1935 preface to his student Kōyama Iwao's book, *Nishidan Philosophy* (*Nishida-tetsugaku*), Nishida writes:

> Since *An Inquiry into the Good* my thinking has arisen neither from the subject nor from the object, but rather from that which precedes the separation of subject and object. That remains unchanged to this day. Yet, with regard to the question of how to philosophically conceive of this immediate and concrete standpoint, and the question of how to think about various problems from such a standpoint, my thought has undergone various changes in the course of its repeated struggles.[3]

As can be seen clearly in this passage, Nishida's basic philosophical comportment, from his earlier to his later writings, remained that of returning to what is most immediate and concrete—to what he says is "prior to the separation of subject and object"—and attempting to grasp the entirety of matters from there. However, precisely with regard to the question of how to conceive of that which is most immediate and concrete, and with regard to the question of how to grasp the entirety of matters from there, it can be said that his thought underwent great changes.

Nevertheless, Nishida's initial thoughts revolving around "pure experience" did unquestionably lay the foundation for the whole of his thinking, and, for that reason, I would like to begin by inquiring into the problem he attempted to address with this concept.

PURE EXPERIENCE

What Is Pure Experience?

In *An Inquiry into the Good*, Nishida gives various explanations of pure experience.[4] For example, in the opening paragraph of the first chapter of the first part of the book,

---

[2] Nishida 2002–2009, 1: 3; Nishida 1990, xxxii–xxxiii, translation modified.
[3] Nishida 2002–2009, 11: 281.
[4] Nishida adopted the term "pure experience" from William James, but rethinks it in his own manner based in no small part on his prolonged and intense practice of Zen. See Fujita 1998, 39–65; Fujita 2007, 38–60; Dilworth 1969; Feenberg and Arisaka 1990; Yusa 2002, 49–102; Ueda 1991, 59–257; and Ueda 1993*b*.—Tr.

Nishida states: "Pure experience is identical with direct experience. When one directly experiences one's own state of consciousness, there is not yet a subject [*shu* 主] or an object [*kyaku* 客], and knowing and its object [*taishō* 対象] are completely unified."[5] He goes on to say: "Without adding the least bit of thought, we can shift our attention within the state where subject and object have not yet separated."[6] And, in the final chapter appended to the book, "Knowledge and Love," he writes: "When we are absorbed in something the self loves, for example, we are almost totally unconscious. We forget the self, and at this point an incomprehensible power beyond the self functions alone in all of its majesty; there is neither subject nor object, but only the true union of subject and object."[7]

Using such expressions as "before there is either subject or object," "prior to the separation of subject and object," and "the unification of subject and object," Nishida is clearly targeting for criticism the dualism that sets what is subjective and objective over against one another. Regarding the positing of such an opposition, Nishida writes:

> With respect to seeing reality directly, there is no distinction between subject and object in any state of direct experience—one encounters reality face to face. . . . The distinction between subject and object is a relative form that arises when the unity of experience has been lost, and to regard subject and object as mutually independent realities is merely an arbitrary view.[8]

Nishida thus avoids what he calls the "arbitrary view" that reifies, on the one hand, the mind, or more precisely the "inner mind" or "consciousness" that represents the outside world, and, on the other hand, the "outside world" that is represented by such a consciousness. He thereby expresses the view that the opposition between subject and object is something that is introduced later by means of the work of reflection, whereas in the original experience there is no such distinction or opposition. Repeated statements about experience that is "prior to the separation of subject and object" indicate the fact that this kind of criticism of the subject–object opposition is the central theme of *An Inquiry into the Good*.

It could be said that what supports the opposition of subject and object is, in a sense, nothing other than our everyday manner of seeing things. In everyday life, we do not see things just as they are perceived, but rather supplement this perception with a supposition of how they would look when situated in three-dimensional space. For example, a coin that appears as an oval when seen from an angle is reconceived as a circle, and moreover as something that has a certain thickness to it. Hence, we see things not only as they appear to our own viewpoint, for at the same time we reconceive of them as things that could be observed from any direction. Expressed otherwise, our manner of

---

[5] Nishida 2002–2009, 1: 9; Nishida 1990, 3–4.
[6] Nishida 2002–2009, 1: 11; Nishida 1990, 6.
[7] Nishida 2002–2009, 1: 157; Nishida 1990, 174–175.
[8] Nishida 2002–2009, 1: 34; Nishida 1990, 31–32, translation modified.

seeing things takes our "private" perceptions and repositions them in "public" space. It goes without saying that the natural sciences are based on this manner of viewing things as positioned in "public" space.

It is conceivable that the framework of the so-called opposition of subject and object is constructed by means of setting in opposition what appears to my perspective and what is repositioned in three-dimensional space—that is, what is private and what is public—in the form of "consciousness" and "the outside world." One conclusion naturally drawn from this kind of opposition is that to be conscious is thought of only as an event internal to consciousness and that the content of consciousness is thought of merely as a mental image or representation of what lies outside of consciousness. A further conclusion drawn is that sensations of things like colors and flavors are thought to be reducible to consciousness, and the object in itself is depicted as belonging to a world without color or fragrance that precedes sensation. This supposition is then linked to a manner of thinking according to which the content of consciousness is not the object itself but rather the product of some sort of transformation of the object. Of course, the process of this transformation then becomes problematic. The history of philosophy reveals how many philosophers have, by beginning with this dualistic presupposition, become stuck in the narrow straits of the mind–body problem.

If the basic stance of dualism is to posit, on the one hand, a world of sensation and, on the other, objects as they are in themselves prior to sensation, to think that these are, as it were, spatially separated, and to think of the relation between them in terms of that which reflects and that which is reflected, then Nishida's critique of such an opposition between subject and object can be said to have hit upon the great discrepancy between this kind of construct and the real nature of our experience. The outside world directly participates in our experience. It is not the case that we feel fear or sense a delicious taste inside of a consciousness that is set off at a distance from the outside world. The delicious thing or the thing that arouses fear is directly engaged therein. Conversely stated, things do not present themselves simply as things but rather, from the start, as things that, for example, provide us with the taste of deliciousness or fill us with fear. There is no distance here between two worlds. In other words, there is no "backside" of a delicious apple or a fearsome angry dog.

In his 1936 preface to *An Inquiry into the Good*, Nishida borrows the language of Gustav Fechner (1801–1887) to characterize the abstractness of a conception of reality that sets the world of sensation over against objects that precede sensation as "the colorless and soundless perspective of night found in the natural sciences," in contrast to "the perspective of daytime, in which truth is things just as they are."[9] Standing in front of grasses, flowers, and trees, we are confronted with "plants imbued with living colors and shapes" and not with "purely physical" plants. Moreover, we do not confront plants merely as perceptual or cognitive objects. Together with being objects of

---

[9] Nishida 2002–2009, 1: 4; Nishida 1990, xxxiii. See Gustav Fechner, *Die Tagesansicht gegenüber der Nachtansicht* (Leipzig: Breitkopf und Härtel, 1879), p. 1.

knowledge, grasses, flowers, and trees are things that provide us with refreshing moisture and sanctuary; that is to say, they are things that are "established through our feeling
and willing."[10] The fact that we see "living colors and shapes" or experience refreshing
moisture and sanctuary in plants is not, according to Nishida, merely something that
happens within consciousness. Situating mental phenomena on the inside and physical
phenomena on the outside is, therefore, avoided by him as an "arbitrary view."

To be sure, in *An Inquiry to the Good* Nishida claims that reality is "the phenomena of
consciousness." That "the phenomena of consciousness are the sole reality" is one of the
principal theses of the book. Yet Nishida is not claiming that experience is internal to
consciousness. He clearly rejects such an understanding as mistaken. What is indicated
by the phrase "the phenomena of consciousness" is not mental phenomena in distinction from physical phenomena. Rather, what is indicated is a knowing of facts merely as
facts, prior to the thought of the existence of external things or the existence of the subject. "If red, then merely red"[11]—that is what is meant by "the phenomena of consciousness." This is also a matter of the direct arising into appearance of an object. When a red
salvia flower is seen, the salvia flower itself is arising into appearance. When the rustling
in the wind of tree leaves is heard, the rustling sound of the leaves itself arises into appearance. Reality does not depart from that place and exist somewhere else. "True reality is not something divided into subjectivity and objectivity, and actual nature is not
a purely objective, abstract concept but rather a concrete fact of consciousness that
includes both subject and object."[12]

We have said that we do not see things as mere objects of perception. We feel them to
be beautiful or see them as evoking tranquility or fright. Things are manifesting there
directly, and, even in the flux of our emotions, we are not locked up inside of consciousness. Objects themselves participate in the arousal of our emotions. When the melan-
cholic notes of a violin move our hearts, it is not that our hearts are moved by thought
associations and analogies that are evoked by the sound. Rather, the reverberation of the
strings itself gives rise to our emotions.

As we have seen, concrete reality can be said to "encompass subject and object" and include "feeling and volition." Any "pure matter" prior to sensation is a thought-construct
formed by means of repositioning this concrete reality in three-dimensional space and,
in that sense, must be said to be "that which is most abstract and most removed from the
true view of reality."[13]

[10] Nishida 2002–2009, 1: 50; Nishida 1990, 49.
[11] Nishida 2002–2009, 15: 99.
[12] Nishida 2002–2009, 1: 71; Nishida 1990, 72, translation modified.
[13] Nishida 2002–2009, 1: 67; Nishida 1990, 69, translation modified.

A Logic of Fluidity

Things that have been repositioned in three-dimensional space can be measured with "public" yardsticks and spoken of in "public" language. Yet the undivided knowledge-emotion-volition (*chi-jō-i* 知情意) of the facts of our direct experience themselves can neither be measured nor spoken of in such public manners. In the fourth chapter of the second part of *An Inquiry into the Good*, entitled "Reality," Nishida expresses this point by saying: "We must personally realize the true view of reality, rather than reflect on it, analyze it, and express it in words."[14] Nishida's critique of positing an opposition of subject and object is thus a critique of the idea that grasping the truth is equivalent to measuring it with public yardsticks and speaking about it in public language.

Let us consider, for example, an exercise such as rotating one's arm or swinging one's leg forward and backward. By measuring the sequential positions of one's arm or leg and the time elapsed between these points, it is no doubt possible to use physics to describe and explain the exercise. But that would not explain the continuity or unity of the exercise, which is precisely how I am conscious of it. Like these exercises, our emotions also have a dynamic quality to them. The emotion of sadness, for instance, is hardly something uniform; its movement is such that at times it tends in the direction of grief, or self-abandonment, or anger. Shifting directions, varying widely, it moves unceasingly. It cannot be summed up in the one word "sadness," nor can it be precisely grasped by breaking it down into components of grief, anger, and so on since then its unity is lost sight of.

We endlessly attempt to analyze and describe in detail that which changes unceasingly. By dividing up and fixing in place a myriad number of parts and then reconstructing the whole, we attempt to understand that which changes unceasingly. Or else we cut it off at a certain point and try to use that segment to represent the whole. Yet what we actually experience is not an assemblage of divided and fixed pieces; it has rather the quality of a continuous movement that resists being divided up. Such a thing can only be, as Nishida puts it, "personally realized" (*jitoku suru* 自得する). To use Bergson's expression, it must be "intuited." As Bergson says, this requires us to enter deeply into a thing, "to probe more deeply into its life, and by a kind of *spiritual auscultation*, to feel its soul palpitate."[15]

The year before the publication of *An Inquiry into the Good*, the same year he began teaching at Kyoto University, Nishida published an essay called "Bergson's Philosophical Method," in which he expresses sympathy with Bergson's notion of "intuition." He explains it as "seeing a thing from within," or "seeing by means of becoming a thing itself," and says that it is the only method with which one can "know the true state of a thing itself."[16] Sympathy with Bergson also appears in Nishida's understanding of "pure

---

[14] Nishida 2002–2009, 1: 52; Nishida 1990, 51, translation modified.

[15] Henri Bergson, *Introduction à la métaphysique*, in *Œuvres*, annotated by André Robinet (Paris: Presses Universitaires de France, 1959, 1408); Henri Bergson, *The Creative Mind*, trans. Mabelle L. Andison (New York: Philosophical Library, 1946, 206).

[16] Nishida 2002–2009, 1: 255. Nishida first encountered Bergson's thought soon after assuming his post at Kyoto University. *An Inquiry into the Good* was published the following year, but the manuscript

experience." In his notes for a lecture course called "A Survey of Philosophy," given at Kyoto University in 1911, Nishida defines pure experience in English as "autonomous, qualitatively continuous change." This clearly reflects Bergson's understanding of "*durée pure*" (pure duration) as "nothing but a succession of qualitative changes, which melt into and permeate one another, without precise outlines, without any tendency to externalize themselves in relation to one another, without any affiliation with number."[17] In fact, in those lecture notes, Nishida refers to Bergson's *durée pure* in the following manner:

> [Reality] *continuously changes* without ceasing for *a moment*. Moreover, the manner of this *change* is such that each *moment* points to the state that is about to arrive and includes the state that has already past. It is what Bergson calls *durée interne, durée pure*. This state is our everyday *exp[erience]*, yet it cannot be exhaustively conveyed by means of external *Analyses* even if millions of words are employed. It can only be directly experienced from within.[18]

In comparison with explanations in *An Inquiry into the Good*, what is striking in these notes is Nishida's stress on the dynamic quality of pure experience. Of course, *An Inquiry into the Good* also speaks of "differentiating development" as "the mode in which true reality is established" and of the autonomous "developmental perfecting" of a thing. In the background of the language of "developmental perfecting" clearly lies Nishida's understanding of Hegel's "concept." By contrast, in these lecture notes, pure experience is understood in a sense that is closer to Bergson's *durée pure*. In an essay written around this same time, "Bergson's Philosophical Method," Nishida writes: "Concrete reality that is directly given to us is fluid, developmental, does not halt for an instant, that is to say, it is something that is alive."[19]

If this "living thing" that does not stop moving for even an instant were to become an object of dissecting analysis, it would presumably "become a kind of dried up, rigidified, and lifeless semiotic intellection."[20] In "Bergson's Philosophical Method," Nishida clearly avoids as an error the attitude of orienting oneself from this kind of "semiotic intellection" and attempting to see the whole of matters from there, in other words, the method of attempting to proceed from analysis to intuition. He claims, on the contrary, that the true philosophical method begins with a "direct experience from within" of that which changes and flows; that is to say, it proceeds from intuition to analysis.

---

was completed prior to his arrival at Kyoto University, and no influence from Bergson's thought can be found in it.

[17] Henri Bergson, *Essai sur les données immédiates de la conscience*, in *Œuvres*, 70; Henri Bergson, *Time and Free Will: An Essay on the Immediate Data of Consciousness*, trans. F. L. Pogson (London: George Allen & Company, 1913, 104).

[18] Nishida 2002–2009, 15: 105. [The italicized words are in English and French in Nishida's notes.—*Tr.*]

[19] Nishida 2002–2009, 1: 256.

[20] Nishida 2002–2009, 1: 261.

If we can call the method that endlessly analyzes and attempts to reconstruct the whole from innumerable rigidified pieces a "logic of rigidification," we can call Nishida's and Bergson's method, which attempts to take hold of that which changes ceaselessly in its very dynamism, a "logic of fluidity" (*ryūdōsei no ronri* 流動性の論理).

PLACE

Toward the Standpoint of "Place"

If we divide the development of Nishida's thought into early, middle, and later periods, the representative text of his middle period is the essay "Place" (*Basho*),[21] published in 1926. Soon thereafter, Sōda Kiichirō published "On the Method of Nishidian Philosophy: A Request for Instruction from Dr. Nishida," which amounted to a scathing critique of Nishida's "Basho" from a Neo-Kantian position that goes so far as to say: "I cannot help but deeply doubt that it is acceptable as scholarship."[22] But Sōda did not simply criticize Nishida's philosophy; in fact, his critique followed upon an acknowledgment that, in "Place" and the preceding essay "That Which Acts" (*Hataraku mono*), Nishida "had entered a realm in which he can be said to have established a distinct system." As can be seen from the title of his essay, Sōda crowned Nishida's discourse with the title "Nishidan Philosophy" (*Nishida-tetsugaku* 西田哲学), and he presumably did this in recognition of the fruition of Nishida's thought in these essays. In the wake of Sōda's essay, Nishida's discourse began to be widely referred to as "Nishidan Philosophy."[23]

Soon after Sōda's critique appeared, Nishida published "Responding to Dr. Sōda" (*Sōda-hakase ni kotau*, 1927). In the beginning of his response, Nishida writes: "At the end of 'Place' I believe I managed to attain to a thought that differs to some degree from previous ones."[24] Here, he expresses his shift to the standpoint of "place" (*basho* 場所) in a rather understated manner. Yet, as we have seen in the statement from the preface to the 1936 edition of *An Inquiry into the Good*—"in the second half of *From That Which Acts to That Which Sees*, through the mediation of Greek philosophy, [my philosophical standpoint] underwent a conversion into the thought of 'place.' At that point I acquired an initial sense of how to make my thought logical"[25]—Nishida realized that during this period his thought accomplished a significant advancement.

[21] Nishida 2012*a*, 49–102.

[22] Sōda Kiichirō, "Nishida-tetsugaku no hōhō ni tsuite: Nishida-hakase no oshie o kou," *Tetsugaku kenkyū* [Research in Philosophy] 117: 3; reprinted in Fujita 1998, 45.

[23] *Nishida tetsugaku* is often translated ungrammatically as "Nishida philosophy." However, the Japanese locution itself is not ungrammatical and is best rendered as "Nishidan philosophy."—*Tr.*

[24] Nishida 2002–2009, 3: 479.

[25] Nishida 2002–2009, 1: 3; Nishida 1990, xxxii–xxxiii, translation modified.

The phrase "underwent a conversion" (*itten shite* 一転して) indicates the enormity of the transformation. The 1936 preface also reveals that this transformation was firmly connected to a "making logical," literally a "logicization" (*ronrika* 論理化) of his thought. By contrast, Nishida writes of the deficiencies of his previous thought with such expressions as "psychologism," "the standpoint of consciousness," and "subjectivism." Nishida was presumably compelled toward such self-critical reflection by the critique of so-called "psychologism" carried out by the Neo-Kantians and Husserl. In an essay included in *Thought and Experience* (*Shisaku to taiken*) entitled "On the Epistemological Claims of the Pure Logic School" (*Ninshikiron ni okeru junronriha no shuchō ni tsuite*, 1911), Nishida groups the Neo-Kantians—especially those belonging to the Southwestern or Baden school—and Husserl under the moniker "the Pure Logic School," and he discusses their critique of psychologism. He takes very seriously their severe criticism of philosophical standpoints that attempt to reduce epistemological issues to experiential and temporal matters.

This problem can be heard reverberating in the preface to *Philosophical Essays III* (*Tetsugaku ronbunshū dai san*, 1939), where Nishida reflects on the course his thought had taken since *An Inquiry into the Good*. He writes:

> Since *An Inquiry into the Good* my aim has been to try to see and think about things from the most immediate and most fundamental standpoint. I have attempted to grasp the standpoint from which everything arises and back to which everything returns. Even though "pure experience" bore a psychological taint, it was nevertheless a standpoint beyond subject and object from which I attempted to think of the "objective world" as well. Nonetheless, through coming into contact with the likes of the Southwestern School of Neo-Kantianism, this standpoint of pure experience had to be thoroughly critiqued. Consequently, I came to adopt a standpoint akin to Fichte's self-awareness.[26]

However, the standpoint of "self-awareness" (*jikaku* 自覚) was also unable to wipe away entirely the "psychological taint." In other words, it did not sufficiently provide the logical quality required for constructing a philosophical system. It is precisely for this reason that the transformation to the standpoint of "place" was necessary. Nishida confirms this in his preface to Kōyama's *Nishidan Philosophy*: "Neither pure experience nor [Fichte's] *Tathandlung* are able to fundamentally break free of subjectivism. Through the mediation of Aristotle's *hypokeimenon*, my thought finally came to demand as its starting point something logical."[27]

Nishida thus recognized that his philosophy can be said to have undergone a significant transformation when it came to assume the standpoint of "place." However, it would be one-sided to see here only a change in his thought. We need to give due consideration to connections with his previous thought. The "logicization" of Nishida's thought, after

---

[26] Nishida 2002–2009, 8: 255.
[27] Nishida 2002–2009, 11: 281.

all, was certainly not a mere application of a different logic that he happened to have come upon. Rather, it was something that his thought itself demanded. As he says in his preface to Kōyama's *Nishidan Philosophy*, guidance for this logicization did come unmistakably from Aristotle's concept of *hypokeimenon*. Nishida says he received therefrom an "initial sense," a "hint," for how to make his thought logical. Yet it is not the case that he adopted Aristotle's concept as is. Rather, as we shall see, he reinterprets it. And what required this reinterpretation was Nishida's own thought. Hence, I would like to first of all focus on the connections between the thought of place and Nishida's previous thought and then turn our attention to what is newly revealed by the thought of place.

It is often said that after *An Inquiry into the Good* the early notion of pure experience, as well as the thought based on that notion, quickly vanished from Nishida's thinking. However, it can be said that Nishida's thinking remained consistently characterized by the attempt to return to an "immediate and concrete standpoint"—that is, to "the standpoint that is most direct and most fundamental"—and to comprehend the entirety of matters from there. In the first essay collected in *From That Which Acts to That Which Sees*, "That Which Is Directly Given" (*Chokusetsu ni ataerareru mono*), Nishida uses the term "pure experience" and expresses this as follows:

> What can be referred to as the truly given direct experience or pure experience ... must be understood as containing an infinite content. The further we delve into its depths, the more there is the reality that is given. If we speak of this subjectively, it is the self that cannot be objectified; and if we speak of it objectively, it is the directly given that cannot be fathomed by reflection. There is there an intuition of the unity of subject and object, a consciousness of pure activity, and the wellspring of all knowledge.[28]

The essays collected in *From That Which Acts to That Which Sees* can be said to revolve around and deepen the thought of what Nishida speaks of in this passage as "pure experience," namely "the self that cannot be objectified" and "the directly given that cannot be fathomed by reflection."

The Problem of Logicization and the Concept of Substance

However, a great problem arose here for Nishida: namely, that of the relation between this kind of direct experience and conceptual knowledge based on judgments. We could say that Nishida first became aware of the task of logicizing—making logical—his thought in the form of this kind of problem.

[28] Nishida 2002–2009, 3: 272.

The first text in which Nishida deals with this problem is the fourth essay in *From That Which Acts to That Which Sees*, "On Internal Perception" (*Naibu chikaku ni tsuite*). In the beginning of its third section, referring to Bernard Bosanquet's (1848–1923) "The Essentials of Logic," Nishida writes: "The grammatical subject of perceptual judgements is originally not the so-called logical subject; rather, it must be reality."[29] He then discusses Aristotle's concept of "substance." His claim here corresponds to that of the following passage from "The Unsolved Issue of Consciousness," an essay written soon after "Place":

> As Bosanquet put it, when we say that "this desk is made of oak," what is truly the grammatical subject is not "this desk" but *reality*. It is the synthetic whole that really becomes Aristotle's substance (*hypokeimenon*).[30]

It could be said that, by introducing the concept of this kind of "reality" or "substance," Nishida is attempting to relate direct experience and conceptual knowledge to one another. Adopting verbatim the Aristotelian definition of "substance" as "that which is always a grammatical subject and never a predicate," Nishida writes of the relation between the two as follows:

> The substance that only ever becomes a grammatical subject and never a predicate must be the unification of a limitless predicate, that is, something that unifies infinite judgements. That which unifies one judgement and another must be something that is beyond judgements. Our acts of judgement endlessly orient themselves toward, and yet can never reach, this object. I think of this something in terms of intuition.[31]

As iterated in this passage, the distinguishing characteristic of Nishida's understanding of "substance" is that he thinks of it in terms of intuition. This is not merely a matter of Aristotle's idea of "the individual thing that is one and not two." Nishida's idea is that at the basis thereof is always "the intuition of something irrational." The "individual substance" or "*individuum*," he thought, is rather a product of the "conceptualization" of this kind of intuition.

In "That Which Acts," Nishida explains the relation between experience and judgment as follows:

> The world of things arises by means of our rationalization of the content of experience. To rationalize (*gōrika suru* 合理化する) experience is a matter of experience itself becoming the grammatical subject, that is to say, becoming the substance that becomes grammatical subject and not predicate. Yet that experience itself becomes the grammatical subject must mean that experience, as a self-identical concrete

[29] Nishida 2002–2009, 3: 325.
[30] Nishida 2002–2009, 7: 221; Nishida 2012*b*, 55. [The italicized words are in English and Greek in Nishida's text.—*Tr.*]
[31] Nishida 2002–2009, 3: 327.

universal, establishes judgements within itself by determining (i.e., delimiting, *gentei suru koto* 限定すること) itself.[32]

The rationalization of experience means that experience, which in itself transcends thought and judgment, is reflectively grasped as a universal that is identical with itself (and thus about which only a judgment of self-identity is possible). In Aristotle's language, this means that it is reconceived as "the substance that becomes grammatical subject and not predicate." The establishment of a judgment within a universal can be understood to take place by means of a "substance that becomes grammatical subject and not predicate" (i.e., the "concrete universal") "reflecting back into itself"; that is to say, by means of that which is in itself unitary "differentiating" and "describing itself."

Self-Awareness and Place

Nishida also thinks of this process of the rationalization of experience in terms of "self-awareness" (*jikaku* 自覚). In "On Internal Perception" he writes: "Judgement … must be the self-awareness of a substance that does not become predicate."[33] Here, substance is understood not merely as a universal, but rather as the "I" (*ware* 我) or "self" (*jiko* 自己) that transcends all activity of judging; that is, as that which "does not act" yet lies at the base of all acting and enables acting. This is "the substance that does not enter into acting" and at the same time that which "knows itself" or "sees itself." In other words, it is that which concretizes the self and maintains the self by means of "reflecting the self inside itself." Judgment is a matter of the "self-expression" of this kind of substance.

In this manner, Nishida attends to the act of "self-awareness" as a matter of "reflecting the self within itself," and, at the same time, he turns his attention to the place in which this act of self-awareness is established. He writes for example:

> To the establishment of the consciousness of self-awareness, the [fact that this takes place] "in oneself" must be added. Self-awareness is a matter of the unity of the I that knows, the I that is known, and the place in which I know me.[34]

This is the first passage in which Nishida uses the term "place" in his distinctive sense.

The establishment of the thought of place is thus intimately connected with Nishida's consideration of the place-character of self-awareness. And it is with this in mind that he takes up the concept of substance and interprets it in his distinctive manner. The essence of self-awareness is a matter of the I—as "the substance that does not enter into the act"—concretizing itself and seeing itself by means of reflecting itself in itself. This is what Nishida means when he writes: "That which transcends and envelops the self is

---

[32] Nishida 2002–2009, 3: 397.
[33] Nishida 2002–2009, 3: 351.
[34] Nishida 2002–2009, 3: 350.

the self itself."[35] When Nishida came to understand the relation between "that which transcends the I" and "the I" in terms of an "enveloping" (*tsutsumu koto* 包むこと), it would seem natural that he was compelled to attend to the place-quality of self-awareness as something that takes place "in oneself." The concept of self-awareness had already played a key role in Nishida's *Intuition and Reflection in Self-Awareness (Jikaku ni okeru chokkan to hansei*, 1917),[36] but now it is rethought not merely as the activity of endless self-development or self-creation, but in the context of a substance that, while not entering into any activity whatsoever, reflects itself within itself, sees itself in itself.

Consciousness that Is Conscious

We have seen how Nishida's reception of Aristotle's concept of "substance" played an important role in the origination of his thought of "place." Yet, as we noted, Nishida did not adopt Aristotle's concept as-is. The fact that Nishida ventured to use the term "place" to give expression to his thought is also relevant to what is at stake here.

Nishida's critique of Aristotle's concept of substance is expressed, for example, in "The Unsolved Issue of Consciousness" as follows:

> Aristotle once defined substance (*ousia*) as that which becomes the grammatical subject of judgement but not the predicate. I have not yet come across a better definition of substance. . . . If this is the case, can we not find that-which-is in a still more profound sense in that which, on the contrary, becomes the predicate but not the grammatical subject? Aristotle sought for the transcendent basis of judgement only in the direction of the grammatical subject; but this basis is truly found not in the direction of the grammatical subject but rather in the direction of the predicate.[37]

As we have seen, Nishida understands "substance" as that which sees and knows itself by means of reflecting itself within itself and, in that sense, is what transcends and envelops the I. In the relation between grammatical subject and predicate in a subsumptive judgment, it is to be sought for all the way in the direction of the predicate. Nishida's critique of Aristotle's concept of substance thus aimed to show that it does not grasp that which truly lies at the foundation of judgments.

Nishida expands on this critique in the preface to *Philosophical Essays III* as follows:

> Aristotle's logic is through and through a logic of the grammatical subject. But the self cannot be conceived of with such a logic. The self is something that cannot be objectified. And yet we do conceive of something called the self. This requires an alternative form of thinking. In contrast to Aristotle's logic, I have spoken of a

---

[35] Nishida 2002–2009, 3: 350–351.
[36] Nishida 1987*a*.
[37] Nishida 2002–2009, 7: 221; Nishida 2012*b*, 54–55, translation modified.

predicative logic. One's self, as a unity of consciousness, is not to be thought of in terms of a grammatical subject, but rather in terms of place as a self-determination of a field of consciousness.[38]

According to Nishida, that which infinitely reflects itself within itself, enabling "infinite beings" [to be]—in other words, that which itself does not act but which sees action—is "the true I" or "self." Even though this true I or self may objectify the self, it itself is not objectified. It is something that can be neither conceptualized nor delimited as a grammatical subject. Nishida expresses this as follows:

> This [i.e., the true I] cannot be said to be either the same or different, either being or nothing. It cannot be determined by so-called logical forms; on the contrary, it is the place that enables the establishment of even logical forms.[39]

It is not the content of knowledge, but rather the place in which knowledge is established. Thought of with regard to the subsumptive relation between grammatical subject and predicate, proceeding all the way in the direction of the predicate, it is the transcendent "dimension of the predicate"; that is, "that which always becomes the predicate and not the subject." It is that which itself can never become the grammatical subject— in other words, the content of knowledge—but can only be thought of as "place."

What in the preface of *Philosophical Essays III* is called the "self that cannot be objectified" is referred to in "The Unsolved Issue of Consciousness" as "consciousness that is conscious" (*ishiki suru ishiki* 意識する意識).[40] With the intention of challenging the epistemology of Kant and the Neo-Kantians, Nishida writes:

> Modern epistemology begins with the opposition between that which knows and that which is known. This is admittedly a feasible epistemological approach. It could even be said that this epistemology, in discussing the constitution of the epistemological object, was able to elucidate the objectivity of knowledge. Yet elucidating the constitution of the epistemological object does not amount to directly elucidating what it means to know. The question of knowing qua consciousness has not yet been deeply reflected upon.[41]

---

[38] Nishida 2002–2009, 8: 255–256.

[39] Nishida 2002–2009, 3: 419.

[40] Nishida is making "consciousness" into a verb. In English, we say "to be conscious" rather than "to conscious." In any case, Nishida's point is that when we talk about "consciousness," we objectify it as "the consciousness that one is conscious of" (*ishiki sareta ishiki* 意識された意識) and, in so doing, fail to attend to "the consciousness that is conscious" (*ishiki suru ishiki* 意識する意識); in other words, the experience of being conscious itself. The point is clearer in English in terms of "seeing." "Seeing that is seen" is not the same as "seeing that sees," no more than the eye that is seen is the same as the eye that sees.—*Tr.*

[41] Nishida 2002–2009, 7: 216–217; Nishida 2012*b*, 52, translation modified.

In other words, previous epistemologies addressed the question of consciousness only insofar as it is objectified, whereas the question of consciousness itself—which Nishida refers to here as "knowing as consciousness" or "consciousness that is conscious"—has not been addressed, and so it remains as an unresolved problem. The essay "Place," we could say, is meant to address this remaining problem of "consciousness that is conscious." As long as we begin with acts of judgment that presuppose an opposition between subject and object—even if this is a "feasible" approach to epistemology—we restrict ourselves to elucidating only a consciousness that has been objectified. In order to get beyond this restriction, Nishida does not begin with the act of judgment but rather, as he says in "Responding to Dr. Sōda," with "a reflection on the judging consciousness itself." In short, Nishida attempts to return to consciousness before it becomes conceived of within the subject-object framework—to return to "knowing as consciousness"—and to think from there.

The Place of Nothingness

We have seen how the concept of "substance" played a very significant role in the development of Nishida's conception of "place." Yet, in the end, Nishida uses the concept of place *rather than* substance to express his thought. The reason for this is presumably related to the fact that "substance" originally refers to Aristotle's primary meaning of *ousia*. By contrast, Nishida asserts that place is a matter, not of being, but of "nothingness" (*mu* 無). However, this nothingness is not a nothingness in contrast or in opposition to being. This is because even a nothingness that negates any and all being, as long as it has something against which it stands in opposition, can be considered to be a kind of being. When Nishida refers to place as "the place of nothingness" (*mu no basho* 無の場所), what he means is "something that envelops being and nothingness," in other words, "that which transcends even the opposition of being and nothingness and enables this opposition to be established within itself."[42] Nishida calls this a "mere place,"[43] since it could never become the content of knowledge and could never be delimited in any sense as being. Yet it is precisely by means of its reflection of itself within itself that the opposition of being and nothingness is established within it.[44] Nishida's concept of place, or the place of nothingness, was evidently meant to include this twofold nature.

It could be said that the basic orientation of Nishida's thought is the attempt not to elucidate matters only insofar as they can be objectified, but rather to see from matters as a whole, in other words, from reality itself. And behind his philosophy of place is the intention to give a logical basis to this way of seeing. It is for this reason that Nishida focused his attention on judgments and, in particular, on the subsumptive relation they evince. In terms of this kind of subsumptive relation, what was just referred to as matters

---

[42] Nishida 2002–2009, 3: 424; Nishida 2012b, 57, translation modified.
[43] Nishida 2002–2009, 3: 436; Nishida 2012b, 67, translation modified.
[44] See Chapter 18 in this volume.

as a whole, or as reality, is found by pursuing the direction of the predicate to its extremity. In short, it is precisely "that which always becomes the predicate and not the subject." Nishida's thought was that judgments arise as self-determinations of matters as a whole or reality. Spoken of from the side of the grammatical subject of a judgment, this entails its being enveloped or subsumed by the predicate. On the other hand, spoken of from the side of the predicate, a judgment entails the determination or delimitation of a universal.

Nishida's aim was to avoid following modern epistemology and setting out from the subject–object opposition, and instead to attempt to grasp matters from reality itself before it gets depicted within this framework. Rather than starting with the presupposition of a substance and seeking to comprehend its relation to its attributes, Nishida understood matters in terms of concrete universals. We might say that, in so doing, he tried to free us from our captivation with "being." He attempted instead to think of matters on the basis of that which cannot be grasped as an object and so can be called "nothingness." In terms of logic, in contrast to a logic that centers on the grammatical subject, he attempted to conceive of a logic that centers on the predicate. With regard to the self, rather than conceiving of it as a substance, Nishida sought to understand it as a place. In the essay "Place" he writes:

> The I must be understood not as the unity of a grammatical subject but rather as a predicative unity. It must be understood not as a point but rather as a circle, not as a thing but rather as a place. That the I cannot know itself is a matter of a predicate not being able to become a grammatical subject.[45]

Nishida's intent was thus to problematize the presuppositions and even the very framework of our thinking. In this sense, his thought can be said to have a genuinely radical character.

ACTION-INTUITION

Looking to the World and Action-Intuition

Let us return to the following passage from the 1936 preface to *An Inquiry into the Good*:

> That which I call in the present book the world of direct or pure experience I have now come to think of as the world of historical reality. The world of action-intuition—the world of *poiesis*—is truly the world of pure experience.[46]

---

[45] Nishida 2002–2009, 3: 469; Nishida 2012b, 95–96, translation modified.
[46] Nishida 2002–2009, 1: 3; Nishida 1990, xxxii–xxxiii.

As is evident here, Nishida characterizes the standpoint of his later thought with the term "action-intuition" (*kōi-teki chokkan* 行為的直観). We could even say that the end point of Nishida's path of thought is the standpoint of action-intuition. Yet, as Nishida himself repeatedly states, action and intuition do not directly unite. What, then, is Nishida attempting to say with this paradoxical expression? By way of responding to this question, in this section, I would like to clarify the particular character and significance of Nishida's later thought.

The development of Nishida's thought from its early and middle periods to its later period can be grasped roughly as a movement from "consciousness" or "self" to "world." For instance, in his 1933 essay "Prolegomenon to Metaphysics" (*Keijijōgaku joron*), contained in *Fundamental Problems of Philosophy* (*Tetsugaku no konpon mondai*), Nishida writes:

> The most concrete and true reality can be understood to be the actual world made up of the mutual determination of individuals. Since it determines itself dialectically as the self-identity of what is absolutely contradictory, it can be thought of as a dialectical reality. The world of our personal activity can thus be said to be the most concrete and true reality.[47]

True reality is here no longer said to be "phenomena of consciousness" but rather "the actual world" (*genjitsu no sekai* 現実の世界); that is, "the world that envelops our personal activity, the world in which we act personally."[48] The development of Nishida's later thought revolved around the "logical structure" of such a world.

In such later works as the two volumes of *Fundamental Problems of Philosophy* and the several volumes of *Philosophical Essays*, this logical structure of the actual world is discussed in terms of the mutual determination of individuals and universals, linear determination and circular determination, as well as one-qua-many (*issokuta* 一即多) and many-qua-one (*tasokuitsu* 多即一). As can be surmised from these expressions, the later Nishida's attention to the "world" certainly did not entail a neglect of the individuals who work or act therein. On the contrary, one could say that Nishida's gaze was turned precisely toward human beings acting in the world. This is evident in the opening lines of an essay entitled "The Logical Structure of the Actual World" (*Genjitsu no sekai no ronri-teki kōzō*, included in the second volume of *Fundamental Problems of Philosophy*, 1934):

> What is the actual world? It must not merely stand in opposition to us, but must rather be the world in which we are born and die. Past philosophies that were unable to shed the standpoint of intellectualism took the so-called objective world to be the world of reality. This was merely the world seen external to us, over against which we are merely those who see. But the truly actual world must be a world that envelops us;

[47] Nishida 2002–2009, 6: 50.
[48] Nishida 2002–2009, 6: 7.

it must be the world in which we work, the world of action. What is the logical structure of such a world?[49]

As can be clearly gleaned from this passage, Nishida's focus on "the truly actual world"
is at once a focus on the self—not the self who sees, but rather the self who acts within
the actual world. We are not "eyes that merely see" the world from the outside. Rather,
we are beings that stand in necessary relations with things. We have bodies and engage
in action. This is the sense of self that Nishida sought to capture with the expression
"action-intuition." Nishida's discourses on action-intuition were connected with—or
developed out of—his critique of the kind of intellectualism that conceives of human
beings as mere cognitive subjects and of the world as the objective world that stands in
opposition to such subjects.

Critique of Modern Western Philosophy

When Nishida speaks of intellectualism, he chiefly has in mind modern Western philosophy since Descartes. A key text for understanding how Nishida situates his thought
of action-intuition in the history of philosophy is the 1933 "Summary and Conclusion"
(Sōsetsu) of the first volume of Fundamental Problems of Philosophy (even though he
does not yet use the expression "action-intuition" in this text). In the opening lines of
this text he writes:

> It seems to me that philosophy has hitherto never once truly thought from the stand-
> point of the active self. Consequently, the nature of the actual world in which we act
> has not been understood from its basis.[50]

Nishida goes on to refer to Descartes, claiming that his "cogito ergo sum" in truth should
be rephrased, such that "it is not a matter of 'I think therefore I am' but rather 'I act therefore I am.'"[51]

On the one hand, Nishida of course recognizes that Descartes, by conceiving of
the "thinking self," attained to a new philosophical standpoint. On the other hand,
for Nishida, Descartes' "thinking self" remains but an entirely "abstract" self since it
overlooks the fact that thinking "bears the significance of acting." In order to express this,
Nishida says "I act therefore I am." Precisely in conceiving of the self from this perspective,
he at the same time conceives of the world as the place in which "subjectivity subjectifies
objectivity" and "contrariwise objectivity objectifies subjectivity"; in other words, as "the
world of personal life, the world from which we are born and into which we die."[52]

---

[49] Nishida 2002–2009, 6: 171; Nishida 1970, 113, translation modified.
[50] Nishida 2002–2009, 6: 135; Nishida 1970, 91, translation modified.
[51] Nishida 2002–2009, 6: 136; Nishida 1970, 91, translation modified.
[52] Nishida 2002–2009, 6: 137; Nishida 1970, 92, translation modified.

From there, Nishida proceeds to comment on Kant. On the one hand, he deeply appreciates Kant's philosophical significance, writing: "Modern physics may have begun with Galileo, but the true laying of a logical foundation for empirical scientific reality must be attributed to the achievements of Kant."[53] On the other hand, he criticizes Kant for having remained stuck in the standpoint of intellectualism as follows:

> Kant's logic … was not a logic of a world of acting beings. It was not a logic of socio-historical reality. Kant's world of empirical scientific reality was an objective world of the intellectual self. It was not the objective world of the acting self, the world of actuality in which we act. Consequently, even Kant's transcendental logic was not a logic of true concrete reality.[54]

Nishida also understood Husserl's phenomenology as an extension of this line of modern Western intellectualism. Already in the 1927 essay "The Unsolved Issue of Consciousness" Nishida levels the following criticism against Husserl:

> Even Husserl's phenomenology does not escape starting from the conception of an opposition between consciousness and objects, and thus it fails to conceive of the true standpoint of consciousness. Even what he calls pure consciousness is nothing but a consciousness that is [the object of] thought.[55]

Again in 1934, in the essay "The World as Dialectical Universal" (*Benshōhō-teki ippansha toshite no sekai*, included in the second volume of *Fundamental Problems of Philosophy*), Nishida criticizes phenomenology with reference to its motto, "To the things [*Sache*] themselves!" as follows: "Phenomenology still does not avoid the standpoint of psychology. *Sache* eliminates the *Tat* [act] from *Tatsache* [fact]."[56] In phenomenology, too, according to Nishida's critique, the self that acts is reduced to a mere "conscious self."

When Nishida criticizes Descartes—saying that "it is not a matter of 'I think therefore I am' but rather 'I act therefore I am'"[57]—he evidently has Maine de Biran's thought in mind, as can be seen from the fact that, in the same paragraph, he goes on to write: "As Maine de Biran has already said, the I is a desiring and acting self rather than Descartes' *cogito ergo sum*."[58]

A few years prior to that, in an essay entitled "Anthropology" (*Ningengaku*, 1931), Nishida comments on this point in greater detail. There, he notes how Biran, in his *New Essays in Anthropology* (1823–1824), conceived of a "kind of anthropology of the inner human being based on the fact of emotional and volitional self-awareness."[59] Biran is

---

[53] Nishida 2002–2009, 6: 138; Nishida 1970, 93, translation modified.
[54] Nishida 2002–2009, 6: 138–139; Nishida 1970, 93–94, translation modified.
[55] Nishida 2002–2009, 7: 223; Nishida 2012b, 56, translation modified.
[56] Nishida 2002–2009, 6: 285; Nishida 1970, 196.
[57] Nishida 2002–2009, 6: 136; Nishida 1970, 91, translation modified.
[58] Nishida 2002–2009, 6: 136; Nishida 1970, 91–92.
[59] Nishida 2002–2009, 7: 229.

said to have done this by way of rethinking Descartes' principle, "I think, therefore I am a thinking thing or substance," as "I act, I will, or I think to myself of action, therefore I know that I am a cause, and I actually am or exist as a cause or force."[60]

Nishida's thought of action-intuition, as we have noted, conceives of the self not as a mere "seeing eye" but rather as an embodied being that acts. Nishida highly esteems Biran as a thinker who began to move in that direction. At the same time, however, he criticizes Biran in the following manner:

> From Maine de Biran, who took as his starting point the facts of interior human exist-
> ence, we can learn that human beings are human beings because of their interior exist-
> ence. Yet a human being does not merely exist within himself, but in flesh and bones.
> Nay, he does not exist just in a body but in society, and not just in society but in history.
> We human beings cannot be thought of merely from within. Hence, anthropology must
> be approached from both directions. Over against an anthropology that starts from the
> inside, an anthropology that starts from the outside must be established.[61]

It could be said that, for Biran, "action" was still conceived as "thinking of action." By contrast, for Nishida, action is thoroughly embodied—that is, enacted in flesh and bones. For this reason, it takes place within a social and historical context. This is evidently what the later Nishida means when he sets out to "think from the standpoint of the active self."[62]

The Expressively Active Body/the Historical Body

Nishida thus stresses the fact that human beings are embodied beings. But this is not meant merely in the sense of biological embodiment. The perspective from which Nishida understands human bodies is well displayed in the following passage from the 1935 essay "The Standpoint of Action-Intuition" (*Kōi-teki chokkan no tachiba*, included in *Philosophical Essays I*)[63]: "What I am referring to here as the body is not merely the bi-ological body; it means rather the expressively active body, the historical body."[64]

To begin with, the body is said to be connected with "expression." The fact that we are not merely consciousness but also embodied beings means first of all that things appear to us "expressively." Nishida writes: "The fact that the things we are faced with appear to us intuitively means that they always impinge upon us expressively, that is to say, they move us with their expressive activity [*hyōgen sayō* 表現作用]."[65] "Intuition" is not

---

[60] Maine de Biran, *Nouveaux essais d'anthropologie*, in *Œuvres*, vol. 10/2, edited by F. Azouvi (Paris: Librairie philosophique J. Vrin, 1989), 77.

[61] Nishida 2002–2009, 7: 230.

[62] See Nishida 2002–2009, 6: 135; Nishida 1970, 91.

[63] Nishida 2012c, 64–143.

[64] Nishida 2002–2009, 7: 143.

[65] Nishida 2002–2009, 8: 408.

simply a matter of seeing a thing as an object; it means rather that something impinges upon us as an "expression." In "The Standpoint of Action-Intuition," Nishida defines the concept of "action-intuition" as follows: "We see things by means of action; things determine us and we also determine things. That is action-intuition."[66] In these terms, the first sense of the phrase "seeing things by means of action" (*kōi ni yotte mono o miru* 行為によつて物を見る) is none other than that things arise into appearance before us expressively. Why is it that being an embodied being is connected with expression? The reason is that embodied beings are beings that desire. As a subject of desire, the self is stimulated by things. As that which stimulates us, things are expressive. As expressive, things stimulate and provoke us to act.

Nishida explains this in his 1939 essay, "Empirical Science" (*Keiken kagaku*). "We can do nothing starting from mere consciousness. Action itself must arise from the world of things. We are necessarily embodied. In the beginning our behavior arises impulsively. It arises from seeing things; it is called forth by things."[67] That action is "called forth" by something expressive can indeed be said to be the second sense of the phrase "seeing things by means of action." Intuition is not merely a matter of seeing a thing, but rather "a matter of my birth from the world of things as a self-negation of the world of things"[68] and is thus connected with "action."

What Nishida means by "action" is not simply embodied movement; he stresses that action has the nature of making things (that is to say, production or *poiesis*):

> Praxis must be a matter of production. Our working is inevitably a matter of making things. There is no praxis apart from production. Praxis is labor, it is creation. Seeing the world from the standpoint of the active self necessarily entails doing so from this standpoint.[69]

The third sense of the phrase "seeing things by means of action" lies in this "making things" or "production."

Once things are made, they once again appear before us as expressive things. This is where "seeing" comes about. Action is connected with intuition. In the 1935 essay "The Self-Identity and Continuity of the World" (*Sekai no jiko-dōitsu to renzoku*, included in *Philosophical Essays I*), Nishida elaborates on this connection as follows:

> Things that appear in the historical world are all necessarily expressive. It is for this reason that our behavior always bears the significance of expressive activity. *Poiesis* must have the character of expressive activity. If it did not, it could not be distinguished from instinctual activity or mere movement. To create things expressively

---

[66] Nishida 2002–2009, 7: 101. One can clearly detect in this account of action-intuition Nishida's sympathy with Marx's notion of praxis. On this point, see Fujita 2011, 176–178.

[67] Nishida 2002–2009, 8: 440.

[68] Nishida 2002–2009, 8: 263.

[69] Nishida 2002–2009, 8: 122.

means that things appear expressively and at the same time that we see them expressively. This must include, on the one side, the sense of intuition.[70]

The fact that we see the things that we ourselves make can be said to be the fourth sense of the phrase "seeing things by means of action." And this intuition moves us once again to act. Earlier, we quoted Nishida as writing: "We see things by means of action; things determine us and we also determine things. That is action-intuition."[71] This definition can be said to express the interconnected entirety of what we have said regarding action-intuition.

We have seen that our bodies are not mere biological organisms insofar as they are expressive. They are moved by expressive things, and they expressively make things. "Production," however, is not merely a response to a stimulus. It has "history" in its background. "Human beings can never escape the infinitely deep ballast of history,"[72] writes Nishida. We do not simply stand in front of things; bearing the burden of history, we stand in the midst of the world. Bearing the burden of determining what should be produced, we stand in the midst of the world. Our action is not only "expressive activity," it also always has the sense of "historical formation" (rekishi-teki keisei 歴史的形成). And this means, as Nishida repeatedly stresses, that our actions are "events in the historical world."

The fact that our actions bear the burden of history entails, on the other hand, that history or the world forms itself through our actions. From this angle, Nishida explains the relation between the world and the actions of individuals in the following manner:

> Our embodied selves are creative elements in the historical world, and historical life realizes itself through our bodies. The historical world forms itself by means of our bodies; our bodies are organs for the rationalization of the irrational.[73]

Nishida is saying that our actions are "creative elements" (sōzō-teki yōso 創造的要素) of the historical world in the sense that they become the means for its self-formation. Put the other way around, this also means that we are charged with the task of rationalizing through our actions a world that is in itself irrational.

Action-Intuition as the Basis of Knowledge

In this concluding section, let us clarify what Nishida's notion of action-intuition does and does not signify by way of considering some criticism of it. The most typical

[70] Nishida 2002–2009, 7: 38–39.
[71] Nishida 2002–2009, 7: 101.
[72] Nishida 2002–2009, 8: 293.
[73] Nishida 2002–2009, 8: 47.

criticism contends that it is a religious or mystical intuition unrelated to actual knowledge.[74] But this criticism can be said to rest on a faulty interpretation. In the opening lines of the 1937 essay "Action-Intuition" (*Kōi-teki chokkan*, included in *Philosophical Essays II*), for instance, Nishida writes:

> My notion of action-intuition is neither Plotinus' intuition nor Bergson's pure duration. On the contrary, it is the opposite of these. It is a standpoint of extremely actual knowledge. It indicates what lies at the basis of all empirical knowledge. It is a standpoint of empirical, exceedingly empirical knowledge.[75]

Of course, Nishida does not entirely reject what Plotinus calls intuition. Before the passage just quoted, he had written that "beginning with Plotinus, intuition is not a mere passivity or state of rapture. Plotinus himself thought that it lay at the extremity of reason and entailed an infinite movement."[76] Yet, for Plotinus, action basically arises when the power of contemplation is weak; action is thought to be the "shadow" of contemplation, and a close connection between the two is not especially affirmed.[77] In this regard, Nishida says that "Plotinus . . . thinks that the more spiritual one becomes the further one moves away from action and toward static intuition."[78]

Of Bergson Nishida writes:

> What Bergson means by life is lacking in reality; it is bodiless life. . . . That which determines itself dialectically—in the sense that the environment determines the individual and in turn the individual determines the environment—must be that which acts. What Bergson thinks of as the life of pure duration must be undergirded by this kind of [dialectical] determination.[79]

Nishida thus claims that Bergson's pure duration departs from "seeing things by means of action," which is the most concrete form of experience.

---

[74] For example, Tanabe Hajime, in his 1935 essay "The Logic of Species and a Diagram of the World" (*Shu no ronri to sekai zushiki*), writes the following with regard to Nishida's thought and with specific reference to the concept of action-intuition: "Speaking in such terms as direct-qua-circular, the so-called 'qua' [*soku* 即] in a logic of nothingness that does not consider unification-through-negation of subject and object is the unity of a mystical intuition that is unable to signify the mutuality of space and time in the unification by way of a negation-qua-affirmation that mediates the subject of praxis as the immediate substance" (*Tanabe Hajime zenshū* [Complete Works of Tanabe Hajime] [Tokyo: Chikuma, 1963–1964], vol. 6, 241). Other texts in which Tanabe criticizes Nishida's action-intuition include his essay "Elucidating the Meaning of the Logic of Species" (*Shu no ronri no imi o akiraka ni su*), in vol. 6 of *Tanabe Hajime zenshū*. [See also Sugimoto 2011, and Chapter 19 in this volume.—Tr.]
[75] Nishida 2002–2009, 8: 215.
[76] Ibid.
[77] See Plotinus, *The Enneads*, translated by Stephen MacKenna, abridged with an introduction and notes by John Dillon (New York, Penguin, 1991), 237; section 3.8.4.
[78] Nishida 2002–2009, 3: 282.
[79] Nishida 2002–2009, 5: 281–282.

Nishida declares that, by contrast, what he means by action-intuition is a thorough-going "standpoint of actual knowledge" that is "the basis for all empirical knowledge." This is indeed the core of Nishida's understanding of action-intuition. We find this crucial point developed in an essay that precedes "Action-Intuition," an essay published in 1937 entitled "Praxis and the Cognition of Objects: The Standpoint of Cognition in the Historical World" (*Jissen to taishō ninshiki: Rekishi-teki sekai ni oite no ninshiki no tachiba*, included in *Philosophical Essays II*). As indicated in the subtitle, this essay discusses the question of how cognition is established in the historical world. It stresses in particular the idea that our knowledge is a kind of praxis, a kind of production. In short: "Knowing must also be a kind of praxis."[80]

According to Nishida, as we have seen, to see is to act; seeing is not something separated from action and the production of things. And this is connected to transforming the historical world. That which is transformed, in turn, stands over against us and provokes us into further action. In this way, seeing is a matter of praxis and production, and this is based on the fact that we "are in this world and are born of this world"[81]; in other words, we are beings with bodies. In the actual world, we "see things bodily."[82]

Seeing in this sense cannot be a mere reflection of the image of an object. Nishida makes this point in "Praxis and the Cognition of Objects" as follows:

> The cognition of objects is not a matter of reflecting reality, but rather a matter of expression in the sense of an expressive activity. That which is depicted is not something that is fixed and inert; it must be something thoroughly alive, indeed it must be historical life. That which is depicted is not an image of reality; it must rather be an expression of life. That is where the objectivity of knowledge is located.[83]

In short, cognition entails a genuine grasping of reality in an active relation, in other words, there where production is taking place. This means that, by way of this grasp, reality vividly manifests itself as "life." The "objectivity" of knowledge is understood to have its basis precisely therein.

What is abundantly clear from all this is that Nishida's action-intuition does not entail a mystical intuition. Rather, it supplies the basis for knowledge; it is what enables the objectivity of knowledge to be established. In the 1939 essay "Absolutely Contradictory Self-Identity" (*Zettai mujun-teki jiko-dōitsu*, included in *Philosophical Essays III*), Nishida writes that "action-intuition must be understood as the most fundamental and concrete manner in which we consciously grasp reality."[84] Even a conceptual grasp of

---

[80] Nishida 2002–2009, 8: 103.
[81] Nishida 2002–2009, 8: 106.
[82] Nishida 2002–2009, 8: 115.
[83] Nishida 2002–2009, 8: 133–134.
[84] Nishida 2002–2009, 8: 403.

things first becomes possible through concretely grasping them; that is to say, through "knowing things by means of *poiesis*."[85]

In short, Nishida's momentous conception of action-intuition includes the following points: cognition entails acts of *poiesis* in the historical world; in this active and bodily context, reality manifests itself as something alive; and it is precisely thereupon that the objectivity of knowledge is based. It is these points in particular that those who are interested in the contemporary significance of Nishida's later thought should examine.

Translated from the Japanese by Bret W. Davis

BIBLIOGRAPHY AND SUGGESTED READINGS

(Suggested readings provided by the translator)

Abe, Masao. (2003) "Nishida's Philosophy of 'Place.'" In Masao Abe, *Zen and the Modern World*, edited by Steven Heine. Honolulu: University of Hawai'i Press, 66–87.

Carter, Robert E. (1998) *The Nothingness Beyond God: An Introduction to the Philosophy of Nishida Kitarō*, second edition. St. Paul: Paragon House.

Cestari, Matteo. (1998) "The Knowing Body: Nishida's Philosophy of Active Intuition." *The Eastern Buddhist* 31/2: 179–208.

Cestari, Matteo. (2006) "From Seeing to Acting: Rethinking Nishida Kitarō's Practical Philosophy." In *Frontiers of Japanese Philosophy 6*, edited by Raquel Bouso and James W. Heisig. Nagoya: Nanzan Institute for Religion & Culture, 273–296.

Davis, Bret W. (2006) "Toward a World of Worlds: Nishida, the Kyoto School, and the Place of Cross-Cultural Dialogue." In *Frontiers of Japanese Philosophy*, edited by James W. Heisig. Nagoya: Nanzan Institute for Religion and Culture, 205–245.

Davis, Bret W. (2011) "Nothingness *and* (not *or*) the Individual: Reflections on Robert Wilkinson's *Nishida and Western Philosophy*." *The Eastern Buddhist* 42/2: 143–156.

Davis, Bret W. (2013) "Nishida's Multicultural Worldview: Contemporary Significance and Immanent Critique." *Nishida Tetsugakkai Nenpō* [The Journal of the Society for Nishida Philosophy] 10: 183–203.

Dilworth, David. (1969) "The Initial Formation of 'Pure Experience' in Nishida Kitarō and William James." *Moumenta Nipponica*, 24/1–2: 93–111.

Dilworth, David. (1973) "Nishida Kitarō: Nothingness as the Negative Space of Experiential Immediacy." *International Philosophical Quarterly*, 13/4: 463–483.

Elberfeld, Rolf. (1999) *Kitarō Nishida (1870–1945): Moderne japanische Philosophie und die Frage nach der Interkulturalität*. Amsterdam: Rodopi.

Elberfeld, Rolf, and Yōko Arisaka (eds.). (2014) *Kitarō Nishida in der Philosophie des 20. Jahrhunderts*. Freiburg/Munich: Alber Verlag.

Feenberg, Andrew, and Yoko Arisaka. (1990) "Experiential Ontology: The Origins of the Nishida Philosophy in the Doctrine of Pure Experience." *International Philosophical Quarterly* 30/2: 173–205.

[85] Ibid.

Fujita Masakatsu (ed.). (1998) *Nishida-tetsugaku senshū, bekkan ni: Nishida tetsugaku kenkyū no rekishi* [Selected Works of Nishida's Philosophy, supplementary volume 2: The History of Studies of Nishidan Philosophy], edited by Fujita Masakatsu. Kyoto: Tōeisha.

Fujita Masakatsu. (1998) *Gendai shisō toshite no Nishida Kitarō* [Nishida Kitarō as a Modern Thinker]. Tokyo: Kōdansha.

Fujita Masakatsu. (2004) "Questions Posed by Nishida's Philosophy," translated by Bret W. Davis. *Synthesis Philosophica* 37: 7–17.

Fujita Masakatsu. (2007) *Nishida Kitarō: Ikiru koto to tetsugaku* [Nishida Kitarō: Being Alive and Philosophy]. Tokyo: Iwanami.

Fujita Masakatsu. (2011) *Nishida Kitarō no shisaku sekai* [Nishida Kitarō's World of Thought]. Tokyo: Iwanami.

Goto-Jones, Christopher S. (2005) *Political Philosophy in Japan: Nishida, The Kyoto School, and Co-Prosperity*. London: Routledge.

Heisig, James W., and John C. Maraldo (eds.). (1994) *Rude Awakenings: Zen, The Kyoto School, and the Question of Nationalism*. Honolulu: University of Hawai'i Press.

Itabashi Yūjin. (2008) *Rekishi-teki genjitsu to Nishida-tetsugaku* [Historical Reality and Nishidan Philosophy]. Tokyo: Hōseidaigaku.

Jacinto Zavala, Agustin (ed.). (2012) *Alternatives Filosóicas: Investigaciones recientes sobre Nishida Kitarō*. Michoacan, Mexico: El Colegio de Michoacan.

Kopf, Gereon. (2002) *Beyond Personal Identity: Dōgen, Nishida and a Phenomenology of No-Self*. New York: Routledge.

Kosaka Kunitsugu. (1991) *Nishida tetsugaku no kenkyū: Basho no ronri no sesei to kōzō* [Studies in Nishida Philosophy: The Genesis and Structure of the Logic of Place]. Kyoto: Minerva.

Kosaka Kunitsugu. (1994) *Nishida tetsugaku to shūkyō* [Nishidan Philosophy and Religion]. Tokyo: Daitō.

Kosaka Kunitsugu. (1995) *Nishida Kitarō: Sono shisō to gendai* [Nishida Kitarō: His Thought and the Contemporary Age]. Kyoto: Minerva.

Kosaka Kunitsugu. (2001) *Nishida-tetsugaku to gendai* [Nishidan Philosophy and the Contemporary Age]. Tokyo: Minerva.

Krummel, John W. M. (2015) *Nishida Kitarō's Chiasmic Chorology: Place of Dialectic, Dialectic of Place*. Bloomington: Indiana University Press.

Maraldo, John C. (2014) "Nishida's *Kōiteki chokkan* and the Notion of Enaction in Cognitive Science." In *Kitarō Nishida in der Philosophie des 20. Jahrhunderts*, edited by Rolf Elberfeld and Yōko Arisaka. Freiburg: Verlag Karl Alber, 342–364.

Maraldo, John C. (2015) "Nishida Kitarō." In *The Stanford Encyclopedia of Philosophy* (Winter 2015 Edition), edited by Edward N. Zalta. http://plato.stanford.edu/archives/win2015/entries/nishida-kitaro/.

Nishida Kitarō. (1958) *Intelligibility and the Philosophy of Nothingness*, translated by Robert Schinzinger. Honolulu: East-West Center Press.

Nishida Kitaro. (1970) *The Fundamental Problems of Philosophy*, translated by David A. Dilworth. Tokyo: Sophia University Press.

Nishida Kitarō. (1987a) *Intuition and Reflection in Self-Consciousness*, translated by Valdo H. Viglielmo, Takeuchi Toshinori, and Joseph S. O'Leary. Albany: State University of New York Press.

Nishida Kitarō. (1987b) *Last Writings: Nothingness and the Religious Worldview*. Translated with an Introduction and Postscript by David A. Dilworth. Honolulu: University of Hawai'i Press.

Nishida Kitarō. (1987–1989) *Nishida Kitarō zenshū* [Complete Works of Nishida Kitarō]. Tokyo: Iwanami. [This is the older edition of Nishida's *Complete Works*.]

Nishida Kitarō. (1990) *An Inquiry into the Good*, translated by Masao Abe and Christopher Ives. New Haven: Yale University Press.

Nishida Kitarō. (1999) *Logik des Ortes: Der Anfang der modernen Philosophie in Japan*, edited and translated by Rolf Elberfeld. Darmstadt: Wiss. Buchges.

Nishida Kitarō. (2002–2009) *Nishida Kitarō zenshū* [Complete Works of Nishida Kitarō], edited by Fujita Masakatsu and Kosaka Kunitsugu. Tokyo: Iwanami. [This is the newer version of Nishida's *Complete Works*.]

Nishida Kitarō. (2012a) *Place and Dialectic: Two Essays by Nishida Kitarō*, translated by John W. M. Krummel and Shigenori Nagatomo. New York: Oxford University Press.

Nishida Kitarō. (2012b) "The Unsolved Issue of Consciousness," translated with an introduction by John W. M. Krummel. *Philosophy East and West* 62/1: 44–59.

Nishida Kitarō. (2012c) *Ontology of Production*, translated and with an introduction by William Harver. Durham and London: Duke University Press.

Nishitani Keiji. (1991) *Nishida Kitarō*, translated by Yamamoto Seisaku and James W. Heisig. Berkeley: University of California Press.

Ōhashi Ryōsuke. (1995) *Nishida-tetsugaku no sekai* [The World of Nishida Philosophy]. Tokyo: Chikuma.

Ōhashi Ryōsuke. (2013) *Nishida Kitarō*. Kyoto: Minerva.

Schultz, Lucy. (2012) "Nishida Kitarō, G. W. F. Hegel, and the Pursuit of the Concrete: A Dialectic of Dialectics." *Philosophy East and West* 62/3: 319–338.

Sugimoto Kōichi. (2011) "Tanabe Hajime's Logic of Species and the Philosophy of Nishida Kitarō." In *Japanese and Continental Philosophy: Conversations with the Kyoto School*, edited by Bret W. Davis, Brian Schroeder, and Jason M. Wirth. Bloomington: Indiana University Press, 52–67.

Tremblay, Jacynthe. (2007) *Introduction à la philosophie de Nishida*. Paris: L'Harmattan.

Ueda Shizuteru. (1991) *Nishida Kitarō o yomu* [Reading Nishida Kitarō]. Tokyo: Iwanami.

Ueda Shizuteru. (1993a) "Pure Experience, Self-Awareness, 'Basho,'" translated by James Fredericks and Jan Van Bragt. *Etudes Phénoménologiques* 18: 63–86.

Ueda Shizuteru. (1993b) "Zen and Philosophy in the Thought of Nishida Kitarō," translated by Mark Unno. *Japanese Religions* 18/2: 162–193.

Ueda Shizuteru. (1995a) "Nishida's Thought," translated by Jan Van Bragt. *The Eastern Buddhist* 28/1: 29–47.

Ueda Shizuteru. (1995b) "The Difficulty of Understanding Nishida's Philosophy," translated by Thomas L. Kirchner. *The Eastern Buddhist* 28/2: 175–182.

Uehara Mayuko (2009) "Japanese Aspects of Nishida's Basho: Seeing the 'Form without Form.'" In *Frontiers of Japanese Philosophy 4*, edited by Lam Wing-keung and Cheung Ching-yuen. Nagoya: Nanzan Institute for Religion & Culture, 152–164.

Wargo, Robert J. J. (2005) *The Logic of Nothingness: A Study of Nishida Kitarō*. Honolulu: University of Hawai'i Press.

Wilkinson, Robert. (2009) *Nishida and Western Philosophy*. Surrey, UK: Ashgate.

Yusa, Michiko. (2002) *Zen & Philosophy: An Intellectual Biography of Nishida Kitarō*. Honolulu: University of Hawai'i Press.

CHAPTER 18

NISHIDA KITARŌ'S PHILOSOPHY

Self, World, and the Nothingness Underlying Distinctions

JOHN C. MARALDO

Is there an ultimate context that encompasses not only the terms in which we conceptualize the world but also everything, every being, even the world itself?[1] This question was a central concern of Nishida Kitarō (1870–1945) in the mature stage of his philosophy. Nishida, widely recognized as the most important Japanese philosopher of the twentieth century and the founder of the Kyoto School, authored some twenty volumes of essays influenced by Buddhist thought and deeply informed by the Anglo-European philosophy that was first introduced into Japan in his youth. Nishida began his work with the notion of "pure experience," the state prior to any distinction between experiencing self and experienced object, as it founds the systematic development of our thinking about the world. After lengthy diversions into Neo-Kantian philosophy, mathematics, and philosophies of life to explain the nature of self-awareness, he turned to German dialectical thinking and to early Greek philosophy to locate its place. Along the way he developed a novel alternative to the ways that philosophers have distinguished self and world and sought ultimate grounds for them.[2]

Nishida's alternative was his notion of "the place of absolute nothingness" (*zettai mu no basho* 絶対無の場所) that underlies all distinctions and contextualizes all grounds. This alternative has profound significance for debates concerning the questions gathered under the labels of internalism and externalism, both cognitive and semantic.

---

[1] This chapter was previously published in Maraldo 2017, 181–198, and is reprinted with permission. It is a revised version of the article that appeared in *The Oxford Handbook of World Philosophy*, edited by Jay Garfield and William Halbfass (Oxford: Oxford University Press, 2011), 361–372.

[2] The notion of pure experience is developed in Nishida's first major work, *Zen no kenkyū* (published in 1911), translated as *An Inquiry into the Good* (Nishida 1992). For a synopsis of the themes and development of Nishida's philosophy, see Maraldo 2015 and Chapter 17 in this volume. Davis 2019 places Nishida's work in the context of the Kyoto School.

Once we see through his often forbidding language, his notion suggests a way to uncover the assumptions that both sides of the debate have in common. It points to the positive role that an obscure context plays in making distinctions. The "dazzling obscurity" that he called the place of absolute nothingness can be understood as the ultimate context of contexts, the common ground that makes distinctions possible—although it requires a modification in our usual conception of a ground or foundation. Just as Nishida's language is clarified by an analysis of distinction-making (as well as by some examples from Chinese Daoist and Zen literature), his own account of absolute nothingness clarifies the relation between self and world.

DISTINCTIONS AND EXTERNALISM VERSUS INTERNALISM

Making distinctions is at the heart of teaching and doing philosophy. Think of the importance of the distinctions—and often of the challenge to the distinctions—between *what is* and *what ought to be*, or between *what* something is and *that* it is, between synthetic and analytic, passive and active, empirical and transcendental, and so on. More specifically, recall the distinctions that underlie disputes about the relation between self and world and between mind and world. Not only are the terms of the relation (*self* and *world*, or *mind* and *world*) distinguished, but so too are the types of relationship in question: Is mind self-contained and solely internal to the individual subject of experience, or are its contents dependent upon the environment and the world in general? In the philosophy of mind, internalism broadly conceived holds that the meaning or content of a thought is contained in the individual mind, whereas externalism argues that mental content relies upon external, environmental factors or even that mental processes are not properly said to take place inside the subject (within one's skin, so to speak).[3] It is important to note that the point of reference here is the individual subject, not the mind as such. That is, externalists are not referring to what may or may not be external to the mind, but rather to the individual, bodily subject. Semantic externalism similarly holds that factors external to the individual speaker determine, at least partially, the meaning of words. To give an example, internalists hold that the psychological state of being jealous and the meaning of the word *jealous* are determined by factors within the individual subject, whereas externalists argue that factors in the world, exterior to the

---

[3] See Parent 2013, McDowell 1994, Rowlands 2003, Zahavi 2004, and Zahavi 2008. I do not focus on the possible meanings of *self* and *mind* here, but take both terms to refer to cognizing subjects, or rather agents, of experience. The primary difference for the dispute would be that *self* refers to the individual but *mind* to a domain not necessarily restricted to the individual subject. Nor do I delve into the many variations and nuances in the dispute between externalism and internalism here, which include further distinctions between narrow and broad mental content and between semantic and cognitive externalism. See McCullock 1995 for a detailed analysis.

individual subject, are decisive. Disputes in the same vein pertain to our beliefs about things and about states of affairs in the world; for example, about what counts as *water*.[4]

A primary interest shared by both sides in this dispute is to resist an overbearing imposition of our fallible minds and mental contents on the world; that is, to allow for resistance from the world as a corrective to our ideas. A second shared concern is to strictly preserve the features of experience that differentiate one individual from another. These concerns in turn imply two underlying distinctions, again shared by both sides of the dispute, namely, some distinction between mind and world—however disputed the bounds of the mind may be—as well as some distinction between individual minds. No matter how external or internal to the individual subject the content of her mind and the meaning of her words may be, the mind is not thought to be wholly internal to the world; its fundamental distinction from world is maintained by both sides. These shared features conceal another, perhaps deeper, unsettled matter for both sides: the nature of the self in the background of this dispute. Is the self "self-contained" within the individual bodily subject, within one's skin so to speak, or does its extension reach beyond the body, at least the body as an object in the world? Is self rather a body-subject that reaches beyond the objective confines of the physical body? Is the "skin" of the self a perceptive organ that interacts with the environment and is not measured by dimensions given by tape measures? Settling the dispute about the bounds of mind and its cognitions would require determining with much more precision the bounds of self and its transactions with the world. Yet again, whatever the position regarding the unsettled bounds of the self, the disputes presuppose its distinction from world. The talk of a "transaction" between perceptions, cognitions, or self on the one hand and world on the other implies this distinction. Even the most expansive notions of bodily self interacting with the world and with others, as we find in Merleau-Ponty for example, assume a distinction between self and world. Heidegger's attempt to undermine commonplace assumptions by reformulating the terms and speaking of being-in-the-world still differentiates between oneself and environment and between oneself and world as the ultimate context of meanings.

This chapter does not attempt to resolve these tangled issues or even describe them with more precision. Nor does it intend to question the fundamental distinction between self and world. Rather, it will present an alternative way, modeled after Nishida, to contextualize the distinctions and to understand the grounds of various levels of distinctions—both the grounds of distinctions like those just mentioned and the grounds of their various levels. It will present the ultimate "ground" as a nothingness with respect to all distinguished terms and will thus call for a modification of the notion of ground. At the same time, it will present a way to understand the meaning and function of *nothingness* in the philosophy of Nishida and his East Asian sources.

---

[4] The reference of water is to Hilary Putnam's famous "twin earth" thought experiment that generated much of the externalism–internalism debate: If *water* played exactly the same role in the thinking of two different societies, but one usage referred to H_2O and the other to some other chemical compound, would the meaning of *water* be the same or not? See Putnam 1975.

SELF AND WORLD IN NISHIDA'S PHILOSOPHY

Nishida developed a layered set of distinctions arranged in levels that he took to be increasingly concrete—that is, increasingly inclusive of the terms abstracted out of their underlying context. Eventually he proposed "absolute nothingness" as the ultimate context.[5] Using his terms, we can begin with language and the logic of judgments and note the distinction between the subjects and predicates of our judgments—without deciding whether or to what degree those predicates are internal or external to the judging individual. In judgments like "John is jealous of Mary" and "Eartheans mean water to be H2O," we ascribe to a particular (grammatical) subject certain qualities or attributes, an emotion and a belief in these examples. The qualities or attributes "belong to" the grammatical subject. At the same time, predicates name universals or at least general items that are not restricted to any particular subject. Judgments then are articulated states of affairs that form the context out of which grammatical subjects and predicates are distinguished. In other words, we can apprehend and then articulate a state of affairs that includes the subject and the predicate and that grounds the distinction between them—again without deciding the necessity or the degree of factors external to the individual who is judging.

Taken as the context that encompasses things and their characteristics or relations, the level of judgments leaves out the acts of mind or of consciousness that formulate the judgments. Mind in the act of judging may be said to take the judgment, the articulated state of affairs (John is jealous of Mary, Eartheans think water is H_2O) as its proposed object for consideration—for confirmation or disconfirmation, for example. For Nishida, we must move to a more concrete context that includes both judgments and the mind as the judging agent that is considering them. In Nishida's view, however, the acting mind is not simply one side of the distinction; rather, it includes both the act's object, the judgment, and the mind itself. This is because mind or consciousness in its very activity is self-reflexive; however fallibly, it is aware of itself as well as of things in the world and thus can both distinguish between itself and things in the world and place them in a unity.[6] Self-reflexive mind or consciousness forms the context out of which mind and things with their attributes are distinguished. The move to include judgments, with their grammatical subjects and predicates, within the context of self-aware mind might seem to imply some form of internalism and suggest that the content articulated in judgments is contained within a individual mind and thus independent of external factors in the world. Nishida's move as such, however, only acknowledges that judgments are the

---

[5] My variation here of Nishida's famous "logic of place" is geared toward an explication of a theory of distinctions and represents one among many interpretations. Nishida himself offered different versions during his career; one of the first is in essays in Nishida 1987–1989, vol. 4. For other accounts, see Wargo 2005, especially 121–178, and Maraldo 2015.

[6] For a more detailed analysis of Nishida's self-reflexive structure of consciousness and world, see Maraldo 2017, 273–298.

sorts of matters that are held, entertained, or proposed by minds. To use the previous example, Eartheans' beliefs about water may or may not depend on factors outside Eartheans' minds, but the judgment that articulates what Eartheans believe is proposed by someone and, for Nishida, belongs to the context of the self-aware mind considering the judgment.[8] The appeal to a more inclusive context is not meant to settle the issue between internalism and externalism, but to show what both sides presuppose. We have seen how both assume a distinction between mind and world and between one mind and another. If self-consciousness names a demarcation between self and others and self and world, then what is the context out of which these distinctions arise? We must proceed to the next level in Nishida's scheme to see their common ground.

The next level of concreteness is that of the world—not in the sense of some extramental reality, nor of a pre-existent, non-human universe, nor of some projection or construction of mind, but rather world as that which creates knowing, embodied selves and is created by them. Nishida came to call this "the historical world" to emphasize the concrete and everyday space in which we live as embodied, enculturated selves immersed in the histories that we make and that make us.[7] The philosophical notion of minds as relatively isolated or self-contained units and of the world as a physical, non-human realm are abstracted from the historical world, as is any evidence supporting such notions. Here, too, we might ask whether the self-aware, judging mind is properly understood as a sole individual subject. To take the individual mind acting alone as the self-aware, judging mind would be to abstract it from its context in a world of shared language, culture, and history—all factors that make judgments possible. Insofar as internalism and externalism both recognize that meanings and beliefs are tied to language, culture, and history, they both can agree on this point. This is not to deny that there are individuals with their own mental features. But even to posit such individuating features requires a context of comparison that cannot be derived from any single such mind. Individual agents living in the historical world differentiate themselves from others and reciprocally are subject to differentiation; they create and are created by the historical world. The historical world thus is the context out of which actual, knowing selves are differentiated. This world displays a self-reflexive structure similar to that of self-aware minds in that it refers to itself as including knowing, embodied selves.

If one were to understand the self-reflexive, historical world as a mind of a higher order, however, Nishida's scheme would amount to a form of panpsychism. This view either extends mind beyond individual subjects to some kind of universal mind or finds mind as a constitutive part of the universe. Mind in some sense is taken to be everywhere.[8] Panpsychism would collapse the distinction between mind and world that

---

[7] Nishida expanded this notion to the political realm when he spoke of a globally realized world, the world of worlds that are oriented to the entire world, which is possible in the present age as a place of unity-in-diversity. See for example Nishida 1987–1989, 12: 427, translated in Arisaka 1996.

[8] Advocates of panpsychism are found on the side of materialism as well as idealism; for an example of the former, see Strawson et. al. 2006. For a survey of different positions, see Goff, Seager and Allen-Hermanson 2017.

internalism and externalism hold in common. Nishida does not take that course, but instead maintains a tentative distinction between individual selves as self-aware minds and the world that differentiates and contextualizes them. The world is "self-aware" in the sense that whatever is "in the world" is a reflection or mirroring of the world. In Nishida's parlance, the world "mirrors itself" in all that is in it, but the individual, self-aware self is a "focal point" of the world. There is no outside to this world. In this respect Nishida's conception shares the assumption common to both internalism and externalism that, whatever the bounds of mind or sources of the mind's content, "world" represents the outermost boundary. Yet if world is the broadest existing context for differentiations, if there is no further existing context out of which terms can be distinguished, then what is the basis of the distinction between world and mind or of the very conception of world?

Nishida's answer is: nothing that exists; indeed, *nothingness*. This obscure and difficult topic need not conjure up metaphysical specters that would be anathema to those who debate about self and world, however. We can clarify nothingness in terms of making distinctions and making distinctions in terms of nothingness. Nishida's implicit account of distinctions casts light not only on his own philosophy but on the working of philosophical distinctions in general and, in particular, their role in debates about the relation between self and world.

AN ANALYSIS OF DISTINCTIONS VIA NISHIDA AND ROBERT SOKOLOWSKI

Robert Sokolowski's illuminating analysis of distinctions in general provides an introduction to Nishida's particular account. Sokolowski notes that making distinctions is not merely a matter of opposing one thing to another. Rather, we make distinctions when some obscurity stands in the way of clarifying an issue. A distinction "needs to be understood against the obscurity that calls for it"; and even when the distinction is meant to hold everywhere and always, it is obscurity that "lets the distinction occur."[9] Making distinctions requires not merely that we separate or exclude terms, but that we first bring them together, "so there is the activity of bringing together along with the annulment of their belonging together." The non-distinction does not come before the distinction; rather, the "ability to hold *two as one comes along with* the ability to hold *two together as distinguished*" from one another.[10] Let us take these two "holds" one at a time. "Holding *two together as one* is holding them precisely as not distinguishable." Holding them together as *one* involves both "the possibility of their being distinguished

---

[9] Sokolowski 1992, 56–57.
[10] Sokolowski 1992, 65, my emphasis.

and the denial [or perhaps the deferral] of that possibility."[11] Holding two together *as distinguished* reaffirms that possibility. Before the possibility of distinction, we have what Sokolowski calls mere assimilation, and we don't see the one *as* one. He calls distinction-making the "emergence of thinking and reasoning."[12]

With some appropriate shifts, to which we will return later, we can employ a similar analysis to understand Nishida's talk of nothingness. Sokolowski's stage of assimilation is actually subsequent to the unitary stage that early Nishida called *pure experience*, which precedes our seeing things as one precisely in that it precedes any separation between us and things. Unitary pure experience is not yet thinking and reasoning in that it is prior to the crucial epistemological distinction between subject experiencing and object experienced. Later, Nishida abandoned the talk of pure experience but retained the same priority of a unity in at least three notions: "knowing by becoming," where self and things in the world are experienced as one; self-awareness as "a seeing without a seer"; and nothingness as a universal notion in which "there is no distinction between that which expresses and that which is expressed."[13] In his first works, Nishida was pressed to explain how distinctions and reflective thought could arise out of a state of unity; thus we see him struggling with the themes of "intuition and reflection in self-awareness," the title of his 1917 collection of articles. He eventually gave up the logical and temporal priority of the assimilated state and moved to a kind of interdependence of unity and plurality, or identity and difference—the one comes along with the other. Nishida tried to express this sort of holding together in the enigmatic phrase, "absolute contradictory self-identity" (*zettai mujun-teki jiko-dōitsu* 絶対矛盾的自己同一), an identity that holds many together as one, both as belonging together and as not belonging together, as bringing them together and negating the ability to keep them together.

This is part of what goes on in making distinctions: when we distinguish one thing from another, we first hold them together as being distinguishable but do not distinguish them. Then, in distinguishing them, we annul their belonging together. This annulment occurs in what Nishida calls the self-negation of nothingness, a negation of its non-duality. To elaborate, nothingness is not simply the initial oneness of the two, or the many, held together. And what holds them together cannot be any one thing; it cannot even be called what all things have in common—that is, "being" as the most universal concept. Nor can it be a second principle, different from being, like becoming, which would still need a third principle holding together these two, being and becoming, and differentiating them. Nothingness for Nishida is not so much a third principle (as in Hegel) as the obscurity that lets that—or any—distinction occur. Nishida calls nothingness *absolute*. Literally, the Sino-Japanese term for absolute, *zettai* (絶対), means breaking through opposition, so absolute nothingness is not opposed to anything; it is the place where all things are held together as one, along with the negation of that oneness. As a universal, it is an attempt to name all things without setting itself in opposition

---

[11] Sokolowski 1992, 65, my emphasis.
[12] Sokolowski 1992, 62.
[13] This is the formulation of Heisig 2001, 83.

to them. Individual things and persons emerge as the "self-determinations of absolute nothingness" (*zettai mu no jiko-gentei* 絶対無の自己限定), to use Nishida's terms, just as items emerge into clarity and distinctness from the obscurity behind their distinction. Sokolowski writes that making distinctions is a way of manifesting, presenting, or making present.[14] This corresponds to Nishida's concept of self-determination.

Sokolowski goes on to say that something in addition to obscurity precedes distinction and identification. They occur not only out of obscurity but also because of something "before and between" them that he calls *urgence*. This is "the urge to distinguish or identify," "like the solicitation of affirmation or denial" behind the question, two or one? Urgence, he proposes, is not distinct from identification and distinction in the way that identification and distinction are differentiated from each other; rather, it enters in both of them. The urgence toward identification or distinction "occurs *within the generic obscurity* that calls for a distinction."[15] Nishida's talk of a self-determining context recognizes the impetus toward distinction that "urgence" is meant to account for. But he does not separately name this impetus or identify it as "occurring within" the obscurity that precedes distinction. Rather, the obscurity (i.e., nothingness) is of itself infinitely determinable. In the term *absolute nothingness* Nishida combines the background obscurity and the cognitive impetus that give rise to distinctions. His talk of absolute nothingness brings to light the fundamental obscurity precisely as obscurity, not clarifying it away, but letting it work to generate clarity and distinctness.[16] Or, as he might say, absolute nothingness brings itself to light in the activity of self-awareness.

Two shifts are required to follow Nishida's moves. First, we must shift from a cognitive to an ontological account or, more precisely, a "me-ontological" account (from the Greek το μεον, nonbeing). That is, we must shift from describing how thinking itself works (by making distinctions, etc.) to describing how reality or the "world" works. Nishida does call his mature philosophy a "logic of place" (*basho no ronri* 場所の論理) or, to use a Greek word Nishida himself referred to, a logic of *khôra* But he articulates this "logic" as a kind of ontology (or me-ontology), not as a cognitive description of how mind or reason should operate. The introduction of me-ontology into debates in the philosophy of mind and language may seem a load that such debates are not meant to bear, yet Nishida's logic is relevant insofar as it questions the assumptions of those debates regarding the means by which we distinguish self and world, for example. His logic of place undermines all anthropomorphic assumptions about the locus of awareness in the individual subject's mind. Making distinctions describes logically—not causally—the emergence of the world out of nothingness as the place of non-distinction. Second, we need to shift from considering obscurity as something we must by all means eliminate to seeing obscurity as something we can appreciate—even if it cannot be the last word.

[14] Sokolowski 1992, 64.
[15] Sokolowski 1992, 65–66, my emphasis.
[16] In his seminal essay "*Basho*" [Place] in 1926, Nishida mentions the "dazzling obscurity" (in English) of Pseudo Dionysius Areopagita. Nishida 1987–1989, 4: 229; trans. Nishida 2012b, 63.

Let us take a closer look at each of these shifts. The first involves the unusual idea of ab-solute nothingness bringing itself to light and evincing self-awareness rather than reflective human minds bringing things to light through the mental activity of making distinctions. Examples may help better explain this shift. Some distinctions imply a third term, as the scholar of Chinese philosophy A. C. Graham points out.[17] Some binary distinctions like *above/below, before/after, up/down,* and *left/right* imply a hidden third term that is a point of reference and so leads indirectly to the person making the distinction. Other binary distinctions, as Victor Hori notes, such as that between *I* and *you* or *I* and *it*, do not allow for this hidden third term "because the maker of the distinction is part of the distinction."[18] Both of these types of distinction hinge directly or indirectly on a self as the point of refer-ence.[19] In the *right/left* kind of distinction, the point or reference is an embodied self that can be moved, so that what was right becomes left, for example—or even removed and not mentioned, so that we speak simply of right/left. But in the second type of distinction, be-tween *I* and *it* for example, the self-reference stays put.[20] Nishida wants to move this self-reference, as it is located in the individual, to the logical space out of which it—along with its oppositions—emerges. The ultimate locus of these distinctions between self and other and between subject and object is his "absolute nothingness." This self-negating name points to the obscurity that gives rise to—and by contrast makes evident—all possible distinctions.

The steps through which Nishida tried to accomplish his shift were summarized earlier as the development of his logic of place, from the context of judgments through the context of self-awareness to that of the historical world and, ultimately, to absolute nothingness. We need not explicate Nishida's philosophy in more detail here to discern how his analysis helps clarify debates about the relation between self and world. What is gained is, first of all, a potential clarification of a element of making distinctions that is taken for granted by Sokolowski—and not only by him but everyone who would clarify philosophizing by starting with the self as a cognizing agent. The place of that self in Sokolowski's analysis of distinctions remains ambiguous in two ways. Sokolowski notes the difference between the thinking, reasoning person who begins to make distinctions and the unthinking person. He states that making distinctions is the emergence, the beginning, of thinking and reasoning, but—and here is the first ambiguity—he also implies that it is an achievement of reasoning. We can place the obscurity behind this emergence/achievement in the properly human self, which for Sokolowski (in another essay) means reason naturally ordered toward truth.[21] Such a self reaches for clarity and

[17] Graham 1992, 211.

[18] Hori 2000, 289.

[19] The difference between the direct and indirect point of reference is my addition to Graham's and Hori's analyses.

[20] The point in Hori (2000) is that the second type does not allow for an "identification of opposites" that can be understood intellectually; rather, "the nonduality of I/it, of subject/object … must be experienced."

[21] Sokolowski 2000, 206. Husserl, whom Sokolowski is interpreting there, would call transcendental subjectivity (or the transcendental ego) the ultimate place of distinction-making; but this name would involve a similar problem, for it alone would not account for the obscurities it encounters.

truth out of an inner "urgence," the second element that Sokolowski must add to the "generic obscurity" to account for the activity of making distinctions. Sokolowski says this urgence is not to be differentiated from distinction in the way that identification is, so a deeper obscurity would not underlie both of them. Nevertheless, we can ask what does hold urgence and generic obscurity together? This, too, is an issue that remains ambiguous in Sokolowski's essay. One might think that urgency indicates a subjective or noetic side, whereas generic obscurity describes the noematic side or matter thought about. In that case, both would be found "in" consciousness; that is, found as moments or non-independent parts of consciousness.

If we recognize that generic obscurity is not merely a matter of the mind, not merely found in a consciousness striving for clarity and articulate speech, then we move in Nishida's direction. In his early attempts to formulate a logic of place, Nishida did in fact consider consciousness as the place or locus of the articulating subject–predicate distinction and even called it "nothingness" (*mu* 無) in the sense that it establishes the being or nonbeing of things.[22] Nishida noted, however, that one's very act of consciousness at any one time always eludes one's own consciousness.[23] Eventually he tried to formulate something more basic, a deeper level, as it were, than the consciousness within which obscurities and distinctions are placed. Nishida's absolute nothingness deliberately conflates Sokolowski's generic obscurity, the self's urge to clarify, and the rational agent self over-against other selves—all into a greater, perhaps darker, background. And what is this background without foreground or opposite? There is simply no way to say—that is, no *what* to indicate. Nishida's talk of nothingness gainsays the notion that the thinking self is the ultimate reference point in making distinctions.

THE LIGHTER SIDE OF OBSCURITY

The second shift mentioned earlier requires a positive assessment of obscurity. We do not understand obscurity adequately when we treat it solely as an undesirable vagueness of expression. Sokolowski describes vagueness as a fog that can conceal inconsistencies or incoherence and lead to speech that is indistinct or makes no sense.[24] He recognizes another side of vagueness when he calls it a kind of absence, where things are given to us indistinctly, "in need of further articulation and possession."[25] Ironically, it is this absence of articulation and self-possession that Nishida appreciates in his talk of

---

[22] See the account of the first formulations of "The Logic of the *Topos* (1924–1926)" in Yusa 2002, 202–204.

[23] I examine this insight further in "What Phenomenologists Can Learn from Nishida about Self-Awareness," in Maraldo 2017, 299–349.

[24] Sokolowski 2000, 105–107.

[25] Sokolowski 2000, 217.

nothingness. We find precedents for such appreciation of obscurity and negativity in classical Chinese Daoist texts and Zen dialogues.

The writings ascribed to the Daoist Zhuangzi are full of examples, although there is no direct evidence that Nishida drew from them. Zhuangzi dares to speak of the Way, the Dao, that "has never known boundaries" and speech that "has no constancy." Boundaries come about when there is recognition of a "this" and a "that." Consider this passage, undoubtedly meant to humor the logicians and the normative philosophers of his day:

> Now I am going to make a statement here. I don't know whether it fits into the category of other people's statements or not. But whether it fits into their category or whether it doesn't, it obviously fits into some category [i.e., it is distinguishable]. So in that respect it is no different from their statements [i.e., it is behind such distinctions]. However, let me try making my statement.
>
> There is a beginning. There is a not yet beginning to be a beginning. There is a not yet beginning to be a not yet beginning to be a beginning. There is being. There is nonbeing. There is a not yet beginning to be nonbeing. There is a not yet beginning to be a not yet beginning to be nonbeing. Suddenly there is being and nonbeing. But between this being and nonbeing, I don't really know which is being and which is nonbeing. Now I have just said something. But I don't know whether what I have said has really said something or whether it hasn't said something.[26]

What Zhuangzi so playfully intimates here is the "dissolution of boundaries,"[27] as he calls it, that still preserves the possibility of distinctions. He also uses the metaphor of a hinge in its socket to express the "state in which 'this' and 'that' no longer find their opposites." "When the hinge is fitted into the socket, it can respond endlessly."[28] Although interpretations of such passages in Zhuangzi differ greatly,[29] we can think of these passages as a precedent to the positive appreciation of the obscurity that underlies distinctions. A good hinge turns freely and takes one appropriately in this direction

---

[26] Zhuangzi 1964, 38–39.

[27] The dissolution of boundaries is also the theme of the famous butterfly passage: Zhuangzi dreams he is a butterfly and then wakes up, but he no longer knows that he isn't perhaps the butterfly dreaming he is Zhuangzi. "Between [Zhuangzi] and a butterfly there must be *some* distinction! This is called the Transformation of Things." Zhuangzi 1964, 45.

[28] Zhuangzi 1964, 35.

[29] Does the *Zhuangzi* teach a radical relativism or perspectivism that replaces the notion of "the Dao" with multiple *daos*, none of which is preferable? Does it advance an asymmetrical relativism that does not reduce Zhuangzi's own speaking to just another equally dismissible *dao*? Does it express a dialectical synthesis of opposites? Here, I would not try to adjudicate the various interpretations but rather point out what they have in common: the positive appreciation of the obscurity behind distinctions. This is not to equate Nishida's absolute nothingness with Zhuangzi's Dao. Graham (1981, 56) notes that Zhuangzi's sequence of statements and of beginnings and non-beginnings "are no doubt intended to lead to an infinite regress." In contrast, Nishida ends (and begins) with absolute nothingness. But both Zhuangzi and Nishida point to the inevitable remainder that gets left out of any distinction and analysis, as Graham mentions in the case of the Chinese classic (Zhuangzi 1981, 55).

rather than that; it articulates the sides. Zhuangzi actually enjoins us to swing the door and use illumination or clarity:

> When the hinge is fitted into the socket, it can respond endlessly. Its right then is a single endlessness and its wrong too is a single endlessness. So I say, the best thing to use is clarity.[30]

Surely, it seems, we would want to distinguish clarity from obscurity. And out of what obscurity would that distinction arise? We are thrown back to the primordial obscurity from which emerges the kind of clarity we ordinarily praise. Zhuangzi does an admirable job in clarifying obscurity without eliminating it.

Many Zen dialogues, which were influenced by Daoist texts and in turn inspired some of Nishida's thoughts, also show an appreciation of obscurity, often in the guise of darkness. The dark refers to a standpoint beyond or behind discriminations. Black and dark are words often used to describe the Buddhist notion of emptiness as the undifferentiated that comes to be manifest only in articulated forms.[31] Again we are reminded not only of making distinctions as a way of manifesting, presenting, or making present—but also of the positive role of the obscurity that underlies distinction-making. That appreciation of obscurity and the negative is what we gain from Nishida's talk of nothingness. And—to end with a distinction—what is gainsaid is the notion that clarity always takes precedence over obscurity in the practice of philosophy.

Distinctions that are crucial to discussions about the relation between self and world or mind and world refer at least implicitly to a common ground underlying the distinctions. In the philosophy of mind and of language, the intricate and often nuanced distinctions made in the debates between internalism and externalism likewise imply a common ground, usually left in the dark, that makes a debate intelligible to both sides. This essay has urged us to reflect on the role that such common ground plays in the specific distinctions at stake and in making distinctions in general. It has presented one attempt to bring to light some assumptions made by different sides of the internalism-externalism debate that rest upon their common ground. Finally, it has attempted to clarify the role that obscurity plays as a ground for making distinctions.

BIBLIOGRAPHY AND SUGGESTED READINGS

Arisaka Yoko. (1996) "The Nishida Enigma: 'The Principle of the New World Order,'" *Monumenta Nipponica*, 51.1: 81–106.

---

[30] Zhuangzi 1964, 35.

[31] According to the famous formula in the Heart Sutra, "form is nothing but emptiness, emptiness nothing but form." The emphasis in the preceding interpretation is that form is necessary to manifest emptiness, just as emptiness is necessary for the existence of forms. The Indian Buddhist philosopher Nāgārjuna stressed the latter point (in chapter 24 of the *Mūlamadhyamakakārikā*); Nishida's disciple, Nishitani (1999, 180), stresses the former point.

Davis, Bret W. (2019) "The Kyoto School," *The Stanford Encyclopedia of Philosophy* (Summer 2019 Edition), edited by Edward N. Zalta, https://plato.stanford.edu/archives/sum2019/entries/kyoto-school/.

Elberfeld, Rolf. (1999) *Kitarō Nishida: Modern japanische Philosophie und die Frage nach der Interkulturalität*. Amsterdam: Rodopi.

Elberfeld, Rolf, and Yōko Arisaka, eds. (2014) *Kitarō Nishida in der Philosophie des 20. Jahrhunderts*. Freiburg: Verlag Karl Alber. An anthology of articles on Nishida with a chronology of his works and a list of their translations.

Goff, Philip, William Seager, and Sean Allen-Hermanson. (2017) "Panpsychism." In *The Stanford Encyclopedia of Philosophy* (Fall 2017 Edition), edited by Edward N. Zalta, https://plato.stanford.edu/archives/fall2017/entries/panpsychism/.

Graham, A. C. (1992) *Unreason Within Reason: Essays on the Outskirts of Rationality*. LaSalle, IL: Open Court.

Heisig, James W. (2001) *Philosophers of Nothingness: An Essay on the Kyoto School*. Honolulu: University of Hawai'i Press.

Hori, Victor Sōgen. (2000) "Kōan and *Kenshō* in the Rinzai Zen Curriculum." In *The Kōan: Texts and Contexts in Zen Buddhism*, edited by Steven Heine and Dale S. Wright. Oxford and New York: Oxford University Press, 280–315.

Hori, Victor Sōgen. (2003) *Zen Sand: The Book of Capping Phrases For Kōan Practice*. Honolulu: University of Hawai'i Press.

Krummel, John W. M., and Shigenori Nagatomo. (2012) *Place & Dialectic: Two Essays by Nishida Kitarō*. Oxford: Oxford University Press. Contains Krummel's essay "Basho, World, and Dialectics" and translations of Nishida's "*Basho*" [place] and "Logic and Life."

Maraldo, John C. (2015), "Nishida Kitarō." *The Stanford Encyclopedia of Philosophy* (Winter 2015 Edition), edited by Edward N. Zalta, https://plato.stanford.edu/archives/win2015/entries/nishida-kitaro/.

Maraldo, John C. (2017) *Japanese Philosophy in the Making 1: Crossing Paths with Nishida*. Nagoya: Chisokudō.

McCullock, Gregory (1995) *The Mind and Its World*. London and New York: Routledge.

McDowell, John. (1994) *Mind and World*. Cambridge, MA and London: Harvard University Press.

Nishida Kitarō. (1987) *Intuition and Reflection in Self-Consciousness*, translated by Valdo H. Viglielmo with Takeuchi Yoshinori and Joseph S. O'Leary. Albany: State University of New York Press.

Nishida Kitarō. (1987–1989) *Nishida Kitarō zenshū* [Complete Works of Nishida Kitarō]. Tokyo: Iwanami.

Nishida Kitarō. (1992) *An Inquiry into the Good*, translated by Masao Abe & Christopher Ives. New Haven: Yale University Press.

Nishida Kitarō. (1996) "The Principles of the New World Order," translated by Yoko Arisaka. *Monumenta Nipponica* 51/1: 81–106.

Nishida Kitarō. (1999) *Logik des Ortes: Der Anfang der modern Philosophie in Japan*, edited and translated by Rolf Elberfeld. Darmstadt: Wissenschaftliche Buchgesellschaft.

Nishida Kitarō. (2012a) *Ontology of Production: 3 Essays*, translated with an introduction by William Haver. Rurham and London: Duke University Press.

Nishida Kitarō. (2012b) "Basho," in *Place and Dialectic: Two Essays by Nishida Kitarō*, translated by J. W. M. Krummel and S. Nagatomo. Oxford: Oxford University Press, 49–102.

Nishitani Keiji. (1991) *Nishida Kitarō*, translated by Yamamoto Seisaku and James W. Heisig. Berkeley: University of California Press.

Nishitani Keiji. (1999) "Emptiness and Sameness," in Michele Marra, *Modern Japanese Aesthetics: A Reader*. Honolulu: University of Hawai'i Press. This is Marra's translation of "Kū to soku," in vol. 13 of *Nishitani Keiji chosakushū* [Collected works of Nishitani Keiji]. Tokyo: Sōbunsha, 1987, 111–118.

Parent, T. (2013) "Externalism and Self-Knowledge." In *The Stanford Encyclopedia of Philosophy* (Summer 2013 Edition), edited by Edward N. Zalta, https://plato.stanford.edu/archives/sum2013/entries/self-knowledge-externalism/.

Putnam, Hilary. (1975) "The Meaning of 'Meaning.'" In *Mind, Language and Reality: Philosophical Papers*, vol. 2. Cambridge: Cambridge University Press, 215–271.

Rowlands, Mark. (2003) *Externalism: Putting Mind and World Back Together Again*. Montreal & Kingston: McGill-Queen's University Press.

Sokolowski, Robert. (1992) "Making Distinctions," in *Pictures, Quotations and Distinctions: Fourteen Essays in Phenomenology*. Notre Dame and London: University of Notre Dame Press, 55–91.

Sokolowski, Robert. (2000) *Introduction to Phenomenology*. Cambridge: Cambridge University Press.

Strawson, Galen, et al. (2006) *Consciousness and Its Place in Nature: Does Physicalism Entail Panpsychism?* Exeter: Imprint Academic.

Wargo, Robert. (2005) *The Logic of Nothingness*. Honolulu: The University of Hawai'i Press.

Yusa, Michiko. (2002) *Zen & Philosophy: An Intellectual Biography of Nishida Kitarō*. Honolulu: University of Hawai'i Press.

Zahavi, Dan. (2004) "Husserl's Noema and the Internalism-Externalism Debate," *Inquiry* 47/1: 42–64.

Zahavi, Dan. (2008) "Internalism, Externalism, and Transcendental Idealism," *Synthese* 160/3: 355–374.

Zhuangzi. (1964) *Chuang Tzu: Basic Writings*, translated by Burton Watson. New York: Columbia University Press.

Zhuangzi. (1981) *Chuang-Tzu: The Inner Chapters*, translated by A. C. Graham. London and Boston: Unwin Publishers.

CHAPTER 19

....

THE PLACE OF GOD IN
THE PHILOSOPHY OF
TANABE HAJIME

....

JAMES W. HEISIG

TANABE HAJIME (1885–1962) was one of the pivotal figures in the Kyoto School that traces its origins back to Japan's first great modern philosopher, Nishida Kitarō (1870–1945). He left behind a massive body of writings whose complexity of argument and subtle shifts of position make it difficult to summarize. The present essay focuses on his idea of God as a gateway to understanding the unfolding of his major philosophical ideas.

As we shall see, despite criticisms of the Christian God, Tanabe gradually adjusted the notion in the light of his rediscovery of Buddhist thought and the elaboration of ideas of absolute nothingness, the cultural specificity of rationality, and historical praxis. After a brief capitulation to nationalist thinking during the Pacific War, he undertook a radical rethinking of the philosophical vocation and embraced a more conciliatory approach to religious faith. As his idea of God transformed into a "nothingness-in-love," an appeal to supporting Christian ideas and a reassessment of mystical thought became regular features in his writings.

As with others in the Kyoto School, Tanabe's idea of God is a staunch ally of his idea of absolute nothingness. At first blush, this seems a point-blank contradiction to Western philosophy's God of being, not to mention the God of Abraham, Moses, and Jesus. But the question of how the one locks out the other is not nearly as interesting as the question of why Tanabe found it necessary to give God a place in his thinking at all. When we have understood that, we will have caught the genius of his philosophical particularity and gained passage into the structure of his complex body of his writings.

There is every good reason for ideas of God bred in the bone of Western culture not to settle easily into Japanese intellectual history. Buddhist, Confucian, and Shintō modes of thought block the way at every turn. Nevertheless, Tanabe realized that thin as the echo of the Western "God" is in the native religiosity of Japan, it clings too tightly to the routines of philosophical discourse to be ignored. At the same time, he was not one to read philosophy without trying to crack open the cultural specificity of its concepts and get to the universally human interest of its conceivers. As we trace the unfolding of Tanabe's idea of God, from a critique of Western Christian thought to its reappropriation from a Buddhist standpoint, we come to understand how his moral concern with the historical world led him, after a series of missteps, to a borderland where philosophy and religion intersect in their profoundest impulses.

THE GOD OF BEING

Tanabe's earliest writings do not have much to say about the idea of God as serving any purpose for Japan. In fact, his ideas about God at the time were generally unsteady and scattered amidst accounts of what a small number of Western philosophers have had to say on the matter.

At the age of twenty-nine, Tanabe saw "God" as another name for the true essence of nature[1] and "love of God" as a sentimental name that the faint of heart give to *amor fati*.[2]

Not all his statements are as simple, however. Tanabe freely acknowledged the transition to science as a renunciation of the claim that "knowledge is to be cloaked in belief and truth enfolded by the holy," but he did not think that science alone could do justice to the whole of the human, including religious ideals of relating to God or reality.[3] In a discussion of moral freedom, clearly written under the influence of Kant and Fichte, he argues that even if religion is understood as the completion and final extinction of the relative freedom of morality in the absolute freedom of abandonment to God's self-love, it cannot bypass human morality.[4] From the context, we can infer that he is not advocating religion as such but only addressing a tendency in modern Western philosophy to complement the role of uncaused cause that Aristotle assigns to a Prime Mover with the role of God in grounding moral freedom.

Other comments at this time on the notion of God in Leibniz[5] and Spinoza are content to wrestle with the underlying logic by which they arrive at a relationship between human free will and the idea of an absolute, whether it be called "God" or "cosmos."[6] That said, one has the sense here and there that Tanabe is about to break free and express his own view. The immediate stimulus was Windelband's remark on Leibniz to the effect that God is actually a "civilized" way of unifying all values. This leads Tanabe to

---

[1] 1914, 14: 347. Throughout this chapter, Tanabe Hajime's *Complete Works* are referenced according to year of publication, volume, and page.

[2] 1921, 14: 336.

[3] 1918, 2: 345–6, 349.

[4] 1917, 1: 128–9.

[5] More than any other philosopher, it was Leibniz whom Tanabe returned to again and again to clarify his notion of God as distinct from a mere pantheism. In one of his very last essays, composed at the age of seventy-five, he contrasted Leibniz with D. T. Suzuki's work on the *Platform Sutra* (1960, 13: 179–98).

[6] 1918, 1: 233; 1918, 1: 262, 269, 273–83.

judge that the further step of arguing for the actual existence of God is an arbitrary and dogmatic form of theology that has no place in critical philosophy.[7] Within a year, he expressed his sympathy with Fichte's idea that knowledge of God is only true knowledge of the self and finds it a required step for critical metaphysics. Viewing the Kantian idea of consciousness in general through the lens of Fichte's *das Ich,* Tanabe concludes that "Consciousness in general is sacred subjectivity; it is nothing other than God."[8]

It was not long before Tanabe came to side with Hegel's idealism in identifying the absolute with the subject, reaffirming his rejection of God—or, for that matter, the pure idea of an absolute, transcendent "reality"—as something existing apart from consciousness or as something whose existence can be proved by examining ideas of God.[9]

Upon returning from two years of studies in Europe, Tanabe composed a lengthy essay on Kant in which he proposed what he called a "teleology of self-awareness" grounded in the same moral reason that views God as its goal.[10] The idea did not take him as far as he must have hoped. For some time, Tanabe had been substituting *self-consciousness (jikoishiki* 自己意識) with *self-awareness (jikaku* 自覚), a Buddhist idea that Nishida Kitarō had reshaped into a hermeneutical tool for his own philosophy.

It was only natural that this would affect his evaluation of God in Western philosophy. His study of Hegel's God over the next few years confirms this. To begin with, it put flesh on his bony idea that God can be understood as another name for the realization of self-awareness. It also reconfirmed his intuition that the Hegelian God supports the overcoming of the subject–object dualism and the traditional philosophical starting point of distinguishing existence from consciousness, which for Tanabe, like Nishida, was foundational for true self-awareness.

His study of Hegel also reconfirmed Tanabe's intuition that questions of theodicy and divine providence are a way of including "teleological necessity in the process of self-awareness." In this connection, he notes that Schelling's dualism of God and nature suggests an important corrective to Hegel's monistic tendency to "quietism" before an all-knowing, all-powerful, objective divine creator. He was convinced that room needed to be made for the individual moral subject as a teleological mediator between the ideal, rational totality represented by God and the concrete, irrational, unfinished reality of nature and history. In this way, aligning with the idea of God to the moral dimension of religion could make sense even to those who do not acknowledge the infinite God of Christianity as necessary for finite subjectivity in the historical world.[11] At the same time, Tanabe's acceptance of Hegel stops short of accepting his "theologizing" of philosophy precisely because he is struggling to preserve the essential philosophical role of the

[7] 1918, 1: 277, 283–4.
[8] 1919, 1: 317, 323. The text adheres to the language of Fichte, but there is little doubt about Tanabe's approval of the conclusion.
[9] 1922, 1: 451–3.
[10] 1924, 3: 66–9. See also 1933, 3: 527. We should add that from a purely metaphysical point of view, Tanabe finds Kant's treatment of God preferable to that of Leibniz (46–7).
[11] 1931, 3: 121–5, 131–2, 150, 156, 201, 220–1, 224, 227–8, 334–5, 363–4, 369.

idea of God without subscribing to the Christian dogma of an omniscient, omnipotent, personal God of being.[12]

THE TURN TO A GOD OF NOTHINGNESS

Tanabe's writing is tangled and repetitious, making it often hard to determine just where he changes direction. Still, there is no mistaking the fact that his turn away from the God of being became more pronounced during the 1930s. He had earlier referred to negative theology and to Eckhart's description of the godhead as a *Nichts*, but without comment. Later in the same work he highlighted Hegel's failure to realize that self-awareness based on the negation of a negation of being has to be founded in "self-awareness of nothingness as the foundation of being." [13] He had also grown dissatisfied with Nishida's "intuitional" and "contemplative" approach to absolute nothingness.[14] In a more direct attack that was fated to sour their relationship forever, he all but accused Nishida of overlooking history and collapsing the standpoint of "self-awareness of absolute nothingness" to religion.[15] These criticisms begged the question of what connection Tanabe himself would find between nothingness and God. He knew that the Augustinian idea of an inner spiritual life relying on the grace of an absolute God made no sense without an understanding of human life in its sociohistorical relativity. He also sensed that historical praxis is at its highest when performed as a "self-awareness of absolute emptiness."[16] How to connect the pieces eluded him. He continued to struggle with Western philosophy's ideas of God, but they did not give him what he needed.

In his first and only sustained treatment of Christian theology on its own grounds, he summarizes Barth and Brunner's debate over knowledge of the divine and locates it in a broader context of comparison with Catholic teachings on knowledge of God by the *lumen naturae* and the challenge of the mystical tradition to the idea of God as *totaliter aliter*. In the end, what he takes from "dialectical theology" is the idea that God and culture belong together. The key passage bears citing at length:

> Religion does not ground culture immediately and positively but rather mediates it indirectly by negating it. Not only does it not regulate culture, it negates it in general, and while doing so affirms it and actualizes the rationality of culture as subject. Or perhaps better, "culture" constructed from an immediately human standpoint is not culture. Just as the true "I" is not the immediately natural human "I" but the "I" that has been negated and sublated, so, too, only when co-called culture has been negated can culture come to be. In this sense, culture is absolute revelation and bears

---

[12] 1931, 3: 111; 1933, 3: 491, 494, 499, 511; 1935, 6: 296.
[13] 1933, 3: 443, 507.
[14] 1931, 3: 17–18.
[15] 1930, 4: 318.
[16] 1931, 4: 367, 378.

the image of God. But this does not mean that culture receives positive regulations from the absolute or is an immediate realization of the will of God. It is just that through the salvation of the human being as subject, culture is mediated by the absolute as a negation-in-affirmation. It is said that "there is no Buddha without deluded thoughts" but also that "the Buddha is in the awakening." Thus if we say that God is God in mediating the activities of human beings, we need also to say that rational culture *is* God. There is no absolute to be sought outside of human culture. Whatever is to be found outside of human culture is neither God nor Buddha nor absolute.[17]

It should be obvious that Tanabe is not expressing his faith in divine revelation or an absolute God whose will oversees the world in the usual Judeo-Christian sense of those terms. But far from simply brushing God-talk aside as a mythical, foreign way of speaking about human rationality, he accepts it as an index of something absolute that transcends culture from within culture and sustains it. All of this will make better sense when we come to the new logic he was busy formulating.

As his attempts to demystify philosophy and restore it to daily life grew bolder, allusions to Buddhist ideas also begin to appear here and there in his writings. This should not be seen as a rebuttal of mysticism which, properly understood, awakens philosophy to its original vocation of grasping the absolute, gives it life, and at the same time provides the demands of religion with a religious form.[18] This is consistent with his view that the world as a whole can be seen as the "ordinary self-revelation of the divine."[19]

Cognates to Tanabe's position that do not require defining the absolute as nothingness abound in Western philosophy. But his attempts to expand his understanding of religion beyond an index of moral ideals were urging him to clarify the ontological status of God. For this reason, he begins to fault theology for oppressing the drive to knowledge and trying to take over the attempts of previous metaphysics to absorb nature and science into its domain.[20]

Here, Tanabe's appeal to Buddhist thought comes to the fore. His first essay on the subject was an extended treatment of Dōgen's *Shōbōgenzō*, in which he contrasts theology's clinging to a mythical worldview whose knowledge opposes science and philosophy with Buddhism's general rejection of mythical explanations.[21] While taking favorable note of the positive attitude toward religious praxis in Kierkegaard and certain existentialist philosophers, he draws a sharp line when it comes to the understanding of the absolute:

---

[17] 1934, 5: 77–8.

[18] 1932, 3: 440; 1936, 6: 224.

[19] 1937, 5: 214–5, 226.

[20] 1937, 5: 291; 1939, 5: 419.

[21] Even outside of the Buddhist context, Tanabe often refers to the God of "absolute negation" as preferable to "mythical religion" and the idea of a "creator God" that stands opposed to "nature" (e.g., 1936, 6: 135, 141, 147, 212).

In western thought the search for unifying the relative and the absolute is nothing more than an annihilation of the relative as it melts it into the absolute . . . . This is called "mysticism." Existential philosophy may not rush in that direction, but seems unable to achieve a true unity of the opposition between *Existenz* and *Transcendenz*. It is different with eastern nothingness, where the opposites of relative and absolute are united in absolute nothingness where going forth to one's own salvation entails a return to care for the world.[22]

On this basis, Tanabe ventures for the first time a redefinition of God as absolute nothingness:

Christianity's religion of revelation does not allow for a view of God as absolute nothingness that would radicalize a dialectics of faith-praxis-enlightenment . . . . For believers, the rebirth of death-in-life, try as it might to enlighten itself on the dialectical structure of faith, its "God" comes to rest as a transcendent entity and does not reach an enlightened faith that correlates to the conversion of the subject through a dialectically immanent rebirth . . . . Awareness of their tribulations as a grace and of the immediate conversion of the God of wrath into a God of love is dependent solely on the fact of Christ's redemptive death. This fact is withdrawn from historical relationships and given a universal human meaning that is generally impossible for all but Christians.[23]

Tanabe's respect for Buddhist awakening is offset by an undisguised animus toward Christian teachings that had not been visible in his earlier writings. While we cannot discount a certain acquiescence to the nationalistic fever that was taking over the country, Tanabe's Dōgen essay represents an important first step toward an idea of God that is more than a pastiche of ideas received from Western philosophy. In fact, he ends the essay declaring that it is necessary to "transcend the theistic tendencies of Western philosophy from a standpoint of absolute nothingness." This, he claims, is part of a more general project to "accept Western philosophy but step beyond its limits."[24]

---

[22] 1938, 7: 22; see also 1940, 7: 131. The last phrase (*ōsōmen-soku-gensōmen* 往相面即還相面) is a Pure Land Buddhist term that will return to play a dominant role in Tanabe's metanoetics.

[23] 1937, 5: 487.

[24] 1937, 5: 493. I have passed over the many references in Tanabe's early writings to the influence of Aristotle's notions of God on Christian philosophy, but it is worth mentioning that he now begins to contrast Aristotle's view and its persistence in Hegel's thought with one that is grounded in a "nothingness of absolute, dialectical negation" that transcends being while being within it (1935, 6: 296; 1937, 5: 304, 464).

THE LOGIC OF THE SPECIFIC AND ITS NATIONALISTIC TRANSGRESSIONS

An important turning point came with his proposal of what he called a "logic of the specific," an idea that helped him coordinate many of his thoughts on the idea of God up to that point. The aim of his new logic was to show that the universal exists in the particular only under the conditions of its social *specificity*. In other words, the individual subject has no direct, intuitive access to universal ideas or ideals. Everything is filtered through culture, including the idea that such direct access is possible. The logic of the specific is not intended to expose pursuit of the truth as self-deluded folly but to make conscious the extent to which that pursuit and whatever truth it thinks it has found are never able to disrobe themselves completely of time, place, and socially conditioned modes of thought. But "as the free will of the individual takes back the specific and reverses its limitations, it restores it to the control of the self and makes it a mediator of self-realization."[25] Hence, the greater the consciousness of the irrational specificity of knowledge, the more transparent the specificity, the more knowledge is demystified and open to change, the humbler the "universal" convictions of the individual subject, and the more open the society to the wider world. In a dialectical negation of negation, an ethnic or national identity that is aware of the specific, "primitive, mythical" way in which it dresses ethical and epistemological principles, and even identifies it with religion, thereby negates pure universality and in that very act affirms its specific form as the only kind of universality that is given us as human beings to know.[26]

The consequences for the idea of God are easy to see. Obviously, it means that God is always and ever a cultural concept. "Each age that approaches God directly must do so realizing an absolute value in its own particularity . . . . The glory of God is not a rose that opens up at the limits of a culture; it is more like a lotus in the fire that blossoms in explosions of historical crisis."[27] Tanabe now has a basis for his claim that reason, understood as a cultural phenomenon aimed at expanded consciousness of the world and of the specific conditions of reason itself, is a suitable name for what we call God. This only holds true if self-awareness is made into an absolute universal and divinity is liberated from the individual attributes of person, transcendent creator, judge, and provident will opposed to human will that we see in Catholic doctrine. For Tanabe, this appears to be a necessary condition for a philosophically alert religion.[28]

---

[25] 1935, 6: 117. "Adaptation body" (*ōjin* 応身) refers to the form in which buddhahood is manifest in diverse, concrete forms, such as the historical Buddha, Shakamuni, in order to accommodate to the capacity and needs of worldly beings.

[26] 1935, 6: 148, 153, 200; 1937, 6: 380, 450. Tanabe notes that the failure to understand this led Hegel to absolutize the ethnic nation (1936, 6: 143, 155; 1935, 6: 296).

[27] 1937, 6: 382, 384.

[28] 1935, 6: 122, 141, 144; 1936, 6: 233; 1937, 6: 378; 1937, 6: 492. The stimulus for these ideas, it should be noted, comes from Bergson's distinction between "open" and "closed" societies and his suggestion that the structure of a closed society supports a restricted idea of divine love (1936, 6: 76).

Allusions to the error of universalizing specific religious symbols are very frequent in Tanabe's nationalistic statements, but there are enough of them to turn his previous new logic into a caricature of itself. A single, particularly offensive example should suffice. After locating the Trinitarian doctrine of Paul and Augustine in Hegel's dialectic, Tanabe comments:

> To those who are not Christian, Christian mythology inevitably makes even this deep, speculative truth a stumbling block. Along with that, the contradiction that vestiges of a Jewish personal theism pose to absolute nothingness is not washed clean by the dialectical method and could not be mediated by the scientific thought to follow. My philosophy of the state places the nation in the position of Christ, as it were, a substrate manifestation of absolute nothingness in the form of an *adaptation body* that radicalizes the dialectical truth of Christianity and liberates it from its mythical constraints.[29]

Convinced that only a "new religious spirit" can provide the kind of unifying principle that the present age needs, Tanabe concluded that Japan cannot stop at being a unified ethnic nation but can absorb ideas from other countries and become universal, beginning with a leading role in the construction of East Asia. The concrete manifestation of this principle is service to the emperor in whose person the idea of a society open to the world is made concrete and visible. Christianity is not suited to express this religiously; Mahāyāna Buddhism is.[30]

Within this context, the criticism of Christianity and Hegel come together in his attempt to rethink the notion of the absolute as both a negation and an affirmation of the relative, something he considers the Christian idea of God incapable of performing because of its insistence on obeying divine commands and "redeeming" the relative in an unmediated manner, both of which stop at negating the self to affirm God.[31] The idea of a metaphysics of "absolute dialectics" or "absolute mediation" goes back to the early 1930s,[32] but it is only now that he adopts it to contrast nothingness with the Christian God of being—whether expressed overtly or in the "hidden" mystical language of *Gottheit*—as a kind of "universal individual" transcending all specificity of the relative, "natural" world.[33] Tanabe prefers the view that "the nation is God on earth, not God in heaven, a relative absolute, not an absolute absolute."[34] Jesus' dual role as teacher of humanity and son of God keeps Christianity locked into a personal mode of thought that needs liberating.[35]

---

[29] 1939, 7: 42. Emphasis added.
[30] 1940, 7: 103–12; 1940, 8: 166–7. Tanabe adds that, although he does not consider himself a "Buddhist believer or someone with connections to Buddhism," its religious spirit contains the elements out of which to build a new age.
[31] 1939, 7: 32, 65; 1940, 7: 191–3, 200; 1941.
[32] 1932, 6: 48; 1935, 6: 248.
[33] 1939, 7: 65–6, 68; 1940, 7: 109, 124; 1941, 7: 246.
[34] 1941, 8: 205.
[35] 1939, 7: 43.

These arguments appear with regularity during his essays of 1939 to 1944 and make us expect that, having rejected the idea of the God-man Christ, he would have no further use of the idea of God. In fact, he retains the term and sets up a "trinitarian unity of God, country, and individual." One has the sense that he needs it to engage Western thought critically and to ensure that his own ideas of the absolute can take the place of God, or rather purify it of its mythology, so that "historical philosophy as absolute self-awareness of history with its characteristic relativity" can advance with no loss of sophistication. There can be little doubt that Tanabe compromised the role of "God" during the years leading up to the war. In a talk to students in 1938, he goes so far as to suggest the identity of God and country.[36]

This seems to be out of character with his earlier insistence that the idea of the nation must never directly become a kind of "God" directly identified with a local mythology, but only indirectly play the role of expressing "eternity in time," a call to transcend private ethics not unlike the way the "fear of God" functions in Christianity. In this sense, religious mythology, including talk of God, can even be said to mediate the way to transcend individuality for the sake of the nation. Within two years, however, his mode of expression was more clearly aligned to the prevalent ideology, resembling more the preaching of a crusade than the ethereal philosophical language we had come to expect of him:[37]

> This is where God comes in to mediate the nation and the individual. To bind oneself directly to the state and its service is a manifestation of the divine. It is God's revelation. We may understand that dedicating oneself to the nation is devotion to God.[38]

As if to remove all doubt of where he stood, the following year, he addressed first-year high school students at his alma mater, repeating his view that service to the nation is a sign of "our own obedience to the absoluteness of God." The Christian idea of the incarnation may be mythical, he went on, but, like the Pure Land teaching of the Buddha's compassionate return to save others, it carries the profound meaning of God's participation in human suffering. But more than these, the emperor, as a living divinity, embodies the trinitarian principle of God, nation, and individual.[39]

THE GOD OF METANOETICS

As the consequences of the war effort became more apparent, Tanabe realized that these views had made a mockery of the spirit of his logic of the specific, but it also pressed him

---

[36] 1943, 14: 416.
[37] 1941, 8: 205–6, 209, 215.
[38] 1943, 8: 260.
[39] 1944, 8: 296, 298–9.

to understand why his rationality had failed him. The brunt of his argument is a self-accusation of hubris with regard to the power of reason. In terms of the facile application of abstract ideas to the concrete historical situation, this is certainly true. But there is another sense in which he had failed to consult the basic principle of his own logic; namely, that there is no absolute in culture that is not subject to the critique of relative specificity.

It is not mere coincidence that *Philosophy as Metanoetics* is a religious tract through and through. Three interlocking ideas had been foundational up to that point. The first is the assumption that some conception of an *absolute* is central to philosophical thought. The second is the idea that *God* is the core index of the absolute in Western philosophy. I suppose that without Hegel's idea of the absolute, the idea of God would not have found such a self-evident slide into Japanese philosophy. But, despite his gradual drift away from Hegel's Christian moorings, he seems not to have been bothered about reading Hegel's original use of *the absolute* as a substantive back into the history of Western philosophy, let alone Eastern thought. On the contrary, its cash value was so great that it is not even clear that he, or others in the Kyoto School, were even aware of the novelty of Hegel's coinage. But it is the third idea that became the focus of his repentance, namely, that *reason* is a more fitting way to describe God than anything that Christianity, Judaism, or ancient philosophy had to offer. Obviously, he was not simply going to forsake critical philosophy for theology or mysticism. This left him with the more radical step: to dethrone reason itself by driving it to the point where its limits are exposed.

Tanabe's whole career had been aimed at showing what disciplined reason can do. What he had failed to see is what even the most critical and self-conscious attempts to be reasonable *cannot* do. "Metanoetics" was his term for a conversion to a standpoint at the threshold of rationality where the mind and heart can be touched by a reality beyond reason. He called it "a philosophy that was not a philosophy." Only by deliberately driving reason to the limits where it would die and crumble in one's hands, he felt, could the last stronghold of the self-centered, self-powered self abandon itself to a power from which reason could be reborn, aware of what it can and cannot do. The first instinct of such reason would be service to others and the building up of a historical community. The consequences for philosophy would be to replace the ideal of "speculation about speculation" with a love of others conscious of the fact that it was the instrument of an other-power not its own. The absolute of reason would thus undergo an "absolute conversion."

After the metanoetics, Tanabe's notion of nothingness sheds its affiliations with the Japanese people and their emperor to return to its previous abstract formulation:

> Nothingness, insofar as it is nothingness, cannot work directly by itself, because what works directly by itself is always being, never nothingness. Nothingness works as nothingness only by mediating being. This is why absolute nothing is absolute mediation.[40]

---

[40] 1946, 7: 261. See also 1945, 9: 35 [PM, 22]. PM refers to the English translation, *Philosophy as Metanoetics*.

From there, he reconstructs the standpoint of nothingness in order to deny the self that does no more than criticize the nation and to enter into a deeper, mutual negation in which both self and nation can be "reborn in the eternal love of God." During these years, the idea of God appears with greater frequency, often in a paraphrase of earlier arguments. The difference is that Tanabe adjusts his view to this kind of "absolute conversion," and the character of God is identified as "absolute nothingness-in-love."[41] Gone is his earlier nationalist idealism, which he now spoke of as "taking the standpoint of the Gods." The focus on Christ's incarnation shifts away from its forfeiture of history to be seen as an "archetype corresponding to an absolute, compassionate return to the relative" and even to a "principle for socialist reconstruction." His trinitarian model is broadened to include world-nation-individual and religion-politics-morality as "mediators of absolute nothingness." He explicitly rejects the model of "a chosen divine land, a unification of worship and politics, a living divinity" and other forms of unmediated unity.[42]

This does not mean that God now conforms to the transcendent God of Christianity or even to the "universal self" of Hegel. He continues to see the Christian God as limited by the "absolute mediation" that characterizes all of reality, but he seeks a way to preserve the identity of God and the absolute without compromising human freedom. Human freedom requires that the absolute nothingness of God be absolutely related to everything:

> Since God, as the absolute, is not being but nothingness, the act of submission or obedience that belongs to freedom represents a spontaneous and self-determining choice on the part of the human person, with no external restrictions. The human individual gains freedom through the mediation of God, while God in turn is realized and made manifest through the mediation of human freedom.[43]

Absolute nothingness is only *real* when relative beings are engaged in historical practice and ethical transformation. In this sense, Tanabe's God of nothingness aims to recover Kierkegaard's view of the practice of "eternity in time" as a counterfoil to the "mystical" views of thinkers as diverse as Eckhart and Heidegger and to recognize the metanoetic element to Nietzsche's nihilism.[44]

He clearly rejects any form of religion that speaks of the unity of the divine and the human, the absolute and the relative. The God of Love, we might say, functions less as a noun than as an adverb qualifying praxis. Love cannot be seen as a mere negation of the self in front of a God, but as a compassionate reliance on other-power. The ideal of uniting with or begging salvation of a God who creates the world by pure thought is

---

[41] 1947, 8: 423, 431–2, 438.
[42] 1947, 8: 343, 354, 356.
[43] 1945, 9: 117 [PM, 118].
[44] 1945, 9: 61, 86–7, 89, 92–3, 96, 115. [PM, 54, 83, 85, 89–90, 94, 115].

reason uncritical of itself, a "mental laziness" that "quickly makes action unnecessary and impossible."[45]

GOD IN THE LATE WRITINGS

Certainly, the years after his metanoetics show Tanabe pursuing the idea that "the philosophy of religion crystallizes the most difficult problems of philosophy,"[46] which turned his interest more and more to religious symbols, and nowhere more clearly than in allusions to God and Christ. Indeed, in the first book of this period, he even felt it necessary to clarify to Pure Land traditionalists that he had not converted to Christianity.[47] The increase in religious vocabulary in general did not mark a religious conversion to any one faith, though his favoritism toward Shinran's thought in his interpretations of Christianity and Zen is evident.[48] On the contrary, questioning his own trust in reason strengthened his rational resolve and helped him to coordinate his thoughts on absolute nothingness, self-awareness, historical praxis, absolute mediation, and even the logic of the specific. It was as if he had finished the *basso ostinato* and had turned all his attention to refining the melody and its orchestration. Certainly, this is true of his idea of God.

Although Tanabe continues to reject religious dogmatism of all sorts and describes himself as not belonging to any particular religion, he has begun to see a purpose in religious myth that can survive its displacement by science and reason.[49] At the same time and despite his rejection of ideological nationalism, he was not so quick to give up the religious significance of the nation, which he felt needed to undergo a metanoia of its own. Thus, he continued to describe the nation of Japan as a specific mediator of the universal that functions like Buddhist *upāya* or "expedient means" to negate the individual self and its direct route to the absolute.[50] This is an important part of his attempt to rehabilitate his logic of the specific by way of metanoetic dialectics and to clarify its goal as a critical foundation to overturn Christianity's medieval subservience of philosophy to theology.

He had earlier remarked parenthetically that, as the self-negation of God, Christ overcomes the duality between the divine and the human, spirit and flesh, but does so in an unmediated fashion that preserves the abstract, nondialectical nature of God as being.[51] In a critical aside, he notes that those who make Jesus an object of faith rather

---

[45] 1946, 7: 268–9, 281–2, 285–90, 322, 326, 344, 369. On the rejection of associating God and country, an idea often repeated in his late writings, see also 1949, 11: 223–7.

[46] 1945, 9: 209 [PM, 226].

[47] 1947, 9: 275.

[48] Near the end of his life, he acknowledged Zen as the best guide to a "philosophy of death" (1958, 13: 168; English translation in Tanabe 1959, 4).

[49] 1945, 9: 267–8 [295]; see also 1949, 11: 307.

[50] 1948, 7: 258.

[51] 1937, 6: 492.

than the God whom Jesus believed in lose the mediating role of Jesus as a religious founder.[52] And yet, consistent with his insistence that a philosophy of nothingness combines myth and logic, he acknowledged in advanced age that the demythologizing movement in Christian theology is indicative of a new trend in religious philosophy toward understanding religious faith in terms of self-awareness by "cleansing" myth and transforming it into meaningful symbols.[53]

Tanabe's rejection of the Pauline transformation of Christ into a redeemer[54] and its accompanying neglect of history remain in place, but he took a more conciliatory stance toward the state of mind of the confessing sinner. This is particularly evident in his reading of Kierkegaard's struggles with faith as a conversion from self-power to other-power and at the same time sympathizes with the "power of his faith" to do battle with organized religion. His extended comments on Christianity's teachings and his free use of its vocabulary is salted with enough of his own philosophy to make it clear that he is, after all, a philosopher using religious language for his own purposes. And yet, the tone of the writing, compared to what he had said about God before, verges at times on what he would surely in earlier years have considered pietistic. An example may help and save us from having to catalog its numerous paraphrases:

> The God who is love makes itself into nothing, gives itself to others exhaustively. In that sense, God is the principle of nothingness and never works immediately and of its own will . . . . The phrase "God is love" only becomes real when it is backed up by the actions of people who love God. And action that mediates deeds of compassionate return is none other than love from absolute nothingness.[55]

In 1951, he also set out to combine Zen and Pure Land Buddhism with an eye to aligning Christianity and Buddhism with Marxist socialism.[56] It is hardly surprising that there is no reference to Shintō in the project. The brief return to Marxism then slides quietly out of the picture as he develops his Buddhist reading of Christian scriptures and contemporary theologians in an attempt to underscore his identification of God and Christ with the working of absolute nothingness in the world of relative being.[57] It is not at all surprising to find him describing himself in this late period as "a Christian in the making" who could never "become Christian."[58]

---

[52] 1946, 7: 284.

[53] 1937, 6: 471; 1947, 10: 295; 1948, 10: 31, 35; 1958, 13: 172; 1959, 14: 441; 1961, 13: 285. An extended appraisal of Rudolf Bultmann appears in 1962, 13: 567–76; see also 1962, 13: 604.

[54] 1948, 10: 12, 76–7.

[55] 1947, 9: 329.

[56] See 1947, 10: 297–307.

[57] A short translation of representative passages from this book can be found in Ozaki 1990, 127–69.

[58] 1948, 10: 260. Tanabe uses a German phrase here, which his disciple Nishitani Keiji would later take up in referring to himself as a *gewordener Buddhist* and a *werdender Christ*.

THE HOLLOW LEGACY OF TANABE'S GOD

Tanabe's ideas of God seem to have made little mark on philosophy or theology inside Japan or out. Indeed his two principal disciples, the Christian Mutō Kazuo and the Pure Land Buddhist Takeuchi Yoshinori, did not even seem to find it essential to Tanabe's idea of absolute nothingness. Yet without God, that idea would never have developed as it did. The simplest explanation is that Tanabe's God talk is tied *too* closely to a forbidding style that make his philosophical writings difficult to approach. I cannot believe that is all there is to it.

Simply put, the problem is that, with the possible exception of the postwar repentance of the *Metanoetics*, Tanabe's readers do not feel a sense of companionship with the questions that drove him. Despite his wide-ranging and often radical criticisms against thinkers whose works he was reading for their failure to address history in the concrete, Tanabe himself shied away from applying his own counterpositions to political, economic, institutional, or spiritual problems of his day in any concrete, moral sense; and the upshot is that the practical application of his ideas was never able to reflect back on the quality of the ideas. One has to know a great deal about the times he was writing to understand what specific issues he was inflicting his abstract terminology on, and, even so, it is not clear what tangible difference his reconstructions were supposed to make. To the reader, Tanabe's questions suffocate in the language of his answers.

I do not mean to say that there is *no* question to which he reckoned the idea of God an essential part of the answer, only that its uncovering is trying in the extreme. Having reviewed his writings from start to finish, I now think that his question comes down to this: *How can I, who feel no need to believe in an other-worldly divine being, recover the impulse to such an idea and describe it, to my own satisfaction, in language that preserves the truth of that impulse without having to compromise my own philosophical impulses?*

As we watch Tanabe move away, cautiously at first but then with more confidence, from merely recording the God talk in Western philosophers to struggling with what lies behind it, we realize that he never found another term to which it could be reduced without remainder. The idea was simply too rich, too multifaceted, too plural in its expression to allow for such a reduction. Of no other idea in his philosophy can this be said. It is not too much of an exaggeration to say that self-awareness, absolute nothingness, other-power, and even love were humbled before a word too overdetermined to be left aside. He realized that for every idea in the history of God talk there was an opposite, but he also realized that this very contradiction had an irreplaceable role to play in intellectual history. He could not bring himself to dismiss it as an empty concept used to fill in logical gaps. Tanabe's philosophy took shape in redefining, adjusting, criticizing, comparing, and then redefining yet again this singular idea. Try as he might, not even his own metanoetic conversion was able to come up with a substitute. In the end, the idea of God got the better his every attempt to translate it into a functional equivalent.

That said, I do not think that Tanabe ever came to a clear conception of what the *impulse* behind the idea of God is or even where it is to be sought. Ritual practice and its symbols did not interest him any more than institutionalized religion did. He seemed to have a natural aversion to mystical silence and confessional literalism alike. His sole access to the urges that drive ideas of God was through the door of written texts, and yet one has the sense that he was aware of there being something more to God than could be rationally chastened of its mythical content and then paraphrased. How else explain the teeter-totter in his late works, exhaling the Judaeo-Christian God in one breath and inhaling the God of selfless love in the next?

None of this, of course, proves anything about the nature of existence of a God beyond the impulse. Nor did Tanabe ever suggest it did. The faith in absolute other-power he came to confess was not a faith that provided information about facts inaccessible to reason. The Anselmian idea of "faith seeking understanding" did not attract him. We might say he was closer to Bernard of Clairvaux in seeing faith as a renunciation of reason in order to experience the impulse that reason obscures.

Were the legacy of Tanabe's idea of God only an unspoken and unanswered question, there would be little more to say. Quite to the contrary, I am convinced that the points at which it intercepts Western ideas of God as a transcendent, supreme being bear a closer look. In particular, the suggestion of nothingness as absolutely and directly interrelated to everything that exists poses a serious metaphysical and moral challenge to the dominant complexion of God in the great monotheistic traditions. More than that, I suspect that once we understand how important Tanabe's idea of God was to his idea of absolute nothingness, as I believe I have demonstrated sufficiently, we can also see the sense in which his radically relative God can refresh the Kyoto School philosophy's idea of nothingness by dispensing altogether with the notion of the absolute it had inherited from Hegel and reshaped, which on balance seems to be more trouble than it is worth.

William James reminds us that we prefer what has developed from within to what has been fashioned from without, that an egg is a higher style of being than a piece of clay that an external modeler has made into the image of a bird.[59] This is certainly true of Tanabe's approach to the idea of God as he met it in Western philosophy. Nevertheless, it was a *Western* idea he had in mind. The gods and spirits of his native literary and religious history were of no interest to him. Tanabe was, after all like the cuckoo that prefers to have its eggs hatched in another's nest rather than build a nest of its own. What Tanabe did not figure out was how then to nudge his fledglings to take wing and migrate homeward.

---

[59] William James, *A Pluralistic Universe, in The Collected Works of William James* (Cambridge: Harvard University Press, 1977), 5: 73.

Bibliography and Suggested Readings

Heisig, James W. (1995) "Tanabe's Logic of the Specific and the Spirit of Nationalism." In *Rude Awakenings: Zen, the Kyoto School, and the Question of Nationalism*, edited by James W. Heisig and John C. Maraldo. Honolulu: University of Hawai'i Press, 255–88.

Heisig, James W. (2001) *Philosophers of Nothingness: An Essay on the Kyoto School*. Honolulu: University of Hawai'i Press, 105–79.

Heisig, James and Taitetsu Unno (eds.). (1990) *The Religious Philosophy of Tanabe Hajime: The Metanoetic Imperative*. Berkeley: Asian Humanities Press.

Himi Kiyoshi. (1990) *Tanabe tetsugaku kenkyū: Shūkyō tetsugaku no kannten kara* [Studies in the Philosophy of Tanabe Hajime: A View from the Philosophy of Religion]. Tokyo: Hokuju Shuppan.

Laube, Johannes. (1984) *Dialektik der absoluten Vermittlung: Hajime Tanabes Religionsphilosophie als Beitrag zum "Wettstreit der Liebe" zwischen Buddhismus und Christentum*. Freiburg: Herder.

Morisato, Takeshi. (2019) *Faith and Reason in Continental and Japanese Philosophy: Reading Tanabe Hajime and William Desmond*. New York: Bloomsbury Academic.

Mutō Kazuo. (2012) "Nothingness-in-Love: The Philosophy of Tanabe Hajime and Christianity." In *Christianity and the Notion of Nothingness: Contributions to Buddhist-Christian Dialogue from the Kyoto school*, edited by Martin Repp and Jan Van Bragt. Leiden: Brill, 183–203.

Ozaki Makoto. (1990) *Introduction to the Philosophy of Tanabe*. Amsterdam: Rodopi.

Sugimoto Kōichi. (2011) "Tanabe Hajime's Logic of Species and the Philosophy of Nishida Kitarō." In *Japanese and Continental Philosophy: Conversations with the Kyoto School*, edited by Bret W. Davis, Brian Schroeder, and Jason M. Wirth. Bloomington: Indiana University Press, 52–67.

Takehana Yōsuke. (2006) "Absolute Nothingness and Metanoetics: The Logic of Conversion in Tanabe Hajime," in *Frontiers of Japanese Philosophy*, edited by James W. Heisig. Nagoya: Nanzan Institute for Religion and Culture, 246–68.

Tanabe Hajime. (1963–1964) *Tanabe Hajime zenshū* [The Complete Works of Tanabe Hajime], 15 vols. Tokyo: Iwanami Shoten.

Tanabe Hajime. (1959) "Memento Mori," *Philosophical Studies of Japan* 1: 1–12.

Tanabe Hajime. (1986) *Philosophy as Metanoetics*, trans. Takeuchi Yoshinori et al. Berkeley: University of California Press.

Tanabe Hajime. (1998) "Christianity, Marxism, and Japanese Buddhism: In Anticipation of a Second Religious Reformation." In *Sourcebook for Modern Japanese Philosophy: Selected Documents*, edited by David Dilworth and Valdo Viglielmo. Westport: Greenwood Press, 115–58.

CHAPTER 20

....

MIKI KIYOSHI

Marxism, Humanism, and the Power of Imagination

....

MELISSA ANNE-MARIE CURLEY

MIKI Kiyoshi (1897–1945) studied with both Nishida Kitarō and Tanabe Hajime, the founding Kyoto School thinkers discussed in earlier chapters in this volume. He was a particular favorite of Nishida's—when the young Miki returned to Japan following an eventful trip to Germany,[1] Nishida had him in mind for a faculty position at Kyoto. However, Miki's philosophical differences with his mentors (and some details of his personal life) soon became the topic of scandalized gossip, and Nishida felt compelled to withdraw his support.[2] While in Kyoto, Miki had begun socializing with a coterie of young leftists; after leaving under a cloud, he became increasingly associated with Marxist thought, establishing himself as a vanguard intellectual.

Miki's emergence as a Marxist in some sense pitted him against his mentor, Nishida. During the late 1920s and early 1930s, Marxism was perceived as more fashionable than Nishida's philosophy. Nishitani Keiji recalls an episode in 1930 when Miki, then holding a faculty position at Hōsei University in Tokyo, was invited back to Kyoto as a visiting speaker. His scheduled lecture on Marx happened to coincide with Nishida's class: "During Professor Nishida's talk, suddenly a huge passionate applause broke out from the nearby lecture hall" where Miki was delivering his address.[3] The same year, Miki's involvement with the Japanese Communist Party led to his arrest and a brief period of imprisonment, which in turn cost him the position at Hōsei; he moved on to a successful career in journalism. In 1938, he joined Konoe Fumimaro's Shōwa Research Association—there is much debate around whether this should be understood as a sign of capitulation to the allure of fascism or a strategic effort to fight the system from within—and is thought to have been the author of the association's "Principles of

---

[1] This period in his life is vividly described in Michiko Yusa's "Philosophy and Inflation: Miki Kiyoshi in Weimar Germany, 1922–1924," *Monumenta Nipponica* 53.1 (1998): 45–71.

[2] Yusa 2002, 212–213.

[3] Yusa 2002, 230.

Thought for a New Japan," which would eventually provide an ideological justification for Japanese imperialism under the banner of the Great East Asia Co-Prosperity Sphere. Miki was drafted in 1942 and served in the occupied Philippines as part of the military's propaganda wing; he returned to Japan in 1943 and was arrested again in 1945, this time for helping a friend associated with the Communist Party evade the police. He was still under detention when Japan surrendered. Miki died of illness in prison before the Allied order to release all political prisoners was carried out.

Despite his somewhat vexed relationship with Nishida, Miki shared with his teacher a guiding interest in the question of creation or production. Miki was critical of Asian thinkers for not attending to the importance of historical change; Nishida in turn was critical of Marxism for not attending to the creative capacity of the individual. In his later work, Nishida would argue that, properly understood, historical materialism had to mean that

> the world of matter is a world that neither moves mechanically nor develops biologically. It is necessarily a world that is continually forming itself in expressive activity, which is to say, in production. Thus we can say that, from the beginning, man makes the milieu and that the milieu makes man, and one can speak of a world of the relations of production.[4]

For Miki, too, the question of how human beings create the environments in which they dwell—or, to introduce a term of art used by both Nishida and Miki, how the embodied subject or agent (*shutai* 主体) makes history—was a fundamental one.

This concern for embodied subjectivity or agency (*shutaisei* 主体性) was something postwar Japanese Marxism had difficulty accommodating. Immediately after the war, there was fierce debate in Marxist circles around making room in Marxism for autonomous subjective intentionality and a self-conscious subject who could freely choose to commit herself to the revolution. The party settled the debate in 1948 by declaring that arguments in support of individual agency were evidence of bourgeois idealism; this had the effect of eliding humanism and idealism and made Miki's prewar interest in the agent look unorthodox as well. But for Miki, Marxism *was* humanism. Like other Marxist humanists, he took Marx to offer a theory of history in which the development of history was identical to the development of the human being toward a total flourishing of the human capacity for creation; on this view, "it is a fundamental principle that in Marxism, man is not reduced to the relations of production but defines himself always in terms of free choice and creative projects."[5]

---

[4] Nishida 2012, 164. This resonates with Marx's assertion in *The German Ideology* that "circumstances make men just as much as men make circumstances"; see Marx 2001, 85. In his introduction to *Ontology of Production*, William Haver suggests that Nishida's later work represents "a sustained and rigorous engagement with Marx's problematic"; see Nishida 2012, 11.

[5] Sève 1974, 83; Christopher Goto-Jones suggests the usefulness of Sève's analysis for understanding Japanese Marxism in "The Left Hand of Darkness: Forging a Political Left in Interwar Japan," in *The Left in the Shaping of Japanese Democracy: Essays in Honor of J.A.A. Stockwin*, edited by Rikki Kersten and David Williams (London: Routledge, 2006), 8. On postwar debates over agency (*shutaisei*) among Japanese Marxists and liberals, see Chapter 28 in this volume.

The creative project, in this case, was an epochal one. In June 1939—with Japanese occupation forces spreading across Asia and the Japanese army in the midst of a series of covert border conflicts with the Soviet Union—Miki published a short essay aimed at a general audience on "History's Reason" (*Rekishi no risei*). In the essay, he directly addresses the contemporary situation:

> Faced with the state of the world today, everyone wants to ask where on earth is the reason within history? Seeing such "terrifying confusion," anyone would become a bit skeptical. But if there were no reason at all within history, upon what foundation would we be able to act?[6]

His claim is that the reason at work within history is the logic of "imagination" (*kōsōryoku* 構想力, literally the power of conception).[7] Those who find themselves caught in the midst of historical upheaval should know that they are participants in the creative activity that defines the human being: "Our task now is the creation of a new culture, which must consist in the conceiving of new forms, the creation of new forms."[8]

In the two years leading up to the publication of "History's Reason," Miki had published a series of essays exploring the topic of imagination through the lenses of myth, institution, and technology. These essays were collected in the first volume of his *Logic of Imagination* (*Kōsōryoku no ronri*), also published in 1939.[9] In the pages that follow, we will take "the creation of a new culture" as a touchstone for working through some of the themes of *Logic of Imagination*, focusing particularly on what it means to conceive the agent as making a new milieu through the power of imagination.

DESIRE MATTERS

Miki opens "History's Reason" with an objection to Hegelian idealism. Hegel, he explains, grants sovereignty over history to transcendent reason alone: "in history, however irrational something may seem, it cannot resist the control of this reason; on the contrary, in the end it works under this control, and so reason always accomplishes its own [ends], realizes its own [ends]."[10] Given this, Hegel cannot but run roughshod over our private passions (*jōnetsu* 情熱), reducing them to tools used by "cunning reason" toward its own ends and so making a puppet of the individual person.[11] Taken to its

---

[6] Miki 1967*b*, 249.
[7] Miki 1967*b*, 260.
[8] Miki 1967*b*, 263.
[9] A second volume of *Logic of Imagination* focused on the question of experience was published posthumously in 1946. Although *Logic of Imagination* has to be read as an unfinished work, it is nonetheless widely recognized as Miki's crowning philosophical achievement.
[10] Miki 1967*b*, 250.
[11] Miki 1967*b*, 250–252.

endpoint, this way of thinking about history would culminate in eradicating whatever activities spring from our individual passions or the passions of the ethnos/nation (*minzoku* 民族), thus clearing a path for the unfettered unfolding of reason.[12]

The mistake here, as Miki sees it, is not just that it is deflating to the person to understand the self as history's puppet, but that eradicating subjective human intention from history is the same as bringing history to halt: "Human beings do not exist outside of history; they stand within history. The subjective (*shukantekina mono* 主観的 なもの) enters into history from the very beginning."[13] There is a reason at work in history, but it is not cunning: it does not take human passions and put them into service in pursuit of its own rational aims. On the contrary, the reason at work in history unifies the subjective (*shukantekina mono*) and the objective (*kyakkantekina mono* 客 観的なもの), the emotional (*kanjōtekina mono na mono* 感情的なもの) and the intellectual (*chitekina mono* 知的なもの), the particular (*tokushutekina mono* 特殊的なも の) and the universal (*ippantekina mono* 一般的なもの).[14] The faculty with the power to accomplish this unification, as Miki understands it, is imagination. Thus, in order to grasp the movement of history, we need to understand imagination, and we cannot understand imagination without understanding the passions—the aspect of our being through which we relate to the material world in terms of appetite or desire.[15] History begins, then, with desire.

This is where Miki begins his account of imagination in *Logic of Imagination*, too. Human beings exist as embodied; everything we apprehend, we apprehend first through the body: "Our encounter with things in their materiality (*busshitsusei* 物質性), with things in themselves, takes place by means of the body (*shintai* 身体). It is as things that we encounter things."[16] The encounter between the material body and the material thing registers in *pathos*. But *pathos* is not mere passive receptivity to sensation. *Pathos* has an active dimension, or "an 'impulsive' character; it urges us to action through our bodies."[17] The manifold passions—hope, fear, desire, fury[18]—are examples of this kind of impulse rousing the body to engage the world; so, too, Miki suggests, are craving and longing

[12] Miki 1967b, 249–250. Miki distinguishes between *minzoku* as ethnos or nation constituted through shared custom and *kokumin* 国民 as formal nation-state. Naoki Sakai explains this distinction and its ramifications; see Sakai 2009, 190–192.

[13] Miki 1967b, 256.

[14] Miki 1967b, 260.

[15] In *The German Ideology*, Marx likewise places this encounter with the sensuous world at the base of history: "men must be in a position to live in order to be able to 'make history.' But life involves before everything else eating and drinking, a habitation, clothing and many other things. The first historical act is thus the production of the means to satisfy these needs, the production of material life itself" (Marx 2001, 70).

[16] Miki 1966, 15.

[17] Fujita 2011, 311. In his analysis of Marx's notion of human nature, Erich Fromm discusses the same distinction in terms of receptivity versus productivity; see *Marx's Concept of Man* (New York: F. Ungar, 1966).

[18] Miki 1966, 49.

pathos, taking form as what Schelling calls "hunger for existence."[19] The desirousness of *pathos* animates the body, making it a subject rather than "simply a material object."[20]

Still, if all we had was *pathos*, we could not speak of a *logic* of imagination; we could only speak of irrationalism or a sheer voluntarism. Imagination is "not simply emotion; it is at the same time the faculty that produces intelligible images (*zō* 像)."[21] Imagination draws images forth from mute emotion by means of the intellect. Because it forms images, imagination is restless:

> Formed images (*keizō* 形像)[22] are dynamic and expansive. The logic of imagination is not a static logic. And the reason that formed images are dynamic and expansive is that they come into existence as a synthesis of the emotional and the intellectual, the subjective and the objective.[23]

Following psychologist Théodule-Armand Ribot, Miki proposes that this dynamic element contained within the image drives toward the objective and external, projecting the image beyond the limits of the self toward the universal,[24] where it connects with *logos*—reason or idea—and acquires objective existence.[25]

So there is no activity without imagination—the logic of action is the logic of imagination; the insight that not just artistic activity but all activity is creative making (*poiesis*) reflects a dawning realization that the logic of imagination goes beyond the merely aesthetic.[26] The historical agent has a body, too—a social body (*shakaiteki shintai* 社会的身体), which likewise exists in an environment. In the *poietic* encounter between the historical agent and its environment, the power of imagination works to synthesize *pathos* and *logos*, giving rise to what Miki calls "historical forms" (*rekishitekina katachi* 歴史的な形), a broad term that seems to include what Marx calls forms of intercourse or relations of production.[27] History is the movement from one historical form to another: "a transformation or metamorphosis from form to form" made possible by the power of imagination and animated by the desire of the historical agent.[28]

---

[19] Miki 1966, 71–72. The reference here is to Friedrich Schelling, *Über die Gottheiten von Samothrace* (Stuttgart: J.G. Cotta, 1815). Elsewhere, Miki suggests that this desire for existence has a fundamentally positive orientation toward happiness; see Miki 1967a, 4.

[20] Fujita 2011, 311.

[21] Miki 1966, 49.

[22] The sense of forming here is distinct from form (*katachi* 形), which refers, for Miki, to historical forms. Elsewhere in *Logic of Imagination*, Miki glosses *keizōka* 形像化 as *Verbildlichung*—visualization, picturing, or coming-into-image; see Miki 1966, 45.

[23] Miki 1966, 46.

[24] Miki 1966, 61–62.

[25] Miki 1966, 49.

[26] Miki 1996, 16. Miki would seem to be indirectly addressing Nishida here.

[27] Miki 1966, 17; Miki 1967b, 259.

[28] Miki 1966, 250; Miki 1967b, 260. Marx also characterizes history in terms of movement from one form of intercourse to another: "in the place of an earlier form of intercourse, which has become a fetter, a new one is put, corresponding to the more developed productive forces and, hence, to the advanced mode of the self-activity of individuals—a form which in its turn becomes a fetter and is then replaced by another" (Marx 2001, 124).

MYTH AND REPRESENTATION: THE PRINCIPLE OF PARTICIPATION

The power of imagination is disclosed in myth, which is itself a product of imagination. Miki's treatment of myth follows on the insight of another unorthodox Marxist, French theorist Georges Sorel—it is Sorel, Miki tells us, who discovers myth as a historical force[29] at work in the present in social myths like the general strike and the socialist revolution. For Miki, to assert that the revolution is a myth is not to assert that it will never happen—on the contrary, it is to assert that it is already in the process of becoming a historical form. To understand this, we need to understand how myth works according to the logic of imagination.

Miki argues that those thinkers who insist on the primacy of *logos* misunderstand myth, mistaking it for a primitive, inadequate science.[30] We should instead recognize myth as something that requires cognition or intellect but is "not simply a product of cognition."[31] Myth traffics not in idea alone, but in representations (*hyōshō* 表象, *répresentations*)—images "saturated" with emotional and kinetic elements.[32] This mingling of *pathos* and *logos* echoes in the "pre-logical" category mixing at the heart of mythic representations.

Miki takes the term "pre-logical" from anthropologist Lucien Lévy-Bruhl. By pre-logical, Lévy-Bruhl meant both that the so-called primitive way of thinking preceded the development of scientific reason and that it was utterly indifferent to the logical principles governing scientific reason[33]; this indifference enabled so-called primitive people to happily tolerate category mixing, organizing their worlds according to the principle of participation (rather than the scientific principle of noncontradiction).[34] The principle of participation allows for a mystical identification between one thing and another or one thing and many things. Miki gives us this example from Lévy-Bruhl:

> the people of the Bororo tribe boast that they are red parakeets, but this does not mean they will become red parakeets after they die or that a person of the Bororo is a red parakeet who has changed its form—it means that the people of the Bororo consider themselves to be, at present, red parakeets: that the two are in essence identical. They are human beings and red-winged birds at the same time.[35]

---

[29] Miki 1966, 47.

[30] Miki 1966, 19.

[31] Miki 1966, 28; Fujita 2011, 316.

[32] Miki 1966, 21.

[33] Mousalimas 1990, 38.

[34] Miki 1966, 26; Mousalimas 1990, 35.

[35] Miki 1966, 22. The reference is to Lucien Lévy-Bruhl's *La mythologie primitive* (Paris: Félix Alcan, 1935).

Miki refuses Lévy-Bruhl's suggestion that the pre-logical precedes the logical, acknowledging only its second sense of indifference to contradiction.[36] According to Miki, "the mind of the primitive person goes beyond simply representing objects (*taishō* 対象)" in the sense of representing them as ideas; rather, "it takes hold of objects, and is taken hold of by objects. It enters into an exchange with objects."[37] We might recognize here a description of the encounter between the self and the world of objects that is at the foundation of imagination. The encounter between the person and the red parakeet gives rise both to a representation (the red parakeet as totem of the Bororo) and an agent (the person of the Bororo tribe). The principle of participation supports a feeling on the part of the individual person that he is a parakeet (one thing identical to another thing) and that he is a person belonging to a tribe (one identical to many).[38] By elaborating on the representation—developing myths, ceremonies, taboos around the totem, for example—it is possible to sustain this feeling of participation even when the direct encounter is no longer taking place. Representations thus allow indirect participation saturated by the feeling of direct communion. Myth is an activity that "borrows the power of an intermediary in order to actualize a participation no longer felt directly ... a means of preserving this connectedness and ceaselessly renewing it."[39] Far from disappearing as societies grow more complex then, we should expect to see myths proliferate because it is through myth that we participate in an imagined community like a nation.

Furthermore, if we look at the essential content of myth, we will find, Miki says, that myths are only about two things: "the creation of the world and the generation of human beings."[40] A myth about the creation of the world necessarily tells the story of creation of the natural by the supernatural or creation of the immanent from the transcendent. In myth, the transcendent element of creation is given symbolic form as an "uncreated creating as the transcendent ground of that which is created,"[41] motivated by its own primordial craving.[42] But every myth about the creation of the world itself, as representation, creates a world—springing forth from imagination, it consolidates and sustains a particular human world; as Fujita Masakatsu describes it, myth-making "is the activity of portraying, or quite literally 'drawing out' (*egakidasu* [描き出す]), a new world (reality) on top of the natural world."[43] Through myth, imagination tells us something true about itself: creation comes from the encounter between the transcendent and the natural, or *logos* and *pathos*. By telling ourselves a story about how the world was created, we not only affirm that we belong to an existing world, but also remind ourselves how

---

[36] Miki 1966, 21. Later, he will note that a pre-logical mentality should in no sense be understood as an antecedent to logical thought, asserting on the contrary that the pre-logical persists alongside and beyond the logical; see Miki 1966, 26.

[37] Miki 1966, 22.

[38] Miki 1966, 23.

[39] Miki 1966, 24.

[40] Miki 1966, 66.

[41] Miki 1966, 66.

[42] Miki 1966, 71.

[43] Fujita 2011, 316.

worlds are made and exercise the power of imagination that allows us to draw out a new world from the old one.

This power continues to be exercised as each age gives birth to its own myths: "freedom and equality were the myths of the eighteenth century. In the modern age, there are modern myths—'myths of the twentieth century.'"[44] Miki has Sorel's *Reflections on Violence* in mind here. Sorel writes:

> When we act we are creating a completely artificial world placed ahead of the present world and composed of movements which depend entirely on us. In this way our freedom becomes perfectly intelligible . . . . These artificial worlds generally disappear from our mind without leaving any trace in our memory; but when the masses are deeply moved it then becomes possible to describe a picture which constitutes a social myth.[45]

Like the mythic representations Miki has already described, Sorel's social myths—the general strike or the socialist revolution—draw power from the emotion of the people, binding them together as a collective (the tribe of the proletariat), which itself rehearses the conditions of the new world of freedom from exploitation yet to come. The myth tells us that the creation of this future world is inevitable, such that even setbacks are understood not as failure but as "preparation."[46] This is easily mistaken for a teleological view of history, in which history directs itself toward a determined end point using the masses for its own purposes. But if we follow Miki's line of interpretation, such a mistaken understanding vaults past the critical point: revolution is "myth" not in the sense of mere fantasy but in the sense of being an act of imagination. Far from representing the impossibility of the embodied subject making history, it is a sign of the embodied subject *already* exercising its power of world creation. Linked as it is to *poiesis* or making, for Miki as for Sorel, the myth explaining that this future world is inevitable asserts our freedom to act within history toward the future and create a new culture in which we will live as human beings.[47]

INSTITUTION AND TECHNOLOGY: THE LAW OF IMITATION

At the same time, myths, like dreams, are insubstantial; history is real and objective.[48] If imagination stopped at representation—if it was strictly limited to images (*imajinari*

---

[44] Miki 1966, 27.
[45] Sorel 1999, 26–27.
[46] Sorel 1966, 31.
[47] Miki 1966, 47.
[48] Miki 1966, 98.

イマジナリ)—it could not be the logic of history. As the logic of history, the logic of imagination must involve not only image but also form.[49] The representations of myth find formal expression in institutions: religious institutions, moral institutions, political institutions, and so on—including, most crucially for our purposes, the social institution of the nation. Miki introduces the institution in terms of *nomos*, in its multiple senses of law, manners (*shūzoku* 習俗), habit (*shūkan* 習慣), and custom (*kanshū* 慣習).[50] It is important to recognize that although the *nomos* presents itself to us as obligatory or natural, it is actually, like the collective representations of myth, an act of shared imagination. The institution operates as a kind of legal fiction (*gisei* 擬製) in which "intelligence (*chisei* 知性) can bind with imagination … without imagination, the institution cannot develop."[51] So, for example, although we might think of the greeting in terms of instinct (*honnō* 本能), in fact, it is an invention (*hatsumei* 発明) born out of an encounter between the embodied subject and a distinctively arrayed world, which we call the milieu or environment (*kankyō* 環境); different environments afford different encounters, leading to the invention of different forms of greeting. Social belonging reflects and is reinforced by means of such invented etiquette.[52] Or, we might think of habit in terms of instinct, and, indeed, there is something instinctive at the base of habit.[53] But habit is not reducible to instinct; it is rather "what takes the place of first nature as 'second nature.'"[54] As "second nature," habit mediates nature and culture, involving both instinct and idea, or both nature and will in neat proportion, which explains why we can speak of habit in terms of natural spontaneity.[55] As something of our own making, habit involves both continuity and creation.[56] Miki reads custom as collective habit.[57] Like habits, customs involve both continuity and creation. Institutions—moral, political, religious, social— emerge from customs.

If the imaginative work of myth-making is structured by the principle of participation, the imaginative work of institution-forming is structured by the law of imitation, described by sociologist Gabriel de Tarde. Tarde holds that our sense of moral obligation is initially restricted to those with whom one shares a blood relation. If we are to widen the sphere of moral interest, rationality is required, but the idea of a morality based in pure rational formalism is not adequate—cultivation of the moral institution requires the cultivation of moral emotion. Tarde argues that we expand our sense of moral obligation on the basis of imitation, extending our care to those who are not blood relations by imagining them as blood relations and so making a leap from familial concern into

[49] Miki 1966, 98.
[50] Miki 1966, 102–103.
[51] Miki 1966, 103.
[52] Miki 1966, 107.
[53] Miki 1966, 109.
[54] Miki 1966, 112.
[55] Miki 1966, 114.
[56] Miki 1966, 117.
[57] Miki 1966, 118.

fraternal concern[58] and thus from the biological to the social.[59] Imitation is generative and creative here, not simply repetitive; just so, we should understand morality itself not as habitual but as creative.[60] As something creative, morality is, like other created things, historical; knowing that it is a historical form, we know that imagination lies at its ground.[61]

The embodied subject imagining morality, however, is not the individual agent. If habit belongs to the creative individual, custom belongs to the creative society; the working of creative society creates the created society called institutional society into which the individual is born, just as the self-creating activity of nature (*natura naturans*) creates created nature (*natura naturata*).[62] This creative society is an embodied subject, too. In fact, "creative society is the true transcendental embodied subject."[63] Thus, it is creative society that is the historical subject, and its body the institution—history unfolds as the self-creating activity of society moving from one historical form to the next. As embodied subject, creative society has the capacity to create itself anew through the power of imagination. For Miki, this means more specifically that the encounter between the existing *nomos* or *Gemeinschaft*—the institutional society we refer to as Japan—and the abstract ideal of the *Gesellschaft* can be a generative one in which a *Gemeinschaft* rooted in *pathos* is not simply overcome by a *Gesellschaft* rooted in *logos* but instead sublates that *Gesellschaft* in order to unfold a new form of *Gemeinschaft*, which Miki thinks of in relation to the notions of both *minzoku*, or ethnos, and *Genossenschaft*, or egalitarian fellowship (in which the one and the many are identical, while each yet preserves its own particularity).[64]

Miki calls the *poiesis* occurring in this transformation of forms "technology."[65] Miki defines the technological form in terms of that which is born out of the agent's working out an accommodation to its environment.[66] The bird is a technological form insofar as it is an embodied subject accommodated to its environment—air—through flight.[67] The human being, too, is a technological form. The example of the bird should give us the sense that, for the human being, too, technology both locates the agent in accommodation to the environment and enables the agent to operate freely and expressively within her environment. As Erich Pauer observes, Miki is writing in the context of a burgeoning technocracy[68] in which both objects and human bodies might be understood as raw

---

[58] Miki 1966, 106ff. The reference here is to Gabriel de Tarde, *Les lois de l'imitation, étude sociologique* (Paris: Félix Alcan, 1907).

[59] Miki 1966, 112.

[60] Miki 1966, 119.

[61] Miki 1966, 136.

[62] Miki 1966, 184.

[63] Miki 1966, 184.

[64] Miki 1966, 10; Miki 1967b, 261–263; Sakai 2009, 191–192.

[65] Miki 1966, 250.

[66] Miki 1966, 5; Miki 1967b, 265–266.

[67] Miki 1967b, 265.

[68] Pauer 1999.

material. Miki's presentation of *Logic of Imagination* as an effort to understand history and nature as a unity in which "human technology continues the work of nature"[69] should be read in this light as connected to an effort to wrest technology away from the technocrats.

Setting up a comparison that seems deliberately provocative, Miki positions technology as magic's counterpart. In myth, magic represents the power of self-creation through which formless *pathos* acquires form:

> Through the power of magic, all things come to acquire form (*keisei* 形成) and reality, but *pathos* alone is not magic—in order for *pathos* to become magic, *logos* or idea must be added. Magic is like technology.[70]

Myth is that element of the institution in which what is mystical (*shinpiteki* 神秘的) dominates, and so magic is imagined as mystical power. Technology is scientific rather than mystical—it has an essential connection to science.[71] And yet, Miki insists, just as magic is not pure *pathos*, technology is not pure *logos*: science cognizes, but technology makes. Science is intellect separated from nature; technology is intellect returning to nature. It thus represents the power of self-creation through which formless *logos* acquires form:

> Although the natural law is always at work within nature, nature does not give birth to the electric light or the electric car. In order for these things to be made, the law of electricity must take on form; in order for them to exist, human desire must be introduced. These technological forms are manufactured as a synthesis of objective law and subjective human will. Everything historical is like this.[72]

If magic is bound up with *eros*,[73] technology, too, is bound up with desire, giving it an embodied, affective dimension such that the technological form is at once subjective and objective.[74] We can see desire concretized in the mechanical working of technology. And just as *eros* represents a generative drive, technology, too, is generative: "Technology is creative, and through it the world takes on new form. The transcendental character of imagination is recognizable in the materiality of the free products of imagination."[75]

Again, there is both continuity and rupture here. Technology responds to a historical environment or accommodates a historical environment. But the essence of technology is invention.[76] The moment of technological invention is a moment of historical

---

[69] Miki 1966, 10. The phrase quoted here is as it appears in Gereon Kopf's translation, in Miki 2011, 707.
[70] Miki 1966b, 72.
[71] Miki 1966b, 221.
[72] Miki 1967b, 72.
[73] Miki 1966, 79.
[74] Miki 1966, 266.
[75] Miki 1966, 229.
[76] Miki 1966, 238.

transformation or metamorphosis: "the crucial point at which a manifold of mediations crystallize into a single form that leaps to life."[77] This means we can read history's reason in terms of a series of technological inventions—here understood humanistically as new forms of historical life, or new institutions. In each new form, objective law and subjective desire are mingled, such that history's reason must be sought in both *logos* and *pathos*. If myth sketches a new world and places it on top of or ahead of the natural world, technology makes a new world through the crafting of new institutions. In this process of world-making, the embodied subject at once makes the world and comes into existence as world-maker. Because human life is understood precisely as *poietic* life,[78] in principle, this technological world-making must inevitably be a process through which the world becomes more and more a human world, or more and more a *Genossenschaft*: not simply a co-operative (*kyōdōtai* 共同体) but a voluntary co-operative within which human beings can realize their species-character.[79]

A Problem and a Possibility

History does not bear this optimistic vision of co-operativism out. Instead, Japan pursued imperialist projects under the banner of co-operativism in the form of the Great East Asia Co-Prosperity Sphere and mobilized its subjects for total war.[80] Certain ideological justifications for expansion and mobilization were developed by the Shōwa Research Association (Shōwa kenkyūkai 昭和研究会)[81]; Miki's work as a member of the association has thus been the subject of some significant criticism. Although he has sometimes been accused of drifting into fascism during this period, the logic of imagination includes some built-in resistance to a fascist organic romanticism. As Graham Parkes points out, Miki maintains that the East Asian community is something manufactured rather than grown;[82] as a collective representation or artificial world, it cannot be construed as a naturally given organic unity. Parkes also maintains that the nationalist impulse to give Japan a "leading role" in the Co-Prosperity Sphere was, in the case of Kyoto School thinkers, "balanced by a thoroughgoing internationalism."[83]

---

[77] Miki 1966, 9. The phrase quoted here is as it appears in Gereon Kopf's translation, in Miki 2011, 707.

[78] As Marx writes in the *Economic and Philosophical Manuscripts of 1844*: "productive life is the life of the species. It is life-engendering life. The whole character of a species, its species-character, is contained in the character of its life activity; and free, conscious activity is man's species-character"; see Marx 1986, 41.

[79] Sakai 2009, 191–92.

[80] Sakai 2009, 192. Sakai identifies this as *Gleichschaltung*, total mobilization or total coordination. Klaus Tenfelde points out the essential conflict between the voluntary association of *Genossenschaft* and the mobilization of *Gleichschaltung*; see Tenfelde 2000, 103.

[81] Duus 1996, 60.

[82] Parkes 2011, 256.

[83] Parkes 2011, 248.

However, Iwasaki Minoru argues that it is precisely here that Miki's logic of imagination reveals a weakness. Miki identifies creative society as a transcendent embodied subject or "metasubject"; this metasubject "takes on a regional identity" in the form of an East Asian bloc led by Japan.[84] Throughout *Logic of Imagination*, Miki insists on participation and imitation as generative principles; rather than simply reproducing the existing order, they propel transformations in that order and so negate institutional society. This suggests that there must be heterogeneity within the collective society because it is only by differing from itself that the creative society creates. If we interpret the Great East Asia Co-Prosperity Sphere as a concrete enacting of the logic of imagination, however, we find a rhetoric of internal heterogeneity attached to actual policies enforcing regional homogeneity—"the bogus 'multi-culturalism' of 'East Asian Community.'"[85] Within this regime, the individual embodied agent is mobilized: subjected to the rhythms[86] of a collective agency. Here even if for the transcendent metasubject, the technological working taking place is creative and self-expressive, for the individual person, it cannot but appear in the form of the rule of the machine: "This is a form of existence which, while being 'technological' and historical, and encompassing all human action, also presences precisely through the denial of that action."[87] The individual person is thus made a puppet of history in a way more brutal than anything Hegel proposes. This dimension of the Great East Asia Co-Prosperity Sphere is not simply a product of the state failing to balance nationalism with internationalism; it is born out of Miki's own insistence on a transcendent metasubject and his ambivalence about how the individual subject's *poietic* activity relates to the metasubject's autopoiesis.

Are there resources available within Miki's *Logic of Imagination* to counteract this kind of mobilization? I have room to suggest one possibility.

One of the signal developments in contemporary critical theory has been the turn to affect—what Lauren Berlant defines as "the body's active presence to the intensities of the present [that] embeds the subject in an historical field." [88] Thinking about history in terms of affect requires a fresh understanding of "being in history as a densely corporeal, experientially felt thing"[89]; in contemporary Marxian thought, this crystallizes as an interest in "everyday life,"[90] pioneered in the work of Henri Lefebvre. Certain elements of Lefebvre's analysis would clearly be congenial to Miki. Everyday life, Lefebvre tells us, is

---

[84] Iwasaki 1998, 177.

[85] Iwasaki 1998, 176; see also Kim 2007. Takashi Fujitani offers a vivid example of the logic of mobilization, describing young Korean soldiers "lining up to have their bodies inspected as 'human bullets for victory' "; see Fujitani 2011, 302.

[86] I take this way of thinking about mobilization from Kurt Meyer's discussion of Miki's contemporary, French Marxist Henri Lefebvre; see Meyer 2008, 152; Lefebvre 2004, 68–69.

[87] Iwasaki 1998, 177.

[88] Berlant 2008, 846. Berlant describes two trajectories converging in the affective turn, one traceable back to Bergson and his study of intuition, the other "a strand within Marxist cultural theory, including everyday life theory." Miki may be understood as drawing on both of these streams of thought in *Logic of Imagination*.

[89] Berlant 2008, 849.

[90] Berlant 2008, 846.

established as a rhythm or a repetition in time and space.[91] This repetition is, however, not merely repetitive; it is creative—within the everyday "there is always something new and unforeseen that introduces itself into the repetitive: difference."[92] And this rhythm is not merely mechanical—"rhythm appears as regulated time, governed by rational laws, but in contact with what is least rational in human being: the lived, the carnal, the body."[93] Everyday life takes place in those moments when the repetitive rhythms of social time are "shot through and traversed by great cosmic and vital rhythms" still pulsing in the body; history unfolds as a series of contests between these two rhythms, with itself constituting a great rhythm.[94] But capital despises the body and the "time of living"[95]; having already taken hold of the work day, it moves to take hold of the everyday: it will kill nature, kill creative capacity, kill social richness.[96] The task Lefebvre assigns the "rhythmanalyst" is to guard against the "death-dealing character of capital"[97] and advance reason by "recovering the sensible"[98]: "Without claiming to *change life*, but by fully reinstating the sensible in consciousnesses and in *thought*, he would accomplish a tiny part of the *revolutionary* transformation of this world and this society in decline."[99]

One benefit of reading Miki in conversation with Lefebvre is that it illuminates the ways in which Miki's late work, often identified as representing a shift away from Marxism back toward Nishida philosophy, resonates with developments in postwar European Marxist theory. For Miki, as for Lefebvre, there is no history without irrationality. Because Miki's logic of history is a logic of imagination, and because imagination requires both *logos* and *pathos*, it must be the case that history unfolds only by means of contact between that which is rational and that which is sensible. This makes it impossible for the historian to discern the movement of history without attending to the sensible and impossible for the historical subject to act creatively without drawing on the sensible. This puts the body at the center of history: it is the body (*shintai* 身体) that we refer to when we talk about *pathos*[100] and the social body (*shakaiteki shintai*) "individualized (*kobetsuka* 個別化) by means of bodiliness (*shintaisei* 身体性)" that is the subject of history.[101] Where the body is simply harnessed to the logic of the machine, we no longer have technology, as Miki defines it; where an abstract, universal reason simply overrides passion and feeling, history gives way to sheer repetition. Early in his career as a Marxist, Miki rallied a defense of religion's role in the proletarian movement by arguing that religion has, at its core, a sensible, phenomenal disposition (*kanseiteki*

---

[91] Lefebvre 2004, 6–7.
[92] Lefebvre 2004, 6.
[93] Lefebvre 2004, 9.
[94] Lefebvre 2004, 55.
[95] Lefebvre 2004, 52.
[96] Lefebvre 2004, 53.
[97] Lefebvre 2004, 53.
[98] Lefebvre 2004, 25.
[99] Lefebvre 2004, 26.
[100] Miki 1966, 15.
[101] Miki 1966, 17.

busshōteki seishitsu 感性的、物象的性質)—"the point of departure for every religion is the desire for happiness."[102] We might say the same in defense of Miki: by emphasizing the sensing, feeling, desiring body, he preserves a place in his logic of imagination for what Lefebvre calls "the living."

At the same time, we could employ Miki's own emphasis on the living body as a way of refiguring the relation between the creative individual and creative society. Miki is ambivalent about this relation, writing, on the one hand, that the individual person is able to be inventive "by becoming one with creative society" and, on the other hand, that the individual person makes society "as something independent" from society[103]— this is the basis for his paradoxical assertion that mobilization itself should recognize the autonomy of the individual intellectual.[104] There is an opening here, I think, to shift away from an understanding of history in terms of the movement of creative society, toward an understanding of history in terms of the flight and recapture of the individual embodied subject. Miki's logic requires him to grant creative society a social body, but he is vague about what this body might be; given his emphasis on *pathos*, however, the social body cannot be understood as merely metaphorical. If we fix our attention on the individual body as the site of the social body, or the site in which rising passions signaling historical change actually register, we can foreground a concern for the individual person in our theory of history. Here, those moments when the transcendent social body thoroughly mobilizes individual bodies toward its own ends— when, as Lefebvre puts it, one experiences the "dispossession of one's own body" in terms of an automatism felt as spontaneity[105]—more plainly register not as the working of creative society but as the hardening of the social apparatus through repetition. In such moments of dispossession, imagination itself is endangered. If we continued to push in this direction, we would be able to use Miki's logic of imagination as a way of critically interrogating the mobilization of individual bodies by the state simply by reiterating his own interest in *pathos*.

Bibliography and Suggested Readings

Berlant, Lauren. (2008) "Intuitionists: History and the Affective Event," *American Literary History* 20.4: 845–860.

Curley, Melissa Anne-Marie. (2017) *Pure Land, Real World: Modern Buddhists, Japanese Leftists, and the Utopian Imagination*. Honolulu: University of Hawai'i Press.

Duus, Peter. (1996) "Imperialism Without Colonies: The Vision of a Greater East Asia Co-Prosperity Sphere," *Diplomacy and Statecraft* 7.1: 54–72.

Fujita Masakatsu. (2011) "*Logos* and *Pathos*: Miki Kiyoshi's Logic of the Imagination," translated by Bret W. Davis with Moritsu Ryū and Takehana Yōsuke. In *Japanese and Continental*

---

[102] Miki 1967*a*, 4.
[103] Miki 1966, 184.
[104] Iwasaki 1988, 177.
[105] Lefebvre 2004, 192.

Philosophy: Conversations with the Kyoto School, edited by Bret W. Davis, Brian Schroeder, and Jason M. Wirth. Bloomington: Indiana University Press.

Fujitani Takashi. (2011) *Race for Empire: Koreans As Japanese and Japanese as Americans During World War II*. Berkeley: University of California Press.

Harrington, Lewis. (2009) "Miki Kiyoshi and the Shōwa Kenkyūkai: The Failure of World History," *positions: east asian cultures critique* 17.1: 43–72.

Iwasaki Minoru. (1998) "Desire for a Poietic Metasubject: Miki Kiyoshi's Technology Theory." In *Total War and 'Modernization'*, edited by Yasushi Yamanouchi, J. Victor Koschmann, and Ryūichi Narita. Ithaca, NY: East Asia Program, Cornell University.

Kim, John Namjun. (2007) "The Temporality of Empire: The Imperial Cosmopolitanism of Miki Kiyoshi and Tanabe Hajime." In *Pan-Asianism in Modern Japanese History: Colonialism, Regionalism, and Borders*, edited by Sven Saaler and J. Victor Koschmann. London: Routledge.

Lefebvre, Henri. (2004) *Rhythmanalysis: Space, Time, and Everyday Life*, translated by Stuart Eldon and Gerald Moore. London: Continuum.

Marx, Karl. (1986) *Karl Marx: A Reader*, edited by Jon Elster. Cambridge: Cambridge University Press.

Marx, Karl and Friedrich Engels. (2001) *The German Ideology*, edited and with an introduction by C. J. Arthur. London: Electric Book Co.

Meyer, Kurt. (2008) "Rhythms, Streets, Cities." In *Space, Difference, Everyday Life: Reading Henri Lefebvre*, edited by Kanishka Goonewardena, Stefan Kipfer, Richard Milgrom, and Christian Schmid. New York: Routledge.

Miki Kiyoshi. (1966) *Kōsōryoku no ronri* [Logic of Imagination]. *Miki Kiyoshi zenshū* [Complete Works of Miki Kiyoshi]. Vol. 8. Tokyo: Iwanami Shoten.

Miki Kiyoshi. (1967a) "Donnani shūkyō wo hihan suru ka" [How Shall We Critique Religion]. *Miki Kiyoshi zenshū* [Complete Works of Miki Kiyoshi]. Vol. 13. Tokyo: Iwanami Shoten, 3–11.

Miki Kiyoshi. (1967b) "Rekishi no risei" [History's Reason]. *Miki Kiyoshi zenshū* [Complete Works of Miki Kiyoshi]. Vol. 14. Tokyo: Iwanami Shoten, 249–269.

Miki Kiyoshi. (1998a) "An Analysis of Man," translated by Valdo H. Viglielmo. In *Sourcebook for Modern Japanese Philosophy: Selected Documents*, edited by David A. Dilworth and Valdo H. Viglielmo with Agustín Jacinto Zavala. Westport, CT: Greenwood Press.

Miki Kiyoshi. (1998) "On Tradition," translated by Agustín Jacinto Zavala. In *Sourcebook for Modern Japanese Philosophy: Selected Documents*, edited by David A. Dilworth and Valdo H. Viglielmo with Agustín Jacinto Zavala. Westport, CT: Greenwood Press.

Miki Kiyoshi. (2011) "The Study of the Human" and "Towards a Logic of Imagination," translated by Gereon Kopf. In *Japanese Philosophy: A Sourcebook*, edited by James W. Heisig, Thomas P. Kasulis, and John C. Maraldo. Honolulu: University of Hawai'i Press.

Mousalimas, S. A. (1990) "The Concept of Participation in Lévy-Bruhl's 'Primitive Mentality.'" *Journal of the Anthropological Society of Oxford* 21.1: 33–46.

Nagatomo, Shigenori. (1995) *A Philosophical Foundation for Miki Kiyoshi's Humanism*. Lewiston, NY: Edwin Mellen Press.

Nakajima Takahiro. (2011) "'Asia' as a 'Relational' Concept from the Perspective of Japanese Marxist Philosophers: Hiromatsu Wataru, Miki Kiyoshi, and Tosaka Jun." In his *Practicing Philosophy Between Japan and China*. Tokyo: UTCP.

Nishida Kitarō. (2012) *Ontology of Production: Three Essays*, translated and with an introduction by William Haver. Durham, NC: Duke University Press.

Parkes, Graham. (2011) "Heidegger and Japanese Fascism: An Unsubstantiated Connection." In *Japanese and Continental Philosophy: Conversations with the Kyoto School*, edited by Bret W. Davis, Brian Schroeder, and Jason M. Wirth. Bloomington: Indiana University Press.

Pauer, Erich. (1999) "Japan's Technical Mobilization in the Second World War." In *Japan's War Economy*, edited by Erich Pauer. London: Routledge.

Sakai Naoki. (2009) "Imperial Nationalism and the Comparative Perspective," *positions: east asia cultures critique* 17.1: 159–205.

Sakuta Keiichi. (1978) "The Controversy over Community and Autonomy." In *Authority and the Individual in Japan: Citizen Protest in Historical Perspective*, edited by J. Victor Koschmann. Tokyo: University of Tokyo Press.

Sève, Lucien. (1974) *Marxisme et theorie de la personnalité*. Paris: Editions Sociales.

Sorel, Georges. (1999) *Reflections on Violence*, edited and translated by Jeremy Jennings. Cambridge: Cambridge University Press.

Townsend, Susan C. (2007) *Miki Kiyoshi, 1897–1945: Japan's Itinerant Philosopher*. Leiden: Brill.

Yusa, Michiko. (2002) *Zen and Philosophy: An Intellectual Biography of Nishida Kitarō*. Honolulu: University of Hawai'i Press.

CHAPTER 21

....

NISHITANI KEIJI: PRACTICING PHILOSOPHY AS A MATTER OF LIFE AND DEATH

....

GRAHAM PARKES

生死大事

"Life and death—the great matter."[1]

IN an essay called "My Philosophical Starting Point," the Kyoto School thinker Nishitani Keiji (1900–90) writes of "one fundamental concern that was constantly at work" in his early interest in figures like Nietzsche and Dostoevsky, on the one hand, and Zen thinkers such as Hakuin and Takuan on the other: "a doubt concerning the very existence of the self, something like the Buddhist 'Great Doubt' (*daigi* 大疑)." In another brief memoir, "The Time of My Youth," Nishitani writes of the utter hopelessness of that period of his life, compounded by the death of his father when he was fourteen. He himself succumbed shortly thereafter to an illness similar to the tuberculosis that had killed his father, in the course of which he felt "the specter of death taking hold." These grim experiences, pervaded by a mood of "nihilism," prompted him to take up the study of philosophy:

> My life as a young man can be described in a single phrase: it was a period absolutely without hope .... My life at the time lay entirely in the grips of nihility and despair .... My decision, then, to study philosophy was in fact—melodramatic as it might sound—a matter of life and death.[2]

---

[1] Chinese Buddhist maxim. My thanks to James Heisig for helpful comments on an earlier draft of this chapter.

[2] Nishitani, cited in Heisig 2001, 191.

This basis in profound existential concern distinguishes Nishitani's thought from the philosophies of the senior Kyoto School thinkers, Nishida and Tanabe, which tend to be more speculative and abstract. It was reinforced by Nishitani's engagement with Zen Buddhist practice (zazen meditation) for more than two decades, a physical practice that grounded his thinking in lived experience.[3] He further distinguishes himself from Nishida and Tanabe, who drew from ideas in Western philosophy mainly to better articulate their own thought, by a deeper engagement with European thinkers that aimed to build bridges between Western and Asian philosophies: "to lay the foundations of thought for a world in the making, for a world united beyond differences of East and West."[4] But Nishitani's existential thinking also poses a radical challenge to mainstream Western philosophy: by comparison with a thinking derived from the Buddhist tradition, most Western thought is superficial, dealing with surface phenomena of consciousness and thereby failing to attain a deep understanding of or engagement with the people and things with which we interact.

To convey the power of this challenge and do justice to Nishitani's concern to philosophize "as a matter of life and death," an introduction to his thinking does well to focus on his understanding of human existence as consisting in three levels, or "fields" (*ba* 場), as explicated in his masterpiece from 1961, *Religion and Nothingness* (original Japanese title: *Shūkyō to wa nanika* 宗教とは何か [What Is Religion?]). The three levels are: the field of consciousness (which embraces what he calls "the field of sensation" and "the field of reason"), below that the field of nihility (*kyomu* 虚無), and underlying that the field of emptiness (Skt. *śūnyatā*; Jp. *kū* 空).[5] These fields are always co-present, and each deeper field is more extensive and encompassing than the one above it. On the field of consciousness (which is where most of us live most of our waking lives) we exist, so to say, in a "life" perspective; the field of nihility represents by contrast a "death" perspective; and the field of emptiness offers a death perspective on life, or a "death-life" perspective. Insofar as existing on the field of emptiness offers us, on the Buddhist view, the most enlightened life, this death-life perspective enables us to understand and live life to the fullest.

The challenge to Western philosophy comes from Nishitani's suggestion that it has mostly been conducted on and has often taken as its topic the field of consciousness, where (in the Kantian terms that Nishitani uses) we have no access to things themselves but only to representations of them to ourselves as subjects of consciousness. By contrast, on the field of emptiness, we can break through how things appear to human subjects and encounter them as they are in themselves, "on their home ground," as Nishitani puts it. The claim that Western philosophy has generally failed to explore two significant fields of human existence is well worth pondering because this failure impoverishes our

---

[3] Heisig 2001, 184. For a discussion of Nishitani's views on "psychosomatic practice," see Davis 2013; and for the centrality of bodily practice to classical Chinese and Japanese philosophy more generally, see Parkes 2012.

[4] Nishitani, writing in the mid-1960s, cited by Jan van Bragt in Nishitani 1982, xxviii.

[5] Nishitani 1982, 108-112.

experience as well as our philosophy: "Ontology needs to pass through nihility and shift to an entirely new field, different from what it has known hitherto."[6]

Because Nishitani doesn't characterize the field of nihility in much detail, and his commentators tend to neglect it in favor of emptiness, the discussion to follow will devote relatively more time to the experience of nihility. But because there are some significant prefigurations of Nishitani's ideas about death and life in earlier thinkers who influenced him, it may help to begin with those.

PRECURSORS IN THE FIELD

Chinese Daoist philosophy understands life and death as interdependent and complementary phenomena, alternating phases in the constant transformations between *yang* and *yin*. The *Daodejing* remarks that ordinary people overlook this, ignoring death because of their preoccupation with life and its largess:

> The people treat death lightly:
> It is because the people set too much store by life
> That they treat death lightly.[7]

The interdependence of life and death is also a prominent theme in the Inner Chapters of the *Zhuangzi*. The Daoist sage is one who can "affirm the rightness" of both life and death, because after all:

> How do I know that delighting in life is not a delusion? How do I know that in hating death I am not like an orphan who left home in youth and no longer knows the way back? ... How do I know that the dead don't regret the way they used to cling to life?[8]

For Zhuangzi, we need to be "released from the fetters" of conventional views of life as good and death as bad so that we can "see life and death as a single string, acceptable and unacceptable as a single thread." After all, "Life and death are fated, and come with the regularity of day and night"; and since the creative process of the cosmos "labors me with life, eases me with old age, and rests me with death," this means that "it is precisely because I consider my life good that I consider my death good."[9]

---

[6] Nishitani, cited in Heisig 2001, 221.

[7] Laozi, *Daodejing*, chapter 75. See also Hans-Georg Moeller, *The Philosophy of the Daodejing* (New York: Columbia University Press, 2006), chapter 9, "Death and the Death Penalty."

[8] *Zhuangzi: The Essential Writings*, trans. Brook Ziporyn (Indianapolis: Hackett Publishing, 2009), chapter 2, 19.

[9] Chapters 5 and 6 of *Zhuangzi*, 35, 43. See also Roger T. Ames, "Death as Transformation in Classical Daoism," in Jeff Malpas and Robert Solomon, eds., *Death and Philosophy* (London: Routledge, 1998), and Hans-Georg Moeller, *Daoism Explained: From the Dream of the Butterfly to the Fishnet Allegory* (Chicago: Open Court, 2004), chapter 2, sec. 3.

The influence of Zhuangzi is palpably evident, across some fifteen hundred years, in the philosophy of the Sōtō Zen master Dōgen (1200–53), who was in turn a powerful influence on Nishitani and is a major presence in *Religion and Nothingness*. Central to Buddhist philosophy is the notion of impermanence (Skt. *anitya*; Jp. *mujō* 無常): a refrain that echoes throughout the tradition is "All dharmas (phenomena) are impermanent." All existence—human life naturally included—is understood as a beginningless and endless cycle of arising and perishing, generation and extinction, being born and dying away. But this impermanence doesn't just mean that things don't last, that everything that comes into being returns to nothing, but also that everything does so in every instant. This "momentariness," by virtue of which everything perishes as soon as it arises, is central to the philosophy of Dōgen, who refers to it as "the law of birth and death in each moment":

> Through causes and conditions, the human body . . . is born and perishes moment by moment without ceasing . . . but because of ignorance we don't notice it . . . . What a pity that although we are born and perish at each moment, we don't notice it![10]

For Dōgen, one Buddhist practice that helps us notice this condition is sitting meditation—which he calls "zazen-only" (*shikantaza*)—a practice that Nishitani engaged in for decades. Dōgen instructs his students to sit upright, vertically aligned, with "the ears in line with the shoulders, and the nose in line with the navel":

> Keep the eyes open and breathe gently through the nose. Having adjusted your body in this manner, take a breath and exhale fully, then sway your body to left and right . . . .
>
> Having received a human life, do not waste the passing moments . . . . Human life is like a flash of lightning, transient and illusory, gone in a moment.[11]

The challenge is to maintain complete relaxation of the body and mind together with fully alert attention: without trying to do anything (especially not attain enlightenment), nevertheless to practice—as Dōgen often says—"as if your head were ablaze." If your hair catches fire you don't pause to speculate on the cause: rather you immediately set about putting it out.

In sitting zazen, one comes to experience the parallels between the rising and falling of the breath, the arising and subsiding of thoughts, and the continual birth and death of human existence along with the arising and perishing of all things. The moments between, the still turning points between exhalation and inhalation, highlight the utter contingency of the breath in its rise and fall, until its inevitable final fall: the lack of necessary connection between exhalation and the next breath, which may always be the last.

---

[10] "Virtue of Home Leaving," in Dōgen 2010, 803.
[11] "Recommending Zazen to All People," in Dōgen 2010, 908–909.

Dōgen has little use for the term "nirvāna," which many regard as the goal of the Buddhist life, since for later, Mahāyāna schools of Buddhism nirvāna is not different from "samsāra" (often referred to in Chinese and Japanese Buddhism as "birth-and-death"):

> Just understand that birth-and-death is itself nirvāna. There is nothing such as birth and death to be avoided; there is nothing such as nirvāna to be sought. Only when you realise this are you free from birth and death.[12]

It's a matter neither of avoiding or detaching oneself from birth and death, nor of clinging to or desiring it—but of practicing what the Buddhists call "nonattachment."

We find a similar idea, framed in terms of a process of departure and return, in the writings of another major influence on Nishitani, the Rinzai Zen master Hakuin Ekaku (1686–1769). Hakuin constantly urged his listeners and readers to "see into their own true nature" (kenshō 見性) by seeing through the illusory nature of the ego-self. This entails being prepared at every moment "to let go your hold when hanging from a sheer precipice, to die and return again to life." In this context, Hakuin recommends a kōan, in the spirit of traditional Buddhist meditations on death:

> If you should have the desire to study Zen under a teacher and see into your own nature, you should first investigate the word shi [死, death] . . . by investigating the koan: "After you are dead and cremated, where has the main character gone?" Then . . . you will obtain the decisive and ultimate great joy.[13]

THE FIELD OF CONSCIOUSNESS

Let us consider our everyday experience on what Nishitani calls "the field of consciousness," which he describes at the beginning of Religion and Nothingness. We tend to regard this mode of experience as one in which we find ourselves, as subjects of consciousness, in a world of objects to which we ordinarily relate (if we think about it) "by means of concepts and representations." On the field of consciousness, we "see things from the standpoint of the self." The talk of "concepts and representations" is a reference to Kant, although Nishitani invokes Plato rather than Kant at this point: when we "sit like spectators in the cave of the self," we are confined to "watching the shadows passing to and fro across its walls, and calling those shadows 'reality.'" Nishitani concludes that "on the field of consciousness, it is not possible really to get in touch with things as they are, that is, to face them in their own mode of being and on their own home-ground."[14]

---

[12] "Birth-Death," in Dōgen 2010, 884.
[13] Hakuin 1971, 135, 219.
[14] Nishitani 1982, 9.

But for Nishitani, it's not only "things as they are" that we can't get in touch with; it's also our own selves:

> We also think of our own selves, and of our "inner" thoughts, feelings, and desires as real. But here, too, it is doubtful whether . . . our feelings and desires and so forth are in the proper sense really present to us as they are . . . . Precisely because we face things on a field separated from things, and to the extent that we do so, we are forever separated from ourselves.[15]

Most of us, it seems, spend most of our time on the field of consciousness and can get all the way to the grave without ever becoming aware of the fields Nishitani says exist beneath it. If we're happy enough with this, why should it matter—unless we happen to be philosophers, who perhaps should follow the Socratic injunction to "know ourselves"—that we aren't able to get in touch with ourselves or "things as they are"? Well, it may not matter at all. But what if, on the verge of the grave, we discover that we've missed something, that we haven't really lived? Then, of course, it will be too late.

Nishitani believes we can avoid such a dismal outcome by "breaking through the field of consciousness" and "overstepping the field of beings," but it remains unclear in *Religion and Nothingness* just how this is to be accomplished.[16] We get a hint of the way, however, if we go back to an earlier text.

Nishitani's first extended philosophical engagement with death and nihilism took place in a series of lectures he gave in Kyoto in 1949, which have been translated into English under the title *The Self-Overcoming of Nihilism*.[17] Just as there is a resistance, especially in modern times, to acknowledging the reality of death, let alone confronting one's own mortality, so there is a reluctance to admit that life lacks inherent meaning. Nishitani engages this issue through discussions of Schopenhauer and Kierkegaard. Paraphrasing Schopenhauer's "Doctrine of the Vanity of Existence," he writes:

> For all our pursuit of happiness, at the moment when our life comes to its end in death, it is all one and the same (*einerlei*) whether our life has been happy or unhappy. This is how Schopenhauer sees the nullity of existence grounded in the will to life.[18]

But human beings have always found ways to get around this preposterous situation:

> Beginning from the basic necessities of clothing and food, life is filled with urgent matters to attend to, and from these some kind of meaning is given to life. Daily work and amusement are its inherent meaning; they divert the boredom that is its essence as "pastimes" that help one forget life's abyssal nihility.[19]

[15] Nishitani 1982, 9–10.
[16] Nishitani 1982, 13, 17.
[17] Nishitani 1990.
[18] Nishitani 1990, 15.
[19] Nishitani 1990, 17.

Daily work—overwork especially—seems to work for many people, but if the boredom should reassert itself, we are faced once again with "the essentially void nature of our existence and the existence of all things, their insubstantiality and nullity."[20] A common response is then

> to seek some transcendent meaning through religion or metaphysics in order to escape life's *ennui* and despair. Having lost its inherent meaning, life is thereby restructured from a transcendent ground and given a purpose. But finally, in time of crisis when even religion, metaphysics, and morality are perceived as null, life becomes *fundamentally* void and boring.[21]

In this context, Nishitani cites Kierkegaard's magnificent characterization of existential boredom as "demonic pantheism":

> Pantheism ordinarily implies the quality of fullness; with boredom it is the reverse: it is built upon emptiness, but for this very reason it is a pantheistic qualification. Boredom rests upon the nothing that interlaces existence; its dizziness is infinite, like that which comes from looking down into a bottomless abyss.[22]

For Schopenhauer, the solution is simply—as Nishitani, following Nietzsche, reads him—to renounce the will to live and thereby gain emancipation; whereas for Kierkegaard it is a matter of "a radical engagement with the nihility within nihilistic existence, and a thoroughly existential confrontation with original sin and the finitude and death rooted in it."[23] But for Nishitani such solutions are themselves nihilistic, and, in any case, after "the death of God" in nineteenth-century Europe, the meaninglessness of mortal life grew to become the meaninglessness of all existence: "With this an abyssal nihility opened up at the ground of history and self-being, and everything turned into a question mark."[24]

Nishitani follows Nietzsche in thinking that we can "live and experience nihilism" by way of "psychological reflection" that "gets behind" traditional values to reveal their psychological origin, which in turn reveals their contingency and lack of ultimate meaning.[25] Such reflection shows us that the metaphysical comforts of a monotheistic God and another, truer world above or beyond this one are just that: comforting fictions to veil the inherent meaninglessness of a world in which all our achievements and projects come to naught with our death.

In a lecture on Heidegger (with whom he had studied for two years in the late 1930s), Nishitani discusses Heidegger's idea of nothingness (*das Nichts*) and his "existential

[20] Nishitani 1990, 14–15.
[21] Nishitani 1990, 18.
[22] Nishitani 1990, 18, citing Kierkegaard, *Either/Or*, I: 291.
[23] Nishitani 1990, 21.
[24] Nishitani 1990, 6.
[25] Nishitani 1990, 32.

conception" of death, both in the light of his own idea of nihility. He takes Heidegger's idea that human beings are "held out into" or "suspended over" nothingness to mean that "human being is exposed to nihility in its very foundation," and he connects this with the notion that "death is already included within life; it is a way of being that human being takes upon itself as soon as it exists."[26]

Nishitani goes on to remark the tension in Heidegger's "being-toward-death" between our being "not yet" at the end of our existence, and, owing to the projective structure of *Dasein*, our also being "always already" at our end—since in projecting possibilities of existence we are "running ahead" and so "come up against death." The experience of *Angst* shows that our fundamental condition is one of being strangely not-at-home (*unheimlich*) in the world, insofar as "nihility reveals itself as the ground of beings-as-a-whole." This revelation comes in "moods" such as *Angst* and boredom, which for Heidegger are modes of *Befindlichkeit*, of finding ourselves disposed in the world in such a way that "the ground of it all is discovered to be nihility."[27] The point is that we *find* ourselves in this or that kind of mood: it's not something that can be consciously willed. This connects with Nishitani's interest in Nietzsche's idea of the "self-overcoming of nihilism": one doesn't overcome nihilism through a summoning of willpower on the part of the heroic ego, but rather by "living nihilism through to the end in oneself."[28] As Nishitani said of his own case: "The fundamental problem of my life ... has always been ... the overcoming of nihilism through nihilism."[29]

Nevertheless, insofar as one is able to respond to the mood of *Angst* by "running ahead" and confronting one's death while still alive, this opens up "the meaning of *being* truly *there* (*Dasein*)." The authentic confrontation with death thus makes possible full existential realization and ontological revelation.[30]

The field of consciousness can also be broken through by an external event, by some kind of stroke of fate—again something that befalls us rather than something we will. As Nishitani writes in *Religion and Nothingness*:

> Take, for example, someone for whom life has become meaningless as a result of the loss of a loved one, or the failure of an undertaking on which he had staked his all. All those things that had once been of use to him become good for nothing. This same process takes place when one comes face to face with death.[31]

In such a condition, we drop through the field of consciousness and find ourselves in a very different world.

---

26 Nishitani 1990, 164–165.
27 Nishitani 1990, 166–167, at 162.
28 Nishitani 1990, 8, 30.
29 Cited in Heisig 2001, 215.
30 Nishitani 1990, 166–167.
31 Nishitani 1982, 3.

THE FIELD OF NIHILITY

At the beginning of *Religion and Nothingness*, Nishitani formulates the lessons of *The Self-Overcoming of Nihilism* with considerable power:

> When one comes face to face with death ... a void appears that nothing in the world can fill; a gaping abyss opens up at the very ground on which one stands .... In fact, that abyss is always just underfoot. In the case of death, we do not face something that awaits us in some distant future, but something that we bring into the world with us at the moment we are born. Our life runs up against death at its every step; we keep one foot planted in the vale of death at all times. Our life stands poised at the brink of the abyss of nihility, to which it may return at any moment.[32]

On the field of nihility, where both the existence of the self and the existence of all things become "a question mark," we encounter "the Great Doubt." Nishitani contrasts this condition with Cartesian doubt, in which the ego is doing the doubting, because the Great Doubt comes about precisely through the death, or annihilation, of the ego. For this reason it's equivalent to what the Zen tradition calls "the Great Death." It's a situation where "it is the same with nihility and death ... the elemental source of beings one and all is transformed into nihility, and the world is transformed into a world of death ... our own utter death."[33]

It's a world of death because it's a world of impermanence, where nothing lasts, especially our selves: everything hovers over the abyss of nihility. "From the very outset life is at one with death. This means that all living things, just as they are, can be seen under the Form of death." It's all a matter of time, and the Zen notion of temporality that Nishitani goes on to elaborate resembles the temporality of Heidegger's "being-toward-death." Death isn't something that happens in the future, because the future isn't real and death is "very real."[34] The only reality is the present moment, because the future is yet to come (just as the past has already gone) and its reality (like that of the past) consists in its entering the present moment.

Nietzsche may have been the first to notice how the noisy and exuberant vitality of the modern city actually intimates, to one who has ears to hear, the silence of the grave to which all its citizens are heading.[35] After moving to Genoa, he found that life in that great bustling port on the Mediterranean coast contrasted delightfully with the sepulchral atmosphere of his homeland in the north of Germany. An aphorism "The Thought

[32] Nishitani 1982, 3–4.
[33] Nishitani 1982, 17–21, 230.
[34] Nishitani 1982, 50, 7.
[35] Friedrich Nietzsche, *The Joyful Science*, aphorism 278; *Kritische Studienausgabe*, edited by Giorgio Colli and Mazzino Montinari (Berlin: Walter de Gruyter, 1998), vol. 3, 523, my translation.

of Death" tinges this delight with sadness, foreshadowing Nishitani's ideas so forcefully that it's worth citing at length:

> It gives me a melancholy pleasure to live in the midst of this jumble of little lanes, of needs, of voices: how much enjoyment, impatience, and desire, how much thirsty life and intoxication with life comes to light at every moment! And yet for all these clamorous, lively, life-thirsty people it will soon be so silent! And behind each one of them his shadow stands, as his dark fellow traveller! It is always as in the last moment before the departure of an emigrant ship: there is more to say than ever before, the hour is at hand, and the ocean with its desolate silence is waiting impatiently behind all this noise—so covetous and certain of its prey.

The clamorous exuberance of the modern city, where desires and lust for life continually gush to the surface, is at a deeper level a defensive, nihilistic reaction against the silent imminence of death. Shadowed by our death-selves, we're already heading for the quiet of the grave, at the last moment before embarking on the voyage out, one foot planted on the bark of death. Modernity's breaking with the past is accompanied by a reduction in mortality rates and a loosening of community ties that removes death from its hitherto central place within everyday life. Nietzsche liked to spend time in the spectacular Monumental Cemetery of Staglieno, on the outskirts of Genoa, a place where community ties to the dead remain close. The aphorism continues:

> And each and every one of them supposes that the heretofore means little or nothing, and that the near future is everything: hence this haste, this clamour, this drowning out and overreaching of each other. Everyone wants to be the first in this future—and yet it is death and deathly silence that are alone certain and common to all in this future! How strange that this sole certainty and commonality does almost nothing for people, and that they are *farthest removed* from feeling that they form a brotherhood of death.

Life is full of uncertainty, but the one certainty we have in common we pretend to ignore: that the mortality rate for being human holds steady at exactly 100 percent. Acknowledging this certainty could do much for us, instead of almost nothing, by way of enriching our lives, but our failure to realize the presence of the future unravels the frail fabric of human fraternity.

In a consideration of the modern metropolis reminiscent of Nietzsche's musings on life in Genoa (with which Nishitani was no doubt familiar), Nishitani invokes a "double vision" of places burgeoning with life, such as the Ginza in Tokyo or Broadway in New York, as being simultaneously "fields of death." Elaborating a traditional Zen image of skulls lying scattered all over the field of existence, he writes:

> A hundred years hence, not one of the people now walking the Ginza will be alive, neither the young nor the old, the men nor the women . . . . In a flash of lightning before the mind's eye, what is to be actual a hundred years hence is already an actuality

today. We can look at the living as they walk full of health down the Ginza and see, in double exposure, a picture of the dead . . . . This kind of double exposure is true vision of reality . . . . The aspect of life and the aspect of death are equally real, and reality is that which appears now as life and now as death.[36]

This idea is prefigured in Heidegger's discussion of death in relation to life in his essay from 1946, "What Are Poets For?" Central to the discussion is the idea that human beings, as "mortals," are now living "in a destitute time" because they "are hardly aware and capable even of their own mortality."[37] Heidegger shows how this theme weaves through the poetry of Rainer Maria Rilke and cites a sentence from one of the poet's "Letters from Muzot" from 1923, where he recommends regarding death as the hidden back-side of life:

Like the moon, so life surely has a side that is constantly turned away from us, and which is not life's opposite but its completion to perfection, to plenitude, to the truly whole and full sphere and globe of *Being*.[38]

The next sentences from this letter are also worth citing because they anticipate with such eloquent clarity Nishitani's idea of "death-*as*-life, life-*as*-death":[39]

I shall not say that one should *love* death; but one should love life with such magnanimity, and without calculating exceptions, that one involuntarily always includes death (as the averted half of life) and loves it along with life . . . . It is thinkable that death stands infinitely nearer to us than life itself.[40]

Although Nishitani claims that the aspects of life and death are equally real, insofar as the acceptance of death opens us to emptiness he will also emphasize that this field opens up "on the near side, more so than what we normally regard as our own self."[41]

In an essay from 1960, "Science and Zen," Nishitani expands his treatment of nihility to cosmic dimensions. He proceeds from the premise that the most profound effect of the rise of the natural sciences in recent centuries has been the destruction of "the teleological worldview," which holds that the world has some purpose to it and is heading toward some end that grants meaning to human existence. The "big picture" presented by the modern scientific worldview is by contrast rather bleak:

---

[36] Nishitani 1982, 51–52.

[37] Martin Heidegger, *Poetry, Language, Thought*, translated by Albert Hofstadter (New York: Harper & Row, 1975), 94.

[38] Letter of January 6, 1923, in Rilke Rainer Maria, *Briefe* (Wiesbaden: Insel Verlag, 1950), 806; cited by Heidegger in *Poetry, Language, Thought*, 121.

[39] Nishitani 1982, 75.

[40] Rilke, *Briefe*, 806–807.

[41] Nishitani 1982, 95, 97.

This view sees matter, in its usual state, as subject to conditions that could never serve as an environment for living beings (for example, in conditions of extremely high or extremely low temperatures). The range of the possibility of existence for living beings is like a single dot surrounded by a vast realm of impossibility: one step out of that range and life would immediately perish. Thus, to this way of thinking, the universe in its usual state constitutes a world of death for living beings.[42]

Recent advances in astrobiology confirm Nishitani's claim concerning the extremely narrow range of conditions that can give rise to and support life.[43] As Nietzsche once wrote: "Let us beware of saying that death is opposed to life. The living is only a species of the dead, and a very rare species at that."[44]

Nishitani then turns, characteristically, to the existential counterpart to the natural scientific account of our situation, which he again presents in a cosmic context:

> Directly beneath the field of man's being-in-the-world, and the field of the very possibility of that being, the field of the impossibility of that being has opened up. The field where man has his being is his teleological dwelling place; it is the place where he has his life with a conscious purpose as a rational being. And yet this is disclosed as a field merely floating for a brief moment within a boundless, endless, and meaningless world governed by mechanical laws (in the broad sense of the term) and devoid of any telos. Our human life is established on the base of an abyss of death.[45]

Contemporary natural science, astronomy in particular, has lent considerable depth and weight to the Buddhist insight into impermanence, where any arising takes place in interdependence with perishing in a field of life-and-death, where life is "a very rare species" indeed.

Nishitani goes on to invoke the eschatological myth of the "cosmic conflagration," found in many cultures, remarking that the Buddhists transformed it from a cosmological doctrine into "an existential problem":

> Seen from this standpoint, this world as it is—with the sun, the moon, and the numerous stars, with mountains, rivers, trees, and flowers—is, as such, the world ablaze in an all-consuming cosmic conflagration. The end of the world is an actuality here and now; it is a fact and a destiny at work directly underfoot.[46]

In Heidegger's terms, transferred from the individual to the cosmic dimension, death as the "possibility of the absolute impossibility of all possibilities" isn't something in the

---

[42] Nishitani, in Franck 2004, 109.

[43] See, for example, NASA (2003), "Astrobiology Roadmap," 2 (retrieved January 4, 2012, from http://astrobiology.arc.nasa.gov/roadmap/g1.html); and K. Kashefi and D. Lovley, "Extending the Upper Temperature Limit for Life," *Science* 301. 5635 (2003): 934.

[44] Nietzsche, *The Joyful Science*, aphorism 109; *Kritische Studienausgabe*, vol. 3, 467, my translation.

[45] Nishitani, in Franck 2004, 110.

[46] Nishitani, in Franck 2004, 117.

future that we need to wait for: it is rather what is "nearest" to us, since death is always "possible at any moment."[47]

Nishitani allows that the myth of the cosmic conflagration "can also be interpreted in a scientific way," saying that "it is at least scientifically possible that the planet on which we live . . . and the whole cosmos itself might be turned into a gigantic ball of fire."[48] Fifty years later we *know* that this is what's happening to the earth: as the sun proceeds toward its Red Giant phase it will boil off the earth's atmosphere, before expanding beyond the planet's orbit to engulf it in a fiery conflagration.[49] The latest models predict that the Earth, even without help from anthropogenic global warming, could fall out of the "habitable zone" in some 1.75 billion years—although our zeal for increasing the rate of global warming could make this happen sooner.[50]

Returning to the field of nihility as experienced by the individual, we find Nishitani characterizing it as a "field of infinite dispersion," a zone of death because everything, including our selves, is cut off from everything else:

> All things appear isolated from one another by an abyss. Each thing has its being as a one-and-only, a solitariness absolutely shut up within itself . . . . On the field of nihility all nexus and unity is broken down and the self-enclosure of things is absolute. All things that are scatter apart from one another endlessly.[51]

It is thus not a place where one can function normally, because the abysses and scattering have a paralyzing effect. And if the scattering makes it hard to walk on the field of nihility, it's just as hard to talk (and not only about it), since language, too, fails to function.

> Seen essentially, that is, as existing in nihility and as manifest in nihility, everything and everyone is nameless, unnamable, and unknowable. Now the reality of this nihility is covered over in an everyday world, which is in its proper element when it traffics in names.[52]

If the idea is to be open to the field of nihility as the way to emptiness, one might wish that Nishitani had described it more fully. (Western philosophers who talk about confronting the abyss, like Kierkegaard, Nietzsche, and Heidegger, also offer minimal description of the experience.) But before concluding that Nishitani's field of nihility derives from a peculiarly East Asian experience inaccessible to those who haven't suffered the Great

---

[47] Martin Heidegger, *Sein und Zeit* (Tübingen: Niemeyer, 1967), §§ 50–53.

[48] Nishitani, in Franck 2004, 118.

[49] K.-P. Schröder and R. C. Smith, "Distant Future of the Sun and Earth Revisited," *Monthly Notices of the Royal Astronomical Society* 3861 (2008): 155–163.

[50] A. Rushby et al., "Habitable Zone Lifetimes of Exoplanets Around Main Sequence Stars," *Astrobiology* 13.9 (2013): 833–849.

[51] Nishitani 1982, 145.

[52] Nishitani 1982, 101.

Doubt, or Zen sickness, we should consider that Western counterparts are indeed to be found, and described, in the field of literature.

In nihility all is "nameless, unnamable, and unknowable." It is not for nothing that the third novel in Samuel Beckett's magnificent trilogy is *The Unnamable*: the entire work (and many passages from other works) can be heard as spoken by a voice, or voices, on the field of nihility.

An earlier, equally magnificent evocation of nihility (with which Nishitani may have been familiar) is to be found in Hugo von Hofmannsthal's famous "Chandos Letter." In this brief text, purportedly addressed to the philosopher Francis Bacon, the writer explains how he has "completely lost the ability to think or speak coherently about anything at all." At first, he had problems with talking about "elevated topics," where "abstract words ... disintegrated in my mouth like rotten mushrooms." But then "the affliction broadened, like spreading rust," so that people in general and their affairs became impossible to understand:

> I could no longer grasp them with the simplifying gaze of habit. Everything came to pieces, the pieces broke into more pieces, and nothing could be encompassed by one idea. Isolated words swam about me; they turned into eyes that stared at me and into which I had to stare back, dizzying whirlpools that spun around and around and led into the void.[53]

After a failed attempt to escape from this condition by immersing himself in the thought of Seneca and Cicero, the writer eventually begins to sense a spontaneous change in his experience, especially with respect to such insignificant things as "a watering can, a harrow left in a field, a dog in the sun, a shabby churchyard, a cripple, a small farmhouse":

> These mute and sometimes inanimate beings rise up before me with such a plenitude, such a presence of love, that my joyful eye finds nothing dead anywhere. Everything seems to mean something.... I feel a blissful and utterly eternal interplay in me and around me, and amid the to-and-fro there is nothing into which I cannot merge. Then it is as if ... we could enter into a new, momentous relationship with all of existence if we began to think with our hearts.[54]

This could be a description of the turn from the field of nihility to the field of emptiness, which now allows the author to get, from the heart, to the heart of things.

Nishitani talks about the "transitional" character of nihility, insofar as it is "not a field one can stand on in the proper sense of the term." If we can't stand on it, perhaps we just need to stand it, until the turn takes place. Or else take a step. Nishitani writes at one point of "the necessity of having nihility go a step further and convert to śūnyatā ...

---

[53] Hugo von Hofmannsthal, *The Lord Chandos Letter and Other Writings* (New York: New York Review Books, 2005), 121, 122.

[54] Hofmannsthal. *Lord Chandos Letter*, 123, 125.

where emptiness appears at one with being." But he also talks of a "step back" from ni-hility to the field of emptiness, to shed light (a Zen expression) on what is underfoot.[55]

THE FIELD OF EMPTINESS

It's not that we can take that further step deliberately, through exercising will—because on the field of nihility, with the death of the ego, willing is no longer possible. In an early discussion of European nihilism, Nishitani talked of the self-overcoming of nihilism as "a turn":

> This "Nothing," without God or Truth actually harbored within itself the seeds of a turn to a great affirmation in which existential nothingness replaced God as the creative force.[56]

The self-overcoming of nihilism thus involves staying with the meaninglessness, the Great Doubt, and Death, hanging in there until the turn comes that opens up the field of emptiness. It turns out to be worth the wait, undergoing the nihility until the self-overcoming takes place.

On the field of emptiness, we experience a complete reversal of the way things were just before:

> In contrast to the field of nihility on which the desolate and bottomless abyss distances even the most intimate of persons or things from one another, on the field of emptiness that absolute breach points directly to a most intimate encounter with everything that exists.[57]

Such intimacy is possible because, on the field of emptiness, we have gone far beyond the superficial encounters we have with things on the field of consciousness, and the network of relationships that make every thing the thing that it is comes to the fore, allowing us to get to the heart of things, to their very "center," where we can experience them "in their truly elemental and original appearances."[58]

In this context, Nishitani cites the well-known advice of the haiku poet Bashō to those who aspire to writing about a pine tree or bamboo (which one could as well extend to those who would paint them):

> From the pine tree
> learn of the pine tree,
> and from the bamboo
> of the bamboo.

---

[55] Nishitani 1982, 137, 123; 4. See Davis 2004 for a discussion of the "step back."
[56] Nishitani 1990, 8; see also 82, 90, 173.
[57] Nishitani 1982, 98, 102.
[58] Nishitani 1982, 130, 140, 110.

Rather than dealing with mere representations on the field of consciousness, we are to undermine the anthropocentric perspective by getting to the heart of the thing and experiencing it from there. (In the case of thinkers like Zhuangzi, or Dōgen, or Nietzsche, we could talk of entering into the perspective of the other.) Nishitani understands Bashō's dictum as an encouragement to shift to

> the dimension where things become manifest in their suchness, to attune ourselves to the selfness of the pine tree and the selfness of the bamboo. The Japanese word for "learn" [*narau* 習う] carries the sense of "taking after" something, of making an effort to stand essentially in the same mode of being as the thing one wishes to learn about.[59]

This kind of learning is possible because we exist in a field of dynamic forces that are patterned by what the Buddhists call "dependent co-arising" (or the Daoists "*dao*"):

> The field of śūnyatā is a field of force. The force of the world makes itself manifest in the force of each and every thing in the world. To return to a terminology adopted earlier on, the force of the world, or "nature" [*physis*], becomes manifest in the pine tree as the *virtus* of the pine, and in the bamboo as the *virtus* of the bamboo. Even the very tiniest thing, to the extent that it "is," displays in its act of being the whole web of circuminsessional interpenetration that links all things together. In its being, we might say, the world "worlds."[60]

Thus, a single pine tree—through its *virtus*, power, 徳 (Ch. *de*; Jp. *toku*)—is not only the center of a world, supported by all other things, or processes, but it also supports and contributes to everything else that's going on. (Readers familiar with Daoism or Neo-Confucianism, Huayan or Tientai Buddhism, or the later Heidegger's ideas about thing and world, will find Nishitani's discussion aptly reminiscent of those earlier philosophies.) To the extent that we ourselves participate in this wondrous process, we do so not as our selves understood as "some thing," but as ourselves a field: "the self has its being as such a field" (*Dasein* as a clearing; *Lichtung*, in Heidegger).[61]

On the question of how we get to the field of emptiness, Nishitani writes of another way later in *Religion and Nothingness*, in discussing Dōgen's idea of "body-and-mind dropping off": "It is said that we take our leave of the darkness of ignorance exclusively by means of just sitting [zazen]."[62] Nishitani seems reluctant to write about zazen, perhaps because he regarded his Zen practice and his philosophical thinking as to some extent separate, although complementary, activities. He spoke of himself "thinking and then sitting, sitting and then thinking." But, of course, they needn't be separate, and for

---

[59] Nishitani 1982, 128.
[60] Nishitani 1982, 150.
[61] Nishitani 1982, 151.
[62] Nishitani 1982, 185.

a thinker like Dōgen, they weren't: "Now sit steadfastly and think not-thinking. How do you think not-thinking? Beyond thinking."[63]

Practice-enlightenment for Dōgen necessarily involves a kind of thinking, but not, of course, anthropocentric conceptual or rational thinking on the field of consciousness. It is a deeper process, like Nietzsche's "it thinks" (*es denkt*) or Heidegger's "meditative thinking"—or what Nishitani calls "existential" thinking, thinking in images or kōans, usually drawn from the Chan and Zen traditions. Because such thinking emerges from or through a mortal body, it's a major component of Nishitani's task of practicing philosophy as a matter of life and death. Yet such practice is by no means morbid: Nishitani frequently emphasizes the profound *joy* that eventually attends it. He suggests that the field of emptiness may be accessed through the practice of zazen as, in Dōgen's words, "the right entrance to free and unrestricted activity in self-joyous samādhi."[64] On this field, the self can ease itself into the joy of the self of the world.

The kind of thinking involved here is not guided by the controlling ego, but by the things themselves as they come and go on the field of emptiness, because these all engage in "preaching the dharma," or expounding the Buddhist teachings:

> Things ... express themselves, and in expressing themselves they give expression, at the same time, to what it is that makes them be, pointing it out and bearing witness to it.... The pine speaks the *koto* [matter, *Sache, logos*] of the pine tree, the bamboo the *koto* of the bamboo .... [They speak from] the place where things are on their own home-ground, just as they are, manifest in their suchness.[65]

Our intimacy with things is enhanced when we not only get to their hearts but also listen to what they have to say to us, as friends and companions on the Way. The only passage from an earlier thinker that Nishitani quotes three times in *Religion and Nothingness* is this one from Dōgen's "Genjōkōan," which intimates the optimal stance toward things:

> To practice and confirm all things [dharmas] by conveying one's self to them, is illusion: for all things to advance forward and practice and confirm the self, is enlightenment.[66]

It's a matter of letting things be (in the middle voice of the verb "let"), what Heidegger calls *Gelassenheit* (releasement), so that our thoughts arise from the things themselves.

---

[63] Heisig 2001, 184; Dōgen, "Recommending Zazen to All People," in Dōgen 2010, 908.

[64] Nishitani 1982, 187–188; see also 199–200, 246–247.

[65] Nishitani 1982, 195. The idea that things "preach the dharma" comes from Kūkai's notion of *hosshin seppō* (法身説法; the Dharmakāya expounds the Dharma), and Dōgen's similar idea of *mujō seppō* (無情説法; insentient beings expound the Dharma). For a discussion of the contemporary significance of these ideas, see Parkes 2013.

[66] Nishitani 1982, 107, 164, 196.

The complex profundity of Dōgen's thought often makes it difficult to fathom, but when he talks to the monks in his monastery about "the great matter," he is straightforward and clear:

> It goes without saying that you must consider the inevitability of death. You should be resolved not to waste time and refrain from doing meaningless things. You should spend your time carrying out what is worth doing. Among the things you should do, what is the most important?[67]

These are existential and not moral "shoulds," and the appropriate response to the question addressed to the individual mortal (like the response to Nietzsche's imagistic presentations of eternal recurrence, or Heidegger's existential conception of death) has no predetermined or specific content. In the face of your imminent death, how are you going to live this moment, and the next, and the one after that? Nishitani doesn't explicitly pose Dōgen's question, but it is implicit throughout his discussions of death, and the response is simply: to open oneself to the field of emptiness.

Just before the end, let us entertain a short metaphysical question about Nishitani's three fields philosophy: why the nihility? Why not just experience on the field of consciousness and then leave open the possibility of enlightened existence on the field of emptiness? Why the necessity for the middle nonground, the transitional zone where everything appears as an absolute inversion of the field of emptiness? Why insist, as Nishitani does, on the reality of the abyssal separation and solitude of everything that is ultimately, on the deeper field beneath, so intimately interconnected?

The simple answer: because of death, the radical impermanence of all things. But then the existential-nihilistic question arises: why bother? Why not stay with the field of consciousness, forget about nihility and death, and simply get on with our lives? If it all comes to naught, why not just enjoy life as much as and while we can? Because that way we can miss so much of it and fail to attain breadth or depth in its enjoyment. But if instead we try to live life more fully by opening down to the field of emptiness and engaging other people and things as they are, then, when we reach the end, we may find we can face it with relative serenity—and perhaps even, with Hakuin, "obtain the decisive and ultimate great joy" on the way.

BIBLIOGRAPHY AND SUGGESTED READINGS

Davis, Bret W. (2004) "The Step Back Through Nihilism: The Radical Orientation of Nishitani Keiji's Philosophy of Zen." *Synthesis Philosophica* 37: 139–159.

Davis, Bret W. (2013) "Psychosomatic Practice and Kyoto School Philosophies of Zen." *Journal of Religious Philosophy* 64: 25–40.

---

[67] Dōgen 1987, 97.

Dōgen. (1987) *Shōbōgenzō-zuimonki*, translated by Shōhaku Okumura. Kyoto: Kyoto Zen Center.

Dōgen. (2010) *Treasury of the True Dharma Eye: Zen Master Dogen's Shobo Genzo*, edited by Kazuaki Tanahashi. 2 vols. Boston: Shambhala.

Franck, Frederick. (2004) *The Buddha Eye: An Anthology of the Kyoto School and Its Contemporaries*. Bloomington, IN.: World Wisdom.

Hakuin, Ekaku. (1971) *The Zen Master Hakuin: Selected Writings*, translated by Philip Yampolsky. New York: Columbia University Press.

Heisig, James W. (2001) *Philosophers of Nothingness: An Essay on the Kyoto School*. Honolulu: University of Hawai'i Press.

Nishitani Keiji. (1982) *Religion and Nothingness*, translated by Jan van Bragt. Berkeley: University of California Press.

Nishitani Keiji. (1984) "The Standpoint of Zen," translated by John C. Maraldo. *The Eastern Buddhist* 18.1: 1–26.

Nishitani Keiji. (1986-95) *Nishitani Keiji chosakushū* [Collected Works of Nishitani Keiji], Tokyo: Sōbunsha.

Nishitani Keiji. (1990) *The Self-Overcoming of Nihilism*, translated by Graham Parkes with Setsuko Aihara. Albany: State University of New York Press.

Nishitani Keiji. (1991) *Nishida Kitarō*, translated by Yamamoto Seisaku and James W. Heisig. Berkeley: University of California Press.

Nishitani Keiji. (1999) "Emptiness and Sameness." In *Modern Japanese Aesthetics*, edited by Michele Marra. Honolulu: University of Hawai'i Press, 179-217.

Nishitani Keiji. (2004) "Science and Zen." In *The Buddha Eye: An Anthology of the Kyoto School and Its Contemporaries*, edited by Frederick Franck, Bloomington, IN: World Wisdom, 107–136.

Nishitani Keiji. (2004) "The I-Thou Relation in Zen Buddhism." In *The Buddha Eye: An Anthology of the Kyoto School and Its Contemporaries*, edited by Frederick Franck, Bloomington, IN: World Wisdom, 39–54.

Nishitani Keiji. (2006) *On Buddhism*, translated by Seisaku Yamamoto and Robert E. Carter. Albany: State University of New York Press.

Parkes, Graham. (2012) "Awe and Humility in the Face of Things: Somatic Practice in East-Asian Philosophies." *European Journal for Philosophy of Religion* 4.3: 69–88.

Parkes, Graham. (2013) "Kūkai and Dōgen as Exemplars of Ecological Engagement." *The Journal of Japanese Philosophy* 1: 85–110.

Unno, Taitetsu, ed. (1989) *The Religious Philosophy of Nishitani Keiji*. Berkeley: Asian Humanities Press.

CHAPTER 22

UEDA SHIZUTERU

The Self That Is Not a Self in a Twofold World

STEFFEN DÖLL

My father taught at Kōya University and also presided over a temple on Mount Kōya. Once, when I was already living in Kyoto, I returned home for the summer holidays. I was around 30 years old and, as a postdoctoral adjunct lecturer, did not yet have a steady job. So I spent my days in my father's office which was located on the ground floor of the University library's splendid prewar four-story building. For lunch I returned to our temple by way of a small mountain path behind the library. It was not only a shorter way than going through town but, much to my liking, was also a narrow path through the standing trees with no trace of anyone to be seen.

One day, I encountered a dog on this mountain path. That happened only once during all those years. I saw this dog coming towards me, but the path was too narrow for more than one man to walk on . . . . I felt somehow awkward and the dog also averted his eyes when we tried to make room and squeeze past one another. Then, after seven or eight steps I felt struck [by a feeling], stopped, and turned around only to find my eyes meeting those of the dog who himself had stopped and turned around. I was surprised and he also gave the impression of feeling slightly unsettled. He looked to the ground and hesitatingly trotted off. Before long, he had vanished down the slope of the mountain path.

Even now I see him before me with his self-conscious expression. And each and every time I see him it strikes me: The one I met that day I had not taken to be a dog at all.

— *Kodachi ni te* ("Among the Trees")

UEDA Shizuteru (1926–2019) is generally regarded as the main representative of the Kyoto School's third generation and one of the most stimulating and influential thinkers of contemporary Japan. His academic research focuses on questions from the fields of modern philosophy, East Asian Buddhism, and Christian religiosity. But, as the epigraph suggests, there is more to his work than detached analysis: he is a suggestive and imaginative essayist as well as a distinguished lecturer. In his books, essays, and talks, he manages to integrate the experiences of an eventful life with a wealth of philosophical knowledge and understanding, as well as compassionate insight into the human condition.

Ueda graduated in 1949 from Kyoto University's Faculty of Philosophy under the guidance of Nishitani Keiji (1900–1990), who may well be said to be the defining influence on Ueda's thought. Ueda then spent the years between 1959 and 1963 at Marburg University in Germany, where he wrote his doctoral dissertation in the field of religious studies.[1] After returning to Japan, he was professor first of German language and literature and later, succeeding his mentor Nishitani, of religious philosophy at Kyoto and Hanazono Universities. He has published extensively[2] on topics such as Christian mysticism, especially that of Meister Eckhart (1260–1328); Buddhism, especially Chan/Zen; philosophy, especially that of Nishida Kitarō (1870–1945); and on the philosophy of language and the phenomenology of spiritual experience, especially as depicted in classical Zen texts such as the *Ten Ox-Herding Pictures*.[3]

There is another facet to his life, however: a steady religious practice that both underlies and informs Ueda's academic career. He is, as his own evocative reminiscence quoted here relates, the son of a Buddhist priest at Mount Kōya in Wakayama prefecture. However, unlike his upbringing in a temple household belonging to the esoteric Shingon denomination of Japanese Buddhism might suggest, Ueda's religious inclinations lie elsewhere, namely with the meditative introspection of Zen Buddhism. He has spent long years training as a lay practitioner at Shōkoku Zen monastery in the city of Kyoto, where abbot Kajitani Sōnin (1914–1995) bestowed upon him official acknowledgment of his awakening (*inka shōmei* 印可証明). Ueda continued his religious praxis at Shōkoku monastery until 2017: he presided over a meditation group of lay practitioners to whom he also lectured regularly on the Zen Buddhist canon. He passed away just before this volume was published in 2019.

---

[1] Ueda 1965.

[2] The *Eastern Buddhist (New Series)* has published several English translations of essays by Ueda, the most important of which are to be found in the bibliography to this chapter. His broad oeuvre in Japanese has been mostly gathered in the twelve volumes of *Ueda Shizuteru shū* [The Ueda Shizuteru Collection] (Ueda 2001–2004) and in the five volumes of *Tetsugaku korekushon* [Philosophical Collection] (Ueda 2007–2008). Many of his articles written in German have been gathered in Ueda 2011c. Quotations in this chapter's notes from *Ueda Shizuteru shū* (Ueda 2001–2004) will be abbreviated as USS.

[3] Numerous translations and commentaries in Western languages exist, the most widespread English translation being Kakuan 1957. A more recent translation along with a commentary by Zen master Yamada Mumon is also available (Yamada 2004). See Section 4 for an overview of Ueda's exegesis of the *Ox-Herding Pictures*.

In this chapter, I examine the thought of Ueda Shizuteru with special reference t conceptualization of self and world. On our way through Ueda's treatments of Descai philosophical meditations, Heidegger's existential analysis, and Zen phenomenol. I will demonstrate that his work posits the interdependency of philosophical analysis and spiritual practice and is concerned first and foremost with an existential transformation of the human subject. Ueda's work therefore also calls into question any rigorous distinction of academic disciplines in favor of a living and practicing philosophy.

WITH AND AGAINST DESCARTES:
MEDITATIONS ON THE SELF

Small essayistic pieces such as the one quoted at the beginning of this chapter are widespread in Ueda's writings and often follow a certain pattern: he portrays some perplexing everyday experience that casts doubt on the basic assumptions we usually have as to our identity, our everyday lives, the world we live in, and the way we function in our multiple roles. Furthermore, in such situations, it becomes apparent that our conception of the world and our place within it is at best preliminary, at worst fundamentally flawed.

We invariably misrepresent and misconceptualize our self and the world we live in—to Ueda, this observation is neither a mere academic exercise nor is it dogmatic in nature; it is meant rather as a sober diagnosis of the existential situation that pervades our everyday lives. Ueda agrees with Heidegger when he defines moments in which our ambitions fail, our expectations remain unfulfilled, or in which we face human frailty and mortality as moments of existential angst from which there can be no easy escape. Then, we are confronted with a ubiquitous insignificance that renders the images we have of ourselves and the self-assumed roles we play in our worlds invalid and leaves us with the question: "Who am I?" Or, to rephrase the question in terms better suited to philosophical analysis: "What is the self?"[4]

Indeed, this question is pivotal to Ueda. To provide an answer, he suggests, it is necessary to return to and start anew from the—phenomenologically speaking—most basic stuff available to us: experience.

When discussing the nature of experience, we usually rely on a dualistic conception of subject and object: someone experiences something, and the observer makes sense of the observed in a hermeneutical act. (This dichotomy claims validity even in the case of purely internal experiences in which we experience different parts of ourselves.) The sovereign subject standing over and against an external world of objects finds its paradigmatic philosophical formulation in the work of René Descartes (1596–1650).

In his quest for truth, Descartes arrived at a rigorous application of methodical doubt, which intends to strip away everything that can in any way be doubted in order to finally

---

[4] See in particular Ueda 2000 and Ueda 2011c.

leave only that which is absolutely certain.[5] This certainty, somewhat counter to our initial, intuitive expectations, he found in the perceiving subject itself. Because although
it may be argued that error and deceit remain possible, especially in perception, even if
that should be the case, we can be certain that there must be something that perceives,
errs, and is deceived. That something can be none other than the self. Since every one of
these processes is located within the subject's mind and its cognition, Cartesian certainty
takes the form of the cogito: "I think, therefore I am." Descartes thus formulates an answer to Ueda's question of "What is the self?" The self is the cogito; that is, the thinking
subject around which every kind of world—be it reality or fantasy—takes place.

For Ueda, this answer is insufficient. Granted, the "cogito ergo sum" is an "extreme
and powerful answer,"[6] the pervasive plausibility of which allows for the human dominance of nature through technology, progress in the sciences and arts, and the steady
growth of material wealth. That these come at a price is a truism that hardly needs elaboration, but it should be emphasized that the problematic nature of a dualistic and antagonistic conception of the human being versus his world begins, for Ueda, at the level
of the basic experience of the self. According to his analysis of the Cartesian subject,
its defining attribute is the recursive character of its cognition: the "I think, therefore
I am" leaves unmentioned, and its deceptive simplicity and superficial clarity obfuscate,
the fact that it is in itself a thought process. Unabridged, the phrase actually implies: "I
think: I think, therefore I am." In its basic structure Descartes's argument is circular in
nature. It aims to prove the certainty of thought on the basis of thought itself: "I think
(cogito B) that I am because I think (cogito A)." Seen from this perspective, Cartesian
analysis does not arrive at certainty at all, which by now is effectively left out of the equation, but at a solipsistic entanglement of the self in its own cognition. As Ueda puts it in
no uncertain terms: Thought thinking itself "comes to realize that thought itself [cogito
B] is more certain than the 'I think, therefore I am' [cogito A] that had been discovered
as something certain. Thought is not satisfied with discovering truth but has the tendency to hyperbolize itself, as that which discovered truth, into truth as such."[7] Then,
"the absoluteness of an absolute existence that has its ground in itself and thus is the
ground of everything existing ... metastasizes onto the side of the human subject"[8]
in an act of false apotheosis. In the end, the thinking self comes to realize itself as the
basis not only of its own existence but of existence as such. The self is then taken as sufficient cause for self and world, and the Cartesian formula may be verbalized as a closed
circle: "I am because I am."

According to Ueda, this narcissistic megalomania is unacceptable for several reasons.
For one, it puts subjects in competition with one another over the position of absolute

---

[5] See René Descartes, "Meditations on First Philosophy," in *Philosophical Essays: Discourse
on Method; Meditations; Rules for the Direction of the Mind*, translated by Laurence J. Lafleur
(Indianapolis: Bobbs-Merrill, 1964).

[6] USS vol. 10, 189.

[7] USS vol. 10, 87.

[8] USS vol. 10, 86.

existence or, more radically, effectively negates the possibility of any other subject in addition to one's own self. Even more problematic for Ueda is this view's hermetic structure: by shutting out everything that is not the self, no room whatsoever is left for experience as the most fundamental constituent of human existence.

THE LAYERED SELF:
A NISHIDAEAN DYNAMISM

In opposition to this recursive conception of self, Ueda understands experience—in the strict sense of the term—to be a primordial dimension underlying the Cartesian cogito. As such, it must constantly elude the framework of subject/object or self/world. Primordial experience is not yet differentiated into subject and object but constitutes an open whole. It is on the basis of this dimension that the possibility of discursive reflection arises only as a secondary development.

It is well known that in his debut study, *Inquiry into the Good* (1911), Nishida's ambition was "to explain all things on the basis of pure experience as the sole reality."[9] The key term in this programmatic statement is, of course, "pure experience"—a term adopted from the writings of William James (1842–1910). The concise description Nishida gives for pure experience is equally well-known and oft-quoted: "The moment of seeing a color or hearing a sound, for example, is prior not only to the thought that the color or sound is the activity of an external object or that one is sensing it, but also to the judgment of what the color or sound might be."[10]

Ueda takes up Nishida's definition in a twofold manner: on the one hand, in the role of the exegete, he explains and illustrates it with concrete examples.[11] In this function, he points out that primordial experience is "pure" precisely because it is not yet "contaminated" with the rift between subject and object. Contrary to our everyday perspective and Cartesian analysis, the subject/object dichotomy is not a precondition of experience but a product of the spontaneous self-unfolding of an underlying experiential unity. It is only on this basis that poetic speech and conceptual thought become possible. These, in turn, then relate to primordial experience and, in the process, regularly misinterpret its self-unfolding in the terminology of a subject/object dualism.

On the other hand, Ueda speaks as a creative philosopher in his own right when he points out that the phrasing of Nishida's ambitious project—"to explain all things on the basis of pure experience as the sole reality"—itself mirrors the self-unfolding structure of pure experience.[12] The experiential fact (*koto* 事: "pure experience") unfolds into

---

[9] Nishida Kitaro, *An Inquiry into the Good*, trans. Masao Abe and Christopher Ives (New Haven, CT: Yale University Press, 1990), xxx.

[10] Ibid., 3.

[11] See Ueda 1991.

[12] See, most recently, Ueda 2006.

self-awareness and primal articulation (*koto* 言: "pure experience [is] the sole reality")
and is developed further self-consciously into a principle of philosophical reflection ("to
explain all things on the basis of pure experience as the sole reality").

Ueda specifies primordial experience as that in which "the framework of subject and
object, in which consciousness was enclosed, is broken through, opening up a [field of]
disclosedness."[13] Consciousness at that point is, in the most radical sense, a factual consciousness in which observer and fact are as yet undifferentiated. Ueda sees instances
of such experiential phenomena in spiritual communion and meditative immersion as
events of pure awareness that form the basis of the subsequent advent of self-awareness.

Out of this event arises spontaneous articulation by way of *poiesis*, an "Ur-
Satz" or primordial phrase. Words begin to structure the original undifferentiated
disclosedness: the self becomes conscious not *as* pure experience (that would be a conceptual contradiction), but *of* pure experience as an initial fracture of the primordial
experiential union. This speech act is truly poietic in the sense of the most fundamental
creativity.[14] The language of the poet and the sage (and perhaps also the madman), inspired by mystic communion, deep meditation, or transcendent inspiration, belongs
here. Although an initial differentiation between subject and object becomes gradually
visible, this is not yet reflective consciousness.

In the subsequent act of conceptualization, in the formulation of a "Grundsatz" or
philosophical principle, subject and object stand over and against one another in the
way Descartes found them to be and in the way we are used to them. It is only from
this perspective that we are able to reflect back on the process by which we went from
immediacy through elementary poietic expression on to the dichotomy of everyday
consciousness. The development then comes full circle: by way of abstraction, analysis, and synthesis, philosophical reflection is initiated, which Ueda defines as "the
self-objectification of pure experience."[15] The centripetal movement in which the self-
development of pure experience reflexively reappropriates itself thus complements the
centrifugal impulse of articulation and conceptualization.

At the same time, philosophical reflection opens up the possibility of seeing these
three dimensions as intimately related to one another: they are phases in the process of
the self-unfolding of pure experience. For this reason, Ueda characterizes them as a "dynamic connection that makes up the layering of (1) awareness, (2) self-awareness, and
(3) understanding self and world."[16] Descending through its own formative layers, the
everyday self eventually reaches the unbroken facticity of pure experience. It discovers
its own ground in a disclosedness that carries the latent seeds not only of the self, but
also of the world—in an as-yet undiscriminated and unarticulated self/world-complex.

But, if this is the case, our initial question as to the nature of the self must also pertain to
the place of the self in its world and, per extension, to the world as such. This is to say that

---

[13] Ueda 1991, 250.
[14] See Ueda 2011*b*.
[15] Ueda 1991, 252.
[16] Ibid., 250.

the self is always a self within a certain world and, as such, a "being-in-the-world." And to Ueda, "being-in-the-world" encompasses the mystical or spiritual dimension of pure experience as well as the reflective or philosophical dimension of a self/world hermeneutics. For this reason, he posits the necessity of religious insight to complement philosophical speculation and establishes Zen as the experiential paradigm: "Zen is the penetration into the origins of the self's self-awareness, whereas philosophy, as an ordering and unifying apprehension of the world, is the self-awareness of the world in which the self is located."[17]

The Twofold World: Totality of Involvements and Nothingness

On the one hand, Ueda often adopts Heidegger's locution and speaks of human being as "being-in-the-world" (*sekai-nai sonzai* 世界内存在). On the other, he asserts: "First and foremost, we understand (or rather misunderstand) the world and the self in a prejudiced way in that we find ourselves within the world."[18] How can we resolve this apparent contradiction?

In the preceding paragraphs, we have established that the self in its basic structure is constituted by a dynamical movement between experience, articulation, and reflection. Seen this way, "self" in the everyday usage of the term is too simple, too unambiguous to be left unqualified. As we have also already indicated, the world derives from the same source as "the self"; namely, the disclosive unity of primordial experience. It might therefore seem prudent to afford it the same reservations as "the self," and, indeed, it comes as no surprise that for Ueda "world" also has a twofold structure.

Ueda follows Heidegger in defining the world as a "totality of involvements":[19] human existence within the world, our *Dasein*, enables us to relate to other beings, attribute them significance, and disclose them in the context of the world. We understand ourselves and the things of our world in terms of this involvement, but the world itself remains beyond the grasp of such existential comportment. Only in moments of anxiety is our everyday worldview fundamentally upset; only then does the totality of involvements slip away into nothingness; only then, as beings are "nihilated" and fall from view, does the world as such become visible. It is revealed as enveloped and permeated by nothingness, and, out of this nothingness, the totality of involvements becomes possible: "On the one hand, nothingness lets beings as a whole slip away in the

---

[17] Ibid., 253.

[18] USS vol. 9, 28.

[19] See Martin Heidegger, *Being and Time*, translated by John Macquarrie and Edward Robinson (New York: Harper & Row, 1962); and Martin Heidegger, "What Is Metaphysics?" in *Basic Writings: From Being and Time (1927) to The Task of Thinking (1964)*, translated by David Farrell Krell (New York: Harper & Row, 1977).

manner of 'having no support in anything'; it exposes Dasein to nothingness and indeed sends it adrift into nothingness. But, on the other hand, nothingness conversely makes human being possible in that it is [only] by transcending beings as a whole that human being can relate to beings."[20]

Thus, every kind of human existence not only finds itself immersed in the world as totality of involvements, but also emplaced in the world as nothingness. Being and nothingness form a complementary unity that renders the world essentially ambiguous. "World" is always already a twofold structure in which a self is surrounded by being as well as by nothingness. This implies that "our existence is a twofold 'within.'"[21]

Let us approach the matter from yet another angle. Drawing on Nishida's theory of "locus" (basho 場所), Ueda employs the term "world" in the sense of a plurality of loci.[22] Every locus is multivalent with regards to time and space: I am writing this sentence late in the afternoon on a kitchen table in my home, not too far from the Oktoberfest chaos, and in an out-of-the-way corner of the Milky Way's Orion arm some billion years after the Big Bang. In relation to each of these definitions, I understand myself differently and choose different interpretations of my role within a specific locus: as family member, university lecturer, Munich resident, and so on. In this sense, "world" is more than a mere container in which beings may (or may not) find their place. Rather, it is the constantly shifting totality of spatially, temporally, functionally, and relationally specific loci. "World," then, is the locus of all loci. That being the case, the question arises: what is the locus of the world? The answer cannot simply be that it has no locus, because it would be unintelligible to say that the world does in fact exist, but it does not exist anywhere. Neither can we "specify" or "define"—in the precise senses of these terms—the locus in which the world exists because then the locus of the world would have to be part of the cumulative totality of loci and thus, paradoxically, be subsumed in the term "world" as well. It follows that the locus of the world defies verbalization, let alone definition, and can only be referred to as a conceptual nothing. Nishida therefore called it "the locus of absolute nothingness" (zettaimu no basho 絶対無の場所), yet Ueda often prefers "empty expanse" (kokū 虚空). The twofold world, then, is the totality of loci and, simultaneously, the openness that surrounds and pervades them.

---

[20] USS vol. 9, 32.

[21] Ibid., 36.

[22] See especially "Jikaku no basho: Zettaimu / shi-zen / nin-gen" [The Locus of Self-awareness: Absolute Nothingness, Natural Being-of-itself, Human Betweenness], in USS vol. 6, 245–278.

THE ELUSIVE OX, OR THE DIALECTICS
OF SELF AND WORLD

The twofold nature of both self and world has profound consequences for the task that Ueda sets for his philosophy. The most distinctive trait of his thought may be the episte-mological and existential paradigm shifts it requires of us. Such shifts are clearly at issue in his interpretation of the *Ten Ox-Herding Pictures* (*Jūgyū-zu* 十牛図).[23]

The *Ox-Herding Pictures* developed as a kind of handbook for Zen students in China roughly during the twelfth century. The work as it is most commonly known today consists of ten pictures with commentary in prose and poetry (in both Chinese and Japanese). The pictures—with the significant exception of numbers eight, nine, and ten—show a young herdsman in the process of searching for, catching, and bringing home the ox that had escaped him; all but one of the plates depict landscapes and natural surroundings; all of them are set in a circular frame.

Although there is vast room for interpretation, we will follow Ueda's working hy-pothesis that the young herdsman symbolizes a Buddhist practitioner in his quest for enlightenment. The ox, consequently, stands for the awakening the student is striving for. Yet because, according to Zen Buddhist doctrine, awakening happens solely by achieving insight into the reality of one's own self, the ox in fact symbolizes nothing other than the self—albeit an aspect or dimension that is radically different from the one symbolized by the herdsman. For this purpose, Ueda introduces the distinction be-tween the true self and the delusional self: our everyday self is deeply entangled in the unwholesome passions that form the matrix of existential anguish, and it is only pos-sible to free oneself from anguish and unwholesome entanglements by seeing through the delusions of the self. Thus, the de(con)struction of our everyday self becomes the primary concern on our way to our true self.

The *Ox-Herding Pictures* depict precisely this process. Although the young herdsman initially gives the impression of having lost something important, he basically does not yet have any idea of what to look for and where to look for it. Only in the second pic-ture does he become aware of the ox's footprints "along the riverbank and under the tress." Ueda sticks with the classical interpretation of this passage when he interprets it as symbolizing the encounter with religion as a set of doctrines that teach the imperfec-tion of human existence and the necessity of aspiring to spiritual maturity. Or, in more Buddhist terms, one has started to read canonical scriptures, commentary literature, or even begun to converse with a Zen master—all these unmistakably point one in the right direction, but the actual searching has yet to be undertaken by oneself.

Surprisingly early in the *Ox-Herding* series, insight into one's true self is symbolized: already in the third picture the herdsman catches a glimpse of the ox. The

---

[23] See USS 6, as well as Döll 2005.

practitioner has by now not only learned second-hand about a fundamental self, but also has actually witnessed its existence. This is as yet but a tentative and partial fulfillment of the search because the texts make it very clear that, if given even a single moment of leniency, the ox will run off again. The various depictions of this stage also express the preliminary and precarious quality of the experience: the ox is shown either beckoning the herdsman from the far shores of a river with no obvious way to cross the water or dashing away from the herdsman's rope with all its speed.

After a hard chase, the herdsman succeeds in throwing a rope around the neck of the ox and tries with all his might to stop it from breaking away once again, while the ox refuses to yield and threatens to escape if given the chance. The tension between the antagonists reaches its climax in the fourth picture, where the rope is taut and seems to be on the verge of breaking. The original self has, so to speak, been acquired for the time being, but still the danger, even the probability, remains that the practitioner strays from the path and suffers a relapse into his inauthentic self. This tension dissolves to a certain degree in the fifth picture. The rope is hanging loose, even though it may not be entirely unnecessary just yet. The herdsman quietly leads, the ox obediently follows. A self-integration has taken place, and the ambiguity of the self, its inner fracturedness or alienation from itself, seem to have been resolved.

The spiritual quest apparently begins to draw to a close in the sixth picture, where there is no longer any tension whatsoever within the self. In perfect harmony, the ox is treading along a set path, while the herdsman is casually playing the flute on its gently swaying back. Everyday self and true self have been harmonized with each other to the extent that the two seem to be more united than separate. The union of the self is taken one step further in the seventh picture. The ox is nowhere to be seen: it has merged with the herdsman and leaves not a trace behind.[24] Subject and object of the search, self and awakening have become one; not just theoretically—as in the Buddhist teachings—or allegorically—as in the Ox-Herding Pictures—but experientially. According to Ueda's interpretation, however, this is not yet the conclusion of the search: each and every stage of practice contains specific hazards, and, in the present stage, the enlightened practitioner runs the risk of taking his enlightenment as the ultimate achievement, as what is most valuable in and of itself. Such presumptuousness implies the danger of relapsing into a sublated form of the same deluded attachments from which he had struggled to free himself since the first picture. An awakening from awakening, a practice at once immanent to and transcendent of practice, is necessary. Otherwise this seventh picture is nothing but "elevated self-indulgence."[25]

The Ox-Herding Pictures may seem intuitively understandable and compelling up to the sixth, maybe even the seventh picture, but the final three pictures pose formidable

---

[24] The Ox-Herding Pictures' symbolism is far from perfect: it could be argued that it seems improbable that the true self would run away from the everyday self's spiritual quest. Also, if and when integration takes place, it seems that it should be the herdsman (our everyday self) that dissolves into the ox (the true self). Ueda takes note of these issues; see USS vol. 6, 104–107.

[25] USS vol. 6, 130.

hermeneutical challenges. Ueda's exegesis is based on the assumption that pictures eight, nine, and ten are no longer stages in a developmental process, but rather interrelated aspects of what Ueda calls the "dynamic trinity"[26] of the true self.

The first seven pictures are a constant, ever-deepening negation of the everyday, delusional self in disciplined spiritual practice (relative negation). This negation itself is then negated in the eighth picture (absolute negation), in which nothing at all is depicted. Our self is shown, in the words of Nishitani Keiji, to be "an existence that has become one with what is not existence at all. Ceaselessly passing away, and ceaselessly regaining its existence, it trembles above nihility."[27] The danger in this stage is to fall into a static condition of nihilism; that is, of taking emptiness to be a kind of "negative substance."[28] In order to avoid this crucial error, Ueda argues that we must understand absolute negation in terms of a "pure movement in two directions at the same time: (1) The negation of negation in the sense of a further denial of negation that does not come back around to affirmation but opens up into an endlessly open nothingness; and (2) the negation of negation in the sense of a return to affirmation without any trace of mediation."[29]

Although the absolute negation symbolized by the eighth picture remains in effect, an affirmation is now layered on its basis: the ninth picture with its blossoming flowers and flowing stream symbolizes the affirmation of being that complements the negation of nothingness. But, as the quotation just given indicates, it would be a mistake to interpret nothingness and being as counterparts of equal ontological status: just as the ninth picture presupposes the disclosing framework of the eighth (more on this topic later), being is neither self-sufficient nor absolute, but rather a function of the creative negativity of nothingness. And the reaffirmation of being through the negation of nothingness becomes possible only in the relational dynamics of the true self—a fact that is emphasized in the tenth picture, which brings us full circle. In this final picture, we see a herdsman in friendly conversation with a pot-bellied and good-humored older monk,[30] but a transformation has taken place. The herdsman we knew from the start of the picture series has grown beyond himself: it is he who is the old monk, a bodhisattva who now in turn inspires the quest for the true self in another young herdsman.

Together, the final three pictures thus form an intelligible set: negation and affirmation relate to one other dynamically and constitute the bodhisattva's play (i.e., a practice

---

[26] Ibid., 246.

[27] Nishitani Keiji, *Nishitani Keiji chosakushū 10: Shūkyō to wa nani ka* [The works of Nishitani Keiji, vol. 10: What Is Religion?] (Tokyo: Sōbunsha, 1987), 6; Nishitani Keiji, *Religion and Nothingness*, translated by Jan van Bragt (Berkeley: University of California Press, 1982), 4, translation modified.

[28] USS vol. 6, 182.

[29] Ueda 1982a, 160–161.

[30] The older monk resembles Hotei (Ch. Budai) who, according to legend, was a Chinese monk during the Tang dynasty (618–907). He is popularly remembered for the sack from which he gave alms to the poor and presents to the children (hence his name, which literally translates as "Sack of Cloth"), his ever-present laugh (hence his nickname, "Laughing Buddha"), and his refusal to take up abode anywhere permanently. Especially in the Chan/Zen tradition, he was understood as a personification of playful nonattachment and an incarnation of the future Buddha, Maitreya. In Japanese popular religion, he is considered to be one of the Seven Gods of Good Fortune.

beyond practice, a pure, ludic, compassionate activity that goes beyond all dualistic divisions, such as that of means vs. ends or subject vs. object). The bodhisattva's self is not actually itself anymore but, as Ueda formulates it, a "self that is not a self" (*jiko narazaru jiko* 自己ならざる自己). Whereas the eighth picture illustrates the radical negation of the self as a culmination of spiritual praxis, the ninth depicts the concrete reality that is "not the self," with the tenth returning once again—in the double sense of herdsman and bodhisattva—to a "self."

If we read the picture series against the grain and start from the back, it immediately becomes apparent that picture nine has always been the setting of each and every one of the pictures (excluding the empty circle). From the willows and pines to the grasses on the riverbanks and the full moon, the *Ox-Herding Pictures* take as their locus the landscapes and environs of the natural world. If we further expand our perspective with regard to the eighth "non-picture," we become aware that, without exception, every single picture is set within the frame of the empty circle. This layering of the specific locus of each individual picture onto its natural surroundings, and furthermore onto the underlying nothingness, is a strikingly apt illustration of Ueda's conception of the self that is not a self within a world that is twofold.

This interpretation throws new light on the question of soteriology: The fact that the self of the tenth, the natural environs of the ninth, and the framing nothingness of the eighth picture are ever present in the series suggests the possibility of a shortcut to the "trinity of the true self." In a way, even in the first picture, numbers eight, nine, and ten are already included. So why would we need to bother to run the full gauntlet and take upon ourselves the painstaking process of getting hold of our ox? And, indeed, the breakthrough to our true self is ever at hand, as the prose commentary to the first picture indicates: "Intrinsically [the ox] has never been lost, so what need is there to go in pursuit?" Whether stepping out of delusion and into truth is necessarily the product of a gradual process or whether it happens suddenly in the blink of an eye is a question that remains. What is clear is that Ueda's interpretation of the herdsman and the ox, far from being merely a scholarly exercise, is meant to suggest that our very existence can, and indeed should, be transformed through religious practice. It is primarily in this soteriological sense that Ueda's is a philosophy of religion.

ON THE USE OF SEARCHING: TOWARD A CRITICAL APPRAISAL OF UEDA'S THOUGHT

Ueda Shizuteru's philosophy has been aptly characterized by Mori Tetsurō: "Its originality lies in its theory of 'being in the twofold world,' which we may characterize as an intriguing encounter of Nishida's 'locus of nothingness' with Heidegger's 'being-in-the-world.'"[31] Yet, given the considerations just described, we may specify that Ueda's

---

[31] Mori Tetsurō, "Zen-Bukkyō to Kyōto gakuha: *Jūgyū-zu* kara mita Kyōto gakuha no basho-ron" [Zen Buddhism and the Kyoto school: The Kyoto School's Theory of Locus as Seen from the *Ten Ox-Herding*

thought aims less at describing the way human existence is related to the world in which it takes place than it is at communicating the necessity of an existential and epistemological shift in perspective. Insofar as such a shift in perspective involves soteriological claims, his philosophy is clearly rooted not only in ontological analysis but also, and perhaps even more importantly, in a religiously informed practice. In fact, Ueda explicitly integrates ontological analysis and performative spirituality. The epistemological shift he writes of brings about an existential conversion that shatters the delusional patterns of our everyday selves and sets us on the way of pursuing our ox. Ueda's philosophy thus presents us with a task: to discover the true self as that which lies at the foundation of both self and world and yet, at the same time, transcends these.

Religion, understood as an attempt to systematize such a spiritual path, is emphatically affirmed and yet is not Ueda's central concern. His own affiliation with Zen Buddhism remains beyond doubt throughout his work and clearly informs his critical analyses of other philosophies and religions. It is, after all, having such a firm foothold in a specific tradition that arguably renders a transconfessional and intercultural encounter meaningful in the first place. This is evident in Ueda's work on Eckhart in particular and Christian mysticism more broadly: although he attributes an astounding profundity to the insights of these Christian thinkers, and although in his interpretations he takes great pains to do justice to the complexities of their thought, Zen's (or more generally Buddhism's) superiority is consistently maintained. It is invariably the notion of the "negation of negation" that underlies this conviction. Whereas Eckhart in the end remains, for Ueda, attached to a conception of the nothing of the Godhead—however subtle and contourless it might be—Zen, he contends, breaks through all figures of transcendence and leaves behind even the Nothing of the mystics and negative theologians.[32]

In terms of the development of his thought through the many decades of his work, Ueda seems to have found his religio-philosophical center very early, and he never strayed from it. There is no trace whatsoever of a "Kehre," a Heideggerian turn (such as one finds in Nishida as well as in Tanabe and, in some respects, even in Nishitani). Ueda's work consists of the constant unfolding—in multiple directions throughout his essays and his studies on mysticism, on philosophy, and on religion—of an unshakable conviction as to the twofold or two-layered nature of both self and world, as well as the fundamental inseparability of these layers.

Ueda's philosophy is thus not merely a set of theses and speculations governed by the laws of logic and rational comprehensibility. Such is only one aspect of what really concerns him. For Ueda, philosophy is a genuine quest for understanding and insight, not just a mundane accumulation and assessment of information. Its claim is less to immediate plausibility than to transformative power, and it is meant to be reenacted and experienced by his readers. Ueda proposes to us that philosophy, in the end, is a

---

Pictures]. *Kyōto sangyō daigaku Nihon bunka kenkyū-jo kiyō* [Newsletter of the Research Institute of Japanese Culture at Kyoto Sangyo University], vol. 7/8 (2003), 20.

[32] See Ueda 1965, 145–169; and Ueda 1982a.

soteriological undertaking that concerns what it actually means to live and to die as a self that is not a self in a world that is twofold.

BIBLIOGRAPHY AND SUGGESTED READINGS

Davis, Bret W. (2008) "Letting Go of God for Nothing: Ueda Shizuteru's Non-Mysticism and the Question of Ethics in Zen Buddhism." In *Frontiers of Japanese Philosophy* 2, edited by Victor Sōgen Hori and Melissa Anne-Marie Curley. Nagoya: Nanzan Institute for Religion and Culture, 226–255.

Davis, Bret W. (2013) "Wer und was bin ich? Zur Phänomenologie des Selbst im Zen-Buddhismus by Shizuteru Ueda (review)." *Monumenta Nipponica* 68.2: 321–327.

Davis, Bret W. (2019) "Expressing Experience: Language in Ueda Shizuteru's Philosophy of Zen." In *Dao Companion to Japanese Buddhist Philosophy*, edited by Gereon Kopf. New York: Springer Publishing, 713–738.

Döll, Steffen. (2005) *Wozu also suchen? Zur Einführung in das Denken von Ueda Shizuteru* [Why Bother Searching? An Introduction to the Thought of Ueda Shizuteru], preface Klaus Vollmer. Munich: Iudicium.

Döll, Steffen. (2011) "Self and World. Ueda Shizuteru in Dialogue with René Descartes, Martin Heidegger and Maurice Merleau-Ponty." In *Japanese and Continental Philosophy. Conversations with the Kyoto School*, edited by Bret W. Davis, Brian Schroeder, and Jason M. Wirth. Bloomington: Indiana University Press, 120–137.

Heisig, James W. (2005) "Approaching the Ueda Shizuteru Collection." *The Eastern Buddhist* 37.1–2: 254–74.

Kakuan. (1957) "Ten Bulls," translated by Nyogen Senzaki and Paul Reps. In *Zen Flesh, Zen Bones: A Collection of Zen and Pre-Zen Writings*, compiled by Paul Reps and Nyogen Senzaki. Boston: Charles E. Tuttle, 163–186.

Suzuki Daisetsu, Ueda Shizuteru. (1973) "The Sayings of Rinzai. A Conversation between Daisetsu Suzuki and Shizuteru Ueda." *The Eastern Buddhist* 6.1: 92–110.

Ueda Shizuteru. (1965) *Die Gottesgeburt in der Seele und der Durchbruch zur Gottheit: Die mystische Anthropologie Meister Eckharts und ihre Konfrontation mit der Mystik des Zen-Buddhismus* [The Birth of God in the Soul and the Break-through to the Godhead: Meister Eckhart's Mystical Anthropology and Its Confrontation with the Mysticism of Zen Buddhism]. Gütersloh: Verlagshaus Gerd Mohn.

Ueda Shizuteru. (1982a) "'Nothingness' in Meister Eckhart and Zen Buddhism: With Particular Reference to the Borderlands of Philosophy and Theology," translated by James W. Heisig. In *The Buddha Eye: An Anthology of the Kyoto School*, edited by Frederick Franck. New York: Crossroad, 157–169.

Ueda Shizuteru. (1982b) "Emptiness and Fullness: Śūnyatā in Mahāyāna Buddhism," translated by James W. Heisig and Frederick Greiner. *The Eastern Buddhist* 15.1: 9–37.

Ueda Shizuteru. (1989) "The Zen Buddhist Experience of the Truly Beautiful," translated by John C. Maraldo. *The Eastern Buddhist* 22.1: 1–36.

Ueda Shizuteru. (1991) *Nishida Kitarō wo yomu* [Reading Nishida Kitarō]. Tokyo: Iwanami.

Ueda Shizuteru. (1992) "The Place of Man in the Noh Play." *The Eastern Buddhist New Series* 25.2: 59–88.

Ueda Shizuteru. (1993) "Zen and Philosophy in the Thought of Nishida Kitaro." *Japanese Religions* 18.2: 162–193.

Ueda Shizuteru. (2000) *Watashi to wa nani ka* [What Is the self?]. Tokyo: Iwanami.

Ueda Shizuteru. (2001) "The Concept of God, the Image of the Human Person and the Origin of the World in Zen Buddhism." In *The Concept of God, the Origin of the World and the Image of the Human in the World Religions*, edited by Peter Koslowski. Dordrecht: Kluwer, 43–56.

Ueda Shizuteru. (2001–2004) *Ueda Shizuteru shū* [The Ueda Shizuteru Collection], 12 vols. Tokyo: Iwanami.

Ueda Shizuteru. (2006) "Sōsetsu: Zen to Kyōtō tetsugaku" [Summary: Zen and Kyoto Philosophy]. In *Kyōtō tetsugaku sensho bekkan: Zen to Kyōtō tetsugaku* [Selected Writings of Kyoto Philosophy, Supplement: Zen and Kyoto Philosophy]. Kyoto: Tōeisha.

Ueda Shizuteru. (2007–2008) *Tetsugaku korekushon* [Philosophical Collection], 5 vols. Tokyo: Iwanami.

Ueda Shizuteru. (2011a) "Contributions to Dialogue with the Kyoto School," translated by Bret W. Davis. In *Japanese and Continental Philosophy. Conversations with the Kyoto School*, edited by Bret W. Davis, Brian Schroeder, and Jason M. Wirth. Bloomington: Indiana University Press, 19–31.

Ueda Shizuteru. (2011b) "Language in a Twofold World," translated by Bret W. Davis. In *Japanese Philosophy: A Sourcebook*, edited by James W. Heisig, Thomas P. Kasulis, and John C. Maraldo. Honolulu: University of Hawai'i Press, 766–784.

Ueda Shizuteru. (2011c) *Wer und was bin ich? Zur Phänomenologie des Selbst im Zen-Buddhismus* [Who and What Am I? On the Phenomenology of the Self in Zen Buddhism]. Freiburg/München: Karl Alber.

Ueda Shizuteru. (2013) *Zen y filosofía* [Zen and Philosophy], translated by Raquel Bouso García and Illana Giner Comín. Barcelona: Herder Editorial.

Yamada Mumon (2004). *The Ten Oxherding Pictures: Lectures by Yamada Mumon Roshi*, translated by Victor Sōgen Hori. Honolulu: University of Hawai'i Press.

OTHER MODERN
JAPANESE
PHILOSOPHIES

CHAPTER 23

···

WATSUJI TETSURŌ

The Mutuality of Climate and Culture and an Ethics of Betweenness

···

ERIN MCCARTHY

WATSUJI TETSURŌ (1889–1960) was a contemporary of the Kyoto School of Japanese philosophy's founder Nishida Kitarō (1870–1945). While considered by some to be on the fringes of the Kyoto School, he was invited by Nishida to teach the ethics courses at Kyoto Imperial University in 1925, and he became a professor there in 1931. In 1934, he became a professor at Tokyo Imperial University where he remained until his retirement in 1949. As was typical of the period in Japan, Watsuji was educated in the Western philosophical tradition. He wrote his graduating thesis for Tokyo Imperial University on Schopenhauer, he was early on deeply interested in Nietzsche and Kierkegaard and published work on each of them, and he subsequently engaged in a study of the philosophical anthropology and phenomenology of his day, especially that of Scheler and Heidegger.[1] But Watsuji also devoted time to Japanese thought and Buddhism; he wrote books on the intellectual history of Japan and on early Buddhism, and his book *Shamon Dōgen* was responsible for reviving modern interest in the medieval Zen monk and philosopher Dōgen in Japan beyond Sōtō Zen temples.[2]

What can be considered Watsuji's first major philosophical work, *Fūdo* (風土) or *Climate and Culture*, was written in 1929 and published in 1935.[3] *Fūdo* also initiated Watsuji's critique of Western individualism, which he first formulated during a trip to Germany in 1927 when he read Heidegger's *Being and Time*. In it, he develops his philosophical interpretation of the traditional Japanese concept of *fūdo* or *milieu*

---

[1] For more on Watsuji's life and career, see Carter and McCarthy 2014.

[2] *Shamon Dōgen* (Watsuji 2011) was published in the series *Nihon seishinshi kenkyū* (*A Study of the History of the Japanese Spirit*), the first volume appearing in 1925 and the second in 1935.

[3] The English translation of *Fūdo* is only of the first half of the book. The rest of the book goes into more detail on the monsoon climates/cultures of China and Japan, looks at art in terms of climate (*fūdo*), and finally surveys the study of climate in Europe, with a focus on Herder and Hegel.

(initially translated into English as "climate"). His discussion lays the groundwork for his concept of ethics and self as *ningen*, the core of his later work. In all his work, Watsuji encourages us to think about our place in the network of relationships comprising our world. Drawing inspiration from Dōgen and the Buddhist concept of co-dependent origination, he emphasizes the extent to which we are all embedded in a network of relationships from the moment we are born—not just human relationships, but also relationships with our planet. We are not solitary individuals but rather beings of what Watsuji calls "betweenness" (*aidagara* 間柄).

WATSUJI'S CRITIQUE OF HEIDEGGER

Fūdo broke new philosophical ground for its emphasis on relationality and spatiality, in contrast to the emphasis on the individual and temporality in Heidegger's *Being and Time*. "I found myself intrigued," Watsuji wrote, "by the attempt to treat the structure of man's existence in terms of time but I found it hard to see why, when time had thus been made to play a part in the structure of subjective existence, at the same juncture space also was not postulated as part of the basic structure of existence."[4] His critique points out an undue subordination of spatiality to temporality in Heidegger's phenomenological description of being-in-the-world, one that Heidegger himself recants and corrects long after *Being and Time*.[5]

From the outset of *Being and Time*, Heidegger had made it clear that temporality is the key to the phenomenological analysis of being-in-the-world. The human being—Da-sein—is to be elucidated first and foremost in temporal terms. And Da-sein's spatiality is clearly subordinated to its temporality. As he wrote:

> Time must be brought to light and genuinely grasped as the horizon of every under-standing and interpretation of being. For this to become clear we need an *original explication of time as the horizon of the understanding of being, in terms of temporality as the being of Da-sein which understands being.*[6]

For Heidegger, temporality reigns supreme in understanding being, and it is this that Watsuji singles out for criticism—the imbalance that results from the prioritizing of temporality over spatiality. Heidegger's, and in general the West's, emphasis on the

---

[4] Watsuji 1988, v.

[5] "The attempt in Being and Time, section 70, to derive human spatiality from temporality is untenable" (Martin Heidegger, "On Time and Being," translated by Joan Stambaugh (New York: Harper & Row, 1972, 23). On Heidegger's later conception of the spatiality of human existence, see, for example, "Building Dwelling Thinking," translated by Albert Hofstadter, in *Poetry, Language, Thought* (New York: Harper and Row, 1971, 143–162). See also McCarthy 2000.

[6] Martin Heidegger, *Being and Time*, translated by Joan Stambaugh (Albany: SUNY Press, 1996, 15/17). References to *Being and Time* are given with German followed by English pagination.

individual nature of human being meant that the concepts of human being arising out of this emphasis, Da-sein among them, lost "touch completely with the vast network of interconnections that serves to make us what we are, as individuals inescapably immersed in the space/time of a world, together with others."[7] As Bret Davis explains, by "spatiality" Watsuji meant in part "a more radical notion of what Heidegger calls 'being-with' (*Mitsein*): the originary sociality or betweenness' (*aidagara*) of human beings."[8]

While in his later work Heidegger moved toward a greater recognition of the importance of relations for the self, his concept of self in *Being and Time* had indeed overly emphasized the individual.[9] Even though he states that "the understanding of others already lies in the understanding of being of Da-sein because its being is being-with,"[10] for the most part Da-sein is not in the world in such a way that it recognizes this understanding of others. Despite breaking with the tradition of positing an isolated subject as the starting point of philosophical investigation into human being in the world—being-with *is* a part of Da-sein after all—"his analysis of Dasein in *Being and Time* leads back insistently to the solitary self."[11] Whereas for Heidegger, being-with-others in the they, *das Man*, hides the true nature of Da-sein, its authentic individuality, for Watsuji being-with-others is part of the *authentic* nature of being human.

While formulating his critique of Heidegger, Watsuji also began to reflect more deeply on the unique qualities of Japanese thought. He began to take a more critical view of the emphasis on the individual not only in Heidegger's work, but in Western thought more generally.

Without taking spatiality into account, Watsuji maintained, Heidegger would not be able to come up with a satisfying account of what it is to be a human-being-in-the-world, one which includes *both* the individual and relational aspects of being-in-the world. Thus began Watsuji's development of the concept that is at the root of his philosophy— the human being as *ningen* (人間)—a relational, embodied, embedded sense of self which takes into account the individual, the spatiality of her relationships, and also the

---

[7] Carter 1996, 329. For a more detailed discussion of how a focus on temporality leads to individuality, particularly in the work of Heidegger and Husserl, see McCarthy 2010. For a discussion of how temporality has led to individuality in the Anglo-American tradition, see Paul Ricoeur, *Oneself As Another* (Chicago: University of Chicago Press, 1992), particularly the introduction.

[8] Davis 2013, 462.

[9] As Carolyn Culbertson points out, in a lecture course prior to the publication of *Being and Time*, *Die Grundbegriffe der aristotelischen Philosophie*, Heidegger had given more attention to the social dimensions of human existence. Watsuji seems to have been unaware of this course, and such attention to this does not appear in *Being and Time*. (Culbertson, "The Genuine Possibility of Being-with: Watsuji, Heidegger, and the Primacy of Betweenness," unpublished paper, presented at *The Heidegger Circle*, Baltimore, MD, 2014).

[10] Heidegger, *Being and Time*, 116/123.

[11] Christopher Fynsk, *Heidegger: Thought and Historicity* (Ithaca: Cornell University Press, 1986), 28. See also, *Being and Time*: "The nonrelational character of death understood in anticipation individualizes Da-sein down to itself. . . . It reveals the fact that any being-together-with what is taken care of and any being-with the others fails when one's ownmost potentiality-of-being is at stake. Da-sein can *authentically* be *itself* only when it makes that possible of its own accord" (243/263).

geographical/climatological and cultural places and spaces, the *fūdo*—the Japanese word meaning "climate-and-culture"—or *milieu* in which she lives and interacts.

By virtue of relegating spatiality to something dependent on temporality in *Being and Time*, Heidegger missed a key aspect of selfhood that the inclusion of spatiality reveals: betweenness, a central element of *ningen*. Once one admits the irreducible spatiality of human beings, the concept of self that arises could never be that of the purely individual consciousness because spatiality includes relationship as fundamental to selfhood.

NINGEN AND BETWEENNESS

In *Fūdo* (*Climate and Culture*), we find the first articulation of what Watsuji later labels *ningen*. He explains that by "human being" he means:

> not the individual (anthropos, homo, homme, etc.) but man both in this individual sense and at the same time man in society, the combination of the association of man. This duality is the essential nature of man . . . . For a true and full understanding, one must treat man both as individual and as whole.[12]

This is the root of Watsuji's notion of *ningen*, the focus of what is perhaps his best known work in English, *Ethics* (*Rinrigaku*). The Japanese character for *ningen* (人間),[13] discussed further by Robert Carter in his chapter in this volume, is made up of two characters: the character for "person," 人; and for "between," 間. This signifies that, as *ningen*, we are both individual and social *at the same time*. As Watsuji conceives it: "*ningen* is the public and, at the same time, the individual human beings living within it. Therefore, it refers not merely to an individual 'human being' nor merely to 'society.' What is recognizable here is a dialectical unity of those double characteristics that are inherent in a human being."[14] For Watsuji, this dialectical unity implies that the self is dynamic insofar as it comprises both individual and social aspects and, as *ningen*, one continually moves back and forth between these two characteristics—neither one has priority over the other.

Watsuji's betweenness goes beyond what we might think of as intersubjectivity—a relation among separate centers of consciousness of the sort found, for example, in the philosophy of Edmund Husserl. As Watsuji makes clear in *Ethics*:

> Betweenness is quite distinct from the intentionality of consciousness. Activity inherent in the consciousness of an "I" is never determined by this "I" alone but is also determined by others. It is not merely a reciprocal activity in that one way conscious

---

[12] Watsuji 1988, 8–9.
[13] Watsuji 1996.
[14] Watsuji 1996, 15.

activities are performed one after another, but, rather, that either one of them is at once determined by both sides; that is, by itself and by the other. Hence, so far as betweenness-oriented existences are concerned, each consciousness interpenetrates the other.[15]

This dialectical unity in betweenness means that, due to the communal or social aspect of *ningen*, we merge with others, they are part of us. Yet, due to the individual aspect of *ningen*, we also emerge out of this merger, are transformed in some way as an individual, only to move back again into relationship. Neither the social nor the individual is more basic to *ningen*. Literally, *ningen* means "between persons," which is a very helpful way to think about Watsuji's concept. *Ningen* is not to be understood as a thing or substance but more like a place or space—yet a fluid, not a fixed place. It is a shifting network of relations that are continually reconfigured in time and space. While fully developed in *Ethics*, this idea has its roots in *Fūdo*.

Fūdo or *Climate and Culture*

In *Fūdo*, Watsuji insists that the betweenness that permeates our being-in-the-world encompasses both human beings (*ningen*) and living nature as well as the world of things. While it is true that in later work on ethics, Watsuji focuses more on the relatedness among human beings, it remains the case that in his ethics, "the individual must be conceived as being situated in a spatial field of relatedness or betweenness not only to human society, but also to a surrounding climate ... of living nature as the ultimate extension of embodied subjective space in which man dwells."[16]

In the first paragraph of the preface to *Fūdo*, Watsuji explains how he understands *fūdo*, "literally 'Wind and Earth' in Japanese,"[17] by drawing an important distinction between climate (*fūdo*) and environment:

> Natural environment is usually understood as an objective extension of "human climate" regarded as a concrete basis. But when we come to consider the relationship between this and human life, the latter is already objectified, with the result that we find ourselves examining the relation between object and object, and there is no link with subjective human existence. ... *it is essential to my position that the phenomena of climate are treated as expressions of subjective human existence and not of natural environment.*[18]

[15] Watsuji 1996, 77.
[16] Steve Odin, "The Japanese Concept of Nature in Relation to the Environmental Ethics and Conservation Aesthetics of Aldo Leopold," *Environmental Ethics* 13 (1991): 351.
[17] Watsuji 1988, 1.
[18] Watsuji 1988, v, emphasis added.

Watsuji distinguishes his interpretation of *fūdo* from what he maintained was its then conventional understanding simply as a term used for natural environment—something that is a resource to be used, or an object separate from or merely alongside our being-in-the-world. He thinks this understanding of *fūdo* merely as an object keeps us apart from our surroundings and, as a result, apart from the fullness of our experience as human beings. Properly construed, *fūdo*, misunderstood by us, according to Watsuji, as "natural environment" only is neither object nor subject, but rather a relation of betweenness—the betweenness of relationships with others as well as betweenness with nature and the world of things. *Fūdo* is at once the ground out of which our self-apprehension arises and, at the same time, an expression of this very self. As Watsuji's last student, Yuasa Yasuo, notes: "Space, prior to a particular subject's spatial experience, exists first (even historically) as the life-space, endowed with various human meanings."[19] In other words, space as a container, or environment considered as something without human subjects in it, is merely an abstraction. When viewed as a subject of inquiry in the natural sciences, environment is analyzed in terms of relations between objects in ways that abstract from our actual experience of space, an experience that is never empty of meanings created by human beings.[20] *Fūdo*, as Watsuji conceives it, cannot be objectified, nor is it merely subjective. It cannot and should not be pinned down as either subject or object, and the relationship between human beings and *fūdo* remains reciprocal. The French geographer Augustin Berque argues that, for Watsuji, there is no human being except under the conditions of *fūdo* and reciprocally, that *fūdo* doesn't exist without human beings in it,[21] for, as we saw earlier, *fūdo* is an expression of "subjective human existence." It is a mutually constituting or co-constituting relationship or interdependence.

In order to more faithfully convey Watsuji's notion of *fūdo*, Berque suggests "milieu" as a more preferable translation than "climate" (as was used in the English translation of the book). *Milieu* more accurately captures the mutual co-constituting at the heart of *fūdo* than the term "climate," which too easily implies the understanding of *fūdo* that Watsuji rejects—the idea of climate as mere object, as something outside of and apart from human beings. For Watsuji, the notion of *fūdo* is supposed to suggest that the spatial, environmental, and collective aspects of human existence are all intertwined in the complex concepts of *fūdosei* or mediance.[22] Etymologically, *milieu* can be traced back to "middle," but it later came to mean one's surroundings, including the environmental and social.[23] The term *milieu* thus better reflects the multiplicity of relationships at work in our relationships both with each other and the places we inhabit that Watsuji analyzes in *Fūdo*. Furthermore, Watsuji stresses that experience associated with inhabiting places

[19] Yuasa 1987, 40.

[20] Berque 1994, 497.

[21] Berque 1994, 498.

[22] Berque 1994, 498.

[23] Oxford English Dictionary online: http://www.oed.com/view/Entry/118407?redirectedFrom=Mili eu#eid.

is inescapably spatial—it is connected with embodied lives lived in particular locations under particular conditions.[24] *Milieu* affects who we are and how, in turn, we affect the spaces and places in which we live. This reciprocal connection involves a cycle that is ongoing, never complete. As Berque observes, Watsuji's concept of *milieu* is more intimately knitted into human being than is the notion of "environment." A milieu is woven out of relations that form the foundation of the existence of the human being as subject.[25] The concept of *milieu* also reflects the importance of betweenness in Wastuji's philosophy—and these relations, we recall, are not merely relations among people, but also relations between people and nature, between people and the world of things in which they live—and the multiplicity of these relations between people and their world is facilitated through their embodied existence.

EMBODIMENT

A crucial aspect of both *ningen* and *milieu* is embodiment. Watsuji, like Heidegger, wanted to avoid the dualism associated with the mind–body problem. He was not so much concerned with questions of mind–body causation or the relation of disparate substances. For him, dualism should be rejected because it does not serve self-understanding. While, as I argue elsewhere,[26] Heidegger chose to ignore the body as a problem, Watsuji takes a different approach: "the crux of the problem becomes the

---

[24] The most unique, enduring, and groundbreaking aspects of *Fūdo* which I focus on here, lie in the introduction and the first chapter. As for the individual studies of climate that follow, I acknowledge that they can seem to tend toward traditional geographic determinism, where the traits of natural climate are seen to determine the traits of the society. Augustin Berque, for example, points out that Watsuji seems to fall prey to the very view he is trying to argue against for, in his analyses of climates, he does seem to do what he expressly states he will not—that is, analyze natural climate and its influence on a people. See Augustin Berque, *Vivre l'espace au Japon* (Paris: PUF, 1982, 496). However, this critique may be too hasty. While it is perhaps true that Watsuji overemphasizes the one direction of climate's influence on culture in the body of the work, his whole point, as he makes clear in the conclusion of *Fūdo*, is that, in becoming aware of climatic influence, we are in a better position to *not* be one-sidedly determined by climate. In the concluding pages of the second part of *Climate and Culture*, Watsuji clearly states (the following passages are from Watsuji 1992, 8:119–120, translated by Bret Davis; the corresponding passages in the existing translation can be found in Watsuji 1988, 116–117): "But I do not claim that this climate was the sole source of European culture. History and climate act as the shield and buckler of culture." And a bit further on: "When humans become aware of the deep roots of their existence and express this awareness in an objective manner, the manner of that expression is not only historically but also climatically determined." Moreover, Watsuji stresses that we can *both* "discover climate within a historical event" *and* "read history within climatic phenomena." Finally, he points out that in this study he has "*focused on the perspective of climate*"; that is, on the heretofore neglected side of this relation of mutual influence, so we can see that Watsuji was deliberate in his focus on this one side of the relation and was not, in fact, unaware of the other side. (I am grateful to Bret Davis for pointing me to these passages and for retranslating them.)

[25] Berque 1994, 497, my translation.

[26] See McCarthy 2010, particularly chapter 2.

realisation that body is not mere matter; in other words, it is the problem of the self-active nature of the body."[27] As he urges, the body cannot be pinned down as mere matter, as an object or tool for the mind; rather, mind and body work in concert. It is a "both/and" rather than an "either-or" relationship—that is, body is part of self just as much as mind. He goes on to state that the "self-active nature of the body has as its foundation the spatial and temporal structure of human life; a self-active body cannot remain in isolation for its structure is dynamic, uniting in isolation and isolated within union."[28] Properly understood as body-mind, the self (as *ningen*) is not an atomistic isolated individual. Every individual body-mind is part of a human community and thus in betweenness with other body-minds. For Watsuji, then, the body is an inherent part of human being-in-the-world. This being-in-the-world encompasses spatiality not only in the form of our own bodies, the bodies through which we experience ourselves and others, but also in the embodied betweenness—that is, the embodied being-with other human beings in *milieu*. This is reinforced when he tells us that

> in its most fundamental significance, the relation between body and spirit lies in the relation between the body and the spirit of "man in his social relationships," the individual and social body-spirit relation which includes the relationship with history and climate.[29]

Our embodied nature thus extends beyond what we normally consider to be corporeal boundaries to include betweenness with nature, the world of things, history, and relationships with other human beings. As *ningen,* we relate to both *milieu* and to other human beings through our bodies. If we take Watsuji's nondualism seriously, we see our body as an extension of ourselves (rather than our "selves" as somehow transcending the body) and view it as including and extending out into an intimate part of the *milieu* in which we live. Commenting on dualistic philosophies that leave out this integral part of human existence on this planet, Watsuji writes: "Climate, too, as part of man's body, was regarded like the body as mere matter, and so came to be viewed objectively as mere natural environment. So the self-active nature of climate must be retrieved in the same sense that the self-active nature of the body has to be retrieved."[30] As we will see in more detail later, dualistic philosophies that separate time from space, mind from body, humans from *milieu* serve to devalue or subordinate the second term in the pair. Watsuji's *ningen* and *fūdo* correct this, not by reversing it, but by retrieving body and *milieu* as subjects as well as objects, giving us a fuller picture of human being in the world, one that is not limited by the constraints of a dualism that is exclusive but is rather embedded in a radical nondualism, rooted, as we will see, in the Buddhist concept of emptiness.

[27] Watsuji 1988, 11.
[28] Watsuji 1988, 11.
[29] Watsuji 1988, 12.
[30] Watsuji 1988, 12.

As noted in the discussion of *ningen*, the idea of betweenness is key for understanding Watsuji's ethics. *Ningen* is "a betweenness oriented being,"[31] and there are at least two layers of betweenness at work in *ningen* and *milieu*. The first is within the individual, where body and mind are not separate. The second is in relation to other humans and to living nature and the world of things in the betweenness of our relationships, all of which are mediated through the body. Discovery of *milieu* is likewise embodied, and Watsuji insists that from "the standpoint of the individual, this becomes consciousness of the body."[32] But such discovery does not stop here: rather, *milieu* continues to reveal itself through the embodied individual's actions—"in the ways of creating communities, and thus in the ways of constructing speech, the methods of production, the styles of building, and so on."[33] Understanding *milieu*, and thus ourselves, is impossible without the body. As Berque also observes, the body is key for mediance, *fūdosei*. According to Berque, Watsuji calls *fūdosei* the "structural moment of human existence." Berque views this as: "the dynamic coupling of two terms, one of which is our animal body, and the other is our social body—I prefer to say our *medial body* (i.e., milieu), because it is not only technical and symbolic, but necessarily also ecological, since it imprints itself into, and is conditioned by, the ecosystems of the biosphere. It is—a human milieu is—eco-techno-symbolic; and this is precisely why human milieu must be differentiated from that mere environment."[34] For Watsuji, *milieu* goes far beyond environment understood from an objective standpoint and encompasses—indeed *is*—an intimate interweaving of self, nature, and the world of things we create and inhabit.

WATSUJI'S NONDUALISM: ROOTED IN EMPTINESS

Watsuji's nondualistic concepts of self and *milieu* stand in sharp contrast to dominant Western notions of self (and ethics), which are dualistic. A view is dualistic if it conceives of the self, and consequently the world, in terms of the dichotomies of mind and body, self and other, and so on. Dualists typically locate the self in some subset of the elements of human being (such as reason, individual consciousness, the brain, or an individual soul) and view these core elements as more authentically human than the others and thereby worthy of more weight, authority, or value. On such a view, cultivation of these elements of the self is essential to becoming fully human in a way that the development of the other elements is not. This sort of view takes the remaining elements to be, if not inimical to human development, at best ancillary to it.

[31] Watsuji 1996, 117.
[32] Watsuji 1988, 12.
[33] Watsuji 1988, 12.
[34] Berque 2004, 392.

Nondualism, on the other hand, rejects the sharp distinctions between body and mind, self and other, and subject and object. In each case, we recall, it is a matter of both/and rather than either/or. That is, nondualism allows for difference to be retained even as it is transcended—in other words, nondualism is not the same as monism or holism, neither the whole nor its parts are given priority. In Watsuji's view then, self is constituted by both mind and body at the same time, and neither is more important or fundamental to the self than the other. Watsuji's nondualistic concept of self also views each person's ethical identity as integrally related to that of others and extends it beyond merely human relations. Self and other, self and nature, are viewed as inseparable from ethical identity and are related to, rather than viewed as opposed to or exclusive of each other.[35] In Watsuji's *ningen*, we find this nondualism lived out in ways that extend ethical identity beyond relations between human beings to encompass the world in which we live—it is part of *milieu*.

Transcending dualities is a fundamental aspect of *ningen*. It implies both the dissolving of individual into community, of self into other, and, at the same time, the resolution of community into the individual, with self being co-constituted by and in community, with both movements proceeding at the same time in a process of construction-deconstruction-reconstruction. For Watsuji, one is not fully human or ethical until one acknowledges the dynamic tension between the individual and social aspects of *ningen* and the necessity of continuing to move between the two poles; that is, negating the individual (collapsing the difference between self and other) and negating the social so as to reassert one's status as an individual. *Ningen* is thus a back-and-forth movement of what Watsuji calls "double negation" (*nijū hitei* 二重否定).[36] As he puts it, "the negative structure of a betweenness-oriented being is clarified in terms of the self-returning movement of absolute negativity through its own negation."[37] Watsuji's talk of self in terms of constant negating of negation might sound nihilistic. In fact, it is anything but. He conceives the self as something rich and dynamic and, contrary to nihilism, as fundamentally linked to others even while at the same time being distinct from them. We can relate both this notion of emptiness or negation in Watsuji's *ningen* and the interdependence we find in his betweenness philosophy of *ningen* and *milieu* to the Mahāyāna Buddhist notions of co-dependent origination and emptiness.

Co-dependent origination means that everything is intricately interconnected and thus that the idea of the independent existence of anything at all, including the supposedly independent existence of the self is, in fact, empty. Genuine existence is dynamic and relational, and realizing this requires letting go of the false idea of the self as an independent, permanent entity. Out of co-dependent origination, then, emerges the notion of no-self (Sk. *anātman*; Jp. *muga* 無我), which we can also see reflected in Watsuji's *ningen*, clearly influenced by his study of Buddhism generally and of Dōgen in particular. The Buddhist belief is that there is no permanent, independent, abiding

---

[35] For more on this, see Chapter 34 in this volume.
[36] See Watsuji 1996, chapter 6.
[37] Watsuji 1996, 117.

self. For practical purposes, we may identify our "selves" as such, but a closer examination reveals that, in fact, there is no *permanent* and *independent* self. What we normally consider to be permanent and as having independent existence is illusory—it is but a construction or a delusion.[38] As we have seen, Watsuji's *ningen* is constantly in flux, never fixed or permanent, continually moving between the poles of individual and social, never, ideally, getting stuck at one pole or the other. For Watsuji, the structure of *ningen*, the betweenness, is emptiness (Sk. *śūnyatā*; Jp. *kū* 空), and this is what provides the ground for the interconnectedness or interdependence of *ningen* that manifests in milieu.

In *Fūdo*, after he articulates the dual nature of what will in his later work be termed *ningen*, Watsuji emphasizes nonduality and emptiness, writing that for "a true and full understanding, one must treat man both as individual and as whole; it is only when the analysis of human existence is made from this viewpoint that it becomes evident that this existence is completely and absolutely negative activity."[39] Watsuji further develops this idea in *Ethics*, where he identifies three moments that the negation or emptiness inherent in *ningen* encompasses: "fundamental emptiness, then individual existence, and social existence as its negative development. These three are interactive with one another in practical reality and cannot be separated. They are at work constantly in the practical interconnection of acts and can in no way be stabilized fixedly at any place."[40] Even though, as Watsuji himself states, these three moments are constantly interactive and inseparable from one another, I will try to elucidate what he means by each. Let's start with individual existence. For Watsuji, the individual has no determinate identity in herself. As he puts it: "Individual persons do not subsist in themselves."[41] Rather, they exist in the between. *Ningen*, as we have seen, implies interdependence both with other human beings and with *milieu*, so the idea of the individual, isolated human being is, in fact, empty (as is the idea of the "environment" or "nature" as an object set apart from what constitutes being human on Watsuji's view). Yet, the individual does exist, by negating the group, by distinguishing itself from those with whom it exists in the between, by stepping away from the group, from that particular *milieu*. One defines oneself as separate or apart from the group, as distinct from it. Think of a toddler beginning to establish her own identity by pushing away, separating herself from her parents with the constant stream of "no," for example. However, in establishing herself by negating the group, the individual *at the same time* admits that there *is* a group to which she is related. So, the individual is also negated in this very act of asserting herself as separate. She admits that she is part of the group, part of the between, which is to negate or deny her existence as an isolated individual.

There is, however, another aspect of emptiness at work here, an aspect which grounds *ningen*. This is the fundamental emptiness that exists in the between, where self and

---

[38] Carter 1996, 350.
[39] Watsuji 1988, 9.
[40] Watsuji 1996, 117.
[41] Watsuji 1996, 101.

other momentarily cease to exist, where the dualism of subject and object is overcome. As noted earlier, the notion of fundamental emptiness at play here comes out of the tradition of Mahāyāna Buddhism. In Buddhism, emptiness is not a void that needs to be filled; rather, it is the source for all being and beings. Even emptiness itself is not something permanent for it, too, is devoid of unchanging characteristics. Whereas a dualistic system is hierarchical and fixed, the flux and impermanence inherent in nondualism precludes such a fixed hierarchy. It thus limits subjugation or domination of one element over another—be it people or nature. On this nondualist view of relation, the becoming of the self is never completed because, according to the doctrine of "no-self," there is no eternal, independently existing self. And yet, each individual is a unique combination of what the Buddha called the five *skandha*s or aggregates (material form, feeling, perception, volitional impulses, consciousness). As such, the embodied form of the particular combination of aggregates matters, so there *is* difference. Emptiness is what makes the subject–object relation, or better, the relation both inherent in *ningen* and between *ningen* possible—for now we must see each subject in its particularity without having to close off its becoming. Thus, difference is not only maintained but fostered. As the Zen saying goes, nonduality is a matter of "not one, not two." And, as Taigen Dan Leighton explains, discussing Dōgen's philosophy, "nonduality is not about transcending the duality of form and emptiness. This deeper nonduality is not the opposite of duality, but the synthesis of duality and nonduality, with both included, and both seen as ultimately not separate, but as integrated."[42] Accordingly, there is still room in this view for difference, but not a difference fixed for all time because all things—selves included—are in flux.

In emptiness, everything is there in its distinctive radiance. Each individual thing—be it a person, a rock, a tree, a mountain, or a blade of grass—appears in its absolute uniqueness: the body, the other, the self. And yet, *prajñā* (wisdom) entails insight into the fact that these things are *at the same time* empty of independent existence. So, emptiness is not a nihilistic idea; rather, it is at the root of everything that exists. It is what allows us to be *ningen* and, as such, is beyond the dualism of individual and social, or human and nature. Just as the individual does not subsist in herself alone, the whole does not subsist in itself. Rather, as Watsuji explains, the whole "appears only in the form of the restriction or negation of the individual."[43]

Ningen continually performs this double movement of negation of the individual and negation of the social whole. This process of becoming never comes to a standstill if one is being *ningen*. If it does, betweenness—and thus the basis of ethics—collapses. If it continues, however, "the movement of the negation of absolute negativity is, at the same time, the continuous creation of human beings."[44] Watsuji maintains that this is the fundamental structure of our existence as ethical human beings. For him, as long as we are being fully human, we are continually becoming. As we saw in the earlier explanation of

---

[42] Taigen Dan Leighton, "Dōgen's Cosmology of Space and the Practice of Self-Fulfillment," *Pacific World* 6 (2004): 35.

[43] Watsuji 1996, 99.

[44] Watsuji 1996, 117–118.

milieu, we are always influencing the world and people we come into contact with, and the world and people we are in the between with are influencing our individual selves and our *milieu*. As Watsuji sees it, being human as *ningen* is not a matter of belonging to a community at the expense of one's individual identity or being an individual at the expense of forging meaningful bonds with others. Concrete human existence, Watsuji argues, is neither an individualistic experience nor an experience of being completely dissolved into society.[45] For him, "*ningen* is the public and, at the same time, the individual human beings living within it."[46] While the concept of relationality is certainly foregrounded in Watsuji's ethics, *neither* of these dimensions of human-being-in-the-world—not the individual nor the social—is privileged in *ningen*. What is more, *ningen* encompasses relations not only between humans, but also between humans and the *milieus* we inhabit.

MILIEU, *NINGEN*, AND ENVIRONMENTAL ETHICS

Augustin Berque has noted the significance of Watsuji's work for rethinking environmental ethics. He maintains that there are two basic approaches in environmental

---

[45] It should be noted that while here I argue for a view of *ningen* where neither individual nor communal takes precedence, as presented in *Rinrigaku* and *Fudō*, in Watsuji's overtly political writings, this is a bit more problematic as he does seem to give more weight to the social whole. See, for example, the essay "The Way of the Japanese Subject" (*Nihon no shindō*, 1944, in English in *A Source Book for Modern Japanese Philosophy*). We do know that, in 1925, the newly formed "*Genri Nipponsha*" or "Japan Principle Society,"whose "founding purpose was to 'denounce democracy and Marxism, both of which go against the spirit of the Japanese national polity'" singled Watsuji out, among others, for being "liberal, pro-democracy, and pro-individualism, and thus 'dangerous' in the eyes of the ultranationalists" (Michiko Yusa "Nishida and Totalitarianism," in *Rude Awakenings: Zen the Kyoto School and the question of Nationalism*, edited by James W. Heisig and John C. Maraldo. Honolulu: University of Hawai'i Press 1994, 119–120). We also know that Nishida was heartened in 1938 that Watsuji was to be on a Ministry of Education "Committee for the Renewal of Education and Scholarship," where he felt they could make their views regarding the period of fascism in the country known. And we know that Watsuji added his voice of support to Nishida's explicit criticism of the aims of the committee. Furthermore, when Tsuda Sōkichi was attacked by the nationalistic right, when his works were banned and he was forced into retirement from teaching in 1940, Watsuji "was among those to defend Tsuda's scholarship during the court trial that resulted" (Minamoto Ryōen "The Symposium on 'Overcoming Modernity,'" in *Rude Awakenings*, 201). Nonetheless, "The Way of the Japanese Subject" is problematic. As Robert Bellah points out, "The humane and gracious figure of Watsuji Tetsurō would not be problematic for Modern Japan were it not for the fact that partly behind the cloak of just such thinking as his, a profoundly pathological social movement brought Japan near to total disaster" (Bellah 1965, 593–594). For his part, John Maraldo maintains that the question of whether Watsuji's work "encouraged subservience to the state, or rather implied resistance (passive and covert to be sure), must remain an open question" (Maraldo 2002, 192–193). For more on Watsuji's politics, see Arima 1969, Sevilla 2014, and Lafleur 1994 and 2001.

[46] Watsuji 1996, 15.

ethics, and "these positions extend between two theoretical extremes, one of which would be humanity's subordination to the biosphere, and the other subordination of environmental issues to humanity's interests. In general the first set of views is labeled holism and the second anthropocentrism."[47] Environmental ethics, he goes on to say, "comes up against a basic *aporia* as soon as it is developed a little further: at one and the same time acknowledging that in a sense the human transcends nature and that in another sense the second subsumes the first."[48] Environmental ethics has not thus far been able to bridge these two theoretical extremes. Yet Berque thinks Watsuji's insights can provide us with an alternative to both views. Watsuji's concepts of *milieu* and *ningen* give us a way to rethink selfhood in a way that takes us beyond the *aporia* because we are not forced to take sides in these untenable debates.[49] In fact, Berque diagnoses the problem—that is, the problem of being forced to choose between setting humans apart from nature or erasing any difference between humans and nature—as arising out of dualism:

> This *aporia* arose from the fact that a being limited by the individual horizon of the Cartesian "I", and even Heidegger's *Dasein*, cannot structurally operate a moral rule requiring that one take account of what is beyond that horizon: the *environment* (or *fūdo* in Watsuji's vocabulary), which, in time as well as space, goes beyond the modern individual's ontological *topos*. However, *seeing this context not as external to our being (in the form of the objectal environment), but as constituting it no less fundamentally than the identity of our topos*, allows us to carry out a decentering process that is as decisive as the one that inaugurated modern times—the Copernican revolution.[50]

To take Berque's idea further, Watsuji's philosophy allows us to "decenter" the self. On his view nature or the environment, from the perspective of *ningen* and *milieu* is *neither outside of us nor identical to us*. In fact, this is a view that characterizes the human/nature relationship in much of Japanese thought. In this, Watsuji is allied with the feminist environmental philosopher Val Plumwood. In her groundbreaking essay, "Nature, Self, and Gender: Feminism, Environmental Philosophy and the Critique of Rationalism," she notes that environmental ethics faces a key problem: "the view of nature as sharply discontinuous or ontologically divided from the human sphere [which leads to the view of] humans as apart from or 'outside of' nature usually as masters or external controllers of it."[51] In other words, like Watsuji and Berque, she sees the dualistic approach of environmental ethics that puts humans outside of and above nature as deeply problematic.

---

[47] Berque 2005, 6.

[48] Berque 2005, 6–7.

[49] Berque 2005, 10.

[50] Berque 2005, 10, emphasis added.

[51] Valerie Plumwood, "Nature Self and Gender: Feminism, Environmental Philosophy and the Critique of Rationalism," *Hypatia* 6.1/1991: 10.

At the same time, she critiques the holistic view of deep ecology along lines similar to Berque, though from a feminist perspective.

Like many other feminist philosophers, Plumwood observes that the traditional dualism of man and nature can be mapped onto the homologous hierarchical dichotomies of male–female, reason–emotion, and so on.[52] In these dichotomies, we recall, each side is set up in opposition to the other, and one term in the pair is always devalued or subordinated to the other. As Plumwood points out, the dominant mode of analysis is reason, and women and nature have been denied possession of such a faculty: "It is in the name of such a reason that these other things—the feminine, the emotional, the merely bodily or the merely animal, and the natural world itself—have most often been denied their virtue and been accorded an inferior and merely instrumental position."[53] This echoes Watsuji's critique of the term "environment" as something outside of the world of human experience. And his main point of contention with dualism echoes that of feminist philosophers and Berque: dualism tends to privilege one of the two dichotomous terms over the other: time over space, mind over body, subject over object, man over woman, self over other, human over nature. Plumwood calls for a concept of self "that enables a recognition of interdependence and relationship without falling into the problems of indistinguishability, that acknowledges both continuity and difference, and that breaks the culturally posed false dichotomy of egoism ... it bypasses both masculine 'separation' and traditional-feminine 'merger' accounts of the self."[54] Watsuji's *fūdo* and *ningen* provide a framework for just such an account of self. On his view of *ningen* and *milieu,* one's individuality is preserved even though it is essentially influenced and informed by another (be it nature or other human beings—by *milieu*). On this view, autonomy and difference do not need to be understood apart from human relationships, the body, or nature.[55] In fact, this nonduality between self, nature, and freedom can be found throughout Japanese thought. For example, as Bret Davis explains, "the freedom (*jiyū* 自由) of the self (*jiko* 自己) is thought to accord with—rather than stand in opposition to—the naturalness (*jinen* 自然) of nature (shizen 自然) .... In taking part in nature, one is naturally free."[56] Nature includes the human, but, at the same time, this does not mean, in Japanese thought, that nature is identical with the human. We can see how this idea threads its way through Watsuji's nondualism. Of particular interest for environmental philosophy is Watsuji's view of how *ningen* (as well as Zen's "not one, not two") works to avoid both the "separation" and "merger" accounts that Berque and feminist environmental philosophers like Plumwood find so troubling. As Davis puts it, "The true self is a part of nature, but it is a part that dynamically stands out from and

---

[52] For more on human/nature nondualism in Japanese philosophy in general, see Chapter 33 in this volume.

[53] Plumwood 1991, 6.

[54] Plumwood 1991, 20.

[55] For more on this, see McCarthy 2010, particularly chapter 4.

[56] Chapter 33 in this volume.

returns to nature. Natural freedom is not a static state of being, but rather a dynamic dialectic of existence and return."[57]

In deep ecology, according to Plumwood, one view of the self is that it is indistinguishable from nature.[58] This, she argues, obliterates important distinctions: "we need to recognize not only our own human continuity with the natural world but also its distinctness and independence from us and the distinctness of the needs of things in nature from ours."[59] Many feminist philosophers are suspicious of this merger or "indistinguishability" account of self and nature, where humans are no different from and do not stand apart in any way from nature. Caring for nature requires a sense of being different from it, or else my caring for nature (or the other) can become ego-driven rather than driven by genuine concern for the other. If differences are merely ignored, one subject would be subsumed by the other and denied its own distinctive subjectivity; in other words, on this view of self, nature's interests are too easily assimilated to my own. This is also partly what Plumwood is getting at when she critiques the merger account of self—too often, women have merged their needs, desires, identities with those they are in relationship with, thus losing a sense of their own subjectivity.[60] Since Watsuji's concepts of *ningen* and *milieu* are rooted in nonduality and emptiness, both relationality and difference, or individual subjectivities, can be preserved and even fostered in their interdependence. Watsuji's betweenness gives us a deep interconnection that does not require assuming identity with nature (something, Plumwood argues, that is impossible anyway).

As betweenness-oriented existences, however, we can maintain, indeed we *must* maintain and foster relationships or connections with nature, but not in ways which are exclusionary or permanent. Rather, from the perspective of *ningen*, one will see those connections as part of what guides us in our ethical decision-making. Using *ningen* and betweenness as a framework, we need not be stuck either in attachment (either assuming an identity with nature or assuming we are outside of it) or in an abstract universalism. On Watsuji's view, we must continually move between the poles of particular and universal, subject and community, and between the poles of self and other, not only in relations with other human beings such as marriage and friendship, but also in our relation to our *milieu*. What this means is that Watsuji's *ningen* and *milieu* avoids these pitfalls and gives a framework for what Plumwood seeks: the recognition of both humans (of all genders, if we enhance our reading of Watsuji with a feminist perspective) and nature as having inherent value and, at the same time, their own subjectivities. If one is truly being *ningen* in one's *milieu*, truly being ethical in all of the variety of "betweennesses" we inhabit on a daily basis, the individual is neither isolated nor subsumed by other individuals or the community at large. Furthermore, the individual neither subsumes

---

[57] Ibid.

[58] Plumwood argues that deep ecologists keep their definitions of self slippery and identifies three different concepts of self at work in deep ecology. See Plumwood 1991.

[59] Plumwood 1991, 13.

[60] For more on this, see McCarthy 2008, and Plumwood 1991, 14.

nor is subsumed by nature in the kind of relationship with the earth that Berque and feminist philosophers of the environment advocate.

As we have seen, Watsuji's concept of *milieu* clearly has the human being embedded in her surroundings. Plumwood states that on the "relational account, respect for the other results neither from the containment of self nor from a transcendence of self, but is an *expression* of self in relationship, not egoistic self as merged with the other but self as embedded in a network of essential relationships with distinct others."[61] This is precisely what happens in Watsuji's account of *milieu* and in human being as *ningen*. In *milieu*, we see that: "individuals are involved in nets of reciprocal relationships and suffer [undergo] constant change. ... In this sense, neither an individual nor society is something fixed. Instead, they determine each other while undergoing transformation."[62] On Watsuji's *ningen* model, self is clearly embedded in a network, is part of nature in the *milieu* that she inhabits, in the way which Plumwood seeks.

Drawing deeply on Buddhist, Chinese, and Japanese sources, Watsuji's work helps us advance toward an understanding of the relationality of human being that Western philosophy has only begun to fathom. While Continental, feminist, and environmental philosophies have struggled to find ways of thinking about selfhood, body, and nature in ways that avoid the pitfalls of dualism and essentialism, they have not been fully successful as these ideas are so well entrenched in most of Western philosophy. Watsuji's philosophy provides us with ways of thinking through who we are and how we inhabit our world in ways that are nondualistic and yet still allow for difference.

BIBLIOGRAPHY AND SUGGESTED READINGS

Abe, Masao. (1985) *Zen and Western Thought*, edited by William R. LaFleur. Honolulu: University of Hawai'i Press.

Arima, Tatsuo. (1969) *The Failure of Freedom: A Portrait of Modern Japanese Intellectuals.* Cambridge, MA: Harvard University Press.

Bellah, Robert N. (1965) "Japan's Cultural Identity: Some Reflections on the Work of Watsuji Tetsurō." *The Journal of Asian Studies* 24/4: 573–594.

Bernier, Bernard. (2001) "De l'ethique au nationalism et au totalitarianisme chez Heidegger et Watsuji." In *Approches Critiques de la pensée japonaise du XXe siècle (Critical Readings in Twentieth Century Japanese Thought)*, edited by Jacynthe Tremblay. Montréal: Les Presses de l'Université de Montréal, 109–162.

Bernier, Bernard. (2008) "Transcendence of the State in Watsuji's Ethics." In *Neglected Themes and Hidden Variations*, edited by Victor Sōgen Hori and Melissa Anne-Marie Curley. Nagoya: Nanzan Institute for Religion and Culture, 94–100.

Berque, Augustin. (1994) "Milieu et logique du lieu chez Watsuji." *Revue Philosophique de Louvain* 92/4: 495–507.

[61] Plumwood 1991, 20.
[62] Watsuji 1996, 109.

Berque, Augustin. (2004) "Offspring of Watsuji's theory of milieu (*Fūdo*)." *GeoJournal* 60: 389–396.

Berque, Augustin. (2005) "A Basis for Environmental Ethics." *Diogenes* 207: 148–151.

Carter, Robert E. (1996) "Interpretive Essay: Strands of Influence." In *Watsuji Tetsurō's Rinrigaku: Ethics in Japan*, translated and edited by Yamamoto Seisaku and Robert E. Carter. Albany: State University of New York Press, 325–354.

Carter, Robert E. (2001) *Encounter With Enlightenment: A Study of Japanese Ethics*. Albany: State University of New York Press.

Carter, Robert E. (2007) "Japanese Philosophy." In *The Edinburgh Companion to Twentieth-Century Philosophy*, edited by Constantin V. Boundas. Edinburgh: Edinburgh University Press Ltd, 675–688.

Carter, Robert E. (2011) "Japanese Ethics." In *The Oxford Handbook of World Philosophy*, edited by Jay L. Garfield and William Edelglass. Oxford: Oxford University Press, 302–316.

Carter, Robert E. (2013) *The Kyoto School: An Introduction*. Albany: State University of New York Press.

Carter, Robert E., and McCarthy, Erin A. (2014) "Watsuji Tetsurō," *The Stanford Encyclopedia of Philosophy* (Winter 2014 Edition), edited by Edward N. Zalta. http://plato.stanford.edu/archives/win2014/entries/watsuji-tetsuro/.

Couteau, Pauline. (2006) "Watsuji Tetsurō's Ethics of Milieu." In *Frontiers of Japanese Philosophy*, edited by James W. Heisig. Nagoya: Nanzan Institute for Religion and Culture, 269–290.

Couteau, Pauline. (2008) "Guiding Principles of Interpretation in Watsuji Tetsurō's History of Japanese Ethical Thought with Particular Reference to the Tension between the Sonno and Bushido Traditions." In *Neglected Themes and Hidden Variations*, edited by Victor Sōgen Hori and Melissa Anne-Marie Curley. Nagoya: Nanzan Institute for Religion and Culture, 101–112.

Davis, Bret W. (2013) "Heidegger and Asian Philosophy." In *The Bloomsbury Companion to Heidegger*, edited by François Raffoul and Eric S. Nelson. New York: Bloomsbury Academic, 459–471.

Dilworth, David. A. (1974) "Watsuji Tetsurō (1889–1960): Cultural Phenomenologist and Ethician." *Philosophy East and West* 24/1: 3–22.

Dilworth, David A., and Valdo H. Viglielmo, with Agustin Jacinto Zavala. (1998) *Sourcebook for Modern Japanese Philosophy: Selected Documents*. Westport CT/London: Greenwood Press. [This anthology contains translations of three essays by Watsuji.]

Furukawa, Tetsushi. (1961) "Watsuji Tetsurō, the Man and His Work." In Watsuji Tetsurō, *Climate and Culture: A Philosophical Study*. Tokyo: The Hokuseido Press, Ministry of Education, 209–235.

Janz, Bruce B. (2011) "Watsuji Tetsurō, Fūdo and Climate Change." *Journal of Global Ethics* 7/2: 173–184.

Johnson, David W. (2019) *Watsuji on Nature: Japanese Philosophy in the Wake of Heidegger*. Evanston: Northwestern University Press.

Keung, Lam Wing. (2008) "Subjectivity, Rinrigaku, and Moral Metaphysics." In *Neglected Themes and Hidden Variations* edited by Victor Sōgen Hori and Melissa Anne-Marie Curley. Nagoya: Nanzan Institute for Religion and Culture, 129–144.

Krueger, Joel. (2013) "Watsuji's Phenomenology of Embodiment and Social Space." *Philosophy East and West* 63/2: 127–152.

LaFleur, William R. (1990) "A Turning in Taishō: Asia and Europe in the Early Writings of Watsuji Tetsurō." In *Culture and Identity: Japanese Intellectuals During the Interwar Years*, edited by J. Thomas Rimer. Princeton, NJ: Princeton University Press, 234–256.

LaFleur, William R. (1994) "An Ethic of As-Is: State and Society in the *Rinrigaku* of Watsuji Tetsurō." In *La société civile face à l'État dans les traditions chinoîse, japonaise, coréenne et vietnamienne*, edited by Léon Vandermeersch. Paris: Études thématiques 3, École française d'Extrême-Orient, 443–464.

LaFleur, William R. (2001) "Reasons for the Rubble: Watsuji Tetsurō's Position in Japan's Postwar Debate About Rationality." *Philosophy East and West* 51/1: 1–25.

Liederbach, Hans Peter. (2001) *Martin Heidegger im Denken Watsuji Tetsurōs: Ein japanischer Beitrag zur Philosophie der Lebenswelt*. Munich: Iudicium.

Maraldo, John C. (2002) "Between Individual and Communal, Subject and Object, Self and Other: Mediating Watsuji Tetsurō's Hermeneutics." In *Japanese Hermeneutics*, edited by Michael Marra. Honolulu: University of Hawai'i Press, 179–183.

Maraldo, John C. (2002) "Watsuji Tetsurō's Ethics: Totalitarian or Communitarian?" In *Komparative Ethik: Das gute Leben zwischen den Kulturen*, edited by Rolf Elberfeld and Günter Wohlfart. Koln: Edition Chōra, 76–86.

Mayeda, Graham. (2006) *Time, Space and Ethics in the Philosophy of Watsuji Tetsurō, Kuki Shuzo, and Martin Heidegger*. New York: Routledge.

McCarthy, Erin. (2000) *The Spatiality of the Self*. Dissertation. Ottawa: University of Ottawa. Print and online.

McCarthy, Erin. (2003) "Ethics in the Between." *Philosophy, Culture, and Traditions* 2: 63–78.

McCarthy, Erin. (2008) "Towards a Transitional Ethics of Care." In *Neglected Themes and Hidden Variations*, edited by Victor Sōgen Hori and Anne-Marie Curley. Nagoya: Nanzan Institute for Religion and Culture, 113–128.

McCarthy, Erin. (2010) *Ethics Embodied: Rethinking Selfhood through Continental, Japanese, and Feminist Philosophies*. Lanham: Lexington Books.

McCarthy, Erin. (2011) "Beyond the Binary: Watsuji Tetsurō and Luce Irigaray on Body, Self and Ethics." In *Japanese and Continental Philosophy: Conversations with the Kyoto School*, edited by Bret W. Davis, Brian Schroeder, and Jason M. Wirth. Bloomington: Indiana University Press, 212–228.

Odin, Steve. (1992) "The Social Self in Japanese Philosophy in Japanese Philosophy and American Pragmatism: A Comparative Study of Watsuji Tetsurō and George Herbert Mead." *Philosophy East and West* 42/3: 475–501.

Odin, Steve. (1996) *The Social Self in Zen and American Pragmatism*. Albany: State University of New York Press.

Piovesana, Gino K. (1969) *Contemporary Japanese Philosophical Thought*. New York: St. John's University Press.

Sakai, Naoki. (1991) "Return to the West/Return to the East: Watsuji Tetsurō's Anthropology and Discussions of Authenticity." In *Japan and the World, a special issue of Boundary*, 2, edited by Masao Miyoshi. Durham, NC: Duke University Press, 157–190.

Schultz, Lucy. (2013) "Creative Climate: Expressive Media in the Aesthetics of Watsuji, Nishida, and Merleau-Ponty." *Environmental Philosophy* 10/1: 63–82.

Sevilla, Anton Luis. (2014) "Watsuji's Balancing Act: Changes in his Understanding of Individuality and Totality from 1937 to 1949." *Journal of Japanese Philosophy* 2: 105–134.

Sevilla, Anton Luis. (2014) "Concretizing an Ethics of Emptiness: The Succeeding Volumes of Watsuji Tetsurō's Ethics." *Asian Philosophy* 24/1: 82–101.

Shields, James M. (2009) "The Art of *Aidagara*: Ethics, Aesthetics, and the Quest for an Ontology of Social Existence in Watsuji Tetsurō's *Rinrigaku*." *Asian Philosophy* 19/3: 265–283.

Toru, Tani (2002) "Watsuji Tetsurō: Beyond Individuality, This Side of Totality." In *Phenomenological Approaches to Moral Philosophy: A Handbook*, edited by J. J. Drummond and Lester Embree. The Netherlands: Kluwer, 497–515.

Watsuji Tetsurō. (1988) *Climate and Culture*, translated by Geoffrey Bownas. New York: Greenwood Press, Inc. in cooperation with Yushodo Co., Ltd.

Watsuji Tetsurō. (1992) *Watsuji Tetsurō zenshū* [Complete Works of Watsuji Tetsurō], 27 vols., edited by Abe Yoshishigo et al. Tokyo: Iwanami Shoten.

Watsuji Tetsurō. (1996) *Watsuji Tetsurō's Rinrigaku: Ethics in Japan*, translated by Yamamoto Seisaku and Robert E. Carter. Albany: State University of New York Press.

Watsuji Tetsurō. (2011) *Purifying Zen: Watsuji Tetsurō's Shamōn Dōgen*, translated by Steve Bein. Honolulu: University of Hawai'i Press.

Watsuji Tetsurō. (2012) *Pilgrimages to the Ancient Temples in Nara*, translated by Hiroshi Nara. Portland, ME: Merwin Asia.

Yuasa, Yasuo. (1987) *The Body: Toward an Eastern Mind-Body Theory*, edited by T. P. Kasulis, translated by Nagatomo Shigenori and T. P. Kasulis. Albany: State University Press of New York.

Yuasa, Yasuo. (1996) "The Encounter of Modern Japanese Philosophy with Heidegger." In *Heidegger and Asian Thought*, edited by Graham Parkes. Honolulu: University of Hawai'i Press, 155–174.

....

CHAPTER 24

KUKI SHŪZŌ

*A Phenomenology of Fate and Chance and an
Aesthetics of the Floating World*

....

GRAHAM MAYEDA

KUKI Shūzō (1888–1941) is one of the most accessible, unique, and interesting Japanese philosophers of the twentieth century. He wrote clearly and in language that was easily comprehensible. He chose subjects of interest to non-philosophers: art, love, fate, life, and death. His texts communicate a sense of the upheaval of Japanese society in the Taishō (1912–26) and early Shōwa (1926–89) periods during which he produced his mature work. And they are useful for understanding aspects of traditional Japanese thought, art, and culture because Kuki reflects on the similarities and differences between Japanese and contemporary European philosophical ideas. Also, the works for which he is best known express how he felt as an outsider, a feeling that we all have at one time or another: his personal life was complex, he studied abroad for many years and experienced the alienation this entails, and he was an artist who experienced the world around him in an intense way.

In this chapter, I interpret Kuki's two most important works: *The Structure of Iki* (*Iki no kōzō* いきの構造), which explores the aesthetics of the "Floating World" of the *geisha* (芸者), and *The Problem of Contingency* (*Gūzensei no mondai* 偶然性の問題), which investigates the role of fate and chance in our lives through a detailed analysis of philosophical concepts of contingency. As we will see, the two works are closely tied together. Drawing on the samurai philosophy of *bushidō* (武士道), Buddhism, and popular Japanese ideas about love and romance, *The Structure of Iki* describes some of the fundamental attitudes that Kuki believes color the way that the Japanese interpret their experience of the world. In *The Problem of Contingency*, he deepens his exploration of fate as a fundamental experience that animates these attitudes. In so doing, Kuki addresses the existentialist question of how one should live knowing the vanity of a life that ends all too soon in death.

The Aesthetic Expression of a Japanese Attitude to Life: The Hermeneutics of *Iki*

When we look at an artist's work, we are often struck by the influence that their cultural heritage and the places they have lived appears to have on their art. The "Group of Seven" Canadian landscape painters expressed something ineffably Canadian through their depictions of the rugged yet beautiful outdoors: an awe of and respect for nature combined with a wellspring of emotion that belies an unsentimental exterior. The art of Henri de Toulouse-Lautrec expresses the night life of Montmartre; Paul Klee, the political and creative atmosphere of the Weimar Republic; Andy Warhol, American popular culture. In *The Structure of Iki*, Kuki analyzes the relationship between the aesthetic expression of a culture[1] and the people living in that culture.

The first part of the text deals with methodology and makes some important points about aesthetics and hermeneutics, the philosophy of interpretation, which he learned from Henri Bergson and Martin Heidegger. The second and third parts of *The Structure of Iki*, in which Kuki describes the aesthetic sensibility of *iki*, provide an insider's perspective on the life of the *geisha* and the relationship between a *geisha* and her clients. Together, all three parts of *The Structure of Iki* discuss ideas and ideologies that are fundamental to Japanese culture more generally: namely, *bushidō* (武士道, the way of the samurai) and Buddhism. In his treatment of these topics, Kuki touches on some themes of universal human interest, such as the nature of suffering, love, and fate. Finally, in describing the relationship between a *geisha* and her patron, Kuki unfolds the ethics that animates their relationship and which emerges from and responds to these fundamental aspects of human life.

Living *Iki* Versus Thinking *Iki*: Capturing Life Through the Hermeneutic Method

If you were asked to describe an aesthetic, you might start with a description of works of art that embody it. For example, a modern "steampunk" aesthetic draws on the images of futuristic inventions as people in the nineteenth century imagined them. This is mixed with the palette and motifs of modern fantasy and horror. Terry Gilliam's 1985 film *Brazil* is an early example of the aesthetic that inspired modern steampunk. If one

---

[1] Nara 2004, 14. References to *The Structure of Iki* (Kuki 1930) will be to Nara's 2004 translation.

were to provide a similar description of the aesthetics of *iki*, one would give examples drawn from the world of the Tokyo *geisha* of the late eighteenth century (the *Meiwa* period, 1764–72), including dress, comportment, architecture, and design. However, Kuki says that it is wrong to begin a hermeneutic study in this way. If we begin by describing and cataloguing instances of the aesthetic of *iki*, we will be tempted to generalize from them.[2] But a generalization will miss the living meaning of the aesthetic and the way that those who embody the aesthetic experience it. As he says, a generalized description of the scent of a rose cannot describe the many different scents of actual roses.[3]

If we do not study aesthetics by generalizing from particular instances that express it, how should we go about it? Kuki says that we should understand an aesthetic as "a phenomenon of consciousness,"[4] which is a general attitude toward life that colors our experiences of it. This is perhaps well captured by what the later Heidegger calls a "frame"—an idea or set of ideas through which we filter or interpret our experience.[5] When we "frame" our experience by conceptualizing it in one way, we often overlook alternative conceptions. Heidegger uses the famous example of a waterfall: when we experience a waterfall through a work of literature, it will be described in poetic language or become a symbol, for instance, of strength or purity.[6] But if we look at it through the eyes of a hydraulic engineer, the same waterfall will be described in quantitative terms: for instance, how many cubic meters of water are falling per second or how much hydroelectric power it could generate.[7] Kuki, like Heidegger, encourages us to be aware of the "frame"—the phenomenon of consciousness—that can structure but also limit the way in which we interpret the world around us.

In the second part of *The Structure of Iki*, Kuki describes the phenomenon of consciousness of *iki*, which consists of attitudes or ideas through which a Japanese person of a particular historical period[8] views his or her experience of the world. A person who experiences the world as the expression of *iki* is characterized by three attitudes: coquetry (*bitai* 媚態), pride (*ikiji* 意気地), and resignation (*akirame* 諦め). These general

---

[2] Ibid., 17–19.

[3] Ibid., 17.

[4] Kuki uses the term "phenomenon of consciousness" in the sense of an "experience of meaning" that reflects a particular "comprehension of being" (Nara 2004, 18). I understand this to mean that a phenomenon of consciousness is a sort of representational framework or an attitude. Even though the term suggests individual experiences rather than the larger structure in which these experiences fit, when Kuki calls "*iki*" a "phenomenon of consciousness," he means to evoke the whole framework by which a geisha and her patron give meaning to the world they inhabit.

[5] Martin Heidegger, "The Question Concerning Technology," in *Basic Writings: Revised & Expanded Edition* (San Francisco: Harper Collins, 1993), 325–326. The term "frame," which translates the German word "Gestell," refers to a way of revealing the world peculiar to technology.

[6] Heidegger refers to Hölderlin's poem "The Rhine" as an example of a literary treatment (Heidegger 1993, 321).

[7] Ibid.

[8] Although "*iki*" commonly refers to the aesthetic of the *Meiwa* period, Kuki is not clear in his essay if his interpretation of *iki* refers to how a Japanese person of that period would have experienced the world or if it refers to how a Japanese person of the early *Shōwa* period, when Kuki was writing *The Structure of Iki*, experiences it.

attitudes that are adopted by the *geisha* and her patron frame or color their experience of each other and of the world. In a sense, they predispose them to favor a certain aesthetic—the aesthetic of *iki*.

The aesthetic of *iki* is slightly bawdy: it is the aesthetic of the pleasure quarters of Edo (Tokyo). It does not correspond to our stereotypes of the refined Japanese aesthetic associated with Zen or even the rarefied world of the Kyoto *geisha*. Moreover, it was an aesthetic of the late Tokugawa era (late eighteenth century), a period associated with the general decline of that regime.[9] Why did Kuki choose this aesthetic to explain what it means to be Japanese?

One possibility is that this choice provided him with an opportunity to critique a Japanese tradition that was quickly disappearing during his lifetime. By treating the aesthetic of the *geisha* as an expression of the essence of contemporary Japanese culture, he rejects traditional Japanese interpretations of how a person ought to behave, both to others and to the world around him or her. The *geisha* who exhibits *iki* lives in tension with those with whom she interacts, not in harmony, a concept so central in traditional Japanese approaches to human relations.[10] She does not fall into the traditional five relationships of Confucianism,[11] which would assign to her a specific role and mode of interaction with others. Instead, the *geisha* maintains a separation between herself and her clients, holding open the possibility of a relationship that is constantly evolving and changing. It is a relationship that does not become formalized into that between a husband and wife, for instance, and so does not fit into the prescriptive Confucian categories. The *geisha* is also plucky (*ikiji*)—she is brave and idealistic, not willing to give up the ideal of love that guides her and yet which she knows cannot be realized in this world. She exhibits a kind of Nietzschean nobility.[12] Finally, she is resigned (*akirame*); she accepts her fate. She does not dwell on past defeats in love nor does she deny them. Rather, her acceptance of the past enables her to bravely confront the fate that manifests

---

[9] Pinkus 1996, 13 and 16–17.

[10] Harmony is one of the ideals of Confucianism, a system of values that underlies much of traditional Japanese culture. Tu Wei-ming expresses this idea as follows: "the Confucian tradition either omits or rejects a large category of Western ideas which is thought to have been the necessary outgrowth of a more refined philosophical understanding of humanity. The category includes ideas of self-interest, private property, spiritual loneliness, and psychological egoism as positive contributions to the formulation of respectively political, economic, religious, and ethical individualism . . . . a conflicting . . . category of ideas assumes great prominence in Confucian thought: for example, duty-consciousness, public service, mutuality between man and Heaven, and a sense of community." "The Value of the Human in Classical Confucian Thought" in Tu Wei-ming, *Confucian Thought: Selfhood as Creative Transformation* (Albany: SUNY Press, 1985), 77.

[11] The five relationships are ruler–minister, husband–wife, parent–child, old–young, friend–friend. *Mencius* 3A:4, in Wing-Tsit Chan, *A Source Book in Chinese Philosophy* (Princeton: Princeton University Press, 1963), 69–70.

[12] As Alphonso Lingis describes it, the noble spirit for Nietzsche does not lie in social, political, or military power but rather "in being different, in incommunicability" ("The Will to Power" in David B. Allison [ed.], *The New Nietzsche* [Cambridge, MA: MIT Press, 1985], 52), in "the power to make of the present its own law" (Ibid., 53). Kuki mentions Nietzsche's "nobility" and "pathos of distance" as examples of the European expression of *ikiji* (Nara 2004, 59).

itself in her life.[13] The aesthetic of *iki* and the life of the *geisha* perhaps expressed to Kuki something both very modern and yet something that long existed as an undercurrent of Japanese life and sensibility.

Kuki traces these three elements of *iki*—coquetry, pride, and resignation—back to non-Confucian currents in Japanese philosophy. He associates the pluckiness of the *geisha* with the ideals of *bushidō*. A samurai does not give up on the ideals of *bushidō* even in extreme poverty or need. Likewise, explains Kuki, the *geisha* exhibits the pride and honor[14] captured by the saying, "A samurai uses a toothpick even when he has not eaten."[15] The resignation with which a *geisha* who is *iki* faces the world is derived from Buddhist ideas: having suffered in this life, the *geisha* accepts that life is this suffering, and, while she may hold to ideals, she is not surprised when it is fate and not her ideals that determines what becomes of her in real life.[16] "[I]*ki*," writes Kuki, "arises from the 'world of suffering' in which 'we are scarcely able to keep afloat, carried down on the stream of *ukiyo*'"[17] (浮き世 the "floating" or "ephemeral" world). The *geisha* is "free of grime, unclinging, disinterested, and free from obstacles" and has removed herself "from any egotistical attachment to reality."[18]

Contrary to expectations, the life of the *geisha* that Kuki describes is highly ethical. The *geisha* accepts her humanity and the suffering inherent to the human condition, but she does not give up on the ideals that guide her. Moreover, she is not content to simply play the role that society assigns to her, and she does not disappear into a relationship with the other in which her individuality (and that of her partner) is abandoned. Kuki's admiration for the ethical relationship between a *geisha* and her patron may be somewhat problematic today because it is tied to heterosexual norms and is highly gendered. Indeed, the ethics of the *geisha* is described from a man's point of view, and this naturally endows it with a certain voyeuristic perspective. Also, Kuki does not examine how the aesthetic is tied to class and, as a form of patronage relationship, to economics. However, Kuki clearly wished to describe an ethical attitude that lies behind the aesthetic sensibility of *iki* and that transcends the relationship of *geisha* and patron. In his view, the ethics of *iki* requires two people to respect the differences between them. To achieve this, the gap between self and other can never and must never be completely overcome, nor must two people relate to each other only through the social roles they are assigned, as some interpretations of Confucianism require. While there are similarities between the ethics of *iki* and the ethics of Emmanuel Levinas, unlike for Levinas, in Kuki's ethics there is no element of justice—no third (God)—before which each is ultimately

---

[13] Lingis also sees this as a characteristic of the Nietzschean noble—the ability to forget: "The source of the great power of the noble life, its welcoming openness to what comes, to what presents itself, lies in that it has the power to forget, to forget the past, to forget what is irrevocable, to let what dies die" (Lingis 1985, 53).

[14] Nara 2004, 21.

[15] Ibid., 20.

[16] Ibid., 21–22.

[17] Ibid., 21.

[18] Ibid., 22.

answerable.[19] The *geisha* is not answerable to anyone except to the reality of this world of suffering.

Having explained the general attitude of a person who displays the attitude (phenomenon of consciousness) that creates the aesthetic of *iki*, Kuki then turns to what he calls the "objective" expression of *iki*—its manifestation in various arts, including both fine art and design. This is an "objective" expression of *iki* presumably because these arts describe a "taste"; that is, they capture elements that all who possess the sensibility of *iki* would recognize.[20] While the hermeneutic method Kuki employed in uncovering the intensional structure of *iki* forbade him from beginning with generalizations, having now finished describing *iki* as phenomenon of consciousness—as an attitude toward human experience—it is fine to resort to generalizations when describing how *iki* expresses itself in the arts. It is not possible within the scope of this chapter to go into all the examples that Kuki discusses. However, a few can be illuminating.

In terms of the dress and comportment of the *geisha*, Kuki contrasts the *geisha* with the European aesthetic. The following captures this contrast:

> An expression embodying *iki* that involves the entire body is the **wearing of very thin fabric.** Take for example this *senryū: Akashi kara honobono to suku hijirimen* "The scarlet crepe chemise from Akashi; how it shows through ever so subtly." Here, the reference is the fact that the undergarment made of scarlet Akashi crepe can be seen through the kimono. The motif of wearing thin fabric is often found in *ukiyoe* [浮世絵 woodblock prints depicting the "floating world"]. There, the relation between material and formal cause is expressed in terms of fabric so translucent it opens a way to a woman by at once veiling her and revealing her. The Venus de Medici expresses coquetry specifically by means of the position of her hands on her naked body, but her gesture is too explicit to be said to represent *iki*. It goes without saying that the scantily clad ladies in the Paris revues have nothing whatever in common with *iki*.[21]

In textiles, parallel lines best express the ethical relationship between a *geisha* and her patron, in which the individuality of each is maintained, neither partner dominating the other.[22] As Kuki explains, "[p]arallel lines are the purest visual objectification of duality, extending on forever, eternally equidistant."[23] Likewise, flashy colors (*hade*) do not express the duality inherent to *iki*.[24] Instead, the *iki* palette includes greys, browns, and

---

[19] For similarities and differences between the philosophies of Levinas and Kuki, see Graham Mayeda, "Time for Ethics: Temporality and the Ethical Ideal in Emmanuel Levinas and Kuki Shūzō," *Comparative and Continental Philosophy* 4:1(2012): 105–124. For a good discussion of the role of the third in Levinas's thought, see Robert Gibbs, *Why Ethics? Signs of Responsibilities* (Princeton: Princeton University Press, 2000).

[20] For a description of how taste can be objective, see Immanuel Kant's discussion of the *sensus communis* in his *Critique of the Power of Judgment*, edited by Paul Guyer (Cambridge: Cambridge University Press, 2000), 173–176.

[21] Nara 2004, 36.

[22] Ibid., 41.

[23] Ibid.

[24] Ibid., 48.

blues.[25] Kuki particularly favors brown, which embodies *iki* "because the opulent characteristic of a color and the loss of saturation express a sophisticated sensuality and a coquetry that knows resignation."[26] "*Iki*," he writes, "allows for being tinged by another color without being muddled by it."[27]

DEEPENING THE ANALYSIS: FROM *THE STRUCTURE OF IKI* TO *THE PROBLEM OF CONTINGENCY*

The ideas that Kuki introduced in *The Structure of Iki* are the embryonic form of those that he went on to develop in his later philosophy. For instance, *The Problem of Contingency* explores the notion of fate that underlies the resignation (*akirame*) that Kuki attributes to the *geisha* in *The Structure of Iki*. In the earlier text, Kuki attributes the *geisha*'s attitudes of resignation (*akirame*) and pride (*ikiji*) to her recognition and affirmation of fate: even though we live in a world in which suffering is necessary and inevitable, the *geisha* "boldly brackets everyday life" and continues on with her ideal "in a manner disinterested and purposeless ... transcending all of life around" her.[28] The plucky *geisha* resigns herself to her fate and does not despair; she does not give up on idealism even though most of us would in her place. An acceptance of fate was clearly important to Kuki: to live freely, he thought, we must accept fate—we must choose to live freely even when it seems impossible to do so. In Kuki's words, fate "forces us to return to freedom."[29]

But what is fate? Is the Japanese conception of *unmei* (運命) similar to European notions of fate? Or to other Asian notions? This is the subject addressed in *The Problem of Contingency*. While fate does not appear to be the primary topic of the book when one first opens it, the reader soon understands that Kuki is interested in contingency and necessity—the putative topic of the work—with the purpose of deepening his understanding how humans can be free in a world in which old age, sickness, and death are inevitable. Kuki's concept of fate is interesting because it departs from our common sense notions of it. One tends to think that one is free when one's future is not fated—that is, when the future is full of endless possibilities among which one is at liberty to choose. But, as we shall see, Kuki thinks the opposite: only Sisyphus is truly free, although he is doomed to eternally repeat the same pointless task.

[25] Ibid.
[26] Ibid.
[27] Ibid.
[28] Ibid., 23.
[29] Ibid.

LEAVE IT TO CHANCE: KUKI'S *THE PROBLEM* *OF CONTINGENCY*

Why was Kuki interested in the nature of contingency and chance? As we have seen, Kuki was interested in fate, and, as he demonstrates in *The Problem of Contingency*, fate is closely linked to chance. How so? People often connect "fate" with chance events. For instance, an opening line like "We just *happened* to be at the same concert" or "Believe it or not, we were on the same bus on a seven-hour trip to Missouri" is often the pre-amble to something like the following, "We hit it off so well—it was like fate brought us together." In popular culture, chance and fate are closely related. Yet fate is also closely linked with necessity, the opposite of contingency. Indeed, one often hears people say, "It just *had* to happen; it was fate." In *The Problem of Contingency*, Kuki undertakes a philo-sophical investigation of the closely related concepts of fate, contingency, and necessity.

His ultimate goal is a phenomenological one: to explore the nature of human ex-istence by starting with our experience of the world. He wishes to uncover what our experiences of contingency and fate tell us about the fundamental structures of human experience such as space and time. But, in addition to exposing these phenomenological structures—the structures of our experience—Kuki is also interested in *how* to live our lives in a world that seems to be beyond our control, a world in which chance and neces-sity appear to remove our freedom to make meaningful choices.

An Overview of Kuki's Analysis of Chance

In *The Problem of Contingency*, Kuki analyzes three kinds of contingency: categorical, hypothetical, and disjunctive. Each of them is a road marker along the way to his goal: to explain how we experience "fate" in what otherwise appears to be a world full of contin-gency and chance.

Categorical contingency deals with the role of chance in how we think. Much of our thought is organized around concepts: "a tree," "a star," "a circle." Many of these concepts have necessary attributes (e.g., trees have a trunk, stars are very hot, every point on the circumference of a circle is equidistant from the center). But, in real life, concrete examples of these concepts also have many contingent attributes (this tree has a crooked trunk; that star is blue, but this one yellow; this circle is small, that large). Thus, necessity and chance—necessary attributes and contingent attributes—play a fundamental role in our cognition.

But Kuki does not end his inquiry into contingency with this study of concepts and our ideas. He also recognizes that we experience contingency concretely in our lives, not just in our thoughts. And so he examines what he calls *hypothetical contingency* to uncover what basic form this experience takes. According to him, the most basic kind of experience of contingency is the experience of the intersection of two causally independent causal chains. Imagine that at the very moment that a man exits a building, he is crushed by the engine of a plane that had exploded in the air minutes before. When something like this occurs, we are struck by how unlikely—how contingent—such a tragedy is. The set of causes that brought the man to exit the building there and then seems completely independent of the set of events that caused the engine to explode in the air. But here, the two causal lines cross. It is the experience of horror and surprise that accompanies the crossing of causal chains that Kuki identifies as the source of our experience of chance. Surprise is thus the fundamental way that we experience contingency in our everyday lives.

Kuki does not stop at identifying the experiential source of our ideas of contingency. Instead, he follows this experiential source back to the wellspring—to the structures of human existence and experience that it uncovers and that make the experience of contingency possible. He wants to understand what the way in which we experience chance and contingency tells us about the nature of human experience and existence. His explanation involves the third kind of contingency, *disjunctive contingency,* which deals with the relationship between a whole and its parts. As we will see, the wellspring that is the source of our experience of contingency is fate, and fate, Kuki explains, has both a spatial and a temporal dimension. Thus, in the last section of *The Problem of Contingency,* Kuki's study of contingency leads him to the topic that really interests him: fate.

In the following sections, I elaborate on each of the three kinds of contingency identified by Kuki.

The Law and the Exception: Categorical Contingency

Categorical contingency is manifest in the relation between an object and its properties. Some of these properties are considered "necessary"; for example, a clover has three leaflets, a bird has feathers, a cloud is made of drops of water or ice particles. These properties are necessary because the very concept of each object includes them. However, specific objects—a particular clover leaf, that seagull, or this cumulonimbus cloud—may have additional properties that are contingent rather than necessary. These properties are not necessarily contained in the concept itself. For instance, while a clover leaf by definition has three leaflets—having three leaflets is contained within the concept of a clover leaf—the size of the leaves fall within a broad range. Thus, the size of a clover leaf is a contingent property of a clover plant.

But Kuki's analysis of categorical contingency does not stop at his exposition of logical relations. Kuki also wants to uncover the *existential meaning* of categorical contingency: that is, he wants to explain what the fact that humans divide the attributes of objects into necessary and contingent tells us about the nature of human existence.[30] Our ideas of objects can be neatly ordered and their properties divided into the necessary

---

[30] Omodaka 1966, 24.

and the contingent, but individual, concrete objects defy the regularity and order of our thoughts: each snowflake is different, each drop of water unique. The concept of a snowflake with its limited number of readily identifiable necessary characteristics is belied by the nearly infinite diversity present in each snowfall.[31] Kuki's examination of categorical contingency thus points out something very important about the nature of reality and human existence: we create general concepts despite the fact that the world is filled only with objects that are exceptions to them.[32] We experience the world as a dizzying array of experiences; what, Kuki wonders, does our need to simplify and conceptualize it tell us about how we habitually live our lives?

Another fundamental question is hidden in Kuki's examination of categorical contingency. The question is: Why do we live in the imperfect world of reality, a world that defies the order of our conceptual world? Near the end of this section of *The Problem of Contingency*, he cites a Buddhist text, the *Milindapanha Sutra*. In it, Milinda asks the sage Nagasena how humans can, on the one hand, all share similarities such as having a head, a body, four limbs, and the like, and yet each have a different fate: some die young, others live until old age, some are sick, some poor, others healthy and rich.[33] This quote addresses a fundamental question in Buddhism: Why do sadness and suffering exist?[34] In the *Milindapanha Sutra*, Nagasena answers by simply providing other examples of contingency; this answer implies that diversity is a basic feature of reality—some of us die early and others later because that is the way of nature. Just as the fruit of some trees is sweet, that of others is sour, so too are some men rich and others poor.[35] Kuki is dissatisfied with this answer, but he delays providing his own alternative until the end of the book. The answer he gives there is not rational or philosophical, but rather experiential: our experience of the everyday world may lead us to think that it is a world of dissatisfaction (*dukkha*), but we also have experiences of transcendence—experiences of a fate that point beyond the mundane.

Chance Occurrences: Hypothetical Contingency

One possible answer to the question Kuki poses about the "why?" of each person's suffering is that there is a discernible, rational reason for it. Each experience of our life is caused by multiple factors, and it is often possible to discern what these factors are. This is the basic attitude of the European sciences. For instance, for a classical Newtonian physicist, we live in a deterministic world in which we can trace back every current state

---

[31] Ibid.

[32] Omodaka 1966, 26. Here, Kuki is indirectly poking holes in the traditional theory of concepts. For instance, the concept of a dog might entail having four legs—but one can still call a three-legged dog a "dog." This suggests that concepts are more like "family resemblances" than descriptions of necessary and sufficient conditions.

[33] Ibid., 24.

[34] Ibid.

[35] Ibid.

of affairs to a previous one and also trace forward what will happen in the future based on our knowledge of the current state. The classical approach promises that, in theory, all states of the universe are knowable if we apply the laws of physics to a complete knowledge of all present states of affairs. Why do I suffer from diabetes? From the mechanistic presumptions of this kind of scientific view, we can answer this question by pointing to a genetic predisposition to diabetes combined with a long period of unhealthy eating and insufficient exercise. But while in theory such explanations should be possible for every present state of affairs, in reality, we often do not know enough to understand what caused it. In this section of his book, Kuki explains this kind of "causal" contingency— the kind in which the connection between various experiences is not evident and so appears to be contingent.

Kuki's first step is to divide hypothetical contingency into three types: rational, causal, and final. These deal roughly with knowing the *reason* that something has occurred (rational hypothetical contingency), identifying the *causal means* by which a thing or state of affairs is brought about (causal hypothetical contingency), and discerning the *purpose* for which it has occurred (final hypothetical contingency). An example of each will illustrate what is meant.

Rational hypothetical contingency is illustrated by a situation in which we do not have sufficient information to understand why something exists or why a state of affairs has come about, in consequence of which it appears irrational. What occurs in a dream or is depicted in a work of art can be irrational in this sense.[36]

Causal hypothetical contingency describes the relationship between experiences in which a state of affairs is brought about, but we do not know the cause. For instance, if we run out of petrol while driving our car from New York to Philadelphia and yet we arrive there nonetheless, we might say that we were "lucky" to have arrived—that it was only chance that saved us. In saying this, we mean either that there was some unknown physical cause at work that continued to propel the car or else that some nonphysical cause (magic?) was at work.[37]

Final causal contingency manifests itself when we cannot perceive the purpose for which an object or state of affairs has come about.[38] For instance, when we come across a double flower that lacks the reproductive organs of an ordinary, single flower, we may ask ourselves why it exists—what its purpose for existing is—and yet we can find no answer.[39] The purpose of flowers is to enable plants to reproduce; why would a plant produce an impotent double flower?

Kuki adopts a phenomenological approach for analyzing hypothetical contingency: he investigates how we *experience* the apparent lack of causal reasons for a thing or state of affairs to exist. Sometimes, we are struck by the apparent absence of a physical cause for a thing or state of affairs—it appears to have come about spontaneously

---

[36] Ibid., 32–35.
[37] Ibid., 50.
[38] Ibid., 51.
[39] Ibid., 52.

without physical or natural cause.[40] This Kuki calls "negative hypothetical contingency." In contrast, sometimes, we are struck "positively" by the existence of a noncausal relationship between two states of affairs. For instance, a tile may fall from the roof and land on a rubber balloon rolling on the ground next to the house, causing it to burst.[41] When we say that the tile fell "by chance" to burst the balloon, we capture this sense of positive causal contingency: two causal chains have intersected, but they have done so fortuitously and not out of necessity.[42] There is no (apparent) reason why they should have done so.

While it may seem appealing to divide our experiences of hypothetical contingency into negative forms (those for which we do not experience the reason for the contingent event having come about) and positive forms (those for which we do have such an experience), Kuki demonstrates that the positive form is more fundamental: all negative forms of hypothetical contingency are ultimately based on a positive form. In the case of negative hypothetical contingency, we may not have experienced the cause of a given state of affairs, we may not be able to provide a logical reason for it having come about, and we may not be able to see that its occurrence serves any purpose. But this ignorance, Kuki says, is only the result of a deficiency of knowledge or experiential power on our part.[43] Ultimately, it is possible to experience or know the cause of every chance occurrence, although we do not do so in certain instances.[44] All experiences of chance events ultimately reduce to experiences (or possible experiences) of the crossing of two apparently independent causal chains.

Why Kuki goes to such trouble to reduce all experiences of chance to the positive form only becomes completely clear in the last section of *The Problem of Contingency*. However, provisionally, Kuki does this in order to identify the way that we experience chance events. Whether we seem ignorant of why a chance event has occurred or whether we have (positively) observed the crossing of two causal chains, what unites our experience of chance in our experiential world is "surprise." When we notice the contingent, we are "struck" by the coincidence.[45] In the next section, Kuki will demonstrate that what we are "struck" by is an order or structure to the world that points to aspects of transcendent reality.

Before moving on to the final section of *The Problem of Contingency*, it is worth noting that Kuki points out that this phenomenological analysis of contingency has a long history in East Asian philosophy. For instance, in the *Book of Changes* (*I Ching*), every change comes about by a different combination of two factors, *yin* and *yang*.[46] The philosophy of the *I Ching*, Kuki writes, is thus "built on the unexpected encounters

---

[40] Ibid., 68.
[41] Ibid., 79.
[42] Ibid.
[43] Ibid., 84.
[44] Ibid.
[45] Ibid., 83.
[46] Ibid., 88.

between the two trigrams A and B that represent" combinations of *yin* and *yang*.[47] The coincidence of causal chains is also of interest to Buddhists. For instance, the jewel net of Indra[48] is a metaphor used to explain why experiences of unexpected causal connections are considered profound. The jewel net is described in the *Avatamsaka Sutra*: the net is composed of jewels, each of which reflects every other jewel. Thus, it is possible—if only ideally—to know how all things are interconnected. The experience of two causal chains coinciding is an important experience because it indicates to us the fundamental interconnection between all things; that is, it is an experience that points to an otherwise hidden (transcendent) aspect of experience.

Chance Encounters: Disjunctive Contingency

The final kind of contingency Kuki discusses in *The Problem of Contingency* is disjunctive contingency. This term refers to a contingent relationship between a whole and its parts.[49] In this section, Kuki intends to use his investigation of disjunctive contingency to deepen his phenomenological analysis and uncover the meaning of our experience of the contingent. In other words, he wants to know what the possibility of this kind of experience tells us about the nature of human existence in general. Since all of our experience is both spatial and temporal, his phenomenological analysis of disjunctive contingency (and disjunctive necessity) must involve the dynamic correlates of these concepts: possibility and impossibility. These are temporal concepts because to say that something is "possible" is to say that, although it is not the case now, it may be in the future. If Kuki can explain how contingency relates to possibility and impossibility, he can describe more fully how we experience the contingent and, more importantly, what such experience means about the nature of human experience and human existence.

Disjunctive contingency involves the relationship between a whole and its parts. What does this have to do with possibility? One common meaning of chance or contingency is that it describes what *could have been otherwise than it is*. When we use the term "contingency" in this way, it means the same as "possibility." A state of affairs can be said to be "contingent" if it is the manifestation of one of a number of possibilities. In this sense, the contingent is opposed to the necessary. Kuki gives the example of the eight schools of Buddhism. Here, Buddhism is the whole; each school a part. The doctrines held by any one school are contingent in the sense that this school chose to promote this doctrine while that school chose that doctrine, but each could have chosen a different guiding doctrine—each school could have chosen among different *possible* doctrines, and so its choice is in some sense contingent.[50]

---

[47] Ibid.
[48] Ibid., 106.
[49] Ibid., 111.
[50] Ibid., 112–113.

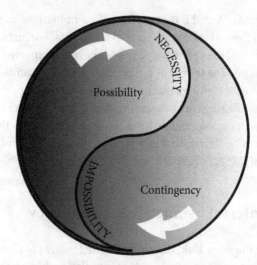

FIGURE 24.1 Once a possibility is born, it develops until it becomes a necessity. Similarly, once a contingency is born, it develops until it becomes impossible (Kuki 1935, 170; Omodaka 1966, 139).

But is chance always the opposite of necessity? According to Kuki, not if the system we are dealing with is dynamic rather than static. In a dynamic system, the contingent and the necessary are closely related because what is contingent can *become* necessary. This can be expressed in temporal terms as follows: as the possible becomes reality, other possibilities become impossible. For example, whether a lamb is white or black is contingent because it is possible for a lamb to be born either white or black.[51] The contingency becomes necessity when the possibility of a lamb being born either white or black becomes reality: it is born black, and so the possibility of a white or black lamb has been realized in the black lamb.[52] Kuki uses a term from mathematics to describe the relationship between necessity and contingency in a dynamic system: "limit." As the possible becomes less and less likely—more and more impossible—contingency decreases and approaches the "limit" of necessity. Likewise, as the contingent becomes more and more possible, the necessity of non-being diminishes toward a limit. Kuki depicts this with a few illuminating diagrams (Figures 24.1 and 24.2).

Thus, for the phenomenologist who is interested in the structures of our experience and what these tell us about the nature of human existence,[53] the contingent and the necessary are not opposites but instead exist in a relationship of "limit": the contingent never becomes necessary, but, as it becomes more and more possible, it approaches the limit of the contingency function, which is necessity.

Is it possible to experience this "limit," that is, the point at which the contingency of a system has decreased so much (as the merely possible becomes more and more likely)

[51] Black sheep are the expression of a recessive gene.
[52] Omodaka 1966, 127.
[53] Ibid., 136.

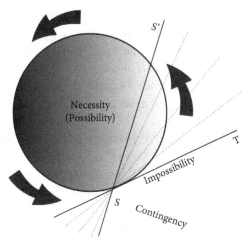

FIGURE 24.2 Necessity is the limit of possibility; impossibility is the limit of contingency (Kuki 1935, 186; Omodaka 1966, 127).

that it is approaching reality and, hence, necessary being? According to Kuki, the answer is "yes." Our experience of the present moment is precisely the experience of the merely possible becoming real and, therefore, necessary. Thus, from a phenomenological standpoint, the contingent is the experience of the present moment when possibility becomes reality.

But how do we experience the present in concrete terms? What feeling do we have when we truly experience the present? Kuki thinks that while other philosophers have accurately explained how we experience the future and the past, they have failed to properly analyze our experience of the present. Martin Heidegger identified our mode of experiencing the future as *anxiety*. Our future is always tinged with the possibility of our own impossibility (i.e., our death).[54] Thus, we naturally experience the uncertainty of the future as anxiety about the possibility that the next moment will be our last. In contrast, we experience the past with *tranquility* because it is necessary and determined[55]: it has already happened, so we need not fear anything unexpected from that quarter. But what of the present? Heidegger does not say; but Kuki fills in the gap: the present is experienced as "surprise" or "wonder."[56]

From the existential phenomenological point of view, then, what is the contingent? It is simply the real—the moment where possibility (future) meets impossibility and therefore necessity (past). It is the diminishing limit of the possible which, as soon as

---

[54] Ibid., 160–161.

[55] Ibid.

[56] Ibid. Here, "wonder" is used in the Cartesian sense—see *The Passions of the Soul*, where he describes wonder as "a sudden surprise of the soul which brings it to consider with attention the objects that seem to it unusual and extraordinary"; AT 380; in John Cottingham, Robert Stoothoff, and Dugald Murdoch, trans., *The Philosophical Writings of Descartes*, vol. 1 (Cambridge: Cambridge University Press, 1985).

we reach the present moment and one contingent reality is established, turns into the necessary and recedes into the past. At the same time as the contingent reality is established, all other possibilities become necessarily impossible. When we truly experience the present, we do so with wonder and surprise. But what is the meaning of this kind of experience? What is so wondrous about the present? The answer, Kuki thinks, is that we experience the present as fate—as an experience of the transcendence of human existence.

At last, we have returned to fate, Kuki's main reason for studying the problem of contingency. The reader will recall that, earlier in this essay, I mentioned two common ways of understanding fate: fate as necessity ("It just *had* to happen; it was fate") and fate as chance ("We just happened to be on the same bus together and we hit it off. It was like fate brought us together"). Kuki's notion of fate does not correspond to the first common understanding—fate as necessity, as that which one cannot escape. This is because this kind of fate is not rooted in any possible human experience. When one thinks of fate as necessity, one must adopt the standpoint of a god, not that of a mere mortal. From the point of view of an omniscient being standing outside the changing world of reality, what happens next may seem necessary and hence "fated." But for a person living in time—a constant succession of present moments—our destiny appears only as a contingency: that is, it appears only by surprise in the present. As Schelling explains, real contingency—contingency from the human perspective—is plunged in the "immeasurable depth" of reality[57] from which it is impossible to gain an omniscient point of view. Perhaps it is this surprise that is expressed in the second common notion of fate—the kind of fate in which a contingent meeting brings together two lovers who are so compatible that it seems as if the meeting was fated. Here, the use of "fate" expresses the idea that meeting was so unexpected that it must be the manifestation of some transcendent order generally inaccessible to human experience.

Kuki thus links our experience of contingency to an experience of transcendence. Because we are plunged in the depth of a temporal world, he explains, we experience ultimate contingency in the present as a limit—that is, as a lack of control over what our present experience may bring. As Nishida Kitarō explains, "there must be some point at which, in our journey, we come up against divine reality which dominates us with its absolute power and decrees that here is the limit that human strength and ingenuity cannot overcome."[58] It is in this way that our experience of fate is also an experience of transcendence. When we experience our fate, we truly experience how we as humans are bound in time. The precondition of such an experience, Kuki argues, is that in the moment of surprise and wonder—the transcendent experience of our fate—we behold the structure of transcendental time itself. When we truly experience the present, otherness—the limit of our human power—becomes apparent.[59] In the present, contingent moment, which we experience with surprise, we experience our limitations as

[57] Omodaka 1966, 171.
[58] Quoted by Kuki at Omodaka 1966, 175.
[59] Omodaka 1966, 175.

temporal beings, but, in experiencing this limit, we also experience the limitless, which Kuki describes as the experience of the eternal manifest in the temporality of reality.[60]

What is the nature of this experience of the moment? And what is the form of temporality revealed by it? It is the manifestation in the present of eternal time as the infinitely recurrent, metaphysical time.[61] This seems quite obscure: What does it mean to experience transcendent time as infinitely recurring? Kuki's discussion of our experience of the contingent aims to provide a very concrete example of how we experience this. In the section of *The Problem of Contingency* on hypothetical contingency (discussed in the previous subsection of this chapter), Kuki pointed out that the kind of coincidence in which we are most clearly struck by an experience of contingency or chance is that in which two similar events succeed each other. For example, we might be struck by the coincidence of seeing, throughout the course of the same day, the same number appear in different contexts. As an example, let's choose the number 8765032. It appears for the first time as a recurrent decimal in the result of a calculation (0.87650328765032). Later that day, the same numbers appear in a license plate, then as the number of a train carriage, and then, finally, in the winning lottery ticket announced in the newspaper. What strikes us in the succession of these events is the *repetition* of the number.

But why does this repetition strike us as a coincidence? Why does it stand out? Kuki explains that this occurs because our experience of repetition is an experience of an order—a pattern—that appears to transcend physical time. It appears as if a moment from the past has occurred again. In turn, this suggests to us an order of time that is perpendicular to everyday physical time. It does not run as a succession of linear moments, but, instead, it has the ability to "hop" from point to point along the line of real time. This experience of recurrence—of the "eternal return of the same" to use a Nietzschean concept, or of time as circular, to draw on Asian traditions—is the source of the wonder and surprise with which we are struck when we truly experience the present. Destiny is the experience in the present of the limit of human power and knowledge: it is the revelation of an order of cause and effect—that is, of temporality—that goes beyond our daily experience of the temporal as a succession of equal moments.[62] And what particularly strikes us is that transcendental time, unlike the linear concept of everyday time, is recurrent, circular.

All of Kuki's examination of contingency is thus in aid of explaining the *experience* of transcendence that he ascribes to the Buddhist notion of destiny (karma)[63] and that Western philosophy describes, through Nietzsche, as the eternal recurrence of the same: the experience of the *Übermensch* who glimpses all of human existence from the vantage point of recurrent time.[64] Ordinary time is linear: it is a progression from point

---

[60] Ibid., 176–177.

[61] Ibid.

[62] Ibid., 168.

[63] One Buddhist view of karma is that it is about self-determination and choice (Harvey 1990, 40). However, Kuki describes it as a kind of necessity: karma, he says, "implies predetermined identity" (see "The Idea of Time and the Repossession [*la reprise*] of Time in the Orient" at p. 204, n. 6).

[64] Omodaka 1966, 163.

A to point B. But in our surprise at the present, we encounter time differently: there is this moment, and now this moment again, unconnected to the last, and now this moment again.... Time is not running from point A to point B, but is piling up "perpendicular" to the arrow of time of our thoughts and experiences.

How Should We Live in a World of Chance?

Kuki concludes *The Problem of Contingency* with a hint at how we ought to live in a world in which we can experience transcendence of this kind. Drawing on a passage from the Buddhist *Pure Land Sutra*, Kuki implores us to live in such a way that the experience of the transcendent in the moment not be in vain.[65] And because the experience of the transcendent in the moment occurs in the chance coincidence of two independent causal lines, we must live in such a way that we value the present and those whom we encounter in it—in other words, we must live such that our chance encounters with others are not in vain.[66] In short, much as in *The Structure of Iki*, Kuki describes the ethical life in *The Problem of Contingency* as a life in which we come face to face with another person—our causal chain crosses with that of the other—and, rather than looking away, we experience the encounter with surprise and wonder and so see that person for what he or she really is, without preconceptions. To ensure this experience of wonder is not in vain, we must treat the other as what he or she is: an opportunity for experiencing the transcendent. Above all, we must not bring down the other to our level—to something we can grasp and understand. Instead, we must respect that we live two parallel lives that just happened to have touched in this present moment of meeting.

BIBLIOGRAPHY AND SUGGESTED READINGS

Clark, John. (1997) *Reflections on Japanese Taste: The Structure of Iki*. Sydney: Power Publications. [Translation of Kuki's *Iki no kōzō* (The Structure of Iki).]
Dilworth, David A., and Valdo H. (1998) Viglielmo with Agustín Jacinto Zavala, eds. *Sourcebook for Modern Japanese Philosophy: Selected Documents*. Westport: Greenwood Press.
Harvey, Peter. (1990) *An Introduction to Buddhism: Teachings, History and Practices*. Cambridge: Cambridge University Press.
Kuki Shūzō. (1930) *Iki no kōzō* [The Structure of Iki]. *Shisō* [Thought] 92 and 93. [Hiroshi Nara and John Clark have both translated this work into English.]

[65] Ibid., 196. For a further explanation on the relationship between chance and ethics, see Graham Mayeda, "Leaving Ethics to Chance: The Ethical Significance of Contingency in the Philosophy of Kuki Shūzō," in Victor Sōgen Hori and Melissa Curley (eds.), *Frontiers of Japanese Philosophy 2: Neglected Themes and Hidden Variations* (Nagoya: Nanzan Institute for Religion and Culture, 2008), 7–35.
[66] Omodaka 1996, 196.

Kuki Shūzō. (1935) *Gūzensei no mondai* [The Problem of Contingency]. Tokyo: Iwanami Shoten, 1935. Reprinted in *Complete Works of Kuki Shūzō*, vol. 2. Tokyo: Iwanami Shoten, 1981.

Kuki Shūzō. (1998) "The Expression of the Infinite in Japanese Art." In *Sourcebook for Modern Japanese Philosophy: Selected Documents*, translated and edited by David A. Dilworth and Valdo H. Viglielmo, with Agustin Jacinto Zavala. Westport, CT: Greenwood Press. Originally published as "L'expression de l'infini dans l'art japonais," in *Kuki Shūzō zenshū* [Complete works of Kuki Shūzō, vol. 1. Tokyo: Iwanami Shoten, 1981]. Given as a lecture at Pontigny on August 17, 1928.

Kuki Shūzō. (1998) "The Idea of Time and the Repossession of Time in the Orient." In *Sourcebook for Modern Japanese Philosophy: Selected Documents*, translated and edited by David A. Dilworth and Valdo H. Viglielmo, with Agustin Jacinto Zavala. Westport, CT: Greenwood Press. Originally published as "La notion du temps et la reprise sur le temps en orient," in *Kuki Shūzō zenshū* [Complete Works of Kuki Shūzō, vol. 1. Tokyo: Iwanami Shoten, 1981]. Given as a lecture at Pontigny on August 11, 1928.

Kuki Shūzō. (2011) "Contingency." In *Japanese Philosophy: A Sourcebook*, edited by James W. Heisig, Thomas P. Kasulis, and John C. Maraldo. Honolulu: University of Hawai'i Press.

Light, Stephen. (1987) *Shūzō Kuki and Jean-Paul Sartre: Influence and Counter-Influence in the Early History of Existential Phenomenology*. Carbondale: Southern Illinois University Press.

Marra, Michael F. (2004) *Kuki Shūzō: A Philosopher's Poetry and Poetics*. Honolulu: University of Hawai'i Press. [Contains translations of some of Kuki's poetry as well as an essay about it.]

Mayeda, Graham. (2006) *Time, Space and Ethics in the Philosophy of Martin Heidegger, Watsuji Tetsurō and Kuki Shūzō*. New York: Routledge.

Nara Hiroshi. (2004) *The Structure of Detachment: The Aesthetic Vision of Kuki Shūzō*. Honolulu: University of Hawai'i Press. [Contains a translation of Kuki's *Iki no kōzō* (The Structure of Iki) and some interpretative essays.]

Okada Minoru. (1999) *Die Struktur von "Iki" von Shūzō Kuki: Eine Einführung in die japanische Ästhetik und Phänomenologie*. New York: Hänsel-Hohenhausen. [German translation of Kuki's *Iki no kōzō* (The Structure of Iki).]

Omodaka Hisayuki. (1966) *Le Problème de la contingence*. Tokyo: Editions de l'Université de Tokyo. [French translation of *The Problem of Contingency*.]

Pinkus, Leslie. (1996) *Authenticating Culture in Imperial Japan: Kuki Shūzō and the Rise of National Aesthetics*. Berkeley and Los Angeles: University of California Press.

Sakabe Megumi. (1990) *Fuzai no uta* [Songs of Absence: The World of Kuki Shūzō]. Tokyo: TBS Britannica.

Sakabe Megumi, Fujita Masakatsu, and Washida Kyokazu, eds. (2002) *Kuki Shūzō no sekai* [The World of Kuki Shūzō]. Kyoto: Minerva.

Tanaka Kyūbun. (1992) *Kuki Shūzō: Gūzen to shizen* [Kuki Shūzō: Chance and Nature]. Tokyo: Perikansha.

....

CHAPTER 25

COMPARATIVE PHILOSOPHY
IN JAPAN

Nakamura Hajime and Izutsu Toshihiko

....

JOHN W. M. KRUMMEL

Two thinkers who cannot be ignored when discussing comparative philosophy in Japan are Nakamura Hajime (1912–1999) and Izutsu Toshihiko (1914–1993). Contemporaries, they emerged during the postwar period and were respected for scholarly accomplishments in their respective fields—Buddhist studies and Indology for Nakamura, Islamic studies for Izutsu. Yet both authors, in their inexhaustible appetite and with their multilingual capacity, expanded their investigations to produce numerous comparative studies. Furthermore, each worked on an explicit and distinct theory of comparison.

Nakamura was versed in Sanskrit and Pali and became initially known in Japan for producing the first Japanese translation of the *Tripitaka*, followed by many other translations and commentaries of Buddhist texts ranging from South to East Asia, as well as of non-Buddhist Indian philosophical texts. His broad knowledge of Asian thought, extending beyond India to include the East Asian traditions, along with his knowledge of Western philosophy and multiple languages, allowed him to author comparative works, many of which were translated into Western languages and won him an international reputation. Astonishingly, his entire oeuvre consists of more than a thousand works, including books and articles he authored and dictionaries and encyclopedias he edited.

Izutsu, on the other hand, first made his mark as a pioneer of Islamic studies in Japan and for the first published translation of the Qur'an from the original Arabic. Based on his knowledge of Middle Eastern languages, he came to author many studies on Islamic thought, especially Persian philosophy and Sufi mysticism and theology. But, in addition, he also studied Western medieval philosophy as well as Jewish thought, and, in his later years and on the basis of his Buddhist background, he expanded his research into the domain of Eastern thought, both East Asian and South Asian. His oeuvre in fact extends beyond the domain of philosophy to include works on literature and the arts, linguistics, history, and Islamic jurisprudence. And his mastery of more than twenty languages enabled him to engage in comparative investigations. His comparative work is unique in providing not only an encounter between East and West, but also between Far East (East Asia) and Near East (Islam, including Arabia and Persia). Both his works on Islamic thought, as well as his comparative studies have been translated and are appreciated the world over.

The comparative project for each is distinct: Nakamura aimed to construct a world history of ideas that uncovers some basic patterns in the unfolding of human "thought." Izutsu aimed to (re-)construct an original "Oriental philosophy" that would encompass the vast terrain of his studies. In this chapter, I examine their respective comparative philosophies, compare and contrast them, and conclude with an assessment of their merits and demerits.

NAKAMURA HAJIME

Project

Why does Nakamura engage in comparative philosophy? Nakamura has been vocal concerning the pitfalls of overspecialization in academia and the need for a comprehensive framework that can clarify the significance of each subject within the contemporary context.[1] He especially expresses opposition to the division in the study of philosophy in Japanese academia between "Indian philosophy," "Chinese philosophy," and so-called *pure philosophy* (*junsui tetsugaku* 純粋哲学) that concentrates on Western philosophy. On the one hand, he criticizes scholars who only research Western philosophy while ignoring other regions. On the other hand, he critiques the predominantly philological approach taken in the other two philosophical fields and their lack of any critical spirit willing to tackle universal philosophical issues.[2] He stresses that Indian and Buddhist philosophies have contemporary relevance, with implications for our lives. Hence, their study belongs within a philosophically broader perspective, a global context that would make their relevance evident. Philosophical claims and ideas in general possess value and meaning for the entire human race, transcending country and period despite the particularities of historical-cultural context. Therefore we ought to overcome traditional boundaries so that we can obtain a comprehensive understanding of certain philosophical issues that may be universal. And this requires both a universal history of thought (*fuhenteki shisōshi* 普遍的思想史) and an investigation into the taxonomy of thought (*shisō keitaironteki kenkyū* 思想形態論的研究).[3]

---

[1] Nakamura 1974, 187; 1992, 4.
[2] Nakamura 1976, 233–235, 299.
[3] Nakamura 1976, 304–305.

Especially in today's world of mass communication and transportation, "our sense of belonging to one world has never been keener than the present."[4] But world peace can only be secured by greater mutual understanding between cultures and nations. Although becoming one in terms of technological civilization, the world is still divided in spirit, involving mutual suspicion and ideological conflict. This makes the comparative study of different currents of philosophy, their different views concerning similar issues, increasingly indispensable.[5] Nakamura laments, however, that there has not yet been any systematic gathering of the facts or features common to the different intellectual traditions within such a comprehensive perspective.[6] And this is the motivation for his own comparative project. Nakamura's hope is that comparison can open the gates to realizing peace and understanding among humanity as a whole.[7] He also states that only through comparison that would connect our lives to the essence of human existence may we hope to reach the truth—a truth that can lead to a new philosophy that corresponds to the world, a "new world philosophy."[8] His comparative project aims to open that possibility.

Method

Nakamura's comparative work is, for the most part, directed toward the analysis of "ways of thinking" or "thought" (shisō 思想) rather than philosophy (tetsugaku 哲学) per se. By "thought" he means the thinking habits of a culture, expressed in "the characteristic popular sayings, proverbs, songs, mythology, and folklore of that people," as opposed to coherent, self-conscious systems of thought that would be "philosophy."[9] As such, it is a cultural phenomenon (bunka genzō 文化現像), involving sociohistorical, psychological, aesthetic, and linguistic phenomena, and so on.[10] He prefers this broader significance of "thought" over the more restrictive connotation of "philosophy" that might exclude religious scriptures and literary works, because thought is the site of concrete issues encountered in everyday life that also serves as the cultural foundation indispensable to the growth of philosophy in the more restrictive sense. It is the link connecting the philosopher to his or her environment, whereby "the ways of thinking of philosophers cannot be freed completely of national or historical traditions."[11] Philosophy has developed within distinct cultural spheres, each with its own mode of thinking. And thus Nakamura takes human thought itself (ningen no shisō sonomono

---

[4] Nakamura 1964, 3.

[5] Nakamura 1976, 1, 232.

[6] Nakamura 1974, 188.

[7] Nakamura 1976, 233, 330–331; 1992, 567.

[8] Nakamura 1976, 231, 161; 1963, 59.

[9] Nakamura 1964, 5, 10.

[10] See the forward by Arthur Frederick Wright in Nakamura 1964, vii–viii, and the editor's preface by Philip P. Wiener in Nakamura 1964, xi.

[11] Nakamura 1964, 9.

人間の思想そのもの) to be the fundamental issue of his comparative analyses.[12] And *thought as such* should be studied regardless of who it belongs to. The focus of the investigation ought not to be on the personalities or authors traditionally regarded as authority figures,[13] because the individual is "strongly influenced by the ways of living and thinking in his own nation and culture,"[14] and it is *thought itself* vaguely diffused throughout society that becomes concentrated and crystallized in that single thinker.[15]

Not only do ways of thinking differ on the basis of the sociocultural environment, they also change as those environing conditions change. We cannot ignore their historical development. The comparative investigation of thought therefore must be undertaken historically.[16] But, in his historical investigations, Nakamura found that comparable modes of thought have emerged in entirely unrelated cultural spheres. On this basis, he also proposes the necessity in the comparative history of thought of a conceptual terminology that can be universally applicable to distinct philosophical currents.[17] Furthermore, he proposes such comparative research to be carried in two distinct directions: particularization and universalization. Particularization will either clarify the philosophical-intellectual tradition of a particular people of a particular region or make conspicuous the philosophical-intellectual particularities of a specific period common to distinct cultural areas (e.g., the medieval periods of both Europe and India). Universalization entails the application of an intellectual taxonomy in order to summarize specific types of philosophical or intellectual positions (e.g., materialism) regardless of the area, period, or developmental stage.[18] This latter might allow us, for example, to compare Buddhist psychology with modern psychology, as Rys-Davis did.[19] Nakamura attempts to realize some of these ideas concerning comparison in two monumental works.

Nakamura's Comparative History of Thought

Two major and massive works from the 1960s, in which Nakamura engages in such a comparative history of thought, are *Ways of Thinking of Eastern Peoples* (*Tōyōjin no shisō hōhō*, 1960 and revised 1964) and *History of World Thought* (*Sekai shisōshi*, 1975 based on 1964 lectures). In his slightly earlier work, *Ways of Thinking of Eastern Peoples*, Nakamura compares the thinking of distinct cultural spheres within the so-called East: India, China, Tibet, and Japan. He follows a common plan by first discussing the language and logic unique to a specific people and then discussing the manifestations

---

[12] Nakamura 1976, 1–2, 241–242.
[13] Nakamura 1976, 236, 238.
[14] Nakamura 1964, 3.
[15] Nakamura 1976, 239–240.
[16] Nakamura 1976, 131, 215, 230.
[17] Nakamura 1976, 238, 242.
[18] Nakamura 1976, 161.
[19] Nakamura 1976, 307.

of those linguistic-logical patterns in concrete cultural phenomena. He argues that the cultural life of a people, including their way of thinking, is intimately related to the grammar and syntax of its language.[20] That mode of thinking is also often made explicit and systematized in a logic (*ronri* 論理), the inductive and deductive modes of inference and judgment. But even logic as such is inseparable from sociocultural conditions. So, characteristic differences in ways of thinking between each people become reflected in patterns of logic.[21]

Nakamura also examines in *Ways of Thinking of Eastern Peoples* how each cultural sphere received and modified Buddhism in different ways. His purpose was to isolate indigenous thought patterns that resisted and endured under Buddhist influence.[22] Throughout his study, he makes comparisons and contrasts with Western ways of thinking as well. But his main focus here seems to be the differences among these peoples of "the East," differences that would undermine the stereotypical notion that there is a monolithic culture of "the Orient" that can then be contrasted with "the Occident." For example, he points out in another work of the same period how Indian thought tends to stress universals and disregard individuals or particulars, leading to the Indian disregard for history. Chinese thinking, however, tends to emphasize the particular while lacking consciousness of the universal, with the consequence that the Chinese are uneasy concerning attempts to abstract fixed laws from particular facts of history.[23] In general, in *Ways of Thinking of Eastern Peoples*, Nakamura underscores the same point he makes in *On Comparative Thought* (*Hikaku shisōron*, 1976, first edition 1960)[24]: there are conspicuous differences in thought due to environing sociocultural conditions that preclude reduction to simplistic dichotomies such as East versus West.

In *History of World Thought*, Nakamura extends his investigation beyond Asia to "the world," by which he actually means the advanced cultures of Eurasia. He maintains his view that thought is influenced by the sociocultural and linguistic setting, but he also attempts to "isolate, describe, and analyze certain key philosophical problems that have appeared historically in almost parallel developments within different cultural areas, East and West."[25] Here, "philosophical problem" has the same broad significance as "thought" in the above-mentioned sense. But by "parallel developments," Nakamura has in mind the fact that similar intellectual core issues have emerged in certain stages of cultural development in culturally unconnected areas and that particular issues characterize particular stages and lead to similar solutions. Because closely related problems were met in similar stages, the developmental process itself proved to be similar among different cultural areas.[26] Similar to how civilizations worldwide have

---

[20] Nakamura 1964, 5–6.
[21] Nakamura 1964, 8–9.
[22] See forward by Wright in Nakamura 1964, p. viii.
[23] Nakamura 1963, 45–49 and 46*n*2.
[24] Nakamura 1976, 230.
[25] Nakamura 1992, 3.
[26] Nakamura 1976, 249; 1974, 185; 1992, 3–5.

generally proceeded through the same stages from Stone Age to Bronze Age to Iron Age, and so on, Nakamura points to common stages in the intellectual history of the major Western and Eastern cultural spheres, moving from (1) ancient thought (in early agricultural societies) to (2) the rise of philosophy to (3) universal thought (with the early universal religions and the ideology of the universal state) to (4) medieval thought, and to (5) modern thought.[27] An example of a core issue emerging in distinct spheres in parallel stages would be the realism-nominalism debate concerning the status of universals that occurred in both Western Europe and in India during their respective medieval periods.[28] Another would be the relativisms of Heraclitus in ancient Greece and of the Jains in ancient India during the second stage of intellectual history.[29] Nakamura does not neglect to point out important contextual differences as well. Nevertheless, his focus here is on the similarity in development of intellectual history and in its stages among unrelated cultural areas.[30] He concludes that human beings, despite distinct traditions, face much the same problems of life, more or less, and have demonstrated comparable responses to them, due to similarity in human nature and human concerns.[31] In *On Comparative Thought*, he had already noticed that there are many philosophical issues universal to humanity and that truth may be discerned among every ethnic group regardless of tradition. But, at the same time, those universal issues, as concrete problems, are dealt with differently in response to different environments.[32]

Nakamura's Rejection of Stereotypes

One point that significantly distinguishes Nakamura from many other comparativists is his rejection of common stereotypes, whether Orientalist essentialism and the purported dichotomy between East and West on the one hand or a simplistic universalism and perennialism on the other. Although his *History of World Thought* was focused on showing the similarities in stages of development in intellectual history among cultures, he was careful to discuss significant differences that are due to linguistic and sociocultural conditions, as he already had in *Ways of Thinking of Eastern Peoples*. His analysis precludes the dichotomization of the world into two hemispheres, East and West. Throughout his comparative works, Nakamura repeatedly critiques such dualist formulas as Western logic versus Eastern intuition, Western individualism versus Eastern collectivism, Western analysis versus Eastern synthesis, Western secularism versus Eastern religiosity, Western materialism versus Eastern spirituality, and the like by providing counterexamples and showing the complex diversity within the so-called

---

[27] Nakamura 1992, 11.
[28] Nakamura 1976, 274–275.
[29] See Nakamura 1992, 170–171.
[30] Nakamura 1992, 565.
[31] Nakamura 1992, 475, 565.
[32] Nakamura 1976, 228–229.

East.[33] He concludes, concerning "Eastern thought," that we are "incapable of isolating a definite trait which can be singled out for contrast with the West" and that "there exists no single 'Eastern' feature."[34] In this regard, he points out the difficulty in Watsuji Tetsurō's theory of summing up the characteristics of the whole of what Watsuji called "the monsoon zone"—India, China, and Japan—and labeling them as "Asiatic."[35] In connection to this, he also criticizes the tendency among Western scholars to take everything east of Marseilles together as "the Orient."[36] And, just as the East is not a cultural unity but rather a diversity, the same can be said of the West, that "as far as ways of thinking are concerned, we must disavow the *cultural unity* of the West."[37] He thus finds the purported East–West dichotomy, according to which each is taken as a monolithic entity, to be conceptually inadequate and believes such commonly repeated clichés need to be reexamined.[38] This point is important to bear in mind as we turn now to examine Izutsu's comparative work.

Izutsu Toshihiko

Project

The trajectory informing Izutsu's comparative work is ultimately the formulation of a new type of "Oriental philosophy" (*tōyō tetsugaku* 東洋哲学) "based on a series of rigorously philological, comparative studies of the key terms of various philosophical traditions in the Near, Middle, and Far East."[39] Whereas Western philosophy, founded upon the two pillars of Hellenism and Hebraism, presents a fairly conspicuous organic uniformity in its historical development, there is no such historical uniformity or organic structure in the East. Instead, Eastern philosophy consists of multiple coexisting traditions with no cohesion that can be juxtaposed to Western philosophy as a whole.[40] Izutsu thus proposes to engage in the systematic study of the philosophies of the East in order to arrive at a comprehensive structural framework—a meta-philosophy of Eastern thought—that could *gather* those philosophies into a certain level of structural uniformity, a single organic and integral philosophical horizon.[41] What initially strikes today's reader, however, is that in his categorization of what is "Eastern" or "Oriental" in philosophy, he includes Islamic thought in conjunction with the South and East

---

[33] See Nakamura 1976, 205–212; 1964, 3–4, 13–15, 17.
[34] Nakamura 1964, 21.
[35] Nakamura 1964, 18–19.
[36] Nakamura 1976, 294.
[37] Nakamura 1964, 24.
[38] Nakamura 1963, 59; 1992, 4.
[39] Izutsu 1984, vii.
[40] Izutsu 1994, 2; 2001, 410.
[41] Izutsu 1994, 2; and see also afterword by Izutsu Toyoko in Izutsu, 1993, 187–188.

Asian traditions. Once having encompassed all the Eastern schools of thought, Izutsu ultimately hopes that such a meta-philosophy can then be broadened to encompass Western philosophy as well.

Izutsu claims that today's world more than ever before is in need of what Henry Corbin has called a "dialogue in meta-history" (*un dialogue dans la métahistoire*) between East and West.[42] And philosophy provides the suitable common ground for opening such intercultural meta-historical dialogue.[43] Comparative philosophy in general thus has the significance of promoting deep understanding between cultures.[44] But we first need better philosophical understanding within the confines of the Eastern traditions. Once this is done, the West can be included in the meta-historical dialogue. He adds that, despite the global dominance of the West, texts of the Orient can stimulate and enrich modern thought and can contribute, ultimately, to the development of a new world philosophy based on the convergence of the spiritual and intellectual heritages of East and West.[45] In other words, meta-historical dialogue, conducted first for the construction of "Oriental philosophy," can eventually be expanded to crystallize into a *philosophia perennis*—"for the philosophical drive of the human mind is, regardless of ages, places and nations, ultimately and fundamentally one."[46] Here, Izutsu, while focusing on "Oriental philosophy," unabashedly assumes the final goal of "perennial philosophy."

Method

In *Creation and the Timeless Order of Things*, Izutsu complains that comparative philosophy has failed hitherto mainly due to its lack of a systematic methodology.[47] He proposes that the comprehensive structural framework that would constitute the hoped-for meta-philosophy would consist of a number of substructures, each consisting of a network of key philosophical concepts abstracted from the major traditions and semantically analyzed.[48] The product should be a complex but "well-organized and flexible conceptual system in which each individual system will be given its proper place and in terms of which the differences as well as common grounds between the major schools of the East and West will systematically be clarified."[49] In his later years, in *Consciousness and Essence* (*Ishiki to honshitsu*; published in 1983), he calls this theoretical operation, "synchronic structuralization" (*kyōjiteki kōzōka* 共時的構造化).[50] He proposes that, on its basis, we can conduct a meta-historical analysis of traditions that

[42] Izutsu 1984, 1–2; 1994, 1.
[43] Izutsu 1984, 469; 1994, 67.
[44] Izutsu 1994, 68.
[45] Izutsu 1994, 66–67, also 185–186.
[46] Izutsu 1984, 469.
[47] Izutsu 1994, 67.
[48] Izutsu 1994, 68.
[49] Izutsu 1994, 68.
[50] Izutsu 2001, 411; also 1993, 11.

would be a meta-philosophy of Oriental philosophies. That is, by abstracting the philosophical traditions from the complexities and contingencies of their historical context and transferring them to an ideal plane—the dimension of what he calls "synchronic thought" (*kyōjiteki shisō* 共時的思想) where they are spatially juxtaposed and temporally co-current—he purports to construct a new "Oriental philosophy as a whole."[51] Within this structural field, the various traditions can be rearranged paradigmatically, enabling us to extract fundamental patterns of thought.[52] He admits that the development of such an organic unity out of disparate traditions would involve a certain artificial, theoretical, and, indeed, creative operation.[53] It requires the imposition of a common linguistic (or conceptual) system that would permit a meta-historical dialogue between the traditions.[54] But he *also* claims that these extracted patterns of thought are primordial and regulative archetypes in the deep layers of philosophical thinking of the "Oriental peoples."[55]

On this basis, the second step of Izutsu's comparative methodology involves a subjectification of that system of extracted patterns by internalizing them into oneself, thereby establishing one's own "Oriental philosophical viewpoint."[56] This existential move can, in turn, contribute to establishing, from out of the philosophical product of "synchronic structuralization," a new philosophy in the world context.[57] The postulation of this second stage seems to have personal significance for Izutsu when he states that the very premise of his comparative project was his self-realization that the root of his own existence lies in "the Orient" (*tōyō* 東洋), although he acknowledges here that what he means is rather vague and incoherent.[58] He says that he began to feel this root only as a participant in the Eranos Conference (1967–82). It was during those years that he decided he ought to pay greater attention to the Eastern traditions.[59]

Izutsu's "Oriental Philosophy"

With the goal of such a meta-philosophy of Eastern thought in view, Izutsu constructs an elaborate ontology using the concepts of existence, essence, and articulation. He begins this in his study of Sufism by taking the Islamic concept of the "oneness/unity of being" (*waḥdat al-wujūd*), stemming from Ibn al-'Arabī and developed in Iran by Mullā Sadrā, as the partial field of such a meta-philosophy.[60] The concept of existence

[51] See Izutsu 2001, 7–8, 411.
[52] Izutsu 2001, 411.
[53] Izutsu 2001, 410–411.
[54] See Izutsu 1984, 472.
[55] Izutsu 2001, 411.
[56] Izutsu 2001, 411.
[57] Izutsu 2001, 412.
[58] Izutsu 2001, 409.
[59] See Yoshitsugu Sawai, "Editor's Essay: Izutsu's Creative 'Reading' of Oriental Thought and Its Development" in Izutsu 2008, 2:215–223, 216.
[60] See Izutsu 1994, 66–68.

or being—*wujud* in Arabic and *existentia* in Latin—has the same basic connotation in the Islamic and Christian traditions. But the issue of identifying this concept is compounded when there is no historical connection between the ideas being compared, as in Sufism and Daoism. In his study comparing the two (*Sufism and Taoism*, 1984, first edition 1966–67) as represented by 'Arabī on the one hand and Laozi and Zhuangzi on the other, he expresses the need to pinpoint a central concept active in both even if having its linguistic counterpart in only one of the systems while remaining implicit in the other. We must then stabilize it with a definite "name," which may be borrowed from the one system in which it is linguistically present.[61] He thinks the concept of "existence/being" from the Arabic *wujud* serves this purpose because it is simple and does not color what it intends with unnecessary connotations.[62] Izutsu believes the Sufi notion of the "unity of being," if structurally analyzed and developed properly, can provide a theoretical framework or basic conceptual model for clarifying the fundamental mode of thinking characterizing Eastern philosophy *in general*, not only Islamic philosophy. As such, it provides a broad conceptual framework or common philosophical ground—an archetypal form—on the basis of which a meta-historical dialogue between Eastern philosophies historically divergent in origin can be established.[63] For example, beyond Islam and Daoism, he includes Buddhism in the mix, with its notion of "suchness" (Sk. *tathatā*; Jp. *shinnyo* 真如), which he interprets to mean "being as it really is."[64] He also includes Western existentialism in its recognition of the fundamental vision of existence itself as primary.[65]

Another conspicuous example of his method of extracting a common concept to construct a meta-philosophy is his examination of the concept of "essence" (*honshitsu* 本質) in his *Consciousness and Essence*. He extracts this notion of the *whatness* of a thing from the context of the scholastic debates that dominated the history of post-Greco philosophy (as *quidditas*, *essentia*, and *māhīyah*) since Aristotle and extends its application into the context of Eastern thought.[66] He does this on the basis of his claim that at least conceptual equivalents to it played a significant role in Eastern philosophies as well. What he stresses as noticeable in all cases is its connection with the semantic function of language and the multilayered structure of human consciousness.[67] In fact, it is the distinction and relationship between the two key concepts of existence (being) and essence, constituting an ontological dynamic, that forms the thematic of the full flowering of Izutsu's entire comparative project of "Oriental philosophy" in his later years.

Whether the focus is on existence or on essence, one fundamental theme that reappears throughout Izutsu's project of "the synchronic structuralization of Oriental

---

[61] Izutsu 1984, 472.

[62] Izutsu 1984, 472–473.

[63] See Izutsu 1994, 66–69, especially 68–69; also 1984, 472–473.

[64] Izutsu 1994, 76.

[65] See Izutsu 1994, 177.

[66] See Izutsu 2001, 61–64.

[67] Izutsu 2001, 7–8.

philosophy" is articulation (*bunsetsu* 分節)—both ontological and semantic (the two being inseparable). Articulation for Izutsu is the process whereby beings are discriminated or differentiated through meaning.[68] Language plays an important role in this process, and it is also inseparably connected with consciousness, whereby "the self-same reality is said to be perceived differently in accordance with different degrees of consciousness."[69]

On the basis of this theme of articulation, involving both existence and essence, he constructs a general ontology for his Oriental philosophy in *Consciousness and Essence*. Accordingly, the source or foundation of reality is originally indeterminate and without form or name (*musō mumei* 無相無名). In different traditions, it is called absolute (*zettai* 絶対), true reality (*shinjitsuzai* 真実在), *dao* (道), emptiness (*kū* 空), nothing (*mu* 無), the one (*issha* 一者), true suchness (*shinnyo*), *al-ḥaqq*, *wujud*, or being/existence (*sonzai* 存在), and more.[70] In its original state prior to any linguistic partitioning, Izutsu calls it "absolute non-articulation" (*zettai mubunsetsu* 絶対無分節).[71] But we find this idea in his earlier comparative works as well, such as in his study of Sufism and Daoism, wherein he identifies the pure act (*actus purus*) of existence in both 'Arabī's "unity of being" and in Zhuangzi's "heavenly leveling" or "chaos" (Ch. *hundun*; Jp. *konton* 混沌) as unconditionally simple, without delimitation, and not a determinate thing, a nothing (in Zhuangzi, *wuwu* 無無).[72] As further references indicative of absolute nonarticulation, he includes Shingon's "originally unborn" (*honpushō* 本不生), Vedānta's Brahman, the nonpolarity (Ch. *wuji*; Jp. *mukyoku* 無極) beyond ultimate polarity (Ch. *taiji*; Jp. *taikyoku* 太極) in Neo-Confucianism, Nāgārjuna's emptiness (*śūnyatā*), Neoplatonism's "the one," Kabbalah's *ein sof*, and the like.[73] In that original state of being an undifferentiated whole, things are without essence.[74]

The vision of that undifferentiated unity of being is obtained in an "abnormal" spiritual state that Izutsu finds exemplified in a variety of traditions, as in the Daoist practice of "sitting in oblivion" (*zuowang*), the Sufi experience of "self-annihilation" (*fanā'*), the Buddhist experience of *nirvāna*, the Zen experience of nothing (*mu*) or emptiness (*kū*), and the *ātman-Brahman* identification in Vedānta.[75] In all of these cases, what takes place is the emptying of the ego into that nonarticulated source. In such a state, consciousness loses its intentionality to correspond to existence in its original nonarticulation. In *Consciousness and Essence* Izutsu takes this state of consciousness to be a meta-consciousness of the profound subtlety of being as absolutely unarticulated.

---

[68] See Sawai in Izutsu 2008, 2: 221.

[69] Izutsu 1994, 7.

[70] See afterword by Izutsu Toyoko in Izutsu, 1993, 188.

[71] Izutsu 2001, 11–12, 392.

[72] See Izutsu 1984, 304–305, 310, 377, 386–387, 389–390, 482–483, 486; 1994, 37n28, 87–88; 2008, 2: 140–143.

[73] See Izutsu 1987, 194; 1994, 33–34; 2001, 277–278; 2008, 2: 167.

[74] See Izutsu 1984, 323, 363.

[75] See Izutsu 1984, 358, 420, 475, 478, 480–481; 1994, 77; 2001, 392.

He asserts this to be a fundamental characteristic of Oriental thought.[76] Moreover, in many of these traditions, this state of world-and-ego annihilation is followed by a return to the manifold, whereby one engages with the world anew, this time with the awareness that everything is an *articulation of the originally unarticulated*. For example, in Sufism, that state following *fanā'* would be *baqā*.[77]

The nothingness of undifferentiation obtained in that vision is at the same time the plenitude of being as the ground of everything.[78] Hence, the empty vessel that is the *dao* in *Laozi* is infinitely full of being[79] and the undivided chaos crumbles into "an infinity of ontological segments."[80] In Shingon Buddhism, emptiness is simultaneously the *dharmakāya* (*hosshin* 法身), symbolized by the letter *A*, meaning *both* negation *and* origination.[81] In Vedānta, that duplicity between nothing and being in the absolute is expressed in the notions of *nirguna Brahman* and *saguna Brahman*. In Sufism, it would be the inner essence of God (*dhat*) and his self-revealing exteriority (*zāhir*), and in Neo-Confucianism, it would be nonpolarity (*wuji*) and ultimate polarity (*taiji*). Izutsu also refers to Zhuangzi, Nāgārjuna, Zen, and the Jewish Kabbalah as exemplifying parallel ideas.[82] He does point out differences, however, such as between Mahāyāna Buddhism's emphasis on the nothingness of all essences of things and Vedānta's emphasis on Brahman as the one true essence behind everything.[83] On the basis of that duplicity of the ontological ground, the world serves as the locus for the continuous and inexhaustible self-articulation of what is originally unarticulated. For example, in 'Arabī, the process moves from the divine essence (*haqq*) to the created world (*khalq*); in Laozi, from the mystery of mysteries to the ten thousand things.[84] Everything in the world is thus indicative of the absolute, as its delimitation, and the many as such eventually returns to ascend back into its source, the one.[85] What unifies the one and the many here is existence itself as the all-comprehensive reality of which things are determining qualities or attributes; hence, Izutsu's generalization of "the oneness of being" (*wadhat al-wujūd*).[86] What characterizes these "Oriental" philosophers for Izutsu is that they have learned to see things simultaneously in those two directions—reality as indeterminate and as determined, as one and as many, as nothing and as being, with "compound eyes."[87] And all of these examples of Eastern thought that he cites indicate, each in its own way, that process of reality as the self-articulation of absolute nonarticulation (*zettai mubunsetsu*)

---

[76] Izutsu 2001, 16.

[77] Izutsu 1994, 79.

[78] Izutsu 1984, 483.

[79] Izutsu 1984, 409.

[80] Izutsu 1987, 193.

[81] Izutsu 2001, 231–232.

[82] See Izutsu 1982, 129–130; 1993, 36–37, 45; 1994, 28, 85–86; 2001, 27, 231, 277; 2008, 2:73–75, 166.

[83] See Izutsu 2001, 28–29; 2008, 2: 19–21.

[84] See Izutsu 1984, 481, 492–493.

[85] See Izutsu 1984, 412, 491–493; 2008, 2: 53.

[86] See Izutsu 1994, 73, 181.

[87] Sawai in Izutsu 2008, 2: 222; also see 158.

into discrete things and events. Through this "articulation" (*bunsetsu*) theory, Izutsu thus extracts what he views to be the common structure behind the disparate texts of the "Eastern" traditions, including those of the Near East, Persia, and Semitic thought.

According to Izutsu, the process of ontological articulation corresponds to psychological states or degrees of awareness.[88] He accordingly takes to be another major characteristic of Eastern thought the notion that consciousness is a multilayered structure in correspondence with the articulation process of being.[89] The mandala in esoteric Buddhism, for example, depicts that dynamic process between nonarticulation and articulation as a matrix not only of cosmological events but also of psychological events.[90] As usual, he refers to multiple sources from distinct traditions as exemplifying this idea: Mullā Sadrā, Śaṅkara, ʿArabī, Yogācāra, and others.[91] In the case of ʿArabī, he cites the middle realm between the absolute and the world, the *mundus imaginalis* or realm of primordial images (*aʿyān thābitah*), where so-called essences unfold as archetypes in the deep structures of both being and consciousness. He finds equivalents in the *Yijing*'s hexagrams and the Kabbalah's *sefirot* as all depicting the dynamic process of articulation, involving degrees or levels, moving from the unarticulated to the articulated, in both being and mind.[92] Izutsu creatively interprets Yogācāra's notion of the *alaya-vijñāna* together with the Buddhist notion of *karma* in correspondence with this theory as well.[93]

Izutsu approaches articulation further in terms of the cultural environment or network of linguistic meanings that contextualizes the emergent entity. Such semantic articulation (*imi bunsetsu* 意味分節) is linguistic; it happens through naming, and this determines—particularizes and specifies—what is thus articulated. Everything—facts and thing-events in the empirical world as well as ourselves—is nothing but ontological units of meaning or meaningful units of being that have been articulated semantically through language. Hence, for Izutsu, "semantic articulation is immediately ontological articulation" (*imibunsetsu soku sonzaibunsetsu* 意味分節即存在分節),[94] and he regards this to be one of the main points of Eastern thought in general. Although this became his thesis concerning "Oriental philosophy," it is interesting to note that even prior to the initiation of his comparative project, in his early anthropological-sociological study from 1956, *Language and Magic: Studies in the Magical Function of Speech*, he states that the grammatical and syntactic structure of language is to a great extent responsible for the way we think and that it constitutes for its speakers a special sort of *meaning*.[95] With his theory of articulation, he extends that early interest in the

---

[88] See Izutsu 1994, 7.
[89] Izutsu 2001, 316–317.
[90] Izutsu 2008, 2: 52.
[91] See Izutsu 1974, 168–170; 1982, 126–127, 152; 1994, 10–11.
[92] See Izutsu 2001, 73, 273–275.
[93] We see this throughout Izutsu 1993 and 2001.
[94] Quoted by Izutsu Toyoko in her afterword in Izutsu 1993, 189.
[95] Izutsu 1956, 89–90.

importance of language in the ontological direction, whereby consciousness draws lines of articulation through the semantic function of words.

In Izutu's mature thought, it is that articulative function of language, in connection with the multilayered structure of consciousness, that gives rise to "essences" (*honshitsu*) in the various traditions.[96] Consciousness is naturally directed toward grasping the "essence" of some thing,[97] and this directedness is connected to the semantic indicative function of language. Through the reception of a name, something X obtains an identity and crystallizes into such and such a *thing*.[98] Thus, in Laozi and Zhuangzi, the originally unarticulated *dao* that is a nothing (Ch. *wu*; Jp. *mu*) transforms into beings by receiving names. Izutsu views that articulation into "essences" to be an a priori occurrence through a cultural and linguistic framework as a kind of transcendental structure, whereby ancient Greece had its own system of "essences" expressed in Socrates' search for the eternal and unchanging *ideas*, and ancient China had a distinct system of "essences" expressed in Confucius' theory of the rectification of names.[99] Every phenomenon receives its form by passing through this culturally or linguistically specific mesh of archetypal semantic articulation.

Borrowing Buddhist terminology, Izutsu calls that culturally specific collective framework, operating in the deep layers of consciousness, "the linguistic *alaya*-consciousness" (*gengo araya-shiki* 言語アラヤ識).[100] As a "linguistic a priori," it is the storehouse of semantic "seeds" (*shuji* 種子) of meaning, as karmic traces of our mental and physical activities, their semantic effects, conditioned by the cultural-linguistic mesh, accumulated and stored, but in constant flux. Eventually, these seeds, as they surface into our conscious states, become objectified, hypostatized, and reified into the concrete images we take to be ontological realities.[101] On this basis, we tend to polarize the subject and object realms as mutually exclusive,[102] and we come to recognize "essences" in the empirical world that had been produced through the activation of the semantic "seeds."[103] In effect, this is a superimposition of essences upon reality, articulating the originally unarticulated into discrete unities with names.

Essences as such, in themselves, are fictions. This is in contrast to the essentialist positions that would reify essences into absolutes. In his view, essentialism alone cannot comprehend the true nature of reality that is originally undifferentiated.[104] Izutsu

---

[96] Izutsu 2001, 7–8.

[97] Izutsu 2001, 8.

[98] Izutsu 2001, 13–14.

[99] Izutsu 2001, 129; see 1956, 66–67.

[100] See Izutsu 2001, 130; also 2008, 2: 125–126.

[101] See Izutsu 2008, 2: 13–14, 127–128; Izutsu Toyoko's afterword in Izutsu 1993, 191–192; and Shinya Makino, "On the Originality of 'Izutsu' Oriental Philosophy" in *Consciousness and Reality: Studies in Memory of Toshihiko Izutsu*, edited by Sayyid Jalāl al-Dīn Āshtiyānī, Hideichi Matsubara, Takashi Iwami, and Akiro Matsumoto (Leiden: Brill, 2000), 251–258, 255–257.

[102] Izutsu 1987, 190.

[103] Izutsu 2001, 130–131.

[104] Izutsu 1984, 358, 365.

notices as common to the Eastern traditions a deep-seated mistrust of language and its function of articulating reality into such essences.[105] He refers to the ontological currents of Mahāyāna Buddhism, such as Madhyamaka, Cittamatra, Zen, and Shingon, as well as Advaita Vedānta, Neo-Confucianism, Daoism, and Sufism, to make his case.[106] He does point out, however, differences among Mahāyāna, 'Arabī, and Śankara concerning the degree of reality essences possess.[107] And he also discusses cases that do not fit his view of the "existentialism" of "Oriental philosophy"; for example, the "essentialisms" of primitive Confucianism's "rectification of names," of Song Neo-Confucianism's notion of *li* (Jp. *ri* 理, "principle"), and of the Nyāya-Vaisesika of India.[108] But he seems to regard them as exceptions to the main current of the East. The main philosophical current is this "existentialism," founded on the intuitive grasp of the "unity of being," existence as it dynamically unfolds essences, as expressed in Izutsu's formula "semantic articulation qua ontological articulation" (*imi bunsetsu soku sonzai bunsetsu*). This also means that essences are not absolutely nonexistent because they are pervaded by existence and are the unfolding of existence.[109] Izutsu finds this ontological dynamism exemplified in the Mahāyāna phrase, "true emptiness, profound being" (*shinkū myōu* 真空妙有).[110] That is to say, essences exist as the articulation of the unarticulated. True suchness thus *both* resists *and* permits articulation.[111]

Izutsu finds that ontology of "true emptiness and profound being"—the semantic qua ontological articulation of the unarticulated—to be the meta-structure common to the various traditions of "Oriental philosophy." According to Nagai, "the Orient" as a philosophical concept signifies for Izutsu nothing other than that negation of the reification of essence and the ontological dynamism between nonarticulation and articulation.[112] According to Izutsu's wife Izutsu Toyoko, this dynamic of articulation is the key perspectival stance and structural hypothesis that Izutsu conceptually designed and intentionally assumed in his attempt to realize "the synchronic integrative structure of Oriental philosophy" (*tōyōtetsugaku no kyōjironteki seigō kōzō* 東洋哲学の共時論的整合構造).[113] With this idea, he attempted to integrate the various cultural-textual horizons he had traversed in his lifelong studies into a single meaningful and organic all-inclusive horizon to bring his philosophical search to closure.[114]

---

[105] Izutsu 1987, 193–194.

[106] See Izutsu 1987, 194–195; 2001, 19.

[107] See Izutsu 2001, 26–33.

[108] See Izutsu, 1984, 382–385; 1987, 188; 2001, 33–35.

[109] Izutsu 1984, 367–368.

[110] Izutsu 2001, 24.

[111] See Izutsu 1993, 45–46.

[112] Shin Nagai, "Phenomenology of the 'Inapparent' and 'Oriental Philosophy': Towards a Phenomenology of 'Emptiness,'" *Journal of the Indian Council of Philosophical Research*, 25 (1) (January–March 2008), 19–30, 26–27.

[113] Izutsu Toyoko in Izutsu 1993, 192.

[114] See Izutsu Toyoko in Izutsu 1993, 193–194.

The last work he completed before his passing, *The Metaphysics of Consciousness in the Philosophy of the Awakening of Faith in the Mahāyāna* (*Ishiki no keijijōgaku—Daijōkishinron no tetsugaku*), published in 1992 was supposed to initiate the full-scale concretization of this "synchronic structuralization of Oriental philosophy." And he allegedly had plans to further incorporate other texts, traditions, and doctrines—*alaya-vijñāna*, Kegon and Tendai, Suhrawardi's Illuminationism (Ishraqi), Platonism, Confucianism, Shingon, and Daoism (of Laozi and Zhuangzi), as well as texts of Jewish thought, Indian philosophy, and the Japanese classics, among others—as key topics in the establishment of such a "synchronic structural horizon" (*kyōjironteki kōzō chihei* 共時論的構造地平).[115] The general sense one gets of his concept of "Oriental philosophy," as we can see, seems expansive enough to include almost anything outside of the mainstream dualist strand of Western philosophy, such that one can find traces of "the East" within "the West" (e.g., Plotinus, Eckhart, etc.) as well as within the Semitic, Persian, and Islamic traditions.

CONCLUSION

We are now in a position summarize the comparative philosophies of each thinker before comparing and contrasting them and discussing their merits and demerits. We might summarize important features of Nakamura's comparative philosophy in the following manner. He claims that his work proves philosophy is not confined to the West.[116] But, at the same time, he prefers the term "thought" (*shisō*) over "philosophy" as having a broader significance to encompass intellectual ideas expressed in religion, literature, and mythology as well. In the historical development of such thought, he recognizes similar patterns throughout the advanced cultures due to our common humanity. And yet he also recognizes important differences that result from distinct sociocultural environments. This makes him reject the stereotypical dichotomy of East versus West that would essentialize each or reduce them to monolithic entities because he recognizes diversity within each hemisphere, as well as commonalities between them. To make his point, Nakamura succeeds in compiling an abundant amount of historical information. But while emphasizing the need to go beyond mere philology or historiology in doing comparative philosophy, Nakamura keeps to a minimum his speculations concerning any metaphysical or ontological implications of his comparative analyses.

The scope of Izutsu's research activities, like Nakamura's, is vast. But the true trait of his comparative work is really in its speculative depth and originality. I believe Izutsu's comparative project of "Oriental philosophy" has merit when read as his creative construction of a unique ontology on the basis of concepts appropriated from a variety of

---

[115] Izutsu Toyoko in Izutsu 1993, 186–187.
[116] Nakamura 1992, 567.

traditions. But his project becomes problematic if we read him as merely a comparativist aiming to unfold the true essence of "the Orient" common to the disparate traditions he groups under the category of "the East." In doing this, he appropriates conceptual schemes from a single tradition and uses them to explicate the others. Izutsu admits, for example, to the Greek origin of the Islamic concept of existence and its relation to the Western scholastic concept, *existentia*.[117] This connection with philosophical schemes stemming from the scholastic traditions of both Islam and the West becomes obvious especially in *Consciousness and Essence* when he refers to the essence-existence contrast and the opposition of essentialism and existentialism. One thus cannot help but ask whether Izutsu is reading Daoism and the other traditions of Asia under a light originally cast by ancient Greece. And, if so, would this undermine his claim that what he is uncovering is a truth unique to "the Orient"? Of course, he often includes "ancient Greece" within what he means by "the Orient," but the essence-existence scheme he borrows was fully developed within Western medieval philosophy. And he never provides an explicit defense or justification for his extension of "the Orient" to ancient Greece, which is commonly referred to as the origin of "the Occident." When he writes that the thought patterns he extracts from his comparative analyses are primordial patterns regulative of the philosophical thinking of Eastern peoples, "the Orientals" (*tōyōjin* 東洋人),[118] one cannot help but ask: Who are "the Orientals"? He includes not only the peoples of East Asia and South Asia, but also the Persians and the Semites and even the ancient Greeks. How can the extraction of "the Orient" out of such disparate traditions and diverse peoples not be arbitrary? Is this not an invention of "the Orient" rather than its discovery? Is he ignoring his own ontological premise of "Oriental philosophy," that is, the linguistic-cultural contingency of essences, by constructing an "essence"—"Orient"—that defies the manifold fluidity of "existence"? Certainly, his project is to construct an ontological standpoint out of the variety of nondualist traditions that fall outside of the mainstream dualist and essentialist current of Western philosophy. But even if we grant this much, why must we call it "Eastern" or "Oriental"? In the end, the question of whether Izutsu's ontological theory of "existentialism" and "Oriental philosophy" is viable depends largely on how one reads Izutsu—as a *comparative* philosopher comparing traditions or as a comparative *philosopher* creating his own ontology.

Both thinkers were incredibly prolific as comparative philosophers, covering a wide range of traditions based on penetrating analyses of major texts. Moreover, they both reflected on the nature of comparison, and each constructed a theory of comparative philosophy. Having examined their work, we are now in a position to compare and contrast their comparative projects and evaluate their strong and weak points. Both possess a firm foundation in their respective fields—Izutsu in Islamic studies and Nakamura in Indology and Buddhist studies—with unsurpassed knowledge of languages permitting them to read texts from multiple traditions. Significantly, both stress the importance

---

[117] Izutsu 1984, 471–472.
[118] Izutsu 2001, 411.

of language and its analysis as a starting point for their comparative work. Nakamura focuses on the differences between languages as a basis for sociohistorical differences in ways of thinking among distinct cultures. Izutsu focuses on the universal function of language as semantic articulation that also leads to culturally specific distinctions. Both speak of the need for a common conceptual terminology in comparing the traditions. But in the intellectual history of distinct cultures, both East and West, Nakamura recognizes a pattern they all follow in their stages of development. Izutsu, on the other hand, discerns within the multiple traditions of "the East" a core sensibility that distinguishes them from Western philosophy. Certainly, Nakamura's project, especially in *History of World Thought*, aims to show those common patterns through which intellectual history unfolds in response to human situations. But he is careful to point out culture-specific sociohistorical conditions that account for important differences as well. It may then be too simplistic to regard his comparative theory as merely a "universalism." On the other hand, Izutsu, while emphasizing "the Orient," attempts to construct a kind of transcultural transhistorical metaphysics that bypasses those cultural-historical specifics that Nakamura is keen on pointing out. Moreover, it encompasses a vast range of traditions that broadens "the Orient" from the Far East to the Near East and includes Semitic, Persian, and even Greek thought. His "relativism" thus harbors within itself a tendency toward "universalism" in its own right. And, like Nakamura, he speaks of the ultimate aim of a "world philosophy," even a *philosophia perennis*. I raise these points to underscore the complexity of each of their comparative theories and to prevent us from simplistically characterizing Nakamura as a universalist and Izutsu as a relativist.

Stylistically, their methods of comparison and philosophizing are quite distinct. Nakamura is meticulous in his examination of the relevant historical and sociocultural data. He seems both historically and sociologically, as well as philologically, well-grounded in his claims. But his claims are modest in speculation and do not extend deep into the realms of metaphysics or ontology. Izutsu, by contrast, is much more speculative and metaphysically bold. But, in his enthusiasm, he tends to overlook significant contextual differences between the traditions as he liberally overlays conceptual schemes borrowed from one tradition upon other traditions. Nakamura was keen in debunking popular stereotypes, such as the reductive dichotomy of East and West. Under Nakamura's penetrating gaze, Izutsu's entire project of "Oriental philosophy" may appear suspect. But Nakamura, while admonishing scholars of Asian thought for being too philological and lacking any philosophical depth, himself seemed to shy away from venturing into the kind of metaphysical speculation that he might have attempted on the basis of his comparative analyses. Although stating that comparison ought to lead to a new world philosophy, he fails to provide one himself. Izutsu, on the other hand, in his zeal to construct the sort of "world philosophy" to which Nakamura thinks comparison ought to lead, ends up committing the fallacies Nakamura warns against. In short, we can say that Nakamura was too cautious and Izutsu was too daring. Nevertheless, comparative philosophers today need to pay attention to these two intellectual giants of

Japan in the field of comparative philosophy. We can learn from both their strengths and weaknesses.

BIBLIOGRAPHY AND SUGGESTED READINGS

Izutsu, Toshihiko (1956). *Language and Magic: Studies in the Magical Function of Speech.* Tokyo: Keio Institute of Philological Studies.

Izutsu, Toshihiko (1974). "The Philosophical Problem of Articulation in Zen Buddhism," *Revue internationale de philosophie 28*: 165–183.

Izutsu, Toshihiko (1982). *Toward a Philosophy of Zen Buddhism*, Boulder, CO: Prajñā Press.

Izutsu, Toshihiko (1984). *Sufism and Taoism: A Comparative Study of Key Philosophical Concepts.* Berkeley: University of California Press.

Izutsu, Toshihiko (1987). "The Ontological Ambivalence of 'Things' in Oriental Philosophy." In *The Real and the Imaginary: A New Approach to Physics*, edited by Jean E. Charon. New York: Paragon House, 187–197.

Izutsu Toshihiko (1993). *Tōyō tetsugaku kakusho—Ishiki no keijijōgaku—Daijōkishinron no tetsugaku* [Notes on Oriental Philosophy: The Metaphysics of Consciousness: The Philosophy of *The Awakening of Faith in the Mahāyāna*]. Tokyo: Chūōkōronsha.

Izutsu, Toshihiko (1994). *Creation and the Timeless Order of Things: Essays in Islamic Mystical Philosophy.* Ashland, OR: Cloud Press.

Izutsu Toshihiko (2001). *Ishiki to honshitsu* [Consciousness and Essence]. Tokyo: Iwanami.

Izutsu, Toshihiko (2008). *The Structure of Oriental Philosophy: Collected Papers of the Eranos Conference*, Vols. 1 & 2. Tokyo: Keio University Press.

Nakamura, Hajime (1963). "Comparative Study of the Notion of History in China, India and Japan," *Diogenes 42* (Summer): 44–59.

Nakamura, Hajime (1960). *Tōyōjin no shisō hōhō* [Ways of Thinking of Eastern Peoples]. Tokyo: Shinkōsha.

Nakamura, Hajime (1964). *Ways of Thinking of Eastern Peoples: India, China, Tibet, Japan*, translated and edited by Philip P. Wiener. Honolulu: East-West Center Press.

Nakamura, Haijme (1967). "Interrelational Existence," *Philosophy East and West 17.1/4* (January–October):107–112.

Nakamura, Hajime (1970). "Pure Land Buddhism and Western Christianity Compared: A Quest for Common Roots of their Universality," *International Journal for Philosophy of Religion 1*, 2(Summer): 77–96.

Nakamura, Hajime (1974). "Methods and Significance of Comparative Philosophy," *Revue internationale de philosophie 28*: 184–193.

Nakamura Hajime (1975). *Sekai shisōshi* [History of World Thought]. Tokyo: Shunkōsha.

Nakamura Hajime (1976). *Hikaku shisōron* [On Comparative Thought]. Tokyo: Iwanami.

Nakamura, Hajime (1992). *A Comparative History of Ideas.* Delhi: Motilal Banarsidass.

Nakamura, Hajime (2002). *History of Japanese Thought 592–1868: Japanese Philosophy before Western Culture Entered Japan.* London: Kegan Paul.

CHAPTER 26

JAPANESE CHRISTIAN PHILOSOPHIES

TERAO KAZUYOSHI

JAPANESE Christianity's encounter with Western philosophy dates back to the late nineteenth century, when the Edo Shogunate opened the country after two centuries of self-imposed isolation. Thus, historically speaking, the encounter belongs to Japan's engagement with "modernity." Christianity itself had arrived in the so-called *kirishitan* period of the sixteenth and seventeenth centuries, but the role of philosophy only came to the fore in the transition from the middle ages period to the early modern period, where it represented an important chapter in the story of the Christian mission in Japan. Although Christianity lacked universities or other suitable facilities to discuss philosophy, a small number of outstanding individuals took the first steps. Among them were the eminent statesman and Confucian scholar Arai Hakuseki (1657–1725) who conducted a respectful examination of Giovanni Battista Sidotti, a Catholic missionary apprehended by government authorities, and Fukansai Habian (1565–1621), a Zen monk who converted to Christianity and became a Jesuit, only later to become a severe critic of his adopted religion.

Here, we concentrate our attention on the historical period beginning with the Meiji restoration of 1868, although it must be said that prior to the end of World War II, Japanese Christian philosophies remained relatively undeveloped. While theologians were clumsily trying to digest denominational doctrines imported into their seminaries from abroad, academics interested in philosophy focused their attention all but exclusively on German philosophies represented by the towering figures of Kant and Hegel. The two camps labored independently and rarely crossed paths. It was only in the postwar years that this began to change. With their new-found freedom of thought, theologians and philosophers were able to establish themselves on more solid ground and initiate an intellectual exchange that has continued to the present.

Not surprisingly, the first Japanese Christian philosophers were young and filled with the enthusiasm of pioneers. Hence, even if "Christian philosophy" was virgin territory, it was blessed with a number of first-rate minds. In what follows, we single out some of these figures and organize them into seven basic types. In doing so, we draw on the broader fields of theology and social thought that border on philosophy in the strict sense.

MUKYŌKAI CHRISTIAN PHILOSOPHY

Mukyōkai Christian philosophy originated with the *Mukyōkai* (無教会) or No-Church movement founded by Uchimura Kanzō (1861–1930) who saw Jesus and Japan as the twin pillars of his Christian faith. A sibling group was begun by Nitobe Inazō, an old friend of Uchimura who was later to join the Quakers. Both of them had participated in Japan's emergence from the feudal society of the Edo shogunate and passed on to their followers a strong sense of the value of asceticism. This is particularly evident in Nitobe's classical work, *Bushidō* (武士道). In addition, most of their disciples were deeply influenced by the writings of Kant and Max Weber. As already mentioned, from the Meiji to the early Shōwa period, academic philosophy in Japan revolved principally around Kant and Hegel. In general, Hegelian philosophy was dominant during World War II and Kant in subsequent years. Thus, for example, the Hegelian brands of nationalism that flourished during World War II were later overshadowed by the more pacifist approach of Kant. This latter is evident in the Christian philosophy of the *Mukyōkai* movement.

The first person of note here is Yanaihara Tadao (1893–1961), an economist who went on to become president of the University of Tokyo. A specialist in colonial management, Yanaihara had a solid knowledge of political philosophy and was in close contact with Nitobe, himself an active "citizen of the world" who had married an American and served as undersecretary-general of the League of Nations. Their contemporary, Nambara Shigeru (1889–1974), maintained close ties to Kantian philosophy throughout his life. Kant's essay on "Perpetual Peace" was one of his favorites, and indeed Nanbara's pacifist idealism proved often to be a source of tension with politicians of the day. The statesman and realist Yoshida Shigeru, for example, dismissed Nambara as an "idiot who twisted the truth to play to the times" (*kyokugaku asei no to* 曲学阿世の徒). Among Nambara's successors we may mention Miyata Mitsuo (1928–) whose pacifist philosophy combined Kantian ideas with biblical thought and the theology of Karl Barth.

The *Mukyōkai* school also produced the talented biblical scholar Sekine Masao (1912–2000) and the advocate of a moral philosophy of education Amano Teiyū (1884–1980), as well as Hakari Yoshiharu (1931–), who adopted a Kantian perspective to provide a philosophical foundation for the *Mukyōkai* movement. Recognizing the importance of Christianity in Kant's philosophy, Hakari struggled against the tendency in the *Mukyōkai* movement to belittle theology.

Perhaps the most celebrated Weberian in Japan, Ōtsuka Hisao (1907–1996) had a historical theory of economics named after him. Like Maruyama Masao (1914–1996), who himself had no connection to the *Mukyōkai* movement but was deeply influenced by

Weber's political theory, Ōtsuka was a leading scholarly voice for postwar democracy. Having studied under Uchimura as a young man, Ōtsuka combined his sympathy for Marx's claim that the United Kingdom was the most developed country of the time with a strong emphasis on Weber's theory of the "Protestant ethic." His "philosophy of democracy" served the intelligentsia with viable arguments for economic development and political democratization.

Although these philosophers and thinkers in the *Mukyōkai* movement had their feet firmly planted in Christianity, they did not so much speculate on their faith as lay the ground for successive generations of Japanese Christian philosophy.

CHRISTIAN PHILOSOPHY AND CLASSICAL PHILOLOGY

The textual focus of classical philology meant that its place in Japanese Christian philosophy has been largely limited to academics working in national universities, where theologians have not had a strong presence. At the same time, since many of the leading figures have been Christian, we cannot rule out the presence of latent theological interests. Katō Shinrō (1926–), a specialist in Platonic philosophy, has tried to link the philosophical thought of church fathers like Augustine to various types of mystical thought, East and West. Sekine Seizō (1950–), a professor of ethics, has sought a philosophical perspective from which to relate the thinking of the Old Testament to pressing issues facing society today. In addition to the department of philosophy, the study of classical philology in the University of Tokyo's faculty of arts has promoted the research and teaching of philology. We may mention the work on Gnostic thought that has gone on there and has played an important role in expanding the view of established Christianity in order to pursue a deeper understanding of the figure of Jesus as a human being. In particular, we single out Arai Sasagu (1930–), who has brought questions of gender and heresy to the fore, and Ōnuki Takashi (1945–), who introduced literary sociology into the field of Christian studies. Insofar as Gnosticism is concerned with an intellectual approach to God and the cosmos, it is seen as one way to stimulate dialogue among individuals and, at the same time, to open intellectual pursuits to greater participation in the public sphere.

In contrast, Kyoto University's specialization in classical philology has generally kept its distance from Christianity, although its focus on the history of Western philosophy has included the study of medieval Christian philosophy. One thinks here of the work of Yamada Akira (1922–2008) on Augustine and Thomas Aquinas. Yamada played a central role in the meticulous translation of the *Summa Theologiae*. That said, he did not accept scholastic thought dogmatically but reserved a role for independent thinking, as his major works, including *Lectures on Augustine* (*Augusutinusu kōwa*), attest. The study of medieval philosophy among Catholic scholars introduced an emphasis on reason in Christian philosophy in Japan to counterbalance the often excessive Protestant tendency to downplay rational thought.

The approach of classical philology, although biased toward Greek and Latin texts and rather weak in its appreciation of Hebraic thought, raised the standard of scholarship and, at the same time, opened the way to public philosophy. Given the rigorous linguistic demands and the limited number of academic posts available to them in Japan, it is not surprising that the number of specialists in the field has been small. Nevertheless, their efforts served to strengthen the ties of Christian philosophy to critical thinking.

MARXIST AND SOCIALIST CHRISTIAN PHILOSOPHY

Along with Marxist and socialist thought, Christianity played a great part in helping fill the spiritual void that overtook Japan after its defeat in World War II. Broadly speaking, all three shared a common humanism. As a capitalist country, in the Meiji era, Japan was quick to participate in the world economy, even though the recognition of human rights was held in check by the older imperial Constitution. The two questions were inseparable, but Japan's role in world history was still peripheral and too overshadowed by emotional and theoretical difficulties to assert itself.

The transition from theory to praxis was far from smooth, as witnessed by the Christian socialist Kagawa Toyohiko (1888–1960), whose mystical temperament combined with a strong activism that characterized him as a core member of the first generation of Japan's Social Democrat Party. Tensions between Christianity and Marxist socialism are still more evident in the case of Akaiwa Sakae (1903–1966). A committed follower of Karl Barth, Akaiwa was no less committed to socialist ideals, which he tried to embody under the dual role of Christian pastor and communist. We see this reflected in a work published just before his death, *The Exodus from Christianity* (*Kirisutokyō dasshutsuki*). In his efforts to pursue demythification of Christian doctrine to its ultimate consequences, his philosophical standpoint remained a loose and undeveloped amalgam of Marxism and existentialism. It was rather Aikawa's lifestyle that influenced many young intellectuals who shared his concerns.

Although most philosophers engaged in these questions displayed a high degree of emotional involvement, there were those who took a more tempered approach. Most notable among them was Matsumoto Masao (1910–1998), an Anglican convert to Catholicism and specialist in medieval philosophy. His interest in ontology led him to wrestle with the thought of Nishida Kitarō (1870–1945), in particular the idea of "creation from nothing," but his work was all but totally ignored by philosophers carrying on the tradition of the Kyoto School. After the war, Matsumoto focused on the socialist thought of Christian activists like Félicité-Robert de Lamennais and the French Catholic republican Antoine-Frédéric Ozanam. Matsumoto also embraced wholeheartedly the commitment to freedom of conscience championed by the Catholic Church in the wake of the Second Vatican Council. In his view, this entailed a rejection of the union of church and state, as well as a repudiation of traditional dogmatic hegemony, but it did not mean a simple acquiescence to Marxist socialism. His foundational idea was that Christianity needs to promote the cause of natural law vigorously in order to bring the maturity it had achieved as a religion to the social dimension as well. To this end, he argued that Christianity should establish closer cooperation with well-intentioned thinkers outside the Christian faith, convinced as he was that leftist ideologies had much to offer by way of criticism of the ecclesiastical rigidity that traced its roots back to Constantine the Great.

Tagawa Kenzō (1935–) represents this type of engaged Christian philosophy that flourished during the 1960s and 1970s. During those years, when Marxism and socialism had reached their peak in Japan, he presented Jesus as a kind of paradoxical rebel. His portrayal of Jesus as a liberator from economical oppression was meant to foster the same internal self-criticism that characterized Christianity's abiding influence in Western civilization.

As interest in Marxism and socialism waned, so did the appeal of leftist Christian philosophies. Today, they are almost entirely passed over, as many Christian intellectuals have grown weary of the pointless and ineffectual squabbles between socialists and evangelicals. Meantime, the Catholic Church has failed to develop critical thinking of its own, with the paradoxical result that the inspiration of Vatican II has become a kind of empty cliché. In short, Christian philosophies of a Marxist and socialist stamp have dwindled into total obscurity.

CHRISTIAN PHILOSOPHIES OF RELIGION

A fourth type of Christian philosophy has to do with the philosophy of religion. To understand this current of thought, we need to look back to the years before and during the war. The most representative figure in this area was Hatano Seiichi (1877–1950). Dissatisfied with the views of the Neo-Kantians who were being widely discussed at the time, Hatano returned to the critical philosophy of Kant himself. On this basis, he examined the religious experience of Jesus, Paul, and other key persons in early Christianity. By focusing on what they had to say on topics like time and eternity, his aim was to rethink the place of religion in human life and its potential for transforming human existence. Hatano made it clear that he did was a philosopher of religion, not a theologian. As he put it, he did not want to theorize about human beings from the perspective of God but rather to discuss God from the viewpoint of the human. Culture, as a communal reality born of interaction among human beings and bearing a fund of symbols, was equipped to manage the conflicts between individuals in their natural state. But without taking a more encompassing reality into account, other persons degenerate into mere objects for the subjective ego. Hatano held that the idea of God as supreme being and absolute other was indispensable for valuing human existence and bringing it to the full flower of *agape*, the highest achievement of creation. Even so, he continued to insist that the concern of philosophy was to examine the essence of religion within the horizon of human activity.

Hatano was the founder and first senior professor in the second department of religion, now the department of Christian studies, in Kyoto University's faculty of letters. He was succeeded in the post by Ariga Tetsutarō (1899–1977), whose approach differed from Hatano's, and then by Mutō Kazuo (1913–1995), who returned to Hatano's interests in the philosophy of religion. Like Hatano, Mutō did not feel bound by conventional theological method but brought a theological sensitivity to bear on preparing the philosophical ground for Christianity's dialogue with other religions. He had studied under Tanabe Hajime and concentrated on Kierkegaard, but he later turned to phenomenology for guidance. Mutō's approach has been linked to the neo-Romanticism of Odagaki Masaya (1929–), who labored to overcome the subject–object dichotomy in theology by focusing on the Holy Spirit as a way to recover faith at the limits of disbelief.

A current of thought known as existential Christian philosophy broke new ground in the Christian philosophy of religion. Although Odagaki may be included here, Noro Yoshio (1925–2010) is a more representative figure. A specialist in the thought of John Wesley, Noro later turned to existential theology. He drew on the philosophical ideas of writers like Carl Michelson, who interpreted biblical thought and its culmination in the events of the eschaton as an existential reading of human being, and the Russian mystical thinker Nicolai Berdyaev. Under their influence, Noro took a positive view of universal salvation while at the same time developing his own theology of *saṃsāra*—the repeating cycle of birth, life, death, and rebirth—by reading theories of metempsychosis in the light of Christian spirituality and cosmology.

These developments in Christian philosophy of religion cleared the path for a more positive reception of Buddhist ideas, reinforcing earlier intimations of the potential of Christian philosophy to appropriate elements of Buddhist philosophy.

CHRISTIAN PHILOSOPHY IN A BUDDHIST KEY

Throughout the history of Christian philosophies in Japan, the influence of Buddhist philosophy stands head and shoulders above everything else. Behind it stand two intellectual giants: Nishida Kitarō, who provided philosophical support, and Takizawa Katsumi (1909–1984), who carried Nishida's thought over into Christian thought. Takizawa worked out his own Christian philosophy by grappling with a broad range of ideas from Zen, Pure Land Buddhism, and Marxism, all of which were popular among postwar thinkers.

Without applying the designation "Buddhist philosophy" too strictly, we may say that Nishida kept Buddhist thought at the core of his speculation from his early days as a Zen practitioner all the way through to his crowning essay on "The Logic of Place and the Religious Worldview" (*Bashoteki ronri to shūkyōteki sekaikan*). Indeed, the ideas of Pure Land Buddhism figured more prominently in that piece than anywhere else in his corpus.

Nishida had encouraged Takizawa to seek out Karl Barth to supervise his studies in Germany rather than work under Martin Heidegger. Although Takizawa spent several years studying philosophy and ethics at Kyūshū University, it was indeed his encounter with the theology of Barth during his time in Bonn and Basel that proved to be the decisive influence.

Even before his baptism at forty-nine, Takizawa can rightly be called a Christian philosopher. His thought revolves around the proto-fact of "Immanuel" (*Immanueru no genjijitsu* インマヌエルの原事実), a relationship between God and human beings that is "inseparable, non-identical, and irreversible" (*fukabun fukadō fukagyaku* 不可分・不可同・不可逆). This proto-fact entails two points of contact: the primary contact of God's unmediated love for human beings, which is present prior to any expectations we place on God, and the secondary contact that results from human attempts to see God. For Takizawa, Jesus is the prototype of this secondary contact and as such holds a place of special importance, but this does not preclude the presence of other concrete models of secondary contact. Barth acknowledged in principle that it would be possible to conceive of salvation in other religions similar to salvation through Christ, but denied that it had actually occurred in reality. In contrast, Takizawa not only held that salvation outside of Christ was *possible* but sought examples in the salvific claims of other religions. For Takizawa and his followers, the challenge of such an open approach to salvation without giving up belief in Christianity was to work out its implications concretely in the context of human life. This, we may say, represents the broadest and deepest current of Christian philosophy in Japan.

The Catholic philosopher Honda Masaaki (1929–) struggled against nihilism in his youth before finding his way to the faith. For a time, he even contemplated entering the priesthood. Unable to abide what he saw as the excessively Western character of world Christianity, Honda grounded his thinking on the "logic of *soku* (即)" (identity based on a mutually defining correlation) as he found it in Zen and Tendai Buddhism. This logic provided him a viewpoint from which to sublate monism and dualism and, at the same time, to put to rest the debate over the reversibility or irreversibility of Takizawa's theory of Immanuel as proto-fact.

Onodera Isao (1929–) has emphasized the spirituality of the earth for which his homeland of Tōhoku has been emblematic. His writings pursue what he calls "immanent Catholicism." While remaining rooted in his native milieu, his philosophy has taken the form of a new pneumatology based on "the place where Trinity is located" (*sanmi ittai no oite aru* 三位一体のおいてある場所), which in turn draws on a notion of "place" (*basho* 場) crucial to Nishida's philosophy of absolute nothingness. In this connection, we may recall the efforts of Odagaki and, more importantly, Nobuhara Tokiyuki (1937–), whose thinking bears the strong imprint of his study of Whitehead thought under John B. Cobb, Jr. In recent years, Nobuhara has turned his attentions to questions of ecology, where he has enriched the tradition of process thought with original reflections on the celebrated Zen monk Ryōkan.

Among Takizawa's disciples and sympathizers, Yagi Seiichi (1932–) stands out for his radical—and often critical—development of Takizawa's thought. Coming from a specialization in New Testament theology, Yagi adopted Takizawa's idea of the proto-fact of Immanuel to draw a fundamental distinction between Jesus and Christ. He argues that *Christ* refers to the true and ultimate self all human beings are endowed with, what Zen master Linji called the "true human without rank" (*mui no shinjin* 無位の真人), whereas *Jesus* is a historical figure who accepted the divine workings of this immanent Christ and incorporated its nondiscriminating love in his own person.

Kitamori Kazō (1916–1998) was conspicuous for his critical approach to these Buddhist formulations of Christian philosophy. He is best known for his *Theology of the Pain of God* (*Kami no itami no shingaku*), in which he sought to counter the tendency to "identification with the divine" in Western theology. Kitamori had great respect for Nishida's claim that a "religion of suffering" embodying the absolute vow of Amida Buddha represents the essence of the "spirit of the present age." At the same time, he resisted Nishida's attempts to constrain God to the ontological category of "nothingness" and to gloss over the reality of divine wrath. When all is said and done, he concluded, Nishida's standpoint eclipses the sense of sinfulness, which is needed to prepare human beings for a divine love that embraces a humanity wholly undeserving of it. Despite his insistence that theology be held accountable for the effect its ideas have on society and his harsh criticisms of philosophy for its failure to assume responsibility in the real world, Kitamori's writings themselves never more than skim the surface of philosophical questions. This is not to say that his instincts were entirely off the mark. For instance, he raised the interesting criticism that the further Nishida's speculations on the *unity* of the many became removed from concrete historical problems, the easier it was for them to slide into the *uniformity* of the many.

GENERATIVE CHRISTIAN PHILOSOPHY

In recent years, a new spiritual trend has begun to take shape in Japanese philosophical circles. Stimulated by the thrust of Kitamori's criticisms but unwilling to relegate them to an academic joust between theology and philosophy, and encouraged by the encounter with Buddhist philosophy to question the overreliance on Greek and Roman modes of thinking, a number of thinkers have tried to wed existential Christian philosophy to Kitamori's emphasis on "pain" by focusing on the memory of historical tragedies.

Miyamoto Hisao (1945–), a Dominican priest and first-rate biblical scholar who is well versed in the philosophy of the Church fathers, has set his sights on a core idea of Western theology: "onto-theo-logia." The view of the world spawned from this idea,

Miyamoto argues, has been the seedbed of totalitarian ideas that dehumanize and de-value the human, ideas that have found their extreme expression in the gas chambers of Auschwitz and the atomic holocausts of Hiroshima and Nagasaki. Taking his cue from the Old Testament narrative of deliverance that galvanized the identity of the Jewish people, he set out to find similar routes of "exodus" for Japanese Christianity to liberate itself from Western ontological thinking. He finds the feelings of ethnic oppression captured in the Korean idea of *han* (恨) sympathetic to his aim of a positively creative or "generative" mode of Christian thought. He suggests shifting the priority from Ariga's focus on objective "hayatology" (a Hebrew notion of existence or *hāyāh* as an alternative to Greek ontology) to a more subjective "ehyehology" (from *ehyeh*, the first-person ap-pellation by which Yahweh identifies himself). His project is underscored by a dynamic pneumatology that relates the power of *ruach*, the breath of life, to public philosophy, and then goes on to re-envision human society from the standpoint of harmony and cooperation.

The concrete application of philosophical ideas to the reconstruction of civilized so-ciety found a dedicated pioneer in the figure of Oshida Shigeto (1922–2003), an older Dominican colleague of Miyamoto's. Oshida was not an academic but a spiritual leader. He carried out his reforms by moving to the Japanese countryside, far away from the supervision of the ecclesiastical establishment, where he set up a largely self-subsistent commune. He stressed a mindset of *koto-kotoba* (コトことば), words embodied in events that precede words. In this way, he hoped to heal the rift between word and act that he saw in modernity and Western civilization, and to carry out, on a modest scale, his own brand of resistance to institutionalization. Oshida's radical "imagination from nothing," whose echoes he found both in Zen and in the Christian spiritual tradition, sought to replace the drive for strength and domination with a community of like-minded but weak individuals seeking harmony with a fragile environment.

POPULAR CHRISTIAN PHILOSOPHY

By and large, Christian philosophies in Japan were born in academia, but there are some important exceptions. The most typical of these was Yamamoto Shichihei (1921–1991), the owner of a small publishing house devoted mainly to biblical studies. From his wide reading in the classics of China and Japan, Yamamoto's own writings were leveled against the self-preoccupation of Japanese culture with its own uniqueness. In a famous book published under the pen name of Isaiah Ben Dasan and entitled *The Japanese and the Jews* (*Nihonjin to Yudayajin*), he characterized the Japanese people as the exact op-posite of the Jews, who defined themselves in terms of a covenant with God. Written as a kind of self-portrait of the Japanese mind, the subtlety of its criticism was lost on many of its readers, among them Takizawa Katsumi, who published a book-length refutation. Yamamoto also dabbled in historical criticism. For example, he traced the "spirit of cap-italism" in Japan back to two Edo-period thinkers, Ishida Baigan and the Zen monk

Suzuki Shōsan, and the Meiji restoration to the seventeenth-century Zen monk turned Neo-Confucian, Yamazaki Ansai. He further advanced his own view of the Japanese emperor, arguing that neglect of political thinkers like Yamazaki had led to the distorted idea of the emperor as a living deity or *arahitogami* (現人神), an idea that brought great suffering to Japanese Christians during the war years.

Tomioka Kōichirō (1957–), a literary critic with a university position, has been deeply influenced by Uchimura's idea of Japan as an "Old Testament" for Japanese Christianity. Tomioka sees Japan neither as a culture nor as a tradition but as a principle and an orthodoxy. This standpoint had been present in the background of the wartime debate on "overcoming modernity" (*kindai no chōkoku* 近代の超克) and, indeed, Tomioka himself took a positive stance toward the Greater East Asian War on the grounds that Japan was able to function as a symbolic presence of principled morality.

Wakamatsu Eisuke (1968–), a Catholic who had been baptized as an infant, studied mystical thinkers like Izutsu Toshihiko (1914–1993) and, in the aftermath of the Great East Japan Earthquake of March 11, 2011, has tried to find meaning in the tragedy by proposing that the dead be viewed as an ongoing, living presence. His efforts form part of more widespread efforts today, including those of established religions, to clarify Japanese thinking on life and death.

In general, popular Christian philosophers have been skeptical of academic culture on the grounds that it all too easily becomes lost in abstractions. On the one hand, they argue that pure scholarship deprives religion of its essentially transcendent dynamism by dissolving it into anthropology. As a result, it both distorts the reality of God and, ironically, impoverishes our view of human life. On the other, they consider the anthropocentric moorings of academic philosophy to be an uncritical import from the modern West. Given the aborted attempts by wartime and postwar Japanese intellectuals to "overcome modernity," these hints from popular Christian philosophy have something important to add to the discussion.

Conclusion

Christian philosophy in Japan has been too diversified to speak of any unified position or even of a common fund of questions. If there has been one unifying factor, it is the awareness that Christianity, as a religious practice or as a body of thought, is insufficiently rooted in the native soil of Japan to blossom in the same manner as it has in the West. For this reason, many Christian philosophers from various specializations have challenged world Christianity to seriously consider the value of forms of thought fundamentally different from those of traditional Western philosophy. The self-examination going on within Western philosophy in recent years suggests that the time is ripe for Japanese Christian philosophy to come into its own.

Despite the minority status of Christianity in Japan, compared with neighboring countries in East Asia like South Korea, where it has taken a strong hold, we need not jump to the conclusion that the Christian mission as such has come to an end in Japan. On the contrary, the intellectual experiments carried out among Japanese thinkers independently of the clerical establishment, clumsy and piecemeal as they have been, hold out the promise of a new beginning. The very marginalized nature of these experiments, together with the fact that they are largely sympathetic to a religious worldview of immanent transcendence and other aspects of the Buddhist heritage they share with the culture at large, has enabled them to lay the foundations of a forum for dialogue. Moreover, there are signs that younger Christian philosophers are eager to navigate more freely among the seven categories outlined herein and to blur the borders of specialization that have hitherto kept them apart. In other words, Christian philosophy in Japan has gradually become a kind of laboratory for developing new strains of Christian self-understanding. Much of this may alarm the gatekeepers of orthodoxy, but if the efforts of Christian thinkers in Japan are not incorporated into local tradition and exposed to similar efforts going on around the world, there is little chance Christianity will get over its chronic isolation from Japanese life and thought.

BIBLIOGRAPHY AND SUGGESTED READINGS

Works in Japanese

Akaiwa Sakae. (1964) *Kirisutokyō dasshutsuki* [Exodus from Christianity]. Tokyo: Rironsha.

Hakari Yoshiharu. (1994) *Kinchō: tetsugaku to shingaku* [Tension: Philosophy and Theology]. Tokyo: Risōsha.

Hatano Seiichi. (1943) *Toki to eien* [Time and Eternity]. Tokyo: Iwanami Shoten.

Kim Seung Chul. (2006) "Ajia no shūkyōteki tagensei to kirisutokyō [Christianity and the Religious Plurality of Asia]." In *Hikaku shūkyōgaku e no shōtai* [An Invitation to the Comparative Study of Religion], edited by Ashina Sadamichi. Tokyo: Kōyō Shobō, 144–67.

Matsumoto Masao. (1968) *Shingaku to tetsugaku no jidai* [The Age of Theology and Philosophy]. Tokyo: Chūō Shuppansha.

Miyamoto Hisao. (2008) *Tasha no yomigaeri* [The Revival of Others]. Tokyo: Sōbunsha.

Nambara Shigeru. (1973) *Nihon no risō* [The Ideal of Japan]. *Nambara Shigeru chosakushū* [Collected Works of Nambara Shigeru], vol. 9. Tokyo: Iwanami Shoten.

Nishida Kitarō. (1989) *Nishida Kitarō tetsugakuronshū* [Collected Philosophical Essays of Nishida Kitarō], vol. 3. Tokyo: Iwana Shoten.

Noro Yoshio. (1964) *Jitsuzonronteki shingaku* [Existential Theology]. Tokyo: Sōbunsha.

Oshida Shigeto. (1983) *Tōi manazashi* [A Distant View]. Tokyo: Jiyūsha.

Ōtuska Hisao. (1966) *Shakaikagaku no hōhō* [The Method of Social Science]. Tokyo: Iwanami Shoten.

Tagawa Kenzō. (1980) *Iesu to iu otoko* [Jesus the Man]. Tokyo: San'ichi Shobō.

Takizawa Katsumi. (1964) *Bukkyō to kirisutokyō* [Buddhism and Christianity]. Kyoto: Hōzōkan.

Yamada Akira. (1986) *Augusutinusu kōwa* [Lectures on Augustine]. Tokyo: Shinchi Shobō.

Yanaihara Tadao. (1946) *Nihon seishin to heiwa kokka* [Japan's Spirit and Peaceful Nation]. Tokyo: Iwanami Shoten.

Works in English and German

Ben Dasan, Isaiah/Yamamoto, Shichihei. (1981) *The Japanese and the Jews*. Tokyo: Tuttle.

Hatano, Seiichi. (1988) *Time and Eternity*. New York: Greenwood Press.

Kitamori, Kazoh. (1965) *Theology of the Pain of God*. Richmond: John Knox Press.

Mutō Kazuo. (2012) *Christianity and the Notion of Nothingness: Contributions to Buddhist-Christian Dialogue from the Kyoto School*. Leiden: Brill.

Takizawa, Katsumi. (1987) *Das Heil im Heute: Texte einer japanischen Theologie*. Göttingen: Vanderhoeck & Ruprecht.

Yagi, Seiichi, and Leonard Swidler. (1988) *A Bridge to Buddhist-Christian Dialogue*. New York: Paulist Press.

CHAPTER 27

··

YUASA YASUO'S PHILOSOPHY OF SELF-CULTIVATION

A Theory of Embodiment

··

SHIGENORI NAGATOMO

AMONG the voluminous writings of YUASA Yasuo (1925–2005), we find essays that thematize and develop a theory of embodiment. These are gathered mainly in Volume Fourteen of *Yuasa Yasuo's Complete Works*,[1] which contains two major works addressing the topic of self-cultivation along with eighteen other essays that supplement them. The two major works are *Shintai: Tōyōteki shinshinron no kokoromi* (*The Body: Toward an Eastern Mind-Body Theory*) (Yuasa 1987c) and *Shintai, Ki, Shugyō* (*The Body, Self-Cultivation and Ki-Energy*) (Yuasa 1992). Judging from the fact that this was the first volume of his *Complete Works* that he had published, it seems that it occupied a central place in his scholarship. It is for this reason that I will focus in this chapter on the two main works contained in that volume.

Why, then, does Yuasa develop a theory of embodiment as one of the most important themes of inquiry in his scholarship? We can probably adduce many reasons for this, including psychological, cultural-geographical, and historical issues,[2] but a short answer—which I think captures his real intent—would be for the purpose of proposing an East Asian view of the body in the context of global philosophy. Or, alternatively, Yuasa presents a theory of embodiment as an attempt to overcome the modern Western paradigm of thinking and offers it as a stepping stone to propose East Asian holistic views of the human being and nature. He believes that his theory of embodiment can open up a new perspective on these holistic views, with the hope that his theory becomes

---

[1] Yuasa 1999–2013.

[2] Yuasa's direct motive for launching an investigation into this topic is indicated in the postscript he wrote to *Kindai nihon no tetsugaku to jitsuzonshisō* [Modern Japanese Philosophy and Existential Thought], in which we find him saying that "Through the research material for this book, I have come to notice that a unique view of the body exists among the Japanese philosophers" (Yuasa 1999–2013, 10: 393).

an impetus to change the direction of the contemporary global situation in a way conducive to fostering a holistic thinking and lifestyle.

When we attempt to articulate his theory of embodiment within the context of the philosophy of self-cultivation, however, we immediately encounter the difficulty of capturing its entirety accurately within a limited space for it incorporates a diversity of academic fields, such as Eastern and Western philosophy, depth psychology, neurophysiology, modern Western medicine, conditioned reflex theory, psychosomatic medicine, Eastern acupuncture medicine, and parapsychology. It also covers theories of sports and artistry. On glancing at the scope of his inquiry, one cannot but be amazed by its breadth because it goes far beyond the average capacity of a single scholar. Only an intellectual giant such as Yuasa could digest these diverse fields and craft them into a unified theory while maintaining thematic consistency and coherence as well as depth of thought. Yuasa's theory is as comprehensive as it is interdisciplinary.

Since it is not possible to thoroughly discuss within a limited space all the multifarious dimensions of Yuasa's theory of embodiment, I will focus on four salient thematic features that I discern in his theory: (1) the predicament of human beings—particularly their everyday epistemological stance, which he characterizes as "commonsensical" dualism; (2) the body scheme he designs to capture the process involved in self-cultivation; (3) a methodological approach to overcoming commonsensical dualism; and (4) certain salient features discernible in the philosophy of self-cultivation that he incorporates into his theory of embodiment. To conclude this short chapter, I will draw a few implications from this theory of embodiment.

COMMONSENSICAL DUALISM

To understand Yuasa's theory of embodiment, we need to first look at how the body is treated in the Western philosophical tradition. Historically, in the tradition of Western philosophy, a concern for how to understand the body surfaced explicitly in the seventeenth century when Descartes declared "*cogito ergo sum*" as *the* principle of philosophical investigation—that is, his claim of the apodictic certainty of the *cogito*—although the germination of this mode of thinking can be traced as far back as the distinction introduced in Greek philosophy between form (*eidos*) and matter (*hylē*).[3] Descartes defines the body as that which is extended—that is, as matter existing in space that is ontologically distinct from the *cogito*—whereas he defines the *cogito* as that which thinks, as well as that which is extensionless: as a disembodied mind (or soul) that stands, as

---

[3] See Nishida Kitarō's criticism concerning this distinction in Nishida Kitarō, *Place and Dialectic: Two Essays*, translated by John W. M. Krummel and Shigenori Nagatomo (New York and Oxford: Oxford University Press, 2011), 49–60. For Nishida's criticism concerning this distinction, see his "*Kōitekichokkan*" [Acting-Intuition] contained in *Nihon no meicho 47: Nishida Kitarō* (Tokyo: Chūōkōron sha, 1976), 417–418.

it were, outside of space. This is the well-known Cartesian dualism.[4] Yuasa questions, however, if the body as understood in Cartesian dualism is not, in fact, the body belonging to an "I."[5] This is, Yuasa reasons, because one's own body as a whole resists total objectification, insofar as "I" rely on "my" external sensory perception for observation, unlike another's body, which "I" can objectify *in toto*.[6] Let us examine Yuasa's critique of Cartesian dualism a little more closely.

In Descartes' mind-body dualism, the concept of the mind-in-general arises by generalizing the *cogito* of an "I" that is anonymized.[7] What should be noted here is the fact that in this generalization others' minds are totally excluded. This is because the concept of the generalized mind is obtained, when considering its ontogenesis, by expanding the scope and content of the *cogito* that belongs to an "I." On the other hand, the concept of the body-in-general is obtained equally by generalizing others' bodies while also rendering them anonymous. Consequently, "my" own body similarly disappears in this generalization because the generalized concept of the body includes only others' bodies as seen from the perspective of an "I." In short, Yuasa's point is that these generalizations ignore a difference in the mode of cognition. To be specific, they ignore the difference between an "I" knowing "my" own body and others' bodies and between an "I" knowing "my" mind and others' minds. For example, when "I" attempt to know another's mind, "I" rely on his or her bodily and/or linguistic expression, but, unlike knowing "my" own mind, another's mind cannot be known *directly* here and now as long as "I" rely on the everyday mode of understanding.

However, when we judge these points in light of the experiential fact that as long as a human being is alive, he or she is *an integrated whole* of the mind and the body (i.e., in light of "I" knowing "my" own body vis-à-vis the state of "my" mind), then it is obvious that Descartes' mind-body dualism is incoherent. For although the mind belongs to an "I," the body that is accordingly thematized is not "my" body but that of others. In other words, when Descartes defines "the mind" as that which is extensionless, he is using the other's body as a referential point that does not belong to an "I," and so we can discern here a discrepancy between the mind and the body in regard to their ownership. This reveals an inconsistency in his thinking. At the same time, it also discloses that his mind-body dualism is disjunctive in nature because "my" mind is cut off from "my" body and is juxtaposed with another's body as if it equally refers to "my" body. If so, it follows that the "therefore I am" that is declared after asserting "I think" comes to mean that "my" mind exists without implying that "my" body exists, which is incoherent in view of the experiential fact that human beings are an integrated whole.

---

[4] As is often observed, in the background of this dualism is an inheritance of the Christian flesh-spirit dualism in a secularized form, along with the faith in the immortality of the soul.

[5] Yuasa 1999–2013, 11: 632–636.

[6] One may argue that since the meaning of the body is that which is thought by the *cogito*, it is correct to understand it as the idea of the body (i.e., as bodyness). Because of this reason, it cannot be understood as that which is perceived by external perception. As the following argument suggests, it is unquestionable, however, that the body thus understood also contains a problem.

[7] Yuasa 1999–2013, 11: 339.

Regardless of this incoherence, the generalized concept of the body, which does not include "my" body, is assumed to be real in the practice of medical science, which is organized by following the Cartesian method of thinking: the body that this science addresses in its research and treatment is a body that is taken as a mere physical object. It is an object-body that is opposed to an "I" who lives "my" subject-body from within. On the other hand, the generalized concept of the mind, which does not include another's mind in Descartes' disjunctive mind-body dualism, is seen in the philosophy of idealism, which regards transcendental subjectivity as an a priori condition for cognition (e.g., in the philosophies of Kant and Husserl).

Why, then, does Descartes' dualism surface in this way? Yuasa argues as follows.[8] In the field of everyday experience, there exists a pre-reflective, practical understanding of communal nature as a condition that exists *prior to* a theoretical investigation concerning the mind-body relationship, and this antecedent condition imposes a structure on how the everyday understanding must occur. In other words, on the strength that we are all humans, there exists a pre-reflective understanding that presupposes an *interchangeability* between "my" mind and another's mind and between "my" body and another's body, and, by accepting this interchangeability as "a matter of fact," we carry out our daily activity. If a person were to deny it, such a person would fall into solipsism. However, the truth that a solipsist holds is ephemeral because it disappears with his or her death. In spite of this pre-reflective, practical, communal understanding as an antecedent condition, however, a "way" to *directly* apprehend another's mind is closed off in the field of everyday experience when relying on "my" sensory perception and "my" discursive mode of reasoning—that is, as long as we rely on the everyday method of cognition. This epistemological closure is a predicament for the human being placed in the field of everyday experience, where "being placed" for Yuasa is a fundamental restriction for the human being as a contingent being. (I will expound this point later in the chapter.) He takes this position on the ground that the human being is an embodied existence. He calls the standpoint that places the human being in such a predicament "commonsensical dualism."[9]

Here, we can discern a reason why Yuasa turns to the philosophy of self-cultivation. We must acknowledge provisionally, he reasons, that the above-mentioned epistemological predicament is *intrinsic* to the everyday standpoint[10] as long as we take a theoretical stance toward understanding the mind-body relationship in which is embedded the aforementioned discrepancy, incoherence, and inconsistency. However, the predicament also gives rise to the thought, born from an inner demand, that the everyday standpoint must be overcome existentially, ethically, and epistemologically if we are to have a holistic understanding of what it means to be human. How, then, can we overcome it? This is the question that drives Yuasa to propose his theory of embodiment. It must be overcome, Yuasa maintains, not through an exercise of pure reason or a discursive mode

---

8 Ibid., 14: 335.
9 Ibid., 14: 636.
10 Ibid., 14: 335.

of theoretical reasoning, but through the practice of self-cultivation. Since this stance forms an integral part of Yuasa's theory of embodiment, we need to keep it in mind. The preceding reflection now takes us to Yuasa's body scheme.

YUASA'S BODY SCHEME

Yuasa's body scheme is more comprehensive in terms of its scope and explanatory power than those that have thus far been proposed (e.g., by Henry Head, Henry Bergson, Maurice Merleau-Ponty, and Ichikawa Hiroshi). This is because Yuasa incorporates in his body scheme (as mentioned at the beginning of this chapter) knowledge he gained from his study of various fields of scholarship. To get a sense of its comprehensiveness, we will examine briefly his body scheme, which consists of four information circuits: (1) the sensory-motor circuit, (2) the circuit of coenesthesis, (3) the emotion-instinct circuit, and (4) the circuit of unconscious quasi-body.[11] One of the salient characteristics of Yuasa's body scheme is that, in the standpoint of everyday experience, one's awareness gradually disappears as one moves from the first circuit to the fourth circuit. However, with a deepening of self-cultivation, one's awareness will, in turn, open up.

The first circuit captures how a sense datum is (centripetally) received through a sense organ (i.e., sensory perception) and how an action is executed (centrifugally) based on it. Physiologically, the first circuit designates the activity of sensory nerves passively receiving stimuli from the external world and the activity of motor nerves actively responding to them. This circuit is proposed by following the models of Bergson's sensory-motor apparatus (*les appareils sensori-moteurs*), Merleau-Ponty's sensory-motor circuit (*un circuit sensori-moteurs*), and Penfield's automatic sensory-motor mechanism. It depicts perception and action as they relate to the field of everyday experience.

The second circuit, the *circuit of coenesthesis*, schematizes the self-apprehension or feeling one has of one's own body, such as a kinetic sensation (i.e., the *circuit of kinesthesis*), as well as sensations regarding the visceral organs (i.e., the *circuit of somesthesis*). Unlike the first circuit, a clear awareness of this circuit cannot be obtained in a healthy state. We become aware of the circuit of kinesthesis through our motor sensation, and this motor sensation is located experientially at the periphery of the Cartesian *cogito*, represented by such mental activities as thinking, willing, feeling, and imagining. Husserl, for example, was aware of the importance of kinesthesis existing at the periphery of sensory awareness, but he never fully incorporated it in his phenomenology. Moreover, in Merleau-Ponty's body scheme (*le scheme corporel*), the first circuit and kinesthesis are extensively investigated in connection with his concept of "habit-body" (*le corps habituel*), but Yuasa notes that he makes no reference to somesthesis.[12]

---

[11] Ibid., 14: 423–435, 498–510.
[12] Ibid., 14: 498–510.

The circuit of somesthesis is comprised, among other things, of splanchnic nerves that inform our brain of the condition of the visceral organs, although our awareness of this circuit is dim due to the small area on the neoencephalon receptive to this condition. The sensation of the circuit of somesthesis is dark and vague and is found further back at the periphery of motor sensation. This circuit is often compared to a biofeedback mechanism, but Yuasa admits that we do not have sufficient understanding of it because we have insufficient knowledge connecting psychological function with the corresponding physiological function.

To explain how the difference in motor capacity arises between a novice and a master of sports and/or performing arts, Yuasa, in this connection, notes that both the circuits of kinesthesis and somesthesis are closely connected through habituation with the sensory-motor circuit in executing actions in athletics or the performing arts. Both the sensory-motor circuit and the circuit of coenesthesis belong to what Yuasa calls the *conscious-cortex order*. It is relegated as "conscious" because information received through these circuits and the execution of an action based on this information can be processed consciously, whereas it is designated as "cortex" because the activity of sensing and executing an action can be mapped neurophysiologically onto the neoencephalon. It should be noted here, however, that the preceding two circuits are a schematization that obtains through an analysis of the everyday, commonsensical standpoint.

The last two circuits in Yuasa's body scheme are the *emotion-instinct circuit* and the *circuit of unconscious quasi-body*. His incorporation of these two circuits in his body scheme is one of his greatest contributions to the theory of the body.[13] The emotion-instinct circuit is psychologically related to the activity of the unconscious and neurophysiologically to the activity of the autonomic nervous system. This circuit converts the stimuli received through a sensory organ into an emotional response (i.e., pleasure or pain) or information about stress, which affects the activity of the visceral organs and then, in turn, holistically affects the whole person. Moreover, if and when any one of the visceral organs controlled by the autonomic nerves fails to function, it leads to death. It is in this literal sense a vital circuit. Yuasa points out that emotions and instincts are psychologically issued from the unconscious, whereas the regions that generate and express emotions and instincts are neurophysiologically located in the midbrain. Considering these points, he observes that the emotion-instinct circuit belongs to the *unconscious-autonomic order*. It is labeled *unconscious* because its activity, psychologically speaking, cannot ordinarily be brought to conscious awareness by exercising the will of ego-consciousness. This is because this information system does not reach the neoencephalon. Moreover, it is *autonomic* because its activity is controlled by the autonomic nervous system that also works independently of the will of ego-consciousness. For this reason, it remains "invisible" to everyday consciousness.

---

[13] Without his knowledge of the practice of self-cultivation, Pavlov's theory of conditioned reflex, and Jung's depth psychology, they would have never been discussed in the field of philosophy.

A question naturally arises whether the unconscious-autonomic order can be connected to the *conscious-voluntary order*. This is where Yuasa introduces the significance of breathing exercises incorporated in any mediation practice. He points out that breathing is ordinarily performed unconsciously or autonomously, but because voluntary muscles are attached to the respiratory organs we can also perform breathing consciously. Meditative self-cultivation takes advantage of this ambiguity through conscious breathing: it brings unconscious or autonomous breathing to conscious awareness and conditions the breathing that is governed by the autonomic nerves. What is surprising is that the physiological center for the activity of breathing and the psychological center that controls the activity of emotions happen to be housed in the same area of the brain—the midbrain.

This suggests that the breathing exercises performed in meditation can correct emotional distortions. Emotion and the pattern and rhythm of breathing are correlated with each other, as we know experientially, for example, in comparing a peaceful state and an angry state. Therefore, the breathing exercises in meditation promote the establishment of a stronger mind-body correlativity than the correlativity operative in the everyday standpoint. Breathing exercises also carry an ethical meaning in that they move one toward perfecting personality because they function to correct the distortion of emotions.

The circuit of unconscious quasi-body, by contrast, is a philosophical recapitulation of the meridians of acupuncture medicine, and it incorporates an energy activity of a psycho-physiological nature (i.e., *ki* energy) that flows in a living body. *Ki* energy is constantly changed by and exchanged with the *ki* energy existing outside of the body by way of the skin. However, as may be surmised from the fact that this circuit exists beneath the third circuit, it cannot be brought to awareness under normal circumstances: it is an invisible circuit also insofar as it is buried in the unconscious. In the everyday standpoint, one can only come to know it indirectly, for example, by way of the refreshing feeling one has after walking through the woods or spending time at a beach. For most people, this feeling is an *unconscious circumspatial awareness* because it operates intuitively or unconsciously. Only through the practice of self-cultivation via meditation or the performing arts can this unconscious circumspatial awareness be brought to clear awareness. Yuasa schematizes this circuit in consideration of the fact that a seasoned meditator and a master martial artist are known to apprehend the flow of *ki* energy in one's own body as well as in others. It is also important to note that developing an awareness of this fourth circuit is correlated with an awareness of establishing synchronistic phenomena, which, according to Yuasa's interpretation of Jung, means a meaningful coincidence between a mental phenomenon and a physical phenomenon (or another mental phenomenon). A condition for synchronistic phenomena is realized when micro-macrocosmic correlativity is established between a person and the activity of nature. In the activity of nature is an expression of *ki* energy as a psychophysiological energy, which creates this capacity for attuning an inner image with the physiological condition of the body that is an expression of nature. The preceding four circuits may be schematically represented as in Figure 27.1.

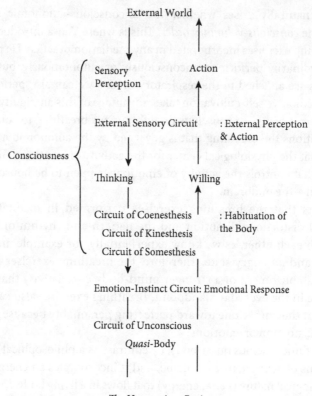

FIGURE 27.1 Yuasa's four circuits.

What is noteworthy here is that the philosophy of self-cultivation regards living nature as filled with *ki* energy, which exists abundantly and pervasively. Unlike the idea of absolute space that Newton held, this philosophy considers space to be a field of energy.[14] Accordingly, it carries an environmental message that living nature must be kept in a pristine condition if humans and all living beings are to survive. Yuasa's philosophy emphasizes that, in order to apprehend the flow of *ki* energy or *divine subtle*-energy, a human being *qua* microcosm must interresonate with the activity of nature *qua* macrocosm. To bring this correlation into clear awareness through the practice of self-cultivation is the goal of this philosophy.

Before we move into Yuasa's philosophy of self-cultivation, we pause here to reflect on the difference between the methodological stances of Cartesian disjunctive dualism and

[14] Newton's absolute space, for example, contains no content and is regarded as homogenous. That there is no content in this idea of space means that it is something that is constructed in thought; it means that it is formally abstracted from lived space. This abstract idea of absolute space carries no meaning experientially for a living human being because a lived spaced is filled with things and is not homogenous. Moreover, lived space is qualitative in the sense that there are places in lived space where one feels good or bad.

the philosophy of self-cultivation. In so doing, we will be able to put the characteristics of Yuasa's theory of embodiment into clear relief while showing how Yuasa attempts to overcome commonsensical dualism, including Cartesian disjunctive dualism, by way of a philosophy of self-cultivation.

REFLECTION ON METHODOLOGICAL STANCES

The preceding inquiry enables us to discuss the following characteristics in Yuasa's methodological reflection.[15] When Western philosophers attempt to question the mind-body relationship, they take a theoretical stance that is anchored in the above-mentioned standpoint of commonsensical dualism, and they often formulate their question as: "What is the relationship between the mind and the body?" In this methodological stance is presupposed—as is seen in the genealogy of idealism in Western philosophy—a prioritization of theory (*theōria*) over practice (*prāxis*). Consequently, this kind of questioning has typically led Western philosophers to an essentialistic or substantialistic ontology because their inquiry is formulated in terms of what-questions that seek essences or substances. Philosophers are duped by the subject-predicate linguistic structure into thinking that it is "natural" and "reasonable" to formulate their inquiry in this way. On the other hand, when philosophers in the tradition of self-cultivation raise a question about this relationship, they ask, "How do a mind and a body *change* through the practice of self-cultivation?" This is because they are interested in practical, lived experience. In this methodological stance, an emphasis is placed on practice, and a theoretical concern for the mind-body relationship is, to use a term from phenomenology, "bracketed" until such practice is brought to completion.

In their endeavors, then, they do not accept essentialistic or substantialistic ontology for, if they did, it would lead them to deny psychophysiological transformations that occur in the course of self-cultivation. To put it differently, practice precedes theory in the methodological stance of this philosophy. Herein is clearly indicated Yuasa's methodological stance of the philosophy of self-cultivation, in which, as we can discern, practice is advocated over theory. The practical philosophy of self-cultivation accepts the prioritization of practice over theory because it acknowledges that, when philosophers take a theoretical orientation to investigate the mind-body problem, the discrepancy, incoherence, and inconsistency intrinsically embedded in the everyday standpoint exist as a starting point of their inquiry. This does not mean, however, that the philosophy of self-cultivation is not interested in theoretical questions. Instead, it understands that a proper perspective on formulating a theoretical question cannot be forthcoming as long as one is anchored in the standpoint of commonsensical dualism because human beings

[15] *Shintai ron: Tōyōteki shintairon to gendai* [The Theory of the Body: An Eastern Mind-Body Theory and the Contemporary Period] in Yuasa 1999–2013, 11.

are in actuality incapable of overcoming the predicament of the everyday standpoint as long as they remain in the everyday standpoint with merely a theoretical interest. (For Yuasa this predicament is as much epistemological as it is existential and ethical, as mentioned earlier.) Accordingly, we must find a "way" that overcomes the everyday standpoint. Yuasa seeks such a way in a philosophy of self-cultivation, based in particular on such practices in the Eastern tradition as meditation. Before we move on to this topic, I would like to discuss how Yuasa schematizes everyday commonsensical dualism and the transformative process of self-cultivation that goes beyond it.

PHILOSOPHY OF SELF-CULTIVATION

As seen earlier, Yuasa incorporates the tradition of self-cultivation as an integral element in his theory of embodiment, and what he has primarily in mind are various meditation methods such as those practiced by *Kuṇḍalini* yoga, Daoism, and Esoteric, Zen, and Pure Land Buddhism. Because meditation is a practice that involves the whole of a person (i.e., both mind and body), it is a holistic pursuit. Yuasa captures a principle common to all of these meditation methods as follows: *one corrects the modality of one's mind by correcting the modality of one's body*.[16] In this formulation, we can see why the philosophy of self-cultivation refrains from asking the essence/substance-seeking what-question concerning the mind-body relationship. This is because this principle is based on the practical knowledge that the capacity of the mind can be positively transformed through training just as a bodily capacity can be enhanced through training.[17] We can understand from this fact that the what-question is a premature question to raise when it is posed from within the everyday standpoint, insofar as it seeks the whatness of a thing. If we are to use the terminology of existentialism, self-cultivation is an "existential project" through which, Yuasa thinks, one can overcome the commonsensical standpoint. This is a cardinal point in Yuasa's philosophy of self-cultivation.

How, then, can it be overcome? Since Daoist categories are easy to understand— because they capture a complex process schematically—I will briefly explicate a process of overcoming commonsensical dualism by using them while keeping in mind Yuasa's explanation. According to Daoist philosophy, meditation transforms sexual energy (*sei* 精) into energy of psychophysiological nature (*ki* 気), which is then transformed into a spiritually subtle divine energy (*shin* 神).[18] In Daoism, the spiritually subtle divine energy is said to be further transformed into the void (*kyo* 虚), which Daoism understands

---

[16] See Yuasa 1999–2013, 11: 237.

[17] We need to be clear about the fact that this differs from the position advanced, for example, by Aristotle. Even though Aristotle assumed an empirical stance, he insisted in his *Metaphysics* that a true, authentic knowledge is a theoretical knowledge of a universal that is obtained through an intellectual generalization.

[18] Yuasa 1999–2013, 14: 462–468.

to be a primal font, though formless, of creative energy and the home of the authentic self. These three transformative processes describe how a Daoist meditator moves to transformed states of consciousness, but when they are interpreted epistemologically, they describe how the commonsensical dualistic perspective of the everyday standpoint is transformed into a non-dualistic, holistic perspective and how thing-events come to be seen from the latter's perspective.

Take, as an example, the *Secret of the Golden Flower*, a well-known Daoist meditation text in which is described an experience of reaching an apex of meditative self-cultivation. This text states: "[I] try to find [my] body, but cannot find it," wherein we can discern that the body opposing the mind is no longer present, which suggests a practical overcoming of the commonsensical dualism. Myōe (1173–1232), who is known to have observed precepts throughout his life in the tradition of Kegon Buddhism, reflectively captured his meditation experience as "mind-body crystallization" (*shinjin gyōnen* 身心凝念). This phrase describes a clear, transparent state of mind that obtains in meditation, wherein the oppositional relationship between the mind and the body is cleared away. Similarly, Dōgen (1200–1253), who is often heralded as one of the most philosophical Zen masters, expressed a similar meditation experience as "dropping off the body and the mind" (*shinjin datsuraku* 身心脱落), wherein the dualistic distinction between the mind and the body disappears. Dōgen's Zen Buddhism and Daoism maintain that the being of the clear transparent mind is at the same time the being of the world, wherein a transparent light is said to be dazzlingly bright and shining.[19] These examples show instances of experience in which the mind and the body are no longer opposed to each other; hence, by overcoming commonsensical dualism, the meditator moves into a non-dualistic state that is holistic in nature.

As these examples indicate, the holistic standpoint is a perspective that opens up only when practically transcending the commonsensical, dualistic standpoint. The philosophy of self-cultivation teaches that since the transformation of the mind is correlated with the transformation of the body, the practice of self-cultivation *practically* transforms the commonsensical dualism, including the Cartesian disjunctive dualism, into the correlative mind-body dualism, and, through the process of this transformation, the meditator reaches a holistic perspective. Herein, we can clearly discern the aforementioned principle of Yuasa's self-cultivation philosophy: namely, that "one corrects the modality of one's mind by correcting the modality of one's body."

More specifically, essential to this transformative process, as exemplified in both the Daoist and the Buddhist schemes, is a transformation of egocentric personality traits—which are formed by emotions, desires, and instincts that are based on the principle of self-preservation—into higher spiritual energy. Because these affective modalities are of the body, the practice of meditation enables a meditator to become consciously aware of complexes of "wandering thoughts" and to learn to dissolve them by letting them dissipate in terms of image experiences, concerns, worries, and fears. In other words,

---

[19] See, for example, Dōgen's *Ikkamyōju* fascicle of *Shōbōgenzō*.

meditation has a function of purifying the source out of which these affective modalities surface. This purification, in turn, has an effect on personality formation because the personality is in part formed by various complexes that are unconsciously defined by one's likes and dislikes. In the tradition of self-cultivation, it is experientially known that such purification has a positive effect on personality formation. Because personality is a habituated pattern of emotional responses, it therefore leads Yuasa to conclude that self-cultivation carries an ethical sense of perfecting a personality.

Because the process of purifying unconscious complexes involves various image-experiences arising out of the unconscious, Yuasa devotes considerable space to examining the texts of yoga, Daoism, and (Esoteric and Pure Land) Buddhism in order to elucidate their depth-psychological meaning by utilizing the knowledge he acquired through his close study of Jung's depth psychology.[20] The unconscious, according to Jung, is a reservoir of images with varying magnitudes and significance. Yuasa interprets the unconscious as forming a stratified, hierarchical constellation that is, for example, well-exemplified in the Womb maṇḍala (Sk. garbhamaṇḍala; Jp. taizōkai-mandara 胎蔵界曼荼羅) of Esoteric Buddhism. This maṇḍala is a formalized, pictorial representation of image-experiences that occur in the course of self-cultivation practice, and these constellated layers of images form "one world." "One world" means that, just as we share one common physical space, we share "one spiritual world" in the dimension of the unconscious or the soul.[21] This "one world," like Zhuangzi's "chaos," is a world in which time and space are indeterminate or rendered zero. For example, in the world of zero time and zero space, it takes no time for information to travel from one place to another because there is no space. When one returns to the home ground of one's own existence, one enters the zone where there is no time and no space. This is ground zero, and it corresponds to Nishida's "place of absolutely nothing" (zettai mu no basho 絶対無の場所). In this primordial zone, it takes no time for information to travel from one place to another because there also is no distance (i.e., no space) to travel.[22]

How does one then approach such a world? The hierarchy of images consists of base and frightening images at its shallow layers, but with a deepening of meditation practice, the meditator experiences being embraced by the divine, the sacred, and by transparent illuminations. This point was exemplified in the foregoing, when I mentioned the Daoist example of not being able to find one's body, Myōe's experience of "body-mind crystallization," and Dōgen's experience of "dropping off the body and the mind."

With a deepening of experience in the course of meditative practice, Yuasa points out that what Jung called "archetypal situations," or what may also be called

[20] See, for example, four volumes Yuasa wrote on Jung's psychology: Jung and Christianity, in Yuasa 1999–2013, 3; Jung and European Spirituality, in Yuasa 1999–2013, 4; and two volumes of Jung and the East, in Yuasa 1999–2013, 6.

[21] Here, we can sense Yuasa's development of the concept of "one world" (unus mundus), which can be traced back to Plato and which Jung incorporated in his psychology.

[22] In contemporary physics, a similar phenomenon has been discussed under the topic "nonlocalization" phenomenon. This was initially proposed as the Einstein-Podolsky-Rosen (EPR) paradox, but it is now recognized as the EPR principle.

parapsychological phenomena, begin surfacing following the *principle of synchronicity*.[23] In the context of the philosophy of self-cultivation, the principle of synchronicity means that the body and the mind become one, wherein an image of a thing-event in the psychological space and an image of a thing-event in the physical space coincide in meaning. For this to occur, we must assume a state in which a physical space and a psychological space become overlapped or correlated. The principle of synchronicity, in other words, presupposes mind-body correlativity or micro-macrocosmic interresonance. This point shows Yuasa's incorporation of the by-products that are known to occur in the course of meditation practice in the traditions of yoga, Buddhism, and Daoism. He concludes that at the apex of such image-experiences is found an authentic self, which is identified, for example, as enlightenment (*satori*) in Zen and as Dao in Daoism. We may now ask: what views of the human being and nature then emerge from Yuasa's philosophy of self-cultivation?

IMPLICATIONS OF YUASA'S THEORY

Yuasa maintains that human beings are fundamentally "passive beings," delimited by their own bodies.[24] What he means by "passive beings" is that they are beings—to borrow Heidegger's terminology—"thrown into the world" (i.e., thrownness). Yuasa's idea also seems to be influenced in part by his teacher, Watsuji Tetsurō (1889–1969), who erected, among other things, an East Asian ethical system based on the examination of the network of "betweenness" that governs interpersonal relationships in the field of everyday experience—a network that "always already" exists prior to one's birth. Because this network exists prior to an individual's birth, an individual is "passively thrown" into the network. This recognition of the fundamental passivity of human beings led Yuasa to take a practical rather than a theoretical approach (e.g., in understanding an authentic self), as seen in the fact that he advocates the philosophy of self-cultivation.

To reflect this utterly contingent aspect of human existence, he defines the human being as a "being-in-nature." By this phrase, he intends to convey the image of a human being living in interresonance with the invigorating activity of nature while at the same time receiving its energy. Here, nature is grasped as "living" nature. He proposes this idea of the human being in order to overcome the modern Western epistemological paradigm that defines the human being, according to Yuasa, as a "being-outside-of-nature." This term refers to Cartesian disjunctive dualism, wherein "my" mind stands outside of "my" body and observes things external to it. If one expands this image, the human being is seen as standing outside of nature, attempting to observe nature as a collection of material substances. This stance designates a theoretical standpoint, like

[23] For Yuasa's excellent treatment of Jung's theory of synchronicity, see Yuasa 2008.
[24] Yuasa 2004, 196.

Descartes' *cogito*, in order to control nature. Nature thus grasped is a "dead" nature that is anthropocentrically understood. By contrast, Yuasa's "being-in-nature" is a phrase that attempts to capture nature holistically. What he means by "holistically" is that the epistemological subject is part and parcel of nature: it does not stand apart from the epistemological object, and, consequently, there is no gap or barrier created between them. According to this scheme, it is through an interresonance via image-experiences between them that a thing-event comes to be known.

Needless to say, Yuasa acknowledges that the human being in the field of everyday experience can be characterized as having this dual nature, and, using Nishida's well-known phrase, he refers to the human being as a "contradictory self-identity" (*mujun-teki jikodōitsu* 矛盾的自己同一). However, he emphasizes "being-in-nature" more than "being-outside-of-nature" because the former is the perspective that opens up fully once the practice of self-cultivation is brought to completion. He also fears that if one emphasizes the latter in disassociation with the former, humanity will undergo a dangerous process of deracination, for example, through the destruction of nature and the manipulation of DNA. For Yuasa, the human being is a being rooted in what has been referred to in the Japanese tradition as "Great Nature" (*daishizen* 大自然).

Yuasa attempts with his theory of embodiment to grasp the human being as a phenomenon that is intimately connected with a great, creative, and living nature.[25] To portray this image, he proposes the idea that an incarnate human being is a microcosm that resonates with the activity of living nature *qua* macrocosm[26]; that is to say, the idea of a micro-macrocosmic correlativity. He advances this idea because he thinks that the human being is born from nature and returns there. This view that connects the human being to living nature holds that if one comes to thoroughly know the activity of the microcosm that is one's own body through the process of self-cultivation, one also comes to know the activity of the macrocosm. There is no "I" in this apprehension. Yuasa's theory of embodiment, in the final analysis, suggests a lifestyle in which an "I" is not posited as the parameter for understanding everything, including one's self, one's interpersonal relationships, and the natural environment.

BIBLIOGRAPHY AND SUGGESTED READINGS

Nagatomo, Shigenori. (1992*a*) "An Eastern Concept of the Body: Yuasa's Body-Scheme." In *Giving the Body Its Due*, edited by Maxine Sheets-Johnstone. Albany: State University of New York Press.

Nagatomo, Shigenori. (1992*b*) "Two Contemporary Japanese Views of the Body: Ichikawa Hiroshi and Yuasa Yasuo." In *Self as Body in Asian Theory and Practice*, edited by T. P. Kasulis. Albany: State University of New York Press.

[25] Ibid., 183.

[26] Historically speaking, this idea is a recapitulation of the idea of "Heaven-Human Correlativity" that Tochujo (Dong Zhongshu) proposed during the early Han dynasty in the second century. See Yuasa 2004, 183.

Yuasa Yasuo. (1987a) "A Cultural Background For Traditional Japanese Gymnastic Philosophy, and A Theoretical Examination of this Philosophy," translated by Shigenori Nagatomo. In *Proceeding of the PSSS Conference*. Tsukuba, Japan: University of Tsukuba Press.

Yuasa Yasuo. (1987b) "An Encounter of Modern Japanese Philosophy with Heidegger," translated by Shigenori Nagatomo & Monte Hull. In *Heidegger and Asian Philosophy*, edited by Graham Parkes. Honolulu: University of Hawai'i Press.

Yuasa Yasuo. (1987c) *The Body: Toward an Eastern Mind-Body Theory*, translated by Shigenori Nagatomo and Thomas P. Kasulis. Albany: State University of New York Press.

Yuasa Yasuo, Shigenori Nagatomo, and David E. Shaner. (1989) *Science & Comparative Philosophy: Introducing Yuasa Yasuo*. Leiden, Holland: Brill.

Yuasa Yasuo. (1990) "Nationalism and Japanese Philosophy," translated by Shigenori Nagatomo and Ruth Tonner, *Obirin Review of International Studies* 2: 9–28.

Yuasa Yasuo. (1992) "A Contemporary Scientific Paradigm and the Discovery of the Inner Cosmos." In *Self as Body in Asian Theory and Practice*, translated by Shigenori Nagatomo and William Allen; edited by T. P. Kasulis. Albany: State University of New York Press.

Yuasa Yasuo. (1993) *The Body, Self-Cultivation & Ki-Energy*, translated by Shigenori Nagatomo and Monte Hull. Albany: State University of New York Press.

Yuasa Yasuo. (1995) "Meditation and the View of Nature in East Asia," translated by Shigenori Nagatomo. *Obirin Review of International Studies* 7: 47–70.

Yuasa Yasuo. (1999–2013) *Yuasa Yasuo zenshū* [The Complete Works of Yuasa Yasuo]. Tokyo: Hakua shobō (vols. 1–12 and 14), Biingu Netto Puresu (vols. 13 and 15–16).

Yuasa Yasuo. (2000) "Meditation and Sexuality: Interpretation of Qìgōng and Its Present-Day Significance," translated by Shigenori Nagatomo. In *Bodywork and Psychotherapy in the East*, edited by Wang Weidong. Delft, The Netherlands: Eburon.

Yuasa Yasuo. (2001) "Foreword" to Robert Carter's *Encounter with Enlightenment: A Study of Japanese Ethics*, translated by Shigenori Nagatomo and Pamela Winfield. Albany: State University of New York Press.

Yuasa Yasuo. (2004) *Tetsugaku no tanjō: Danseisei to jyoseisei no shinri* [The Birth of Philosophy: Psychology of Masculinity and Femininity]. Kyoto: Jinbun shoin.

Yuasa Yasuo. (2005) "Image-Thinking: Understanding of 'Being': The Psychological Basis of Linguistic Expression," translated by Shigenori Nagatomo and Jacques Fasan. *Philosophy East and West* 55(2): 179–208.

Yuasa Yasuo. (2008) *Overcoming Modernity: Synchronicity and Image-Thinking*, translated by Shigenori Nagatomo and John W. M. Krummel. Albany: State University of New York Press.

CHAPTER 28

POSTWAR JAPANESE POLITICAL PHILOSOPHY

Marxism, Liberalism, and the Quest for Autonomy

RIKKI KERSTEN

THE TRANS-WAR DYNAMIC IN POSTWAR JAPAN

IN depicting periods of dramatic change in history, there is a natural tendency to adopt a bifurcated perspective. There is a "before" and an "after," where a temporal shift, however short, is exaggerated by an overwhelming awareness of the new. Discontinuity rules, but the "new" identity cannot establish foundations—and thus legitimacy—without a history that incorporates the artificial division of lived or recorded experience. In the case of war, and even more so of defeat in war, the temporal and psychological barriers are more formidable still. Defeat represents a level of personal and national trauma that compounds the complexity of integrating this experience into a postwar identity. For a defeated nation and its people, a discredited past neatly underscores the psychological and temporal legitimacy of the "after," but it also reveals an uncomfortable notion that the ethical coherence of the present comes at the cost of subjective and historical incoherence.

The rhetoric of historical discontinuity was rampant in Japan's postwar intellectual life. Discontinuity and disassociation underpinned the logic of the war crimes trials, intellectual debates over war responsibility, and the appraisal of wartime collaboration or apostasy (known in Japanese as *tenkō* 転向). In the Tokyo War Crimes Trials, the state and the military were blamed for the deeds of war, with wartime society implicitly designated as victims of the state[1] and postwar society positioned as the ethical locus of

---

[1] The Potsdam Declaration was more explicit, stating that the people of Japan had been "deceived and misled" by their militaristic leaders.

postwar democracy.[2] The entities of state and self that were ideologically intertwined in wartime were consequently wrenched apart in postwar discourse on war responsibility, denying an active association of state and self in the past for the sake of normative integrity in the postwar present.

For this reason, when examining political philosophy in post-1945 Japan, we must acknowledge that the postwar philosophical landscape was fundamentally a trans-war one. Narratives that sought to rationalize the past war laid the foundations for a divided consciousness in postwar that entrenched antagonistic opposites as the parameters for postwar discourse. State versus self, politics versus ethics, theory versus value, ideas versus action, and intellectuals versus "ordinary" people were all manifestations of the desire in the postwar era to establish ethical legitimacy through the dynamics of normative distancing. Paramount in this endeavor was an insistence by Japan's postwar thinkers on creating and maintaining a hostile separation between civil society and the state as the proof of a rehabilitated ethos for postwar democracy.

Here we will scrutinize some of the key ideas and thinkers that emerged in this vibrant yet polarized intellectual arena of postwar Japan between 1945 and 1970. Delivered in the form of debates between individual thinkers across and within an array of popular journals and intellectual associations, intellectuals sparred over fundamental notions such as responsibility for the war, autonomy, democracy, and pacifism. How they did so exemplified both the persistence of trans-war thinking after 1945 and the normative inversion that constituted its generative core. Though it may appear as overly simplistic, the parameters of postwar discourse were framed as antonyms. For instance, postwar democracy was defined by default as the value opposite of wartime fascism, and the performance of war responsibility after 1945 involved embracing pacifism in an antagonistic attitude toward the state. This conceptual framing had consequences for postwar thought and how it was articulated. In effect, the retrospective fragmentation of subjective responsibility led to the alienation of politics and value in the postwar era, preventing the coherence of subjectivity and responsibility upon which the integrity of the trans-war narrative depended.

The compulsion to explain collusion with the wartime state and the failure of intellectuals effectively to resist or oppose an authoritarian regime were major preoccupations for many thinkers after 1945.[3] The so-called "war responsibility" (*sensō sekinin* 戦争責任) discourse involved explaining the failures of prewar thought and intellectuals with the primary purpose of protecting postwar democracy. It was in the debates over *tenkō* (political apostasy) and *shutaisei* (主体性, autonomy) that autonomous value judgment and intellectual consistency emerged as key intellectual themes in postwar Japanese political thought.

---

[2] Kersten 1994, 1–9.
[3] See, for instance, Ienaga 1985; Oguma 2002; Dower 1999.

In his first postwar writings, the political scientist Maruyama Masao (1914–1996) posited the relationship between value creation and agency as an essential concern for those seeking to understand war responsibility, asking his fellow citizens "what are the intellectual structures and psychological foundations ... that drove us to wage war against the rest of the world?"[4] His answer to this question—indeed the question itself—ran counter to the thrust of the Potsdam Declaration and the Tokyo war crimes trials in that he implicitly rejected victimhood as an adequate explanation for collusion, insisting instead that agency be considered when examining war responsibility. Under the guise of deconstructing Japanese ultra-nationalism, Maruyama identified the propensity of the wartime state to make value definition and morality its exclusive preserve (rather than something that is forged according to an individual's conscience) as a primary reason for why it was necessary to quarantine the post-1945 state from the realm of value creation.[5] Thereafter autonomous value creation on the part of civil society became a central concern for Japan's postwar thinkers across the ideological spectrum.

The experience of defeat left many intellectuals determined to intervene as active subjects in the making of history in the future. Marxist historian Tōyama Shigeki declared that, through defeat in 1945, he had lost an association both with the idea of the citizen (*kokumin* 国民) and the self (*jiko* 自己). He felt that the history of defeat ought to be rewritten as the history of the ethnic nation (*minzoku* 民族) and, that for his part, he would be an actor in history after the experience of August 15, 1945, declaring "8.15 is not history for me."[6] Maruyama also celebrated the fact that history had been reclaimed from the grip of the state through defeat in 1945, but, in his numerous postwar writings on democracy, he was most concerned to find evidence of what he called "the spirit of internal values." "Ideas are ends in themselves," he wrote in October 1945, "but the spirit that through internal values helps us to respect ideas is at present impoverished in our country."[7] For Maruyama, then, a pristine separation from the state after the war was only part of the equation required in order to deliver democracy to the postwar nation; the other part involved what he called the development of an "internal spiritual structure," a topic that elicited much controversy in the early postwar years in the form of debates on *shutaisei*.

THE *SHUTAISEI* DEBATE

It was not surprising that the prioritization of agency and subjective value definition after 1945 would clash with notions of historical materialism. The subordination of consciousness and value that is implied in theories of historical materialism dramatized

---

[4] Maruyama 1964, 11.
[5] Maruyama 1964, 14.
[6] Tōyama 1955, 104–105, 110.
[7] Maruyama 1998, 11.

the underlying dissonance of postwar visions held by so-called progressive thinkers and communist thinkers, dividing the intellectual community of postwar Japan into hostile camps depicted as "modernists" or "idealists" versus "materialists." As early as 1947, debates over autonomy (*shutaisei*) exposed this philosophical discord underpinning postwar thought. For communist and leftist thinkers, defeat was confirmation that wartime Japan had been semi-feudal and therefore not yet ripe for socialist revolution. Accordingly, the Kōza (講座 Lecture) group of Marxist theorists was poised to complete the revolutionary trajectory in postwar Japan. This structural logic of incompleteness was complemented by the so-called modernists, who had found incomplete modernity to be one of the underlying causes for Japan's turn to war (and for the weakness of liberalism). This framing of the postwar era as something founded on prewar deficiency made postwar thought into a quest for sufficiency in terms of Japan's level of socio-intellectual development as well as socio-economic progress.

The pivotal *shutaisei* debates of the late 1940s and 1950s were conducted not only between emblematic opposed positions, but also in symbolic language. Instead of "idealism" the term "worldview" was used, implying a Neo-Kantian attention to humankind's role as maker of its history. Determinism appeared under the guise of "science," implying an objective yet theoretical certainty concerning what moved history. Seething beneath the surface was a battle between the historical inevitability of revolution and a historical consciousness centered on human agency. In the postwar era, the imperative of gaining control over the making of history reflected a pervasive assumption that war had been an act of state. Communist intellectuals needed to reassert the theory of inevitable revolution and the collapse of capitalism after the war because this would help make sense of the signal failure of communism as a movement to resist the Emperor System in wartime. The war could then be explained as part of the historical process whereby capitalism was overreaching and ultimately destroying itself. The imperial state's suppression of communism became the focus in the search for war responsibility, rather than the failure of the movement theoretically to overcome the Emperor System ideology. In this way, 1945 could become "Year Zero" in terms of communist integrity, and historical materialism could be rescued from the rubble of the movement's wartime collapse. The trauma of mass political apostasy on the part of the Communist Party membership in the 1930s thus had the effect of hardening the communist tendency toward theoretical orthodoxy in the postwar period.

The idea of *shutaisei* resonated with the same concerns that accompanied the shifts in historical consciousness that arose in late eighteenth- and nineteenth-century Europe. As C. Wright Mills has indicated, shifts in historical consciousness have been preoccupied with identifying a relationship between human agency and ideals. In his view, this was the catalyst for much of the revisionist activity in Marxian circles after the death of Marx.[8] Isaiah Berlin has been even harsher, stating baldly that "vulgar historical materialism denies the power of ideas."[9] In postwar Japan, *shutaisei* connoted a

---

[8] C. Wright Mills, *The Marxists* (Harmondsworth: Penguin, 1962), 81.
[9] Berlin 1969, 119.

subject-centered view of history. *Shutaisei* was premised on individuals who were free and able to engage in active value creation, which was invariably expressed through action in accordance with those values. The theme of the "emancipation of the self" was code for the type of modernity that many thinkers believed was required for postwar Japan, representing a reflex opposite to the war-era experience that had been facilitated by what was portrayed as a "feudal" mentality. In this way. both the prescription for postwar democracy and the rationale for wartime collusion became entangled in debates over history, mobilizing terminologies associated with modernity and premodernity that subsumed the imperatives of agency and autonomy within ideological strictures.

The representative debate on *shutaisei*, which appeared in the Iwanami journal *Sekai* in February 1948,[10] saw a gathering of intellectuals who were meant to symbolize the respective standpoints of the day. The Marxist philosophers Kozai Yoshishige and Matsumura Kazuto were the advocates for the materialist skepticism concerning autonomy and subjectivity; the social theorist Mashita Shinichi waved the banner for anti-determinism; social psychologist Miyagi Otoya insisted on subjective engagement in social change; Maruyama Masao and Shimizu Ikutarō approximated between them the progressive commitment to agency and value; with Hayashi Kentarō representing a hybrid view that recognized the logic of historical materialist theory but could not endorse it without reservation. The debate was a snapshot of the elemental trans-war angst that could neither wholeheartedly put faith in the common man nor invest unqualified confidence in a theory that presented itself as orthodoxy. In the *shutaisei* roundtable debate, Maruyama's pleas for Marxists to recognize that value-consciousness had a place in Marxist aspirations for humanity fell on deaf ears.

Shimizu Ikutarō

Part of the problem with *shutaisei* in the minds of some postwar thought leaders was that it invested extraordinary faith in the capacity of the common man to engage in informed value creation free from manipulation or intimidation, whether conscious or subconscious. This concern was articulated most clearly by the social scientist Shimizu Ikutarō (1907–1988). Shimizu entered the postwar debate culture harboring serious doubts about the common man. In 1946, he referred to Japanese society as a "drainage ditch" or a "sewer," comprising a repository of unreflective, unconscious, custom-driven behavior on the part of the community: "Trends like customs are a drainage ditch for social behaviour; people live not like individuals but are obscured through social behaviour."[11] Shimizu deplored the enlightenment impulse of Japan's postwar thinkers because they appeared to believe mediated reality (ideas) could connect with the actual

---

[10]   *Sekai*, February 1948. Reproduced in Maruyama Masao, *Maruyama Masao zadan* [Round Table Discussions with Maruyama Masao] Vol. 1 (Tokyo: Iwanami Shoten, 1998), 89–141.

[11]   Shimizu Ikutarō, "Jishusei no kaifuku" [The Restoration of Autonomy], reproduced in *Waga seishin no hōrōki, Vol. 1 Nihon no toppakō* (Tokyo: Chūō Kōronsha, 1975), 10.

reality of the people. But for Shimizu, what he called "the repository of anonymous thought" first needed to be comprehended for what it was.

In his signature 1950 essays "Anonymous Thought" and "The Common Man," Shimizu laid blame for wartime compliance squarely with the "behaviourial drainage ditch" within the people themselves: "while being something that demanded service to the State, it was also something that freed the self from troublesome reflection and responsibility."[12] The task for postwar democracy, in Shimizu's view, was to "find a way to introduce democracy into the world of customs and the unconscious."[13] For Shimizu, this could be achieved if the common man could acquire rationality, or what Shimizu called "science," and thereby select from the multiple and competing value sets of the modern world and juggle memberships of multiple collectives. Thus, in the throes of the *shutaisei* debate, Shimizu sought to set a middle course by advocating the necessity of both subjectivity *and* science. The first priority, argued Shimizu, was to help the people achieve transcendence over those things that can command one from within: "trusting science is nothing other than trusting the ability to externalise."[14] Shimizu argued that if the pursuit of meaning and value smothered the objective appraisal of reality and if philosophical subjectivity hindered scientific objectivity, the common man would not emerge from the premodern urge to obliterate the self in an all-powerful, transcendental collective.

The doubts that coursed through the *shutaisei* debate played themselves out in the splintering intellectual trajectories of various thinkers as the postwar era moved into its second decade. But there was also urgency attached to this intellectual exercise, with the concerns over *shutaisei* being aired against the backdrop of the so-called *reverse course* in Occupation policy and the outbreak of the Korean War. The Cold War not only added an additional layer of polarization to the mix; it also revived deeply held fears concerning the imperative of intellectual consistency when confronted by existential crisis. This was particularly acute in the community of postwar Marxists, who were wrenched from an immediate postwar after-glow of wartime heroism into an anti-determinist, pro-capitalist intellectual environment, not to mention the Occupation-led Red Purge of 1950.

Umemoto Katsumi

Umemoto Katsumi (1912–1974) was a Marxist philosopher who felt compelled by the circumstances of trans-war Japan to try to find a way to reconcile value consciousness in the form of *shutaisei,* with Marxist theory. For his pains, he was labeled a revisionist

---

[12] Shimizu Ikutarō, "Tokumei no shisō" [Anonymous Thought] 1950, reproduced in Shimizu 2006–2007, 8: 210.

[13] Shimizu Ikutarō, "Kyō no kyōiku" [Education Today], *Sekai* 7 (July 1946): 48.

[14] Shimizu Ikutarō, "Shutaisei no kyakkanteki kōsatsu" [An Objective Appraisal of Autonomy], Shimizu 2006–2007, 8: 182.

by his communist peers, and was targeted by the US-led Occupation in the Red Purge of 1950. But Umemoto saw himself as acting from a position of "loyal dissent" from Marxist theoretical orthodoxy. In his 1947 essay, "The Limits of Human Freedom," Umemoto presented Marxism as an essentially humanist philosophy whose goal was the emancipation of humankind. In the postwar world, this did not mean that individuals were not "free"; rather, it meant that these free modern individuals had been deprived of their humanity. Political liberation through democracy was one thing, but the accompanying oppression of capitalism was another. In Umemoto's view, democracy was "a means for humanism, without being the end goal in its own right."[15] His chosen focus of "humanity," and his association of Marxism with humanism, was a well-disguised but unmistakable challenge to historical materialism.

Umemoto hereafter embarked on a tortured philosophical route in his attempt to reconcile the poles of postwar discourse without doing violence to either one. He insisted that material freedom be accompanied by ethical subjectivity, "but of course this also is premised on each individual first achieving self-direction in a material sense."[16] Umemoto argued his case by emphasizing that history was as much a march toward autonomy as it was a march toward freedom. Indeed, human history featured a move from humankind's emancipation from nature to their emancipation from societal and material oppression. Whereas the first emancipation was achieved objectively, it was the element of consciousness and intent that transformed "the objective existence of freedom to the inevitable existence of freedom" in the case of the second.[17] In an attempt to stay within accepted hermeneutical parameters, Umemoto portrayed this historical process as a dialectical movement between the material and the spiritual realms.

> No matter how often we are told that opposing elements synthesize, it is built on the premise of the transformation from the material to the spiritual, and the spiritual to the material, moreover this premise is itself premised on self-consciousness[18]

The ethical expression of consciousness was to choose emancipation and to acknowledge that humanity played a subjective role in achieving this ethical goal of human liberation. "Science" would help by proving the fact of oppression to those whose task it was to fight against that oppression.

Umemoto did not doubt the validity of the end goal, but he insisted on the presence of an ethical motivation for those who were to carry out the imperatives of history. In his seminal 1947 essay "Materialism and Humanity," Umemoto was prompted to look beyond the category of class to the relationship between individuals and society. Given that individuals were the point of departure in modern thinking, wrote

---

[15] Umemoto Katsumi, "Ningenteki jiyū no genkai" [The Limits of Human Freedom], in Umemoto 1977, 1: 12.

[16] Umemoto, "Ningen jiyū no genkai," 11.

[17] Umemoto, "Ningenteki jiyū no genkai," 17.

[18] Umemoto, "Ningenteki jiyū no genkai," 22.

Umemoto, it was not historical coherence delivered by theory that mattered, so much as ethical coherence within each individual: "From the nature of the position that it occupies in history, modernity demands that new individuals should discover within themselves as real individuals the principle for unity."[19] Relations of production were no doubt one cause for rupture between the individual and the whole (note the absence of the word "class"), but these relations also offered the opportunity for individuals to rebel, thereby enabling humanity to realize its true self. In positing a dialectical relationship between ethics and class, Umemoto was attempting to approximate Nishida Kitarō's concept of "*mu*" (無 nothingness).[20] Specifically, Umemoto argued that individuals (*ko* 個) and the whole (*zen* 全) could be reunified when individuals used ethics to contradict and ultimately transcend class. Finally, Umemoto nailed his revisionist colors to the mast. In "Materialism and Humanity," Umemoto openly identified a gap in Marxism, namely the failure of the scientific to incorporate the ethical.

For Umemoto, the fight for a new social whole preceded the recognition of the need for class warfare. So why should anyone want to fight for a new social whole?

> At its axis, [this desire] comes from the desire to contribute to the self-emancipation of the special class that occupies the historical position of liberating the whole of humankind. It is a contribution to this entire whole. Furthermore, this contribution to the entire whole is a conscious recognition [on the part of individuals] that they are contributing to the emancipation of humanity as a whole ... but this kind of self-recognition cannot emanate from a scientific investigation.[21]

Umemoto maintained that relations of production were also human relations. "Relations are human relations, they are where the self truly and consciously recognizes the self."[22] Science could not possibly deliver this kind of ethical motivation, argued Umemoto, without which the retrieval of unity for humanity would not be possible.

Matsumura Kazuto

Umemoto's terminology—"self" and "whole"—was interpreted by orthodox Marxists as a declaration of war on historical materialism. Fellow Marxist philosopher Matsumura Kazuto (1905–1977) led the charge against Umemoto's heresy. And yet, even though Matsumura left the reader in no doubt of his low opinion of Umemoto's revisionism,

---

[19] Umemoto Katsumi, "Yuibutsuron to ningen" [Materialism and humanity], Umemoto 1977, 1: 38.
[20] On Nishida's concept of nothingness (*mu*), see Chapters 17 and 18 in this volume. On the political aspects of his and other Kyoto School members' thought, see Chapters 16 and 36.
[21] Umemoto, "Yuibutsuron to ningen," 49.
[22] Umemoto, "Yuibutsuron to ningen," 51.

he nonetheless understood why Umemoto had been driven to embrace ethics. He knew that the war experience had led many thinkers to a subject-focused, diagnostic view of society. During the war. people were deprived of the freedom of thought; what was required in the postwar era was more self-awareness, the engagement of social life with value consciousness, and the value autonomy from the state that this implied. But to Matsumura, this mind-set insinuated alien elements into Marxist thinking, making ethical revisionism "the distortion of the fundamental spirit of Marxism."[23] There would be no place for the subject in Japan's postwar Marxist orthodoxy. Umemoto had meant well, but he was wrong. From this time onward, Japanese Marxism turned not only against one philosopher, but against a core concern of Japanese postwar thought.

Matsumura clarified Marxist orthodoxy in his rebuttal: Umemoto's attention to "self" and "whole" amounted to a supra-class position, and this fundamentally negated an essential element of historical materialism. By using abstract notions of humanity and an undifferentiated society as his basis, Umemoto was depriving history of its revolutionary catalyst, the disaffected and oppressed working class. In searching for the triumph of "sociality" (shakaisei 社会性) over individuality (kojinsei 個人性), Umemoto was distorting the true nature of conflict; namely, that it was an irreconcilable conflict between classes.

In response, Umemoto engaged in a series of "clarifications" in an attempt to remain within the orthodox Marxist fold without abandoning his ideas. He insisted that shutaisei was already immanent in historical materialism. The awareness of historical inevitability on the part of the proletariat was in effect a manifestation of shutaisei:

> The establishment of the autonomy of the proletariat depends on the recognition of this unshakable historical inevitability. At the very least, this recognition connects directly with their class consciousness. When we say that there is autonomy within this inevitability, we mean nothing less than that we recognize ourselves as the agents of this inevitability[24]

This combination of materialism and autonomy (shutaisei) was the very engine of historical inevitability, argued Umemoto. He subsequently rephrased this as the "shutaisei of historical materialism," arguing that this amounted to a philosophical expression of materialism itself. In effect, historical materialism was a worldview and ought to be understood as such. After all,

> How can people of today who cannot experience the best way to promote the welfare of future generations sacrifice their lives to this end?

---

[23] Matsumura Kazuto, "Tetsugaku ni okeru shūseishugi" [Revisionism in Philosophy], Sekai 31 (July 1948): 43.
[24] Umemoto, "Shutaisei to nihirizumu" [Shutaisei and Nihilism], Umemoto 1977, 1: 132.

Because

> The historical consciousness of materialism is not just consciousness but a con-
> sciousness that incorporates judgement and is led by practical determination, and in
> this regard the self is clearly distinguished from all neutral consciousness.[25]

In the end, Umemoto continued to believe that "Marxists tacitly hold a moralistic
ideal as a premise"; only through understanding this ideal could communists fashion
Marxism into a "complete worldview."[26] After all, "if Marxism is simply positivistic social science then it is unrelated to the people who will change the world."[27]

In his pursuit of meaning in history, Umemoto was not rejecting historical materialism, but instead—in his own opinion—he was providing postwar Marxism
with its "missing link." In this, Umemoto epitomized the historical consciousness
of trans-war Japan, and his revisionism was a powerful expression of the changed
historical consciousness that was in the air all around him. In the aftermath of the
Greater East Asian War, Umemoto was unable to relinquish his conviction that
ethics and existence were inseparable.[28] History and the movement toward greater
emancipation for humankind only gained momentum through the concurrent en-
hancement of consciousness. What Umemoto failed to understand, though, was the
underlying concern beneath Matsumura's harsh and unequivocal rejection of ethical socialism. Matsumura saw in Umemoto's attempts to build a bridge between the
material and the spiritual aspects of existence the spectre of wartime Japanese in-
doctrination. Specifically, Matsumura reacted violently against Umemoto's invocation of the concept of *mu*—nothingness—the philosophical contribution of Japan's
greatest modern philosopher, Nishida Kitarō (1870–1945). In postwar Japan, and
even up to the present day, Nishida and the Kyoto School of philosophy had been
derided as collaborators, whose philosophy provided intellectual legitimation for
the imperialist war. Matsumura saw in Umemoto's calls for *shutaisei* the same potential for life to be subsumed into one amorphous whole, where the material and
the spiritual became indistinguishable and thereby infinitely malleable and con-
trollable. Matsumura drew from the crisis the opposite lesson to the one drawn by
Umemoto: namely, that the separation of science and value was essential for the task
of liberating the proletariat.

---

[25] Umemoto Katsumi, "Yuibutsushikan to dōtoku" [Historical Materialism and Ethics], Umemoto
1977, 1: 213.

[26] Umemoto, "Yuibutsushikan to dōtoku," 213.

[27] Umemoto, "Yuibutsushikan to dōtoku," 220.

[28] Umemoto Katsumi, "Benshōhōteki tokushitsu to sono jikaku no ronri—Matsumura Kazuto shi
no hihan ni kotaete" [The Character of Dialectics and the Logic of Consciousness—A Response to
Matsumura Kazuto's Critique], Umemoto 1977, 1: 183–184.

Tenkō

....

While the *shutaisei* debates focused on the question of consciousness and subjectivity, postwar debates over wartime collusion and complicity were more concerned with the question of intellectual consistency. In modern Japanese history, *tenkō* (political apostasy) is normally associated with the 1930s and 1940s mass defections of communists from the Japan Communist Party, triggered by the spectacular defections on the part of two leading figures in the Japan Communist Party Central Committee, Sano Manabu (1892–1953) and Nabeyama Sadachika (1901–1979).[29] After 1945, communists who had committed *tenkō* in the 1930s were initially cast as victims of the state, whereas those communists who had endured imprisonment throughout the war without betraying their belief system emerged as heroes of postwar social democracy, even though communism as a movement had failed to mount an effective challenge against militarism. Although the debates over war responsibility broadened in the 1950s to include constituencies beyond the state and the military,[30] the prevailing assumption in postwar thinking until the mid-1970s was that the problem of intellectual inconsistency that had occurred in wartime could be resolved in postwar Japan if the causes and pathways of this intellectual betrayal could properly be understood.[31] This was the primary thrust of the debates over *tenkō* in the postwar years.

Commentators and scholars have defined *tenkō* with uncanny consistency. In most cases, *tenkō* was seen to involve rejecting Comintern-defined communism and instead declaring a kind of accommodation with the Emperor System state in circumstances of physical and/or psychological intimidation. Betrayal (of the communist party) appears in the company of compulsion; ideas are abandoned in favor of identity. Consequently, the values and ideas that motivate the individual apostate enter a subjective void. The negative act of *tenkō* is rendered comprehensible by the presence of force and by the magnetism of nationalism. *Tenkō-sha* （転向者 those who committed tenkō）are transformed into victims of circumstance and culture, and the communists who renounce the party are implicitly excused (because they were compelled).[32] The inherent dissonance of ideas and identity, and the denial of subjective decision-making on the part of autonomous actors, ran counter to the concurrent postwar philosophical preoccupation with retrieving subjective value definition and agency for non-state actors.

---

[29] The seminal work in English on wartime *tenkō* is Steinhoff 1991. In Japanese, the first comprehensive postwar assessment of wartime *tenkō* is presented in Shisō no Kagaku Kenkyūkai 1959–1962.

[30] For example see Maruyama Masao, "Sensō sekinin no mōten" [The Blindspots of War Responsibility], in Maruyama 1976, 596–602.

[31] This assumption characterized the landmark postwar study of wartime *tenkō* by the Shisō no Kagaku Kenkyūkai (1959–1962) group of scholars.

[32] This point is made by Sumiya 1976, 16.

Compulsion is part of the definition of *tenkō* posited by the standard Japanese publication, the three volumes compiled by the Shisō no Kagaku Kenkyūkai (Research Group for the Science of Thought) between 1959 and 1962, *Kyōdō Kenkyū Tenkō* (Joint Research on *Tenkō*).[33] While trans-war *tenkō* is the subject of these multiauthored volumes, the underlying concern throughout is another question altogether, namely: Why wasn't there significant resistance among Japanese intellectuals during the war? The main theoretical contributions in these volumes are provided by Tsurumi Shunsuke (1922–2015) and Fujita Shōzō (1927–2003). Both nominated force as an essential element of *tenkō*, though in his introductory essay Tsurumi includes "voluntarism" as part of the equation. Tsurumi's basic definition of *tenkō* as "a change of thought that occurs because of pressure"[34] is qualified by his acknowledgment of subjective decision-making, making *tenkō* "a combination of pressure and voluntary compliance" (*kyōsei to jihatsusei no karami-ai* 強制と自発性 の絡み合い).[35] In the mid-1950s, Tsurumi had led the charge among the so-called progressive intellectual community by questioning war responsibility of intellectuals in general.[36] Yet, in the context of the *tenkō* study, Tsurumi was preoccupied with the phantom of intellectual resistance, and he appeared to regard the *tenkō* study as a contribution to unraveling this deeply troubling void in Japan's intellectual culture. In Sumiya's view, the void could be filled by *shutaisei*: "where the sense of self (*shutaisei*) is weak, the situation determines thought and behaviour."[37] For this reason, postwar debates over *tenkō* can justifiably be seen as an extension of the debates over autonomy in the late 1940s.[38]

Somewhat contrary to the thrust of Tsurumi's pursuit of intellectual inconsistency, Maruyama posited value consistency as something that could tolerate or accommodate intellectual inconsistency. Believing that *tenkō* could occur within the confines of a consistent ideological position, Maruyama asked whether individuals in the 1930s and 1940s had retained essential subjective consistency with their own value system when confronted with changing political circumstances. "Thus when we look at Japan's position it is really a matter of whether or not there was a strong subjective sense of fundamental values or integrity. The answer must be that there was not."[39] As for postwar *tenkō*, it is once again value consistency that preoccupied Maruyama, especially the question of self-definition of values that inspire action. Given that after the war the element of state compulsion was absent, Maruyama identified the danger of conformism with the state as the instrument of intellectual degradation in the postwar era. "When

---

[33] Shisō no Kagaku Kenkyūkai 1959–1962.

[34] Tsurumi Shunsuke, in Shisō no Kagaku Kenkyūkai 1959–1962, 1: 5.

[35] Tsurumi Shunsuke, in Shisō no Kagaku Kenkyūkai 1959–1962, 1: 2.

[36] Tsurumi Shunsuke, "Chishikijin no sensō sekinin" [Intellectuals' War Responsibility], *Chūō Kōron* 71/1 (January 1956): 57–63.

[37] Sumiya 1976, 26.

[38] Nakajima makes this point in Nakajima Makoto, *Tenkō ron yosetsu: Senchū to sengo o tsunagu mono* [Introduction to Tenkō: The Link Between War and Postwar]. (Tokyo: Mineruba Shobō, 1980), 197.

[39] Maruyama Masao et al., "Gendai sekai to tenkō" [The Contemporary World and *Tenkō*], in Shisō no Kagaku Kenkyūkai 1959–1962, 3: 403.

we think of *tenkō* in the postwar era, surely it is revealed at the moment we conform with authority?"[40]

Together, these ideas contributed to a postwar intellectual culture that struggled between war and postwar mind-sets. When postwar thinkers insisted on resistance to the postwar state, they were slaying demons that they had failed to annihilate in the past. When they explored the idea of autonomy (*shutaisei*) as a companion to resistance as proof of democracy, they were trying to give space to value definition in political history. The attempts to confirm value as a vital component of *tenkō* has led to a greater incidence being placed on history and on how individuals juggle ideas and values in times of intense historical dislocation. It is the interplay of thought and value in the *shutaisei* and *tenkō* debates that reveals the underlying drivers behind the debate culture of postwar Japanese political thought. Rather than ideological representations of reality, it was how individuals located themselves vis-á-vis the value centers of the state, the nation, and the self that mattered. Accordingly, we often find *tenkō-sha* referring to the "internal" and "external" facets of political apostasy, implying realignment of the self in relation to the state and the nation during times of existential dislocation or crisis. During the course of postwar discussions on wartime *tenkō*, intellectuals stood accused of alienation from the people (the ethnic nation, *minzoku* 民族), of having collaborated with the Emperor System (the state, *kokka* 国家), and of weak subjective adherence to imported ideas (Marxism or liberalism).

Yoshimoto Takaaki

Yoshimoto Takaaki (1924–2012) erupted into the traumatized intellectual environment of the first postwar decades in Japan with a diametrically opposed mindset that privileged subjective and historical coherence over all other considerations. Whereas his peers saw *shutaisei* and *tenkō* as vehicles to underscore discontinuity from an undesirable past, Yoshimoto instead embraced the trauma of defeat as the very essence of trans-war subjective coherence and historical integration. This set Yoshimoto against the prevalent thrust of thinking in his time. His assault on the notion that intellectual consistency is normatively superior shook the foundations of postwar intellectual ethics and forced his peers to scramble in defence of their adherence to a bifurcated identity as the touchstone of intellectual legitimacy in postwar Japan. It also caught the attention of the youth who would drive the New Left movement in the late 1960s, in the process severely weakening the status of the Japan Communist Party as a leader of the left in the postwar era. Yoshimoto was himself a multiple (and proud) *tenkō-sha* (apostate). He not only shifted his own political identification radically in 1945, 1960, and 1982, but he was also a major catalyst in debates during the 1950s on wartime *tenkō* in the

---

[40] Maruyama, in "Gendai sekai to tenkō," 421.

world of Japanese literature.[41] Yoshimoto's works such as "Gisei no shūen" (The End of Fiction),[42] "Kyōdō Gensō Ron" (Our Shared Delusions),[43] and "Maruyama Masao Ron" (On Maruyama Masao)[44] were the companion texts for radical activist students in the late 1960s. In the explosion of youth-led activism in 1968–69, Yoshimoto led the charge against the intellectuals who had defined democracy after 1945 in terms of *shutaisei*, instead lumping them all into the category of "the establishment."

Yoshimoto's distinctive approach to conceptualizing the postwar era was based on two analytical perspectives: a temporal axis of generational consciousness and a spatial axis of "the internal" and "the external." For Yoshimoto, the temporal layers of experience defined by the war were an indispensable differential in the postwar world; no amount of common intellectual orientation could or should ignore this shared generational experience.[45] Most significantly, for Yoshimoto, *tenkō* was a phenomenon that embodied the essential continuity between prewar, war, and postwar. As a trans-war concept, *tenkō* actually served in Yoshimoto's view as a unifying conceptual marker for modern Japan's history.

When Hirohito's high-pitched tones crackled over the radio waves at noon on August 15, 1945, and suggested that Japan had been defeated, Yoshimoto was a twenty-year-old conscripted laborer working in the Japan Carbide factory in Tōyama. His first reaction was to go back to his dormitory, crawl inside his futon, and cry like a baby.[46] Yoshimoto claims to have lived his late teen years resigned to the likelihood that he would not live longer than that.[47] Yoshimoto's memories of his wartime youth were not painted in sombre hues; rather, he remembered it as a time of vitality and purpose. He later scoffed at writers who referred to the war as a "dark valley," dismissing them as "massive liars."[48] Yoshimoto described himself in retrospect as a *"gunkoku shōnen"* (軍国少年 militarist youth),[49] someone who had been completely behind the war effort. In the nastier phases of the war responsibility debate, communist writer Hanada Kiyoteru (1910–1974) concentrated on what he saw as the discrepancy between Yoshimoto's actual wartime experience and his postwar credentials: "It would be best if he [Yoshimoto] stopped acting like the representative of his young peers who died in battle,"[50] wrote Hanada, as "there are many aspects of Yoshimoto's self-appointed role as spokesman for those soldiers who died with bitterness in their hearts, that reminds one of Hitler."[51]

---

[41] See Yoshimoto 1995, 7–29; and Tsuzuki 1995, 505n29.

[42] Yoshimoto 1968–1975, 13: 47–71.

[43] Yoshimoto 1968–1975, vol. 11, entire volume.

[44] Yoshimoto Takaaki 1968–1975, 12: 3–96.

[45] Tsurumi Shunsuke also observed this aspect of Yoshimoto's thinking, though he regarded it as "abnormal." See Tsurumi, "Tenkōron no tembō," in Shisō no Kagaku Kenkyūkai 1959–1962, 3: 350. Tsuzuki comments in a more considered manner on the significance of defeat for intellectuals in Tsuzuki 1995, 253.

[46] Yoshimoto 1999, 207.

[47] Yoshimoto Takaaki, *Isho* [Testament] (Tokyo: Kadokawa Haruki Corporation, 1998), 173.

[48] Yoshimoto 2002, 196.

[49] Yoshimoto 2002, 190.

[50] Hanada 1977–1980, 8: 48.

[51] Hanada 1977–1980, 8: 25.

In his articulation of the significance of defeat, Yoshimoto imposed his own temporal logic by associating critical continuity with the very axis of bifurcated experience, with August 1945. Instead of embracing discontinuity with a negative past, where 1945 signified the end of Emperor-centered authoritarianism and the liberation of anti-establishment thought, Yoshimoto argued for ethical continuity through his critical treatment of "prewar generation" intellectuals. Instead of allocating "war responsibility" to the militarists and the fascist leadership of the wartime State, Yoshimoto demanded accountability from those people who were celebrated in the postwar era as paragons of wartime resistance—the communists who did not *tenkō* (*hi-tenkō sha* 非転向者), the communists who merely pretended to commit *tenkō* (*gisō-tenkō sha* 偽装転向者), and the prewar generation of progressive thinkers. Yoshimoto wore his generational category of "war generation" (*sensō-sedai* 戦争世代) like a badge of honor, but his idea of generations was inherently paradoxical.[52] Yoshimoto referred to those who were adults when war broke out and were actively confronted with participating in the war effort as "the prewar generation" (*senzen-ha* 戦前派), whereas those like him who were still in their teens during the war were the "wartime generation" (*senchū-ha* 戦中派). The prewar generation had for the most part participated actively in the war and had been directly in the line of fire, whereas the war generation had stayed at home, eligible for conscripted labor duty (and only called up into the military upon completion of their education). And yet, Yoshimoto accused the prewar generation of being mere "voyeurs" of war, while the wartime generation had been "wholeheartedly committed" to the war effort. This is because, in the postwar era, those who had experienced war retrospectively distanced themselves from that experience. In Yoshimoto's, eyes they remained unreflective after the war of the discrepancy between their ideas and their actions in wartime. For Yoshimoto this meant that their education had comprised little more than "irresponsible ideas":

> The prewar generation, having been mere spectators during the war or even co-operative in a *tenkō-sha* kind of way, have existed to this day without ever having assimilated the substantial experience surrounding the structure of thought in wartime. For this generation, the war was nothing but a nightmare.[53]

For Yoshimoto, war and defeat had been "internal experiences" (*naiteki keiken* 内的経験).[54] He believed that intellectuals, poets, and writers were the people who should ensure that ideas resonated with life. In his first writings on this question, Yoshimoto employed the category of the "war generation" as the mechanism through which he could attack those who had failed to deliver that resonance. Here emerged the theme of the unacceptability of the gap between life and thought, between the "external" and

---

[52] Oguma 2002, 619, 629.

[53] Yoshimoto Takaaki, "Sengo sedai no seiji shisō" [The political thought of the postwar generation], *Chūō Kōron* 75/1 (January 1960): 32–33.

[54] Yoshimoto 1968–1975, 8: 137.

the "internal," that Yoshimoto would wield in fierce debates with his peers and with members of the prewar generation throughout the second postwar decade. We can also see what Yoshimoto meant by his taunt of "spectator" when he wrote about the prewar generation thinkers. Yoshimoto believed that, despite being at war and in battle, those who emerged in the postwar era preaching democracy had in wartime quarantined their ideas from their real-world experience, merely observing the war instead of intellectually engaging, either in collaboration with or in opposition to that war.

Yoshimoto began with a simple but heart-felt conviction that defeat ought to be regarded as a significant event for those thinkers and activists who were adults in August 1945. Through his essays on the wartime poet and propagandist Takamura Kōtarō (1883–1956), Yoshimoto made it clear that, in his view, this significance stemmed from the fact that August 1945 offered the opportunity for the prewar generation to engage in essential self-criticism and self-transformation. This would enable their postwar ideas to resonate with trans-war life. Failure to engage in this reflection would mean that the significance of defeat would be lost. His thinking on *tenkō* had little in common with the line taken by the Shisō no Kagaku Kenkyūkai group. In fact, Yoshimoto took part in some of the discussions in the later stages of the project. He was also part of its subject matter, as when his acrimonious debate with Hanada Kiyoteru was featured. The Shisō no Kagaku group's emphasis had been on the top-down dynamics of *tenkō*; Yoshimoto, on the other hand, side-lined the external impulses behind the act of *tenkō* altogether: "I do not think that official force or pressure was the greatest factor. Rather, the axis of my thinking is that isolation from the masses (*taishū* 大衆) was the greatest factor."[55] Yoshimoto's search for intellectual accountability among intellectuals themselves, rather than in the objective environment of war and authoritarianism, prepared the way for a clash between postwar opinion leaders over the substance not only of *tenkō*, but also of war responsibility.

Almost twenty years after defeat, Yoshimoto was able clearly to articulate what had niggled at him during his fierce debates during the late 1950s: the reason why defeat was such a vitally important element in his thinking. In recalling successive defeats in his life to date—1945, the defeats he experienced as a union activist in the early 1950s, and the "defeat" of the anti-security treaty protests in 1960—Yoshimoto spoke of defeat as a process instead of a watershed event. "No matter how big or how small the fight," wrote Yoshimoto, "from the time the trouble starts through to the aftermath of defeat ... I trust the fact that I have experienced this entire process."[56] This clarification of a core concept was entangled with Yoshimoto's idealization of "fighting to the bitter end" (or "wholeheartedness"), but it was Yoshimoto's commitment to experiencing multiple defeats, as processes that included implementing the lessons of those defeats, that remained a cornerstone of his writing thereafter. In 1964, Yoshimoto was very clear about this:

[55] Yoshimoto 1968–1975, 13: 9–10.
[56] Yoshimoto Takaaki, "Kako ni tsuite no jichū" [Notes on the past] in *Shoki Nōto* [Early notes]. (Tokyo: Kōbunsha Bunko, 2006), 557–558.

> ... what is important is not pretending there has been a victory after accumulated
> attempts, but rather to learn from what comes out of the depths of experiencing de-
> feat after defeat.[57]

With this transformation of defeat from a particular event into a metaphor for the life–
thought nexus, Yoshimoto was able to invoke his 1945 experience in numerous postwar
contexts without introducing the specific context of what he called the Pacific War.
Yoshimoto's discomfort with conventional interpretations in the postwar era of wartime
tenkō began with the fact that the pivotal significance of defeat was not recognized in
this discourse. He noted that wartime *tenkō-sha* showed no sign of the experience of war
at all in their approach to their postwar work.[58] In the case of those who had only pretended to undergo *tenkō* during the war, this meant that their "fake fascism" was being
followed after the war by "fake democracy." Failure to integrate the war into their intellectual worldview meant that they had overlooked the historical axis of defeat. They
were carrying on their intellectual activity as though nothing important had happened,
either to them or to their readers. Yoshimoto found this not only unacceptable, but dangerous. The association of wartime pretend-*tenkō* (*gisō tenkō* 偽装転向) with active or
passive wartime resistance appalled Yoshimoto further still. "I was appalled when the
generation that had supposedly opposed the war emerged. If such a generation exists,
one would think that I would have met them before."[59]

Yoshimoto identified the existence of a life–thought nexus as essential for an integrated, trans-war philosophy. Controversially, he accused the communists and the wartime state for their alienation from this nexus. The alienated space between intellectuals
and society was the very space that the wartime state had recognized, and abused, and
that the communists had failed to see at all. In "Geijutsuteki teikō to zasetsu" (Artistic
Resistance and Despair) Yoshimoto identified what he called "the dark zone," which
represents the gap between intellectuals' internal thought structures and reality as
perceived by their audience, the people.

> If we examine the history of revolutionary movements in Japan, we can say that the
> absolutist authorities utilised this dark zone that existed between the parallel layers
> of vanguard consciousness and popular consciousness, and absorbed it.[60]

The internal–external paradigm also helps explain in structural terms why, in
Yoshimoto's view, wartime communist intellectuals failed to overcome this alienation
from the people with their own ideas. He argued that their own structure of thought had
been built around an internal–external frame that served to enforce incoherence between political consciousness (*seiji ishiki* 政治意識) and the consciousness of everyday

---

[57] Yoshimoto, "Kako ni tsuite," 558.
[58] Yoshimoto quoted in Tsuzuki 1995, 258.
[59] Yoshimoto quoted in Tsuzuki, 1995, 256.
[60] Yoshimoto 1968–1975, 4: 165.

life (*seikatsu ishiki* 生活意識). The incoherence began not between themselves and society, but within their own thought processes. In Yoshimoto's mind, this incoherence was born from spiritual and ideological disconnection. For Yoshimoto, the link between external reality and internal emotion had to exist somewhere for ideology to acquire personal resonance. When so-called thought leaders such as Maruyama Masao hailed the 1960 popular protests against the revision of the US–Japan Security Treaty as a victory for democracy, Yoshimoto saw only the compounded disgrace of thought alienated from life, an insult to the transformative trans-war opportunity afforded by defeat.

JAPAN AND 1968

Japan's version of 1968 resonated with the youth-led protests that exploded around the world that year.[61] In their rejection of technocracy, bureaucracy, and alienation that accompanied the advent of advanced industrial capitalism, and in their protest against the revision of the US–Japan Security treaty in 1960, Japan's New Left youth exhibited profound skepticism concerning the integrity of the postwar world. In the whirlwind of rage that erupted on university campuses around the nation at the end of the decade, Japan's student protestors were also rejecting the formula for postwar society that had been posited by both the communist left and the progressive idealist thinkers after 1945. In performing their nihilist variation of *shutaisei* in 1968–69, they transcended the trans-war discourse that had been constrained by the normative disintegration of war and postwar value and subjectivity. Yoshimoto's credo of "wholeheartedness" was manifest in the violence performed by students with staves and helmets and in the evolution of postwar *shutaisei* from value autonomy toward individual atomization and self-criticism.[62] Yoshimoto's thought inspired both the rejection of postwar measures of legitimacy and its aftermath.

In the midst of violent protest, Yoshimoto invented an alternative version of autonomy or independence—*jiritsu* (自立)—that was premised on normative distancing from the postwar Establishment that included intellectuals from both sides of the spectrum as well as the state. For Yoshimoto, in the age of mass society, true autonomy could only be found within the apolitical everyday. To this end, *jiritsu* meant "independence from enlightenment attitudes, vanguardism, and the composite category of modern rationalism."[63] Through the notion of *jiritsu*, Yoshimoto hoped to decontaminate autonomy from its association with discredited elites and illusory democratic freedoms, to realize true autonomy in a post-postwar era. In his reading of the nature of postwar modernity and capitalism, Yoshimoto declared redundant the "dead terminologies" of

---

[61] See Okamoto 1995.

[62] See Kersten 2009.

[63] See Washida 1992, 218. For Yoshimoto's exposition on *jiritsu*, see "Jiritsu no shisōteki kyoten" [The Intellectual Basis of *Jiritsu*], in Yoshimoto 1968–1975, 13: 240–274.

postwar discourse along with the rationalizations of postmodern life that they implied. In this he shared the view of Herbert Marcuse that rationality was being utilized in the postwar, advanced industrial era to integrate individuals into a self-legitimizing system, in effect suppressing autonomy to create the impression of consensus.[64] Yoshimoto's solution was to return to the grassroots, this time identified as the masses (*taishū*), in what amounted to a negative variant of autonomy; that is, autonomy from the Establishment (to paraphrase Isaiah Berlin).

In the wake of the 1968–69 maelstrom, Maruyama Masao emerged with quite a different response to the dilemma confronting postwar thought. Instead of value-based action quarantined from state interference, Maruyama instead called for a return to universalism as the best way to instill the "spirit of autonomy" in the postwar nation. But it seemed that the weight of war and war responsibility still permeated his problem consciousness. Universalism and utopian aspiration was required in his view because "it is born of pressure from reality, of a consciousness of total resistance."[65] Yoshimoto's furious denunciation in the late 1960s of progressive renderings of a pristine postwar ethos emanated from his own core value—authenticity—which for him was the integral link between life and thought. It was a similar clarion call for authenticity connected to a prewar ethic that novelist Mishima Yukio evoked with his gruesome ritual suicide in 1970. For many, Mishima's violent demonstration of connectivity with a prewar ethos symbolized the redundancy of the trans-war momentum in postwar Japan. But as Maruyama's repost to Yoshimoto reveals, the searing presence of war remained stubbornly and forcefully embedded in the thought of many trans-war thinkers:

> Was it better for Japan to lose the war, or to win it? In order to answer this question, we have a responsibility to scream out our answer to the question of whether or not Japan's postwar democracy is an illusion. Do we say then that the prewar imperial state was not illusion, but reality? If so, then rather than the reality of imperial Japan, I choose the illusion of Japanese democracy.[66]

BIBLIOGRAPHY AND SUGGESTED READINGS

Berlin, Isaiah. (1969) "Two concepts of liberty." In *Four Essays on Liberty*. Oxford: Oxford University Press, 118–172.

Conrad, Sebastian. (2010) *The Quest for the Lost Nation: Writing History in Germany and Japan in the American Century*. Berkeley: University of California Press.

Dower, John. (1999) *Embracing Defeat: Japan in the Wake of World War II*. New York: W. W. Norton and Company.

Hanada Kiyoteru. (1977–1980) *Hanada Kiyoteru zenshū* [Complete Works of Hanada Kiyoteru]. 17 Vols. Tokyo: Kōdansha.

[64] See, in particular, Herbert Marcuse, *One Dimensional Man* (Boston: Beacon Press, 1964).
[65] Maruyama 1982, 128.
[66] Maruyama 1998, 246.

Ienaga Saburō. (1985) *Sensō sekinin* [War Responsibility]. Tokyo: Iwanami Shoten.

Iida Momo. (2003) *Nijū-isseiki no "ima-koko": Umemoto Katsumi no shōgai to shisōteki isan* [The "Here and Now" of the 21st Century: Umemoto Katsumi's Life and Legacy]. Tokyo: Kobushi Shobō.

Joly, Jacques. (2011) "Maruyama Masao: From Autonomy to Pacifism." In *Japan's Postwar*, edited by M. Lucken, A. Bayard-Sakai, and E. Lozerand, translated by J. A. A. Stockwin. London: Routledge, 65–83.

Kajiwara Nobutoshi. (2004) *Yoshimoto Takaaki ron: Sensō taiken no shisō* [On Yoshimoto Takaaki: His Thought on War Experience]. Tokyo: Shinpūsha.

Kersten, Rikki. (1994) "The War in Postwar Japanese Politics." *Bulletin of the Japanese Studies Association of Australia* 15(3)/3: 1–9.

Kersten, Rikki. (1996) *Democracy in Postwar Japan: Maruyama Masao and the Search for Autonomy.* London: Routledge.

Kersten, Rikki. (2009) "The Intellectual Culture of Postwar Japan and the 1968–1969 University of Tokyo Struggles: Repositioning the Self in Postwar Thought." *Social Science Japan Journal.* 12/2: 227–245.

Koschmann, J. Victor. (1996) *Revolution and Subjectivity in Postwar Japan.* Chicago: Chicago University Press.

Maruyama, Masao. (1963) *Thought and Behaviour in Modern Japanese Politics.* Expanded edition. Oxford: Oxford University Press.

Maruyama, Masao. (1964) *Gendai seiji no shisō to kōdō* [Thought and Behaviour in Modern Japanese Politics]. Expanded edition. Tokyo: Miraisha.

Maruyama, Masao. (1976) *Senchū to sengo no aida* [Between Wartime and Postwar]. Tokyo: Misuzu Shobō.

Maruyama, Masao. (1982) *Kōei no ichi kara* [From the Rearguard]. Tokyo: Misuzu Shobō.

Maruyama, Masao. (1996) *Maruyama Masao shū* [Works of Maruyama Masao]. 16 vols. Tokyo: Iwanami Shoten.

Maruyama, Masao. (1998) *Jikonai taiwa: 3 satsu nōtō kara* [Internal Conversations: Extracts from 3 Notebooks]. Tokyo: Misuzu Shobō.

Mishima Yukio, Tōdai Zenkyōtō. (1969) *Bi to kyōdōtai to tōdai tōsō* [Beauty, Community and the Tokyo University Struggles]. Tokyo: Kadokawa Shoten.

Okamoto Hiroshi. (1995) *1968 nen: Jidai tenkan no kiten* [1968: The Starting Point for the Change of Era]. Kyoto: Hōritsu Bunkasha.

Oguma Eiji. (2002) *Minshū to aikoku* [The People and Patriotism]. Tokyo: Shinyōsha.

Oguma Eiji. (2009) *1968.* 2 vols. Tokyo: Shinyōsha.

Otake Hideo. (2007) *Shinsayoku no isan: nyū refuto kara posuto modān e* [The Legacy of the New Left: From the New Left to Post-modern]. Tokyo: Tokyo Daigaku Shuppankai.

Seraphim, Franziska. (2006) *War Memory and Social Politics in Japan, 1945–2005.* Cambridge, MA: Harvard University Press.

Shimizu Ikutarō. (2006-2007) *Shimizu Ikutarō chosakushū* [Collected Works of Shimizu Ikutarō]. 19 vols. Tokyo: Kōdansha.

Shisō no Kagaku Kenkyūkai, ed. (1959–1962) *Kyōdō kenkyū tenkō* [Joint Research on Tenkō]. 3 Vols. Tokyo: Heibonsha.

Shōji Takeshi. (2015) *Shimizu Ikutarō: isai no gakushō no shisō to jissen* [Shimizu Ikutarō: The Thought and Practice of a Scholar of a Different Hue]. Kyoto: Mineruba.

Steinhoff, Patricia G. (1991) *Tenko: Ideology and Societal Integration in Prewar Japan.* New York: Garland.

Sumiya Mikio. (1976) "Tenkō no shinri to ronri" [The Psychology and Logic of Tenkō]. *Shisō* 624/June: 15–30.

Tōyama Shigeki (1955) "Haisen no rekishi o dō uketomeru ka" [How Should We Interpret the History of Defeat]. *Sekai* 116/August: 103–110.

Tsuzuki Tsutomu. (1995) *Sengo Nihon no chishikijin: Maruyama Masao to sono jidai* [Postwar Japan's Intellectuals: Maruyama Masao and His Era]. Tokyo: Seori Shobō.

Umemoto Katsumi. (1977–1978) *Umemoto Katsumi chosakushū* [Collected Works of Umemoto Katsumi]. 10 Vols. Tokyo: Sanichi Shobō.

Washida Koyata. (1992) *Yoshimoto Takaaki ron* [On Yoshimoto Takaaki]. Tokyo: Sanichi Shobō.

Watanabe Kazuyasu. (2010) *Yoshimoto Takaaki no 1940 nendai* [Yoshimoto Takaaki's 1940s]. Tokyo: Perikansha.

Watanabe Kazuyasu. (2012) *Yoshimoto Takaaki no 1950 nendai no kiseki* [Yoshimoto Takaaki's Trajectory in the 1950s]. Tokyo: Perikansha.

Watanabe Kazuyasu. (2013) *Tatakau Yoshimoto Takaaki: 60 nen anpo kara 70 nen anpo e* [Yoshimoto Takaaki Fights: From the 1960 Security Treaty to the 1970 Security Treaty]. Tokyo: Perikansha.

Yasumaru Yoshio. (2004) *Gendai Nihon shisō ron: Rekishi ishiki to ideorogii* [On Contemporary Japanese Thought: Historical Consciousness and Ideology]. Tokyo: Iwanami Shoten.

Yoshimoto Takaaki. (1968–1975) *Yoshimoto Takaaki zenchosakushū* [Complete Collected Works of Yoshimoto Takaaki]. 15 vols. Tokyo: Keiso Shobō.

Yoshimoto Takaaki. (1995) *Waga tenkō* [My apostasy]. Tokyo: Bungei Shunjū.

Yoshimoto Takaaki. (1999) *Watashi no "sensōron"* [My "War Theory"]. Tokyo: Bunkasha.

Yoshimoto Takaaki. (2012) *Dai ni no haisen ki* [The Second Era of Defeat]. Tokyo: Shunjūsha.

CHAPTER 29

....

RAICHŌ: ZEN AND THE FEMALE BODY IN THE DEVELOPMENT OF JAPANESE FEMINIST PHILOSOPHY

....

MICHIKO YUSA AND LEAH KALMANSON

PART I: ZEN-FEMINST RAICHŌ IN THE CONTEXT OF MEIJI SPIRITUALITY (BY MICHIKO YUSA)

....

THE elegant and colorful figure of Hiratsuka Haru, better known by her pen name of Raichō (1886–1971), has been familiar to Western scholars of feminism for some time now. She initiated a venue for multiple, often competing, female and feminist voices in the early twentieth century by establishing the Bluestocking Society or Seitōsha in 1911 (the 44th year of the Meiji period, 1868–1912). In the post-World War II period, she became actively involved in the call for the removal of American military bases in Japan, as well as for the banning of the manufacture and deployment of nuclear weapons.[1] Through her lifelong engagement in social concerns, she came to earn wide public respect as a critic to be reckoned with. What is relatively unknown, however, is that her impetus for social engagement came from her Zen practice and her *kenshō* experience, which profoundly shaped her life and thought.[2] She remarked in her very last years: "Had I not practiced Zen, I would have led a life utterly unrelated to social activism."[3]

---

[1] Hiratsuka 2006, 314.

[2] Hiroko Tomida's study of Raichō, however, dismisses the essential significance of her Zen practice, concluding that Raichō's "religious leanings" were inconsistent at best. See Tomida Hiroko, *Hiratsuka Raichō and Early Japanese Feminism* (Leiden and Boston: Brill, 2004), 373.

[3] Recorded by Kobayashi Tomie, who assisted Raichō's project of writing her autobiography. See Kobayashi, "Postscript" to Hiratsuka 1971–73, 3:310.

The question of how "Zen practice" led to her social activism and the formation of her original thought touches on how contemplation is related to action and to philosophy, a question shared by many Kyoto School thinkers. Raichō's original thinking, buttressed by her conviction of the fundamental importance of discovering one's "spiritual identity," contains a message relevant to contemporary feminism. In her case, the mental and spiritual flexibility she gained through her Zen practice enabled her to look deeply into the predicament of women in a critical manner, and spurred her along on the path of independent thinking concerning women's subjectivity, all with an open-mindedness that characterized her thought. Her philosophical view evolved as her life experience expanded—from that of an inexperienced young woman to that of a woman capable of love as a wife and a mother. She came to view herself as a *sexed body* and not merely a conceptual abstract person devoid of physical reality, and in this way her analysis of life deepened as her life unfolded. She faced an inner conflict that was taking place between her ego and the self—the self belonging to a larger life transcending her ego—and out of this struggle she gained a deeper understanding and appreciation of dynamic ever-unfolding *life*.

Zen Awakening as the Source of Insight and Action

Raichō initially turned to Zen when she was about twenty years old. In those days, the young Meiji students, both male and female, were typically engrossed in the question of their spirituality (which was directly tied to their self-understanding and sense of self-identity in a period of transition from old Japan to new). Accounts by Tsunashima Ryōsen (né Tsunashima Eiichirō, 1873–1907) of his mystical experience drew wide attention.[4] A well-known scholar and religious seeker in his time, in July 1904 Ryōsen had an experience of "his self melting into the divine," which he also described as "seeing God" in the depths of his inner self. The young men and women of his day enthusiastically read Ryōsen's account.[5] Because Ryōsen's writings are hard to find today, let us quote this account in full from one of Raichō's essays:

> If I were to describe the state of my consciousness [at the very moment of my mystical experience], it was something like this: I was working on my essay with a writing brush in my hand. In the next moment, lo! this "I" was profoundly tucked into the

---

[4] See Itō Tomonobu, "Tsunashima Ryōsen," in *Kindai nihon tetsugaku shisōka jiten* [Dictionary of Modern Japanese Philosophers and Thinkers], edited by Nakamura Hajime and Takeda Kiyoko (Tokyo: Tokyo Shoseki, 1982), 370–2.

[5] Nishida Kitarō was among those who enthusiastically read Ryōsen's essays. See diary of February 17, 1905, "I read Mr. Tsunashima's 'Religious Rapture' (*Shūkyōjō no kōyō* 宗教上の光耀), which spoke to me"; and March 2, 1905, "Today I read Mr. Tsunajima's essay published in the *Taiyō*. Deeply touched." *Nishida Kitarō zenshū* [Collected Works of Nishida Kitarō], vol. 17 (Tokyo, Iwanami Shoten, 1980), 135–36. Unless otherwise noted, translations in this chapter are by Michiko Yusa.

bosom of heaven and earth. "I," the ego, disappeared, and God was actually holding the brush. I intuited this moment as absolute, transcendent, and utterly astonishing. I don't know any other way to describe my state of consciousness of that experience. I saw God in this way; I encountered God in this way. But to put it in terms of "seeing" or "encountering" is still superficial and external, and does not sufficiently convey my spiritual state of that moment. It is the meeting and fusing of my ego into God (*jinga no yūkai* 神我融会), the two becoming one (*gōitsu* 合一). At that instant, I had melted into God's presence. I became God.[6]

Ryōsen was familiar with both Buddhism and Christianity, and he freely drew from both traditions as they shaped his religious experience.

His words remained in Raichō's consciousness as she set about looking deeply into her own ego so that she could find God.[7] She wrote:

By reading the account of Tsunashima Ryōsen's religious experience, I came to understand that the exploration of my ego (*jiga no tankyū* 自我の探求) *is* the surest way to "seeing God" (*kenshin* 見神). I no longer doubted. God is at the foundation of my self, and it is not a mere God of concept .... I began my *zazen*, with the hunch that what Zen masters speak of as "awakening to the true nature of the self, and attaining enlightenment" (*kenshō gonyū* 見性悟入) is the same thing as the experience of "seeing God."[8]

Raichō began her formal Zen practice in 1906 under Shaku Sōkatsu (1870–1951), who was a dharma heir of Shaku Sōen (1859–1919). The *kōan* that Master Sōkatsu gave Raichō was: "What is *your* original face before your father and mother were yet to be born?"[9] She was to meditate on this mind-boggling "homework" not only while she sat in meditation (*zazen*), but at all times. The "solution" to this question is not found in any book but by each student coming up with his or her own answer in and through their *zazen* meditation practice. Raichō first needed to clear her mental slate by discarding all the preconceived ideas that she had accumulated. Through *kōan* study and *zazen*, she came to discover her body not only as the *instrument* but also the very *faculty* of thinking and

---

[6] Qtd. in Hiratsuka 1983–84, 6:24–5. The original essay by Tsunashima Ryōsen, "*Yo ga kenshin no jikken*" [The Experiment of My Seeing God], is compiled in his *Byōkanroku* [Records of My Illness and Convalescence].

[7] Like Tsunashima, Raichō expresses an openness to various paths of religious faith as equally authentic. When her daughter chose to become a Christian, Raichō spoke these words of assurance: "You need not worry about the fact that your faith is something different from that of your family members. The fact that it is gradually becoming a non-issue for you shows that you are spiritually maturing. It may seem funny and strange to you that your mother recites a *norito* (Shintō prayer) in front of the family alter that enshrines Shintō gods, and chants a *sutra* in front of the Buddhist altar. But in my mind, I see no contradiction whatsoever in my action, just as I can accept your Christian faith without any sense of contradiction. Christianity, Buddhism, and Shintō may still appear to be different to you, but for a person who sees the truth of life (the 'great way' *daidō* 大道), they are one." Hiratsuka 1983–84, 6:33.

[8] Hiratsuka 1983–84, 7:25.

[9] On the *kōan* she was given, see Hiratsuka 1983–84, 6:27.

understanding. After about six months of intensive *zazen* practice, in July 1906, she had the breakthrough experience known as *kenshō* (見性), in which her conceptual barriers totally broke down, bringing her directly to the reality of pulsating life (*inochi* いのち).

At that crucial moment of her spiritual awakening, the following hymn by Hakuin, known as *Zazen wasan*, touched her so profoundly that she broke into uncontrollable tears:

> Sentient beings are originally Buddha.
>> It is like ice and water.
>> Apart from water, there is no ice,
>> And apart from sentient beings, there is no Buddha ....
>> At this moment, what is there more for you to seek, with *nirvāna* itself manifest before you?
>> This very place, this is the Land of Lotus (*rengekoku* 蓮華国); this very body, this is Buddha.[10]

She clearly saw that life, the stuff the real "self" is made up of, was God, and that this divine reality extended far beyond the confines of the limited ego. This recognition constituted her *kenshō* experience, in which Zen students come to grasp the spiritual reality of the "self" as life itself, beyond concepts and ideas. What makes Raichō a thinker and not just a student of Zen is that she reflected on the content of her *kenshō* experience to explain it in a language that would make sense to ordinary people who may have never practiced Zen. Years later, addressing a young readership, she spoke about her understanding of the deep unity of life, self, and God—the experience that had come to her in a flash of intuition—as follows:

> You may think that your young beautiful body is "you." But in fact, you already know that your body is just an "organ" created and animated by life (*inochi*). And this life is actually the real "you." ... This "you"—life—lives on without fatigue, old age, or death, regardless of what happens to your organ. It was there even before your body appeared from the womb of your mother; and even after your body will have perished and only bones remain, life will continue to be. Life freely creates another body and gives birth to it. "You" are this eternal life—you are God.[11]

Human beings are born of eternal life, but we habitually attribute "divinity" to an objectified notion of Buddha or God.

Raichō's *kenshō* experience liberated her from the conventions that had earlier bound her and worked deeply on her psyche to spur her into action. However, she had to learn how to channel this newly discovered exuberant energy that was unleashed in the wake

[10] Hiratsuka 1983–84, 7:21. The last four lines are quoted in Hiratsuka Raichō 2006, 92.
[11] "*Anata jishin o shire*" [Know thyself] (1947), Hiratsuka 1983–84, 7:20.

of her *kenshō*. Her youthful inexperience caused her to equate the real self or "no-self" (*muga* 無我) with an abstractly conceptualized self that transcended the distinction of male and female. This led to her reckless action in 1908; she participated in the experiment of "love suicide" with a male writer who was anxious to realize his literary ideals. They were safely rescued in the snowy mountains near Shiobara and taken into custody by the local police. This happening was widely publicized by the media, which made her a kind of "celebrity."[12] Many young women of her generation secretly admired her courage and became her fans. A Jungian analyst would say that without the audacity to be playful, one does not fully savor life.[13] From her dealings with the insatiable appetite of a curious press, Raichō learned that it was best to make her personal life an open book. Moreover, she perceived that an authentic person is a "public" person, for private affairs essentially are the expressions of a universally human experience. Therefore she wrote about her personal affairs and offered them to the public readership. This culminated in the autobiography compiled in her last years.

Raichō's *kenshō* experience galvanized her into action with a hitherto untapped energy, both physical and mental, and directed her to social activism. But Zen practice alone would not produce a social activist or a philosopher. In Raichō's case, it was the combination of her rather unique modern upbringing,[14] her native intelligence, her poetic imagination, a certain psychic makeup, and her desire for learning that made her a "perfect vessel, in which the explosion, the unleashing, of women's life force, which had been suppressed and pent-up for many generations in a society controlled by men, could take place."[15] Lest her message be narrowly construed by the public, she deliberately did not foreground the influence of Zen in her writings, but she remained convinced of its essential power to liberate and transform women. She wrote:

> By a pure karmic connection I took up *zazen*, underwent the spiritual experience called "*kenshō*," and entered the world of Zen. But because I believe that different spiritual approaches eventually lead to the same endpoint, I consciously avoided the mention of the word "Zen" so that the reader would not misconstrue my words narrowly.... Women ... over time had lost, or at least weakened, this power of spiritual concentration, and became dispirited spineless creatures. But we must not give up.... I had great hopes and expectations for the future of women, and advocated that each and every woman undergo her inner transformation.[16]

---

[12] On the "Shiobara Incident," see Hiratsuka Raichō 2006, 104–18.

[13] Cf. Marie-Louise von Franz, *The Golden Ass of Apuleius: The Liberation of the Feminine in Man* (Boston & London: Shambhala, 1992), 39.

[14] Her father was sent to Germany by the Meiji government to study the new method of accounting; he gave his two daughters the highest education available to young women.

[15] Hiratsuka 1971–73, 3:300–1.

[16] Hiratsuka 1971–73, 1:336.

From Zen Practice to the Life of Social Activism

As mentioned above, in 1911 together with like-minded female colleagues, Raichō established the Bluestocking Society, which started out as a platform to showcase contemporary women's creative writings, but which soon turned into a forum for early Japanese feminists to criticize the perceptions of women in the past and present and to debate various new possibilities. The society's journal, *Seitō*, running from 1911 to 1916, published frank discussions of topics ranging from the protection of mothers and children to sexuality, abortion, and the abolition of prostitution.[17] The notoriety that Raichō inadvertently gained following the "Shiobara Incident" helped to bring the Society's journal to public attention and contributed to its robust sales.

As Raichō became progressively involved in the running of Seitōsha, she gradually left behind her formal Zen practice. But she continued to "sit" in meditation, whenever she found herself in a tight situation.[18] Her habit of independent thinking nurtured by her Zen practice liberated her from the yoke of hackneyed conventional concepts and ready-made ideas. Her development as a critical thinker was sustained by her religious awareness of the reality of the ego in view of the boundlessness of life. This explains, for instance, Raichō's negative response to Henrik Ibsen's *A Doll's House*, which was translated into Japanese and staged in Tokyo in 1911 to wide public acclaim. Her colleagues of the Seitōsha generally expressed their approval of the female protagonist Nora, hailing her as exemplifying new possibilities for women.[19] But to Raichō, it appeared that Nora's actions were rash, hasty, and juvenile, and that both Nora and her husband needed to surmount serious spiritual questions before they could become truly authentic persons.[20]

RAICHŌ'S PHILOSOPHY OF THE SEXED BODY

Raichō developed her philosophical reflection on the full reality of the human body as sexed. As we saw earlier, she first viewed the true self in abstract terms by overlooking the presence of the sexed body. But later on, as she responded to her life's experiences of falling in love, sharing the life of love with her husband, and becoming a mother of two children, she came to embrace the richer and concrete reality woven out of the body as sexed. At first, facing her reality of being a woman was for her the source of a struggle

---

[17] For a sample of works available in English see Bardsley 2007.

[18] Hiratsuka 1983–84, 5:274–76.

[19] For the special section on *A Doll's House* see the journal *Seitō* 2.1 (January 1912). See also the collection of *Seito* essays in Horiba 1991, 31–79.

[20] Horiba 1991, 62–9. The original is Hiratsuka Raichō's "*Nora-san ni*" [To Miss Nora], *Seitō* 2.1 (January 1912), 133–41. Cf. *Seitō sōmokuji-sakuin* [The complete table of contents and indices *of Seitō*] (Tokyo: Ryūkei Shosha, 1980). It is interesting that Nishida Kitarō made a similar remark a few years earlier on this play by Ibsen: "Nora has abandoned her home, and now what kind of life is she going to seek? If she is to have another 'awakening,' I have the feeling that she has to come back home." See Letter no. 75 to Tanabe Ryūji, March 14, 1908, *Nishida Kitarō zenshū*, 18:95.

between her drive to preserve her self-identity as her ego and her willingness to accept forces beyond her control, which eventually opened up a new interrelational horizon of human existence. Her path of discovery may be sketched in three phases or stages.

Phase 1: The Universal View of the Sexes

Raichō's early view on the sexed body is found in her celebrated 1911 manifesto in the inaugural issue of *Seitō*.[21] Therein, she proclaims her unbridled belief in women's "hidden genius" by emphasizing "heaven-given talent" (*tensai* 天才, which in today's Japanese means "genius," but for Raichō meant "a talent bestowed by heaven") as follows:

> In the beginning, woman was truly the sun, an authentic person (*shinsei no hito* 真正の人).
>
> Now she is the moon, a pale and sickly moon, dependent on another, reflecting another's brilliance....
>
> Together with all women, I want to believe in women's hidden heaven-given talent. I want to place my trust in this unique potential and rejoice in our good fortune of being born a woman. Our savior is the heaven-given talent within us.[22]

As she goes on, evidence of her spiritual convictions comes to the fore. She brushes off the sexual distinction between male and female as insignificant in the larger scheme of "universal spirituality," and, accordingly, she relegates sexual difference to the lower rungs of consciousness:

> I shall seek genius through spiritual concentration.
>
> Heaven-given talent is mystery; it is the authentic person.
>
> *Heaven-given talent has nothing to do with one's being a male or a female.*
>
> Male or female—this sexual distinction belongs to the level of intermediate or lower rung of the "self," the tentative "ego," which ought to die and perish. This distinction of male and female does not exist at the highest level of the "self," of the "true ego" (*shinga* 真我) that is immortal and imperishable.[23]

In this manifesto, we notice already a variety of positions on gender—at times advocating the overcoming of constructed gender identities and at times celebrating the uniqueness of women's spiritual potential. It also must be added that Raichō in this early period harbored prejudice against men as a vestige of her negative experience regarding the Shiobara Incident.[24] By elevating the "true self" beyond all gender distinctions, she in fact refused to see any positive value in the sexed body, either male or female. She was

---

[21] Hiratsuka 1987, 9–24.

[22] Hiratsuka 2006, 157 and 159.

[23] Hiratsuka 1987, 11, emphasis added.

[24] See Raichō's discussion of the Shiobara Incident and her feelings surrounding men and sexuality in Hiratsuka Raichō 2006, 104–29. She came to acknowledge that this prejudice hindered her from squarely facing women's issues.

not yet ready to see herself in the particular, and she stuck to the dimension of the universal. In Buddhist parlance, she privileged the aspect of universality (*byōdō* 平等) over that of particularity (*shabetsu* 差別).

Phase 2: "Encounter" with Ellen Key and Sexual Difference

This all was to change when, in August 1912, Raichō encountered her future husband, Okumura Hiroshi, a painter five years her junior. Around this time, Raichō was reading *Love and Marriage*, just published in 1911 by the Swedish feminist Ellen Key (1848–1926).[25] In this book, Key treated the controversial topic of the complex sexual and spiritual aspects of love, criticizing the traditional institution of marriage in favor of marriage based on love, which was still a novel idea around the turn of the twentieth century in many northern European countries.[26] The timing of the encounter with Key's work was "providential" to Raichō,[27] because it opened her eyes to "women's issues" for the first time and made her think about "many things and raise many questions."[28] Well-bred young Japanese women of the Meiji period were so sheltered that they were provided with almost no knowledge of sexuality or sexual relations. So, for Raichō, Key became a guide through the unfamiliar terrain of love and partnership.

Key, today a mostly forgotten figure even in her native land, was quite well known in Europe during her lifetime, even dubbed as "a humane, practical, female counterpart of Nietzsche."[29] She advocated the individual's happiness as "the most important condition" in life, where happiness is understood as the free and voluntary formation of one's own moral values (and not as "wanton promiscuity," as her opponents were wont to depict it).[30] Key's position on women's liberation was different from that of the universal suffrage movement of her time, and for that she was viciously attacked by the proponents of the latter.[31] Key questioned the premise of the suffragist movement, which in her view tacitly accepted androcentric values as the measure over against which women's worth was evaluated. Key's position aimed at *more* than mere equality of the sexes and was directed toward the liberation of women *qua* women. By nurturing their nature and participating in the betterment of society, women would help create a more peaceful and egalitarian community. In Key's eyes, the suffragists tended to obscure women's uniqueness in their slogans advocating the equality of the sexes, which even tended to

[25] Hiratsuka 1971–73, 2:491.

[26] Ellen Key, *Love and Marriage*, trans. A. Chater (New York and London: G. P. Putnam, 1911), 15: "The doctrine that love is the moral ground of sexual relations is thus as yet only an unendorsed sequence of words." There was the traditional view that "marriage and love were mutually exclusive" (ibid., 23).

[27] Hiratsuka 1971–73, 2:491.

[28] Hiratsuka 1971–73, 1:179.

[29] Quoted by Berenice A. Carroll, in her introduction to Ellen Key, *War, Peace, and the Future*, trans. Hildegard Norberg (New York & London: Garland Publishing, 1972), 6. This work by Ellen Key was originally published in America in 1916.

[30] Ellen Key, *Love and Marriage*, 55. See also Louise Nyström-Hamilton, *Ellen Key: Her Life and Her Works*, trans. A. E. B. Fries (New York and London: G. P. Putnam's Sons, 1913), 102.

[31] Louise Nyström-Hamilton, *Ellen Key: Her Life and Her Works*, esp. 106–9.

"masculinize women." Havelock Ellis, in agreement with Key, succinctly clarified the latter's unique position: "it was not enough to claim woman's place as a human being— especially in an age when man was regarded as the human being par excellence, but it also became necessary to claim woman's place in the world as a woman. That was not, as it might at first seem, a narrower but a wider claim."[32]

Key called for the social protection of motherhood by maintaining that the state ought to recognize the significance of the work of mothering as the source of creating domestic happiness, which becomes the building block of a good society. For Raichō, this intersection of the personal and the public, so persuasively articulated by Key, be- came essential to her reassessment of the sexed body and its social role.

Phase 3: Transition from the Universal to the Particular

Feeling the need to build for herself a solid philosophical foundation concerning women's issues, Raichō took Key's *Love and Marriage* as her textbook. In order to un- derstand Key's position better, she decided to translate it into Japanese and published it in installments in *Seitō*.[33] In her introduction to the first installment of her translation, she frankly admitted the conflict between the new ideas appearing on the horizon of her thinking and her earlier position: "When I engage in thinking or writing, and even when I am in romantic love, my awareness as a woman is hardly present. I only have the aware- ness of my ego (*jiga*), and I am aware of this ego's fundamental desire . . . to live fully by developing and expanding my energy in the world of higher reality."[34] Nevertheless, Key's influence on Raichō turned out to be "quite fundamental, along with the influence of *kenshō* through *zazen*—although not as profound a transformation for me as *kenshō* effected," she admitted.[35] While working on her translation of Key's book, Raichō's love for Okumura grew significant and serious. Also, Key's philosophy convinced her to ac- cept marriage and bear children. After half a year of courtship, the two lovers moved into the arrangement of "common living," as opposed to officially getting married. Until 1947, according to the old civil code, married women in Japan had no legal property rights or financial independence, and the wife was treated as the possession of the hus- band. In defiance of this civil code, Raichō established a branch of the Hiratsuka family and registered herself as its head, and she willingly bore the humiliation of registering their children "born out of wedlock" or "bastard."

After moving in with Okumura, her view of romantic love and the sexed body under- went a further transformation:

---

[32] Havelock Ellis, "Introduction," *Love and Marriage* by Ellen Key, xiii–xiv.

[33] Dina Lowy criticizes Raichō for using Key's eugenic arguments "to promote legislation [that] appealed to a state increasingly concerned with national pride and racial purity" and "made strategic use of them [i.e., Key's ideas of love, marriage, and motherhood] and converted Key's universal ideas into nationalist terms." See Lowy, "Love and Marriage: Ellen Key and Hiratsuka Raichō Explore Alternatives," *Women's Studies* 33 (2004), 370 and 377. However, no textual substantiation can be found in Raichō's writings for this criticism.

[34] Hiratsuka 1983–84, 1:178–79.

[35] Hiratsuka 1971–73, 2:492–93.

Romantic love became something solemn and significant that I had to look at with completely different eyes. I had to think long and hard about what it means to live as a woman and what value there is for a woman to live a life of love . . . . In the process I came to see *the need to liberate women not only as human persons but also as sexed women.* This was a totally new philosophical problem for me. My guide and moral support at the time, my source of ideas and hints as to how to proceed, was the book by Ellen Key [*Love and Marriage*]. During these two years of living with Okumura, I have slowly awakened to myself as a mature, integrated woman. At the same time, my life of love conflicted with my inner life—with my eagerness to continue to work, and the cry of my soul for solitude.[36]

Raichō's need for solitude—time for contemplation and writing about it—was further challenged during her first pregnancy, which forced her to face a serious existential quandary. She wondered: "Could I attain equilibrium between my life, in which I try to develop my personality, and the life of a mother? — these uncertainties aroused fear in me."[37]

She described this inner conflict as a battle between the preservation of her "ego" and the instinct for altruism and self-sacrifice occasioned by her becoming a mother. The latter, she saw, was issuing from the "imperative power of life," the transcendent force of nature that was operating inside her. Raichō now saw that self-liberation was taking place enabled not by an abstract genderless self, but by a concrete sexed body that is always connected to others through physical, mental, emotional and spiritual bonds. About five months into her pregnancy, she reflected:

Recently, I came to recognize that the desire to have my own baby and to be a mother are both latent in me . . . . How could I deny a baby, which is the creation of love—of that love that I affirmed when I entered into a life of love? . . . In this way, the fleeting idea that crossed my mind about aborting the fetus vanished completely. Although I am filled with fear and anxiety, along with an immense sense of responsibility, as I approach this unfamiliar world step by step, I am also beginning to experience a certain attachment, unexpected hope, and even joy. Not only that, the bond between my lover and me has grown deeper and more sincere, and our commitment to each other has strengthened.[38]

The birth of a baby girl in December 1914 sharpened Raichō's reflection on motherhood. She wondered, "Where did that strange new strength well up inside me, the strength that so easily overcame my egoism, which was inveterately rooted within me, and that made me want to raise the baby, regardless of all possible difficulties and sacrifices I may have to make, and despite all the contradicting feelings within me?"[39]

---

[36] Hiratsuka, 1983–84, 2:49–51; also Yusa 2011, 1125. Emphasis added.
[37] Hiratsuka 1971–73, 2:557.
[38] Hiratsuka 1983–84, 2:49–51. See also Yusa 2011, 1124–25.
[39] Hiratsuka 1983–84, 2:268.

Even then, the sense of being a mother and her love for the child did not come to her right away, but "only after the baby began to laugh, and recognized me as the mother and started to seek me out."[40]

Her motherly instinct, however, did not completely eradicate the pull of egoism, which remained in her as the dissatisfaction with having been thrown into the life of a mother and the many sacrifices it required of her. In this "constant battle between her egoism (or individualism) and altruism (her love for others)," a larger horizon of her life's meaning emerged:

> I affirmed my romantic love initially in order to assert my individual identity and develop it. But love rooted in self-affirmation and self-development turned out to be gateway to the love of others, the other side of life. In no time the whole panorama of love of the other unfolded in front of me, first through the love I bore my lover, and then through my love for my child. I ended up experiencing all sorts of contradictions in my life, but I can no longer dismiss them as merely "life's contradictions." I have rather come to think of them as gateways that open out into a wider, larger, and deeper life. And the real harmonization of these two orientations may well be the subtle and ultimate flavor of life itself.[41]

The truth of the matter is that Raichō continued to struggle with these contradictions until her two children reached the age of independence. Nonetheless, we discern in Raichō's personal conflicts a movement of philosophical development: from a disembodied abstract self to a sexed self, and then to the integrated personal and social self bonded by love and respect. All the while, her need for contemplation and critical and honest inner reflection—a habit she cultivated through her *zazen* and *kōan* practice—continued to mature and sustain her life of social activism.

PART II: RAICHŌ IN THE WIDER CONTEXT OF FEMINIST PHILOSOPHY (BY LEAH KALMANSON)

In Part I, we highlighted the importance of Zen practice to Raichō's life and work; in Part II, we elaborate on the significance of her ideas in the larger context of feminist philosophy. Many of the central concerns of Raichō and other early Japanese feminists overlap considerably with issues still relevant for feminism today. Raichō and her colleagues faced two interrelated problems: (1) Are the categories of gender and sexual

[40] Ibid.
[41] Ibid., 274–275. See also Yusa 2011, 1125–26.

identity purely constructed, or are they at least partly rooted in biology or an innate nature? (2) Are members of the women's movement working toward a new understanding of both humanity and equality that cuts across, or possibly transcends, gender and sex distinctions? Or, are they working at least in part to showcase women's uniqueness, and hence to develop a vision of equality that prioritizes gender particularity?[42]

In navigating these dilemmas, Raichō's Zen practice invites the insight that women's liberation, or any liberation, is as much *from* the self as it is *for* the self. In other words, while Raichō prioritizes greater autonomy for women and hence liberation *for* women's self-directed pursuits, she also acknowledges a sense of spiritual liberation *from* the limitations of the ego.

As both her writing and her actions show, liberation is not freedom for a generic subject; a deeper sense of liberation empowers the particular, embodied person and enables the capacity to work actively on behalf of others in society. This commitment is seen across a spectrum of feminist voices in Japan, both in Raichō's lifetime and today.

Raichō and Feminist Discourse in Japan

In Raichō's day, questions of motherhood, women's social roles, and the construction of women's identities divided the feminist movement while at the same time providing a rich source of debate and discussion. Of note is a series of exchanges in 1918 between Raichō and her contemporary Yosano Akiko (1878–1942). In the background of this debate is Raichō's own experience of raising her first baby alone while her husband—a painter with no steady income—was recovering from tuberculosis. During this time, Raichō was, in effect, a single mother who wrote essays and short novels to earn a living for the entire family. Hence she questioned Yosano's opposition to state aid for mothers and determination to accept nothing short of total financial independence for women. Raichō worried that Yosano's vision of equality obscured gender differences and devalued the unique contributions to society of women's work as mothers. Raichō was supported in this debate by fellow feminist Yamada Waka, who was also a reader of Ellen Key. Another important voice in the discussion, Yamakawa Kikue, linked the underprivileged status of women to other economic disparities, holding that only a systemic change from capitalism to socialism would address the root of women's problems.[43]

Despite differences among all of these thinkers, they do share a common conviction that liberation for a given woman does not mean simply greater personal freedom but also greater personal responsibility within a community. Of course, the fight for women's rights is on the agenda for feminists in Japan as elsewhere, but many voices

---

[42] Written works on these topics are too numerous to list, but for a good overview of some fairly recent material, see Barbara S. Andrew, Jean Keller, and Lisa H. Schwartzman, eds., *Feminist Interventions in Ethics and Politics* (Oxford: Roman and Littlefield, 2005).

[43] Yusa 2011, 1123.

in Raichō's time converge on the key point that women are fighting for their *duties* as much as for their *rights*. For example, when Yosano declares five conditions for reform, the fourth is "the principle of classless solidarity in taking responsibility for humanity at large." She explains: "When it comes to the creation of cultural life, all human beings bear the responsibility to act in solidarity. As women, we desire an equal share in this responsibility."[44] For Yosano, as well as for Raichō, freedom is not the pursuit of egotistical desires but the unhindered capacity to fulfill meaningful responsibilities and to participate fully in community life. Likewise, although Yamakawa joins Yosano in rejecting the idealization of motherhood, she, too, echoes Raichō's general insight that liberation for the self is liberation *from* petty individualism *for* greater social responsibilities. She writes: "Rather than companions or subsidiaries, women are peers of men . . . . it is only proper that they should work diligently towards the construction of an autonomous culture. It is as much a duty as it is a right for women."[45] Yamakawa goes on to emphasize that the women's movement must not be sidetracked by fighting for economic access to a privileged leisure class in the guise of the fight for equal rights.[46]

In more recent years, these questions of women's identity and the meaning of equality are seen, for example, in a well-known disagreement between cultural critic Aoki Yayoi and influential sociologist Ueno Chizuko. Aoki is associated with an eco-feminism that embraces the female principle as a powerful force in nature and society, to which Ueno responds with concerns about overly romanticizing the feminine. Yet, neither woman's position is simplistic or easily classifiable. For example, Aoki's understanding of the feminine principle is not reducible to a naïve, socially constructed femininity. She writes:

> if all [feminism] achieves is the right of passage of women into the existing male social structures and practices, I don't know that we have achieved very much . . . . I don't believe we can achieve any real liberation for women until we have some vision of an alternative lifestyle, some other way of existing, not just between man and woman but between humans and the environment.[47]

Ueno herself notes that she, too, values the importance of the "maternal function" while qualifying this statement with the idea that both men and women can learn to be effective nurturers.[48] Moreover, both Aoki and Ueno would agree that studies of female identity in Japan today cannot be divorced from the history of Japan's encounters with various imperialisms, including its own emperor system, as well as deep-rooted relations with China and more recent relations with the United States and Europe. In particular, Ueno notes that arguments once deployed to define Japanese uniqueness against Chinese cultural hegemony are now deployed to undermine the influence of feminist critique as one more imperialist importation from the West.

[44] Yosano 2011, 1144.
[45] Yamakawa 2011, 1160.
[46] Ibid., 1162.
[47] Buckley, ed. 1997, 15.
[48] Buckley, ed. 1997, 281–83.

Ueno resists this move, saying: "Japanese feminism has its own raison d'être, its own history, and its own voice, and the charge of being an import was created to attack feminism by reducing it to mere Western influence."[49] In particular, Ueno characterizes American feminism as being overly focused on the language of individual rights and at times undervaluing domestic work as an important social function. She expresses admiration for Japanese feminism's historical engagement with issues of maternity and femininity, noting emphatically that all notions of "freedom" need not be cast in a Western mold: "Asian women do have significant power, although it is not a form of power recognized by non-Asian feminists . . . . It is possible for Asian women to develop a feminism that is the product of their own cultural context and meaningful to them."[50]

We look back to the early twentieth-century Japanese feminists as setting the stage for a reading of "liberation" that accommodates the personal as much as the interpersonal and that thereby recognizes forms of power and freedom beyond liberal individualism. Here, we see the potential of Raichō's work to contribute to contemporary discourses surrounding the meaning of liberalism for feminist ethics and politics.

Raichō and Feminist Discourse in Western Scholarship

Feminism in Western scholarship is divided over the values of liberal individualism, such as autonomy, equality, and freedom, which are widespread in moral theory at large. On the one hand, many feminists advocate these values as central to obtaining and sustaining rights for women in society. For example, Martha Nussbaum, one of the most well known feminists of the liberal tradition, writes:

> Personhood, autonomy, rights, dignity, self-respect: These are the terms of the liberal Enlightenment. Women are using them, and teaching other women to use them when they did not use them before. They treat these terms as though they matter, as though they are the best terms in which to conduct a radical critique of society, as though using them is crucial to women's quality of life.[51]

On the other hand, despite the successes of liberalism in gaining political rights for women across the globe, some feminists question liberal values for being overly individualistic, indebted to a traditionally patriarchal picture of the subject, or reflective of Western hegemony. For example, Eva Feder Kittay argues that liberalism "fosters a fiction that the incapacity to function as a fully cooperating societal member is an exception in human life, not a normal variation."[52] Kittay counters that periods of dependency—as

---

[49] Ueno 2005, 232.
[50] Buckley, ed. 1997, 278.
[51] Martha Nussbaum, *Sex and Social Justice* (Oxford: Oxford University Press, 1999), 56.
[52] Eva Feder Kittay, *Love's Labor* (New York: Routledge, 1999), 92.

in childhood, old age, and extended illness—are inevitable and normal. Liberalism, she continues, not only obscures the normalcy of dependency but also devalues the work of those caretakers in charge of dependents, relegating such work to the private sphere and hence shielding it from political critique. Kittay is associated with a field of feminist theory known as "care ethics," which argues for an understanding of personhood at odds with the rational, independent, self-interested subject of liberalism. As Virginia Held writes: "It is characteristic of the ethics of care to view persons as relational and as interdependent . . . . [T]o many care theorists, persons are at least partly constituted by their social ties."[53] Nussbaum criticizes care ethics for romanticizing women's social roles and privileging motherly devotion over self-determination, a point that recalls similar objections to Ellen Key's work several generations earlier.

Although there is little (if any) direct influence of Ellen Key on contemporary care ethics, they do share similar concerns about the undervalued status of women's work in the family and the home. These similarities situate Raichō fruitfully within contemporary feminist discourses surrounding liberalism, especially her frank reflections on the tensions between what she called her "egoism" and her "altruism." As we have seen, she acknowledges that the body has a life and power of its own, one that frustrates the agency of her ego while at the same time providing a source of liberation and creativity. Similarly, society and family relations at times stand in her way while also providing her with a larger sense of self. Although Raichō's work gives no easy answers to the problems of identity and autonomy that she raises, the influence of Buddhism on her understanding of liberation is instructive. Feminists, not only in care ethics, but in other areas of moral theory and philosophy, critique the individualistic, substantive, or overly rational ego of the Cartesian tradition; yet, at times, they also struggle to articulate a vision of autonomy or empowerment suitable for the post-Cartesian subject. How might Raichō's political as well as spiritual insights be relevant to this articulation?

Perhaps recent work in Womanist–Buddhist dialogue has already begun answering this question.[54] For example, social ethicist Melanie Harris comments on the relevance of Buddhist practices for black women, in words that recall Raichō:

> The imagined path from Womanism to the Gospel of Mary into the gardens of Buddhism suggests that self-love is part of the process of coming to know the self, of realizing the "inner deity" that merges the boundary lines between being human and divine. These two gifts of Buddhism, building confidence and meditation upon the divine self, echo calls that Womanists also answer, to reestablish a sense of wholeness in black women.[55]

---

[53] Virginia Held, *The Ethics of Care* (Oxford: Oxford University Press, 2006), 46. Beyond care ethics, the idea of a relational or a "social self" is popular in other areas of feminist moral theory that are critical of liberal individualism. See Catriona Mackenzie and Natalie Stoljar, eds., *Relational Autonomy: Feminist Perspectives on Autonomy, Agency, and the Social Self* (Oxford: Oxford University Press, 2000).

[54] The Womanist-Buddhist Consultations, which ran from 2009 to 2011 at Harvard Divinity School, University of Georgia, and Texas Christian University, gathered a variety of Womanist scholars together to read and discuss Buddhist texts. See Wakoh Shannon Hickey, "Editor's Introduction," *Buddhist-Christian Studies* 32.1 (2102): vi–viii.

[55] Melanie Harris, "Buddhist Meditation for the Recovery of the Womanist Self, or Sitting on the Mat Self-Love Realized," *Buddhist-Christian Studies* 32 (2012): 70.

Following on the work of pioneering black feminist and Buddhist practitioner Jan Willis, Harris recommends Buddhist meditation as a healing practice that not only sustains personal well-being but also enables the ongoing work of social justice.

For thinkers such as Harris, spiritual reflection is not merely passive and contemplative—rather, it is a call to compassionate action and a foundation for social activism. Such progressive voices undoubtedly find a supportive ally in a figure such as Raichō. Her commitment to both spiritual and political liberation for women conveys a powerful message that brings added perspective to ongoing concerns in feminism today.

BIBLIOGRAPHY AND SUGGESTED READINGS

Bardsley, Jan. (2007) *The Bluestockings of Japan: New Woman Essays and Fiction from Seitō, 1911–16.* Ann Arbor: University of Michigan.

Buckley, Sandra, ed. (1997) *Broken Silence: Voices of Japanese Feminism.* Berkeley: University of California Press.

Hiratsuka Raichō. (1971–73) *Hiratsuka Raichō jiden: Genshi josei wa taiyō de atta* [Hiratsuka Raichō's Autobiography: In the Beginning Woman was the Sun], 4 vols. Tokyo: Ōtsuki Shoten.

Hiratsuka Raichō. (1983–84) *Hiratsuka Raichō chosakushū* [Collected writings of Hiratsuka Raichō], 8 vols., edited by Hiratsuka Raichō Chosakushū Henshū Iinkai. Tokyo: Ōtsuki Shoten.

Hiratsuka Raichō. (1987) *Hiratsuka Raichō hyōronshū* [Critical Writings of Hiratsuka Raichō], edited by Kobayashi Tomie & Yoneda Sayoko. Tokyo: Iwanami Shoten.

Hiratsuka Raichō. (2006) *In the Beginning, Woman Was the Sun: The Autobiography of a Japanese Feminist,* translated by Teruko Craig. New York: Columbia University Press.

Horiba Kiyoko, ed. (1991) *"Seitō": Josei kaihōronshū* ["Seitō": Essays on Women's Liberation], Tokyo: Iwanami Shoten.

Kitagawa Sakiko. (2009) "Living as a Woman and Thinking as a Mother in Japan: A Feminine Line of Japanese Moral Philosophy." In *Frontiers of Japanese Philosophy 6: Confluences and Cross-Currents,* edited by R. Bouso and J. W. Heisig. Nagoya: Nanzan Institute for Religion and Culture, 141–54.

Mackie, Vera. *Feminism in Modern Japan: Citizenship, Embodiment, and Sexuality.* Cambridge: Cambridge University Press, 2003.

Robins-Mowry, Dorothy. (1983) *The Hidden Sun: Women of Modern Japan.* Boulder, Colorado: Westview Press.

Rodd, Laurel Rasplica. (1991) "Yosano Akiko and the Taishō Debate over the 'New Women.'" In *Recreating Japanese Women, 1600–1945,* edited by G. L. Bernstein. Berkeley, Los Angeles, Oxford: University of California Press, 175–98.

Ueno Chizuko. (2005) "In the Feminine Guise: A Trap of Reverse Orientalism." *Contemporary Japanese Thought,* edited by Richard F. Calichman. New York: Columbia University Press.

Yamakawa Kikue. (2011) "An Inquiry into Feminism," translated by Robin Fujikawa. In *Japanese Philosophy: A Sourcebook,* edited by J. Heisig, J. Maraldo, and T. Kasulis. Honolulu: University of Hawai'i Press, 1159–64.

Yosano Akiko. (2011) "Conditions for Reform," translated by Michiko Yusa. In *Japanese Philosophy: A Sourcebook,* edited by J. Heisig, J. Maraldo, and T. Kasulis. Honolulu: University of Hawai'i Press, 1143–45.

Yusa, Michiko. (2009) "Women Rocking the Boat: A Philosophy of the Sexed Body and Self-Identity." In *Frontiers of Japanese Philosophy 6: Confluences and Cross-Currents*, edited by R. Bouso and J. W. Heisig. Nagoya: Nanzan Institute for Religion and Culture, 155–69.

Yusa, Michiko. (2011) "Women Philosophers Overview." In *Japanese Philosophy: A Sourcebook*, edited by J. Heisig, J. Maraldo, and T. Kasulis. Honolulu: University of Hawaiʻi Press, 1115–26.

Yusa, Michiko. (2017) "Affirmation via Negation: Zen Philosophy of Life, Sexual Desire, and Infinite Love." In *Bloomsbury Research Handbook of Contemporary Japanese Philosophy*, edited by M. Yusa. London & New York: Bloomsbury, 333–64.

Yusa, Michiko. (2018) "Dōgen and the Feminine Presence: Taking a Fresh Look into His Sermons and Other Writings." In Special Issue of "Women in Buddhism," *Religions* 9. http://wwu.mdpi.com/207-1444/9/8/232/htm

Yusa, Michiko, Robin Fujikawa, and Craig Teruko, trans. (2011) "Women Philosophers: Yosano Akiko, Hiratsuka Raichō, and Yamakawa Kikue." In *Japanese Philosophy: A Sourcebook*, edited by J. Heisig, J. Maraldo, and T. Kasulis. Honolulu: University of Hawaiʻi Press, 1138–64.

CHAPTER 30

....

JAPANESE PHENOMENOLOGY

....

TANI TŌRU

PHENOMENOLOGY was established by Edmund Husserl (1859–1938) not as an unchange-able system, but rather, in accordance with the motto "to the things themselves," as an ongoing philosophical movement of "breaking through" theoretical presuppositions to concrete experience.[1] As such, it spread beyond its original German-speaking sphere and eventually took root in Japan, where it became a major current of modern Japanese philosophy. Why and how did this happen? The present chapter focuses on the theories of four contemporary phenomenologists, but, before we embark on this subject, let me provide a rough sketch of how phenomenology came to Japan.

First, there is the historical fact of its arrival, not too long after Japan opened its doors to the West in the late nineteenth century, after two and a half centuries of political and cultural seclusion. The Edo Shogunate (1603–1867), which initiated and enforced that policy, secretly collected information from abroad even during the years of isolation. For most Japanese, however, the sudden encounter with the "outside" and "otherness" came as a great shock and revelation. The new Meiji government (1868–1912) proceeded to embrace a radical policy of speedy Westernization, and this included the introduc-tion of "philosophy," for which a brand-new word, *tetsugaku* 哲学, was coined. Nishida Kitarō (1870–1945), an early follower of the new discipline, realized the importance of Husserl's work at an early stage and pressed his students to study phenomenology. They and many other young scholars were dispatched to Europe, one after another, to sit at the feet of Husserl and Martin Heidegger (1889–1976). In fact, so many scholars visited Freiburg in the 1920s that the expression *Freiburg-mode* was coined—*mode* being a pun on the German *Mode* ("fashion") and *mō-de* in Japanese, which means "worship at a shrine."

Pilgrims to the Freiburg "shrine" included Yamauchi Tokuryū (1890–1982) in 1920 and 1922–24, Itō Kichinosuke (1885–1961) (who apparently employed Heidegger as a private

---

[1] Edmund Husserl, *Logical Investigations* vol. 1, translated by J. N. Findlay (London/New York: Routledge, 2003), 3.

tutor[2]) in 1921–22, Tanabe Hajime (1885–1962) in 1922, Takahashi Satomi (1886–1964) and Mutai Risaku (1890–1974) in 1926–27, Kuki Shūzō (1888–1941) and Watsuji Tetsurō (1889–1960) in 1927–28, and Miyake Gōichi (1895–1982) and Otaka Tomoo (1899–1956) in 1930–32.[3] After World War II, a younger generation of scholars visited not only Heidegger, but also Eugen Fink and carried their new knowledge back to Japan.

In addition to these historical events, there was a philosophical and phenomenological context to the eager reception of phenomenology in Japan. The most simplistic explanation is that Japanese thought, even before its encounter with Western philosophy, had an original "affinity" to phenomenology. This may be so, but we must be careful to consider the meaning of this "affinity." Although the general framework of Western philosophy was met with acceptance, certain points caused some discomfort: notably, the dualism of subject and object. The notion of "being-in-itself" was also viewed with suspicion. "Being" seemed too strong a concept, and this distaste extended to a subject-object relationship in which subject and object were regarded as separate entities.

The new-fangled ideas from the West made their way into the Japanese mind through linguistic expressions: neologisms, odd emphases, strange combinations, sentences that strayed from traditional grammar, and the like. Encountering these novel expressions, the Japanese sensed that this language, along with the ideas themselves, was different from "their own." But, in fact, "their own" appeared to them for the first time, *as such*, only after the encounter with strangeness. Prior to the encounter, "their own" had been too familiar to be noticeable.

In contrast to other philosophical methods, phenomenology conducted an *epoché*, or "bracketing," of the belief in "being-in-itself." Japanese scholars considered this methodology and other phenomenological concepts to have an affinity with or at least provide a possible bridge to traditional ideas like "nothingness" and "emptiness." Ideas like "nothingness" and "emptiness" were Chinese or Indian in origin (although firmly rooted in Japan for more than a millennium), but scholars also had access to old terms in the ancient Yamato language, which forms the linguistic nucleus of modern Japanese. Both the grammar and core vocabulary of modern Japanese are based in the indigenous Yamato language, although an enormous number of words and concepts were imported over the centuries from China and later from the West.

Grappling with the Western concept of being, scholars referred to the common term for "being," *ari*, which is an old Yamato word. *Ari* derives from *aru*, which originally meant "arise, spring up, grow" and also "appear." When *aru* persists, then it is *ari*, or "being." Without *aru*, *ari* is not possible; *ari* implies *aru*. The implication is now buried

---

[2] As reported in: Tokita Masakatsu, "Sakata-shusshin no tetsugakusha, Itō Kichinosuke no jiseki" [The Footsteps of Itō Kichinosuke, Philosopher from Sakata], in *Forum 21*, vol.14 (Tōhoku-kōeki-bunka University, June 30, 2008), 30. Itō visited Berlin in 1920, and Hamburg and Freiburg in 1921.

[3] Another visitor, Haga Mayumi, recounts that Miyake, Otaka, Usui Jihei, and Haga himself studied privately with Eugen Fink. See Haga Mayumi, "Kleine Begegnung," in *Edmund Husserl und die phänomenologische Bewegung*, edited by Hans Rainer Sepp (München: Verlag Karl Alber, 1988).

and sometimes forgotten, but it remains. So when philosophers pondered the meaning of "being," they referred to *ari*, where "being" always implies an "appearing."

If "being" is seen as objective and substantial, and "appearing" as subjective and transient, the two appear antithetical. But if *ari* is taken as the starting point, the very idea of a "being" without "appearing"—as a "being-in-itself"—becomes dogmatic. The same can be said of causal arguments that assert that a thing "appears" because it already "is" something "in itself." Avoiding a dogmatic belief in "being" is an old Japanese habit and a primary reason for the perceived affinity between traditional and phenomenological thinking.

However, it was the actual encounter with Western philosophy—and considerations of concepts like "being"—that made the distinctive aspects of Japanese thinking perceptible. Something of "one's own" is not so from the start; it appears as such, for the first time, by being "reflected" in the other, the foreign, or the alien. The idea of a Japanese way of thinking "in itself" was discovered only retrospectively, after encountering this reflection. In the same way, the affinity between Japanese thinking and phenomenology is also something that appeared only afterward.

To return to history: World War II radically changed Japanese society and the thinking of its people. Many Japanese philosophers initially responded to the upheaval by committing themselves to existentialism or Marxism, but, after the 1970s, many turned back to phenomenology, turned newly to deconstructionism, or focused on the problem of the other.

Representative phenomenologists after World War II include Takiura Shizuo (1927–2011), Kida Gen (b. 1928), Nitta Yoshihiro (b. 1929), Watanabe Jirō (1931–2008), and Tatematsu Hirotaka (b. 1931). In applied phenomenology, we find scholars like Ueda Shizuteru (1926–2019) (religious philosophy), Kobata Junzō (1926–84) (aesthetics), and Kimura Bin (b. 1931) (psychiatry). I would like to add Sakabe Megumi (1936–2009) to this list, although he is not commonly regarded as a phenomenologist. A younger generation includes Yamagata Yorihiro (1943–2010), Ōhashi Ryōsuke (b. 1944), Murata Jun'ichi (b. 1948), Noé Keiichi (b. 1949), and Washida Kiyokazu (b. 1949). There are many others, but this chapter will focus on just four—Sakabe, Nitta, Noé, and Washida—as being exemplary of the development of phenomenology in Japan.

SAKABE MEGUMI: BETWEENNESS, ENCOUNTER, REFLECTION

Sakabe Megumi was born in 1936 and studied at the University of Tokyo, where he spent most of his teaching career. He is noted in Japan primarily for his unique interpretation of Kant,[4] but his studies cover a wide range of intellectual history that encompasses

[4] Sakabe 1976.

both the West and Japan. His philosophical tendency is, roughly speaking, more hermeneutical than phenomenological. Nevertheless, I focus on him as a phenomenologist because I find his analyses of *awai* (betweenness) and *utsushi* (transfer, reflection) to be quintessentially phenomenological and, furthermore, to be indispensable in understanding the character of Japanese phenomenology as a whole.

Sakabe perceives the essence of Japanese thinking in the following way: "in traditional Japanese thinking, there is no Cartesian category of substance, nor are there any firmly established and unyielding dualisms of mind and body, inside and outside, visible and invisible, etcetera."[5]

The essence of dualism lies in the positing of two independent terms, but Sakabe and his contemporary Kimura Bin point out that the two terms are necessarily in a relationship. They refer to this relationship as *aida*: "betweenness" or "in-between." *Aida* is not an empty space between two substances; it is something that precedes them and makes them possible. The concept of *aida* is also found in Watsuji, although he uses the form *aidagara*, which has the same meaning but is applied primarily to human relationships. Sakabe himself prefers the word *awai*, an older word that is nearly synonymous with *aida*. Why the preference? Sakabe explains his usage in the following way:

> The everyday meaning of this word [*awai*] is "*Zwischenraum*" [interspace] in German. But it is not a static or inert betweenness. *Awai* is the nominalization of the verb *au* [encounter], just as *katarai* [conversation] is formed from *katari* [telling] and *hakarai* [discretion] from *hakari* [measuring, planning, guessing]. Thus *awai* is dynamic rather than static in meaning, its nuance being very verbal, very predicative from the very start. I see a coincidence with Nishida's key term *basho* [topos], which is also dynamic and predicative. To express *awai* in the European languages, I use *Zwischenheit-Begegnung* in German, *Betweenness-Encounter* in English, and *entreté-rencontre* in French. In this way, I try to communicate the nuance of *awai* in Japanese.[6]

Awai is both a place and a movement. We should pay special attention to the dynamism of this term. In another text, Sakabe refers to the European tradition of translating the Greek word *logos* into Latin as *verbum*, which means not only "word" but "verb." Sakabe regards the verbal aspect of language to be more important than its nominal. The verbal aspect of "betweenness" (*awai*) is "to encounter" (*au*), and this means that someone or something encounters the "other" in the betweenness. This is why Sakabe translates *awai* as "betweenness-encounter."

What occurs when someone or something encounters the other? Sakabe writes:

> In the world of modern people, who are imprisoned and confined to a self-identical I and [its] world, and who are, one might say, species-schizophrenic [= separated

---

[5] Sakabe 1989, 49.
[6] "Sei to shi no awai" [Between Life and Death]. In Sakabe 2006–7, 3: 308.

from intersubjectivity] with no living contact to reality; who are, in another context, split into subject and object and imprisoned in the two poles—for them there can be no true metamorphosis or *metaphora* (*métaphore*), which is a "carrying" (*phoreo*) "beyond" (*meta-*) into another realm.[7]

Meta-phoreo (carrying someone or something beyond) is the verbal significance of the word *awai*. It is what happens when someone or something encounters the other. *Awai* can be considered a phenomenological concept in that it describes the way something "appears." The other keywords of Sakabe's philosophy—*utsushi* (reflecting), *shirushi* (signifying), *katari* (telling), *furumai* (behaving)—all have to do with the way things "appear" and, as such, can be characterized as "phenomenological" notions.

The most fundamental of these is *utsushi*. The word *utsushi* can be variously translated as "transition," "transfer," "change," or "reflection." Sakabe illustrates its meaning by citing an old poem:

> When autumn comes
>   (*Aki kureba* 秋くれば)
> Even the pine wind from Tokiwa Mountain
>   (*Tokiwa no yama no matsukaze mo* 常磐の山の松風も)
> Seems to change [with the season]
>   (*Utsuru bakarini* うつるばかりに)
> And penetrates my body
>   (*Minizo shimikeru* みにぞしみける)[8]

The key word is *utsuru* in the third line: "Seems to change [with the season]." It is the verb form of *utsushi* and is still used in modern Japanese with various meanings that include "to change," which is what I have used for my provisional translation. The common interpretation of the poem straightforwardly accepts *matsukaze* (wind in the pines) as the subject of *utsuru* and reads: "the pine wind itself seems to change." That is, "with the transition (also *utsuru*) of time (i.e., with the coming of autumn), the wind itself changes." But Sakabe has a more complex idea of *utsuru/utsushi* and reads: "the coldness of the wind (which blows outside me) appears by transferring itself into my body (and into my mind). At the same time, the sadness of my mind (inside me) transfers itself to the wind (outside me), appearing as the coldness of that wind." There is an encounter; there is a mutual transference; there is a mutual reflection of the inside and outside. The sadness in my mind "appears" as such by being "transferred" to the wind outside me (therefore, by being transferred to the "other"). The former is "reflected" in the latter and vice versa. *Awai* is the betweenness where reflection (*utsushi*) occurs, when something encounters another.

---

[7] "Omote no kyōi" [Dimension of *Omote*]. In Sakabe 2006–7, 3: 4.

[8] A well-known poem by the tenth-century poetess Izumi-shikibu, included in the thirteenth-century anthology *Shinkokin-wakashu*. Cited in "Utsushimi" [The Possessed] in Sakabe 2006–7, 4: 65.

Something appears in the betweenness, but it has no substance. There is only appearance, which is a kind of movement. Sakabe writes: "There is nothing but 'projection,' 'transfer,' 'change,' and an endlessly metamorphosing 'reflection.'" [9]

Applying this to temporality, we can say that the present does not exist in itself, but appears only as a reflection in the "non-present"—the past or future—and that the non-present appears only by being reflected in the present. Time is the *awai*—betweenness-encounter—where this occurs.

This also holds for spatiality. According to the mythical geography of Japan, *Takama-no-hara* (the Heavenly Land, where the gods reside) appears by *utsushi* in *Ashihara-no-nakatsukuni* (the Middle Land, where humans reside). The emperor who lives in the Middle Land is an *utsushi* (reflection) of (the intention of) the gods in the Heavenly Land. Thus, he is called *utsushi-omi*, where *omi* means "subject" or "vassal. " There is no dualism here because no line is drawn between reality and imagination.

Sakabe extends the idea of *utsushi* to human relationships, with the concept of *furumai*. *Furu-mai* (behavior) is the Japanese word for a human act, and Sakabe focuses on *mai*, which means "dance." *Mai* is a form of *mimesis*, where people imitate one another and where behavior functions as a kind of *utsushi*. *Mai* is a precondition for intersubjectivity. But *mai* is inseparable from *senuhima* (time of not dancing; pause), such that the two are in a relationship of figure and ground, one supporting the other. Similarly, *katari* (telling) is founded on *uta* (singing), which makes possible the linguistic mimesis that becomes linguistic communication. This, in its turn, is inseparable from *shijima* (time of not telling; pause), such that the two are also related as figure and ground.

Mai is inseparable from *senuhima*, and *uta* from *shijima*. They are interdependent in such a way that, when one appears, the other disappears. Nevertheless, that which appears "reflects" the other that has disappeared. What makes this complementary and dynamic relationship possible? Sakabe writes:

> What is it that makes all beings "reflect" one other, but does not in itself appear anywhere? What is this, at the foundation of all being? What is called *Dao* (by Laozi and Zhuangzi) or "emptiness" or "nothingness" [in Buddhist thought] was implicitly understood and experienced in Japanese culture, particularly in the traditions of common folk, as something that can be expressed only through mediation or in metaphor.[10]

Sakabe's notion of *awai* indicates a dimension that cannot be directly expressed. Nevertheless, his analyses lead us not only to a dimension fundamental to the Japanese psyche, but to a dimension of great importance to phenomenology.

---

[9] Sakabe 1989, 55.
[10] Ibid., 56.

Nitta Yoshihiro: Transcendental Mediality as Verticality

Nitta Yoshihiro is one of Japan's most eminent phenomenologists and is also well known to the German-speaking world. He was born in 1929, studied at Tohoku University in Sendai, and taught for many years at Toyo University in Tokyo. Two early books, *Genshōgaku towa nanika* [What Is Phenomenology?] in 1968 and *Genshōgaku* [Phenomenology] in 1978, were the fruit of painstaking studies of Husserl and Heidegger and greatly influenced the direction of Japanese phenomenological research. He also re-examined Nishida from the phenomenological viewpoint in books such as *Gendai no toi toshiteno Nishida-tetsugaku* [Nishida's Philosophy as a Contemporary Inquiry] and helped to revitalize the study of Nishida in Japan. *Sekai to seimei* (World and Life), published in 2001, is a presentation of Nitta's distinctive form of phenomenology.

Nitta's phenomenology is characterized by the single-minded pursuit of the athematic—that is, that which does not explicitly appear to consciousness. His approach to the problem is defined by the distinction he makes between the "horizontal" and the "vertical."

What Nitta calls the "horizontal" is analogous to the "ground" in relation to a "figure." When an object appears as a figure against a ground, the appearance of the figure is correlative to the disappearance of the ground. Without the disappearance of the latter, nothing appears; everything appearing at once would be equivalent to nothing appearing at all. Temporally, something that appeared before can later become the ground against which something else appears. This also holds for meaning—for the meaning of objects as well as for meanings in history. What appears meaningful in the historical present is always complemented by something that has disappeared or is hidden. This idea was formulated by Husserl as "horizon" and further elaborated by hermeneutics. Nitta read Gadamer with great care[11] and studied narrative theory in the same context as he worked out his own theory.

Nitta is attentive to the horizontal but ultimately believes the athematic aspect of the vertical to be more important. What he calls "verticality" is, roughly speaking, the "function" or "act" of appearing. That is, the function of appearing—what phenomenology calls the "noetic"—is more important in Nitta's view than that which appears by means of the function.

Nitta begins by considering Husserl's analyses of temporality, corporality, and intersubjectivity. With regard to temporality, he ponders the anonymity of the world-constituting I of the "living present," which Gerd Brand and especially Klaus Held clarified through an analysis of Husserl's late theory of time. The living present is not

---

[11] Nitta 1997.

illuminated by the gaze of the reflecting I and is therefore anonymous. Nevertheless, it is "known." This is a riddle at the deepest dimensions of phenomenology. Husserl defines the living present as both "streaming and standing still." "Streaming" and "standing" are its two moments. Both Brand and Held understand the moment of "streaming" to be a "disappearing" of the present or a "flowing away" into a no-longer-visible past. Correspondingly, "standing" is comprehended to be the "appearance" of the present. Nitta, on the other hand, proposes that it is the constitutive function that "stands" and that this function is anonymous and athematic. It is "streaming," in fact, that is the moment of "appearing." In other words, it is in "streaming away" from the present that the constituting function first appears and is thematized. When it appears, it has already streamed away, which means that the constitutive function in the present is always hidden. The constituting function of the I in the living present does not appear as such, thematically, although the "appearing" and "disappearing" are inseparable from each other.

Corporality (or kinesthetic consciousness) has two aspects: it is noematic in the broad sense, but also part of the noetic function. The latter does not appear thematically while it is functioning. For example, eyes cannot appear to themselves while they make the world appear. The other is also a function that, together with the I, makes the world appear. But when the I appears thematically, the other disappears, and when the other is thematized, the I is a-thematic and hidden from itself. Both the I and the other are functions that make something appear only when they themselves do not appear. Nevertheless, Nitta looks for a way to see them even as they function.

How can this be done? Husserl's method is based on "reflection." At least after *Ideas I*, this reflection is said to occur when the I—usually forgetful of itself and attentive only to the world—turns around and thematizes itself. Phenomenological reflection is not an external thematization, like that undertaken by the natural sciences. It is the self-forgetful I appearing to itself. Nevertheless, in thematization, the I splits itself into the thematizing-I and the thematized-I, and this engenders a kind of dualism. The I, in the moment of reflection, is divided in itself.

Nitta regards this as a severe limitation of Husserl's method of phenomenological reflection, and one that is of a different dimension from the difficulty of thematizing horizontal phenomena because horizontal phenomena fundamentally belong to the order of the noematic and are not part of the constituting function itself. He declares that, in order to overcome this limitation, that is, "in order for philosophical thinking to go back to its own roots, the movement of thinking must break away from its horizontal character and change direction, proceeding vertically into the movement itself."[12] Indeed, a change of this type actually occurred in the phenomenological movement, particularly in the thinking of Heidegger. How did this occur? Because thinking does not control itself as entirely as the Western ideal of autonomy would have it, phenomenology was prompted, from the bottom up, by the "things themselves" to change direction.

---

[12] Nitta 1998, 17.

Thinking is not only "subjective" in the sense of being autonomous; it is also "subject" to things—although this does not make it an "object." The German word *Medium* sometimes refers to *mediale Diathese* or "middle voice" in the grammatical sense. Thinking is neither merely active nor passive, but operates in the middle voice, "responding" to the call of the things themselves.[13] Although Nitta does not say so explicitly, this sense of *Medium* appears to be an important aspect of what he calls "mediality."

To go beyond the reflection in which the I splits into subject and object, Nitta descends into the depths of the constituting function. In those depths, it is no longer an I-as-subject reflecting on an I-as-object, divided from itself. Nitta speaks of the nondualistic constituting function by which something is "known" nonthematically—in which a thing appears and conceals itself at the same time. This function is also called "life" or "living," in the verbal or dynamic sense. It makes the world appear in a nonreflective, nonthematic way, but nevertheless knows itself prereflectively and athematically as it functions.

Nitta calls this function "transcendental mediality," and he looks for evidence of this idea in the intellectual history in Europe. The notion of mediality can be found in early modernity, he says. For example, Nicolaus Cusanus analyzed the function of the prism, which makes visible the different colors of light. The prism is a type of "medium" or "mediator" that mediates worldly appearance (in this case, visible color). Meanwhile, the prism itself is transparent and invisible and therefore does not appear. It is athematic, and, as such, Nitta regards it as a model for transcendental mediality. He also discovers an analysis of the way mediality functions in Fichte's late theory of the image (*Bild*). Closer to home, he believes that Nishida's philosophy provides a firm ground for a philosophy of mediality.

Nitta underscores the importance of Nishida's theory of knowledge and particularly his analysis of how knowledge is formed. The starting point for Nitta is the basic structure of Nishida's methodology, in which "the self is reflected in the self," which we have seen to be the structure of *utsushi*. Rephrased in the Husserlian terms of noesis and noema (which Nishida appropriated and reinterpreted), the noesis "reflects" itself in the noema; the noema is an "expression" of the noesis. The same structure can also be applied to *poiesis* (making): in *poiesis*, the noesis reflects itself in the world, and the world is "made" by the noesis. The world has (visible) forms—like the colors in Cusanus's example—that belong to the noema. Is it "our self" that "makes" this world? But the "self" was not there before the world was "made." And the world is not a mere object. Self and world stand in a reciprocal and medial relation. In making each other, they

---

[13] The act that is neither active nor passive shares common ground with the notion of "nature" in the Japanese/East-Asian tradition. When something occurs neither actively nor passively but "of itself," the occurrence is said to be "natural." There seems to be an affinity between the middle voice (*Medium*) and the Japanese/East-Asian notion of "nature." See Chapter 33 in this volume. On the philosophical implications of the middle voice in the Japanese language, see Rolf Elberfeld, "The Middle Voice of Emptiness: Nishida and Nishitani," in *Japanese and Continental Philosophy: Conversations with the Kyoto School*, edited by Bret W. Davis, Brian Schroeder, and Jason M. Wirth (Bloomington: Indiana University Press, 2011), and also Chapter 32 in this volume.

reflect each other, and this reflection is a kind of knowing or a "making conscious." It is in this context that Nitta quotes Nishida: "When the world becomes conscious, our self becomes conscious."[14]

Neither the self nor the world predominates in this relationship of mutual reflection. The relationship is neither simply egologically teleological nor worldly causal. Lying "between" the two in their mutual relationship is "life," which is a word that Nishida also likes to use. But "life" is not something that pre-exists with specific determinations. Nitta concurs with Nishida that it is in the relationship that "formless life en-forms itself."[15] This is also a kind of *utsushi*, but it does not mean that formless life transfers itself entirely into its forms. Identifying "formless life" with noesis and "en-formed life" with noema, Nitta writes: "it so happens that the noesis reflects itself in the noema, and conceals itself precisely because it does so. The noema is not a function of the noesis itself, but only its image. In fact, it is the 'not' of the above statement, that is, its negativity, that operates as the moment of a movement toward the formation of knowledge or knowing."[16]

The noesis, which is verbal, reflects itself in the noema, which is nominal, but it can never completely reflect its verbal character, which remains hidden. Nitta therefore does not recognize the possibility of a perfect coincidence between the noetic and the noematic, or between the self and the world. (A coincidence of this kind might be possible in the religious, but not in the philosophical dimension.) In fact, the two terms are characterized by their negativity, or their *difference*—that is, by their *not* being the other. More radically, life itself—or mediality—is a movement of differentiation. As such, it is the basis of knowledge or knowing in general, and of philosophy. Nitta's insight is that philosophy operates not in identification, but in the differentiation of life.

The inner workings of such a philosophy cannot be grasped by mere observation, so Nitta tries to enter the movement itself and, so to speak, live through it. This is his turn toward verticality. Heidegger attempted a similar turn, but Nitta sees another possibility in the notion of *narikiru* (なり切る): "to invest oneself wholeheartedly." In this case, it means to throw oneself entirely into the movement of life. A complete identification with life being impossible, Nitta introduces the idea of a "spiral" descent into its murky depths.

Nishida once wrote: "To transcend in the direction of the noesis is to transcend into the depths of the acting self."[17] Nitta rewords this phenomenologically: "To transcend into the noetic act [= function] through the mediation of the noematically circumscribed aspects that reflect the act, is to make a spiral descent into the depths of the act itself."[18]

---

[14] Nitta 1998, 74.

[15] Ibid., 39.

[16] Ibid., 196.

[17] Nishida Kitarō, "*Eichiteki sekai*" [The Intelligible World], in *Nishida Kitarō zenshū* [Collected Works of Nishida Kitarō] (Tokyo: Iwanami Shoten, 2003), vol. 4, 121.

[18] Ibid., 25.

This vertical descent into the act is the essence of Nitta's phenomenological method, in that it is a "reduction" to the original or the originating function of the world. Moved by the movement of life, Nitta descends to the origin itself (life), whereby the insight gained in the descent ascends as a "self-demonstration" (*jishō* 自証) or "self-expression" of that life. We see here a double movement of in-sight and ex-pression, of descending and ascending, which is a movement of differentiation. It is a movement neither of subjectivity nor of objectivity, but of mediality.

How should we understand Nitta, since neither his thinking nor his words can be separated from this movement of differentiation? Do his words "reflect" something? Yes and no. What they reflect is a functioning: something that can be expressed only negatively or differentially. Whereas language normally reflects something that appears, we might say that Nitta's words reflect "nonappearance," or that language and life stand in a relationship of negative differentiation in his philosophy. This is precisely why they resonate so strongly with those who make a serious attempt to descend into the depths of life.

Noé Keiichi: Narrative and Experience

Noé was born in 1949 and belongs to a younger generation than Sakabe and Nitta. This is the generation of baby boomers, who are also called the "militant generation" because they matured in an era of social activism. Other new leaders of the phenomenological movement in Japan, such as Murata Jun'ichi and Washida Kiyokazu, also belong to this generation. They differ from the earlier generation of phenomenologists in their strong response to social issues and are, in this sense, "socio-philosophical." Murata began from a phenomenological theory of perception and advanced toward a theory of ecology and technology. Washida formulated a theory of fashion and launched a "clinical philosophy" that shares common ground with the theories of psychiatrist-philosopher Kimura Bin. Noé began with phenomenology and the philosophy of science, studied with Sakabe and Nitta, and went on to develop a philosophy of narrative.

Noé was born and raised in Sendai, a major city in the northeastern region of Japan that was devastated by the great earthquake and tsunami of 2011. This latter experience resulted in a further deepening of his philosophy, which was already wide in scope. He began his academic career by studying physics at Tohoku University in Sendai, but soon turned to philosophy. He was initially drawn to the philosophy of science and was attracted to Husserlian phenomenology as a possible grounding for that science. He also studied with Hiromatsu Wataru (1933–1994), who was most widely known for his Marxist theories but who was also interested in phenomenalism and the early phenomenology of Ernst Mach. Noé went on to study at Princeton University in the United States and became familiar with the philosophical tendencies of the English-speaking world.

In the philosophy of science, Noé paid particular attention to the paradigm theory of Thomas Kuhn. This theory, along with Norwood Russell Hanson's theory of theory-ladenness, has a clear affinity with hermeneutics, and Noé later wove these theories into a distinctive theory of narrative presented in his 1993 book *Kagaku no kaishakugaku* [The Hermeneutics of Science].[19]

Generally speaking, Noé works not only "between" European and American philosophy, but also between "rationality" (as represented by natural science, or, more broadly, by *logos* and logical language) and the "lived experience" that is the basis of rationality but is not always rational. His philosophy of narrative lies in that betweenness, yet also encompasses traditional Japanese thought, especially as articulated by Nishida and the folklorist Yanagita Kunio (1875–1962).

In *Monogatari no tetsugaku* [Philosophy of Narrative],[20] Noé refers to American philosopher Arthur Danto (1924–2013). The ideal chronicler, according to Danto, describes history from the viewpoint of God—from outside of history. But no one actually has such a viewpoint; no one can escape being laden with a personal viewpoint or being bound to a historical perspective. History can be described only from the inside of history. Noé compares this to Mach's famous sketch, where we see the subject's legs, arms, and other parts but nothing of his face except the nose, the fringe of his eye, and mustache. It is what Mach himself sees. Noé says that this is what a frontal view of history looks like, whereas the ideal chronicler would have a side view. This is an idea that Noé appropriates from Mach and develops through his study of Husserl. One might call it a "historically expanded" version of the phenomenological reduction. So-called historical facts cannot be confirmed from the side view (i.e., from the viewpoint of an omniscient God), but are constituted (through each appearance) from a frontal viewpoint. A historical fact does not exist "in itself." But what then is the frontal viewpoint? The eyes of Mach's sketch are not drawn in. The viewpoint itself is not described but "shown," says Noé in a reference to Wittgenstein.

Noé puts forward six propositions in his philosophy of history:

1. Events or facts of the past do not exist objectively, but are reconstituted hermeneutically through "recollection." [Nonrealism of history]
2. Historical events (*Geschichte*) and historiography (*Historie*) are inseparable; the former do not exist outside the context of the latter. [Phenomenalism of history]
3. Historiography is none other than a linguistic creation (*poiesis*) that "communalizes" and "structuralizes" memories. [History as narrative]
4. The past is incomplete, and no historiography is exempt from correction. [Holism of history]
5. Time does not flow. It accumulates from moment to moment. [Suntory thesis]
6. What we cannot narrate, we must pass over in silence. [Pragmatics of history][21]

---

[19] Noe 1993c. In addition to this book, *Gengo-kōi no genshōgaku* [Phenomenology of Speech Acts] (1993a) and *Mukonkyo kara no shuppatsu* [Starting from Groundlessness] (1993b) were also published in the same year. These almost simultaneous publications greatly influenced philosophical research at that time.

[20] Noé 1992.

[21] Noé 1996, 147–148.

These propositions are derived from the frontal view of history and are quite different from any that might be derived from the viewpoint of the ideal chronicler. (The fifth is called the "Suntory thesis" because it is a quote from a popular commercial for Suntory Whisky.)

Noé's book provoked a lively response, including the following objection to Proposition 1: but what happens to what is not recollected? This question relates to what Hannah Arendt called "holes of oblivion." Noé responded that our memories are like islands on the surface of the ocean. What surrounds them are not holes, but an ocean. Historiography can save only a small portion of historical facts, most of which are forgotten. We weave our stories with what we have. His position is that of a "low narrativist," in contrast to "high narrativists," who assert that all experience can be worked into the story.

Proposition 3 has to do with the character of the narrator. Noé avoids the idea of a strong and absolute "I" who constitutes the story in a unifying manner. Instead, he refers to the Japanese word *monogatari* (narrative, story), which is a combination of *mono* (thing) and *katari* (which becomes *gatari* for phonetic reasons). *Katari* (telling) is related to *kata* (figure, form, frame) and means: "to give form to something obscure."[22] History as a narrative is not a sum of facts, but a "form-giving," he says. Who gives the form? Noé emphasizes the anonymity of *mono*, which means an unidentified something. Such is the author of the telling: not a strong and active subjectivity, but an anonymous intersubjectivity. This is especially the case with folktales, where it is impossible to identify a specific author. Even an identified author is affected by his or her (anonymous) intersubjectivity and by his or her own history, without which the story cannot be told.

Proposition 6 is, of course, a parody of Wittgenstein. One possible criticism of this statement is that lived experience essentially contains something that cannot be narrated. A second is that the act of narration, in making something appear explicitly, necessarily conceals something else. When Noé personally encountered the earthquake and tsunami of 2011, he said it was an experience that left him "wordless." Yet narratives often begin anew after such wordlessness, instead of passing over them in silence. How does that happen, and what role do they play? Noé speaks of the necessity of inquiring more deeply into these problems, especially into the relationship between experience and language. As his theory directs itself toward the roots of narration itself, there is a possibility that it will grow closer to Nitta's philosophy of mediality.

[22] Sakabe also discusses this point. See *"Katari to shijima"* [Telling and Silence] in Sakabe 2006–7, 4: 181–182.

Washida Kiyokazu: Reversibility and Transgression

Washida Kiyokazu is one of Japan's most well-known and popular philosophers. Openness to the layman is a trait shared by many philosophers of his generation, but even among them Washida stands out for his readability and popular appeal.

He has written many "theoretical" tomes[23] but tends to be critical of such writing and is more inclined toward essays.[24] Moreover, he is strongly committed to various practical undertakings. Not least among these is the founding of a program in clinical philosophy at Osaka University.

Washida was born in Kyoto and studied at Kyoto University. He taught for most of his career at Osaka University and was president of that institution from 2007 to 2011. His initial philosophical interest lay in Husserl and William James, but his focus soon shifted to Merleau-Ponty. He was interested in the various interpretations of phenomenology, but Merleau-Ponty ultimately became the base for his own philosophy, which tends toward "ambiguity" in correlation with its openness. The ambiguity is particularly marked in his position toward Husserl, which is that of "with Husserl, against Husserl."

Husserl was in search of the ultimate basis for all knowledge, including mathematics, geometry, and the sciences in general. Washida asserts: "The configuration of knowledge does not have an ultimate basis from which all knowledge derives, and is therefore not a closed or self-contained system."[25] This critical attitude toward closure and self-containment is one of the chief aspects of Washida's thinking.[26]

Whereas Husserl regards the "I" to be the starting point of philosophy, Merleau-Ponty regards corporality as the foundation of the I and places intercorporality at the starting point of philosophy. Washida embraces this idea and says the "half-darkness of the corporal or communal anonymous medium"[27] is where philosophy should begin. Precisely because the medium is not clear to the I, the I is open to the other. (Let us note here that "medium" relates not only to Merleau-Ponty, but also signals a common ground with Nitta.) The I is not a Cartesian consciousness, but corporality and, what is more, an intercorporal intersubjectivity. "The 'I' is always in a relationship with the other,"[28] he says. If "experience" is where the relationship takes place, we might say that philosophy begins by "thinking about experience." But philosophy, too, is a type of "experience"— an experience "squared" or "to the second power." If the latter can also be considered

---

[23] Particularly in Washida 1989, 1995, and 2007.
[24] Washida 1999 is a good example.
[25] Washida 1989, 178.
[26] He is also critical of "pureness," as expressed in concepts like "pure phenomenology."
[27] Ibid., 137.
[28] Ibid., i.

as part of the "I," it would seem that everything and anything can be gathered up into the "I." But Washida says: "Philosophy is not an event that occurs within the I; rather (to borrow from Kierkegaard), the I is embedded in a relationship called experience, and philosophy is a relationship with relationship itself." In this "squared" (and therefore self-relating) relationship, "experience generates other relationships within itself, so that it diverges from itself."[29] Starting from relationships and transforming experience from within experience: these are the basic precepts of Washida's phenomenological philosophy.

After arriving at these principles, Washida applied his study of corporality to a theory of fashion. Fashion is normally regarded as an external matter—as something occurring outside the mind and therefore unimportant and inessential to philosophy. Washida, however, rejects the dualism of the internal and external[30]—a dualism parallel to that of subject and object—and treats fashion as an external expression that directly involves the interior (although the words "interior" and "exterior" are actually inadequate). He sees the exterior as an essential expression of inner being, in a Sakabe-like rejection of the interior-exterior divide.

Washida's "I" is not a substance, but a relationship to the other. Whatever it is, it is "open" to the other and the mimesis of the other is an indispensable moment in its constitution. Correspondingly, the I is defined not so much by its self-ness, as by its *hoka-naranu*-ness—*hoka-naranu* being a Japanese idiom meaning "none other [than]." "None other [than]" usually means "identical," as in "I am none other than I." But Washida points out that this expression already presupposes the other. The "I" is "what is not the other." That is, the "identity" of an "I" who is open to the other can be defined only in its "difference" from the other. "Difference" and "negativity" are indispensible in defining the I of an open relationship.

Yet the relationship itself is not negative, but positive. It places the I and the other in a give-and-take alliance that Washida depicts in his observations on "care." Normally, "care" refers to a self-sufficient person providing unilateral support to someone who is not. Washida denies that this is the case: "In care, a reversal often occurs such that the person who provides care is given care by the person who is cared for. When a caregiver devotes too much of him/herself, it sometimes happens that the devotion reverses itself into a grudge: 'I'm doing so much for this person.' "[31] That is, in order for the act of caring to be successful, it is necessary for the caregiver to receive something in return: love, gratitude, a mere response.

---

[29] Ibid., ii.

[30] Sakabe criticized this dualism through an analysis of the Japanese notion of *omote* (which means "persona" and also "surface"). *Omote* has the same etymological root as *omou* (to think), which is normally considered to be an internal act. The relationship between *omote* and *omou* is clearly not a dualistic relationship of external and internal. *Omote* and *omou* are directly linked. Even if *omote* is regarded as an "appearance," there is no "substance" hiding behind it. Washida develops a similar argument, but based mainly on Merleau-Ponty.

[31] From a newspaper column by Washida in *The Asahi Shimbun*, December 10, 2010.

Giving and taking are normally considered to be opposites, but Washida asserts that a unilateral giving or taking can be tragic, whereas a reversible or reciprocal relationship is indispensable to true care. Washida appropriates this idea from Merleau-Ponty's concept of *réversibilité*, which, in a Japanese context, could be regarded as an *utsushi* occurring in a betweenness-encounter. The betweenness must not be closed, and Washida is ready to open it to any new encounters.

Washida is zealous in collaborating with colleagues in other fields. A particularly important achievement is his founding of a program in clinical philosophy at Osaka University. The goal is to transgress the borders of the university and to step out into the real world (i.e., clinics) where the philosopher can "hear" the words of those who need to be listened to. Whereas traditional philosophy "speaks," Washida emphasizes the importance of "listening." Heidegger also emphasized listening, but he was mostly listening to Being. Washida, on the other hand, tries to listen to the other person. To listen to the other is to accept that person. Acceptance can sometimes be realized by simply repeating the words of the other in a kind of mimesis, which is the first step toward a reversible relationship. Washida's clinical philosophy is an attempt to transgress the border between theory and practice and, in doing so, to enable a transformation—to quote Merleau-Ponty, a "coherent transformation"—of the mundane, everyday-life world.

Conclusion

Phenomenology came to Japan almost immediately after its formulation in the early twentieth century and continues to develop and contribute to Japanese philosophy. This chapter has focused on four philosophers of the postwar period whom I believe to represent certain unique tendencies of Japanese phenomenology. There are many others no less important: the Marxist theory of Hiromatsu Wataru, Takiura Shizuo's attempted dialogue with analytic philosophy, the aesthetic phenomenology of Kobata Junzo, and Murata Jun'ichi's theory of perception and technology, to name just a few. Younger phenomenologists are working in even more various directions: phenomenology and ecology, robotics, caring, religion, and interculturality are some examples. Many investigations are directed at global problems shared by scholars all over the world; others are unique to the region (Japan or, more broadly, East Asia) and are increasingly studied with reference to history and to classical systems of thought. Phenomenology is a tree with deep roots, some of which have burrowed far and wide in the field of Japanese scholarship. By retaining the original spirit of moving toward "the things themselves" by way of "breaking through" theoretical presuppositions, it is a tree from which healthy new branches are sure to grow in Japan as elsewhere.

BIBLIOGRAPHY AND SUGGESTED READINGS

Japanese Sources

Nitta Yoshihiro. (1968) *Genshōgaku towa nanika* [What is Phenomenology?]. Tokyo: Kinokuniya Shinsho. (Reprinted by Tokyo: Kōdansha, 1992; Tokyo: Kinokuniya Shoten, 1996.)

Nitta Yoshihiro. (1978) *Genshōgaku* [Phenomenology]. Tokyo: Iwanami-shoten. (Reprinted by Tokyo: Kōdansha, 2013.)

Nitta Yoshihiro. (1997) *Genshōgaku to kaishakugaku* [Phenomenology and Hermeneutics] Tokyo: Hakuseisha. (Reprinted by Tokyo: Chikuma-shobō, 2006.)

Nitta Yoshihiro. (1998) *Gendai no toi toshiteno Nishida-tetsugaku* [Nishida's Philosophy as a Contemporary Inquiry]. Tokyo: Iwanami-shoten.

Nitta Yoshihiro. (2001) *Sekai to seimei,* [World and Life]. Tokyo: Seidosha.

Noé Keiichi. (1993*a*) *Gengo-kōi no genshōgaku* [Phenomenology of Speech Acts]. Tokyo: Keisō-shobō.

Noé Keiichi. (1993*b*) *Mukonkyo kara no shuppatsu* [Starting from Groundlessness]. Tokyo: Keisō-shobō.

Noé Keiichi. (1993*c*) *Kagaku no kaishakugaku* [Hermeneutics of Science]. Tokyo: Shinyōsha. (Reprinted by Tokyo: Chikuma-shobō, 2007.)

Noé Keiichi. (1996) *Monogatari no tetsugaku* [Philosophy of Narrative]. Tokyo: Iwanami-shoten.

Sakabe Megumi. (1976) *Risei no fuan* [Uneasiness of Reason]. Tokyo: Keiso-shobō.

Sakabe Megumi. (1989) *Kagami no naka no nihongo* [Japanese Language in the Mirror]. Tokyo: Chikuma-shobō.

Sakabe Megumi. (2006–2007) *Sakabe Megumi shū* [Collected Works of Sakabe Megumi]. Vols. 1–5. Tokyo: Iwanami-shoten.

Washida Kiyokazu. (1989) *Bunsan suru risei* [Dispersing Rationality]. Tokyo: Keisō-shobō. (Republished under a new title: *Genshōgaku no shisen* [The Gaze of Phenomenology]. Tokyo: Kōdansha, 1997.)

Washida Kiyokazu. (1995) *Ninshō to kōi* [Person and Behavior]. Kyoto: Shōwadō.

Washida Kiyokazu. (1999) *Kikukoto no chikara* [The Power of Listening]. Tokyo: TBS-Britannica.

Washida Kiyokazu. (2007) *Shikō no eshikkusu* [Ethics of Thinking]. Kyoto: Nakanishiya.

Suggested Readings in Western Languages

Kojima Hiroshi. (2000) *Monad and Thou: Phenomenological Ontology of Human Being.* Athens, GA: Ohio University Press.

Nitta Yoshihiro, ed. (1984) *Japanische Beiträge zur Phänomenologie.* Freiburg/München: Verlag Karl Alber.

Nitta Yoshihiro. (1984) "Phänomenologie als Theorie der Perspektive und die Aporie des Gesichtspunkts." In *Japanische Beiträge zur Phänomenologie,* edited by Nitta Yoshihiro. Freiburg/München: Verlag Karl Alber.

Nitta Yoshihiro. (2006) "Welt und Leben, Das Selbstgewahren des Lebens bei Nishida Kitarō." In *Leben als Phänomen,* edited by Hans Rainer Sepp and Ichiro Yamaguchi. Würzburg: Königshausen & Neumann.

Nitta Yoshihiro. (2011) "Zur Phänomenologie der transzendentale Medialität." In *Aufnahme und Antwort, Phänomenologie in Japan I*, edited by Nitta Yoshihiro and Tani Toru. Würzburg: Königshausen & Neumann.

Nitta Yoshihiro and Tatematsu Hirotaka, eds. (1979) *Japanese Phenomenology*, in *Analecta Husserliana 8*. Boston: Reidel.

Noé Keiichi. (1993) "Husserl and the Foundations of Geometry." In *Japanese and Western Phenomenology*, edited by P. Blosser et al. Dordrecht: Kluwer Academic Publishers.

Noé Keiichi. (1994) "The Non-Cartesian Subject in Japanese Philosophy." In *Discours Social/ Social Discourse*, Vol. 6, No. 1–2. Montreal: Chaire McGill/Université McGill.

Noé Keiichi. (2009) "Nishida Kitaro as Philosopher of Science." In *Facing the 21st Century*, edited by Lam Wing-keung and Cheung Ching-yuen. Nagoya: Nanzan Institute for Religion and Culture.

Ōhashi Ryōsuke. (1999) *Japan im interkulturellen Dialog*. Munich: Iudicium.

Ogawa Tadashi, Michael Lazarin, and Guido Rappe, eds. (1998) *Interkulturelle Philosophie und Phänomenology in Japan*. Munich: Iudicium.

Sakabe Megumi. (1999a) "Mask and Shadow in Japanese Culture: Implicit Ontology in Japanese Thought." In *Modern Japanese Aesthetics: A Reader*, translated and edited by Michael F. Marra. Honolulu: University of Hawai'i Press.

Sakabe Megumi. (1999b) "*Modoki*: The Mimetic Tradition in Japan." In *Modern Japanese Aesthetics: A Reader*, translated and edited by Michael F. Marra. Honolulu: University of Hawai'i Press.

Ueda Shizuteru. (2011) *Wer und was bin ich: Zur Phänomenologie des Selbst im Zen-Buddhismus*. Freiburg: Verlag Karl Alber.

Steinbock, Anthony, ed. (1998) *Phenomenology in Japan*. Dordrecht: Klewer.

Washida Kiyokazu. (1984) "Handlung, Leib und Institution—Perspektiven einer phänomenologischen Handlungstheorie." In *Japanische Beiträge zur Phänomenologie*, edited by Nitta Yoshihiro. Freiburg/München: Verlag Karl Alber.

Washida Kiyokazu. (2002) "The Past, the Feminine, the Vain." In *Talking to Myself* by Yohji Yamamoto. Green Bay, WI: Seidl.

Washida Kiyokazu. (2009) "The Art of Passivity: Introducing My Books *The Power of 'Listening'* and *Waiting*," translated by Judy Wakabayashi. In *Special Issue of the Annals of Ethics 2009* of the Japanese Society for Ethics.

CHAPTER 31

THE KOMABA QUARTET

A Landscape of Japanese Philosophy in the 1970s

KOBAYASHI YASUO

SINCE philosophy inquires into a "truth" that somehow transcends the present, its activity has an atemporal aspect. The true worth of a philosopher is not necessarily understood in his or her own time, the history of philosophy showing that often the profundity of a philosopher's thoughts is discovered only much later. That is why it can be so difficult to evaluate a contemporary philosopher with any high degree of objectivity, a difficulty compounded when one has to select for a foreign audience which ongoing philosophical projects are likely to be continued in the future. We must live our present era through our subjectivity and cannot, in essence, draw an accurate map of the culture of the times in which we live. As a result, I will not attempt to map the whole of "recent currents" in Japanese philosophy.[1] Rather, accepting the risk of being somewhat arbitrary, I will choose one *season* or period and one *place*, displaying the diversity of philosophical thoughts that bloomed then and there and the horizon they shared.

A PHILOSOPHICAL SEASON, A PHILOSOPHICAL PLACE

The season I choose is the 1970s. Japan had undergone reconstruction at a remarkable pace since its defeat in WWII 1945, enduring fierce internal political conflicts. Careful observers of the history of postwar Japanese culture will note that, around 1970, Japanese culture underwent a discontinuous break or turn. At least on the surface, the so-called postwar period ended. Yet, there remained a number of contradictions. In that euphoric

---

[1] I was originally asked by the editor of this volume to write a chapter on recent currents in Japanese philosophy outside of the Kyoto School.

season, which continued until about 1989, Japan shifted from a culture led by politics and literature to one led by what can be broadly called *design-technique* and *fantasy*. New philosophical ideas, cultivated for a quarter century in the soil of the postwar culture, began to bloom, replacing the earlier political orientation of thought. Furthermore, in the global theater of philosophy in the 1970s, existentialism began to recede from its leading role, as structuralism and so-called poststructuralism moved to the front of the stage. Japanese philosophy in the '70s, whether obviously or not, resonated with that global movement shift in philosophy.

As for the *place* on which I will focus, it is Komaba, a campus of the University of Tokyo. Although Komaba does offer higher level undergraduate and graduate courses, more importantly, it is where all students who come to the university spend their first two years in the liberal arts curriculum. Whereas the Hongo campus, which is regarded as the main campus, is an aggregation of specialized faculties, the Komaba campus is a place for studying a wide range of liberal arts, thus producing in students a broad knowledge of the arts and sciences that form the foundation of knowledge. If philosophy is to question the very foundation of academic disciplines, Komaba has to serve as the *place* for doing it. Insofar as philosophy precedes all other disciplines in that sense, it can be considered more "youthful" than the others, and it is young people who can truly aspire to it.

Among those who taught in the Komaba campus in the '70s were philosophers whom we can retrospectively see as the sources of our philosophical thinking in today's Japan. Having different tendencies and styles, they did not form a "school," however. Komaba is literally a *campus* (i.e., a *field*) full of different flowers blooming freely. I will pick four flowers and present their unique *color* and *scent*, focusing mainly on their works in the 1970s.

The following is a list of the members of what I call the "Komaba Quartet." As I will show, each philosopher has his own distinctive coloration that he brings to the collection. This is a list of their dates and the years they joined and left Komaba.[2]

Hiromatsu Wataru	(1933–1994)	[1976–94]
Sakabe Megumi	(1936–2009)	[1973–76]
Ōmori Shōzō	(1921–1997)	[1953–82]
Inoue Tadashi	(1926–2014)	[1957–87]

[2] The list shows the periods during which the four philosophers taught at Komaba full-time. The periods exclude their years as part-time lecturers or as assistants. Sakabe transferred to the Faculty of Letters of the University of Tokyo in 1976. The other three were affiliated with Komaba until their retirement.

HIROMATSU WATARU: INTERSUBJECTIVITY AND THE RELATIONAL (*KOTO-TEKI* 事的) WORLDVIEW

The *color* of Hiromatsu Wataru's philosophy is undeniably Marxist. He threw himself into a political movement at a very young age, when he was still in middle school. He spent the 1960s, the years of harsh political battles, as an activist and theorist. As a theorist, he read Marx's *The German Ideology* from a new perspective, discovering the fundamental mechanism of reification. That became the point of departure for Hiromotsu's philosophy as a whole, one that advocates the conversion from substantialism to relationalism. In Marx's analysis of commodification, Hiromatsu discovered the mechanism through which human social relations are reified as relations among things or values among things. In maintaining that this mechanism applies not only to commodities but to the general structure of existence, Hiromatsu established a novel foundation for philosophy, replacing altogether the modern framework of epistemology that is founded in the dualism of subjectivity and objectivity.

In 1972, Hiromatsu published *The Intersubjective Ontological Structure of the World*. In that book, which became the groundwork for his later philosophy, he referred to the "world as it appears to pre-reflective consciousness"[3] as the *phenomenal world*, and he developed an epistemology that posits its composition as a "four-limbed structure" consisting of a duality in the subject's part and a duality in the object's part. The object's duality, on the one hand, is the "integrated two-limbed structure of the ideal and the real." The subject's duality, on the other, is that of the "I" and "someone as someone" or "the 'I' that is *more than* the simple 'I'"; it is also the duality of the "I" and "the 'I' as we," which is a duality of the "self-disintegrative self-integration."

As is clear from the terms used, the basic attitude of Hiromatsu's epistemology is similar in tone to phenomenology. I would like to suggest that, as we will see in the other philosophers of the Quartet as well, the Japanese philosophy of the 1970s can be understood as a response to the phenomenological tradition leading from Husserl to Merleau-Ponty, although the four philosophers were not always explicit about that connection. The philosophers from the earlier Kyoto School commonly responded to the ontological tradition from German Idealism to Heidegger. In a parallel fashion, the philosophers in the '70s began raising questions concerning the "phenomena" or "appearances" of the world under the impact of, but with a clear demarcation from, phenomenology. Illustrating that demarcation, even when discussing such terms as "phenomenal," "phenomenon," "ideal," and "real" in Japanese, Hiromatsu did not use the standard convention of sinographs (*kanji*), but instead wrote the words phonetically, spelling them out in the syllabary form of *katakana*. That orthographic strategy expresses not so much a

---

[3] Hiromatsu 1972, 22.

reverence for European languages, but rather an assertion that his work is not simply following so-called phenomenology in a derivative, standard way. (When Hiromatsu later co-authored *Merleau-Ponty*, published in 1983, he thematized that confrontation.[4])

It is also revealing that, in the period following the publication of his first main work *The Intersubjective Ontological Structure of the World*, Hiromatsu wrote for a political magazine of the new left in serial form "The 'Overcoming of Modernity' and Japanese Remnants" (which was later revised and published in 1980 as *Discourses on the "Overcoming of Modernity": A Fragmentary Reflection on the Shōwa History of Ideas*). "The Overcoming of Modernity" refers, of course, to the symposium held as a feature article of the literary magazine *Bungakukai* during the war in 1942. The participants were thirteen scholars and literary critics, among whom was Nishitani Keiji from the Kyoto School as a representative of philosophy. From the postwar perspective, the symposium is generally read as symptomatic of the Japanese intelligentsia, including the philosophers of the Kyoto School, in their attempt to overcome Western "modernity" while relying on the war-mongering Japanese fascist ideology to complement their own ideas.

That symposium exposed the philosophy of the Kyoto School running up against its historical limitations. To put it in a somewhat exaggerated way, Japanese philosophy, having faced such limitations or "failures," found itself trapped in a dysfunctional state for a quarter century after the war. Only in the '70s do we find the launching of a new philosophy arising from the confrontation and re-examination of that "negative legacy."

Analyzing in detail how that project of "overcoming modernity" consistently motivated Japan's prewar intellectual efforts, Hiromatsu declared at the end of *Discourses on the "Overcoming of Modernity"* that the "philosophical anthropology" at the base of the Kyoto School was, after all, merely "a form of a typical modern philosophy and a typical modern ideology corresponding to the horizon of the modern age *qua* the so-called 'age of anthropocentrism.'"[5] That assessment was inextricably linked with his emphatic assertion that a true "overcoming of modernity" that frees itself of the snares of such a philosophical anthropology can only arise through a relationalist epistemology based on a Marxist standpoint aimed at the overcoming of capitalism itself.[6]

---

[4] Hiromatsu Wataru and Minatomichi Takashi, *Meruro-Pontī* [Merleau-Ponty] (Tokyo: Iwanami Shoten, 1983).

[5] Hiromatsu 1980, 248.

[6] On March 16, 1994, Hiromatsu published an essay in the newspaper *Asahi Shimbun* shortly before his untimely death. (Hiromatsu Wataru, "Tōhoku Ajia ga rekishi no shuyaku ni: Nitchū o jiku ni 'Tōa no shin-taisei o!" [North East Asia as the Central Actor of History: Japan and China as the axis of a New East Asian Regime!], in *Hiromatsu Wataru shosaku-shū* [Collected Works of Hiromatsu Wataru] [Tokyo: Iwanami Shoten], pp. 497–500). He declared that "a new worldview and ethics will, after all, come from Asia, and will sweep the world," and made the appeal "Japan and China as the axis of a new East Asian regime!" which was nearly indistinguishable from the prewar theories on the "overcoming of modernity." That stunned many people, including those close to him. We should say, however, that his determination to "overcome modernity" was consistent with his previous thought.

For Hiromatsu, this "overcoming" is made possible by a thoroughgoing relationalism in opposition to the substantialism and subject-object dualism constituting the horizon of modern European philosophy. The key arena for this oppositional stance is language. Language by itself, Hiromatsu claimed, has the "peculiar ontological character of being 'both real and ideal,'"[7] and the relational (*koto-teki* 事的) worldview opens up only when we understand language fundamentally as the ontological emergence (*tachiaraware* 立ち現われ) of the world, rather than as a mere projection of the objectified world.[8]

In the 1970s, there were multiple intellectual and cultural currents pouring into Japan. Among them were structuralism and other linguistic theories growing out of Saussure's linguistics as one of their sources, as well as the so-called linguistic turn in philosophy that began with the early Wittgenstein. In response, the Japanese philosophers of that period, including Hiromatsu, had to address the issue of language, but that, in turn, led them to the problem of having to inquire into the language of their own philosophy (i.e., the Japanese language).

In 1979, Hiromatsu published *Mono, koto, kotoba* (*Things, Occurrences, and Words*). It is hardly possible to translate this title, for the three words are written in the *hiragana* syllabary rather than sinographs. That is, the words (which I have tentatively translated as "thing," "occurrence," and "word") are investigated as *concepts* rooted in the soil of the Japanese language, where "occurrence" and "word," for example, sound homonymous from the beginning. Hiromatsu begins by investigating the distinction made in Japanese between the concept "thing" and the concept "occurrence," and he argues that the world, from the outset, emerges into consciousness as something linguistic, as a "super-grammatical subject-predicate state (*koto* こと)" or as an "occurrence (*koto* こと)."[9] In so doing, he presented a significant intersubjective ground for his philosophical view of the world.

Sakabe Megumi: Toward a Poetics of "In-betweenness" (*awai* あわい)

If Hiromatsu's "color" was Marxism, I would say Sakabe's was poetry. In 1976, Sakabe Megumi published two books. One was *The Anxiety of Reason: The Genesis and Structure of Kant's Philosophy*, which was the sum of his studies after his doctoral thesis, and the other was *The Hermeneutics of the Mask*. The former, as indicated in its title,

---

[7] Hiromatsu 2007, 123.

[8] This relational (*koto-teki*, which literally means something like "occurrence-based") worldview, for Hiromatsu, was tied to the Buddhist worldview (in particular to the interrelational worldview of the *Avatamsaka Sutra*). See the book he co-authored with the Buddhist scholar Yoshida Hiroki: Hiromatsu Wataru and Yoshida Hiroaki, *Bukkyō to koto-teki sekai-kan* [Buddhism and the Relational Worldview] (Tokyo: Asahi Shuppan-sha, 1979).

[9] Hiromatsu 2007, 246.

was a startling work in which Sakabe's reading of Kant's precritical texts, especially his *Dreams of a Spirit-Seer*, revealed how Kant's critical philosophy, the cornerstone of modern Western philosophy, owed its genesis to reason's fundamental anxiety over the external. Sakabe's critical analysis argued that modern philosophy came into being by discarding a domain that, like dreams, stands equivocally between the rational and irrational. In response, Sakabe emphatically asserted that we need to construct a more comprehensive philosophy that can incorporate the "shadow" disregarded by the modern. Rather than overcoming modernity by opening up a new horizon, Sakabe reconsidered the philosophical possibility that what has been forgotten and discarded by modernity is precisely the most fundamental dimension of being human. With that initial insight, it was a natural progression for Sakabe's philosophy to explore the dimension of what is "*between* reason and insanity," "*between* reality and surreality," "*between* self and other," "*between* life and death," or "*between* logic and images."

In the other book, Sakabe's original philosophical idea began to crystallize further. The "mask," to which the title of the book refers, means, of course, not only an ordinary mask but the *persona*. Thus, the book undoubtedly owes its problematique to Watsuji Tetsurō's *Mask and Persona*. Watsuji was related to the Kyoto School in terms of his personal connections, but, philosophically, he distinguished himself from it by developing a unique anthropology that defines the human as essentially a "betweenness between people." That anthropology of "betweenness" served a critical role in bridging the gap between the face that emerges from betweenness and the person itself. Although indebted to Watsuji's thought, Sakabe aimed to deconstruct its modern mold by returning to the genesis of the persona, which precedes the starting point of Watsuji's analysis.

Inspired by such theories as Jacques Lacan's psychoanalysis, Claude Lévi-Strauss's anthropology, and Jacques Derrida's philosophy of deconstruction, Sakabe proceeded along the lines of seeing the fundamental otherness of the self in the mechanism of the persona. As if following the natural course of that trajectory, Sakabe arrived at the integration of duality, in particular through what he thought of as a predicative integration. "The 'persona' embodies as its necessary moment the structure of the 'mask' (i.e., the persona)—in other words, the structure of the predicative determination of selfness by otherness, or the structure of integration of the separated self and other."[10]

It should be noted that Sakabe's integration of duality is not Hiromatsu's duality of the "ideal" and the "real," but rather (to put it in Lacanian terminology) the duality of the "imaginary" (*imaginaire*) and the "symbolic" (*symbolique*). As Lacan says, the "real" (*le réel*) is not possible. In that respect, Sakabe was always attentive to the fundamental significance of the "imaginary." In fact, Sakabe followed the passage I have just quoted with reference to Arthur Rimbaud's so-called "Letter of the Seer," taking its famous line "I is another" to mean "I am another person." At that point, philosophy and poetry meet.

Moreover, in his *Hermeneutics of the Mask*, Sakabe developed and wove together his philosophical thoughts in dialogue not only with Rimbaud but also with Hagiwara

---

[10] Sakabe 2009, 87.

Sakutarō, Izumi Shikibu, and Kawabata Yasunari's novel *The Sound of the Mountain*, as well as poetry from Zeami's *Noh*, *Man'yōshū*, and Shintō prayers. Through that approach, Sakabe could investigate the philosophical potential of the Japanese language even more radically than had Hiromatsu. Sakabe held that whereas the European and American languages basically follow a subject-predicate structure that is primarily assimilating in character, the Japanese language, which is exclusively predicative, is essentially "differential" (*différentiel*).[11] The Japanese language stubbornly eludes the logic of assimilation per se and is open to "the space of the infinite polysemy of metaphors" or "the space of the infinite overlapping of masks and the world whose bare face will never be reached."[12] Pointing out that in traditional Japanese thinking the "word" (*kotoba* こと ば or *koto-no-ha* ことのは) is "one leaf (*ha* は) of occurrence (*koto*)" or "one edge (*ha* は) of occurrence (*koto*)," Sakabe came to affirm the essential correlation between "word" (*kotoba* or *koto-no-ha*) and "occurrence" (*koto*).

By that route, Sakabe's hermeneutic thinking, whose departure point was the polysemous character of the Japanese word *omote* (おもて) as meaning both a "mask" and a "surface," came to consider the polysemy of *utsutsu* (うつつ). The word *utsutsu* is an archaic word for "reality," its root *utsu* (うつ) being shared also by *utsuri* (うつり) meaning "copying" and "transferring," and by *utsushi* (うつし) meaning "reflecting" and "emerging." Based on this, Sakabe continuously thematized *awai* (あわい), or "in-betweenness," which starts out *transferring* and *reflecting* but comes to be *emerging*. The character of this *utsutsu* is completely unlike the "(immediate and vivacious) presence" that Derrida was in those same years criticizing and trying to dismantle as the Western metaphysics underlying discourse. Sakabe repeatedly thematized the boundary where such oppositions as life and death, self and other, sacred and secular, or dreams and reality reverberate with each other.

Sakabe wrote about the mask as the very *person* we are: "The mask is none other than what emerges in, as it were, a sort of anti-*utsutsu*, a surreal world born in the depths of the lower layer of the world, possessing a different kind of constitutive principle (or code) from which the world of *utsutsu* emerges, but being reflected in the world of *utsutsu*."[13]

With Sakabe, a new philosophy was born. It is a philosophy that views the person not only as emerging "between" persons, but, above all, as the very emerging of the "in-betweenness" of the "real reality" and the "imaginary surreality."

[11] Sakabe 2009, 145.
[12] Sakabe 2009, 146.
[13] Sakabe 2009, 205.

ŌMORI SHŌZŌ: THE MONISM OF EMERGENCE
(*TACHIARAWARE*)

Also in 1976, Ōmori Shōzō published what could be called his main work, *Mono to kokoro* (*Objects and Mind*). Since he is the oldest of the four philosophers discussed in this chapter, the book does not necessarily record the departure point for a later philosophy, but it can be said that his own original philosophy really did begin to bloom in the '70s. The reason is that Ōmori had taken a detour, graduating from the physics department of the prewar Tokyo Imperial University and then earning a degree from the philosophy department of the University of Tokyo after the war. Consistent with his study at Stanford and Harvard Universities, his philosophy was influenced by Wittgenstein and Anglo-American analytical philosophy, critically reconsidering the scientific worldview and the "commonsensical" worldview supporting it. Ōmori did so by using ordinary language without the preconceptions of existing philosophical concepts. In his terms, he hoped to escape the "trap of science" and the "trap of common sense." In that respect, we can say Ōmori's *color* is that of "science" (and "common sense").

Therefore, Ōmori kept his focus on ordinary, commonplace experiences such as "I see a lamp" in its complete concreteness. He said that although natural science can speak of all the data, such as those concerning the room where the lamp is, the light rays, the physiological reaction of the body, and the electrochemical transition in cerebral cortex cells, such an accumulation of data will never add up completely to the fact that "I see a lamp."[14] Natural science only "superposes" scientific descriptions or pictures on my "raw experience." How, then, is it possible to locate the raw experience itself, the "fundamental fact," without losing it in its entirety? This was Ōmori's persistent question.

Ōmori tried to respond by pursuing a radical monism that completely avoids the restraints imposed by dualistic "core schemata"[15] such as subject and object, object and meaning, objects and mind, or the body and the mind—dualisms to which philosophical thinking along with common-sense thinking are easily susceptible. He thereby provided a "more appropriate" *description* or *picture* of the entirety of raw experience as it actually is. Ōmori's book *Mono to kokoro* (*Objects and Mind*) is a collection of essays aiming to break through the core schemata of the dualism of "objects" (*mono* 物) and "mind" (*kokoro* 心), the greatest obstacle to his monism. For that purpose, he made the bold proposal of reducing "perceptual representations" and "nonperceptual representations," which require that "objects" be beyond the veil of representations inside the "mind," to an "adverbial" difference on a single continuous spectrum, such that the difference is that between "objects' emerging *in the mode of perception*" and "objects' emerging *in the mode of thinking*."[16] He then extended this to claim that all the instances

[14] Ōmori 1976, 16.
[15] Ōmori 1976, 117.
[16] Ōmori 1976, 120.

of "emerging" that we generally judge to be falsity, fantasy, fancy, and dreams, "exist on the same footing as reality."[17]

The implication is that, for Ōmori, the world of experience in which we live, whether it is a world of perception or thinking, is ultimately the emergence of the world equally in every case. It is the emergence of the "four-dimensional universe" prior to the distinction between true and false, right and wrong, or real and unreal, and without the distinction among past, present, and future. Even in a trivial situation where "I see a lamp," the "four-dimensional universe" is continuously emerging. At each time, "one space-time is particularly strongly illuminated," and it is, in one case, merely a thing called a "lamp." There is the emergence at each time, and it is only that the "figure-aspect" of it comes to differ.[18]

The following objection could be raised: it should always be possible to posit the "reality" of a numerically identical object—the "reality" that persists through the myriad instances of an "emergence." Here, Ōmori makes no concession at all, responding that such positing simply arises from the "order of identity systematized conventionally."[19] That is, it is because the "order of identity" of "meaning" is conventionally systematized that the distinction is made between "real" and "unreal," "things" (mono もの) and "occurrences" (koto), and so on. Originally, there is the "emerging" simply and uniformly. Ōmori's account is a "naïve ontology"[20] that "strangles" and discards the highly philosophical notion "existence." By the same point, his account also discards the highly common-sense notion "meaning." "When we see something, conceive of something, and think of something, things that are seen, conceived of, and thought of are immediately seen, conceived of, and thought of."[21] Ōmori himself calls such a linguistic view the kotodama (ことだま) view. Kotodama is an ancient Japanese linguistic view that language has the magical power to summon the reality of what is spoken. Language is not a "copy" or a rehash, but is that which makes the world immediately emerge.

Thus, Ōmori's argument smashes all our "common-sense ideas" and "preconceptions," concentrating instead on approximating the fundamental factuality of the "emergence of the world." Of course, there is an aporia here: Ōmori endeavors to make pure raw experience emerge through "descriptions" in language, even though, with respect to such experience, even the secondariness of "descriptions" already lacks "meaning." However, although Ōmori does not explicitly say this, philosophy should be nothing other than the act of "staking one's life" on such an endeavor.

At the end of the chapter on kotodama, discussing the "order of identity systematized conventionally," Ōmori stresses that it is not fixed at all, but is "constantly reorganized" and is "constantly wavering."[22] He further says that its system is not systematized from

---

[17] Ōmori 1976, 153.
[18] Ōmori 1976, 195.
[19] Ōmori 1976, 153.
[20] Ōmori 1976, 154.
[21] Ōmori 1976, 176.
[22] Ōmori 1976, 153.

the viewpoint of the "truth" or "reality," but is a "pragmatic system" for "living," a "system for living" we call "truth" or "reality" after the fact. If so, philosophy has to be a ceaseless effort to shake up the existing order of identity and rewrite it. Here, Ōmori fully displays his philosophy of radical pragmatism.[23]

INOUE TADASHI: THE WAY OF THE
ENCOUNTER-IDEA (*IDEAI* イデアイ)

Every quartet requires the bass to play a thorough-bass and to beat out the fundamental rhythm. If so, the cello part of our "Komaba Quartet" is played by the philosophy of Inoue Tadashi. In terms of an area of specialty within the academic framework, he specializes in ancient Greek philosophers such as Parmenides, Plato, and Aristotle. However, Inoue goes far beyond being just a philologist. For him, philosophy is a genuine "seeking," a genuine "way." What he calls the "Ground" (*konkyo* 根拠) is the "Idea," "behind" which is our world of facts. [24] To engage in philosophy is to go toward an encounter with this Idea and to "engrave" one's own existence in the world of facts as a "work" (*ergon*). Thus, Inoue's *color* can only be that of the "Idea." There is, however, the reservation that we—even in Plato's context—can never answer the question "what is the Idea?" Better stated, the Idea, to begin with, can only be the very emergence of the question "what is this?"

In 1973, Inoue published *A Challenge from the Ground: An Investigation of Greek Philosophy*, a collection of essays related to Greek philosophy written over a period of more than twenty years. A major motivation for the book, as Inoue himself stated repeatedly, is articulated in his sentence "a fact is not the Ground." Although we live through and through in the world of facts, no fact can ever be our *Ground* because every fact is but a fragment or part, lacking in wholeness. Yet, as Plato said in *Parmenides*, "a part is always *part of the whole*."[25] Inspired by that statement, Inoue concluded that Plato's *methexis*, which is the relation between the Idea and the world of facts, cannot (as it is often interpreted) mean simply "partaking" or "participating." According to Inoue, *methexis* is *meta-echein*, with *meta* meaning "behind" and *echein* meaning "to hold," and

---

[23] From our present vantage point, we might be able to see Ōmori's personal or existential belief as that of one who graduated from the prewar Tokyo Imperial University, entered the Navy, experienced defeat in war, and immediately "converted" to philosophy. It would be a "belief" that resists all the beliefs in the constantly wavering "truth" and searches for the absoluteness of life free from contamination by such "truth."

[24] "Ideai" is a term coined by Inoue based on the homonymy between the Greek word "idea" and the Japanese word "*Ideai*" (出逢い), which means encounter.

[25] Inoue 1974, 133. Inoue refers to the following parts of Plato's *Parmenides*: 157e, 137e, 142d. See *Plato's Parmenides, The Dialogues of Plato*, volume 4, revised edition, translated by Reginald E. Allen (New Haven: Yale University Press, 1997), 18, 26, 50.

therefore it is a "background relation." In the background of every part, there is invisible darkness, which is nonetheless essentially the total effulgence of existence, the Idea as the Ground spreading out in the background. Inoue says that "*moira* (part) is *moira* (fate)." He then goes on to say that to our world

> a part was sent as a fate, and since it is a part of the whole, it is not a mere flake of desultory flux (i.e. a part of the many), but is, if seen as a fact of a single occurrence in history, in Aristotle's wording, an *ergon* copying the eternal *energeia* in the fashion of *analogia*, or a "work," and is *energeia* in the course of this, that is, "being on the way of a work."[26]

Thus, Inoue listened for the truth of the Idea in the "resonance" of Plato and Aristotle.

That landscape is at the core of Inoue's philosophy. And, when a human being seeks to take charge of his own fate as if to almost reverse the fated "way of a work," that is, when "one, weighing one's life by placing it on the palm, risks and stakes the whole of oneself, and 'human being' per se, on the step-by-step way," the work, or *each* work, *in its own way*, "takes on the character of being one whole." That is precisely what Inoue thinks of as the way of philosophy, a way that is a staking of one's life. Yet, it is inevitable that such a staking would fall into self-attachment, and Inoue is aware of this. He asserts that the way of philosophy is the "activity of self-attachment" and says that it is through self-attachment that one can completely open oneself "to that free background the Ground inhabits."

What is interesting for us is that, in the part of the chapter titled "*Ideai e no kunren*" (Training for Encounter-Idea), at the conclusion of the chapter, Inoue describes an exchange with Ōmori who said to him:

> Then what is the Ground? Please give me an example. If you can give an example, it is tantamount to a fact. If the Ground is not a fact, what is the Ground? Please show that to me. If you can speak about it, I would like to listen to you to understand it without prejudice.[27]

In response Inoue only wrote "(Silence)."

Nonetheless, as any reader of A Challenge from the Ground is likely to remember, at one point in the book, Inoue did speak about one such encounter in poetic prose, in a style quite different from the work's main discussion. He spoke of a singularly striking encounter he had one day, an encounter that would be almost irreducible to being a mere fact. It happened when he was walking on a mountain path on a rainy day and crossed the ridge of Shinshū-tōge. Suddenly, there was a shape of a mountain (Mizugaki-yama) that he had not seen before.

---

[26] Inoue 1974, 142.
[27] Inoue 1974, 157.

It was a tremendous moment. It was that moment at which all of our functions were absorbed solely into the world of vision, or, precisely, into another world that resembled vision, and were dissolved. I gasped. *That*, which emerged from the grand shape of the mountain, was certainly *something* that instantaneously faded out the landscape of nature before our eyes as well as the existence of the humans facing it, shattering them into shadows.[28]

It was over in an instant. In fact, it was only a mountain that emerged. Yet—whether people believe it or not—he encountered *that*. *That* struck him.[29]

IN-BETWEEN *KOTO* (WORD) AND *KOTO* (OCCURRENCE)

Hiromatsu, expecting a historical revolution in the world, conceived a philosophy to cognize the world structurally from the perspective of intersubjectivity. Sakabe sought to have a glimpse of the existence of the human by descending to the boundary of *awai*, where reality and surreality intermingle with each other. Ōmori strove to secure the monism of the emergence of life as a world underlying the world of facts. Conversely, Inoue insisted that the sole mission of philosophy is to encounter the wholeness of the Idea, the Ground, behind which is the world of facts. Of course, it is impossible to briefly summarize each of their complex philosophical journeys. My descriptions do not give the entire picture of each philosophy, but only present its *color* and *scent*, slightly sketching the space of the philosophical quartet that rose unexpectedly from the utterly different flowers in one place and in one time.

The Komaba Quartet did not form a "school," but they did teach the common lesson that philosophy is not just doctrines. Although it does not despise doctrine, philosophy cannot stay at the level of doctrine. To borrow Inoue's words, philosophy is to accept one's own "solitude" and one's "part" as an "individual" and to inquire into the *Ground* of "being human" through the way of the Logos. One has to be a soloist. A true quartet can rise only from soloists, at least to the ear listening for that.

The *color* and *scent* of that time was strongly influenced by the quartet. Even though the four philosophers' pursued their journeys in quite different directions, they made their ways in the same landscape of the age. If I were to accentuate the "*color and scent*" of the time, I would refer to *koto*. All of the four developed their thinking in their own ways

---

[28] Inoue 1974, 39.

[29] Inoue was born in Hiroshima Prefecture. In a note in his paper "The Dead Come Back to Life," he writes, "Twenty years ago, a shot of ominous flame shone in the 'military city' Hiroshima. I witnessed *that*." (Inoue Tadashi, "Shisha wa yomigaeru" [The Dead Come Back to Life], in Inoue 1985, 122.) Similar to Ōmori, after graduating from the Department of Political Science of the Faculty of Law of the University of Tokyo, Inoue re-enrolled in the Department of Philosophy of the Faculty of Letters.

by reflecting on the association between *koto* (occurrence) and *koto* (word), an association enabled by the homonymy of the two words in Japanese. They were each aware of using the Japanese language as a resource for their philosophy, and, although they each saw the world as occurrence in quite different ways, the "philosophy of *koto*" in which occurrence and language are inseparable was the common horizon of their thinking. In the 1970s, the wind of *koto* was blowing across a "field" of philosophy known as Komaba.

BIBLIOGRAPHY AND SUGGESTED READINGS

For a selection of passages translated from works by Ōmori Shūzō, Hiromatsu Wataru, and Sakabe Megumi, see *Japanese Philosophy: A Sourcebook*, edited by James W. Heisig, Thomas P. Kasulis, and John C. Maraldo (Honolulu: University of Hawai'i Press, 2011), pp. 936–942, 973–978, and 979–992.

Sources in Japanese

Hiromatsu Wataru. (1972) *Sekai no kyōdō-shukan-teki sonzai-kōzō* [The Intersubjective Ontological Structure of the World]. Tokyo: Keisō Shobō.

Hiromatsu Wataru. (1980) *"Kindai no chōkoku" ron: Shōwa shishōshi e no ichi-dansō* [Discourses on the "Overcoming of Modernity": A Fragmentary Reflection on the Shōwa History of Ideas]. Tokyo: Asahi Shuppan-sha.

Hiromatsu Wataru. (1982) *Sonzai to imi: Koto-teki sekai-kan no teiso, Dai-ikkan* [Being and Meaning: Laying the Cornerstone of the Relational Worldview, Vol. 1]. Tokyo: Iwanami Shoten.

Hiromatsu Wataru. (1989) *Hyōjō* [Countenance]. Tokyo: Kōbundō.

Hiromatsu Wataru. (1993) *Sonzai to imi: Koto-teki sekai-kan no teiso, Dai-nikan* [Being and Meaning: Laying the Cornerstone of the Relational Worldview, Vol. 2]. Tokyo: Iwanami Shoten.

Hiromatsu Wataru. (1994) *Marukusu no konpon-isō wa nan de attaka* [What Were Marx's Fundamental Thoughts?]. Tokyo: Jōkyō-shuppan.

Hiromatsu Wataru. (2007) *Mono, koto, kotoba* [Things, Occurrences, and Words]. Tokyo: Chikuma Shobō.

Inoue Tadashi. (1974) *Konkyo yori no chōsen: Girisha-tetsugaku kyūkō* [A Challenge from the Ground: An Investigation of Greek Philosophy]. Tokyo: Tōkyō Daigaku Shuppan-kai.

Inoue Tadashi. (1985) *Tetsugaku no kizami 1: Sei to shi o koeru mono* [The Engraving of Philosophy 1: What Goes Beyond Sex and Death]. Kyoto: Hōzōkan.

Ōmori Shōzō. (1976) *Mono to kokoro* [Objects and Mind]. Tokyo: Tōkyō Daigaku Shuppan-kai.

Ōmori Shōzō. (1982) *Shin-shikaku-shinron* [A New Essay Towards a New Theory of Vision]. Tokyo: Tōkyō Daigaku Shuppan-kai.

Ōmori Shōzō. (1992) *Jikan to jiga* [Time and the Self]. Tokyo: Seidosha.

Ōmori Shōzō. (1994) *Jikan to sonzai* [Time and Existence]. Tokyo: Seidosha.

Ōmori Shōzō. (1996) *Toki wa nagarezu* [Time Does Not Flow]. Tokyo: Seidosha.

Sakabe Megumi. (1976) *Risei no fuan: Kanto tetsugaku no seisei to kōzō* [The Anxiety of Reason: The Genesis and Structure of Kant's Philosophy]. Tokyo: Keisō Shobō.

Sakabe Megumi. (1997) *"Furumai" no shigaku* [The Poetics of "Behaviour"]. Tokyo: Iwanami Shoten.

Sakabe Megumi. (1989) *Perusona no shigaku: Katari, furumai, kokoro* [The Poetics of Persona: Narration, Behaviour, and Mind]. Tokyo: Iwanami Shoten.

Sakabe Megumi. (2000) *Watsuji Tetsurō: Ibunka kyōsei no katachi* [Watsuji Tetsurō: A Form of Cross-Cultural Co-existence]. Tokyo: Iwanami Shoten.

Sakabe Megumi. (2009) *Kamen no kaishaku-gaku [Shinsō-ban]* [The Hermeneutics of the Mask (New Edition)]. Tokyo: Tōkyō Daigaku Shuppan-kai.

PART V

PERVASIVE TOPICS IN JAPANESE PHILOSOPHICAL THOUGHT

CHAPTER 32

....

PHILOSOPHICAL
IMPLICATIONS OF THE
JAPANESE LANGUAGE

....

ROLF ELBERFELD

LANGUAGE as it is spoken and written is the basic medium of philosophical thinking. Yet language never exists independently from a plurality of particular natural, artificial, or formal languages. It is thus the case that every instance of philosophizing is realized in a concrete particular language. Reflection on the philosophical significance of this fact began in European philosophy in the sixteenth century.[1] In the twentieth century, discussion of this matter congealed in the opposition between universalism (Chomsky) and relativism (Whorf). The following reflections on the Japanese language belong to neither of these orientations. Neither can a universal structure beyond particular languages be ascertained, nor are philosophers locked up in a particular language. Both languages and thinking transform themselves, such that thinking develops within the parameters of various languages. Since 1868, a process of translation from European languages has taken place in Japan, a process that has altered the Japanese language, including the language of philosophy. This chapter will attempt to show, with examples selected from both older and newer contexts, which structures in particular of the Japanese language are philosophically significant.

---

[1] On the history of the inclusion of a consideration of the plurality of languages in philosophical thinking, see Elberfeld 2013, 19–86.

THE JAPANESE LANGUAGE

Japanese is still considered to be an isolated language whose origins remain lost in the darkness of the distant past. Attempts to unequivocally assign it to a language family have not been successful. Extensive research has shown that Japanese does contain a host of loan words from Korean; yet this fact, together with some shared structures, has not proved sufficient to constitute a common language family. It has furthermore been claimed that there are indications of a proximity to the Altaic language family, to which Korean is also ascribed by some scholars. Japanese appears to share several phonetical elements in common with Turkic, Mongolic, and Tungusic.[2]

Japanese is not related to the Chinese language. The structural constitution of Japanese is fundamentally different from that of Chinese. Nevertheless, starting in the fifth century CE, at the latest, the Chinese script was introduced to Japan, which at the time did not have a script for its spoken language. Because of the vast linguistic differences—Chinese is mainly an isolating language, whereas Japanese is an agglutinative language—it took several more centuries and the invention of two supplementary phonetic alphabets (Hiragana and Katakana) until the Japanese language could be written in a satisfactory manner. In addition to the combination of Chinese characters and newly invented phonetic alphabets used to write indigenous Japanese words, a comprehensive vocabulary of loan words was adopted from Chinese along with the characters. It thus seems amazing that the two languages are nonetheless not considered to be "related." The reason for this is that, in most cases, for two languages to be designated "relatives," a common primordial language must be presupposed.

Since Japanese is an agglutinative language, there exists in it neither conjugation of verbs nor declination of nouns as there are in English. In comparison to English, much in Japanese is grammatically formed either differently or not at all.

WORD TYPES IN JAPANESE

It is not initially obvious how types of words in Japanese are to be distinguished and understood. Neither the number of types nor their exact functions can be straightforwardly grasped in terms of Latin. Even the difference between noun and verb in the context of Classical Japanese lies in question. In his study, *Einige Grundzüge des japanischen Sprachbaus* [Some Fundamental Traits of the Linguistic Structure of Japanese], Peter Hartmann goes so far as to deny for the most part the distinction between noun and verb:

[2] Lewin 1996, 3–5.

On the basis of an absence of differentiation between noun and verb in Classical Japanese, it seems justified to suppose that an object and the process enacted by it are perceived as a unity, that is, as not separated from one another.[3]

If we take this claim seriously, then we can assume that, before the separation of noun and verb, there might exist a level of language that expresses objects as pure processes, such that a distinction between noun and verb could not be made. Only once they are regarded as separated from one another can the object become something persisting that can play a role in the context of an action or activity. Hartmann goes on to write:

> If the stem—the kernel of the word which supports its meaning—is employed without additions (suffixes, etc.), then it dispenses with all formal characteristics of a verb, whose essence is after all to represent a process in some modified manner. In this case only the basic meaning can determine the conceptual category—if any at all is to be found—to which such a word belongs. This is especially the case in Japanese, where the structure of word stems for nouns and verbs is the same, and where one must be satisfied with the ascertainment that a word conveys content either of an object or a process.[4]

It seems necessary to question anew the word categories not only for each language, but also for each stage in the historical development of a language. Just as the distinction between noun and verb must be called into question, it is also the case that the distinction between verb and adjective, as it is typically found in Indo-European languages, cannot simply be applied to the Japanese language. In the meantime, a threefold division has come to be accepted: verbs (*dōshi* 動詞), qualitatives (*keiyōshi* 形容詞), and verbal qualitatives (*keiyōdōshi* 形容動詞).[5] Together, these three word categories are called *yōgen* (用言).[6] The *yō* in this term is an old Chinese character whose basic meaning is "to function," on the one hand in the sense of "to function as a quality" and, on the other, in the sense of "functioning as being operative." Both meanings indicate something active, yet in different *manners*. What is at issue, however, is not merely an *action*, but rather a *functioning* in both of the senses given. One could even translate *yōgen* as "function words."

On account of their common denotation, verbs and adjectives are brought into close proximity, yet they are nevertheless distinguished. The word category *keiyōdōshi* (verbal qualitatives) was introduced by Ōtsuki Fumihiko (1847–1928) "with regard to the qualitatives in general, in order to stress their verbal character in contradistinction to English adjectives."[7] In discussing Japanese grammar, the way in which the European distribution into verbs and adjectives stands in the way of understanding and describing

---

[3] Hartmann 1952, 34.

[4] Ibid., 36.

[5] On these grammatical distinctions, see Lewin 1996, §§117, 145, 152.

[6] Lewin translates *yōgen* as "action words" (*Aktionswörter*), in ibid., §117.

[7] Ibid., §152.

the linguistic function of the Japanese words in question must be borne in mind constantly. An older term used by philologists in the Edo period for "qualitatives" can perhaps offer some assistance: *arikata-no-kotoba* (あり方の言葉).[8] The word *arikata* is used today as a translation of Heidegger's *Seinsweise* (manner of being). The original meaning is simply *the manner in which something exists*. With this oblique reference to Heidegger, we can describe a "qualitative" as a *manner of functioning* (*Wirkweise*). This cannot be understood as an accident of a substance; rather, it shows the whole, which is specified further by means of a "qualitative," in its *manner of functioning*. Thus is expressed the fact that the qualities actively participate in the actuality of events and actively contribute (*wirken*) to their manner (exert a *yō*) such that they closely approximate verbs. In this sense, the grass is not *green* as an accidental property, but rather the grass *greens*. If we attempt to construct verbal formulations of adjectives that in English do not have verb forms, this may provide us with an impression of the qualitative difference at stake here: rather than "The rose is red," "The rose reds." Or still more unusual: instead of "The flower is beautiful," "The flower beautys."

Analogous to the case with Classical Chinese, it can be said of Japanese that a sharp distinction does not exists between verb and adjective and that the qualitatives should not be understood according to the model of substance and accidents. This suggests that the predicate plays a central role in the Japanese language and so, too, in the language of Japanese philosophy.

Subject and Predicate

Although the grammatical structures of Japanese and Chinese are dissimilar, there exists an important structural similarity with respect to the meaning of the subject. Similar to Classical Chinese, the predicate plays the central role in the sentence construction of Japanese:

> The essential element in a Japanese sentence is the predicate, since it can contain more sense determinations in a statement than any other element. By comparison, the subject in a Japanese sentence is less significant; it often even remains undesignated and thus can only be discerned from the predicate or context.[9]

We are also struck by the fact that the subject in a Japanese sentence is of minor significance, and its use tends to be avoided. When Lewin speaks of the "predicate" being of central significance, this, too, is philosophically relevant. Yet when one speaks of the "predicate" here, this should not be understood in the framework of English grammar since in the latter the predicate is tightly bound up with the subject of the sentence.

[8] Ibid., §145.
[9] Ibid., §199.

Rather, in the case of Japanese, the predicate is seen as its own center, a center to which, in certain situations, a subject can be linked:

> The [Japanese] predicate, which arranges its determinations before itself, is however not a predicate in the Indo-Germanic[10] sense; it does not bear a stamp from a subject. It is rather the master in the sentence, which all the other things referenced merely further determine. Hence, the Japanese sentence is a conjunction of modifiers that are arranged in respect to the predicate, such that the predicate is more specifically determined in relation to them.[11]

In the English language—and above all in the discourse of philosophy in English—predication is always related to a grammatical (and in this case also logical) subject. In the sentence, "Socrates is mortal," what is of primary concern is *who* is mortal; of less concern is the meaning of "mortality." In the sentence, "I think," Descartes and Kant attend above all to the "I" as subject and less to "thinking" as an occurrence. One can clearly recognize how the subject rules in the thinking that takes place in the English language. What would it mean, conversely, for the "predicate" to take over the leading and central place in the sentence? In terms of our examples, the occurrences of "mortality" and "thinking" would become the points of departure for what could—but need not—place itself in a subordinate relation to a subject. In English and other European languages, the grammatical subject of many statements often remains a construction that is necessitated by grammar even though it is logically superfluous.[12] By contrast, if the predicate stands in the center, one is less concerned with always locating the subject of the statement and more concerned with the inner differentiation of the statement or of the process itself. The process or the experience of a matter itself is thus the central concern. Whether a "subject" for this process or experience can be found is of secondary importance; it can, when necessary, be provided, but usually is left out[13]:

> While an effort to clearly demonstrate logical categories (e.g., singular/plural) and logical relations (e.g., subject and predicate) governs Indo-Germanic [i.e., Indo-European] languages, Japanese is less shaped by a logical compulsion as it is by an immediate reproduction of impressions; its grammatical means are used to indicate which representations in experience form a unity. The logical relations among the array of experiential unities are specifically articulated only when necessary, and

---

[10] Hartmann still uses here the old terminology. Today, one no longer speaks of "Indo-Germanic" langauges, but rather of "Indo-European." The Indo-European language family can be traced back to what is now referred to as "Proto-Indo-European." The latter, however, can only be reconstructed at this point since no textual documentation of it has survived.

[11] Hartmann 1952, §101.

[12] The "essentially subjectless" sentences that are spoken of in regard to Classical Chinese can be given here as examples. [An example of a sentence in which English grammar necessitates an otherwise logically superfluous subject is: "It is raining."—*Tr.*]

[13] It must be stressed that Classical Japanese was entirely capable of formulating logical connections in the sense of logical propositions. This linguistic form, however, did not dominate philosophical texts.

generally this is deferred to an affective disclosure from the context. Three levels of grammatical relation are to be distinguished:

(1) experiential unity (the impressions taken from experience as a unity): (a) verbal (i.e. process-) unity, a verb as a kernel of representation, clarified or supplemented by other words; (b) adjectival (i.e., impressional-) unity; (c) substantive (i.e., object-) unity.

(2) experiential chains (various experiences that are linked as a series): (a) verbal and adjectival chains (the links that stand before the last link in a chain); (b) substantive chains.

(3) sharp division between unities that are bound together only in thought and not in experience (in secondary clauses and statements regarding a logical subject with [the suffix particle (*joshi* 助詞)] *wa*).[14]

Similar to the grammar of Classical Chinese, in this classification, the designation of a grammatical and logical subject is *a special case*, which even then remains oriented toward the predicate as center and not the other way around. The third point of the analysis can be further differentiated in that the experiential unities and chains undergo a reflective articulation in which certain moments of experience are stressed and become themselves the topic of the sentence. Corresponding to divisions also made in the Chinese language,[15] the third point can be better grasped in terms of the "theme/rheme" or "topic/comment" relation. In this relation, rather than something being predicated of a subject, a topic is drawn out from an experiential unity, accentuated, and described in more detail with regard to that experiential unity.

This can be also be illustrated with regard to the so-called verbal suffixes (*jodōshi* 助動詞), which play an important role in Japanese. They have a different function than postpositions "since they do not supply the content of a statement with order and precision, but rather concretize it according to manner and place."[16] Lewin provides us with illuminating formulations for distinguishing the various functions of verbal suffixes. They indicate the grammatical categories for designating the following: the place of the subject in an occurrence, the relationship between speaker and partner, the position in a temporal sequence, the phases in a temporal process, one's emotional involvement, one's volitional involvement, and one's judicative involvement.[17] This clearly illustrates how the *concrete situation* essentially and even *structurally* determines an event of speech.

In light of this finding that in Classical and also in Modern Japanese the predicate stands in the foreground of the sentence, producing a variety of possibilities for formulating "subjectless sentences," we can inquire into the relevance of this for thinking. In what follows, I will demonstrate this relevance for both ancient and modern thinking by means of an analysis of some prominent examples.

---

[14] Hartmann 1952, 34–35.
[15] See, in this regard, Li and Thompson 1976, 457–490.
[16] Lewin 1996, §159.
[17] Ibid., §161–193.

This first example, from ancient Japan, is a brief passage from Dōgen (1200–1253), who is not only one of the greatest Japanese Zen masters but also an important thinker. In contrast to the denial of language that is attributed to Zen especially in the West, Dōgen uses language in such a pointed manner that, precisely through the use of language, the limits of language are made apparent. Upon closer inspection, his use of language on the whole can evoke a deepened refection on linguisticality and language use.

In a short text entitled *Uji*—often considered to be one of the most difficult writings in all of Japanese literature—Dōgen succinctly expresses his conception of time. The title already eludes unambiguous translation since without a context it admits of various interpretations. The combination of the two Chinese characters 有時 (Ch. *you-shi*; Jp. *u-ji*)[18] was quite common in Classical Chinese. A German dictionary gives "*zuweilen*" ("sometimes" or "at times") as a definition for *you-shi*, which however only imprecisely reveals its meaning. Typical translations of the title *Uji* in Western languages are: *Existence-Time* (Nishijima), *Being Time* (Abe/Waddel), *Being-Time* (Heine), *Living Time* (Wright), and *Sein = Zeit* (Tsujimura). These translations of the title indicate its polysemic possibilities, which for Dōgen's use of language are not detrimental but rather intentionally employed for the sake of thinking. In *Uji*, Dōgen thematizes the relation between what is collectively given as being and time in general. The "I" also plays a role here, though not as subject but rather as an occurrence. In the text, we find the following sentence:

> われを排列しおきて盡界とせり、この盡界の頭頭物物を時時なりと覷見す
> べし。
>
> To let I-arraying be the entire world; each single thing of this entire world is to be seen in each case as time (*jiji* 時時).[19]

The sentence begins with the word *ware* (I), the first person personal pronoun, yet not as the subject of the sentence but rather as the object of "to array." There is moreover no subject indicated in the sentence. If one wanted to assert nevertheless that the logical subject is included implicitly, one would be faced with the problem that the sentence is concerned with the emergence of the subject itself. In Buddhism, after all, the subject is not presupposed; one proceeds rather from a non-ego that underlies all talk of an ego. In the Indian context during the time of its origination in the fourth and third centuries BCE, it was precisely with the teaching of *anātman* (non-ego, no-self; Ch. *wuwo*; Jp. *muga* 無我) that Buddhism set itself apart from other Indian philosophies. The Buddhist

---

[18] While *you-shi* is the Chinese pronunciation of the two characters, *u-ji* is one particular Japanese pronunciation of them. [*U-ji* is the *onyomi* or "phonetic reading" of the characters in Japanese, whereas *aru toki* is the *kunyomi* or "indigenous reading" of the characters.—*Tr.*]

[19] Ōhashi and Elberfeld 2006, 95. [Ōhashi and Elberfeld's German translation reads: "Ich Anordnen als die gesamte Welt wirken lassen; jede einzelne Sache dieser gesamten Welt ist jeweils als Zeit (*jiji*) einzusehen."—*Tr.*] For a detailed interpretation of the text *Uji*, see Elberfeld 2004. On Dōgen's thought, see Ōhashi and Elberfeld 2006, as well as Chapters 8 and 9 in this volume.

doctrine of *anātman* consists of the insight that there exists no "I" as substance since the idea of an "I" arises only through the interplay of various factors of existence (*skandhas*) without there being any continuously abiding element. The idea of the "I," which at first seems indubitable as the fixed reference point of my personal identity, is unremittingly deconstructed in the early Buddhist practices by means of meditation on the individual factors of existence. Every examination realizes that the "I" is *anātman*, that is to say, an interplay of the factors of existence. Yet already here we are driven to the limits of our language since our grammatical demand for a subject compels us to attribute to the realization of the *anātman* a subject who realizes. When one says that the "I" realizes itself as *anātman*, there is always the danger that the "I" who realizes this is once again understood as a fixed point in the realization. But if one more radically understands the "I" *as anātman*, the insight may occur that the *anātman* can only realize *itself* as *I* and only ever as an occurrence of the factors of existence. For how else could the *anātman* realize itself, other than as *the ever renewed self-constellating I*?

We face peculiar problems when attempting to translate Dōgen's sentence. There is no clear subject named in the first part of the sentence. We are presented with the possibility of forming subjectless sentences in order to approach the thought in a philosophically subtle manner. "I-arraying" is indeed the "subject," whereby the entire world arises. Yet, in principle, we can no longer speak of a "subject" but rather of an occurrence, out of which both "I" and also "world" emerge as integral parts of the structure of the occurrence that cannot be separated from one another. "I-arraying" as the constellating of factors of existence is also the constellating of the interconnections of the world. As a continual process, this constellating is something *temporal*, such that every single thing of the entire world emerges always as *time* in the sense of a processuality. Yet since every single thing comes in its own manner of temporal processuality, each thing is *in its own manner* time. Each moment of time is, as constellation, nevertheless also a moment of the time of the I, since the temporal arraying of the I corresponds exactly to the temporal course of states of affairs. The I *as arraying* is time, whereby the entire world arises as time.

By means of the structural possibilities of the Japanese language, Dōgen can reflect on subjectless occurrences with patently more ease than is possible in European languages. One reason that Heidegger, especially in his later work, used formulations that strike German readers as strange lies in the grammatical structure of the German language itself, which makes it difficult to construct philosophically significant subjectless sentences.

THE MIDDLE VOICE

In addition to the active and passive voices, the Japanese language possesses a grammatical form for the middle voice, even if, presumably under the influence of Latin-centric grammar paradigms, it may not be characterized as such in modern grammar books. Regarding the grammar of Classical Japanese, however, the following is generally accepted:

> The middle voice in Japanese is formally and semantically very close to the passive, in that it presents a verbally designated occurrence or state of affairs that affects the subject, yet without being caused by an agent and regardless of whether or not through one's own intuition. . . . The medial forms of Japanese are ancient and can be traced back to the beginning of the written tradition. . . . (The passive voice in Japanese is probably merely a semantic development of the middle voice by means of designating the agent that brings about the affect or experience.) . . . In the course of the Heian period [794–1185], the ancient form of the middle voice also took on the sense of potentiality.[20]

This description of the middle voice by a German Japanologist manifests the influence of explanations of the middle voice in Classical Greek. The being-affected of the subject in an occurrence or state of affairs is understood to be the semantic content of the middle voice. The final part of the first sentence, however, brings about a shift in the description that is not to be found in Classical Greek. With the statement that the middle voice in Japanese occurs "without being caused by an agent," that is, without a subject or doer, the explanation of the middle voice in Japanese is connected with the question concerning the subject in the sentence. As we have seen, in Japanese, the subject can be left out without further ado since it does not stand in the center of the sentence. It is the occurrence or situation that appears in the foreground, wherein it is not the subject but rather the quality of the occurrence itself that is central.

The final sentence of the preceding quotation states that in Japanese the middle voice also took on the meaning of "potentiality," that is, the form of capability. This indicates yet another semantic level of the middle voice that is not found in Indo-European languages. All together, the middle voice in Japanese possesses, according to standard descriptions, four basic meanings. The following quotation is from a Japanese grammarian who does not interpret the middle voice within the horizon of Classical Greek but rather understands it from the Japanese tradition:

1. Spontaneity, an action which occurs without prior intention. (In this sense *ru*, *raru* shows that a certain action occurs naturally, or a certain condition naturally arises. The original meaning of *ru*, *raru* was spontaneity, and the other meanings developed from it.)
2. Passive voice. (This passive shows that a certain action is suffered from another person and as a general rule it is used only for people and animals.)
3. Potential. (In this sense the ending shows that a certain action is possible. In the Heian period *ru*, *raru* was used with the negative auxiliary verb *zu*, when it expressed potential; but with the arrival of the Kamakura period it was used

---

[20] Lewin 1996, 152–153.

independently. It is important to note that the potential meaning also includes the sense that a condition naturally arises (spontaneity).)

4. Respect. (It is used to show respect with regard to the action of the person who is the topic of a sentence [. . .]. *Ru, raru* did not express respect until the Heian period when many respectful usages were developed.)[21]

The basic meaning of the middle voice, according to this explanation, is the "spontaneity" of an occurrence that happens in a natural manner. Nothing is said in the explanation about the subject who is affected by the occurrence or in some way related to it. The description puts the quality of the occurrence itself directly in the center and stresses that the three other meanings are derived from this basic meaning. The middle voice in Classical Japanese thus combines in itself four different levels of meaning, all of which are interwoven and still obtain today.[22]

The first and oldest meaning of the middle voice is a process that arises and proceeds entirely from itself and, in this sense, naturally. In Japanese, this level of meaning is called *jihatsu* (自発), literally, "to come forth of itself." In this explanation, it is above all the self-referentiality of the occurrence that takes center stage in the description the middle voice, without there being anything said of a subject that is affected in the process. From this meaning of a process that occurs of its own accord is derived the meaning of the passive voice by means of the designation of a participant upon whom the occurrence befalls: *ukemi* (受身). That the passive voice derives from the middle voice was already noted earlier in the general characterization of the middle voice. It is important to note that this is also the case in Japanese, which developed without any relation to Sanskrit or other Indo-European language.

A further meaning that derives from the self-generating process is that of possibility. For as soon as something comes forth and proceeds of its own accord, its full possibility emerges of itself: *kanō* (可能). In this sense, the middle voice designates an occurrence that is accompanied by possibility, such that something in particular is or becomes possible.

The forth meaning of the middle voice is a form of respectfulness: *sonkei* (尊敬). Japanese contains a wide range of forms of polite and respectful speech. The fact that the middle voice came to be tied to respectful speech is probably due to the fact that it stresses the relationality—especially in the sense of reciprocity—of the speakers involved. This is directly connected with the concept of "between-humans" (*kanjin* 間人) or "between-human-ness" (*ningen* 人間).

---

[21] Ikeda 1975, 112.

[22] The *genus verbi* is designated in the Japanese language by means of the verbal suffix. The active form is not formally designated. Designated are the middle voice, which gets diffused into various meanings, and the factitive, which expresses an "instigating" or a "permitting." In Classical Japanese, since the Heian Period, the verbal suffixes for the middle voice are "*ru*" and "*raru*" (the variations of which cannot be treated here). In Modern Japanese, one mostly finds the suffixes "*reru*" and "*rareru*" used.

The four basic meanings of the middle voice in Japanese can be summarized as follows:

1. *jihatsu*, an occurrence that unfolds entirely naturally and of itself.
2. *ukemi*, the construal as passive, when something befalls a given subject in an occurrence.
3. *kanō*, the construal as possibility, when something is or becomes possible by means of the interplay of the occurrence.
4. *sonkei*, the construal as a form of respect.

Since the Meiji period (1868–1912), some Japanese scholars have drawn on the European tradition as well as on their own tradition in order to develop a suitable manner of describing the grammar of the Japanese language. One of the most famous Japanese grammarians is Yamada Yoshio (1875–1958), who has brought the two traditions together in a unique manner. In his Japanese grammar, the middle voice is called *shizensei* (自然勢, which can also be read as *shizen no ikioi*), a locution that means something like "the verve and movement of what is natural," or simply "natural movement." With this description, Yamada connects the middle voice with an ancient basic word of the Sino-Japanese tradition, 自然 (Ch. *ziran*; Jp. *shizen* or *jinen*), a word that played a decisive role already in the earliest stages of Chinese philosophy. At this point, it becomes clear how the explanation of grammatical forms and philosophical thoughts can be brought together in order to indicate new ways of explaining the semantic content of grammatical forms. While, on the one hand, the subject and its being affected stand first and foremost in the center of explanations of the middle voice in the context of the European tradition, on the other hand, self-referentiality in the form of a natural occurrence occupies the center of attention in explanations of the middle voice from within the horizon of the Japanese language. This demonstrates how the middle voice itself is weighed differently in each language depending on language usages and, above all, on the use of the subject (grammatical and logical).

In order to shed further light on the middle voice in Japanese, let us turn to an example from an ancient piece of literature. In the famous *Tsurezuregusa* [Essays in Idleness], written in the fourteenth century, we find the following sentence: *fude wo toreba, mono kakare* (筆を取ればものかかれ). The individual words have the following meanings: *fude* = "brush"; *wo* = an accusative particle; *toreba* = "to grasp" or "to take" in the conditional form; *mono* = "a matter" or "a thing"; *kakare* = "to write" in the grammatical form of the middle voice. No grammatical subject is named in the sentence. The logical subject, insofar as it makes sense to distinguish one at all, is the person holding the brush.

A German Japanologist translates the sentence with obvious reference to the description of the middle voice in Classical Greek: "When I clasp the brush, *I write something down (for myself)*."[23] In this translation, the reflexive relation to the subject of the writing

---

[23] Lewin 1996, 152. [Lewin's German translation reads: "Wenn ich den Pinsel ergreife, *schreibe ich (so für mich) etwas hin.*"—Tr.]

is added in parentheses. Presumably, the translator thought of the direct or indirect middle voice in Classical Greek, in which an activity is related back to an actor or is performed in the interest of the actor. The "I" as subject is inserted into the first clause, and the verb "to write" is also added. The translated sentence sounds rather plain and not particularly interesting as literature.

Another translation gives us the following sentence: "If one grasps the brush, the desire to write sets in."[24] In the first clause, instead of naming an "I" as subject, the indefinite pronoun "one" is placed in the subject position so that the sentence becomes a more general statement. In the second clause, the middle voice is interpreted presumably in the sense of a dynamic middle voice since "desire," which is not mentioned in the Japanese sentence, is supposed to express a particular involvement in the process by the subject. The "matter" or "thing" that is written is left out of the sentence in this translation.

An alternative translation that attempts to do justice to the sense of the middle voice in Classical Japanese might read: "Clasping the brush, the writing of something proceeds of its own accord."[25] The word "*kakare*" designates an attunement of writing in which, without clear intention, something writes itself down, something that afterward may surprise the writer her- or himself. If one takes seriously the description of the middle voice as a spontaneous occurrence, then the naming of a subject should be avoided, and the "of itself" or "of its own accord" (*von selbst*) of the occurrence should be stressed. It is difficult to accomplish both of these things when translating into a European language since, on the one hand, the compulsion to name a subject can hardly be evaded and, on the other hand, the quality of "of its own accord" is not particularly weighted in the intellectual history of the West. In the translation attempted here, because it is not the person writing but rather the writing that becomes the subject, the occurrence of the writing itself can be placed in the foreground.

The middle voice can be found not only in ancient Japanese texts, but also in texts from modern Japanese philosophy, for example in those of Nishitani Keiji (1900–1990). In an essay entitled "On Awareness," Nishitani writes about the process of seeing and hearing in relation to the middle voice:

> In the original place that brings about what is called sensibility, that is to say, in the locale of appearing wherein sensibility in its pure simplicity first originates just as it is, there is no distinction between the "something" that senses and the "something" that is sensed. The activity of seeing is immediately one with the being visible [*mieru to iu koto* 見えるということ] of the thing, and the activity of hearing is immediately one with the being audible [*kikoeru to iu koto* 聞こえるということ] of the sound. When it is said that subject and object are undivided, or that thing and ego

---

[24] Yoshida 1991, 100. [Benl's German translation reads: "Greift man zum Pinsel, stellt sich die Lust zum Schreiben ein."—*Tr.*]

[25] [The author's German translation reads: "Den Pinsel ergreifend stellt sich von selbst das Schreiben von etwas ein."—*Tr.*]

forget one another, this refers to this place. We say, "the sea is visible" or "the bell is audible." In these cases, " ... visible [*ga mieru* が見える]" is something other than either "to see [*wo miru* を見る]" the sea, or the sea "is seen [*ga mirareru* が見られる]." Rather, [it] expresses both sides inseparably as one.[26]

In order to express his thoughts, Nishitani is able to resort directly to the medial forms *mieru* and *kikoeru* without being especially aware that he is thereby resorting to a very ancient grammatical form in the Japanese language, a form that still, even if often remaining unrecognized, centrally informs the speaking and writing of modern Japanese. What is at stake in Nishitani's account is the description of a place in which seer and seen are immersed in a process uninterrupted by a split between subject and object.

THE JAPANESE SCRIPT

In the sixth century BCE, the Chinese script was introduced to Japan and adopted by the Japanese. On account of the difficulty of integrating this script with the Japanese language, several centuries later, two syllabic alphabets were extracted from the Chinese characters so that the Japanese language could be written down without dependence on the Chinese characters. Yet these syllabic alphabets did not, in the end, become established as an independent script; rather, their use was combined in a certain manner with the use of Chinese characters. Today, the Latin alphabet is also at times included, such that in some cases four different scripts can be found in a single Japanese text. Over the course of centuries the Chinese characters have been slightly modified in Japan, but they remain essentially compatible with the characters of ancient China. Yet increasingly fewer characters overall have been used in Japan in comparison with China because, over time, it became less necessary to use Chinese characters for all grammatical purposes in Japanese since this could be accomplished with the new syllabic alphabets. Here are the two syllabic alphabets of Japanese:

---

[26] Nishitani 1987, 106. [The author's German translation reads: "In dem ursprünglichen Ort, der die so genannte Sinnlichkeit hervorbringt bzw. im Ort des Erscheinens, in dem Sinnlichkeit in reiner Einfachheit, so wie sie von sich her ist, anfänglich entsteht, ist kein Unterschied zwischen dem empfindenden ‚Etwas' und dem empfundenen ‚Etwas' enthalten. Die Tätigkeit des Sehens ist mit dem Sichtbarsein (mieru to iu koto) des Dinges und die Tätigkeit des Hörens ist mit dem Hörbarsein (kikoeru to iu koto) des Tones unmittelbar eins. Wenn es früher hieß, Subjekt und Objekt sind ungeschieden oder Dinge und Ich vergessen einander, so verwies das auf diesen Ort. Wir sagen: ‚Das Meer ist sichtbar' oder ‚Die Glocke ist hörbar'. In diesem Falle ist , ... sichtbar' etwas anderes als das Meer ‚sehen' oder das Meer ‚wird gesehen'. Vielmehr drückt [es] beide Seiten ungeschieden ineins aus."—*Tr.*]

Hiragana					Katakana					Phonetic transcription				
あ	い	う	え	お	ア	イ	ウ	エ	ヲ	a	i	u	e	o
か	き	く	け	こ	カ	キ	ク	ケ	コ	ka	ki	ku	ke	ko
さ	し	す	せ	そ	サ	シ	ス	セ	ソ	sa	shi	su	se	so
た	ち	つ	て	と	タ	チ	ツ	テ	ト	ta	chi	tsu	te	to
な	に	ぬ	ね	の	ナ	ニ	ヌ	ネ	ノ	na	ni	nu	ne	no
は	ひ	ふ	へ	ほ	ハ	ヒ	フ	ヘ	ホ	ha	hi	fu	he	ho
ま	み	む	め	も	マ	ミ	ム	メ	モ	ma	mi	mu	me	mo
や		ゆ		よ	ヤ		ユ		ヨ	ya		yu		yo
ら	り	る	れ	ろ	ラ	リ	ル	レ	ロ	ra	ri	ru	re	ro
わ	を	ん			ワ	ヲ	ン			wa	wo	n		

An analysis of the opening sentence of Nishida Kitarō's *Inquiry into the Good* (1911) will, among other things, serve to elucidate the manner in which Chinese characters are combined with a syllabic alphabet in modern Japanese:

経験するといふのは事実其侭に知るの意である 。

keiken suru to iu no wa jijitsu sono mama ni shiru no i de aru.[27]

keiken (経験) consists of two Chinese characters and is used as the translation of the noun "experience."

suru (する) means "to do" and appears here in its "final form," that is, in its undetermined basic form. Since in this case *keiken* is followed by *suru*, the former is made into a verb: "to experience."

to iu (といふ) is an expression that follows verbs or other content words and means "is called," "signifies," or "is designated as."

no (の) can come after verbs, in which case it nominalizes them. Here it is attached to *keiken suru*, such that "to experience" becomes a nominalized verb.

wa (は) is a topic particle, by means of which even a lengthy clause can be made to function equivalent to a subject. In this case, it indicates that "to experience" is the main topic and also subject of the sentence.

jijitsu (事実) consists of two Chinese characters and is the philosophical translation for "reality" or "actuality."

sono mama (其侭) is an idiom that is made up of the Chinese characters meaning "this" and "as it is," and thus it means "such as it is of itself."

ni (に) means, following the previous phrase, "in this manner."

shiru (知る) is the verb "to know" in its final form and so without any further grammatical determinations.

no (の) is in this case a genitive particle, which sets the subsequent word in a genitive relation with the preceding phrase.

i (意) means "meaning," yet could also be translated here as "to mean."

[27] Nishida 1987, 9. [Abe and Ives translate this sentence as: "To experience means to know facts just as they are." (Nishida 1990, 3)—*Tr.*]

de aru (である) is sometimes characterized as the Japanese copula. Yet the original meaning is "being like" or "manner of being."

No person is named in the entire sentence; no temporal tense is directly expressed; and no
distinction is made between singular and plural. Basically, two verbal processes are set in
relation to one another: "To experience means to know what is real as it is of itself [*Erfahren
bedeutet Wirkliches, so wie es von sich her ist, zu wissen*]." This sentence clearly shows how
the verbal dimension determines the main semantic content without there having to be a
person designated along with it. Later, Nishida speaks of how it is not the case that the individual has or performs experiences, but rather the other way around: that the individual
emerges and gets determined out of the process of experiencing.[28] Nishida thus uses the
structural possibilities of the Japanese language in order to express his thoughts. Yet, from
another perspective, it could be said that the Japanese language made available to Nishida
certain ways of thinking, which he then unfolded in the context of that language.

We can discern something very similar going on in Zen master Dōgen's use of language. He denounces Buddhists who don't understand the significance of language
use: "They don't understand that contemplation happens in words and that words
liberatingly pervade contemplation."[29] The philosophical fruitfulness achieved in
Dōgen's use of language will be explained here only in terms of four linguistic and textual strategies. The Chinese and Japanese characters will need to be provided since
without them the movement of the language cannot reveal itself:

1. *In playing with combinations of Chinese characters, time and again Dōgen manages to
   bring an astounding movement into linguistic expression.* Combinations of two, three,
   or four characters are in the process played out in a manner that is not possible in
   any European language. In one passage, after referring to the Chinese phrase 即心
   是佛 (pronounced in Japanese: *soku shin ze butsu*), Dōgen proceeds to formulate the
   following combinations: 心即佛是 *(shin soku butsu ze)*, 佛即是心 *(butsu soku ze
   shin)*, 即心佛是 *(soku shin butsu ze)*, 是佛心即 *(ze butsu shin soku)*. By letting the
   characters occupy different positions in this manner, a semantic shift takes place in
   each new combination. By means of these combinations, the characters achieve a degree of interpenetration that is only possible on the basis of the particular script and
   structure of the Chinese language. In the play of semantic components, the sense is
   made fluid and thereby becomes itself a medium of awakening. The passage just referred to in which this occurs can be translated as follows:

We concretely fathom that "the heart is at once Buddha"; we concretely fathom the
"the heart, which is at once Buddha, is this"; we concretely fathom that "the Buddha is

---

[28] See Nishida 1987, 4; Nishida 1990, xxx.
[29] Ōhashi and Elberfeld 2006, 130. [Ōhashi and Elberfeld's German translation reads: "Sie wissen
nicht, dass Nachdenken in Worten geschieht und Worte das Nachdenken loslösend durchdringt."—Tr.]
Language and speaking are extraordinarily important for the practice of Zen Buddhism. See also
Chapters 9 and 10 in this volume.

at once this heart"; we concretely fathom that "the at once of heart and Buddha is the case"; we concretely fathom that "this Buddha-heart is the at once."[30]

2. *Dōgen achieves semantic reinterpretations by means of syntactically innovative readings of combinations of Chinese characters.* The expression, 此法起時 (Ch. *ci fa qi shi*), which sounds rather simple in Chinese, becomes in Dōgen's hands 此法は起時なり (Jp. *kono hō wa kiji nari*). Whereas the Chinese phrase can be translated, "When these dharmas[31] arise...," Dōgen's iteration can be rendered, "These dharmas are the time of emergence." By means of a slight shift made on the syntactical level of the Japanese language, the innocuous "when" in the Chinese becomes a philosophical thought that explains "time" in association with the emergence of dharmas. This kind of puzzling conjunction of everyday concretion and elevated abstraction is among Dōgen's preferred devises for transporting a linguistic expression onto a plane where the differentiation between concrete and abstract seems to be overcome.

3. *Dōgen constantly employs the polysemic nature of Chinese characters to enhance the expressive power of his writing.* Whereas in European philosophy ambiguity is considered a great impediment to the construction of unambiguous meaning, with Dōgen—just as with various older traditions of Chinese philosophy—ambiguity becomes an element of the dynamic quality of language as such. This is clearly displayed in certain titles of his texts, such as *Kūge* (空華) and *Dōtoku* (道得).

The compound *Kūge* consists of two characters. The former character 空 (*kū*) first of all simply means "sky." Yet it is also the translation of the Sanskrit word, *śūnyatā*, a basic concept of Buddhism that can be translated as "emptiness." According to this thought, which was above all developed by Nāgārjuna in India in the second and third centuries CE, all things are seen through as "empty" in the Buddhist sense. The second character 華 (*ge* or *ka*) means "flower" or "blossom." Hence, with the word *kūge* Dōgen is playing with the meanings "sky" and "emptiness," so that that the word speaks both of "empty blossom" and also of "sky blossom," and thus the concrete image of the openness of the sky converts into "emptiness" in the sense of the Buddhist teaching.

The compound *Dōtoku* also consists of two characters. The first character, pronounced *dō* in Japanese, is the Chinese word *dao* (道), often translated as "way." It can, however, also mean "to say" or "to speak." The second character, *toku* (得), means "to attain" or "to achieve." *Dōtoku* can thus, on the one hand, mean the "attaining of the way" and, on the other hand, can signify the "achieving of speaking." In a very subtle manner Dōgen links the Way of Buddhism together with speaking and language. Between the "attaining of the way" and the "achieving of speaking" lies a difference that resembles a picture puzzle. We see in it one figure without at the same time being

---

[30] This passage can be found in the *Sokushinzebutsu* fascicle of Dōgen's *Shōbōgenzō*. [Ōhashi and Elberfeld's German translation reads: "Wir ergründen konkret, dass ,das Herz zugleich Buddha ist'; wir ergründen konkret, dass ,das Herz, das zugleich Buddha ist, dies ist'; wir ergründen konkret, dass ,der Buddha zugleich dieses Herz ist'; wir ergründen konkret, dass ,das Zugleich von Herz und Buddha zutreffend ist'; wir ergründen konkret, dass ,dieses Buddha-Herz das Zugleich ist'"—*Tr.*]

[31] This is a Buddhist term that simply means "all things and beings."

able to see the other. Only when we leap over to the other figure do we realize that another figure simultaneously abides in the same drawing, and yet we cannot see both at the same time. It is thus above all the *leaping over* and the movement of the picture puzzle that affords it a deep significance. With his puzzling use of language, Dōgen is able to let language—even in its specific expressions—unfold its efficaciousness always only in leaping and moving, such that every substantialization of thoughts and concepts is constantly undercut by means of the pragmatics of language.

4. *Dōgen drives the self-reflexivity of linguistic expressions into a movement that repeatedly leaps out beyond itself.* A passage from the text *Sansuikyō* (山水経) reads:

> There are some who, living in water, catch fish, catch people, and catch ways. . . . Going further, there should be those who catch themselves; there should be those who catch the fishing rod; there should be those who are caught by the fishing rod; there should be those who are caught by the Way.[32]

In this brief passage, the process of "catching" is turned this way and that, such that everything is caught by everything. Sharpening the point, one could say that everything hangs on the "hook" of everything, and, in just this way, movement occurs as the practice of awakening.

In another passage self-reflexivity is driven still further toward the extreme. In the text *Uji* (有時) we read:

> 礙は礙をさへ、礙をみる。礙は礙を礙するなり、これ時なり。
> Obstructing obstructs obstructing and [thereby] sees obstructing. Obstructing obstructs obstructing – this is time.[33]

This passage—which admittedly has been torn out of its context—sets in motion a movement of language and thought that possesses no unambiguous aim, but rather turns back again and again on itself without thereby becoming simply meaningless. With regard to the word "obstructing," it should be recalled that "non-obstructing" (Ch. *wu-ai* 無礙) plays a central role in Huayan Buddhism. "Non-obstructing" means that everything can be just what it is, without being obstructed by something else. In other words, since everything is what it is, it also lets other things be what they are, without obstructing them. In the word "non-obstructing," however, there is also contained an "obstructing," in the sense that each single thing obstructs other things from being it, and it thereby sets itself over against other things. "Obstructing" thus converts into an enabling of concrete movement, which can never be "stated"

---

[32] Ōhashi and Elberfeld 2006, 152. [Ōhashi and Elberfeld's German translation reads: "Es gibt einige, die im Wasser wohnend Fische angeln, Menschen angeln, und Wege angeln. [. . .] Weiter voranschreitend soll es die geben, die sich selbst angeln, soll es die geben, die die Angel angeln, soll es die geben, die von der Angel geangelt werden, soll es die geben, die vom Weg geangelt werden."—*Tr.*]

[33] Ibid., 112. [Ōhashi and Elberfeld's German translation reads: "Verhindern verhindert Verhindern und sieht [dadurch] Verhindern. Verhindern verhindert Verhindern—dies ist Zeit."—*Tr.*]

[*festgestellt*, fixed in place with a static statement] since it only takes place [*zustande kommt*] in the various layers and processes of "obstructing." In this sense, a word also obstructs another word and thereby becomes precisely this word. The other word, for its part, occurs in the same manner, such that negating and positing thoroughly interpenetrate. Adumbrated here is a use of language that does not consist merely in negation and deferral, but rather that always, together with radical negation, at the same time in a positive manner allows full, concrete "singularities" to emerge and at no point to cling to themselves.

The examples given here will have to suffice to suggest a use of language that can be further developed for the sake of philosophizing in a contemporary intercultural context. Especially suggestive is the fact that all of the examples, in their own ways, display a nonsubstantializing pragmatics of language and thus support an interest in further stressing and cultivating a sense of "between-ness" and "movement" in contrast to univocal ascriptions and fixed ascertainments. Analogous to the way in which, starting in the second century BCE, the translation of ancient Greek philosophy into the Latin language brought about many fundamental changes and developments in philosophical thinking, the process of philosophizing in the Chinese and Japanese languages since the end of the nineteenth century has already given rise to philosophical initiatives that have remained largely unnoticed in Europe and North America.

Translated from the German by Bret W. Davis

References

Elberfeld, Rolf. (2004) *Phänomenologie der Zeit im Buddhismus: Methoden interkulturellen Philosophierens*. Stuttgart/Bad Cannstatt: Frommann-Holzboog.

Elberfeld, Rolf. (2013) *Sprache und Sprachen: Eine philosophische Grundorientierung*, second edition. Freiburg: Verlag Karl Alber.

Hartmann, Peter. (1952) *Einige Grundzüge des japanischen Sprachbaus, vorgezeigt an den Ausdrücken für das Sehen*. Heidelberg: Winter Heidelberg.

Ikeda, Tadashi. (1975) *Classical Japanese Grammar Illustrated with Texts*. Tokyo: The Toho Gakkai.

Yoshida Kenkō. (1991) *Betrachtungen aus der Stille*, translated by Oscar Benl. Frankfurt: Insel.

Lewin, Bruno. (1996) *Abriß der japanischen Grammatik auf der Grundlage der klassischen Schriftsprache*. Wiesbaden: Harrassowitz.

Li, Charles N., and Sandra A. Thompson. (1976) "Subject and Topic: A New Topology of Languages." In *Subject and Topic*, edited by Charles N. Li. New York: Academic Press, 457–490.

Nishida Kitarō. (1987) *Zen no kenkyū* [An Inquiry into the Good], *Nishida Kitarō zenshū* [Complete Works of Nishida Kitarō], vol. 1. Tokyo: Iwanami.

Nishida Kitarō. (1990) *An Inquiry into the Good*, translated by Masao Abe and Christopher Ives. New Haven, CT: Yale University Press.

Nishitani Keiji. (1987) "Kaku ni tsuite" [On Awareness]. In *Nishitani Keiji chosakushū* [Collected Works of Nishitani], vol. 13. Tokyo: Sōbunsha, 97–110.

Ōhashi, Ryōsuke, and Rolf Elberfeld, eds. and trans. (2006) *Dōgen: Shōbōgenzō: Ausgewählte Texte: Anders Philosophieren aus dem Zen*. Tokyo/Stuttgart: Keio University Press/ Frommann-Holzboog.

Further Reading

Asari Makoto. (2008) *Nihongo to Nihon-shisō* [The Japanese Language and Japanese Thought]. Tokyo: Fujiwara Shoten.

Elberfeld, Rolf. (2011) "The Middle Voice of Emptiness: Nishida and Nishitani," translated by Jason M. Wirth. In *Japanese and Continental Philosophy: Converstations with the Kyoto School*, edited by Bret W. Davis, Brian Schroeder, and Jason Wirth. Bloomington: Indiana University Press, 269–285.

Fujita Masakatsu. (2011) "Kotoba to shisaku: Nihongo de shisaku suru koto no imi" [Language and Thought: The Significance of Thinking in Japanese]. In *Nishida Kitarō no shisaku sekai* [Nishida Kitarō's World of Thought], by Fujita Masakatsu. Tokyo: Iwanami, 97–120.

Fujita Masakatsu. (2013) "The Significance of Japanese Philosophy," translated by Bret W. Davis, *Journal of Japanese Philosophy* 1: 5–20.

Heine, Steven. (1994) *Dōgen and the Kōan Tradition: A Tale of Two Shōbōgenzō Texts*. Albany: State University of New York Press.

Kim, Hee-Jin. (2007) "The Reason of Words and Letters." In *Dōgen on Meditation and Thinking: A Reflection on His View of Zen*, by Hee-Jin Kim. Albany: State University of New York Press, 59–78.

Marra, Michael F. (2011) *Japan's Frames of Meaning: A Hermeneutics Reader*. Honolulu: University of Hawai'i Press.

Nakamura Yūjirō. (1983) "Basho: 'Mu no ronri'" [Place: "Logic of Nothingness"]. In *Nishida Kitarō*, by Nakamura Yūjirō. Tokyo: Iwanami, 77–111.

Takeuchi Seiichi. (2012) *Yamato kotoba de tetsugaku suru* [Philosophizing in the Indigenous Japanese Language]. Tokyo: Shunjūsha.

Takeuchi Seiichi. (2015) *Yamato kotoba de "Nihon" wo shisō suru* [Thinking "Japan" in the Indigenous Japanese Language]. Tokyo: Shunjūsha.

Ueda Shizuteru. (2008) *Kotoba* [Language]. Tokyo: Iwanami.

Ueda Shizuteru. (2011) "Language in a Twofold World," translated by Bret W. Davis. In *Japanese Philosophy: A Sourcebook*, edited by James W. Heisig, Thomas P. Kasulis, and John C. Maraldo. Honolulu: University of Hawai'i Press, 766–784.

CHAPTER 33

....

NATURAL FREEDOM

Human/Nature Nondualism in Zen
and Japanese Thought

....

BRET W. DAVIS

Follow the creative transformations of nature; return to the creative transformations of nature!

—Bashō (1644–1694)

If one has engaged in this practice for a long period of time, no matter in which direction one lets the mind go, it moves in a state of freedom.

—Takuan Sōhō (1574–1645)

"How should one live?"[1]
"One should live freely and naturally."

An intuitively compelling response. And yet, can one have it both ways? Can one be both free and natural?

In fact, strong currents in the Western tradition tell us no. According to long-standing metaphysical dualisms, just as the mind or soul is distinct from the body, freedom is of an essentially different order than nature. While transcendently oriented religion tells us that we must free our supernatural souls from their embodiment in nature or, as Plato suggests, their entombment or imprisonment in the body,[2] modern (or, at least,

---

[1] An earlier and much shorter version of this chapter appeared as "Natural Freedom: Human/Nature Non-Dualism in Japanese Thought," in *The Oxford Handbook of World Philosophy*, edited by Jay Garfield and William Edelglass (New York: Oxford University Press, 2011), 334–347.

[2] For the idea of *soma-sema* (body as tomb), see Plato's *Gorgias* 493a, *Cratylus* 400c, *Phaedo* 62b, and *Phaedrus* 250c.

Newtonian) science tells us that nature is governed by deterministic laws that would seem to be the very antithesis of freedom as autonomy or self-determination.

To be sure, quantum physics now suggests that the material world consists, not of atomistic particles interacting like billiard balls according to deterministic laws of causality, but rather of nondeterministic actualizations that take place within a thoroughly interrelational field of potentiality.[3] Yet, if we understand the indeterminacy of quantum events merely in terms of "randomness" and "chance," all we have done is swap determinism for arbitrariness, and the latter is hardly less antithetical to our sense of freedom than is (absolute or probabilistic) determinism. In any case, should we even be looking to physics for an understanding of psychological, social, and spiritual freedom? Moreover, is "nature" in the highest and broadest sense reducible to the phenomena objectified and explained by our modern natural sciences?[4]

In his *Freedom* essay of 1809, Schelling complained that "the whole of modern European philosophy since its inception (through Descartes) has this common deficiency—that nature does not exist for it and that it lacks a living basis."[5] In other words, the modern objectification of nature by the scientific worldview renders us incapable of appreciating nature as the "living ground" in which our freedom is rooted. Despite the efforts of Schelling and others, however, the apparent gap between human

---

[3] The parallels between the interconnected event ontology of quantum physics, on the one hand, and Asian philosophies such as Buddhism and Daoism, on the other, have often been noted, especially since the publication of Fritjof Capra, *The Tao of Physics: An Exploration of the Parallels between Modern Physics and Eastern Mysticism*, fourth edition (Boston: Shambhala, 2000, first published in 1975).

[4] In *Quantum Questions: Mystical Writings of the World's Greatest Physicists* (Boston: Shambhala, 2001), Ken Wilber collects works by Heisenberg, Schroedinger, Einstein, and other foundational physicists of the twentieth century, seeking to demonstrate that they all "rejected the notion that physics proves or even supports mysticism, and *yet every one of them was an avowed mystic*" who thought that reality cannot be reduced to the objective phenomena studied by physics (ix). Wilber himself argues for a "nested" relation between ascending levels of physics, biology, psychology, theology, and mysticism, where each higher level transcends and includes the levels beneath it (12–17).

[5] Schelling 1936, 30. This is not the place to comment extensively on Schelling's exceptional treatise. Yet since in certain respects it provides one of the nearest Western approximations to the understanding of the relation between freedom and nature (and the divine) we find prevalent in Japanese thought, let me sketch some of its key points. Schelling inherits the pantheistic legacy of Spinoza's identification of God and Nature (*deus sive natura*), but claims that Spinoza falls into deterministic fatalism because he fails to understand that God is a *life* rather than a system ordered by invariable rational laws (22, 78). Schelling understands nature as the *basis* or *ground* for God's existence, a ground that is in God but is not yet God himself in his existence (*Existenz*) (31–33). Like all things, humans have their ground in nature which is in God (33). God is not an eternal unchanging entity but rather a life, and a life as such entails growth and suffering (84). Specifically, God becomes God by way of revealing himself through the travails of human freedom (19–20). Hence, human freedom is rooted in divine freedom, even though they differ insofar as evil is a real option for the latter (26, 39, 41–42). Schelling places "man and his freedom in the divine being, by saying that man exists not outside God but in God, and that man's activity itself belongs to God's life" (11). Although Schelling's dogged struggle with the problem of theodicy betrays his indebtedness to a theological tradition that is quite foreign to Japan, the notion that nature is not a creation separate from a transcendent creator, and especially the notion that human freedom is rooted in nature, bring Schelling into proximity to the Japanese ways of thinking we will be pursuing in this chapter.

freedom and the processes of nature has continued to divide us, cloaked only by our increasingly tenuous efforts to technologically impose our will on nature.[6]

Where does this leave us? For those of us who can neither swallow the metaphysical dogma that would separate our souls from the natural world nor bite the bullet of either determinism or randomness and renounce our longing for—and inner sense of—freedom, the question is: Can we find a path that leads beyond these apparent conflicts between freedom and nature? One thing seems clear: if there is such a path of reconciliation, it would entail along the way a radical rethinking of the very concepts of "nature" and "freedom."

What I mean to demonstrate in this essay is that Zen Buddhism and related strands of Japanese thought have much to contribute to precisely such a rethinking of nature and freedom, a rethinking which sees them as nondually interrelated in their origins and as ultimately reconcilable through practice. I will draw on a number of traditional (pre-Meiji) and modern (post-Meiji) texts and teachings, mainly those of Zen, but, in addition, some from Shintō, Shin Buddhism, Japanese Confucian thought, and the "ways" (dō 道) of Japanese poetry and other Japanese cultural and martial arts, as well as a number of Japan's modern philosophies that bring these East Asian traditions into dialogue with Western thought. My intent here is not to treat the full breadth of Zen thought or to fully address its relation to other sometimes complementary and sometimes competing strands of Japanese thought.[7] Rather, in conversation with Western thinkers and their concerns, I aim to plumb various traditional and modern Japanese sources for the sake of recognizing and realizing the possibility of a *natural freedom*.

---

[6] Along with "the denaturing effects released through a technology" that is "governed by the politics of unlimited production and consumption," John Sallis has decried the "capitalist rhetoric" that coopts a genuine search for ways of "returning to nature" with its "cynical course of invoking nature in order to stave off the public reaction against the total industrialization of the things of everyday life" (Sallis 2016a, 8). What is truly needed, he goes on to write, is a rethinking of nature that proceeds both by "retrieving antecedent senses and determinations of nature—as, for example, among the Greeks—and also thinking the sense of nature anew in a way that takes account of such distinctively modern developments as—to give a prime example—those of recent astronomy, which now reveal the expanse of the cosmos on a scale far exceeding any that could previously have been envisioned and which cannot but bring about a transformation of our conception of the place of the human" (8). Sallis's work is exemplary in his rethinking of the sense of nature (*phusis*) in Greek philosophy and also in his call for a "cosmological turn" that would take into account developments in contemporary astronomy. More recently, he has also assisted in opening doorways to dialogue with East Asian traditions of philosophy and art; see *Cao Jun: Hymns to Nature*, edited by John Sallis (Boston: McMullen Museum of Art, 2018).

[7] It is beyond the scope of this chapter to discuss the parallels, influences, and differences between Japanese and Chinese (especially Daoist and Chan) conceptions of the intimacy of freedom and nature. It is also not the specific intent of this chapter to examine variations within Japanese thought; the intent here is rather to explicate and reflect on a more or less shared sense of "natural freedom" that pervades much of this tradition. Nevertheless, it should be mentioned that, just as the Daoists who pleaded for a return to naturalness had their critics in the Legalists and some Confucians (notably Xunzi and Hanzi) who stressed an artificial reshaping of human nature, the prominent theme of recovering natural freedom was not always universally accepted in Japan. We shall see how, in the Edo or Tokugawa period (1603–1868), Confucian thinkers such as Ogyū Sorai stressed the need for human "invention" (*sakui* 作為) rather than emulation of the principles of nature.

REDISCOVERING THE INTIMACY
OF FREEDOM AND NATURE

The modern Japanese philosopher Kuki Shūzō (1888–1941) wrote the following succinct and striking account of the fundamental differences between typically Western and typically Japanese conceptions of the relation between freedom and nature.

> In the Japanese ideal of morality, "nature" in the sense of what is "so of itself" [*onozukara na shizen* 自ずからな自然] has great significance . . . . If one does not reach the point of naturalness [*jinen* 自然], then morality is not seen as completed. This is quite distinct from the West. Indeed, in Western conceptual configurations nature is often thought in opposition to freedom. By contrast, in Japanese practical experience there is a tendency for nature and freedom to be understood as fused together and identified. Freedom is something that naturally springs forth of itself. Freedom is not born as the result of a strained self-assertiveness. When the heart/mind of heaven and earth naturally comes forth of itself just as it is, that is freedom.[8]

According to traditional Japanese thought, then, freedom is not something gained by separating ourselves from nature, but rather is itself an expression of naturalness. It is not a freedom from nature, but rather a freedom in nature, a freedom of naturalness or a natural freedom.

This intimacy between freedom and nature is in fact reflected in the very language used to speak of "nature" and "freedom" in Japan. The *ji* of *jiyū* 自由 ("freedom" or, more literally, "arising-from-oneself") or of *jizai* 自在 ("freedom" or, more literally, "abiding-of-oneself") is written with the same character as the *shi* of *shizen* 自然 ("nature" or, more literally, "what-is-just-so-of-itself"). The compound 自然 can also be read as *jinen* ("naturalness" or, more literally, "being-just-so-of-itself"). Moreover, the same character 自 (*shi* or *ji*)—a prefix meaning "self-" or "auto-" and originally a preposition meaning "from"—is also used, with only a slight variation in its phonetic extension, to write both *onozukara* 自ずから and *mizukara* 自ら. *Onozukara* is used as a noun or as an adjective signifying what is—or that something is—originally "so-of-itself," or as an adverb signifying that something occurs naturally "of-itself." *Mizukara*, on the other hand, can be used as a first-person pronoun or as a noun meaning "oneself," and it is often used as an adverb signifying that something is done "of-oneself," "by-oneself," or "from-oneself." The root meaning of "self" can also be found in these expressions in the *ono* 己, which refers generally to the self (*onore* 己 or *jiko* 自己), and in the *mi* 身, which refers more specifically to the "personal embodied self" (as in *mibun* 身分 or *jibunjishin* 自分自身).

---

[8] Kuki 1980, 3: 276; see also Kuki 1980, 2: 102. Unless otherwise noted, translations from Japanese sources are my own. On Kuki's thought, see Chapter 24 in this volume.

Mizukara and *onozukara* are indigenous Japanese expressions that are sometimes written entirely in phonetic script (*hiragana*); more often, however, they are written in part with the *kanji* or ideogram adopted from China: 自. "That the Japanese believe they can express these seemingly autonomous terms by means of a single character," write Hubert Tellenbach and Kimura Bin, "points toward a deeper insight by which they apprehended *Onozukara* and *Mizukara, nature* and *self,* as originating from the same common ground."[9] As we shall see, what is striking in Japanese thought is precisely the *nonduality* between the personal initiative implied in the expression *mizukara* and the impersonal naturalness implied in the expression *onozukara.* In other words, the freedom (*jiyū* 自由) of the self (*jiko* 自己) is thought to accord with—rather than to stand in opposition to—the naturalness (*jinen* 自然) of nature (*shizen* 自然). Only by way of finding one's place of participation in what is naturally "so-of-itself" (*onozukara* 自ずから) can one recover the authentic ability to be freely "of-oneself" and to act freely "from-oneself" (*mizukara* 自ら). In taking part in nature, one is naturally free.

As with the Western terms "freedom" and "liberty," Japanese words such as *jiyū* and *jizai* also imply, at least to begin with, a *freedom from* constraints. However, a liberation merely from external restrictions can all too easily give way to an arbitrariness and even egoistic wantonness. In fact, the Japanese linguist Yanabu Akira informs us that, prior to its adoption as a translation for the Western terms "freedom" and "liberty," the primary everyday connotation of the term *jiyū* in Japanese in the nineteenth century was that of selfish egoism (*wagamama katte* 我まま勝手).[10] This negative connotation of *jiyū*, Yanabu argues, gave rise to misunderstandings when *jiyū* was used to translate the positive Western notions of freedom and liberty, as can be seen in debates that took place in late nineteenth century Japan between conservative critics and liberal proponents of the newly imported idea of the civil right to individual liberty. However, Yanabu also notes as an exception to the popular negative sense of *jiyū* the positive use of this term by Zen monks, who linked it with the idea of spiritual liberation (*gedatsu* 解脱); he also notes how this positive Zen sense of *jiyū* had long been used to translate the freedom spoken of in Christian texts.[11]

Given his familiarity with the variety of connotations borne by these terms in both English and Japanese, it is thus not surprising that the cross-cultural Zen thinker D. T. Suzuki (Jp. Suzuki Daisetsu, 1870–1966) takes pains to draw a sharp distinction between a true sense of "freedom" (*jiyū*) on the one hand and mere "licentiousness" (*hōitsu* 放逸) on the other. Indeed, he claims that these are opposites, insofar as the latter involves a lack of self-control that leads to a slavery to the passions.[12] It is worth noting that Suzuki criticizes in this context the "Beat Generation" of the 1950s—many of whom ironically claimed to be inspired by Suzuki's own writings on Zen—for failing to make this crucial

---

[9] Tellenbach and Kimura 1989, 154–155.
[10] Yanabu 1982a, 178. The entry for *jiyū* in *Kōjien* (Tokyo: Iwanami, 1991) traces this meaning back to a fourth century Chinese text.
[11] Yanabu 1982a, 179.
[12] Suzuki 1997, 68.

distinction between genuine freedom and merely following one's whims. In a well-known essay from the period, Alan Watts pointed out that many proponents of what he calls "Beat Zen" were wont to self-consciously flaunt their antinomianism. Watts contrasts the licentious rebelliousness of Beat Zen with the all too formalized and institutionalized practice of "Square Zen." The freedom of true Zen may be approached by either path, he admits, but to reach it one has to go beyond all self-defensive attempts to justify oneself, either by way of following or rebelling against the rules of the establishment.[13] To be sure, following the prescriptions of ritualistic discipline is certainly prevalent in the institutionalized practice of Zen, but it is not the ultimate point of the practice, which is the realization of wisdom, compassion, and natural freedom.[14]

Nietzsche writes of three stages of the "transformations of the spirit"—from the "camel" who obediently takes on the burdens and the disciplines of a tradition, to the

---

[13]   Alan Watts, "Beat Zen, Square Zen, and Zen," *Chicago Review* 42.n3 (Summer–Fall 1996): 48–55, reprinted in http://www.thezensite.com/ZenEssays/Miscellaneous/Beat_Zen_Square_Zen.html (accessed Feb. 2, 2018). Watts is careful to distinguish between authors such as Jack Kerouac and Gary Snyder. After all, the latter, in contrast to the former, was and still is a serious student and practitioner of Zen as well as an original poet and writer (see Wirth 2017). In the same essay, Watts writes: "To the Westerner in search of the reintegration of man and nature there is an appeal far beyond the merely sentimental in the naturalism of Zen." He thus indicates how Zen seems to answer a question and a quest that Westerners were already struggling with. Coming from Japan and meeting Westerners halfway, D. T. Suzuki borrows heavily, as David McMahan demonstrates (McMahan 2008), from such Western currents of thought as German Idealism, German and English Romanticism, and American Transcendentalism in his presentation and interpretation of the Zen view of "nature" (Suzuki 2015; see also Suzuki 1959). In contrast to the tendency in the West to dichotomize humans and nature, to set humans over nature as something to be conquered and transcended, Suzuki writes that "Man is, after all, part of Nature itself. . . . Man must be after all an insider . . . . Man cannot be outside of Nature, he still has his being rooted in Nature . . . . Nature is the bosom whence we come and whither we go" (Suzuki 2015, 116, 119, 134). While critical of Suzuki's assertions of cultural superiority and his downplaying of his Western sources, McMahan, unlike many contemporary critics of Suzuki, acknowledges the productive manner in which Suzuki borrowed from currents of Western thought so as to reinterpret selective elements of the Zen tradition in a manner that allows them to "address some of the dominant concerns of modernity" (McMahan 2008, 128). The present chapter might be viewed as contributing to a similar kind of project. Yet I am attempting to do this transparently, with reference to the Western as well as East Asian sources that inform my interpretive stance and without falling into the traps of overgeneralizing, essentializing, or ethnocentric privileging. On the problem of ethnocentric nationalism in "theories of Japanese-ness" (*Nihonjin-ron* 日本人論), see the Introduction and Chapter 36 in this volume.

[14]   This does not mean that practice ends when this freedom in attained. On the contrary, Dōgen's teaching of the "oneness of practice and enlightenment" (*shushō ittō* 修証一等) entails that true freedom is realized as true practice (Dōgen 1990, 1: 28; Dōgen 2002, 19). To be sure, practitioners of Sōtō Zen are susceptible to falling into a rigidly formalistic "Square Zen" insofar as they obediently follow the letter rather than the spirit of Dōgen's teaching that "Dignified decorum is the Buddha Dharma, formal etiquette is the essential teaching" (*igi soku buppō, sahō kore shūshi* 威儀即仏法、作法是宗旨). Nishitani acknowledges that the Rinzai tradition has also tended to fall into a formalistic "mannerism" (Nishitani 1986–1995, 19: 110–3). On the other hand, and despite his critique of the "Beat Zen" which his own works, along with those of D. T. Suzuki, ironically helped inspire, Alan Watt's interpretation of Zen questionably sidelines the roles that ritual, doctrinal worldview, and communal regulations play in Zen as it is practiced in Japan and elsewhere in East Asia, and, like Suzuki, does not always duly recognize and critically reflect on the Western sources and presuppositions that, to a significant degree, shape his own interpretive approach to Zen.

"lion" who rebelliously says "No!" and thereby gains a negative freedom from externally imposed decrees, and finally to the "child" who, free from rebellion as well as from subservience, is positively free for new creations.[15] Similarly, Zen and the Japanese "ways" of the cultural and martial arts speak of the three stages of "preserving" (shu 守), "breaking with" (ha 破), and finally "departing from" (ri 離) the inherited forms of a tradition.[16] The freedom that enables a genuine creativity is found on the other side of both the discipline of letting go of the ego in order to learn from a tradition and the still dependent because egoistically oppositional rebellion of breaking with a tradition.[17]

The realization of true freedom, according to Zen, requires more than just surpassing one's teacher or innovatively reforming an old or originating a new tradition. It requires more than just a "gymnastics of the will" which defiantly asserts that whatever does not kill one makes one stronger.[18] It requires a more radical self-overcoming that entails passing through not only a discipline of self-mastery, but ultimately through an existential "great death" (daishi 大死) of the ego as the internal source of bondage. As a classic Zen formulation puts it: "First of all—the great death; after cutting off completely—once again coming back to life."[19] Suzuki refers in this regard to both the Biblical notion of dying to oneself so as to be reborn in Christ (Mathew 10:39, 16:24–25; Mark 8:34–35), as well as to a famous saying by the seventeenth-century Japanese Zen master Shidō Munan (or Bunan): "Become a dead person while alive; die completely; then do what you will [omou ga mama ni suru 思ふがままにする]; all your acts are then good."[20]

Unlike humans, inanimate things and non-human animals have no need for such an existential death and rebirth since they are all along not alienated from their own specific forms of natural freedom. Suzuki writes: "The pine tree is not the bamboo, and the bamboo is not the pine tree; each dwells in its own place, and this is the freedom of the pine tree and the bamboo."[21] To call this "necessity" rather than "freedom," he remarks, is to take an outsider's perspective. For the pine tree to be a pine tree is the expression of its specific kind of natural freedom, not the result of a denial of its desire to be something else. Natural necessity, experienced from within, is natural freedom. The Zen philosopher Nishitani Keiji (1900–1990) also suggests a kind of compatiblism between natural freedom and natural necessity when he writes: "when someone tosses a crust of bread and a dog leaps up in the air to catch it, every 'thing' involved ... [is] subject to certain

---

[15] Friedrich Nietzsche, Thus Spoke Zarathustra, trans. Graham Parkes (New York: Oxford University Press, 2005), 23–24. Regarding Nietzsche's proximity to and distance from Zen, see Davis 2004a as well as Graham Parkes's critique of this essay and my response in Journal of Nietzsche Studies 46/1 (2015): 42–88.

[16] See Fujiwara Ryōzō, Shu ha ri no shisō [The Thought of Shu Ha Ri] (Tokyo: Bēsubōru-magajinsha, 1993).

[17] On the cultivation of what I am calling natural freedom in the traditional Japanese artistic and martial "ways," see Chapters 14 and 34 in this volume, and Carter 2008.

[18] See Davis 2004a, 120–121.

[19] Kusumoto Bunyū, Zengonyūmon [Introduction to Zen terms] (Tokyo: Daihōrinkaku, 1982), 104.

[20] Suzuki 1997, 68; Shidō Munan Zenji shū [The collected writings of Zen Master Shidō Munan], edited by Kōda Rentarō (Tokyo: Shunshūsha, 1968), 31.

[21] Suzuki 1997, 67.

physico-chemical laws . . . . [And yet,] the dog and the man *live* the laws of nature . . . . [Moreover,] their activities in some sense also imply an *appropriation* of the laws of nature."[22] Suzuki writes that "Zen would say that Nature's necessity and Man's freedom are not such divergent ideas as we might imagine but that necessity is freedom and freedom is necessity."[23] Indeed, in an autobiographical essay Suzuki relates that his initial experience of enlightenment (*kenshō* 見性) remained opaque until sometime afterward when "suddenly the Zen phrase *hiji soto ni magarazu*, 'the elbow does not bend outward,' became clear to me." While the inability of the elbow to bend outward "might seem like a kind of necessity," he writes, "suddenly I saw that this restriction was really freedom, the true freedom, and I felt that the whole question of free will had been solved for me."[24]

In fact, as we shall see, in the Japanese tradition, human freedom is thought to be compatible not only with the lawful regularity, but also with the radical indeterminacy and contingency of nature's unfathomable ways. In this crucial respect, the "compatibilism" at issue here differs from the versions of compatibilism in recent Western philosophical discourse that mainly seek to reconcile freedom with deterministic causality.[25]

In any case, the nondualistic compatibilism at issue in the Japanese sense of natural freedom we are discussing is not something that is simply given or guaranteed. Paradoxically, our most natural way of being is something that must be attained; our most proper way of being must be appropriated. Humans, and apparently humans alone, are capable not only of naturalness but also of "falsity," that is, of a distorted and distorting view of their own place in the world and the range of possibilities open to this place. We are not supernatural creatures, and yet we purport to be. To be sure, we humans are not pine trees; we have certain unique abilities and responsibilities for cooperatively shaping our environment. But it is a hubristic falsification for us to think of ourselves as supernatural masters of the natural world. Neither genuine human freedom nor an intimate understanding of nature is gained by artificially forcing nature to divulge its secrets and serve our purposes, as suggested by the scientific method proposed by Francis Bacon in the sixteenth century and followed by much of Western civilization

---

[22] Nishitani 1986–1995, 10:89–90; Nishitani 1982, 79–80. On Nishitani's thought, see Chapter 21 in this volume.

[23] Suzuki 2015, 135.

[24] D. T. Suzuki, "Early Memories," in *Selected Works of D. T. Suzuki, volume 1, Zen*, edited by Richard M. Jaffe (Oakland: University of California Press, 2015), 210. Suzuki apparently inherits the view of his teacher, Zen master Shaku Soen, who wrote (in lectures translated and edited by Suzuki) that just as the Christian God should be understood to be "perfectly free in following the laws of nature," insofar as He is their maker, "I see, then, no obstacles, no hampering, no discordant jarring in my following the laws of my being." Soyen Shaku, *Zen for Americans*, trans. D. T. Suzuki (La Salle: Open Court, 1974 [original edition 1906], 100.

[25] See McKenna, Michael, and Coates, D. Justin, "Compatibilism," *The Stanford Encyclopedia of Philosophy* (Summer 2015 Edition), Edward N. Zalta (ed.), http://plato.stanford.edu/archives/sum2015/entries/compatibilism/. The question of the compatibility of free will with determinism dominates contemporary debates on the topic of freedom in analytic philosophy. See Fischer, Kane, Pereboom, and Vargas 2007.

ever since.[26] Insofar as we, too, have our own specific freedom within nature, not outside or opposed to it, the attainment of freedom happens not in a transcendence of, but rather in a return to nature.

Artistic Participation in the Creativity of Nature

When the Japanese poet Matsuo Bashō (1644–1694) says to "follow the creative transformations of nature (*zōka* 造化); return to the creative transformations of nature,"[27] he is telling his fellow poets to reattune themselves to nature understood as "the spontaneous process of creation and transformation, of which all things, including human beings, are an integral part."[28]

However, this is not a rejection of culture, much less a return to animality. Bashō stresses that the part human beings are meant to play in the natural ways of the world includes learning to see and poetically depict the astonishing beauty and truth in everything, such that one sees the "flower" and the "moon"—epitomes of beauty in Japanese poetry—in the most mundane and even morose phenomena. For example, upon spending an unpleasant night in a rural dwelling on one of his travels, Bashō composed the following haiku:

> fleas, lice
>   a horse peeing
>   by my pillow[29]

Cultivating the quintessentially human ability for poetic appreciation and expression of all facets of life experience, according to Bashō, demands "going beyond the barbarians and departing from animals."[30] He is thus adamantly *not* counseling a return to nature or animality in the sense of a rejection of culture and humanity. Barbarians, who do not rise above the level of animals, are not properly cultured. Bashō is in effect suggesting that it is not human culture as such, but rather a lack of the right kind of culture that alienates humans from nature. As is the case with most forms of traditional Japanese art, Bashō's poetry is a specifically human way of regaining and *cultivating* an original intimacy with the beauty of nature as a process of creative transformations. A negative

---

[26] See Francis Bacon, *The New Organon*, ed. Lisa Jardine and Michael Silverthorne (Cambridge: Cambridge University Press, 2000); Hadot 2006, 93–4; and Oelschlaeger 1991, 80–85.

[27] Matsuo 1962–1969, 6: 75.

[28] Qiu 2005, 129. The term *zōka* (pronounced *zaohua* in Chinese) can be traced back to chapter six of the *Zhuangzi*.

[29] *nomi shirami* 蚤虱 / *uma no shitosuru* 馬の尿する / *makura moto* 枕もと. Matsuo 2004, 94.

[30] Matsuo 1962–1969, 6: 75.

freedom from remaining immersed in animality or barbarity is necessary in order to actualize one's *natural* human capacities, that is to say, in order to *cultivate* the positive *freedom for* participation in the creativity of nature.

Bashō translator and scholar David Landis Barnhill insightfully comments on the predominant East Asian view of nature in contrast to the predominant Western views. He writes that "the West has been informed by two major notions of nature": on the one hand a "dualistic" view according to which "nature and the natural refer to whatever humans have not manipulated, controlled, or despoiled" and, on the other hand, the "comprehensive" view of the natural sciences according to which everything, without exception, obeys "the laws of nature." "The dominant East Asian view of nature," Barnhill contends, "tends to be different than either of these."

> What is natural is what exist according to its true nature. It is an "adverbial" sense of natural, since it refers to a way of being. Humans are fully part of nature: *essentially* we are natural. However, we have the distinctive ability to act contrary to our nature: *existentially* we usually live unnaturally. We do this by acting on a [deluded] sense of the personal ego and its desires and will. One of the primary religious goals in East Asia is to act according to one's nature, which (paradoxically to us) requires spiritual cultivation and discipline. In this view, we have neither a separation of humans from nature as in the dualistic view, nor the view that everything humans do is natural as in the comprehensive view of nature.[31]

Barnhill goes on to say that great artists, according to the East Asian view, "create out of their deepest nature, in concert with the creativity of nature itself." "The greatest poet, then, is not only the most cultured but also the most natural, because to be fully cultured is to follow the processes of nature."[32]

Although Barnhill insightfully contrast this East Asian view with the dominant dualistic and scientific views of the West, there is yet another long-standing tradition in the West that is much more consonant with the East Asian nondualistic understanding of the relation between art and nature. Pierre Hadot calls this the "Orphic attitude," which he contrasts with the "Promethean attitude." Hadot sums up the differences between these two attitudes toward nature in the following passage:

> If man feels nature to be an enemy, hostile and jealous, which resists him by hiding its secrets, there will then be opposition between nature and human art, based on human reason and will. Man will seek, through technology, to affirm his power, domination, and rights over nature . . . . If, on the contrary, people consider themselves a part of nature because art is already present in it, then there will no longer be opposition between nature and art; instead, human art, especially in its aesthetic aspect, will be in a sense the prolongation of nature, and then there will no longer be any relation of dominance between nature and mankind. The occultation of nature

[31] David Landis Barnhill, translator's introduction to Matsuo 2005, 7.
[32] Barnhill in Matsuo 2005, 8.

will be perceived not as a resistance that must be conquered but as a mystery into which human beings can be gradually initiated.[33]

If the former (Promethean) attitude provides us with a stark contrast to the predominant traditional Japanese attitude toward nature, the latter (Orphic) attitude presents us with the closest Western approximation to it. While the Promethean attitude dominates much of the Western tradition, especially in the modern scientific and technological worldview heralded by Bacon and Descartes, the Orphic attitude has been a significant counterpoint throughout the history of the Western tradition, as seen in such philosophers as Rousseau,[34] Schelling,[35] Nietzsche,[36] Emerson,[37] Heidegger,[38] and Merleau-Ponty,[39] and in such poets and artists as Goethe, Wordsworth, Albert Bierstadt, and Cezanne.

Hadot's remarkable treatment of the changing and competing conceptions of nature in the Western tradition needs to be supplemented, as he acknowledges, by ecofeminist treatments of the topic, such as Carolyn Merchant's *The Death of Nature: Women,*

---

[33] Hadot 2006, 92. Hadot calls the latter attitude "Orphic" on account of the theogonic poems and the seductive power of music ascribed to Orpheus (96), yet this designation strikes me as infelicitous given that the idea of a supernatural soul entombed in the natural body (*soma-sema*) is also of Orphic origin.

[34] Rousseau can be said to have inaugurated the Romantic tradition of returning to nature as "the universal being that embraces all things," inner as well as outer, for the source of morality, freedom, and creativity. See Hadot 2006, 86–87, 263–264; and David L. McMahan *The Making of Buddhist Modernism* (New York: Oxford University Press, 2008), 79–80.

[35] For a contemporary pursuit of Schelling's project of rethinking the human–nature relation, see Jason M. Wirth, *Schelling's Practice of the Wild* (Albany: State University of New York, 2015).

[36] See Graham Parkes, "Human/Nature in Nietzsche and Taoism," in Callicott and Ames 1989, 79–97.

[37] Ralf Waldo Emerson, *Nature*, in *Essays and Lectures* (New York: The Library of America, 1983), 1–230. For an insightful interpretation of Emerson's conceptions of nature in relation to those of German Idealism, see Sallis 2016a, chapter 1.

[38] For Heidegger's retrieval of the Greek notion of *phusis*, which the Romans translated as *natura*, see Martin Heidegger, *Introduction to Metaphysics*, 2nd ed., trans. Gregory Fried and Richard Polt (New Haven: Yale University Press, 2014), 15–20. He writes that the Greeks understood *phusis* as first of all "what emerges from itself (for example, the emergence, the blossoming, of a rose), the unfolding that opens itself up, the coming-into-appearance in such unfolding, and holding itself and persisting in appearance—in short, the emerging-abiding-sway" (15–16). Before becoming restricted to a designation of a specific realm of entities—natural as opposed to divine or human beings—"*phusis* originally means both heaven and earth, both the stone and the plant, both the animal and the human, and human history as the work of humans and gods; and finally and first of all, it means the gods who themselves stand under destiny" (16). For Heidegger, *phusis* is one of the primary Greek words for being (*Sein*) rather than a delimited realm of beings (*Seienden*). However, in *Introduction to Metaphysics*, Heidegger thinks of the relation of human being to *phusis* or being in confrontational and even violent terms—the human must willfully bring to a stand the onslaught of *phusis* lest he be overwhelmed by it—whereas he later thinks in more pastoral terms of dwelling within the clearings afforded by the healing "forest" of the open-region of being. See Davis 2014a.

[39] See Ted Toadvine, *Merleau-Ponty's Philosophy of Nature* (Evanston, IL: Northwestern University Press, 2009).

[40] See Hadot 2006, x; and Carolyn Merchant, *The Death of Nature: Women, Ecology, and the Scientific Revolution*, reprint edition (New York: Harper & Row, 1980). In Chapter 23 of the present volume, Erin McCarthy brings Watsuji into dialogue with the ecofeminist philosopher Valerie Plumwood.

tradition of thinking about nature in the United States that runs from Emerson and Thoreau to John Muir, Aldo Leopold, and the Zen poet Gary Snyder; nor does he discuss either Whitehead's process philosophy or the Deep Ecology movement.[41] Thankfully, other scholars have recently been bringing such Western figures and schools of environmental philosophy into fruitful conversation with traditional and modern Japanese thinkers such as Saigyō, Kūkai, Dōgen, Watsuji Tetsurō, and Imanishi Kinji.[42]

Although Hadot endeavors to give a fair treatment of both Promethean and Orphic attitudes toward nature in the Western tradition, in the concluding paragraph of his book he confesses to having been seduced by two themes, both of which resonate deeply with the Japanese conception of the relation between humans and nature that we are discussing: "An idea: nature is art and art is nature, human art being only a special case of the art of nature." And "an experience that consists in becoming intensely aware of the fact that we are a part of nature, and that in this sense we ourselves are this infinite, ineffable nature that completely surrounds us."[43] He closes with a quote from Hölderlin and another from Nietzsche, each of which expresses such an experience of unity with nature. Earlier in the book, he cites artists, among them Paul Klee, who speaks of "terrestrial rootedness" and "cosmic participation."[44] Such a painter, Hadot says, "may paint in a state in which he feels his deep unity with the earth and the universe." The point is not to unlock the secrets of nature from without, but rather "to undergo an experience of identification with the creative movement of forms, or with *phusis* in the original sense of the word."[45]

Experiences such as this, Hadot admits, "are perhaps not very frequent in a pictorial context [in the West]. They appear [only] at specific periods in the West, for instance, in the Romantic period or at the end of the nineteenth century"—"or, by contrast," he adds, "in a traditional way in the East." Hadot then ventures a brief excursion into some discourses on Chinese and Japanese art. The eleventh-century Chinese literati Su Zhe, he notes, "speaks of an artist who, while painting a stalk of bamboo, loses consciousness of himself and abandons his own body. He himself becomes bamboo."[46] We may add that, six centuries later, the Japanese poet Bashō echoes this artistic practice of empathetic identification with natural phenomena when he writes:

---

[41] For some incisive and insightful reflections on nature and the contemporary ecological crisis in light of the Zen writings of Gary Snyder and Dōgen, see Wirth 2017. On the Deep Ecology movement, see Sessions 1995. With respect to many of these figures and movements, Hadot 2006 is well supplemented by Oelschlaeger 1991. For an anthropological critique of the concepts of "wilderness" and "nature" as Western constructs set in dualistic opposition to civilization or culture, an opposition not found in most other traditions around the world, see Descola 2012.

[42] See Callicott and McRae 2017; section three of Callicott and McRae 2014; and Imanishi 2002.

[43] Hadot 2006, 319.

[44] Hadot 2006, 225.

[45] Hadot 2006, 225–226.

[46] Hadot 2006, 226.

From the pine tree
learn of the pine tree,
And from the bamboo
of the bamboo[47]

According to Bashō's disciple Dohō, "learn" here means that the poet must "detach the mind from his own self" in order "to enter into the object, perceive its delicate life, and feel its feeling, whereupon a poem forms itself."[48] Bashō praises in this way a naturally "grown" poem as superior to an artificially "made" poem.

Vincent van Gogh was among those Western artists at the end of nineteenth century who were deeply inspired by their exposure to Japanese art. In a letter to his brother Theo, he wrote:

> If one studies the Japanese painters, then one sees a man indisputably wise, philo-
> sophical, and intelligent, who spends his time doing what? Studying the distance
> from the earth to the moon? No. Studying Bismarck's politics? No, he studies a single
> blade of grass. Yet this blade of grass leads him to draw all plants, then the seasons,
> the great aspects of landscapes, finally animals, then the human figure . . . . Let us
> see: is it not almost a real religion that we are taught by these oh-so-simple Japanese,
> who live within nature as if they themselves were flowers?[49]

In fact, as we have seen, for Japanese artists and poets such as Bashō, it is by "returning to the creative transformations of nature" that one first learns to truly live, among the flowers and fleas, as a fully cultivated and naturally free human being.

FREEDOM: NEGATIVE AND POSITIVE, SUPERNATURAL AND NATURAL

We have come to see how, in Japan, art and culture are not typically seen as essentially opposed to nature and naturalness. It is not surprising, then, that the modern Zen phi-losopher Hisamatsu Shin'ichi (1889–1980) lists "naturalness" (*jinen*) as one of the distinctive characteristics of the aesthetics of Zen art and culture. Like Bashō, moreover, Hisamatsu is careful to distinguish this naturalness from mere unrefined "naïveté or in-stinct." The artistic naturalness at issue here is "never forced or strained," and yet that does not mean that it simply occurs in nature without human intention or effort. "On

---

[47] *Matsu no koto wa matsu ni narae, take no koto wa take ni narae* 松のことは松に習へ 、 竹のことは竹に習へ. See Nishitani 1982, 195.

[48] As quoted in Makoto Ueda, "Bashō on the Art of the Haiku: Impersonality in Poetry," in *Japanese Aesthetics and Culture: A Reader*, ed. Nancy G. Hume (Albany: State University of New York Press, 1995), 161.

[49] Quoted in Hadot 2006, 228.

the contrary," writes Hisamatsu, "it is the result of a full, creative intent that is devoid of anything artificial or strained—[it is the outcome] of an intention so pure and so concentrated ... that nothing is forced." It "results when the artist enters so thoroughly into what he is creating that no conscious effort, no distance between the two, remains." It is a naturalness that lies on the thither, rather than the hither, side of arduous efforts of cultivation and training. Hence, Hisamatsu concludes that it "is not found either in natural objects or in children. True naturalness is the 'no mind' or 'no intent' that emerges from the negation both of naïve or accidental naturalness and ordinary intention."[50] Culture allows us to actualize our humanity, and cultivation requires refraining from acting according to the arbitrary beck and call of every impulse and desire. And yet, the process of culturation and humanization is not simply a departure from nature; it is rather the development of a specifically human participation in nature. This requires a double negation: first a negation of uncultivated nature and, second, a negation of cultivated artificiality. Becoming naturally free requires in this sense both a surmounting of and a return to nature—a circuitous path proper to human nature.

While Suzuki somewhat polemically claims that the (modern liberal) West has failed to think beyond a negative sense of freedom or liberty, in fact there have long been debates in Western philosophy surrounding what political theorist Isaiah Berlin has referred to as "two concepts of liberty,"[51] namely, a "negative freedom" from constraints and a "positive freedom" for self-actualization. Moreover, it is not the case that negative freedom has only been thought in the sense of freedom from *external* constraints. According to Kant, for example, morality demands a freedom from *internal* compulsions (sensuous or natural "inclinations"), a negative freedom which in turn enables a positive freedom, namely, the "autonomy" of giving the super-sensuous or super-natural law of practical reason to oneself.[52]

Nevertheless, while Kant thinks of autonomy dualistically as requiring a super-sensuous will free from natural inclinations, Suzuki thinks in nondualistic terms of an autonomous naturalness. Suzuki defines freedom as "the activity that naturally

---

[50] Hisamatsu 1971, 32–33.

[51] See Isaiah Berlin, "Two Concepts of Liberty," in *Four Essays on Liberty* (London: Oxford University Press, 1969). Berlin argues for a pluralistic society in which individuals are at liberty to choose their own ends, that is to say, a society in which individuals are "negatively free" from external constraints so that they can choose and pursue their own positive values and visions of the good life. He claims that the notion of "positive freedom" in the political sphere has been responsible for inspiring totalitarian ideologies that end up denying such individual freedom. Although the essays in Suzuki 1997 are from the 1950s and 60s, Berlin would presumably be suspicious of the prewar and wartime political context in which Suzuki formulated some of his ideas. Suzuki, for his part, is more interested in psychological and spiritual freedom, and he would presumably include Berlin among the Western thinkers who pay insufficient attention to the internal constraints on freedom that are left unaddressed by the external liberties afforded by liberal democracies.

[52] See Immanuel Kant, *Foundations of the Metaphysics of Morals*, 2nd ed., trans. Lewis White Beck (New York: Macmillan, 1990), 70 [452]. When Kant uses the term "nature" in the "widest sense" to mean "the existence of things under laws," he opposes the intelligible world of "supersensuous nature" to the empirical world of "sensuous nature." He claims that these worlds, or views of the world, are strictly distinct and yet somehow coexist in a manner incomprehensible to us. See Immanuel Kant, *Critique of Practical Reason*, trans. Lewis White Beck (New York: Macmillan, 1956), 44 [43], 102–103 [99–100].

comes forth as it is—without any direction from another and without restriction—from the principle of nature."[53] Far from seeing autonomy as an independence from nature, he stresses the linguistic as well as semantic intimacy between freedom or "arising-from-oneself" (*jiyū* 自由), autonomy in the sense of acting on one's own accord or "from-oneself" (*mizukara* 自ら), and naturalness as a spontaneous activity that happens "of-itself" (*onozukara* 自ら).[54] On the one hand, then, Suzuki would agree with Kant that positive freedom requires a negative freedom, not just from external constraints, but also from internal compulsions. On the other hand, however, he would disagree with the idea that autonomy is gained by means of a super-natural freedom from and rational control of *all* natural inclinations. Autonomy is not gained by means of a complete independence from the supposed heteronomy of nature, but rather by means of harmonizing oneself with the truly natural Way that is the very source of the self. Freedom is realized not by way of a dualistic disengagement from nature, but rather by way of a nondualistic engagement in nature.

In an early work, Nishitani articulates a dialectical path that leads through a disengagement from egoistic self-will (what we might call our inauthentic, alienated, and alienating self-nature) to a recovery of genuine naturalness (our authentic self-nature).[55] He acknowledges Kantian rational autonomy as a significant step on a way which ultimately, however, should lead back to a realization of the nonduality of our authentic self with a radical naturalness. In his later attempts to think this human/nature nonduality, according to which the self freely participates in nature, Nishitani increasingly turns his attention to the tradition of Zen Buddhism. He quotes, for instance, the following passages from Zen master Musō Kokushi (1275–1351):

> Hills and rivers, the earth, plants and trees, tiles and stones, all of these are the self's own original part.... Out of the realm of the original part have arisen all things: from the wisdom of Buddhas and saints to the body-and-mind of every sentient being, and all lands and worlds.[56]

When the self awakens to its own "original part," the core and source of its being, it realizes its participation in the dynamically interconnected whole of nature.

---

[53] Suzuki 1997, 65.

[54] Suzuki 1997, 65. Note that Suzuki writes here *mizukara* and *onozukara* exactly the same, distinguishing them only by appended phonetic script (*furigana*).

[55] See Nishitani 1986–1995, 1: 85–90.

[56] Nishitani 1986–1995, 10: 121; Nishitani 1982, 108.

THE INDIGENOUS WAY OF THE GODS (*SHINTŌ*) AND THE CONFUCIAN WAY OF HEAVEN (*TENDŌ*)

The Zen understanding of the intimate relation between self and nature took root in Japan alongside the indigenous beliefs and practices that came to be called Shintō or the "Way of the Gods" (神道). A contemporary head priest and scholar of this tradition, Yamakage Motohisa, stresses that "we are part of nature, rather than above or beyond it," and so we should strive "to live within nature rather than attempting to dominate or destroy it." In Shintō, he goes on to say, "heaven, earth, and humanity are different manifestations of one life energy."[57] According to the tradition of Yamakage Shintō that he represents, "our universe (or the big circle of the universe) is a current of whirling spirits springing out of *daigenrei* [大源霊] (great original spirit). In this spiritual current individuals with their own identity are generated, like sparks of energy, which are also manifested as a vortex."[58] And so, "in their innermost essence, human beings, animals, plants, and all natural matter are the offspring of the great original spirit Kami of the universe."[59]

Robert Carter writes that "Shintō is about directly experiencing one's kinship with the world around one" by means of "purifying oneself in order to experience once more the divinity of one's own inner depths."[60] While Shintō teaches the inherent goodness of nature and thus of human nature, life is a constant process of improvement via purification, such that one's spirit returns to its originary source by way of becoming ever more "clean, bright, right, and straight" (*seimei seishoku* 清明正直). Yamakage writes that "human error and uncleanliness are considered coterminous," that "error and fault are mistakes committed by immature souls,"[61] and that "the basic religious idea of Shintō is the continuous process of creation."[62] In the same vein, Carter suggests that while, according to Shintō, "human beings (and in Shintō, Nature itself) are basically good," the divine spirit of which they are manifestations "encounters obstacles due to lack of experience and these obstacles we call 'evil.'"[63] Evil is thus a problem of alienation and imperfection, but, in contrast to Abrahamic monotheism, for Shintō the problem is that of the self-alienation of the ever evolving spirit of nature itself, which is still in the process

---

[57] Yamakage 2006, 14, 16.

[58] Yamakage 2006, 141.

[59] Yamakage 2006, 27.

[60] Carter 2001, 39.

[61] Yamakage 2006, 123.

[62] Yamakage 2006, 126.

[63] Carter 2001, 39, 43. In the latter passage Carter is quoting J. W. T. Mason, *The Meaning of Shintō: The Primaeval Foundation of Creative Spirit in Modern Japan* (Port Washington, NY: Kennikat Press, 1967), 117.

of learning through experience how to manifest its originary purity. And we humans, in our departures and returns to naturalness, are part of this learning process.[64]

In early modern times, that is to say, during the Edo or Tokugawa period (1603–1867), Neo-Confucianism and then the school of Ancient Learning (*Kogaku* 古学)—which called for a return to the ancient Confucian sages and their teachings—gained philosophical preeminence in Japan.[65] Although their main focus is on ethical and political matters, these Confucian schools of thought also bring with them an understanding of nature in terms of "Heaven" (*ten* 天) or the "Way of Heaven" (*tendō* 天道) as well as teachings regarding how humans are to live in accord with this way. Intellectual historian Sagara Tōru (1921–2000) elucidates the continuities between Japanese Confucian conceptions of the proper human relation to the Way of Heaven and the indigenous Japanese conceptions of the relation between *mizukara* and *onozukara* that, he claims, had already decisively influenced Japanese Shintō and Buddhist thought.[66] To begin with, he notes the tendency already present among Neo-Confucian thinkers such as Hayashi Razan (1583–1657) to reject the canonical twelfth-century Neo-Confucian Zhu Xi's metaphysical elevation of the "Principle of Heaven" (Ch. *tianli*; Jp. *tenri* 天理) over the "psycho-physical energy" (Ch. *qi*; Jp. *ki* 気) that constitutes the natural world.[67] Whereas Zhu Xi may have at least equivocated on this point, his Japanese followers insisted that the governing principles of the cosmos were to be found only immanently pervading the cosmos itself.[68]

The question, then, becomes how to bring the self into accord with this immanent Way of Heaven. Sagara shows how two lines of thought diverge in response to this question, both of which start with rejecting the intellectualist approach that attempts to rationally fathom the principles of Heaven. The first line, taken by Satō Issai (1772–1859), is the more traditional Japanese approach of "negating the ego and its desires" (*mushi muyoku* 無私無欲) so as to "naturally accord with the Way of Heaven" (*onozukara tendō ni kanau* おのずから天道にかなう) and thus to "recover the Unity of Human and Heaven" (*ten-jin ittai no kaifuku* 天人一体の回復).[69] One can find an early twentieth-century iteration of this approach in Natsume Sōseki's notion of "adhering to Heaven,

---

[64] On Shintō, see Chapter 2 in this volume.

[65] See Chapters 12 and 13 in this volume.

[66] Sagara 1989, 56–59, 102, 226.

[67] Although Zhu Xi's view of "principle" (*li* 理) as having priority and in some sense being prior to the "vital force" (*qi* 氣) that constitutes the material universe goes further in the direction of metaphysical transcendence than most Chinese schools of thought, in fact he, too, says that "principle is not a separate entity. It exists right in material force [*qi*]" (*A Sourcebook in Chinese Philosophy*, trans. Wing-Tsit Chan [Princeton, NJ: Princeton University Press, 1963], 634). While Maruyama Masao compares Zhu Xi's thought to the natural law theory of medieval European society, he acknowledges that "in Chu Hsi [Zhu Xi] philosophy, any concept of a personal god outside and transcending even the all-embracing world known as heaven and earth is totally lacking. In this sense its organic mode of thought, essentially an immanentism, is more thoroughgoing than that of scholasticism" (Maruyama 1974, 231).

[68] Sagara 1989, 104–107. According to Tu Wei-Ming, such an immanent "continuity of being" also characterizes the predominant Chinese view of nature; see Tu 1989.

[69] Sagara 1989, 109, 112.

removing the ego" (*sokuten-kyoshi* 則天去私).[70] The second approach is the novel one taken by the scholars of Ancient Learning led by Itō Jinsai (1627–1705) and Ogyū Sorai (1666–1728). Rather than an ascetic practice of negating the ego, they stressed the need for study (*gakumon* 学問); namely, study of the teachings of the ancient Chinese sages, since purportedly only they have authoritatively discerned the principles of Heaven.

Political theorist and intellectual historian Maruyama Masao (1914–1996) has traced the manner in which Sorai and subsequent Ancient Learning scholars asserted the priority of human "making" or "invention" (*sakui* 作為) over "nature" (*shizen* 自然) in the human affairs of ethics and politics. Specifically, Sorai was critical of the "Natural Way of Heaven and Earth" (*ten-chi shizen no michi* 天地自然の道) to which Neo-Confucian scholars, especially those of the prevailing Zhu Xi school, appealed in justifying the Confucian social order and, by extension, that of the feudal regime of the Tokugawa Bakufu. For example, whereas Razan had explained the proper relations between ruler and subject, father and son, and husband and wife in terms of the relation between *yang* (Jp. *yō* 陽) and *yin* (Jp. *in* 陰), Sorai "firmly rejected the practice of importing into the social system the concepts of yin and yang, which are categories of the natural world."[71] Sorai insists that the Way (*michi* or *dō* 道) human beings are to follow is not "the Natural Way of Heaven and Earth" but rather "a way that was founded by *the Sages*" whose teachings form the basis of the Confucian tradition.[72] Sorai's intent was to argue "that the Tokugawa founder, Ieyasu, had been entrusted with the basic task of establishing institutions [*seido* 制度] in accordance with the Way of the Sages."[73] Yet, according to Maruyama, despite this conservative attempt to restore the stability of the feudal social order, Sorai inadvertently opened the door to the "modernization" of Japan into a *Gesellschaft* based on human agency rather than obedience to the "natural law" dictated by the Way of Heaven.[74] All that remained was to claim that not only the ancient sages, and not only the contemporary rulers, but *all* humans have the power and the right to establish the order of society, and the way is prepared for Meiji Enlightenment thinkers and proponents of Westernization such as Fukuzawa Yukichi (1835–1901) and Ueki Emori (1857–1892) to assert, in the words of the latter: "When heaven created man, it made everybody equal under heaven . . . . That is why all men have equal rights."[75]

At this point, however, Maruyama makes a crucial point which calls for further consideration. He notes that:

> the theoretical basis for this doctrine of liberty and popular rights is the natural law of the Enlightenment. Since the latter taught that the rights of men are natural rights, it would seem superficially that we should classify it as a theory of natural order. But

[70] See Ueda Shizuteru, "Sōseki and Buddhism: Reflections on His Later Works," *Eastern Buddhist* 29/2 (1996): 172–206.

[71] Maruyama 1974, 196, 208.

[72] Maruyama 1974, 207.

[73] Maruyama 1974, 218–9.

[74] Maruyama 1974, 222, 239, 242–3, 275.

[75] Quoted from Ueki's *Minken inaka-uta* in Maruyama 1974, 313.

a more careful examination shows directly that the opposite is true. The "rights of man" in question are not rights embedded in any actually existing social order. On the contrary, they are concrete embodiments of the autonomy of man, who can establish a positive social order. Thus the theory's insistence on the a priori character of natural law necessarily implies the view that any positive law derives its validity from its original establishment by man.[76]

The line of thought that Maruyama does *not* pursue is that, just as universal natural human rights need to be distinguished from the specific positive rights conferred on citizens by a government (where, in the case of a democracy, the latter derive their authority from the former), we need to distinguish between a sense of nature as governed by static laws or principles, which humans are to either emulate or distinguish themselves from, and nature as a wellspring of creativity and freedom. Maruyama tends to understand "nature" in the first of these senses, and specifically in the sense of the "Natural Way of Heaven and Earth" that the Tokugawa Neo-Confucians relied on in their justifications of the social hierarchies of the feudal regime that needed to be overcome for Japan to eventually become a modern democracy. In so doing, he presents us with a limited choice between a feudal ideology based on a supposedly natural order and democracy based on the overcoming of nature by invention. Yet, must we choose between naturalness on the one hand and creativity and agency on the other? Might there be a third way that would allow us to recover a source of natural freedom without succumbing to an ideology of natural servitude?

Although Maruyama's specialty is the political thought of the Tokugawa and Meiji periods, in an influential essay he argues that the most "ancient layer" of Japanese historical consciousness—discernable already in the opening lines of the earliest texts of the Japanese tradition, the Shintō classics *Kojiki* and *Nihon shoki*, and continuing to implicitly determine Japanese thought to the present day as a kind of *basso ostinato*—is expressed in the phrase *tsugi-tsugi ni nari-yuku ikioi* (つぎつぎになりゆくいきほひ), which can be translated as "impulse of continual becoming" or as "energetic movement forward from one moment to the next."[77] Linking this baseline of Japanese thought and experience to that of *onozukara* (naturalness), Maruyama endeavors to show how this Japanese sense of the natural flow of existence colored the reception of Confucian concepts. He claims that, unlike the Chinese concept of "nature" (Ch. *ziran* 自然), and also unlike the Western concept of "nature," *onozukara* does not have the secondary sense of "essence," and thus does not point beyond the immanent flux of becoming to a transcendent order.[78] Moreover, Maruyama cites a Tokugawa period text that contrasts the "natural impulses" (*shizen no sei* 自然の勢) of mercurial human emotions to Zhu Xi's conception of the abiding "Principles of Heaven and Earth Nature" (*tenchi shizen no ri* 天地自然の理).[79] Yet, while in this case his critique is aimed not at

---

[76] Maruyama 1974, 313.

[77] Maruyama 1992, 334.

[78] Maruyama 1992, 339. Also see Sagara 1989, 40–41, 104.

[79] Maruyama 1992, 336.

early Tokugawa period Neo-Confucianism and its philosophy of an unchanging natural order but rather at the legacy of Shintō's root conception of natural organic growth,[80] once again Maruyama's intent is apparently to demonstrate and lament the lack of a "modern" historical consciousness and political philosophy based on human initiative and agency (a historical consciousness and political philosophy epitomized by the Western Enlightenment and its Meiji importers and successors) that looks constructively toward the future rather than abandoning oneself—with a sigh of Buddhist resignation or Shintō enjoyment—to the natural processes occurring in the present.

Given his admirable liberal political agenda in postwar Japan,[81] Maruyama's textual foci and interpretive lens are certainly understandable. And yet today one must ask: Can one adequately treat the topic of naturalness (*onozukara*) in Japanese intellectual history without paying serious attention to Zen Buddhist thinkers such as Dōgen (1200–1253) and the Pure Land Buddhist Shinran (1173–1263)? Moreover, can one treat *onozukara* (of-itself) without giving due attention to its at once contrasting and complementary concept of *mizukara* (from-oneself)?

Sagara disagrees with Maruyama's assertion that Ogyū Sorai breaks with the Japanese tradition of attempting to reconcile the tension between *onozukara* and *mizukara*. While he agrees that Jinsai and especially Sorai increasingly stress human agency and innovation, he points out that this human activity is still thought of in terms of participatory assistance (*san-san* 参賛) of—rather than in terms of acting outside, much less against—the Natural Way of Heaven. The innovations of the ancient sages, after all, were meant to properly respond to the Way of Heaven. Innovation is, as it were, the natural way of being human. In short, Sagara finds still at work in the otherwise innovative thinking of these Ancient Learning scholars "the traditional [Japanese] thought of living out the natural of-itself (*onozukara*) in a manner that is properly from-oneself (*mizukara*)."[82]

NATURE AS A WAY OF NATURALNESS

Pursuing the question of freedom has taken us back once again to the question of nature. The contemporary Japanese psychoanalyst Kimura Bin (b. 1931) draws a broad distinction between, on the one hand, a conception of nature that sets it in opposition to human culture and, on the other, a conception of nature that sees it as "pertaining to the

[80] Maruyama 1992, 309.

[81] Maruyama 1992, 35–51. On the postwar context of Maruyama's intense concern with human agency (*shutaisei* 主体性), see Chapter 28 in this volume.

[82] Sagara 1989, 56–58, 119–123. This traditional connection and tension between *onozukara* and *mizukara* persists, Sagara goes on to argue, even in thinkers such as Ueki Emori (1857–1892) who, at the end of the Tokugawa period and beginning of the Meiji period, and under the influence of Western liberal thought, attempt to reject the transcendence and authority of Heaven by way of identifying themselves with Heaven (137–140).

innermost psychic reality" of human beings. The former conception, Kimura contends, prevails in the Western tradition, whereas the latter is typified in the traditional Japanese understanding of nature.[83] Suzuki also claims that "Western 'nature' is dualistic and is set over against 'the human,'" while "Eastern '*shizen*' includes 'the human.'"[84] Even while there are resonances between the ancient Greek sense of *phusis* as "what emerges from itself" and the Japanese notions of *shizen/jinen* and *onozukara*, the Greeks did often set *technē* (art/craft) and *nomos* (convention) over against *phusis* (nature) in a way that the Japanese did not set human action over against natural processes (at least not until the Tokugawa period); and the strict dualistic distinction between the natural body (*soma*) and the supernatural soul (*psuchē*) that gets repeated in one form or another from Plato's *Phaedo* through medieval Christian theology to Descartes is foreign to the main streams of Japanese thought. Of course, as we have seen, countercurrents to such dualisms can be found throughout the Western tradition, beginning with the Presocratic natural philosophers (*phusikoi*) and extending to many contemporary philosophers of nature.[85] But it is true that, in Japan, a radical human/nature nondualism has always been the main current of thinking. As Yanabu writes, the traditional Japanese notion of "nature" (*shizen*) signifies a world which either precedes the subject–object split or which entails the unification of subject and object.[86]

What, then, is this "nature" in which humans nondually participate? Today, *shizen* is used as a translation of the Western term "nature."[87] In premodern (that is, pre-Westernized) Japan, however, "nature" as the amalgamation of all natural things was referred to with such expressions as "mountains-rivers-grasses-trees" (*sansensōmoku* 山川草木) and "the interwoven variety [literally the 'forest web'] of the myriad phenomena" (*shinrabanshō* 森羅万象). On the other hand, "nature" as the ordered whole of the cosmos, or as a dynamic cosmological principle of transformation, was expressed

---

[83] Kimura 1988, 4.

[84] Suzuki 1997, 220.

[85] On the Presocratics and for a rethinking of *phusis* in Plato's thought, see Sallis 2016b. For Whitehead's critique of the "bifurcation of nature" into subjective and objective domains, see Alfred North Whitehead, *The Concept of Nature* (Cambridge: Cambridge University Press, 1920). With reference to Whitehead and pursuing James Lovelock's "Gaia theory," sociologist of science Bruno Latour criticizes the "unwarranted generalization that gave rise to the strange opinion that has made it possible to deanimate one sector of the world, deemed objective and inert, and to overanimate another sector, deemed to be subjective, conscious, and free" (*Facing Gaia: Eight Lectures on the New Climate Regime*, trans. Catherine Porter [Cambridge: Polity, 2017], 85). A host of recent philosophers have embarked on rethinking the human–nature relation under the banners of "speculative realism" or "transcendental materialism." See Peter Gratton, *Speculative Realism: Problems and Prospects* (New York: Bloomsbury, 2014).

[86] Yanabu 1982b, 133.

[87] Note, however, that *shizen* only translates "nature" in the sense of the natural world; it does not translate "nature" in the sense of "essence," which is translated as *honshitsu* (本質) or *honsei* (本性, also read as *honshō*), meaning the root quality that is native to something. The Western equivocation regarding the meaning of "nature" is arguably rooted in the Greek tendency to think of the *kosmos* as an ordered whole whose principles can be rationally fathomed. In effect, nature is thought to consist of beings whose essences can be discerned by the intellect.

with such ancient Chinese terms as "Heaven and Earth" (Ch. *tiandi*; Jp. *tenchi* 天地), the Way (Ch. *dao*; Jp. *dō* or *michi* 道), and, as we have seen, "creative transformation" (Ch. *zaohua*; Jp. *zōka* 造化). Nature in the Japanese tradition is thus an inherently dynamic and creative whole unto itself. It is not the product of a transcendent Creator; indeed, even the Shintō gods are said to have emerged from mysterious yet natural processes.[88]

In many respects, this Japanese sense of "nature" does resemble a Greek sense of *kosmos*: that is to say, a self-contained world that includes the gods as well as all animate and inanimate beings and in which humans are to find their proper place. But the Japanese did not attempt to develop a "cosmology" in the sense of a thoroughly logical account (*logos*) of a thoroughly rationally ordered world (*kosmos*). While nature is not thought of as simply chaotic—that is, while there are indeed principles or, more literally, "patterns" (*ri* or *kotowari* 理) that permeate the phenomenal flux—the rhyme and reason of nature's Way ultimately exceeds human calculation and intellectual reasoning. Nevertheless, while the principles of this fluid Way cannot be fixed in place by the objectifying intellect, they can be existentially realized by means of a holistically engaged praxis that includes, but is not limited to and ultimately goes beyond or beneath, discursive reasoning.

In the Japanese tradition, nature is thus not so much an object of study as it is a way of life. The Japanese were concerned less with "nature" as the object of a theory of being, and more with "naturalness" as a principle of becoming and as a practical way of living. In fact, as we have seen, the Japanese word that is used today to translate the Western concept of "nature"—自然 read as *shizen*—was originally used as an adjective (natural) or as an adverb (naturally) rather than as a substantive (nature).[89] Rather than a noun indicating an essence or a realm of entities (as when Westerners speak of the "nature" of a thing or of the things that belong to "nature" rather than culture or human artifice), 自然 was originally used as an adjective or adverb expressing the natural occurrence of a process. Naturalness—自然 read still today as *jinen*—is an adverb describing the authentic way in which things, animals, and, ideally, people exist. The human task is therefore not to learn to completely predict and externally control nature by fathoming its fixed rational laws, but rather to bring oneself into accordance with the fluid principle of its Way.

A Way Beyond Both Licentious Naturalism and Dualistic Supernaturalism

As we have seen, in traditional Japanese thought, freedom is not found in a victorious or tragic struggle against nature, but rather in the naturalness of a harmonious participation

---

[88] See Sagara 1989, 43–44, 58; Sagara 1995, 148–149; and Maruyama 1992.
[89] Sagara 1989, 33; Yanabu 1882b, 134.

in nature. But this free participation in nature is not in fact a given; the source of natural freedom must be recovered. And the path back to the radical wellspring of naturalness must avoid the pitfall of a superficial "naturalism." At the same time, Japanese thinkers attempted to avoid this pitfall without diverting the path away from a nondualistic this-worldly naturalness toward a dualistic otherworldly supernaturalism.

An affirmation of the soteriological efficacy of nature is a recurrent theme in Japanese Buddhism as well as in indigenous Shintō thought.[90] The Buddha Way is thought not to lead to a transcendence of nature, but rather to entail a return to naturalness; and natural phenomena themselves help teach us this Way. Dōgen claims that "grass and trees" are the Buddha-nature[91] and that "the present mountains and waters are actualizations of the Way of the ancient Buddhas."[92] "The sutras," he says, "are the entire universe, mountains and rivers and the great earth, plants and trees," and we are counseled to listen to "the voices and figures of streams and the sounds and shapes of mountains" as they "bounteously deliver eighty-four-thousand gāthās [verses]."[93]

And yet, Dōgen was also keenly aware that the then prevalent doctrine of the "original enlightenment" (hongaku 本覚) of all beings can easily mislead one to embrace a superficial "naturalism" that permits a wanton indifference to practice.[94] In this regard, he cites his teacher Rujin's warning: "If one says all sentient beings are from the first Buddhas, that would fall under the teaching of the non-Buddhist school of Naturalism [jinen gedō 自然外道]."[95]

That a genuinely radical naturalness is not to be confused with the egoistic abandon of so-called naturalism is also clearly apparent in Shinran's ideal of "dharmic naturalness" (jinen-hōni 自然法爾). For Shinran, such genuine naturalness is achieved precisely by disposing of all egoistic workings of "self-power" (jiriki 自力) and opening oneself to the "other-power" (tariki 他力) of Amida Buddha's grace. According to the Tannishō, Shinran taught:

> If the entrusting heart [shinjin 信心] is established, birth [in the Pure Land] will be brought about by Amida's design, so there must be no calculating on our part . . . . Our not calculating is called naturalness [jinen 自然]. It is itself other-power.[96]

---

[90] See Lafleur 1989.

[91] Dōgen 1990, 1: 106; Dōgen 2002, 85.

[92] Dōgen 1990, 2: 184; Dōgen 2007b, 217, translation modified.

[93] Quoted from the "Jishō zammai" and "Keiseisanshoku" fascicles of the Shōbōgenzō in Hee-Jin Kim, Dōgen Kigen: Mystical Realist (Tucson: University of Arizona Press, rev. ed., 1987), 97, 256.

[94] According to Takeuchi Seiichi, the "naturalism" (shizenshugi 自然主義) of the "I novels" of early twentieth-century Japanese literature also fell into an analogous pitfall. See Takeuchi 2004, 11–13, 20–21.

[95] "Dōgen's Hōkyō-ki (1)," trans. Norman Waddell, The Eastern Buddhist New Series 10/2 (October 1977): 121. On Dōgen's thought, see Chapters 8 and 9 in this volume.

[96] Shinran 1997, 1: 676, translation modified. On Shinran and his legacy, see Chapters 6 and 7 in this volume.

To Western ears, this may initially sound like a familiar sacrifice of naturalistic egoism for the sake of supernatural fideism; in other words, a giving up of self-will for the sake of faithful obedience to the "higher power" of God's Will. As with the *Gelassenheit* of Christian mystics, the naturalness spoken of here would be a matter of "Let not my will but Thy Will be done."[97] However, in a letter written at the end of his life, Shinran went so far as to suggest that the personified transcendence of Amida is ultimately to be understood as an "expedient means" for returning to a natural spontaneity and effortless compassion. In that letter Shinran writes:

> The Supreme Buddha is formless, and being formless, is called *jinen* [自然, naturalness]. When this Buddha is shown as having form, it is not called the Supreme Nirvāna [i.e., the Supreme Buddha]. In order to make us realize that true Buddha is formless, it is expressly called Amida Buddha; so I have been taught. Amida Buddha is the medium through which we are made to realize *jinen* [naturalness].[98]

Would not, in the end, this dharmic naturalness lie radically beyond the very duality of self-power and other-power that purportedly separates the paths of Zen and Shinran's Shin Buddhism?[99]

Nishida Kitarō (1870–1945), who not only intensely practiced Zen but who also was deeply sympathetic to the teachings of Shin Buddhism, writes that "in dharmic naturalness, we see God in a place where God is not,"[100] and he explicitly suggests that dharmic naturalness must be understood neither in terms of the egoistic arbitrariness of an immanent naturalism nor in terms of a deferential obedience to a supernatural being.

> Something such as what Shinran calls dharmic naturalness is not what is thought of as natural [*shizen*] in Western thought. It is not a matter of behaving arbitrarily and just following one's impulses. It is not a matter of so-called "naturalism" [*shizenshugi* 自然主義]. Dharmic naturalness must involve exhaustively exerting the self in the face of things. It must include infinite effort, and must not merely be a matter of going with the flow. And yet, it should be recognized that one's efforts are themselves not one's own. There is something which of itself naturally allows things to happen [*onozukara shikarashimeru mono* 自ら然らしめるもの] . . . . [This] must not be [thought of as] something that moves the self either from the outside or from the inside, but rather [as] something that envelopes the self.[101]

True naturalness is not gained by simply passively submitting oneself to the Will of a transcendent being outside the self, any more than it can be gained by simply acting on the

---

[97] On the question of whether this conception suffices for an understanding of the *Gelassenheit* of Meister Eckhart, who coined the term, see Davis 2007*a*, chapter 5.

[98] Shinran 1997, 1: 530, translation modified. See also Sagara 1995, 136–7; and Unno 2002.

[99] See Davis 2014*b*.

[100] Nishida 1987–1989, 11: 462.

[101] Nishida 1987–1989, 12: 369.

willfulness found immanent in the surface layers of the self. Rather, according to Nishida, the true individual discovers him- or herself to be "enveloped" by the "place of absolute nothingness"; and, realizing oneself as a "focal point" of the self-determination of this dynamic place, one truly becomes what one is, "a creative element in a creative world."[102]

THE DYNAMIC OF HUMAN/NATURE NONDUALITY: EXISTENCE AND RETURN

Nondualism is sometimes taken to be synonymous with distinctionless monism. However, while this may apply to the Parmenidean One or the Nirguna Brahman of the Advaita Vedānta school of Hindu philosophy, in East Asian thought, and in Zen Buddhism in particular, nonduality (*funi* 不二) tends to be thought rather in terms of "neither one nor two" (*fuichi-funi* 不一不二). As seen in the passage quoted earlier, Nishida was satisfied neither with a philosophy of sheer immanence nor with one of dualistic transcendence. Rather, he thought that the nondual relation between the self and the absolute must be understood in terms of what he calls "immanent transcendence" (*naizai-teki-chōetsu* 内在的超越).[103] Precisely because the finite self is "enveloped by" rather than externally opposed to the absolute, the absolute is found at the very heart of the finite self. Insofar as we understand nature to be the encompassing whole of reality in which we participate,[104] it is helpful to think in terms of a relation of immanent transcendence. The self is not simply submerged in or indistinguishable from nature; but neither is it something dualistically separate or separable from nature.

Kimura interprets the relation between the self and nature in terms of a literal sense of "existence." "The self, *mizukara*, is nothing but an 'existence' in the sense of a 'standing

---

[102] See Nishida 1987–1989, 8: 314. On Nishida's thought, see Chapters 17 and 18 in this volume.

[103] See Nishida 1987–1989, 11: 434, 448, 463, and my "Ethical and Religious Alterity: Nishida After Levinas," in *Kitarō Nishida in der Philosophie des 20. Jahrhunderts*, edited by Rolf Elberfeld and Yōko Arisaka (Freiburg/Munich: Alber Verlag, 2014), 313–341.

[104] Nishida himself does not in fact usually speak of the absolute or the ultimately enveloping and self-determining world as "nature." Indeed, James Heisig has forcefully argued that nature is a crucially "missing *basho* [place]" in Nishida's thought from beginning to end (James W. Heisig, "*An Inquiry into the Good* and Nishida's Missing *Basho*," in *Much Ado About Nothingness: Essays on Nishida and Tanabe* [Nagoya: Chisokudō, 2016], 150–152). It is true that, even in his later thought, Nishida tends to limit "nature" (*shizen*) per se to the realms of biology and physics, which he generally claims are enveloped by what he calls the historical world (Nishida 1987–1989, 14: 211). However, in an important text from his later period, Nishida writes of the dialectically self-determining world in terms of "historical nature" (*rekishi-teki shizen* 歴史的自然) (Nishida 1987–89, 8: 273–394). In an early essay, Nishida had written that "nature and culture are not opposed to one another; nature is the root of culture. An artificial culture separated from a profound and vast nature cannot but degenerate" (Nishida 1987–89, 13: 129). While it can be said that Nishida did not explicitly or at least sufficiently develop his early sense of a "profound and vast nature" that is "the root of culture" or fully clarify the relation between human history and this profound and vast sense of nature, these have been central concerns for Nishida's successor Nishitani as well as for Nishitani's successor Ueda Shizuteru. In an essay on Nishida's lifelong penchant for gazing at

out' or 'emerging' of the intrinsic nature, *onozukara*, into the outer intersubjective reality of human life through the 'ex-it' of one's own body, *mi*."[105] The personal embodied self is thus an *ek-stasis*, a standing out, insofar as it is an emergence from "the overall spontaneous activity of nature" that is the "very origin of the inner self."

Kimura suggests that mental health requires a dynamic balance between individuating existence and staying in touch with one's natural origins. While on the one hand the schizophrenic is unable to first achieve an individuating existence from nature, on the other hand the Zen practitioner seeks to radically return to the creative source of (human) nature. "If the goal of endeavor in Zen Buddhism is gaining access to the true Self before the differentiation of *mizukara* from *onozukara*, the basic disturbance of the schizophrenic psychosis can be seen in a difficulty to differentiate them."[106] While the schizophrenic fails to become an individual in the first place, the Zen practitioner attempts to transcend—or, as Nishitani would say, trans-descend—individual egoism and alienation by returning to the natural roots of humanity.

Freedom is thus not simply an innate given, but rather the achievement of a *regained* naturalness. The true self is a part of nature, but it is a part that dynamically stands out from and is called upon to return to its natural origin. Natural freedom is not a static state of being, but rather an ongoing dynamic of existence and return.

THE UNFATHOMABILITY OF NATURE AND FREEDOM

Insofar as we humans are nondually inseparable from nature—in other words, insofar as we come from nature and can return to nature—we can holistically attune ourselves to the fluid principle of its Way. And yet, insofar as we stand out from nature as existing finite

and writing poems about the ocean, Ueda suggests that the ocean was for Nishida a sensible incarnation of the infinite place that encompasses our finite historical worlds (Ueda 2001–4, 1: 335–8). For three essays grouped under the section title "Basho toshite no shizen" [Nature as Place], see Ueda 2001–4, 9: 211–322. For Ueda's comments on the natural scene depicted in the ninth of the *Ten Oxherding Pictures* as a "concrescence of the non-egoity of the true self"; that is, as the place of nature in which the self loses itself so as to find itself, breaking out of the shell of its ego so as to no longer separate itself from all things, see Ueda 2001–4, 6: 161–187, 236–239, 258–262. For his claim that, despite their proximities, Zen offers a more direct and explicit openness to the place of nature and empathetic appreciation of natural phenomena than does the still too transcendently oriented Christian mysticism of Meister Eckhart, see Ueda 2001–4, 8: 77.

[105] Kimura 1988, 6.

[106] Kimura 1988, 10. Ueda Shizuteru sees true freedom as rooted in "the place of absolute nothingness," which alone can reconcile the impersonal of-itself (*onozukara*) of nature with the personal agency (*mizukara*) of humans (Ueda 2001–2003, 6: 251).

individuals who intellectually objectify (the rest of) nature, we can neither fathom its every rhyme and reason nor control every twist and turn of its flow.

As we have seen, the same characters 自然 can be read either as *jinen* or as *shizen*. While the former reading was used in the past, as it is still today, in the sense of "natural," without artificial intervention, the latter reading was traditionally used to refer to events that were unexpected, "one in ten thousand" (*man-ichi* 万一). Analogously, the expression *onozukara* was used not only to refer to events that were "natural," that happen as a matter "of course," but also to events that occur "perchance" (*hyottosuruto* ひょっとすると or *tamatama* たまたま).[107] Hence, the expressions *onozukara* and *shizen* evince, not a nature that is exhaustively ruled by laws of necessity that can be epistemologically fathomed and technologically manipulated, but rather a nature that can manifest itself also in radically contingent and surprising events.[108] Such events, that of death in particular, are beyond our ken and control—and yet they, too, are natural.[109] Returning to a life of naturalness thus requires more than comprehending and attuning ourselves to the lawful regularities of nature; it also demands an openness to nature's unfathomable contingencies and a recognition of our own finitude and mortality in particular.

This conjunction of what is natural ("of course") with what is contingent and surprising is paradoxical only if we assume that the ways of nature can be reduced to the laws of human understanding and submitted to the calculations of egoistic desire. Yet, while this noncalculable contingency means that the natural world is beyond our control, the indeterminacy of nature is in fact also the source of our own freedom. An acknowledgment of the ultimate unfathomability of natural processes is at the same time an affirmation of the nondeterministic freedom of our participation in these processes. The spontaneity and creativity of nature and freedom is the complement of their contingency and unpredictability.

After all, freedom by definition cannot be defined. It cannot be explained, for to explain freedom would be to explain it away.[110] What can be determined in advance is, strictly speaking, nothing new, but rather merely the mechanistic or teleological unfolding of what was already there. However situated and finite it may be, freedom is precisely what cannot be exhaustively determined by predefined causes and conditions. Indeed, freedom (*jiyū* 自由) is as such an origin; it is a source from (自) which

---

[107] See the entries for "*shizen*" and "*onozukara*" in *Kōjien* (Tokyo: Iwanami, 1991) and in *Iwanami kogojiten* (Tokyo: Iwanami, 1992). Also see Sagara 1989, 46.

[108] It is not surprising that Kuki's philosophical investigation of "contingency" (*gūzen* 偶然) led him through European existentialism back to the Japanese conception of nature. See Tanaka 1992, chapter 5.

[109] See Sagara 1995, 124–125, 151–153. Sagara elsewhere stresses that, unlike the Western notions of *phusis* and *natura*, and also, he claims, 自然 (Ch. *ziran*) for the Chinese, the Japanese do not tend to understand 自然 (*shizen*, *jinen*) as expressing the nature of something as an essence or principle (Ch. *li* 理) that can be fathomed by reason (Sagara 1989, 40–41, 104).

[110] Heidegger writes: "Kant says that the fact of freedom is incomprehensible. The only thing that we comprehend is its incomprehensibility." He goes on say that freedom resists comprehension because it is freedom that "transposes us into the occurrence of Being" (Martin Heidegger, *Schelling's Treatise on the Essence of Human Freedom*, trans. Joan Stambaugh [Athens: Ohio University Press, 1985], 162).

712   BRET W. DAVIS

something new arises (由). It is not a predictable becoming based on determinate being, but rather a creative emergence out of an indeterminate "nothingness."[111]

The traditional Japanese conception of the Way of nature that we are pursuing thus entails a nondeterministic, uncontrollable, incalculable excess of originality and creativity. This natural Way both exceeds the control of our egos and is the very source of the freedom of our authentic selves. For, as Nishida puts it, we become true individuals when we realize ourselves as "creative elements in a creative world."

THE PRACTICE OF REGAINING
NATURAL FREEDOM

As is implied in Bashō's call for us to "*return* to the creative transformations of nature," natural freedom is not simply a given; it must be achieved. This achievement, however, is a matter of radical re-gress rather than linear progress; that is to say, it entails stepping back to our forgotten roots, getting back in touch with the hidden source of spontaneous creativity and compassionate responsibility that lies underfoot. The quest for natural freedom in Japanese thought thus always starts with a paradox of self-alienation: to begin with, we are not who we are most originally.

Dōgen opens his *Fukanzazengi* with a version of this paradox: "From the beginning the Way circulates everywhere; why the need to practice and verify it? . . . And yet, if there is the slightest discrepancy, heaven and earth are vastly separated; if the least

---

Heidegger follows Schelling, who claims that "freedom is . . . not the property of man, but the other way around: Man is at best the property of freedom . . . . freedom itself is a determination of true Being in general, a determination that surpasses all human being. Insofar as man is as man, he must participate in this determination of Being" (9). This thought is close to the Japanese sense of natural freedom we are pursuing, yet the "participation" in the last line must be stressed, otherwise we may end up, contrary to Heidegger's best intentions, simply reversing the modern metaphysics of subjectivity so as to revert from a hubristic humanistic voluntarism to a medieval theism that commands an abandonment of self-will for the sake of becoming a passive vehicle for a transcendent Will (see Davis 2007, 122–126, 298–301). Jean-Luc Nancy also discusses this ambiguity in Heidegger's later thought. Agreeing with Heidegger's critique of the modern metaphysics that views freedom as a property or act of the sovereign subject, Nancy affirms that "thinking does not appear to itself in a subject, but receives (itself) from a freedom that is not present to it . . . . it is given over to and delivered for what from the beginning exceeded it, outran it, and overflowed it" (Nancy 1993, 8). Yet Nancy stresses that freedom as "the archi-originary bursting of pure being" happens only ever as "a singularity of existence" (57–58), which is always an exposure to and a sharing with other singularities of existence. Nancy also stresses the ungraspability of freedom, since "the burst of freedom," as "that by which thought thinks," cannot itself be represented as an object of thought (59). This means that a discourse on freedom, such as his own, can only hope to evoke the experience that is freedom, which is for Nancy first and foremost the experience of thought. In a note appended to the "Fragments" that constitute the final chapter of his book, Nancy writes: "There is not a 'thinking' of freedom, there are only prolegomena to a freeing of thinking" (206n2).

[111] See Nishitani 1986–1995, 14: 120; Nishitani 2005, 67–68.

disorder arises, the heart and mind get lost in confusion."[112] Although the natural Way is everywhere, its ubiquity must be realized—that is, awakened to and actualized. Dōgen's solution to the initiated enlightenment (*shikaku* 始覚) versus original enlightenment (*hongaku* 本覚) dilemma is found in his key teaching of "the oneness of practice and enlightenment" (*shushō ittō* 修証一等).[113] With this doctrine, he manages to avoid the pitfall of a superficial naturalism that excuses humans from the task of *realizing* the originary ubiquity of the Buddha-nature. Practice is not a means by which we acquire a new essence; yet it is a way of expressly verifying our true being. As he tells us in *Bendōwa*: "Although the Dharma [cosmic law] amply inheres in every person, without practice, it does not presence; if it is not verified, it is not attained."[114] The natural freedom of our Buddha-nature is always already underfoot, and yet it must be appropriated by means of holistic practice (*shugyō* 修行).

While there is no end to this practice of the realization of natural freedom (insofar as what one realizes is that "practice is realization"), one does pass from a more or less artificially forced discipline to what Takuan Sōhō (1574–1645) calls a state of "samadhic freedom" (*jiyū zammai* 自由三昧).[115] The practice (*keiko* 稽古) of serious discipline, Takuan writes, leads to a "state of freedom [*jiyū*]" in which one can let the mind go in any direction.[116] If one has learned to "throw the mind away in the entire body, not stopping it here or there," then, "when it does inhabit these various places, it will realize its function and act without error."[117] Freed from internal compulsion by means of strict external discipline, one finally lets go of the latter to realize a genuinely natural freedom in the midst of everyday activity.[118]

As we have seen, the nonduality of this natural freedom does not imply a licentious naturalism. Neither does it imply a distinctionless monism into which singular differences are dissolved and ethical responsibility abnegated. Although Takuan is sometimes accused of abolishing ethical distinctions, insofar as in his "lessons to the sword master" he says that the self, the opponent, and the sword are all to be viewed as "empty [of independent substantiality],"[119] in fact the spontaneous freedom he teaches does contain significant ethical implications. It is necessary to cast off the dualistic discriminations of the ego, not in order to attain a blanket state of non-discrimination,

---

[112] *Dōgen Zenji goroku*, ed. Kagamishima Genryū (Tokyo: Kōdansha, 1990), 171.

[113] Dōgen 1990, 1: 28; Dōgen 2002, 19. See my "The Enlightening Practice of Nonthinking: Unfolding Dōgen's *Fukanzazengi*," in *Engaging Dōgen's Zen: The Philosophy of Practice as Awakening*, edited by Tetsuzen Jason M. Wirth, Shūdō Brian Schroeder, and Kanpū Bret W. Davis (Somerville, MA: Wisdom Publications, 2016), 207–215. The attempt to steer through the horns of initiated versus original enlightenment dualism did not remain unique to Dōgen. As Takeuchi Seiichi points out, Ippen spoke of "the nonduality of initiated and original enlightenment [*shihon-funi* 始本不二]" (Takeuchi 2004, 19).

[114] Dōgen 1990, 1: 11; Dōgen 2002, 8, translation modified.

[115] Takuan 1970, 181; Takuan 1986, 82. Wilson translates *jiyū zammai* as "freedom in a meditative state."

[116] Takuan 1970, 70; Takuan 1986, 36.

[117] Takuan 1970, 45, 57; Takuan 1986, 26, 31, translation modified.

[118] The great jazz musician Charlie Parker is said to have remarked: "You've got to learn your instrument. Then, you practice, practice, practice. And then, when you finally get up there on the bandstand, forget all that and just wail."

[119] Takuan 1970, 74; Takuan 1986, 37.

but rather in order to discriminate—that is, to make practical distinctions and ethical judgments—*freely and naturally*. This freedom from (artificial and egoistic) discrimination and freedom for (natural and non-egoistic) discrimination is presumably what Takuan means when he says: "Without looking at right and wrong, he is able to see right and wrong well; without attempting to discriminate, he is able to discriminate well."[120] One finds the ultimate source of practical wisdom not by intellectually disengaging oneself from the everyday world and transcending it to a supernatural realm of reason, but rather by means of a holistic practice of intimately engaging oneself with the everyday world, by nondually attuning oneself to the fluid principle—the natural Way—that pervades the singular events of the here and now.

To be sure, Zen masters and other Japanese thinkers in the past and in the present do not always live up to their ideal practices of returning to a free and responsible naturalness. At their worst, these teachers and thinkers have inhibited individual autonomy by conflating non-egoistic naturalness with conformity to the status quo of the community or obedience to the dictates of an authority.[121] On the path toward recovering a nondual spontaneity, there are certainly perilous sidetracks that would confuse nonduality with homogeneity and pitfalls that would simply replace self-assertive activity with deferential passivity. But such aberrations and crude reversals should not divert our attention from indications of genuine pathways for recovering a natural freedom. At their best, Zen masters and other Japanese thinkers have conveyed ways of casting off both collective and individual egoism through practices of returning ever again to the nondual wellsprings of spontaneously compassionate responsibility and naturally creative freedom.

BIBLIOGRAPHY AND SUGGESTED READINGS

Callicott, J. Baird, and Roger T. Ames, eds. (1989) *Nature in Asian Traditions of Thought*. Albany: State University of New York Press.

Callicott, J. Baird, and James McRae, eds. (2014) *Environmental Philosophy in Asian Traditions of Thought*. Albany: State University of New York Press.

Callicott, J. Baird, and James McRae, eds. (2017) *Japanese Environmental Philosophy*. New York: Oxford University Press.

Carter, Robert E. (2001) *Encounter with Enlightenment: A Study of Japanese Ethics*. Albany: State University of New York Press.

Carter, Robert E. (2008) *The Japanese Arts and Self-Cultivation*. Albany: State University of New York Press.

Davis, Bret W. (2004a) "Zen after Zarathustra: The Problem of the Will in the Confrontation Between Nietzsche and Buddhism." *Journal of Nietzsche Studies* 28: 89–138.

---

[120] Takuan 1970, 178; Takuan 1986, 81, translation modified.

[121] See Takeuchi 2004, 14, 26. On the uses and abuses of a disciplined cultivation of spontaneity within the variety of conceptions of *bushidō*, see Chapter 14 in this volume. See also Brian (Daizen) A. Victoria, *Zen at War* (New York: Weatherhill, 1997), and Christopher Ives, *Imperial-Way Zen: Ichikawa Hakugen's Critique and Lingering Questions for Buddhist Ethics* (Honolulu: University of Hawai'i Press, 2009).

Davis, Bret W. (2004*b*) "Rethinking the Rational Animal: The Question of Anthropologocentrism in Heidegger, Bergson, and Zen." *Interdisziplinäre Phänomenologie—Interdisciplinary Phenomenology* 1: 173–187.

Davis, Bret W. (2007*a*) *Heidegger and the Will: On the Way to Gelassenheit*. Evanston, IL: Northwestern University Press.

Davis, Bret W. (2007*b*) "Does a Dog See Into Its Buddha-nature? Re-posing the Question of Animality/Humanity in Zen Buddhism." In *Buddha Nature and Animality*, edited by David Jones. Fremont, CA: Jain Publishing, 83–126.

Davis, Bret W. (2014*a*) "Returning the World to Nature: Heidegger's Turn from a Transcendental-Horizonal Projection of World to a Releasement to the Open-Region." *Continental Philosophy Review* 47/3: 373–397.

Davis, Bret W. (2014*b*) "Naturalness in Zen and Shin Buddhism: Before and Beyond Self- and Other-Power." *Contemporary Buddhism* 15/2: 433–447.

Davis, Bret W. (2018) "Seeing into the Self in Nature: Awakening Through Cao Jun's Paintings." In *Cao Jun: Hymns to Nature*, edited by John Sallis. Chicago: University of Chicago Press, 25–34.

Davis, Bret W. (2022) *Zen Pathways: An Introduction to the Philosophy and Practice of Zen Buddhism*. New York: Oxford University Press.

Descola, Philippe. (2012) *Beyond Nature and Culture*, translated by Janet Lloyd. Boston: McMullen Museum of Art, Boston College.

Dōgen. (1990) *Shōbōgenzō* [The Treasury of the True Dharma Eye], four volumes, edited by Mizuno Yaoko. Tokyo: Iwanami.

Dōgen. (2002) *The Heart of Dōgen's Shōbōgenzō*, translated by Norman Waddell and Masao Abe. Albany: State University of New York Press.

Dōgen. (2007*a*) "*Keisei-sanshiki*: The Voices of the River Valley and the Form of the Mountains," translated by Gudo Wafu Nishijima and Chodo Cross. In *Shōbōgenzō: The True-Dharma Eye Treasury*, volume 1. Berkeley, CA: Numata Center for Buddhist Translation and Research, 109–125.

Dōgen. (2007*b*) "*Sansuigyō*: The Sutra of Mountains and Water," translated by Gudo Wafu Nishijima and Chodo Cross. In *Shōbōgenzō: The True-Dharma Eye Treasury*, volume 1. Berkeley, CA: Numata Center for Buddhist Translation and Research, 217–234.

Fischer, John Martin, Robert Kane, Derk Pereboom, and Manuel Vargas. (2007) *Four Views on Free Will*. Malden, MA: Blackwell.

Hadot, Pierre. (2006) *The Veil of Isis: An Essay on the History of the Idea of Nature*, translated by Michael Chase. Cambridge, MA: Harvard University Press.

Hisamatsu, Shin'ichi. (1971) *Zen and the Fine Arts*, translated by Gishin Tokiwa. Tokyo: Kodansha.

Imanishi, Kinji. (2002) *A Japanese View of Nature: The World of Living Things*, edited by Pamela J. Asquith, translated by Pamela J. Asquith et al. New York: RoutledgeCurzon.

Kimura Bin. (1988) "Self and Nature—An Interpretation of Schizophrenia." *Zen Buddhism Today* 6: 1–10.

Kuki Shūzō. (1980) *Kuki Shūzō zenshū* [Complete Works of Kuki Shūzō]. Tokyo: Iwanami.

Maruyama, Masao. (1974) *Studies in the Intellectual History of Tokugawa Japan*, translated by Mikiso Hane. Tokyo: University of Tokyo Press.

Maruyama Masao. (1992) "Rekishi-ishiki no 'kosō'" [The Ancient Layers of Historical Consciousness]. In *Chūsei to hangyaku* [Fidelity and Rebellion]. Tokyo: Chikuma, 295–351.

Matsuo Bashō. (1962–1969) *Kōhon Bashō zenshū* [Complete Works of Bashō]. Tokyo: Kadokawa Shoten.

Matsuo, Bashō. (2004) *Bashō's Haiku: Selected Poems of Matsuo Bashō*, translated by David Landis Barnhill. Albany: State University of New York Press.

Matsuo, Bashō. (2005) *Bashō's Journey: The Literary Prose of Matsuo Bashō*, translated by David Landis Barnhill. Albany: State University of New York Press.

McMahan, David L. (2008) "Buddhist Romanticism: Art, Spontaneity, and the Wellsprings of Nature." In *The Making of Buddhist Modernism*. New York: Oxford University Press, 117–147.

Lafleur, William R. (1989) "Saigyō and the Buddhist Value of Nature." In *Nature in Asian Traditions of Thought*, edited by J. Baird Callicott and Roger T. Ames. Albany: State University of New York Press, 183–209.

Nancy, Jean-Luc. (1993) *The Experience of Freedom*, translated by Bridget McDonald. Stanford, CA: Stanford University Press.

Nishida, Kitarō. (1987) *Last Writings: Nothingness and the Religious Worldview*, translated by David A. Dilworth. Honolulu: University of Hawai'i Press.

Nishida Kitarō. (1987–1989) *Nishida Kitarō zenshū [Complete Works of Nishida Kitarō]*. Tokyo: Iwanami.

Nishitani, Keiji. (1982) *Religion and Nothingness*, translated by Jan Van Bragt. Berkeley, CA: University of California Press.

Nishitani Keiji. (1986–1995) *Nishitani Keiji chosakushū* [Collected Works of Nishitani Keiji]. Tokyo: Sōbunsha.

Nishitani, Keiji. (2005) "On Nature," translated by Setsuko Aihara and Graham Parkes. In *Confluences: Studies from East to West in Honor of V. H. Viglielmo*, edited by William Ridgeway and Nobuko Ochner. Honolulu: University of Hawai'i Press, 56–73.

Oelschlaeger, Max. (1991) *The Idea of Wilderness: From Prehistory to the Age of Ecology*. New Haven: Yale University Press.

Qiu, Peipei. (2005) *Bashō and the Dao: The Zhuangzi and the Transformation of Haikai*. Honolulu: University of Hawai'i Press.

Sagara Tōru. (1989) *Nihon no shisō* [Japanese Thought]. Tokyo: Perikansha.

Sagara Tōru. (1995) *Chōetsu, Shizen* [Transcendence, Nature], *Sagara Tōru chosakushū* [The Collected Works of Sagara Tōru], volume 6. Tokyo: Perikansha.

Sallis, John. (2016a) *The Return of Nature*. Bloomington: Indiana University Press.

Sallis, John. (2016b) *The Figure of Nature: On Greek Origins*. Bloomington: Indiana University Press.

Schelling, F. J. W. (1936) *Philosophical Inquiries into the Nature of Human Freedom*, translated by James Gutman. La Salle, IL: Open Court.

Sessions, George, ed. (1995) *Deep Ecology for the 21st Century*. Boston: Shambhala.

Shaner, David Edward. (1989) "The Japanese Experience of Nature." In *Nature in Asian Traditions of Thought*, edited by J. Baird Callicott and Roger T. Ames. Albany: State University of New York Press, 163–182.

Shinran. (1997) *The Collected Works of Shinran*, two volumes. Edited and translated by Dennis Hirota et al. Kyoto: Jōdo Shinshū Hongwanji-ha.

Suzuki, Daisetz T. (1959) "Love of Nature." In *Zen and Japanese Culture*. Princeton, NJ: Princeton University Press, 331–395.

Suzuki Daisetsu. (1997) *Tōyō-teki-na mikata* [The Eastern Point of View]. Tokyo: Iwanami.

Suzuki, D. T. (2015) "The Role of Nature in Zen Buddhism." In *Selected Works of D. T. Suzuki, volume 1, Zen*, edited by Richard M. Jaffe. Oakland: University of California Press, 113–135.

Takeuchi Seiichi. (2004) *"Onozukara" to "mizukara": Nihonshisō no kiso* ["Of Itself" and "From Oneself": The Basis of Japanese Thought]. Tokyo: Shunjūsha.

Takuan Sōhō (1970) *Fudōchishinmyōroku*, edited by Ikeda Satoshi. Tokyo: Tokuma Shoten.

Takuan, Sōhō (1986) *The Unfettered Mind*, translated by William Scott Wilson. Tokyo: Kodansha.

Tanaka Kyūbun. (1992) *Kuki Shūzō: Gūzen to shizen* [Kuki Shūzō: Contingency and Nature]. Tokyo: Perikansha.

Tellenbach, Hubertus and Bin Kimura. (1989) "The Japanese Concept of 'Nature.'" In *Nature in Asian Traditions of Thought*, edited by J. Baird Callicott and Roger T. Ames. Albany: State University of New York Press, 153–162.

Tu, Wei-Ming. (1989) "The Continuity of Being." In *Nature in Asian Traditions of Thought*, edited by J. Baird Callicott and Roger T. Ames. Albany: State University of New York Press, 67–97.

Ueda Shizuteru. (2001–2004) *Ueda Shizuteru shū* [Collected Works of Ueda Shizuteru], twelve volumes. Iwanami Shoten, Tokyo.

Unno, Taitetsu. (2002) "Life as Naturalness: Jinen." In *Shin Buddhism: Bits of Rubble Turned into Gold*. New York: Double Day, 154–159.

Wirth, Jason M. (2017) *Mountains, Rivers, and the Great Earth: Reading Gary Snyder and Dōgen in an Age of Ecological Crisis*. Albany: State University of New York Press.

Yamakage, Motohisa. (2006) *The Essence of Shintō: Japan's Spiritual Heart*, edited by Paul de Leeuw and Aidan Rankin, translated by Mineko S. Gillespie et al. New York: Kodansha.

Yanabu Akira. (1982*a*) "Jiyū: Yanagida Kunio no hanpatsu" [*Jiyū*: Yanagida Kunio's Resistance], in *Honyakugo seiritsu jijō* [How Translations of Terms Were Established]. Tokyo: Iwanami, 173–191.

Yanabu Akira. (1982*b*) "Shizen: Honyakugo no unda gokai" [*Shizen*: A Misunderstanding Originating in Translation], in *Honyakugo seiritsu jijō* [How Translations of Terms Were Established]. Tokyo: Iwanami, 125–148.

CHAPTER 34

....

JAPANESE ETHICS

....

ROBERT E. CARTER

MANY philosophers working in the field of "Western" ethics find it difficult to come to grips with those approaches to ethics taken by the Japanese.[1] To begin with, the Japanese perceive no hard and fast dividing line between religion and philosophy. While philosophy in Japan is grounded on evidence and rigorous thinking, much of the evidence comes from four major religious influences: Shintō, Confucianism, Buddhism, and Daoism. It would also not be wrong to include Zen Buddhism as a separate and distinctive source. In each of these religious traditions, a particular emphasis is placed on the transformation of the individual: a self-cultivation that requires following pathways to enlightenment marked out by these traditions, usually involving various meditative practices. Thus, not only are these pathways normative, but, more significantly, they are also transformative. Furthermore, for the Japanese, the "norm" in normative refers not to the average person but to those few, in any practice, who have reached excellence. As exemplars, these people act spontaneously out of a profound sense of compassion, which itself is based on the enlightened awareness of the fact that all things, human and nonhuman, are somehow connected. The comprehending of the "oneness of all things" grants sensitivity to the well-being of others that is not the result of mere ethical calculation or the following of rules. Rather, even though the results of calculated action may not seem to differ from those actions resulting from this deep sense of compassion, the source for each is radically different. However, "true" ethics is spontaneous caring and concern for others that has been achieved by lifelong practice yielding a transformation of both understanding and action. Thus, true ethical action results from being ethical through and through. For those who are en route, there are still rules, regulations, calculations, and precepts, but the goal and heart of ethics is the spontaneous and selfless expression of human-heartedness.

---

[1] An earlier version of this chapter was published in *The Oxford Handbook of World Philosophy*, edited by Jay Garfield and William Edelglass (New York: Oxford University Press, 2011), 302–316.

PAST AND PRESENT

In looking for answers to his central question, "How are we to live?," Peter Singer explores the textual traditions of scholarship on ethics as well as examining present-day societies in his attempt to discover what is and is not working, ethically speaking. To his great credit, he includes a chapter on "How the Japanese Live" in which he assesses whether or not Japanese society stands as a successful social experiment that the rest of the world ought to adopt. Singer concludes that, while there are numerous achievements in the way the Japanese live their lives, there are also ethical shortcomings to consider as well. Such a conclusion is both measured and unsurprising, insofar as one could safely say the same of almost any society. Less evident, however, is the particular list of shortcomings that he offers and the nature of the sources used to confirm them.

Just as it is illegitimate to conclude that there is nothing in Western philosophy to temper the rampant selfishness that so often manifests in the guise of individuality, so it would be wrong to conclude, as Singer does, approvingly quoting John David Morley, that "there is in Japanese ethics nothing corresponding to the key Christian injunction 'thou shall love thy neighbor as thyself.'"[2] But what is the basis of this conclusion? Surely it cannot be Morley's expertise, for his study is of the Japanese sex trade, in the form of a novel, with only the briefest analysis of Japanese ethics as casual observation.[3] A Japanese making a similar observation in New York, London, or Berlin might well conclude that such admonitions as to turn the other cheek or to love one's neighbor are, in any significant sense, ideals completely absent in Western ethics since they are almost nowhere practiced. Rather than a casual observation of behavior in the Ginza in Tokyo or Soho in London, it is, I will argue, both imperative and instructive to seek out those underlying values that, taken together, serve as the background infusing ethics in contemporary Japan. That theory is not sufficiently put into practice is a fact common to both East and West. Nevertheless, the wellsprings of any society, to the extent that ethics is a concern at all, are to be found in the rich philosophical and religious traditions of that culture.

To begin, and in partial agreement with Singer, Hajime Nakamura (Jp. Nakamura Hajime, 1911–1999), in *Ways of Thinking of Eastern Peoples*, has argued convincingly that the Japanese mindset has long given precedence to social relationships over that of individual concerns.[4] The primary good is that which profits the social group, and the group is usually a "limited social nexus." While loyalty to the Emperor, to one's community, or to one's family is strong enough to result in significant altruistic sacrifice, "only a few cases" of such sacrifice are made "for the sake of something universal, something that transcends a particular human nexus."[5] Nakamura concludes that Western people

---

[2] Singer 1995, 125.
[3] Morley 1985.
[4] Nakamura 1964, 409.
[5] Nakamura 1964, 414.

are more aware of the importance of transcending limited social human relationships in making moral judgments.[6] Nakamura's work in this area remains definitive with respect to Japanese culture, and yet it is less than obvious that Western peoples are as different as he intuits them to be. To take an example, Lawrence Kohlberg (1927–1987), whose study of the stages of moral development remains foundational, concluded that only at stage five of his six-level moral development scale does universalization in moral reasoning occur. Prior to that, it is preconventional and conventional moral reasoning that prevails, and the contexts of such reasoning range from one other person in one's group, to one's peer group, to one's country (right or wrong). Each of these is a limited social nexus. Only about five percent of US citizens, Kohlberg concluded, are ever firmly at stage five of moral universalization.[7] Therefore, even though the US Constitution is written in stage five language, it must be conceded that, at most, only a small portion of the population can understand it in a way that exceeds or transcends a limited social nexus. While the theory is stage five, the practice is stage one to four. The theory transcends any of the restrictions, while the practice is deeply entrenched in one of the limited nexuses. His longitudinal studies brought him to much the same conclusion for other Western countries. In short, most people operate from a limited social nexus. But now what both Singer and Kohlberg fail to appreciate is that universalization itself plays little or no role in ethics as conceived in Japan or in classical China. Ethical decisions are concretely based, not abstractly rule- or principle-based, and are dependent on the character development of the ethical actor. More about this shortly.

Still, what is different in Nakamura's analysis is a de-emphasis of the importance of the individual in Japanese ethics and an increased emphasis on the importance of the group. About this I will also say more later. However, it is important to understand here that it is not the case that the individual is unimportant in Japan, but rather that the individual is always both an individual and a member of social groups. It is not an either/or logic that applies but a both/and logic that must be conceded. To be a human person requires both individuality and social loyalty and cohesiveness.

On the basis of its Confucian background, it is certainly not accurate to conclude that a concern for the well-being of an ever-widening circle of people is rare or even absent in Japanese culture. This conclusion becomes even more convincing when the Buddhist and Shintō traditions are considered. Historically, Japanese ethics results from the confluence of three streams of thought and influence: indigenous Shintōism, Confucianism from China, and Buddhism from India, again by way of China. Chinese Daoism is a lesser, though important, influence as well, particularly in Zen Buddhism. Only Shintō originated in Japan, while the other spiritual traditions underwent the Japanese alchemy of transformation, with aspects of the original importation altered to better fit Japan's

---

[6] Nakamura 1964, 415.

[7] Kohlberg 1981, 237. Kohlberg offered these percentages to me in a conversation. However, he was optimistic that the moral developmental level of US citizens would improve. See Lawrence Kohlberg, *The Philosophy of Moral Development: Moral Stages and the Idea of Justice, Vol. 1 of Essays on Moral Development* (San Francisco, CA: Harper and Row Publishers, 1981), p. 237.

cultural environment. Nevertheless, the bulk of the imported traditions remained basically what they were. Although Confucianism is often viewed as the primary source of Japanese ethical values, to my mind this understanding is too simplistic for ethics in Japan is a complex mixture of these, and, in more recent times, Western influences must be added to the mix as well.

Nevertheless, the importance of Confucian teachings is not to be minimized. Perhaps the first thing to note is that moral concern for an extended, if not universal, social nexus is paramount in Confucianism. Confucius emphasized that *ren* (Jp. *jin* 仁, human-heartedness or benevolence) is the cornerstone of his philosophy. Centuries before the Christian era, Confucius taught that the meaning of *ren* is "do not impose on others what you yourself do not desire."[8] The *ren* person, or authoritative person, displays five attitudes: "respect, tolerance, living up to one's word, diligence, and generosity."[9] It is reasonable to conclude that the essence of Confucian ethical teaching is a selfless concern for others, without restriction, and a subsequent acting "on behalf of others" as one's duty as a conscientious moral being. Thus, the goal of one's self-development is to become spontaneously and effortlessly human-hearted. David Hall and Roger Ames point out that "Confucius does insist that the dissolution of the limiting ego-self is a necessary precondition for *ren* action."[10] The *ren* person shows concern for "the widest possible range of interests."[11] A related insight from within the Zen Buddhist tradition is offered by the Zen teacher and scholar, Richard DeMartino, who succinctly summed up the issue when he wrote: "It is not that the ego *has* a problem. The ego *is* the Problem."[12]

Given this brief review of the teachings of Confucius, and granted that Confucianism remains a major source of ethical thinking in Japan, it is impossible to conclude that there is nothing in Japanese ethics that corresponds to the Christian injunction to love one's neighbor as oneself.

The Buddhist emphasis in ethics is on a heartfelt, and eventually spontaneous, impulse toward compassionate identification with the joys and sorrows of others. The core teaching of co-dependent origination (Sk. *pratītya samutpāda*; Jp. *engi* 縁起) makes amply clear that everything arises and exists in relation to and interconnected with everything else. As radical empiricists, Buddhists in their epistemology have always rejected universals as "unreal" and were usually very careful to contextualize generalized claims. The Buddha clearly saw that universality is closely connected to rigidity while simultaneously recognizing the pragmatic need for generalized statements. The compassion of Buddha does not exclude any being in immediate experience, but not because of some universal principle. The Buddha simply *is* compassionate as evidenced by the constancy of his actions. Ethically speaking, what we have in place here is a "declaration of interdependence." We simply are connected to others, and to our environment, for we exist

---

[8] Hall and Ames 1987, 123 [12/2].
[9] Hall and Ames 1987, 122 [17/6].
[10] Hall and Ames 1987, 117.
[11] Hall and Ames 1987, 117.
[12] DeMartino 1960, 154.

co-dependently from an experiential perspective. Psychologically, this translates into a strong feeling of kinship with other human beings and with our environment as well. If I am not an independent, rigidly demarcated center of consciousness but rather an aggregate of forces that persists only so long as the greater context of forces keep me afloat in a sea of nonsubstantial energy, then this so-called "I" really has no boundary but extends out into the dynamic force field of nature. "I" am an energy center seemingly separate from but actually inextricably connected with and related to other things. In this sense, other things are a part of me, and I am a part of them. We are each other, and so it is only rational that I should treat others as I would be treated because they *are* me! Thus, rather than a limited social nexus at work, we have a field-like vision of the mutual interconnectedness of all "things" (each seemingly independent centers of awareness but in reality nonsubstantial) whereby each center is but a focus of awareness or consciousness in a seamless field of becoming. The Buddha went so far as to "advocate the treatment *of all beings* as ends in themselves."[13] What is given is not a theory of ethics, but, instead, a path leading to one becoming ethical.

Likewise, Shintō does not provide an explicit catechism of rules for ethical living. Rather, it charts a pathway (*michi* 道) to follow in becoming naturally who one is that involves a cluster of attitudes defining what it means to be truly human. These attitudes include sincerity (*makoto* まこと, whose meaning includes acting in accordance with the will of the universal divine energy), honesty or trustworthiness, purity, courtesy, group harmony, thankfulness, cheerfulness, and benevolence. The bite in all of this is that if one falls significantly short of these virtuous attitudes or ways of walking with others in the world, one brings dishonor to oneself, to one's family, and to the group with which one is affiliated. Thus, it is honor that binds one to the ethical world. And while Singer concedes that it is impossible to say whether a culture is better in terms of its likelihood to put the interests of the group ahead of individual interests,[14] he does conclude that the Japanese are able to eradicate the false dilemma between group and individual interests by believing that "the satisfaction of the individual is only to be found in commitment to the group."[15] While it is true that, for a Japanese, ethical satisfaction cannot be achieved if it does not include commitment to the group, it is simply incorrect to say that it is only to be found in such commitment or that such commitment is ethically insignificant. The writings of Watsuji Tetsurō, which are still considered to be the definitive studies of Japanese ethics, make this abundantly clear.[16] While Watsuji's account of Japanese ethics is primarily descriptive of Japanese ethics as it is lived and does not propose a theory of ethics, it lays the foundation for understanding the Japanese take on the nature of the individual in society.

[13] Dharmasari 1989, 20.
[14] Singer 1995, 123.
[15] Singer 1995, 122.
[16] On Watsuji, see also Chapter 23 in this volume.

WATSUJI TETSURŌ (1889–1960)

Nothing is more important to the Japanese than relationships. It is as though their ethics is a wholesale application of the Buddhist theory of co-dependent origination, with decidedly Confucian overtones. To the Japanese, an ethical person stands in the center of a complex intersection of relationships, such as father or mother, son or daughter, buyer or seller, teacher or learner, physician or patient, friend or enemy, nurturer or nurtured. Indeed, each of us is often both sides of these pairs at one and the same time; we can be fathers or mothers to our children but also the children of our own mothers and fathers. Watsuji begins his analysis with the Confucian cardinal relationships of parent and child, lord and vassal, husband and wife, young and old, and friend and friend. Important as these relationships are in Japanese life, Watsuji himself went through a period of rejecting such seeming social conformity while taking on a "Western" sense of the centrality of individualism. The more he came to live the life of individualism, however, the less satisfying he found it. In due course, he returned to his birth culture's emphasis on community for he found that, in an ethics of individualism, the individual loses touch with the vast network of interconnections that serves to make us individuals immersed in the world with others. Individualism is isolating, and the way around this was to get beyond the hard shell of the ego, becoming open to the countless possibilities of social interaction and interconnection. Thus, one becomes oneself within a community which, further, is found in the "betweenness" (*aidagara* 間柄) between people, the space in which people interact with other people.

Ethics (*rinri* 倫理) is, for Watsuji, the study of the human being, and the word he uses for "human being" is *ningen* (人間), which is composed of two characters. The first, *nin* (人), means "human being" or "person," and the second, *gen* (間), means "space" or "between." Watsuji explicates the *gen* in *ningen* in terms of *aidagara* (間柄) in order to draw out the fact that what is being referred to is the space or place in which people are located and socially interact. This space is always already etched with the crisscrossings of social interaction, past and present. Furthermore, *nin* indicates that human beings exist both as independent individuals and as socially imbedded members of a community. *Ningen*, then, makes plain that human beings are both individuals and social beings within a space as the betweenness in which social interaction occurs. Betweenness includes all of the various human relationships in our life; it is the network that provides humanity with social meaning.

Thus, human beings have a "dual-nature" for we are individuals with individual personalities and unique histories, and yet we are inextricably connected to many others for we exist in community from our first breath. It is not that individuality is lacking among the Japanese, but that the Japanese concept of a human being must never leave out the social dimension: we are both individuals and, at the same time, socially embedded in many different ways. It is Western individualism that is one-sided, for it assumes the priority of the individual, often to the exclusion of the social. For the

Japanese, becoming an individual is an achievement, however, and not a fundamental starting point. Individuality emerges from within social relationships. Individuality arises last, rather than first. Society and culture provide the necessary resources (from emotional to physical needs; from language to customs) for realizing an individuality that is never created *ex nihilo* or *sui generis*.

In attempting to make clear what is distinctively Japanese about "human being" as *ningen*, Watsuji adopts a way of thinking originally provided by his colleague, Nishida Kitarō: contradictory self-identity (*mujun-teki jiko-dōitsu* 矛盾的自己同一). In order to be an individual, it is necessary to reject the group, to stand against it; and yet there must also be a group or groups against which an individual stands. Similarly, in order to be a member of a group, one must relinquish one's radical individuality; and yet there must already be such individuality to set aside in becoming a member of a group. Each of us is both an individual as isolated and necessarily interconnected with others in some community or other. We are *both*, in mutual interactive negation: as well as being determined by the group, we determine and shape this community as well. As such, we are living self-contradictions and, therefore, living identities of self-contradiction or unities of seeming opposites in mutual interactive negation. The Japanese give more weight to participation in society than do those of us who have been brought up on a heavy dose of individualism. Yet it is important to notice that the Japanese do not emphasize the group at the expense of individuality—or at least they need not. It can be that one becomes swamped by the group, just as one can exaggerate one's individualism at the expense of others to the point of becoming egoistically antisocial. The ideal, however, is to be an individual in the world who is thoroughly comfortable in the various communities through which one is connected to others.

Watsuji also carried the idea of *nothingness* (*mu* 無) into his analysis of ethics in Japan. Just as individuality and sociality are apparent self-contradictions preserved in the broader context of "a human person" that includes both in continual tension, so individuals and social groups are now understood to rest on a deeper ground that, itself, is neither individual nor social but is that greater context out of which both the individual and the social arise; namely, nothingness, or that which is prior to all distinctions. Nothingness is the silence out of which sound arises, against which sound is contrasted, and in which sound becomes possible. In this nothingness, the ego-self disappears, and it is this annihilation of the self that "constitutes the basis of every selfless morality since ancient times."[17] To lose one's self in this way is to become authentically who one is; namely, a self-expression of the One as creative formless energy becomes formed. The result is the experience of a non-dualistic connection between self and others that actually negates any trace of opposition; non-differentiation replaces distinction-making, and non-discrimination replaces the ever widening discrimination of ordinary consciousness. Dualistically comprehended, both the self and other are preserved, but

[17] Watsuji 1996, 134.

non-dualistically: each *is* the other, and together these constitute the basis for selfless, compassionate interaction with others.

What is clear from Watsuji's description is that the interests of the group ought not to deny the interests of the individual, not because the interests of the individual are taken to be the interests of the group, but because the interests of the group and the interests of the individual are both essential aspects of dual-natured human persons. Perhaps this accounts for some of the extraordinary pressures of Japanese life that Singer refers to;[18] not only are they the result of having to walk the narrow lines of group approval that are so important in Japan but of trying to be a good citizen while maintaining one's own individual path in the short term. It may be easier for a confirmed individualist to live simply because she or he can more or less ignore group responsibility. The "me" generation in North America has had just such a reputation.

PRAXIS

And how well do the Japanese live up to the standards of Confucian, Buddhist, and Shintō ethical traditions? Is the answer to such a question to be easily found? How well do Christians live up to the ideals of Christianity; Muslims to the ideals of Islam; or Jews to the teachings of Judaism? Few societies come even close to living up to their ethical ideals. It may be that the world is experiencing the great difficulties of the present precisely because the wise teachings of tradition are being ignored—or at least bent out of shape. Thus, it is unlikely that one will discover how we ought to live by examining how most people in a given society actually do live.

There is another possible approach: reconstruct or recover the ideals of a nation, culture, or religious tradition as *resources* for the ethical improvement of society. But what are the ethical wellsprings of a tradition, and how might they be employed to improve and enrich a people's understanding? In this chapter, I have already begun this enquiry by looking more closely at the Confucian, Buddhist, and Shintō perspectives on the individual's relationship to humanity at large and to the environment. But another distinctive aspect of the Japanese approach to ethics is to be found in the practice of the great arts. Some of this can be found in other East Asian societies, but the Japanese have honed such practices to a degree rarely found elsewhere. What is less understood is that these arts are ethically drenched: while they teach a specific set of skills, they also strive to bring about the transformation of the individual's character. Such self-cultivation moves one along the path of enlightenment, inescapably nourishing in the individual an awareness of one's interconnection with others, with nature, and with the cosmos. Such awareness supplies the lubrication that makes easier effective and appropriate interaction with others, ideally yielding a community of harmony, cooperation,

---

[18] Singer 1995, 124.

good-heartedness, and nurturing. And the arts teach these indirectly, through the practice of something else entirely. Moreover, all of the arts, as meditative practices, gently but inexorably lead one to overcome the ego-self, replacing it with an expanding range of concern. Such a transformation of the person is central to ethics in Japan. Francisco Varela makes this point clearly when he writes that "an attitude of all-encompassing, decentered, responsive, compassionate concern" can only be "developed and embodied through *disciplines* that facilitate the letting-go of ego-centered habits and enable compassion to become spontaneous and self-sustaining."[19] So, true self-cultivation involves casting off the ego-dominated self, and this is achieved through the stilling of the ordinary mind by means of various meditative practices, with a resultant expansion of compassion and concern to an increasingly wider field of application.

An inquiry into ethics as praxis in the Japanese arts might allow a glimpse of how practical ethics is taught in the present while drawing on centuries of past tradition.[20] The arts (the Way of Tea, the Way of Flowers, the martial arts, haiku poetry, calligraphy, and so on) in Japan convey not only cultural specifics, but also are meant to lead to self-transformation and provide ethical teachings about how one should relate to others. These "Ways" (*dō* 道) are unlike sports, or hobbies, or even vocational and commercial activities as we know them in the West. Each of the arts is a pathway, a road, a way of life. Not mere entertainment or distraction, they are all ways of self-development leading to the transformation of the participant. In short, each of these arts is, if seriously engaged in, itself a path to enlightenment and to ethical behavior.

The word *shugyō* (修行), when applied to the practice of a "Way," indicates a lifelong practice and is never a casual undertaking but a serious journey leading, hopefully, to some form of spiritual awakening or realization. For this reason, true understanding is not just theory in Japan but is meant to be everyday practice. Ethics is not a theoretical, intellectual "meta" search for the criterion of right or wrong but a way of "walking" (or being) in the world. Because this kind of approach to ethics is focused on the journey to enlightenment, it involves a recognition that we are not only inextricably intertwined with others but with the entire cosmos. It is a manifestation of the aforementioned "declaration of interdependence" that serves as the basis of all ethical action. Thus, if I am one with my brothers and sisters, insofar as the enlightenment experience informs us that all that exists is a self-manifestation of the original creative energy called "nothingness," then to do harm to another human being is simply unthinkable. Varela says of nothingness that it is both threatening and paradoxical for "it is no ground whatsoever; it cannot be grasped as ground, reference point, or nest for a sense of ego. It does not exist—nor does it not exist . . . . When the conceptual mind tries to grasp it, it finds nothing, and so it experiences it as emptiness. It can be known (and can only be known) directly."[21] Nothingness, emptiness (*kū* 空), Buddha-nature (*busshō* 仏性), no-mind (*mushin* 無心),

---

[19] Varela 1992, 73.

[20] Those who wish to read more about Japanese ethics as theory might turn to my earlier work, *Encounter With Enlightenment* (Carter 2001).

[21] Varela 1992, 68.

and the like all refer to this same state of awareness. Out of this emptiness, compassion arises. This is an enlightened state which yields a "warmth towards the world" and a compassionate concern for others. Once the surface mind is quieted and the ego has "fallen off," there is then room for compassion to arise. One simply *is* other-concerned now. One's horizon is far wider than ever before, and it manifests as specific action in specific situations. Enlightenment is not separate from practice, even though it is also an achievement (or a series of achievements) yielding a level of realization beyond the ordinary. In this way, ethics in Japan is not separate from the arts, or from the practice of religion, or from the everyday living of one's life. Self-cultivation means a transformation of personality, and it is from this that the strongest ethical insights arise: to see the "other," whether human or not, as a source of wonder and delight, of worth and as a potential friend, as inseparable from oneself, is a profound foundation for acting ethically. It is a way of being in the world that seeks to preserve and nurture, to embrace and assist whenever appropriate. To exemplify how the arts achieve this transformation, I will use examples from several of the Japanese arts.

THE JAPANESE ARTS

The Japanese arts are "ways of living" and providing discipline in specific techniques that are meant to be generalized as habits for living all of the aspects of one's life. These techniques, when regularly practiced, become internalized as spontaneous reactions to the varied occurrences of everyday life.

For example, learning to make tea is also a means to one's own self-cultivation because it is an act leading to increased spiritual awareness and a magnificent expression of courteous and compassionate behavior toward others. The former grandmaster of the Urasenke school of Tea, Dr. Soshitsu Sen XIV, stated that "Tea teaches us how to approach the people around us, and how to get along with them."[22] The Way of Tea (*chadō* or *sadō* 茶道) teaches that the world as ordinarily seen, as full of separate objects, is a fantasy created by the ego in its attempt to stabilize and solidify what is, in reality, ever-changing and impermanent. This insight—that the ordinary way of comprehending the world as made up of more or less independent, fixed, and permanent objects is a delusion—brings compassion to the fore since the recognition that nothing exists separately means that it is interconnected with everything else in this flux of impermanence. The result is that everything and everyone is kindred in a sense far deeper even than blood ties. Furthermore, the Japanese Buddhist sense of the impermanence (*mujō* 無常) of all things is a central teaching of Tea as well: make tea as though this was your last opportunity to celebrate with others in this deliciously intimate way. Hōnen (1133–1212), in

---

[22] From an interview with Dr. Sen, at the Urasenke Foundation Headquarters, Kyoto, Japan, in October 2003.

his *One Page Testament*, viewed the Way of Tea as an art "motivated and informed by a compassion for things and for one's fellows. In the love termed *suki*, artistic and religious aspirations are one . . . . [and] this love takes as its model the compassion of Buddha."[23] The Buddha committed himself to the elimination of suffering for all beings by bringing them to enlightened awareness. To follow the Buddha's example is to abandon the self-centered perspective, which is also Singer's ethical goal.

Dr. Sen serves as a fine example of how the Japanese have moved away from the extremely limited social nexus perspective of feudal times and have joined Singer and others in adopting a more comprehensive perspective. As an ambassador of peace for the United Nations and as President of the United Nations Association of Japan, he remarks that he has "toured the world for more than a quarter of a century with the goal of 'Peace through sharing a bowl of tea.' The simple act of serving tea and receiving it with gratitude is the basis for a way of life called *Chadō*, the Way of Tea."[24] "Tea is a way of communicating," he said to me in an interview in 2003. "Tea is *kokoro* to *kokoro*," or mind and heart to mind and heart, or soul to soul, or "from thou to thou" in Martin Buber's terms. This way of being with others "is contagious, for as the host attends meticulously to the feelings of his guests, then everyone else begins to attend to the feelings of the other guests." It is this quality, Dr. Sen urged, that gives Tea such an important role to play in the development of world peace. The sharing of tea is a communal act and that, if successful, lifts each participant to a higher level of awareness, kindness, and appreciation where everyone is not only of equal rank but of no rank whatsoever.

Ethics is a part of the martial art of *aikidō* (合気道): *ai* (合) means harmony, *ki* (気) means energy, *dō* (道) means way or path. Developed by Ueshiba Morihei (1883–1969) in the past century, *aikidō* has now spread all over the world. Ueshiba taught that *aikidō* is about the cultivation of body and mind and is based on the insight that each of us is already one with the universal (the ultimate source of all that exists). Influenced by both Shintō and Buddhist teachings, *aikidō* encourages human beings to become aware of this oneness with the cosmos. The term *michi* (道) refers to the cosmic vitalizing force or energy, the spirit of the cosmos, and "is probably the most expressive term in the Japanese vocabulary of ethics and religion," for it can refer not only to a person of character or integrity, but it links also "the subject in some awe-inspiring way with the height and depth of the great All."[25] A second key term is *makoto* (まこと or 誠 or 真), which means sincerity or integrity. It is the root of truthfulness, honesty, and trustworthiness, all of which are necessary for anything resembling dependable and worthwhile social interaction, and, as such, it is the foundation of all human relationships.[26] One who *is* *makoto* is genuine, honest, and self-reflective such that one is vigilant in facing one's shortcomings and steadfast in working toward continuous character development. Such integrity inevitably leads to benevolence, faithfulness, and loyalty since it is the

---

[23] Hirota 1995, 110.
[24] Sen 1979, front cover.
[25] Herbert 1967, 45.
[26] Watsuji 1996, 48.

fastidious attempt to keep oneself unsullied by selfish desire, hatred, ill will, or a shriveled sense of reality as purely material. One *aikidō* scholar and practitioner, Saotome Mitsugi, writes that "The laws of nature have come into being through the function of love, the absolute harmony found in the unfolding process of creation. It is imperative that those on the path of *Aikidō* practice with these things held deep within their hearts."[27] Ueshiba further taught that "we all share the same divine origin. There is only one thing that is wrong or useless. That is the stubborn insistence that you are an individual, separate from others."[28] Expanding on this very theme, Saotome writes that "The truth of I AM is that I am the other. I am a part of God. I am a part of the cosmos. I am a part of the earth. I am part of you. I Am is [the] true God [of] Consciousness, Universal Ego."[29]

A major part of ethics is being able to recognize the value and worth of another. This is, in fact, the fundamental starting point of ethics, and education must be aimed at bringing this out, the ability to perceive the innate worth of another, an ability that arises from an attitude of human-heartedness or fellow-feeling. We are kin in that we all come from the same cosmic womb. And, as surprising as this might be coming from a martial artist, Ueshiba taught that any worthy martial art teaches the art of loving. Even in swordsmanship, the spilling of blood and the aggressive behavior of the samurai gave way to the teachings of Zen Buddhism which held that the sword is no-sword. That is to say, that swords should be carried but not used. The metal sword was to be used for protection only. In *kendō* (剣道, the Way of Swordsmanship), the metal sword gave way to a practice sword of bamboo, split into several strands and yielding a broken sound when struck. The Zen love of paradox manifests in this way—the sword that killed can now be used to bring about nonaggression. One must be able to use the sword not as a sword. Through learning the use of the sword and following the path of self-cultivation and enlightenment one can now live a life without ever having to draw a sword!

Perhaps the greatest modern-day teacher of *aikidō*, the late Tōhei Kōichi, taught that it is incumbent upon us not to fight (unless there is no other alternative, and even then it is "fighting" with the purpose of helping the other person; i.e., not allowing the other to hurt or be hurt), not to focus on winning or losing, and not to egoistically rank oneself as superior but rather to "correct each other as whetstones, and mirror each other's actions."[30] He stresses such character traits as openness, frankness, humility, perseverance, generosity, courtesy, harmony, fearlessness, wisdom, friendship, reconciliation, cooperation, empathy, respect, patience, having a calm mind, and being in control of one's anger. While this approach does not advocate a single rational criterion for recognizing what a right action is, it does emphasize, in the predictable Japanese way, what it will take to be an ethical and well-developed person in a demanding world. The focus is on character development, personal growth, and spiritual realization. It is little

[27] Saotome 1993, 67.
[28] Gleason 1995, 6.
[29] Saotome 1993, 152.
[30] Tohei 1966, 197.

wonder, then, that those who practice *aikidō* do not speak of opponents, but only of "partners."

Likewise, in Japanese landscape gardening and design, the garden is much more than a garden: it is an expression of eternity, of the originary nothingness. The late Professor Nishitani Keiji (1900–1990), during a visit I had with him at his home in Kyoto, told me that most people who visit the great landscape gardens merely "look at the surface . . . at the beautiful rocks, the rippled patterns in the sand, the moss, and the earth-colored walls. But the garden is an expression of the landscape architect's own enlightenment! . . . Underneath our feet, where we stand in the garden, the garden is looking at us, for we are now a part of the actual manifestation of the garden architect's own personal self-transformation."

Masuno Shunmyō, a Sōtō Zen priest and one of Japan's foremost landscape architects, designed the Zen garden at the Canadian Museum of Civilization in Ottawa. He writes, "It is called *Wakei No Niwa* [和敬の庭], which, roughly translated, means to understand and respect all cultures—their history, spirit, and people—which leads to cultural harmony."[31] This stands as yet another indication that the Japanese, too, are becoming citizens of the world and not merely of some small in-group. In designing a garden, Masuno first meditates and then establishes a "dialogue" with the space assigned to the garden, as well as with the rocks, plants and trees. To accomplish this, one must empty the self in order to "hear" the garden elements speak. In discussions with him, he articulated his perspective on the ethics of gardening. Landscape gardening brings about a gentleness in the designer, the builders, and the caretakers. The garden teaches the suchness or intrinsic value of each thing, the connectedness, harmony, tranquility, and the sacredness of the everyday. Developing a sense of respect for all things is no small step in becoming an ethical human being, both with respect to other humans and the environment at large. The garden teaches that we are always in relationship, and gardening requires us to respect the *kokoro* (こころ or 心) of each component of the garden. He added that the garden teaches by example: "the most important things cannot be expressed in words, and so the physical manifestations of the *dō* teach by example, rather than through abstract words—it is like pouring liquid from one cup to another." The garden raises you to a higher level of awareness and self-integration. The experience of the garden can convey to people a physical, emotional, and spiritual sense of how to live one's life in a very different way than before. One now lives as though walking or meditating in a garden. One is thereby engaged in practice, in self-cultivation, attempting to emulate the enlightenment experience of the designer. The result is far more than an intellectual lesson, for the resultant awareness involves the whole person in a gentle affirmation of one's connection with all of existence—a sense of genuine relationship with rocks and ferns, trees and insects, people and pets. And to viscerally experience one's kinship with all of these is a giant step toward becoming an ethical person, one who works in harmony with the things that exist in order to create beauty, to offer a glimpse of truth, and

---

[31] Masuno 1999, 53.

to express goodness. The landscape garden, in all of its forms, encourages each of us to cherish and nurture this world of which we are an integral part.

CONCLUSION

In *The Japanese Arts and Self-Cultivation*, I wrote the following: "If the Japanese approach to ethics is to develop the desired attitudes with which to face and greet life, then the practice of the various arts is central to the learning of these attitudes."[32] Rather than a single-minded focus on either the individual or membership in a group, Watsuji stressed both. And rather than an almost exclusive emphasis on theoretical reason that has no, or very little, impact on one's living, the Japanese way is to cultivate the heart through meditation and specific other-directed activities. In an abstract, intellectual approach to living, it is possible to think one knows what to do, ethically speaking, but so often either one does not act on that knowledge or takes no joy in doing so.

An ethical person will likely have a passion for acting well, for not causing undue pain to others, and for nurturing and protecting the environment at large. This passion arises out of the awareness that we are all interconnected, that we are one, that we are kinfolk, and the most powerful insight into this way of being is the experience of one's own empty self, which opens out to an interest in and concern for others. Varela contends that "authentic care resides at the very ground of Being," of nothingness.[33] And while such passion may be no more universal among the Japanese than is observance of the Ten Commandments or the teachings of Jesus, Kant, or John Stuart Mill in Western cultures, it would be a colossal mistake to imagine that either Japan or the Western peoples are devoid of traditions that teach how one ought to live ethically in the fullest sense. Perhaps the surprise is that the Japanese have been able to create a modern-day culture in which guns play almost no part, where it is still remarkably safe to walk the streets and alleys at any time during the day or night. It is a culture that shows a high degree of respect for others in day-to-day encounters. Yet Singer also addresses the many shortcomings of Japanese society. The crucial mistake, however, is to assume that a particular culture is missing essential resources in its depths rather than to recognize the advantages that might come from weaving insights from that culture into our own. Japanese culture and ethics are both deep and ancient. When explored in depth, rather than superficially, they offer new horizons of understanding that both nourish and offer insights into one's own culture and way of being in the world. Such a fusion of horizons, in the many ways that it might occur, may cause a rethinking of one's most cherished beliefs and ethical assumptions. And, if such a fusion occurred, it could further manifest that vital self-cultivation and personal growth along a pathway leading toward self-transformation and enlightenment.

---

[32] Carter 2008, 143.
[33] Varela 1992, 73.

Confucius, whose ethical teachings are still highly regarded in Japan and in Japanese education, remarked that at sixty years of age his ears were attuned to the biddings of heaven. To be in harmony with the macrocosm (heaven) is the ethical ideal. At seventy, he was able simply to follow his heart's desire without transgressing the ethical norm (*Analects*, 2.4). He had become a steadfastly good man, a man of *ren*; that is, dependably human-hearted. Proper ethical action was now internalized such that to be ethical took no thinking and was utterly spontaneous. So, too, the self-actualized person in Japan will not only act compassionately, but also will want to so act: to be ethical is now his or her nature.[34] Such a person is the ideal in Japan, a self-actualized individual who spontaneously acts for the well-being of all that exists, at least to the greatest extent possible. The norm is for the microcosm to act in harmony with the macrocosm in Confucianism, and the enlightened person in Japan is one with the whole of existence.

BIBLIOGRAPHY AND SUGGESTED READINGS

Carter, Robert E. (2001) *Encounter With Enlightenment: A Study of Japanese Ethics.* Albany: State University of New York Press.

Carter, Robert E. (2008) *The Japanese Arts and Self-Cultivation.* Albany: State University of New York Press.

DeMartino, Richard. (1960) "The Human Situation and Zen Buddhism." In *Zen Buddhism and Psychoanalysis*, edited by D. T. Suzuki, Erich Fromm, and Richard De Martino. New York: Harper and Brothers, 142–171.

Dharmasiri, Gunapala. (1989) *Fundamentals of Buddhist Ethics.* Antioch, CA: Golden Leaves Publishing Co.

Gleason, William. (1995) *The Spiritual Foundations of Aikidō.* Rochester, VT: Destiny Books.

Hall, David L., and Roger T Ames. (1987) *Thinking Through Confucius.* Albany: State University of New York Press.

Herbert, Jean. (1967) *Shintō: At the Fountain-head of Japan.* London: George Allen and Unwin Ltd.

Hirota, Dennis. (1995) *Wind in the Pines: Classic Writings of the Way of Tea as a Buddhist Path.* Fremont, CA: Asian Humanities Press.

Kohlberg, Lawrence. (1981) *The Philosophy of Moral Development: Moral Stages and the Idea of Justice. Vol. 1 of Essays on Moral Development.* San Francisco: Harper & Row, Publishers.

Masuno, Shunmyo. (1995) "Landscapes in the Spirit of Zen: A Collection of the Work of Shunmyo Masuno," *Process Architecture*, Special Issue 7.

Masuno, Shunmyo. (1999) *Ten Landscapes*, edited by J. G. Truelove. Rockport, MA: Rockport Publishers Inc.

Morley, John David. (1985) *Pictures from the Water Trade: Adventures of a Westerner in Japan.* New York: Perennial Library.

Nakamura, Hajime. (1964) *Ways of Thinking of Eastern Peoples: India-China-Tibet-Japan*, edited by Philip P. Wiener. Honolulu: East-West Center Press.

---

[34] For more on the theme of natural spontaneity in Japanese philosophy, see Chapter 33 in this volume.

Saotome, Mitsugi. (1993) *Aikidō and the Harmony of Nature*. Boston and London: Shambhala.

Sen, Soshitsu XV. (1979) *Tea Life, Tea Mind*. New York: Weatherhill, Published for the Urasenke Foundation, Kyoto.

Singer, Peter. (1995) *How Are We to Live?: Ethics in an Age of Self-Interest*. Amherst, NY: Prometheus Books.

Tohei, Koichi. (1966) *Aikidō in Daily Life*. Tokyo: Rikugei Publishing House.

Varela, Francisco J. (1992) *Ethical Know-How: Action, Wisdom, and Cognition*. Stanford: Stanford University Press.

Watsuji, Tetsurō. (1996) *Watsuji Tetsuro's Rinrigaku: Ethics in Japan*, translated by S. Yamamoto and Robert E. Carter. Albany: State University of New York Press.

CHAPTER 35

....

JAPANESE (AND AINU) AESTHETICS AND PHILOSOPHY OF ART

....

MARA MILLER AND YAMASAKI KŌJI

SITTING in a Philadelphia diner I overheard a conversation about the difficulties of learning Japanese.[1] I discovered the speakers were trying to teach themselves this (notoriously difficult) language; when I eventually turned around to look, I was surprised to see three African-American teenagers struggling with a bilingual *manga* (Japanese comic book). Japanese aesthetics has lost none of its power, I realized, though the immediate stimuli, the categories of Japanese aesthetics that appeal, and their audiences have changed. In fact, no place has had a more illustrious, far-reaching, influential, or penetrating impact on global arts and aesthetics than Japan. Such claims apply *prima pares* to the traditional, distinctively Japanese aesthetic categories ("categorical aesthetics")[2] and to qualities such as vagueness, irregularity and asymmetry, spontaneity, "closeness to

[1] Mara Miller is the primary author of this chapter, which treats different issues from her 2011 article "Japanese Aesthetics" in the *Oxford Handbook of World Philosophy*. Yamasaki Kōji contributed substantially to the section on Ainu aesthetics, including all its basic research. We thank Austin Rooks for his editorial help with this manuscript and Prof. John Zuern, University of Hawai'i-Manoa, for sponsoring the English Department's Internship Program.

[2] Miller 2011 addresses types of aesthetic pleasure ("categorical aesthetics"), their objectives, such as enlightenment via aesthetic shock (Pali *samvega* संवेग < *sam*=with, together + *vega*=force, agitation, dismay; Chinese *yanbu*, Japanese *enfu* 厭怖 <厭=loathe, tire of + 怖=shudder, terror, dread); and contrasts Japanese and Western definitions of aesthetics and the applicability of the term to Japan. It also discusses the alleged uniqueness of Japanese aesthetics and its role in constructing national identity; aesthetics and everyday life; self-cultivation and self-realization; and implications of aesthetics for relationship intersubjectivity, and/or co-subjectivity. Because the field is developing rapidly (see Nguyen, 2017), because aesthetics and arts accomplish more in Japanese than in Western philosophy, and because new translations of classical Japanese aestheticians are now published, the present chapter covers different issues so as to understand philosophically how Japanese aesthetics function, what they accomplish, and why they are so compelling internationally. For studies of the uses of aesthetics in Japanese literature to probe ethical issues, see Miller 2002, 2014*b*, 2015, and 2020.

„nature," and the like,[3] many of which are based in Zen.[4] But they apply equally to some new aesthetics with different origins and to pre-Zen aesthetics such as *mononoaware*.[5]

The importance of Japanese aesthetics is not only a function of their popularity and influence, however. Rather, they are popular and influential because they (sometimes) do things that nothing else does and that we badly need. What, then, do Japanese aesthetics (and arts manifesting those aesthetics) do? They make us more joyful. They enable us to notice—and enjoy—change, especially seasonal, but also topographical and other kinds of change; to acknowledge and comprehend the ineffable; to see just how much information and knowledge can be conveyed outside language; to bear the unbearable (in the words of Emperor Hirohito's 1945 radio broadcast); to survive atomic destruction; to see the beauty in folk arts; to create beauty in the everyday and enhance what is already there; to simplify under increasingly confusing, even overwhelming, conditions; to lessen our cravings for stuff, for bling, for ostentation, for luxury, even for purported "necessities"; to express individuality and experience community—outside the paradigm of adversarial individuals and society's relationships; and to become better persons through self-cultivation, enhanced experience, and fresh insight.

Japanese aesthetics and the arts instantiating them offer us extraordinary ways of being alive, introduce new ways of perception, thinking, and feeling. They teach us ways of loving, ways of understanding and encountering the other including the land that may not otherwise be available, as well as new approaches to our very selves, to the very constitution of selfhood and self-consciousness. They offer new ways of recognizing what it can mean to be oneself.[6] They provide countless windows on modernization— what we gain, what we lose, and by what processes—and provide as well medicine for some of its ills, for coping with loneliness, isolation, alienation. (But are they cures or palliatives, painkillers? And how are they related to fascism, to the "spiritual and cultural crisis: the dead end of modernity and the loss of guiding cultural and existential myths ... [and the] desperate need to ease the ache of those losses ... "?[7]) They suggest new ways of conceptualizing, understanding, and relating to natural and built environments. The arts embodying these aesthetics serve as cognitive prostheses, ways

[3] Keene 1971.
[4] Robert E. Carter reports that Hisamatsu Shin'ichi lists seven Zen-based characteristics of the Japanese sense of beauty: "asymmetry, simplicity, austere sublimity or lofty dryness, naturalness, subtle profundity or deep reserve, freedom from attachment, and tranquility. Within these categories such qualities as *wabi, sabi,* and *yūgen* [appear]" ("A Philosophic Grounding for Japanese Aesthetics," in Nguyen 2017). See Hisamatsu 1971. Early work in English is found in Daisetz T. Suzuki, *Zen and Japanese Culture* (New York: Pantheon Books, 1959; new edition with an introduction by Richard M. Jaffe, Princeton: Princeton University Press, 2010). On the related aesthetic of the "indistinct," see Cooper 2018.
[5] Valdo H. Viglielmo, "The Aesthetic Interpretation of Life in *The Tale of Genji,*" in *Analecta Husserliana* 17, *Phenomenology of Life*, edited by A. -T. Tymieniecka (Dordrecht: D. Reidel, 1984), 347–359.
[6] So do the aesthetics of other cultures, of course—for instance, Confucian, with its *essentially* relational self.
[7] Tansman 2009a, 51.

of extending and/or enhancing our cognitive abilities on both individual and societal levels.[8]

To assert such claims is not to deny there can be perfidious, insidious, demeaning, amoral or anti-ethical, and even dangerous applications of Japanese aesthetics (by Japanese or outsiders). Even as Japanese aesthetics retain their popularity and power, they have come under suspicion, internationally and within Japan. Their early reception abroad is now often seen as a type of orientalism (condescending and self-serving), although this recognition of the objectification and sometimes "feminization" of Japan by the "colonial gaze" (Japan was never colonized) often underestimates both the force and variety of Japanese contestation and agency, and sometimes overlooks the fact that there are differences between being forced to trade and being colonized.[9] At the same time, Japanese and Western theorists and historians increasingly acknowledge the economic and political agendas underlying Japanese aesthetics and their modern exportation—agendas that have been all the more puzzling and hard to spot given Western assumptions about the supposed "disinterestedness" and transcendence of art. Finally, aesthetics was complicit in the undermining of individual agency and independent thought and action as part of fascism; in Alan Tansman's words,

> Fascism was one means to enchant a culture stripped of its magic by modernity. Intellectuals [in the 1930s] argued for, and creative artists made attractive, the abandonment of individuality—an abstract modern notion, seen as perniciously Western, festering at the core of the crisis—and searched for an identity grounded in native culture and life, mediated through absolute identification with "the people" (*minzoku*) and the state. The individual came to be viewed not only as selfish but also as an inadequate source of meaning.[10]

This problem will be discussed later.

This chapter has four aims: indicating some accomplishments of Japanese aesthetics so we can better understand them and ourselves, analyzing their complexities, highlighting some of the special challenges Japanese aesthetics presents to Western thinking about art and aesthetics, and introducing some emerging aesthetics and new analyses of traditional aesthetics. To distinguish the field of study from the qualities and experiences studied, we term the qualities (the kinds of pleasure) "categorical aesthetics."[11]

---

[8] This list is not exhaustive. Nor are these functions confined to *Japanese* aesthetics—or to Japanese *aesthetics*. No single aesthetic category or art does it all—especially since some aesthetics are at crosspurposes with others.

[9] Female agency and contestation in pre- and early modern Japan are similarly underrecognized, and for similar reasons.

[10] Tansman 2009a, 9. Tansman recommends Kevin Michael Doak's "Ethnic Nationalism and Romanticism in Early Twentieth-Century Japan," *Journal of Japanese Studies* 22(1): 1966): 77–103, Tansman, 2009a, 287n22.

[11] For the several meanings of the English term "aesthetics," see Miller 2011, 496. Susan Buck-Morss points out a fourth, early twentieth-century sense, closer to Japanese usage: "... a form of cognition, achieved through taste, touch, hearing, seeing smell—the whole corporeal sensorium." Susan Buck-Morss, "Aesthetics and Anaesthetics: Walter Benjamin's Artwork Essay Reconsidered," *October* 62 (autumn 1992): 6.

META-AESTHETICS (ANALYSIS
OF AESTHETICS ANALYSIS)

Japan began selectively adopting and adapting foreign (at the time, Chinese) cultures some 1,500 years ago. This means it presents the nearly unprecedented example of modernizing (and, later, to some extent Westernizing) with the advantage of a millennium and a half of practice in the conscious and deliberate adaptation of foreign cultures[12]—a practice that elicited nearly as long a history of "meta-aesthetics" and philosophy of art.[13] It demanded examination of differences between Japanese and Chinese arts and aesthetics, conceptualized in binary oppositions for native/Chinese (and male/female) versions of painting and writing, and later for native/Western and Japanese/Asian culture. Recently, studies of the "open[ing] up of [what had been] the binary positioning of Japan and the Occident into the three-way positioning of the Occident-Japan-Orient" during modernization are emerging.[14] In addition, new ways of recovering Ainu aesthetics are being discovered (discussed later).

The Complexities of Japanese Aesthetics

As the variety of categorical aesthetics suggests, Japanese aesthetics—under any definition—is no unified phenomenon. (Much less should it be understood as essentializing or definitive of the Japanese.[15]) The situation is complex, given that categorical aesthetics apply on several levels: the aesthetics and/or theories in accordance with which works are created (artists' intentions, heritage, and/or *milieu*), the categorical aesthetics and/or theories exhibited by the works, and the aesthetics predominating in works of art referred to or shown within another work of art (e.g., the *wabi* of a tea bowl in a novel). Depth increases with the facts that philosophy in the Western sense did not exist in Japan until the Meiji era (1868–1912) because metaphysical, epistemological, ethical, and other philosophical questions were typically addressed within Buddhist or Confucianist frameworks and that many theorists of art were also artists. In addition, we should eventually (I cannot attempt it here) recognize more fully the ways in which visual and performing arts do some of the work that is in the West done only in language. (At some point, we need to examine how works of art express new philosophical positions or question/challenge existing positions.)

---

[12]   Shōtoku Taishi's *Seventeen-Article Constitution* of 604 combined principles from Chinese Confucianism and Buddhism. See Heisig et al. 2011, 33–39, 1018, and Chapter 1 in this volume.

[13]   This meta-aesthetics began with Kūkai (Kōbō Daishi) and was soon followed by the preface to the Kokinshū.

[14]   Yuko Kikuchi, "Visualizing Oriental Crafts: Contested Notion of 'Japaneseness' and the Crafts of the Japanese Empire," in Inaga 2010.

[15]   Miller 2011, 493–495.

Historically, Japanese aesthetics demonstrate complexity on four levels:

1. The maintenance of earlier aesthetics and artistic styles even after new ones are created—in contrast to Western practices, in which new forms often supplant existing ones
2. The length and complexity of the aforementioned Japanese history of accommo-dating themselves to features of foreign cultures that seemed important in some way (sometimes to the point where they threatened to dominate native culture) and of experimenting with ways of internalizing and/or modifying what they wanted and rejecting what they did not want
3. The complexity of the arts themselves in a culture where aesthetics have often served military purposes (as well as the various political and religious ends ac-knowledged in the West), where folk traditions were endorsed by and within the fine arts since the sixteenth century, and where, in addition to the tripartite elite of imperial court, shogunate/lords, and temples, each of which supported different aesthetics, the urban middle class has supported its own arts for four centuries
4. Japanese recognition after World War II of the desperation of their position and of the demands placed on arts in their unprecedented situation.[16]

These complexities appear in every artistic field. We need to remember several things, though. First, at the same time, many Japanese were intensely ambivalent toward mod-ernization (often conceptualized as "Westernization"—as is sometimes appropriate).[17] Second, influences went both ways, so the "success" of Japanese aesthetics sometimes rested on its absorption of foreign values and formulations. Third, nostalgia seem-ingly informed much of Japanese art: a yearning for an idealized past now sacrificed (or sold out) that prompted some of Japan's greatest modern scholarly, political, and artistic movements to recover and subsidize traditional crafts and arts, as well as—in the wake of the atomic bombings, no less—artists' return to the land with its (aes-thetically informed) local significance and the recovery of ancient, even Neolithic, artistic techniques (with *their* distinctive aesthetics).[18] Finally, while Frankfurt School philosophers have dominated thinking about nostalgia, nostalgia is now being reconsidered;[19] thus, views of its role in twentieth-century Japanese arts and aesthetics will need to be reevaluated as well (though not here).

This points up the complexity of Japanese aesthetics and of the task of understanding them. There are five tasks. First and second, how do we understand Japanese aesthetics in both senses: what do we understand it to be, and how do we go about this process? We

[16] Miller 2010.

[17] And was "modernization" to include socialism and/or communism? Some thought so, and some of them were incarcerated or killed. The stakes of modernization were high.

[18] Mara Miller, "Beauty, Religion and Tradition in Post-Nuclear Japanese Arts and Aesthetics," in *Artistic Visions and the Promise of Beauty: Cross-Cultural Perspectives*, edited by Kathleen Higgins, Shakti Maira, and Sonia Sikka (Dordrecht: Springer, 2016).

[19] See Svetlana Boym, *The Future of Nostalgia* (New York: Basic Books, 2002).

cannot begin to answer those two questions, however, until we answer the most important (third) question: how do Japanese aesthetics (with their various purposes and in
varying contexts) enhance life?

Fourth, how should we understand the roles of aesthetics in shaping (a) Japan (contemporary, modern, and "traditional") and our understanding of them; (b) modern and
contemporary Western/American society; and (c) American–Japanese relations since
1868? Finally, what does Japanese aesthetics have to offer the world in terms of critiques
of philosophical positions and of existing ways of constructing and making sense of our
world? This is an intriguing question, and, while widely intuited and often asserted by
artists, it is little studied by philosophers. These questions cannot be answered here, but
they are worth mentioning. This quintuple task is only one of several complexities facing
us here: in the context of Japanese discussions of aesthetics, what it means to be Japanese
is itself at issue—although this issue is not purely philosophical but also social, historical, and psychological—and surfaces again with the aesthetics of the Ainu.

The Female Voice and Gaze and Feminist Aesthetics

Japanese women provide the only example in any literate culture of persistent female
voices in the literary and philosophical mainstream over a long time (1,500 years—
since the poems in the first written anthology based partly on oral tradition).[20] Donald
Keene's analysis stands out for its recognition that "feminine" and "masculine" are social rather than biological attributions and do not correlate with the sex of the human
subject and acknowledgment of the importance of these women, whose contributions
comprise a crucial female voice.[21] No culture has a stronger history of interweaving
aesthetics and nation-building; scholars therefore recognize profound impacts of
the female voice on national identity and nationalism as men came to identify with
women and with the feminine, and the identification evolved into a sense of national
identity.[22] Tomiko Yoda explicates the intricate interrelationships among sex/gender
and the ideologies of Japanese identity asserted by major Japanese scholars over the
past 300 years, arguing that, from the eighteenth century on, "modernizing discourses
on literature in Japan used gender difference as a foundational asymmetry—a vitally

[20] For a critique of the use of the anachronistic term "feminist" in regard to classical Japan, see Mara
Miller 2020. In spite of the obvious problems, I identify twelve ways in which Murasaki Shikibu's and Sei
Shonagon's aesthetics (ca. 1000 C.E.) can be considered harmonious with contemporary feminism and
vice versa.

[21] He characterized it as "almost modern in tone," p. 117. Miller 2020 analyzes Keene's views in the light
of contemporary feminism.

[22] Chance 2000; Henitiuk 2005 and 2011; Schalow and Walker 1996. Chino Kaori made her lifework
the study of the ways in which the visual arts made the feminine central to Japanese identity; see Chino
2010; Kano Ayako. "Women? Japan? Art?: Chino Kaori and the Feminist Art History Debates" *Review of
Japanese Culture and Society*, December 2003; and Melissa McCormick, "On the Scholarship of Chino
Kaori," *Review of Japanese Culture and Society* (2003) 15: 1–24.

interconnected and hierarchically differentiated binary," arguing that "Through the manipulation of this gendered structure, . . . literature was constituted as the expression of a unified and autonomous national subject"[23]

In Japan, the female gaze, a notion derived from Laura Mulvey's seminal work on the male gaze and elaborated by (among others) Margaret Whitford in her study of Luce Irigaray, [24] manifests itself since at least the Heian period (794–1185) both through women's and men's artistic creations and in depictions as viewing subjects within images and literature (by both men and women).[25] The female gaze establishes the agency of looking by women as opposed to passively occupying the position of object of the male gaze and thus establishes a female subject position within hegemonic male power structures.

These two forces, the female voice and the female gaze, studied so far primarily in relation to the theory of Japanese national identity and (through the lenses of feminist theory) to contestations of male hegemony, also have implications *for* global feminist theory (often mistakenly construed as universal). Their implications in regard to the mistrust of language and the elaborations of "gender-independent co-subjectivity"[26] are still unexplored, as are their implications for gendered space, for understanding the aesthetics of women architects,[27] and for work in contemporary feminist aesthetics.

CATEGORICAL AESTHETICS AND SPECIAL TOPICS

Recovering Ainu Aesthetics

The Ainu, an indigenous people now of northern Japan, are geographically and politically part of Japan but ethnically and culturally distinct.[28] Ainu aesthetics developed

[23] Tomiko Yoda, *Gender and National Literature: Heian Texts in the Construction of Japanese Modernity* (Durham, NC: Duke University Press, 2004), 7.

[24] Laura Mulvey, "Visual Pleasure and Narrative Cinema," *Screen* 16, 3 (Autumn, 1975); Margaret Whitford, *Luce Irigaray: Philosophy in the Feminine* (New York: Routledge, 1991).

[25] See the Special Section "In Her Voice: Interrogating Gendered Notions of Gaze and Body," edited by Kelly Hansen, with articles by Monika Dix, Kelly Hansen, Irena Hayter, and Catherine Ryu, *Japanese Language and Literature* 48, 1 (April 2014); Melissa McCormick's work on illustrations of women discussing *The Tale of Genji*, "Monochromatic *Genji*: The Hakubyō Tradition and Female Commetarial Culture," in *Envisioning the* Tale of Genji: *Media, Gender, and Cultural Production*, edited by Haruo Shirane (New York: Columbia University Press, 2008); and Mara Miller, "Identity, Identification, and Temperament in Emblematic Portraits of Edo Japanese Literati Artists Taiga & Gyokuran," *MingQing Yanjiu* (Napoli: Universita degli Studi di Napoli, 2007), 65–111, and Miller 1998.

[26] Miller 1993.

[27] As of 2014 Kazuyo Sejima (in 2010) was fifty percent of the women who have won the Pritzker Prize.

[28] For a solid introduction to the current state of the field regarding studies of the Ainu, see Mark J. Hudson, ann-elise lewallen, and Mark K. Watson, *Beyond Ainu Studies: Changing and Public Perspectives* (Honolulu: University of Hawai'i Press, 2014).

independently, differing both from Japanese notions and particularly from the Western view that beauty is absolute, transcends time, and is ideally free of instrumental functions and interests.[29] All Dennis Dutton's twelve criteria for defining art ("direct pleasure, skill and virtuosity, style, novelty and creativity, criticism, representation, special focus, expressive individuality, emotional saturation, intellectual challenge, arts traditions and institutions, and imaginative experience") apply to the Ainu case.[30]

A recent experiment at Hokkaido University initiated the rediscovery of Ainu aesthetics.[31] The experiment and its resulting exhibition had two objectives: encouraging more people, particularly Ainu artists, to make use of the specimens in an Ainu ethnological collection and exploring the works' present-day significance through their utilization. The study opened up the renowned collection of Ainu art and handcrafts to Ainu artists so they could study—and *handle*—Ainu museum objects in order to make replicas, encouraging tactile and *kinesthetic* contact (for touch does not exhaust the full experience of physical contact with objects); it then enabled the artists to replicate works they had selected; and, finally, it facilitated their discussion with each other, recording and publishing their observations about both the objects and their processes of discovery.

The results of this experiment were as follows. First, a sense of spiritual connection resurfaced in many ways: connection with earlier artists (through replicating their choices and movements), with materials and tools, with the selected objects, with future generations, with local animals, and with specific locales and/or their communities. Second, aesthetics were revealed to be gendered (women continued women's work and styles, identifiable as distinctively women's, and men men's) and elicited different observations. Third, artists spoke repeatedly about learning from the observed objects, from their reproduction processes, and from the materials they used, which were often different from the modern materials they used customarily. These (traditional) materials often required different ways of working; the experiment thus allowed the artists to reconstruct traditional techniques and values. Aesthetic values in the earlier works noted by artists include a beauty that seems to have been equated with efficacy in its intended use; freedom of expression; "sensitivity and sharpness of our ancestors toward nature"; and haptic, textural, and kinesthetic values. Fourth, individuality appeared in many guises: it was sometimes seen as failure or inability, sometimes as self-expression. Fifth, artists' comments as well as completed works show that Ainu aesthetics link persons and the community to the environment through connections to local spirits and to the animals who live in particular locales, through the use of local materials, and through connoisseurs' recognition and selection of (and artists' use of) regionally specific styles. These findings reinforce the findings regarding gender and cloth/clothing of Tsuda Nobuko and ann-elise lewallen

[29] Pierre Bourdieu, *The Rules of Art: Genesis and Structure of the Literary Field* (in Japanese), translated by Yojirō Ishii (Tokyo: Fujiwara Shoten, 1996).

[30] Miller 2014a; Denis Dutton, *The Art Instinct: Beauty, Pleasure, and Human Evolution* (New York: Bloomsbury Press, 2009), 52–59.

[31] It took place at the Hokkaido Botanic Garden, Field Science Center for Northern Biosphere at Hokkaido University. See Yamasaki, Kato, and Amano 2012 and Yamasaki and Miller 2017.

[sic], authors who also underscore the changing nature of Ainu arts and aesthetics (as opposed to an eternal "traditional") over at least the past several hundred years. (Tsuda pioneered the "restor[ation of] the embodied knowledge of textile making to the Ainu community" through replication and participatory engagement in the arts.[32])

This experiment challenges received notions in the philosophy of art, especially about the value of replication; the nature of originality—which, outside mechanical and digital production, may (as in East Asian calligraphy) be almost inevitable—and the nature and value of "copying"; and the supposed dichotomy between original and forgery. It questions the validity of relying solely on vision to understand even so-called visual art, presenting some major challenges to museum practice.[33] It is invaluable for what it suggests about relations between art and collective and distributed memory. Finally, the experiment calls into question the primacy and hegemony of language in collective memory, transmission of values, and aesthetic thinking.

Modern Aesthetics

New art historical studies of historic Buddhist temples and Noh masks raise important philosophical issues[34] relating to principles and themes that underlie Japan's famous categorical aesthetics,[35] such as the interest in "everyday aesthetics,"[36] minimalism, gestural art, and the female gaze and voice. An increasing body of research-based theory relates to modernization and Westernization, the impact of colonialism on Japan's understanding of its mission in Asia, the mutual views ("gaze") of Japan and the West,[37] and modern changes in personal identity.[38] This section examines new aesthetics rather than traditional aesthetics encountered by the twentieth century.[39]

---

[32] Tsuda Nobuko, "Our Ancestors' Handprints: The Evolution of Ainu Women's Clothing Culture;" and ann-elise lewallen [sic], "The Gender of Cloth: Ainu Women and Cultural Revolution," in *Beyond Ainu Studies: Changing and Public Perspectives*, edited by Mark J. Hudson, ann-elise lewallen, and Mark K. Watson (Honolulu: University of Hawai'i Press, 2014).

[33] Yamasaki and Miller 2017.

[34] Philosophical dimensions are analyzed in my reviews of Sherry D. Fowler's *Muroji: Rearranging Art and History at a Japanese Buddhist Temple* and Gregory P. A. Levine's *Daitokuji: The Visual Cultures of a Zen Monastery, Journal of Aesthetics and Art Criticism* 68(2: Spring), 177–178; and of Stephen E. Marvin's *Heaven Has a Face, So Does Hell: The Art of the Noh Mask, Journal of Aesthetics and Art Criticism*, 72 (1: Winter 2014), 176–79.

[35] Saito 2018; anthropologist Richard L. Anderson's Japan chapter in *Calliope's Sisters: A Comparative Study of Philosophies of Art* (Englewood Cliffs, NJ: Prentice Hall, 1990) is especially good at explicating these principles.

[36] Yuriko Saito, *Everyday Aesthetics* (Oxford: Oxford University Press, 2008).

[37] Shigemi Inaga, *Questioning Oriental Aesthetics and Thinking: Conflicting Visions of "Asia" Under the Colonial Empires* (Kyoto: International Research Center for Japanese Studies, 2010).

[38] See Miller 2011, 325–330; Miller 1997; Janet Walker, *The Japanese Novel of the Meiji Period and the Ideal of Individualism* (Princeton: Princeton University Press, 1979); Washburn 1995; and Heisig et al., "Culture and Identity," in Heisig et al. 2011; the latter discuss the "I-novel," *watakushi-shōsetsu* (私小説)

[39] Other influential aesthetics, including presentational theatre; *ma* (間, space or interval); *umami* (旨味, 旨み, or 旨), a fifth category of taste contributing to the deliciousness of savory foods; and *mitate* (見立て, layered meanings), are omitted here for reasons of space.

Furusato

The arts of photography, folk tales, popular song, and advertising together created the aesthetic and concept of *furusato* (古里, 故郷, 旧跡): hometown, birthplace, or native village. Originating with Yanagita Kunio's 1910 compilation of folktales, *Legends of Tono*,[40] it refers to modern city-dwellers' cherishing of one's idealized home village now left behind in the wake of late Meiji urbanization. It links ethics, society, aesthetics—and travel marketing—into a seemingly unified sensibility, that "prov[es] to be a labile and shifting one, open to conservative political uses as well as to sharply antiauthoritarian attempts to reimagine the democratic possibilities of community."[41] Evolving theory about nostalgia requires reevaluation of *furusato*. *Furusato*, a theme suggestive of categorical aesthetics, is related to but should not be confused with meta-analyses of Japanese aesthetics of space.[42]

Aesthetics of Fascism and War

Japanese aesthetics and arts moved in many directions during the modernizing years of Meiji, Taisho (1912–1926), and early Showa (1926–1989), since the modernization project required the invention of new sentence structures[43] and shapes of narrative for fiction, such as the *watakushi shōsetsu* or "I-novel", new forms of consciousness and recognitions of individualism,[44] and new architectural styles and ways of constructing to accommodate new forms of political and physical action. Literary and artistic movements proliferated.[45] As modernity's early promise began to fail in the late '20s and '30s, however, reactionary and fascist movements developed.[46] Since national identity was traditionally defined through aesthetics—and had been by disparate thinkers (Yoda 2004, Shirane 2000)—aesthetics played a prominent role in the dissemination of what became twentieth-century fascism.[47]

---

[40] Kunio Yanagita, *Legends of Tono*, translated by Ronald A. Morse (Tokyo: The Japan Foundation, 1975). Photographer Daido Moriyama's legendary book of photographs, *Tales of Tono*, was reissued with essays by Moriyama, on the concept of *furusato* by Lena Fritsch (translator), and on Moriyama's photography (London: Tate Publishing, 2012).

[41] Ivy 2010, 103. See also Gerbert 1998.

[42] See Tadahiko Higuchi, *The Visual and Spatial Structure of Landscapes* (Cambridge, MA: MIT Press, 1983) and Thorsten Botz-Bornstein, *Aesthetics and Politics of Space in Russia and Japan: A Comparative Philosophical Study* (Lanham, MD: Rowman & Littlefield, 2009). Botz-Bornstein discusses Watsuji Tetsurō and others.

[43] See Atsuko Ueda, "*Bungakuron* and 'Literature' in the Making" in *Japan Forum* vol. 20, no. 1, March, 2008.

[44] By individualism, I refer to the premise that the individual comprises a basic unit of value within a political system. This sense of individualism was new—and highly problematic—in Japan. Individuality in the sense of recognition of the personal styles and consciousness of individual artists, on the other hand, had been part of the aesthetic ethos for centuries, in spite of oft-repeated assertions to the contrary.

[45] See Ito 2008; and Jonathan M. Reynolds, "The Bunriha and the Problem of 'Tradition' for Modernist Architecture in Japan, 1920–1928," in Minichiello 1998, 228–246.

[46] For a summary of the debate regarding whether Japanese politics during this period can be characterized as fascist, see Tansman 2009*a*, 283–285*n*9 and 292*n*60.

[47] The eighteenth-century mode of "*chic*" called *iki*, revisited by Kuki Shūzō during this period, is frequently blamed (unfairly) for fascism. For a fuller discussion of the problems with this assessment

Alan Tansman has pioneered the study of uses of aesthetics to inculcate fascism in the prewar years, offering a definitive analysis of the forces at play during the war years.[48] He argues that

> ... fascist aesthetics—including artistic evocations of beauty and the aesthetic re-sponse to them— ... attempted to resolve the conflicts of modernity by calling for complete submission, either to absolute order or to an undifferentiated but liberating experience of violence. Such an aesthetics exalted mindlessness and glamorized death.[49]

Anyone arguing that (some) Japanese aesthetics are fascist must account for the facts that the same aesthetics are used (in different contexts) to decidedly nonfascist effect and that at least some of the artists and theorists evidently had no fascist intention. Tansman shows how the effects are achieved through the incantatory use of language and an appeal to *kotodama* (the sense of language as efficacious and/or spiritual). He insists that it is not the content of the aesthetic per se but the use of it to avoid or prevent logical thought and questioning, combined with the attempt to fuse the individual with the state, the circumventing of individual responsibility, and the accompanying glori-fication of and incitement to violence, that make an aesthetic fascist. The results are in-sidious precisely because they seem so apolitical: Tansman is at pains to point out that (a) "writers can aesthetically sow the seeds of a fascist atmosphere without intending to do so"; (b) "this atmosphere was produced by a fascist aesthetic whose language was often complex and carried within it the seeds of its own undoing"; (c) "it is precisely those creations ... most resistant to political reading that best reveal the aesthetic strains of fascism"; (d) " ... a beautiful novel or a recondite essay could help form a fascistic sensibility precisely because fascist moments, embedded in literary or cultural works, emerged from within a medium that appeared to writers and readers as apolitical"; and (e) not all of the aesthetics associated with mid-twentieth century traditional Japanese beauty are part of this movement, citing the fiction of Yasunari Kawabata (1899–1972) as such an exception.[50] Tansman's interpretations of Okakura Tenshin's 1906 *The Book of Tea*[51] and of the use the fascist essayist Yasuda Yojūrō made of it in his paradigmatic and

---

and a summary of views of national identity and *iki*, see Miller 2011 and Tansman 2009*a*, 14–15; Tansman also has the broader and deeper analysis required for the relations between fascism and aesthetics. On aesthetics and the crisis of identity after the war, see Miller 2010. For new interpretations of *iki*, see Caroline Steinberg Gould, "*Iki* and Glamour as Aesthetic Properties of Persons: Glancing in a Cross-Cultural Mirror"; David Bell, "Finding *Iki*: *Iki and the Floating World*"; and Peter Leech, "Scents and Sensibility: Kuki Shūzō and Olfactory Aesthetics," all in Nguyen 2017. Also see Chapter 24 in this volume. On women writers' role in the creation of national identity, see Yoda 2004.

[48] Tansman 2009*a* and 2009*b*.

[49] Tansman 2009*a*, 2.

[50] Tansman 2009*a*, 1–2; regarding Kawabata, 121.

[51] Okakura Tenshin, *The Book of Tea* (New York: Dover, 1964; originally published New York: Fox, Duffield and Company, 1906).

influential essay "Japanese Bridges" should be required reading for anyone interested in this issue.

Art and War in Japan and Its Empire 1931–1960[52] discusses philosophical issues such as relations between religion, consumer culture, tradition/history, and the core of the war and colonization efforts; the social responsibility of artists; the role of arts in reimagining society; the body as the locus of subjective autonomy (*shishitsu* 資質); contingency; the meaning of abstraction; ideology; autonomy of the artwork and of artists; the role artists play in transcending values; and mass consumption.

Zen Aesthetics and War

Not a few authors attribute to Zen everything distinctive about Japanese aesthetics and interpret as the very core of Japanese identity[53] what they see as Zen-inspired love of beauty and of Nature (capitalized), grounded in an obliteration of the illusory sense of the self-in-opposition-to objects and others, citing as evidence tea ceremony and poetry. Tea, cultivated by Zen monks, adumbrates temporality and temporal positioning—in the long course of human history (referring to the masters who made and used the utensils) and in the season of year, emphasizing the transience of life while reconciling us to transience through the beauty of the moment. Zen aesthetics are renowned for their subtle and subdued colors, avoidance of unnecessary movement or busy patterning, and other features conducive to calm serenity. Zen also informs *yūgen* (幽玄), "mystery and depth," a sad beauty espoused in poetry by Fujiwara Shunzei (1114–1204), and developed by Zeami (1363?–1443?). Underlying Noh drama and medieval poetry, *yūgen* comprises "something that is in the heart but is not expressed in words" (Shōtetsu [1381–1459]) that therefore contributes to the ongoing valuation of the ineffable.[54]

This religio-aesthetic nexus reveals connections between Zen aesthetics and war in Japan. To my knowledge, Zen arts and aesthetics have never celebrated war or violence (despite frequent religious and political support of leaders by Zen temples and monks). Nonetheless, the same personnel and aesthetics were often involved in political, military, and aesthetic spheres. While fundamentally pacific in their underlying philosophy, implementation, and effects (nonviolence and serenity being both means and goal), Zen aesthetics were developed (through Noh, tea ceremony, painting, and poetic and other

---

[52] Ikeda, Asato, Aya Louisa McDonald, and Ming Tiampo 2013.

[53] See Carter in Nguyen 2017. Carter cites Charles A Moore, Hisamatsu Shin'ichi, Nishida Kitarō, Yanagi Sōetsu, and Nishitani Keiji to this effect, although D. T. Suzuki was also influential in this regard—as was the openness of the Daitokuji abbot to American poets and artists after World War II. See Suzuki, *Zen and Japanese Culture* (Princeton: Princeton University Press, 1938), Goldberg 2006, and Pearlman 2012. While Zen has contributed in these ways, this is but one of a number of independent strands, some of which, such as *miyabi*, are quite at odds with aspects of the Zen aesthetic; others , such as *mononoaware*, predate Zen by centuries.

[54] Quoted and discussed by Kusanagi Masao in Michele Marra, *Modern Japanese Aesthetics: A Reader* (Honolulu, HI: University of Hawai'i Press, 1999).

aesthetics) during the medieval period (1336–1600), a time of almost constant warfare. During that time, Zen temples gave religious and political support to the power structure—and vice versa. New research shows similar support during World War II.[55] This mutual support is not entirely arbitrary.

For compared to some other forms of Buddhism (Jōdoshū, Jōdoshinshū, and the esoteric Tendai and Shingon, for instance), Zen places relative emphasis on detachment through meditation (as opposed to the intercession of Buddhas or bodhisattvas, or to chanting, dancing, or ritual).[56] Both the detachment and the ability to concentrate, which eliminates emotions and other distractions, are especially valuable in war (as recent writings on personal/business management suggest they are in these arenas). The historic connection was brought home to me through an exhibit at Honnouji Temple in Kyoto of the pack of tea-ceremony utensils that the great warlord/daimyo and national unifier Oda Nobunaga (1534–1582) took with him to the battlefield. We don't ordinarily associate tea ceremony with battle, but two features make tea ceremony and war intimate. First, as a Zen-influenced art, tea teaches concentration and brings about a sense of calm originating in a focused mind. What would be more calming to a commander's nerves before battle (presumably *after* he had decided strategy and tactics)? Second, tea ceremony is a cultivation of human relationships, the host demonstrating every consideration for the needs and enjoyment of the guests, to develop the relationship and to register his appreciation of his guests. What could be more meaningful to Nobunaga and his guests as he prepared for battle, where he might well lose kin, friends, and allies, than to serve them tea beforehand?

The famous tea writer Okakura drew explicit connections between tea and war:

> In the thoroughness and minutiae of our preparations for war, we recognize the same hands whose untiring patience gave its exquisite finish to our lacquer. In the tender care bestowed upon our stricken adversary of the battlefield will be found the ancient courtesy of the samurai, who knew the "poignancy of things" [*mononoaware*] and looked to his enemy's wound before his own.[57]

This is not to say, however, that there is any *necessary* connection between Zen/tea ceremony principles and aesthetics on the one hand and war; indeed, they would be equally or more useful for hospital workers. And, working to opposite ends, Urasenke's retired head, Sen Genshitsu XV, gives public tea ceremonies dedicated to world peace to legislatures.

---

[55] Marilyn Ivy, *Discourses of the Vanishing: Modernity, Phantasm, Japan* (Chicago: University of Chicago Press, 2010) and Brian (Daizen) A. Victoria, *Zen at War* (New York: Weatherhill, 1997), 18–28, 102–144.

[56] All forms of Buddhism seek "salvation" or "enlightenment;" some prioritize other means such as faith or action—and creating stupas or statues or paintings of Buddhas, as in the Mahāyāna *Lotus Sutra*.

[57] Tansman 2009a, 71; Okakura 1964, 1, 4.

Post-Atomic Categorical Aesthetics

Japanese aesthetics offer some of the best evidence we have for how lives, communities, and values are reconstituted after mass trauma such as carpet- and atomic bombings.[58] The literature, dance, and film that confront the topic most directly also prove excruciating for readers and viewers, although there are excellent studies, such as John Treat's, which address the difficulties of putting traumatic experiences into language.[59] After pondering for thirty years the remark of Kawabata Yasunari, aesthetics commentator, art collector, and Japan's first Nobel Prize-winning novelist, that (at least in the aftermath of the atomic bombings) "looking at old works of art is a matter of life and death" (*sekkan na seimei de aru*), I concluded that he meant this quite literally, and I summarized the ways in which this might be true as inspiration, pleasure, knowledge, access to truth, and the facilitation of wisdom (defined as the ability to apply information and objective knowledge to personally challenging *subjective* situations)—though this list is not exhaustive.[60]

Although work by some artists who were victims (calligrapher Inoue Yūichi) or witnesses (Iri and Toshi Maruki)[61] is so extreme it seems to have no "lessons" the rest of us can apply (we can only stand in awe), other Japanese visual artists' contributions, along with those of musicians and performance artists, particularly the Ankoku Butō (暗黒舞踏, "dance of darkness") or Butō (舞踏) and Gutai (具体) "embodiment" movements,[62] helped define post-War avant-garde art internationally.[63]

---

[58] There were surprisingly few studies of how the Japanese accomplished this, admirable exceptions (in English) being Robert Jay Lifton, *Death in Life: Survivors of Hiroshima* (New York: Random House, 1967); Lifton and Greg Mitchell, *Hiroshima in America: A Half Century of Denial* (New York: Avon Books, 1995); and some films. The field of disaster management is young; new knowledge will emerge due to research on the March 11, 2011 earthquake, tsunami, and nuclear power plant partial meltdown. See Koichi Haga, *The Earth Writes: The Great Earthquake and the Novel in Post-3/11 Japan* (Lanham, MD: Lexington Books, 2019).

[59] Treat 1995.

[60] For Kawabata's and my reasoning, see Miller 2014b, 261–275. Donald Keene translated Kawabata's remark in *Dawn to the West: Japanese Literature in the Modern Era*, Volume I (New York: Holt Rinehart and Winston, 1984), 827; (1st ed. Holt, Rinehart & Winston, 1984), 805. For further thoughts on the role of wisdom regarding the atomic bombings and subsequent nuclear weapons and technology, see Mara Miller, "Atomic/Nuclear Weapons and Energy Technologies (ANWETs): The Need for Wisdom," in *Practical Wisdom in the Age of Technology: Insights, Issues and Questions for a New Millennium*, edited by Nikunj Dalal, Ali Intezari, and Marty Heitz (New York: Routledge and UK: Gower Publishing: Series: The Practical Wisdom in Leadership and Organization Series, 2016).

[61] For Inoue's work, see Munroe 1994; the Maruki Gallery website is http://www.aya.or.jp/~marukimsn/gen/gen1e.html.

[62] Christine Greiner, "Butō: A Dance Experience to Recreate the Body Beyond the East–West Dichotomies," in Inaga 2010.

[63] This is demonstrated by Alexandra Munroe, *Japanese Art After 1945: Scream Against the Sky* (New York: Harry N. Abrams, 1994).

Post-Modern Aesthetics: Haikyo

The "historically dark and impoverished Tono [that] now identifies itself as a generic *furusato* relates closely to its transformation from a dystopia into a utopia, from the vanishing marginal into the centrally Japanese," as Marilyn Ivy describes it, and her characterization of *furusato* as including "diffuse, publicly acknowledged traces of ancient sites"[64] lead us to the brink of the fascinating poignancy of contemporary ruins (*haikyo* 廃墟, abandoned places) analyzed by Hirofumi Katsuno. Such sites— decrepit factories, abandoned resorts—are popular subjects for painting and creative photography and are romanticized in film, literature, and mass media, providing scenic backdrops while being used as metaphors for other forms of decline or decay. They occur as "past ruins and post-apocalyptic ruins," "romanticized, revered, and monumentalized as the embodiment of history, which is usually [an] idealized past . . . discontinuous with the present." They comprise "sites of affective investment" among young people:

> Representing the loss of modern and post-modern utopian dreams, the decaying places paradoxically appear as a zone of comfort in the era of uncertainty and anxiety. More specifically, the disorderly, fragmental, and marginal nature of abandoned spaces evokes an intensive reality of death and failure, in which the young explorers cynically but melancholically observe modernity's excess and the faded and congealed dreams of commodity capitalism. At the same time, they nostalgically feel the ruins are signs of natural and sacred cycle of birth and death and rebirth when seeing man-made buildings return to nature.[65]

This is reminiscent of Ivy's conclusions about *furusato*:

> Precisely because of the eerie character of its tales, Tono became a particularly haunting and complex example of a generalized ideal. Many of the tales . . . were marked by extremes of violence, suffering, crime, and poverty. Yet these extremes have been vividly juxtaposed . . . with their opposites: the warm, homey, authentic, natural, and beautiful . . . Tono thus confronts Japanese and others with these questions: How do the terrifying and mysterious become objects of detached appreciation?[66]

---

[64] Ivy 2010, 103.

[65] Hirofumi Katsuno, "Chasing Paradise Lost: Formation of Ruinophilia in Post-Industrial Japan," unpublished paper presented at the Association for Asian Studies 2014 conference.

[66] Ivy 2010, 105. Though there is no room to comment on it here, Rene Girard's mimetic theory suggests a path by which the apparently oppositional tendencies might require their opposites. See Jeremiah L. Alberg, editor, *Apocalypse Deferred: Girard and Japan* (Notre Dame, Indiana: University of Notre Dame Press, 2017).

Post-Atomic Horror and Post-Industrial Kawaii and Moe

The pre-eminent aesthetic genre of the post-atomic era is horror, terror born of technology gone wrong, starring Godzilla, who encapsulates fears of atomic destruction.[67] That the popularity of many postmodern aesthetics is assisted by sophisticated technologies, institutions, and marketing campaigns means neither that they can go without scrutiny nor that they lack legitimacy, but that they demand theoretical examination of their relations to late capitalism, new technologies, and changing political and social realities. Kawaii (可愛い, darling, cute), an aesthetic denoting childlike, innocent, vulnerable things that make us love and want to protect them, typified by Hello Kitty, is the best known of the contrasting aesthetics.[68] (Disturbingly for feminists, the feminine Hello Kitty has no mouth or hands, denying her agency.) Sharon Kinsella shows how the "cute style betrays a lack of confidence in the very notion of the individual, and cannot muster the energy and optimism necessary for rebellion. It is a soft revolt."[69]

The everyday words moe and moeru (燃える, to burn; 萌える, to bud or sprout, nominalized as moe) emerged in the 1990s to refer to "a euphoric response to fantasy characters or representations of them." [70]
Like kawaii, moe is a mass-culture rebellion against growing up in the postindustrial economy. It refers not to a specific style or character type but to the interaction between the person and his or her two-dimensional "object" of attraction, as well as to the ability to arouse affect ("a moment of unformed and unstructured potential") rather than feelings, defined as "personal, or emotions, the social expression of feelings." Both kawaii and moe seem to be aesthetic versions of the well-documented psychosocial phenomenon amae(ru) (甘え(る)), the ability to appeal for nurturance—a quality that has

---

[67] The critical study is Susan J. Napier's "Panic Sites: The Japanese Imagination of Disaster from Godzilla to Akira," Journal of Japanese Studies 19:2 (Summer 1993): 327–351; Peter H. Brothers explores the linkage to nuclear weapons in Mushroom Clouds and Mushroom Men—The Fantastic Cinema of Ishiro Honda (Bloomington, IN: AuthorHouse, 2009). The genre originated with Horace Walpole's 1764 novel, considered a founding document in modern political thinking due to its paranoia regarding the oppressive patriarch.

[68] Christine R. Yano, Pink Globalization: Hello Kitty's Trek Across the Pacific (Durham: Duke University Press, 2013); Gabrielle Lukacs, "The Labor of Cute: Net Idols, Cute Culture, and the Digital Economy in Contemporary Japan," Positions 23:3 (2015): 487–513; and Gabrielle Lukacs, "The Labor of Cute: Net Idols, Cute Culture, and the Social Factory in Contemporary Japan," unpublished paper.

[69] Kitty Hauser, "Cute," London Review of Books 26:8 (2004, April 15). I thank members of the Japan Art History Forum, especially Gabriella Lukacs, for their assistance with kawaii references.

[70] Patrick W. Galbraith notes that the term means "to bud or sprout" and is homophonous with the verb "to burn." In the 1990s, the word appeared on the bulletin board website 2channel in a discussion of young, cute and innocent anime girls and a burning passion for them. See Patrick Macias and Tomohiro Machiyama, Cruising the Anime City: An Otaku Guide to Neo Tokyo (Berkeley: Stone Bridge Press, 2004), in "Moe: Exploring Virtual Potential in Post-Millennial Japan," Electronic Journal of Contemporary Japanese Studies, Article 5 in 2009. Galbraith cites Brian Massumi's "Notes on the Translation and Acknowledgements," in Gilles Deleuze and Felix Guattari, A Thousand Plateaus (Minneapolis: University of Minnesota Press 1987) and Parables for the Virtual (Durham: Duke University Press, 2002); he summarizes psychoanalytic analyses of moe.

had strong aesthetic appeal since at least the *Tale of Genji*.[71] Yet both are symptomatic of the resurgent anomie of consumer culture.

CONCLUSION

Far more has been happening in Japanese aesthetics recently than can be indicated here: the development of subfields (sports aesthetics), expansion of both traditional and brand-new aesthetics to new audiences via mass media and information and communications technologies, reinterpretation of familiar aesthetics by different criteria, and application of theory to artworks, arts practices, and even arts-related businesses. Closer ties, better access, and improved multilingual literacy skills among international philosophers, theorists, collectors, museum professionals, audiences, and historians and practitioners of the arts are opening up Japanese aesthetics in new ways, demanding that we relinquish some comfortable views of our favorite aesthetics. But the appeal— or rather, the multifarious kinds of appeal—continue to enrapture us, to enlighten us, to open us up to new possibilities. And because conviction of the primacy of arts to religion, ethics, communication, and personal and group identity lies at the heart of Japanese aesthetics thinking and practice, the aesthetics of Japan are arguably among the most important in the modern/postmodern world.

BIBLIOGRAPHY AND SUGGESTED READINGS

Chance, Linda H. (2000) "*Zuihitsu* and Gender: *Tsurezuregusa* and *The Pillow Book*." In *Inventing the Classics: Modernity, National Identity, and Japanese Literature*, edited by Haruo Shirane and Tomi Suzuki. Palo Alto: Stanford University Press, 120–147.

Chino Kaori. (2010) *Chino Kaori chosakushū* [Collected Works of Chino Kaori], edited by Shinobu Ikeda, Akiko Mabuchi, and Wakana Kamei. Tokyo: Brucke Publishing.

Cooper, David E. (2017) "Cloud, Mist, Shadow, Shakuhachi." In *New Studies in Japanese Aesthetics*, edited by A. Minh Nguyen. Lanham, MD: Lexington Books.

Dower, John W. and John Junkerman. (1985) *The Hiroshima Murals: The Art of Iri Maruiki and Toshi Maruki*. Tokyo: Kodansha Intl.

Eubanks, Charlotte. (2009) "The Mirror of Memory: Constructions of Hell in the Marukis' Nuclear Murals." PMLA, vol. 124, no. 5, pp. 16–22.

Galbraith, Patrick. (2009) "*Moe*: Exploring Virtual Potential in Post-Millennial Japan," *Electronic Journal of Contemporary Japanese Studies*, Article 5.

Gerbert, Elaine. (1998) "Space and Aesthetic Imagination." In *Japan's Competing Modernities: Issues in Culture and Democracy, 1900–1930*, edited by S. A. Minichiello. Honolulu: University of Hawai'i Press, 70–90.

---

[71] Takeo Doi, *The Anatomy of Dependence* (Tokyo: Kodansha, 1973; Japanese edition *Amae no kōzō*, 1971); Margaret H. Childs, "The Value of Vulnerability: Sexual Coercion and the Nature of Love in Japanese Court Literature," *The Journal of Asian Studies* 58:4 (November 1999): 1059–1079.

Goldberg, Michael. (2006) *A Zen Life: D.T. Suzuki*. Tokyo: International Videoworks, Japan Inter-Culture Foundation, and Nihon Kokusai Seinen Bunka Kyokai.

Harper, Thomas J. (1971) *Motoori Norinaga's Criticism of the Genji Monogatari: A Study of the Background and Critical Content of His Genji Monogatari Tama no Ogushi*. Ann Arbor: University of Michigan.

Heisig, James W., Thomas P. Kasulis, and John C. Maraldo, eds. (2011) *Japanese Philosophy: A Sourcebook*. Honolulu: University of Hawai'i Press.

Henitiuk, Valerie. (2005) "Virgin Territory: Murasaki Shikibu's Ōigimi Resists the Male." In *Feminism in Literature: Vol. 1: Antiquity-18th Century*, edited by J. Bomarito and J. W. Hunter. Farmington Hills, MI: Thomson Gale, 90–96.

Henitiuk, Valerie. (2011) "Prefacing Gender: Framing Sei Shônagon for a Western Audience, 1875–2006." In *Translating Women*, edited by L. von Flotow. Ottawa: University of Ottawa Press, 247–269.

Hisamatsu Shinichi. (1971) *Zen and the Fine Arts*, translated by Tokiwa Gishin. Tokyo: Kodansha.

Ikeda Asato, Aya Louisa McDonald, and Ming Tiampo, eds. (2013) *Art and War in Japan and Its Empire 1931–1960*. Leiden: Brill.

Inaga, Shigemi, ed. (2010) *Questioning Oriental Aesthetics and Thinking: Conflicting Visions of "Asia" under the Colonial Empires*. Kyoto: International Research Center for Japanese Studies.

Ito, Ken. (2008) *An Age of Melodrama: Family, Gender, and Social Hierarchy in the Turn-of-the-Century Japanese Novel*. Stanford: Stanford University Press.

Ivy, Marilyn. (2010) *Discourses of the Vanishing: Modernity, Phantasm, Japan*. Chicago: University of Chicago Press.

Kasulis, Thomas P. (1998) "Zen and Artistry." In *Self as Image in Asian Theory and Practice*, edited by Roger T. Ames with Thomas P. Kasulis and Wimal Dissanayake. Albany, NY: SUNY Press, 357–371.

Keene, Donald. (1971) "Feminine Sensibility in the Heian Era," in *Appreciations of Japanese Culture*. Tokyo: Kodansha Intl. Ltd.; reprinted in Nancy G. Hume, ed., *Japanese Aesthetics and Culture: A Reader*. Albany, NY: SUNY Press, 1995.

Marra, Michael F., ed. (2002) *Japanese Hermeneutics: Current Debates on Aesthetics and Interpretation*. Honolulu, HI: University of Hawai'i Press.

Matsumoto, Koji. (2007) *Japanese Spirituality and Music Practice: Art as Self-cultivation*. New York: Springer International Handbooks of Education.

Meli, Mark. (2002) "Motoori Norinaga's Hermeneutics of *Mono no Aware*: The Link between Ideal and Tradition." In *Japanese Hermeneutics: Current Debates on Aesthetics and Interpretation*, edited by M. F. Marra. Honolulu, HI: University of Hawai'i Press, 60–75.

Miller, Mara. (1993) "Canons and the Challenge of Gender: Women in the Canon of Japan," *The Monist* 76(4): 477–493.

Miller, Mara. (1996) "Teaching Japanese Aesthetics: Whys & Hows for Non-Specialists." *Newsletter of the American Society for Aesthetics* 16, 2.

Miller, Mara. (1997) "Views of Japanese Selfhood: Japanese and Western Perspectives." In *Culture and Self: Philosophical and Religious Perspectives, East and West*, edited by Douglas Allen with Ashok Malhotra.

Miller, Mara. (1998) "Art and the Construction of Self and Subject in Japan." In *Self as Person in Asian Theory and Practice*, edited by Wimal Dissanayake et al. Albany: State University of New York Press, 421–460.

Miller, Mara. (2002) "Ethics in the Female Voice: Murasaki Shikibu and the Framing of Ethics for Japan." In *Varieties of Ethical Perspectives*, edited by Michael Barnhart. Lanham, MD: Lexington Books, 175–202.

Miller, Mara. (2004) "Four Approaches to Emotion in Japanese Art." In *Emotion in Asia*, edited by Paolo Santangelo. Naples: Universita degli Studi di Napoli L'Orientale, 265–313.

Miller, Mara. (2010) "Japanese Aesthetics and the Disruptions of Identity after the Atomic Bombings." *kritische berichte. zeitschrift für kunst- und kulturwissenschaften* 2(2010): 73–82. [Special issue on Japanese identity after the atomic bombings.]

Miller, Mara. (2011) "Japanese Aesthetics." In *Oxford Handbook to World Philosophy*, edited by Jay Garfield and William Edelglass. Oxford: Oxford University Press, 317–333.

Miller, Mara. (2012) "*Genji*'s Gardens: From Symbolism to Personal Expression and Emotion: Gardens and Garden Design." In *The Tale of Genji*. In *Concepts and Categories of Emotion in East Asia*, edited by Giusi Tamburello. Rome: Carocci editore, 105–141.

Miller, Mara. (2014*a*) "*The Art Instinct*: Evolutionary and Cross-Cultural Perspectives for Aesthetics." *Philosophy and Literature* (Summer 2014) [Supplementary Issue on the work of Denis Dutton].

Miller, Mara. (2014*b*) "'A Matter of Life and Death:' Yasunari Kawabata on the Value of Art After the Atomic Bombings." *Journal of Aesthetics and Art Criticism* 74 (2: Summer 2014): 261–275.

Miller, Mara. (2015, October) "Aesthetics as Investigation of Self, Subject, and Ethical Agency Under Trauma in Kawabata's Post-War Novel *The Sound of the Mountain*." *Philosophy and Literature* 39 [Special issue, Ethical Criticism in Practice].

Miller, Mara. (2017) "Agency, Identity, and Aesthetic Experience in Three Post-Atomic Japanese Narratives: Yasunari Kawabata's *The Sound of the Mountain*, Rio's *Thread Hell*, and the *Anime* Film *Barefoot Gen*." In *New Essays in Japanese Aesthetics: Philosophy, Politics, Culture, Literature, and the Arts*, edited by A. Minh Nguyen. Lanham, MD: Lexington Books.

Miller, Mara. (2020) "Early Feminist Aesthetics in Japan: Murasaki Shikibu, Sei Shōnagon, and A Thousand Years of the Female Voice in Japan." In *Feminist Aesthetics and Philosophy of Art: Critical Visions, Creative Engagements*, edited by L. Ryan Musgrave. New York: Springer Press.

Minichiello, Sharon A., ed. (1998) *Japan's Competing Modernities: Issues in Culture and Democracy, 1900–1930*. Honolulu: University of Hawai'i Press.

Munroe, Alexandra, ed. (1994) *Japanese Art After 1945: Scream Against the Sky*. New York: Harry N. Abrams, in association with the Yokohama Museum of Art, the Japan Foundation, the Guggenheim Museum, and San Francisco Museum of Art.

Nguyen, Minh A., ed. (2017) *New Essays in Japanese Aesthetics: Philosophy, Politics, Culture, Literature, and the Arts*. London and Lanham, MD: Lexington Books.

Okakura Tenshin. (1906) *The Book of Tea*. New York: Dover, 1964; originally published New York: Fox, Duffield and Company.

Pearlman, Ellen. (2012) *Nothing & Everything: the Influence of Buddhism on the American Avant-Garde, 1942–1962*. Berkeley, CA: Evolver Editions.

Reynolds, Jonathan M. (1998) "The Bunriha and the Problem of 'Tradition' for Modernist Architecture in Japan, 1920–1928." In *Japan's Competing Modernities: Issues in Culture and Democracy, 1900–1930*, edited by S. A. Minichiello. Lanham, MD: Lexington Books, 228–246.

Saito, Yuriko. (2018) "Historical Overview of Japanese Aesthetics." In *New Essays in Japanese Aesthetics*, edited by A. Minh Nguyen. Lanham, MD: Lexington Books, xxx–xlviii.

Schalow, Paul G., and Janet Walker, eds. (1996) *The Woman's Hand: Gender and Theory in Japanese Women's Writing*. Stanford: Stanford University Press.

Shirano, Haruo and Tomi Suzuki, eds. (2000) *Inventing the Classics: Modernity, National Identity, and Japanese Literature*. Palo Alto: Stanford University Press.

Suzuki, Tomi. (1996) *Narrating the Self: Fictions of Japanese Modernity*. Palo Alto, CA: Stanford University Press.

Tansman, Alan. (2009a) *The Aesthetics of Japanese Fascism*. Durham, NC: Duke University Press.

Tansman, Alan, ed. (2009b) *The Culture of Japanese Fascism*. Durham, NC: Duke University Press.

Treat, John Whittier. (1995) *Writing Ground Zero: Japanese Literature and the Atomic Bomb*. Chicago: University of Chicago Press.

Ueda, Atsuko. (2007) *Concealment of Politics, Politics of Concealment*. Stanford University Press.

Ueda, Atsuko and Michael K. Bourdaghs, eds. (2018) *Literature among the Ruins, 1945–1955: Postwar Japanese Literary Criticism*. Lanham, Maryland: Lexington Books.

Ueda, Atsuko, Michael K. Bourdaghs, Richi Sakakibara, and Hirokazu Toeda, eds. (2018) *The Politics and Literature Debate in Postwar Japanese Criticism, 1945–52*. Lanham, MD: Lexington Books.

Washburn, Dennis C. (1995) *The Dilemma of the Modern in Japanese Fiction*. New Haven: Yale University Press.

Yamasaki, Koji, and Miller, Mara. (2017) "Ainu Aesthetics and Philosophy of Art: Replication, Remembering, Recovery." In *New Studies in Japanese Aesthetics*, edited by A. Minh Nguyen. Lanham, MD: Lexington Books.

Yamasaki, Koji, Masaru Kato, and Tesuya Amano, eds. (2012) *Teetasinrit Tekrukoci: The Handprints of Our Ancestors: Ainu Artifacts Housed at Hokkaido University—Inherited Techniques*. Sapporo, Japan: Hokkaido University Museum/Hokkaido University Center for Ainu and Indigenous Studies.

Yoda, Tomiko. (2004) *Gender and National Literature: Heian Texts in the Constructions of Japanese Modernity*. Durham, NC: Duke University Press.

CHAPTER 36

....

THE CONTROVERSIAL CULTURAL IDENTITY OF JAPANESE PHILOSOPHY

....

YOKO ARISAKA

As our global awareness grows, Japanese philosophy has also become more visible in academia over the past twenty years. If one is a newcomer to the field of Japanese philosophy—whether one comes via the non-Western, cultural, or comparative philosophy route or through Buddhism or Zen—one may be surprised to learn that the very field of "Japanese philosophy," and in particular the "Kyoto School," remains today shrouded in controversy. Or, one may have learned about modern Japanese philosophy in the context of mostly American critiques of Japanese imperialism and cultural nationalism during the Pacific War, as a philosophy to be critiqued and rejected. At any rate, beyond the technicalities of its discourses, one cannot pretend today that Japanese philosophy is "merely" a philosophical tradition that developed in Japan.

UNIVERSALISM, PARTICULARISM, AND DEVELOPMENTAL THINKING

....

Before exploring the controversial case of Japanese philosophy on the topic of its "identity and distinctness," let me begin with a reflection on today's global intellectual context in order to situate the discussion. Even today, the term "Japanese philosophy" raises some eyebrows in the company of Euro-American philosophers—the veiled question, often not asked out of politeness, is: "But is it really *philosophy*?" Obviously, when one speaks of "philosophy" in the United States or Europe, the referent is clear: it unambiguously and unproblematically means the history of Western philosophy, and, in the Anglo-American context, "philosophy" most often means "analytic philosophical methods and traditions." In any case, so-called non-Western philosophies, if acknowledged at all, are still not seriously considered "sufficiently philosophical." Philosophers grounded in Euro-American traditions feel no need to acknowledge their lack of knowledge regarding other traditions, yet philosophers specialized in any other tradition, if they are to be taken seriously at all, must also demonstrate knowledge of Euro-American philosophies.[1]

In our century, globalization has advanced to the point where transnationalism and global cultural exchange are ubiquitous. Nevertheless, and despite well-known critiques of Eurocentrism, the discipline of philosophy obstinately retains the center-margin paradigm, with its dominant markers and standards of measurement still firmly grounded in Euro-American contexts. As much as we would like to celebrate the cosmopolitan, global, egalitarian, multicultural, intercultural, progressive network of world citizenry and knowledge exchange today, the stark reality paints another picture: Our world still carries the weight and legacies of the 400-year history of European imperialism and colonialism that shaped (and reinforces) today's *neo-colonial* global geopolitics. And, unfortunately, philosophy has not, for the most part, moved beyond this neo-colonial state of affairs.

This is not only a politico-historical story. It has also shaped our current worldviews and consciousness in subtle yet destructive ways. Thomas McCarthy analyzes and critiques the metaphysical notion of "development"—the idea that human beings and civilizations "develop" from uncivilized to more civilized states over time, that there is a "progress" to be made in an imaginary linear development in human conditions, and that some cultures are ahead of others, an idea that has justified colonialism and long-standing global racism prevalent still today.[2] In the European tradition since the eighteenth century, it was taken for granted, by intellectuals such as Kant, that the most enlightened civilizational (and philosophical) center of truth and the most universal, advanced culture was that of Christian Europe.[3] Hegel asserted that History and Knowledge were only fully developed in Europe, and though Asia had some hopes (if they were able to imitate Europe), Africa had none at all. The heathen non-West (including Japan) was simply outside the realm of truth or "behind and backwards" in the timeline of civilizational development. Those that are "not yet enlightened" are still mired in feudalism/despotism, fundamentalism, cosmic thinking, and the like. This way of understanding civilizations in the world was standard up until the twentieth

---

[1]   On questions surrounding the definitions of "philosophy" and "Japanese philosophy," see Bret W. Davis's introduction to this volume.

[2]   See McCarthy 2009.

[3]   Kant's anthropology, according to which Caucasian white Europeans were understood to be the most advanced race, is quite appallingly racist from today's standards, but, at the time, it was viewed as the most scientific theory of race. See his "Von der verschiedenen Rassen der Menschen," 1775, and *Observations of the Feeling of the Beautiful and the Sublime*, 1764. Hegel's "Anthropology" (see section 393 of the *Encyclopaedia of the Philosophical Sciences*) as well as his philosophy of history (*Vorlesungen über die Geschichte der Philosophie*) blatantly endorse the superiority of the "Caucasian peoples" and denigrate "Africans and Mongols" for their utter lack of capacity for development.

century, and, even today, we still refer to some cultures as "barbaric" or "uncivilized," by which we mean they exhibit culturally specific practices that are either "no longer" observed in Europe or in the United States or simply foreign to Judeo-Christian cultural practices (some common targets today include the caricature of the status of women in Muslim cultures or the practice of polygamy in some African contexts). The civilizational "universal-particular" mapping still locates the "particulars" to be largely non-Western (and non-white). While European and American philosophies enjoy their taken-for-granted universality claims, Japanese philosophy still suffers from a legitimation process. Grim as it may seem, this is the current context in which we reflect on past and present debates regarding the identity of Japanese philosophy.

ORIGINS AND CONTEXTS OF MODERN JAPANESE PHILOSOPHY

Let us turn the clock back to the nineteenth century and move to Japan. The birth of modern Japanese philosophy is particularly interesting because it could be seen as one of the first serious responses to the Western hegemony and self-appointed supremacy discussed in the previous section. From 1639 until the mid-1800s, Japan remained isolated from the rest of the world. In order to control the spread of Christianity, the Tokugawa Shōgunate closed all the ports in the mid-seventeenth century, except the port of Nagasaki in the southernmost island of Kyushu, and only China and Holland were allowed to continue trade under strictly controlled conditions. By the time the American "Black Ships" arrived in 1853 and demanded the opening of the country, Japan had missed out on the amazing industrial advancements and revolutions that had occurred in Europe and America during the eighteenth century, as well as on the developmental thinking discussed earlier that was by then taken for granted in Europe and America. Facing modern American weaponry and superior military power, Japan had two alternatives: either become a victim of Western expansionism or open itself up to modernization and protect itself. So began the period of rapid modernization with the official Meiji Restoration of 1868.

The daunting processes of change reached all aspects of life: social, political, economic, educational, technological, cultural, aesthetic, and, of course, intellectual.[4] It is not an exaggeration to say that the history of post-Meiji Japan is shaped by the cultural understanding of a *difference* between "Japanese versus Western," or more commonly, "East and West (*seiyō to tōyō* 西洋と東洋)," where the East (*tōyō*) represents what is traditional, spiritual, indigenous, cultural, backward, and particular (to Japan or Asia), and the West (*seiyō*) represents its contrast: namely, what is modern, materialistic, foreign,

---

[4] For some fascinating accounts of the transformation processes, see Samson 1984, Jansen 1965, and Irowaka and Jansen 1985.

scientific, advanced, and universal (as science and technology, the chief markers of modernity, were said to be based on the principles of universal truth).[5]

Modern Japanese philosophy was born in this conflicted milieu of negotiating East and West, and it, too, was preoccupied with the theme of developing a philosophy based on Japanese culture yet embodying the systematic universality of the Western philosophical tradition.[6] In fact, the term "philosophy" (*tetsugaku* 哲学) had to be coined in Japanese as this particular form of systematized, scientific philosophy did not exist in the traditional Neo-Confucian or Buddhist traditions.[7] As the Meiji intellectuals became more aware of the differences between Western modes of rational thinking and "traditional Japanese values," philosophy became a site of intellectual negotiation among rationality, systematicity, and logic, on the one hand (universality), and spirituality, holistic thinking, artistic thinking, and cultural thinking (particularity), on the other. Japanese thinkers thought that there are also unique elements in their own tradition that must also be universal and that they, too, could be given philosophical expression.

In this mood of optimism, some thinkers and cultural leaders (such as the founder of "Japanese arts," Okakura Tenshin) began to critique Western developmentalism and its inherent Eurocentrism. Theoretically, philosophical universalism is supposed to apply to all human beings, yet practically all Western thinkers took it for granted that only Euro-American civilization represents universal truth. Meiji intellectuals were dissatisfied with such arrogance and aspired to develop a philosophy that is "Japanese yet universal"; *if* Japan could develop a culturally non-Western yet universal form of philosophy, then that would be proof that European civilization is not the only center of universal truth. If such a philosophy is indeed universal, then this would necessarily mean that European and American minds must be able to understand it as also applicable to the nature of the human mind, the self, or reality as such. If this could be achieved, then Japan could contribute to the creation of a more globally balanced world culture, offering the possibility of a counterbalance and a conception of an "alternative, non-Western modernity" to the Western-dominated world.

Note that the very way in which Japanese thinkers conceived of themselves as belonging to a particular culture (versus the universal West) itself reinforces the Western metaphysics of universality and particularity. As Sakai Naoki notes, Japan cannot possibly appear as a particular without reference to the universal which would define it as such; but this is just to reinstitute such a metaphysics—and thereby reinforce the West

---

[5] I shall use the contested terms "East and West" (or the expression "the West") here as they were used by Japanese intellectuals at the time.

[6] See Chapter 15 in this volume. For a brief introduction of Japanese philosophy in the post-Meiji context, see also Arisaka 2014b. For overviews of and translated essays by Japanese thinkers from the seventh to twentieth centuries, see Heisig, Kasulis, and Maraldo 2011. This comprehensive 1,300-page volume is a *tour-de-force* on the major thinkers of Japan.

[7] Nishi Amane (1829–1897), who traveled to Holland and brought back Comte's and Mill's philosophies, coined the term in 1862.

as the primary reference point.[8] Yet this issue did not concern Japanese thinkers at the time since they were not trying to *reject* Western metaphysics in search of an alternative. Rather, they were interested in making their own claims to universality in terms of what was perceived as their identity in particularity.

Such a search for self-identity and recognition of universal validity occurred in many anticolonial movements later in the century as well. Négritude movements in the 1930s, for example, developed a critique of racist European/French colonialism and tried to create, by way of adopting Marxism, a pan-African identity/movement as anticolonial resistance.[9] Civil rights movements could not have been possible without the notion of the universality of human dignity; claiming rightful status for a neglected particular was also a common strategy among many variants of liberation politics and resistance.

Universalism of Japanese Philosophy: Nishida's Case

In what way, specifically, has Japanese philosophy succeeded in producing a particularly Japanese yet universal system of thought? In what way was it a critical response to the Western hegemonic world order? Let me briefly focus on Nishida Kitarō (1870–1945), who is generally considered the father of modern Japanese philosophy. I will not review here his vast philosophical oeuvre; many of its elements are indeed universal in their philosophical scope, as chapters by Fujita Masakatsu and John Maraldo in this volume have shown. Beyond his metaphysics and epistemology, however, he also developed a political theory of globalization; this is the aspect of his philosophy that gets mired in controversies.

Up until the mid- to late 1930s, Nishida's theory was rather strictly metaphysical and epistemological—and apolitical.[10] However, as Japan expanded its empire in the late 1930s into the early '40s, Nishida began to lecture as well as write about the political application of his theory. In 1938, at Kyoto University, he delivered the lecture series *The Problem of Japanese Culture*, which was published in 1940. In 1943, at the request of the

---

[8] See Sakai 1989. He elaborates these reflections further in Sakai 1993, in the context of discussing Watsuji Tetsurō. Both are groundbreaking essays on the "production" of the East–West framework.

[9] Césaire of Martinique, a Marxist poet and one of the key figures in the Négritude movements, wrote in 1955: "the so-called European civilization—'Western' civilization—as it has been shaped by two centuries of bourgeois rule, is incapable of solving the two major problems to which its existence has given rise: the problem of the proletariat and the colonial problem; that Europe is unable to justify itself either before the bar of 'reason' or before the bar of 'conscience'; and that, increasingly, it takes refuge in a hypocrisy which is all the more odious because it is less and less likely to deceive. *Europe is indefensible*" (9).

[10] It was criticized by his Marxist student Tosaka Jun to be a bourgeois idealism, "merely phenomenological and historically insignificant." *Tosaka Jun zenshū* (1966, *Collected Works of Tosaka Jun*, Tokyo: Keisō-Shobō, 3, 172–173).

Tōjō Government and its Imperial Army, which was seeking a theoretical formulation for Japan's role in the construction of the Greater East Asian Co-Prosperity Sphere (*Dai tōa kyōeiken* 大東亜共栄圏), Nishida (who by then was considered to be the most important philosopher in Japan) wrote his controversial essay, "The Principle of the New World Order" (*Sekai shinchitsujo no genri*).[11] That Nishida did not approve of the actions of the Imperial Army was known, but, as one might surmise, the contents (and especially the language) of the essay became a target of criticism in the postwar era.

In "The Principle of the New World Order," the metaphysical-dialectical theory of Nishida's "Historical World," which posits that all entities are mediated through the process of historical action-creation-mediation, was applied to a theory of the "Age of the Self-Realization of the World" through nation-building. Every nation, in order to establish itself, would do so through a negation of itself (in the recognition of alterity/difference) as well as a negation of the other (to establish itself as the other of the other), and, through this dialectic, each nation would affirm itself in relation to others. In this process, the particularities of cultures would be preserved and the essential interdependence of nations would be recognized. Through this process taking place on a global scale, the "realization of the Global-World" (*sekaiteki sekai no jikaku* 世界的世界の自覚) would be achieved.

In his vision of the Global-World, Eurocentric hegemony is rejected, and the philosophically non-Western element that is added is the role of "absolute nothingness." The distinct cultures appear as such, dialectically negating and defining themselves against one another, but the whole interactive process occurs on a world scene which must itself be empty. Nishida understands this empty "place" (*basho* 場所) of the Global-World as "absolute nothingness" (*zettai mu* 絶対無).

The universalism of this theory should be clear enough. Before discussing the complications and controversies specific to this theory in its historical context, let me turn to some broader problems that contextualize the issues of distinctness, essentialism, and nationalism.

THE "PROBLEMS" OF DISTINCTNESS, ESSENTIALISM, NATIONALISM, AND *NIHONJIN-RON*

The complex of "problems with Japanese philosophy" is at least threefold. The first aspect consists of the contemporary philosophical issues surrounding notions of identity, distinctness, uniqueness, and "essentialism." The second aspect is a bad offshoot of the first: distinctness claims easily degenerate into the discourses of racial essentialism,

---

[11] See Arisaka 1996 for a translation of the essay as well as a summary of the debates surrounding it.

cultural exclusionism, uniqueness, and superiority. The third aspect, the most problematic, is the political context; it has generated what I call the problem of "the double-edge of universalism" and expanded the second problem to produce a version of what might be taken as neo-nationalism and cultural essentialism.[12] Let me initially address the first problem.

The problems with essentialism are numerous, but the critiques known as deconstruction and poststructuralism have swept through American academia since the 1980s. Any expression that indicated some kind of an "identity" or a "grand narrative" became suspect—it was "essentialist." So an expression like "Japanese philosophy" is essentialist in that it assumes a purported identity, "Japan," to which some "philosophy" must belong; but this is all a metaphysical confusion. There is no ontologically coherent "entity with an essence" called "Japan" or "philosophy" (or anything else, for that matter); it is all a question of linguistic differences and historical narratives that produce a simulacrum of an identity. Identity claims are necessarily politico-cultural productions, with power driving the formation of discourses (and silencing practices); "Japan," and its history and culture, are just such constructions.[13] Essentialized identities are outdated grand substance ontology to be transcended. If one had to refer to Japan, the country, for example, it was safer to put it in quotes or write in lower case: "japan," to indicate that one is aware of the problems of essentializing discourse. Likewise for anything to do with "East and West," comparative philosophy, culture, history, universalism, and the like. Granted that many significant theoretical horizons opened up in the wake of deconstruction (such as deconstructive feminisms, queer theories, race theories), but, in cases of the philosophies of other traditions, the philological policing became rather cumbersome and annoying, and at times even intellectually silly, as if one could debunk all traditional discourses merely by labeling them essentialistic. Philosophically speaking, one should know that by referring to a country or a tradition by name, one is using a metonomic device that does not usually indicate an essentialized, substantialized entity. Some cultural discourses were and are indeed essentialistic and politically problematic (see later discussion), but their contents need to be criticized in a historically coherent manner (and not as a target of false substance ontology—that is not their primary evil).

Some culturally specific reflections can be interesting, thought-provoking, or insightful, and they can be much loved as a part of getting to know the other's difference or oneself through the eyes of the other. For example, Lafcadio Hearn's *Kokoro: Hints and Echoes of Japanese Inner Life*, first published in 1896, is much appreciated by Japanese readers as well as by readership outside Japan. One could complain that the book is anachronistic, hopelessly essentialist, orientalist (sexist and racist), an embarrassing exoticization by a European—and it is, if one reads it through the deconstructionist-poststructuralist lens. But such a critique smacks of neo-colonial arrogance—as if only

---

[12] A detailed discussion of the double-edge of universalism can also be found in Arisaka 1997.

[13] Interesting accounts of the constructivist production of "modern Japan" can be found in, among others, Gluck 1985, for the late Meiji Period, and Harootunian 2000, for the 1920s–1930s. See also Tanaka 1993, for an account of reverse-orientalist discourse used in Japan in order to construct its identity.

the most dominant European discourse to date may sit in judgment of other discourses. It seems to lack the intellectual generosity of appreciating other discourses that occupy ontologically and epistemologically different spaces.

As the antiessentialists would agree, *doing* philosophy is inevitably grounded in culture and history, no matter what the abstract claims are, no matter how "universal" it is in its philosophical aim and construction. Doing philosophy, in this sense, is always a historical particular being made by philosophers steeped in their worlds. The production of knowledge is a robust politico-historical process (ideologies included), and it is surely true that Eurocentrism carries with it the legacies of colonialism and imperialism, with its racial and cultural essentialisms, claims of supremacy, and hegemonic discourses, to which the notion of universalism contributed as a historical particular. The birth of Japanese philosophy is no exception. It was in the context of the Meiji negotiation with Western encroachment that the particularities of Japanese philosophy developed in the way they did. So, in this trivial sense, Japanese philosophy is distinctly Japanese, distinctly post-Meiji; one could also understand how Thoreau's philosophy is American in its distinctness, and Fanon's philosophy cannot be what it is without its postcolonial political context. This sort of historical contingency that produces a distinct identity should not be confused with the philosophical question of essentialism. But how should we understand this "distinctness?" Real historicity does produce uniqueness or singularity as a matter of historical contingency, but can such a contingency be called an "identity?"

The second problem is indeed the problem of cultural essentialism. Following the Shintō-inspired nativism that developed in the post-Meiji era as a reaction against foreign influences,[14] there has in fact been a populist tradition that tried to construct what is "essential" to the identity of Japaneseness. Historical and even geographical contingencies are "appropriated" in order to construct a representation of that which is unique, and, in Japan's case, such endeavors produced what is known as *Nihonjin-ron* (日本人論; *Nihon*: Japan, and *ron*: theory), so theories of Japanese-ness.[15] Although there had long been such theorizing, it enjoyed a renewed surge during the postwar

[14] For instance, Ōkuni Takamasa wrote in 1861: "The highest ambition of all among the different kinds of 'uprightness in adhering to the origin' is for those who are born in our land of Japan to adhere to the ancient facts concerning the age of the *kami*, handed down as the ancestral lineage of our emperor, and to preserve this land for all time. If all the people of Japan embrace this ambition, we will never be defeated even if we are attacked by foreign countries" (in Heisig, Kasulis, Maraldo 2011, 525).

[15] *Nihonjin-ron* theorists claim that the "facts" seem to prove the nation's purported singularity: the Japanese language is spoken only in Japan; Japan was the only country able to isolate itself deliberately from the rest of the world for 250 years; Japan was the only country onto which the atomic bombs were dropped; no other country in the world has an imperial lineage that goes back to the origin of the nation; Japan's unique "vertical" organizational and familial structures made the postwar economic miracle possible (see Nakane 1972); Japan's unique aesthetic sensibilities for smallness made the global technological breakthrough possible; Japanese psychoanalysis shows a unique pattern of mother–child relations which also functions to regulate social relations (see Doi 1973); and the list goes on. Two good treatments of *Nihonjin-ron* in English are Befu's anthropological account (2001) and Yoshino's sociological analyses (1992).

economic boom. Numerous scholars (from the natural sciences to sociology, politics, arts and humanities, cultural geography, literature) have been inspired to speculate on the uniqueness of being Japanese. Especially through the neo-nationalist sensibilities that prevail today, it has become nearly a matter of common sense for Japanese to think of their nation as unique, often superior even, among the nations in world. Needless to say, such theories of cultural essentialism have been severely criticized.[16]

Japanese philosophy, in its claim to be a unique hybrid of Japanese culture and European philosophy, became a target of criticisms against such *Nihonjin-ron* and cultural essentialism. To elaborate, let me turn to the third problem, the political story, in more detail. What propelled this problem was the rising nationalism of the post-Meiji Era. The victories of the Sino-Japanese War (1894–1895) and Russo-Japanese War (1905) had instilled confidence that Japan was a modern nation capable of nation-building and defending itself against the West. As Western expansions into Asia progressed in the late 1800s, Japan, too, began its expansion into the East-Asian continent. With the victory of the first Sino-Japanese War in 1895, the colonization of Formosa (Taiwan) started; the colonization of Korea began in 1910; the Manchurian government north of the Korean peninsula was established in 1931; and the invasion of China began in 1937.[17] During this time, the intellectual currents that favored the combination of modernity and Japanese culture became more dominant. By the time Nishida's political writings appeared, the nation was swept up in the general fervor of nationalism, equipped with a full-blown Japanese Imperial Army with its colonialization program. Since political philosophizing and historical context cannot be separated clearly, we need to return to Nishida's essay in the nationalist context of the time.

NISHIDA'S THEORY OF JAPAN AS LEADER OF ASIA

At the abstract and universal level, Nishida's ontological theory of globalized cultures is not in itself politically problematic; it simply describes a dialectical process through which nations become what they are. What made it problematic was Japan's purported position in this dialectic at the time of Japanese colonialist expansion in Asia: it so happens that, according to Nishida, it was Japan that most fully expressed this universally applicable, globally significant, world-making dialectic, and, as such, it was the "historical mission of Japan" to bring this insight to the greater world ravaged by Euro-American imperialism and materialism (which Nishida criticized to be operating under the principle of the egoistic expansionism of the nineteenth century that merely dominates and subjugates others for one's own purposes). The creation of the Greater

---

[16] Although perhaps idiosyncratic, a critique of *Nihonjin-ron* is found in Dale 2011.
[17] See Myers and Peattie 1984, for a detailed history.

East-Asian Co-Prosperity Sphere was said to be a step toward consolidating the world-historical expressions of the peoples of East Asia (against Euro-American domination), and Japan was to self-appoint itself as the leader of this mission.

Nishida uses the wartime slogans, such as the Greater East-Asian Co-Prosperity Sphere, National Polity (*kokutai* 国体—literally "national body"), the Imperial House (*kōshitsu* 皇室), "Oneness of the Emperor and his people" (*kunmin ittai* 君民一体), and "All the people assisting the Emperor" (*banmin yokusan* 万民翼賛), but he gives a philosophical reinterpretation of these phrases in accord with his theory. The Imperial House of Japan is said to embody the universal principle of "world-formation," yet since it is an "empty" subject (referring to his theory of Place as Absolute Nothingness, in turn suggesting that the Japanese Polity should be seen as a Place of Nothingness in which all entities show themselves), metaphysically speaking, Japan itself could not be an oppressive force and a dominating particular, as England or America was.

The metaphysical placement of the universal of Absolute Nothingness in the particular nation of Japan is ingenious and to a certain extent made sense, given the fact that it was the only East-Asian nation that succeeded in modernizing at the time. However, the problem is that the presumed universality of "Absolute Nothingness" becomes identified with a historical particular, the Japanese National Polity, which was in fact the agent of atrocious colonial expansion in Asia during the Pacific War, and the formative principles of Nishida's dialectic are presented as Japan's "logic" for the establishment of the New World Order. This in effect supported standard imperialist discourses of the time.

Here is the "double-edge of universalism": just as Europe used its own universalist discourse to justify its imperialism and colonialism (by "liberating" and "enlightening" those who are merely stuck in their backward particularities, to lead them into modernity, a universal culture), Japan used an analogous discourse in its attempt to colonize Asia, with the language of "liberating East-Asia" through modernization. At this point, the philosophical universal collapses into a standard wartime imperialist narrative, regardless of its original metaphysical meaning or ethical intent.

Apart from whether it was practically possible to do so, theoretically Nishida could have used his world-historical dialectic in order to *oppose* the Imperial House (which cannot but be a historical particular). In fact, that would have been more consistent with his theory. This would be to produce an immanent critique.[18] If the concretization/self-determination of Absolute Nothingness occurs everywhere (as it in fact does, given the theory), then there is no logical or metaphysical necessity that *Japan* would have to embody the principle.[19] Every nation is theoretically an individual that affects others in the

---

[18] Bret Davis also writes that it is possible to read Nishida "against Nishida" in order to develop such a self-criticism. See his discussion of immanent critique in Davis 2013*a*. See also Arisaka 2014*a* for a discussion of this point.

[19] Kopf 2009*b* makes a similar point: "Most of all, however, his arguments in support of nationalist beliefs belie the subversive potential of his non-dualist philosophy, which, if taken seriously, subverts rather than reifies conceptual tokens such as the nation state and the orientalist bifurcation of the world" (79).

dialectic, and the particular "hierarchy" of powers comes from the particular power relations that are at work in the particular situation. In addition, the metaphysical connection which allowed the theory to work perniciously was precisely the notion of Absolute Nothingness, the most "universal" of all notions—in fact, it is strictly speaking no "notion" at all but a metaphysical postulate "in which" or "through which" all notions can appear: as such, it can only be negatively "postulated." The notion of "nothingness" or "emptiness" allowed Nishida to claim that his theory differs from the European colonialist discourse; if the Japanese Polity, in essence, is absolutely empty, then it merely serves as a metaphysical "placeholder" and cannot be an aggressive force. But here the theory contradicts itself if one tries to make it a theory of historical development, with *one leading nation* as the ultimate Place through which the world realizes itself. The connection to Japan was made externally in that it was the most modern and most powerful nation in East Asia at the time, but the idea that the most advanced nation should lead and liberate the less advanced peoples belongs to the standard developmentalist European colonial thinking and procedure (which Japan adopted). It was not a *necessary* component of the theory.

The Controversy Surrounding the Kyoto School

However, the most infamous case from the postwar perspective came from the participation of Nishida's students in the *Chūōkōron* and Overcoming Modernity (*Kindai no chōkoku*) symposia in 1941–1942, which were published in major journals and then as books.[20] Some members of the Kyoto School (Nishitani Keiji, Kōsaka Masaaki, Suzuki Shigetaka, Shimomura Toratarō, and Kōyama Iwao) actively defended the role the Japanese Imperial Army played in the Pacific War in order to "overcome" the Euro-American form of modernity and its domination across the globe. The hitherto dominant version of modernity was criticized as being mired in materialism, rationalism, individualism, selfishness, pursuit of profit, power, and the like; it lacked spiritual wholeness, community, progressive thinking, and ground. They had hoped that the newly emerging "non-Western modernity" and its emphasis on culture, as represented by Japan, could provide a positive alternative that is "modern yet spiritual." The ideas reflected the contents of Nishida's Principle of the New World Order essay, among others, with a much stronger language of cultural essentialism, Asian racial unity, and the legitimation of support for the Imperial Army.

---

[20] Translations of the symposia are available in English: see Calichman 2008, Williams 2014, and Heisig, Kasulis, and Maraldo 2011, 1059–1084. For various analyses on the topic of nationalism and the Kyoto School thinkers, see also Heisig and Maraldo 1995, Goto-Jones 2008, Williams 2004, 2014, and Chapters 16, 19, and 20 in this volume.

After the war, most of the Kyoto School participants in the round table discussions were forced to resign from their academic posts. Once prominent, the Kyoto School thus acquired the notorious image of an ultranationalist enclave and gradually declined and became isolated after the late 1940s. Nishida never participated in the round table discussions, but since his students' ideas were heavily influenced by his philosophy, among left-leaning circles he is often held "guilty by association." During the postwar period, Japanese philosophy was thus forced into oblivion, and, just as at the beginning in the Meiji Period, "philosophy" in Japan became "Western philosophy" again, and Eurocentrism was even thought justified in the face of Japan's defeat.

Needless to say, it is this political alignment of the Kyoto School thinkers that became the target of postwar critique, primarily among US scholars of Japanese intellectual history, including H. D. Harootunian, Tetsuo Najita, John Dower, Robert Sharf, Ben-Ami Shillony, Peter Dale, Bernard Faure, and Pierre Lavelle who produced a most trenchant criticism of Nishida.[21] The critiques were often quite severe in their political charges and accusative language. For example, Faure writes that "Nishida eventually placed the formulas borrowed from Western philosophy and Buddhism in the service of nationalism, apparently [sic] espousing the Kokutai ideology."[22] Sharf says "Nishida was himself guilty of the most spurious forms of nihonjinron speculation."[23] And Najita and Harootunian go so far as to claim that "no group helped defend the state more consistently and enthusiastically than did the philosophers of the Kyoto faction, and none came closer than they did to defining the philosophic contours of Japanese fascism."[24]

Dower contends:

[T]he Kyōto School also made it clear that the current conflict represented Japan's ascension as the leading "world-historical race." To them as to all other Japanese patriots, the war in Asia and the Pacific was a "holy war," and represented an unprecedented struggle for the attainment of a transcendent Great Harmony (Taiwa).[25]

Graham Parkes responds with a sharp corrective to these polemics, which were often published in highly visible venues. Parkes shows that they were mostly delivered without rigorous philosophical analyses and justification (or even understanding), and therefore they are even academically irresponsible.[26] Much more nuanced and philosophically

---

[21] According to Lavelle 1994: "Nishida's political ideas belong to the common base of ultra-nationalism" (164).

[22] Faure 1995, 249, 253.

[23] Sharf 1993, 23.

[24] Najita and Harootunian 1988, 741.

[25] Dower 1986, 227.

[26] See Parkes 1997: "Indeed, the scholarship behind these criticisms is, in general, poor—and in some cases even irresponsible, given how seriously accusations of fascism or ultranationalism need to be taken in the current global-political climate. And since most of the people attacking the Kyoto School thinkers are prominent in their fields, and in the relevant writings published by respectable university presses, their criticisms call all the more urgently for a response" (305).

cogent criticisms are in fact available, such as those by Andrew Feenberg and John Maraldo.[27]

FROM THE POSTWAR PERIOD
TO THE PRESENT

Let us now examine the historical context from the postwar period to the present. After the postwar recovery period of the 1960s into the 1980s, as Japan again emerged as a global economic success story, national confidence grew and leading elites again began to represent Japan as a unique center of non-Western modernity. This time, the kind of universalism Japan spread to the world was not via philosophy or cultural discourse but rather through consumer technology and pop culture; nevertheless, Japan finally succeeded in having a globally recognized presence and power. In this milieu of optimism, there was a renewed interest in the themes of the interwar Overcoming Modernity debates. The new interest was not so much in rekindling the old debate as such but rather in thinking anew the possibility of "overcoming" the West by studying some unique features of the "Japanese mind and behavior" which purportedly gave the Japanese a special cultural advantage. *Nihonjin-ron* flourished with renewed vigor. For instance, Umehara Takeshi, known as one of the "New Kyoto School" thinkers, developed his own theory of Japanese culture ("Umehara Japanology," *Umehara Nihongaku*) based on Buddhism and Shintō, set against the scientific culture of Europe that was seen as reaching an impasse.[28] Without much actual study of the old debate, the phrase "Overcoming Modernity" was resurrected and popularized again in the renewed atmosphere of cultural neo-nationalism.

After the growth period of the 1970s, interest in Japanese philosophy, including Nishida, was rekindled and a new generation of scholars appeared who wanted to develop original theories that reflected elements of Japanese culture. For example, Nakamura Yujirō's 1987 book, *Nishida tetsugaku no datsu-kōchiku* (*Deconstruction in Nishidan Philosophy*) opened up a new circle of Nishida scholarship, updating Nishida's antiessentialism to match poststructuralist thought.[29] Other notable developments include Kimura Bin's psychoanalyses that are inspired by Watsuji's theory

---

[27] See, for example, Feenberg 1995 and Maraldo 1995 and 2006.

[28] For example, Umehara argues for the superiority of Japanese culture and its pantheistic religious beliefs in contrast to European monotheism and scientism. In his *Nihon bunka ron* (1976, *Theory of Japanese Culture*), he criticizes nuclear power as a product of the European culture based on anger (in contrast to the Japanese culture of peace).

[29] Nakamura Yujirō, *Nishida tetsugaku no datsu-kōchiku* (Tokyo: Iwanami Shoten, 1987). Unfortunately, there is no English translation of this work yet.

of "in-between-ness" (*aidagara* 間柄)[30]; French geographer Augustin Berque's theory of "*milieu*" and "*écoumène*," which expand on Watsuji's theory of *fūdo* (風土, which Berque translates as *milieu*)[31]; and Sakabe Megumi's phenomenological aesthetics,[32] which draws on Kuki Shūzo as well as on Watsuji. Since these developments did not specifically try to articulate Japanese *uniqueness*, but rather aimed for culturally informed yet universal philosophical articulations, they are not usually considered *Nihonjin-ron* theories (though this point might be disputed).

The tendency toward cultural nationalism continued to grow, particularly into the 1980s, this time with the idea that Japan is the genuine postmodern nation.[33] The underlying reverse-orientalist claim is still that Japan is somehow positively different (Buddhist-postmodern), the real Other of the West, and that this accounts for Japan's amazing civilizational recovery since World War II, an event unprecedented in world history. According to this reasoning, what makes Japan so special culturally are the supposedly indigenous notions of "emptiness" and "harmony." As Karatani Kōjin notes:

> In the context of the economic development of the 1970s, the fact that a self did not exist was highly valued. It is precisely because of this fact that Japan was able to become a cutting-edge super-Western consumer and information society. Indeed, there was no self (subject) or identity, but there was a predicative identity with the capacity to assimilate anything without incurring any shock or giving rise to any confusion. This is what Nishida Kitaro read as "predicative logic" or "the logic of place," in which he identified the essence of the emperor system.[34]

Because of its emptiness, Japan is supposedly able to absorb advanced technologies readily, and it is also perfectly suited for the internationalized "information society" which is to prevail in the coming century vis-á-vis the material-industrial civilization of the past. As the "post-Western" world arrived in the late twentieth century, with its multiple global power centers, Japan would be able to offer a leading paradigm of world-civilization for the next millennium. Note the contemporary iterations of ideas expressed by Nishida in the New World Order essay in such a rhetoric. This sort of neo-nationalist discourse was consciously promoted by the Ohira and Nakasone cabinets during the early to mid-1980s, with their optimistic portrayal of Japan as the leader of the internationalization movement. Thus, as cultural critic Asada Akira notes, far from being an embarrassing memory, today the issues raised in the Overcoming Modernity

---

[30] See, for example, Kimura 1972. There is no translation of this work in English, but it is translated into German: see Kimura 1995.

[31] Berque has an extensive publication list in French and Japanese; in English, see Berque 1997*a*, 1997*b*. In French, Berque 2000. On Watsuji and Berque's work, see Chapter 23 in this volume.

[32] On Sakabe, see Chapters 30 and 31 in this volume.

[33] See, for example, Wei-hsun Fu and Heine 1995; for critical essays, see also Miyoshi and Harootunian 1989 and 1993.

[34] Karatani 1993, 298.

debate are "ideologized and revived like ghosts" in contemporary Japan's "groundless self-confidence."[35] Influenced by poststructuralism and Neo-Marxism, Karatani also criticizes the facile comparison of deconstruction and Japanese capitalist expansion in the postwar period.[36]

The cultural-nationalist sentiments continued to grow in the 1990s, and, as Japan commemorated the fiftieth anniversary of the end of the Pacific War in 1995, the issue of how to account for its colonial activities in Asia attracted renewed interest in the public sphere. Although the stories of atrocities are no longer a secret, the once-sloganized justification, the "liberation of Asia from Western imperial powers," still enjoyed (and continues to enjoy) considerable support among the conservative sector of society. Although Prime Minister Murayama finally issued a formal apology on August 15, 1995, the event was shrouded in controversy and resistance; the preferred national discourse is that of being a victim (of the atom bombings), and in fear of humiliation there is considerable resistance to recognizing Japan as the *perpetrator* of violence. The official apologies by the Koizumi Cabinet followed well into the 2000s, yet Prime Minister Koizumi visited the controversial Yasukuni Shrine, regarded by Korea and China as the symbol of Japanese militarism, in 2005 and 2006, aggravating political relations with both of these countries.[37] As recently as the spring of 2016, the Japanese government still refuses to acknowledge the Imperial Army's coercion of "comfort women" in Korea and China. Apart from what the government officials do or do not do, the sentiments of the majority of Japanese still support the neo-nationalist line that Japan need not keep apologizing. The issue is far from settled.

There are three currents of thought underlying such resistance: (1) Japan's *intent* to liberate Asia from the encroachment of Western hegemony in the war is thought to have been in itself noble (and necessary). (2) War (and its associated atrocities) is simply a part of history, and, as Buddhist metaphysics would have it, there is no ultimate good and evil that can be judged—everything mirrors everything else in an ever-shifting process: war is one of these shifting moments, and what would be "evil," if anything at all, would be to make the mistake of fixing something as "evil" (e.g., war) when in fact there is ultimately no such fixed thing. (3) Japan should not be "singled out" for its violent actions; war crimes are part of war, lamentable as this might be. Retrospectively, one could read all of these ideas already expressed in the Overcoming of Modernity debates. Critics on the left continued to be wary of the use of depersonalizing historicism to

---

[35] Hiromatsu et al. 2004: 10. See also Miyoshi and Harootunian 1989, for essays in English by Asada, Karatani, and other critics of *Nihonjin-ron*. See also Miyoshi and Harootunian 1993 for a good collection of critical essays on Japanese identity formation, essentialism, postwar US–Japan relations, and so on.

[36] Karatani, who studied with Paul de Man and Frederic Jameson at Yale, is one of the contemporary Japanese philosophers known outside Japan. His works have been recognized by thinkers like Derrida and Žižek, which has brought him international recognition. His 1985 work, *Hihyō to posutomodan* (Critique and Postmodernism), is perhaps among the best known of his works in Japan, but there are several translations of his other works available in English, such as *Transcritique* (2003), another one of his well-known theories.

[37] See Takahashi 2005, for the controversies surrounding the Yasukuni Shrine, as well as his critique.

evade responsibilities and worried about the reaffirmation of nationalist sentiments that its resurgence implies; nevertheless, the once-forgotten giants of Japanese philosophy and the cultural ideas they represented also became a focus of attention again.

After nearly fifty years of silence, in 1995, Kyoto University officially re-established "Japanese Philosophy" in the graduate curriculum. After the war, descendants of the Kyoto School, most notably students of Nishitani, had continued to work, primarily in religious philosophy in an academically isolated environment; now, they have gained a recognized institutional center again where they are continuing the tradition. Nishida scholarship has enjoyed a resurgence, although criticism from the left continues.[38] It is still the case that among certain circles the image of the "right" is attributed to those who study Japanese philosophy today, but it is no longer a shunned field in the academy. There is indeed excellent scholarship emerging from the new generation of Kyoto School scholars, as well as from scholars in the West who specialize in Kyoto School philosophies. The renewed focus is on intercultural or global modes of philosophizing, which takes up traditional themes of the Kyoto School in today's contexts, such as multiculturalism, global pluralism, intercultural exchange, and diversity, applying the antiessentialist, dialectic insights of the original thinkers of the Kyoto School to today's problems and concerns.[39] In addition to intercultural and global-multicultural philosophy, critiques of Eurocentrism and Western hegemony are still very relevant in our neo-colonial global context. In this regard, David Williams offers a new defense of the Kyoto School thinkers, aligning their thinking with the anticolonial critique of millennial white supremacy; he notes the significance of the "post-White thinking" of the Kyoto School thinkers in today's geopolitics:

> During the twenty-first century, White West hegemony, the racial imbalance that has defined our global society for half a millennium, seems almost certain to pass away. Tanabe, Kōyama, Suzuki, Nishitani and Kōsaka were among the earliest thinkers to sense the enormous opportunity but also the great test facing those who would seek to realize this change. American hegemony now stands in the way of this renaissance. For any society that would take up this challenge, the Kyoto thinker's gift for metaphysical vision and historical realism has provided future generations with the philosophical tools to dream forward.[40]

Thus, according to Williams, the Kyoto School thinkers of the Overcoming Modernity notoriety "were right but fatally ahead of their times, and thus prophets without honour, at home or abroad."[41]

---

[38] See the interesting works by the "decendents" of the Kyoto School, such as Ueda Shizuteru, Ōhashi Ryōsuke, and Fujita Masakatsu. Critics in Japan include Hiromatsu Wataru and Takahashi Tetsuya, among others. See Hiromatsu 1989 and Takahashi 1995.
[39] For collections of essays on the contemporary relevance of Japanese philosophy, see Fujita and Davis 2005 and Heisig 2006. On the topic of cross-cultural dialogue and philosophy in the contemporary global context, see Maraldo 1995; Kopf 2009a, 2009b, 2011, and 2014; Davis 2006, 2010, 2013b, and 2014b.
[40] Williams 2004, 91.
[41] Ibid.

BEYOND GLOBAL MULTICULTURALISM: THE POSSIBILITY OF A DECOLONIZED WORLD ORDER

Having chronicled the turbulent history of modern Japanese philosophy, we now return to the contemporary global context discussed at the outset of this chapter, that is to say, the neo-colonial world order—the world ravaged by uncontrolled transnational neo-capitalism, continuing (or perhaps even worsening) global racism and sexism, the environmental crisis, and the gaping breach between those who control and those who are controlled. Not that we are ambitious enough to take on all these issues here, but what *would* be a constructive way to move forward with Japanese philosophy today, given that doing philosophy is a historical activity? Let me make three points to conclude the chapter. (1) For pragmatic reasons we *must* go beyond defending or attacking Nishida and the Kyoto School and move our assessments to the current context. (2) Japanese philosophy must go beyond the borders of Japan; it must participate in philosophizing globally. (3) Articulating the de-essentialized dialectic at play in the interactive mutual creations of different cultural groups (such as Nishida has done and as has been refreshed by Bret Davis, John Maraldo, Gereon Kopf, and others) has much contemporary significance in the contexts of liberal multicultural democratic politics and cosmopolitanism. Yet, given the global power inequities, the discourse of liberal multiculturalism can actually mask the recalcitrant problem of global racism.[42] Even though it is necessary to start with multiculturalism, what we need today is to move beyond multiculturalism to a *decolonized* world order. Can Nishida's theory, for example, offer a theoretical framework to go forward in this direction? Perhaps yes, but this will happen not merely through textual exegesis or application, but only through a reinterpretation and expansion.

To the first point: as stated earlier, from the global perspective, the current political mood in Japan still appears rather neo-nationalist and myopically Japanocentric and Japanosupremacist in that, when it comes to the issue of war crimes and moral demands for recognition, issues that come to the political fore (as well as the tendency among the citizens witnessed in countless blog entries) are the refusal to see Japan as a perpetrator, historical amnesia, playing the victim, blaming the victim, self-justification, self-pity, evasion of responsibility, criticizing the critics, and intra-Asian racism. Japan's political relations to Korea and China continue to be tense under such self-denial. What is taught at schools about the Pacific War, censored and approved by the Ministry of Education, is woefully lacking in any non-Japanese perspectives. This is not just a "background scene" against which we, as philosophers and academics and citizens, theorize, teach, converse, and live; it *is* what makes up the very stuff of our historicity today. As citizens

---

[42] For a discussion of this problem in a context of racism and multiculturalism, see Arisaka 2010.

and educators, critics and evaluators, *we* are also not "above or below" history, as if we could assume a neutral ground in order to produce our critique. Our voices are themselves creators and interlocutors within and beyond the narratives of philosophy (politics, ethics, and life in general), and our words are not the final words.

In this sense, our reconstruction and interpretation of the politics of the Kyoto School, for example, are not really about the past but rather about the *present and the future*; they are part of our *current, continuous, ongoing creation* of an academic narrative today. Defending (or attacking) the Kyoto School, therefore, is not really about defending or attacking per se, but rather about participating in the current production of knowledge. We participate in writing history, and what we endorse and what we disregard, what we choose to discuss and what we ignore, what we communicate to our students and colleagues, what and how we discuss or do not discuss, what and how we teach, all become part of the process of knowledge production and have consequences in the long run, perhaps even making a moral difference.[43] We may actually not have as much choice as we think we do in this matter, for whatever narrative we produce, we are implicated in a *positioning*, a "realization" and the concretization of a moment (a "self-determination") within the dialectical universal, if one were to use the language of Nishida's theory.

For example, although philosophical universalism can legitimately buttress liberatory agendas (obvious cases are universal rights discourse or civil rights claims, but Nishida's New World Order essay also can certainly be read in this liberatory vein),[44] it ought not be used to *justify* the pernicious outcome of history *in retrospect*. Even though it was a standard narrative until the early twentieth century, Europe can no longer use the language of enlightenment and paternalistic liberation to justify European colonialism because we regard colonialism to be something that we ought not to attempt to justify at all today. (What would be the *point* of such a justification?) It hardly matters in this context that universalism can be theoretically used to liberate because that never happened in the history of colonialism, anywhere.

Let me make a pragmatic point. Justice demands recognition, retribution, and reconciliation; pragmatically speaking, *if* intra-Asian justice is important at all, then that is a *goal* toward which we ought to be theorizing, rather than theorizing in a direction that hinders it.[45] The self-appointed and supposed supremacy of Japan was a problem then

[43] In this sense, it is interesting to contrast the culture of postwar German national guilt to that of the relatively guilt-free Japanese national self-understanding. As Habermas once made clear in the "historians debate" in the 1980s in Germany (in which some right-leaning historians argued that Germany ought to get over its dark past of National Socialism to move forward), the ongoing narratives of guilt and the recognition of past wrongs are important, precisely because they recreate and reinstitute over and over in the current discourse a *continued* awareness. It is therefore for the *future*, not for the past. See McCarthy 2009, 99–105, for further analysis of this debate.

[44] See Ueda 1995, Yusa 1995, and Krummel 2015, for good presentations of Nishida's universalism as a liberatory theory.

[45] One could, of course, regard intra-Asian justice as unimportant; or be a right-leaning cultural essentialist or a Japanosupremacist; or be so embedded in the lineage of the Kyoto School that one must abstain from criticizing the forbearers out of respect; or decide to abstain from any political commentary. My particular take on this issue thus represents only one possible view.

and it still is now, not just diplomatically but also morally. How, then, would it help to re-peat such a discourse from the past and claim today that it had its own merits? The retro-spective, historical, or textual defense, even in the name of "truth," misses the point that such analyses are themselves *participating in the current production of power discourse* embedded in the current historical context.[46] This is why it does not suffice to say, "well, but the historical context back then was so different and everything must be read in that context"—because this statement is itself uttered now in our already contentious *present* context. (Think of how impossible it would be today to make such a historicized defense of National Socialism in Germany and remain "neutral" in the current context.)

Following from the first is the second point. What is the *place* of Japanese philosophy today, and what should it be? Until now, Japanese philosophy has remained confined pri-marily to those who can read and write the Japanese language. Of course, knowing the language is extremely important, but I would argue that Japanese philosophy harbors a great many philosophical potentialities that could be meaningfully made available to the global scene of doing philosophy, such that it is a shame if Japanese philosophy re-mains a rather specialized and isolated, even "guarded," discourse in Japan just because of its linguistic inaccessibility. Indeed, this smacks of cultural protectionism and even, to some extent, academic chauvinism. Let me repeat the point James Heisig recently made:

> The future of Nishida's philosophy is not served by treating it like Shakespeare's tragedies or Dante's Divine Comedy. It has rather to be read like all great philosophers: diffused and adapted to as many questions of human life and to as many different historical and linguistic contexts as possible, stretching his ideas to the breaking point until they deliver on their full promise.[47]

Nishida (and the Kyoto School thinkers) aimed for an antiessentialist, dialectical con-crete universal in the making, here and now. To remain stuck in historical analyses and exegesis in a narrow scholarly Japanese context would, in fact, belie his own theory. As Heisig notes, Nishida's thought is a kind of place that must be contextualized in the ever-broader place of thought today.[48] Following this suggestion, we must "update" Nishida's theory by testing it against the "questions of the day—questions like the maldistribu-tion of wealth, the enslavement of the poor, the research into ever more powerful killing machines, the deliberate infection of the air and the water—and then try to set [these contemporary questions] in the context and vocabulary of Nishida's philosophy."[49]

---

[46] The attacks would then have to be read in the current context of Japan-bashing, US neo-colonialism, Chinese domination, intra-Asian politics of power negotiations, and so on. The point remains the same—it is not about the past but the present/future.

[47] Heisig 2016, 223.

[48] Heisig 2016, 236: "Nishida's thought is not a self-enclosed universe nor can it be understood simply as a part of Japan's intellectual history. Only by seeing it as located in the wider *basho* of world philosophy are we able to understand it."

[49] Heisig 2016, 238. In Heisig's view, the ultimate *basho*, which should be focused on rather urgently today, is the Earth.

In this vein, let me turn to the third point, my own attempt to tease out a theoretical strain in Nishida with the aim of becoming able to address such contemporary issues. Let me suggest two possible ways to reconstruct his theory as a whole: from a "third-person perspective" and from a "first-person-perspective."[50] In the third person, one describes the formal process of the dialectic, as if to see it from a bird's-eye view; for instance, nations determine one another through self-negation and appropriation, as Nishida describes in his New World Order essay. History develops as the process of such a concrete dialectic, and this process contains peaceful as well as contentious relations and developments, including war. As such, one cannot say that the dialectic and the resulting situation is "good" or "bad." Today, our global-geopolitical situation is obviously not what it was in the 1940s, but there are patterns of domination and exchange, claims for self-determination, shifting movements of capital, competition and alliance, and there is still war. Nishida's theory could certainly be used to describe and give us insight into how such patterns dialectically produce the development of global history. If one approaches and interprets Nishida's political theory in this vein, then it could indeed appear that all the moral charges are overblown in that he simply produced an ontologically descriptive account. This is by far the most common reading of Nishida in the scholarship.

However, there is another interpretive strand which may be possible—that of the first-person perspective—which can be traced from his early theory of "pure experience" to his theory of "personality" and "action-intuition" (kōiteki chokkan 行為的直観) in the historical dialectic. From the standpoint of action-intuition, the subject is not simply "one of the actors" seen from above but the *self as the I*, with thoughts, body, will, and plans (a "personality"), in existential and *free* dialectical interactions with others and with itself, including self-negation-in-affirmation-of-the-other. What *I* choose or do not choose to do alters and influences and "forms" the environment/the Other, and, through this interaction, *I* am changed accordingly. I am, as a subject, not simply an object, an "event" in history, but an *acting co-creator* in the dialectical process of the historical world. What I choose or do not choose to do makes a difference in the environment/history in which I am involved; by concretizing a particular situation (among numerous possible realities), my choices "determine" a particular direction. Here, one cannot say "and this too is neither good nor bad," as I am not an automaton simply determined by the environment. I am rather an *agent* who deliberates and contemplates the actions (even though some of this deliberation and contemplation may not be at a conscious level). The historical world of such agents ("personalities") is full of responsibilities connected with decisions, and since we are always making-in-the-made-environment, the sense of our responsibilities is always relational, for the other, for the larger context.[51]

[50] More on the third-person versus first-person perspectives in Arisaka 2014a, Feenberg 1999, and Feenberg and Arisaka 1990.
[51] See Takahashi and Lee 2007, for the importance of philosophizing with a sense of responsibility for the other (as a critique of neo-liberal–individualist elitism).

The shift to the first-person perspective brings with itself an *ethical-moral* dimension which was not present in the third-person description of history.[52]

From the first-person perspective, since my decisions are situated and implicated in the concrete processes of history, my dialectical involvement with others and with the wider environment is *always already* moral-political. In this sense, history does not "just happen" but rather is dialectically created through its participants and their decisions, actions, projections, reflections, interpretations, moral sensibilities, compassion, understanding, will, and freedom. From the first-person perspective, Nishida's theory highlights this existential dimension in the dialectical-historical process and such a dimension includes *us today*: pure experience and action-intuition, the dialectical universal and its self-determination are not in "books" or in "Nishida's philosophy" but are still very much the articulations of the very processes in which we live, theorize, and communicate, here and now. We continue a living tradition, a concrete universal in the process of unfolding. It is a dialectic in the making, and not only our current geopolitics of radical power inequities and racism, but also, as Heisig and Krummel point out, our environmental crisis as a whole seems to demand that we develop a new discourse of a common future.[53]

We are, as Nishida reminds us, historical agents, material "personalities" that co-create the world, and what we do and think, or fail to do and think, matter in the long run. Literally as we speak, the global scene is changing. Perhaps Nishida's theory could still be used to produce an embodied theory of resistance, an *existential critical theory*, to empower the subjects of history and action, to subvert and transcend the injustices that subjugate, to rethink and extend our sense of compassion and responsibility, and to imagine critically and create a common future, a new, *humane*, world order—this time, a globally decolonized one.[54]

BIBLIOGRAPHY AND SUGGESTED READINGS

Arisaka, Yoko. (1996) "The Nishida Enigma: 'The Principle of the New World Order.'" *Monumenta Nipponica* 51(1): 81–99.

Arisaka, Yoko. (1997) "Beyond East and West: Nishida's Universalism and a Postcolonial Critique." *The Review of Politics* 59(3): 541–560.

Arisaka, Yoko. (2010) "Paradox of Dignity: Everyday Racism and the Failure of Multiculturalism." *Ethik und Gesellschaft* 2/2010. http://www.ethik-und-gesellschaft.de/ojs/index.php/eug/article/view/2-2010-art-3/107

Arisaka, Yoko. (2014a) "Action, History, and the Dialectical Universal in Nishida's Philosophy." In *Kitaro Nishida in der Philosophie der 20. Jahrhunderts*, edited by R. Elberfeld and Y. Arisaka. Freiburg: Alber Verlag, 146–170.

[52] Krummel 2015 notes that Nishida's dialectic could accommodate an ethic of "mutual self-negation, an ethics calling for humility vis-á-vis one's others" (221).

[53] See Heisig 2016, 237; Krummel 2015, 224.

[54] I would like to thank Bret Davis for his extensive comments and helpful suggestions—not to mention his patience and encouragement.

Arisaka, Yoko. (2014b) "Modern Japanese Philosophy: Historical Contexts and Cultural Implications." In *Philosophical Traditions*, edited by Anthony O'Hear. Cambridge: Cambridge University Press, 3–25.

Befu, Harumi. (2001) *Hegemony of Homogeneity: An Anthropological Analysis of "Nihonjinron."* Melbourne: Trans Pacific Press.

Berque, Augustin. (1997a) *Japan: Nature and Artifice*. London: Pilkington Press.

Berque, Augustin. (1997b) *Japan: Cities and Social Bonds*. London: Pilkington Press.

Berque, Augustin. (2000) *Écoumène: Introduction à l'étude des milieux humains*. Paris: Belin.

Buruma, Ian. (1994) *The Wages of Guilt: Memories of War in Germany and Japan*. New York: Farrar Straus Giroux.

Calichman, Richard, ed. and trans. (2008) *Overcoming Modernity: Cultural Identity in Wartime Japan*. New York: Columbia University Press.

Césaire, Aimé. (1972) *Discourse on Colonialism*. New York: Monthly Review Press.

Dale, Peter. (1986, 2011) *The Myth of Japanese Uniqueness*. London: Croom Helm, 1986; London and New York: Routledge, 2011.

Davis, Bret W. (2006) "Toward a World of Worlds: Nishida, the Kyoto School, and the Place of Cross-Cultural Dialogue." In *Frontiers of Japanese Philosophy*, edited by James W. Heisig. Nagoya: Nanzan Institute for Religion and Culture, 205–245.

Davis, Bret W. (2008) "Turns to and from Political Philosophy: The Case of Nishitani Keiji." In *Re-Politicising the Kyoto School as Philosophy*, edited by C. Goto-Jones. London and New York: Routledge, 26–45.

Davis, Bret W. (2010) "Dialogue and Appropriation: The Kyoto School as Cross-Cultural Philosophy." In *Japanese and Continental Philosophy: Conversations with the Kyoto School*, edited by Bret W. Davis, Brian Schroeder, and Jason M. Wirth. Bloomington: Indiana University Press, 33–51.

Davis, Bret W. (2013a) "Nishida's Multicultural Worldview: Contemporary Significance and Immanent Critique." *Nishida tetsugaku Nenpō* 10: 183–203.

Davis, Bret W. (2013b) "Opening Up the West: Toward Dialogue with Japanese Philosophy." *Journal of Japanese Philosophy* 1: 57–83.

Davis, Bret W. (2014a) "Ethical and Religious Alterity: Nishida after Levinas." In *Kitaro Nishida in der Philosophie der 20. Jahrhunderts*, edited by R. Elberfeld and Y. Arisaka. Freiburg: Alber Verlag, 313–341.

Davis, Bret W. (2014b) "Conversing in Emptiness: Rethinking Cross-Cultural Dialogue with the Kyoto School." In *Philosophical Traditions*, edited by Anthony O'Hear. Cambridge: Cambridge University Press, 171–194.

Davis, Bret W., Brian Schroeder, and Jason M. Wirth, eds. (2010) *Japanese and Continental Philosophy: Conversations with the Kyoto School*. Bloomington: Indiana University Press.

Doi, Takeo. (1973, 1989) *The Anatomy of Dependence*. Tokyo: Kodansha International.

Dower, John. (1986) *War Without Mercy: Race and Power in the Pacific War*. New York: Pantheon Books.

Elberfeld, Rolf, and Yoko Arisaka, eds. (2013) *Kitaro Nishida in der Philosophie der 20. Jahrhunderts*. Freiburg: Alber Verlag.

Faure, Bernard. (1995) "The Kyoto School and Reverse Orientalism." In *Japan in Traditional and Postmodern Perspectives*, edited by C. Wei-shun Fu and S. Heine. Albany: SUNY Press, 245–281.

Feenberg, Andrew, and Yoko Arisaka. (1990) "Experiential Ontology: The Origins of the Nishida Philosophy in the Doctrine of Pure Experience." *International Philosophical Quarterly* 30: 173–205.

Feenberg, Andrew. (1995) "The Problems of Modernity in the Philosophy of Nishida." In *Rude Awakenings: Zen, the Kyoto School and the Question of Nationalism*, edited by J. W. Heisig and J. C. Maraldo. Honolulu: University of Hawai'i Press, 151–173.

Feenberg, Andrew. (1999) "Experience and Culture: Nishida's Path 'To the Things Themselves.'" *Philosophy East and West* 49/1: 28–44.

Fujita Masakatsu, and Bret Davis, eds. (2005), *Sekai no naka no Nihon no tetsugaku* [*Japanese Philosophy in the World*] Kyoto: Showa-dō.

Gluck, Carol. (1985) *Japan's Modern Myths: Ideology in the Late Meiji Period*. Princeton, NJ: Princeton University Press.

Goto-Jones, Christopher. (2005) *Political Philosophy in Japan: Nishida, the Kyoto School, and Co-Prosperity*. London and New York: Routledge.

Goto-Jones, Christopher, ed. (2008) *Re-Politicising the Kyoto School as Philosophy*. London and New York: Routledge.

Harootunian, Harry. (2000) *Overcome by Modernity: History, Culture, and Community in Interwar Japan*. Princeton, NJ: Princeton University Press.

Hearn, Lafcadio. (1972) *Kokoro: Hints and Echoes of Japanese Inner Life*. Tokyo: Charles Tuttle.

Heisig, James, ed. (2006) *Nihon tetsugaku no kokusai-sei* [The Global Significance of Japanese Philosophy]. Kyoto: Sekai Shisō-sha.

Heisig, James W. (2016) *Much Ado About Nothingness: Essays on Nishida and Tanabe*. Nagoya: Chisokudō.

Heisig, James W., Thomas P. Kasulis, and John C. Maraldo, eds. (2011) *Japanese Philosophy: A Sourcebook*. Honolulu: University of Hawai'i Press.

Heisig, James W., and John C. Maraldo, eds. (1995) *Rude Awakenings: Zen, the Kyoto School and the Question of Nationalism*. Honolulu: University of Hawai'i Press.

Hiromatsu Wataru. (1989) *Kindai no chōkoku-ron* [Theory of the Overcoming of Modernity] Tokyo: Kodansha.

Hiromatsu Wataru, Asada Akira, Ichikawa Hiroshi, and Karatani Kōjin. (2004) "Kindai no chōkoku to Nishida tetsugaku" ["Overcoming of Modernity" and Nishidan Philosophy], a round table discussion. In *Kikan Shichō 4 "Kindai no chōkoku" to Nishida tetsugaku* ["Overcoming of Modernity" and Nishidan Philosophy], edited by Asada Akira. Tokyo: Shichōsha, 6–38.

Irowaka, Daikichi. Jansen, M. ed. (1985) *The Culture of the Meiji Period*. Princeton, NJ: Princeton University Press.

Jansen, Marius, ed. (1965) *Changing Japanese Attitudes Toward Modernization*. Tokyo: Charles Tuttle.

Karatani Kōjin. (1985) *Hihyō to posutomodan* [Critique and Postmodernism]. Okayama: Fukutake Shoten/Benesse.

Karatani Kōjin. (1993) "The Discursive Space of Modern Japan." In *Japan in the World*, edited by M. Miyoshi and H. D. Harootunian. Durham, NC: Duke University Press, 288–315.

Karatani, Kōjin. (2003) *Transcritique: On Kant and Marx*, translated by S. Kohso. Cambridge, MA: MIT Press.

Kimura Bin. (1972) *Hito to hito to no aida: Seishin byōri-gaku-teki nihonjin-ron* [Between Person and Person: A Psychiatric Theory of Japanese-ness]. Tokyo: Kobundo.

Kimura Bin. (1995) *Zwischen Mensch und Mensch: Strukturen japanischer Subjektivität.* Darmstadt: Wissenschaftliche Buchgesellschaft.

Kopf, Gereon. (2009*a*) "Between the Global and the Local: Applying the Logic of the One and the Many to a Global Age." In *Frontiers of Japanese Philosophy 4: Facing the 21st Century*, edited by Wing-keung Lam and Cheung Ching-yuen. Nagoya: Nanzan Institute for Religion and Culture, 76–89.

Kopf, Gereon. (2009*b*) "Nationalism, Globalism, and Cosmopolitanism: An Application of Kyoto School Philosophy." In *Frontiers of Japanese Philosophy 6: Confluences and Cross-Currents*, edited by Raquel Bouso and James W. Heisig. Nagoya: Nanzan Institute for Religion and Culture, 170–189.

Kopf, Gereon. (2011) "Ambiguity, Diversity and an Ethics of Understanding: What Nishida's Philosophy Can Contribute To the Pluralism Debate." *Culture and Dialogue* 1/1: 21–44.

Kopf, Gereon. (2014) "Philosophy as Expression: Towards a New Model of Global Philosophy." *Nishida Tetsugaku Nenpo* 11: 155–181.

Krummel, John W. M. (2015) *Nishida Kitarō's Chiasmatic Chorology: Place of Dialectic, Dialectic of Place.* Bloomington: Indiana University Press.

Lavelle, Pierre (1994) "The Political Thought of Nishida Kitaro." *Monumenta Nipponica* 49/2: 139–165.

Maraldo, John. (1995) "The Problem of World Culture: Towards an Appropriation of Nishida's Philosophy of Nation and Culture." *The Eastern Buddhist* 28/2: 183–197.

Maraldo, John. (2006) "The War Over the Kyoto School," *Monumenta Nipponica* 61/3 (Autumn 2006): 375–401.

McCarthy, Thomas. (2009) *Race, Empire, and the Idea of Human Development.* Cambridge: Cambridge University Press.

Miyoshi, Masao, and H. D. Harootunian, eds. (1989) *Postmodernism and Japan.* Durham, NC: Duke University Press.

Miyoshi, Masao, and H. D. Harootunian, eds. (1993) *Japan in the World.* Durham, NC: Duke University Press.

Myers, Ramon, and Mark Peattie, eds. (1984) *The Japanese Colonial Empire, 1895–1945.* Princeton, NJ: Princeton University Press.

Najita, Tetsuo, and H. D. Harootunian. (1988) "Japanese Revolt against the West: Political and Cultural Criticism in the Twentieth Century." In *The Cambridge History of Japan*, edited by Peter Duus. Cambridge: Cambridge University Press, 711–774.

Nakane, Chie (1972) *Japanese Society.* Oakland: University of California Press.

Nishida Kitarō. (2012) *Ontology of Production: Three Essays.* Translated and with an introduction by William Haver. Durham, NC: Duke University Press.

Parkes, Graham. (1997) "The Putative Fascism of the Kyoto School and the Political Correctness of the Modern Academy." *Philosophy East and West* 47/3: 305–336.

Sakai, Naoki. (1989) "Modernity and Its Critique: The Problem of Universalism and Particularism." In *Postmodernism and Japan*, edited by M. Miyoshi and H. D. Harootunian. Durham, NC: Duke University Press, 93–122.

Sakai, Naoki. (1993) "Return to the West/Return to the East: Watsuji Tetsuro's Anthropology and Discussions of Authenticity." In *Japan in the World*, edited by M. Miyoshi and H. D. Harootunian. Durham, NC: Duke University Press, 237–270.

Sakai, Naoki. (1997) *Translation and Subjectivity: On Japan and Cultural Nationalism.* Minneapolis: Minnesota University Press.

Sakai, Naoki. (1997) *Nihon shisō to iu mondai: Honyaku to shutai* [The Problem of Japanese Thought: Translation and Subject]. Tokyo: Iwanami Shoten.

Samson, G. B. (1984) *The Western World and Japan*. Tokyo: Charles Tuttle.

Sharf, Robert. (1993) "The Zen of Japanese Nationalism." *History of Religions* 33/1: 1–43.

Takahashi Tetsuya. (1995) *Kioku no echika: Sensō, tetsugaku, Aushubittsu* [Ethics of Memory: War, Philosophy, Auschwitz]. Tokyo: Iwanami Shoten.

Takahashi Tetsuya. (2005) *Yasukuni mondai* [The Yasukuni Shrine Issue]. Tokyo: Chikuma Shobō.

Takahashi, Tetsuya, and H. D. Lee. (2007) "Philosophy as Activism in Neo-Liberal, Neo-Nationalist Japan." *The Asia Pacific Journal* 5/11/0: 1–22.

Tanaka, Stefan. (1993) *Japan's Orient: Rendering Past into History*. Berkeley: University of California Press.

Ueda, Shizuteru. (1995) "Nishida, Nationalism, and the War Question," translated by Jan Van Bragt. In *Rude Awakenings: Zen, the Kyoto School and the Question of Nationalism*, edited by J. W. Heisig and J. C. Maraldo. Honolulu: University of Hawai'i Press, 77–106.

Umehara Takeshi (1976) *Nihon bunka ron* [Theory of Japanese Culture]. Tokyo: Kodansha.

Wakabayashi, Bob Tadashi. (1986) *Anti-Foreignism and Western Learning in Early-Modern Japan: The New Theses of 1825*. Cambridge, MA: Harvard University Press.

Wakabayashi, Bob Tadashi, ed. (1998) *Modern Japanese Thought*. Cambridge: Cambridge University Press.

Wei-hsun Fu, Charles, and Steven Heine, eds. (1995) *Japan in Traditional and Postmodern Perspectives*. Albany: SUNY Press.

Williams, David. (2004) *Defending Japan's Pacific War: The Kyoto School Philosophers and Post-White Power*. London and New York: Routledge.

Williams, David. (2014) *The Philosophy of Japanese Wartime Resistance: A Reading, with Commentary, of the Complete Texts of the Kyoto School Discussions of "The Standpoint of World History and Japan."* London and New York: Routledge.

Yoshino, Kosaku (1992) *Cultural Nationalism in Contemporary Japan*. London and New York: Routledge.

Yusa, Michiko. (1995) "Nishida and Totalitarianism: A Philosopher's Resistance." In *Rude Awakenings: Zen, the Kyoto School and the Question of Nationalism*, edited by J. W. Heisig and J. C. Maraldo. Honolulu: University of Hawai'i Press, 107–131.

Index